McDOUGAL LITTELL

Creating America

A History of
the United States

**Beginnings
through
Reconstruction**

ONLINE EDITION @
CLASSZONE.COM

Zitkala-Ša
Native American author

Elizabeth Cady Stanton
Leader of the women's rights movement in the 1800s

Abigail Adams
Supporter of women's rights; married to President John Adams

Sam Houston
A hero of the Texas Revolution and the first president of the Republic of Texas

Juan Seguín
A hero of the Texas Revolution

Andrew Jackson
Seventh president of the United States

Harriet Tubman
Abolitionist and conductor on the Underground Railroad

Abraham Lincoln
Sixteenth president of the
United States

Crispus Attucks
American colonist killed
in the Boston Massacre

George Washington
First president of
the United States

Creating America

A History of
the United States

**Beginnings
through
Reconstruction**

Jesus Garcia

Donna M. Ogle

C. Frederick Risinger

Joyce Stevos

Winthrop D. Jordan

McDougal Littell

Evanston, Illinois • Boston • Dallas

Senior Consultants

Jesus Garcia is Professor of Curriculum and Instruction at the University of Kentucky. A former social studies teacher, Dr. Garcia has co-authored many books and articles on subjects that range from teaching social studies in elementary school to seeking diversity in education. Dr. Garcia will serve as President of the National Council for the Social Studies in 2004–2005.

Donna M. Ogle is Professor of Reading and Language Arts at National-Louis University in Evanston, Illinois, and is a specialist in reading in the content areas with an interest in social studies. She is past president of the International Reading Association. A former social studies teacher, Dr. Ogle is also Director of a Goals 2000 grant for Reading and Thinking in the Content Areas for four Chicago high schools. She developed the K-W-L reading strategy that is so widely used in schools.

C. Frederick Risinger is Director of Professional Development and Coordinator for Social Studies Education at Indiana University. He is past president of the National Council for the Social Studies. Mr. Risinger also served on the coordinating committee for the National History Standards Project. He writes a monthly column on technology in the social studies classroom for *Social Education.*

Joyce Stevos is the Director of Social Studies and Fine Arts for the Providence, Rhode Island, Public Schools. She is also an adjunct faculty member at Rhode Island College. Previously, she served 15 years as the social studies area supervisor in Providence, in which position she developed programs on Holocaust studies, the Armenian genocide, character education, voter education, and government and law.

Winthrop D. Jordan is the William F. Winter Professor of History and Professor of Afro-American Studies at the University of Mississippi, where he has taught since 1982. Since 1998, he has been the Frederick A. P. Barnard Distinguished Professor at that university. Dr. Jordan is the author of several books, including the highly acclaimed *White Over Black.*

C, 2, 4

Copyright © 2002 by McDougal Littell, a division of Houghton Mifflin Company. All rights reserved.

The USA TODAY® service mark has been licensed by USA TODAY® for use for certain purposes by McDougal Littell, a division of Houghton Mifflin Company. USA TODAY® charts, articles and photographs incorporated in these reading materials are displayed for informational and promotional purposes only. The USA TODAY® charts, articles and photographs incorporated herein are solely for private, personal and noncommercial use. Any other use of the USA TODAY® charts, articles and photographs incorporated herein, without prior express written permission of USA TODAY®, is strictly prohibited.

Maps on pages A1–A21 © Rand McNally & Company. All rights reserved.

No part of this work may be reproduced or transmitted in any form or by any means, electronic or mechanical, including photocopying and recording, or by any information storage or retrieval system, without the prior written permission of McDougal Littell, a division of Houghton Mifflin Company, unless such copying is expressly permitted by federal copyright law. Send inquiries to Manager, Rights and Permissions, McDougal Littell, a division of Houghton Mifflin Company, P.O. Box 1667, Evanston, IL 60204.

Acknowledgments begin on page R84.

ISBN 0-618-16254-2

Printed in the United States of America

4 5 6 7 8 9 – DWO – 07 06 05 04 03

Consultants and Reviewers

Content Consultants

The content consultants reviewed the manuscript for historical depth and accuracy and for clarity of presentation.

Roger Beck
Department of History
Eastern Illinois University
Charleston, Illinois

David Farber
Department of History
University of New Mexico
Albuquerque, New Mexico

Cheryl Johnson-Odim
Department of History
Loyola University
Chicago, Illinois

Joseph Kett
Department of History
University of Virginia
Charlottesville, Virginia

Jack N. Rakove
Department of History
Stanford University
Stanford, California

Virginia Stewart
Department of History
University of North Carolina,
   Wilmington
Wilmington, North Carolina

Christopher Waldrep
Department of History
Eastern Illinois University
Charleston, Illinois

Nancy Woloch
Department of History
Barnard College
New York, New York

Multicultural Advisory Board

The multicultural advisors reviewed the manuscript for appropriate historical content.

Betty Dean
Social Studies Consultant
Pearland, Texas

Tyrone C. Howard
College of Education
The Ohio State University
Columbus, Ohio

Jose C. Moya
Department of History
University of California
   at Los Angeles
Los Angeles, California

Pat Payne
Office of Multicultural Education
Indianapolis Public Schools
Indianapolis, Indiana

Betto Ramirez
Former Teacher, La Joya, Texas
Social Studies Consultant
Mission, Texas

Jon Reyhner
Department of Education
Northern Arizona University
Flagstaff, Arizona

Ronald Young
Department of History
Georgia Southern University
Statesboro, Georgia

Consultants and Reviewers

Teacher Consultants

The following educators contributed activity options for the Pupil's Edition and teaching ideas and activities for the Teacher's Edition.

Paul C. Beavers
J. T. Moore Middle School
Nashville, Tennessee

Holly West Brewer
Buena Vista Paideia Magnet School
Nashville, Tennessee

Ron Campana
Social Studies Consultant
New York, New York

Patricia B. Carlson
Swanson Middle School
Arlington, Virginia

Ann Cotton
Ft. Worth Independent School
    District
Ft. Worth, Texas

Kelly Ellis
Hamilton Junior High School
Cypress, Texas

James Grimes
Middlesex County Vocational–
Technical High School
Woodbridge, New Jersey

Brent Heath
De Anza Middle School
Ontario, California

Suzanne Hidalgo
Serrano Middle School
Highland, California

Barbara Kennedy
Sylvan Middle School
Citrus Heights, California

Pamela Kniffin
Navasota Junior High School
Navasota, Texas

Tammy Leiber
Navasota Junior High School
Navasota, Texas

Lori Lesslie
Cedar Bluff Middle School
Knoxville, Tennessee

Brian McKenzie
Dr. Charles R. Drew Science
    Magnet School
Buffalo, New York

W. W. Bear Mills
Goddard Junior High School
Midland, Texas

Lindy Poling
Millbrook High School
Raleigh, North Carolina

Jean Price
T. H. Rogers Middle School
Houston, Texas

Meg Robbins
Wilbraham Middle School
Wilbraham, Massachusetts

Philip Rodriguez
McNair Middle School
San Antonio, Texas

Leslie Schubert
Parkland School
McHenry, Illinois

Robert Sisko
Carteret Middle School
Carteret, New Jersey

Marci Smith
Hurst-Euless-Bedford Independent
    School District
Bedford, Texas

James Sorenson
Chippewa Middle School
Des Plaines, Illinois

Nicholas G. Sysock
Carteret Middle School
Carteret, New Jersey

Lisa Williams
Lamberton Middle School
Carlisle, Pennsylvania

Michael Yell
Hudson Middle School
Hudson, Wisconsin

Teacher Panels

The following educators provided ongoing review during the development of prototypes, the table of contents, and key components of the program.

Bill Albright
Wilson Southern Junior High School
Sinking Spring, Pennsylvania

Henry Assetto
Gordon Middle School
Coatesville, Pennsylvania

James Berry
Kennedy Middle School
Grand Prairie, Texas

Ralph Burnley
Roosevelt Middle School
Philadelphia, Pennsylvania

Mary Ann Canamar
Garner Middle School
San Antonio, Texas

Zoe Carter
San Jacinto Junior High School
Midland, Texas

Stephen Cicero
Butler Area Junior High School
Butler, Pennsylvania

Charles Crescenzi
Dover Intermediate School
Dover, Pennsylvania

Sharon McDonald
Cook Junior High School
Houston, Texas

Phil Mifsud
Roosevelt Middle School
Erie, Pennsylvania

Joel Mumma
Centerville Middle School
Lancaster, Pennsylvania

September Olson
Richardson Middle School
El Paso, Texas

Donald Roberts
Frick International Studies Academy
Pittsburgh, Pennsylvania

Mary Rogers
Brookside Intermediate School
Friendswood, Texas

Lucy Sanchez
John F. Kennedy High School
San Antonio, Texas

Steve Seale
Hamilton Middle School
Houston, Texas

Yolanda Villalobos
Dallas Independent School District
Dallas, Texas

Diane Williams
Hill-Freedman Middle School
Philadelphia, Pennsylvania

Lisa Williams
Lamberton Middle School
Carlisle, Pennsylvania

Student Board

The following students reviewed pages for the textbook.

Adam Backhaus
Parkland School
McHenry, Illinois

Ben Barney
Hamilton Junior High School
Cypress, Texas

Amanda Berrier
Lamberton Middle School
Carlisle, Pennsylvania

Debra Hurwitz
T. H. Rogers Middle School
Houston, Texas

Reginald Jones
Dr. Charles R. Drew Science
    Magnet School
Buffalo, New York

Brendon Keinath
Wilbraham Middle School
Wilbraham, Massachusetts

Daniel MacDonald
Carteret Middle School
Carteret, New Jersey

Cameron Mote
Serrano Middle School
Highland, California

Kim Nguyen
Sylvan Middle School
Citrus Heights, California

Arianna G. Noriega
De Anza Middle School
Ontario, California

Nicholas Tofilon
Burlington Middle School
Burlington, Wisconsin

Emmanuel Zepeda
Haven Middle School
Evanston, Illinois

UNIT
1

Three Worlds Meet BEGINNINGS TO 1763

Pontiac

JOIN, or DIE.

UNIT 2

Creating a New Nation 1763 – 1791

George Washington

x

A Changing Nation   1810 – 1860

California gold miner

Frances Ellen
Watkins Harper

Abraham Lincoln

Buzz Aldrin

Features

CITIZENSHIP TODAY

Economics *in* History

America's HERITAGE

AMERICA'S HISTORY MAKERS

Features

Voices from the Past

A VOICE FROM THE PAST

The land is the finest for cultivation that I ever in my life set foot upon, and it also abounds in trees of every description.

Henry Hudson, quoted in *Discoverers of America*

A VOICE FROM THE PAST

These, with the pictures, busts [sculptures of the head and shoulders], and prints (of which copies upon copies are spread everywhere), have made your father's face as well known as that of the moon.

Benjamin Franklin, letter to his daughter Sally

Voices from the Past

A VOICE FROM THE PAST

I overtook many sloops and schooners, beating to the windward, and parted with them as if they had been at anchor. The power of propelling boats by steam is now fully proved.

Robert Fulton, quoted in *Robert Fulton and the "Clermont"*

A VOICE FROM THE PAST

The determination of our slaveholding President to prosecute the war, and the probability of his success in wringing from the people men and money to carry it on, is made evident,...None seem willing to take their stand for peace at all risks; and all seem willing that the war should be carried on in some form or other.

Frederick Douglass,
The North Star, January 21, 1848

A VOICE FROM THE PAST

The red coat was changed for one of blue and buff, a sword was held in the hand instead of a sceptre [staff of authority], the head was decorated with a cocked hat, and underneath was painted in large characters, GENERAL WASHINGTON.

Washington Irving,
"Rip Van Winkle"

A VOICE FROM THE PAST

"A house divided against itself cannot stand." I believe this government cannot endure, permanently half slave and half free. I do not expect the Union to be dissolved—I do not expect the house to fall—but I do expect it will cease to be divided. It will become all one thing, or all the other.

Abraham Lincoln,
Springfield, Illinois, June 16, 1858

Voices from the Past

A VOICE FROM THE PAST

I have a dream that my four little
children will one day live
in a nation where they will not
be judged by the color of their skin
but by the content of their character.
I have a dream today.

Dr. Martin Luther King, Jr.,
"I Have a Dream,"
August 28, 1963

Visual Primary Sources for Assessment

Historical Maps

Charts and Graphs

Causes of the War of 1812

Impressment of U.S. Citizens

Interference with American shipping

British support of Native-American resistance

WAR

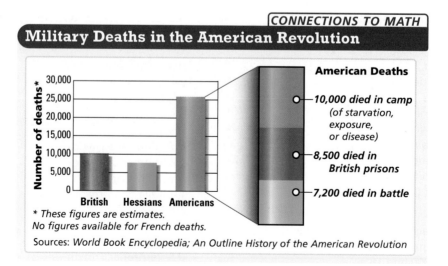

CONNECTIONS TO MATH

Military Deaths in the American Revolution

Number of deaths*

British   Hessians   Americans

* These figures are estimates.
No figures available for French deaths.

American Deaths

10,000 died in camp (of starvation, exposure, or disease)

8,500 died in British prisons

7,200 died in battle

Sources: *World Book Encyclopedia; An Outline History of the American Revolution*

Time Lines and Infographics

The Rise and Decline of Feudalism

In feudalism, nobles offered to protect peasants from invaders. In return, the peasants farmed the nobles' lands.

Feudalism made people feel safe enough to travel. Trade increased and towns grew.

Then many peasants ran away to towns, where they could live more freely. Feudalism declined. Trade continued to grow.

THEMES of AMERICAN HISTORY

Imagine life in Jamestown, America's first permanent English settlement. The nation we inhabit now is a much different place than it was then, more than three centuries ago. Yet there are repeating themes—ideas and issues—in American history that tie the past and present together. This book focuses on nine significant themes in U.S. history. Understanding these themes will help you to make sense of American history.

Democratic Ideals

From the day they declared themselves citizens of a new nation, Americans have built their society around the principles of democracy. In a democracy, power lies with the people, and every individual enjoys basic rights that cannot be taken away. Throughout the nation's history, however, some Americans—mainly women and minorities—have had to struggle to gain their full rights. Still, the ideals of democracy remain the guiding principles of this land.

What right or freedom do you consider the most important? Why?

Citizenship

The citizens of the United States enjoy rights and freedoms found in very few other places in the world. Yet Americans know that with such freedoms come responsibilities and duties. Whether they stand in line to vote or spend a weekend to clean up a local river, Americans recognize that citizen participation is what keeps a democracy strong.

How do citizens that you know contribute to your community?

Dr. Martin Luther King, Jr.

Impact of the Individual

The history of the United States is the story not only of governments and laws but of individuals. Indeed, individuals have made the United States what it is today through their extraordinary achievements. American history provides a variety of examples of the impact of the individual on society in both the United States and the world.

Name several individuals who have an impact on American society today. What impact do they have?

A young Asian immigrant

Diversity and Unity

The United States has been a land of many peoples, cultures, and faiths. Throughout the nation's history, this blend of ethnic, racial, and religious groups has helped to create a rich and uniquely American culture. The nation's many different peoples are united in their belief in American values and ideals.

What things do you enjoy that came to the United States from other cultures?

Immigration and Migration

The movement of people has played a vital role in American history. The first Americans migrated from Asia thousands of years ago. Millions more have immigrated in the past five centuries. Even within the United States, large numbers of people have migrated to different regions of the country. However, movements to and within the United States have not always been voluntary. Africans were brought against their will to this country. Native Americans were forced from their homelands in order to make room for European settlers.

Why do you think people continue to immigrate to the United States?

Expansion

When the United States declared its independence from Great Britain, it was only a collection of states along the Atlantic Ocean. But the new country would not remain that way for long. Many Americans shared a sense of curiosity, adventure, and a strong belief that their destiny was to expand all the way to the Pacific Ocean. Driven by this belief, they pushed westward. Americans' efforts to increase the size of their nation is a recurring theme in early U.S. history.

Where do you predict that the exploration of space—the final frontier—will lead?

Poster for Buffalo Bill's Wild West show

America and the World

As the power and prestige of the United States have grown, the nation has played a much more active role in world affairs. Indeed, throughout the 20th century, the United States focused much of its energy on events beyond its borders. The nation fought in two world wars and tried to promote democracy, peace, and economic growth around the globe. As one of the world's political and economic leaders, the United States will continue to be a key player in world affairs throughout the new century.

What do you think the role of the United States in the world should be today?

Science and Technology

Americans have always been quick to embrace inventions and new ways of doing things. After all, this country was settled by people who turned away from old ways and tried new ones. In the past two centuries, new inventions, new technologies, and scientific breakthroughs have transformed the United States—and will continue to do so in the new century.

What recent inventions or innovations affect your life?

Economics in History

Economics has had a powerful impact on the course of U.S. history. For example, the desire for wealth led thousands to join the California Gold Rush in 1849. The nation as a whole has grown wealthy, thanks to its abundant resources and the hard work of its citizens. An important economic issue, however, has been how to make sure that all people have opportunities to share fully in the nation's wealth. This issue will continue to be important in the 21st century.

What do you think are the most exciting economic opportunities for Americans today?

Thomas Edison's first light bulb

STRATEGIES FOR TAKING STANDARDIZED TESTS

This section of the textbook helps you develop and practice the skills you need to study history and to take standardized tests. Part 1, **Strategies for Studying History,** takes you through the features of the textbook and offers suggestions on how to use these features to improve your reading and study skills.

Part 2, **Test-Taking Strategies and Practice** offers specific strategies for tackling many of the items you'll find on a standardized test. It gives tips for answering multiple-choice, constructed-response, extended-response, and document-based questions. In addition, it offers guidelines for analyzing primary and secondary sources, maps, political cartoons, charts, graphs, and time lines. Each strategy is followed by a set of questions you can use for practice.

CONTENTS

Part 1: Strategies for Studying History

Reading is the central skill in the effective study of history or any other subject. You can improve your reading skills by using helpful techniques and through practice. The better your reading skills, the more you'll remember what you read. Below you'll find several strategies that involve built-in features of *Creating America*. Careful use of these strategies will help you learn and understand history more effectively.

Preview Chapters Before You Read

Each chapter begins with a two-page chapter opener and a one-page **Setting the Stage** feature. Study the materials to help you get ready to read.

1 Read the chapter and section titles and study the chapter-opening visual. Look for clues that indicate what will be covered in the chapter.

2 Preview the time line. Note the years that the chapter covers. What important events took place during this time period?

3 Study the **Interact with History** feature. Experience what it was like to live in the past by answering **What Do You Think?** questions.

4 Read the **Setting the Stage** feature (see page S3). **What Do You Want to Know?** and **Read and Take Notes** will help focus your reading.

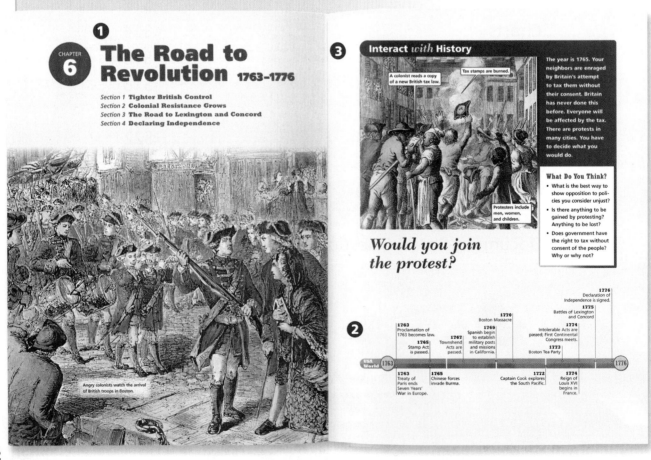

1

CHAPTER **6**
The Road to Revolution 1763–1776

Section 1 **Tighter British Control**
Section 2 **Colonial Resistance Grows**
Section 3 **The Road to Lexington and Concord**
Section 4 **Declaring Independence**

Angry colonists watch the arrival of British troops in Boston.

3 **Interact** *with* **History**

A colonist reads a copy of a new British tax law.

Tax stamps are burned.

Protesters include men, women, and children.

The year is 1765. Your neighbors are enraged by Britain's attempt to tax them without their consent. Britain has never done this before. Everyone will be affected by the tax. There are protests in many cities. You have to decide what you would do.

What Do You Think?

- What is the best way to show opposition to policies you consider unjust?
- Is there anything to be gained by protesting? Anything to be lost?
- Does government have the right to tax without consent of the people? Why or why not?

Would you join the protest?

2

1763 Proclamation of 1763 becomes law.

1765 Stamp Act is passed.

1767 Townshend Acts are passed.

1769 Spanish begin to establish military posts and missions in California.

1770 Boston Massacre

1773 Boston Tea Party

1774 Intolerable Acts are passed; First Continental Congress meets.

1775 Battles of Lexington and Concord

1776 Declaration of Independence is signed.

U.S. / World — 1763 ... 1776

1763 Treaty of Paris ends Seven Years' War in Europe.

1765 Chinese forces invade Burma.

1772 Captain Cook explores the South Pacific.

1774 Reign of Louis XVI begins in France.

Preview Sections Before You Read

Each chapter consists of three, four, or five sections. These sections focus on shorter periods of time or on particular historical themes. Use the section openers to help you prepare to read.

5 Study the sentences under the headings **Main Idea** and **Why It Matters Now**. These tell you what's important in the material that you're about to read.

6 Preview the **Terms & Names** list. This will give you an idea of the issues and personalities you will read about in the section.

7 Read **One American's Story** and **A Voice from the Past**. These provide one individual's view of an important issue of the time.

8 Notice how the section is divided into smaller chunks, each with a red headline. These headlines give you a quick outline of the section.

TERMS & NAMES
King George III
Quartering Act
revenue
Sugar Act
Stamp Act
Patrick Henry
boycott
Sons of Liberty

4

Chapter **6** SETTING THE STAGE

BEFORE YOU READ

Previewing the Theme
Impact of the Individual From 1763 to 1776, American colonists changed from loyal subjects of the British king to revolutionaries. This chapter explains how this dramatic change took place. It also discusses the individuals who led America to independence.

Protest

War

Independence

What Do You Know?
What do you already know about the time before the Revolution? What were the issues that caused the colonists to choose independence?

THINK ABOUT
• what you have learned about this period from movies, television, or historical fiction
• reasons people in history have chosen to fight for freedom from oppression

What Do You Want to Know?
What questions do you have about the issues and events that pushed the American colonists toward rebellion? Record them in your notebook before you read the chapter.

READ AND TAKE NOTES

Reading Strategy: Sequencing Events
Sequencing means putting events in the order in which they happen in time. In learning about how the American colonies moved toward independence, it would be helpful to list the important events.

Place them in the order in which they occurred. You might record the event and its date in a graphic organizer such as the one below. Copy this organizer in your notebook. Fill it in as you read the chapter.
See Skillbuilder Handbook, page R4.

Proclamation of 1763 →

Declaration of Independence, 1776

1 Tighter British Control

TERMS & NAMES
King George III
Quartering Act
revenue
Sugar Act
Stamp Act
Patrick Henry
boycott
Sons of Liberty

6

5

MAIN IDEA	WHY IT MATTERS NOW
Americans saw British efforts to tax them and to increase control over the colonies as violations of their rights.	Colonial protests were the first steps on the road to American independence.

7 ONE AMERICAN'S STORY

James Otis, Jr., a young Massachusetts lawyer, stormed through the streets of Boston one day in 1760. He was furious. His father had just been denied the post of chief justice of the Massachusetts colony by the royal governor. To Otis, this was one more example of Britain's lack of respect for colonial rights. Another example was its use of search warrants that allowed customs officers to enter any home or business to look for smuggled goods. Otis believed these searches were illegal.

Otis took up a case against the government that involved these search warrants. In court in February 1761, Otis spoke with great emotion for five hours about the search warrant and its use.

A VOICE FROM THE PAST
It appears to me the worst instrument of arbitrary power, the most destructive of English liberty and the fundamental principles of law, that was ever found in an English law-book.
James Otis, Jr., quoted in *James Otis: The Pre-Revolutionist* by J. C. Ridpath

Spectators listened in amazement. One of them, a young lawyer named John Adams, later wrote of Otis's performance: "Then and there, in the old Council Chamber, the child Independence was born."

In making the first public speech demanding English liberties for the colonists, James Otis planted a seed of freedom. In this section, you will read more about the early protests against Britain's policies in America.

James Otis, Jr., argues in court against illegal search warrants in 1761.

8 The Colonies and Britain Grow Apart

During the French and Indian War, Britain and the colonies fought side by side. Americans took great pride in being partners in the victory over the French. However, when the war ended, problems arose. Britain wanted to govern its 13 original colonies and the territories gained in the war in a uniform way. So the British Parliament in London imposed new laws and restrictions. Previously, the colonies had been allowed to develop largely on their own. Now they felt that their freedom was being limited.

What Do You Want to Know?
What questions do you have about the issues and events that pushed the American colonists toward rebellion? Record them in your notebook before you read the chapter.

Use Active Reading Strategies As You Read

Now you're ready to read the chapter. Read one section at a time, from beginning to end.

1 Ask and answer questions as you read. Look for the **Reading History** questions in the margin. Answering these will show whether you understand what you've just read.

2 Try to visualize the people, places, and events you read about. Studying the pictures and any illustrated features will help you do this.

3 Read to build your vocabulary. Use the marginal **Vocabulary** notes to find the meaning of unfamiliar terms.

4 Look for the story behind the events. Read **Background** notes in the margin for additional information on people, places, events, and ideas.

Reading **History**
A. Summarizing
Who was upset by the Proclamation of 1763?

The first of Parliament's laws was the Proclamation of 1763. (See Chapter 5.) It said that colonists could not settle west of the Appalachian Mountains. Britain wanted this land to remain in the hands of its Native American allies to prevent another revolt like Pontiac's Rebellion.

The proclamation angered colonists who had hoped to move to the fertile Ohio Valley. Many of these colonists had no land of their own. It also upset colonists who had bought land as an investment. As a result, many ignored the law.

Reading **History**
A. Summarizing
Who was upset by the Proclamation of 1763?

British Troops and Taxes

King George III, the British monarch, wanted to enforce the proclamation and also keep peace with Britain's Native American allies. To do this, he decided to keep 10,000 soldiers in the colonies. In 1765, Parliament passed the **Quartering Act**. This was a cost-saving measure that required the colonies to quarter, or house, British soldiers and provide them with supplies. General Thomas Gage, commander of these forces, put most of the troops in New York.

Britain owed a large debt from the French and Indian War. Keeping troops in the colonies would raise that debt even higher. Britain needed more **revenue**, or income, to meet its expenses. So it attempted to have the colonies pay part of the war debt. It also wanted them to contribute toward the costs of frontier defense and colonial government.

In the past, the king had asked the colonial assemblies to pass taxes to support military actions that took place in the colonies. This time, however, Parliament voted to tax the Americans directly.

In 1764, Parliament passed the **Sugar Act**. This law placed a tax on sugar, molasses, and other products shipped to the colonies. It also called for strict enforcement of the act and harsh punishment of smugglers. Colonial merchants, who often traded in smuggled goods, reacted with anger.

Colonial leaders such as James Otis claimed that Parliament had no right to tax the colonies, since the colonists were not represented in Parliament. As Otis exclaimed, "Taxation without representation is tyranny!" British finance minister George Grenville disagreed. The colonists were subjects of Britain, he said, and enjoyed the protection of its laws. For that reason, they were subject to taxation.

3
Vocabulary
tyranny:
absolute power
in the hands of
a single ruler

Britain Passes the Stamp Act

The Sugar Act was just the first in a series of acts that increased tension between the mother country and the colonies. In 1765, Parliament passed the **Stamp Act**. This law required all legal and commercial documents to carry an official stamp showing that a tax had been paid. All diplomas, contracts, and wills had to carry a stamp.

2
The colonial view of the hated stamp tax is shown by the skull and crossbones on this emblem (above); a royal stamp is pictured at right.

Even published materials such as newspapers had to be written on special stamped paper.

The Stamp Act was a new kind of tax for the colonies. The Sugar Act had been a tax on imported goods. It mainly affected merchants. In contrast, the Stamp Act was a tax applied within the colonies. It fell directly on all colonists. Even more, the colonists had to pay for stamps in silver coin—a scarce item in the colonies.

Colonial leaders vigorously protested. For them, the issue was clear. They were being taxed without their consent by a Parliament in which they had no voice. If Britain could pass the Stamp Act, what other taxes might it pass in the future? Samuel Adams, a leader in the Massachusetts legislature, asked, "Why not our lands? Why not the produce of our lands and, in short, everything we possess and make use of?" **Patrick Henry**, a member of Virginia's House of Burgesses, called for resistance to the tax. When another member shouted that resistance was treason, Henry replied, "If this be treason, make the most of it!"

The Colonies Protest the Stamp Act

Colonial assemblies and newspapers took up the cry—"No taxation without representation!" In October 1765, nine colonies sent delegates to the Stamp Act Congress in New York City. This was the first time the colonies met to consider acting together in protest. Delegates drew up a petition to the king protesting the Stamp Act. The petition declared that the right to tax the colonies belonged to the colonial assemblies, not to Parliament. Later, colonial merchants organized a **boycott** of British goods. A boycott is a refusal to buy.

Meanwhile, some colonists formed secret societies to oppose British policies. The most famous of these groups was the **Sons of Liberty**. Many Sons of Liberty were lawyers, merchants, and craftspeople—the colonists most affected by the Stamp Act. These groups staged protests against the act.

Not all of their protests were peaceful. The Sons of Liberty burned the stamped paper whenever they could find it. They also attacked customs officials, whom they covered with hot tar and feathers and paraded in public. Fearing for their safety, many customs officials quit their jobs.

The protests in the colonies had an effect in Britain. Merchants thought that their trade with America would be hurt. Some British political leaders, including

Reading **History**
B. Making Inferences Why did the colonists boycott goods?

Background
To voice their protests, the Sons of Liberty in Boston met under a huge, 120-year-old elm tree that they called the Liberty Tree.

4

2

Colonists protest the Stamp Act.

Vocabulary
tyranny:
absolute power
in the hands of
a single ruler

Background
To voice their
protests, the
Sons of Liberty in
Boston met
under a huge,
120-year-old elm
tree that they
called the Liberty
Tree.

Review and Summarize What You Have Read

When you finish reading a section, review and summarize what you've read. If necessary, go back and reread information that was not clear the first time through.

5 Reread the red headlines for a quick summary of the major points covered in the section.

6 Study any charts, graphs, and maps in the section. These visual materials usually provide a condensed version of information in the section.

7 Review the pictures and note how they relate to the section content.

8 Complete all the questions in the **Section Assessment.** They will help you think critically about what you have just read.

---

immediately offered Massachusetts their support. They sent food and money to Boston. The committees of correspondence also called for a meeting of colonial delegates to discuss what to do next.

5 ### The First Continental Congress Meets

In September 1774, delegates from all the colonies except Georgia met in Philadelphia. At this meeting, called the **First Continental Congress,** delegates voted to ban all trade with Britain until the Intolerable Acts were repealed. They also called on each colony to begin training troops. Georgia agreed to be a part of the actions of the Congress even though it had voted not to send delegates.

The First Continental Congress marked a key step in American history. Although most delegates were not ready to call for independence, they were determined to uphold colonial rights. This meeting planted the seeds of a future independent government. John Adams called it "a nursery of American statesmen." The delegates agreed to meet in seven months, if necessary. By that time, however, fighting with Britain had begun.

Reading History
A. Evaluating Why do you think the First Continental Congress was important?

Between War and Peace

The colonists hoped that the trade boycott would force a repeal of the Intolerable Acts. After all, past boycotts had led to the repeal of the Stamp Act and the Townshend Acts. This time, however, Parliament stood firm. It even increased restrictions on colonial trade and sent more troops.

By the end of 1774, some colonists were preparing to fight. In Massachusetts, John Hancock headed the Committee of Safety, which had the power to call out the militia. The colonial troops continued to train.

6

CAUSE AND EFFECT: Growing Conflict Between Britain and America

DATE	BRITISH ACTION		COLONIAL REACTION
1763	Proclamation of 1763 issued	▶	Proclamation leads to anger
1765	Stamp Act passed	▶	Boycott of British goods; Stamp Act Resolves passed
1766	Stamp Act repealed; Declaration Act passed	▶	Boycott ended
1767	Townshend Acts passed	▶	New boycotts; Boston Massacre (March 1770)
1770	Townshend Acts repealed (April)	▶	Tension between colonies and Britain reduced
1773	Tea Act passed	▶	Boston Tea Party
1774	Intolerable Acts passed	▶	First Continental Congress bans trade; militias organized
1775	Troops ordered to Lexington and Concord, Massachusetts	▶	Militia fights British troops; Second Continental Congress; Continental Army established

SKILLBUILDER Interpreting Charts
1. What British action caused the first violence in the growing conflict between Britain and America?
2. How might the Intolerable Acts be seen as a reaction as well as an action?

When the British moved, so did Revere and Dawes. They galloped over the countryside on their "midnight ride," spreading the news. In Lexington, they were joined by Dr. Samuel Prescott. When Revere and Dawes were stopped by a British patrol, Prescott broke away and carried the message to Concord.

Lexington and Concord

At dawn on April 19, some 700 British troops reached Lexington. They found Captain John Parker and about 70 militiamen waiting. The British commander ordered the Americans to drop their muskets. They refused. No one knows who fired first, but within a few minutes eight militiamen lay dead. The British then marched to Concord, where they destroyed military supplies. A battle broke out at a bridge north of town, forcing the British to retreat.

Nearly 4,000 Minutemen and militiamen arrived in the area. They lined the road from Concord to Lexington and peppered the retreating redcoats with musket fire. "It seemed as if men came down from the clouds," one soldier said. Only the arrival of 1,000 more troops saved the British from destruction as they scrambled back to Boston.

Background
British losses totaled 273 soldiers compared to 95 militiamen.

Lexington and Concord were the first battles of the Revolutionary War. As Ralph Waldo Emerson later wrote, colonial troops had fired the "shot heard 'round the world." Americans would now have to choose sides and back up their political opinions by force of arms. Those who supported the British were called **Loyalists.** Those who sided with the rebels were **Patriots.** The conflict between the two sides divided communities, families, and friends. The war was on!

Reading History
C. Drawing Conclusions Why did Emerson call it the "shot heard 'round the world"?

7 Now *and* then

PATRIOTS' DAY
The "shot heard 'round the world" is celebrated every year in Massachusetts and Maine. Patriots' Day, as it is called, is the third Monday of April. In Concord and nearby towns, modern-day Minutemen like those below reenact the battle that began the Revolution on April 19, 1775. The Boston Marathon is also run on Patriots' Day.

---

8 ### Section 3 Assessment

1. Terms & Names
Identify:
• militia
• Minuteman
• Intolerable Acts
• First Continental Congress
• Paul Revere
• Lexington and Concord
• Loyalist
• Patriot

2. Taking Notes
Use a diagram like the one below to show events that led to the Revolutionary War.

☐ → ☐ → ☐

☐ → Revolution

3. Main Ideas
a. Why did Britain pass the Intolerable Acts?

b. Who took part in the First Continental Congress?

c. What was the purpose of the "midnight ride"?

4. Critical Thinking
Supporting Opinions
Do you think the fighting between Britain and the colonies could have been avoided? Why or why not?

THINK ABOUT
• Britain's attitude toward the colonies
• colonial feelings about Britain

ACTIVITY OPTIONS
GEOGRAPHY
MATH
Research the Battles of Lexington and Concord. Draw a map of key events or create a chart showing statistics from the battles.

Part 2: Test-Taking Strategies and Practice

Improve your test-taking skills by practicing the strategies discussed in this section. Read the tips on the left-hand page. Then apply them to the practice items on the right-hand page.

Multiple Choice

A multiple-choice question consists of a stem and a set of choices. The stem is usually in the form of a question or an incomplete sentence. One of the choices correctly answers the question or completes the sentence.

1 Read the stem carefully and try to answer the question or complete the sentence without looking at the choices.

2 Pay close attention to key words in the stem. They may direct you toward the correct answer.

3 Read each choice with the stem. Don't jump to conclusions about the correct answer until you've read all of the choices.

4 Think carefully about questions that include *All of the above* among the choices.

5 After reading all of the choices, eliminate any that you know are incorrect.

6 Use modifiers to help narrow your choice.

7 Look for the best answer among the remaining choices.

stem

1 1 At the beginning of the Revolution, (most) **2** Americans were

Most is a key word here. Replacing it with *all* or *some* changes the sentence and calls for a different answer.

3 choices

  A united in support of the war.
  B Patriots who wanted independence from Great Britain.
  C against a war with Great Britain.
  D Loyalists who supported the British point of view.

2 Which of the following present-day states was ceded to the United States in the Treaty of Guadalupe Hidalgo?

  A Arizona
  B California
  C New Mexico
  D All of the above **4**

If you select this answer, be sure that all of the choices are correct.

3 At the outset of the Civil War, both the Union and the Confederacy wanted the support of the border states

  A Delaware, Maryland, Kentucky, and Oklahoma.

5 You can eliminate **A** if you remember that Oklahoma was not a state at the time of the Civil War.

  B Delaware, Maryland, Kentucky, and Missouri.

  C Delaware, Maryland, West Virginia, Kentucky, and Missouri.

  D (all) the states bordering the Missouri Compromise line.

6 Absolute words, such as *all, never, always, every,* and *only,* often signal an incorrect choice.

7 In **C**, West Virginia did lie on the border between the Union and the Confederacy. However, it broke away from Virginia early in the war and became a state in 1863. Therefore, **B** is the correct answer.

answers: 1 (C), 2 (D), 3 (B)

Directions: Read the following questions and choose the *best* answer from the four choices.

1 New inventions that helped open the Great Plains to farming included

  A the steel windmill.

  B barbed wire.

  C the spring-tooth harrow.

  D All of the above

2 The movement of Puritans from England to North America in the 1620s and 1630s is known as the Great

  A Awakening.

  B Compromise.

  C Debate.

  D Migration.

3 During the presidency of Thomas Jefferson, the United States was able to foster westward expansion when it acquired territory in what is known as

  A Seward's Folly.

  B the Missouri Compromise.

  C the Kansas-Nebraska Act.

  D the Louisiana Purchase.

4 Who commanded the Texan forces at the Alamo?

  A James Fannin

  B David Crockett

  C William Travis

  D Sam Houston

Primary Sources

Primary sources are materials written or made by people who took part in or witnessed historical events. Letters, diaries, speeches, newspaper articles, and autobiographies are all primary sources. So, too, are legal documents, such as wills, deeds, and financial records.

1 Look at the source line and identify the author. Consider what qualifies the author to write about the events discussed in the passage.

2 Skim the document to form an idea of what it is about.

3 Note special punctuation. Ellipses indicate that words or sentences have been removed from the original passage. Brackets indicate words that were not in the original. Bracketed words often are replacements for difficult or unfamiliar terms.

4 Carefully read the passage and distinguish between facts and the author's opinions. (That the groups of soldiers were wandering in all directions is a fact. The reasons for their wandering offered by Madison are her opinions.)

5 Consider for whom the author was writing. The intended audience may influence what and how an author writes.

6 Before rereading the passage, skim the questions to identify the information you need to find.

answers: 1 (D), 2 (B)

The Flight from the White House

2 *Wednesday Morning, twelve o'clock.* Since sunrise I have been turning my spy-glass in every direction, . . . but alas! I can **3** see **4** only groups of military, wandering in all directions, as if there was a lack of arms, or of spirit to fight for their own fireside.

Three o'clock. Will you believe it, my sister? we have had a battle, or skirmish, near Bladensburg, and here I am still, within sound of the cannon!. . . Two messengers covered with dust come to bid me fly. . . . At this late hour a wagon has been [found], and I have had it filled with plate and the most valuable portable articles belonging to the house. Whether it will reach its destination . . . or fall into the hands of British soldiery, events must determine. Our kind friend, Mr. Carroll, has come to hasten my departure, and is in a very bad humor with me, because I insist on waiting until the large picture of General Washington is secured. . . . It is done! and the precious portrait placed in the hands of two gentlemen of New York, for safe keeping. And now, dear sister, I must leave this house. . . . When I shall again write to you, or where I shall be tomorrow, I cannot tell!

1 The author is Dolley Madison, the wife of President James Madison. She personally oversaw the evacuation of the White House in 1814.

—Dolley Madison, in a letter to her sister describing her flight from the White House in August 1814

5 This is a letter. If it were an official report to Congress, the style and content would be much different.

6 **1** Dolley Madison's letter describes her preparations to flee the White House in advance of a British attack. In which war did this attack take place?

A War of Jenkins' Ear

B French and Indian War

C Revolutionary War

D War of 1812

2 Why might Dolley Madison be considered a good source of information on the British attack on Washington, D.C.?

A She was the wife of President James Madison.

B She was an eyewitness to the attack.

C She helped her husband develop military policy.

D She had intercepted British war plans.

Directions: Read the following passage written in the 1800s. Use the passage and your knowledge of U.S. history to answer the questions below.

Life in Texas, Mid-1800s

I wish that I could emphasize this feature of our early Texan life. *The spirit of helpfulness and friendly fellowship always prevailed. It was one of the best of the good things of the new country.* We were all strangers together, always willing to lend or borrow. . . . Once Mr. Van Zandt was called away from home . . . [and] another man came and took our gun and killed a deer, for he knew we needed meat. . . . When our need for things was pressing, we usually found a way for making them. One time Mr. Van Zandt needed a saddle—he made it, having only a drawing knife from which to fashion the saddle-tree from a dead sassafras tree which he cut down for the purpose. His shoes were gone and he could get no others. He bought some red leather, made a last [a foot-shaped, wooden block] and manufactured some very respectable shoes.

—Frances Cook Lipscomb Van Zandt,
Texas settler, 1839–1846

1 What was a good thing about the new Texas country that the author writes was important to her?

A Being hungry

B Being a stranger

C The spirit of helpfulness and friendliness

D Getting deer meat whenever she wanted it

2 Mr. Van Zandt used leather, wood, and simple tools to

A build a wagon.

B make goods to trade for meat.

C build a spinning wheel.

D make a saddle and shoes.

3 According to the passage, the Van Zandts and their Texas neighbors got their supplies in all of the following ways *except* by

A lending or borrowing things.

B making them by hand with simple tools.

C buying them from mail-order catalogs.

D volunteering to help each other.

4 Frances Van Zandt wrote, "We were all strangers together," to explain that hardships on the Texas frontier

A left people isolated and alone.

B drew people together to help each other.

C were shared only by close friends and relatives.

D made people suspicious of one another.

Passage from "Frances Cook Lipscomb Van Zandt Reminisces About the Early Years in Texas, 1839–1846," from the Van Zandt Folder, Mary Daggett Lake Papers, series IV, box 3, Fort Worth Public Library, Fort Worth, Texas. Courtesy of the Fort Worth Public Library, Fort Worth, Texas.

Secondary Sources

Secondary sources are descriptions or interpretations of historical events made by people who were not at those events. The most common types of written secondary sources are history books, encyclopedias, and biographies. A secondary source often combines information from several primary sources.

1 Read titles to preview what the passage is about.

2 Look for topic sentences. These, too, will help you preview the content of the passage.

3 As you read, use context clues to help you understand difficult or unfamiliar words. (You can tell from the description of the battle in the previous sentences that the word *fiasco* must mean something like "disaster," "failure," or "blunder.")

4 As you read, ask and answer questions that come to mind. You might ask: Why would the Washington raid embarrass and anger Americans? Why did the Washington raid achieve little?

5 Before rereading the passage, skim the questions to identify the information you need to find.

1 **The British Offensive**

2 Ironically, Britain's most spectacular success began as a diversion from [its main] offensive [in the North]. A British army that had come up from Bermuda entered Chesapeake Bay and on August 24, 1814, met a larger American force . . . at Bladensburg, Maryland. The Battle of Bladensburg deteriorated into the "Bladensburg Races" as the American troops fled, virtually without firing a shot. The British then descended on Washington, D.C. Madison, who had witnessed the **3** Bladensburg fiasco, fled into the Virginia hills. His wife, Dolley, loaded her silver, a bed, and a portrait of George Washington onto her carriage before joining him. British troops ate the supper prepared for the Madisons and then burned the presidential mansion **4** and other public buildings in the capital. Beyond embarrassing and angering Americans, the Washington raid accomplished little, for after a failed attack on Baltimore, the British broke off the operation.

—Paul S. Boyer, et al., *The Enduring Vision*

5 1 Why do you think the authors refer to the Battle of Bladensburg as a "fiasco"?

A Because the American forces fled almost without a fight

B Because President Madison had to flee the White House

C Because it allowed the British to attack Washington, D.C.

D Because it was a famous victory for the British forces

2 What, according to the authors, did the British raid on Washington, D.C., accomplish?

A It paved the way for the British capture of Baltimore.

B It burned down all the public buildings in the city.

C It helped the British offensive in the North.

D It embarrassed and angered many Americans.

Remember to be wary of choices that contain absolutes, such as *all*, *every*, or *only*.

answers: 1 (A), 2 (D)

S10

Directions: Use the passage and your knowledge of U.S. history to answer the questions below.

African-American Sailors

African Americans contributed greatly to the growth of maritime commerce in the United States. Beginning in colonial times, slaves, with their masters' permission, hired themselves out as sailors. Some served as translators on slave ships. Merchant ships also offered a means of escape for runaway slaves. A few escapees even took to the sea as pirates.

Seafaring was one of the few occupations open to free African Americans. They served on clippers, naval vessels, and whaling ships from the 1700s into the late 1800s. Federal crew lists from Atlantic seaports show that during this time African Americans made up 10 percent or more of sailors on American ships. Seafaring was an especially dangerous line of work for free blacks. They risked capture in southern ports, where they were often thrown in jail or sold into slavery.

1   What records show that African Americans made up 10 percent or more of sailors on American ships?

A Shipyard records

B Family Bibles

C Federal crew lists

D Ships' logs

2   The passage implies that free and enslaved African Americans went to sea for all of the following reasons *except* to

A escape slavery.

B live as pirates.

C earn wages as sailors.

D discover new lands.

3   The author states that life was especially dangerous for free African-American sailors because

A American prosperity depended on their work alone.

B the worst jobs on board ship were always assigned to them.

C they ran the risk of capture and enslavement in southern ports.

D they were more likely than white sailors to contract scurvy.

Political Cartoons

Political cartoons are drawings that express views on political issues of the day. Cartoonists use symbols and such artistic styles as caricature—exaggerating a person's physical features—to get their message across.

1 Identify the subject of the cartoon. Titles and captions often indicate the subject matter.

2 Identify the main characters in the cartoon. Here, the main character is Horace Greeley, a candidate in the 1872 presidential election.

3 Note the symbols—ideas or images that stand for something else—used in the cartoon.

4 Study labels and other written information in the cartoon.

5 Analyze the point of view. How cartoonists use caricature often indicates how they feel. The exaggeration of Greeley's physical appearance—short and overweight—makes him appear comical.

6 Interpret the cartoonist's message.

The cartoonist shows Tammany Hall, New York's Democratic political machine, as a tiger. Uncle Sam, a symbol for the United States, is shown looking on.

The writing on the wall suggests that Tammany Hall wants reform. The "Whitewash" label on the bucket suggests that the tiger's true, corrupt, stripes are just being covered up.

Thomas Nast, *Harper's Weekly*, August 31, 1872

1 "What are you going to do about it, if 'Old Honesty' lets him loose again?"

1 Based on the cartoon, what do you think was Horace Greeley's major issue in the 1872 presidential campaign?

A Political reform

B States' rights

C Abolition

D Temperance

2 Which one of the following statements do you think *best* represents the cartoonist's point of view?

A Horace Greeley is an honest man.

B Tammany Hall supports political reform.

C Tammany Hall, regardless of Greeley's view, is still corrupt.

D Horace Greeley, like most Tammany politicians, is corrupt.

answers: 1 (A), 2 (C)

Directions: Use the cartoon and your knowledge of U.S. history to answer the questions below.

Anonymous, 1858

THE LITTLE GIANT.. IN THE CHARACTER OF THE GLADIATOR.

1   Stephen A. Douglas is portrayed as a
     gladiator armed with the sword and
     shield of

   A Congress and the rule of law.

   B freedom of speech and of the press.

   C constitutional and property rights of
     slaveholders.

   D voting rights and self-government for
     the territories.

2   Popular sovereignty was used in the
     1850s to address the issue of

   A states' rights.

   B federalism.

   C slavery.

   D voting rights.

3   The cartoon illustrates the fight over
     whether to

   A admit Kansas into the Union as a free
     state or a proslavery state.

   B grant freedom of the press to
     newspapers in the territories.

   C allow sword fighting and dueling as
     legal activities in the 1850s.

   D replace a system of majority rule with
     a monarchy.

Charts

Charts present information in a visual form. History textbooks use several types of charts, including tables, flow charts, Venn diagrams, and info-graphics. The type of chart most commonly found in standardized tests is the table. It organizes information in columns and rows for easy viewing.

❶ Read the title and identify the broad subject of the chart.

❷ Read the column and row headings and any other labels. This will provide more details about the subject of the chart.

❸ Compare and contrast the information from column to column and row to row.

❹ Try to draw conclusions from the information in the chart. Ask yourself: What patterns are apparent in the chart?

❺ Read the questions and then study the chart again.

❶ **Trails West, 1850**

❷

Trail	Start/End Point	Distance	Time Taken	Average Daily Distance	Best Time to Travel
California Trail	Fort Hall, Id./Sutter's Fort, Calif.	700 miles	About 6 weeks	15 miles	Summer months
Mormon Trail	Iowa/Great Salt Lake, Ut.	1,300 miles	2–3 months	15–20 miles	May–September
Old Spanish Trail	Santa Fe/Los Angeles	1,200 miles	10–12 weeks	12–15 miles	Spring–early summer
Oregon Trail	Missouri/Oregon	2,000 miles	4–6 months	10–15 miles	April–September
Santa Fe Trail	Missouri/Santa Fe	800 miles	6–8 weeks	12–20 miles	Early spring–early summer

❹

Compare and contrast the distance, time taken, and average daily distance traveled for each trail. ❸

❺ **1** What was the best time of year for travel on most of the trails?

    A Spring and summer

    B Summer and fall

    C April

    D September

2 On which trails did travelers sometimes average 20 miles per day?

    A California and Oregon trails

    B Santa Fe and Old Spanish trails

    C Mormon and Santa Fe trails

    D Oregon and Mormon trails

answers: 1 (A), 2 (C)

Directions: Use the charts and your knowledge of U.S. history to answer the questions below.

Percentage of Population Free and Enslaved, by States and Territories, 1790

North		
State/Territory	Free	Enslaved
Connecticut	98.9	1.1
Delaware	85.0	15.0
Maine	100.0	0.0
Massachusetts	100.0	0.0
New Hampshire	99.9	0.1
New Jersey	93.8	6.2
New York	93.8	6.2
Pennsylvania	99.1	0.9
Rhode Island	98.6	1.4
Vermont	100.0	0.0

South		
State/Territory	Free	Enslaved
Georgia	64.5	35.5
Kentucky	83.1	16.9
Maryland	67.8	32.2
North Carolina	74.5	25.5
South Carolina	57.0	43.0
Virginia	60.9	39.1

Source: Inter-University Consortium for Political and Social Research

1 The state with the highest percentage of enslaved people was

A New Hampshire.

B North Carolina.

C Rhode Island.

D South Carolina.

2 Which of the following *best* describes most states in the North?

A The population was more than 98 percent free.

B More than 10 percent of the population was enslaved.

C Less than 60 percent of the population was free.

D The population was more than 20 percent enslaved.

3 Which statement about the percentage of enslaved people is true?

A It was much lower in the South.

B It was much higher in the South.

C There was no difference between the regions.

D There was a slight difference between the regions.

4 What economic factor *best* explains the population differences between the regions?

A The North focused on manufacturing.

B The North was wealthy enough to free enslaved people.

C The South focused on plantation agriculture.

D The South needed enslaved people for factory work.

Line and Bar Graphs

Graphs show statistics in a visual form. Line graphs are particularly useful for showing changes over time. Bar graphs make it easy to compare numbers or sets of numbers.

① Read the title and identify the broad subject of the graph.

② Study the labels on the vertical and horizontal axes to see the kinds of information presented in the graph. Note the intervals between amounts and between dates. This will help you read the graph more efficiently.

③ Look at the source line and evaluate the reliability of the information in the graph. Government statistics on population tend to be reliable.

④ Study the information in the graph and note any trends.

⑤ Draw conclusions and make generalizations based on these trends.

⑥ Read the questions carefully and then study the graph again.

① United States Population, 1800–1850

Grid lines make the information on the graph easier to read.

③ Source: *Historical Statistics of the United States*

⑥ 1 The United States population rose above 10,000,000 between

    A 1810 and 1820.

    B 1820 and 1830.

    C 1830 and 1840.

    D 1840 and 1850.

① United States Urban Population, 1800–1850

A generalization you might make here is that urban population grew markedly between 1840 and 1850.

③ Source: *Historical Statistics of the United States*

⑥ 2 Which of the following sentences *best* describes the trend shown in the bar graph?

    A United States urban population steadily increased.

    B United States urban population showed little change.

    C United States urban population rose and fell.

    D United States urban population decreased steadily.

answers: 1 (B), 2 (A)

Directions: Use the graphs and your knowledge of U.S. history to answer the questions below.

Growth of the African-American Population, 1820–1860

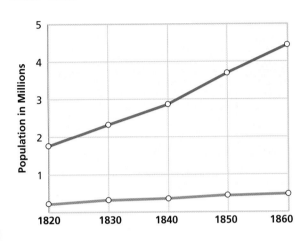

■ Total Population
■ Free Population

Source: Gilder Lehrman Institute of American History

Churches by Denomination, 1750

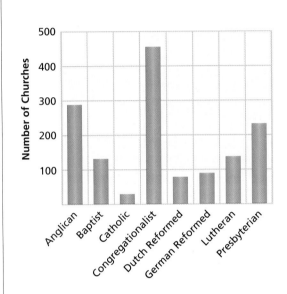

Source: Gilder Lehrman Institute of American History

1 In which decade did the total African-American population first exceed 3.5 million?

  A 1820–1830

  B 1830–1840

  C 1840–1850

  D 1850–1860

2 About how many times larger than the enslaved population was the free population in 1860?

  A Four

  B Five

  C Six

  D Eight

3 Which one of the following statements accurately reflects information in the graph?

  A There were more Congregationalist churches than all other denominations combined.

  B There were more Presbyterian churches than Anglican churches.

  C The Baptists had the fewest churches.

  D The Congregationalists had the most churches.

4 In which colony might you expect the most Catholics to live?

  A Georgia

  B Maryland

  C Massachusetts

  D Virginia

Pie Graphs

A pie, or circle, graph shows relationships among the parts of a whole. These parts look like slices of a pie. The size of each slice is proportional to the percentage of the whole that it represents.

1 Read the title and identify the broad subject of the pie graph.

2 Look at the legend to see what each slice of the pie represents.

3 Read the source line and note the origin of the data shown in the pie graph.

4 Compare the slices of the pie and try to make generalizations and draw conclusions from your comparisons.

5 Read the questions carefully and review difficult or unfamiliar terms.

6 Eliminate choices that you know are wrong.

1 **The Popular Vote in the 1860 Presidential Election**

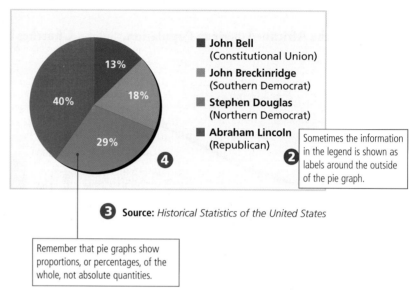

■ **John Bell** (Constitutional Union)
■ **John Breckinridge** (Southern Democrat)
■ **Stephen Douglas** (Northern Democrat)
■ **Abraham Lincoln** (Republican)

2 Sometimes the information in the legend is shown as labels around the outside of the pie graph.

3 **Source:** *Historical Statistics of the United States*

Remember that pie graphs show proportions, or percentages, of the whole, not absolute quantities.

1 In the 1860 presidential election, Abraham Lincoln won

A by a landslide.

B a majority of the votes cast.

C a plurality of the votes cast.

D by a narrow margin.

5 In electoral terms, the word *landslide* refers to an overwhelming victory, *majority* means "more than 50 percent," and *plurality* means "the most but less than 50 percent."

2 What political situation in 1860 does the pie graph show?

A The Democratic Party was split into northern and southern wings before the 1860 election.

B The Republican Party was not yet an important force in national politics.

C Douglas won fewer popular votes than Lincoln but won more electoral votes.

D Because no candidate won a majority of the popular votes, the House of Representatives decided the election.

6 You can eliminate **B** when you notice that the Republican Party received more votes than any other.

answers: 1 (C), 2 (A)

Directions: Use the pie graph and your knowledge of U.S. history to answer the questions below.

Ethnic Makeup of the Colonial Population, 1775

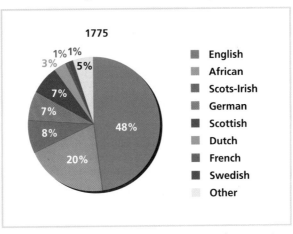

Source: Gilder Lehrman Institute of American History

1 The largest ethnic group in the colonial population of 1775 was

A African.

B Dutch.

C English.

D French.

2 What percentage of the colonial population arrived mostly against its own will?

A 5%

B 8%

C 20%

D 48%

3 The area between the Connecticut and Delaware rivers, now known as New York, was first colonized in the 1600s by the

A Dutch.

B English.

C Swedes.

D Germans.

4 What was the largest group of non-English-speaking Europeans to settle in the colonies?

A Swedes

B Dutch

C Germans

D French

Political Maps

Political maps show countries and the political divisions within countries—states, for example. They also show the location of major cities. In addition, political maps often show physical features, such as rivers, seas, oceans, and mountain ranges.

1 Read the title to determine the subject and purpose of the map.

2 Read the labels on the map. This will reveal information about the map's subject and purpose.

3 Study the legend to find the meaning of symbols used on the map.

4 Look at the lines of latitude and longitude. This grid makes locating places much easier.

5 Use the compass rose to determine directions on the map.

6 Use the scale to estimate the distances between places shown on the map.

7 Read the questions and then carefully study the map to determine the answers.

1 Middle Colonies to 1700

Instead of a compass rose, some maps have a North arrow.

Map scales typically show distances in both miles and kilometers.

7 1 Which of the following bodies of water formed part of the border between New Netherland and the English middle colonies?

   A Lake Erie

   B Lake Huron

   C Delaware River

   D Hudson River

2 Which entire English colony was once part of New Netherland?

   A New York

   B New Jersey

   C Pennsylvania

   D All of the above

answers: 1 (C), 2 (B)

Directions: Use the map and your knowledge of U.S. history to answer the questions below.

New States, 1816–1848

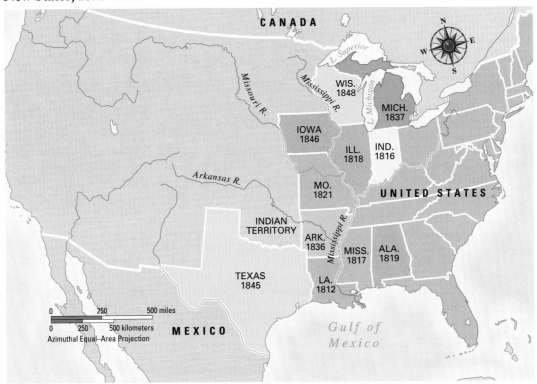

1 Which state joined the Union in 1845?

  A Iowa

  B Illinois

  C Wisconsin

  D Texas

2 The Mississippi River forms the western border of which of the following states?

  A Missouri, Arkansas, and Louisiana

  B Illinois and Mississippi

  C Iowa and Missouri

  D Iowa, Missouri, and Arkansas

3 A barge filled with logs from Wisconsin is going to the Gulf of Mexico. It is most likely traveling

  A south on the Mississippi River.

  B west across the Great Plains.

  C north on the Arkansas River.

  D southwest through Indian Territory.

4 The states admitted to the Union in the 1840s were

  A Missouri, Wisconsin, and Illinois.

  B Kansas, Texas, and Iowa.

  C Texas, Wisconsin, and Iowa.

  D Illinois, Texas, and Wisconsin.

Thematic Maps

A thematic map, or special-purpose map, focuses on a particular topic. The location of baseball parks, a country's natural resources, election results, and major battles in a war are all topics you might see illustrated on a thematic map.

1 Read the title to determine the subject and purpose of the map.

2 Examine the labels on the map to find more information about the map's subject and purpose.

3 Study the legend to find the meaning of the symbols and colors used on the map.

4 Look at the colors and symbols on the map and try to identify patterns.

5 Read the questions and then carefully study the map to determine the answers.

1 **Southern Military Districts, 1867**

3 While a thematic map focuses on one topic, it often offers several kinds of information on that topic. Therefore, the legend for a thematic map is usually very detailed.

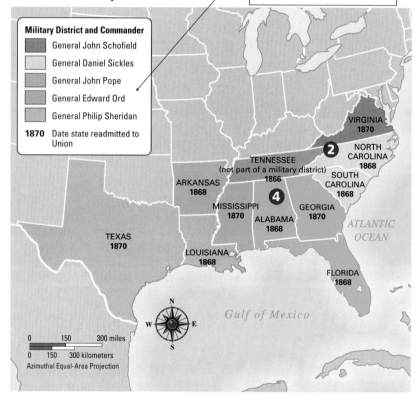

Military District and Commander
- General John Schofield
- General Daniel Sickles
- General John Pope
- General Edward Ord
- General Philip Sheridan

1870 Date state readmitted to Union

VIRGINIA 1870
NORTH CAROLINA 1868
TENNESSEE (not part of a military district) 1866
SOUTH CAROLINA 1868
ARKANSAS 1868
MISSISSIPPI 1870
ALABAMA 1868
GEORGIA 1870
ATLANTIC OCEAN
TEXAS 1870
LOUISIANA 1868
FLORIDA 1868
Gulf of Mexico

0   150   300 miles
0   150   300 kilometers
Azimuthal Equal-Area Projection

5 **1** Which former Confederate state was the first to be readmitted to the Union?

A Tennessee

B South Carolina

C Florida

D Alabama

2 The military district in which Texas was located was commanded by

A General Edward Ord.

B General John Pope.

C General Philip Sheridan.

D General Daniel Sickles.

answers: 1 (A), 2 (C)

Directions: Use the map and your knowledge of U.S. history to answer the questions below.

The Battle of San Jacinto, 1836

1 The Texan camp was located in what type of area?

A Swamp

B Ridge

C Woods

D Open plains

2 In which direction did the Texan forces move to attack the Mexican army?

A Directly south

B Northeast

C Directly east

D Southeast

3 An attack was launched on the Mexican forces from the west by

A Texan artillery.

B Texan cavalry.

C Texan infantry.

D All of the above

4 What was the importance of the Battle of San Jacinto?

A Texas won its independence from Mexico.

B It avenged the defeats at Goliad and the Alamo.

C Texas gained U.S. support in the struggle for freedom.

D It proved that the Texans were better fighters than the Mexicans.

Time Lines

A time line is a type of chart that lists events in the order in which they occurred. In other words, time lines are a visual method of showing what happened when.

1 Read the title to discover the subject of the time line.

2 Identify the time period covered by the time line by noting the earliest and latest dates shown. On vertical time lines, the earliest date is shown at the top. On horizontal time lines, it is on the far left.

3 Read the events and their dates in sequence. Notice the intervals between events.

4 Use your knowledge of history to develop a fuller picture of the events listed in the time line. For example, you might try to identify some of the leading individuals involved in the events.

5 Note how events are related to one another. Look particularly for cause-effect relationships.

6 Use the information you have gathered from the above strategies to answer the questions.

1 The Road to Revolution, 1765–1775

1765
Stamp Act passed, imposing first direct tax on American colonies; Sons of Liberty founded to oppose the act.

1773
Tea Act passed; colonists dumped tea in Boston Harbor at Boston Tea Party.

The Coercive Acts essentially placed Boston under military rule.

1774
Coercive Acts passed; First Continental Congress met in Philadelphia.

1767
Townshend Acts passed, imposing taxes on many imports; colonists began boycott of British goods.

1768
British troops sent to Boston to keep order.

1770
Boston Massacre

1775
Battles of Lexington and Concord

Boycotts were the major weapon that the colonists used to combat the actions of the British government.

6 1 How did the colonists respond to the passage of the Townshend Acts?

A They founded the Sons of Liberty.

B They dumped British tea in Boston Harbor.

C They began a boycott of British goods.

D They called the First Continental Congress.

2 About how much time passed between the Coercive Acts and the first battles of the Revolutionary War?

A One year

B Three years

C Seven years

D Nine years

answers: 1 (C), 2 (A)

Directions: Use the time line and your knowledge of U.S. history to answer the questions below.

The Erie Canal, 1816–1840s

1816
Former New York City Mayor DeWitt Clinton proposes building a canal to connect the Great Lakes to Albany.

1825
Erie Canal completed; shipping time from New York City to Buffalo reduced from 3 weeks to 8 days.

1836
Toll receipts exceed entire cost of construction; work begins to enlarge canal.

1840
New York City is now the busiest port in the U. S.

1815

1845

1817
New York state authorizes $7 million to build the 363-mile-long Erie Canal; construction begins.

1819
Mid-section of canal completed; first boat travels from Rome to Utica.

1829
3,640 bushels of wheat shipped down the canal.

1837
500,000 bushels of wheat transported down the canal.

1841
One million bushels of wheat shipped down the canal.

1 The Erie Canal was completed and ready for water traffic between Buffalo and Albany in

   A 1817.

   B 1819.

   C 1825.

   D 1840.

2 About how many years after the canal was finished did work begin to enlarge it?

   A 4 years

   B 6 years

   C 11 years

   D 21 years

3 Which of the following statements about the Erie Canal is *not* true?

   A The canal greatly reduced the time it took to ship goods between the Great Lakes and New York.

   B From 1837 to 1841, the volume of wheat shipped through the canal doubled.

   C The cost of building the canal was greater than the amount of tolls collected.

   D The mid-section of the canal was completed in 1819.

Constructed Response

Constructed-response questions focus on various kinds of documents. Each document usually is accompanied by a series of questions. These questions call for short answers that, for the most part, can be found directly in the document. Some answers, however, require knowledge of the subject or time period addressed in the document.

1 Read the title of the document to discover the subject addressed in the questions.

2 Study and analyze the document. Take notes on what you see.

3 Read the questions and then study the document again to locate the answers.

4 Carefully write your answers. Unless the directions say otherwise, your answers need not be complete sentences.

1 List of Purchases Made by Meriwether Lewis for the Expedition to the West

Item	Cost
Mathematical Instruments	$ 412.95
Arms, Ammunition, & Accouterments	182.08
Medicine, etc.	94.49
Clothing	317.73
Provision, etc.	366.70
Indian Presents	669.50
Camp Equipage	116.68
	$2,160.13

Source: National Archives and Records Administration

2 Constructed-response questions use a wide range of documents, including short passages, cartoons, charts, graphs, maps, time lines, posters, and other visual materials. The information in this chart is taken from the records kept by Meriwether Lewis.

3 1 What was the largest expense for Lewis and Clark's expedition to the West?

4 _Indian presents_

2 Why were arms and ammunition needed for the expedition?

for protection and for hunting for food

3 Why did Lewis and Clark carry mathematical instruments with them on their expedition to the West?

President Thomas Jefferson asked Lewis and Clark to make charts and to carry out scientific studies during the expedition.

Directions: Use the chart and your knowledge of U.S. history to answer the questions below.

First Amendment Rights: the Five Basic Freedoms

Freedom of Religion	People have the right to practice the religion of their choice.
Freedom of Speech	People have the right to state their ideas.
Freedom of the Press	People have the right to publish their ideas.
Freedom of Assembly	People have the right to meet peacefully in groups.
Freedom to Petition	People have the right to petition the government.

1   Does the first amendment guarantee you the right to belong to any religion you like?

2   You write a letter to the mayor asking for a stop sign to be placed at an intersection near your school. Which of the five basic freedoms are you exercising?

3   What specific activities are covered by freedom of speech, and what activities are covered by freedom of the press? How are the two freedoms related?

Extended Response

Extended-response questions, like constructed-response questions, usually focus on one kind of document. However, they are more complex and require more time to complete than typical short-answer constructed-response questions. Some extended-response questions ask you to complete a chart, graph, or diagram. Still others ask you to write an essay, a report, or some other lengthier piece based on the document.

① Read the title of the document to get an idea of the subject.

② Study and analyze the document. Take notes on your ideas.

③ Carefully read the extended-response questions. (Question 1 asks you to present the information in the chart in a time line. Question 2 asks you to write an essay by applying your knowledge of history to information in the chart.)

④ If the question calls for some type of diagram, make a rough sketch on scrap paper first. Then make a final copy of your diagram on the answer sheet.

⑤ If the question requires an extended piece of writing, jot down ideas in outline form. Use this outline to write your answer.

① **Ratifying the Constitution**

State	Date Ratified
Connecticut	January 9, 1788
Delaware	December 7, 1787
Georgia	January 2, 1788
Maryland	April 28, 1788
Massachusetts	February 6, 1788
New Hampshire	June 21, 1788
New Jersey	December 18, 1787
New York	July 26, 1788
North Carolina	November 21, 1789
Pennsylvania	December 12, 1787
Rhode Island	May 29, 1790
South Carolina	May 23, 1788
Virginia	June 25, 1788

②

④ For time lines and other diagrams, remember to include a title and all appropriate labels.

③ **1** Use the information in the chart and your knowledge of U.S. history to create a time line for the ratification of the Constitution.

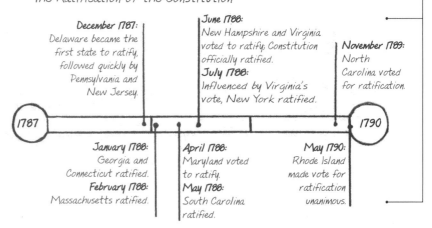

The Ratification of the Constitution

December 1787: Delaware became the first state to ratify, followed quickly by Pennsylvania and New Jersey.

June 1788: New Hampshire and Virginia voted to ratify; Constitution officially ratified.

July 1788: Influenced by Virginia's vote, New York ratified.

November 1789: North Carolina voted for ratification.

1787

1790

January 1788: Georgia and Connecticut ratified.
February 1788: Massachusetts ratified.

April 1788: Maryland voted to ratify.
May 1788: South Carolina ratified.

May 1790: Rhode Island made vote for ratification unanimous.

③ **2** Write a brief essay explaining the significance of the Bill of Rights to the ratification of the Constitution.

⑤ **Essay Rubric** The best essays will point out that the promise of a Bill of Rights was key to getting enough support to ensure ratification of the Constitution. The vote for ratification by Virginia—the largest of the states—was contingent upon the passage of a Bill of Rights.

For more test practice online . . .
i TEST PRACTICE
CLASSZONE.COM

Directions: Read the following passage and study the chart. Then follow the directions beneath the chart to write a short essay.

A Country Dividing

As the United States grew during the 1800s, Congress and the people argued about what form of government each new territory and state would have. The differences of opinion centered on one issue more than any other: slavery. Eventually, those sectional arguments led to the Civil War.

The chart below lists three acts of Congress that addressed the issue of slavery in the West. On the right are the provisions of each of these acts.

Act	Provisions
Missouri Compromise, 1820	1. Slavery was to be prohibited in the Louisiana territory north of the 36° 30′ parallel. 2. Missouri would enter the Union as a slave state. 3. Maine would enter the Union as a free state.
Compromise of 1850	1. The territories of New Mexico and Utah were created without restrictions on slavery. 2. California would enter the Union as a free state. 3. The slave trade would be prohibited in Washington, D.C. 4. Congress would pass a strong fugitive slave law for mandatory return of escaped slaves.
Kansas-Nebraska Act, 1854	1. Two new territories, Kansas and Nebraska, were created. 2. The people residing in the Kansas and Nebraska territories would have the right to decide whether their territory would enter the Union as a free or slave state (popular sovereignty). 3. The Kansas-Nebraska Act repealed the Missouri Compromise of 1820, which prohibited slavery in territories north of 36° 30′.

1 Write an essay explaining how the Missouri Compromise, the Compromise of 1850, and the Kansas-Nebraska Act promoted sectionalism.

Document-Based Questions

A document-based question focuses on several documents—both visual and written. These documents often are accompanied by short-answer questions. You then use the answers to these questions and information from the documents to write an essay on a specified subject.

1 Carefully read the "Historical Context" to get an indication of the issue addressed in the question.

2 Note the action words used in the "Task" section. These words tell you exactly what the essay question requires.

3 Study and analyze each document. Think about how the documents are connected to the essay question. Take notes on your ideas.

4 Read and answer each of the document-specific questions.

Introduction

1 **Historical Context:** During President George Washington's first term, political parties started to develop around the beliefs of two members of Washington's cabinet, Secretary of the Treasury Alexander Hamilton and Secretary of State Thomas Jefferson. Despite Washington's opposition to political parties, they had a great influence in American domestic and foreign policy.

2 **Task:** (Discuss) the role of the Federalist and the Democratic-Republican parties in the early republic, and (explain) why George Washington believed that political parties were divisive.

Part 1: Short Answer

Study each document carefully and answer the questions that follow.

Document 1: A Warning on Political Parties

3 Let me . . . warn you in the most solemn manner against the baneful [harmful] effects of the spirit of party generally. This spirit, unfortunately, is inseparable from our nature, having its root in the strongest passions of the human mind. . . .

It serves always to distract the public councils and enfeeble [weaken] the public administration. It agitates the community with illfounded jealousies and false alarms; kindles the animosity [hatred] of one part against another; foments occasionally riot and insurrection. It opens the door to foreign influence and corruption, which find a facilitated access [easy entry] to the government itself through the channels of party passions.

—George Washington, Farewell Address

4 **Why did Washington believe that political parties would harm the nation?**

He believed that political parties would have a bad effect on the nation by playing upon the jealousies of different factions and stirring up considerable trouble for the nation. Foreign governments might also find it easy to use political parties to influence our national affairs.

Document 2: Positions of the First United States Political Parties

Federalist Party	Democratic-Republican Party
Strong central government	Weak central government
Loose interpretation of the Constitution	Strict interpretation of the Constitution
Government should pay states' Revolutionary War debts	Each state should pay its own debts
Favored a national bank	Opposed a national bank
Favored business interests	Favored agricultural interests
Pro-British foreign policy	Pro-French foreign policy

How were the policies favored by the Federalists different from those favored by the Democratic-Republicans?

The parties held opposite views on major policy issues.

Document 3: Policy Dispute in Congress Hall, Philadelphia

The cartoon shows the two parties fighting over foreign policy. What does it imply about their ability to settle disagreements?

Their disputes, if not settled by debate, threatened to destroy the federal government.

Part 2: Essay

5 Using information from the documents, your answers to the questions in Part 1, and your knowledge of U.S. history, write an essay in which you discuss the different views the first political parties held on major issues between 1789 and 1801, and explain why Washington believed that political parties were divisive. **6**

5 Carefully read the essay question. Then write an outline for your essay.

6 Write your essay. Be sure that it has an introductory paragraph that introduces your argument, main body paragraphs that explain it, and a concluding paragraph that restates your position. In your essay, include extracts or details from specific documents to support your ideas. Add other supporting facts or details that you know from your study of American history.

Essay Rubric The best essays will point out the differences between the Federalists and the Democratic-Republicans (Document 2) and will show how political disagreements, such as those portrayed in the cartoon (Document 3), supported Washington's warning in his Farewell Address (Document 1). Essays should draw upon information not specifically included in the documents that illustrates an understanding of the political debate during the Washington and Adams administrations. Students may also refer to the Alien and Sedition Acts passed by the Federalist Congress during Adams's presidency and the opposing viewpoint expressed in the Kentucky and Virginia Resolutions authored by Jefferson and Madison, respectively.

Introduction

Historical Context: In 1775, Great Britain had an army of 48,647 men located throughout the world, about 8,000 of them in the Americas. A rebellion by the small group of 13 colonies in America did not scare the keepers of such a large colonial empire.

Task: Discuss how the colonists' beliefs and military actions contributed to their victory in the Revolution. Include the significance of the American alliances with European nations.

Part 1: Short Answer

Study each document carefully and answer the questions that follow.

Document 1: First Georgia Regiment of Infantry Continental Line, 1777

The hunting shirt, or rifle dress, shown here was recommended by George Washington in his general order of July 24, 1776. Declaring it a practical item to be given to the troops, he also claimed that ". . . it is a dress justly supposed to carry no small terror to the enemy, who think every such person a complete marksman."

Source: New-York Historical Society

What unusual military tactics did patriots like the man in the picture use to surprise and outsmart the British during the Revolution?

Document 1: *Uniforms of the American Revolution: 1st Georgia Regiment Continental Infantry, 1777, Private Field Dress,* Charles Lefferts. Watercolor, gouache on paper. Copyright © Collection of the New-York Historical Society.

Document 2: Philadelphia, September 12, 1777

> I close this paper with a short address to General Howe. . . . We know the cause which we are engaged in, and though a passionate fondness for it may make us grieve at every injury. . . . We are not moved by the gloomy smile of a worthless king, but by the ardent glow of generous patriotism. We fight not to enslave, but to set a country free, and to make room upon the earth for honest men to live in. In such a case we are sure that we are right; and we leave to you the despairing reflection of being the tool of a miserable tyrant.
>
> —Thomas Paine, *The American Crisis No. IV*

Although this excerpt is addressed to the British General Howe, how might it also have encouraged the colonists to continue their fight against the British?

Document 3: The Battle of Yorktown, 1781: Winning the American Revolution

Estimated American, French, and British Forces and Casualties		
Generals and Their Divisions	Forces	Casualties
General Washington (American colonies)	11,100	90
General Rochambeau (France)	7,800	250
General Cornwallis (Britain)	8,900	550

Estimated French and British Naval Strength*		
French and British Fleets	Ships	Guns on Board Ship
Admiral Graves (Britain)	25	1,450
Lieutenant General DeGrasse (France)	35	2,610

*Does not include small craft or transport ships

Source: U.S. Army Center of Military History

What support was provided by the French in the Battle of Yorktown?

Part 2: Essay

Using information from the documents, your answers to the questions in Part 1, and your knowledge of U.S. history, write an essay that discusses how the colonists' beliefs and military actions contributed to their victory in the Revolution. Include in your essay the significance of American alliances with European nations.

The Landscape of America

The best place to begin your study of American history is with the geography of America. Geography is more than the study of the land and people. It also involves the relationship between people and their environment.

The United States is part of the North American continent. The United States ranks third in both total area and population in the world. It is filled with an incredible variety of physical features, natural resources, climatic conditions, and people. This handbook will help you to learn about these factors and to understand how they affected the development of the United States.

A timber company collects logs in the Northwest.

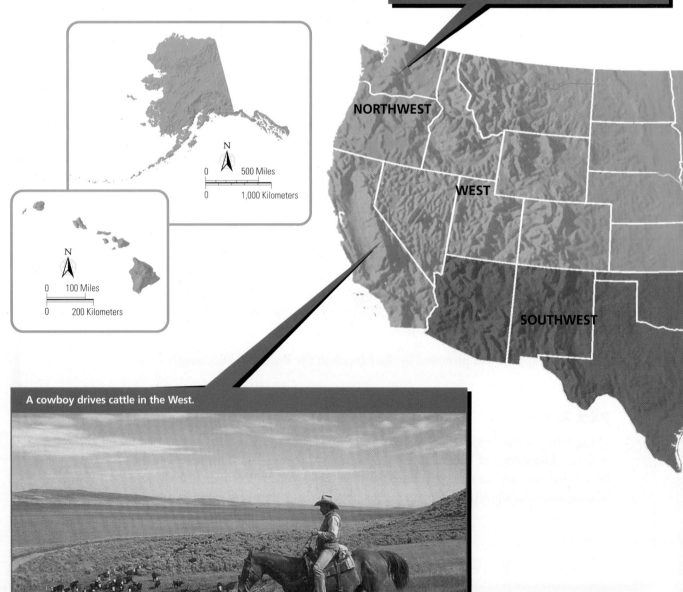

NORTHWEST

WEST

SOUTHWEST

N
0   500 Miles
0   1,000 Kilometers

N
0   100 Miles
0   200 Kilometers

A cowboy drives cattle in the West.

A combine harvests wheat in the Midwest.

TABLE OF CONTENTS

NORTHEAST

MIDWEST

SOUTHEAST

Fishers haul their catch toward shore in the Northeast.

N

| 0 | 500 Miles |
| 0 | 1,000 Kilometers |

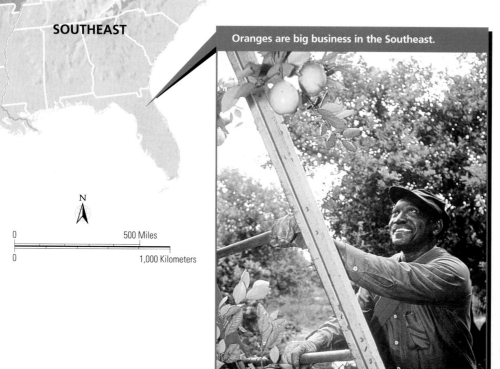
Oranges are big business in the Southeast.

The Landscape of America **3**

Themes of Geography

One useful way to think about geography is in terms of major themes or ideas. These pages examine the five major themes of geography and show how they apply to Boston, Massachusetts. Recognizing and understanding these themes will help you to understand all the different aspects of geography.

Boston is located on the shores of the Atlantic Ocean.

Location

"Where am I?" Your answer to this question is your *location*. One way to answer it is to use *absolute* location. That means you'll use the coordinates of longitude and latitude to give your answer (see page 8). For example, if you're in Boston, its absolute location is approximately 42° north latitude and 71° west longitude.

Like most people, however, you'll probably use *relative* location to answer the question. Relative location describes where a certain area is in relation to another area. For example, Boston lies in the northeast corner of the United States, next to the Atlantic Ocean.

THINKING ABOUT GEOGRAPHY What is the relative location of your school?

Place

"What is Boston like?" *Place* can help you answer this question. Place refers to the physical and human factors that make one area different from another. Physical characteristics are natural features, such as physical setting, plants, animals, and weather. For example, Boston sits on a hilly peninsula.

Human characteristics include cultural diversity and the things people have made—including language, the arts, and architecture. For instance, Boston includes African Americans, as well as people of Irish, Italian, Chinese, and Hispanic ancestry.

THINKING ABOUT GEOGRAPHY What physical and human characteristics make where you live unique?

Boston has grown and changed since this 1722 map.

Region

Geographers can't easily study the whole world at one time. So they break the world into regions. A *region* can be as large as a continent or as small as a neighborhood. A region has certain shared characteristics that set it apart. These characteristics might include political division, climate, language, or religion. Boston is part of the northeast region. It shares a climate—continental temperate—with the cities of New York and Philadelphia.

THINKING ABOUT GEOGRAPHY What characteristics does your city or town share with nearby cities or towns?

Airplanes from Boston's Logan International Airport move people and ideas around the globe.

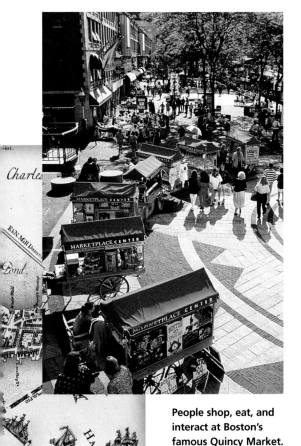

People shop, eat, and interact at Boston's famous Quincy Market.

Movement

Movement refers to the shifting of people, goods, and ideas from one place to another. People constantly move in search of better places to live, and they trade goods with one another over great distances. Movement also causes ideas to travel from place to place. In recent years, technology has quickened the movement of ideas and goods.

Boston became known as the *Cradle of Liberty* because of the movement of ideas. The concepts of freedom and self-government that developed in Boston spread to the other colonies and helped to start the American Revolution.

THINKING ABOUT GEOGRAPHY What are some of the different ways you spread information and ideas?

Human-Environment Interaction

Human-environment interaction refers to ways people interact with their environment, such as building a dam, cutting down a tree, or even sitting in the sun.

In Boston, human-environment interaction occurred when officials filled in swampy areas to make the city larger. In other ways, the environment has forced people to act. For example, people have had to invent ways to protect themselves from extreme weather and natural disasters.

THINKING ABOUT GEOGRAPHY What are ways that people in your city or town have changed their environment?

Themes of Geography Assessment

1. Main Ideas

a. What is the relative location of your home?

b. What are three characteristics of the region in which you live?

c. What are at least three ways in which you have recently interacted with the environment?

2. Critical Thinking

Forming and Supporting Opinions Which aspect of geography described in these themes do you think has most affected your life? Explain.

THINK ABOUT
• ways that you interact with your environment
• how you travel from place to place

Map Basics

Geographers use many different types of maps, and these maps all have a variety of features. The map on the next page gives you information on a historical event—the War of 1812. But you can use it to learn about different parts of a map, too.

Types of Maps

Physical maps Physical maps show mountains, hills, plains, rivers, lakes, oceans, and other physical features of an area.

Political maps Political maps show political units, such as countries, states, provinces, counties, districts, and towns. Each unit is normally shaded a different color, represented by a symbol, or shown with a different typeface.

Historical maps Historical maps illustrate such things as economic activity, migrations, battles, and changing national boundaries.

Tools of Geography

The ancient Greeks developed some of the first ways to study geography. Today, geographers and map makers use advanced technology to study geography.

GPS
A Global Positioning System (GPS) is a navigational system that uses at least three satellites to identify a person's absolute location. It is also used to study other aspects of geography.

Surveyors
An American surveys the land in the 19th century.

Computers
Computers can create electronic maps in which geographers can quickly add or remove features that keep the map current. Computers can also be used to monitor environmental problems such as deforestation and global warming.

Reading a Map

A **Lines** Lines indicate political boundaries, roads and highways, human movement, and rivers and other waterways.

B **Symbols** Symbols represent such items as capital cities, battle sites, or economic activities.

C **Labels** Labels are words or phrases that explain various items or activities on a map.

D **Compass Rose** A compass rose shows which way the directions north (N), south (S), east (E), and west (W) point on the map.

E **Scale** A scale shows the ratio between a unit of length on the map and a unit of distance on the earth. A typical one-inch scale indicates the number of miles and kilometers that length represents on the map.

F **Colors** Colors show a variety of information on a map, such as population density or the physical growth of a country.

G **Legend or Key** A legend or key lists and explains the symbols, lines, and colors on a map.

H **Lines of Longitude** These are imaginary, north-south lines that run around the globe.
Lines of Latitude These are imaginary, east-west lines that run around the globe. Together, latitude and longitude lines form a grid on a map or globe to indicate an area's absolute location.

The War of 1812

Longitude Lines (Meridians)

Latitude Lines (Parallels)

Northern Hemisphere

Southern Hemisphere

Western Hemisphere

Eastern Hemisphere

Longitude lines

- are imaginary lines that run north to south around the globe and are known as meridians
- show the distance in degrees east or west of the prime meridian

The prime meridian is a longitude line that runs from the North Pole to the South Pole. It passes through Greenwich, England, and measures 0° longitude.

Latitude lines

- are imaginary lines that run east to west around the globe and are known as parallels
- show distance in degrees north or south of the equator

The equator is a latitude line that circles the earth halfway between the North and South poles. It measures 0° latitude.

The tropics of Cancer and Capricorn are parallels that form the boundaries of the Tropics, a region that stays warm all year.

Latitude and longitude lines appear together on a map and allow you to pinpoint the absolute location of cities and other geographic features. You express this location through coordinates of intersecting lines. These are measured in degrees.

Hemisphere

Hemisphere is a term for half the globe. The globe can be divided into Northern and Southern hemispheres (separated by the equator) or into Eastern and Western hemispheres. The United States is located in the Northern and Western hemispheres.

Projections

A projection is a way of showing the curved surface of the earth on a flat map. Flat maps cannot show the size, shape, and direction of a globe all at once with total accuracy. As a result, all projections distort some aspect of the earth's surface. Some maps distort distances, while other maps distort angles. On the next page are four projections.

Mercator Projection

The Mercator projection shows most of the continents as they look on a globe. However, the projection stretches out the lands near the North and South poles. The Mercator is used for all kinds of navigation.

Azimuthal Projection

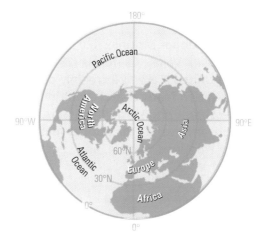

An azimuthal projection shows the earth so that a straight line from the central point to any other point on the map gives the shortest distance between the two points. Size and shape of the continents are also distorted.

Homolosine Projection

This projection shows the accurate shapes and sizes of the landmasses, but distances on the map are not correct.

Robinson Projection

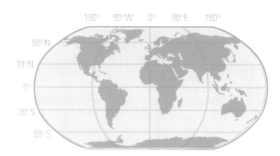

Textbook maps commonly use the Robinson projection. It shows the entire earth with nearly the true sizes and shapes of the continents and oceans. However, the shapes of the landforms near the poles appear flat.

Map Basics Assessment

1. Main Ideas

a. What is the longitude and latitude of your city or town?

b. What information is provided by the legend on the map on page 7?

c. What is a projection? Compare and contrast Antarctica on the Mercator and the Robinson projections.

2. Critical Thinking

Making Inferences Why do you think latitude and longitude are so important to sailors?

THINK ABOUT

• the landmarks you use to find your way around

• the landmarks available to sailors on the ocean

Physical Geography of the United States

From the heights of Mount McKinley (20,320 feet above sea level) in Alaska to the depths of Death Valley, California (282 feet below sea level), the geography of the United States is incredibly diverse. In between these extremes lie such varied features and conditions as scorching Arizona deserts, lush Oregon forests, freezing Vermont winters, and sunny Florida beaches. Physical geography involves all the natural features on the earth. This includes the land, resources, climate, and vegetation.

Flowers and brush cover the Coral Pink Sand Dunes in southern Utah.

Land

Separated from much of the world by two oceans, the United States covers 3,717,796 square miles and spans the entire width of North America. To the west, Hawaii stretches the United States into the Pacific Ocean. To the north, Alaska extends the United States to the Arctic Circle. On the U.S. mainland, a huge central plain separates large mountains in the West and low mountains in the East. Plains make up almost half of the country, while mountains and plateaus make up a quarter each.

An abundance of lakes—Alaska alone has three million—and rivers also dot the landscape. Twenty percent of the United States is farmed, providing the country with a steady food supply. Urban areas cover only about two percent of the nation. Refer to the map on the next page for a complete look at the U.S. landscape.

THINKING ABOUT GEOGRAPHY What is the land like around your city or state?

Resources

The United States has a variety of natural resources. Vast amounts of coal, oil, and natural gas lie underneath American soil. Valuable deposits of lead, zinc, uranium, gold, and silver also exist. These resources have helped the United States become the world's leading industrial nation—producing nearly 21 percent of the world's goods and services.

These resources have also helped the United States become both the world's largest producer of energy (natural gas, oil, coal, nuclear power, and electricity) and the world's largest consumer of it. Other natural resources include the Great Lakes, which are shared with Canada. They contain about 20 percent of the world's total supply of fresh surface water. Refer to the map on the next page to examine the nation's natural resources.

THINKING ABOUT GEOGRAPHY What are the different natural resources that you and your family use in your daily lives?

Oil drilled from Alaska helps power the nation's planes, trains, cars, and factories.

Land and Resources

N

0   250 Miles
0   500 Kilometers

Miners extract such minerals as gold, silver, and copper from the Rocky Mountains.

PACIFIC OCEAN

ATLANTIC OCEAN

The Appalachians are among the earth's oldest mountains.

Aluminum	Lumber
Coal	Natural gas
Copper	Oil
Gold	Silver
Iron ore	Uranium
Lead	Zinc

Elevation Key

Feet	Meters
13,120	4,000
9,840	3,000
6,560	2,000
3,280	1,000
1,640	500
656	200
0	0
Below sea level	

Physical Geography of the United States **11**

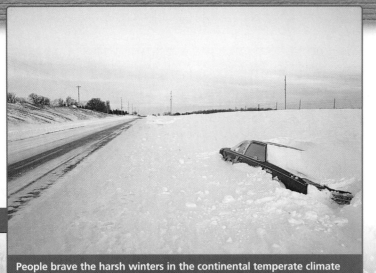

People brave the harsh winters in the continental temperate climate of the upper Midwest.

Climate

Mount Washington in New Hampshire has experienced one of the world's lowest recorded wind chills of over −100° F, one of the world's highest wind speeds at 231 miles per hour, and a three-day snow fall of 8 feet.

CANADA

WASH.
OREGON
IDAHO
MONTANA
N. DAK.
MINN.
S. DAK.
WIS.
MICH.
WYO.
NEBR.
IOWA
NEV.
UTAH
COLO.
CALIF.
ARIZ.
N. MEX.
KANS.
MO.
OKLA.
ARK.
TEXAS
LA.
ILL.
IND.
OHIO
KY.
TENN.
MISS.
ALA.
GA.
W. VA.
VA.
N.C.
S.C.
FLA.
PA.
N.Y.
VT.
MAINE
N.H.
MASS.
R.I.
CONN.
N.J.
DEL.
MD.

PACIFIC OCEAN
ATLANTIC OCEAN
Great Lakes
Gulf of Mexico

50°N
40°N
30°N
20°N
120°W
110°W
100°W
90°W
80°W
70°W

Marine (mild year-round)
Highland (cool year-round)
Mediterranean (warm summers, and rainy, mild winters)
Steppe (hot summers, cold winters, dry)
Desert (very hot summers, with cold nights, very dry)
Continental temperate (mild-to-hot summers, cold winters)
Humid subtropical (hot summers, mild winters, rainy)
Tropical (very hot summers, warm winters)
Tundra (bitterly cold winters, freezing summers)
Subarctic (very cold winters, cold summers)

Sequoia National Park in California contains the world's largest tree, the General Sherman, a giant sequoia. It measures 103 feet around at its base and is 275 feet high. It weighs about 6,167 tons—over 12 million pounds!

Rain and humidity nourish the lush forests in the humid subtropical climate of the Southeast.

ALASKA
70°N
60°N
160°W
140°W

HAWAII
20°N
160°W
155°W

N
0   500 Miles
0   1,000 Kilometers

Climate

The United States contains a variety of climates. For example, the mean temperature in January in Miami, Florida, is 67° F, while it is 11° F in Minneapolis, Minnesota. Most of the United States experiences a continental climate, or distinct change of seasons. Some regional climatic differences include hot and humid summers in the Southeast versus hot and dry summers in the Southwest. Harsh winters and heavy snow can blanket parts of the Midwest, the Northeast, and the higher elevations of the West and Northwest. Refer to the map on the previous page to see the nation's climatic regions.

Human activities have affected the climate, too. For example, pollution from cars and factories can affect local weather conditions and may be contributing to a dangerous rise in the earth's temperature.

THINKING ABOUT GEOGRAPHY How would you describe the climate where you live?

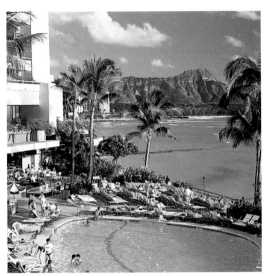
Tourists and residents bask in the sunshine of Waikiki Beach in Hawaii.

Vegetation

Between 20,000 and 25,000 species and subspecies of plants and vegetation grow in the United States—including over 1,000 different kinds of trees. Climate often dictates the type of vegetation found in a region. For instance, cold autumns in the Northeast contribute to the brilliantly colored autumn leaves. Rain nourishes the forests in the Northwest and Southeast. The central plains, where rainfall is less heavy, are covered by grass. Cactus plants thrive in the dry southwestern deserts.

Along with natural vegetation, climate dictates the nation's variety of planted crops. For example, temperate weather in the Midwest helps wheat to grow, while warm weather nourishes citrus fruit in Florida and California.

THINKING ABOUT GEOGRAPHY What kinds of trees or plants grow in your region?

This mountainside burns with the autumn foliage of New Hampshire.

Physical Geography Assessment

1. Main Ideas
a. What are the different aspects of physical geography?
b. Which state contains the largest variety of climates?
c. What two states contain most of the country's oil resources?

2. Critical Thinking
Drawing Conclusions What do you think are the advantages of living in a country with diverse physical geography?

THINK ABOUT
• the different resources available in your region
• the variety of recreational activities in your region

Physical Geography of the United States **13**

Geographic Dictionary

volcano
an opening in the earth, usually raised, through which gasses and lava escape from the earth's interior

strait
a narrow strip of water connecting two large bodies of water

cape
a pointed piece of land extending into an ocean or lake

sea level
level of the ocean's surface, used as a reference point when measuring the height or depth of the earth's surface

bay
part of an ocean or lake partially enclosed by land

harbor
a sheltered area of water, deep enough for docking ships

(river) mouth
the place where a river flows into a lake or ocean

marsh
soft, wet, low-lying, grassy land that serves as a transition between water and land

island
a body of land surrounded by water

delta
a triangular area of land formed from deposits at the mouth of a river

flood plain
flat land near the edges of rivers formed by mud and silt deposited by floods

swamp
an area of land that is saturated by water

desert
a dry area where few plants grow

butte
a raised, flat area of land with steep cliffs, smaller than a mesa

oasis
a spot of fertile land in a desert, fed by water from wells or underground springs

prairie
a large, level area of grassland with few or no trees

steppe
a wide, treeless plain

mountain
natural elevation of the earth's surface with steep sides and greater height than a hill

valley
low land between hills or mountains

glacier
a large ice mass that moves slowly down a mountain or over land

mesa
a wide, flat-topped mountain with steep sides, larger than a butte

cataract
a large, powerful waterfall

canyon
a narrow, deep valley with steep sides

cliff
the steep, almost vertical edge of a hill, mountain, or plain

plateau
a broad, flat area of land higher than the surrounding land

15

Human Geography of the United States

Human geography focuses on people's relationships with each other and the surrounding environment. It includes two main themes of geography: human-environment interaction and movement. The following pages will help you to better understand the link between people and geography.

Humans Adapt to Their Surroundings

Humans have always adapted to their environment. For example, in North America, many Native American tribes burned forest patches to create grazing area to attract animals and to clear area for farmland. In addition, Americans have adapted to their environment by building numerous dams, bridges, and tunnels. More recently, scientists and engineers have been developing building materials that will better withstand the earthquakes that occasionally strike California.

THINKING ABOUT GEOGRAPHY What are some of the ways in which you interact with your environment on a daily basis?

Early Americans of the Southwest protected themselves from the weather by building cliff dwellings.

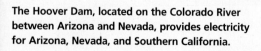

The Hoover Dam, located on the Colorado River between Arizona and Nevada, provides electricity for Arizona, Nevada, and Southern California.

An oil spill from the ship *Exxon Valdez* harmed wildlife, such as this bird, in Prince William Sound, Alaska, in 1989.

Destruction of Original Forests

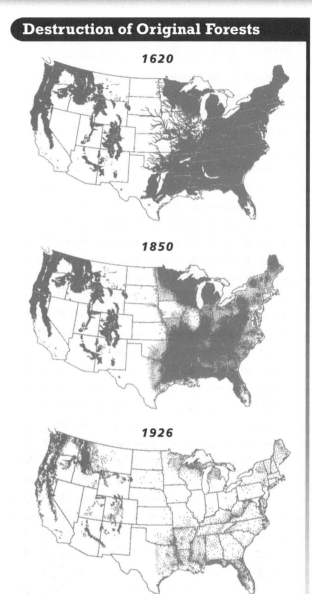

1620

1850

1926

These maps show that, over the years, human beings have nearly cut down all the original forests in the United States. Each dot represents 25,000 acres.

Humans Affect the Environment

When humans interact with the environment, sometimes nature suffers. In the United States, for example, major oil leaks or spills occur each year—fouling shorelines and harming wildlife. Building suburbs and strip malls has also destroyed forests, farmland, and valuable wetlands.

THINKING ABOUT GEOGRAPHY What are some of the environmental problems in your city or town?

Children plant trees along a Chicago expressway.

Preserving and Restoring

Americans—as well as people all over the world—have been working hard to balance economic progress with conservation. For example, car companies in the United States and around the world are working to develop pollution-free vehicles. In 1994, the average American family of four recycled around 1,100 pounds of waste. And, in the 1990s, Americans have planted more than two million acres of new trees each year.

THINKING ABOUT GEOGRAPHY What are some of the ways in which you help the environment?

Human Movement

In prehistoric times, people roamed the earth in search of food. Today in the United States, people move from place to place for many different reasons. Among them are cost of living, job availability, and climate. Since the 1970s, many Americans—as well as many new immigrants—moved to the Sunbelt. This region runs through the southern United States from Virginia to California. Between 1950 and 1990, that region's population soared from 52 million to 118 million.

THINKING ABOUT GEOGRAPHY Has your family ever moved? If so, what were some of the reasons?

This map shows human movement in the 1970s. The information below explains some of the results of this movement in the 1990s.

Americans on the Move, *1970s*

NORTHWEST

NORTHEAST
N.Y.

311,000

67,000

472,000

MIDWEST

WEST

964,000

CALIFORNIA

790,000

A

75,000

SOUTHWEST

SOUTHEAST

C

•Phoenix

B

D

TEXAS

FLORIDA

N

0 | 500 Miles
0 | 1,000 Kilometers

A By 1996, the Phoenix-Mesa metropolitan area reached a population of 2.75 million, more than the number of people living in the entire state in 1980.

B Between 1990 and 1994, Texas overtook New York as the nation's second most populous state, behind California.

C One of the nation's fastest growing areas was the Southeast, where population growth ranged from six to nine percent between 1990 and 1994. Jobs grew in the area by 14 percent.

D Florida's population is growing so much that it could become as populous as New York state by around 2020.

New home developments cover the desert in Las Vegas, Nevada.

In the late 19th century, millions of immigrants arrived on the shores of the United States.

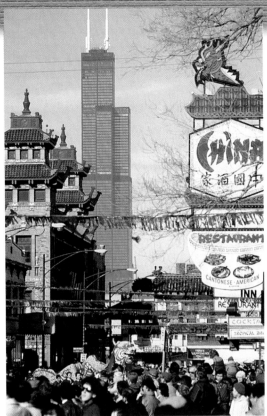

The Sears Tower overlooks Chinatown in Chicago.

Humans Spread Ideas and Information

Throughout U.S. history, people from all over the world have come to the United States. They have brought with them food, music, language, technology, and other aspects of their culture. As a result, the United States is one of the most culturally rich and diverse nations in the world. Look around your town or city. You'll probably notice different people, languages, and foods.

Today, the spreading of ideas and customs does not rely solely on human movement. Technology—from the Internet to television to satellites—spreads ideas and information throughout the world faster than ever. This has created an ever-growing, interconnected world. As the 21st century opens, human geography will continue to play a key role in shaping the United States and the world.

THINKING ABOUT GEOGRAPHY How have computers and the Internet affected your life?

Human Geography Assessment

1. Main Ideas

a. What are some of the ways that people have helped to restore the environment?

b. What are some of the ways that residents of your region have successfully modified their landscape?

c. What are some of the reasons that people move from place to place?

2. Critical Thinking

Recognizing Effects In what ways has technology helped bring people in the world together?

THINK ABOUT

- the different ways in which people communicate today
- the speed in which people today can communicate over long distances

GEOGRAPHY HANDBOOK ASSESSMENT

TERMS

Briefly explain the significance of each of the following.

1. physical map
2. political map
3. longitude
4. latitude
5. hemisphere
6. projection
7. flood plain
8. sea level
9. human geography
10. human movement

REVIEW QUESTIONS

Themes of Geography (pages 4–5)

1. What is the difference between *absolute* location and *relative* location?
2. What is meant by the theme of place?
3. What are the themes of movement and human-environment interaction?

Map Basics (pages 6–9)

4. What do you think are some of the benefits of using technology to study geography?
5. What are the three major kinds of maps?
6. What are latitude and longitude lines?

Physical Geography (pages 10–13)

7. How have the natural resources in the United States helped its economic development?
8. What are the different climates within the United States?

Human Geography (pages 16–19)

9. How is human geography different from physical geography?
10. What aspects of human geography might cause people to move?

CRITICAL THINKING

1. **Forming and Supporting Opinions** Which of the five themes of geography do you think has had the most impact on history? Why?
2. **Analyzing Causes** How do the climate and natural resources of an area affect its economy?
3. **Drawing Conclusions** How have computers helped geographers make more accurate maps?
4. **Making Inferences** Why do you think the Mercator projection is used for all types of navigation?
5. **Recognizing Effects** How does a diverse landscape help or hurt the economy of an area?

GEOGRAPHY SKILLS

1. INTERPRETING MAPS: Movement

Basic Map Elements

a. What region of the United States is shown?
b. Compare the number of teams on the 1987 map and the 2000 map. How many more teams are on the 2000 map?

Interpreting the Map

c. What geographic theme(s) is most responsible for the increase in sports teams in this region?
d. According to the map, which sport enjoyed the biggest surge in popularity in this region?

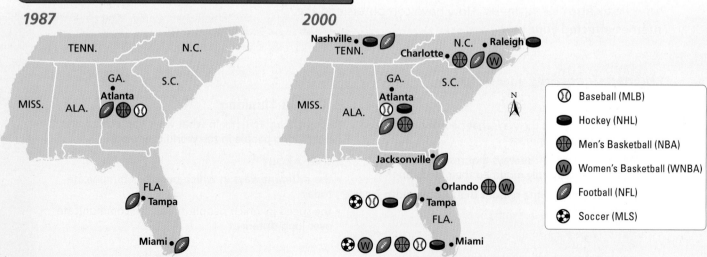

Major League Sports in Southeast Cities

GEOGRAPHY SKILLS

2. INTERPRETING MAPS: Region

Study the map and then answer the questions.

California: Cross section at 38° N

Basic Map Elements

a. What are the different landforms on the map?

Interpreting the Map

b. What is the level of the San Joaquin Valley? How many miles does it take to get from there to the highest point in California at the 38th parallel?

3. INTERPRETING PRIMARY SOURCES

In 1803, President Thomas Jefferson appointed Meriwether Lewis to explore the lands of the Louisiana Purchase. Jefferson gave him these instructions:

> The object of your mission is to explore the Missouri river . . . by its course & communication with the waters of the Pacific Ocean, may offer the most direct & practicable water communication across this continent, for the purposes of commerce. . . .
>
> Other objects worthy of notice will be the soil & face of the country, its growth & vegetable productions . . . the mineral productions of every kind. . . . climate as characterized by the thermometer . . . the dates at which particular plants put forth or lose their flowers, or leaf, times of appearance of particular birds, reptiles, or insects.
>
> **Thomas Jefferson,** quoted in *The Journals of Lewis and Clark*

a. What was Jefferson expecting to find in the West?

b. Why might the president want to know about the land's soil and vegetable production?

c. What aspect of human geography might be of interest to the president?

ALTERNATIVE ASSESSMENT

1. INTERDISCIPLINARY ACTIVITY: Math

Plotting Latitude and Longitude On a piece of graph paper, sketch a map of the United States. Be sure to draw in state boundaries, too. Then, using an atlas as a reference, draw and mark the latitude and longitude lines that cross the nation at five degree intervals. Plot the estimated longitude and latitude location of your city or town. Determine at which degrees the lines intersect where you live. Repeat this exercise for at least five different places you have visited or would like to visit within the United States.

2. COOPERATIVE LEARNING ACTIVITY

Making a Map How well do you know the neighborhood around your school? Form groups of three to four students. Then work together to draw a map of the neighborhood around your school. Include:

- streets
- residences
- stores
- geographic features
- important landmarks

The map should be accurate but not too cluttered with unnecessary details. Compare your group's map with those of the other groups in the class.

3. TECHNOLOGY ACTIVITY

Writing Directions Several Internet sites provide detailed maps of the United States. They also provide driving directions to most places in the country.

- Locate one of these map sites on the Internet.
- Think of a place in the United States that you would like to visit.
- Work with the computer to find the best route for reaching it.

Write out clear directions as well as the total mileage of your trip. Also, note the type of map it is and the features it highlights.

For more important geography sites . . .

INTERNET ACTIVITY
CLASSZONE.COM

4. HISTORY PORTFOLIO

Review your alternative assessment activities. Use comments made by your teacher or classmates to improve your work.

Additional Test Practice, pp. S1–S33

TEST PRACTICE
CLASSZONE.COM

Three Worlds Meet

The ruins of the Anasazi Cliff Palace, in modern-day Colorado, stand as a reminder of the Native American societies that existed before the arrival of Europeans.

"The story of my people and the story of this place are one single story."

—*Taos Pueblo man*

CHAPTER 1

The World in 1500 Beginnings–1500

Imagine how these Native Americans might feel at their first sight of strange ships.

This picture is an artist's idea of the first meeting between European explorers and Native Americans.

The Europeans will plant this flag and claim the island for Spain.

The Native Americans offer a tray of the island's fruit as a welcome gift.

The Native Americans may wonder if this long object is a walking stick or a weapon.

The year is 1492, and you live on an island in the Caribbean. One day you see a giant boat topped by strange white cloths. Men climb into smaller boats and row toward you. You have never seen men like this. They have pale skin and wear heavy, colorful clothing. You wonder what will happen when they land.

What Do You Think?

- What can different societies learn from each other?
- What might they want to gain from each other?
- What positive and negative things might happen when they meet?

What happens when different societies meet?

Americas
World

100 B.C.

A.D. 1500

200s
The Maya are using hieroglyphic writing.

800s
Maize is widely grown in what is now the southeastern United States.

1100s
The city of Cahokia flourishes in what is now Illinois.

1200s
The Aztecs conquer much of central Mexico.

1492
The European explorer Columbus lands in the Americas.

About 6 B.C.
Jesus of Nazareth is born. His teachings become the basis for Christianity.

476
Western Roman Empire ends. Over time, Europe splits into small kingdoms.

Early 600s
Muhammad begins the religion of Islam in Arabia.

1096
Europeans begin the Crusades to capture the Holy Land from followers of Islam.

1324
Mansa Musa, emperor of Mali, travels to Islam's holy city. Word of his gold spreads to Europe.

1481
Portuguese traders begin to build a fort near Benin in Africa.

BEFORE YOU READ

Previewing the Theme

Diversity and Unity Chapter 1 explains that by 1500, diverse societies had developed in the Americas, West Africa, and Europe. After 1500, economic, political, social, and religious forces brought West Africans and Europeans to the Americas. Those people and Native Americans helped create the United States.

CENTRAL AMERICA This pyramid at Chichén Itzá, in what is now Mexico, was built between the 900s and 1200s.

AFRICA This Muslim mosque in Timbuktu, Mali, was built in the 1300s and 1400s.

EUROPE St. Peter's Basilica (a Christian church) in Vatican City, Italy, was built in the 1500s and early 1600s.

What Do You Know?

What do you know about the history of the Americas, West Africa, and Europe? How technologically advanced must a society be to build large structures like the ones at the left?

THINK ABOUT

• what you know about other societies, such as Egypt, that built large structures
• what you've read in books

What Do You Want to Know?

What questions do you have about the past societies of the Americas, West Africa, and Europe? What do you want to know about how they met? Record those questions in your notebook before you read the chapter.

READ AND TAKE NOTES

Reading Strategy: Categorizing One way to make better sense of what you read is to categorize. To categorize is to sort information into groups. The chart below will help you record information about the societies of the Americas, West Africa, and Europe. As you read, look for information relating to the categories of trade, technology, religion, and art. Record that information on your chart.

See Skillbuilder Handbook, page R6.

	Trade	Technology	Religion	Art
AMERICAS				
WEST AFRICA				
EUROPE				

TERMS & NAMES
culture
domestication
civilization
Mound Builders
technology
slash-and-burn
  agriculture
Iroquois League

MAIN IDEA	WHY IT MATTERS NOW
Ancient peoples came from Asia to the Americas and over time established many diverse Native American societies.	Some Americans today claim one or more of these cultures as part of their heritage.

ONE AMERICAN'S STORY

To do her work, Solveig Turpin must climb rugged cliffs, step over rattlesnakes, and dodge sharp cactus spines. For more than 20 years, she has searched the caves and cliffs of Texas for paintings that ancient people left on rock walls. Turpin is an archaeologist, a scientist who studies the human past by examining the things people left behind. One painting that Turpin found shows a red, 9-foot-long panther. She believes it shows a religious leader who turned himself into an animal.

A VOICE FROM THE PAST

This is the Shaman [religious leader] who transforms into the largest and most powerful animal here. . . . I like to call [the shamans] supramen because they were over everything.

Solveig Turpin, quoted in *In Search of Ancient North America*

Archaeologist Solveig Turpin wears a shirt displaying the rock paintings of ancient peoples as she discusses her work.

Archaeologists make theories about the past based on what they learn from bones and artifacts. Artifacts are tools and other objects that humans made. They give clues about who ancient people were and how they lived. This section discusses some theories about early Americans.

The First People in America

Scientists believe that the first Americans migrated, or moved, to the Americas from Asia. They disagree, however, about how and when this movement took place. Some ancient people may have crossed a land bridge, known as Beringia, that joined Asia and North America during the last Ice Age. The Ice Age, which lasted for thousands of years, was a period of extreme cold in which glaciers trapped so much water that ocean levels dropped. The scientists who hold this theory believe the earliest Americans arrived 12,000 years ago.

Other scientists believe humans came to the Americas much earlier. They have found artifacts in South America that tests show to be 30,000 years old. These scientists believe that people came to the Americas by many routes, including by boat, over thousands of years.

The Emergence of Civilizations

A **culture** is a way of life that people share, including arts, beliefs, and customs. The first people to live in the Americas thousands of years ago lived in hunting and gathering cultures. They hunted animals and gathered wild seeds, nuts, fruits, and berries.

In time, people in different parts of the world began planting seeds. This was the beginning of agriculture. About 5,000 years ago, humans began to domesticate plants and animals. **Domestication** is the practice of breeding plants or taming animals to meet human needs. People in central Mexico learned to grow corn, which became an important food source. Agriculture spread throughout the Americas.

Having a stable food supply changed the way people lived. Once they no longer had to travel to find food, they built permanent villages and focused their energy on many different activities. Slowly, some cultures grew complex and became civilizations. A **civilization** has five features: (1) cities that are centers of trade, (2) specialized jobs for different people, (3) organized forms of government and religion, (4) a system of record keeping, and (5) advanced tools.

*Reading*History
A. Drawing Conclusions Why would a culture need to learn agriculture before it could develop a civilization?

About 1200 B.C., an advanced civilization arose in Mesoamerica, a region that stretches from central Mexico to present-day Nicaragua. For 800 years, a people called the Olmec thrived in this region along the Gulf of Mexico. The Olmec built large cities, set up a network of trade routes, and constructed earthen mounds shaped like pyramids. Around 400 B.C., the Olmec mysteriously vanished. By then, their culture had spread along trade routes and influenced others.

By A.D. 250, about 650 years after the Olmec vanished, the Maya had developed a great civilization. Their cities were in southern Mexico and Guatemala, where they built pyramid mounds topped by temples. By 900, the Maya had abandoned many of their cities. Scientists think that revolts, disease, or crop failures may have caused their society to fail.

Early Native American Civilizations

Ancient peoples of the American Southwest used images like this to communicate with each other. Such images are called petroglyphs.

During the Mayan period, various groups of people built civilizations in the areas that would become the present-day United States. The Hohokam created a flourishing society from about 300 B.C. to A.D. 1400 in what is now Arizona. In order to farm the dry land, the Hohokam dug hundreds of miles of canals to irrigate, or water, their crops. The Hohokam also traded with peoples in neighboring regions.

Beginning about A.D. 100, the Anasazi lived in the area where Utah, Arizona, Colorado, and New Mexico now meet. Like the Hohokam, the Anasazi were mainly farmers who traded widely. Around 1300, drought or warfare caused the Anasazi to leave their homes.

In the eastern part of what is now the United States lived several groups of people called Mound Builders. The **Mound Builders** were Native Americans who built large earthen structures as burial mounds and temples. Mound Builder cultures included the Adena, the Hopewell, and the Mississippians. The Mississippians, who lived from A.D. 800 to 1700, built some of the first cities in North America. By the 1700s, most of the Mississippians had died from diseases they caught from Europeans.

By 1500, North America was home to hundreds of cultural groups, speaking perhaps 2,000 languages. One reason Native Americans were so diverse was that each group adapted to its own environment—whether subzero ice fields, scorching deserts, or dense forests.

Environment shaped each group's way of life. In some regions, Native Americans based their economy on farming. In others, they relied on hunting or fishing. Different environments caused technology to vary. **Technology** is the use of tools and knowledge to meet human needs. In coastal areas, farmers made tools from shells. In deserts, they used irrigation, the bringing of water to land. Environment affected religion, too. Native Americans strongly believed that certain places were sacred—and that animals, plants, and natural forces had spiritual importance.

Peoples of the North and West

The Aleut (uh•LOOT) and the Inuit (IHN•yoo•iht) lived in the frozen lands of the far North. The Aleut lived on islands off Alaska, and the Inuit lived near the coast. Because their climate was too cold for farming, the Inuit and Aleut were hunters. Farther south, Northwest Coast people, such as the Haida and the Kwakiutl (KWAH•kee•OOT•uhl), hunted sea mammals and fished for salmon. Living by forests, they used wood for houses, boats, and carved objects.

The peoples of the West included tribes in California, the Columbia Plateau, and the Great Basin. Much of the West is not suitable for farming. The people who lived there existed mainly by hunting and gathering. To the south, in what is now the American Southwest, lived the Pueblo people. Their ancestors were the ancient Hohokam and Anasazi. Like their ancestors, the Pueblo used irrigation to alter their desert region for farming. The Navajo and the Apache were nomadic, or wandering, hunter-gatherers who came to the region later than the Pueblo. Over time, the Navajo adopted farming and other Pueblo practices.

daily*life*

KACHINA DANCES

Every year in summer the Hopi, Zuni, and other Pueblo Indians held a religious celebration. The ceremony called on the kachinas, or spirits of the ancestors, to bring a plentiful harvest. At the festival, masked dancers played the role of different kachinas. They danced and sang songs to bring rain in the year ahead. Today, the Pueblo also carve kachina dolls, shown below, as well as hold dances.

Reading **History**

B. Reading a Map On the map on page 30, locate the cultures of California, the Plateau, and the Great Basin. Notice why these three together are called the peoples of the West.

North America, 1500

Haida
Kwakiutl
Blackfoot
Nez Perce
Crow
Mandan
Cree
Ojibwa
Ottawa
Algonquin
Chinook
PACIFIC OCEAN
Shoshone
Cheyenne
Dakota (Sioux)
Sauk
Potawatomi
Huron
Iroquois
Wampanoag
Pequot
Pomo
Pawnee
Iowa
Miami
Delaware
Paiute
Arapaho
Kansas
Shawnee
Susquehanna
Powhatan
ATLANTIC OCEAN
40°N
Chumash
Kiowa
Osage
Tuscarora
Navajo
Apache
Chickasaw
Cherokee
Hopi
Zuni Pueblo
Choctaw
Creek
Pima

Huichol
Gulf of Mexico
Tropic of Cancer
Seminole

Aztec
Taino

N
0   500 Miles
0   1,000 Kilometers

Native American Cultures
- Subarctic
- Northwest Coast
- California
- Plateau
- Great Basin
- Mesoamerican
- Southwest
- Plains
- Eastern Woodlands
- Southeastern
- Caribbean
- Major trade routes

GEOGRAPHY SKILLBUILDER
Interpreting Maps
1. **Movement** Which Native American culture was able to trade directly with the Aztecs?
2. **Location** Which culture lived around the Great Lakes?

Peoples of Mexico

Far to the south, the Aztecs created a great civilization in what is now central Mexico. In 1325, they began to build their capital city, Tenochtitlán (teh•NAWCH•tee•TLAHN), on islands in Lake Texcoco. Two things helped the Aztecs build a strong empire. First, they drained swamps and built an irrigation system. This enabled them to grow plenty of food. Second, they were a warlike people who conquered most of their neighbors.

The Aztecs had a complex society. Rulers were the highest class. Priests and government workers ranked next. Slaves and servants were at the bottom. The Aztecs had elaborate religious ceremonies linked to their calendar and their study of the sun, moon, and stars.

Peoples of the Great Plains and East

The Great Plains of North America is a region of flat grasslands stretching from the Mississippi River west to the Rocky Mountains. The Native Americans that inhabited this land were a diverse group. Some were nomads. Others lived in villages by rivers, where land was easier to farm. Many Plains tribes relied on the buffalo for much of their food, clothing, and tools.

The Southeast, which stretches from east Texas to the Atlantic Ocean, has mild winters and warm summers with plentiful rainfall. The long growing season allowed the Choctaw (CHAHK•taw), Chickasaw (CHIHK•uh•SAW), and other southeastern groups to become farmers.

Like the Southeast, the Northeast had plenty of fish, game, and rain. But the climate was colder with snowy winters. Forests covered much of the region, so it is called the Eastern Woodlands. Most of the people living there spoke either an Iroquoian or Algonquian language. The Iroquois adapted the forest for farming by using slash-and-burn agriculture. In **slash-and-burn agriculture,** farmers chopped down and then burned trees on a plot of land. The ashes from the fire enriched the soil.

The Iroquois often raided each other's villages for food and captives. In the late 1500s, five northern Iroquois nations took the advice of a peace-seeking man named Deganawida. They stopped warring with each other and formed an alliance. This alliance of the Cayuga, Mohawk, Oneida, Onondaga, and Seneca was the **Iroquois League.** The League brought a long period of peace to the Iroquois. A council of leaders from each nation governed the League. Women played important roles in Iroquois society. They nominated members of the tribal council. And if a leader did something wrong, the women of his clan could vote him out of office.

Across the Atlantic, the peoples of West Africa and Europe were also building impressive civilizations. You will read about these people and cultures in the next section.

Section 1 Assessment

1. Terms & Names

Explain the significance of:
- culture
- domestication
- civilization
- Mound Builders
- technology
- slash-and-burn agriculture
- Iroquois League

2. Taking Notes

Use a chart like the one below to list ancient cultures of Mesoamerica and North America and their locations.

Ancient Culture	Location

Which of these cultures was closest to where you live?

3. Main Ideas

a. How did the development of farming lead to the growth of civilization?

b. How were the Pueblo like their ancestors, the Hohokam and Anasazi?

c. How did the formation of the Iroquois League benefit its member nations?

4. Critical Thinking

Comparing How did tribes such as the Hohokam and the Iroquois adapt to living in their environment?

THINK ABOUT
- Hohokam agriculture
- Iroquois farming

ACTIVITY OPTIONS

GEOGRAPHY
TECHNOLOGY

Review the map on page 30. Create a **map** or **electronic presentation** showing the Native American cultures and trade routes that existed in your home state.

The Iroquois Great Law of Peace

Setting the Stage The five nations of the Iroquois League created a constitution, called the Great Law of Peace, that had 117 laws and customs. These laws governed all aspects of life and war. In this excerpt, Deganawida introduces the Great Law by describing a tree that symbolizes the permanence and stability of the league. **See Primary Source Explorer**

1 I am Deganawida and with the Five Nations' Confederate **Lords**[1] I plant the Tree of Great Peace. I plant it in your territory, **Adodarhoh,**[2] and the Onondaga Nation, in the territory of you who are Firekeepers.

I name the tree the Tree of the Great Long Leaves. Under the shade of this Tree of the Great Peace we spread the soft white feathery down of the globe thistle as seats for you, Adodarhoh, and your cousin Lords.

We place you upon those seats, spread soft with the feathery down of the globe thistle, there beneath the shade of the spreading branches of the Tree of Peace. There shall you sit and watch the Council Fire of the **Confederacy of the Five Nations,**[3] and all the affairs of the Five Nations shall be transacted at this place before you, Adodarhoh, and your cousin Lords, by the Confederate Lords of the Five Nations.

2 Roots have spread out from the Tree of the Great Peace, one to the north, one to the east, one to the south, and one to the west. The name of these roots is The Great White Roots and their nature is Peace and Strength.

If any man or any nation outside the Five Nations shall obey the laws of the Great Peace and make known their disposition to the Lords of the Confederacy, they may trace the Roots to the Tree and if their minds are clean and they are obedient and promise to obey the wishes of the Confederate Council, they shall be welcomed to take shelter beneath the Tree of the Long Leaves.

1. **Lords:** chiefs.

2. **Adodarhoh:** the name of the office of the Onondaga chief.

3. **Confederacy of the Five Nations:** the Iroquois League.

A CLOSER LOOK

THE COUNCIL FIRE

The council fire of the Iroquois League was kept burning for about 200 years.

1. What do you think it would mean if the council fire were allowed to die?

A CLOSER LOOK

THE GREAT WHITE ROOTS

The roots of a tree help to anchor it in the ground, and they draw water and food from the soil.

2. Why might Deganawida say the nature of the roots is "Peace and Strength"?

Interactive Primary Source Assessment

1. Main Ideas

a. In what territory was the Tree of the Great Peace planted?

b. Where will the affairs of the Five Nations be conducted?

c. Where have the Tree's roots spread?

2. Critical Thinking

Making Inferences Were outsiders welcome to join the Iroquois League? Explain.

THINK ABOUT

• the phrase *they may trace the Roots to the Tree*

• the phrase *take shelter beneath the Tree*

② Societies of West Africa and Europe

TERMS & NAMES
Muslim
Islam
European Middle Ages
feudalism
Crusades
Renaissance
Reformation

MAIN IDEA	WHY IT MATTERS NOW
By 1500, the peoples of West Africa and Europe developed sophisticated civilizations.	The changes taking place in West Africa and Europe helped shape European exploration of the Americas.

ONE AFRICAN'S STORY

King Tenkaminen (TEHN•kah•MEE•nehn) of the West African empire of Ghana was a powerful ruler. He grew rich by taxing gold traders who traveled through his land. His wealth impressed visitors to his kingdom. In 1067, a geographer described the royal court.

A VOICE FROM THE PAST

The king adorns himself . . . wearing necklaces round his neck and bracelets on his forearms. . . . Behind the king stand ten pages holding shields and swords decorated with gold and on his right are the sons of the vassal [lower] kings of his country wearing splendid garments and their hair plaited [braided] with gold.

al-Bakri, quoted in *The Horizon History of Africa*

Kumasi, a modern West African chief, wears gold to show his status, just as the ancient king of Ghana did.

West Africa had several other kingdoms and empires that grew powerful through trade. Meanwhile, trade also played an increasingly significant role in Europe. This section examines life in both lands on the eve of the European explorations that would bring their worlds into contact with the Americas.

Africa in 1500

Africa is the world's second largest continent. (See the map on page 34.) It is home to a variety of land forms and climates. Dense rain forests stretch along the equator in central and western Africa. North and south of the rain forests are broad savannas, or flat grasslands. Beyond the savannas to the north and south are miles of desert.

By A.D. 1500, coastal ports had linked Africa with the rest of the world for many centuries. Ships from ports on the Mediterranean and the Red Sea carried goods to Arabia and Persia. On Africa's eastern coast, city-states carried on a brisk trade with ports across the Indian Ocean.

Like other parts of Africa, West Africa has rain forest along the equator and savanna to the north. Along its northern edge, West Africa borders the Sahara Desert. By A.D. 500, camel caravans led by eager merchants made regular journeys across the desert. This trade helped West African kingdoms grow wealthy.

Ghana and Islam

Ghana became the first West African kingdom to grow rich through trade. From the 700s to the mid 1000s, Ghana became a marketplace for traders going north and south in search of salt and gold. Salt was important because it helps the human body retain water in hot weather. Traders carried salt from the Saharan salt mines in the north. In Ghana's markets, they met other traders offering gold from the forests of West Africa.

Ghana's king benefited from this trade. He imposed taxes on all gold and salt passing through his kingdom. The king then used the resulting wealth to pay for an army and build an empire.

Many of the traders who came to Ghana from North Africa were **Muslims.** Muslims are followers of the religion of Islam. Founded by the prophet Muhammad in the 600s, **Islam** teaches that there is one God, named Allah. Muslims must perform such duties as praying five times a day and making a visit to the holy city of Mecca in Arabia.

The Muslim empires of North Africa sought to convert Ghana's people to Islam and to control Ghana's gold trade. In 1076, Muslim armies began invading Ghana's frontier region and the empire weakened.

Reading **History**
A. Clarifying
What did Islam preach?

Mali and Songhai

By the 1200s, another West African kingdom, Mali, had taken over most of Ghana's territory. Its wealth also came from control of the gold-salt trade. By 1312, Mali had become one of the largest empires in the world.

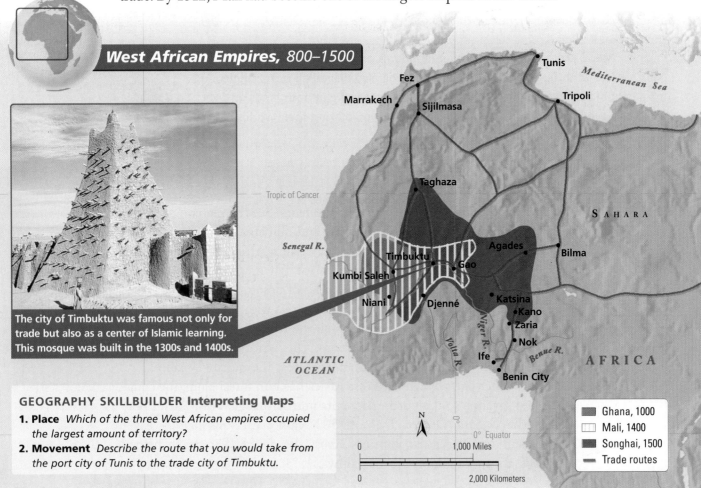

West African Empires, 800–1500

The city of Timbuktu was famous not only for trade but also as a center of Islamic learning. This mosque was built in the 1300s and 1400s.

Legend:
- Ghana, 1000
- Mali, 1400
- Songhai, 1500
- Trade routes

GEOGRAPHY SKILLBUILDER Interpreting Maps
1. **Place** *Which of the three West African empires occupied the largest amount of territory?*
2. **Movement** *Describe the route that you would take from the port city of Tunis to the trade city of Timbuktu.*

Vocabulary
devout: very religious

Its leader during this period was a devout Muslim named Mansa Musa (MAHN•sah moo•SAH). Under his rule, Islamic culture spread throughout the empire. After Mansa Musa's death in 1337, Mali slowly weakened.

As the power of Mali decreased, the Songhai (SAWNG•HY) people living near the Niger River broke away from the empire's control. In 1464, under the leader Sunni Ali, they created their own empire. Sunni Ali was a Muslim, but he also practiced the traditional Songhai religion. After Sunni Ali died in 1492, Askia Muhammad rose to power. A devoted Muslim, Muhammad ably governed the empire for 35 years. He chose officials who made the government run smoothly. He also expanded trade and set up an efficient tax system. Askia Muhammad used his wealth to build mosques and support Muslim scholars. After Muhammad's reign, several weak rulers succeeded him. Eventually, the empire collapsed.

Reading **History**

B. Recognizing Effects How would Askia Muhammad's actions promote Islam in Songhai?

As empires rose and fell in some parts of West Africa, small city-states arose in other parts of the region. The Hausa (HOW•suh) states emerged after A.D. 1000 in what is now Nigeria. The Yoruba (YAWR•uh•buh) lived in the forests southwest of the Niger River. They were gifted artists who carved prized wood, ivory, and metal sculptures. In the river's delta region, near a crossroad of trade routes, the kingdom of Benin emerged.

In the late 1400s, Europeans reached Benin. Portuguese arrived in ships and set up a trade center near the capital, Benin City. Trade was just one reason Europeans were sailing far beyond their lands. A number of social changes were occurring in Europe—changes that would push them to explore the world.

Now and then

AFRICAN HERITAGE

One way many African Americans show pride in their heritage is by wearing kente cloth. Kente cloth, shown below, is a colorful fabric woven by the Akan and Ewe people of Ghana.

Some African Americans celebrate the holiday of Kwanzaa in December. Based on traditional African harvest festivals, Kwanzaa lasts a week. Each day honors a value held by Africans: unity, self-determination, collective responsibility, cooperative economics, purpose, creativity, and faith.

Europe Undergoes Great Change

The period from the late 400s, when the Western Roman Empire collapsed, to about the 1300s, is known in Europe as the **European Middle Ages.** It was a time of great social and political instability and warfare. To survive such difficult times, Europeans developed feudalism. **Feudalism** is a political system in which a king allows nobles, or lords, to use lands that belong to him. In return, the lords owe the king military service and protection for the people living on the land.

Along with feudalism, Europeans developed the manor system. In this system, lords divided their lands into manors, or large estates, that were farmed mostly by serfs. Serfs were landless peasants who were not

In feudalism, nobles offered to protect peasants from invaders. In return, the peasants farmed the nobles' lands.

Feudalism made people feel safe enough to travel. Trade increased and towns grew.

Then many peasants ran away to towns, where they could live more freely. Feudalism declined. Trade continued to grow.

allowed to leave the manor. In return for the serfs' work, the lord promised to protect them.

Christianity was the dominant religion of Europe, and Europeans were greatly influenced by Judeo–Christian beliefs. "Judeo" refers to Judaism—the religion of the Jews. Judeo–Christian beliefs include the worth of the individual and the importance of ethical behavior. The central code of behavior is the Ten Commandments. Judeo–Christian beliefs have played an important role in the United States.

By the 1000s, feudalism had brought more stability to European society. As strong lords gained more control over their lands, long periods of peace and security followed. Merchants increasingly felt safe to travel, and trade increased. Old towns near busy trade routes revived, and new towns grew up near manor houses and churches.

War also spurred trade. In 1096, European Christians launched the **Crusades,** a series of wars to capture the Holy Land—the biblical region of Palestine in southwest Asia—from the Muslims. They ultimately failed to keep the Holy Land, but the Crusades changed European life. During the years of fighting, Europeans encountered a variety of Asian goods. After the war, they continued to demand these items.

The growth of trade and towns weakened feudalism as serfs left the manors to live in the growing towns. Beginning in 1347, a deadly disease known as bubonic plague also weakened feudalism by reducing the number of workers. Lords had to compete for laborers by paying wages to peasants.

As feudal lords lost power, kings grew stronger. Kings won the support of townspeople because they could raise large armies to enforce order. This process contributed to the gradual rise of nations.

The Renaissance and Reformation

Italy, which was thriving because of trade, became the birthplace of the **Renaissance**—a time of increased interest in art and learning. Renaissance is a French term meaning "rebirth." Lasting from the 1300s to 1600, the Renaissance spread from Italy throughout Europe.

*Reading***History**
C. Identifying Problems What problems were Europeans trying to solve with feudalism and the manor system?

*Reading***History**
D. Analyzing Causes What three causes led to the decline of feudalism?

Several forces led to the Renaissance. As feudalism weakened and the plague brought great suffering, Europeans began to question what life meant. In their search for new answers, some people turned to old sources. They studied the classical writings and art of the ancient Greeks and Romans. As a result of these studies, European ideas changed.

Vocabulary
philosophy: the study of the meaning of life

1. The Greeks had praised human achievement. European scholars developed humanism, the study of human value and ideas.
2. Classical education stressed such subjects as history, philosophy, and literature. Europeans spent more time studying those subjects.
3. From classical art, Renaissance artists learned to make art more realistic. These artists created some of the world's finest paintings and statues.
4. Muslim scholars had saved classical manuscripts about science. Also, Muslim mathematicians had invented algebra. Contact with Muslim societies influenced European science and mathematics.

In about 1455, a German named Johannes Gutenberg invented the printing press. This invention prompted an increase in book printing and helped to spread Renaissance ideas more quickly.

By the early 1500s, Renaissance ideas and other forces weakened the Roman Catholic Church. Many Church leaders were corrupt. Martin Luther, a German monk, publicly posted 95 statements that criticized a number of Church practices. This protest began the **Reformation,** a movement to correct problems in the Church. The Reformation split the Church into two groups in western Europe—Catholics and Protestants. In time, Protestants divided into many different churches.

HISTORY *through*ART

This painting, *School of Athens* by Raphael, shows many aspects of Renaissance art and culture.

- Like much Renaissance art, it looks more realistic than the art of the Middle Ages.
- It honors the Greek thinkers Aristotle and Plato, who are the two men in the center arch.
- It also honors Renaissance artists. Raphael himself is in the group to the right.

Why might Raphael have wanted to include himself in a painting with famous Greeks?

CAUSE & EFFECT: *Causes of Exploration*

After the Crusades, Europeans want Asian goods.

CAUSE

↓

EFFECT
Italy dominates trade because it developed a network during the Crusades.

CAUSE

↓

EFFECT
Other European nations want a share of Italy's profits.

CAUSE

↓

EFFECT
Other nations seek water route to Asia.

SKILLBUILDER Interpreting Charts
What economic activity was the primary cause of exploration?

Changes in Trade

The Renaissance period saw not only changes in learning and religion but also in trade. As trade grew, Italian merchants needed to improve the way they did business. They began to use more exact ways of keeping track of a business's income and its costs. By subtracting the costs from the income, the merchants determined the profit.

Italian merchants made huge profits by trading in Asian goods. Italians had done business with Muslims for centuries. Thus, they had developed a special relationship. In addition, the Italians used their military strength to control the trade on the Mediterranean and did not allow other Europeans to take part in it.

Merchants in other European countries envied the profits made by Italian merchants. As a result, other Europeans began to want a share of the rich trade in Asian goods. They had to find different routes to Asia from the ones controlled by the Italians and Muslims. Other European countries began to search for a non-Mediterranean water route to Asia, as you will read in Section 3.

*Reading*History
E. Making Generalizations
If a country tries to completely dominate trade in a certain area, how will other countries respond?

Section 2 Assessment

1. Terms & Names

Explain the significance of:
• Muslim
• Islam
• European Middle Ages
• feudalism
• Crusades
• Renaissance
• Reformation

2. Taking Notes

On a web like the one below, list how the Renaissance changed art and learning.

Renaissance

3. Main Ideas

a. How did Ghana's ruler benefit from controlling the gold-salt trade?

b. How did Islam spread within West Africa?

c. What caused feudalism to develop?

4. Critical Thinking

Contrasting How did the Renaissance differ from the European Middle Ages?

THINK ABOUT
• the economy
• how power was distributed
• the authority of the church

ACTIVITY OPTIONS

TECHNOLOGY

MUSIC

Design a **Web site** or compose a **song** advertising the great new Renaissance invention—the printing press.

Early European Explorers

MAIN IDEA

As Europeans searched for sea routes to Asia, Christopher Columbus reached the Americas.

WHY IT MATTERS NOW

Columbus's journey permanently linked the Americas to the rest of the world.

ONE EUROPEAN'S STORY

Sailors seeking a route to Asia depended on the skill of their navigator. A **navigator** plans the course of a ship by using instruments to find its position. In the 1400s, Portugal had a famous prince called Henry the Navigator. Yet, Henry wasn't a navigator. He never sailed on any of the ships trying to find Asia. So how did he earn his name?

Henry lived at Sagres, on the southwestern tip of Portugal. It was a site that overlooked the Atlantic Ocean. He invited astronomers, mathematicians, mapmakers, and navigators to Sagres. There he began a school of navigation.

Henry decided to organize and pay for sailing expeditions to explore the Atlantic and the west coast of Africa. He was hoping to find African gold, to learn more about geography, and to spread Christianity. His ships traveled farther down the African coast than Europeans had ever gone. Because Henry sponsored the voyages, the English named him "the navigator." Those voyages began Europe's age of discovery. As you will read in this section, this age of discovery eventually led Europeans to the Americas.

Henry the Navigator sponsored voyages that helped Portugal find a water route to Asia.

A Water Route to Asia

Under Prince Henry, the Portuguese developed an improved ship called the **caravel**. The caravel had triangular sails as well as square sails. Square sails carried the ship forward when the wind was at its back. Triangular sails allowed the caravel to sail into the wind. The caravel was better than other European ships of the time at this type of sailing.

In January 1488, the Portuguese explorer Bartolomeu Dias (DEE•uhs) reached the southern tip of Africa. After sailing around it, he returned to Portugal at the urging of his crew. Portugal's king named the tip the Cape of Good Hope because he hoped they had found a route to Asia.

Ten years later, another Portuguese explorer, Vasco da Gama, followed Dias's route around the cape. He continued north along the eastern coast of Africa. Then he sailed east across the Indian Ocean to India. At last, someone had found an all-water route from Europe to Asia.

CHRISTOPHER COLUMBUS
1451–1506

Christopher Columbus's son Ferdinand wrote that his father "took to the sea at the age of 14 and followed it ever after."

Columbus's early voyages nearly cost him his life. When he was 25, pirates off the coast of Portugal sank his ship. Columbus survived by grabbing a floating oar and swimming to shore.

But he also learned a lot from sailing on Portuguese ships. The sailors taught Columbus about Atlantic wind patterns. This knowledge later helped him on his history-making voyage.

What character traits, shown in Columbus's early life, might have made him a good leader?

That route meant that the Portuguese could now trade with Asia without dealing with the Muslims or Italians. Portugal took control of the valuable spice trade. The merchants of Lisbon, Portugal's capital, grew rich. Spain and other European rivals wanted to take part in this profitable trade. They began to look for their own water routes to Asia.

Columbus's Plan

By the time of da Gama's voyage, an Italian sailor named **Christopher Columbus** thought he knew a faster way to reach Asia. Europeans had known for centuries that the earth is round. Columbus decided that instead of sailing around Africa and then east, he would sail west across the Atlantic. He calculated that it would be a short journey.

But Columbus made several mistakes. First, he relied on the writings of two people—Marco Polo and a geographer named Paolo Toscanelli—who were wrong about the size of Asia. They claimed that Asia stretched farther from west to east than it really did.

Second, Columbus underestimated the distance around the globe. He thought the earth was only two thirds as large as it actually is! Because of Polo and Toscanelli, Columbus thought that Asia took up most of that distance. Therefore, he believed that the Atlantic Ocean must be small. And a voyage west to Asia would be short.

In 1483, Columbus asked the king of Portugal to finance a voyage across the Atlantic. The king's advisers opposed the plan. They argued that Columbus had miscalculated the distance to Asia. They also reminded the king of the progress that Portuguese explorers had made sailing down the coast of Africa looking for a route to Asia. The advisers persuaded the king not to finance the voyage. So in 1486, Columbus turned to Portugal's rival, Spain.

Help from Spain's Rulers

Spain's rulers, King Ferdinand and Queen Isabella, liked Columbus's plan because they wanted a share of the rich Asian trade. As a strong Catholic, the Queen also welcomed a chance to spread Christianity. But there were also reasons not to support Columbus. First, a royal council had doubts about Columbus's calculations and advised Ferdinand and Isabella not to finance him. Second, the Spanish monarchs were in the middle of a costly war to drive the Muslims out of Spain. Third, Columbus was asking a high payment for his services.

The years of waiting had made Columbus determined to profit from his explorations. As a reward for his efforts, he demanded the high title

*Reading*History
A. Comparing
Compare what happened after Portugal began to control the spice trade to what happened when Italy controlled it.

Vocabulary
monarch: a king or queen

Admiral of the Ocean Sea and a percentage of any wealth he brought from Asia. He also expected to be made the ruler of the lands he found.

Finally in January of 1492, the Spanish conquered the last Muslim stronghold in Spain. The Spanish monarchs could now afford to finance Columbus but still had doubts about doing so. Columbus left the palace to return home. But after listening to a trusted adviser, the king and queen changed their minds and sent a rider on horseback to bring Columbus back. He and the rulers finally reached an agreement.

*Reading*History

B. Drawing Conclusions Did this agreement give Columbus what he was asking for? Explain.

A VOICE FROM THE PAST

Your Highnesses . . . accorded me great rewards and ennobled me so that from that time henceforth I might . . . be high admiral of the Ocean Sea and perpetual Governor of the islands and continent which I should discover.

Christopher Columbus, letter to King Ferdinand and Queen Isabella

Preparing to sail, Columbus assembled his ships—the *Niña*, the *Pinta*, and the *Santa María*—at the port of Palos de la Frontera in southern Spain.

Setting Sail

At first, Columbus had trouble finding a crew. Then a respected local shipowner agreed to sign on as captain of the *Pinta*. Other crew members soon followed. About 90 men loaded the ships with enough food for one year, casks of fresh water, firewood, and other necessities.

Exploration Leads to New Sea Routes, 1487–1504

→ Route of Dias, 1487–1488
→ Route of da Gama, 1497–1498
Routes of Columbus:
→ 1492–1493
→ 1493–1496
→ 1498–1500
→ 1502–1504

EUROPE

NORTH AMERICA

ATLANTIC OCEAN

PORTUGAL SPAIN

SAN SALVADOR

CUBA

HISPANIOLA

PACIFIC OCEAN

SOUTH AMERICA

AFRICA

ASIA

INDIAN OCEAN

Tropic of Cancer

0° Equator

Tropic of Capricorn

40°N

40°W

40°E

80°E

40°S

N

0   1,000 Miles

0   2,000 Kilometers

GEOGRAPHY SKILLBUILDER Interpreting Maps

1. **Movement** *Approximately how many miles did Columbus sail before he reached San Salvador on his first voyage?*
2. **Human-Environment Interaction** *Why do you suppose that Dias stayed close to the west coast of Africa during his voyage, while da Gama sailed farther out?*

41

The tiny fleet of wooden ships glided out of the harbor on August 3, 1492. First they sailed southwest toward the Canary Islands off the northwest coast of Africa. From there, Columbus was relying on trade winds that blew toward the west to speed his ships across the ocean.

Once aboard ship, Columbus kept a log, or daily record of each day's sailing. In fact, he kept two logs. One he showed to his men and one he kept secret. Columbus's secret log recorded the truth about the journey.

> **A VOICE FROM THE PAST**
>
> [We] made 15 leagues [this] day and . . . [I] decided to report less than those actually traveled so in case the voyage were long the men would not be frightened and lose courage.
>
> **Christopher Columbus,** quoted in *Columbus and the Age of Discovery*

Reading **History**
C. Analyzing Causes What caused Columbus to decide to keep two logs?

By October 10, the men had lost both courage and confidence in their leader. They had been at sea for almost ten weeks and had not seen land for over a month. Afraid that they would starve if the trip went on longer, they talked of returning home. To avoid mutiny, Columbus and the crew struck a bargain. The men agreed to sail on for three more days, and Columbus promised to turn back if they had not sighted land by then. Two days later in the early morning hours of October 12, a sailor on the *Pinta* called out "Tierra, tierra" [Land, land].

Reaching the Americas

By noon, the ships had landed on an island in the Caribbean Sea. Columbus believed that he had reached the Indies, islands in Southeast Asia where spices grew. The islanders who greeted Columbus and his men were Taino (TY•noh) people, but Columbus mistakenly called them Indians.

Columbus named the island San Salvador. After unfurling the royal banner and flags, he ordered his crew to "bear witness that I was taking possession of this island for the King and Queen." Eager to reach the rich country of Japan, which he believed was nearby, he left San Salvador. He took six or seven Taino with him as guides. For the next three months, he visited several of the Caribbean islands.

Finally, he reached an island that he named Española, which we call Hispaniola today. (See map on page 41.) On that island, Columbus and his men found some gold and precious objects such as pearls. This convinced Columbus that he had reached Asia. He decided to return home, leaving 39 of his men on Hispaniola. Even before Columbus left, his men had angered the Taino people by stealing from them and committing violence. By the time Columbus returned ten months later, the Taino had killed the men.

Background
Today, the Indies are called the East Indies. The islands of the Caribbean are called the West Indies.

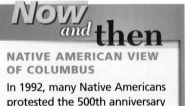

NATIVE AMERICAN VIEW OF COLUMBUS

In 1992, many Native Americans protested the 500th anniversary of Columbus's voyage. Suzan Shown Harjo, who is Cheyenne and Creek, explained why.

As Native American peoples in this red quarter of Mother Earth, we have no reason to celebrate an invasion that caused the demise [death] of so many of our people and is still causing destruction today.

The Spanish enslaved the Taino, who nearly all died from disease and bad treatment. This statue is one of the few Taino artifacts left from the 1500s.

In January 1493, he sailed back to Spain. Firmly believing that he had found a new water route to Asia, he wrote to Ferdinand and Isabella. The Spanish rulers called him to the royal court to report on his voyage. Neither Columbus nor the king and queen suspected that he had landed near continents entirely unknown to Europeans.

A French mapmaker uses an instrument to learn his exact position on the globe.

An Expanding Horizon

Columbus made three more voyages to the Americas, but never brought back the treasures he had promised Spain's rulers. He also failed to meet Queen Isabella's other goal. She wanted Christianity brought to new people. When she learned that Columbus had mistreated and enslaved the people of Hispaniola, she became angry.

After the fourth voyage, Spain's rulers refused to give Columbus any more help. He died in 1506, still believing he had reached Asia and bitter that he had not received the fame or fortune that he deserved.

In time, the geographic knowledge Columbus brought back changed European views of the world. People soon realized that Columbus had reached continents that had been unknown to them previously. And Europeans were eager to see if these continents could make them rich.

Reading **History**

D. Making Inferences How did the Atlantic become a bridge connecting Europe, Africa, and the Americas?

For centuries, Europeans had seen the ocean as a barrier. With one voyage, Columbus changed that. Instead of a barrier, the Atlantic Ocean became a bridge that connected Europe, Africa, and the Americas. As you will learn in Chapter 2, Columbus's explorations began an era of great wealth and power for Spain. As Spain grew rich, England, France, and other European countries also began to send ships to the Americas.

Section 3 Assessment

1. Terms & Names

Explain the significance of:
- navigator
- caravel
- Christopher Columbus

2. Taking Notes

On a diagram like the one shown, list the effects of Columbus's voyages.

Columbus's Voyages			
Effect	Effect	Effect	Effect

Which effects were negative and which were positive?

3. Main Ideas

a. Why was Prince Henry eager to find an all-water route to Asia?

b. Why did Spain's king and queen decide to support Columbus's first voyage?

c. Why was Columbus disappointed by the outcome of his four voyages to the Americas?

4. Critical Thinking

Analyzing Points of View Explain how each of the following people might have viewed Columbus's first voyage. Give reasons for their points of view.

THINK ABOUT
- Columbus
- Queen Isabella
- a Taino chief

ACTIVITY OPTIONS

GEOGRAPHY

MATH

Use the map on page 41. Create an enlarged **map** of Columbus's first voyage, or measure the distance of each voyage to list on a **table**.

The World in 1500

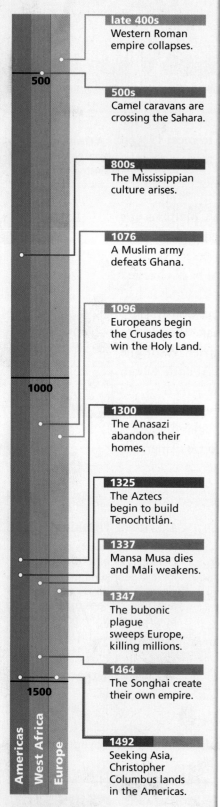

late 400s
Western Roman empire collapses.

500

500s
Camel caravans are crossing the Sahara.

800s
The Mississippian culture arises.

1076
A Muslim army defeats Ghana.

1096
Europeans begin the Crusades to win the Holy Land.

1000

1300
The Anasazi abandon their homes.

1325
The Aztecs begin to build Tenochtitlán.

1337
Mansa Musa dies and Mali weakens.

1347
The bubonic plague sweeps Europe, killing millions.

1464
The Songhai create their own empire.

1500

1492
Seeking Asia, Christopher Columbus lands in the Americas.

Americas / West Africa / Europe

TERMS & NAMES

Briefly explain the significance of each of the following.

1. civilization
2. Mound Builders
3. technology
4. Iroquois League
5. Islam
6. feudalism
7. Crusades
8. Renaissance
9. navigator
10. Christopher Columbus

REVIEW QUESTIONS

Societies of North America (pages 27–32)

1. What are two theories about migration to the Americas?
2. For what purposes did the Mound Builders construct earthen mounds?
3. What enabled the Aztecs to build a strong empire?
4. How did the Iroquois League come about?

Societies of West Africa and Europe (pages 33–38)

5. What enabled Ghana, Mali, and Songhai all to grow rich?
6. Did Islam become more or less influential in West Africa from the 700s to the 1400s? Explain.
7. How did the manor system work during the Middle Ages?
8. How did the Crusades increase European interest in trade?

Early European Explorers (pages 39–43)

9. Why did non-Italian Europeans seek new trade routes to Asia?
10. How did Columbus miscalculate the distance to Asia?

CRITICAL THINKING

1. USING YOUR NOTES

Using your completed chart, answer the questions below.

	Trade	Technology	Religion	Art
AMERICAS (Sections 1)				
WEST AFRICA (Section 2)				
EUROPE (Sections 2 and 3)				

a. What was one example of how trade spread knowledge?
b. Which of the technologies that you listed are still used today?
c. Which religions were practiced in each of the three regions?

2. ANALYZING LEADERSHIP

Do you think Columbus was a good leader or a bad one? Use details from the chapter to explain your answer.

3. THEME: DIVERSITY AND UNITY

How have Native Americans, Africans, and Europeans all influenced American culture? Give examples from your own experience.

4. MAKING GENERALIZATIONS

What types of goods are people most likely to seek through trade? Think about the trade goods mentioned in the chapter and why people wanted them.

5. APPLYING CITIZENSHIP SKILLS

Compare the Iroquois League to what you know of the U.S. government. How are they similar?

Interact *with* History

Think about the various encounters between societies mentioned in the chapter. What do you think happened when more Europeans came to the Americas and met Native Americans?

HISTORY SKILLS

1. INTERPRETING MAPS: HUMAN-ENVIRONMENT INTERACTION

Study the map. Answer the questions.

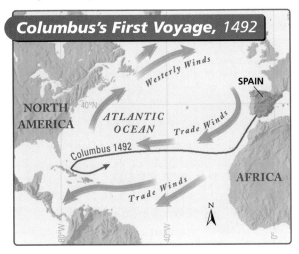

Columbus's First Voyage, 1492

Basic Map Elements

a. What is the name of the winds blowing west across the Atlantic? blowing east?

b. In what direction did Columbus sail on his first journey from Europe?

Interpreting the Map

c. How did the winds affect Columbus's journey?

d. If Columbus's route had been farther north, would his voyage have taken more or less time? Explain.

2. INTERPRETING PRIMARY SOURCES

Drawn in 1570, this is the earliest map to show North America and South America as separate continents.

a. What are the names of any places that you recognize on this map?

b. Compare this map to the map of the world on page 41. Which continent on this map do you think looks more accurate? Explain why.

ALTERNATIVE ASSESSMENT

1. INTERDISCIPLINARY ACTIVITY: Literature

Retelling a Folk Tale Many North American Indian tales give insight into the relationship between Native Americans and their environment. Select a tale from a collection of Native American literature and retell the tale for the class.

2. COOPERATIVE LEARNING ACTIVITY

Creating a Sound Collage Columbus's log of his first voyage can be found in many public libraries. Have one or two members of your group select portions of the log for audiotaping. Other members of the group can decide on sound effects to be heard in the background. Consider using some of the following:

- sounds of the ocean or of storms
- shipboard sounds, such as bells, clanking chains, and flapping sails
- shouted commands to the crew
- seafaring songs or other music

You may want to use a sound effects tape, available in many libraries, or create your own sounds.

3. PRIMARY SOURCE EXPLORER

Choosing a Symbol Countries and alliances often use a symbol to represent who they are. The Iroquois League chose a tree. Think of a group you belong to and choose a symbol to represent it. Before you choose, use the CD-ROM, library, or Internet to find out more about why the Iroquois chose a tree.

- Think about what your group stands for. Write a list of adjectives to describe it.
- Brainstorm animals, plants, or objects that share those qualities. Choose one to be your symbol.
- Write an explanation of your symbol and why you chose it.

4. HISTORY PORTFOLIO

Review the questions that you wrote for What Do You Want to Know? on page 26. Then write a short report in which you explain the answers to your questions. If any questions were not answered, do research to answer them. Be sure to use standard grammar, spelling, sentence structure, and punctuation in your report. Add your report to your portfolio.

Additional Test Practice, pp. S1–S33

TEST PRACTICE
CLASSZONE.COM

Create and Decode a Pictograph

Native Americans of the Southwest created thousands of images to communicate with each other. These images, known as pictographs, helped people recall certain events, ideas, or information. Even if the people who created them were no longer present, others could read the messages. Most images were painted or carved on the surfaces of rock. There are three types of pictographs: petroglyphs, petrograms, and geoglyphs. (See HELP DESK on the next page.)

ACTIVITY Create a pictograph that other students will decode, or figure out. Then, acting as an anthropologist, interview students in one other group about their pictograph.

TOOLBOX

Each group will need:

drawing paper or poster board	watercolor paints and brushes (optional)
markers	an envelope
regular and colored pencils	

The Fremont culture carved this petroglyph. It is currently located in Dinosaur National Monument—most of which sits in northwestern Colorado.

STEP BY STEP

1 **Form a group of 4 or 5 students.** Together, think of a message to tell someone living in the future. What might you want future generations to know about your culture, or way of life? If you're having trouble coming up with a message, copy the chart below into your notebook. Write information for each category that you think would be interesting to future generations. Then choose one of these categories for your message.

Sports	
Politics	
Fashion	
Music	
Entertainment	
Weather	
Daily Life	

2 **Examine reference materials.** In the library or on the Internet, research Native American pictographs. Use the information you find to help start your project. (See HELP DESK on the next page.)

3 **Create your pictograph.**
Communicate your message with symbols like the ones that you have researched. Sketch your pictograph on the drawing paper or poster board with a pencil first. Make the pictograph simple so that the decoders will understand your message. Remember to use symbols—not letters.

4 **Decorate your pictograph.**
Use markers or watercolor paints to finish your pictograph. Also, record the translation of your pictograph in your notebook.

5 **Exchange your pictograph with another group of students.** Try to decode the message in the pictograph that the other group of students has given you. Write your translation and place it in your envelope. Give the envelope to the group whose pictograph you decoded.

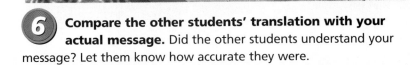

6 **Compare the other students' translation with your actual message.** Did the other students understand your message? Let them know how accurate they were.

WRITE AND SPEAK

Using the information in the pictograph that you decoded, write a description of the people who created the message. Use the symbols as well as the message itself to help you in your description. Explain to the class how you came to your conclusions.

 HELP DESK

For related information see Chapter 1, p. 28.

Researching Your Project

• *On the Trail of Spider Woman: Petroglyphs, Pictographs, and Myths of the Southwest* by Carol Patterson-Rudolph. Shows variety of actual pictographs.

• *21 Kinds of American Folk Art and How to Make Each One* by Jean and Cle Kinney. Explains process of making pictographs.

For more about pictographs . . .

RESEARCH LINKS
CLASSZONE.COM

Did You Know?

Petroglyphs are images carved into a rock using stone tools. **Petrograms** are images painted on a rock. **Geoglyphs** are images formed on the ground by scraping away soil or by arranging stones to form an image.

REFLECT & ASSESS

• Which symbols in your pictograph were clear to the decoders? Which were not clear?

• What methods did you use to decode the messages of others?

• What did you learn about language and communication from doing this pictograph decoding activity?

CHAPTER 2

European Exploration of the Americas

1492–1700

Section 1 **Spain Claims an Empire**

Section 2 **European Competition in North America**

Section 3 **The Impact of Colonization**

Ships in a harbor in Lisbon, Portugal, are preparing for a voyage of exploration.

Vasco Núñez de Balboa led expeditions to explore the Americas for Spain.

Balboa claimed the Pacific Ocean for Spain.

Balboa crossed Panama to reach the Pacific Ocean.

The year is 1510. You live in a European port town and have heard exciting tales about mysterious lands across the sea. You decide to join a voyage of exploration in search of fortune.

Would you join a voyage of exploration?

What Do You Think?

- What do you think led people like Balboa to explore distant lands?
- What reasons would make you want to join a voyage of exploration?
- What reasons would keep you from joining such a voyage?

1535 Cartier leads expedition up St. Lawrence River.

1539–1542 Coronado, de Soto, and Cabrillo explore different parts of North America.

1609 Hudson searches for Northwest Passage.

1680 Popé leads Pueblo Revolt and forces Spanish from New Mexico.

1497 Cabot searches for Northwest Passage.

1521 Cortés conquers Mexico.

1565 Spanish found St. Augustine.

1626 Dutch buy Manhattan Island.

N. America World   1492   1700

1494 Spain and Portugal agree to Treaty of Tordesillas.

1542 King of Spain issues laws for better treatment of Native Americans.

1588 English navy defeats Spanish Armada.

1644 Manchus establish Qing Dynasty in China.

1651 English Parliament passes Navigation Act.

BEFORE YOU READ

Previewing the Theme

Immigration and Migration From the 15th century to the 18th century, millions of people came to the Americas from other continents. Chapter 2 discusses why people came to the Americas and the effect that these migrations had on the people who already lived there.

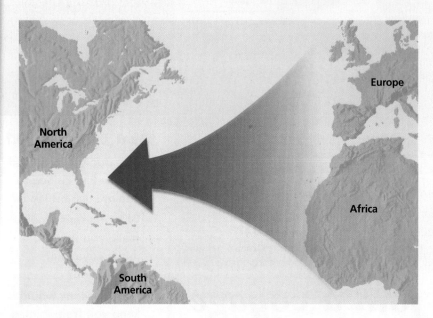

What Do You Know?

What comes to mind when someone uses the word *explorer*? Why do you think people explored different territories?

THINK ABOUT

• what you've learned about explorers from movies, school, or your parents

• reasons that people travel throughout the world today

What Do You Want to Know?

What questions do you have about exploration or the early colonization of the Americas? Write those questions in your notebook before you read the chapter.

READ AND TAKE NOTES

Reading Strategy: Taking Notes To help you remember what you read, take notes about the events and ideas discussed in the chapter. Taking notes means writing down important information.

The chart below lists the major events and ideas covered in the chapter. Use the chart to take notes about these important events and ideas.

 See Skillbuilder Handbook, page R3.

Event/Idea	Notes
Exploration	
Establishing Colonies	
European Competition	
Columbian Exchange	
Origins of Slavery	

1 Spain Claims an Empire

TERMS & NAMES
Treaty of Tordesillas
mercantilism
conquistador
Hernando Cortés
Montezuma
Francisco Pizarro

MAIN IDEA	WHY IT MATTERS NOW
Spain claimed a large empire in the Americas.	The influence of Spanish culture remains strong in modern America.

ONE EUROPEAN'S STORY

Pope Alexander VI had an important decision to make. In 1493, the rulers of Spain and Portugal wanted him to decide who would control the lands that European sailors were exploring. Ferdinand and Isabella of Spain expected Alexander VI to give Spain the rights over many of these lands. But King John II of Portugal claimed territories, too. What would the new pope do?

In May 1493, the pope issued his ruling. He drew an imaginary line around the world. It was called the Line of Demarcation. Portugal could claim all non-Christian lands to the east of the line. Spain could claim the non-Christian lands to the west. In this section, you will learn how Spain and Portugal led Europe in the race to gain colonies in the Americas.

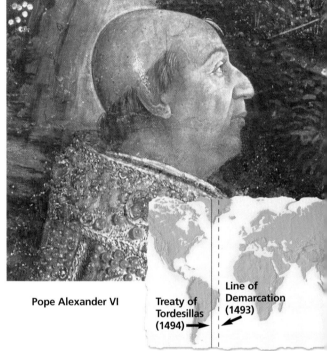

Pope Alexander VI

Treaty of Tordesillas (1494)

Line of Demarcation (1493)

Spain and Portugal Compete

King John II was unhappy with the pope's placement of the line. He believed that it favored Spain. So he demanded that the Spanish rulers meet with him to change the pope's decision. In June 1494, the two countries agreed to the **Treaty of Tordesillas** (tawr•day•SEEL•yahs). This treaty moved the Line of Demarcation more than 800 miles farther to the west. The change eventually allowed Portugal to claim much of eastern South America, which later became the Portuguese colony of Brazil. Following this agreement, Spain and Portugal increased their voyages of exploration.

European countries had three main goals during this age of exploration. First, they wanted to spread Christianity beyond Europe. Second, they wanted to expand their empires. Third, they wanted to become rich.

By increasing their wealth, European countries could gain power and security. An economic system called **mercantilism** describes how Europeans enriched their treasuries. (See Economics in History on page 52.) Colonies helped nations grow rich in several ways. Colonies provided

Economics *in* History

Mercantilism

The main goal of mercantilism was to increase the money in a country's treasury by creating a favorable balance of trade. A country had a favorable balance of trade if it had more exports than imports. Colonies helped a country have the goods to maintain a favorable balance of trade.

For example, say Spain sold $500 in sugar to France, and France sold $300 in cloth to Spain. France would also have to pay Spain $200 worth of precious metals to pay for all the sugar. Spain would then have a favorable balance of trade because the value of its exports (sugar) was greater than the value of its imports (cloth). Spain would become richer because of the precious metals it received from France.

Sugar $500

Spain

France

Cloth $300

Gold & Silver $200

CONNECT TO HISTORY

1. **Finding Main Ideas** Under mercantilism, what did a country need to do to become rich? Discuss the way colonies enriched a country according to mercantilism.

 See Skillbuilder Handbook, page R5.

CONNECT TO TODAY

2. **Making Inferences** Think about your own family budget. What do you think would happen if your family collected less money than it paid for goods for several years? Do you think this situation would be the same for a nation as it would for a family?

For more information on mercantilism . . .

RESEARCH LINKS
CLASSZONE.COM

---

various raw materials as well as mines that produced gold and silver. In addition, colonies served as markets for goods made in the home country.

Europeans Explore Foreign Lands

After Columbus's first voyage, many explorers went to sea. Italian sailor Amerigo Vespucci (vehs•POO•chee) set out in 1501 to find a sea route to Asia. Vespucci realized that the land he saw on this voyage was not Asia. A German mapmaker was impressed by Vespucci's account of the lands, so he named the continent "America" after him. Another famous explorer was the Spaniard Vasco Núñez de Balboa. In 1513, he led an expedition through the jungles of Panama and reached the Pacific Ocean.

In 1519, Portuguese sailor Ferdinand Magellan set out to reach Asia by sailing west around South America. During the long journey, he and his fellow sailors suffered great hardship. A member of the crew described what they ate.

A VOICE FROM THE PAST

We were three months and twenty days without . . . fresh food. We ate biscuit, which was no longer biscuit, but powder of biscuits swarming with worms. . . . We drank . . . water that had been putrid for many days.

Antonio Pigafetta, quoted in *The Discoverers*

Although Magellan died during the trip, his crew carried on and became the first people to sail around the world.

Background
Magellan was killed after becoming involved in a local war in the Philippines.

The Invasion of the Americas

While Magellan's crew was sailing around the world, the Spanish began their conquest of the Americas. Soldiers called ***conquistadors*** (kahn•KWIHS•tuh•DAWRZ), or conquerors, explored the Americas and claimed them for Spain. **Hernando Cortés** was one of these conquistadors. After landing in Central America in 1519, Cortés and his army of 508 men set their sights on conquering the mighty Aztec Empire.

The Spaniards marched inland and formed alliances (agreements with friendly peoples) with the native peoples who hated Aztec rule. Upon reaching the Aztec capital, Tenochtitlán (teh•NAWCH•tee•TLAHN), Cortés received a warm greeting from the Aztec emperor, **Montezuma**. Relations between the two sides quickly collapsed, however, as Cortés sought to take control of the empire. After several fierce clashes, the Aztecs drove the Spanish out.

Despite this defeat, the Spaniards and their allies regrouped. In May 1521, Cortés led his forces back to Tenochtitlán. At this point, the Spaniards got help from an invisible ally. Many Aztecs fell victim to an outbreak of smallpox, which severely weakened their ranks. The germs that caused this disease had been brought to America by the Europeans. After months of fighting, Cortés conquered the empire.

Reading **History**

A. Clarifying
Why did relations between the Spanish and Aztecs quickly break down?

AMERICA'S HISTORY MAKERS

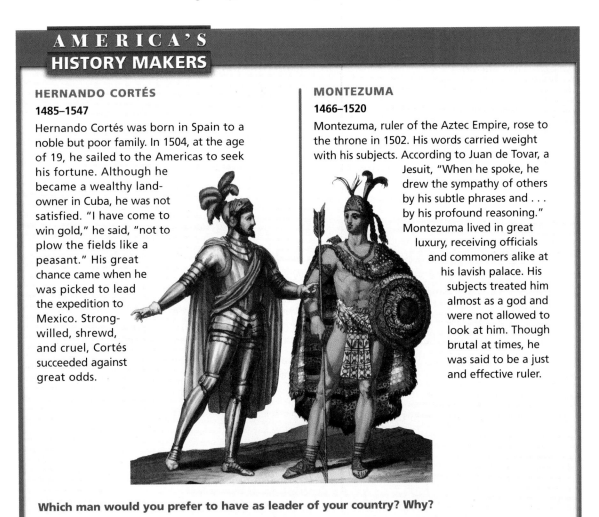

HERNANDO CORTÉS
1485–1547
Hernando Cortés was born in Spain to a noble but poor family. In 1504, at the age of 19, he sailed to the Americas to seek his fortune. Although he became a wealthy land-owner in Cuba, he was not satisfied. "I have come to win gold," he said, "not to plow the fields like a peasant." His great chance came when he was picked to lead the expedition to Mexico. Strong-willed, shrewd, and cruel, Cortés succeeded against great odds.

MONTEZUMA
1466–1520
Montezuma, ruler of the Aztec Empire, rose to the throne in 1502. His words carried weight with his subjects. According to Juan de Tovar, a Jesuit, "When he spoke, he drew the sympathy of others by his subtle phrases and . . . by his profound reasoning." Montezuma lived in great luxury, receiving officials and commoners alike at his lavish palace. His subjects treated him almost as a god and were not allowed to look at him. Though brutal at times, he was said to be a just and effective ruler.

Which man would you prefer to have as leader of your country? Why?

In 1531, a *conquistador* named **Francisco Pizarro** marched on the Incas. The Incas had built a powerful and wealthy empire centered in the Cuzco Valley in what is now Peru. With an army of only 180 men, Pizarro conquered the Inca.

People have long been amazed that the great Aztec and Incan empires fell to such small groups of Spanish *conquistadors*. But Spanish success can be explained by three major reasons.

1. The spread of European diseases killed millions of Native Americans.
2. The Spanish were excellent soldiers and sailors. They also had superior weapons, such as guns.
3. Spain made alliances with Native Americans who were enemies of the Aztecs and Incas.

Having conquered the major Native American empires in Central and South America, the Spaniards began to explore other parts of North and South America.

Estevanico was a slave who helped the Spanish explore parts of North America. He was killed during Coronado's search for golden cities.

*Reading*History
B. Drawing Conclusions
What was the most important reason for the Spanish success in conquering territory in the Americas?

Other Spanish Explorers

The Spaniards hoped to collect treasures from North America as they had from Mexico and Peru. Rumors of golden cities kept Spanish hopes high. For example, the Spaniard Álvar Núñez Cabeza de Vaca and Estevanico, a slave of North African descent, wandered across the continent and heard Native American stories about cities of gold.

Between 1539 and 1542, three expeditions set out to find these cities. Francisco Vázquez de Coronado traveled through present-day Arizona and New Mexico. Hernando de Soto set out from Florida to explore the southeast. Juan Rodríguez Cabrillo sailed up the California coast. But all three failed to find the fabled cities of gold.

For a while, it seemed that the Spaniards would explore the Americas all by themselves. As you will read in the next section, however, the Spanish would soon face competition from other Europeans.

Section 1 Assessment

1. Terms & Names

Explain the significance of:
- Treaty of Tordesillas
- mercantilism
- *conquistador*
- Hernando Cortés
- Montezuma
- Francisco Pizarro

2. Taking Notes

Review the section and find four events to place on a time line that shows how Spain built its empire.

Spain Builds an Empire

Which event do you think is the most important? Why?

3. Main Ideas

a. Why did Europeans explore different territories?

b. Why did Spain succeed in conquering so much of the Americas?

c. What was significant about the Magellan expedition?

4. Critical Thinking

Comparing What was similar about the conquests of Mexico and Peru?

THINK ABOUT
- the *conquistadors*
- the size of their armies

ACTIVITY OPTIONS

ART

LANGUAGE ARTS

Use the library or Internet to find a photograph of an Aztec or Incan artifact. Create a **replica** or write a **description** of the object.

② European Competition in North America

TERMS & NAMES
Henry Hudson
John Cabot
Giovanni da Verrazzano
Jacques Cartier
Spanish Armada
Samuel de Champlain
New France

MAIN IDEA	WHY IT MATTERS NOW
Other European countries competed with Spain for control over territory in the Americas.	European culture has strongly influenced American culture.

ONE EUROPEAN'S STORY

In 1609, an Englishman named **Henry Hudson** set sail from Europe. He sailed under the Dutch flag and hoped to find a route to China. Arriving at the coast of present-day New York, he sailed up the river that now bears his name. In his journal, Hudson described what he saw.

A VOICE FROM THE PAST

The land is the finest for cultivation that I ever in my life set foot upon, and it also abounds in trees of every description. The natives are a very good people; for, when they saw that I would not remain, they supposed that I was afraid of their bows, and taking the arrows, they broke them in pieces and threw them into the fire.

Henry Hudson, quoted in *Discoverers of America*

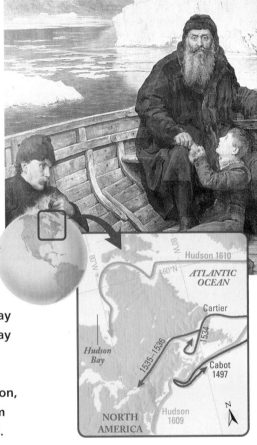

Hudson did not find a passage to Asia, but he led another expedition in 1610, this time sailing for the English. He made his way through ice-clogged waters in Canada and entered a large bay, today called Hudson Bay. There he sailed for months, but still found no westward passage.

After enduring a harsh winter, his crew rebelled. They put Hudson, his young son, and several loyal sailors in a small boat and set them adrift (shown at right). Hudson's party was never heard from again.

The Search for the Northwest Passage

Hudson's voyages showed that some European countries hoped to find a westward route to Asia as late as the 1600s. While Spain was taking control of the Americas, other Europeans were sending out expeditions to find the Northwest Passage, a water route through North America to Asia.

One of the first explorers to chart a northern route across the Atlantic in search of Asia was the Italian sailor **John Cabot.** In 1497, Cabot crossed the Atlantic Ocean to explore for the English. He landed in the area of Newfoundland, Canada. He was certain that he had reached Asia and claimed the land for England. The next year he set sail once more, hoping

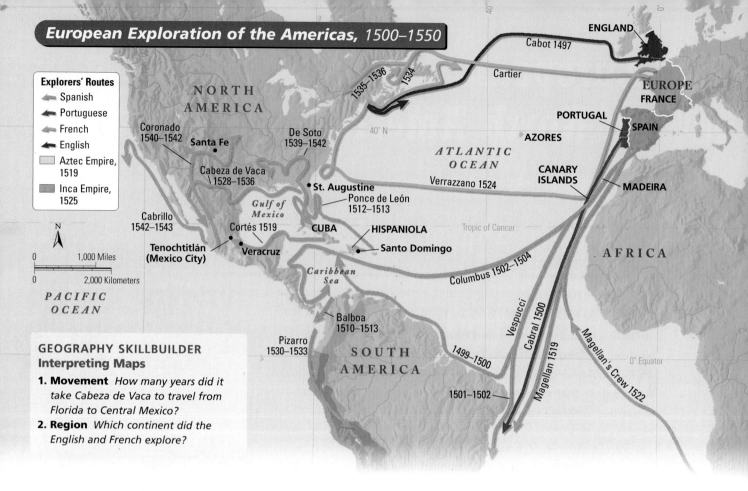

European Exploration of the Americas, 1500–1550

Explorers' Routes
- Spanish
- Portuguese
- French
- English
- Aztec Empire, 1519
- Inca Empire, 1525

ENGLAND
Cabot 1497
Cartier
EUROPE
FRANCE
PORTUGAL
SPAIN
AZORES
CANARY ISLANDS
MADEIRA
AFRICA

NORTH AMERICA
1535–1536
1534
40° N
ATLANTIC OCEAN
Verrazzano 1524

Coronado 1540–1542
Santa Fe
Cabeza de Vaca 1528–1536
De Soto 1539–1542
St. Augustine
Ponce de León 1512–1513
Cabrillo 1542–1543
Cortés 1519
Tenochtitlán (Mexico City)
Veracruz
Gulf of Mexico
CUBA
HISPANIOLA
Santo Domingo
Tropic of Cancer

Caribbean Sea
Balboa 1510–1513
Pizarro 1530–1533
SOUTH AMERICA
1499–1500
1501–1502
Columbus 1502–1504
Vespucci 1500
Cabral 1500
Magellan 1519
Magellan's Crew 1522
0° Equator

PACIFIC OCEAN

N
0   1,000 Miles
0   2,000 Kilometers

GEOGRAPHY SKILLBUILDER
Interpreting Maps
1. **Movement** *How many years did it take Cabeza de Vaca to travel from Florida to Central Mexico?*
2. **Region** *Which continent did the English and French explore?*

to reach Japan. He was never seen again. Even so, his voyages were the basis for future English colonies along the Atlantic shore of North America.

In 1524, another Italian, **Giovanni da Verrazzano,** set out under the French flag to find the Northwest Passage. He explored the Atlantic coastline of North America, but there was no passage to be found.

France tried again between 1534 and 1536 with the voyages of **Jacques Cartier** (ZHAHK kahr•TYAY). Cartier traveled up the St. Lawrence River to the site of present-day Montreal. At that point, rapids blocked the way and ended his search for the Northwest Passage. It would be almost 75 years before the French would return to colonize the region.

Reading **History**
A. Reading a Map
Use the maps on pages 55 and 56 to see the areas Cabot, Hudson, Verrazzano, and Cartier visited.

Spain Responds to Competition

French and English claims to North America angered Spain, which had claimed the land under the Treaty of Tordesillas. The tensions between Spain, England, and France stemmed from religious conflicts in Europe, such as the Reformation, which you read about in Chapter 1. These conflicts also led to fighting in the Americas.

Florida was one of the battlegrounds between the Spanish and the French. In 1564, a group of French Protestants, called Huguenots (HYOO•guh•NAHTS), founded a colony called Fort Caroline. Before long, Spanish troops under the command of Pedro Menéndez de Avilés arrived in that area. "This is the armada of the King of Spain," he announced, "who has sent me [here] to burn and hang the Lutheran [Protestant] French." Menéndez built a fort, St. Augustine, a short distance away. Then he brutally massacred the French.

Vocabulary
armada: a fleet of warships

Spain and England Clash

Religious differences and the quest for national power also led to conflict between Spain and England. In 1558, Queen Elizabeth I, a Protestant, came to the English throne. Spain, which was Catholic, plotted to remove the Protestant queen. But Elizabeth fought to defend England and challenge Spain's power at sea.

Although England's navy was not as powerful as Spain's, the English fleet had many speedy ships with skillful sailors. Daring sailors, known as sea dogs, used these ships to attack the Spanish. The Spanish sailed bulky, slow-moving ships called galleons. These galleons brought gold and silver from the Americas to Spain.

Sir Francis Drake became the most famous of the sea dogs because of his bold adventures and attacks against the Spanish. In 1577, Drake began a three-year voyage that took him around the world. During this voyage, he raided Spanish ports and ships in South America. He stole great amounts of treasure from them. When he arrived home in 1580, he was a national hero. Not only had Drake and his men hounded the Spanish, but they were also the first Englishmen to sail around the world.

The Defeat of the Spanish Armada

The attacks of Drake and other sea dogs enraged Philip II, the Spanish king. Determined to teach the English a lesson, Philip sent the **Spanish Armada** to conquer England and restore Catholicism to that nation. This fleet, made up of 130 ships, set out for England in the summer of 1588.

The English and Spanish navies met in the English Channel, which separates England from the European continent. In their smaller but faster craft, the English darted among the Spanish warships, firing deadly rounds with their cannons. Confused and crippled, the armada was retreating when it was hit by a severe storm. With half of its ships destroyed, the armada barely made it home.

Spain was still quite strong after the defeat of the armada. It quickly rebuilt its navy and maintained its large colonial possessions. But Spain would never again be as powerful as it was in 1588.

The English victory over Spain had two important effects. First, it ensured that England would remain independent and Protestant. Although England was less powerful than Spain, England proved that it could defend itself. Second, Spain's image suffered. The world saw that Spain could be beaten. Other nations joined England in challenging Spain.

America's
HERITAGE

ST. AUGUSTINE

The thick stone walls of the fort at St. Augustine (shown below) still stand guard over the Florida coast today. Founded in 1565, St. Augustine is the oldest permanent European settlement in the United States. For more than two centuries, St. Augustine was an important outpost of Spain's empire in the Americas. Many Spanish colonial buildings remain at the site. The fort is now a national monument.

*Reading*History

B. Drawing Conclusions
Why was the defeat of the Spanish Armada important?

English adventurers like Drake continued to attack Spanish interests abroad. In addition, England challenged Spanish claims to lands in North America, such as California and Newfoundland. Even so, England took a cautious approach to overseas expansion. The English government refused to provide money to start colonies. Instead, private citizens had to provide the money for colonization. As a result, England did not establish a successful colony in America until after 1600.

The French and Dutch Seek Trade

France and the Netherlands were also looking for ways to gain wealth through exploration and colonization. At first, their goal in the Americas was to find the Northwest Passage to Asia. When that search failed, they began to focus on North America itself.

The Frenchman **Samuel de Champlain** (sham•PLAYN) explored the St. Lawrence River. In 1608, he founded a fur-trading post at Quebec. This post became the first permanent French settlement in North America. Champlain's activities opened a rich fur trade with local Native Americans. After a couple of decades, **New France**, as the colony was called, began to thrive.

At the same time, the Dutch were building a colony called New Netherland. It was located along the Hudson River in present-day New York. After Hudson's voyage up the river in 1609, the Dutch built Fort Nassau in 1614, near the site of the modern city of Albany.

In 1626, the Dutch bought Manhattan Island from Native Americans. The Dutch then founded the town of New Amsterdam on that site, where New York City is currently located. New Netherland was soon thriving from the fur trade with Native Americans.

These early French and Dutch colonies, however, were small compared to the large empire Spain was building in the Americas. You will read about Spain's empire and the impact of colonization in the next section.

Reading History
C. Making Inferences Why do you think it took France and the Netherlands so long to set up colonies in the Americas?

Section **2** Assessment

1. Terms & Names
Explain the significance of:
• Henry Hudson
• John Cabot
• Giovanni da Verrazzano
• Jacques Cartier
• Spanish Armada
• Samuel de Champlain
• New France

2. Taking Notes
Use a chart like the one below to show how European nations competed for power.

England	
France	
Netherlands	
Spain	

3. Main Ideas
a. What were the English, French, and Dutch searching for in their early voyages of exploration?

b. How did England defeat the Spanish Armada?

c. Where did the French and Dutch set up their first American colonies?

4. Critical Thinking
Making Inferences Why do you think England founded colonies later than Spain did?

THINK ABOUT
• conditions in Spain and England
• the lands each country discovered

ACTIVITY OPTIONS

MUSIC
TECHNOLOGY

Research the life of one of the explorers discussed in this section. Compose a **song** or design a **Web page** about that person.

③ The Impact of Colonization

TERMS & NAMES
encomienda
plantation
slavery
African Diaspora
middle passage
racism
Columbian Exchange

MAIN IDEA	WHY IT MATTERS NOW
Spanish rule in the Americas had terrible consequences for Native Americans and Africans.	The effects of slavery, including racism, helped shape attitudes and social conditions in the United States.

ONE AMERICAN'S STORY

Huamán Poma, a Peruvian Native American, was angry about the abuse the Spanish heaped upon Native Americans. He wrote to King Philip III of Spain to complain about the bad treatment.

A VOICE FROM THE PAST

It is their [the Spanish] practice to collect Indians into groups and send them to forced labor without wages, while they themselves receive the payment for the work. . . . The royal administrators and the other Spaniards lord it over the Indians with absolute power.

Huamán Poma, *Letter to a King*

In his letter, Poma asked the king to help the Native Americans and uphold the rule of law in Peru. Regardless, the Spanish colonists continued to mistreat Native Americans as the Spaniards expanded their empire in the Americas. In time, colonists from Spain and other European nations would import millions of Africans to the Americas and enslave them as well. For the members of these subjected groups, American colonization was devastating.

A Spanish priest forces a Native American woman to work at a loom.

Life in Spanish America

The Spanish Empire grew rapidly, despite efforts by other European countries to compete with Spain. By 1700, it controlled much of the Americas. Spain took several steps to establish an effective colonial government. First, it divided its American empire into two provinces called New Spain and Peru. Each province was called a viceroyalty. The top official of each viceroyalty was called the viceroy. He ruled in the king's name.

The Spaniards made sure that people with Spanish backgrounds held power in the colonies. Just below the Spanish were the Creoles—people of Spanish descent who were born in the colonies. The next step down

European Exploration of the Americas **59**

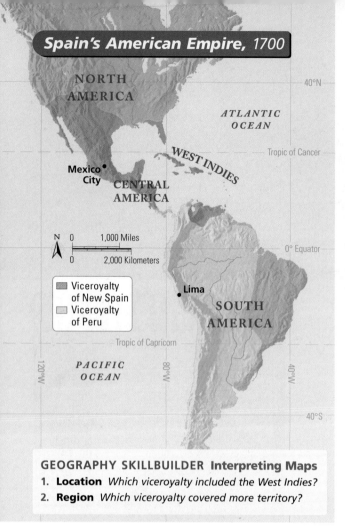

Spain's American Empire, 1700

NORTH AMERICA

ATLANTIC OCEAN

40°N

Tropic of Cancer

Mexico City

WEST INDIES

CENTRAL AMERICA

0° Equator

Lima

SOUTH AMERICA

Tropic of Capricorn

PACIFIC OCEAN

40°S

N

0   1,000 Miles

0   2,000 Kilometers

■ Viceroyalty of New Spain
■ Viceroyalty of Peru

120°W   80°W   40°W

GEOGRAPHY SKILLBUILDER Interpreting Maps
1. **Location** *Which viceroyalty included the West Indies?*
2. **Region** *Which viceroyalty covered more territory?*

the social order were the *mestizos.* *Mestizos* are people of mixed Spanish and Native American ancestry. The people with the least power and fewest rights were Native Americans and enslaved Africans.

The Catholic Church played an important role in Spanish colonial society. In places like New Mexico and California, the church built missions, settlements that included a church, a town, and farmlands. The goal of the missions was to convert Native Americans to Christianity. The missions also increased Spanish control over the land.

Some Spanish colonists received *encomiendas* to help them make the colonies productive. An **encomienda** was a grant of Native American labor. The Spanish rulers also created large estates, called *haciendas,* to provide food for the colony. *Haciendas* often became **plantations,** large farms that raised cash crops, such as sugar, coffee, and cotton, which were in great demand in Europe. The Spanish forced Native Americans to work on these plantations.

Background
In precolonial America, forms of slavery were practiced by some Native Americans and differed greatly among different peoples.

Most Spaniards treated the Native Americans as little more than beasts of burden, forcing countless numbers of them to work in the fields and mines. In addition, some missionaries mistreated them by forcing them to work terrribly hard. Other missionaries, though, tried to protect Native Americans from being treated cruelly.

One missionary in particular who fought for better treatment of Native Americans was Bartolomé de Las Casas. Las Casas, a Catholic priest, fought against the abuse of Native Americans, earning the title "Protector of the Indians." Due largely to his efforts, Spanish authorities passed laws providing greater protection for Native Americans. Most colonists, however, ignored the laws.

In 1680, a man named Popé led the Pueblo Indians in a rebellion against the Spanish. His forces surrounded the Spanish settlement at Santa Fe, in present-day New Mexico, and forced the colonists to flee temporarily from the region.

Reading History
A. Summarizing In what ways did the Spanish mistreat Native Americans?

The Emergence of American Slavery

As more and more Native Americans died from overwork and European diseases, the Spanish and Portuguese turned to another source for labor: enslaved Africans. **Slavery** is the practice of holding a person in bondage

The images above show how slave traders packed enslaved Africans onto slave ships for the middle passage.

for labor. The Europeans enslaved Africans for four basic reasons. First, Africans were immune to most European diseases. Second, Africans had no friends or family in the Americas to help them resist or escape enslavement. Third, enslaved Africans provided a permanent source of cheap labor. Even their children could be held in bondage. Fourth, many Africans had worked on farms in their native lands.

In the early 1500s, European traders began bringing Africans to the Americas for slave labor. This forced removal has become known as the **African Diaspora.** Before the slave trade ended in the late 1800s, approximately 12 million Africans had been enslaved and shipped to the Western Hemisphere.

Vocabulary
diaspora: the scattering of people outside their homeland

The voyage of the slave ships from Africa to the Americas was called the **middle passage.** The voyage was given this name because it was the middle leg of the triangular trade. The triangular trade refers to the movement of trade ships between Europe, Africa, and the Americas. You will learn more about the triangular trade in Chapter 4.

Olaudah Equiano (oh•LOW•duh EHK•wee•AHN•oh) was one of these kidnapped Africans. He made this journey in the 1700s. He was about 11 years old when he was sold into slavery. Later, after he bought his freedom, he wrote his life story and described the terror of the middle passage.

A VOICE FROM THE PAST

The first object which saluted my eyes when I arrived on the coast, was the sea, and a slave ship . . . waiting for its cargo. These filled me with astonishment, which was soon converted into terror, when I was carried on board.

Olaudah Equiano, quoted in *Great Slave Narratives*

It is estimated that perhaps two million Africans died during the middle passage. Those who survived faced a hard life in the Americas. Some were taken to large homes where they worked as servants. Most were forced to do hard labor in *haciendas* or mines.

61

Many slaves resisted slavery by running away or rebelling. To prevent rebellion, the Spanish government passed slave codes, laws to regulate the treatment of slaves. Some of these laws tried to soften the harsh conditions of slavery, but most were designed to punish slaves and keep them in bondage.

Over time, Europeans came to associate slavery with black Africans. To many Europeans, dark skin color became a sign of inferiority. Slavery, which developed to provide a labor force, led to racism. **Racism** is the belief that some people are inferior because of their race.

The slave trade lasted 400 years, from the 1500s until the 1800s. By the 1700s, all the American colonies of European countries had African slaves.

Despite the horrors of slavery, Africans survived in part by clinging to their African cultures, including their artistic heritage of dance, music, and storytelling. The slave trade brought together people from different parts of Africa with different cultural traditions. The experience of slavery helped create a common African-based culture in the Americas. African culture would become one of the forces that shaped life in the American colonies.

*Reading*History

B. Analyzing Causes What could have caused slave traders to treat other humans with such cruelty?

The Columbian Exchange

The arrival of Europeans in the Americas brought more than a clash of peoples and cultures. It also brought a movement of plants, animals, and diseases between the Eastern and Western hemispheres. This movement of living things between hemispheres is called the **Columbian Exchange**.

One result of the Columbian Exchange was the transfer of germs from Europe to the Americas. When Europeans came to America, they brought with them germs that caused diseases such as smallpox, measles, and influenza. Native Americans had no immunity to them.

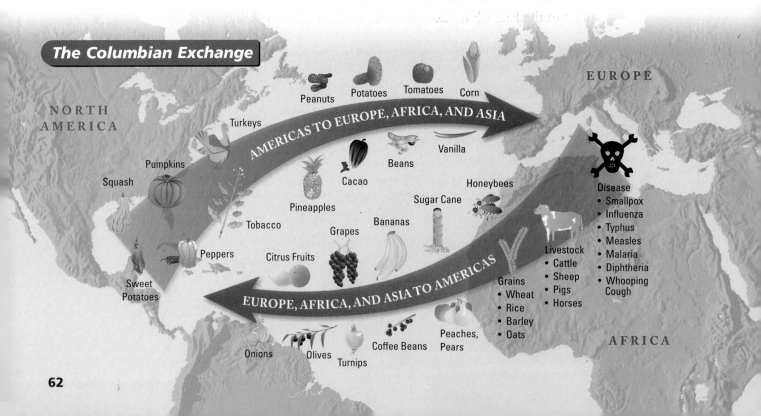

The Columbian Exchange

NORTH AMERICA

EUROPE

AMERICAS TO EUROPE, AFRICA, AND ASIA

EUROPE, AFRICA, AND ASIA TO AMERICAS

AFRICA

Peanuts · Potatoes · Tomatoes · Corn · Turkeys · Pumpkins · Squash · Cacao · Beans · Vanilla · Pineapples · Tobacco · Bananas · Honeybees · Grapes · Sugar Cane · Peppers · Citrus Fruits · Sweet Potatoes · Onions · Olives · Turnips · Coffee Beans · Peaches, Pears

Grains
• Wheat
• Rice
• Barley
• Oats

Livestock
• Cattle
• Sheep
• Pigs
• Horses

Disease
• Smallpox
• Influenza
• Typhus
• Measles
• Malaria
• Diphtheria
• Whooping Cough

Reading **History**

C. Making Inferences What might have happened if Native Americans had been immune to European diseases?

Although exact numbers are unknown, historians estimate that diseases brought by Europeans killed more than 20 million Native Americans in Mexico in the first century after conquest. Many scholars agree that the population of Native Americans in Central America decreased by 90 to 95 percent between the years 1519 and 1619. The result was similar in Peru and other parts of the Americas. A Spanish missionary in Mexico described the effects of smallpox on the Aztecs.

A VOICE FROM THE PAST

There was a great havoc. Very many died of it. They could not walk. . . . They could not move; they could not stir; they could not change position, nor lie on one side; nor face down, nor on their backs. And if they stirred, much did they cry out. Great was its destruction.

Bernardino de Sahagún, quoted in *Seeds of Change*

Other effects of the Columbian Exchange were more positive. The Spanish brought many plants and animals to the Americas. European livestock—cattle, pigs, and horses—all thrived in the Americas. Crops from the Eastern Hemisphere, such as grapes, onions, and wheat, also thrived in the Western Hemisphere.

The Columbian Exchange benefited Europe, too. Many American crops became part of the European diet. Two that had a huge impact were potatoes and corn. They helped feed European populations that might otherwise have gone hungry. Potatoes, for example, became an important food in Ireland, Russia, and other parts of northern Europe. Without potatoes, Europe's population might not have grown as rapidly as it did during the last five centuries.

By mixing the products of two hemispheres, the Columbian Exchange brought the world closer together. Of course, people were also moving from one hemisphere to the other. The next chapter discusses the movement of the English to the Americas and their efforts to build an empire.

Section 3 Assessment

1. Terms & Names

Explain the significance of:
- *encomienda*
- plantation
- slavery
- African Diaspora
- middle passage
- racism
- Columbian Exchange

2. Taking Notes

Use a diagram like the one below to compare the experience of Native Americans and Africans under slavery.

Native Americans	Africans

3. Main Ideas

a. What were the four levels of Spanish colonial society?

b. Why did Europeans bring Africans to the Americas?

c. How did enslaved Africans respond to their enslavement in the Americas?

4. Critical Thinking

Recognizing Effects What were the positive and negative effects of the Columbian Exchange?

THINK ABOUT
- disease
- food
- livestock

ACTIVITY OPTIONS

ART

MATH

Research some aspect of the slave trade, such as the middle passage or the number of people enslaved. Paint a **picture** or draw a **graph** to show what you learned.

TERMS & NAMES

Briefly explain the significance of each of the following.

1. mercantilism
2. *conquistador*
3. Hernando Cortés
4. Montezuma
5. Spanish Armada
6. New France
7. *encomienda*
8. African Diaspora
9. middle passage
10. Columbian Exchange

REVIEW QUESTIONS

Spain Claims an Empire (pages 51–54)

1. What were three reasons for the European voyages of exploration in the 1400s and 1500s?
2. Who conquered the Aztecs and Incas?
3. What three reasons explain Spain's success in building an empire in the Americas?

European Competition in North America (pages 55–58)

4. What was the Northwest Passage?
5. Why did the Spanish Armada attack England?
6. What did the French and Dutch colonists trade?

The Impact of Colonization (pages 59–63)

7. How did Spanish rule affect Native Americans?
8. How did the middle passage get its name?
9. Why did the Spanish and Portuguese use slave labor in their colonies?
10. How did the Columbian Exchange affect Europe?

CRITICAL THINKING

1. USING YOUR NOTES

Event/Idea	Notes
Exploration	
Establishing Colonies	
European Competition	
Columbian Exchange	
Origins of Slavery	

Using your completed chart, answer the questions below.

a. What causes did European competition and exploration have in common?
b. How did the establishment of colonies in the Americas lead to slavery?
c. Which concept in the chart contributed most to the Columbian Exchange?

2. ANALYZING LEADERSHIP

Think about the explorers and *conquistadors* discussed in this chapter. What qualities did they possess that made them successful in their efforts?

3. THEME: IMMIGRATION AND MIGRATION

What were the causes and effects of the migration of Europeans and Africans to the Americas?

4. APPLYING CITIZENSHIP SKILLS

What kind of values did Bartolomé de Las Casas demonstrate in his actions? How effective was he in improving his society?

Interact *with* History

Have your answers about whether or not you would join a voyage of exploration changed after reading the chapter? Explain.

VISUAL SUMMARY

European Exploration of the Americas

Causes

- National Competition
- Desire for Wealth
- Spread Christianity

→ European Exploration of the Americas →

Effects

- Destruction of Aztec and Incan Empires
- The Columbian Exchange
- European Colonies in the Americas
- Slavery

HISTORY SKILLS

1. INTERPRETING CHARTS

Slaves Imported to the Americas (in thousands)	1601–1810	
REGION/COUNTRY	1601–1700	1701–1810
British N. America	*	348
British Caribbean	263.7	1,401.3
French Caribbean	155.8	1,348.4
Spanish America	292.5	578.6
Dutch Caribbean	40	460
Danish Caribbean	4	24
Brazil (Portugal)	560	1,891.4

*=less than 1,000

Source: Philip D. Curtin, *The Atlantic Slave Trade*

Basic Chart Elements

a. What is the subject of the chart?

b. How many years are covered in each column?

Interpreting the Chart

c. Which European nation imported the most slaves in the Americas?

d. Which region imported less than 1,000 slaves before 1700?

2. INTERPRETING PRIMARY SOURCES

Bernal Díaz del Castillo was a *conquistador* who accompanied Cortés during the conquest of Mexico. Díaz described what he saw when Cortés and Montezuma met. Read the passage. Then answer the questions.

> On our arrival we entered the large court, where the great Montezuma was awaiting our Captain [Cortés]. Taking him by the hand, the prince led him to his apartment in the hall where he was to lodge, which was very richly furnished. . . . Montezuma had ready for him a very rich necklace, made of golden crabs, a marvelous piece of work, which he hung round Cortés's neck. His captains were greatly astonished at this sign of honour.
>
> **Bernal Díaz del Castillo,** from *The Conquest of New Spain*

a. What can you tell about Montezuma from this passage?

b. How would you describe the relationship between Montezuma and Cortés?

ALTERNATIVE ASSESSMENT

1. INTERDISCIPLINARY ACTIVITY: Language Arts

Writing a News Report Research an event in the conquest of the Americas, such as *La Noche Triste* or the death of Atahualpa, the Inca ruler. Write a news report about the event that explains what happened and who was involved. You should also explain when, where, why, and how the event occurred. Be sure to use standard grammar, spelling, sentence structure, and punctuation in your news report.

2. COOPERATIVE LEARNING ACTIVITY

Creating a Diorama With a group of classmates, research the communities of Spanish America in the 1600s. Then create a diorama of one of those settlements, including a mission, a hacienda, roads, and mines or sugar mills. Use elements such as drawings, maps, and written text to show significant features of life there. Display your diorama and discuss it in class.

3. TECHNOLOGY ACTIVITY

Making a Class Presentation The Columbian Exchange refers to the movement of plants and animals around the world as a result of exploration. Today, species of plants and animals continue to move across the planet. Using the library or the Internet, find diaries and news articles about the effects of this continued movement of plants and animals.

For more information on the migration of plants and animals . . .

INTERNET ACTIVITY
CLASSZONE.COM

Create a class presentation about the movement of plants and animals around the world, using the suggestions below.

- Choose a specific species of plant or animal. Use a map or globe to show where that species has moved in recent years.

- Choose one specific place, and list any species that are new to the area as well as their effects on the ecology.

4. HISTORY PORTFOLIO

Review your section and chapter assessment activities. Select one that you think was your best work. Then revise your work based on the comments of your teacher or classmates and add your work to your portfolio.

Additional Test Practice, pp. S1–S33

TEST PRACTICE
CLASSZONE.COM

The English Establish 13 Colonies 1585–1732

Early settlers build the fort at Jamestown.

The settlers at Jamestown, Virginia, built a fort with three walls rather than four to make it easier to defend.

military training

gate

houses

cannon

water well

The year is 1607. You have just sailed across the ocean and arrived in a strange land. Your family has traveled to the eastern coast of North America in search of freedom and prosperity. Your first task in the new land is to decide what you need to do to survive.

What Do You Think?

- What do you need to survive in the wilderness?

- This settlement is actually a fort, with an armed force and high fences. What reasons might there be for building a fort?

- What kind of settlement would you build?

What dangers would you face as a settler?

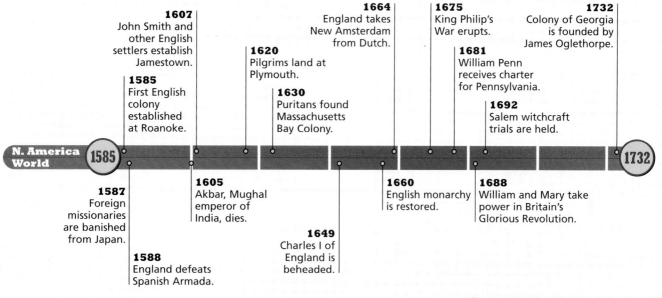

1607
John Smith and other English settlers establish Jamestown.

1664
England takes New Amsterdam from Dutch.

1675
King Philip's War erupts.

1732
Colony of Georgia is founded by James Oglethorpe.

1620
Pilgrims land at Plymouth.

1681
William Penn receives charter for Pennsylvania.

1585
First English colony established at Roanoke.

1630
Puritans found Massachusetts Bay Colony.

1692
Salem witchcraft trials are held.

N. America
World

1585

1732

1587
Foreign missionaries are banished from Japan.

1605
Akbar, Mughal emperor of India, dies.

1660
English monarchy is restored.

1688
William and Mary take power in Britain's Glorious Revolution.

1649
Charles I of England is beheaded.

1588
England defeats Spanish Armada.

BEFORE YOU READ

Previewing the Theme Impact of the Individual

Beginning in 1585, English settlers started colonies along the eastern coast of North America. This chapter explains how the determination of a few leaders led to new colonies. It also explains how the colonies survived, gained more diverse settlers, and began to drive Native Americans (shown in the map below) off the land.

What Do You Know?

What do you already know about the American colonies? What sort of person might choose to leave his or her native country and cross the ocean to settle in a new land?

THINK ABOUT

- what you've learned about American settlers from movies, television, historical fiction, or science fiction about space travel
- opportunities and challenges offered in a new land

What Do You Want to Know?

What questions do you have about the Europeans who settled in North America? about those who were already here? Record your questions in your notebook before you read this chapter.

READ AND TAKE NOTES

Reading Strategy: Sequencing Events

Sequencing means putting events in order. In learning about the early colonies, for example, it will be useful to you to list the 13 original colonies and an important early date mentioned for each in the chapter. You might record the name and a date for each colony in a graphic organizer such as the one below. Copy this organizer in your notebook. Fill it in as you read the chapter.

S See Skillbuilder Handbook, page R4.

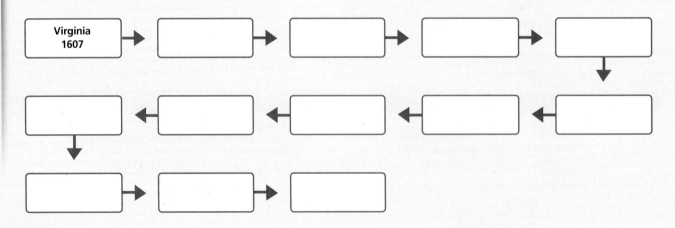

Virginia 1607

1 Early Colonies Have Mixed Success

TERMS & NAMES

joint-stock company

charter

Jamestown

John Smith

indentured servant

House of Burgesses

Bacon's Rebellion

MAIN IDEA

Two early English colonies failed, but Jamestown survived—partly through individual effort and hard work.

WHY IT MATTERS NOW

Jamestown's survival led to more English colonies and a lasting English influence in the United States.

ONE AMERICAN'S STORY

John White was a talented artist. He traveled with the first English expedition to Roanoke, an island off North Carolina, in 1585. While there, he painted scenes of Native American villages. White sailed back to England in 1586 and then returned to Roanoke as governor the next year, bringing with him more than 100 settlers. White's daughter Elinor gave birth to a baby girl, Virginia Dare, during their stay. John White described the event.

A VOICE FROM THE PAST

On August 18 a daughter was born to Elinor, . . . wife of Ananias Dare. . . . The child was christened on the following Sunday and was named Virginia because she was the first Christian born in Virginia.

John White, *The New World*

Drawing by John White of an old man of the Pomeiock tribe.

In 1587, White was forced to sail back to England a second time to get needed supplies. He left the colonists, including his granddaughter, Virginia, in Roanoke. Delayed by the Spanish Armada (a fleet of ships that attempted to invade England in 1588), White did not return to Roanoke until 1590.

To his shock and grief, he found no trace of the colonists or his granddaughter, all of whom had disappeared. The only clues to their whereabouts were the letters *CRO* carved in a tree and the word *Croatoan* carved in a doorpost. White never discovered the fate of his family and the other colonists. In this section, you will learn why English settlers such as White came to America despite such hardships. You'll also learn how they lived and what they believed.

The English Plan Colonies

As you read in Chapter 2, religious and political rivalries increased between England and Spain in the late 1500s. Spain had many colonies in the Americas, but England had none. England began directing its resources toward establishing colonies after its defeat of the Spanish Armada in 1588.

Richard Hakluyt (HAK•LOOT), an English geographer, urged England to start a colony. Hakluyt thought that colonies would provide a market for English exports. They also would serve as a source of raw materials. By having colonies, England hoped to increase its trade and build up its gold supply. This is the economic theory of mercantilism (see page 52). In mercantilism, the state controls trade and attempts to transfer wealth from colonies to the parent country. Hakluyt also thought that English colonies would help to plant the Protestant faith in the Americas.

The earliest English colonists had many reasons for going to America. The lack of economic opportunity in England forced many to seek their fortunes abroad. Stories of gold mines lured some to leave England. Others left to escape religious persecution.

*Reading*History
A. Summarizing Why did English colonists settle in America?

Two Early Colonies Fail

Sir Walter Raleigh was a soldier, statesman, and adventurer who served under Queen Elizabeth I of England. She gave him permission to sponsor the colony at Roanoke. He named England's first colony Virginia after the unmarried, or virgin, queen. Financed by Raleigh, the colony began in 1585 on Roanoke Island. The colonists relied on the Native Americans for food. But when the Native Americans realized that the settlers wanted their land, they cut off the colonists' food supply. Those who survived returned to England in 1586.

Vocabulary
financed: paid for; raised funds for

In 1587, artist John White convinced Raleigh to try again to establish the Roanoke colony, with the disastrous results described in One American's Story (page 69). To this day, no one knows for sure what happened. Some historians think that the colonists mingled with the neighboring Native Americans. Others believe that they moved to Chesapeake Bay and were killed by Native Americans defending their land.

In 1607, the Plymouth Company sponsored the Sagadahoc colony at the mouth of the Kennebec River in Maine. Some of the settlers were English convicts. One colonist wrote of George Popham, the governor, "He stocked or planted [the colony] out of all the jails of England." Within the first year, arguments among colonists, a harsh winter, fights with Native Americans, and food shortages forced most of the colonists to return to England.

Now *and* then

THE LUMBEE AND THE LOST COLONISTS

The Lumbee tribe lives mainly in North Carolina. Some of the Lumbee believe they are descendants of the lost colonists of Roanoke. Among the evidence cited is the fact that 41 of the 95 last names of the Lumbee were last names of the colonists.

Other Lumbee don't believe that they are descended from English ancestors. The Lumbee are trying to win federal recognition as a Native American tribe. English ancestry might weaken their claim for federal financial support.

Financing a Colony

Raleigh had financed the colony at Roanoke. When the colony failed, he lost his investment. The English learned from Raleigh's financial loss at Roanoke that one person could not finance a colony. To raise money, they turned to the **joint-stock company**. Joint-stock companies were backed by investors, people who put money into a project to earn profits. Each investor received pieces of ownership of the company called shares of stock. In this way, the investors split any profits and divided any losses.

Merchants organized the Virginia Company of London and the Virginia Company of Plymouth. King James I of England granted charters to both companies in 1606. A **charter** was a written contract, issued by a government, giving the holder the right to establish a colony.

Jamestown Is Founded in 1607

In 1607, the Virginia Company of London financed an expedition to Chesapeake Bay that included more than 100 colonists. They sailed up the James River until they found a spot to settle. They named the first permanent English settlement **Jamestown** in honor of King James.

From the start, the Jamestown colonists endured terrible hardships. The site of the colony was swampy and full of malaria-carrying mosquitoes. This disease made the colonists sick with fever. Many also became ill from drinking the river water. To make matters worse, the London Company had incorrectly told the settlers that the colony would be rich in gold. They spent their days searching for gold rather than building houses and growing food.

The climate was also a hardship. The colonists soon learned that the summers were hot and humid and the winters bitter cold. As one colonist recalled, "There were never Englishmen left in a foreign country in such misery as we were in this newly discovered Virginia."

Jamestown Grows

By January 1608, only 38 colonists remained alive. Later that year, **John Smith,** a soldier and adventurer, took control. To make sure the colonists worked, Smith announced, "He that will not work shall not eat." Smith's methods worked. He ordered an existing wall extended around Jamestown. He also persuaded the Powhatan tribe to trade their corn to the colonists. In 1609, Smith was injured in a gunpowder explosion and returned to England. That same year, 800 more English settlers arrived in Jamestown.

Background
Historians used to believe that the colony's original site had been flooded by the James River. Recent archaeological digs, however, have discovered the site on higher ground.

Reading **History**
B. Solving Problems If you had been John Smith, how would you have forced the colonists to work?

This is a computer reconstruction of the face of Mistress Forrest, believed to be the first English woman to come to Jamestown.

Early English Settlements, 1585–1607

Sagadahoc R. (Kennebec)

Sagadahoc, 1607

Massachusetts Bay

Hudson R.

ATLANTIC OCEAN

Potomac R.

Chesapeake Bay

James R.

Jamestown, 1607

Roanoke R.

Roanoke I., 1585, 1587

0   100 Miles
0   200 Kilometers

45°N
40°N
35°N
30°N

GEOGRAPHY SKILLBUILDER Interpreting Maps
1. **Location** *Which colony was located northeast of Jamestown? How many miles northeast was it?*
2. **Human-Environment Interaction** *Why did the colonists settle near the coast?*

Because of growing tensions between the settlers and Native Americans, the Powhatan stopped trading food and attacked the settlers. The settlers did not dare leave the fort. During the "starving time," the colonists ate rats, mice, and snakes. Only 60 of the colonists were still alive when two ships arrived in 1610. Lord De La Warr, the new governor, imposed discipline, and the "starving time" ended.

In 1612, John Rolfe developed a high-grade tobacco that the colonists learned to grow. It quickly became very popular in England. The success of tobacco growing changed Jamestown in many ways. The Virginia Company thought of the colonists as employees. The colonists, however, wanted a share of the profits.

The company responded by letting settlers own land. Settlers worked harder when the land was their own. The company offered a 50-acre land grant for each man, woman, or child who could pay his or her way to the colony. In 1619, the first African Americans arrived in Jamestown. The population of Virginia jumped from about 600 in 1619 to more than 2,000 in 1621.

*Reading*History
C. Analyzing Causes What was the main reason for the various arrangements the Virginia Company came up with to bring people to America?

Even more laborers were needed. Those who could not afford passage to America were encouraged to become **indentured servants**. These men and women sold their labor to the person who paid their passage to the colony. After working for a number of years, they were free to farm or take up a trade of their own.

The colonists soon became annoyed at the strict rule of the governor, who represented the Virginia Company's interests back in London. To provide for more local control, the company decided that burgesses, or elected representatives, of the colonists would meet once a year in an assembly. The **House of Burgesses**, created in 1619, became the first representative assembly in the American colonies.

Conflicts with the Powhatan

Cultural differences put the Powhatan and the English on a collision course. At first, the Powhatan traded food with the colonists. Then, as more colonists arrived and wanted land, relations grew worse. In an effort to improve relations between the English colonists and the Powhatan, John Rolfe married Chief Powhatan's daughter, Pocahontas, in 1614.

For a time, there was an uneasy peace. The colonists learned from the Powhatan how to grow corn, catch fish, and capture wild fowl. However, the expanding tobacco plantations took over more and more Powhatan land. In 1622, in response to land grabs by the colonists, the Powhatan killed hundreds of Jamestown's residents.

*Reading*History
D. Finding Main Ideas What was the central dispute between the Powhatan and the settlers?

POCAHONTAS
1595?–1617

Pocahontas met John Smith when she was about 12 years old. Smith taught her English and admired her spirit. She admired Smith's bravery and saved his life twice. After Smith returned to England, she married the colonist John Rolfe in 1614. Shown below is a portrait of Pocahontas, done in 1616.

Two years later, the Rolfes went to England to raise money for the Jamestown colony. While getting ready to sail home, Pocahontas died of smallpox.

How did Pocahontas show that Native Americans and white settlers might live in peace?

Bacon's Rebellion in 1676

As you have seen, many of the English colonists who came to Virginia during the 1600s fought with the Native Americans. They also battled one another. By the 1670s, one-fourth of the free white men were former indentured servants. These colonists, who did not own land, resented the wealthy eastern landowners. The poor settlers lived mostly on Virginia's western frontier, where they battled the Native Americans for land.

Nathaniel Bacon and a group of landless frontier settlers opposed Governor William Berkeley. They complained about high taxes and Governor Berkeley's favoritism toward large plantation owners. Bacon demanded that Berkeley approve a war against the Native Americans to seize their land for tobacco plantations. Governor Berkeley's refusal of Nathaniel Bacon's demand sparked **Bacon's Rebellion** in 1676.

Bacon marched into Jamestown, took control of the House of Burgesses, and burned Jamestown to the ground. Bacon's sudden illness and death ended the rebellion. Berkeley hanged Bacon's followers. Angered by Berkeley's actions, King Charles II recalled the governor to England. After that incident, the House of Burgesses passed laws to prevent a royal governor from assuming such power again. The burgesses had taken an important step against tyranny. In the next section, you will read about the New England colonies and their steps toward independence.

Vocabulary
tyranny: a government in which a single ruler has absolute power

Nathaniel Bacon (right) confronts Virginia governor William Berkeley at Jamestown in 1676.

Section 1 Assessment

1. Terms & Names

Explain the significance of:
- joint-stock company
- charter
- Jamestown
- John Smith
- indentured servant
- House of Burgesses
- Bacon's Rebellion

2. Taking Notes

Use a series-of-events chain to review events that led to the founding of Jamestown.

What were reasons England wanted colonies in America?

3. Main Ideas

a. Why did the first English settlement at Roanoke fail?

b. How did the English finance their colonies after 1606?

c. What was the outcome of Bacon's Rebellion?

4. Critical Thinking

Drawing Conclusions
What were the main reasons that Jamestown survived and prospered?

THINK ABOUT
- how, after the "starving time," Lord De La Warr took control
- John Rolfe's development of a high-grade tobacco plant

ACTIVITY OPTIONS

ART
LANGUAGE ARTS

You need indentured servants to work on your plantation. Draw a **poster** or write an **advertisement** that will attract people to your plantation.

Report from the New World

You are a settler who has landed on the wild eastern shore of North America. You and your 93 fellow colonists survived a frightening nine-week Atlantic voyage. Now you are struggling to build a new home in the wilderness. There are no roads, inns, or towns in this land. The game, berries, and fish here taste strange, sometimes unpleasant. Your only neighbors are small groups of Native Americans.

COOPERATIVE LEARNING On these pages are challenges you face as you put down roots in America. Working with a small group, decide how to deal with each challenge. Choose an option, assign a task to each group member, and do the activity. You will find useful information in the Data File. Be prepared to present your solutions to the class as part of a report to your sponsors back in England.

CIVICS CHALLENGE

"They had little or no care of any other thing, but to pamper their bellies."

As your colony takes root, most members work hard to farm, cook, wash, mend, trade, and defend the colony. But a few colonists think only of their own comfort. You call a meeting to set some rules about work. Present your solution to this problem using one of these options:

- Make a poster for the meeting hall that states the new work rules and punishments.

- Write a report describing the problem and how the colony solved it.

ECONOMICS CHALLENGE

"A bright tin dish most pleased him."

By the time spring arrives, your stores of English foods are running low. You and your friends decide to try trading with the neighboring Native Americans. They could provide a steady supply of meat, fish, and vegetables until your harvest comes in. Develop a plan for opening trade. Present your plan using one of these options:

- As a group, role-play the meeting in which you create your trading plan.
- Write instructions for the team of colonists who will open trade with the Native Americans.

The Journey

Distance: more than 5,000 nautical miles from Europe to the east coast of North America

Length: 6–14 weeks

Dangers: storms, scurvy, dysentery, malnutrition, seasickness, overcrowding

Food and Livestock Taken

barrels of salted beef, oatmeal, dried grains, cheese, oil, vinegar, and salt; seeds for peas, barley, herbs, and other crops; cows, horses, goats, pigs, sheep, and chickens

Equipment Taken

axes, hoes, nails, hooks for doors, hammers, chisels, hatchets, spades, pickaxes, iron pots, copper kettles, skillets, platters, dishes, wooden spoons, rugs

Weapons Taken

swords, muskets, daggers, gunpowder, light armor, cannon

Clothes Taken

shirts, several pairs of shoes, leather for mending, waistcoats, caps, skirts, jackets, trousers

Dangers in America

Biggest killers: typhoid, dysentery, famine

Other dangers: pneumonia, malaria, and other diseases; exposure to harsh weather; fire; wild animals; attacks by Native Americans

Benefits in America

religious and political freedom; opportunity to own land; abundant timber for shelters, forts, heat, ships, and trade; rich food resources

For more about the American colonies . . .

🛈 **RESEARCH LINKS**
CLASSZONE.COM

ACTIVITY WRAP-UP

Present to the class As a group, review your solution to each challenge. Consider the following:

- How well each solution meets its particular challenge
- Which solution shows the most creativity

Once you have made your decision, present your solutions to the class. Each group member should take part in the presentation.

TERMS & NAMES
Pilgrims
Mayflower Compact
Puritans
Great Migration
Fundamental Orders
  of Connecticut
Roger Williams
Anne Hutchinson
King Philip's War

MAIN IDEA	WHY IT MATTERS NOW
Religion influenced the settlement and government of the New England colonies.	The Puritan work ethic and religious beliefs influence American culture today.

ONE AMERICAN'S STORY

In 1605, English fishermen captured and enslaved a Native American named Squanto and took him to England. While there, he learned to speak English. After a series of misadventures, including serving as a slave in Spain, Squanto returned to America in 1619. There he discovered that his Pawtuxet tribe had been wiped out by disease in the years 1616–1618. In 1621, Squanto set about helping the English plant corn, beans, and pumpkins on tribal lands. Colonist William Bradford made the following comment about Squanto.

> **A VOICE FROM THE PAST**
>
> Squanto . . . was a special instrument sent of God for their [the colonists'] good beyond their expectation. . . . He directed them how to set their corn, where to take fish, and to procure other commodities, and was also their pilot to bring them to unknown places.
>
> **William Bradford,** quoted in *The Pilgrim Reader*

Squanto teaches the Pilgrims how to grow corn.

Thanks to Squanto, the first settlers in New England prospered and lived in peace with the Native Americans. In this section, you will learn about the Pilgrims and Puritans, their relations with the Native Americans, and their settlement of the New England colonies.

The Voyage of the *Mayflower*

In the early 1500s, King Henry VIII of England broke that country's ties with the Catholic Church and established the Church of England, an official state church under his control. In the early 1600s, a religious group called the Separatists called for a total break with the Church of England. They thought it was too much like the Catholic Church.

The **Pilgrims** were a Separatist group. King James attacked them for rejecting England's official church. To escape this harsh treatment, the Pilgrims fled to Holland, a country known for its acceptance of different opinions. Eventually, the Pilgrims became dissatisfied with life in Holland. They approached the Virginia Company and asked if they could settle in America "as a distinct body by themselves." The Virginia

Company arranged for them to settle on land within its boundaries on the eastern coast of North America.

On a cold, raw November day in 1620, a ship called the *Mayflower* arrived off Cape Cod on the Massachusetts coast. Blown north of its course, the *Mayflower* landed in an area that John Smith had mapped and called New England. They landed at a site that had been named Plymouth.

Because the Pilgrims landed outside the limits of the Virginia Company, their charter did not apply. For the sake of order, the men aboard the *Mayflower* signed an agreement called the **Mayflower Compact.** In it, they vowed to obey laws agreed upon for the good of the colony. The Mayflower Compact helped establish the idea of self-government and majority rule. (See Interactive Primary Sources, page 82.)

The Pilgrims Found Plymouth

Like the early settlers at Jamestown, the Pilgrims at Plymouth endured a starving time. That first winter, disease and death struck with such fury that "the living were scarce able to bury the dead." Half the group had died by spring.

However, energy, hope, and help returned. One day a Native American walked up to a group of colonists. To their astonishment, he called out, "Welcome, Englishmen." This was Samoset, a Pemaquid who had learned to speak English from European fishermen. Samoset introduced the settlers to another Native American named Squanto, a Pawtuxet, who also spoke English.

"Welcome, Englishmen."
Samoset

Reading History
A. Making Inferences
Why do you think Squanto was so helpful to the Pilgrims?

The Pilgrims had angered the Native Americans by taking their corn. Squanto acted as an interpreter between the Pilgrims and Chief Massasoit. He helped them to negotiate a peace treaty and showed them how to plant, hunt, and fish. While their crops grew, the colonists began trading with the Native Americans for furs and preparing lumber to ship back to England in order to make a profit.

Sometime in the fall—no one knows exactly when—the Plymouth settlement celebrated the blessings of a good harvest by holding a three-day feast. It was the first Thanksgiving. This Thanksgiving came to represent the peace that existed at that time between the Native Americans and Pilgrims.

Thanks to the help of Squanto and other Native Americans, the Pilgrims learned to survive in their new environment. Soon more people would sail to New England seeking religious freedom.

The Puritans Come to Massachusetts Bay

Between about 1630 and 1640, a religious group called the **Puritans** left England to escape bad treatment by King James I. Unlike the Separatists, who wanted to break away from the Church of England, the Puritans wanted to reform, or "purify," its practices. By the thousands, Puritan families left for the Americas. Their leaving is known as the **Great Migration**. Many thousands of Puritans left their homeland to found new settlements around the world. Of these settlers, about 20,000 crossed the Atlantic Ocean to New England.

Many Puritan merchants had invested in the Massachusetts Bay Company. In 1629, the company received a royal charter to settle land in New England. In 1630, 11 well-supplied ships carried about 1,000 passengers to the Massachusetts Bay Colony. Unlike earlier colonists, the Puritans were well prepared and did not suffer through a starving time. John Winthrop was the colony's Puritan governor. He stated that the new colony would be a commonwealth, a community in which people work together for the good of the whole.

Background During the Great Migration, the Puritans also went to Ireland, the Netherlands, the Rhineland, and the West Indies.

> **A VOICE FROM THE PAST**
>
> So shall we keep the unity of the spirit, in the bond of peace. . . . Ten of us will be able to resist a thousand of our enemies. . . . For we must consider that we shall be as a City upon a Hill, the eyes of all people are on us.
>
> **John Winthrop**, *"Model of Christian Charity"*

*Reading*History
B. Making Inferences After Winthrop, politicians sometimes spoke of America as "a city upon a hill." What does this phrase suggest about America's role in the world?

The New England Way

The basic unit of the commonwealth was the congregation—a group of people who belong to the same church. Each Puritan congregation set up its own town. The meetinghouse was the most important building in each town. There people gathered for town meetings, a form of self-government in which people made laws and other decisions for the community. In the Massachusetts Bay Colony, only male church members could vote or hold office. They elected representatives to a lawmaking body called the General Court, which in turn chose the governor.

By law, everyone in town had to attend church services held in the meetinghouse. The sermon, the most important part of the church service, provided instruction in the "New England Way." This was a term

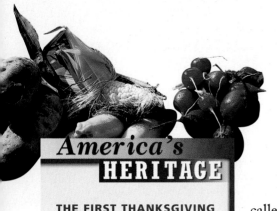

America's HERITAGE

THE FIRST THANKSGIVING
It is hard to believe, but turkey was not on the menu at the first Thanksgiving. The Pilgrims and Native Americans ate venison (deer), roast duck, roast goose, clams and other shellfish, and eel (shown below). Other treats were white bread and corn bread, leeks, watercress, and salad herbs. The guests topped off their meal with wild plums and dried berries for dessert.

Vocabulary
godliness: piety, reverence

used by the Puritans to describe both their beliefs and their society, which emphasized duty, godliness, hard work, and honesty. The Puritans thought that amusements such as dancing and playing games would lead to laziness. They believed that God required them to work long and hard at their vocation.

The Puritan work ethic helped contribute to the rapid growth and success of the New England colonies. The New England Way also depended on education. Because the Puritans wanted everyone to be able to read the Bible, laws required that all children learn to read.

Reading **History**
C. Summarizing
What were some important elements of the New England Way?

Some Puritan congregations set up new colonies. In 1636, Thomas Hooker moved his congregation to the Connecticut Valley. There they wrote and adopted the **Fundamental Orders of Connecticut** in 1639 (see page 82). In effect, these laws were a

Settlements shown in modern state boundaries.

NEW HAMPSHIRE

Portsmouth (1623)

ATLANTIC OCEAN

Connecticut River

Hudson River

MASSACHUSETTS

Massachusetts Bay

Plymouth (1620)

Providence (1636)

Hartford (1636)

CONNECTICUT

RHODE ISLAND

N   0   50 Miles

0   100 Kilometers

GEOGRAPHY SKILLBUILDER Interpreting Maps
1. **Location** *Which of these early colonies does the Connecticut River not flow through or touch?*
2. **Place** *What was the earliest major English settlement in the New England colonies?*

constitution. The Fundamental Orders extended voting rights to non-church members and limited the power of the governor. They expanded the idea of representative government.

The first European settlement in New Hampshire was a village near Portsmouth in 1623. In 1638, John Wheelwright established the town of Exeter. The town's founders drew up the Exeter Compact, which was based on the Mayflower Compact.

Anne Hutchinson preaches in her home in Boston.

Challenges to Puritan Leaders

Not everyone agreed with the New England Way. **Roger Williams** was a minister in Salem, Massachusetts, who founded the first Baptist church in America. He opposed forced attendance at church. He also opposed the English colonists' taking of Native American lands by force. Because of his beliefs, the General Court forced Williams to leave the colony. In 1636, he fled southward and founded the colony of Rhode Island, which guaranteed religious freedom and the separation of church and state.

Anne Hutchinson believed that a person could worship God without the help of a church, minister, or Bible. She conducted discussions in her home that challenged church authority. Hutchinson was brought to trial and forced to leave Massachusetts. In 1638, she fled to Rhode Island.

Another religious group was the Quakers. Their name came from an early leader's statement that they should "tremble [quake] at the word of the Lord." Opponents coined the name as an insult. Quakers challenged the Massachusetts commonwealth. They believed that each person could know God directly through "an inner light." Neither ministers nor the Bible was needed. Quakers also believed in treating Native Americans fairly, which set them apart from other colonists. For such beliefs, Quakers were whipped, imprisoned, and hanged. Many left for Rhode Island.

Reading **History**
D. Forming Opinions Why is it odd that the Puritans persecuted certain individuals and groups for their religious beliefs?

King Philip's War

The growing population of colonists began to force the Native Americans from their land. Europeans and Native Americans defined land ownership differently. To Europeans, land could be owned by individuals. To Native Americans, land belonged to everyone. Conflict over land resulted in warfare.

In 1675–1676, the Puritan colonies fought a brutal war with the Native Americans. This was known as **King Philip's War.** "King Philip" was the English name of Metacom, leader of the Wampanoag. To help fight the war, Metacom organized an alliance of tribes. The Wampanoag lost the war. Many were killed, while others were sold into slavery in the West Indies. Those who remained lost their land and were forced to become laborers. English settlers expanded even farther into Native American land.

Background Metacom was the son of Massasoit, friend of the Pilgrims.

CAUSE & EFFECT: *King Philip's War, 1675–1676*

Reasons for Conflict
• Land ownership
• Religion
• Increased population of Europeans

KING PHILIP'S WAR

Native American Losses
• Approximately 3,000 killed
• King Philip (Metacom) killed
• About 500 Native Americans enslaved

European Losses
• About 600 settlers killed
• More than 45 villages attacked
• About 12 villages destroyed

Sources: *Encyclopedia Britannica, World Book Encyclopedia*

SKILLBUILDER Interpreting Charts
1. *Was there a greater loss of life among the settlers or the Native Americans?*
2. *How might the growing population of Europeans have created more conflict with the Native Americans?*

The Salem Witchcraft Trials

Puritan New England was originally a society centered on the church. By the late 1600s, however, this had begun to change. Societal changes in Puritan New England had led to an atmosphere of fear and suspicion. Then, several Salem village girls were told frightening stories about witches by Tituba, a slave from the West Indies. Pretending to be bewitched, the girls falsely accused others of witchcraft. The witch-hunts began in 1692. The clergy viewed the Salem witch-hunts and trials as a sign from God for the village to return to a strict Puritan lifestyle.

This mid-nineteenth-century oil painting, *The Trial of George Jacobs, August 5, 1692,* was painted by T. H. Matteson in 1855. It captures the horrors of the Salem witch trials. As the young women cry out, the accused tries to defend himself against charges that he bewitched them.

Jacobs's own granddaughter testified against him. He was tried and convicted on August 5, 1692, and executed two weeks later along with four neighbors.

How accurately do you think the painting shows the strong emotions in the courtroom?

Vocabulary
scapegoat: one that is made to bear the blame of others

Hysteria spread through Salem. Those accused were forced to name others as witches. More than 100 people were arrested and tried. Of those, 20 were found guilty and put to death. Nineteen persons were hanged, and another was pressed to death by heavy stones when he refused to enter a plea in response to the charge of witchcraft. The panic was short-lived, and Salem came to its senses. The experience showed, however, how a society can create scapegoats for its problems.

In the next section, you will read about the Middle and Southern colonies, how they were founded, and how they provided the new settlers with economic opportunities.

Section 2 Assessment

1. Terms & Names

Explain the significance of:
- Pilgrims
- Mayflower Compact
- Puritans
- Great Migration
- Fundamental Orders of Connecticut
- Roger Williams
- Anne Hutchinson
- King Philip's War

2. Taking Notes

Use a cluster diagram to review details about the New England Way.

New England Way

Which parts would you find easy to accept? Which difficult?

3. Main Ideas

a. What is the Mayflower Compact?

b. What is the meaning of the term the "Great Migration"?

c. What were some of the causes of King Philip's War?

4. Critical Thinking

Recognizing Effects What impact did the arrival of the English in New England have on the Native Americans?

THINK ABOUT
- Squanto
- Chief Massasoit
- King Philip's War

ACTIVITY OPTIONS

Choose one of the Puritan dissenters from this section and retell his or her story. Either write a **newspaper article** about the person or give an **oral history**.

The Mayflower Compact

Setting the Stage In 1620, 41 of the colonists aboard the *Mayflower* drew up the Mayflower Compact. This document refers to the area where they landed as "Virginia" because the land grants of the Virginia Company extended into New England. The colonists provided for self-government under majority rule of the male voters. **See Primary Source Explorer**

A CLOSER LOOK

REASONS FOR VOYAGE

The three reasons the colonists give for their voyage to the eastern seaboard of North America are the glory of God, the advancement of Christianity, and the honor of the king.

1. Why might sailing to new lands advance Christianity?

A CLOSER LOOK

GUIDING PURPOSE

The general good of the colony is the guiding purpose of the colonists in signing the compact.

2. What does this suggest about the relationship between the individual and the community?

We, whose names are underwritten, . . . having undertaken for the glory of God, and advancement of the Christian faith, and the honor of our King and country, a voyage to plant the first colony in the northern parts of Virginia, do by these presents, solemnly and mutually in the presence of God and one another **covenant**[1] and combine ourselves together into a civil **body politic,**[2] for our better ordering and preservation; and furtherance of the ends afore-said . . . do enact, constitute, and frame such just and equal laws, ordinances, acts, constitutions, and offices from time to time as shall be thought most [proper] and convenient for the general good of the colony unto which we promise all due submission and obedience. In witness whereof we have here-unto subscribed our names at Cape Cod the eleventh of November, in the year of our **sovereign**[3] lord King James of England . . . Anno Domini 1620.

From B. P. Poore, ed., *The Federal and State Constitutions*, Part I, p. 931.

1. **covenant:** promise in a binding agreement.
2. **body politic:** the people of a politically organized group.
3. **sovereign:** supreme.

The Fundamental Orders of Connecticut

Setting the Stage In January 1639, male citizens of three townships in Connecticut (Hartford, Windsor, and Wethersfield) assembled and drew up the Fundamental Orders of Connecticut. This document is often called the first written constitution in America. It contains a preamble, or introduction, and a set of laws. **See Primary Source Explorer**

Preamble

Forasmuch as it has pleased the Almighty God by the wise disposition of His Divine Providence so to order and dispose of things that we, the inhabitants and residents of Windsor, Hartford, and Wethersfield are now cohabiting and dwelling in and upon the river of Conectecotte [Connecticut] and the lands thereunto adjoining; and well knowing where a people are gathered together the Word of God requires that, to maintain the peace and union of such a people, there should be an orderly and decent government established according to God, to order and dispose of the affairs of the people at all seasons as occasion shall require; do therefore associate and **conjoin**[1] ourselves to be as one public state or commonwealth. . . . As also in our civil affairs to be guided and governed according to such laws, rules, orders, and decrees as shall be made, ordered and decreed, as follows:

Laws, Rules, and Orders

1. It is ordered, sentenced, and decreed that there shall be yearly two general assemblies or courts. . . . The first shall be called the Court of Election, wherein shall be yearly chosen . . . so many magistrates and other public officers as shall be found **requisite**.[2] . . .

4. It is ordered . . . that no person be chosen governor above once in two years, and that the governor be always a member of some approved congregation. . . .

5. It is ordered . . . that to the aforesaid Court of Election the several towns shall send their deputies. . . . Also, the other General Court in September shall be for making of laws, and any other public occasion which concerns the good of the Commonwealth. . . .

7. It is ordered . . . that after there are warrants given out for any of the said General Courts, the constable or constables of each town shall forthwith give notice distinctly to the inhabitants of the same . . . that at a place and time . . . they meet and assemble themselves together to elect and choose certain deputies to be at the General Court then following to [manage] the affairs of the Commonwealth. . . .

1. **conjoin:** unite.
2. **requisite:** required.

A CLOSER LOOK

GOOD GOVERNMENT

Good government is pleasing to God in the eyes of the colonists. An orderly and decent government helps to maintain peace and order within a community and between people.

3. How would you define good government today?

A CLOSER LOOK

THE GOVERNOR'S ROLE

The person serving as governor can serve only once every two years and must be a member of an approved congregation.

4. Why might the colonists have wished to limit the power of the chief executive?

A CLOSER LOOK

THE COURTS

The Court of Election chooses officials to serve; the General Court makes laws.

5. Why might it be a good idea to separate these two functions?

Interactive Primary Sources Assessment

1. Main Ideas

a. Whose rights did the Mayflower Compact protect?

b. Why are written documents useful in setting up a government?

c. How were the Fundamental Orders based on religion?

2. Critical Thinking

Supporting Opinions
How do you think these documents reflect the English contribution to American democracy?

THINK ABOUT
• self-government
• majority rule

Founding the Middle and Southern Colonies

TERMS & NAMES
Peter Stuyvesant
patroon
Duke of York
proprietary colony
William Penn
Quaker
royal colony
James Oglethorpe

MAIN IDEA	WHY IT MATTERS NOW
The founding of the Middle and Southern colonies provided settlers with many economic opportunities.	America is still a place where immigrants seek freedom and economic opportunity.

ONE AMERICAN'S STORY

The Dutch had founded the colony of New Netherland (later New York) on the eastern coast of North America in 1624. **Peter Stuyvesant**, the new governor, arrived in the city of New Amsterdam in May 1647. Because of his harsh personality and rough manner, he soon lost the support of the Dutch colonists. In 1664, a British fleet ordered the city of New Amsterdam to surrender itself to British control. Stuyvesant was unable to gain the support of the Dutch colonists against the British. He surrendered and then defended his decision to his superiors back in the Netherlands.

A VOICE FROM THE PAST

Powder and provisions failing, and no relief or reinforcements being expected, we were necessitated [forced] to come to terms with the enemy, not through neglect of duty or cowardice . . . but in consequence of an absolute impossibility to defend the fort, much less the city of New Amsterdam, and still less the country.

Peter Stuyvesant, quoted in *Peter Stuyvesant and His New York*

Peter Stuyvesant, governor of the Dutch colony of New Netherland, lost his leg in 1644 during a military action against the island of St. Martin in the Caribbean.

After the surrender, Stuyvesant retired to his farm. This land later became part of New York City. In this section, you will read about the founding of the Middle Colonies (such as New York) and the Southern Colonies. You will learn who settled there and why they came.

The Middle Colonies

The Middle Colonies were New York, New Jersey, Pennsylvania, and Delaware. They were located between New England to the north and the Chesapeake region to the south. (See the map on page 86.) Swedes, Dutch, English, Germans, and Africans were among the groups who came to these colonies.

Religious freedom attracted many groups, including Protestants, Catholics, Quakers, and Jews. The Hudson and Delaware rivers supported shipping and commerce. The river valleys had rich soil and mild winters. These conditions were favorable for farming and raising livestock.

New Netherland Becomes New York

In 1624, Dutch settlers financed by the Dutch West India Company founded the colony of New Netherland. New Netherland included the Hudson River valley, Long Island, and the land along the Delaware River.

To attract more settlers, the Dutch West India Company employed the patroon system. A **patroon** was a person who brought 50 settlers to New Netherland. As a reward, a patroon received a large land grant. He also received special privileges in hunting, fishing, and fur trading on his land.

In the early years, many different kinds of people settled in New Netherland. Twenty-three Jewish settlers arrived in 1654, and others soon followed. Later, Africans were brought to the colony as slaves and indentured servants. Many Puritans also came.

Peter Stuyvesant, the colony's governor, wanted to add land to New Netherland. He attacked the nearby charter colony of New Sweden in 1655. This colony was located along the Delaware River. The main settlement was Fort Christina (later named Wilmington, Delaware). It had been settled by Swedes in 1638. After an attack by the Dutch, the Swedes surrendered Fort Christina.

England's King Charles II decided that his brother, the **Duke of York,** should drive the Dutch out of New Netherland. The Dutch colony was a threat to England because of its trade. It was also a threat because of its expanding settlements and its location. There were English colonies in New England to the north and Virginia to the south. As you have seen, when the duke's ships appeared off New Amsterdam in August 1664, the colony surrendered. New Netherland became the **proprietary colony** of New York. The Duke of York was now the proprietor, or owner, of the colony.

New Jersey, Pennsylvania, and Delaware

The Duke of York had become the largest single landowner in America. He gave part of his claim, the province of New Jersey, to his friends Sir George Carteret and Lord John Berkeley in 1664. They encouraged settlers to come by promising freedom of religion. They also promised large grants of land and a representative assembly.

William Penn became another large landowner in America. Born into a wealthy English family, Penn joined the **Quakers,** to his father's disapproval. The young Penn was attacked for his Quaker beliefs. King Charles II owed the Penn family money. In repayment, in 1681 he gave Penn a large piece of land in America that came to be called Pennsylvania. The name means "Penn's woods."

America's HERITAGE

THE LOG CABIN

Swedish colonists living in Delaware built the first log cabin in America in 1638. The log cabin was the perfect house to build where there were many trees. Settlers needed few tools to build such cabins, which were made of round logs with curved notches at the ends. After the ends were placed in the notches, the logs were secured. After 1780, the log cabin became the typical frontier home.

Reading **History**

A. Forming Opinions Why might the promise of religious freedom encourage a diverse population in a colony?

The 13 English Colonies, 1732

FRENCH TERRITORY

- New England colonies
- Middle colonies
- Southern colonies

MAINE (part of MASS.)

Claimed by N.Y & N.H.

N.H.

MASS.
- Boston, 1630
- Plymouth, 1620
- Providence, 1636

N.Y.

Hartford, 1636

R.I.

CONN.

PENNSYLVANIA

N.J.
- Philadelphia, 1682
- Wilmington, 1664 (Ft. Christina)

DEL.

MD.

ATLANTIC OCEAN

VIRGINIA
- Jamestown, 1607

Roanoke Island

NORTH CAROLINA

SOUTH CAROLINA

GEORGIA

Charles Town, 1670 (Charleston)

APPALACHIAN MOUNTAINS

SPANISH TERRITORY

0 250 Miles
0 500 Kilometers

GEOGRAPHY SKILLBUILDER
Interpreting Maps
1. **Region** What geological feature formed a logical western boundary for the colonies?
2. **Location** For approximately how many miles did the colonies extend along the eastern coast of North America?

Penn used this land to create a colony where Quakers could live according to their beliefs. Among other things, the Quakers believed that all people should live in peace and harmony. They welcomed different religions and ethnic groups. In Pennsylvania, Penn extended religious freedom and equality to all. He especially wanted the Native Americans to be treated fairly. In a letter to them in 1681, Penn said, "May [we] always live together as neighbors and friends."

Penn's policies helped make Pennsylvania one of the wealthiest of the American colonies. Many settlers came to Pennsylvania seeking religious freedom and a better life. In 1704, Penn granted the three lower counties of Delaware their own assembly. The counties later broke away to form the colony of Delaware.

*Reading*History
B. Comparing and Contrasting How did Penn's policies toward Native Americans compare with those of other colonies you have read about?

The Southern Colonies

The new Southern Colonies were Maryland, the Carolinas, and Georgia. The Appalachian Mountains bordered parts of these colonies in the west. In the east, the colonies bordered the Atlantic Ocean. The soil and climate of this region were suitable for warm-weather crops such as tobacco, rice, and indigo.

Maryland and the Carolinas

Lord Baltimore established Maryland in 1632 for Roman Catholics fleeing persecution in England. To attract other settlers besides Catholics, Lord Baltimore promised religious freedom. In 1649, Maryland passed the Toleration Act.

Maryland based its economy on tobacco, which required backbreaking work. Every three or four years, the tobacco crop used up the soil, and workers had to clear new land. Most laborers came as either servants or slaves. Maryland attracted few women as settlers.

In 1663, Carolina was founded as a colony. English settlers from Barbados built Charles Town, later called Charleston, in 1670. They busied themselves cutting timber, raising cattle, and trading with the Native Americans. After 1685, Charleston became a refuge for Huguenots, French Protestants seeking religious freedom.

Carolina's colonists needed laborers to grow rice and indigo. The English settlers encouraged the use of enslaved Africans. They also sold local Native Americans into slavery. As a result, wars broke out between the settlers and the Tuscarora and Yamasee tribes. The settlers' taking of tribal lands also fueled the wars.

Carolina's proprietors, or owners, refused to send help to stop a threatened Spanish attack on Charleston. Because of this, the colonists overthrew the colony's proprietary rule in 1719. In 1729, Carolina became a **royal colony**. Then it was ruled by governors appointed by the king. The colony was divided into North Carolina and South Carolina.

Vocabulary
Carolina: The name of the colony is based on a Latin form of "Charles," in honor of King Charles II.

Georgia

In 1732, **James Oglethorpe** founded Georgia as a refuge for debtors. The English government wanted to use the colony as a military outpost against Spanish Florida to the south and French Louisiana to the west. In 1739, during a war between England and Spain, the Spanish tried to force the English colonists out of Georgia but were unsuccessful. English, German, Swiss, and Scottish colonists settled in Georgia. All religions were welcome. As the colony's leader, Oglethorpe set strict rules that upset the colonists. The king, in response to unrest, made Georgia a royal colony in 1752.

By the early 1700s, there were 13 English colonies along the eastern coast of North America. In the next chapter, you will read about how these colonies developed.

*Reading*History
C. Reading a Map
Use the map on page 86 to check the location of Georgia in relation to the Spanish territory of Florida.

James Oglethorpe was the founder of Georgia.

Section 3 Assessment

1. Terms & Names
Explain the significance of:
- Peter Stuyvesant
- patroon
- Duke of York
- proprietary colony
- William Penn
- Quaker
- royal colony
- James Oglethorpe

2. Taking Notes
Identify an effect for each cause listed in the chart below.

Cause	Effect
New Netherland threat to English	
English attacked Quakers	
Laborers needed in Carolinas	
Oglethorpe too strict in Georgia	

3. Main Ideas
a. What were the goals of the patroon system?

b. What three Middle Colonies offered religious freedom?

c. What were three crops grown in the Southern Colonies?

4. Critical Thinking
Analyzing Causes Why did colonists in Maryland and the Carolinas enslave Native Americans and use African slaves?

THINK ABOUT
- the crops being grown
- the nature of farm work

ACTIVITY OPTIONS

LANGUAGE ARTS
SCIENCE

What are the health effects of tobacco? Write a **news article** or give a **television report** for a science show about the effects of tobacco on the body.

The English Establish 13 Colonies **87**

TERMS & NAMES

Briefly explain the significance of each of the following.

1. joint-stock company
2. Jamestown
3. John Smith
4. House of Burgesses
5. Pilgrims
6. Mayflower Compact
7. Great Migration
8. Fundamental Orders of Connecticut
9. proprietary colony
10. William Penn

REVIEW QUESTIONS

Early Colonies Have Mixed Success (pages 69–75)

1. What were the reasons given by Richard Hakluyt that England should start a colony?
2. Why were Jamestown and Plymouth financed by joint-stock companies?
3. How did John Rolfe change the Virginia colony?

New England Colonies (pages 76–83)

4. What was John Winthrop's vision for Massachusetts Bay?
5. What was the system of government in the Massachusetts Bay Colony?
6. What were some of the effects of King Philip's War?

Founding the Middle and Southern Colonies (pages 84–87)

7. Why did Charles II want New Netherland?
8. What were relations like between Native Americans and settlers in Pennsylvania?
9. What was the Toleration Act of 1649?
10. What ethnic and racial groups settled in the Middle Colonies and why did they do so?

VISUAL SUMMARY

CRITICAL THINKING

1. USING YOUR NOTES

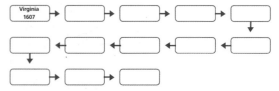

Using your completed chart, answer these questions:

a. Which was the earliest successful settlement in Virginia?
b. Which colony was founded last?

2. ANALYZING LEADERSHIP

Why do you think William Penn was a more successful leader than Peter Stuyvesant?

3. APPLYING CITIZENSHIP SKILLS

What were some of the common ideals that link the Mayflower Compact, the establishment of the House of Burgesses, and town meetings?

4. THEME: IMPACT OF THE INDIVIDUAL

How did individual effort help ensure the success of England's colonies in America?

5. ANALYZING CAUSES

What were the political, economic, and social causes for the founding of the different British colonies in North America?

Interact *with* History

How do the dangers you discussed before you read this chapter compare with the dangers people actually faced?

The 13 Colonies

		Important Early Dates	Founder(s)
New England Colonies	Massachusetts	Plymouth,1620; Mass. Bay, 1630	Pilgrims; Puritans
	New Hampshire	Portsmouth, 1623	Proprietors
	Rhode Island	Providence, 1636	Roger Williams
	Connecticut	Hartford, 1636	Thomas Hooker
Middle Colonies	New York (New Netherland)	Dutch settlers arrive, 1624	Dutch West India Company
	Delaware	Fort Christina, 1638	Swedes
	New Jersey	Duke of York establishes, 1664	George Carteret, John Berkeley
	Pennsylvania	Charles II bestows land, 1681	William Penn
Southern Colonies	Virginia	Jamestown, 1607	Virginia Company of London
	Maryland	Founded as religious haven, 1632	Lord Baltimore
	North Carolina	Founded, 1663	Proprietors
	South Carolina	Founded, 1663	Proprietors
	Georgia	Founded as debtors' refuge, 1732	James Oglethorpe

HISTORY SKILLS

1. INTERPRETING GRAPHS

Study the graph and then answer the questions.

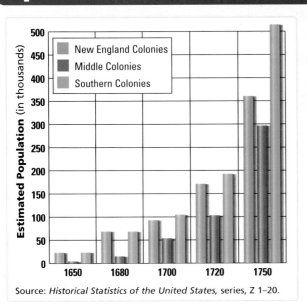

Population of the Colonies

New England Colonies
Middle Colonies
Southern Colonies

Source: *Historical Statistics of the United States*, series, Z 1–20.

a. How much did the population of the Southern colonies increase between 1720 and 1750?

b. What was the increase in the population of the New England colonies between 1700 and 1720?

c. Ask and answer a question about the geographic patterns shown in the graph.

2. INTERPRETING PRIMARY SOURCES

The early colonists used a surveyor's compass (below) to divide up the land they had come to settle.

a. What attitudes about ownership of the land are revealed by the use of a surveyor's compass?

b. How might the use of a surveyor's compass reflect differences in attitudes toward the land between European settlers and Native Americans?

ALTERNATIVE ASSESSMENT

1. INTERDISCIPLINARY ACTIVITY: Geography

Drawing a Map Draw a map of the New England, Middle, and Southern colonies. Place on the map the major cities and rivers of each colony. Show also the colonies in which people of different racial and ethnic groups settled. Explain how each region's geographic location contributed to the colonies' economic activities. Share your map with the class.

2. COOPERATIVE LEARNING ACTIVITY

Performing a Scene from a Play The "lost colonists" of Roanoke disappeared sometime between 1588 and 1590. Write and perform a play depicting a meeting of the colonists in which they try to decide what to do. John White has not returned with the supplies he promised to bring. How are the colonists to deal with food shortages, illness, and relations with the Native Americans?

Take the roles of Elinor Dare and her husband, Ananias; their child, Virginia; and other colonists. Come up with different solutions to their problems. Then vote on your preferred course of action.

3. 💿 PRIMARY SOURCE EXPLORER

Planning a Government As with any group of people living in a community, some sort of government was needed in Plymouth. The Pilgrims devised the Mayflower Compact. Using the CD-ROM, library, and Internet, find out more about the Mayflower Compact.

Create your own plan for a government using the following suggestions:

• Draw up a plan for a government that will apply to your class.

• Adapt ideas from the Mayflower Compact that you think will work for the class.

• Decide what rules are needed in your government. Decide who will hold office, how they will be appointed or selected, and how long they will serve.

• Decide whether there should be limits on majority rule in your government.

4. HISTORY PORTFOLIO

📘 Review the chapter and write a brief report describing how different racial, ethnic, and religious groups resolved their differences in 17th- and 18th-century America. Be sure to use standard grammar, spelling, sentence structure, and punctuation in your report. Add your report to your portfolio.

Additional Test Practice, pp. S1–S33

INTERNET ACTIVITY
CLASSZONE.COM

CHAPTER 4

The Colonies Develop 1700–1753

In 1702, a vast countryside surrounded Philadelphia. Most colonists earned their living in the country. Fewer than one in ten lived in cities.

Boston

Boston was the largest colonial city until the mid-1700s.

American cities depended on trade.

Many craftspeople, such as this shoemaker, made a living in cities.

It is the early 1700s when you arrive in one of America's larger port cities. After nearly a month of ocean travel, you are thrilled to see land. As you leave the ship, you wonder where you will live and how you will earn a living.

Would you settle on a farm or in a town?

What Do You Think?

- Will you choose to live where other people from your homeland live? Or will you try somewhere new?

- How did you make a living in your old country? Will this influence your choice?

1742
First European settlement west of Allegheny Mountains is established.

1718
French found city of New Orleans at mouth of Mississippi River.

Spanish priests build Alamo in Texas.

c. 1750
Population of the English colonies passes the one million mark.

c. 1700
Colonial population reaches 257,000.

1712
Slave uprising occurs in New York City.

1739
Enslaved Africans revolt in Stono Rebellion.

USA
World **1700** — **1753**

1701
War of the Spanish Succession begins in Europe.

1707
Act of Union unites England with Scotland and creates Great Britain.

1727
George II becomes King of Great Britain.

1747
Slave trading African kingdom of Dahomey is defeated by Oyo.

1752
China suppresses Tibetan rebellion and forces Dalai Lama to accept its authority.

BEFORE YOU READ

NEW ENGLAND COLONIES

MIDDLE COLONIES

Backcountry

SOUTHERN COLONIES

Previewing the Theme

Economics in History When immigrants came to the Americas, they settled in places with different climates and resources. These conditions affected the economic choices made by colonists. As Chapter 4 explains, those choices contributed to the formation of four different colonial regions.

What Do You Know?

What ideas and pictures come to mind when you hear people talk about "the South" or "the North"? Why do you think these distinct regions developed?

THINK ABOUT

• what you have learned about these regions from books or movies
• the way geography affects people's choices

What Do You Want to Know?

What questions do you have about how the four colonial regions developed? Record these questions in your notebook before you read the chapter.

READ AND TAKE NOTES

Reading Strategy: Analyzing Causes and Recognizing Effects As you read about history, it is important to understand not only what happened in the past, but also the reasons why it happened. Clue words that indicate cause—such as *because* and *since*—can help you look for causes of historical events. Use the chart below to list causes that contributed to the different economic developments in each of the colonial regions.

See Skillbuilder Handbook, page R11.

		NEW ENGLAND COLONIES	MIDDLE COLONIES	SOUTHERN COLONIES	BACKCOUNTRY
CAUSES	Climate				
	Resources				
	People				
EFFECT	Economic Development				

① New England: Commerce and Religion

TERMS & NAMES
Backcountry
subsistence farming
triangular trade
Navigation Acts
smuggling

MAIN IDEA	WHY IT MATTERS NOW
Fishing and trade contributed to the growth and prosperity of the New England Colonies.	Coastal cities in New England continue to engage in trade.

ONE AMERICAN'S STORY

Peleg Folger, a New England sailor, was only 18 years old when he began whaling. Folger kept a journal that describes what whaling was like in the 1750s. In one journal entry, Folger explained what happened after whales were sighted and small boats were launched to pursue them.

A VOICE FROM THE PAST

So we row'd about a mile and a Half from the [ship], and then a whale come up under us, & [smashed in] our boat . . . and threw us every man overboard [except] one. And we all came up and Got Hold of the Boat & Held to her until the other boat (which was a mile and half off) came up and took us in, all Safe, and not one man Hurt, which was remarkable, the boat being threshed to pieces very much.

Peleg Folger, quoted in *The Sea-Hunters*

Whales hunted by New Englanders, such as Peleg Folger, might weigh as much as 50 tons and be over 60 feet in length.

When Folger and his mates did manage to kill a whale, they cut a hole in its head. Then "a man got in up to his armpits and Dipt out [barrels] of clear oil." When the ship returned to port, this oil was sold to colonists, who used it as fuel in their lamps.

Many settlers in the New England Colonies—Massachusetts, New Hampshire, Connecticut, and Rhode Island—turned to the Atlantic Ocean to make a living. The majority of New Englanders, however, were farmers.

Distinct Colonial Regions Develop

Between 1700 and 1750, the population of England's colonies in North America doubled and then doubled again. At the start of the century, the colonial population stood at about 257,000. By 1750, more than 1,170,000 settlers called the English colonies home.

By the 1700s, the colonies formed three distinct regions: the New England Colonies, the Middle Colonies, and the Southern Colonies. Another area was the **Backcountry**. It ran along the Appalachian Mountains through the far western part of the other regions.

Several factors made each colonial region distinct. Some of the most important were each region's climate, resources, and people.

1. New England had long winters and rocky soil. English settlers made up the largest group in the region's population.
2. The Middle Colonies had shorter winters and fertile soil. The region attracted immigrants from all over Europe.
3. The Southern Colonies had a warm climate and good soil. There, some settlers used enslaved Africans to work their plantations.
4. The Backcountry's climate and resources varied, depending on the latitude. Many Scots-Irish immigrants settled there.

During the colonial era, the majority of people made their living by farming. However, the type of agriculture they practiced depended on the climate and resources in the region where they settled.

The Farms and Towns of New England

Life in New England was not easy. The growing season was short, and the soil was rocky. Most farmers practiced **subsistence farming**. That is, they produced just enough food for themselves and sometimes a little extra to trade in town.

Most New England farmers lived near a town. This was because colonial officials usually did not sell scattered plots of land to individual

Vocabulary
latitude: the distance north or south of the equator, measured in degrees

The New England Colonies, 1750

Cattle
Fish
Shipbuilding
Timber
Whaling

St. Lawrence R.
MAINE (part of MASS.)
Claimed by N.Y. and N.H.
Falmouth
NEW HAMPSHIRE
Portsmouth
Connecticut R.
Hudson R.
Salem
Boston
Plymouth
Newport
MASSACHUSETTS
CONNECTICUT
New Haven
RHODE ISLAND
Lake Ontario
ATLANTIC OCEAN

0   100 Miles
0   200 Kilometers

GEOGRAPHY SKILLBUILDER Interpreting Maps
1. **Location** *All of the New England Colonies are to the east of what major river?*
2. **Region** *What ocean-related products was colonial New England known for?*

This New England meetinghouse is located in Sturbridge Village, Massachusetts.

farmers. Instead, they sold larger plots of land to groups of people—often to the congregation of a Puritan church. A congregation then settled the town and divided the land among the members of its church.

This pattern of settlement led New England towns to develop in a unique way. Usually, a cluster of farmhouses surrounded a green—a central square where a meetinghouse was located and where public activities took place. Because people lived together in small towns, shopkeepers had enough customers to make a living. Also, if the townspeople needed a blacksmith or a carpenter, they could pool their money and hire one.

Reading **History**
A. Recognizing Effects How did the way land was sold in New England affect the way people lived?

Harvesting the Sea

New England's rocky soil made farming difficult. In contrast, the Atlantic Ocean offered many economic opportunities. In one story, a group of settlers was standing on a hill overlooking the Atlantic. One of them pointed out to sea and exclaimed, "There is a great pasture where our children's grandchildren will go for bread!"

The settler's prediction came true. Not far off New England's coast were some of the world's best fishing grounds. The Atlantic was filled with mackerel, halibut, cod, and many other types of fish.

New England's forests provided everything needed to harvest these great "pastures" of fish. The wood cut from iron-hard oak trees made excellent ship hulls. Hundred-foot-tall white pines were ideal for masts. Shipbuilders used about 2,500 trees to produce just one ship!

Background
In 1742, over 16,000 people lived in Boston.

New England's fish and timber were among its most valuable articles of trade. Coastal cities like Boston, Salem, New Haven, and Newport grew rich as a result of shipbuilding, fishing, and trade.

Atlantic Trade

New England settlers engaged in three types of trade. First was the trade with other colonies. Second was the direct exchange of goods with Europe. The third type was the triangular trade.

Triangular trade was the name given to a trading route with three stops. For example, a ship might leave New England with a cargo of rum

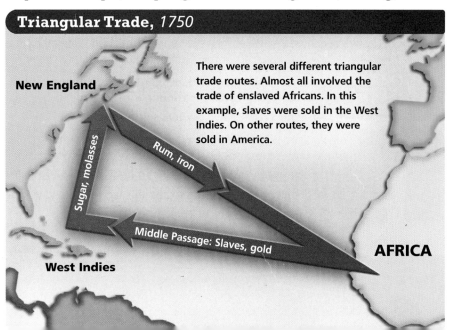

Triangular Trade, *1750*

There were several different triangular trade routes. Almost all involved the trade of enslaved Africans. In this example, slaves were sold in the West Indies. On other routes, they were sold in America.

New England

Sugar, molasses

Rum, iron

Middle Passage: Slaves, gold

West Indies

AFRICA

and iron. In Africa, the captain would trade his cargo for slaves. Slaves then endured the horrible Middle Passage to the West Indies, where they were exchanged for sugar and molasses. Traders then took the sugar and molasses back to New England. There, colonists used the molasses to make rum, and the pattern started over.

Background
See Olaudah Equiano's descriptions of the Middle Passage on page 62.

New England won enormous profits from trade. England wanted to make sure that it received part of those profits. So the English government began to pass the **Navigation Acts** in 1651. The Navigation Acts had four major provisions designed to ensure that England made money from its colonies' trade.

1. All shipping had to be done in English ships or ships made in the English colonies.
2. Products such as tobacco, wood, and sugar could be sold only to England or its colonies.
3. European imports to the colonies had to pass through English ports.
4. English officials were to tax any colonial goods not shipped to England.

But even after the passage of the Navigation Acts, England had trouble controlling colonial shipping. Merchants ignored the acts whenever possible. **Smuggling**—importing or exporting goods illegally—was common. England also had great difficulty preventing pirates—like the legendary Blackbeard—from interfering with colonial shipping.

STRANGE but True

BLACKBEARD THE PIRATE

Of all the pirates who attacked colonial ships, Blackbeard (shown below) was the most famous. He was a fearsome man known to stick matches in his hair to light up his face during battle.

Blackbeard's pirate career finally came to an end in 1718, when Virginia's governor sent an expedition against him. Nearly half the expedition's men died in the key battle. Blackbeard himself did not fall until he had suffered nearly 25 wounds. Before sailing back to port, sailors cut off his head and put it on the front of their ship.

African Americans in New England

There were few slaves in New England. Slavery simply was not economical in this region of small farms. Also, because the growing season was short, there was little work for slaves during the long winter months. Farmers could not afford to feed and house slaves who were not working.

Even so, some New Englanders in larger towns and cities did own slaves. They worked as house servants, cooks, gardeners, and stable-hands. In the 1700s, slave owners seldom had enough room to house more than one or two slaves. Instead, more and more slave owners hired out their slaves to work on the docks or in shops or warehouses. Slave owners sometimes allowed their slaves to keep a portion of their wages.

Occasionally, some enslaved persons were able to save enough to buy their freedom. In fact, New

Reading **History**
B. Analyzing Causes Why were there relatively few enslaved workers in New England?

England was home to more free blacks than any other region. A free black man might become a merchant, sailor, printer, carpenter, or landowner. Still, white colonists did not treat free blacks as equals.

Changes in Puritan Society

*Reading*History
C. Making Inferences Why might an interest in material things compete with the Puritan religion?

The early 1700s saw many changes in New England society. One of the most important was the gradual decline of the Puritan religion. There were a number of reasons for this decline.

One reason was that the drive for economic success competed with Puritan ideas. Many colonists, especially those who lived along the coast, seemed to care as much about business and material things as they did about religion. One observer had this complaint.

"[Boston] is so conveniently Situated for Trade."

An observer in 1713

A VOICE FROM THE PAST

[Boston] is so conveniently Situated for Trade and the Genius of the people are so inclined to merchandise, that they seek no other Education for their children than writing and Arithmetick.

An observer in 1713, quoted in *A History of American Life*

Another reason for the decline of the Puritan religion was the increasing competition from other religious groups. Baptists and Anglicans established churches in Massachusetts and Connecticut, where Puritans had once been the most powerful group.

Political changes also weakened the Puritan community. In 1691, a new royal charter for Massachusetts guaranteed religious freedom for all Protestants, not just Puritans. The new charter also granted the vote based on property ownership instead of church membership. This change put an end to the Puritan churches' ability to control elections.

To the south of New England were the Middle Colonies, which developed in quite different ways—as the next section shows.

Section 1 Assessment

1. Terms & Names

Explain the significance of:
• Backcountry
• subsistence farming
• triangular trade
• Navigation Acts
• smuggling

2. Taking Notes

Use a chart like the one shown to record how New Englanders prospered from the Atlantic Ocean.

Economic Activity	Benefits to Colonists

How did some profit illegally from the ocean?

3. Main Ideas

a. How did most people in New England earn a living?

b. Why did England pass the Navigation Acts?

c. What factors led to the decline of the Puritan religion in New England?

4. Critical Thinking

Making Inferences What advantages might there be in living near other people in small towns, such as those in New England?

THINK ABOUT
• the transportation options available to colonists
• why shopkeepers chose to open businesses in towns

ACTIVITY OPTIONS

ART
TECHNOLOGY

Read more about whaling. Make a **mobile** that shows different kinds of whales or plan a **multimedia presentation** on whaling today.

2 The Middle Colonies: Farms and Cities

TERMS & NAMES
cash crop
gristmill
diversity
artisan
Conestoga wagon

MAIN IDEA	WHY IT MATTERS NOW
The people who settled in the Middle Colonies made a society of great diversity.	States in this region still boast some of the most diverse communities in the world.

ONE AMERICAN'S STORY

Elizabeth Ashbridge was only 19 years old when she arrived in America from England in the 1730s. Even though she was young, she had already been married and widowed. And although she was an indentured servant, she hoped to earn her freedom and find a way to express her strong religious feelings.

After several years, Elizabeth did gain freedom. She started to search for a religion that she could devote her life to. Finally, in the colony of Pennsylvania, she found what she was looking for—the Society of Friends, or Quakers. The new Quaker longed to share her beliefs openly.

A VOICE FROM THE PAST

I was permitted to see that all I had gone through was to prepare me for this day; and that the time was near, when it would be required of me, to go and declare to others what the God of mercy had done for my soul.

Elizabeth Ashbridge, *Some Account . . . of the Life of Elizabeth Ashbridge*

A woman speaks out at a Quaker meeting. The Society of Friends allowed women a more active role than other religions.

The Quakers believed that people of different beliefs could live together in harmony. They helped to create a climate of tolerance and acceptance in the Middle Colonies of New York, New Jersey, Pennsylvania, and Delaware. These colonies began to attract a wide variety of immigrants, as you will read in this section.

A Wealth of Resources

The Middle Colonies had much to offer in addition to a climate of tolerance. A Frenchman named Michel Guillaume Jean de Crèvecoeur (krehv•KUR) praised the region's "fair cities, substantial villages, extensive fields . . . decent houses, good roads, orchards, meadows, and bridges, where an hundred years ago all was wild, woody, and uncultivated."

The prosperity that Crèvecoeur described was typical of the Middle Colonies. Immigrants from all over Europe came to take advantage of this region's productive land. Their settlements soon crowded out Native Americans, who had lived in the region for thousands of years.

Among the immigrants who came to the Middle Colonies were Dutch and German farmers. They brought the advanced agricultural methods of their countries with them. Their skills, knowledge, and hard work would soon result in an abundance of foods.

The Middle Colonies boasted a longer growing season than New England and a soil rich enough to grow **cash crops.** These were crops raised to be sold for money. Common cash crops included fruits, vegetables, and, above all, grain. The Middle Colonies produced so much grain that people began calling them the "breadbasket" colonies.

The Importance of Mills

Vocabulary
grist: another name for grain, the one-seeded fruit of cereal grasses like wheat and rye

After harvesting their crops of corn, wheat, rye, or other grains, farmers took them to a **gristmill.** There, millers crushed the grain between heavy stones to produce flour or meal. Human or animal power fueled some of these mills. But water wheels built along the region's plentiful rivers powered most of the mills.

The bread that colonists baked with these products was crucial to their diet. Colonists ate about a pound of grain in some form each day—nearly three times more than Americans eat today. Even though colonists ate a great deal of grain, they had plenty left over to send to the region's coastal markets for sale.

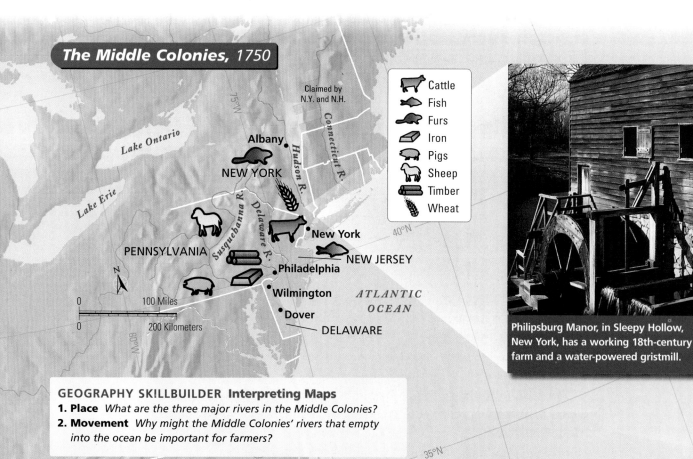

The Middle Colonies, 1750

Claimed by N.Y. and N.H.

Cattle
Fish
Furs
Iron
Pigs
Sheep
Timber
Wheat

Lake Ontario
Lake Erie
Albany
NEW YORK
Hudson R.
Connecticut R.
Susquehanna R.
Delaware R.
PENNSYLVANIA
New York
NEW JERSEY
Philadelphia
Wilmington
Dover
DELAWARE
ATLANTIC OCEAN
40°N
35°N
75°W
80°W

0   100 Miles
0   200 Kilometers

N

Philipsburg Manor, in Sleepy Hollow, New York, has a working 18th-century farm and a water-powered gristmill.

GEOGRAPHY SKILLBUILDER Interpreting Maps
1. Place *What are the three major rivers in the Middle Colonies?*
2. Movement *Why might the Middle Colonies' rivers that empty into the ocean be important for farmers?*

The Cities Prosper

The excellent harbors along the coasts of the Middle Colonies were ideal sites for cities. New York City grew up at the mouth of the Hudson River, and Philadelphia was founded on the Delaware River. The merchants who lived in these growing port cities exported cash crops, especially grain, and imported manufactured goods.

Because of its enormous trade, Philadelphia was the fastest growing city in the colonies. The city owed its expansion to a thriving trade in wheat and other cash crops. By 1720, it was home to a dozen large shipyards—places where ships are built or repaired.

The city's wealth also brought many public improvements. Large and graceful buildings, such as Philadelphia's statehouse—which was later renamed Independence Hall—graced the city's streets. Streetlights showed the way along paved roads. In 1748, a Swedish visitor named Peter Kalm exclaimed that Philadelphia had grown up overnight.

*Reading*History
A. Reading a Map Locate New York and Philadelphia on the map on page 99. Note the rivers next to which they were built.

daily *life*

NAMES AND OCCUPATIONS
Many English colonists had names like Miller and Smith—names that reflected how their families had made a living in England. For example, a colonist named Miller probably had an ancestor who had operated a mill. Similarly, Smith probably had an ancestor who had been a blacksmith.

Sometimes colonists continued in the same occupations as their ancestors. But as time went on, colonists turned to other occupations, and their names no longer reflected how they earned a living. Yet names like Smith and Miller remain common in the United States, reflecting the country's past as English colonies.

A VOICE FROM THE PAST

And yet its natural advantages, trade, riches and power, are by no means inferior to any, even of the most ancient towns in Europe.

Peter Kalm, quoted in *America at 1750*

New York could also thank trade for its rapid growth. This bustling port handled flour, bread, furs, and whale oil. At midcentury, an English naval officer admired the city's elegant brick houses, paved streets, and roomy warehouses. "Such is this city," he said, "that very few in England can rival it in its show."

Background
In 1742, New York City's population was about 11,000, and nearly 13,000 people lived in Philadelphia.

A Diverse Region

Many different immigrant groups arrived in the port cities of the Middle Colonies. Soon, the region's population showed a remarkable

A. Cooper

A. Sawyer

A. Smith

A. Potter

diversity, or variety, in its people. One of the largest immigrant groups in the region, after the English, was the Germans.

Many of the Germans arrived between 1710 and 1740. Most came as indentured servants fleeing religious intolerance. Known for their skillful farming, these immigrants soon made a mark on the Middle Colonies. "German communities," wrote one historian, "could be identified by the huge barns, the sleek cattle, and the stout workhorses."

Germans also brought a strong tradition of craftsmanship to the Middle Colonies. For example, German gunsmiths first developed the long rifle. Other German **artisans,** or craftspeople, became iron-workers and makers of glass, furniture, and kitchenware.

Germans built **Conestoga wagons** to carry their produce to town. These wagons used wide wheels suitable for dirt roads, and the wagons' curved beds prevented spilling when climbing up and down hills. The wagons' canvas covers offered protection from rain. Conestoga wagons would later be important in settling the West.

The Middle Colonies became home to many people besides the Germans. There were also the English, Dutch, Scots-Irish, African, Irish, Scottish, Welsh, Swedish, and French. Because of the diversity in the Middle Colonies, different groups had to learn to accept, or at least tolerate, one another.

Background
By the second half of the 1700s, more than one in three colonists in Pennsylvania claimed German ancestry.

Reading **History**
B. Summarizing
How would you describe the population of the Middle Colonies?

The Middle Colonies, *1750*

Population Diversity

- French **2%**
- Swedish **3%**
- Welsh **3%**
- Scottish **4%**
- Irish **5%**
- African **7%**
- Scots-Irish **9%**
- Dutch **10%**
- German **18%**
- English **39%**

Source: *Population of the British Colonies in America Before 1776,* 1975

SKILLBUILDER Interpreting Graphs
1. *What group made up nearly one-fifth of the population in the Middle Colonies?*
2. *What were the two main languages spoken in the Middle Colonies?*

A Climate of Tolerance

While the English Puritans shaped life in the New England Colonies, many different groups contributed to the culture of the Middle Colonies. Because of the greater number of different groups, it was difficult for any single group to dominate the others. Thus, the region's diversity helped to create a climate of tolerance. Some of the region's religious groups also helped to promote tolerance.

The Middle Colonies' earliest settlers, the Dutch in New York and the Quakers in Pennsylvania, both practiced religious tolerance. That is, they honored the right of religious groups to follow their own beliefs without interference. Quakers also insisted on the equality of men and women. As a result, Quaker women served as preachers, and female missionaries traveled the world spreading the Quaker message.

OBSERVATIONS
On the Inslaving, importing and purchasing of

Negroes;

With some Advice thereon, extracted from the Epistle of the Yearly-Meeting of the People called Quakers, held at *London* in the Year 1748.

Anthony Benezet

When ye spread forth your Hands, I will hide mine Eyes from you, yea when ye make many Prayers I will not hear; your Hands are full of Blood. Wash ye, make you clean, put away the Evil of your Doings from before mine Eyes Isai. 1, 15.

Is not this the Fast that I have chosen, to loose the Bands of Wickedness, to undo the heavy Burden, to let the Oppressed go free, and that ye break every Yoke, Chap. 58, 7.

Second Edition.

GERMANTOWN:
Printed by Christopher Sower. 1760.

Most Quakers were opposed to slavery. Shown here is a Quaker antislavery pamphlet printed in the Middle Colonies.

Quakers were also the first to raise their voices against slavery. Quaker ideals influenced immigrants in the Middle Colonies—and eventually the whole nation.

African Americans in the Middle Colonies

The tolerant attitude of many settlers in the Middle Colonies did not prevent slavery in the region. In 1750, about 7 percent of the Middle Colonies' population was enslaved. As in New England, many people of African descent lived and worked in cities.

New York City had a larger number of people of African descent than any other city in the Northern colonies. In New York City, enslaved persons worked as manual laborers, servants, drivers, and as assistants to artisans and craftspeople. Free African-American men and women also made their way to the city, where they worked as laborers, servants, or sailors.

Tensions existed between the races in New York City, sometimes leading to violence. In 1712, for example, about 24 rebellious slaves set fire to a building. They then killed nine whites and wounded several others who came to put out the fire. Armed colonists caught the suspects, who were punished horribly. Such punishments showed that whites would resort to force and violence to control slaves. Even so, the use of violence did little to prevent the outbreak of other slave rebellions.

Force would also be used in the South, which had far more enslaved Africans than the North. In the next section, you will learn how the South's plantation economy came to depend on the labor of enslaved Africans.

*Reading*History
C. Forming Opinions Why do you think that force was needed to keep Africans enslaved?

Section 2 Assessment

1. Terms & Names
Explain the significance of:
• cash crop
• gristmill
• diversity
• artisan
• Conestoga wagon

2. Taking Notes
Use a cluster diagram like the one shown to indicate where different immigrants in the Middle Colonies came from.

Middle Colonies' Population

What was the third largest group in the region?

3. Main Ideas
a. What attracted settlers to the Middle Colonies?

b. What service was performed at gristmills?

c. Why might enslaved Africans be able to join in rebellion more easily in the city than the country?

4. Critical Thinking
Analyzing Causes What factors allowed large coastal cities to develop in the Middle Colonies?

THINK ABOUT
• geography
• people
• trade

ACTIVITY OPTIONS
MATH
GEOGRAPHY

Read more about Philadelphia. Create a **database** of the city's population growth in the 1700s or draw a **map** that shows its physical growth.

③ The Southern Colonies: Plantations and Slavery

TERMS & NAMES
indigo
Eliza Lucas
William Byrd II
overseer
Stono Rebellion

MAIN IDEA	WHY IT MATTERS NOW
The economy of the Southern Colonies relied heavily on slave labor.	The existence of slavery deeply affected the South and the nation.

ONE AMERICAN'S STORY

George Mason was born to a wealthy Virginia family in 1725. Mason—who later described the slave trade as "disgraceful to mankind"—wrote about the contributions of enslaved persons on his family's plantation.

A VOICE FROM THE PAST

My father had among his slaves carpenters, coopers [barrel makers], sawyers, blacksmiths, tanners, curriers, shoemakers, spinners, weavers and knitters, and even a distiller. . . . His woods furnished timber and plank for the carpenters and coopers, and charcoal for the blacksmith; his cattle killed for his own consumption and for sale supplied skins for the tanners, curriers, and shoemakers, and his sheep gave wool and his fields produced cotton and flax for the weavers and spinners, and his orchards fruit for the distiller.

George Mason, quoted in *Common Landscape of America*

George Mason was active in local affairs in Virginia. He would later play a role in the drafting of the United States Constitution.

Because the Masons and other wealthy landowners produced all that they needed on their own plantations, they appeared to be independent. But their independence usually depended on the labor of enslaved Africans. Although planters were only a small part of the Southern population, the plantation economy and slavery shaped life in the Southern Colonies: Maryland, Virginia, the Carolinas, and Georgia.

The Plantation Economy

The South's soil and almost year-round growing season were ideal for plantation crops like rice and tobacco. These valuable plants required much labor to produce, but with enough workers they could be grown as cash crops. Planters had no trouble transporting their crops because the region's many waterways made it easy for oceangoing ships to tie up at plantation docks.

Like George Mason's boyhood home, most plantations were largely self-sufficient. That is, nearly everything that planters, their families, and their workers needed was produced on the plantation. Because plantations were so self-sufficient, large cities like those in the North were rare

The Southern Colonies, 1750

Corn
Indigo
Naval stores
Pigs
Rice
Tobacco

MARYLAND
Baltimore
Potomac R.
Chesapeake Bay
VIRGINIA
Richmond
James R. Jamestown
Roanoke R.
NORTH CAROLINA
APPALACHIAN MOUNTAINS
Wilmington
SOUTH CAROLINA
ATLANTIC OCEAN
Savannah R.
GEORGIA
Charles Town (Charleston)
Altamaha R.
Savannah

0   100 Miles
0   200 Kilometers

40°N
35°N
75°W
85°W
N

The Orton plantation, south of Wilmington, North Carolina, was founded around 1725. Such plantations were representative of the economic and political power held by Southern planters.

GEOGRAPHY SKILLBUILDER Interpreting Maps
1. **Location** The Southern Colonies were south of what latitude?
2. **Place** Which Southern Colonies grew crops of both rice and indigo?

Southern Colonies. The port city of Charles Town (later called Charleston) in South Carolina was an early exception.

As the plantation economy continued to grow, planters began to have difficulty finding enough laborers to work their plantations. Toward the end of the 1600s, the planters began to turn to enslaved Africans for labor.

Background
In 1742, Charles Town's population was 6,800.

The Turn to Slavery

For the first half of the 1600s, there were few Africans in Virginia, whether enslaved or free. In 1665, fewer than 500 Africans had been brought into the colony. At that time, African and European indentured servants worked in the fields together.

Starting in the 1660s, the labor system began to change as indentured white servants started to leave the plantations. One reason they left was the large amount of land available in the Americas. It was fairly easy for white men to save enough money to buy land and start their own farms. White servants could not be kept on the plantations permanently. As Bacon's Rebellion showed, it was also politically dangerous for planters to try to keep them there (see page 73). As a result, the landowners had to find another source of labor.

U.S. Slave Population

Percentage of Population

40
30
20
10
0
1650 1670 1690 1710 1730 1750

■ North   ■ South

Source: Fogel and Engerman, *Time on the Cross*, 1974

Reading **History**

A. Reading a Graph Ask and answer a question about the geographic pattern of changes in the slave population.

Planters tried to force Native Americans to work for them. But European diseases caused many Native Americans to die. Those who survived usually knew the country well enough to run away.

*Reading*History

B. Analyzing Causes What factors led to the importation of enslaved Africans into the South?

To meet their labor needs, the planters turned to enslaved Africans. As a result, the population of people of African descent began to grow rapidly. By 1750, there were over 235,000 enslaved Africans in America. About 85 percent lived in the Southern Colonies. Enslaved Africans made up about 40 percent of the South's population.

Plantations Expand

The growth of slavery allowed plantation farming to expand in South Carolina and Georgia. Without slave labor, there probably would have been no rice plantations in the region's swampy lowlands.

Enslaved workers drained swamps, raked fields, burned stubble, and broke ground before planting. They also had to flood, drain, dry, hoe, and weed the same fields several times before the harvest.

The cultivation of rice required not only back-breaking labor but also considerable skill. Because West Africans had these skills, planters sought out slaves who came from Africa's rice-growing regions.

On higher ground, planters grew **indigo,** a plant that yields a deep blue dye. A young woman named **Eliza Lucas** had introduced indigo as a successful plantation crop after her father sent her to supervise his South Carolina plantations when she was 17.

The Planter Class

Slave labor allowed planters, such as the Byrd family of Virginia, to become even wealthier. These families formed an elite planter class. They had money or credit to buy the most slaves. And because they had more slaves, they could grow more tobacco, rice, or indigo to sell.

Small landowners with just one or two slaves simply could not compete. Many gave up their land and moved westward. As a result, the powerful planter class gained control of the rich land along the coast. The planter class was relatively small compared to the rest of the population. However, this upper class soon took control of political and economic power in the South. A foreign traveler in the South commented that the planters "think and act precisely as do the nobility in other countries."

Some planters, following the traditions of nobility, did feel responsible for the welfare of their enslaved

*Reading*History

C. Recognizing Effects How did the growth of slavery affect political power in the South?

AMERICA'S HISTORY MAKERS

WILLIAM BYRD II
1674–1744

William Byrd II was one of the best known of the Southern planters. His family owned a large estate in Virginia. After his father died, Byrd took on his father's responsibilities, including membership in the House of Burgesses.

But Byrd is best remembered for his writing. His most famous work is *History of the Dividing Line betwixt Virginia and North Carolina.* In it, Byrd celebrates the land and climate of the South. At times, however, he is critical of its people. Even today, the book creates a vivid picture of life in the Southern Colonies.

How did William Byrd II demonstrate his leadership abilities?

workers. Power, they believed, brought with it the responsibility to do good. Many planters, though, were tyrants. They held complete authority over everyone in their households. Planters frequently used violence against slaves to enforce their will.

Vocabulary
tyrant: harsh ruler

Life Under Slavery

On large Southern plantations, slaves toiled in groups of about 20 to 25 under the supervision of **overseers.** Overseers were men hired by planters to watch over and direct the work of slaves. Enslaved persons performed strenuous and exhausting work, often for 15 hours a day at the peak of the harvest season. If slaves did not appear to be doing their full share of work, they were often whipped by the overseer.

Enslaved people usually lived in small, one-room cabins that were furnished only with sleeping cots. For a week's food, a slave might receive only around a quarter bushel of corn and a pound of pork. Some planters allowed their slaves to add to this meager ration by letting them raise their own potatoes, greens, fruit, or chicken.

In spite of the brutal living conditions, Africans preserved many customs and beliefs from their homelands. These included music, dances, stories, and, for a time, African religions—including Islam. African kinship customs became the basis of African-American family culture. A network of kin was a source of strength even when families were separated.

Reading **History**
D. Finding Main Ideas What customs and beliefs from their homelands provided strength for enslaved Africans?

Resistance to Slavery

At the same time that enslaved Africans struggled to maintain their own culture, they fought against their enslavement. They sometimes worked slowly, damaged goods, or purposely carried out orders the wrong way. A British traveler in 1746 noted that many slaves pretended not to understand tasks they often had performed as farmers in West Africa.

A VOICE FROM THE PAST

You would really be surpriz'd at their Perseverance; let an hundred Men shew him how to hoe, or drive a wheelbarrow, he'll still take the one by the Bottom, and the other by the Wheel; and they often die before they can be conquer'd.

Edward Kimber, quoted in *White over Black*

At times, slaves became so angry and frustrated by their loss of freedom that they rose up in rebellion. One of the most famous incidents was the **Stono Rebellion.** In September 1739, about 20 slaves gathered at the Stono River just south of Charles Town. Wielding guns and other weapons, they killed several planter families and marched south, beating drums and loudly inviting other slaves to join them in their plan to seek freedom in Spanish-held Florida. By late that afternoon, however, a white militia had surrounded the group of escaping slaves. The two sides clashed, and many slaves died in the fighting. Those captured were executed.

Background
Slave codes were laws designed to control slaves and keep them in bondage.

Stono and similar revolts led planters to make slave codes even stricter. Slaves were now forbidden from leaving plantations without permission. The laws also made it illegal for slaves to meet with free blacks. Such laws made the conditions of slavery even more inhumane.

The Southern Colonies' plantation economy and widespread use of slaves set the region on a very different path from that of the New England and Middle Colonies. In the next section, you will learn how settlers used the unique resources of the Backcountry to create settlements there.

Section 3 Assessment

1. Terms & Names

Explain the significance of:
• indigo
• Eliza Lucas
• William Byrd II
• overseer
• Stono Rebellion

2. Taking Notes

Use a diagram like the one shown to review the factors that led to the use of slaves in the South.

Causes		Effect

Why didn't planters use Native American workers?

3. Main Ideas

a. What percentage of the South's population was enslaved in 1750?

b. What crops did plantations in Georgia and South Carolina grow?

c. How did enslaved persons resist their slavery?

4. Critical Thinking

Contrasting How did geographic differences between the Southern Colonies and the New England Colonies affect their labor systems?

THINK ABOUT
• the climate of the regions
• the nature of the soil

ACTIVITY OPTIONS

ART
SCIENCE

Do more research on rice plantations. Draw a **diagram** of a typical plantation or write a **report** on how rice is cultivated today.

Differences Among the Colonies

Many factors shape a region's economy and the way its settlers make a living. One of the most important is its physical geography—the climate, soil, and natural resources of the region. The geography of the American colonies varied from one colony to another. For example, in some areas, farmers could dig into rich, fertile soil. In others, they could not stick their shovels in the ground without hitting rocks.

Major Regional Exports (by export value*)

NEW ENGLAND COLONIES

New England had a short growing season and rocky soil. Colonists took advantage of other opportunities in the region, especially fishing and whaling.

■ Dried Fish and Whale Oil	44%
■ Livestock	17%
■ Wood Products	13%
■ Other	26%

MIDDLE COLONIES

The longer growing season of the Middle Colonies—the "breadbasket colonies"—allowed farmers to grow cash crops of grain.

■ Grain	73%
■ Iron	5%
■ Wood Products	5%
■ Other	17%

SOUTHERN COLONIES

The South had a nearly year-round growing season. The use of enslaved Africans allowed Southern planters to produce cash crops of tobacco and rice.

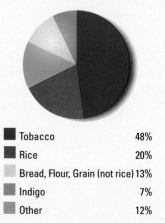

■ Tobacco	48%
■ Rice	20%
■ Bread, Flour, Grain (not rice)	13%
■ Indigo	7%
■ Other	12%

*Export Value in Pounds Sterling (Five-Year Average, 1768–1772)

Source: James F. Shepherd and Gary M. Walton, *Shipping, Maritime Trade, and the Economic Development of Colonial North America* (Cambridge: Cambridge University Press, 1972.)

ARTIFACT FILE

Farmer's Plow Middle colonists relied on the heavy blades of plows to cut seed rows into the region's fertile soil.

Indigo On some plantations in the South, planters grew crops of indigo plants—like the one pictured here—to produce the rich blue dyes used to color this yarn.

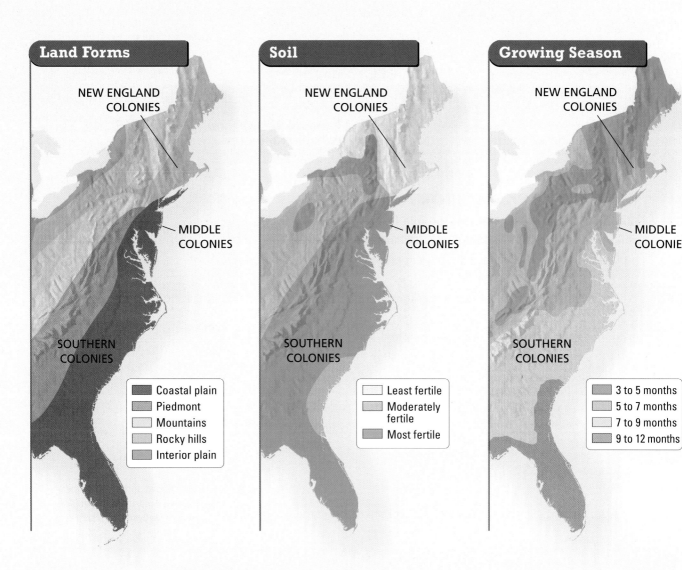

Land Forms

NEW ENGLAND COLONIES

MIDDLE COLONIES

SOUTHERN COLONIES

- Coastal plain
- Piedmont
- Mountains
- Rocky hills
- Interior plain

Soil

NEW ENGLAND COLONIES

MIDDLE COLONIES

SOUTHERN COLONIES

- Least fertile
- Moderately fertile
- Most fertile

Growing Season

NEW ENGLAND COLONIES

MIDDLE COLONIES

SOUTHERN COLONIES

- 3 to 5 months
- 5 to 7 months
- 7 to 9 months
- 9 to 12 months

Physical Geography The maps above show the different types of land forms, soil, and growing seasons that were found in the different colonial regions. These factors helped to shape the economies of each of the regions, which were quite different, as the pie graphs show on the previous page.

On-Line Field Trip

The New Bedford Whaling Museum in Massachusetts has many objects related to whaling, including bone or ivory objects called scrimshaws. A sailor carved this whale's tooth with a jackknife or sail needle and colored the design with ink.

For more about whaling . . .

RESEARCH LINKS
CLASSZONE.COM

CONNECT TO GEOGRAPHY

1. **Region** How long was the growing season in most of the Southern Colonies?
2. **Human-Environment Interaction** How might the soil quality in the Middle Colonies have influenced the region's population?

   See Geography Handbook, pages 10–13.

CONNECT TO HISTORY

3. **Analyzing Causes** Why did the land forms and soil of New England cause many to turn to the Atlantic Ocean for a living?

4 The Backcountry

TERMS & NAMES

Appalachian
  Mountains
fall line
piedmont
clan

MAIN IDEA	WHY IT MATTERS NOW
Settlers moved to the Backcountry because land was cheap and plentiful.	Backcountry settlers established a rural way of life that still exists in certain parts of the country.

ONE AMERICAN'S STORY

Alexander Spotswood governed Virginia from 1710 to 1722. He believed that the future of English colonists lay to the west. To prove his point, he led a month-long expedition over the crest of the Blue Ridge Mountains in August 1716.

During the 400-mile journey, adventurers braved dense thickets, muddy streams, and rattlesnakes. At night, they feasted on the deer, wild turkeys, and bear they had shot. John Fontaine, who accompanied Spotswood, kept a diary of the trip.

Alexander Spotswood meets Native Americans in the Blue Ridge Mountains—a segment of the Appalachians Mountains.

A VOICE FROM THE PAST

We had a rugged way; we passed over a great many small runs of water, some of which were very deep, and others very miry. Several of our company were dismounted, some were down with their horses, others under their horses, and some thrown off.

John Fontaine, quoted in *Colonial Virginia*

After the expedition, Spotswood gave each of his companions a golden horseshoe. His journey with the "Knights of the Golden Horseshoe" is considered a symbol of Virginia's westward expansion.

Geography of the Backcountry

Just as Spotswood predicted, settlers soon began to move into the Backcountry. This was a region of dense forests and rushing streams in or near the **Appalachian Mountains.** The Appalachians stretch from eastern Canada south to Alabama.

In the South, the Backcountry began at the **fall line.** The fall line is where waterfalls prevent large boats from moving farther upriver. Beyond the fall line is the **piedmont.** Piedmont means "foot of the mountains." It is the broad plateau that leads to the Blue Ridge Mountains of the Appalachian range.

The Backcountry's resources made it relatively easy for a family to start a small farm. The region's many springs and streams provided water, and forests furnished wood that settlers could use for log cabins and fences.

Backcountry Settlers

The first Europeans in the Backcountry made a living by trading with the Native Americans. Backcountry settlers paid for goods with deerskins. A unit of value was one buckskin or, for short, a "buck."

Vocabulary
buck: an adult male deer; the adult female is called a *doe*

Farmers soon followed the traders into the region, but they had to be cautious. As the number of settlements grew, the farmers often clashed with the Native Americans whose land they were taking.

Farmers sheltered their families in log cabins. They filled holes between the logs with mud, moss, and clay. Then they sawed out doors and windows. Lacking glass, settlers used paper smeared with animal fat to cover their windows.

Reading **History**
A. Analyzing Points of View
What was William Byrd's attitude toward Backcountry settlers?

William Byrd—on his expedition to establish the southern border of Virginia—described a long night that he spent in one such cabin. He complained that he and at least ten other people were "forct to pig together in a Room . . . troubled with the Squalling of peevish, dirty children into the Bargain."

Backcountry life may have been harsh, but by the late 1600s many families had chosen to move there. Some of them went to escape the plantation system, which had crowded out many small farmers closer to the seacoast. Then, in the 1700s, a new group of emigrants—the Scots-Irish—began to move into the Backcountry.

Backcountry, 1750

This log cabin is typical of the dwellings in the Backcountry.

GEOGRAPHY SKILLBUILDER Interpreting Maps
Region *What geographical feature did the northern and southern areas of the Backcountry have in common?*

The Scots-Irish

The Scots-Irish came from the borderland between Scotland and England. Most of them had lived for a time in northern Ireland. In 1707, England and Scotland merged and formed Great Britain. The merger caused many hardships for the Scots-Irish. Poverty and crop failures made this bad situation even worse.

Vocabulary
clan: comes from an Old Irish word that means offspring, or descendants

As a result, Scots-Irish headed to America by the thousands. After they arrived, they quickly moved into the Backcountry. The Scots-Irish brought their clan system with them to the Backcountry. **Clans** are large groups of families—sometimes in the thousands—that claim a common ancestor. Clan members were suspicious of outsiders and banded together when danger threatened. These clans helped families to deal with the dangers and problems of the Backcountry.

Now and then

BACKCOUNTRY SPORTS TODAY

Three centuries ago, crowds in the Backcountry were thrilled by some of the same games that are now part of track and field competitions.

One of these games is the hammer throw. In this event, an athlete swings around a 16-pound metal ball on a wire-rope handle. After whirling around several times, the athlete lets go of the hammer, hoping it will travel the farthest distance.

The Scots-Irish brought other games to America, including the shotput, high jump, and long jump.

Backcountry Life

Life in the Backcountry was very different from life along the seaboard. Settlers along the coast carried on a lively trade with England. But in the Backcountry, rough roads and rivers made it almost impossible to move goods.

As a result, Backcountry farmers learned quickly to depend on themselves. They built log cabins and furnished them with cornhusk mattresses and homemade benches and tables. They fed their families with the hogs and cattle they raised and with the fish and game they killed. They grew yellow corn to feed their livestock and white corn to eat. Popcorn was probably their only snack food. To protect their precious corn from pests, daytime patrols of women, children, and the elderly served as human scarecrows.

Women in the Backcountry worked in the cabin and fields, but they also learned to use guns and axes. An explorer who traveled in the region described one of these hardy Backcountry women.

A VOICE FROM THE PAST

She is a very civil woman and shows nothing of ruggedness or Immodesty in her carriage, yett she will carry a gunn in the woods and kill deer, turkeys, etc., shoot doun wild cattle, catch and tye hoggs, knock down [cattle] with an ax and perform the most manfull Exercises.

A visitor to the Backcountry, quoted in *A History of American Life*

Settlers in the Backcountry often acted as if there were no other people in the region, but this was not so. In the woods and meadows that surrounded their cabins, settlers often encountered Native Americans and other groups that had made America their home.

Other Peoples in North America

The Backcountry settlers started a westward movement that would play a critical role in American history. Most settlers' motivation to move west was simple—the desire for land.

Yet the push to the west brought settlers into contact with other peoples of North America. Native Americans had made their homes there for thousands of years. In addition, France and Spain claimed considerable territory in North America.

Sometimes this contact led to changes in people's cultures. For instance, North America had no horses until the Spanish colonists brought them into Mexico in the 1500s. Horses migrated north, and Native Americans caught them and made them an important part of their culture.

Reading **History**

B. Making Inferences How would you describe the way people in the Backcountry lived?

Reading **History**

C. Summarizing As England's colonies expanded westward, what groups did they encounter?

112 CHAPTER 4

Contact also led to conflict. As English settlers pushed into the Backcountry, they put pressure on Native American tribes. Some tribes reacted by raiding isolated homesteads and small settlements. White settlers struck back, leading to more bloodshed.

This painting shows Native Americans catching wild horses. Many would later use the horses to hunt buffalo on the Great Plains.

The English colonists also came into conflict with the French. The French had colonized eastern Canada and had moved into the territories, rich with fur, along the Mississippi River. French fur traders wanted to prevent English settlers from moving west and taking away part of the trade. One Native American told an Englishman, "You and the French are like two edges of a pair of shears, and we are the cloth that is cut to pieces between them."

Vocabulary
shears: scissors

Spain also controlled large areas of North America—including territories that today form part or all of the states of Arizona, California, Colorado, Florida, Nevada, New Mexico, Texas, Utah, and Wyoming. Spanish settlers were farmers, ranchers, and priests. Priests, who established missions to convert Native Americans, built forts near the missions for protection. In 1718, Spaniards built Fort San Antonio de Bexar to guard the mission of San Antonio de Valero, later renamed the Alamo.

These different groups continued to compete—and sometimes fight—with one another. Frequently, England's colonies had to unite against these other groups. As a result, a common American identity began to take shape, as you will read in Chapter 5.

Section 4 Assessment

1. Terms & Names
Explain the significance of:
- Appalachian Mountains
- fall line
- piedmont
- clan

2. Taking Notes
Use a chart like the one shown to list some of the geographic characteristics of the Backcountry.

Backcountry Geography
1.
2.
3.
4.

3. Main Ideas
a. Which settlers migrated to the Backcountry?

b. How did clans help the Scots-Irish survive?

c. What economic activities did women carry out in the region?

4. Critical Thinking
Identifying Problems As England's colonies expanded farther west, what problems would they face?

THINK ABOUT
- other inhabitants of the Americas
- the resources desired by the colonists

ACTIVITY OPTIONS

LANGUAGE ARTS
ART

Read an account of the Backcountry written in the 1700s. Write a **newspaper article** or draw a series of **cartoons** that describe what you have read.

VISUAL SUMMARY

The Colonies Develop

NEW ENGLAND COLONIES

MIDDLE COLONIES

Backcountry

SOUTHERN COLONIES

New England: Commerce and Religion

New England was distinguished by its small farming towns and profitable fishing and trade.

The Middle Colonies: Farms and Cities

The Middle Colonies' farms produced large cash crops that fueled trade in its coastal cities.

The Southern Colonies: Plantations and Slavery

The South's plantation economy and large number of enslaved Africans made it different from the other regions.

The Backcountry

The Backcountry was distant from the denser coastal populations, so settlers there developed an independent and rugged way of life.

TERMS & NAMES

Briefly explain the significance of the following.

1. Backcountry
2. subsistence farming
3. triangular trade
4. Navigation Acts
5. cash crop
6. gristmill
7. Conestoga wagon
8. overseer
9. Stono Rebellion
10. Appalachian Mountains

REVIEW QUESTIONS

New England: Commerce and Religion (pages 93–97)

1. How would you describe the life of a New England farmer?
2. In what ways did settlers in the region take advantage of the Atlantic Ocean?
3. How were New England towns settled?

The Middle Colonies: Farms and Cities (pages 98–102)

4. How were farms in the Middle Colonies different from those in New England?
5. What characterized the population of the Middle Colonies?

The Southern Colonies: Plantations and Slavery (pages 103–109)

6. Why did Southern planters infrequently travel to towns to sell their crops or to buy food and supplies?
7. Why did planters turn to enslaved Africans for labor?
8. In what ways did slaves resist?

The Backcountry (pages 110–113)

9. Where was the Backcountry located in the 1700s?
10. How was life in the Backcountry different from that along the coast?

CRITICAL THINKING

1. USING YOUR NOTES

Using your completed chart, answer the questions below.

	NEW ENGLAND COLONIES	MIDDLE COLONIES	SOUTHERN COLONIES	BACKCOUNTRY
CAUSES — Climate				
Resources				
People				
EFFECT — Economic Development				

a. How was the Middle Colonies' climate different from the Backcountry's?
b. How did the South's labor system differ from the North's?
c. How did the resources of New England affect its economy?

2. ANALYZING LEADERSHIP

How did the South's plantation economy influence who became leaders in the region?

3. THEME: ECONOMICS IN HISTORY

What factors influenced the economic development of each of the four colonial regions?

4. APPLYING CITIZENSHIP SKILLS

How did the Quaker influence in the Middle Colonies contribute to the behavior of citizens of the region?

5. SEQUENCING EVENTS

What changes took place in the population and treatment of African Americans between 1650 and 1750?

Interact with History

How would the choice that you made at the beginning of the chapter have varied according to the region in which you lived? Would you still make the same choice?

HISTORY SKILLS

1. INTERPRETING MAPS: Human-Environment Interaction

Study the map. Answer the questions.

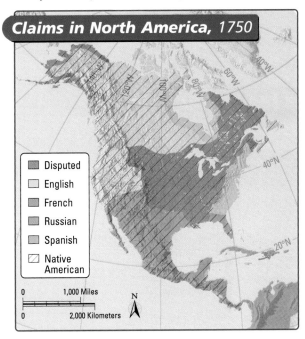

Claims in North America, 1750

Legend:
- Disputed
- English
- French
- Russian
- Spanish
- Native American

0 — 1,000 Miles
0 — 2,000 Kilometers

N

Basic Map Elements

a. What is the subject of the map?

Interpreting the Map

b. Which of the groups shown inhabited the largest area of North America?

c. Which groups claimed the northernmost territory?

2. INTERPRETING PRIMARY SOURCES

In the backwoods of North Carolina, William Byrd met a family he suspected of being escaped slaves. Read the selection below and answer the questions.

> [They] called themselves free, though by the shyness of the master of the house, who took care to keep least in sight, their freedom seemed a little doubtful. . . . Many slaves [hide] in this obscure part of the world, nor will any of their righteous neighbors discover them. On the contrary, [their neighbors profit by] settling such fugitives on some out-of-the-way corner of their land to raise stocks for a mean and inconsiderable share, well knowing their condition makes it necessary for them to [accept any pay they are offered].
>
> **William Byrd,** from *Secret History of the Dividing Line*

a. Why does Byrd suspect the family members are escaped slaves?

b. Why don't their neighbors turn them in?

ALTERNATIVE ASSESSMENT

1. INTERDISCIPLINARY ACTIVITY: Geography

Making a Map Using the library or the Internet, read more about the history of the slave trade in the 1700s. Create a map of Africa that shows countries that were major sources of enslaved persons.

For more about the history of Africa . . .

INTERNET ACTIVITY
CLASSZONE.COM

2. COOPERATIVE LEARNING ACTIVITY

Building a Log Cabin Do some more research on the Backcountry and the history of log cabins. Work with others to record details about the location where you will build your cabin. Then design and construct a model of a log cabin that could be compared to the cabins in which Backcountry settlers lived.

3. TECHNOLOGY ACTIVITY

Making a Class Presentation Life on a farm in colonial New England was a real challenge. Using the library or the Internet, find accounts of how New England farm families lived. Then design a multimedia presentation about a typical New England farmer and his family. Be sure to include the social and economic contributions of women in your presentation.

For more about daily life during colonial times . . .

INTERNET ACTIVITY
CLASSZONE.COM

- Create a map of the town in which the farmer and his family lived.
- Dress up like a farmer to discuss the challenges of New England agriculture.
- Create a chart that lists the differences between your family's lifestyle and the colonial family's.

4. HISTORY PORTFOLIO

Option 1 Review your section and chapter assessment activities. Select one that you think is your best work. Then use comments made by your teacher or classmates to improve your work and add it to your portfolio.

Option 2 Review the questions that you wrote for What Do You Want to Know? on page 92. Then write a short report in which you explain the answers to your questions. Add your report to your portfolio.

Additional Test Practice, pp. S1–S33

TEST PRACTICE
CLASSZONE.COM

CHAPTER

5

Beginnings of an American Identity 1689–1763

Section 1 **Early American Culture**
Section 2 **Roots of Representative Government**
Section 3 **The French and Indian War**

Conflicts with the British government helped shape a separate identity for British colonists. Here, Patrick Henry argues against the king in 1763.

Interact *with* History

Conflicts with Native Americans and French colonists also helped shape the identity of British colonists. In response to attacks on the Pennsylvania frontier, Benjamin Franklin published this cartoon in 1754 urging the colonies to unite for defense.

You have seen this cartoon in the *Pennsylvania Gazette*. You are outraged by the attacks on British traders and settlers. You wonder whether it is wise to join with other colonies, though. Will it mean that Virginians or New Englanders will be able to make laws for Pennsylvania?

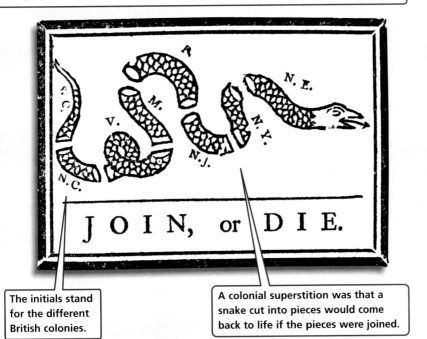

The initials stand for the different British colonies.

A colonial superstition was that a snake cut into pieces would come back to life if the pieces were joined.

What do you have in common with other British colonists?

What Do You Think?

- What are some good reasons to join with the other British colonies?

- How great are the differences between the British colonies?

- What separates British colonists from French colonists?

1689
Massachusetts colonists overthrow royal governor Andros.

1704
Boston Newsletter is founded.

1735
Decision in the Zenger trial supports freedom of the press.

1759
Quebec falls to the British.

1754
French and Indian War begins.

1738
Minister George Whitefield arrives in Georgia.

1763
French and Indian War ends.

USA / World 1680   1763

1689
William and Mary replace James II as rulers of England.

1707
England and Scotland join to form Great Britain.

1709
About 13,500 people leave the German states and emigrate to England.

1756
Seven Years' War between France and Britain is declared.

Chapter 5 SETTING THE STAGE

BEFORE YOU READ

Previewing the Theme

Democratic Ideals In the 1700s and even earlier, American colonists demanded protection of their "rights as Englishmen." Among these was the right to elect representatives to government. Chapter 5 explains how a heritage of English rights was one of many forces drawing the different British colonies together.

What Do You Know?

What beliefs do you consider American? How do you think people in Britain's American colonies saw themselves?

THINK ABOUT

• your own beliefs as an American
• what you know about the regions where the colonies were established
• what you know about the backgrounds and beliefs of colonists in different regions

What Do You Want to Know?

What questions do you have about colonial America in the early and middle 1700s? Write them down in your notebook before you read this chapter.

READ AND TAKE NOTES

Reading Strategy: Finding Main Ideas To recognize a main idea, you must notice how smaller details are connected. In your notebook, copy a web like the one shown here. Write brief notes about the main things people in the British colonies had in common—the beliefs and experiences that formed an American identity.

• Read and remember the Main Idea at the beginning of each section.
• At the end of each group of paragraphs under a heading, ask yourself, "Have I learned about something that united the colonists?"

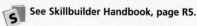 See Skillbuilder Handbook, page R5.

Economy

Education

Religion

American Identity

Publishing

Political Ideas

War

① Early American Culture

TERMS & NAMES
apprentice
Great Awakening
Jonathan Edwards
George Whitefield
Enlightenment
Benjamin Franklin
John Locke

MAIN IDEA	WHY IT MATTERS NOW
The British colonies were shaped by prosperity, literacy, and new movements in religion and thought.	These forces began to create an American identity that is still developing today.

ONE AMERICAN'S STORY

On October 2, 1704, Sarah Kemble Knight set out on horseback from her home in Boston. She was riding all the way to New Haven, Connecticut. Today the ride is two hours by car, but then it took five days.

In her journal, Madam Knight described her travel hardships and commented on people she met—country girls, tobacco-chewing farmers, and rude housewives.

A VOICE FROM THE PAST

We hoped to reach the french town and Lodg there that night, but unhapily lost our way about four miles short. . . . A surly old shee Creature, not worthy the name of woman, . . . would hardly let us go into her Door, though the weather was so stormy none but shee would have turnd out a Dogg.

Sarah Kemble Knight, *The Journal of Madam Knight*

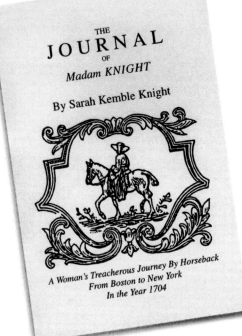

THE
JOURNAL
OF
Madam KNIGHT

By Sarah Kemble Knight

*A Woman's Treacherous Journey By Horseback
From Boston to New York
In the Year 1704*

This reprint of *The Journal of Madam Knight* is a 1920 edition.

Her attitude toward people from other colonies was typical. In the early 1700s, people of the different British colonies did not think of themselves as living in one country. They were separated by distance and customs. In this section, you will learn what began to draw the colonies together.

Land, Rights, and Wealth

At the time of Madam Knight's journey, the colonies were thriving. Cheap farmland and plentiful natural resources gave colonists a chance to prosper. They would have had less opportunity in Europe. In England, fewer than 5 percent of the people owned land. In fact, land rarely went up for sale. By contrast, in the colonies, land was plentiful—once Native American groups were forced to give up their claims. Colonists who owned land were free to use or sell whatever it produced.

Land ownership gave colonists political rights as well as prosperity. Generally, only white male landowners or property owners could vote. There were some exceptions. City dwellers could vote by paying a fee.

Colonial Social Ranks

HIGH
- large landowners
- church officials
- government officials
- wealthy merchants

UPPER MIDDLE
- small farmers
- tradespeople

LOWER MIDDLE
- renters
- unskilled workers

LOW
- indentured servants
- slaves

Land ownership also helped determine colonists' social position. Unlike England, America had no class of nobles whose titles passed from parent to child. But people were still divided into high, middle, and low ranks, as they were in England. Large landholders were high in rank. Small farmers who owned their land were in the middle rank. Most colonists fit this category. People who did not own land, such as servants, slaves, or hired workers, were low in rank. Colonial women held the same rank as their husbands or fathers.

Colonists showed respect to their "betters" by curtsying or tipping a hat, for example. Seats in church were assigned by rank, with wealthy families in the front pews and poor people in the back. Despite such divisions, the wealthy were expected to aid the poor.

Reading **History**
A. Finding Main Ideas What did colonists gain by owning land?

Women and the Economy

Although women were not landholders, their work was essential to the colonial economy. As you learned in Chapter 4, enslaved African women helped raise cash crops such as tobacco and indigo. Most white women were farm wives who performed tasks and made products their families needed. They cooked, churned butter, made soap and candles, spun fibers, wove cloth, sewed and knitted clothes, and did many other chores. They usually tended a garden and looked after farm animals. At harvest time, they often worked in the fields alongside men and older children.

Because cash was scarce, farm wives bartered, or traded, with their neighbors for goods and services. For example, a woman who nursed a sick neighbor or helped deliver a baby might be paid in sugar or cloth.

Women in towns and cities usually did the same types of housework that rural women did. In addition, some urban women ran inns or other businesses. Madam Knight, whose journey was described in One American's Story on page 119, sold writing paper, taught handwriting, and rented rooms to guests. A few women, usually the wives or widows of tradesmen, practiced trades themselves.

Reading **History**
B. Finding Main Ideas In what ways was women's work essential to the economy?

Although women contributed to the colonial economy, they did not have many rights. Women could not vote. In most churches, they could not preach or hold office. (Quaker meetings were an exception.) A married woman could not own property without her husband's permission. By law, even the money a woman earned belonged to her husband.

Young People at Work

Children's work also supported the colonial economy. Families were large. New England families, for example, had an average of six to eight children. More children meant more workers. Children as young as three or four were expected to be useful. They might help look after farm animals, gather berries, and watch younger children.

Around age six, boys were "breeched." This meant that they no longer wore the skirts or smocks of all young children but were given a pair of pants. They then began to help their fathers at work. Sons of farmers worked all day clearing land and learning to farm. Sons of craftsmen tended their fathers' shops and learned their fathers' trades.

Around age 11, many boys left their fathers to become apprentices. An **apprentice** learned a trade from an experienced craftsman. The apprentice received food, clothing, lodging, and a general education, as well as training in the specific craft or business. He worked for free, usually for four to seven years, until his contract was fulfilled. Then he could work for wages or start his own business.

*Reading*History
C. Contrasting
How did the training of boys and girls differ?

Girls rarely were apprenticed. They learned sewing and other household skills from their mothers. In New England, girls of 13 or 14 often were sent away to other households to learn specialized skills such as weaving or cheese making. Orphaned girls and boys worked as servants for families who housed and fed them until adulthood.

Colonial Schooling

If land, wealth, and hard work were valued across the colonies, so was education. Most children were taught to read so that they could understand the Bible. Only children from wealthy families went beyond reading to learn writing and arithmetic. These children learned either from private tutors or in private schools. Poorer children sometimes learned to read from their mothers.

HISTORY *through*ART

This drawing shows the inside of an 18th-century one-room schoolhouse.

What does the picture suggest to you about colonial schooling?

daily *life*

THE SCHOOL OF MANNERS

Colonial children learned proper behavior from *The School of Manners,* a book published in 1701. Here are examples of rules and an illustration from the book.

"Spit not in the Room, but in a corner, and rub it out with thy Foot, or rather go out and do it abroad."

"If thou meetest the scholars of any other School jeer not nor affront them, but show them love and respect and quietly let them pass along."

Or they attended "dame schools," where women taught the alphabet and used the Bible to teach reading. Most children finished their formal education at age seven.

Children's textbooks emphasized religion. The widely used *New England Primer* paired the letter *A* with the verse "In *Adam's* fall / We Sinned all." Beside the letter *B* was a picture of the Bible. The primer contained the Lord's Prayer and *The Shorter Catechism,* more than 100 questions and answers about religion.

Colonial America had a high literacy rate, as measured by the number of people who could sign their names. In New England, 85 percent of white men were literate, compared with 60 percent of men in England. In the Middle Colonies, 65 percent of white men were literate, and in the South, about 50 percent were. In each region of the colonies, roughly half as many white women as men were literate. Most colonists thought schooling was more important for males. Educated African Americans were rare. If they were enslaved, teaching them to read was illegal. If they were free, they were often kept out of schools.

*Reading*History

D. Contrasting
How was colonial education different from education today?

Newspapers and Books

Colonial readers supported a publishing industry that also drew the colonies together. In the early 1700s, the colonies had only one local newspaper, the *Boston News-letter.* But over the next 70 years, almost 80 different newspapers appeared in America. Many were published for decades.

Most books in the colonies were imported from England, but colonists slowly began to publish their own books. Almanacs were very popular. A typical almanac included a calendar, weather predictions, star charts, farming advice, home remedies, recipes, jokes, and proverbs. In 1732, Benjamin Franklin began to publish *Poor Richard's Almanack.* It contained sayings that are still repeated today, such as "Haste makes waste."

Colonists also published poetry, regional histories, and autobiographies. Most personal stories told of struggles to maintain religious faith during hard times. A form of literature unique to the Americas was the captivity narrative. In it, a colonist captured by Native Americans described living among them.

*Reading*History

E. Categorizing
What were some types of colonial literature?

Mary Rowlandson's 1682 captivity narrative, *The Sovereignty and Goodness of God,* was one of the first colonial bestsellers. Native Americans attacked Rowlandson's Massachusetts village in 1676, during King Philip's War. They held her hostage for 11 weeks. During that time, she was a servant to a Narragansett chieftain, knitting stockings and making shirts for his family and others. "I told them it was Sabbath day," she recalled, "and desired them to let me rest, and told them I would do as much more tomorrow. To which they answered me, they would break my face." After townspeople raised money to ransom Rowlandson, she was released. Although she mourned a young daughter who had died in captivity, she praised God for returning her safely.

The Great Awakening

Mary Rowlandson's religious faith was central to her life. But in the early 1700s, many colonists feared they had lost the religious passion that had driven their ancestors to found the colonies. Religion seemed dry, dull, and distant, even to regular churchgoers.

In the 1730s and 1740s, a religious movement called the **Great Awakening** swept through the colonies. The traveling ministers of this movement preached that inner religious emotion was more important than outward religious behavior. Their sermons appealed to the heart and drew large crowds. **Jonathan Edwards,** one of the best-known preachers, terrified listeners with images of God's anger but promised they could be saved.

A VOICE FROM THE PAST

And now you have an extraordinary opportunity, a day wherein Christ has thrown the door of mercy wide open, and stands in calling and crying with a loud voice to poor sinners. . . . How awful it is to be left behind at such a day!

Jonathan Edwards, "Sinners in the Hands of an Angry God"

The Great Awakening lasted for years and changed colonial culture. Congregations argued over religious practices and often split apart. People left their old churches and joined other Protestant groups such as Baptists. Some of these groups welcomed women, African Americans, and Native Americans. Overall, churches gained 20,000 to 50,000 new members. To train ministers, religious groups founded colleges such as Princeton and Brown.

The Great Awakening inspired colonists to help others. **George Whitefield** (HWIT·feeld) drew thousands of people with his sermons and raised funds to start a home for orphans. Other ministers taught Christianity and reading to Native Americans and African Americans. The

George Whitefield preaching to a crowd

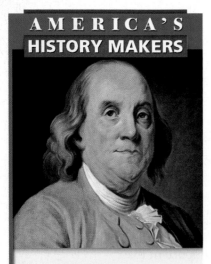

BENJAMIN FRANKLIN
1706–1790

As an Enlightenment thinker, Benjamin Franklin used reason to improve society. At 42, he retired from business to devote his life to science and public service. He proved that lightning was a form of electricity. Then he invented the lightning rod to protect buildings. The Franklin stove and bifocal eyeglasses were also his inventions. He organized a fire department, a lending library, and a society to discuss philosophy. Later he helped draft the Declaration of Independence.

How did Franklin help improve colonial society?

Great Awakening encouraged ideas of equality and the right to challenge authority. In this way, the movement contributed to the revolutionary fervor of the colonists when they declared independence from England years later.

The Enlightenment

Unlike the Great Awakening, which stressed religious emotion, the **Enlightenment** emphasized reason and science as the paths to knowledge. **Benjamin Franklin** was a famous American Enlightenment figure. This intellectual movement appealed mostly to wealthy, educated men. But it, too, had far-reaching effects on the colonies.

The Enlightenment began in Europe, as scientists discovered natural laws governing the universe. Isaac Newton, for example, explained the law of gravity.

Other Enlightenment thinkers applied the idea of natural law to human societies. The English philosopher **John Locke** argued that people have natural rights. These are rights to life, liberty, and property. People create governments to protect their natural rights, he claimed. If a government fails in this duty, people have the right to change it. Locke challenged the belief that kings had a God-given right to rule.

Enlightenment ideas of natural rights and government by agreement influenced leaders across Europe and the colonies. As you will see in Section 2, colonists began to wonder whether the British government protected their rights and freedoms. Eventually, they would rebel and form a new government.

*Reading*History
F. Recognizing Effects What were five effects of the Great Awakening?

Background
Locke argued against the idea that the kings had a God-given right to rule. But he still believed that the natural rights of individuals came from God.

Section 1 Assessment

1. Terms & Names

Explain the significance of:
• apprentice
• Great Awakening
• Jonathan Edwards
• George Whitefield
• Enlightenment
• Benjamin Franklin
• John Locke

2. Taking Notes

Describe the parts of colonial culture in a chart.

Economy	
Education	
Publishing	
Religion	

Why was each important in colonial culture?

3. Main Ideas

a. Why was land ownership so important to the colonists?

b. How did women and young people contribute to the colonial economy?

c. How did the Great Awakening affect the colonies?

4. Critical Thinking

Contrasting How were the Great Awakening and the Enlightenment different?

THINK ABOUT
• the ideas each movement promoted
• the people to whom each movement appealed

ACTIVITY OPTIONS

LANGUAGE ARTS

ART

Make up a **saying** that reflects some part of colonial culture, or draw an **illustration** of a saying from colonial times.

2 Roots of Representative Government

TERMS & NAMES
Magna Carta
Parliament
Edmund Andros
Glorious Revolution
English Bill of Rights
salutary neglect
John Peter Zenger

MAIN IDEA	WHY IT MATTERS NOW
Colonists expected their government to preserve their basic rights as English subjects.	U.S. citizens expect these same rights, such as the right to a trial by jury.

ONE AMERICAN'S STORY

On April 7, 1688, the famous Puritan minister Increase Mather set sail for England. He was to speak to King James II to get relief for the Massachusetts colony. The English government had canceled the charter of Massachusetts and sent a royal governor to rule.

The colonists thought that the governor trampled their rights as English subjects. Mather stayed in England for four years. During this time, he saw the king driven out and replaced by new rulers. In the end, he came home with a new charter that he hoped would satisfy the New England colonists.

A VOICE FROM THE PAST

For all English liberties are restored to them: No Persons shall have a Penny of their Estates taken from them; nor any Laws imposed on them, without their own Consent by Representatives chosen by themselves.

Increase Mather, quoted in *The Last American Puritan*

This is a detail of *Increase Mather* by Jan van der Spriett.

Mather called the new charter "a Magna Carta for New England." In this section, you will learn about the rights of English people set forth in the Magna Carta and later documents. These rights are the basis for the rights Americans enjoy today, such as the right not to be jailed without cause and the right to a jury trial.

The Rights of Englishmen

English colonists expected certain rights that came from living under an English government. These "rights of Englishmen" had developed over centuries.

The first step toward guaranteeing these rights came in 1215. That year, a group of English noblemen forced King John to accept the **Magna Carta** (Great Charter). The king needed the nobles' money to finance a war. This document guaranteed important rights to noblemen and freemen—those not bound to a master. They could not have their property seized by the king or his officials. They could not be taxed, in most cases, unless a council of prominent men agreed. They could not be put to trial based only on an official's word, without witnesses. They could be punished only by a jury of their peers, people of the same social rank.

A VOICE FROM THE PAST

No freeman shall be seized, imprisoned, dispossessed, outlawed, or exiled, . . . nor will we proceed against or prosecute him except by the lawful judgment of his peers, or by the law of the land.

Magna Carta, translated in *A Documentary History of England*

Reading **History**

A. Comparing
What rights from the Magna Carta remain rights in America today?

The Magna Carta limited the powers of the king. Over time, the rights it listed were granted to all English people, not just noblemen and freemen.

Parliament and Colonial Government

One of the most important English rights was the right to elect representatives to government. **Parliament,** England's chief lawmaking body, was the colonists' model for representative government. Parliament was made up of two houses. Members of the House of Commons were elected by the people. Members of the House of Lords were nonelected nobles, judges, and church officials.

The king and Parliament were too far away to manage every detail of the colonies. Also, like the citizens of England, English colonists in America wanted to have a say in the laws governing them. So they formed

CITIZENSHIP TODAY

The Importance of Juries

The right to a trial by jury, established in the Magna Carta, is an important legal right. When you become an adult, you will likely be asked to serve on a jury.

Many young people in Knox County, Illinois, have already served as jurors on a teen court (shown below, with an advisor). They decide the best punishment for other teenagers who have admitted breaking a law. For example, shoplifters might be sentenced to write an apology to the store. Knox County is one of more than 500 U.S. communities that have teen courts.

How Can You Serve on a Teen Court?

1. Search the library or Internet to learn more about teen courts.
2. Ask the police department whether your town has a teen court. If it does, volunteer.
3. If you want to start a teen court, seek advice from a community that has one.
4. Invite a lawyer to your class to talk about a juror's role.
5. Find a group to sponsor your court, and get support from youth officers and judges.

See the Citizenship Handbook, page 264.

For more about courts and juries . . .

RESEARCH LINKS
CLASSZONE.COM

Knox County Teen Court volunteers

their own elected assemblies, similar to the House of Commons. Virginia's House of Burgesses was the first of these. In Pennsylvania, William Penn allowed colonists to have their own General Assembly. These Virginia and Pennsylvania assemblies imposed taxes and managed the colonies.

Although the colonists governed themselves in some ways, England still had authority over them. The king appointed royal governors to rule some colonies on his behalf. Parliament had no representatives from the colonies. Even so, it passed laws that affected the colonies. The colonists disliked these laws, and they began to clash with royal governors over how much power England should have in America. These conflicts became more intense in the late 1600s.

*Reading*History
B. Making Inferences Why did the colonists dislike laws passed by Parliament?

A Royal Governor's Rule

The reign of James II threatened the colonies' tradition of self-government. James became king in 1685. He wanted to rule England and its colonies with total authority. One of his first orders changed the way the Northern colonies were governed. These colonies, especially Massachusetts, had been smuggling goods and ignoring the Navigation Acts (see Chapter 4). When challenged, the people of Massachusetts had claimed that England had no right to make laws for them. The previous king, Charles II, had then canceled their charter.

"You have no more privileges left you."

a Boston court official

The colonists hated Governor Andros.

*Reading*History
C. Recognizing Effects How did James II weaken self-government in the colonies?

King James combined Massachusetts and the other Northern colonies into one Dominion of New England, ruled by royal governor **Edmund Andros.** Andros angered the colonists by ending their representative assemblies and allowing town meetings to be held only once a year.

With their assemblies outlawed, some colonists refused to pay taxes. They said that being taxed without having a voice in government violated their rights. Andros jailed the loudest complainers. At their trial, they were told, "You have no more privileges left you than not to be Sould [sold] for Slaves."

The colonists sent Increase Mather to England to plead with King James (see One American's Story on page 125). However, a revolution in England swept King James and Governor Andros from power.

England's Glorious Revolution

Background
England had become Protestant in the 16th century. Catholics were kept out of high office.

The English Parliament had decided to overthrow King James for not respecting its rights. Events came to a head in 1688. King James, a Catholic, had been trying to pack his next Parliament with officials who would overturn anti-Catholic laws. He had dismissed the last Parliament in 1685. The Protestant leaders of Parliament were outraged. They offered the throne to James's Protestant daughter, Mary, and her husband, William of Orange. William was the ruler of the Netherlands. Having little support from the people, James fled the country at the end of 1688. Parliament named William and Mary the new monarchs of England. This change in leadership was called England's **Glorious Revolution.**

After accepting the throne, William and Mary agreed in 1689 to uphold the **English Bill of Rights.** This was an agreement to respect the rights of English citizens and of Parliament. Under it, the king or queen could not cancel laws or impose taxes unless Parliament agreed. Free elections and frequent meetings of Parliament must be held. Excessive fines and cruel punishments were forbidden. People had the right to complain to the king or queen in Parliament without being arrested.

Background
The English Bill of Rights was the model for the Bill of Rights in the U.S. Constitution.

The English Bill of Rights established an important principle: the government was to be based on laws made by Parliament, not on the desires of a ruler. The rights of English people were strengthened.

The American colonists were quick to claim these rights. When the people of Boston heard of King James's fall, they jailed Governor Andros and asked Parliament to restore their old government.

Shared Power in the Colonies

After the Glorious Revolution, the Massachusetts colonists regained some self-government. They could again elect representatives to an assembly. However, they still had a governor appointed by the crown.

Background
Massachusetts colonists also gained more religious freedom. They no longer had to be church members to vote.

The diagram on this page shows how most colonial governments were organized by 1700. Note how the royal governor, his council, and the colonial assembly shared power. The governor could strike down laws passed by the assembly, but the assembly was responsible for the governor's salary. If he blocked the assembly, the assembly might refuse to pay him.

During the first half of the 1700s, England interfered very little in colonial affairs. This hands-off policy was called **salutary neglect.** Parliament passed many laws regulating trade, the use of money, and even apprenticeships in the colonies. But governors rarely enforced these laws. The colonists got used to acting on their own.

Vocabulary
salutary: healthful or beneficial

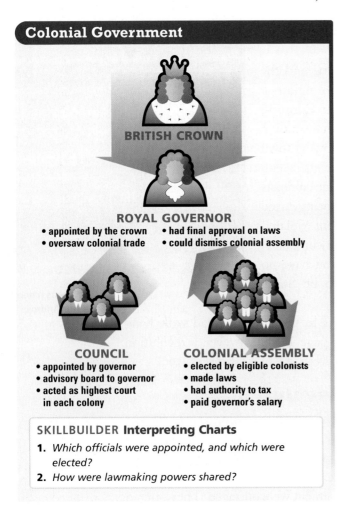

Colonial Government

BRITISH CROWN

ROYAL GOVERNOR
• appointed by the crown
• oversaw colonial trade
• had final approval on laws
• could dismiss colonial assembly

COUNCIL
• appointed by governor
• advisory board to governor
• acted as highest court in each colony

COLONIAL ASSEMBLY
• elected by eligible colonists
• made laws
• had authority to tax
• paid governor's salary

SKILLBUILDER Interpreting Charts
1. Which officials were appointed, and which were elected?
2. How were lawmaking powers shared?

Government officials burn the *New-York Weekly Journal.*

The Zenger Trial

Colonists moved toward gaining a new right, freedom of the press, in 1735. That year, **John Peter Zenger,** publisher of the *New-York Weekly Journal,* stood trial for printing criticism of New York's governor. The governor had removed a judge and tried to fix an election.

A VOICE FROM THE PAST

A Governor turns rogue [criminal], does a thousand things for which a small rogue would have deserved a halter [hanging], and because it is difficult . . . to obtain relief against him, . . . it is prudent [wise] to . . . join in the roguery.

New-York Weekly Journal, quoted in *Colonial America, 1607–1763*

Reading **History**

D. Drawing Conclusions Why was the Zenger trial a step toward freedom of the press?

At that time, it was illegal to criticize the government in print. Andrew Hamilton defended Zenger at his trial, claiming that people had the right to speak the truth. The jury agreed, and Zenger was released.

English rights were part of the heritage uniting people in the British colonies. In the next section, you will read about another unifying force—a war against the French and their Indian allies.

Section 2 Assessment

1. Terms & Names

Explain the significance of:

• Magna Carta
• Parliament
• Edmund Andros
• Glorious Revolution
• English Bill of Rights
• salutary neglect
• John Peter Zenger

2. Taking Notes

In the boxes, show how the rights of English people developed in the three years mentioned.

```
          English Rights
     ┌─────────┼─────────┐
  [     ]   [     ]   [     ]
   1215      1689      1735
```

Which right is most important to you?

3. Main Ideas

a. What were three of the traditional rights expected by English colonists?

b. In what ways did the English government anger the colonists in the late 1600s?

c. How did England's policies toward the colonies change after the Glorious Revolution?

4. Critical Thinking

Supporting Opinions
In your opinion, who had the most power—the royal governor, the council, or the assemblies? Defend your opinion.

THINK ABOUT

• their roles in making laws
• their roles in raising money
• who had final approval in matters

ACTIVITY OPTIONS

SPEECH

ART

Deliver **closing arguments** or create a **leaflet** defending John Peter Zenger and freedom of the press.

The French and Indian War

TERMS & NAMES
French and Indian War
Albany Plan of Union
Battle of Quebec
Treaty of Paris
Pontiac's Rebellion
Proclamation of 1763

MAIN IDEA	WHY IT MATTERS NOW
Britain's victory in the French and Indian War forced France to give up its North American colonies.	British influence spread over North America, though French populations and place names still exist here.

ONE AMERICAN'S STORY

Charles de Langlade, born in 1729, was the son of a French fur trader and his Ottawa wife. His family controlled the fur trade around what is now Green Bay, Wisconsin.

In 1752, Charles commanded 250 Ottawa and Chippewa warriors in an attack on the village of Pickawillany, in present-day Ohio. His reason: the Miami people who lived there had stopped trading with the French and were now trading with the British. Charles and his men destroyed the village's British trading post and killed the Miami chief. This attack helped lead to the French and Indian War.

This section describes the war, in which French forces fought British forces in North America. Each side had Native American allies. Charles de Langlade led several successful attacks against the British. But in the end, he saw the British drive French armies from the continent.

This 1903 painting by Edward Deming shows Charles de Langlade attacking British forces in 1755.

France Claims Western Lands

As you learned in Chapters 2 and 4, the French were exploring the North American interior while English colonists were settling the eastern coast. By the late 1600s, French explorers had claimed the Ohio River valley, the Mississippi River valley, and the entire Great Lakes region. The French territory of Louisiana, claimed by the explorer La Salle in 1682, stretched from the Appalachian Mountains to the Rocky Mountains.

The French built their main settlements, Quebec and Montreal, along the St. Lawrence River in Canada. (See the map on page 132.) They also built forts along the Great Lakes and along rivers draining into the Mississippi. By 1760, the French colony, New France, had a European population of about 80,000. By contrast, the British colonies had more than a million settlers.

Some Europeans in New France were Jesuit priests. They wanted to convert Native Americans to Christianity. Other Europeans in New France worked as fur traders. Native Americans brought furs to French forts and

Background
Often French
traders lived
among and
married Native
Americans.

exchanged them for goods such as iron pots and steel knives. Many French traders carried goods by canoe into remote parts of New France.

Native American Alliances

The English competed with the French for furs. Also, different Native American groups competed to supply furs to the Europeans. The fur trade created economic and military alliances between the Europeans and their Native American trading partners. The Huron and Algonquin peoples of the Great Lakes region were allied with the French. The Iroquois of upper New York often were allied with the Dutch and, later, the English.

Alliances between Europeans and Native Americans led to their involvement in each other's wars. For example, by the mid-1600s, the Iroquois had trapped all the beavers in their own lands. To get more furs, they made war on their Huron and Algonquin neighbors, driving them west. Eventually the Iroquois controlled an area ranging from Maine west to the Ohio Valley and north to Lake Michigan. Iroquois expansion threatened the French fur trade. In response, the French armed the Huron and Algonquin peoples to fight the Iroquois. The Iroquois were armed by the English.

A French trader visits a Native American family.

When France and England declared war on each other in Europe in 1689, French and English colonists in America also began to fight. With their Native American allies, they attacked each other's settlements and forts. During the 1700s, two more wars between France and England fueled wars in their colonies. Neither side won a clear victory in these wars. A final war, the **French and Indian War** (1754–1763), decided which nation would control the northern and eastern parts of North America.

Conflict in the Ohio River Valley

The seeds for the French and Indian War were planted when British fur traders began moving into the Ohio River valley in the 1750s. British land companies were also planning to settle colonists there. The French and their Native American allies became alarmed. To keep the British out of the valley, Charles de Langlade destroyed the village of Pickawillany and its British trading post (see One American's Story on page 130).

*Reading***History**
B. Making
Inferences Why
was the Ohio
River Valley
important to the
French and British
governments?

The British traders left, and the French built forts to protect the region linking their Canadian and Louisiana settlements. This upset the Virginia colony, which claimed title to the land. In 1753, the lieutenant governor of Virginia sent a small group of soldiers to tell the French to leave. Their leader was a 21-year-old major named George Washington. Washington reported the French commander's reply.

> **A VOICE FROM THE PAST**
>
> He told me the Country belong'd to them, that no English Man had a right to trade upon them Waters; & that he had Orders to make every Person Prisoner that attempted it on the Ohio or the Waters of it.
>
> **George Washington,** *"Journey to the French Commandant"*

Virginia's lieutenant governor sent about 40 men to build a fort at the head of the Ohio River, where Pittsburgh stands today. French and Native American troops seized the partially built fort in April 1754 and completed it themselves. The French named it Fort Duquesne (du•KAYN).

War Begins and Spreads

George Washington was on his way to defend Fort Duquesne when he learned of its surrender. He and his men pushed on and built another small fort, Fort Necessity. Following Washington's surprise attack on a French force, the French and their allies attacked Fort Necessity on July 3, 1754. After Washington surrendered, the French let him march back to Virginia. The French and Indian War had begun. This war became part of the Seven Years' War (1756–1763), a worldwide struggle for empire between France and Great Britain.

Background
The Seven Years' War was fought not only in North America but also in the Caribbean, throughout Europe, and in India and Africa.

French and Indian War, 1754–1763

GEOGRAPHY SKILLBUILDER
Interpreting Maps

1. **Place** *Which nation controlled territory along the St. Lawrence and Ohio rivers?*
2. **Place** *Which forts were the sites of British victories?*

Louisbourg 1758
Acadia
Ft. Beauséjour 1755
Quebec 1759
Nova Scotia
Halifax
MAINE (part of MASS.)
Montreal (Surrendered, 1760)
Lake Champlain
Ft. Ticonderoga 1758, 1759
Ft. Frontenac 1758
N.H.
Ft. William Henry 1757
Boston
MASS.
ATLANTIC OCEAN
Lake Ontario
Ft. Oswego 1756
Ft. Niagara 1759
N.Y.
Hudson R.
CONN. R.I.
Lake Erie
Allegheny R.
N.J. New York
PENN.
Philadelphia
Ft. Duquesne 1755
MD.
Ft. Necessity 1754
DEL.
Ohio R.
Monongahela R.
VA.
NEW FRANCE
St. Lawrence R.

British territory
French territory
Disputed territory
British victory
French victory

0 100 Miles
0 200 Kilometers

While Washington was surrendering Fort Necessity, representatives from the British colonies and the Iroquois nations were meeting at Albany, New York. The colonists wanted the Iroquois to fight with them against the French. The Iroquois would not commit to this alliance.

Benjamin Franklin, who admired the union of the six Iroquois nations, suggested that the colonies band together for defense. His **Albany Plan of Union** was the first formal proposal to unite the colonies. The plan called for each colony to send representatives to a Grand Council. This council would be able to collect taxes, raise armies, make treaties, and start new settlements. The leaders in Albany supported Franklin's plan, but the colonial legislatures later defeated it because they did not want to give up control of their own affairs.

Braddock's Defeat

Britain realized that to win the war, it could not rely solely on the colonists for funding or for troops. Therefore, the British sent General Edward Braddock and two regiments to Virginia. In 1755, Braddock marched toward the French at Fort Duquesne. George Washington was at his side. Their red-coated army of 2,100 moved slowly over the mountains, weighed down by a huge cannon.

On July 9, on a narrow trail eight miles from Fort Duquesne, fewer than 900 French and Indian troops surprised Braddock's forces. Washington suggested that his men break formation and fight from behind the trees, but Braddock would not listen. The general held his position and had four horses shot out from under him. Washington lost two horses. Four bullets went through Washington's coat, but, miraculously, none hit him. In the end, nearly 1,000 men were killed or wounded. General Braddock died from his wounds. American colonists were stunned by Braddock's defeat and by many other British losses over the next two years.

*Reading*History
C. Drawing Conclusions Why was Braddock defeated by a smaller enemy force?

The British Take Quebec

In 1757, Britain had a new secretary of state, William Pitt, who was determined to win the war in the colonies. He sent the nation's best generals to America and borrowed money to pay colonial troops for fighting. The British controlled six French forts by August 1759, including Fort Duquesne (rebuilt as Fort Pitt). In late summer, the British began to attack New France at its capital, Quebec.

Background Because the British seemed likely to win the war, some Iroquois had joined them as allies.

America's HERITAGE

ACADIANS TO CAJUNS
Braddock's defeat and other early losses in the war increased British concern about the loyalty of the French people in Acadia (now Nova Scotia). The British had won Acadia from France in 1713.

In 1755, British officers forced out 6,000 Acadians who would not take a loyalty oath. The British burned Acadian villages and spread the people to various British colonies, as shown. Eventually, some Acadians made their way to the French territory of Louisiana. There they became known as Cajuns.

Quebec sat on cliffs 300 feet above the St. Lawrence River. Cannon and thousands of soldiers guarded its thick walls. British general James Wolfe sailed around the fort for two months, unable to capture it. Then, in September, a scout found a steep, unguarded path up the cliffs to the plains just west of Quebec. At night, Wolfe and 4,000 of his men floated to the path and secretly climbed the cliffs.

When the French awoke, the British were lined up on the plains, ready to attack. In the short, fierce battle that followed, Wolfe was killed. The French commander, Montcalm, died of his wounds the next day. Quebec surrendered to the British. The **Battle of Quebec** was the turning point of the war. When Montreal fell the next year, all of Canada was in British hands.

*Reading*History
D. Finding Main Ideas How were the British able to capture Quebec?

The Treaty of Paris

Britain and France battled in other parts of the world for almost three more years. Spain made a pact in 1761 to aid France, but its help came too late. When the Seven Years' War ended in 1763, Britain had won.

By the **Treaty of Paris,** Britain claimed all of North America east of the Mississippi River. To reward Spain for its help, France gave it New Orleans and Louisiana, the French territory west of the Mississippi. Britain, which had seized Cuba and the Philippines from Spain, gave them back in exchange for Florida. The treaty ended French power in North America.

Background
France kept only a few islands near Newfoundland and in the West Indies.

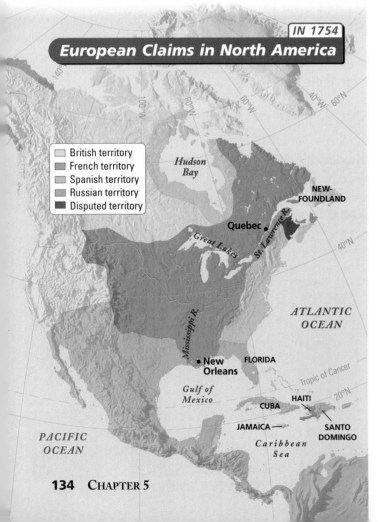

IN 1754
European Claims in North America

- British territory
- French territory
- Spanish territory
- Russian territory
- Disputed territory

Hudson Bay

NEW-FOUNDLAND

Quebec

Great Lakes

St. Lawrence R.

40°N

Mississippi R.

ATLANTIC OCEAN

New Orleans   FLORIDA

Tropic of Cancer

Gulf of Mexico

HAITI

20°N

CUBA

JAMAICA

SANTO DOMINGO

Caribbean Sea

PACIFIC OCEAN

AFTER 1763
European Claims in North America

GEOGRAPHY SKILLBUILDER
Interpreting Maps
1. **Region** *Which nations lost territory after 1763?*
2. **Region** *Which nations gained territory after 1763?*

Hudson Bay

NEW-FOUNDLAND

Quebec

Great Lakes

St. Lawrence R.

40°N

Proclamation Line of 1763

Mississippi R.

PACIFIC OCEAN

N

New Orleans

Gulf of Mexico

ATLANTIC OCEAN

Tropic of Cancer

CUBA   HAITI   20°N

JAMAICA   SANTO DOMINGO

Caribbean Sea

0   500 Miles
0   1,000 Kilometers

Pontiac's Rebellion

After French forces withdrew, the British took over their forts. They refused to give supplies to the Native Americans, as the French had. British settlers also moved across the mountains onto Native American land. In the spring and summer of 1763, Native American groups responded by attacking settlers and destroying almost every British fort west of the Appalachians. They surrounded the three remaining forts. This revolt was called **Pontiac's Rebellion,** although the Ottawa war leader Pontiac was only one of many organizers.

British settlers reacted with equal viciousness, killing even Indians who had not attacked them. British officers came up with a brutal plan to end the Delaware siege at Fort Pitt.

Pontiac

*Reading*History

E. Analyzing Points of View
Why did the Native Americans attack the British?

A VOICE FROM THE PAST

Could it not be contrived to send the Small Pox among those disaffected [angry] tribes of Indians? We must on this occasion use every stratagem in our power to reduce them.

Major General Jeffrey Amherst, quoted in *The Conspiracy of Pontiac*

*Reading*History

F. Reading a Map
Find the Proclamation Line of 1763 on the map on page 134.

The officers invited Delaware war leaders in to talk and then gave them smallpox-infected blankets as gifts. This started a deadly outbreak.

By the fall, the Native Americans had retreated. Even so, the uprising made the British government see that defending Western lands would be costly. Therefore, the British issued the **Proclamation of 1763,** which forbade colonists to settle west of the Appalachians.

The colonists were angry. They thought they had won the right to settle the Ohio River Valley. The British government was angry at the colonists, who did not want to pay for their own defense. This hostility helped cause the war for American independence, as you will read.

Section 3 Assessment

1. Terms & Names

Explain the significance of:

- French and Indian War
- Albany Plan of Union
- Battle of Quebec
- Treaty of Paris
- Pontiac's Rebellion
- Proclamation of 1763

2. Taking Notes

Write the month and year each battle occurred. Classify each as a French or British victory.

Date	Incident	Victor
	Seizure of Fort Duquesne	
	Surrender of Fort Necessity	
	Braddock's defeat	
	Battle of Quebec	

Which was most important?

3. Main Ideas

a. How did the fur trade contribute to the French and Indian War?

b. Why did the British begin to win the war after 1758?

c. What were some causes and effects of Pontiac's Rebellion?

4. Critical Thinking

Analyzing Points of View
Why did the French, British, and Native Americans fight over the Ohio River Valley?

THINK ABOUT

- how the British viewed the valley
- how the French viewed it
- how the Native Americans viewed it

ACTIVITY OPTIONS

GEOGRAPHY

MUSIC

Learn more about the Battle of Quebec and its setting. Make a three-dimensional **model** of the battle or write a **song** about it.

Beginnings of an American Identity

Separate Colonies

Early American Culture

English colonists shared certain values, such as land ownership and hard work. The Great Awakening and the Enlightenment also drew colonists together.

Roots of Representative Government

English colonists expected the right to elect representatives to government and other political rights that had developed in England over centuries.

The French and Indian War

English colonists were also drawn together as they fought against common enemies—the French and their Native American allies.

Common Identity

TERMS & NAMES

Briefly explain the significance of each of the following.

1. Great Awakening
2. Enlightenment
3. John Peter Zenger
4. Magna Carta
5. Parliament
6. Glorious Revolution
7. Edmund Andros
8. French and Indian War
9. Treaty of Paris
10. Proclamation of 1763

REVIEW QUESTIONS

Early American Culture (pages 119–124)

1. Why did colonists want to own land?
2. What was women's role in the colonial economy?
3. What were the effects of the Great Awakening on colonial culture and politics?

Roots of Representative Government (pages 125–129)

4. Why did colonies have representative assemblies?
5. What was one important right granted in the Magna Carta?
6. How did the Zenger trial help lead to freedom of the press?
7. How was the English Bill of Rights related to the Glorious Revolution?

The French and Indian War (pages 130–135)

8. What was George Washington's role in the French and Indian War?
9. What did England gain as a result of the French and Indian War?
10. What was one reason for Pontiac's Rebellion?

CRITICAL THINKING

1. USING YOUR NOTES

Using your completed chart, answer the questions below.

a. What were some political ideas shared by people in the American colonies?
b. How was religion important to American identity?
c. How did publishing help build an American identity?

2. THEME: DEMOCRATIC IDEALS

What democratic ideals did Americans inherit from England?

3. APPLYING CITIZENSHIP SKILLS

Why is jury duty an example of responsible citizenship?

4. CONTRASTING

How did colonial government differ from present-day government in the United States?

5. ANALYZING CAUSES

What do you think was the most important cause of the French and Indian War?

6. ANALYZING LEADERSHIP

Give an example of bad military or political leadership from the chapter. What mistake was made?

Interact with History

Now that you have read the chapter, what would you say British colonists in America had in common?

HISTORY SKILLS

1. INTERPRETING MAPS: Movement

Study the map. Answer the questions.

French Explorers on the Mississippi

Basic Map Elements

a. What do the colors indicate?

Interpreting the Map

b. Who traveled earlier?

c. Who reached the Gulf of Mexico?

d. Along whose route were Fort Detroit and New Orleans later founded?

2. INTERPRETING PRIMARY SOURCES

An unnamed Frenchman who knew Pontiac quotes a speech Pontiac gave to support an attack on British soldiers. Read the quote carefully. Answer the questions.

> When I go to see the English commander and say to him that some of our comrades are dead, instead of bewailing their death, as our French brothers do, he laughs at me and at you. If I ask anything for our sick, he refuses with the reply that he has no use for us. From all this you can well see that they are seeking our ruin. Therefore, my brothers, we must all swear their destruction and wait no longer.
>
> **Journal of Pontiac's Conspiracy,** 1763

a. Why does Pontiac want to attack the English?

b. What is Pontiac's attitude toward the French?

ALTERNATIVE ASSESSMENT

1. INTERDISCIPLINARY ACTIVITY: Language Arts

Making a Speech Do research to learn more about freedom of the press. Then make a speech to convince people that it is important.

2. COOPERATIVE LEARNING ACTIVITY

Holding a Diplomatic Council Working in a small group, review the causes of the French and Indian War, and do further research. Then hold a diplomatic council to try to prevent the war. Role-play representatives from the following groups.

- officials of the English government
- officials of the French government
- English settlers
- French fur traders
- English-allied Iroquois
- French-allied Huron or Algonquin

3. TECHNOLOGY ACTIVITY

Making a Class Presentation Colonial American culture was not like modern American culture. Using the library or the Internet, find images, literature, and informative articles that tell you about daily life in the early and middle 1700s.

For more about colonial American culture . . .

INTERNET ACTIVITY
CLASSZONE.COM

Create a class presentation about colonial culture using the suggestions below.

- Stage a fashion show that illustrates what people of different ranks and ethnic backgrounds wore.
- Create a dramatic play based on the experiences of an interesting figure from the chapter, such as Madam Sarah Knight, Benjamin Franklin, or Pontiac.
- Illustrate sayings from *Poor Richard's Almanack*.
- Give an oral book report on a colonial captivity narrative. For example, find out what happened to Mary Rowlandson among the Narragansett.

4. HISTORY PORTFOLIO

Review your section and chapter assessment activities. Select one that you think is your best work. Then use comments made by your teacher or classmates to improve your work and add it to your portfolio.

Additional Test Practice, pp. S1–S33

TEST PRACTICE
CLASSZONE.COM

Creating a New Nation

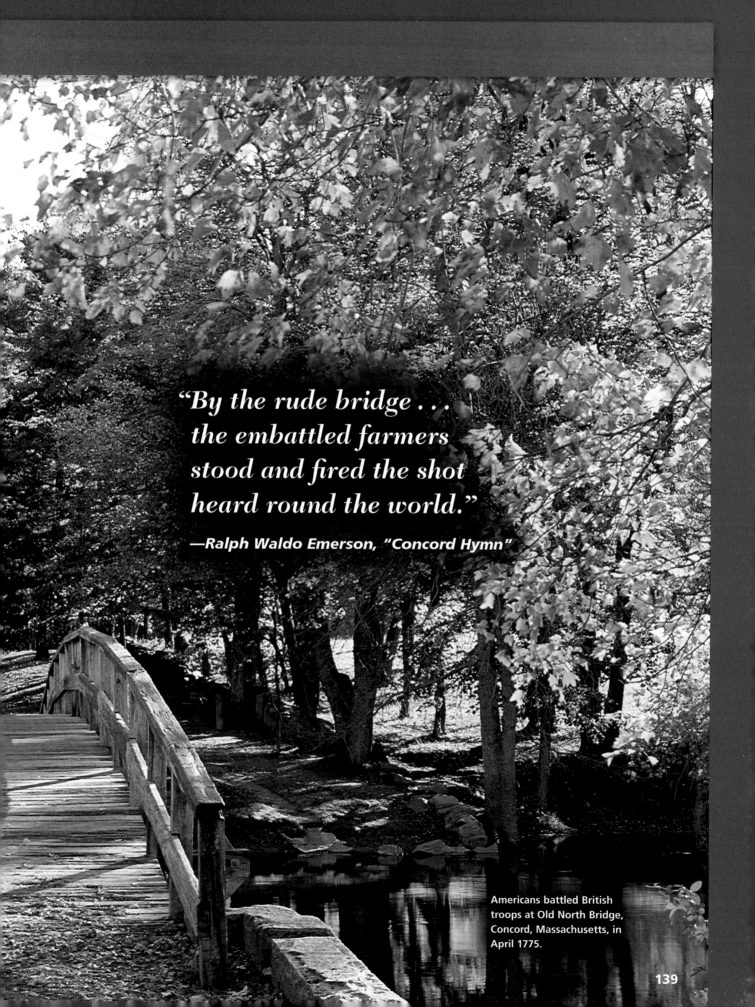

"*By the rude bridge . . .
the embattled farmers
stood and fired the shot
heard round the world.*"

—*Ralph Waldo Emerson, "Concord Hymn"*

Americans battled British
troops at Old North Bridge,
Concord, Massachusetts, in
April 1775.

CHAPTER 6

The Road to Revolution 1763–1776

Angry colonists watch the arrival of British troops in Boston.

A colonist reads a copy of a new British tax law.

Tax stamps are burned.

Protesters include men, women, and children.

The year is 1765. Your neighbors are enraged by Britain's attempt to tax them without their consent. Britain has never done this before. Everyone will be affected by the tax. There are protests in many cities. You have to decide what you would do.

What Do You Think?

- What is the best way to show opposition to policies you consider unjust?

- Is there anything to be gained by protesting? Anything to be lost?

- Does government have the right to tax without consent of the people? Why or why not?

Would you join the protest?

1776
Declaration of Independence is signed.

1775
Battles of Lexington and Concord

1770
Boston Massacre

1774
Intolerable Acts are passed; First Continental Congress meets.

1763
Proclamation of 1763 becomes law.

1769
Spanish begin to establish military posts and missions in California.

1765
Stamp Act is passed.

1767
Townshend Acts are passed.

1773
Boston Tea Party

USA
World

1763

1776

1763
Treaty of Paris ends Seven Years' War in Europe.

1765
Chinese forces invade Burma.

1772
Captain Cook explores the South Pacific.

1774
Reign of Louis XVI begins in France.

BEFORE YOU READ

Protest

War

Independence

Previewing the Theme

Impact of the Individual From 1763 to 1776, American colonists changed from loyal subjects of the British king to revolutionaries. This chapter explains how this dramatic change took place. It also discusses the individuals who led America to independence.

What Do You Know?

What do you already know about the time before the Revolution? What were the issues that caused the colonists to choose independence?

THINK ABOUT
- what you have learned about this period from movies, television, or historical fiction
- reasons people in history have chosen to fight for freedom from oppression

What Do You Want to Know?

What questions do you have about the issues and events that pushed the American colonists toward rebellion? Record them in your notebook before you read the chapter.

READ AND TAKE NOTES

Reading Strategy: Sequencing Events
Sequencing means putting events in the order in which they happen in time. In learning about how the American colonies moved toward independence, it would be helpful to list the important events.

Place them in the order in which they occurred. You might record the event and its date in a graphic organizer such as the one below. Copy this organizer in your notebook. Fill it in as you read the chapter.

S See Skillbuilder Handbook, page R4.

```
Proclamation of 1763 → [    ] → [    ] → [    ]
                                              ↓
[    ] ← [    ] ← [    ] ← [    ]
  ↓
[    ] → [    ] → [    ] → Declaration of Independence, 1776
```

① Tighter British Control

TERMS & NAMES
King George III
Quartering Act
revenue
Sugar Act
Stamp Act
Patrick Henry
boycott
Sons of Liberty

MAIN IDEA	WHY IT MATTERS NOW
Americans saw British efforts to tax them and to increase control over the colonies as violations of their rights.	Colonial protests were the first steps on the road to American independence.

ONE AMERICAN'S STORY

James Otis, Jr., a young Massachusetts lawyer, stormed through the streets of Boston one day in 1760. He was furious. His father had just been denied the post of chief justice of the Massachusetts colony by the royal governor. To Otis, this was one more example of Britain's lack of respect for colonial rights. Another example was its use of search warrants that allowed customs officers to enter any home or business to look for smuggled goods. Otis believed these searches were illegal.

Otis took up a case against the government that involved these search warrants. In court in February 1761, Otis spoke with great emotion for five hours about the search warrant and its use.

A VOICE FROM THE PAST

It appears to me the worst instrument of arbitrary power, the most destructive of English liberty and the fundamental principles of law, that was ever found in an English law-book.

James Otis, Jr., quoted in *James Otis: The Pre-Revolutionist* by J. C. Ridpath

Spectators listened in amazement. One of them, a young lawyer named John Adams, later wrote of Otis's performance: "Then and there, in the old Council Chamber, the child Independence was born."

In making the first public speech demanding English liberties for the colonists, James Otis planted a seed of freedom. In this section, you will read more about the early protests against Britain's policies in America.

James Otis, Jr., argues in court against illegal search warrants in 1761.

The Colonies and Britain Grow Apart

During the French and Indian War, Britain and the colonies fought side by side. Americans took great pride in being partners in the victory over the French. However, when the war ended, problems arose. Britain wanted to govern its 13 original colonies and the territories gained in the war in a uniform way. So the British Parliament in London imposed new laws and restrictions. Previously, the colonies had been allowed to develop largely on their own. Now they felt that their freedom was being limited.

The first of Parliament's laws was the Proclamation of 1763. (See Chapter 5.) It said that colonists could not settle west of the Appalachian Mountains. Britain wanted this land to remain in the hands of its Native American allies to prevent another revolt like Pontiac's Rebellion.

The proclamation angered colonists who had hoped to move to the fertile Ohio Valley. Many of these colonists had no land of their own. It also upset colonists who had bought land as an investment. As a result, many ignored the law.

*Reading*History
A. Summarizing
Who was upset by the Proclamation of 1763?

British Troops and Taxes

King George III, the British monarch, wanted to enforce the proclamation and also keep peace with Britain's Native American allies. To do this, he decided to keep 10,000 soldiers in the colonies. In 1765, Parliament passed the **Quartering Act.** This was a cost-saving measure that required the colonies to quarter, or house, British soldiers and provide them with supplies. General Thomas Gage, commander of these forces, put most of the troops in New York.

Britain owed a large debt from the French and Indian War. Keeping troops in the colonies would raise that debt even higher. Britain needed more **revenue,** or income, to meet its expenses. So it attempted to have the colonies pay part of the war debt. It also wanted them to contribute toward the costs of frontier defense and colonial government.

In the past, the king had asked the colonial assemblies to pass taxes to support military actions that took place in the colonies. This time, however, Parliament voted to tax the Americans directly.

In 1764, Parliament passed the **Sugar Act.** This law placed a tax on sugar, molasses, and other products shipped to the colonies. It also called for strict enforcement of the act and harsh punishment of smugglers.

Colonial merchants, who often traded in smuggled goods, reacted with anger.

Colonial leaders such as James Otis claimed that Parliament had no right to tax the colonies, since the colonists were not represented in Parliament. As Otis exclaimed, "Taxation without representation is tyranny!" British finance minister George Grenville disagreed. The colonists were subjects of Britain, he said, and enjoyed the protection of its laws. For that reason, they were subject to taxation.

Vocabulary
tyranny:
absolute power in the hands of a single ruler

Britain Passes the Stamp Act

The Sugar Act was just the first in a series of acts that increased tension between the mother country and the colonies. In 1765, Parliament passed the **Stamp Act.** This law required all legal and commercial documents to carry an official stamp showing that a tax had been paid. All diplomas, contracts, and wills had to carry a stamp.

The colonial view of the hated stamp tax is shown by the skull and crossbones on this emblem (above); a royal stamp is pictured at right.

144

Even published materials such as newspapers had to be written on special stamped paper.

The Stamp Act was a new kind of tax for the colonies. The Sugar Act had been a tax on imported goods. It mainly affected merchants. In contrast, the Stamp Act was a tax applied within the colonies. It fell directly on all colonists. Even more, the colonists had to pay for stamps in silver coin—a scarce item in the colonies.

Colonial leaders vigorously protested. For them, the issue was clear. They were being taxed without their consent by a Parliament in which they had no voice. If Britain could pass the Stamp Act, what other taxes might it pass in the future? Samuel Adams, a leader in the Massachusetts legislature, asked, "Why not our lands? Why not the produce of our lands and, in short, everything we possess and make use of?" **Patrick Henry,** a member of Virginia's House of Burgesses, called for resistance to the tax. When another member shouted that resistance was treason, Henry replied, "If this be treason, make the most of it!"

The Colonies Protest the Stamp Act

Colonial assemblies and newspapers took up the cry—"No taxation without representation!" In October 1765, nine colonies sent delegates to the Stamp Act Congress in New York City. This was the first time the colonies met to consider acting together in protest. Delegates drew up a petition to the king protesting the Stamp Act. The petition declared that the right to tax the colonies belonged to the colonial assemblies, not to Parliament. Later, colonial merchants organized a **boycott** of British goods. A boycott is a refusal to buy.

Reading **History**
B. Making Inferences Why did the colonists boycott goods?

Background To voice their protests, the Sons of Liberty in Boston met under a huge, 120-year-old elm tree that they called the Liberty Tree.

Meanwhile, some colonists formed secret societies to oppose British policies. The most famous of these groups was the **Sons of Liberty**. Many Sons of Liberty were lawyers, merchants, and craftspeople—the colonists most affected by the Stamp Act. These groups staged protests against the act.

Not all of their protests were peaceful. The Sons of Liberty burned the stamped paper whenever they could find it. They also attacked customs officials, whom they covered with hot tar and feathers and paraded in public. Fearing for their safety, many customs officials quit their jobs.

The protests in the colonies had an effect in Britain. Merchants thought that their trade with America would be hurt. Some British political leaders, including

Colonists protest the Stamp Act.

Bostonians Paying the Taxman

In this British political cartoon, Americans are depicted as barbarians who would tar and feather a customs official, or tax collector, and pour hot tea down his throat.

A Liberty Tree as a gallows

B Stamp Act posted upside down

C Protesters in Boston

D Customs official tarred and feathered

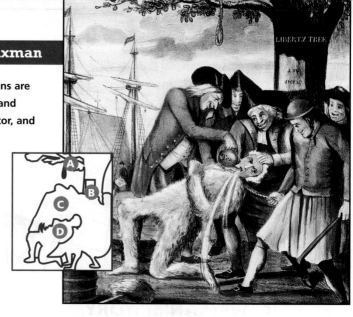

the popular parliamentary leader William Pitt, agreed with American thinking about taxing the colonies. Pitt spoke out against the Stamp Act.

A VOICE FROM THE PAST

The Americans have not acted in all things with prudence and [good] temper. They have been driven to madness by injustice. Will you punish them for the madness you have [caused]? . . . My opinion . . . is that the Stamp Act be repealed absolutely, totally and immediately.

William Pitt, quoted in *Patriots* by A. J. Langguth

Parliament finally saw that the Stamp Act was a mistake and repealed it in 1766. But at the same time, Parliament passed another law—the Declaratory Act. This law said that Parliament had supreme authority to govern the colonies. The Americans celebrated the repeal of the Stamp Act and tried to ignore the Declaratory Act. A great tug of war between Parliament and the colonies had begun. The central issue was control of the colonies, as you will learn in the next section.

Reading **History**

C. Drawing Conclusions Why was it important for Parliament to pass the Declaratory Act?

Section 1 Assessment

1. Terms & Names

Explain the significance of:
- King George III
- Quartering Act
- revenue
- Sugar Act
- Stamp Act
- Patrick Henry
- boycott
- Sons of Liberty

2. Taking Notes

Use a cluster diagram like the one below to review points of conflict between Britain and the colonies.

Points of Conflict

Which do you think was the most serious? Explain.

3. Main Ideas

a. Why did the Proclamation of 1763 anger colonists?

b. How did colonists react to the Stamp Act?

c. What was the goal of secret societies such as the Sons of Liberty?

4. Critical Thinking

Analyzing Points of View What were the two sides in the debate over British taxation of the colonies?

THINK ABOUT
- how Parliament viewed the colonies
- what concerned the colonists about taxes

ACTIVITY OPTIONS

ART

MUSIC

Imagine that you are a colonial leader who wants to get your fellow colonists to protest British policy. Design a **poster** or write a **song of protest**.

② Colonial Resistance Grows

TERMS & NAMES
Crispus Attucks
Townshend Acts
writs of assistance
Samuel Adams
Boston Massacre
John Adams
committee of correspondence
Boston Tea Party

MAIN IDEA	WHY IT MATTERS NOW
Many Americans began to organize to oppose British policies.	Americans continue to protest what they view as wrongs and injustices.

ONE AMERICAN'S STORY

Crispus Attucks knew about the struggle for freedom. The son of an African-American father and a Native American mother, Attucks was born into slavery in Framingham, Massachusetts, around 1723. As a young man, Attucks escaped by running away to sea. He spent the next 20 years as a sailor, working on whaling boats. To avoid recapture, he used a false name, calling himself Michael Johnson.

In March 1770, Attucks found himself in Boston, where feelings against British rule were reaching a fever pitch. The words *freedom* and *liberty* seemed to be on everyone's lips. One night Attucks heard about a disturbance involving colonists and British troops and decided to investigate. He had no idea that he was about to play a key role in American history—losing his life to a British bullet in a protest that came to be known as the Boston Massacre. In this section, you will read how the tension between Britain and its colonies led to violence.

Crispus Attucks, a sailor of African-American and Native American ancestry, was an early hero of America's struggle for freedom.

The Townshend Acts Are Passed

After the uproar over the Stamp Act, Britain hoped to avoid further conflict. Even so, it still needed to raise money to pay for troops and other expenses in America. The Quartering Act was not working. Most of the British army was in New York, and New York saw that as an unfair burden. Its assembly refused to pay to house the troops.

The king's finance minister, Charles Townshend, told Parliament that he had a way to raise revenue in the colonies. So in 1767, Parliament passed his plan, known as the **Townshend Acts.**

The first of the Townshend Acts suspended New York's assembly until New Yorkers agreed to provide housing for the troops. The other acts placed duties, or import taxes, on various goods brought into the colonies, such as glass, paper, paint, lead, and tea. Townshend thought that duties, which were collected before the goods entered the colonies, would anger the colonists less than the direct taxes of the Stamp Act. The money raised would be used to pay the salaries of British governors and other officials in the colonies. To enforce the acts, British officers

The Road to Revolution **147**

would use **writs of assistance,** or search warrants, to enter homes or businesses to search for smuggled goods.

The Reasons for Protest

Protests immediately broke out at news of the Townshend Acts. New Yorkers were angry that their elected assembly had been suspended. People throughout the colonies were upset that Britain was placing new taxes on them. "The issue," said John Dickinson, an important Pennsylvania lawyer, was "whether Parliament can legally take money out of our pockets without our consent." He explained his opposition to the Townshend Acts in essays called *Letters from a Farmer in Pennsylvania,* published in 1767.

A VOICE FROM THE PAST

Let these truths be . . . impressed on our minds—that we cannot be happy without being free—that we cannot be free without being secure in our property—that we cannot be secure in our property if without our consent others may . . . take it away—that taxes imposed on us by Parliament do thus take it away—that duties laid for the sole purpose of raising money are taxes—that attempts to lay such duties should be instantly and firmly opposed.

John Dickinson, quoted in *A New Age Now Begins* by Page Smith

*Reading*History
A. Making Inferences Why does Dickinson believe that taxes interfere with happiness?

The colonists were also angry about the writs of assistance. Many believed, as James Otis had argued (see page 143), that the writs went against their natural rights. These rights had been described by English philosopher John Locke during the Enlightenment. The law of nature, said Locke, teaches that "no one ought to harm another in his life, health, liberty, or possessions." The colonists felt that the Townshend Acts were a serious threat to their rights and freedoms.

Tools of Protest

To protest the Townshend Acts, colonists in Boston announced another boycott of British goods in October 1767. The driving force behind this protest was **Samuel Adams,** a leader of the Boston Sons of Liberty. Adams urged colonists to continue to resist British controls.

The boycott spread throughout the colonies. The Sons of Liberty pressured shopkeepers not to sell imported goods. The Daughters of Liberty called on colonists to weave their own cloth and use American products. As a result, trade with Britain fell sharply.

Colonial leaders asked for peaceful protests. Articles in the *Boston Gazette* asked the people to remain calm—

daily life

WOMEN AND PROTEST

Women were not allowed to participate in political life in the colonies. So their role in protesting British actions was not as prominent as that of men. However, women made their beliefs known by taking part in demonstrations.

Also, some women formed the Daughters of Liberty. This was a patriotic organization that joined in the boycott of British tea and other goods. The refusal of these colonial women to use British imports caused them personal hardship. They were forced to make many of the boycotted items, such as clothing, themselves.

This engraving, *The Bloody Massacre Perpetrated in King Street* by Boston silversmith Paul Revere, appeared in the *Boston Gazette*.

"no mobs.... Constitutional methods are best." However, tempers were running high. When customs officers in Boston tried to seize the American merchant ship *Liberty*, which was carrying smuggled wine, a riot broke out. The rioters forced the customs officers to flee.

Fearing a loss of control, officials called for more British troops. A defiant Samuel Adams replied, "We will destroy every soldier that dares put his foot on shore.... I look upon them as foreign enemies."

The Boston Massacre

In the fall of 1768, 1,000 British soldiers (known as redcoats for their bright red jackets) arrived in Boston under the command of General Thomas Gage. With their arrival, tension filled the streets of Boston.

Since the soldiers were poorly paid, they hired themselves out as workers, usually at rates lower than those of American workers. Resentment against the redcoats grew. Soldiers and street youths often yelled insults at each other. "Lobsters for sale!" the youths would yell, referring to the soldiers' red coats. "Yankees!" the soldiers jeered. *Yankee* was supposed to be an insult, but the colonists soon took pride in the name.

On March 5, 1770, tensions finally exploded into violence. A group of youths and dockworkers—among them Crispus Attucks—started trading insults in front of the Custom House. A fight broke out, and the soldiers began firing. Attucks and four laborers were killed.

Reading **History**

B. Recognizing Propaganda How did the use of the word *massacre* show an anti-British view?

The Sons of Liberty called the shooting the **Boston Massacre.** They said that Attucks and the four others had given their lives for freedom. The incident became a tool for anti-British propaganda in newspaper articles, pamphlets, and posters. The people of Boston were outraged.

Meanwhile, the redcoats who had fired the shots were arrested for murder. **John Adams,** a lawyer and cousin of Samuel Adams, defended them in court. Adams was criticized for taking the case. He replied that the law should be "deaf... to the clamors of the populace." He supported

SAMUEL ADAMS
1722–1803

Samuel Adams was a Harvard graduate. But unlike his cousin John, also a Harvard graduate, he showed little skill for the law. Later, when he took control of the family business, he lost his father's fortune. Yet he succeeded in one important undertaking—moving America toward independence.

Adams's true talent lay in rousing people to action in support of a cause. A fiery orator and a master of propaganda, he used words as a weapon. One British official said that "every dip of his pen stings."

JOHN ADAMS
1735–1826

John Adams, unlike Samuel, was considered a moderate in the struggle against Britain. He was an important voice of reason and at first opposed resisting by force.

Adams believed in the rule of law. He called his defense of the soldiers in the Boston Massacre "one of the best pieces of service I ever rendered my country."

Eventually, Adams became convinced that only outright resistance would gain liberty for America. He said, "Britain has at last driven America, to the last Step, a compleat Seperation from her."

How did the cousins John and Samuel Adams differ in the way they protested British actions?

the colonial cause but wanted to show that the colonists followed the rule of law. Adams argued that the soldiers had acted in self-defense. The jury agreed. To many colonists, however, the Boston Massacre would stand as a symbol of British tyranny.

The Tea Act

The colonists were unaware that on the day of the Boston Massacre, Parliament proposed the repeal of the Townshend Acts. One month later, all the acts except the tax on tea were repealed. The colonial boycott had been effective—British trade had been hurt. But Parliament kept the tea tax to show that it still had the right to tax the colonists. For most Americans, the crisis was over.

Samuel Adams, however, wanted to make sure people did not forget the cause of liberty. He started a drive to form **committees of correspondence** in various towns in Massachusetts. These groups exchanged letters on colonial affairs. Before long, committees throughout Massachusetts were corresponding with one another and with committees in other colonies.

Then, in 1773, Parliament opened up old wounds when it passed the Tea Act. Tea was very popular in the colonies, but much of it was smuggled in from Holland. The Tea Act gave the British East India Company control over the American tea trade. The tea would arrive in the colonies only in the trading company's ships and be sold there by its merchants. Colonists who had not been paying any tax on smuggled tea would now have to pay a tax on this regulated tea. This enraged colonial shippers and merchants. The colonists wondered what Parliament would do next.

*Reading*History
C. Drawing Conclusions
Why did Samuel Adams think that the colonists might forget the cause of liberty?

The Boston Tea Party

Protests against the Tea Act took place all over the colonies. In Charleston, South Carolina, colonists unloaded tea and let it rot on the docks. In New York City and Philadelphia, colonists blocked tea ships from landing. In Boston, the Sons of Liberty organized what came to be known as the **Boston Tea Party**.

Colonists dumped hundreds of chests of tea into Boston Harbor in 1773 to protest the Tea Act.

On the evening of December 16, 1773, a group of men disguised as Native Americans boarded three tea ships docked in Boston Harbor. One of the men, George Hewes, a Boston shoemaker, later recalled the events.

*Reading*History

D. Reading a Map Find Boston Harbor on the map on page 156.

A VOICE FROM THE PAST

We then were ordered by our commander to open the hatches and take out all the chests of tea and throw them overboard. . . . In about three hours from the time we went on board, we had thus broken and thrown overboard every tea chest to be found on the ship, while those in the other ships were disposing of the tea in the same way, at the same time.

George Hewes, quoted in *A Retrospect of the Boston Tea-Party*

That night, Hewes and the others destroyed 342 chests of tea. Many colonists rejoiced at the news. They believed that Britain would now see how strongly colonists opposed taxation without representation.

*Reading*History

E. Recognizing Effects How did Britain react to the Tea Party?

Others doubted that destroying property was the best way to settle the tax debate. Some colonial leaders offered to pay for the tea if Parliament would repeal the Tea Act. Britain rejected the offer. It not only wanted repayment, but it also wanted the men who destroyed the tea to be brought to trial. The British reaction to the Boston Tea Party would fan the flames of rebellion in the 13 colonies, as you will read in the next section.

Section 2 Assessment

1. Terms & Names

Explain the significance of:
- Crispus Attucks
- Townshend Acts
- writs of assistance
- Samuel Adams
- Boston Massacre
- John Adams
- committee of correspondence
- Boston Tea Party

2. Taking Notes

Create a time line like the one below to show the significant people and events described in this section.

1767   1773

Which event do you think was the most important? Explain.

3. Main Ideas

a. Why did colonists oppose the Townshend Acts?

b. Why were British troops sent to Boston?

c. What prompted the Boston Tea Party?

4. Critical Thinking

Drawing Conclusions Do you think colonial outrage over the Boston Massacre was justified? Explain.

THINK ABOUT
- how the British troops were taunted
- whether troops have the right to fire on citizens

ACTIVITY OPTIONS

SPEECH

TECHNOLOGY

Read more about the Boston Massacre or the Boston Tea Party. Present an **oral report** or plan a **multimedia presentation** about the event.

Fight for Representative Government!

You are a colonist living in Boston on the eve of the American Revolution. Nearly a decade of protest against British policies has failed to secure American rights. Redcoats continue to be quartered in the city. The Tea Act still stands. Now the dumping of tea in Boston Harbor by some Patriots has charged the atmosphere with tension. Trouble lies ahead, but you are determined to fight for a government that will protect your rights.

COOPERATIVE LEARNING On this page are two challenges that you face as the conflict with Britain unfolds. Working with a small group, decide how to deal with each challenge. Choose an option, assign a task to each group member, and do the activity. You will find useful information in the Data File. Present your solutions to the class.

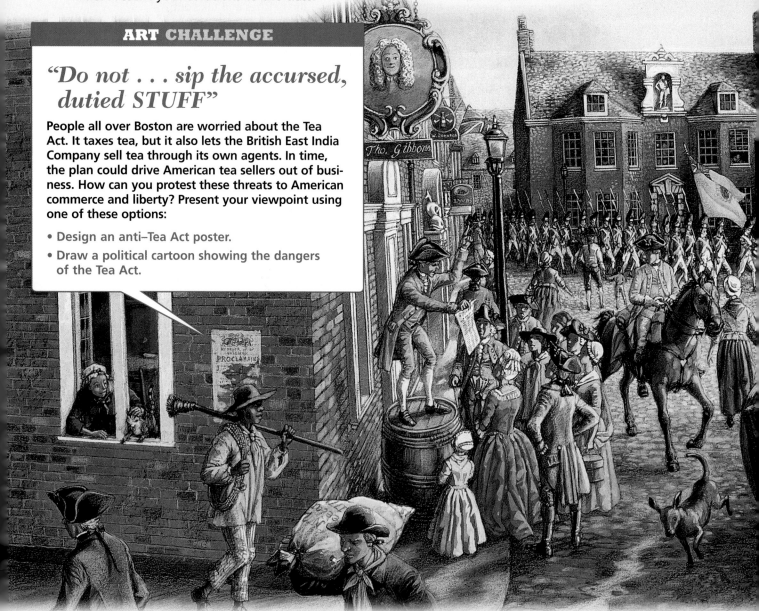

ART CHALLENGE

"Do not . . . sip the accursed, dutied STUFF"

People all over Boston are worried about the Tea Act. It taxes tea, but it also lets the British East India Company sell tea through its own agents. In time, the plan could drive American tea sellers out of business. How can you protest these threats to American commerce and liberty? Present your viewpoint using one of these options:

• Design an anti–Tea Act poster.
• Draw a political cartoon showing the dangers of the Tea Act.

MATH CHALLENGE

"Wear none but your own country linen"

Years of struggle have taken their toll on Boston. People are tired of soldiers and of boycotting British goods, such as clothing. But the Tea Act presents a huge threat. The Boston Tea Party took care of only one shipment. How can you help encourage the boycott of other British goods, such as clothing? Look at the Data File for help. Present your appeal using one of these options:

• Make a graph showing the effect of colonial boycotts on imports of British goods to America.

• Write an editorial using statistics to show how American boycotts have hurt the British.

Population in 1774–1775
Britain: 7,860,000
 London: 700,000

The 13 colonies: 2,350,000
 Philadelphia: 33,000
 New York: 22,000
 Boston: 16,000

North American Imports from Britain
(in millions of pounds sterling)

Year	Value	Year	Value
1763	1.6	1770	1.9
1764	2.3	1771	4.2
1765	1.9	1772	3.0
1766	1.8	1773	2.1
1767	1.9	1774	2.6
1768	2.2	1775	0.2
1769	1.3	1776	0.1

North American Exports to Britain
(in millions of pounds sterling)

Year	Value	Year	Value
1763	1.1	1770	1.0
1764	1.1	1771	1.3
1765	1.2	1772	1.3
1766	1.0	1773	1.4
1767	1.1	1774	1.4
1768	1.3	1775	1.9
1769	1.1	1776	0.1

Key Boycott Dates
1764 Boycott after passage of Sugar Act

1765 Boycott after passage of Stamp Act

1766 Boycott relaxed after Stamp Act repealed

1767 Boycott after passage of Townshend Acts

1770 Townshend Acts repealed

1774 Boycott after passage of Intolerable Acts

Sales and Consumption of Tea at the Time of the Boston Tea Party

British sales: fourth most important product shipped to America
American consumption: 1.2 million pounds per year

For more on Revolutionary America . . .

RESEARCH LINKS
CLASSZONE.COM

ACTIVITY WRAP-UP

Present to the Class Meet as a group to review your responses to British attacks on American liberty. Pick the most creative solution for each challenge and present these solutions to the class.

③ The Road to Lexington and Concord

TERMS & NAMES
militia
Minuteman
Intolerable Acts
First Continental Congress
Paul Revere
Lexington and Concord
Loyalist
Patriot

MAIN IDEA	WHY IT MATTERS NOW
The tensions between Britain and the colonies led to armed conflict in Massachusetts.	Americans at times still find themselves called upon to fight for their principles.

ONE AMERICAN'S STORY

At dawn on April 19, 1775, some 70 militiamen gathered on the grassy common at the center of Lexington, Massachusetts, a small town near Boston. Captain John Parker, a veteran of the French and Indian War, was their commander. The **militia** was a force of armed civilians pledged to defend their community. About one-third of the Lexington militia were **Minutemen,** trained to be "ready to act at a minute's warning." Everyone had heard the news—the British were coming!

Each militiaman was equipped with a musket, a bayonet, and ammunition. Parker had spent months drilling his troops, but they had never faced British soldiers. Soon they would meet the British on Lexington Green in the first battle of the Revolutionary War. According to tradition, Parker told his men, "Stand your ground; don't fire unless fired upon, but if they mean to have war, let it begin here."

In this section, you will read how colonial protests eventually turned into violent revolution.

This statue of Captain John Parker stands in Lexington, Massachusetts.

The Intolerable Acts

The Boston Tea Party had aroused fury in Britain. One British official said that the people of Boston "ought to be knocked about their ears." King George III declared, "We must master them or totally leave them to themselves and treat them as aliens." Britain chose to "master" the colonies.

In 1774, Parliament passed a series of laws to punish the Massachusetts colony and to serve as a warning to other colonies. The British called these laws the Coercive Acts, but they were so harsh that the colonists called them the **Intolerable Acts.**

One of the acts would close the port of Boston until colonists paid for the destroyed tea. Others banned committees of correspondence, allowed Britain to house troops wherever necessary, and let British officials accused of crimes in the colonies stand trial in Britain. To enforce the acts, Parliament appointed General Thomas Gage governor of Massachusetts.

In 1773, Sam Adams had written, "I wish we could arouse the continent." The Intolerable Acts answered his wish. Other colonies immediately offered Massachusetts their support. They sent food and money to Boston. The committees of correspondence also called for a meeting of colonial delegates to discuss what to do next.

The First Continental Congress Meets

In September 1774, delegates from all the colonies except Georgia met in Philadelphia. At this meeting, called the **First Continental Congress,** delegates voted to ban all trade with Britain until the Intolerable Acts were repealed. They also called on each colony to begin training troops. Georgia agreed to be a part of the actions of the Congress even though it had voted not to send delegates.

Reading **History**

A. Evaluating Why do you think the First Continental Congress was important?

The First Continental Congress marked a key step in American history. Although most delegates were not ready to call for independence, they were determined to uphold colonial rights. This meeting planted the seeds of a future independent government. John Adams called it "a nursery of American statesmen." The delegates agreed to meet in seven months, if necessary. By that time, however, fighting with Britain had begun.

Between War and Peace

The colonists hoped that the trade boycott would force a repeal of the Intolerable Acts. After all, past boycotts had led to the repeal of the Stamp Act and the Townshend Acts. This time, however, Parliament stood firm. It even increased restrictions on colonial trade and sent more troops.

By the end of 1774, some colonists were preparing to fight. In Massachusetts, John Hancock headed the Committee of Safety, which had the power to call out the militia. The colonial troops continued to train.

CAUSE AND EFFECT: *Growing Conflict Between Britain and America*

DATE	BRITISH ACTION		COLONIAL REACTION
1763	Proclamation of 1763 issued	▶	Proclamation leads to anger
1765	Stamp Act passed	▶	Boycott of British goods; Stamp Act Resolves passed
1766	Stamp Act repealed; Declaration Act passed	▶	Boycott ended
1767	Townshend Acts passed	▶	New boycotts; Boston Massacre (March 1770)
1770	Townshend Acts repealed (April)	▶	Tension between colonies and Britain reduced
1773	Tea Act passed	▶	Boston Tea Party
1774	Intolerable Acts passed	▶	First Continental Congress bans trade; militias organized
1775	Troops ordered to Lexington and Concord, Massachusetts	▶	Militia fights British troops; Second Continental Congress; Continental Army established

SKILLBUILDER Interpreting Charts

1. *What British action caused the first violence in the growing conflict between Britain and America?*
2. *How might the Intolerable Acts be seen as a reaction as well as an action?*

Most colonial leaders believed that any fight with Britain would be short. They thought that a show of force would make Britain change its policies. Few expected a war. One who did was Patrick Henry.

> ### A VOICE FROM THE PAST
>
> Gentlemen may cry peace, peace—but there is no peace. The war is actually begun! The next gale that sweeps from the north will bring to our ears the clash of resounding arms! Our brethren are already in the field! Why should we idle here? . . . I know not what course others may take. But as for me, give me liberty or give me death.
>
> **Patrick Henry,** quoted in *Patriots* by A. J. Langguth

Henry delivered what became his most famous speech in the Virginia House of Burgesses in March 1775.

The Midnight Ride

Meanwhile, spies were busy on both sides. Sam Adams had built a spy network to keep watch over British activities. The British had their spies too. They were Americans who were loyal to Britain. From them, General Gage learned that the Massachusetts militia was storing arms and ammunition in Concord, about 20 miles northwest of Boston. He also heard that Sam Adams and John Hancock were in Lexington. On the night of April 18, 1775, Gage ordered his troops to arrest Adams and Hancock in Lexington and to destroy the supplies in Concord.

The Sons of Liberty had prepared for this moment. **Paul Revere,** a Boston silversmith, and a second messenger, William Dawes, were charged with spreading the news about British troop movements. Revere had arranged a system of signals to alert colonists in Charlestown, on the shore opposite Boston. If one lantern burned in the Old North Church steeple, the British troops were coming by land; if two, they were coming by water. Revere would go across the water from Boston to Charlestown and ride to Lexington and Concord from there. Dawes would take the land route.

Reading **History**
B. Recognizing Effects What effect might spying have had on the people of Boston?

Background
The signals were a backup system in case Revere was captured.

The Revolution Begins, *1775*

Concord
Concord R.
North Bridge
Revere captured.
Prescott joins Dawes and Revere.
Lexington
Boston
MASS.
Prescott goes forward.
Sudbury R.
Dawes escapes and turns back.
Mystic River
Old North Church
Charlestown
Cambridge
Boston
Charles River
Boston Harbor

0 2 Miles
0 4 Kilometers

GEOGRAPHY SKILLBUILDER
Interpreting Maps

1. **Location** *Where were battles fought?*
2. **Movement** *What was the distance between Lexington and Concord?*

— Revere's route
— Dawes's route
— Prescott's route
— British advance
- - British retreat
✷ Battle

156

When the British moved, so did Revere and Dawes. They galloped over the countryside on their "midnight ride," spreading the news. In Lexington, they were joined by Dr. Samuel Prescott. When Revere and Dawes were stopped by a British patrol, Prescott broke away and carried the message to Concord.

Lexington and Concord

At dawn on April 19, some 700 British troops reached Lexington. They found Captain John Parker and about 70 militiamen waiting. The British commander ordered the Americans to drop their muskets. They refused. No one knows who fired first, but within a few minutes eight militiamen lay dead. The British then marched to Concord, where they destroyed military supplies. A battle broke out at a bridge north of town, forcing the British to retreat.

Nearly 4,000 Minutemen and militiamen arrived in the area. They lined the road from Concord to Lexington and peppered the retreating redcoats with musket fire. "It seemed as if men came down from the clouds," one soldier said. Only the arrival of 1,000 more troops saved the British from destruction as they scrambled back to Boston.

Lexington and Concord were the first battles of the Revolutionary War. As Ralph Waldo Emerson later wrote, colonial troops had fired the "shot heard 'round the world." Americans would now have to choose sides and back up their political opinions by force of arms. Those who supported the British were called **Loyalists.** Those who sided with the rebels were **Patriots.** The conflict between the two sides divided communities, families, and friends. The war was on!

Background
British losses totaled 273 soldiers compared to 95 militiamen.

Reading **History**
C. Drawing Conclusions
Why did Emerson call it the "shot heard 'round the world"?

Now and then

PATRIOTS' DAY
The "shot heard 'round the world" is celebrated every year in Massachusetts and Maine. Patriots' Day, as it is called, is the third Monday of April. In Concord and nearby towns, modern-day Minutemen like those below reenact the battle that began the Revolution on April 19, 1775. The Boston Marathon is also run on Patriots' Day.

Section 3 Assessment

1. Terms & Names
Explain the significance of:
- militia
- Minuteman
- Intolerable Acts
- First Continental Congress
- Paul Revere
- Lexington and Concord
- Loyalist
- Patriot

2. Taking Notes
Use a diagram like the one below to show events that led to the Revolutionary War.

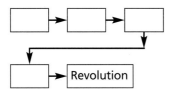

3. Main Ideas
a. Why did Britain pass the Intolerable Acts?

b. Who took part in the First Continental Congress?

c. What was the purpose of the "midnight ride"?

4. Critical Thinking
Supporting Opinions
Do you think the fighting between Britain and the colonies could have been avoided? Why or why not?

THINK ABOUT
- Britain's attitude toward the colonies
- colonial feelings about Britain

ACTIVITY OPTIONS

GEOGRAPHY

MATH

Research the Battles of Lexington and Concord. Draw a **map** of key events or create a **chart** showing statistics from the battles.

From
JOHNNY
TREMAIN
by Esther Forbes

In 1775, 16-year-old Johnny Tremain lives in Boston and works as a delivery boy for a newspaper. Because he travels so much around the city, he is able to help the Patriots gather information about what the British are doing.

On the night of April 18, Johnny learns that British troops will be leaving on an expedition to seize the gunpowder at Lexington and Concord. He rushes to tell this news to Dr. Joseph Warren, who is a Patriot. Then Johnny goes to bed, wondering if the war has started and worried about his friend Rab, who has gone to join the Minutemen at Lexington.

So Johnny slept. It was daylight when he woke with Warren's hand upon his shoulder. Outside on Tremont Street he could hear the clumping of army boots. A sergeant was swearing at his men. The soldiers were paraded so close to the house, which stood **flush**[1] with the sidewalk-less street, that Johnny at first thought they must be in the room.

Doctor Warren dared speak no louder than a whisper.

"I'm going now."

"Something's happened?"

"Yes." He motioned Johnny to follow him into the kitchen. This room was on the back of the house. They could talk without danger of being overheard by the troops in the street.

Doctor Warren had on the same clothes as the day before. He had not been to bed. But now his hat was on his head. His black bag of instruments and medicines was packed and on the table. Silently he put milk, bread, herrings beside it, and gestured to Johnny to join him.

"Where did it begin?" asked Johnny.

"Lexington."

"Who won?"

"They did. Seven hundred against seventy. It wasn't a battle. It was . . . just target practice . . . for them. Some of our men were killed and the British **huzzaed**[2] and took the road to Concord."

"And did they get our supplies there?"

"I don't know. Paul Revere sent for me just after the firing on Lexington Green."

The young man's usually fresh-colored face was **haggard**[3]. He knew the seriousness of this day for himself and for his country.

"But everywhere the alarm is spreading. Men are grabbing their guns—marching for Concord. Paul Revere did get through in time last night. Billy Dawes a little later. Hundreds—maybe thousands—of Minute Men are on the march. Before the day's over, there'll be real fighting—not target practice. But Gage doesn't know that it's begun. You see, long before Colonel Smith got to Lexington—just as soon as he heard that Revere had warned the country—he sent back for reinforcements. For Earl Percy. You and I, Johnny, are just about the only people in Boston who know that blood has already been shed."

"Were many killed—at Lexington?"

"No, not many. They stood up—just a handful. The British fired on them. It was dawn."

Johnny licked his lips. "Did they tell you the names of those killed?"

---

1. **flush:** in a line with.

2. **huzzaed:** cheered.
3. **haggard:** tired.

"No. Did Rab get out in time?"

"Yes. Last Sunday."

The Doctor's clear blue eyes darkened. He knew what was in Johnny's mind. He picked up his bag. "I've got to get to them. They'll need surgeons. Then, too, I'd rather die fighting than on a gallows. Gage won't be so **lenient**[4] now—soon as he learns war has begun."

"Wait until I get my shoes on."

"No, Johnny, you are to stay here today. Pick up for me any information. For instance, out of my bedroom window I can see soldiers standing the length of the street 'way over to the Common. You find out what regiments are being sent—and all that. And today go about and listen to what folk are saying. And the names of any the British arrest. We know Gage expects to move his men back here tonight. If so, there'll be a lot of confusion getting them into town. You watch your chance and slip out to me."

"Where'll I find you?"

" . . . Ask about."

"I will do so."

"They've begun it. We'll end it, but this war . . . it may last quite a long time."

---

4. **lenient:** not strict.

5. **surgery:** operating room.

They shook hands silently. Johnny knew that Warren was always conscious of the fact that he had a crippled hand. Everybody else had accepted and forgotten it. The back door closed softly. Warren was gone.

Johnny went to the **surgery**,[5] put on his boots and jacket. The wall clock said eight o'clock. It was time to be about. There was no leaving by the front door. The soldiers were leaning against it. Through the curtains of the windows he could see the muskets. He noticed the facings on their uniforms. The Twenty-Third Regiment. The narrow course of Tremont Street was filled to the brim and overflowing with the waiting scarlet-coated men. Like a river of blood. He left by the kitchen.

CONNECT TO HISTORY

1. **Recognizing Effects** What was Johnny's reaction to the news about Lexington? Discuss what roles Johnny and Dr. Warren were to play in the early days of the Revolutionary War.

    See Skillbuilder Handbook, page R11.

CONNECT TO TODAY

2. **Researching** Where are there revolutions in the world today?

For more about revolutions . . .

RESEARCH LINKS
CLASSZONE.COM

British troops fire on the Lexington militia on April 19, 1775. The war begins here!

Declaring Independence

TERMS & NAMES
Ethan Allen
artillery
Second Continental Congress
Continental Army
Benedict Arnold
Declaration of Independence
Thomas Jefferson

MAIN IDEA	**WHY IT MATTERS NOW**
Fighting between American and British troops led the colonies to declare their independence.	The United States of America was founded at this time.

ONE AMERICAN'S STORY

In May 1775—one month after the battle at Lexington and Concord—Abigail Adams wrote to her husband, John Adams. "The house is a Scene of Confusion," she said. Colonial militiamen were camped outside. Everyone was preparing for war. John Adams was away in Philadelphia at the time, meeting with other Patriot leaders at the Second Continental Congress.

Abigail and John Adams would spend most of the Revolutionary War apart. In his absence, she ran the household and farm in Braintree, Massachusetts, and raised their four children. During their separation, they exchanged many letters. Abigail was a very sharp observer of the political scene. In one letter, she shared her concerns about the future of the American government.

Abigail Adams was an early advocate of women's rights and one of the great letter writers in history.

A VOICE FROM THE PAST

If we separate from Britain, what Code of Laws will be established? How shall we be governed so as to retain our Liberties? Can any government be free which is not administered by general stated Laws? Who shall frame these Laws? Who will give them force and energy?

Abigail Adams, quoted in *Abigail Adams: Witness to a Revolution* by Natalie S. Bober

These questions would be answered later. First, a war had to be fought and won.

The Continental Army Is Formed

After the fighting at Lexington and Concord, militiamen from Massachusetts and other colonies began gathering around Boston. Their numbers eventually reached some 20,000. General Gage decided to move his soldiers from the peninsula opposite Boston to the city itself. Boston was nearly surrounded by water. This fact, he thought, made a colonial attack by land almost impossible.

Not long after, on May 10, 1775, Americans attacked Britain's Fort Ticonderoga on the New York side of Lake Champlain. **Ethan Allen** led this band of backwoodsmen known as the Green Mountain Boys. They captured the fort and its large supply of **artillery**—cannon and large guns. These guns would be used later to drive the British from Boston.

Also on May 10, the **Second Continental Congress** began meeting in Philadelphia. Delegates included John and Samuel Adams, John Hancock, Benjamin Franklin, George Washington, and Patrick Henry. They agreed to form the **Continental Army.** Washington, who was from Virginia, was chosen as its commanding general. He had served as a colonial officer with the British during the French and Indian War. Congress also authorized the printing of paper money to pay the troops. It was beginning to act as a government.

The Battle of Bunker Hill

Background
The battle was called Bunker Hill because the original plan was to fight the battle there.

Meanwhile, tensions were building in Boston in June 1775. Militiamen seized Bunker Hill and Breed's Hill behind Charlestown. They built fortifications on Breed's Hill. Alarmed, the British decided to attack.

General William Howe crossed the bay with 2,200 British soldiers. Forming in ranks, they marched up Breed's Hill. On the hilltop, the militia waited. According to the legend, Colonel William Prescott ordered, "Don't fire until you see the whites of their eyes!" When the British got close, the militia unleashed murderous fire. The British fell back and then charged again. Finally, they forced the militia off the hill.

"Don't fire until you see the whites of their eyes!"
Colonel William Prescott

The redcoats had won the Battle of Bunker Hill, but at tremendous cost. More than 1,000 were killed or wounded, compared with some 400 militia casualties. "The loss we have sustained is greater than we can bear," wrote General Gage. The inexperienced colonial militia had held its own against the world's most powerful army.

The bloody fighting between militiamen and British troops is shown in *The Death of General Warren at Bunker Hill* by John Trumbull (1786).

A Last Attempt at Peace

Despite this deepening conflict, most colonists still hoped for peace. Even some Patriot leaders considered themselves loyal subjects of the king. They blamed Parliament for the terrible events taking place.

In July 1775, moderates in Congress drafted the Olive Branch Petition and sent it to London. This document asked the king to restore harmony between Britain and the colonies. Some members opposed the petition but signed it anyway as a last hope.

The king rejected the petition, however, and announced new measures to punish the colonies. He would use the British navy to block American ships from leaving their ports. He also would send thousands of hired German soldiers, called Hessians, to fight in America. "When once these rebels have felt a smart blow, they will submit," he declared.

The colonial forces were not going to back down, though. They thought they were equal to the British troops. George Washington knew otherwise. The British soldiers were professionals, while the colonial troops had little training and were poorly equipped. The Massachusetts militia barely had enough gunpowder to fight one battle.

During the summer of 1775, Washington arrived at the militia camp near Boston. He immediately began to gather supplies and train the army. In the fall, Washington approved a bold plan. Continental Army troops would invade Quebec, in eastern Canada. They hoped to defeat British forces there and draw Canadians into the Patriot camp. One of the leaders of this expedition was **Benedict Arnold**. He was an officer who had played a role in the victory at Fort Ticonderoga.

After a grueling march across Maine, Arnold arrived at Quebec in November 1775. By that time, however, winter had set in. Under harsh conditions, the Americans launched their attack but failed. After several months, they limped home in defeat.

The British Retreat from Boston

In Massachusetts, the Continental Army had surrounded British forces in Boston. Neither side was able or willing to break the standoff. However, help for Washington was on the way. Cannons were being hauled from Fort Ticonderoga. This was a rough job, since there were no roads across the snow-covered mountains. It took soldiers two months to drag the 59 heavy weapons to Boston, where they arrived in January 1776.

Background
The olive branch is considered a symbol of peace.

Reading **History**
A. Analyzing Points of View Why did King George reject the petition?

Armed with these cannons, Washington moved his troops to Dorchester Heights, overlooking Boston. The Americans threatened to bombard the city. General Howe, who was now in charge of the British forces, decided to withdraw his troops. On March 17, about 9,000 British soldiers departed Boston in more than 100 ships. Boston Patriots joyfully reclaimed their city. Although the British had damaged homes and destroyed possessions, Boston was still standing.

More than 1,000 Loyalist supporters left along with the British troops. Anti-British feeling in Boston was so strong that the Loyalists feared for their safety. Some Patriots even called for Loyalists to be hanged as traitors. This did not happen, but Loyalists' homes and property were seized.

Reading **History**
B. Forming Opinions Did the Loyalists deserve punishment? Explain.

Common Sense Is Published

In early 1776, most Americans still wanted to avoid a final break with Britain. However, the publication of a pamphlet titled *Common Sense* helped convince many Americans that a complete break with Britain was necessary. Written by Thomas Paine, a recent immigrant from England, this pamphlet made a strong case for American independence.

Paine ridiculed the idea that kings ruled by the will of God. Calling George III "the Royal Brute," Paine argued that all monarchies were corrupt. He also disagreed with the economic arguments for remaining with Britain. "Our corn," he said, "will fetch its price in any market in Europe." He believed that America should follow its own destiny.

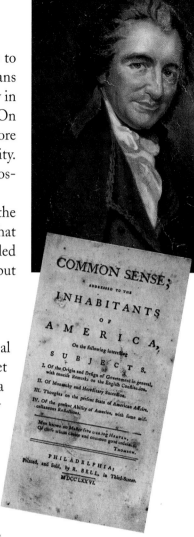

This is the front page of *Common Sense* by Thomas Paine (above). It was one of the most influential political documents in history.

A VOICE FROM THE PAST

Everything that is right or natural pleads for separation. The blood of the slain, the weeping voice of nature cries, "'Tis time to part." Even the distance at which the Almighty has placed England and America is a strong and natural proof that the authority of the one over the other was never the design of heaven.

Thomas Paine, *Common Sense*

Common Sense was an instant success. Published in January, it sold more than 100,000 copies in three months. The call for independence had become a roar.

A Time of Decision

The Continental Congress remained undecided. A majority of the delegates still did not support independence. Even so, in May 1776, Congress adopted a resolution authorizing each of the 13 colonies to establish its own government.

On June 7, Richard Henry Lee of Virginia introduced a key resolution. It called the colonies "free and independent states" and declared that "all political connection between them and the state of Great Britain is . . . totally dissolved."

Congress debated the resolution, but not all the delegates were ready to vote on it. They did, however, appoint a committee to draft a **Declaration of Independence**. The committee included Benjamin Franklin, John Adams, Roger Sherman, Robert Livingston, and **Thomas Jefferson**.

The group chose Jefferson to compose the Declaration. Two reasons for selecting Jefferson were that he was an excellent writer and that he came from Virginia. The members knew that no independence movement could succeed without Virginia's support. Jefferson immediately went to work. In two weeks, he had prepared most of the Declaration. (See pages 166–169.) On July 2, 1776, Congress considered Lee's resolution again. Despite some strong opposition, the measure passed. From this point forward, the colonies considered themselves independent.

The Declaration Is Adopted

Two days later, on July 4, 1776, Congress adopted the document that proclaimed independence—the Declaration of Independence. John Hancock, the president of the Congress, was the first to sign the Declaration. According to tradition, he wrote in large letters and commented, "There, I guess King George will be able to read that." The core idea of the Declaration is based on the philosophy of John Locke. This idea is that people have unalienable rights, or rights that government

The Liberty Bell was rung to announce the first public reading of the Declaration of Independence, in Philadelphia on July 8, 1776.

cannot take away. Jefferson stated this belief in what was to become the Declaration's best-known passage.

A VOICE FROM THE PAST

We hold these truths to be self-evident, that all men are created equal, that they are endowed by their Creator with certain unalienable Rights, that among these are Life, Liberty and the pursuit of Happiness.

Thomas Jefferson, The Declaration of Independence

*Reading*History
C. Summarizing
When does the Declaration say it is right to overthrow an established government?

If a government disregards these rights, Jefferson explained, it loses its right to govern. The people then have the right to abolish that government, by force if necessary. They can form a new government that will protect their rights. When Jefferson spoke of "the people," however, he meant only free white men. Women and enslaved persons were left out of the Declaration.

The Declaration also explained the reasons for breaking with Britain. It then declared the colonies to be free and independent states. This was a very serious action—treason from the British point of view—and the delegates knew it. John Hancock urged the delegates to stand together in mutual defense. Each realized that if the war were to be lost, they would most likely be hanged.

The Declaration closed with this pledge: "And for the support of this Declaration, with a firm reliance on the protection of divine Providence, we mutually pledge to each other our Lives, our Fortunes, and our sacred Honor."

Americans had declared independence. Now they had to win their freedom on the battlefield.

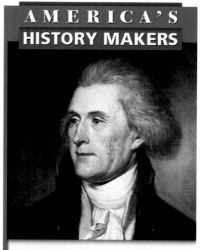

AMERICA'S HISTORY MAKERS

THOMAS JEFFERSON
1743–1826
Jefferson was just 33 when chosen to write the Declaration of Independence. He was already a brilliant thinker and writer and a highly respected political leader. Jefferson came from a wealthy Virginia family. As a child, he was interested in everything, and he became an inventor, scientist, and architect, among other things. In 1769, he began his political career in the House of Burgesses.

Jefferson felt that writing the Declaration was a major achievement of his life. He had that fact carved on his tombstone.

Why do you think Jefferson felt the Declaration was one of his greatest achievements?

Section 4 Assessment

1. Terms & Names

Explain the significance of:
• Ethan Allen
• artillery
• Second Continental Congress
• Continental Army
• Benedict Arnold
• Declaration of Independence
• Thomas Jefferson

2. Taking Notes

Use the chart below to explain colonial views for and against independence.

Views About Independence

For	
Against	

What is the strongest reason for independence? against independence?

3. Main Ideas

a. What challenges did George Washington face in forming the army?

b. What forced the British to leave Boston?

c. What is *Common Sense*?

4. Critical Thinking

Drawing Conclusions
Why did it take colonists so long to declare independence?

THINK ABOUT

• the colonists' British traditions

• the risk of revolution

ACTIVITY OPTIONS

ART

LANGUAGE ARTS

Find out more about a person discussed in this section. Create a **trading card** or write a **biography** of that person.

The Declaration of Independence

Setting the Stage On July 4, 1776, the Second Continental Congress adopted what became one of America's most cherished documents. Written by Thomas Jefferson, the Declaration of Independence voiced the reasons for separating from Britain and provided the principles of government upon which the United States would be built. **See Primary Source Explorer**

[Preamble]

When in the Course of human events, it becomes necessary for one people to dissolve the political bands which have connected them with another, and to assume among the powers of the earth, the separate and equal station to which the Laws of Nature and of Nature's God entitle them, a decent respect to the opinions of mankind requires that they should declare the causes which impel them to the separation.

[The Right of the People to Control Their Government]

We hold these truths to be self-evident, that all men are created equal, that they are **endowed**[1] by their Creator with certain **unalienable**[2] Rights, that among these are Life, Liberty and the pursuit of Happiness; that, to secure these rights, Governments are instituted among Men, deriving their just powers from the consent of the governed; that whenever any Form of Government becomes destructive of these ends, it is the Right of the People to alter or to abolish it, and to institute new Government, laying its foundation on such principles and organizing its powers in such form, as to them shall seem most likely to effect their Safety and Happiness. Prudence, indeed, will dictate that Governments long established should not be changed for light and transient causes; and accordingly all experience hath shewn that mankind are more disposed to suffer, while evils are sufferable, than to right themselves by abolishing the forms to which they are accustomed. But when a long train of abuses and **usurpations**,[3] pursuing invariably the same Object, evinces a design to reduce them under absolute **Despotism**,[4] it is their right, it is their duty, to throw off such Government, and to provide new Guards for their future security.

Such has been the patient sufferance of these Colonies; and such is now the necessity which constrains them to alter their former Systems of Government. The history of the present King of Great Britain is a history of repeated injuries and usurpations, all having in direct object the establishment of an absolute Tyranny over these States. To prove this, let facts be submitted to a **candid**[5] world.

A CLOSER LOOK

RIGHTS OF THE PEOPLE

The ideas in this passage reflect the views of John Locke. Locke was an English philosopher who believed that the natural rights of individuals came from God, but that a government's power comes from the consent of the governed. This belief is the foundation of modern democracy.

1. In what way can American voters bring about changes in their government?

---

1. **endowed:** provided.
2. **unalienable:** unable to be taken away.
3. **usurpations:** unjust seizures of power.
4. **Despotism:** rule by a tyrant with absolute power.
5. **candid:** fair, impartial.

[Tyrannical Acts of the British King]

He has refused his Assent to Laws, the most wholesome and necessary for the public good.

He has forbidden his Governors to pass Laws of immediate and pressing importance, unless suspended in their operation till his assent should be obtained; and, when so suspended, he has utterly neglected to attend to them.

He has refused to pass other Laws for the accommodation of large districts of people, unless those people would **relinquish**[6] the right of Representation in the Legislature, a right inestimable to them, and formidable to tyrants only.

He has called together legislative bodies at places unusual, uncomfortable, and distant from the depository of their public Records, for the sole purpose of fatiguing them into compliance with his measures.

He has dissolved Representative Houses repeatedly, for opposing with manly firmness his invasions on the rights of the people.

He has refused for a long time, after such dissolutions, to cause others to be elected; whereby the Legislative powers, incapable of Annihilation, have returned to the people at large for their exercise; the State remaining in the mean time exposed to all the dangers of invasions from without, and **convulsions**[7] within.

He has endeavoured to prevent the population of these States; for that purpose obstructing the Laws for **Naturalization**[8] of Foreigners; refusing to pass others to encourage their migration hither, and raising the conditions of new Appropriations of Lands.

He has obstructed the Administration of Justice, by refusing his Assent to Laws for establishing Judiciary powers.

He has made Judges dependent on his Will alone, for the **tenure**[9] of their offices, and the amount and payment of their salaries.

He has erected a multitude of New Offices, and sent hither swarms of Officers to harass our people and **eat out their substance.**[10]

He has kept among us, in times of peace, Standing Armies, without the Consent of our legislatures.

He has affected to render the Military independent of and superior to the Civil power. He has combined with others to subject us to a jurisdiction foreign to our constitution and unacknowledged by our laws; giving his Assent to their Acts of pretended Legislation:

For **quartering**[11] large bodies of armed troops among us;

For protecting them, by a mock Trial, from punishment for any Murders which they should commit on the Inhabitants of these States;

For cutting off our Trade with all parts of the world;

A CLOSER LOOK

GRIEVANCES AGAINST BRITAIN

The list contains 27 offenses by the British king and others against the colonies. It helps explain why it became necessary to seek independence.

2. Which offense do you think was the worst? Why?

A CLOSER LOOK

LOSS OF REPRESENTATIVE GOVERNMENT

One of the Intolerable Acts of 1774 stripped the Massachusetts Legislature of many powers and gave them to the colony's British governor.

3. Why was this action so "intolerable"?

A CLOSER LOOK

QUARTERING TROOPS WITHOUT CONSENT

The Quartering Act of 1765 required colonists to provide housing and supplies for British troops in America.

4. Why did colonists object to this act?

---

6. **relinquish:** give up.

7. **convulsions:** violent disturbances.

8. **Naturalization:** process of becoming a citizen.

9. **tenure:** term.

10. **eat out their substance:** drain their resources.

11. **quartering:** housing or giving lodging to.

A CLOSER LOOK

TAXATION WITHOUT REPRESENTATION

The colonists believed in the long-standing British tradition that Parliament could tax only those citizens it represented—and the colonists claimed to have no representation in Parliament.

5. How do persons today give consent to taxation?

For imposing Taxes on us without our Consent;

For depriving us, in many cases, of the benefits of Trial by Jury;

For transporting us beyond Seas to be tried for pretended offenses;

For abolishing the free System of English Laws in a neighboring Province, establishing therein an **Arbitrary**[12] government, and enlarging its Boundaries so as to render it at once an example and fit instrument for introducing the same absolute rule into these Colonies;

For taking away our Charters, abolishing our most valuable laws, and altering fundamentally the Forms of our Governments;

For suspending our own Legislatures, and declaring themselves invested with power to legislate for us in all cases whatsoever.

He has **abdicated**[13] Government here, by declaring us out of his Protection and waging War against us.

He has plundered our seas, ravaged our Coasts, burnt our towns, and destroyed the lives of our people.

He is at this time transporting large Armies of **foreign Mercenaries**[14] to compleat the works of death, desolation, and tyranny, already begun with circumstances of Cruelty & **perfidy**[15] scarcely paralleled in the most barbarous ages, and totally unworthy the Head of a civilized nation.

He has constrained our fellow Citizens, taken Captive on the high Seas, to bear Arms against their Country, to become the executioners of their friends and Brethren, or to fall themselves by their Hands.

He has excited **domestic insurrections**[16] amongst us, and has endeavoured to bring on the inhabitants of our frontiers the merciless Indian Savages, whose known rule of warfare is an undistinguished destruction of all ages, sexes and conditions.

[Efforts of the Colonies to Avoid Separation]

In every stage of these Oppressions We have **Petitioned for Redress**[17] in the most humble terms; Our repeated Petitions have been answered only by repeated injury. A Prince, whose character is thus marked by every act which may define a Tyrant, is unfit to be the ruler of a free people.

Nor have We been wanting in attentions to our British brethren. We have warned them from time to time of attempts by their legislature to extend an unwarrantable jurisdiction over us. We have reminded them of the circumstances of our emigration and settlement here. We have appealed to their native justice and **magnanimity,**[18] and we have conjured them by the ties of our common kindred, to disavow these usurpations, which would inevitably interrupt our connections and correspondence. They too have been deaf to

A CLOSER LOOK

PETITIONING THE KING

The colonists sent many petitions to King George III. In the Olive Branch Petition of 1775, the colonists expressed their desire to achieve "a happy and permanent reconciliation." The king rejected the petition.

6. Why did the colonists at first attempt to solve the dispute and remain loyal?

---

12. **Arbitrary:** not limited by law.

13. **abdicated:** given up.

14. **foreign Mercenaries:** professional soldiers hired to serve in a foreign army.

15. **perfidy:** dishonesty, disloyalty.

16. **domestic insurrections:** rebellions at home.

17. **Petitioned for Redress:** asked for the correction of wrongs.

18. **magnanimity:** generosity, forgiveness.

the voice of justice and of **consanguinity**.[19] We must, therefore, **acquiesce**[20] in the necessity, which denounces our Separation, and hold them, as we hold the rest of mankind, Enemies in War, in Peace Friends.

[The Colonies Are Declared Free and Independent]

We, therefore, the Representatives of the United States of America, in General Congress, Assembled, appealing to the Supreme Judge of the world for the **rectitude**[21] of our intentions, do, in the name, and by the Authority of the good People of these Colonies solemnly publish and declare, That these United Colonies are, and of Right ought to be, Free and Independent States; that they are Absolved from all Allegiance to the British Crown, and that all political connection between them and the State of Great Britain is, and ought to be, totally dissolved; and that as Free and Independent States, they have full Power to levy War, conclude Peace, contract Alliances, establish Commerce, and do all other Acts and Things which Independent States may of right do.

And for the support of this Declaration, with a firm reliance on the protection of divine Providence, we mutually pledge to each other our Lives, our Fortunes, and our sacred Honor. [Signed by]

John Hancock *President, from Massachusetts*

[Georgia] Button Gwinnett; Lyman Hall; George Walton

[Rhode Island] Stephen Hopkins; William Ellery

[Connecticut] Roger Sherman; Samuel Huntington; William Williams; Oliver Wolcott

[North Carolina] William Hooper; Joseph Hewes; John Penn

[South Carolina] Edward Rutledge; Thomas Heyward, Jr.; Thomas Lynch, Jr.; Arthur Middleton

[Maryland] Samuel Chase; William Paca; Thomas Stone; Charles Carroll

[Virginia] George Wythe; Richard Henry Lee; Thomas Jefferson; Benjamin Harrison; Thomas Nelson, Jr.; Francis Lightfoot Lee; Carter Braxton

[Pennsylvania] Robert Morris; Benjamin Rush; Benjamin Franklin; John Morton; George Clymer; James Smith; George Taylor; James Wilson; George Ross

[Delaware] Caesar Rodney; George Read; Thomas McKean

[New York] William Floyd; Philip Livingston; Francis Lewis; Lewis Morris

[New Jersey] Richard Stockton; John Witherspoon; Francis Hopkinson; John Hart; Abraham Clark

[New Hampshire] Josiah Bartlett; William Whipple; Matthew Thornton

[Massachusetts] Samuel Adams; John Adams; Robert Treat Paine; Elbridge Gerry

19. **consanguinity:** relationship by a common ancestor; close connection.

20. **acquiesce:** accept without protest.

21. **rectitude:** moral uprightness.

A CLOSER LOOK

POWERS OF AN INDEPENDENT GOVERNMENT

The colonists identified the ability to wage war and agree to peace; to make alliances with other nations; and to set up an economic system as powers of a free and independent government.

7. What other powers are held by an independent government?

A CLOSER LOOK

DECLARATION SIGNERS

The Declaration was signed by 56 representatives from the 13 original states.

8. Which signers do you recognize? Write one line about each of those signers.

Interactive Primary Source Assessment

1. Main Ideas

a. What is the purpose of the Declaration of Independence as stated in the Preamble?

b. What are the five main parts of the Declaration?

c. What are three rights that all people have?

2. Critical Thinking

Drawing Conclusions Why did the colonies feel that they had to declare their independence?

THINK ABOUT

• colonial grievances against Britain

• Britain's response to these grievances

VISUAL SUMMARY

The Road to Revolution

1763 —○
Proclamation of 1763

○— **1764**
Sugar Act

1765
Quartering Act; Stamp Act; Sons of Liberty; Stamp Act Congress

○— **1766**
Repeal of Stamp Act; Declaratory Act

1767
Townshend Acts; Suspension of New York Assembly

○— **1768**
Occupation of Boston by British troops

1769 —○
Daughters of Liberty

○— **1770**
Boston Massacre; Repeal of all Townshend Acts except tea tax

1772 —○
Committees of Correspondence

○— **1773**
Tea Act; Boston Tea Party

1774
Intolerable Acts; First Continental Congress; Boycott of British goods

1775
Battles of Lexington and Concord; Second Continental Congress; Appointment of Washington as commander of Continental Army; Battle of Bunker Hill; Olive Branch Petition

1776 —○
Common Sense; Declaration of Independence

TERMS & NAMES

Briefly explain the significance of each of the following.

1. Stamp Act
2. Sons of Liberty
3. writs of assistance
4. Samuel Adams
5. Boston Tea Party
6. militia
7. Lexington and Concord
8. Loyalist
9. Declaration of Independence
10. Thomas Jefferson

REVIEW QUESTIONS

Tighter British Control (pages 143–146)

1. How did relations between Britain and the colonies change after the Seven Years' War?
2. Why did Britain try to tax the colonies?
3. Why did the colonists cry, "No taxation without representation"?

Colonial Resistance Grows (pages 147–153)

4. How did the colonists protest the Townshend Acts?
5. How was the Boston Massacre used for propaganda purposes?
6. How did the committees of correspondence help keep people informed?

The Road to Lexington and Concord (pages 154–159)

7. Why was the First Continental Congress held?
8. What was the Midnight Ride?

Declaring Independence (pages 160–169)

9. What was the Battle of Bunker Hill?
10. What was the core idea of the Declaration of Independence?

CRITICAL THINKING

1. USING YOUR NOTES

Using your completed chart, answer the questions below.

a. What city was the site of early protest activity?
b. What event happened after the Tea Act?

2. ANALYZING LEADERSHIP

How did colonial leaders differ in their methods of defending and securing basic rights for the colonies?

3. APPLYING CITIZENSHIP SKILLS

Did colonial leaders have a responsibility to include women, African Americans, and other groups in the Declaration of Independence? Explain.

4. THEME: IMPACT OF THE INDIVIDUAL

How did John Adams's role as lawyer for the British soldiers involved in the Boston Massacre help set a tone for the Revolutionary cause?

5. DRAWING CONCLUSIONS

What factors and events led the colonies to seek independence?

6. SUPPORTING OPINIONS

Do you think the American Revolution would have occurred if Britain had not taxed the colonies? Why or why not?

Interact *with* History

Now that you have read about the road to revolution, do you consider your decision made at the beginning of the chapter to join or not join the protest a wise choice or a poor choice? Explain.

HISTORY SKILLS

1. INTERPRETING MAPS: Location

Study the map and then answer the questions.

United States and Britain, *1776*

GREAT BRITAIN

NORTH AMERICA

40°N

ATLANTIC OCEAN

13 original states

AFRICA

N 0 1,000 Miles
0 2,000 Kilometers

80°W

40°W

0°

Basic Map Elements

a. What is the subject of the map?

b. What do the colors yellow and orange represent?

Interpreting the Map

c. What is the approximate distance between Great Britain and the United States?

d. Who do you think had the advantage in a war fought on the North American mainland?

2. INTERPRETING PRIMARY SOURCES

This British political cartoon is titled *Poor Old England Endeavoring to Reclaim His Wicked Children.* Study the cartoon carefully. Answer the questions.

THE ATLANTIC OCEAN

a. How is England pictured? America?

b. Does the cartoon suggest England will be successful? Explain.

ALTERNATIVE ASSESSMENT

1. INTERDISCIPLINARY ACTIVITY: World History

Giving a Report Do research about another country, colony, or region of the world during the 1760s and 1770s. Give a brief oral report, comparing and contrasting events and conditions there with those in the British colonies.

2. COOPERATIVE LEARNING ACTIVITY

Debating During discussion of the Declaration of Independence, members of the Continental Congress held heated debates on the issue of independence and whether to abolish the slave trade. Imagine that you and your classmates are delegates to the Congress. Hold a debate on these issues, choosing one of the following roles to play:

- a strong supporter of independence and of an end to the slave trade (such as Samuel Adams or John Adams)

- a supporter of independence but an opponent of ending the slave trade (such as George Washington)

- an independence opponent (such as John Dickinson)

3. 💿 PRIMARY SOURCE EXPLORER

Writing a Play The Declaration of Independence announced to the world that the colonies had chosen independence and why. Using the CD-ROM, your textbook, and library research, find out more about the Declaration and the people and events surrounding it. Then write a one-act play using the suggestions below. Be sure to use standard grammar, spelling, sentence structure, and punctuation in your play.

- Set the play after the Declaration has been drafted.

- Have Thomas Jefferson, as the author, answer questions about what he included and perhaps did not include in the Declaration.

- Have Jefferson questioned by delegates to the Congress, or have him appear before a town meeting of ordinary citizens.

- Prepare introductory material to describe the setting and write dialogue for the characters.

4. HISTORY PORTFOLIO

Review your section and chapter assessment activities. Select one that you think was your best work. Then give consideration to suggestions made by your teacher or classmates and revise your work. Add it to your portfolio.

Additional Test Practice, pp. S1–S33

🌐 **TEST PRACTICE**
CLASSZONE.COM

Raise the Liberty Pole

In 1765, the Sons of Liberty gathered around a huge elm tree in Boston that they named the Liberty Tree. It became a meeting place where people voiced their protests against British policies. Replicas of the Liberty Tree—giant poles sometimes decorated with the flags of the colonies— were raised throughout the colonies. These liberty poles represented the unity of the American colonies as they struggled to break away from British rule.

ACTIVITY Like the American Patriots, each group of students will raise its own liberty pole. Each group also will write and deliver a persuasive speech supporting the cause of the American colonies.

TOOLBOX

Each group will need:

scissors	3 cardboard tubes from wrapping paper
poster board	construction paper
pencil	twine
markers	stapler
masking tape	

STEP BY STEP

1 Form groups. Each group should consist of four or five students. The members of your group will do the following jobs:

- research each colony
- design and create flags
- construct a pole
- write and deliver a speech

2 Do research on the 13 colonies. For each colony, your group should find a person, place, or object that represents that colony. For example, a Pilgrim's hat might represent Massachusetts. The 13 colonies are listed below.

New England Colonies	Middle Colonies	Southern Colonies
Massachusetts (including Maine)	New York	North Carolina
New Hampshire	Delaware	Virginia
Connecticut	New Jersey	Maryland
Rhode Island	Pennsylvania	South Carolina
		Georgia

Members of the Sons of Liberty raise a liberty pole in July 1776 to celebrate America's independence.

3 **Design and create 13 flags for the colonies.** Decide what person, place, or object you will use on your flag for each colony. Cut each flag out of the poster board. Sketch your design on the flag with a pencil. Then use markers to decorate it. On the back of each flag, explain how your design portrays the characteristics of that colony.

4 **Construct the pole.** Using masking tape, fasten the three cardboard tubes together to form one long tube. Then reinforce the tube by taping construction paper around it.

5 **String the flags on the pole.** Feed a piece of twine through the open ends of the long tube. Tie the ends of the twine together to form a tight loop. Now staple all 13 flags to the twine.

6 **Raise your liberty pole.** Lean your liberty pole next to a small table or desk. Take turns with members of your group and visit other liberty poles. As students visit your station, explain the significance of your flag designs.

WRITE AND SPEAK

Write a persuasive speech to recruit others to join the cause of liberty. In your speech, explain what is wrong with British policies. Give reasons why the colonies should become independent. Then read your speech to the other groups as part of the recruitment process.

HELP DESK

For related information on the Liberty Tree, see pages 145–146 in Chapter 6.

Researching Your Project
- *The Revolutionary War* by Bart McDowell
- *The American Revolutionaries* edited by Milton Meltzer

For more about the American Revolution . . .

RESEARCH LINKS
CLASSZONE.COM

Did You Know?
The numbers 45 and 92 played an important part in the history of these liberty poles. The 45th issue of a British newspaper openly criticized the king in 1763 and was reprinted in the colonies. In 1768, 92 members of the Massachusetts General Assembly voted against canceling a letter to the other 12 colonies that called for action against Britain. To represent the numbers, 92 members of the Sons of Liberty would often raise liberty poles to a height of about 45 feet.

REFLECT & ASSESS
- How well do your flags represent the colonies?
- How clearly does your speech explain grievances against the British?
- Why do you think the practice of raising liberty poles spread to many of the colonies?

CHAPTER 7

The American Revolution 1776–1783

This painting shows General Washington and his ragged troops traveling to their winter camp at Valley Forge.

Interact *with* History

The British army is on the other side of this hill and coming fast.

These are the family and servants of the American general Philip Schuyler.

Mrs. Schuyler sets fire to her harvest to prevent the British from taking it.

It is 1777. Your brother is an American soldier. In his last letter to you, he wrote that the army has no shoes or bullets and little food. But he plans to keep fighting.

Now, a British army is coming toward your farm. You hear that the soldiers are stealing crops to feed themselves and their horses.

What Do You Think?

- What sacrifices do civilians like Mrs. Schuyler make during wartime?
- What sacrifices do soldiers make?
- Is it worth such sacrifices to win independence for your country? Why or why not?

What would you sacrifice to win freedom?

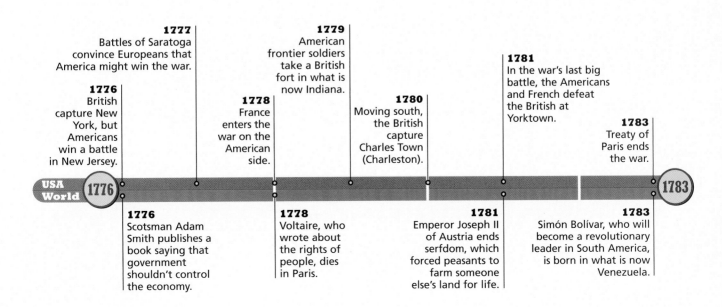

1777
Battles of Saratoga convince Europeans that America might win the war.

1776
British capture New York, but Americans win a battle in New Jersey.

1779
American frontier soldiers take a British fort in what is now Indiana.

1778
France enters the war on the American side.

1780
Moving south, the British capture Charles Town (Charleston).

1781
In the war's last big battle, the Americans and French defeat the British at Yorktown.

1783
Treaty of Paris ends the war.

USA
World
1776

1783

1776
Scotsman Adam Smith publishes a book saying that government shouldn't control the economy.

1778
Voltaire, who wrote about the rights of people, dies in Paris.

1781
Emperor Joseph II of Austria ends serfdom, which forced peasants to farm someone else's land for life.

1783
Simón Bolívar, who will become a revolutionary leader in South America, is born in what is now Venezuela.

BEFORE YOU READ

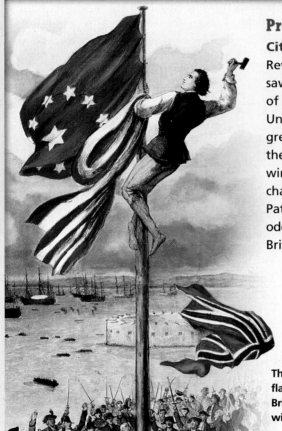

This Patriot has climbed a flagpole to tear down the British flag and replace it with an American one.

Previewing the Theme

Citizenship During the Revolution, many Americans saw themselves as citizens of a new country—the United States. They made great sacrifices and risked their lives and fortunes to win independence. This chapter explains how those Patriots overcame enormous odds to defeat the powerful British Empire.

What Do You Know?

What stories do you know about the people or events of the Revolution? How do people display courage and self-sacrifice during wartime?

THINK ABOUT

• what you've learned about the American Revolution from books, movies, and other classes

• news stories you've heard about revolutions or civil wars in other countries today

What Do You Want to Know?

What would you like to learn about the steps that people took to win the American Revolution? In your notebook, record what you hope to learn from this chapter.

READ AND TAKE NOTES

Reading Strategy: Sequencing Events To sequence is to put events in the order in which they happened. You learned this skill in Chapter 6 by sequencing the events that led to the American Revolution. Now as you read Chapter 7, practice sequencing again. Put the major battles and events of the war in order by recording them on a time line. Copy the time line below in your notebook. You may want to make it bigger.

 See Skillbuilder Handbook, page R4.

| 1776 | 1778 | 1780 | 1783 |

| 1776 | 1777 | 1778 | 1779 | 1780 | 1781 | 1782 | 1783 |

| 1777 | 1779 | 1781 |

① The Early Years of the War

TERMS & NAMES
George Washington
mercenary
strategy
rendezvous
Battles of Saratoga

MAIN IDEA

The American desire to gain rights and liberties led them to fight for independence from Britain.

WHY IT MATTERS NOW

Today those same rights and liberties are protected by the U.S. Constitution.

ONE AMERICAN'S STORY

In search of liberty, Haym Salomon moved from eastern Europe to America sometime between 1764 and 1775. He was a Jew from Poland. Arriving in New York City, Salomon soon became a successful merchant and banker. After the war broke out, Salomon supported the Patriot cause.

When the British captured New York in 1776, many Patriots fled but Salomon stayed. The British arrested him as a spy. Salomon spoke many languages. The British thought he could help their supply officers deal with foreign merchants, so they let him out of prison. Salomon used this opportunity to help other prisoners escape.

In 1778, the British wanted to arrest Salomon again, so he fled to Philadelphia. His earlier time in the cold, damp prison had permanently damaged his health. Even so, he continued to aid the Patriots. He loaned the new government more than $600,000, which was never repaid.

Haym Salomon sacrificed his health and his fortune to help his new country.

Like Salomon, many people made hard choices about which side to support during the Revolutionary War. This section discusses those choices and the obstacles Americans faced in the war's early years.

Americans Divided

The issue of separating from Great Britain divided American society. Opinion polls did not exist in the 1700s, so we don't know exactly how many people were on each side. But historians estimate that roughly 20 to 30 percent of Americans were Loyalists, roughly 40 to 45 percent were Patriots, and the rest remained neutral. Most Americans did not support the Revolution.

Both Patriots and Loyalists came from all walks of life and all parts of America. In general, New England and Virginia had high numbers of Patriots. Loyalists were numerous in cities, in New York State, and in the

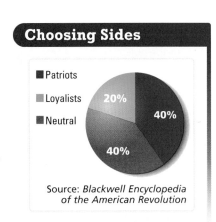

Choosing Sides

- Patriots
- Loyalists
- Neutral

20%
40%
40%

Source: *Blackwell Encyclopedia of the American Revolution*

South. Many Loyalists worked for the British government or were clergy in the Church of England. Some Quakers were Loyalists, although many wanted peace. (Their faith taught that war was wrong.)

The war divided Native Americans, too. For instance, some Iroquois nations fought with the British and others with the Americans. Those Native Americans who joined the British feared that if the Americans won, they would take Native American land. Some Native Americans who lived near colonists and interacted with them sided with the Americans.

African Americans also fought on both sides. At first, slave owners feared that African Americans who had guns might lead slave revolts. Therefore, few states allowed African Americans to enlist, or sign up with the army. Then a British governor offered freedom to any enslaved person who joined the British army. Many slaves ran away to fight for the British. In response, most states began to accept African-American soldiers. In all, about 5,000 African Americans served in the Continental Army. Many African Americans who did so hoped that American independence would bring greater equality.

Differences over the war split families, too. For example, Benjamin Franklin's son William took Britain's side. The father and son stopped speaking.

Background
The Iroquois League had generally kept peace among the Iroquois nations for about 200 years—until the American Revolution.

Creating an Army

Because not everyone supported the war, raising an army was difficult. The army also faced other problems. In June 1775, **George Washington** became the commander of the Continental Army. At first, this new national army was formed from state militias, made up of untrained and undisciplined volunteers.

After Congress created the Continental Army, men began to enlist, but most of them didn't stay long. At the start of the war, Congress asked men to enlist only for one year. Later Congress did lengthen the term of service. When the soldiers' time was up, they went home. As a result, Washington's army never numbered more than 17,000 men.

Congress's inability to supply the army also frustrated Washington. The soldiers needed everything—blankets, shoes, food, and even guns and ammunition. Angrily, Washington wrote, "Could I have foreseen what I have, and am likely to experience, no consideration upon earth should have induced [persuaded] me to accept this command."

Many women tried to help the army. Martha Washington and other wives followed their husbands to army camps. The women cooked, did laundry, and

Reading **History**
A. Analyzing Causes Why would the lack of agreement about the war make it hard to raise an army?

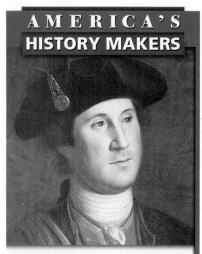

AMERICA'S HISTORY MAKERS

GEORGE WASHINGTON
1732–1799

At the age of 16, George Washington worked as a surveyor, setting land boundaries in the wilderness. He learned to handle hardship by hunting for food and sleeping outdoors.

In the French and Indian War, Washington had many brushes with death. Yet he wrote, "I heard the bullets whistle, and, believe me, there is something charming in the sound."

That war made him the most famous American officer. People loved him for his courage. As commander of the Continental Army, Washington's popularity helped unite Americans.

How did Washington's early life prepare him to lead the army?

nursed sick or wounded soldiers. A few women even helped fight. Mary Hays earned the nickname "Molly Pitcher" by carrying water to tired soldiers during a battle. Deborah Sampson dressed as a man, enlisted, and fought in several engagements.

Building an army was crucial to Washington's plan. To the British, the Americans were disorganized, inexperienced rebels. The British thought that if they won a decisive battle, the Americans would give up. By contrast, Washington's main goal was to survive. To do so, he needed to keep an army in the field, win some battles—no matter how small—and avoid a crushing defeat. He knew he could not hope to win a major battle until he had a large, well-equipped army.

*Reading*History
B. Solving Problems How did Washington try to solve the problem of leading a small, inexperienced force against a large professional army?

These Hessian boots weighed about 12 pounds a pair.

Struggle for the Middle States

As Chapter 6 explains, Washington had forced the British to retreat from Boston in March 1776. He then hurried his army to New York City, where he expected the British to go next. One British goal was to occupy coastal cities so that their navy could land troops and supplies in those cities. From there, they could launch their military campaigns.

Washington's hunch was correct. In July 1776, Britain's General William Howe arrived in New York with a large army. Then in August, more soldiers arrived, including about 9,000 Hessian mercenaries. A **mercenary** is a professional soldier hired to fight for a foreign country. British soldiers usually signed up for life—which discouraged enlistment. So Britain needed mercenaries, whom it hired from the German states.

Background
The British-hired mercenaries came from a part of Germany called Hesse, which is the origin of the term *Hessian*.

For several months, the British and American armies fought for New York State. Finally, the British forced Washington to retreat through New Jersey. By December, when the American army crossed the Delaware River into Pennsylvania, it was in terrible condition. Charles Willson Peale, a Philadelphia painter who watched the crossing, saw one muddy soldier who "had lost all his clothes. He was in an old, dirty blanket jacket, his beard long, and his face so full of sores he could not clean it." To Peale's shock, the soldier called his name. He was Peale's brother!

Political writer Thomas Paine also witnessed the hard conditions and the soldiers' low spirits on the retreat. To

War in the Middle States, 1776–1777

← American forces
← British forces
✳ American victory
✳ British victory

GEOGRAPHY SKILLBUILDER Interpreting Maps
1. **Place** *In what state did the American victories take place?*
2. **Movement** *How did the British general Howe travel from New York to Brandywine?*

179

Thomas Sully's _Passage of the Delaware_ shows Washington at the Delaware River, leading to the American attack on the British at Trenton, New Jersey.

urge them to keep fighting, Paine published the first in a series of pamphlets called _The American Crisis._

A VOICE FROM THE PAST

These are the times that try men's souls. The summer soldier and the sunshine patriot will, in this crisis, shrink from the service of their country; but he that stands it *now,* deserves the love and thanks of man and woman.

Thomas Paine, *The American Crisis*

Reading **History**
C. Recognizing Propaganda How does this passage promote the American cause?

Washington hoped a victory would encourage his weary men. He also knew that he must attack the British quickly because most of his soldiers would leave once their enlistments ended on December 31.

Late on December 25, 1776, Washington's troops rowed across the icy Delaware River to New Jersey. From there, they marched in bitter, early-morning cold to Trenton to surprise the Hessians, some of whom were sleeping after their Christmas celebration. The Americans captured or killed more than 900 Hessians and gained needed supplies. Washington's army won another victory at Princeton eight days later. These victories proved that the American general was better than the British had thought. The American army began to attract new recruits.

Britain's Strategy

Meanwhile, the British were pursuing a **strategy**—an overall plan of action—to seize the Hudson River Valley. If successful, they would cut off New England from the other states. The strategy called for three armies to meet at Albany, New York. General John Burgoyne would lead a force south from Canada. Lieutenant Colonel Barry St. Leger would lead his army from Lake Ontario down the Mohawk Valley. Burgoyne expected General Howe to follow the Hudson north from New York City.

Burgoyne left Canada in June 1777 with an army that included British, Hessians, and Iroquois. In July, they captured Fort Ticonderoga.

Called "Gentleman Johnny" by his soldiers, Burgoyne enjoyed traveling slowly and throwing parties to celebrate victories. After Ticonderoga, his delays gave the Americans time to cut down trees to block his route. They also burned crops and drove off cattle, leaving the countryside bare of supplies for the British troops.

Things grew rougher during the last 25 miles of Burgoyne's march to Albany. On a map, the route looked easy, but it really crossed a swampy wilderness. The army had to build bridges and roads. Burgoyne took four weeks to reach the Hudson. Still confident, he looked forward to the **rendezvous,** or meeting, with St. Leger and Howe in Albany.

On August 4, Burgoyne received a message from Howe. He would not be coming north, Howe wrote, because he had decided to invade Pennsylvania to try to capture General Washington and Philadelphia—where the Continental Congress met. "Success be ever with you," wrote Howe. Yet Burgoyne needed Howe's soldiers, not his good wishes.

Reading**History**
D. Evaluating
Review Howe's two goals for his invasion of Pennsylvania. Was he successful?

Howe did invade Pennsylvania. In September 1777, he defeated but did not capture Washington at the Battle of Brandywine. Howe then occupied Philadelphia. In October, Washington attacked Howe at Germantown. Washington lost the battle, however, and retreated.

Battles Along the Mohawk

As Burgoyne received Howe's message, St. Leger faced his own obstacle in reaching Albany. In the summer of 1777, he was trying to defeat a small American force at Fort Stanwix in the Mohawk River valley of New York. St. Leger's forces included Iroquois led by Mohawk chief Joseph Brant, also called Thayendanegea (THĪ•ehn•DAHG•ee).

Vocabulary
convert: a person who changes religions

Brant and his sister, Molly, had strong ties to the British. Molly was a British official's wife, and Joseph was a convert to the Church of England. Both Joseph and Molly tried to convince the Iroquois to fight for the British, who upheld Iroquois rights to their land.

During August 1777, American general Benedict Arnold led a small army up the Mohawk River. He wanted to chase the British away from

War in the North, 1777

0 — 100 Miles
0 — 200 Kilometers

← American forces
← British forces
✳ American victory
✳ British victory

Quebec
Montreal
MAINE (part of Mass.)
St. Lawrence R.
Burgoyne
Lake Champlain
St. Leger
Lake Ontario
Mohawk R.
Ft. Ontario
Ft. Ticonderoga
Saratoga
N.H.
Ft. Stanwix
Oriskany
Arnold
Bennington
Gates
MASS.
NEW YORK
Albany
Boston
Hudson R.
CONN.
Delaware R.
PENNSYLVANIA
R.I.
ATLANTIC OCEAN

GEOGRAPHY SKILLBUILDER Interpreting Maps
1. **Place** _From which two cities did the British invade the United States?_
2. **Movement** _What did St. Leger want to capture by taking the longer route by way of Lake Ontario?_

The Iroquois chief Joseph Brant was a British ally.

Fort Stanwix. Arnold sent a captured Loyalist and some Iroquois who were American allies to spread the rumor that he had a large army.

The trick worked. St. Leger's troops were afraid they were about to be outnumbered. The army retreated so fast that it left behind tents, cannon, and supplies. Because of St. Leger's flight and Howe's refusal to follow the strategy, no one was left to rendezvous with Burgoyne.

Saratoga: A Turning Point

By this time, Burgoyne's army was running out of supplies, and it needed horses. The general sent a raiding party into Vermont to see what it could find. The raiding party encountered New England troops, who badly defeated it at the Battle of Bennington on August 16, 1777.

Despite this setback, Burgoyne's army headed slowly toward Albany. On the way, it met a powerful Continental Army force led by General Horatio Gates. Gates's soldiers were waiting on a ridge called Bemis Heights, near Saratoga, New York. There the Americans had created fortifications, or built-up earthen walls, behind which to fight. The Polish engineer Tadeusz Kosciuszko (TAH•deh•oosh KAWSH•choosh•kaw) had helped the Americans do this.

Burgoyne would have to break through the fortifications to proceed to Albany. On September 19, he attacked. While Gates commanded the Americans on the ridge, Benedict Arnold led an attack on nearby

*Reading*History
E. Reading a Map
Find Saratoga on the map on page 181. Notice how close it is to Burgoyne's goal of Albany.

CITIZENSHIP TODAY

Exercising Free Speech

The British could have charged Thomas Paine with a crime for writing *The American Crisis.* The crime was sedition, or stirring up rebellion. By saying what he thought, Paine risked going to prison. Today U.S. citizens have the right to speak freely without fear of jail.

Like Thomas Paine, some students have used free speech to urge people to take action. For example, the Sidney Lanier Middle School in Houston, Texas, has published its school newspaper on the Internet. In October 1996, one writer urged other students to get involved in that year's election, saying, "Even though you will not be able to vote yet, you can still influence your parents to do so."

These students are working together to produce a school newspaper.

How Do You Exercise Free Speech?

1. Working in a small group, choose an issue that you care about. Look through newsmagazines for ideas.

2. Use a cluster diagram to record your feelings and opinions about the issue.

3. As a group, decide what action you think people should take on the issue.

4. Write an article expressing the group's opinion. Each member should read the article and suggest changes. Revise the article.

5. Send the revised article to the editorial page of your school or local newspaper.

See Citizenship Handbook, page 266.

For more about free speech . . .

RESEARCH LINKS
CLASSZONE.COM

Freeman's Farm. His men repeatedly charged the British and inflicted heavy casualties. Still, the British held their position.

On October 7, another battle broke out. Again Arnold led daring charges against the British. Although hundreds of muskets were firing at him, he galloped through the battlefield "like a madman," a sergeant later said. Frightened, Burgoyne's Hessian mercenaries began to fall back. Eventually, a bullet tore into Arnold's leg and stopped him. Even so, the Americans forced Burgoyne to retreat.

Burgoyne's army moved slowly through heavy rain to a former army camp at Saratoga. By the time they arrived, the men were exhausted. Some fell in the mud and slept in their wet uniforms. The Continental Army then surrounded Burgoyne's army and fired on it day and night without stopping. Burgoyne decided to surrender. The series of conflicts that led to this surrender is known as the **Battles of Saratoga.**

The Battles of Saratoga had two very different consequences. As Benedict Arnold was recovering from his wound, he married a woman who was a Loyalist. Over time, Arnold came to feel that Congress had not rewarded him enough for his heroic actions at Saratoga and other battles. Influenced by his bitterness and his wife, he betrayed his army. In 1780, he agreed to turn over an American fort to the British. Although his plot was discovered before he could carry it out, he escaped. Even today, the name *Benedict Arnold* is used to mean traitor.

On the positive side, the victory at Saratoga was a turning point in the Revolution. It caused European nations to think that the Americans might win their war for independence. As you will read in Section 2, several European nations decided to help America in its struggle.

*Reading*History
F. Forming and Supporting Opinions Which of the two consequences of the Battles of Saratoga was more significant? Why?

America's HERITAGE

THE FIRST FLAG
June 14 is Flag Day in the United States. On June 14, 1777, the Continental Congress adopted the stars and stripes design for the U.S. flag. According to legend, a Philadelphia seamstress named Betsy Ross designed the first flag, illustrated below. Historians have found no evidence to support this legend. However, Ross did make flags for the Pennsylvania navy.

Section 1 Assessment

1. Terms & Names

Explain the significance of:
• George Washington
• mercenary
• strategy
• rendezvous
• Battles of Saratoga

2. Taking Notes

Use a cluster diagram like the one shown to list the difficulties Americans faced in the early years of the war.

American Difficulties

Which difficulty do you think was hardest to overcome?

3. Main Ideas

a. How were Americans divided over the issue of separating from Great Britain?

b. Why was it difficult for George Washington to form and keep a large army?

c. How did the Battles of Saratoga mark a turning point in the war?

4. Critical Thinking

Contrasting How did the British and American strategies differ during the early years of the war?

THINK ABOUT
• what the British expected from the Americans
• Washington's main goals for the American army
• why Burgoyne invaded from Canada

ACTIVITY OPTIONS

LANGUAGE ARTS

ART

Learn more about a Revolutionary War leader. Write a brief **biography** or create a **trading card** with a picture on one side and important facts on the other.

TERMS & NAMES
ally
Marquis de
  Lafayette
bayonet
desert
privateer
James Forten
John Paul Jones

MAIN IDEA	WHY IT MATTERS NOW
Some Europeans decided to help America. As the war continued, it spread to the sea and the frontier.	This was the beginning of the United States' formal relationships with other nations.

ONE AMERICAN'S STORY

To defeat the mighty British Empire, the United States needed a foreign ally. An **ally** is a country that agrees to help another country achieve a common goal. The ideal ally would share America's goal of defeating Britain. It also had to be able to provide money, troops, and ships. So the United States turned to France—Britain's long-time enemy.

In the fall of 1776, Congress sent Benjamin Franklin to the French capital, Paris. His job was to persuade France to be the ally of the United States. Franklin was already famous for his experiments with electricity. When he reached Paris, he became a celebrity. He wrote to his daughter, saying that medallions with his likeness were popular there.

A VOICE FROM THE PAST

These, with the pictures, busts [sculptures of the head and shoulders], and prints (of which copies upon copies are spread everywhere), have made your father's face as well known as that of the moon.

Benjamin Franklin, letter to his daughter Sally

Franklin's simple Quaker coat and fur hat amused the French. The clothes fit the image they had of him—a wise, noble man from a wild country.

In spite of his popularity, Franklin couldn't convince the French to become America's formal ally until after the victory at Saratoga. Then the French agreed to an alliance. This section explains how the war expanded after foreign allies joined the American side.

Help from Abroad

France was still bitter over its defeat by Britain in the French and Indian War, in which France lost its North American colonies. The French hoped to take revenge on the British by helping Britain's American colonies break free. In 1776, France began to give secret aid to the Americans. However, the French didn't want to lose to Britain a second time. That is why they didn't publicly ally themselves with the United States until after the Americans had proved they could win battles.

After hearing of the American victory at Saratoga, King Louis XVI of France recognized U.S. independence. In 1778, France signed two treaties of alliance with the United States. By doing so, France went to war with Britain. As part of its new alliance, France sent badly needed funds, supplies, and troops to America.

In 1779, France persuaded its ally Spain to help the Americans. Spain was also Britain's rival. The Spanish governor of Louisiana, General Bernardo de Gálvez, acted quickly. He captured the British strongholds of Natchez and Baton Rouge in the lower Mississippi Valley.

From there, his small army went on to take Mobile, and in 1781 Pensacola in West Florida. These victories prevented the British from attacking the United States from the southwest. In addition, Britain had to keep thousands of troops fighting Gálvez—instead of fighting the Americans. However, like France, Spain's motives were not simply to help the United States. Gálvez's victories helped extend Spain's empire in North America.

By entering the war on America's side, France and Spain forced the British to fight a number of enemies on land and sea. The British had to spread their military resources over many fronts. For example, they were afraid they might have to fight the French in the West Indies, so they sent troops there. This prevented the British from concentrating their strength to defeat the inexperienced Americans.

Europeans Help Washington

The Americans gained some of the military experience they needed from Europe. Several European military officers came to Washington's aid, including men from France, Poland, and the German states.

The **Marquis de Lafayette** (LAF•ee•EHT) was a 19-year-old French nobleman who volunteered to serve in Washington's army. He wanted a military career, and he believed in the American cause. He quickly gained Washington's confidence and was given the command of an army division. Lafayette won respect and love from his men by sharing their hardships. Called "the soldier's friend," he used his own money to buy warm clothing for his ragged troops. Washington regarded him almost as a son.

Lafayette fought in many battles and also persuaded the French king to send a 6,000-man army to America. He became a hero in both France and the United States. Later he took part in France's own revolution.

Along with Lafayette came the Baron de Kalb, a German officer who had served in the French army. He became one of Washington's generals and earned a reputation for bravery. In 1780, he received 11 wounds in the Battle of Camden and died.

Another German, Baron von Steuben, helped turn the inexperienced Americans

Background
Galveston, Texas, is named for Gálvez.

Reading**History**
A. Recognizing Effects How did America's allies prevent Britain from focusing all its might on the Americans?

Background
Many of these European officers were professional soldiers looking for an army that would hire them. Some, like Lafayette, also believed in the American cause.

Lafayette stands with the slave James Armistead, whose owner allowed him to spy for Lafayette. After the war, the state of Virginia set Armistead free. Armistead then took Lafayette's last name as his own.

into a skilled fighting force. Washington asked him to train the army. In 1778, Steuben began by forming a model company of 100 men. Then he taught them how to move in lines and columns and how to handle weapons properly. Under Steuben's direction, the soldiers practiced making charges with **bayonets**—long steel knives attached to the ends of guns. Within a month, the troops were executing drills with speed and precision. Once the model company succeeded, the rest of the army adopted Steuben's methods.

Winter at Valley Forge

Help from Europeans came at a time when the Americans desperately needed it. In late 1777, Britain's General Howe forced Washington to retreat from Philadelphia. Beginning in the winter of 1777–1778, Washington and his army camped at Valley Forge in southeast Pennsylvania.

On the march to Valley Forge, Washington's army was so short on supplies that many soldiers had only blankets to cover themselves. They also lacked shoes. The barefoot men left tracks of blood on the frozen ground as they marched. The soldiers' condition did not improve at camp. The Marquis de Lafayette described what he saw.

A VOICE FROM THE PAST

The unfortunate soldiers were in want of everything; they had neither coats, nor hats, nor shirts, nor shoes; their feet and their legs froze till they grew black and it was often necessary to amputate them. . . . The Army frequently passed whole days without food.

Marquis de Lafayette, quoted in *Valley Forge: Pinnacle of Courage*

Reading History
B. Identifying Facts and Opinions Is Lafayette mainly recounting facts or expressing opinions? Explain.

Because of this, the name *Valley Forge* came to stand for the great hardships that Americans endured in the Revolutionary War. Over the winter, the soldiers at Valley Forge grew weak from not having enough food or warm clothing. Roughly a quarter of them died from malnutrition, exposure to the cold, or diseases such as smallpox and typhoid fever.

daily *life*

CAMP LIFE IN WINTER

At Valley Forge, soldiers slept in small huts, 12 men to a hut. They slept in shifts so they could take turns using the scarce blankets. The men also shared clothing. If one went on guard duty, the others lent him their clothes and stayed by the fire in the hut until he came back. Guards had to stand in old hats to keep their shoeless feet warm.

The soldiers cooked on hot stones, in iron kettles, or on portable iron braziers. Often the only food they had was fire cakes—a bread made of flour and water paste.

These iron kettles were so heavy that soldiers often threw them away on a march.

This surgeon's kit includes a saw, used to perform amputations.

Soldiers would place burning coals in braziers like this. Braziers were used to cook food and heat huts.

Washington appealed to Congress to send the soldiers supplies, but it was slow in responding. Luckily, private citizens sometimes came to the soldiers' aid. According to one story, on New Year's Day 1778, a group of Philadelphia women drove ten teams of oxen into camp. The oxen were pulling wagons loaded with supplies and 2,000 shirts. The women had the oxen killed to provide food for the men.

*Reading*History
C. Analyzing Points of View
What are two different explanations for why American soldiers did not desert?

Despite the hardships, Washington and his soldiers showed amazing endurance. Under such circumstances, soldiers often **desert,** or leave military duty without intending to return. Some soldiers did desert, but Lieutenant Colonel John Brooks wrote that the army stayed together because of "Love of our Country." The men also stayed because of Washington. Private Samuel Downing declared that the soldiers "loved him. They'd sell their lives for him."

War on the Frontier

Elsewhere, other Americans also took on difficult challenges. In 1777, a 24-year-old frontiersman named George Rogers Clark walked into the office of Virginia's governor, Patrick Henry. Clark said he had come to take part in defending the Western frontier. He lived in Kentucky, which was claimed by Virginia. Clark wanted Virginia to defend that region against British soldiers and their Native American allies in what is now Indiana and Illinois. "If a country is not worth protecting," he said, "it is not worth claiming."

"If a country is not worth protecting, it is not worth claiming."
George Rogers Clark

Background
In the late 1700s, the Western frontier was the region between the Appalachian Mountains and the Mississippi River.

Clark was difficult to ignore. He stood six feet tall, had red hair, and displayed a dramatic personality. He persuaded Governor Henry that he was right. The governor told Clark to raise an army to capture British posts on the Western frontier.

In May of 1778, Clark and a group of frontiersmen began to travel down the Ohio River. He recruited others on the way, until he had a force of 175 to 200. They went by boat and later on foot to Kaskaskia, a British post on the Mississippi River. They captured Kaskaskia without a fight.

Then they moved east to take Fort Sackville at Vincennes, in present-day Indiana. Earlier, a small force sent by Clark had taken Vincennes, but British forces under Henry Hamilton had recaptured it. Settlers called Hamilton the "Hair Buyer" because he supposedly paid rewards for American scalps.

War on the Frontier, 1778

In 1778, George Rogers Clark captures British outposts on the American frontier without firing a shot. Though the British retake Vincennes, Clark regains it after a short battle in 1779.

American forces
British forces
American victory
American fort
British fort

GEOGRAPHY SKILLBUILDER Interpreting Maps
1. **Movement** From what fort did British general Hamilton travel to Vincennes?
2. **Region** What rivers form the boundaries of the region captured by Clark and his men?

Determined to retake Fort Sackville, Clark and his men set out for Vincennes from Kaskaskia in February 1779. Hamilton wasn't expecting an attack because the rivers were overflowing their banks and the woods were flooded. Clark's men slogged through miles of icy swamps and waded through chest-deep water. They caught the British at Vincennes by surprise.

When Hamilton and his troops tried to remain in the fort, Clark pretended to have a larger force than he really had. He also found a way to frighten the British into leaving. Clark and his men had captured several Native Americans, who were allies of the British and had American scalps on their belts. Clark executed some of them in plain view of the fort. He promised to do the same to Hamilton and his men if they didn't surrender immediately. The British gave up.

Clark's victory gave the Americans a hold on the vast region between the Great Lakes and the Ohio River. This area was more than half the total size of the original 13 states. However, Fort Detroit on Lake Erie remained in the hands of the British.

Reading **History**
D. Making Decisions What factors do you think influenced Clark's decision to execute his prisoners?

War at Sea

The war expanded not only to the frontier but also to the sea. By 1777, Britain had about 100 warships off the American coast. This allowed Britain to control the Atlantic trade routes. There was no way the Americans could defeat the powerful British navy.

But American privateers attacked British merchant ships. A **privateer** is a privately owned ship that a wartime government gives permission to attack an enemy's merchant ships. After capturing a British merchant ship, the crew of a privateer sold its cargo and shared the money. As a result, a desire for profit as well as patriotism motivated privateers. The states and Congress commissioned more than 1,000 privateers to prey on the British. During the war, they captured hundreds of British ships. This disrupted trade, causing British merchants to call for the war to end.

Many men answered the privateers' call for volunteers. Among them was 14-year-old **James Forten,** who was the son of a free African-American sail maker. In 1780, Forten signed up to sail on the *Royal Louis* to earn money for his family after his father died. When a British ship captured the *Royal Louis* in 1781, the British offered Forten a free trip to England. Reportedly, Forten refused, saying he would never betray his country. Released from a British prison after the war, Forten walked barefoot from New York to his home in Philadelphia. He later became famous for his efforts to end slavery.

Vocabulary
merchant ship: a ship used in trade

STRANGE *but* True

THE FIRST COMBAT SUBMARINE

During the Revolution, the Americans built the first combat submarine—the *Turtle,* shown below. It held only a pilot, who steered with one hand and cranked a propeller with the other. To submerge, the pilot used a foot pump to let in water.

In 1776, the *Turtle* failed on its mission to attach a bomb to a British warship in New York harbor. It reached the ship but couldn't drill through its copper-clad hull. The *Turtle* failed at later missions, too.

A Naval Hero

Though outnumbered, the Continental Navy scored several victories against the British. An officer named **John Paul Jones** won the most famous sea battle.

In 1779, Jones became the commander of a ship named *Bonhomme Richard*. With four other ships, he patrolled the English coast. In September, Jones's vessels approached a convoy in which two British warships were guarding a number of supply ships.

Jones closed in on the *Serapis*, the larger of the two warships. At one point, the *Bonhomme Richard* rammed the better-armed British vessel. As the two ships locked together, the confident British captain demanded that Jones surrender. In words that have become a famous U.S. Navy slogan, Jones replied, "I have not yet begun to fight!"

The two warships were so close together that the muzzles of their guns almost touched. They blasted away, each seriously damaging the other. On the shore, crowds of Britons gathered under a full moon to watch the fighting. After a fierce three-and-a-half-hour battle, the main mast of the *Serapis* cracked and fell. The ship's captain then surrendered. The *Bonhomme Richard* was so full of holes that it eventually sank, so Jones and his crew had to sail away in the *Serapis*!

Jones's success against the best navy in the world angered the British and inspired the Americans. Even so, the Americans knew that the war had to be won on land. The next section discusses the major land battles in the closing years of the war.

Vocabulary
convoy: a group of ships traveling together for safety

AMERICA'S HISTORY MAKERS

JOHN PAUL JONES
1747–1792

The most famous naval officer of the Revolution is known by a fake name. He was born John Paul in Scotland and first went to sea as a 12-year-old. By age 21, he had command of a merchant ship.

In 1773, Paul killed the leader of a mutiny on his ship. To avoid a murder trial, he fled to America and added Jones to his name.

Bold and daring, Jones scored many victories against the British. But his battle with the *Serapis* is what earned his place in history.

What are the two words that you think best describe Jones's character? Explain.

Section 2 Assessment

1. Terms & Names
Explain the significance of:
- ally
- Marquis de Lafayette
- bayonet
- desert
- privateer
- James Forten
- John Paul Jones

2. Taking Notes
Use this diagram to list the effects of the entry of France and Spain into the war.

```
Cause: France and Spain
enter the war.
   ↓        ↓        ↓
[Effect] [Effect] [Effect]
```

3. Main Ideas
a. What role did Benjamin Franklin play in helping America win the Revolution?

b. How did European officers such as Lafayette aid America in the Revolutionary War?

c. What was John Paul Jones's major contribution during the war, and why was it important?

4. Critical Thinking
Analyzing Points of View
Why do you think George Rogers Clark thought the frontier was important to defend?

THINK ABOUT
- why General Hamilton was called "Hair Buyer"
- why America might have wanted the frontier region after the war

ACTIVITY OPTIONS

ART

SPEECH

Imagine yourself at Valley Forge in the winter of 1777–1778. Create a **comic strip** or give a **talk** describing your response to the harsh conditions.

3 The Path to Victory

MAIN IDEA	WHY IT MATTERS NOW
Seeking Loyalist support, the British invaded the South—but ultimately lost the war there.	For more than two centuries, the American Revolution has inspired other people to fight tyranny.

ONE AMERICAN'S STORY

Patriot Nancy Hart glared at the five armed Loyalists who burst into her Georgia cabin. Tradition says that the men had shot her last turkey and ordered her to cook it for them. Raids like this were common in the South, where feuding neighbors used the war as an excuse to fight each other. Both Patriots and Loyalists took part in the raids. Many women and children had moved out of Georgia, but the six-foot-tall, freckled Hart chose to stay and fight. She could shoot a gun as accurately as any man.

As she prepared the food, Hart planned her attack. When dinner was ready, the men sat down to eat. Seizing one of their muskets, Hart quickly shot and killed one man and wounded another. She kept the gun aimed on the others as her daughter ran for help. A group of nearby Patriots arrived and hanged the Loyalists.

As Nancy Hart's story demonstrates, the fighting between Patriots and Loyalists in the South was vicious. In this section, you will learn why the British war effort shifted to the South and why it failed.

The state of Georgia named a county after Nancy Hart, who is shown here holding Loyalists prisoner.

Savannah and Charles Town

The British believed that most Southerners were Loyalists. Because of this, in 1778 the British decided to move the war to the South. After three years of fighting in the North, the British were no closer to victory. Although they had captured Northern cities, they couldn't control the countryside because they did not have enough troops to occupy it. The British believed that if they gained territory in the South, Southern Loyalists would hold it for them.

The British also expected large numbers of Southern slaves to join them because they had promised to grant the slaves freedom. Although thousands of African Americans did run away to join the British, not all of them were set free. Instead, some British officers sold African Americans into slavery in the West Indies.

*Reading*History

A. Drawing Conclusions Why was it an advantage to be able to move troops between the West Indies and the South?

Britain's West Indian colonies were a third reason the British invaded the South. Southern seaports were closer to the West Indies, where British troops were stationed. If the British captured Southern ports, they could move troops back and forth between the two regions.

In December 1778, the British captured the port of Savannah, Georgia. Using Savannah as a base, they then conquered most of Georgia. In 1780, a British army led by General Henry Clinton landed in South Carolina. They trapped American forces in Charles Town (now Charleston), which was the largest Southern city. When the city's 5,000 defenders surrendered, the Americans lost almost their entire Southern army. It was the worst American defeat of the war.

The Swamp Fox and Guerrilla Fighting

After that loss, Congress assigned General Horatio Gates—the victor at Saratoga—to form a new Southern army. Continental soldiers led by Baron de Kalb formed the army's core. Gates added about 2,000 new and untrained militia. He then headed for Camden, South Carolina, to challenge the army led by the British general **Lord Cornwallis.**

On the way, a band of Patriots from South Carolina approached Gates. "Their number did not exceed 20 men and boys, some white, some black, and all mounted, but most of them miserably equipped," wrote an officer. Their leader was Francis Marion, called the "Swamp Fox." He provided Gates with helpful knowledge of South Carolina's coastal swamplands. Gates sent Marion to destroy boats on the Santee River behind Camden. (See the map on page 193.) This would cut off British communications with Charles Town.

In August 1780, Gates's army ran into British troops outside Camden. The Americans were in no condition to fight. They were out of supplies and half-starved. Even worse, Gates put the inexperienced militia along part of the frontline instead of behind the veterans. When the British attacked, the militia panicked and ran. Gates also fled, but Kalb remained with his soldiers and received fatal wounds. This second defeat in the South ended Gates's term as head of an army and caused American spirits to fall to a new low.

After Camden, a small British force set out for Charles Town with a column of American prisoners. Marion's band overwhelmed the British and freed the prisoners. Fighting from a base in the swamps, Marion's men cut the British supply line that led inland and north from Charles Town. Marion used the methods of a guerrilla. **Guerrillas** are small bands of fighters who weaken the enemy with surprise raids and hit-and-run attacks. Both Patriots and Loyalists formed guerrilla bands in the South. They carried out vicious raids.

*Reading*History

B. Evaluating What do you think was most responsible for the American loss at Camden?

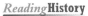

BATTLE TACTICS

A difference in battle tactics affected future warfare. British soldiers marched shoulder to shoulder in three rows. When they neared the enemy, the first row knelt, the second crouched, and the third remained standing. They all fired without aiming.

The Americans were better shots. They often marched in rows, but sometimes they hid in woods or behind walls to take aim. Guerrillas attacked swiftly, then fled into the countryside. Those tactics succeeded and are still used today. This photograph shows modern U.S. soldiers learning guerrilla tactics.

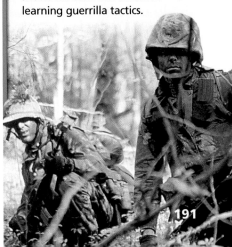

Artillery of the Revolution

Artillery—large guns and cannon—played a key role in the American Revolution. The ability of these guns to kill and destroy from a distance made them essential in war. One witness of a battle described the destruction: "Many men were badly injured and mortally wounded by the fragments of bombs, . . . their arms and legs severed or themselves struck dead." Most cannon used in the Revolution were made of cast bronze. During the 1700s, artillery design did not change significantly. However, artillery became more mobile (more easily moved).

After each shot, a soldier sponged the inside of the barrel. This put out sparks and cleaned away any dirt left from the last shot.

A soldier loaded the cannon with gunpowder and a cannonball. He did so by ramming them down the barrel.

Soldiers aimed the gun by turning the entire carriage. An instrument called a quadrant told them how high to raise the barrel to reach their target.

Cannon were classified by the weight of the iron ball they fired. American artillery ranged from 3-pounders to 32-pounders.

Soldiers lit the cannon by applying a red-hot wire or a tube of burning powder to a touchhole drilled through the back of the barrel, where the gunpowder lay. The gunpowder exploded, forcing the projectile out of the open end of the barrel.

In the 1700s, most cannon were accurate at ranges of up to 1,000 yards. That is the length of ten football fields laid end to end.

CONNECT TO HISTORY

1. **Recognizing Effects** Why would it be an advantage to an army to have mobile artillery?

   S See Skillbuilder Handbook, page R11.

CONNECT TO TODAY

2. **Researching** Find information about modern artillery in an encyclopedia or on the Internet. How did artillery change in the 20th century?

For more about artillery . . .

RESEARCH LINKS
CLASSZONE.COM

The Tide Turns

Even battles in the South sometimes turned vicious. One example was the Battle of Kings Mountain, fought on the border of North and South Carolina in October 1780. After surrounding a force of about 1,000 Loyalist militia and British soldiers, the Americans slaughtered most of them. James P. Collins, a 16-year-old American, described the scene.

A VOICE FROM THE PAST

The dead lay in heaps on all sides, while the groans of the wounded were heard in every direction. I could not help turning away from the scene before me with horror and, though exulting in victory, could not refrain from shedding tears.

James P. Collins, quoted in *The Spirit of Seventy-Six*

Many of the dead had been shot or hanged after they surrendered. The Americans killed them in revenge for Loyalist raids and an earlier incident in which the British had butchered Americans. Kings Mountain was one of Britain's first losses in the South. It soon suffered more.

After Gates's defeat at Camden, Washington put a new general, Nathanael Greene, in charge of the Southern army. Greene was one of Washington's most able officers. He had been a Quaker, but his church had cast him out because of his belief in the armed struggle against the British. Most Quakers are **pacifist,** or opposed to war.

Under Greene's command, the American army avoided full-scale battles, in which the British had the edge because of superior firepower. So the American forces let the British chase them around the countryside and wear themselves out. When the Americans did fight, they did their best to make sure the British suffered heavy losses.

*Reading*History
C. Contrasting
How did Greene's strategy as a general differ from that of Gates at Camden?

As the fighting dragged on into its sixth year, opposition to the war grew in Britain. As a result, some British leaders began to think that American independence would not be so bad.

The End of the War

In 1781, most of the fighting took place in Virginia. In July of that year, the British general Cornwallis set up his base at Yorktown, located on a peninsula in Chesapeake Bay. From there, his army could receive supplies by ship from New York.

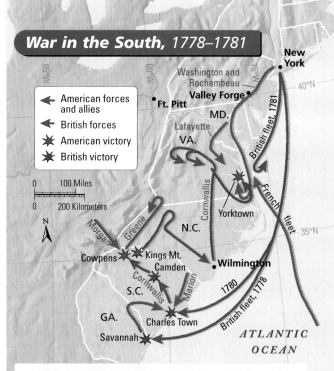

War in the South, *1778–1781*

American forces and allies
British forces
American victory
British victory

0   100 Miles
0   200 Kilometers

New York
Washington and Rochambeau
Valley Forge
Ft. Pitt
MD.
Lafayette
VA.
Cornwallis
Yorktown
French fleet
British fleet, 1781
N.C.
Morgan
Greene
Cowpens
Kings Mt.
Camden
Cornwallis
Marion
Wilmington
1780
British fleet, 1778
S.C.
GA.
Charles Town
Savannah
ATLANTIC OCEAN

GEOGRAPHY SKILLBUILDER Interpreting Maps
1. **Place** *What ports did the British use to invade the South?*
2. **Movement** *Who traveled from Wilmington to Yorktown, and who traveled from New York?*

193

The victorious American forces accept the British surrender at Yorktown. George Washington is to the left of the American flag.

Washington saw Cornwallis's decision as a golden opportunity. In August 1781, a large French fleet arrived from the West Indies and blocked Chesapeake Bay. These ships prevented the British from receiving supplies—and from escaping. They also allowed Washington to come from the North and trap Cornwallis on the peninsula. Washington had enough men to do this because a large French force led by General Jean Rochambeau had joined his army.

Washington and Rochambeau moved south. When British ships tried to reach Cornwallis, French ships drove them back. In the **Battle of Yorktown,** the American and French troops bombarded Yorktown with cannon fire, turning its buildings to rubble. Cornwallis had no way out. On October 19, 1781, he surrendered his force of about 8,000.

Vocabulary
bombard: to attack with artillery

Although some fighting continued, Yorktown was the last major battle of the war. When the British prime minister, Lord North, heard the news, he gasped, "It is all over!" Indeed, he and other British leaders were soon forced to resign. Britain's new leaders began to negotiate a peace treaty, which is discussed in the next section.

Section 3 Assessment

1. Terms & Names

Explain the significance of:
- Lord Cornwallis
- guerrillas
- pacifist
- Battle of Yorktown

2. Taking Notes

Use a chart like the one below to list the geographic factors that made the British move their war effort to the South.

Physical factors, such as location	Human factors, such as who lived there

Were the human factors as helpful as the British hoped?

3. Main Ideas

a. Why did the fighting between Patriots and Loyalists in the South turn vicious?

b. What type of warfare did Francis Marion and his men employ?

c. How did Gates's errors in leadership contribute to the American loss at Camden?

4. Critical Thinking

Analyzing Causes How did each of the following help bring about the British defeat at Yorktown?

THINK ABOUT
- the location chosen by Cornwallis
- the French fleet
- the French troops under Rochambeau
- Washington's planning

ACTIVITY OPTIONS

TECHNOLOGY

MUSIC

Imagine that Congress has asked you to commemorate the Battle of Yorktown. Design a **Web page** or write a **song** celebrating the U.S. victory.

4 The Legacy of the War

TERMS & NAMES
Treaty of Paris
of 1783
republicanism
Elizabeth Freeman
Richard Allen

MAIN IDEA	WHY IT MATTERS NOW
After the war, the new nation faced issues such as a high national debt and calls for equality.	To promote liberty, some states passed laws outlawing slavery and protecting religious freedom.

ONE AMERICAN'S STORY

In 1776, 15-year-old Joseph Plumb Martin of Connecticut signed up to fight for the Americans. He stayed with the army until the war ended and rose in rank from private to sergeant. Among his experiences were the terrible winter at Valley Forge and the winning battle at Yorktown.

One of the hardest things Martin faced was leaving the army after the war was over. Many years later, he wrote about that day.

A VOICE FROM THE PAST

There was as much sorrow as joy. . . . We had lived together as a family of brothers for several years, setting aside some little family squabbles, like most other families, had shared with each other the hardships, dangers, and sufferings incident to a soldier's life; had sympathized with each other in trouble and sickness; had assisted in bearing each other's burdens. . . . And now we were to be . . . parted forever.

Joseph Plumb Martin, quoted in *The Revolutionaries*

At war's end, Martin and his country faced an uncertain future. How would the United States recover from the war? What issues would confront the new nation? Section 4 discusses those questions.

Although this painting is not of Joseph Plumb Martin himself, he may have dressed like this American soldier.

Why the Americans Won

In November 1783, the last British ships and troops left New York City, and American troops marched in. As Washington said good-bye to his officers in a New York tavern, he hugged each one. Tears ran down his face. He became so upset that he had to leave the room.

Earlier in the fall, Washington had written a farewell letter to his armies. In it, he praised them by saying that their endurance "through almost every possible suffering and discouragement for the space of eight long years, was little short of a standing miracle."

By their persistence, the Americans won independence even though they faced many obstacles. As you have read, they lacked training and experience. They were often short of supplies and weapons. By contrast, the British forces ranked among the best trained in the world. They were experienced and well-supplied professional soldiers. Yet the Americans had certain advantages that enabled them to win.

*Reading*History

A. Evaluating
What do you think was Washington's best characteristic as a leader?

1. **Better leadership.** British generals were overconfident and made poor decisions. By contrast, Washington learned from his mistakes. After early defeats, he developed the strategy of dragging out the war to wear down the British. Despite difficulties, he never gave up.
2. **Foreign aid.** Britain's rivals, especially France, helped America. Foreign loans and military aid were essential to America's victory.
3. **Knowledge of the land.** The Americans knew the land where the war took place and used that knowledge well. The British could control coastal cities but could not extend their control to the interior.
4. **Motivation.** The Americans had more reason to fight. At stake were not only their lives but also their property and their dream of liberty.

The Treaty of Paris

As the winners, the Americans won favorable terms in the **Treaty of Paris of 1783,** which ended the Revolutionary War. The treaty included the following six conditions:

1. The United States was independent.
2. Its boundaries would be the Mississippi River on the west, Canada on the north, and Spanish Florida on the south.
3. The United States would receive the right to fish off Canada's Atlantic Coast, near Newfoundland and Nova Scotia.
4. Each side would repay debts it owed the other.
5. The British would return any enslaved persons they had captured.
6. Congress would recommend that the states return any property they had seized from Loyalists.

Neither Britain nor the United States fully lived up to the treaty's terms. Americans did not repay the prewar debts they owed British merchants or return Loyalist property. For their part, the British did not return

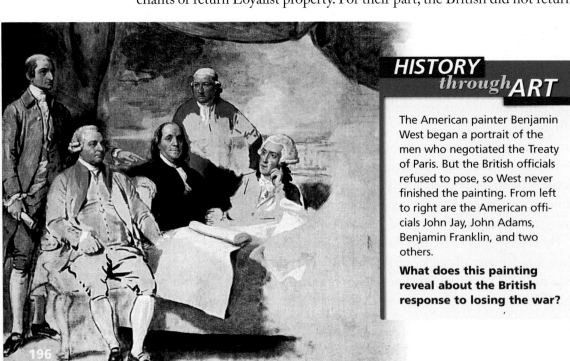

HISTORY *through*ART

The American painter Benjamin West began a portrait of the men who negotiated the Treaty of Paris. But the British officials refused to pose, so West never finished the painting. From left to right are the American officials John Jay, John Adams, Benjamin Franklin, and two others.

What does this painting reveal about the British response to losing the war?

Background
Even after
George Rogers
Clark's Western
victories, the
British stayed at
Fort Detroit.

runaway slaves. They also refused to give up military outposts in the Great Lakes area, such as Fort Detroit.

Costs of the War

No one knows exactly how many people died in the war, but eight years of fighting took a terrible toll. An estimated 25,700 Americans died in the war, and 1,400 remained missing. About 8,200 Americans were wounded. Some were left with permanent disabilities, such as amputated limbs. The British suffered about 10,000 military deaths.

Many soldiers who survived the war left the army with no money. They had received little or no pay for their service. Instead of back pay, the government gave some soldiers certificates for land in the West. Many men sold that land to get money for food and other basic needs.

Both the Congress and the states had borrowed money to finance the conflict. The war left the nation with a debt of about $27 million—a debt that would prove difficult to pay off.

*Reading*History

**B. Analyzing
Causes** Why do
you think the
Loyalists left the
United States?

The losers of the war also suffered. Thousands of Loyalists lost their property. Between 60,000 and 100,000 Loyalists left the United States during and after the war. Among them were several thousand African Americans and Native Americans, including Joseph Brant. Most of the Loyalists went to Canada. There they settled new towns and provinces. They also brought English traditions to areas that the French had settled. Even today, Canada has both French and English as official languages.

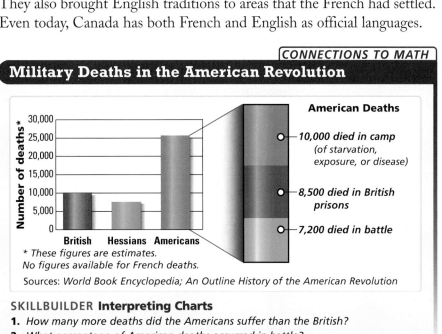

Postwar Boundaries, 1783

RUSSIAN TERRITORY
BRITISH TERRITORY
Hudson Bay
Claimed by Great Britain, Spain, and Russia
QUEBEC
Claimed by U.S and Great Britain
Claimed by U.S and Great Britain
SPANISH TERRITORY
UNITED STATES
ATLANTIC OCEAN
PACIFIC OCEAN
Claimed by U.S. and Spain
MEXICO
Gulf of Mexico
FRENCH TERRITORY
0   500 Miles
0   1,000 Kilometers

CONNECTIONS TO MATH

Military Deaths in the American Revolution

Number of deaths*
30,000
25,000
20,000
15,000
10,000
5,000
0
British   Hessians   Americans
* These figures are estimates.
No figures available for French deaths.

American Deaths

10,000 died in camp (of starvation, exposure, or disease)

8,500 died in British prisons

7,200 died in battle

Sources: *World Book Encyclopedia; An Outline History of the American Revolution*

SKILLBUILDER Interpreting Charts
1. *How many more deaths did the Americans suffer than the British?*
2. *What percentage of American deaths occurred in battle?*

Issues After the War

The American Revolution was not just a war, but a change in ideas about government. Before the war, Americans had demanded their rights as English citizens. But after declaring their independence, they replaced that goal with the idea of **republicanism.** This idea stated that instead of a king, the people would rule. The government would obtain its authority from the citizens and be responsible to them.

For this system to work, individuals would have to place the good of the country above their own interests. At first, only men were allowed to take part in governing by voting or holding public office—and not even all men. However, women could help the nation by teaching their children the virtues that benefited public life. Such virtues included honesty, duty, and the willingness to make sacrifices.

Economics *in* History

Free Enterprise

One cause of the Revolution was the colonists' resentment of British mercantilism. Parliament passed laws to discourage the colonists from developing their own manufacturing and to force them to buy British goods. During the war, British economic control weakened. British exports of woolens to the colonies dropped from £645,900 in 1774 to only £2,540 in 1776. As a result, the colonists were able to make more economic choices—for example, they could choose to manufacture wool clothing.

The end of Britain's mercantilist control allowed free enterprise to begin to develop in the United States. In a free-enterprise system, business can be conducted freely based on the choices of individuals. The government does not control the system, but only protects and regulates it.

CONNECT TO HISTORY
1. **Analyzing Causes** Why do you think the colonists were able to manufacture their own wool clothing during the war?

   See Skillbuilder Handbook, page R11.

CONNECT TO TODAY
2. **Comparing** Think about a mall where you shop. Name examples of businesses that compete with each other. Compare the methods they use to attract customers.

For more about free enterprise . . .

RESEARCH LINKS
CLASSZONE.COM

A Competition encourages businesses to improve goods and services and to keep prices down.

B Property is owned by individuals and businesses.

C The desire to make a profit motivates businesspeople.

D Individuals, not the government, decide what to buy and what to manufacture and sell.

E The government protects private property and makes sure businesses operate fairly.

THE FREE ENTERPRISE MALL

THE BARGAIN STORE

PAY LESS GET MORE STORE

As part of their liberty, Americans called for more religious freedom. Before the war, some laws discriminated against certain religions. Some states had not allowed Jews or Catholics to hold public office. After the war, states began to abolish those laws. They also ended the practice of using tax money to support churches.

Many people began to see a conflict between slavery and the ideal of liberty. Vermont outlawed slavery, and Pennsylvania passed a law to free slaves gradually. Individual African Americans also tried to end slavery. For example, **Elizabeth Freeman** sued for her freedom in a Massachusetts court and won. Her victory in 1781 and other similar cases ended slavery in that state. Freeman later described her desire for freedom.

Elizabeth Freeman fought a court case that helped end slavery in Massachusetts.

Background
Only Northern states ended slavery after the war. In the North, slavery was not as important a part of the economy as in the South.

A VOICE FROM THE PAST

Anytime while I was a slave, if one minute's freedom had been offered to me, and I had been told I must die at the end of that minute, I would have taken it—just to stand one minute on God's earth a free woman.

Elizabeth Freeman, quoted in *Notable Black American Women*

Reading **History**
C. Solving Problems How did free African Americans take on the responsibility of trying to improve their lives?

With freedom, African Americans began to form their own institutions. For example, the preacher **Richard Allen** helped start the Free African Society. That society encouraged African Americans to help each other. Allen also founded the African Methodist Episcopal Church, the first African-American church in the United States.

Perhaps the main issue facing Americans after the war was how to shape their national government. American anger over British taxes, violation of rights, and control of trade had caused the war. Now the United States needed a government that would protect citizens' rights and economic freedom. In Chapter 8, you will read how U.S. leaders worked to create such a government.

Section 4 Assessment

1. Terms & Names

Explain the significance of:
• Treaty of Paris of 1783
• republicanism
• Elizabeth Freeman
• Richard Allen

2. Taking Notes

Use a chart like the one below to classify the terms of the Treaty of Paris according to which side they favored. (Do not list terms that don't favor either side.)

Terms of the Treaty of Paris	
Favorable to America	Favorable to Britain

3. Main Ideas

a. What advantages helped the Americans win the Revolutionary War?

b. How did the end of the war affect Loyalists?

c. What were the economic costs of the war to individuals and to the government?

4. Critical Thinking

Recognizing Effects How did republicanism shape the United States after the war?

THINK ABOUT
• American ideas about government
• the roles men and women could play in public life
• religious freedom
• the antislavery movement

ACTIVITY OPTIONS

SPEECH

MATH

Look up the U.S. population in 1780. Calculate what percentage of American people died in the war. Report your findings in a **speech** or a **pie graph**.

Chapter ⑦ ASSESSMENT

TERMS & NAMES

Briefly explain the significance of each of the following.

1. George Washington
2. mercenary
3. Battles of Saratoga
4. ally
5. Marquis de Lafayette
6. John Paul Jones
7. Lord Cornwallis
8. Battle of Yorktown
9. Treaty of Paris of 1783
10. republicanism

REVIEW QUESTIONS

The Early Years of the War (pages 177–185)

1. What motives led African Americans to fight for the British? The Americans?
2. How did women help the American war effort?
3. What events led to the British defeat at Saratoga?

The War Expands (pages 184–189)

4. What foreign countries helped America? How?
5. What were conditions like at Valley Forge?

The Path to Victory (pages 190–194)

6. What two Southern ports did the British capture?
7. How did America's ally France contribute to the victory at Yorktown?

The Legacy of the War (pages 195–199)

8. For what did Washington praise his army in his farewell letter?
9. What land did the United States acquire from Britain as a result of the Treaty of Paris?
10. What three states outlawed slavery after the war?

CRITICAL THINKING

1. USING YOUR NOTES

Using your completed time line, answer the questions below.

a. What were the main events of 1776 and 1777?
b. While George Rogers Clark was capturing Kaskaskia, what was happening in the South?

2. ANALYZING LEADERSHIP

George Washington was the most beloved American leader of his time. What qualities do you think made him such a respected leader?

3. THEME: CITIZENSHIP

What Revolutionary leaders displayed civic virtue by putting the good of the nation ahead of their own interests? Explain your answer.

4. RECOGNIZING EFFECTS

How did Britain's loss in the war allow free enterprise to develop in the United States?

5. APPLYING CITIZENSHIP SKILLS

How was the writing of *The American Crisis* an example of good U.S. citizenship?

Interact *with* History

How did the sacrifices you discussed before you read the chapter compare with what Patriots really did?

VISUAL SUMMARY

The American Revolution

People and Events of the Revolution

Military		Civilian	
George Washington	commanded the Continental Army.	Haym Salomon	helped finance the war for America.
Marquis de Lafayette	fought for the Americans.	Molly Pitcher	aided soldiers by bringing them water in battle.
John Burgoyne	surrendered to the Americans at Saratoga.	Thomas Paine	wrote *The American Crisis* to inspire Americans.
John Paul Jones	won a major naval victory for America.	Benjamin Franklin	was a diplomat to France and Britain.
George Rogers Clark	helped hold the Western frontier for America.	James Forten	was captured by the British but would not betray America.
Lord Cornwallis	surrendered at Yorktown, ending the war.	Nancy Hart	defended her Georgia home against Loyalist raiders.

HISTORY SKILLS

1. INTERPRETING MAPS: Movement

Study the map, then answer the questions.

Battle of Yorktown, 1781

Basic Map Elements

a. In what state was the Battle of Yorktown fought?

b. In what battle did De Grasse's fleet defeat the British fleet led by Graves and Hood?

Interpreting the Map

c. Describe the route Washington took to reach Yorktown.

d. What British force tried to come to Cornwallis's aid?

2. INTERPRETING PRIMARY SOURCES

Read the passage below, which is a longer version of the quotation you read on page 180.

> These are the times that try men's souls. The summer soldier and the sunshine patriot will, in this crisis, shrink from the service of their country; but he that stands it *now*, deserves the love and thanks of man and woman. Tyranny, like hell, is not easily conquered; yet we have this consolation with us, that the harder the conflict, the more glorious the triumph. What we obtain too cheap, we esteem too lightly: it is dearness only that gives everything its value.
>
> **Thomas Paine,** *The American Crisis*

a. In your own words, explain who "the summer soldier and the sunshine patriot" are.

b. What does Paine promise will be the reward of a hard conflict?

ALTERNATIVE ASSESSMENT

1. INTERDISCIPLINARY ACTIVITY: Science

Creating a Poster Two of the diseases that killed American soldiers in camp were typhoid fever and smallpox. Do research to learn the following about one of these diseases: its cause, its symptoms, its treatment, and how common it is today. Use the information to create a public health poster to inform people about the disease.

2. COOPERATIVE LEARNING ACTIVITY

Performing a Talk Show In a small group, prepare to hold a talk show in which the guests discuss which side to take in the Revolutionary War. One member of your group should be the talk show host. The others should play the roles of various Americans. Each person should explain the reasons for his or her position. Perform the talk show before the class. Students might choose from the following roles:

a. the wife of an American soldier

b. an enslaved African American

c. an Iroquois chief

d. a Quaker minister

e. an employee of the British government

3. TECHNOLOGY ACTIVITY

Creating a Multimedia Presentation Use the Internet, books, and other reference materials to create a multimedia presentation on one of the major battles of the Revolution. Consider including the following:

• paintings of the conflict and photographs of artifacts

• quotations from participants and witnesses

• music of the time period

• recorded sound effects

• graphs showing battle statistics

Show your presentation to the class.

For more about Revolutionary battles . . .

INTERNET ACTIVITY
CLASSZONE.COM

4. HISTORY PORTFOLIO

Review this chapter and write a short report identifying the era it covers and describing the era's defining characteristics. Be sure to use standard grammar, spelling, sentence structure, and punctuation in your report. Add your report to your portfolio.

Additional Test Practice, pp. S1–S33

TEST PRACTICE
CLASSZONE.COM

CHAPTER 8 Confederation to Constitution

1776–1791

Delegates to the Constitutional Convention in 1787 gathered in Philadelphia. They held their meetings in the Pennsylvania State House, now known as Independence Hall.

Delegates kept the windows closed during meetings so that the proceedings would be secret.

Some of the most respected men in the nation served as delegates, including Alexander Hamilton and Benjamin Franklin.

The delegates chose George Washington, hero of the Revolutionary War, to be president of the convention.

The year is 1787, and your young country needs to reform its government. Now everyone is wondering what the new government will be like. You have been called to a convention to decide how the new government should be organized.

What Do You Think?

- What will be your main goal in creating a new government?
- How will you get the people at the convention to agree on important issues?

How do you form a government?

1777
Patriots win Battles of Saratoga.

Continental Congress passes the Articles of Confederation.

1779
Spain declares war on Britain.

1781
Articles of Confederation go into effect.

British surrender at Yorktown.

1781
Joseph II allows religious freedom for Christians in Austria.

1783
Treaty of Paris formally ends the Revolutionary War.

1786–1787
Daniel Shays leads a rebellion of Massachusetts farmers.

1787
Constitutional Convention is held in Philadelphia.

1787
Freetown, Sierra Leone, is made a home for freed slaves.

1788
U.S. Constitution is ratified.

1789
George Washington becomes the first president of the United States.

1789
French Revolution begins.

1791
Bill of Rights is ratified.

USA World 1776 — 1791

BEFORE YOU READ

Previewing the Theme

Democratic Ideals Between 1776 and 1791, the United States struggled to set up a national government. The Articles of Confederation established the first federal government. Chapter 8 explains how the weaknesses of the Articles led Americans to write a new constitution for the United States.

What Do You Know?

What do you think of when people talk about the U.S. government? Why do nations have governments? What does the U.S. government do?

THINK ABOUT

- what you've learned about the U.S. government from the news or your teachers
- what the purpose of a government is
- how the government affects your everyday life

What Do You Want to Know?

What questions do you have about the creation of the U.S. Constitution? Write those questions in your notebook before you read the chapter.

READ AND TAKE NOTES

Reading Strategy: Solving Problems When you read history, look for how people solved problems they faced in the past. Copy the chart below in your notebook. Use it to identify the methods that

Americans used to solve the problems faced by the nation after declaring its independence.

 See Skillbuilder Handbook, page R18.

Problems	Solutions
Western lands	
Postwar depression	
Representation in the new government	
Slavery	

The Confederation Era

TERMS & NAMES
Wilderness Road
republic
Articles of
    Confederation
Land Ordinance
    of 1785
Northwest Territory
Northwest
    Ordinance
Shays's Rebellion

MAIN IDEA	WHY IT MATTERS NOW
The Articles of Confederation were too weak to govern the nation after the war ended.	The weakness of the Articles of Confederation led to the writing of the U.S. Constitution.

ONE AMERICAN'S STORY

In 1775, Daniel Boone and 30 woodsmen cut a road over the Appalachian Mountains into Kentucky. They hacked through brush, chopped down trees, and bridged creeks. They labored like this for about 250 miles. Eventually, they arrived in a grassy meadow along the banks of the Kentucky River. Felix Walker, a member of Boone's party, described what they saw.

A VOICE FROM THE PAST

On entering the plain we were permitted to view a very interesting and romantic sight. A number of buffaloes . . . supposed to be between two and three hundred, made off . . . in every direction. . . . Such a sight some of us never saw before, nor perhaps ever may again.

Felix Walker, quoted in *The Life and Adventures of Daniel Boone*

Early travel to Kentucky is shown in this detail of *Daniel Boone Escorting Settlers Through the Cumberland Gap* (1851–1852) by George Caleb Bingham.

Boone was one of the earliest American settlers in Kentucky. In the late 1700s, most Americans thought of Kentucky as the wild frontier. Some, like Boone, looked at the frontier and saw a world of opportunity. Exploring and governing these lands was only one of the many challenges that faced the new government of the United States.

Moving West

The trail into Kentucky that Daniel Boone helped build was called the **Wilderness Road.** This road was not easy to travel. It was too narrow for carts or wagons, but it became the main road into Kentucky. The settlers came on foot or on horseback. Settlers were drawn to Kentucky's rich river valleys, where few Native Americans lived. But some Native Americans, such as the Shawnee, did live, hunt, and fish in the area.

Tensions between Native Americans and settlers led to violent confrontations. But the settlers did not stop coming. By the early 1790s, about 100,000 Americans lived there. While settlers headed into the Western territories, the people in the East began to create new state governments.

New State Governments

Once the American colonies declared independence, each of the states set out to create its own government. The framers, or creators, of the state constitutions did not want to destroy the political systems that they had had as colonies. They simply wanted to make those systems more democratic. Some states experimented with creating separate branches of government, giving different powers to different branches. By creating separate branches, Americans hoped to prevent the government from becoming too powerful.

Some states included a bill of rights in their constitutions as a way to keep the government under control. The idea of a bill of rights came from the English Bill of Rights of 1689. This was a list of rights that the government guaranteed to English citizens.

Although not all the states had a bill of rights, all of them did have a republican form of government. In a **republic,** the people choose representatives to govern them.

Background Two states, Connecticut and Rhode Island, kept their old colonial charters as their constitutions. The other 11 states wrote new constitutions.

The Articles of Confederation

While the states were setting up their governments, Americans also discussed the form of their national government. During the Revolutionary War, Americans realized that they needed to unite to win the war against Britain. As Silas Deane, a diplomat from Connecticut, wrote, "United we stand, divided we fall."

In 1776, the Continental Congress began to develop a plan for a national government. Congress agreed that the government should be a republic. But the delegates disagreed about whether each state should have one vote or voting should be based on population. They also disagreed about whether the national government or the individual states should control the lands west of the Appalachians.

The Continental Congress eventually arrived at a final plan, called the **Articles of Confederation.** In the Articles, the national government had few powers, because many Americans were afraid that a strong government would lead to tyranny, or oppressive rule. The national government was run by a Confederation Congress. Each state had only one vote in the Congress. The national government had the power to wage war, make peace, sign treaties, and issue money.

But the Articles left most important powers to the states. These powers included the authority to set taxes and enforce national laws. The Articles proposed to leave the states in control of the lands west of the Appalachian Mountains.

"United we stand, divided we fall."
Silas Deane

*Reading*History

A. Reading a Map Look at the map on page 207 to see which states claimed territories in the West.

The Continental Congress passed the Articles of Confederation in November 1777. It then sent the Articles to the states for ratification, or approval. By July 1778, eight states had ratified the Articles. But some of the small states that did not have Western land claims refused to sign.

Reading History

B. Finding Main Ideas Why did the states without Western land claims want the other states to give up their claims?

These states felt that unless the Western lands were placed under the control of the national government, they would be at a disadvantage. The states with Western lands could sell them to pay off debts left from the Revolution. But states without lands would have difficulty paying off the high war debts.

Over the next three years, all the states gave up their claims to Western lands. This led the small states to ratify the Articles. In 1781, Maryland became the 13th state to accept the Articles. As a result, the United States finally had an official government.

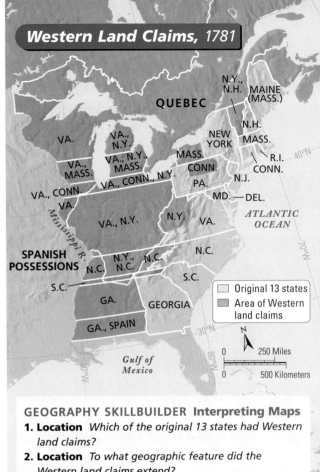

Western Land Claims, 1781

Original 13 states
Area of Western land claims

0   250 Miles
0   500 Kilometers

GEOGRAPHY SKILLBUILDER Interpreting Maps
1. **Location** Which of the original 13 states had Western land claims?
2. **Location** To what geographic feature did the Western land claims extend?

The Northwest Ordinance

One of the most important questions that the Confederation Congress faced was what to do with the Western lands that it now controlled. Congress passed important laws on how to divide and govern these lands—the Land Ordinance of 1785 and the Northwest Ordinance (1787). (See Geography in History on pages 210–211.)

The **Land Ordinance of 1785** called for surveyors to stake out six-mile-square plots, called townships, in the Western lands. These lands later became known as the **Northwest Territory.** The Northwest Territory included land that formed the states of Ohio, Indiana, Michigan, Illinois, and Wisconsin and part of Minnesota.

The **Northwest Ordinance** (1787) described how the Northwest Territory was to be governed. As the territory grew in population, it would gain rights to self-government. When there were 5,000 free males in an area, men who owned at least 50 acres of land could elect an assembly. When there were 60,000 people, they could apply to become a new state.

Background According to the Northwest Ordinance, Native Americans were to be treated fairly, and their lands were not to be taken from them.

The Northwest Ordinance also set conditions for settlement in the Northwest Territory and outlined the settlers' rights. Slavery was outlawed, and the rivers were to be open to navigation by all. Freedom of religion and trial by jury were guaranteed.

The Northwest Ordinance was important because it set a pattern for the orderly growth of the United States. As the nation grew, it followed this pattern in territories added after the Northwest Territory.

Weaknesses of the Articles

Aside from its handling of land issues, however, the Confederation Congress had few successes. By the end of the Revolutionary War, the United States faced serious problems, and the Confederation Congress did not have enough power to solve them.

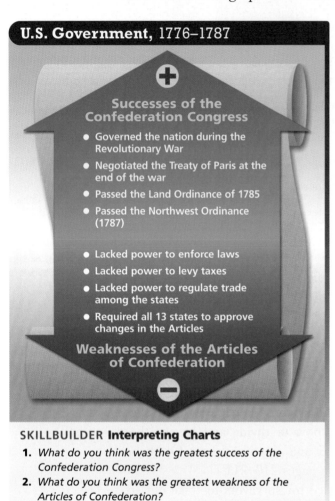

U.S. Government, 1776–1787

➕

Successes of the Confederation Congress

- Governed the nation during the Revolutionary War
- Negotiated the Treaty of Paris at the end of the war
- Passed the Land Ordinance of 1785
- Passed the Northwest Ordinance (1787)

- Lacked power to enforce laws
- Lacked power to levy taxes
- Lacked power to regulate trade among the states
- Required all 13 states to approve changes in the Articles

Weaknesses of the Articles of Confederation

➖

SKILLBUILDER Interpreting Charts

1. *What do you think was the greatest success of the Confederation Congress?*
2. *What do you think was the greatest weakness of the Articles of Confederation?*

Debt was a critical problem for the government. Congress had borrowed large sums to pay for the Revolutionary War. Much of that money was owed to soldiers of its own army. Upset at not being paid, several hundred soldiers surrounded the Pennsylvania State House where Congress was meeting in June 1783. The soldiers threatened the legislators, thrusting their bayonets through the windows. The delegates were forced to flee the city. The event was a clear sign of Congress's weakness.

Even if Congress wanted to pay the soldiers, it did not have the power to levy taxes. The national government depended on the states to send money to Congress. But the states sent very little money.

Congress was not alone in facing economic crises. People throughout the nation faced hard times. In Massachusetts, the economy was so bad that people rose up in arms against the government.

Reading **History**

C. Analyzing Causes How did debt cause problems for the U.S. government under the Articles of Confederation?

Shays's Rebellion

In the mid-1780s, Massachusetts faced economic problems, as did other states. People had little money, but the state continued to levy high taxes. The average family owed $200 in taxes per year—more money than most farmers made. Many Massachusetts farmers fell deeply into debt. Debt laws at the time were strict. Anyone who could not repay his debts would have his property auctioned off. If the auction didn't raise enough money to settle the debts, the debtor could be put in jail. In western Massachusetts, many jails were packed with debtors.

Farmers asked the Massachusetts legislature to provide debt relief. But the legislature refused—and the farmers rebelled. One of the leaders of the rebellion was a Revolutionary War veteran named Daniel Shays. He commanded a group of about 1,500 men.

In January 1787, Shays and his men marched on a federal arsenal, a place to store weapons. The arsenal was defended by 900 soldiers from the state militia. The militia quickly defeated Shays's men. But even though the militia put down **Shays's Rebellion,** as the uprising came to be known, the farmers won the sympathy of many people. America's leaders realized that an armed uprising of common farmers spelled danger for the nation.

Some leaders hoped that the nation's ills could be solved by strengthening the national government. In the next section, you'll read how Americans held a convention to change the Articles of Confederation.

Background
In 1788, Daniel Shays was pardoned for his actions.

Shays's rebels take over a Massachusetts courthouse. A stone marker rests on the spot of the rebellion.

Section 1 Assessment

1. Terms & Names

Explain the significance of:
- Wilderness Road
- republic
- Articles of Confederation
- Land Ordinance of 1785
- Northwest Territory
- Northwest Ordinance
- Shays's Rebellion

2. Taking Notes

Use a diagram like the one below to list some of the challenges Americans faced in shaping a new government.

Challenges

Which challenge do you think was the toughest? Why?

3. Main Ideas

a. What issues affected the Western territories between 1775 and 1787?

b. What were three successes of the Continental Congress?

c. What were the strengths and weaknesses of the Articles of Confederation?

4. Critical Thinking

Forming and Supporting Opinions Which side would you have supported during Shays's Rebellion—the farmers or the officials who called out the militia? Why?

THINK ABOUT
- the farmers' problems
- the farmers' march on the arsenal
- the job of the government

ACTIVITY OPTIONS

CIVICS

GEOGRAPHY

Write an **opinion article** about how the United States should govern the Western territories or draw a **map** showing how you would have divided the lands.

The Northwest Territory

The Northwest Territory was officially known as "the Territory Northwest of the River Ohio." In the mid-1780s, Congress decided to sell the land in the territory to settlers. The sale of land solved two problems. First, it provided cash for the government. Second, it increased American control over the land.

The Land Ordinance of 1785 outlined how the land in the Northwest Territory would be divided. Congress split the land into grids with clearly defined boundaries. It created townships that could be divided into sections, as shown on the map below. Each township was six miles by six miles. This was an improvement over earlier methods of setting boundaries. Previously, people had used rocks, trees, or other landmarks to set boundaries. There had been constant fights over disputed claims.

The Land Ordinance of 1785

TOWNSHIP, 1785

36	30	24	18	12	6
35	29	23	17	11	5
34	28	22	16	10	4
33	27	21	15	9	3
32	26	20	14	8	2
31	25	19	13	7	1

Each township contained 36 sections. Each section was one square mile.

ARTIFACT FILE

The Theodolite The theodolite is a surveying tool. It consists of a telescope that can be moved from side to side and up and down. A theodolite measures angles and determines alignment. These functions are necessary for land surveyors to establish accurate boundaries for land claims.

Township Map Congress reserved several plots (outlined on map) for special purposes. A few were set aside for later sale to raise money for the government. One plot was reserved to support a local school.

1. The first things settlers needed were food and shelter. Cutting trees provided fields for crops and wood for log cabins. The first crop most farmers planted was corn. Even if the land was not fully cleared of trees, farmers planted corn between the stumps.

2. A shortage of labor meant that a farmer working alone was doing well if he cleared several acres a year. As a result, few farms were completely fenced in, and forest covered most of the property. Hogs were allowed to find food in the woods. Farmers collected apples from trees and used sap to make syrup.

3. Over time, families planted fruits and vegetables. Cattle raising also became more common. Beef cattle supplied families with meat. Dairy cattle provided milk. Families could sell extra fruits, vegetables, and dairy products, such as butter and cheese.

CONNECT TO GEOGRAPHY

1. **Region** What was the land in the Northwest Territory like before Americans settled there?

2. **Human-Environment Interaction** How did American settlers affect the landscape in the territory?

G See Geography Handbook, pages 4–5.

CONNECT TO HISTORY

3. **Making Inferences** Why did so many people buy land in the new territory?

On-Line Field Trip

The Ohio Historical Society is located in Columbus, Ohio. It maintains a Web site called Ohio History Central that includes information on the Ohio portion of the Northwest Territory.

For more about the Northwest Territory . . .

RESEARCH LINKS
CLASSZONE.COM

Confederation to Constitution **211**

2 Creating the Constitution

TERMS & NAMES
Constitutional Convention
James Madison
Virginia Plan
New Jersey Plan
Great Compromise
Three-Fifths Compromise

MAIN IDEA	WHY IT MATTERS NOW
The states sent delegates to a convention to solve the problems of the Articles of Confederation.	The Constitutional Convention formed the plan of government that the United States still has today.

ONE AMERICAN'S STORY

On the afternoon of May 15, 1787, Edmund Randolph, the young governor of Virginia, arrived in Philadelphia for the Constitutional Convention. The young nation faced violence and lawlessness, as Shays's Rebellion had shown. And now delegates from throughout the states were coming to Philadelphia to discuss reforming the government.

Randolph knew the serious task he and the other delegates were about to undertake. Early in the convention, Randolph rose to speak. He looked squarely at the delegates and reminded them of their grave responsibility.

A VOICE FROM THE PAST

Let us not be afraid to view with a steady eye the [dangers] with which we are surrounded. . . . Are we not on the eve of [a civil] war, which is only to be prevented by the hopes from this convention?

Edmund Randolph, quoted in *Edmund Randolph: A Biography*

Edmund Randolph (left) and the other delegates gathered in the Pennsylvania State House (above) to discuss creating a new government for the United States.

Over the next four months, the delegates debated how best to keep the United States from falling apart. In this section, you will read about the Convention of 1787 and the creation of the U.S. Constitution.

A Constitutional Convention Is Called

In 1786, a series of events began that would eventually lead to a new form of government for the United States. In September of that year, delegates from five states met in Annapolis, Maryland, to discuss ways to promote trade among their states. At the time, most states placed high taxes on goods from other states. The delegates believed that creating national trade laws would help the economies of all the states.

Making such changes required amending the Articles of Confederation, because the national government had been granted no power to regulate trade among the states. The Annapolis delegates, led by Alexander Hamilton of New York, called for the states to send representatives to

Philadelphia the following May to discuss such changes.

At first, many Americans doubted that the national government needed strengthening. But news of Shays's Rebellion in late 1786 and early 1787 quickly changed many people's minds. Fearing that rebellion might spread, 12 states sent delegates to the meeting in Philadelphia in the summer of 1787. Only Rhode Island refused to participate.

Background
Rhode Island did not send delegates because it feared that a strong national government would force people to repay the war debts on difficult terms.

The Convention's Delegates

The 55 delegates to the **Constitutional Convention,** as the Philadelphia meeting became known, were a very impressive group. About half were lawyers. Others were planters, merchants, and doctors. Three-fourths of them had been representatives in the Continental Congress. Many had been members of their state legislatures and had helped write their state constitutions. Along with other leaders of the time, these delegates are called the Founders, or Founding Fathers, of the United States.

America's most famous men were at the Constitutional Convention. George Washington, the hero of the Revolution, came out of retirement for the meeting. Benjamin Franklin, the famous scientist and statesman, lent his wit and wisdom to the convention. One of the ablest delegates was **James Madison.** Madison had read more than a hundred books on government in preparation for the meeting. When Thomas Jefferson, serving as ambassador to France, read the list of delegates, he wrote, "It is really an assembly of demigods."

*Reading*History
A. Evaluating
How well do the characteristics of the Founders serve as models of civic virtue?

Not everyone was at the Constitutional Convention. Thomas Jefferson and John Adams were overseas at their diplomatic posts. But they wrote home to encourage the delegates. Others had a less positive outlook on the convention. For example, Patrick Henry, who had been elected as a delegate from Virginia, refused to attend. He said he "smelled a rat in Philadelphia, tending toward monarchy."

Also, the convention did not reflect the diverse U.S. population of the 1780s. There were no Native Americans, African Americans, or women among the delegates. The nation's early leaders did not consider these groups of people to be citizens and did not invite any of them to attend. However, the framework of government the Founders established is the very one that would eventually provide full rights and responsibilities to all Americans.

The Delegates Assemble

Most of the delegates arrived at the Constitutional Convention without a clear idea of what to expect. Some thought they would only draft

America's HERITAGE

INDEPENDENCE HALL

The Pennsylvania State House, where the Constitutional Convention took place, is now called Independence Hall. It is protected as part of a national park in Philadelphia.

The State House itself was the site where George Washington received his commission to lead the Continental Army and where the Declaration of Independence was signed. The Liberty Bell is nearby. Many visitors come to Philadelphia to stand in the building where much of America's early history as a nation was made.

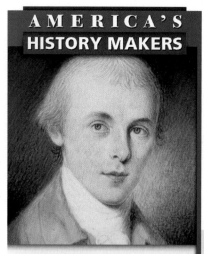

JAMES MADISON
1751–1836

James Madison was a short, soft-spoken man, but he may have made the greatest contribution of any of the Founders at the Constitutional Convention. He took thorough notes of the convention's proceedings. His notes are the most detailed picture we have of the debates and drama of the convention.

But Madison did not just observe the convention. He was perhaps the most important participant. One of the other delegates called him "the best informed Man of any point in debate." Madison was so important that he earned the title "Father of the Constitution."

How did Madison contribute to the Constitutional Convention?

amendments to the Articles of Confederation. Others thought they would design an entirely new plan for the government. But they all agreed that the government should protect people's rights.

Back in 1776, many Americans thought that government was the main threat to people's rights. But by 1787, many realized that the people often came into conflict and needed a government that could maintain order. As a result, the government had to be strong enough to protect people's rights but not too strong to be controlled. Madison later wrote about this problem.

A VOICE FROM THE PAST

If men were angels, no government would be necessary. If angels were to govern men, neither external nor internal controls on government would be necessary. In framing a government which is to be administered by men over men, the great difficulty lies in this: you must first enable the government to control the governed; and in the next place oblige it [the government] to control itself.

James Madison, *The Federalist* "Number 51"

*Reading*History
B. Using Primary Sources
According to Madison, what is the central problem in framing a government?

This was the challenge that faced the delegates: how to set up a strong but limited federal government. By May 25, 1787, at least two delegates from each of seven states had arrived in Philadelphia. With 29 delegates in attendance, the convention was officially under way.

The Convention Begins

The first order of business was to elect a president for the convention. Robert Morris of Pennsylvania nominated George Washington. No American was more respected or admired than Washington. Every delegate voted for him. Washington's quiet and dignified leadership set a solemn and serious tone for the convention.

At their next meeting, the delegates decided on the rules for the convention. They wanted to be able to consider all ideas and to be able to change sides in any debate. They did not want to be pressured by the politics of the day. For these reasons, they decided that their discussions would remain secret. To ensure privacy, the windows in their meeting room were kept shut even though it was summer. Guards were posted outside the door. Whenever the door was opened, the delegates stopped talking. With the secrecy rule approved, they got down to business.

*Reading*History
C. Making Decisions Do you agree with the Founders' decision to keep the convention secret? Why or why not?

The Virginia Plan

On May 29, the delegates began the real work of designing a new national government. Presiding over the convention, George Washington

The delegates at the Constitutional Convention debated the Constitution intensely.

recognized Edmund Randolph as the first speaker. Randolph offered a plan for a whole new government. The plan became known as the **Virginia Plan.** Madison, Randolph, and the other Virginia delegates had drawn up the plan while they waited for the convention to open.

The Virginia Plan proposed a government that would have three branches. The first branch of government was the legislature, which made the laws. The second branch was the executive, which enforced the laws. The third branch was the judiciary, which interpreted the laws.

"If men were angels, no government would be necessary."
James Madison

*Reading*History
D. Summarizing What was the Virginia Plan?

The Virginia Plan proposed a legislature with two houses. In both houses, the number of representatives from each state would be based on the state's population or its wealth. The legislature would have the power to levy taxes, regulate commerce, and make laws "in all cases where the separate states are incompetent [unable]."

The Virginia Plan led to weeks of debate. Because they had larger populations, larger states supported the plan. It would give them greater representation in the legislature. The smaller states opposed this plan. They worried that the larger states would end up ruling the others. Delaware delegate John Dickinson voiced the concerns of the small states.

A VOICE FROM THE PAST

Some of the members from the small states wish for two branches in the general legislature and are friends to a good [strong] national government; but we would sooner submit [give in] to a foreign power than submit to be deprived, in both branches of the legislature, of an equal suffrage [vote], and thereby be thrown under the domination of the larger states.

John Dickinson, quoted in *Mr. Madison's Constitution*

The Great Compromise

In response to the Virginia Plan, New Jersey delegate William Paterson presented an alternative on June 15. The **New Jersey Plan** called for a legislature with only one house. In it, each state would have one vote. In providing equal representation to each state, the New Jersey Plan was similar to the Articles of Confederation.

Even though the New Jersey Plan gave the legislature the power to regulate trade and to raise money by taxing foreign goods, it did not offer the broad powers proposed by the Virginia Plan. The delegates

The Great Compromise

VIRGINIA PLAN

- The legislative branch would have two houses.
- Both houses in the legislature would assign representatives according to state population or wealth.

NEW JERSEY PLAN

- The legislature would have one house.
- Each state would have one vote in the legislature.

THE GREAT COMPROMISE

- The Senate would give each state equal representation.

The legislature would have two houses.

- The House of Representatives would have representation according to state population.

SKILLBUILDER Interpreting Charts

1. *Which plan appealed more to the small states?*
2. *Did the Great Compromise include more of what the large states wanted or more of what the small states wanted?*

voted on these two plans on June 19. The Virginia Plan won and became the framework for drafting the Constitution.

During the rest of June, the delegates argued over representation in the legislature. Emotions ran high as the delegates struggled for a solution. In desperation, the delegates selected a committee to work out a compromise in early July. The committee offered the **Great Compromise**. (Some people also refer to it as the Connecticut Compromise.)

To satisfy the smaller states, each state would have an equal number of votes in the Senate. To satisfy the larger states, the committee set representation in the House of Representatives according to state populations. More than a week of arguing followed the introduction of the plan, but on July 16, 1787, the convention passed it.

Background
Roger Sherman of Connecticut is widely credited with proposing the Great Compromise.

Slavery and the Constitution

Because representation in the House of Representatives would be based on the population of each state, the delegates had to decide who would be counted in that population. The Southern states had many more slaves than the Northern states. Southerners wanted the slaves to be counted as part of the general population for representation but not for taxation. Northerners argued that slaves were not citizens and should not be counted for representation but should be counted for taxation.

On this issue, the delegates reached another compromise, known as the **Three-Fifths Compromise**. Under this compromise, three-fifths of the slave population would be counted when setting direct taxes on the states. This three-fifths ratio also would be used to determine representation in the legislature.

The delegates had another heated debate about the slave trade. Slavery had already been outlawed in several Northern states. All of the Northern states and several of the Southern states had banned the

ReadingHistory
E. Forming and Supporting Opinions Did the delegates do the right thing in agreeing to the Three-Fifths Compromise? Explain.

importation of slaves. Many Northerners wanted to see this ban extended to the rest of the nation. But Southern slaveholders strongly disagreed. The delegates from South Carolina and Georgia stated that they would never accept any plan "unless their right to import slaves be untouched." Again, the delegates settled on a compromise. On August 29, they agreed that Congress could not ban the slave trade until 1808.

Regulating Trade

Aside from delaying any ban on the slave trade, the Constitution placed few limits on Congress's power "to regulate commerce with foreign nations, and among the several states, and with the Indian tribes." Most delegates were glad that Congress would regulate—and even promote—commerce. After all, commercial problems were the main cause of the Annapolis Convention in 1786. Southerners, however, succeeded in banning Congress from taxing exports because Southern economies depended on exports. The commerce clause also showed the shadowy status that Native Americans had under the Constitution. They were neither foreign nations nor part of the separate states.

The Constitutional Convention continued to meet into September. On Saturday, September 15, 1787, the delegates voted their support for the Constitution in its final form. On Sunday, it was written out on four sheets of thick parchment. On Monday, all but three delegates signed the Constitution. It was then sent, with a letter signed by George Washington, to the Confederation Congress, which sent it to the states for ratification, or approval. In the next section, you will read about the debate over ratification.

Now and **then**

PRESERVING THE CONSTITUTION

The National Archives is responsible for preserving the 200-year-old sheets of parchment on which the original Constitution was first written.

The Archives stores the document in an airtight glass case enclosed in a 55-ton vault of steel and concrete. Every few years, scientists examine the pages with the latest technology. For the last examination in 1995, they used fiber-optic light sources and computer-guided electronic cameras designed for space exploration.

Section 2 Assessment

1. Terms & Names

Explain the significance of:
- Constitutional Convention
- James Madison
- Virginia Plan
- New Jersey Plan
- Great Compromise
- Three-Fifths Compromise

2. Taking Notes

Use a chart like the one below to take notes on the contributions made by the leading delegates at the Constitutional Convention.

Delegate	Contribution

3. Main Ideas

a. What was the relationship between the Annapolis Convention and the Constitutional Convention?

b. What is the significance of the date 1787?

c. How did the Constitutional Convention reach a compromise on the issue of slavery?

4. Critical Thinking

Analyzing Points of View How did the delegates at the convention differ on the issue of representation in the new government?

THINK ABOUT
- the large states and the small states
- the Virginia Plan
- the New Jersey Plan
- the Great Compromise

ACTIVITY OPTIONS

TECHNOLOGY

ART

Think about the Three-Fifths Compromise. Make an **audio recording** of a speech or draw a **political cartoon** that expresses your views on the issue.

3 Ratifying the Constitution

TERMS & NAMES
federalism
Federalists
Antifederalists
The Federalist papers
George Mason
Bill of Rights

MAIN IDEA

Americans across the nation debated whether the Constitution would produce the best government.

WHY IT MATTERS NOW

American liberties today are protected by the U.S. Constitution, including the Bill of Rights.

ONE AMERICAN'S STORY

For a week in early January 1788, a church in Hartford, Connecticut, was filled to capacity. Inside, 168 delegates were meeting to decide whether their state should ratify the U.S. Constitution. Samuel Huntington, Connecticut's governor, addressed the assembly.

Samuel Huntington

A VOICE FROM THE PAST

This is a new event in the history of mankind. Heretofore, most governments have been formed by tyrants and imposed on mankind by force. Never before did a people, in time of peace and tranquillity, meet together by their representatives and, with calm deliberation, frame for themselves a system of government.

Samuel Huntington, quoted in *Original Meanings*

The governor supported the new Constitution and wanted to see it ratified. Not everyone agreed with him. In this section, you will learn about the debates that led to the ratification of the Constitution.

Federalists and Antifederalists

By the time the convention in Connecticut opened, Americans had already been debating the new Constitution for months. The document had been printed in newspapers and handed out in pamphlets across the United States. The framers of the Constitution knew that the document would cause controversy. They immediately began to campaign for ratification, or approval, of the Constitution.

The framers suspected that people might be afraid the Constitution would take too much power away from the states. To address this fear, the framers explained that the Constitution was based on federalism. **Federalism** is a system of government in which power is shared between the central (or federal) government and the states. Linking themselves to the idea of federalism, the people who supported the Constitution took the name **Federalists.**

People who opposed the Constitution were called **Antifederalists.** They thought the Constitution took too much power away from the

Vocabulary
aristocracy:
a group or class considered superior to others

states and did not guarantee rights for the people. Some were afraid that a strong president might be declared king. Others thought the Senate might turn into a powerful aristocracy. In either case, the liberties won at great cost during the Revolution might be lost.

Antifederalists published their views about the Constitution in newspapers and pamphlets. They used logical arguments to convince people to oppose the Constitution. But they also tried to stir people's emotions by charging that it would destroy American liberties. As one Antifederalist wrote, "After so recent a triumph over British despots [oppressive rulers], . . . it is truly astonishing that a set of men among ourselves should have had the effrontery [nerve] to attempt the destruction of our liberties."

The Federalist Papers

The Federalists did not sit still while the Antifederalists attacked the Constitution. They wrote essays to answer the Antifederalists' attacks. The best known of the Federalist essays are ***The Federalist* papers.** These essays first appeared as letters in New York newspapers. They were later published together in a book called *The Federalist*.

Three well-known politicians wrote *The Federalist* papers—James Madison, Alexander Hamilton, and John Jay, the secretary of foreign affairs for the Confederation Congress. Like the Antifederalists, the Federalists appealed to reason and emotion. In *The Federalist* papers, Hamilton described why people should support ratification.

Reading **History**
A. Making Inferences What does Hamilton think will happen if the Constitution is not ratified?

A VOICE FROM THE PAST

Yes, my countrymen, . . . I am clearly of opinion it is in your interest to adopt it [the Constitution]. I am convinced that this is the safest course for your liberty, your dignity, and your happiness.

Alexander Hamilton, *The Federalist* "Number 1"

Federalists and Antifederalists

FEDERALISTS	ANTIFEDERALISTS
• Supported removing some powers from the states and giving more powers to the national government	• Wanted important political powers to remain with the states
• Favored dividing powers among different branches of government	• Wanted the legislative branch to have more power than the executive
• Proposed a single person to lead the executive branch	• Feared that a strong executive might become a king or tyrant
	• Believed a bill of rights needed to be added to the Constitution to protect people's rights

SKILLBUILDER Interpreting Charts
1. *Which group wanted a stronger central government?*
2. *If you had been alive in 1787, would you have been a Federalist or an Antifederalist?*

John Jay

George Mason

Supporters of the Constitution turned out in parades like this one in New York in 1788. The "Ship of State" float has Alexander Hamilton's name on it to celebrate his role in creating the Constitution.

What does the picture indicate about the importance of the Constitution in people's lives?

HAMILTON HAMI

The Federalists had an important advantage over the Antifederalists. Most of the newspapers supported the Constitution, giving the Federalists more publicity than the Antifederalists. Even so, there was strong opposition to ratification in Massachusetts, North Carolina, Rhode Island, New York, and Virginia. If some of these states failed to ratify the Constitution, the United States might not survive.

The Battle for Ratification

The first four state conventions to ratify the Constitution were held in December 1787. It was a good month for the Federalists. Delaware, New Jersey, and Pennsylvania voted for ratification. In January 1788, Georgia and Connecticut ratified the Constitution. Massachusetts joined these states in early February.

By late June, nine states had voted to ratify the Constitution. That meant that the document was now officially ratified. But New York and Virginia had not yet cast their votes. There were many powerful Antifederalists in both of those states. Without Virginia, the new government would lack the support of the largest state. Without New York, the nation would be separated into two parts geographically.

Virginia's convention opened the first week in June. The patriot Patrick Henry fought against ratification. **George Mason,** perhaps the most influential Virginian aside from Washington, also was opposed to it. Mason had been a delegate to the Constitutional Convention in Philadelphia, but he had refused to sign the final document. Both Henry and Mason would not consider voting for the Constitution until a bill of rights was added. A bill of rights is a set of rules that defines people's rights.

James Madison was also at Virginia's convention. He suggested that Virginia follow Massachusetts's lead and ratify the Constitution, and he recommended the addition of a bill of rights. With the addition of a bill of rights likely, Virginia ratified the Constitution at the end of June.

*Reading***History**
B. Drawing Conclusions How did the lack of a bill of rights endanger the Constitution?

The news of Virginia's vote arrived while the New York convention was in debate. The Antifederalists had outnumbered the Federalists when the convention had begun. But with the news of Virginia's ratification, New Yorkers decided to join the Union. New York also called for a bill of rights.

It was another year before North Carolina ratified the Constitution. In 1790, Rhode Island became the last state to ratify it. By then, the new Congress had already written a bill of rights and submitted it to the states for approval.

The Bill of Rights

Background
The seven states that asked for a bill of rights were Massachusetts, South Carolina, New Hampshire, Virginia, New York, North Carolina, and Rhode Island.

At the same time that seven of the states ratified the Constitution, they asked that it be amended to include a bill of rights. Supporters of a bill of rights hoped that it would set forth the rights of all Americans. They believed it was needed to protect people against the power of the national government.

Madison, who was elected to the new Congress in the winter of 1789, took up the cause. He proposed a set of changes to the Constitution. Congress edited Madison's list and proposed placing the amendments at the end of the Constitution in a separate section.

The amendments went to the states for ratification. As with the Constitution, three-quarters of the states had to ratify the amendments for them to take effect. With Virginia's vote in 1791, ten of the amendments were ratified and became law. These ten amendments to the U.S. Constitution became known as the **Bill of Rights.** (See the Constitution Handbook, pages 250–252.)

The passage of the Bill of Rights was one of the first acts of the new government. In the next chapter, you will read about other issues that faced the new government.

America's HERITAGE

RELIGIOUS FREEDOM

Freedom of religion was an important part of the First Amendment. Jefferson and Madison believed that government enforcement of religious laws was the source of much social conflict. They supported freedom of religion as a way to prevent such conflict.

Even before Madison wrote the Bill of Rights, he worked to ensure religious liberty in Virginia. In 1786, he helped pass the Virginia Statute for Religious Freedom, originally written by Jefferson in 1777.

Section 3 Assessment

1. Terms & Names

Explain the significance of:
- federalism
- Federalists
- Antifederalists
- *The Federalist* papers
- George Mason
- Bill of Rights

2. Taking Notes

Use a diagram like the one below to compare and contrast the Federalists and the Antifederalists.

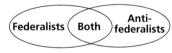

Which group do you think made the stronger argument about ratification? Why?

3. Main Ideas

a. What were Patrick Henry's and George Mason's views on ratification?

b. How did the Federalists and the Antifederalists try to convince people to take their sides in the debate over the Constitution?

c. What was the significance of the Bill of Rights?

4. Critical Thinking

Recognizing Propaganda Reread the quotation by Hamilton on page 219. Is it an example of propaganda? Why or why not?

THINK ABOUT
- Hamilton's use of the word *countrymen*
- Hamilton's reference to liberty, dignity, and happiness

ACTIVITY OPTIONS

SPEECH

LANGUAGE ARTS

Review the major arguments for and against ratification of the Constitution. Hold a **press conference** or write a **news report** on the ratification debate.

The Federalist "Number 51"

Setting the Stage James Madison wrote 29 essays in *The Federalist* papers to argue in favor of ratifying the Constitution. In *The Federalist* "Number 51," Madison explains how the government set up by the Constitution will protect the rights of the people by weakening the power of any interest, or group, to dominate the government. **See Primary Source Explorer**

It is of great importance in a republic not only to guard the society against the oppression of its rulers, but to guard one part of the society against the injustice of the other part. Different interests necessarily exist in different classes of citizens. If a majority be united by a common interest, the rights of the minority will be insecure. There are but two methods of providing against this evil: the one by creating a will in the community independent of the majority—that is, of the society itself; the other, by **comprehending**[1] in the society so many separate descriptions of citizens as will render an unjust combination of a majority of the whole very improbable, if not **impracticable.**[2] . . .

Whilst[3] all authority in it will be derived from and dependent on the society, the society itself will be broken into so many parts, interests and classes of citizens, that the rights of individuals, or of the minority, will be in little danger from interested combinations of the majority. In a free government the security for civil rights must be the same as that for religious rights. It consists in the one case in the multiplicity of interests, and in the other in the **multiplicity of sects.**[4] . . .

In the extended republic of the United States, and among the great variety of interests, parties, and sects which it embraces, a **coalition**[5] of a majority of the whole society could seldom take place on any other principles than those of justice and the general good. . . .

It is no less certain than it is important . . . that the larger the society, provided it lie within a practicable sphere, the more duly capable it will be of self-government. And happily for the republican cause, the practicable sphere may be carried to a very great extent by a **judicious modification**[6] and mixture of the *federal principle*.

—*James Madison*

1. **comprehending:** understanding.
2. **impracticable:** not practical or realistic.
3. **whilst:** while.
4. **multiplicity of sects:** large number of groups.
5. **coalition:** alliance of groups.
6. **judicious modification:** careful change.

Objections to the Constitution

Setting the Stage George Mason was one of the leading Antifederalists. In "Objections to the Constitution of Government Formed by the Convention," he listed his reasons for opposing ratification. Above all, he feared that the Constitution created a government that would destroy democracy in the young nation. **See Primary Source Explorer** 💿

There is no Declaration of Rights; and the Laws of the general Government being **paramount**[1] to the Laws and Constitutions of the several States, the Declaration of Rights in the separate States are no Security. Nor are the people secured even in the Enjoyment of the Benefits of the common-Law. . . .

In the House of Representatives, there is not the Substance, but the Shadow only of Representation; which can never produce proper Information in the Legislature, or inspire Confidence in the People; the Laws will therefore be generally made by Men little concern'd in, and **unacquainted**[2] with their Effects and Consequences.

The Senate have the Power of altering all Money-Bills, and of originating Appropriations of Money and the **Sallerys**[3] of the Officers of their own Appointment in **Conjunction**[4] with the President of the United States; altho' they are not the Representatives of the People, or **amenable**[5] to them. . . .

The President of the United States has the unrestrained Power of granting Pardon for Treason; which may be sometimes exercised to screen from Punishment those whom he had secretly **instigated**[6] to commit the Crime, and thereby prevent a Discovery of his own Guilt.

This Government will **commence**[7] in a moderate **Aristocracy**;[8] it is at present impossible to foresee whether it will, in [its] Operation, produce a **Monarchy**,[9] or a corrupt oppressive Aristocracy; it will most probably vibrate some Years between the two, and then terminate in the one or the other.

—*George Mason*

1. **paramount:** most important.
2. **unacquainted:** unfamiliar.
3. **sallerys:** salaries.
4. **conjunction:** joining.
5. **amenable:** agreeable.
6. **instigated:** caused.
7. **commence:** begin.
8. **aristocracy:** rule by a few, usually nobles.
9. **monarchy:** rule by one, usually a king.

Interactive Primary Sources Assessment

1. Main Ideas

a. Why does Madison believe that a society broken into many parts will not endanger minority rights?

b. What does Mason argue might happen if the president had the power to pardon people?

c. For each writer, what is one example of a fact and one example of an opinion?

2. Critical Thinking

Drawing Conclusions Who do you think makes the stronger argument? Explain your reasons.

THINK ABOUT
- what you know about the history of the United States
- the evidence used by each writer

VISUAL SUMMARY

Confederation to Constitution

Articles of Confederation

1777
Continental Congress passes the Articles of Confederation.

1777–1781
States debate ratification of the Articles of Confederation.

1781
Articles of Confederation go into effect.

1786
Annapolis Convention is held.

1786–1787
Shays's Rebellion occurs.

1787
Constitutional Convention is held in Philadelphia.

1788
U.S. Constitution is ratified.

1789
Government created by the new Constitution takes power.

1791
Bill of Rights is added to the Constitution.

Constitution

Bill of Rights

TERMS & NAMES

Briefly explain the significance of each of the following.

1. republic
2. Articles of Confederation
3. Northwest Ordinance
4. Shays's Rebellion
5. Constitutional Convention
6. James Madison
7. Great Compromise
8. Federalists
9. George Mason
10. Bill of Rights

REVIEW QUESTIONS

The Confederation Era (pages 205–211)

1. What is the Wilderness Road, and where did it lead?
2. What problems did the Confederation Congress successfully address?
3. What powers did the government have under the Articles of Confederation?
4. How did Shays's Rebellion affect people's views on the Articles of Confederation?

Creating the Constitution (pages 212–217)

5. What groups of people were not represented at the Constitutional Convention?
6. What were some things the delegates agreed on at the convention?
7. What compromises did the delegates make during the convention?

Ratifying the Constitution (pages 218–223)

8. What is federalism?
9. Why were Virginia and New York important in the battle for ratification of the Constitution?
10. Why did some states think that it was necessary to add a bill of rights to the Constitution?

CRITICAL THINKING

1. USING YOUR NOTES

Problems	Solutions
Western lands	
Postwar depression	
Representation in the new government	
Slavery	

Using your completed chart, answer the questions below.

a. What were the major problems facing the nation during the Confederation Era?

b. How well did the nation solve these problems? Explain.

2. ANALYZING LEADERSHIP

Think about the leaders discussed in this chapter. Based on their actions, which leader do you think made the greatest contribution to the Constitutional Convention? Why?

3. THEME: DEMOCRATIC IDEALS

How do the Articles of Confederation and the Constitution each carry out democratic ideals?

4. APPLYING CITIZENSHIP SKILLS

Do you think the Founders were right to make the compromises they did in the Constitution on the issues of representation and slavery? What might have happened if they had not compromised?

5. RECOGNIZING EFFECTS

How might U.S. history be different if Virginia had refused to ratify the Constitution? If New York had refused? If both had refused?

Interact *with* History

How did your ideas about how you would form a government change after reading this chapter?

HISTORY SKILLS

1. INTERPRETING MAPS: Region

Study the map and then answer the questions.

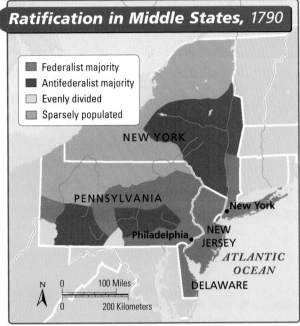

Ratification in Middle States, 1790

- ■ Federalist majority
- ■ Antifederalist majority
- □ Evenly divided
- ■ Sparsely populated

NEW YORK

PENNSYLVANIA

New York

Philadelphia

NEW JERSEY

ATLANTIC OCEAN

DELAWARE

N   0   100 Miles
     0   200 Kilometers

Source: *American Heritage Pictorial Atlas of United States History*

Basic Map Elements

a. Which states are identified on the map?

b. In which states did the Federalists have statewide majorities?

Interpreting the Map

c. Why do you think the two cities on the map were strong Federalist supporters?

2. INTERPRETING PRIMARY SOURCES

The following law was put into effect in Virginia in 1786. Read the law and answer the questions.

> *Be it enacted by the General Assembly,* That no man shall be compelled to frequent or support any religious worship, place, or ministry, whatsoever . . . but that all men shall be free to profess, and by argument maintain, their opinion in matters of religion, and that the same shall in no way diminish, enlarge, or affect their civil capacities.
>
> *The Statute of Virginia for Religious Freedom, 1786*

a. How would you summarize this law?

b. Which right in the Bill of Rights was based on this law?

c. Based on what you know about colonial history, how had American society changed between the early 1600s and the late 1700s?

ALTERNATIVE ASSESSMENT

1. INTERDISCIPLINARY ACTIVITY: Government

Making a Chart Do research to learn how the U.S. Constitution has been used as a model by other nations. Make a chart to summarize the information you find about one specific nation. Include the country, the date the country's constitution was ratified, and two ways in which that nation's constitution is similar to and different from the U.S. Constitution.

2. COOPERATIVE LEARNING ACTIVITY

Staging a Debate Stage a debate between a Federalist and an Antifederalist. Work in small groups to read some of the different arguments each side used. Look for discussions of one or more of the issues listed below. Pick one of the issues and stage a debate, using the strongest arguments from each side. Let the class determine who won the debate and why.

a. the representation of people in Congress

b. the strength of the president and Senate

c. the need for a bill of rights

3. 💿 PRIMARY SOURCE EXPLORER

Creating a Museum Exhibit The creation of the U.S. Constitution was one of the most important events in the nation's history. There is a great amount of information about the Constitution. Using the Primary Source Explorer CD-ROM and your local library, collect information on different topics relating to the Constitution.

Create a museum exhibit about the Constitution using the suggestions below.

- Include information on the historical background of the Constitutional Convention, such as Shays's Rebellion and Enlightenment ideas about government.
- Find biographies about the delegates to the convention, including portraits.
- Collect important primary sources, such as Madison's notes and *The Federalist* papers.
- Include photographs or facsimiles of the documents.
- Draw a diagram that shows a layout for the exhibit.

4. HISTORY PORTFOLIO

Review your section and chapter assessment activities. Select one that you think shows your best work. Then use comments made by your teacher or classmates to improve your work and add it to your portfolio.

Additional Test Practice, pp. S1–S33

ⓘ TEST PRACTICE
CLASSZONE.COM

The Living Constitution

The Framers of the Constitution created a flexible plan for governing the United States far into the future. They also described ways to allow changes in the Constitution. For over 200 years, the Constitution has guided the American people. It remains a "living document." The Constitution still thrives, in part, because it echoes the principles the delegates valued. Each generation of Americans renews the meaning of the Constitution's timeless ideas. These two pages show you some ways in which the Constitution has shaped events in American history. **See Primary Source Explorer**

"In framing a system which we wish to last for ages, we should not lose sight of the changes which ages will produce."

—JAMES MADISON, CONSTITUTIONAL CONVENTION

1787

Delegates in Philadelphia sign the Constitution.

1965

Civil rights leaders protest to end the violation of their constitutional rights. Dr. Martin Luther King, Jr., Coretta Scott King, and others march from Selma toward Montgomery, Alabama, to gain voting rights.

1971

The 26th Amendment to the Constitution gives young people "18 years of age or older" the right to vote.

PCT. 423

1981

A Supreme Court decision rules that Congress can exclude women from the draft. Still, many women who have joined the armed forces have served in combat.

TABLE OF CONTENTS

HOW TO READ THE CONSTITUTION

The complete text of the Constitution of the United States begins on page 232. The main column has the actual text. Some of the spellings and punctuation have been updated for easier reading. Headings and subheadings have been added to the Constitution to help you find specific topics. Those parts of the Constitution that are no longer in use have been crossed out. "A Closer Look" notes and charts will help you understand issues related to the Constitution.

The New York Times

National Edition
Midwest: Mostly sunny, breezy and seasonable in the Great Lakes area and Ohio Valley. Becoming very warm after a cold start in the western Plains. Weather map is on page A6.

"All the News That's Fit to Print"

Printed in Chicago ONE DOLLAR

SATURDAY, FEBRUARY 13, 1999

VOL. CXLVIII .... No. 51,432 Copyright © 1999 The New York Times

CLINTON ACQUITTED DECISIVELY: NO MAJORITY FOR EITHER CHARGE

CENSURE IS BARRED

President Says He Is Sorry And Seeks Reconciliation

By JAMES BENNET and JOHN M. BRODER

But Rebuke From Both Sides of Aisle Dilutes President's Victory

By ALISON MITCHELL

Two hours after the Senate voted yesterday, President Clinton spoke in the Rose Garden of the White House.

The Fallout Of the Trial

Effects on the Office Are Far From Certain

By R. W. APPLE Jr.

'Senators, How Say You?'

	GUILTY	NOT GUILTY		GUILTY	NOT GUILTY
Article 1			Article 2		
Republicans	45	10	Republicans	50	5
Democrats			OBSTRUCTION OF JUSTICE		
			Democrats	0	45

1999

The Senate tries President Bill Clinton for the impeachment charges brought against him by the House of Representatives. As required by the Constitution, the Senate needs a two-thirds majority vote to convict him. This rule saves his presidency.

Seven Principles of the Constitution

The Framers of the Constitution constructed a new system of government. Seven principles supported their efforts. To picture how these principles work, imagine seven building blocks. Together they form the foundation of the United States Constitution. In the pages that follow, you will find the definitions and main ideas of the principles shown in the graphic below.

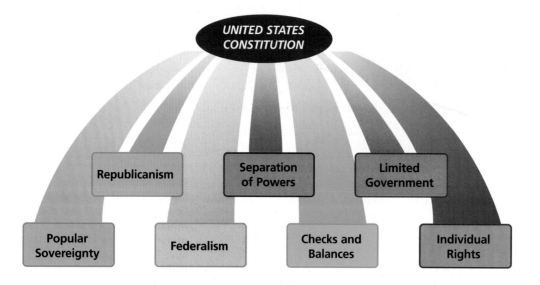

UNITED STATES CONSTITUTION

Republicanism   Separation of Powers   Limited Government

Popular Sovereignty   Federalism   Checks and Balances   Individual Rights

① Popular Sovereignty
Who Gives the Government Its Power?

"We the people of the United States . . . establish this Constitution for the United States of America." These words from the Preamble, or introduction, to the Constitution clearly spell out the source of the government's power. The Constitution rests on the idea of **popular sovereignty**—a government in which the people rule. As the nation changed and grew, popular sovereignty took on new meaning. A broader range of Americans shared in the power to govern themselves.

In 1987, Americans gathered in Washington, D.C., to celebrate the 200th anniversary of the Constitution. The banner proudly displays that the power to govern belongs to the people.

In a republican government, voting citizens make their voices heard at the polls. The power of the ballot prompts candidates to listen to people's concerns.

2 Republicanism
How Are People's Views Represented in Government?

The Framers of the Constitution wanted the people to have a voice in government. Yet the Framers also feared that public opinion might stand in the way of sound decision making. To solve this problem, they looked to republicanism as a model of government.

Republicanism is based on this belief: The people exercise their power by voting for their political representatives. According to the Framers, these lawmakers played the key role in making a republican government work. Article 4, Section 4, of the Constitution also calls for every state to have a "republican form of government."

3 Federalism
How Is Power Shared?

The Framers wanted the states and the nation to become partners in governing. To build cooperation, the Framers turned to federalism. **Federalism** is a system of government in which power is divided between a central government and smaller political units, such as states. Before the Civil War, federalism in the United States was closely related to dual sovereignty, the idea that the federal government and the states each had exclusive power over their own spheres.

The Framers used federalism to structure the Constitution. The Constitution assigns certain powers to the national government. These are *delegated powers*. Powers kept by the states are *reserved powers*. Powers shared or exercised by national and state governments are known as *concurrent powers*.

Federalism

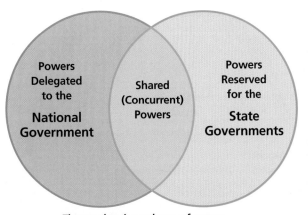

The overlapping spheres of power bind the American people together.

4 Separation of Powers
How Is Power Divided?

The Framers were concerned that too much power might fall into the hands of a single group. To avoid this problem, they built the idea of **separation of powers** into the Constitution. This principle means the division of basic government roles into branches. No one branch is given all the power. Articles 1, 2, and 3 of the Constitution detail how powers are split among the three branches.

Separation of Powers

```
              UNITED STATES
              CONSTITUTION
```

Article 1	Article 2	Article 3
Legislative Branch	**Executive Branch**	**Judicial Branch**
Congress makes the laws.	President enforces the laws.	Supreme Court interprets the law.

5 Checks and Balances
How Is Power Evenly Distributed?

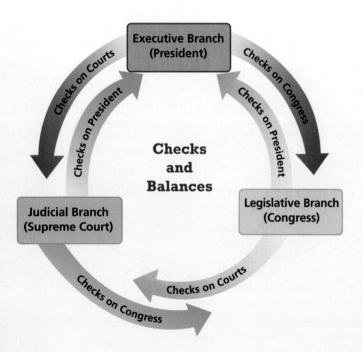

Baron de Montesquieu, an 18th-century French thinker, wrote, "Power should be a check to power." His comment refers to the principle of **checks and balances.** Each branch of government can exercise checks, or controls, over the other branches. Though the branches of government are separate, they rely on one another to perform the work of government.

The Framers included a system of checks and balances in the Constitution to help make sure that the branches work together fairly. For example, only Congress can pass laws. Yet the president can check this power by refusing to sign a law into action. In turn, the Supreme Court can declare that a law, passed by Congress and signed by the president, violates the Constitution.

6 Limited Government
How Is Abuse of Power Prevented?

The Framers restricted the power of government. Article 1, Section 9, of the Constitution lists the powers denied to the Congress. Article 1, Section 10, forbids the states to take certain actions.

The principle of **limited government** is also closely related to the "rule of law": In the American government everyone, citizens and powerful leaders alike, must obey the law. Individuals or groups cannot twist or bypass the law to serve their own interests.

'I AM THE LAW!'

In this political cartoon, President Richard Nixon shakes his fist as he defies the "rule of law." Faced with charges of violating the Constitution, Nixon resigned as president in 1974.

Students exercise their right to protest. They urge the community to protect the environment.

7 Individual Rights
How Are Personal Freedoms Protected?

The first ten amendments to the Constitution shield people from an overly powerful government. These amendments are called the Bill of Rights. The Bill of Rights guarantees certain **individual rights,** or personal liberties and privileges. For example, government cannot control what people write or say. People also have the right to meet peacefully and to ask the government to correct a problem. Later amendments to the Constitution also advanced the cause of individual rights.

Assessment: Principles of the Constitution

1. Main Ideas

a. What are the seven principles of government?

b. How does the Constitution reflect the principle of separation of powers?

c. Why did the Framers include a system of checks and balances in the Constitution?

2. Critical Thinking

Forming Opinions How do the rights and responsibilities of U.S. citizenship reflect American national identity?

THINK ABOUT

• what it means to be an American

• the rights and responsibilities of U.S. citizens

The Constitution of the United States

See Primary Source Explorer

" In 1787, I was not included in that 'We the people.' ... But through the process of amendment, interpretation, and court decision, I have finally been included in 'We the people.' "

—BARBARA JORDAN, 1974
The first African-American congresswoman from the South (Texas)

Preamble. *Purpose of the Constitution*

We the people of the United States, in order to form a more perfect Union, establish justice, insure domestic tranquility, provide for the common defense, promote the general welfare, and secure the blessings of liberty to ourselves and our posterity, do ordain and establish this Constitution for the United States of America.

A CLOSER LOOK Goals of the Preamble

PREAMBLE	EXPLANATION	EXAMPLES
"Form a more perfect Union"	Create a nation in which states work together	• Interstate road network • U.S. coins, paper money
"Establish justice"	Make laws and set up courts that are fair	• Court system • Jury system
"Insure domestic tranquility"	Keep peace within the country	• National Guard • Federal marshals
"Provide for the common defense"	Safeguard the country against attack	• Army • Navy
"Promote the general welfare"	Contribute to the happiness and well-being of all the people	• Safety in the workplace • Aid to the poor
"Secure the blessings of liberty to ourselves and our posterity"	Make sure future citizens remain free	• Commission on Civil Rights • Federal Election Commission

SKILLBUILDER Interpreting Charts
1. *Which goal of the Preamble do you think is most important? Why?*
2. *How does the Preamble reflect the principle of popular sovereignty?*

Article 1. *The Legislature*

> **MAIN IDEA** The main role of Congress, the legislative branch, is to make laws. Congress is made up of two houses—the Senate and the House of Representatives. Candidates for each house must meet certain requirements. Congress performs specific duties, also called delegated powers.
>
> **WHY IT MATTERS NOW** Representatives in Congress still voice the views and concerns of the people.

Section 1. Congress All legislative powers herein granted shall be vested in a Congress of the United States, which shall consist of a Senate and House of Representatives.

Section 2. The House of Representatives

1. Elections The House of Representatives shall be composed of members chosen every second year by the people of the several states, and the **electors** in each state shall have the qualifications requisite for electors of the most numerous branch of the state legislature.

2. Qualifications No person shall be a Representative who shall not have attained to the age of twenty-five years, and been seven years a citizen of the United States, and who shall not, when elected, be an inhabitant of that state in which he shall be chosen.

3. Number of Representatives Representatives and direct taxes shall be apportioned among the several states which may be included within this Union, according to their respective numbers, which shall be determined by adding to the whole number of free persons, including those bound to service for a term of years, and excluding Indians not taxed, three-fifths of all other Persons. The actual **enumeration** shall be made within three years after the first meeting of the Congress of the United States, and within every subsequent term of ten years, in such manner as they shall by law direct. The number of Representatives shall not exceed one for every thirty thousand, but each state shall have at least one Representative; and until such enumeration shall be made, the state of New Hampshire shall be entitled to choose three, Massachusetts eight, Rhode Island and Providence Plantations one, Connecticut five, New York six, New Jersey four, Pennsylvania eight, Delaware one, Maryland six, Virginia ten, North Carolina five, South Carolina five, and Georgia three.

4. Vacancies When vacancies happen in the representation from any state, the executive authority thereof shall issue writs of election to fill such vacancies.

5. Officers and Impeachment The House of Representatives shall choose their Speaker and other officers; and shall have the sole power of **impeachment.**

A CLOSER LOOK

ELECTIONS

Representatives are elected every two years. There are no limits on the number of terms a person can serve.

1. What do you think are the advantages of holding frequent elections of representatives?

A CLOSER LOOK

REPRESENTATION

Some delegates, such as Gouvernor Morris, thought that representation should be based on wealth as well as population. Others, such as James Wilson, thought representation should be based on population only. Ultimately, the delegates voted against including wealth as a basis for apportioning representatives.

2. How do you think the United States would be different today if representation were based on wealth?

Section 3. The Senate

1. Numbers The Senate of the United States shall be composed of two Senators from each state, ~~chosen by the legislature thereof,~~ for six years; and each Senator shall have one vote.

2. Classifying Terms Immediately after they shall be assembled in consequence of the first election, they shall be divided as equally as may be into three classes. The seats of the Senators of the first class shall be vacated at the expiration of the second year, of the second class at the expiration of the fourth year, and of the third class at the expiration of the sixth year, so that one-third may be chosen every second year; ~~and if vacancies happen by resignation, or otherwise, during the recess of the legislature of any state, the executive thereof may make temporary appointments until the next meeting of the legislature, which shall then fill such vacancies.~~

3. Qualifications No person shall be a Senator who shall not have attained to the age of thirty years, and been nine years a citizen of the United States, and who shall not, when elected, be an inhabitant of that state for which he shall be chosen.

A CLOSER LOOK Federal Office Terms and Requirements

POSITION	TERM	MINIMUM AGE	RESIDENCY	CITIZENSHIP
Representative	2 years	25	state in which elected	7 years
Senator	6 years	30	state in which elected	9 years
President	4 years	35	14 years in the U.S.	natural-born
Supreme Court Justice	unlimited	none	none	none

SKILLBUILDER Interpreting Charts

Why do you think the term and qualifications for a senator are more demanding than for a representative?

4. Role of Vice-President The Vice-President of the United States shall be President of the Senate, but shall have no vote, unless they be equally divided.

5. Officers The Senate shall choose their other officers, and also a President **pro tempore**, in the absence of the Vice-President, or when he shall exercise the office of President of the United States.

6. Impeachment Trials The Senate shall have the sole power to try all impeachments. When sitting for that purpose, they shall be on oath or affirmation. When the President of the United States is tried, the Chief Justice shall preside: and no person shall be convicted without the concurrence of two-thirds of the members present.

7. Punishment for Impeachment Judgment in cases of impeachment shall not extend further than to removal from office, and disqualification to hold and enjoy any office of honor, trust or profit under the United States; but the party convicted shall nevertheless be liable and subject to **indictment**, trial, judgment and punishment, according to law.

Section 4. Congressional Elections

1. Regulations The times, places and manner of holding elections for Senators and Representatives shall be prescribed in each state by the legislature thereof; but the Congress may at any time by law make or alter such regulations, except as to the places of choosing Senators.

2. Sessions The Congress shall assemble at least once in every year, ~~and such meeting shall be on the first Monday in December, unless they shall by law appoint a different day.~~

Section 5. Rules and Procedures

1. Quorum Each house shall be the judge of the elections, returns and qualifications of its own members, and a majority of each shall constitute a **quorum** to do business; but a smaller number may adjourn from day to day, and may be authorized to compel the attendance of absent members, in such manner, and under such penalties as each house may provide.

2. Rules and Conduct Each house may determine the rules of its proceedings, punish its members for disorderly behavior, and, with the concurrence of two-thirds, expel a member.

3. Congressional Records Each house shall keep a journal of its proceedings, and from time to time publish the same, excepting such parts as may in their judgment require secrecy; and the yeas and nays of the members of either house on any question shall, at the desire of one-fifth of those present, be entered on the journal.

4. Adjournment Neither house, during the session of Congress, shall, without the consent of the other, adjourn for more than three days, nor to any other place than that in which the two houses shall be sitting.

Section 6. Payment and Privileges

1. Salary The Senators and Representatives shall receive a compensation for their services, to be ascertained by law, and paid out of the treasury of the United States. They shall in all cases, except treason, felony and breach of the peace, be privileged from arrest during their attendance at the session of their respective houses, and in going to and returning from the same; and for any speech or debate in either house, they shall not be questioned in any other place.

2. Restrictions No Senator or Representative shall, during the time for which he was elected, be appointed to any civil office under the authority of the United States, which shall have been created, or the emoluments whereof shall have been increased during such time; and no person holding any office under the United States, shall be a member of either house during his continuance in office.

Section 7. How a Bill Becomes a Law

1. Tax Bills All bills for raising **revenue** shall originate in the House of Representatives; but the Senate may propose or concur with amendments as on other Bills.

2. Lawmaking Process Every bill which shall have passed the House of Representatives and the Senate, shall, before it become a law, be presented to the President of the United States; if he approves he shall sign it, but if not he shall return it, with his objections to that house in which it shall have originated, who shall enter the objections at large on their journal, and proceed to reconsider it. If after such reconsideration two-thirds of that house shall agree to pass the bill, it shall be sent, together with the objections, to the other house, by which it shall likewise be reconsidered, and if approved by two-thirds of that house, it shall become a law. But in all such cases the votes of both houses shall be determined by yeas and nays, and the names of the persons voting for and against the bill shall be entered on the journal of each house respectively. If any bill shall not be returned by the President within ten days (Sundays excepted) after it shall have been presented to him, the same shall be a law, in like manner as if he had signed it, unless the Congress by their adjournment prevent its return, in which case it shall not be a law.

3. Role of the President Every order, resolution, or vote to which the concurrence of the Senate and House of Representatives may be necessary (except on a question of adjournment) shall be presented to the President of the United States; and before the same shall take effect, shall be approved by him, or being disapproved by him, shall be repassed by two-thirds of the Senate and House of Representatives, according to the rules and limitations prescribed in the case of a bill.

A CLOSER LOOK How a Bill Becomes a Law

Introduction	Committee Action	Floor Action

The House introduces a bill and refers it to a committee.

The House committee may approve, rewrite, or kill the bill.

The House debates and votes on its version of the bill.

House and Senate committee members work out the differences between the two versions.

The Senate introduces a bill and refers it to a committee.

The Senate committee may approve, rewrite, or kill the bill.

The Senate debates and votes on its version of the bill.

Section 8. Powers Granted to Congress

1. Taxation The Congress shall have power to lay and collect taxes, duties, imposts and excises, to pay the debts and provide for the common defense and general welfare of the United States; but all duties, imposts and excises shall be uniform throughout the United States;

2. Credit To borrow money on the credit of the United States;

3. Commerce To regulate commerce with foreign nations, and among the several states, and with the Indian tribes;

4. Naturalization, Bankruptcy To establish a uniform rule of <u>naturalization,</u> and uniform laws on the subject of bankruptcies throughout the United States;

5. Money To coin money, regulate the value thereof, and of foreign coin, and fix the standard of weights and measures;

6. Counterfeiting To provide for the punishment of counterfeiting the securities and current coin of the United States;

7. Post Office To establish post offices and post roads;

8. Patents, Copyrights To promote the progress of science and useful arts, by securing for limited times to authors and inventors the exclusive right to their respective writings and discoveries;

9. Federal Courts To constitute <u>tribunals</u> inferior to the Supreme Court;

10. International Law To define and punish piracies and <u>felonies</u> committed on the high seas, and offenses against the law of nations;

11. War To declare war, grant letters of marque and reprisal, and make rules concerning captures on land and water;

12. Army To raise and support armies, but no <u>appropriation</u> of money to that use shall be for a longer term than two years;

13. Navy To provide and maintain a navy;

Final Approval

5 Both houses of Congress pass the revised bill.

Enactment

President signs the bill.
OR
President vetoes the bill.

6

7 Two-thirds majority vote of Congress is needed to approve a vetoed bill.

8 Bill Becomes Law.

LAW

SKILLBUILDER Interpreting Charts
1. *How can a president block a bill?*
2. *What examples of checks and balances are shown in the chart?*

14. Regulation of Armed Forces To make rules for the government and regulation of the land and naval forces;

15. Militia To provide for calling forth the **militia** to execute the laws of the Union, suppress insurrections and repel invasions;

16. Regulations for Militia To provide for organizing, arming, and disciplining the militia, and for governing such part of them as may be employed in the service of the United States, reserving to the states respectively the appointment of the officers, and the authority of training the militia according to the discipline prescribed by Congress;

17. District of Columbia To exercise exclusive legislation in all cases whatsoever, over such district (not exceeding ten miles square) as may, by cession of particular states, and the acceptance of Congress, become the seat of the government of the United States, and to exercise like authority over all places purchased by the consent of the legislature of the state in which the same shall be, for the erection of forts, magazines, arsenals, dockyards, and other needful buildings;—and

18. Elastic Clause To make all laws which shall be necessary and proper for carrying into execution the foregoing powers, and all other powers vested by this Constitution in the government of the United States, or in any department or officer thereof.

A CLOSER LOOK The Elastic Clause

ELASTIC CLAUSE

1787

13 states
• agricultural
• rural
about 4 million people
POP.

The elastic clause allows future generations to expand the meaning of the Constitution. Congress can take action on issues not spelled out in the Constitution.

TODAY

50 states
• industrial
• high-tech
• urban
POP. about 250 million people

A CLOSER LOOK

HABEAS CORPUS

A writ of habeas corpus is a legal order. It protects people from being held in prison or jail without formal charges of a crime. In 1992, the Supreme Court recognized that "habeas corpus is the [basic] instrument for safeguarding individual freedom."

8. How does habeas corpus help ensure fairness and justice?

Section 9. Powers Denied Congress

1. Slave Trade ~~The migration or importation of such persons as any of the states now existing shall think proper to admit, shall not be prohibited by the Congress prior to the year one thousand eight hundred and eight, but a tax or duty may be imposed on such importation, not exceeding ten dollars for each person.~~

2. Habeas Corpus The privilege of the writ of habeas corpus shall not be suspended, unless when in cases of rebellion or invasion the public safety may require it.

3. Illegal Punishment No **bill of attainder** or **ex post facto law** shall be passed.

4. Direct Taxes No capitation, ~~or other direct,~~ tax shall be laid, ~~unless in proportion to the census or enumeration herein before directed to be taken.~~

5. Export Taxes No tax or duty shall be laid on articles exported from any state.

6. No Favorites No preference shall be given by any regulation of commerce or revenue to the ports of one state over those of another: nor shall vessels bound to, or from, one state be obliged to enter, clear, or pay duties in another.

7. Public Money No money shall be drawn from the treasury, but in consequence of appropriations made by law; and a regular statement and account of the receipts and expenditures of all public money shall be published from time to time.

8. Titles of Nobility No title of nobility shall be granted by the United States: and no person holding any office of profit or trust under them shall, without the consent of the Congress, accept of any present, emolument, office, or title, of any kind whatever, from any king, prince, or foreign state.

Section 10. Powers Denied the States

1. Restrictions No state shall enter into any treaty, alliance, or confederation; grant letters of marque and reprisal; coin money; emit bills of credit; make anything but gold and silver coin a **tender** in payment of debts; pass any bill of attainder, ex post facto law, or law impairing the obligation of contracts, or grant any title of nobility.

2. Import and Export Taxes No state shall, without the consent of the Congress, lay any imposts or duties on imports or exports, except what may be absolutely necessary for executing its inspection laws; and the net produce of all duties and imposts, laid by any state on imports or exports, shall be for the use of the treasury of the United States; and all such laws shall be subject to the revision and control of the Congress.

3. Peacetime and War Restraints No state shall, without the consent of Congress, lay any duty of tonnage, keep troops or ships of war in time of peace, enter into any agreement or compact with another state, or with a foreign power, or engage in war, unless actually invaded, or in such imminent danger as will not admit of delay.

A CLOSER LOOK

DIRECT TAX

In 1913, the 16th Amendment allowed Congress to collect an income tax—a direct tax on the amount of money a person earns. Americans today pay much more in taxes than their ancestors would have imagined.

9. Why do you think the issue of taxes is so important to people?

A CLOSER LOOK

TITLES OF NOBILITY

The Framers disapproved of titles of nobility. The list of grievances in the Declaration of Independence included numerous examples of King George III's abuses of power. Symbols of these abuses included English titles of nobility, such as "king," "queen," and "duke." The Framers said clearly that there would be no such titles in the new republic.

10. How do TV news reporters address members of Congress and the president?

Article 1 Assessment

1. Main Ideas

a. What is the main job of the legislative branch?

b. What role does the vice-president of the United States play in the Senate?

c. Why are there more members in the House of Representatives than the Senate?

d. What is one of the powers denied to Congress?

2. Critical Thinking

Drawing Conclusions How does Article 1 show that the Constitution is a clearly defined yet flexible document?

THINK ABOUT

• the powers of Congress

• the "elastic clause"

VOCABULARY

natural-born citizen a citizen born in the United States or a U.S. commonwealth, or to parents who are U.S. citizens living outside the country

affirmation a statement declaring that something is true

Article 2. *The Executive*

> **MAIN IDEA** The president and vice-president are the leaders of the executive branch. Their main role is to enforce the laws. The president commands the military and makes foreign treaties with the Senate's approval.
>
> **WHY IT MATTERS NOW** As the United States has become a world power, the authority of the president has also expanded.

Section 1. The Presidency

1. Terms of Office The executive power shall be vested in a President of the United States of America. He shall hold his office during the term of four years, and, together with the Vice-President, chosen for the same term, be elected, as follows:

2. Electoral College Each state shall appoint, in such manner as the Legislature thereof may direct, a number of electors, equal to the whole number of Senators and Representatives to which the State may be entitled in the Congress; but no Senator or Representative, or person holding an office of trust or profit under the United States, shall be appointed an elector.

A CLOSER LOOK Electoral College *(based on 2000 Census)*

American voters do not choose their president directly. Members of a group called the electoral college actually elect the president. Each state has electors. Together they form the electoral college. In most states, the winner takes all. Except for Maine and Nebraska, all the electoral votes of a state go to one set of candidates.

number of electors for each state =
total number of its senators and representatives

WA 11 · OR 7 · MT 3 · ND 3 · MN 10 · NH 4 · VT 3 · ME 4 · ID 4 · WY 3 · SD 3 · WI 10 · NY 31 · MA 12 · RI 4 · NV 5 · UT 5 · CO 9 · NE 5 · IA 7 · MI 17 · PA 21 · CT 7 · NJ 15 · DE 3 · DC 3 · IL 21 · IN 11 · OH 20 · WV 5 · VA 13 · MD 10 · CA 55 · AZ 10 · KS 6 · MO 11 · KY 8 · NC 15 · NM 5 · OK 7 · AR 6 · TN 11 · SC 8 · HI 4 · TX 34 · LA 9 · MS 6 · AL 9 · GA 15 · FL 27 · AK 3

SKILLBUILDER Interpreting Maps

1. *How many electoral votes does your state have?*
2. *In which states would a presidential candidate campaign most heavily? Why?*

3. Former Method of Electing President ~~The electors shall meet in their respective states, and vote by ballot for two persons, of whom one at least shall not be an inhabitant of the same state with themselves. And they shall make a list of all the persons voted for, and of the number of votes for each; which list they shall sign and certify, and transmit sealed to the seat of the government of the United States, directed to the President of the Senate. The President of the Senate shall, in the presence of the Senate and House of Representatives, open all the certificates, and the votes shall then be counted. The person having the greatest number of votes shall be the~~

President, if such number be a majority of the whole number of electors appointed; and if there be more than one who have such majority, and have an equal number of votes, then the House of Representatives shall immediately choose by ballot one of them for President; and if no person have a majority, then from the five highest on the list the said House shall in like manner choose the President. But in choosing the President, the votes shall be taken by States, the representation from each state having one vote; a quorum for this purpose shall consist of a member or members from two-thirds of the states, and a majority of all the states shall be necessary to a choice. In every case, after the choice of the President, the person having the greatest number of votes of the electors shall be the Vice-President. But if there should remain two or more who have equal votes, the Senate shall choose from them by ballot the Vice-President.

4. Election Day The Congress may determine the time of choosing the electors, and the day on which they shall give their votes, which day shall be the same throughout the United States.

5. Qualifications No person except a **natural-born citizen,** or a citizen of the United States at the time of the adoption of this Constitution, shall be eligible to the office of President; neither shall any person be eligible to that office who shall not have attained to the age of thirty-five years, and been fourteen years a resident within the United States.

6. Succession In case of the removal of the President from office, or of his death, resignation, or inability to discharge the powers and duties of the said office, the same shall devolve on the Vice-President, and the Congress may by law provide for the case of removal, death, resignation or inability, both of the President and Vice-President, declaring what officer shall then act as President, and such officer shall act accordingly, until the disability be removed, or a President shall be elected.

7. Salary The President shall, at stated times, receive for his services, a compensation, which shall neither be increased nor diminished during the period for which he shall have been elected, and he shall not receive within that period any other emolument from the United States, or any of them.

8. Oath of Office Before he enter on the execution of his office, he shall take the following oath or **affirmation:**—"I do solemnly swear (or affirm) that I will faithfully execute the office of President of the United States, and will to the best of my ability, preserve, protect and defend the Constitution of the United States."

Chief Executive

Like a business executive, the president solves problems and makes key decisions. President John F. Kennedy is shown in the oval office in 1962.

Commander in Chief

As a military leader, President Abraham Lincoln meets with his generals during the Civil War.

Chief Diplomat and Chief of State

As a foreign policy maker, President Richard M. Nixon visits the People's Republic of China in 1972.

Legislative Leader

President Lyndon Johnson signs the Civil Rights Act of 1964. All modern presidents have legislative programs they want Congress to pass.

Head of a Political Party

President Ronald Reagan rallies support at the 1984 Republican Convention. By this time, Reagan had put together a strong bloc of voters who supported the Republican Party's policies. During his presidency (1981–1989), Reagan helped build new unity among party members.

Section 2. Powers of the President

1. Military Powers The President shall be commander in chief of the Army and Navy of the United States, and of the militia of the several states, when called into the actual service of the United States; he may require the opinion, in writing, of the principal officer in each of the executive departments, upon any subject relating to the duties of their respective offices, and he shall have power to grant **reprieves** and pardons for offenses against the United States, except in cases of impeachment.

2. Treaties, Appointments He shall have power, by and with the advice and consent of the Senate, to make treaties, provided two-thirds of the Senators present concur; and he shall nominate, and by and with the advice and consent of the Senate, shall appoint ambassadors, other public ministers and consuls, judges of the Supreme Court, and all other officers of the United States, whose appointments are not herein otherwise provided for, and which shall be established by law; but the Congress may by law vest the appointment of such inferior officers, as they think proper, in the President alone, in the courts of law, or in the heads of departments.

3. Vacancies The President shall have power to fill up all vacancies that may happen during the recess of the Senate, by granting commissions which shall expire at the end of their next session.

Section 3. Presidential Duties
He shall from time to time give to the Congress information of the State of the Union, and recommend to their consideration such measures as he shall judge necessary and expedient; he may, on extraordinary occasions, **convene** both houses, or either of them, and in case of disagreement between them, with respect to the time of adjournment, he may adjourn them to such time as he shall think proper; he shall receive ambassadors and other public ministers; he shall take care that the laws be faithfully executed, and shall commission all the officers of the United States.

Section 4. Impeachment
The President, Vice-President and all civil officers of the United States shall be removed from office on impeachment for, and conviction of, treason, bribery, or other high crimes and **misdemeanors**.

VOCABULARY

reprieves delays or cancellations of punishment

convene call together

misdemeanors violations of the law

A CLOSER LOOK

SUPREME COURT APPOINTMENTS

Recent presidents have used their power of appointment to add minorities and women to the Supreme Court. In 1967, President Lyndon Johnson appointed the first African-American justice, Thurgood Marshall. In 1981, President Ronald Reagan appointed the first woman, Sandra Day O'Connor.

12. What do you think influences a president's choice for a Supreme Court justice?

A CLOSER LOOK

STATE OF THE UNION

Major TV networks broadcast the State of the Union address to the whole nation. In this yearly message, the president urges Congress to achieve certain lawmaking goals. The president's speech also must gain the attention of TV viewers.

13. Why is the president's power to persuade an important political skill?

Article 2 Assessment

1. Main Ideas

a. What is the chief purpose of the executive branch?

b. What are the requirements for becoming president?

c. How does the Constitution limit the president's power to make appointments and treaties?

2. Critical Thinking

Analyzing Issues Why do you think the Constitution states that the president must seek approval from the Senate for most political appointments and treaties?

THINK ABOUT
• the abuse of power
• the will of the voters

inferior courts courts with less authority than the Supreme Court

appellate having power to review court decisions

A CLOSER LOOK

ORGANIZING FEDERAL COURTS

The Judiciary Act of 1789, passed by the First Congress, included establishing a Supreme Court with a chief justice and five associate justices and other lower federal courts.

14. How many Supreme Court justices are there today?

A CLOSER LOOK

JUDICIAL POWER

Judicial power gives the Supreme Court and other federal courts the authority to hear certain kinds of cases. These courts have the power to rule in cases involving the Constitution, national laws, treaties, and states' conflicts.

15. What federal cases have you seen reported on TV?

Article 3. *The Judiciary*

> **MAIN IDEA** The judicial branch interprets the laws. This branch includes the Supreme Court, the highest court in the nation, and other federal courts.
>
> **WHY IT MATTERS NOW** Supreme Court rulings can shape government policies on hotly debated issues.

Section 1. Federal Courts and Judges
The judicial power of the United States shall be vested in one Supreme Court, and in such **inferior courts** as the Congress may from time to time ordain and establish. The judges, both of the Supreme and inferior courts, shall hold their offices during good behavior, and shall, at stated times, receive for their services a compensation, which shall not be diminished during their continuance in office.

Section 2. The Courts' Authority

1. General Authority The judicial power shall extend to all cases, in law and equity, arising under this Constitution, the laws of the United States, and treaties made, or which shall be made, under their authority;—to all cases affecting ambassadors, other public ministers and consuls;—to all cases of admiralty and maritime jurisdiction;—to controversies to which the United States shall be a party;—to controversies between two or more states;— between a state and citizens of another state;—between citizens of different states;—between citizens of the same state claiming lands under grants of different states, and between a state, or the citizens thereof, and foreign states, citizens or subjects.

A CLOSER LOOK Judicial Review

Judicial review allows the Supreme Court and other federal courts to play a key role in lawmaking. The judges examine a law or government activity. They then decide whether it violates the Constitution. The Supreme Court established this important right in the case of *Marbury* v. *Madison* (1803). (See Chapter 10.)

2. Supreme Court In all cases affecting ambassadors, other public ministers and consuls, and those in which a state shall be party, the Supreme Court shall have original jurisdiction. In all the other cases before mentioned, the Supreme Court shall have **appellate** jurisdiction, both as to law and fact, with such exceptions, and under such regulations, as the Congress shall make.

A CLOSER LOOK   Checks and Balances

CHECKS ON COURTS
- Appoints federal judges
- Can grant reprieves and pardons for federal crimes

Executive Branch
(President)

CHECKS ON CONGRESS
- Can veto acts of Congress
- Can call special sessions of Congress
- Can suggest laws and send messages to Congress

CHECKS ON PRESIDENT
- Can impeach and remove the president
- Can override veto
- Controls spending of money
- Senate can refuse to confirm presidential appointments and to ratify treaties

Legislative Branch
(Congress)

CHECKS ON COURT
- Can impeach and remove federal judges
- Establishes lower federal courts
- Can refuse to confirm judicial appointments

CHECKS ON PRESIDENT
- Can declare executive acts unconstitutional
- Judges, appointed for life, are free from executive control

Judicial Branch
(Supreme Court)

CHECKS ON CONGRESS
- Judicial review—Can declare acts of Congress unconstitutional

SKILLBUILDER Interpreting Charts
1. *Why is judicial review an important action of the Supreme Court?*
2. *Which check do you think is most powerful? Why?*

3. Trial by Jury The trial of all crimes, except in cases of impeachment, shall be by jury; and such trial shall be held in the state where the said crimes shall have been committed; but when not committed within any state, the trial shall be at such place or places as the Congress may by law have directed.

Section 3. Treason

1. Definition Treason against the United States shall consist only in levying war against them, or in adhering to their enemies, giving them aid and comfort. No person shall be convicted of treason unless on the testimony of two witnesses to the same overt act, or on confession in open court.

2. Punishment The Congress shall have power to declare the punishment of treason, but no attainder of treason shall work corruption of blood, or forfeiture except during the life of the person attained.

Article 3 Assessment

1. Main Ideas

a. What is the main purpose of the judicial branch?

b. What is judicial review?

c. What are two kinds of cases that can begin in the Supreme Court?

2. Critical Thinking

Drawing Conclusions Why might the Supreme Court feel less political pressure than Congress in making judgments about the Constitution?

THINK ABOUT
- the appointment of Supreme Court justices
- Congress members' obligation to voters

A CLOSER LOOK Federalism

Americans live under both national and state governments.

NATIONAL POWERS
- Maintain military
- Declare war
- Establish postal system
- Set standards for weights and measures
- Protect copyrights and patents

SHARED POWERS
- Collect taxes
- Establish courts
- Regulate interstate commerce
- Regulate banks
- Borrow money
- Provide for the general welfare
- Punish criminals

STATE POWERS
- Establish local governments
- Set up schools
- Regulate state commerce
- Make regulations for marriage
- Establish and regulate corporations

SKILLBUILDER Interpreting Charts
What do you think is the purpose of dividing the powers between national and state governments?

Article 4. *Relations Among States*

> **MAIN IDEA** States must honor one another's laws, records, and court rulings.
>
> **WHY IT MATTERS NOW** Article 4 promotes cooperation, equality, and fair treatment of citizens from all the states.

Section 1. State Acts and Records Full faith and credit shall be given in each state to the public acts, records, and judicial proceedings of every other state. And the Congress may by general laws prescribe the manner in which such acts, records and proceedings shall be proved, and the effect thereof.

Section 2. Rights of Citizens

1. Citizenship The citizens of each state shall be entitled to all privileges and **immunities** of citizens in the several states.

2. Extradition A person charged in any state with treason, felony, or other crime, who shall flee from justice, and be found in another state, shall on demand of the executive authority of the state from which he fled, be delivered up, to be removed to the state having jurisdiction of the crime.

3. Fugitive Slaves ~~No person held to service or labor in one state, under the laws thereof, escaping into another, shall, in consequence of any law or regulation therein, be discharged from such service or labor, but shall be delivered up on claim of the party to whom such service or labor may be due.~~

Section 3. New States

1. Admission New states may be admitted by the Congress into this Union; but no new state shall be formed or erected within the jurisdiction of any other state; nor any state be formed by the junction of two or more states, or parts of states, without the consent of the legislatures of the states concerned as well as of the Congress.

2. Congressional Authority The Congress shall have power to dispose of and make all needful rules and regulations respecting the territory or other property belonging to the United States; and nothing in this Constitution shall be so construed as to prejudice any claims of the United States, or of any particular state.

Section 4. Guarantees to the States

The United States shall guarantee to every state in this Union a republican form of government, and shall protect each of them against invasion; and on application of the legislature, or of the executive (when the legislature cannot be convened) against domestic violence.

Article 5. *Amending the Constitution*

> **MAIN IDEA** The Constitution can be amended, or formally changed.
>
> **WHY IT MATTERS NOW** The amendment process allows the Constitution to adapt to modern times.

The Congress, whenever two-thirds of both houses shall deem it necessary, shall propose amendments to this Constitution, or, on the application of the legislatures of two-thirds of the several states, shall call a convention for proposing amendments, which, in either case, shall be valid to all intents and purposes, as part of this Constitution, when ratified by the legislatures of three-fourths of the several states, or by conventions in three-fourths thereof, as the one or the other mode of ratification may be proposed by the Congress; provided that no amendment which may be made prior to the year one thousand eight hundred and eight shall in any manner affect the first and fourth clauses in the ninth section of the first article; and that no state, without its consent, shall be deprived of its equal **suffrage** in the Senate.

A CLOSER LOOK

ADMISSION TO STATEHOOD

In 1998, Puerto Ricans voted against their island becoming the 51st state. A lawyer in Puerto Rico summed up a main reason: "Puerto Ricans want to have ties to the U. S., but they want to protect their language and culture." Also, as a U.S. commonwealth, Puerto Rico makes its own laws and handles its own finances.

17. Do you think Puerto Rico should become a state? Why or why not?

A CLOSER LOOK Process for Amending the Constitution

Proposing Amendments

| 2/3 vote of both houses of Congress | 2/3 state legislatures' call for a national convention |

Ratifying Amendments

| 3/4 approval of state legislatures | 3/4 approval at a state convention |

SKILLBUILDER Interpreting Charts
Why do you think more votes are needed to ratify an amendment than to propose one?

A CLOSER LOOK

PAYING DEBTS

The U.S. government agreed to pay all debts held under the Articles of Confederation. For example, the United States still owed money from the costs of the Revolutionary War.

18. What problems might arise in a country that has a huge national debt?

Article 6. *Supremacy of the National Government*

> **MAIN IDEA** The Constitution, national laws, and treaties are the supreme, or highest, law of the land. All government officials must promise to support the Constitution.
>
> **WHY IT MATTERS NOW** The authority of federal laws over state laws helps keep the nation unified.

Section 1. Valid Debts All debts contracted and engagements entered into, before the adoption of this Constitution, shall be as valid against the United States under this Constitution, as under the Confederation.

Section 2. Supreme Law This Constitution, and the laws of the United States which shall be made in pursuance thereof; and all treaties made, or which shall be made, under the authority of the United States, shall be the supreme law of the land; and the judges in every state shall be bound thereby, anything in the constitution or laws of any state to the contrary notwithstanding.

A CLOSER LOOK

In 1957, the "supreme law of the land" was put to a test. The governor of Arkansas defied a Supreme Court order. The Court ruled that African-American students could go to all-white public schools. President Dwight D. Eisenhower then sent federal troops to protect the first African-American students to enroll in Central High School in Little Rock, Arkansas.

Section 3. Loyalty to Constitution The Senators and Representatives before mentioned, and the members of the several state legislatures, and all executive and judicial officers, both of the United States and of the several states, shall be bound by oath or affirmation to support this Constitution; but no religious test shall ever be required as a qualification to any office or public trust under the United States.

The CENTINEL   VOL IX

REDEUNT SATURNIA REGNA.

On the erection of the Eleventh PILLAR of the great National DOME, we beg leave most sincerely to felicitate "OUR DEAR COUNTRY."

The FEDERAL EDIFICE.

A CLOSER LOOK

This political cartoon shows that New York was the 11th state to ratify the Constitution. Each of the 13 states is represented by a pillar.

Article 7. Ratification

MAIN IDEA Nine of the 13 states had to ratify, or approve, the Constitution before it could go into effect.

WHY IT MATTERS NOW The approval of the Constitution launched a new plan of government still followed today.

The **ratification** of the conventions of nine states shall be sufficient for the establishment of this Constitution between the states so ratifying the same. Done in convention by the **unanimous consent** of the states present, the seventeenth day of September in the year of our Lord one thousand seven hundred and eighty-seven and of the independence of the United States of America the twelfth. In witness whereof we have hereunto subscribed our names.

George Washington—President and deputy from Virginia

New Hampshire: *John Langdon, Nicholas Gilman*

Massachusetts: *Nathaniel Gorham, Rufus King*

Connecticut: *William Samuel Johnson, Roger Sherman*

New York: *Alexander Hamilton*

New Jersey: *William Livingston, David Brearley, William Paterson, Jonathan Dayton*

Pennsylvania: *Benjamin Franklin, Thomas Mifflin, Robert Morris, George Clymer, Thomas FitzSimons, Jared Ingersoll, James Wilson, Gouverneur Morris*

Delaware: *George Read, Gunning Bedford, Jr., John Dickinson, Richard Bassett, Jacob Broom*

Maryland: *James McHenry, Dan of St. Thomas Jenifer, Daniel Carroll*

Virginia: *John Blair, James Madison, Jr.*

North Carolina: *William Blount, Richard Dobbs Spaight, Hugh Williamson*

South Carolina: *John Rutledge, Charles Cotesworth Pinckney, Charles Pinckney, Pierce Butler*

Georgia: *William Few, Abraham Baldwin*

A CLOSER LOOK

THE SIGNERS

The 39 men who signed the Constitution were wealthy and well-educated. About half of them were trained in law. Others were doctors, merchants, bankers, and slaveholding planters. Missing from the list of signatures are the names of African Americans, Native Americans, and women. These groups reflected the varied population of the United States in the 1780s.

19. How do you think the absence of these groups affected the decisions made in creating the Constitution?

Articles 4–7 Assessment

1. Main Ideas

a. What rights does Article 4 guarantee to citizens if they go to other states in the nation?

b. What are two ways of proposing an amendment to the Constitution?

c. What makes up "the supreme law of the land"?

2. Critical Thinking

Forming and Supporting Opinions Should the Framers of the Constitution have allowed the people to vote directly for ratification of the Constitution? Why or why not?

THINK ABOUT

• the idea that the government belongs to the people

• the general public's ability to make sound political decisions

The Bill of Rights and Amendments 11–27

In 1787, Thomas Jefferson sent James Madison a letter about the Constitution. Jefferson wrote, "I will now add what I do not like . . . [there is no] bill of rights." He explained his reasons: "A bill of rights is what the people are entitled to against every government on earth . . . and what no just government should refuse." Jefferson's disapproval is not surprising. In writing the Declaration of Independence, he spelled out basic individual rights that cannot be taken way. These are "life, liberty, and the pursuit of happiness." The Declaration states that governments are formed to protect these rights.

Several states approved the Constitution only if a list of guaranteed freedoms was added. While serving in the nation's first Congress, James Madison helped draft the Bill of Rights. In 1791, these first ten amendments became part of the Constitution.

AMENDMENTS 1–10. *The Bill of Rights*

> **MAIN IDEA** The Bill of Rights protects citizens from government interference.
> **WHY IT MATTERS NOW** Issues related to the Bill of Rights are still being applied, tested, and interpreted.

AMENDMENT 1. Religious and Political Freedom (1791)

Congress shall make no law respecting an establishment of religion, or prohibiting the free exercise thereof; or **abridging** the freedom of speech, or of the press; or the right of the people peaceably to assemble, and to petition the Government for a redress of grievances.

A CLOSER LOOK The Five Freedoms

Freedom of Religion
Right to worship

Freedom of Speech
Right to state ideas

Freedom of the Press
Right to publish ideas

Freedom of Assembly
Right to meet peacefully in groups

Freedom to Petition
Right to protest the government

SKILLBUILDER **Interpreting Charts**
1. *Why is freedom of speech and the press important in a democratic society?*
2. *What impact has religious freedom had on the American way of life?*

AMENDMENT 2. Right to Bear Arms (1791)

A well-regulated militia, being necessary to the security of a free state, the right of the people to keep and bear arms, shall not be infringed.

AMENDMENT 3. Quartering Troops (1791)

No soldier shall, in time of peace be **quartered** in any house, without the consent of the owner, nor in time of war, but in a manner to be prescribed by law.

AMENDMENT 4. Search and Seizure (1791)

The right of the people to be secure in their persons, houses, papers, and effects, against unreasonable searches and seizures, shall not be violated, and no warrants shall issue, but upon probable cause, supported by oath or affirmation, and particularly describing the place to be searched, and the persons or things to be seized.

AMENDMENT 5. Rights of Accused Persons (1791)

No person shall be held to answer for a capital, or otherwise infamous crime, unless on a presentment or indictment of a Grand Jury, except in cases arising in the land or naval forces, or in the militia, when in actual service in time of war or public danger; nor shall any person be subject for the same offense to be twice put in jeopardy of life or limb; nor shall be compelled in any criminal case to be a witness against himself, nor be deprived of life, liberty, or property, without **due process of law;** nor shall private property be taken for public use, without just compensation.

AMENDMENT 6. Right to a Speedy, Public Trial (1791)

In all criminal prosecutions, the accused shall enjoy the right to a speedy and public trial, by an impartial jury of the State and district wherein the crime shall have been committed, which district shall have been previously ascertained by law, and to be informed of the nature and cause of the accusation; to be confronted with the witnesses against him; to have **compulsory process** for obtaining witnesses in his favor, and to have the assistance of **counsel** for his defense.

A CLOSER LOOK

SEARCHES

Metal detectors at airports search passengers. Airline workers search all carry-on luggage. Do these actions violate the 4th Amendment? The courts say no. They have cited many situations that allow for searches without a warrant, or written order. A person's right to privacy is balanced against the government's need to prevent crime.

20. **What does the right to privacy mean to you at home and at school?**

A CLOSER LOOK

In 1966, the Supreme Court made a decision based on the 5th and 6th Amendments. The warnings outlined in this ruling are often called "Miranda rights." Miranda rights protect suspects from giving forced confessions. Police must read these rights to a suspect they are questioning. For example:

- "You have the right to remain silent."
- "Anything that you say can and will be used against you in a court of law."
- "You have the right to an attorney."

A CLOSER LOOK

Protesters such as the young woman at left claim that the death penalty violates the 8th Amendment, which protects people against "cruel and unusual punishment." Supporters (above) believe that the death penalty is a justly deserved punishment.

A CLOSER LOOK

STATES' POWERS

The 10th Amendment gives the states reserved powers. Any powers not clearly given to the national government by the U.S. Constitution or denied to the states in Article I, Section 10, belong to the states. State constitutions sometimes assume authority in unexpected areas. For example, California's constitution sets rules for governing the use of fishing nets.

21. What are some common areas in which states have authority?

AMENDMENT 7. Trial by Jury in Civil Cases (1791) In suits at **common law,** where the value in controversy shall exceed twenty dollars, the right of trial by jury shall be preserved, and no fact tried by a jury, shall be otherwise reexamined in any court of the United States, than according to the rules of the common law.

AMENDMENT 8. Limits of Fines and Punishments (1791) Excessive **bail** shall not be required, nor excessive fines imposed, nor cruel and unusual punishments inflicted.

AMENDMENT 9. Rights of People (1791) The enumeration in the Constitution of certain rights shall not be construed to deny or disparage others retained by the people.

AMENDMENT 10. Powers of States and People (1791) The powers not delegated to the United States by the Constitution, nor prohibited by it to the States, are reserved to the States respectively, or to the people.

Bill of Rights Assessment

1. Main Ideas

a. Which amendment protects your privacy?

b. Which amendments guarantee fair legal treatment?

c. Which amendment prevents the federal government from taking powers away from the states and the people?

2. Critical Thinking

Forming and Supporting Opinions The 4th, 5th, 6th, 7th, and 8th Amendments protect innocent people accused of crimes. Do you think these five amendments also favor the rights of actual criminals? Explain.

THINK ABOUT

- criminals who go free if valuable evidence is found after their trials
- criminals released on bail

Amendments 11–27

> **MAIN IDEA** The Constitution has adapted to social changes and historical trends.
> **WHY IT MATTERS NOW** Amendments 11–27 show that the Constitution is a living document.

AMENDMENT 11. Lawsuits Against States (1798)

Passed by Congress March 4, 1794. Ratified February 7, 1795. Proclaimed 1798.
Note: Article 3, Section 2, of the Constitution was modified by Amendment 11.

The Judicial power of the United States shall not be construed to extend to any suit in law or **equity**, commenced or prosecuted against one of the United States by citizens of another state, or by citizens or subjects of any foreign state.

AMENDMENT 12. Election of Executives (1804)

Passed by Congress December 9, 1803. Ratified June 15, 1804.
Note: Part of Article 2, Section 1, of the Constitution was replaced by the 12th Amendment.

The electors shall meet in their respective states and vote by ballot for President and Vice-President, one of whom, at least, shall not be an inhabitant of the same state with themselves; they shall name in their ballots the person voted for as President, and in distinct ballots the person voted for as Vice-President, and they shall make distinct lists of all persons voted for as President, and of all persons voted for as Vice-President, and of the number of votes for each, which lists they shall sign and certify, and transmit sealed to the seat of the government of the United States, directed to the President of the Senate;—the President of the Senate shall, in the presence of the Senate and House of Representatives, open all the certificates and the votes shall then be counted;—the person having the greatest number of votes for President, shall be the President, if such number be a majority of the whole number of electors appointed; and if no person have such majority, then from the persons having the highest numbers not exceeding three on the list of those voted for as President, the House of Representatives shall choose immediately, by ballot, the President. But in choosing the President, the votes shall be taken by states, the representation from each state having one vote; a quorum for this purpose shall consist of a member or members from two-thirds of the states, and a majority of all the states shall be necessary to a choice. And if the House of Representatives shall not choose a President whenever the right of choice shall devolve upon them, before the fourth day of March next following, then the Vice-President shall act as President, as in the case of the death or other constitutional disability of the President. The person having the greatest number of votes as Vice-President, shall be the Vice-President, if such number be a majority of the whole number of Electors appointed, and if no person have a majority, then from the two highest numbers on the list, the Senate shall choose the Vice-President; a quorum for the purpose shall consist of two-thirds of the whole number of Senators, and a majority of the whole number shall be necessary to a choice. But no person constitutionally ineligible to the office of President shall be eligible to that of Vice-President of the United States.

VOCABULARY

common law a system of law developed in England, based on customs and previous court decisions

bail money paid by arrested persons to guarantee they will return for trial

equity a system of justice not covered under common law

A CLOSER LOOK

SEPARATE BALLOTS

The presidential election of 1800 ended in a tie between Thomas Jefferson and Aaron Burr. At this time, the candidate with the most votes became president. The runner-up became vice-president. The 12th Amendment calls for separate ballots for the president and vice-president. The vice-president is specifically elected to the office, rather than being the presidential candidate with the second-most votes.

22. Why do you think it's important for a presidential election to result in a clear-cut winner?

AMENDMENT 13. Slavery Abolished (1865)

Passed by Congress January 31, 1865. Ratified December 6, 1865.

Note: A portion of Article 4, Section 2, of the Constitution was superseded by the 13th Amendment.

Section 1. Neither slavery nor involuntary **servitude**, except as a punishment for crime whereof the party shall have been duly convicted, shall exist within the United States, or any place subject to their jurisdiction.

Section 2. Congress shall have power to enforce this article by appropriate legislation.

AMENDMENT 14. Civil Rights (1868)

Passed by Congress June 13, 1866. Ratified July 9, 1868.

Note: Article 1, Section 2, of the Constitution was modified by Section 2 of the 14th Amendment.

Section 1. All persons born or **naturalized** in the United States, and subject to the jurisdiction thereof, are citizens of the United States and of the state wherein they reside. No state shall make or enforce any law which shall abridge the privileges or immunities of citizens of the United States; nor shall any state deprive any person of life, liberty, or property, without due process of law; nor deny to any person within its jurisdiction the equal protection of the laws.

Section 2. Representatives shall be apportioned among the several states according to their respective numbers, counting the whole number of persons in each state, excluding Indians not taxed. But when the right to vote at any election for the choice of electors for President and Vice-President of the United States, Representatives in Congress, the executive and judicial officers of a state, or the members of the legislature thereof, is denied to any of the male inhabitants of such state, being twenty-one years of age, and citizens of the United States, or in any way abridged, except for participation in rebellion, or other crime, the basis of representation therein shall be reduced in the proportion which the number of such male citizens shall bear to the whole number of male citizens twenty-one years of age in such state.

A CLOSER LOOK

The 14th Amendment laid the groundwork for many civil rights laws, such as the Americans with Disabilities Act (1990). This act gave people with mental or physical disabilities "equal protection of the laws." For example, public places had to be designed for wheelchair use. Wider doors and ramps allow disabled people to go in and out of buildings.

Section 3. No person shall be a Senator or Representative in Congress, or elector of President and Vice-President, or hold any office, civil or military, under the United States, or under any state, who, having previously taken an oath, as a member of Congress, or as an officer of the United States, or as a member of any state legislature, or as an executive or judicial officer of any state, to support the Constitution of the United States, shall have engaged in **insurrection** or rebellion against the same, or given aid or comfort to the enemies thereof. But Congress may, by a vote of two-thirds of each house, remove such disability.

Section 4. The validity of the public debt of the United States, authorized by law, including debts incurred for payment of pensions and **bounties** for services in suppressing insurrection or rebellion, shall not be questioned. But neither the United States nor any state shall assume or pay any debt or obligation incurred in aid of insurrection or rebellion against the United States, or any claim for the loss or emancipation of any slave; but all such debts, obligations and claims shall be held illegal and void.

Section 5. The Congress shall have power to enforce, by appropriate legislation, the provisions of this article.

AMENDMENT 15. Right to Vote (1870)

Passed by Congress February 26, 1869. Ratified February 3, 1870.

Section 1. The right of citizens of the United States to vote shall not be denied or abridged by the United States or by any state on account of race, color, or previous condition of servitude.

Section 2. The Congress shall have power to enforce this article by appropriate legislation.

A CLOSER LOOK Reconstruction Amendments

The 13th, 14th, and 15th Amendments are often called the Reconstruction Amendments. They were passed after the Civil War during the government's attempt to rebuild the Union and to grant rights to recently freed African Americans.

Amendment 13

1865

• Ended slavery in the United States

Amendment 14

1868

• Defined national and state citizenship
• Protected citizens' rights
• Promised "equal protection of the laws"

Amendment 15

1870

• Designed to protect African Americans' voting rights

SKILLBUILDER Interpreting Charts
What problems did these amendments try to solve?

A CLOSER LOOK

VOTING RIGHTS

The Voting Rights Act of 1965 extended the 15th Amendment. To qualify as voters, African Americans were no longer required to take tests proving that they could read and write. Also, federal examiners could help register voters. As a result, the number of African-American voters rose sharply.

23. What effect do you think the Voting Rights Act had on candidates running for office?

People below the poverty level, as defined by the federal government, do not have to pay income tax. In 1997, the poverty level for a family of four was $16,400 per year. About 13.3 percent of all Americans were considered poor in 1997.

24. Why do you think people below the poverty level do not pay any income tax?

AMENDMENT 16. Income Tax (1913)

Passed by Congress July 12, 1909. Ratified February 3, 1913.

Note: Article 1, Section 9, of the Constitution was modified by the 16th Amendment.

The Congress shall have power to lay and collect taxes on incomes, from whatever source derived, without apportionment among the several states, and without regard to any census or enumeration.

AMENDMENT 17. Direct Election of Senators (1913)

Passed by Congress May 13, 1912. Ratified April 8, 1913.

Note: Article 1, Section 3, of the Constitution was modified by the 17th Amendment.

Section 1. The Senate of the United States shall be composed of two Senators from each state, elected by the people thereof, for six years; and each Senator shall have one vote. The electors in each state shall have the qualifications requisite for electors of the most numerous branch of the state legislatures.

Section 2. When vacancies happen in the representation of any state in the Senate, the executive authority of such state shall issue writs of election to fill such vacancies: Provided, that the legislature of any state may empower the executive thereof to make temporary appointments until the people fill the vacancies by election as the legislature may direct.

Section 3. This amendment shall not be so construed as to affect the election or term of any Senator chosen before it becomes valid as part of the Constitution.

AMENDMENT 18. Prohibition (1919)

Passed by Congress December 18, 1917. Ratified January 16, 1919. Repealed by the 21st Amendment.

Section 1. After one year from the ratification of this article the manufacture, sale, or transportation of intoxicating liquors within, the importation thereof into, or the exportation thereof from the United States and all territory subject to the jurisdiction thereof for beverage purposes is hereby prohibited.

Section 2. The Congress and the several states shall have concurrent power to enforce this article by appropriate legislation.

Section 3. This article shall be inoperative unless it shall have been ratified as an amendment to the Constitution by the legislatures of the several states, as provided in the Constitution, within seven years from the date of the submission hereof to the states by the Congress.

Under Prohibition, people broke the law if they made, sold, or shipped alcoholic beverages. Powerful crime gangs turned selling illegal liquor into a big business. This photo shows federal agents getting ready to smash containers of illegal whiskey. The 21st Amendment ended Prohibition.

A CLOSER LOOK

At left, marchers campaign for the 19th Amendment—woman suffrage. Since winning the right to vote in 1920, women have slowly gained political power. Pictured below are Congress members who belong to the Congressional Caucus for Women's Issues.

AMENDMENT 19. Woman Suffrage (1920)

Passed by Congress June 4, 1919. Ratified August 18, 1920.

Section 1. The right of citizens of the United States to vote shall not be denied or abridged by the United States or by any state on account of sex.

Section 2. Congress shall have power to enforce this article by appropriate legislation.

AMENDMENT 20. "Lame Duck" Sessions (1933)

Passed by Congress March 2, 1932. Ratified January 23, 1933.

Note: Article 1, Section 4, of the Constitution was modified by Section 2 of this amendment. In addition, a portion of the 12th Amendment was superseded by Section 3.

Section 1. The terms of the President and Vice-President shall end at noon on the 20th day of January, and the terms of Senators and Representatives at noon on the 3rd day of January, of the years in which such terms would have ended if this article had not been ratified; and the terms of their successors shall then begin.

Section 2. The Congress shall assemble at least once in every year, and such meeting shall begin at noon on the 3rd day of January, unless they shall by law appoint a different day.

Section 3. If, at the time fixed for the beginning of the term of the President, the President elect shall have died, the Vice-President elect shall become President. If a President shall not have been chosen before the time fixed for the beginning of his term, or if the President elect shall have failed to qualify, then the Vice-President elect shall act as President until a President shall have qualified; and the Congress may by law provide for the case wherein neither a President elect nor a Vice-President elect shall have

A CLOSER LOOK

THE EQUAL RIGHTS AMENDMENT

In 1920, the 19th Amendment took effect, guaranteeing women the right to vote. Nevertheless, many women have continued to face discrimination in the United States. In 1923, the National Women's Party supported the passage of an equal rights amendment to protect women. Congress did not pass such an amendment until 1972. In 1982, however, the amendment died after it failed to be ratified by enough states to be added to the Constitution.

25. Why do you think the 19th Amendment failed to create equality for women?

qualified, declaring who shall then act as President, or the manner in which one who is to act shall be selected, and such person shall act accordingly until a President or Vice-President shall have qualified.

Section 4. The Congress may by law provide for the case of the death of any of the persons from whom the House of Representatives may choose a President whenever the right of choice shall have devolved upon them, and for the case of the death of any of the persons from whom the Senate may choose a Vice-President whenever the right of choice shall have devolved upon them.

Section 5. Sections 1 and 2 shall take effect on the 15th day of October following the ratification of this article.

Section 6. This article shall be **inoperative** unless it shall have been ratified as an amendment to the Constitution by the legislatures of three-fourths of the several states within seven years from the date of its submission.

AMENDMENT 21. Repeal of Prohibition (1933)
Passed by Congress February 20, 1933. Ratified December 5, 1933.

Section 1. The eighteenth article of amendment to the Constitution of the United States is hereby repealed.

Section 2. The transportation or importation into any state, territory, or possession of the United States for delivery or use therein of intoxicating liquors, in violation of the laws thereof, is hereby prohibited.

Section 3. This article shall be inoperative unless it shall have been ratified as an amendment to the Constitution by conventions in the several states, as provided in the Constitution, within seven years from the date of the submission hereof to the states by the Congress.

AMENDMENT 22. Limit on Presidential Terms (1951)
Passed by Congress March 21, 1947. Ratified February 27, 1951.

Section 1. No person shall be elected to the office of the President more than twice, and no person who has held the office of President, or acted as President, for more than two years of a term to which some other person was elected President shall be elected to the office of the President more than once. But this article shall not apply to any person holding the office of President when this article was proposed by the Congress, and shall not prevent any person who may be holding the office of President, or acting as President, during the term within which this article becomes operative from holding the office of President or acting as President during the remainder of such term.

Section 2. This article shall be inoperative unless it shall have been ratified as an amendment to the Constitution by the legislatures of three-fourths of the several states within seven years from the date of its submission to the states by the Congress.

A CLOSER LOOK

George Washington set the tradition of limiting the presidency to two terms. Franklin Roosevelt broke this custom when he was elected president four terms in a row—1932, 1936, 1940, and 1944. His record-long presidency led to the 22nd Amendment. A two-term limit, written into the Constitution, checks the president's power.

AMENDMENT 23. Voting in District of Columbia (1961)

Passed by Congress June 17, 1960. Ratified March 29, 1961.

Section 1. The district constituting the seat of government of the United States shall appoint in such manner as Congress may direct: a number of electors of President and Vice-President equal to the whole number of Senators and Representatives in Congress to which the district would be entitled if it were a state, but in no event more than the least populous state; they shall be in addition to those appointed by the states, but they shall be considered, for the purposes of the election of President and Vice-President, to be electors appointed by a state; and they shall meet in the district and perform such duties as provided by the twelfth article of amendment.

Section 2. The Congress shall have power to enforce this article by appropriate legislation.

AMENDMENT 24. Abolition of Poll Taxes (1964)

Passed by Congress August 27, 1962. Ratified January 23, 1964.

Section 1. The right of citizens of the United States to vote in any **primary** or other election for President or Vice-President, for electors for President or Vice-President, or for Senator or Representative in Congress, shall not be denied or abridged by the United States or any state by reason of failure to pay any poll tax or other tax.

Section 2. The Congress shall have power to enforce this article by appropriate legislation.

AMENDMENT 25. Presidential Disability, Succession (1967)

Passed by Congress July 6, 1965. Ratified February 10, 1967.

Note: Article 2, Section 1, of the Constitution was affected by the 25th Amendment.

Section 1. In case of the removal of the President from office or of his death or resignation, the Vice-President shall become President.

Section 2. Whenever there is a vacancy in the office of the Vice-President, the President shall nominate a Vice-President who shall take office upon confirmation by a majority vote of both houses of Congress.

Section 3. Whenever the President transmits to the President pro tempore of the Senate and the Speaker of the House of Representatives his written declaration that he is unable to discharge the powers and duties of his office, and until he transmits to them a written declaration to the contrary, such powers and duties shall be discharged by the Vice-President as Acting President.

A CLOSER LOOK

POLL TAX

The poll tax was aimed at preventing African Americans from exercising their rights. Many could not afford to pay this fee required for voting.

26. How do you think the 24th Amendment affected elections?

A CLOSER LOOK

PRESIDENTIAL DISABILITY

President John F. Kennedy's death in 1963 signaled the need for the 25th Amendment. The Constitution did not explain what to do in the case of a disabled president. James Reston, a writer for *The New York Times,* summed up the problem: Suppose Kennedy was "strong enough to survive [the bullet wounds], but too weak to govern." The 25th Amendment provides for an orderly transfer of power.

27. What do you think can happen in a country where the rules for succession are not clear?

SUCCESSION

Who takes over if a president dies in office or is unable to serve? The top five in the line of succession follow:

• vice-president

• speaker of the house

• president pro tempore of the Senate

• secretary of state

• secretary of the treasury

28. Why should voters know the views of the vice-president?

Section 4. Whenever the Vice-President and a majority of either the principal officers of the executive departments or of such other body as Congress may by law provide, transmit to the President pro tempore of the Senate and the Speaker of the House of Representatives their written declaration that the President is unable to discharge the powers and duties of his office, the Vice-President shall immediately assume the powers and duties of the office as Acting President. Thereafter, when the President transmits to the President pro tempore of the Senate and the Speaker of the House of Representatives his written declaration that no inability exists, he shall resume the powers and duties of his office unless the Vice-President and a majority of either the principal officers of the executive department[s] or of such other body as Congress may by law provide, transmit within four days to the President pro tempore of the Senate and the Speaker of the House of Representatives their written declaration that the President is unable to discharge the powers and duties of his office. Thereupon Congress shall decide the issue, assembling within forty-eight hours for that purpose if not in session. If the Congress, within twenty-one days after receipt of the latter written declaration, or, if Congress is not in session, within twenty-one days after Congress is required to assemble, determines by two thirds vote of both houses that the President is unable to discharge the powers and duties of his office, the Vice-President shall continue to discharge the same as Acting President; otherwise, the President shall resume the powers and duties of his office.

A CLOSER LOOK Amendments Time Line *1791–1992*

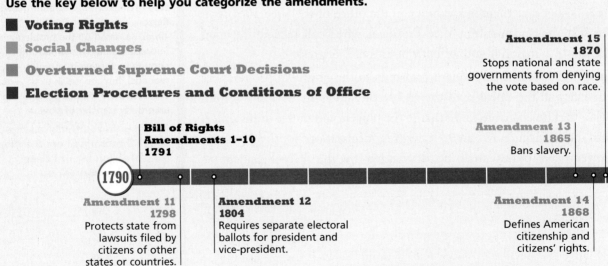

Use the key below to help you categorize the amendments.

■ **Voting Rights**

■ **Social Changes**

■ **Overturned Supreme Court Decisions**

■ **Election Procedures and Conditions of Office**

**Bill of Rights
Amendments 1–10
1791**

1790

**Amendment 15
1870**
Stops national and state governments from denying the vote based on race.

**Amendment 13
1865**
Bans slavery.

**Amendment 11
1798**
Protects state from lawsuits filed by citizens of other states or countries.

**Amendment 12
1804**
Requires separate electoral ballots for president and vice-president.

**Amendment 14
1868**
Defines American citizenship and citizens' rights.

AMENDMENT 26. 18-year-old Vote (1971)

Passed by Congress March 23, 1971. Ratified July 1, 1971.

Note: Amendment 14, Section 2, of the Constitution was modified by Section 1 of the 26th Amendment.

Section 1. The right of citizens of the United States, who are eighteen years of age or older, to vote shall not be denied or abridged by the United States or by any state on account of age.

Section 2. The Congress shall have power to enforce this article by appropriate legislation.

AMENDMENT 27. Congressional Pay (1992)

Passed by Congress September 25, 1789. Ratified May 7, 1992.

No law, varying the compensation for the services of the Senators and Representatives, shall take effect, until an election of Representatives shall have intervened.

A CLOSER LOOK

Members of the recording industry founded Rock the Vote. They urge young people to vote in elections.

Amendments 11–27 Assessment

1. Main Ideas

a. Which amendments affected the office of president?

b. Which pair of amendments shows the failure of laws to solve a social problem?

c. Which amendments corrected unfair treatment toward African Americans and women?

2. Critical Thinking

Summarizing What is the purpose of amending the Constitution?

THINK ABOUT

• the purpose of the Constitution

• problems and issues that Americans have faced throughout U.S. history

---

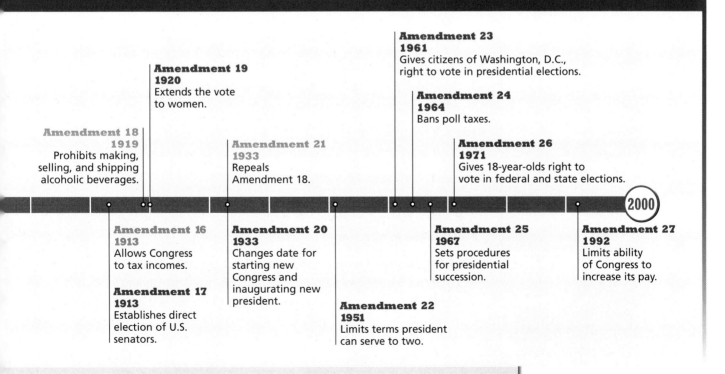

Amendment 18
1919
Prohibits making, selling, and shipping alcoholic beverages.

Amendment 16
1913
Allows Congress to tax incomes.

Amendment 17
1913
Establishes direct election of U.S. senators.

Amendment 19
1920
Extends the vote to women.

Amendment 21
1933
Repeals Amendment 18.

Amendment 20
1933
Changes date for starting new Congress and inaugurating new president.

Amendment 22
1951
Limits terms president can serve to two.

Amendment 23
1961
Gives citizens of Washington, D.C., right to vote in presidential elections.

Amendment 24
1964
Bans poll taxes.

Amendment 26
1971
Gives 18-year-olds right to vote in federal and state elections.

Amendment 25
1967
Sets procedures for presidential succession.

Amendment 27
1992
Limits ability of Congress to increase its pay.

2000

VISUAL SUMMARY

The Constitution of the United States

Preamble

WE THE PEOPLE

Article 1   Article 2   Article 3

The Branches of Government

Executive   Judicial
President   Supreme
             Court

Legislative

Senate   House of
          Representatives

Article 4   Article 6

The Federal System

Powers of   Powers of
the State   the National
                   Government

"Supreme law
of the land"

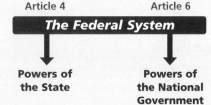

Article 5

Amending the Constitution

Making Changes

*Bill
of
Rights*

Amendments 1–10

Personal   Personal   Rights of
Freedoms   Security   the Accused

Amendments 11–27

*The living Constitution
changes with the times.*

VOCABULARY

Briefly explain the significance of each of the following.

1. electors
2. impeachment
3. naturalization
4. felonies
5. bill of attainder
6. ex post facto law
7. suffrage
8. due process of law
9. servitude
10. primary

SEVEN PRINCIPLES OF THE CONSTITUTION

Make a chart like the one shown. Then fill it in with a definition of each principle and an example from the Constitution.

Principle	Definition	Example
1. popular sovereignty		
2. republicanism		
3. federalism		
4. separation of powers		
5. checks and balances		
6. limited government		
7. individual rights		

REVIEW QUESTIONS

Article 1 (pages 233–239)

1. What are the requirements for becoming a member of the House of Representatives and the Senate?
2. What are two military powers granted to Congress?

Article 2 (pages 240–243)

3. How does the electoral college choose the president?
4. What are three powers of the president?

Article 3 (pages 244–245)

5. What are the two most important powers of the federal courts?

Articles 4–7 (pages 246–249)

6. How can the Constitution be changed?
7. If a state law and a federal law conflict, which law must be obeyed? Why?
8. How was the Constitution ratified?

Bill of Rights and Amendments 11–27 (pages 250–261)

9. What five freedoms are guaranteed in the First Amendment?
10. Which amendments extend voting rights to a broader range of Americans?

CRITICAL THINKING

1. DRAWING CONCLUSIONS

In a two-column chart, summarize the processes for changing the Constitution. Then use your completed chart to answer the questions below.

Proposing Amendments	Ratifying Amendments
1.	1.
2.	2.

a. What role can citizens play in proposing amendments?

b. What do you think are the main reasons for changing the Constitution?

2. MAKING INFERENCES

Explain how the "elastic clause" in Article 1 gives Congress the authority to take action on other issues unknown to the Framers of the Constitution.

3. ANALYZING LEADERSHIP

Think about the president's roles described in the Constitution. What qualities does a president need to succeed as a leader in so many different areas?

4. RECOGNIZING EFFECTS

How would you describe the impact of the 14th, 15th, and 16th Amendments on life in the United States?

5. APPLYING CITIZENSHIP

Suppose you and your family go on a road trip across several states. According to Article 4 of the Constitution, what citizens' rights do you have in the states you are visiting?

HISTORY SKILLS

INTERPRETING PRIMARY SOURCES

In 1937, President Franklin D. Roosevelt gave a speech over the radio. He used interesting comparisons to explain how the government works.

> I described the American form of government as a three-horse team provided by the Constitution to the American people so that their field might be plowed. The three horses are, of course, the three branches of government—the Congress, the Executive, and the Courts. . . . It is the American people themselves who are in the driver's seat. It is the American people themselves who want the furrow plowed.
>
> **Franklin D. Roosevelt,** Radio Address

- How does Roosevelt describe the separation of powers?
- How does Roosevelt explain popular sovereignty?

ALTERNATIVE ASSESSMENT

1. INTERDISCIPLINARY ACTIVITY: Government

Creating a Database Review the grievances against King George III listed in the Declaration of Independence. Then create a database that shows how specific sections of the U.S. Constitution addressed those grievances. Write a brief summary stating how well the Constitution addressed the grievances.

2. COOPERATIVE LEARNING ACTIVITY

Drafting a Constitution Imagine you are asked to write a constitution for a newly formed country. Working with a group, use the outline below to organize and write your constitution.

 I. Purpose of the Constitution (Preamble)

 II. Making Laws (Legislative Branch)

 III. Carrying Out the Laws (Executive Branch)

 IV. Making Laws Fair (Judicial Branch)

 V. Choosing Leaders

 VI. Citizens' Rights (Bill of Rights)

3. PRIMARY SOURCE EXPLORER

Making a Learning Center Creating the U.S. Constitution was one of the most important events in the nation's history. Use the CD-ROM and the library to collect information on different topics related to the Constitution.

Create a learning center featuring the suggestions below.

- Find biographies and portraits of the Framers.
- Collect important primary sources such as James Madison's notes and *The Federalist* papers.
- Gather recent pictures and news articles about the Congress, the president, the Supreme Court, and the Bill of Rights.

4. HISTORY PORTFOLIO

Review your draft of the constitution you wrote for the assessment activity. Choose one of these options below.

 Option 1 Use comments made by your teacher or classmates to improve your work.

 Option 2 Illustrate your constitution. Add your work to your history portfolio.

Additional Test Practice, pp. S1–S33

 TEST PRACTICE CLASSZONE.COM

The Role of the Citizen

Citizens of the United States enjoy many basic rights and freedoms. Freedom of speech and religion are examples. These rights are guaranteed by the Constitution, the Bill of Rights, and other amendments to the Constitution. Along with these rights, however, come responsibilities. Obeying rules and laws, voting, and serving on juries are some examples.

Active citizenship is not limited to adults. Younger citizens can help their communities become better places. The following pages will help you to learn about your rights and responsibilities. Knowing them will help you to become an active and involved citizen of your community, state, and nation.

In this book you will find examples of active citizenship by young people like yourself. **Look for the Citizenship Today features.**

Citizen → **KNOW YOUR RIGHTS** → **BE RESPONSIBLE** → **STAY INFORMED** → **MAKE GOOD DECISIONS** → **PARTICIPATE IN YOUR COMMUNITY** → **Model Citizen**

President John F. Kennedy urged all Americans to become active citizens and work to improve their communities.

The weather was sunny but cold on January 20, 1961—the day that John F. Kennedy became the 35th president of the United States. In his first speech as president, he urged all Americans to serve their country. Since then, Kennedy's words have inspired millions of Americans to become more active citizens.

"Ask not what your country can do for you—ask what you can do for your country!"

—JOHN F. KENNEDY

What Is a Citizen?

A citizen is a legal member of a nation and pledges loyalty to that nation. A citizen has certain guaranteed rights, protections, and responsibilities. A citizen is a member of a community and wants to make it a good place to live.

Today in the United States there are a number of ways to become a citizen. The most familiar are citizenship by birth and citizenship by naturalization. All citizens have the right to equal protection under the law.

CITIZENSHIP BY BIRTH A child born in the United States is a citizen by birth. Children born to U.S. citizens traveling or living outside the country, such as military personnel, are citizens. Even children born in the United States to parents who are not citizens of the United States are considered U.S. citizens. These children have dual citizenship. This means they are citizens of two countries—both the United States and the country of their parents' citizenship. At the age of 18, the child may choose one of the countries for permanent citizenship.

CITIZENSHIP BY NATURALIZATION A person who is not a citizen of the United States may become one through a process called naturalization. The steps in this process are shown below. To become a naturalized citizen, a person must meet certain requirements.

- Be at least 18 years old. Children under the age of 18 automatically become naturalized citizens when their parents do.
- Enter the United States legally.
- Live in the United States for at least five years immediately prior to application.
- Read, write, and speak English.
- Show knowledge of American history and government.

See Citizenship Today: Becoming a Citizen, p. 411

Steps in the Naturalization Process

1. File an application.
2. Take an examination.
3. File a legal petition for naturalization.
4. Appear at a court hearing.
5. Take an oath of allegiance.

Hundreds of people become new citizens at a single ceremony in San Antonio, Texas.

What Are Your Rights?

Citizens of the United States are guaranteed rights by the U.S. Constitution, state constitutions, and state and federal laws. All citizens have three kinds of rights: basic freedoms, protection from unfair government actions, and equal treatment under the law.

Citizens' basic rights and freedoms are sometimes called **civil rights**. Some of these rights are personal, and others are political.

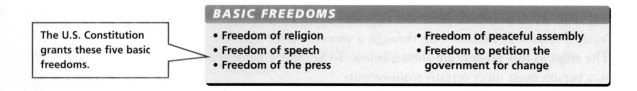

The U.S. Constitution grants these five basic freedoms.

BASIC FREEDOMS

- Freedom of religion
- Freedom of speech
- Freedom of the press
- Freedom of peaceful assembly
- Freedom to petition the government for change

The second category of rights is intended to protect citizens from unfair government actions.

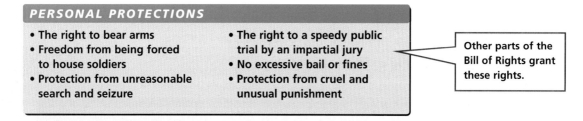

PERSONAL PROTECTIONS

- The right to bear arms
- Freedom from being forced to house soldiers
- Protection from unreasonable search and seizure
- The right to a speedy public trial by an impartial jury
- No excessive bail or fines
- Protection from cruel and unusual punishment

Other parts of the Bill of Rights grant these rights.

The third category is the right to equal treatment under the law. The government cannot treat one individual or group differently from another.

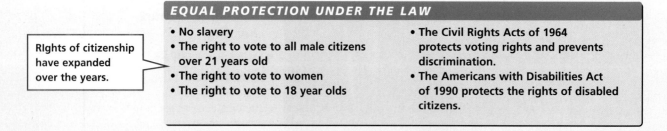

Rights of citizenship have expanded over the years.

EQUAL PROTECTION UNDER THE LAW

- No slavery
- The right to vote to all male citizens over 21 years old
- The right to vote to women
- The right to vote to 18 year olds
- The Civil Rights Acts of 1964 protects voting rights and prevents discrimination.
- The Americans with Disabilities Act of 1990 protects the rights of disabled citizens.

LIMITS TO RIGHTS The rights guaranteed to citizens have sensible limits. For example, the right to free speech does not allow a person to falsely shout, "Fire!" at a crowded concert. The government may place limits on certain rights to protect national security or to provide equal opportunities for all citizens. And rights come with responsibilities.

What Are Your Responsibilities?

For American democracy to work, citizens must carry out important responsibilities. There are two kinds of responsibilities—personal and civic. Personal responsibilities include taking care of yourself, helping your family, knowing right from wrong, and behaving in a respectful way.

Civic responsibilities are those that involve your government and community. They include obeying rules and laws, serving on juries, paying taxes, and defending your country when called upon. One of the most important responsibilities is voting. When you turn 18, you will have that right.

As a young person, you can be a good citizen in a number of ways. You might work with other people in your community to make it a fair and just place to live. Working for a political party or writing to your elected officials about issues that concern you are some other examples.

The chart below shows how responsibilities change with a citizen's age. Notice that all citizens share the responsibility to obey the laws of their communities.

See Citizenship Today: Obeying Rules and Laws, p. 284

Responsibilities of a Citizen

UNDER 18
- Receive an education, either at school or at home.
- Take responsibility for one's behavior.
- Help one's family.

ALL AGES
- Obey rules and laws.
- Be tolerant of others.
- Pay taxes.
- Volunteer for a cause.
- Stay informed about issues.

OVER 18
- Vote.
- Serve on a jury.
- Serve in the military to defend country.

Currently both men and women can serve in the military. Only men must register for the draft.

CITIZENSHIP ACTIVITIES

1. Interview a recently naturalized citizen. Ask about the test he or she took to become a U.S. citizen. Write a report of your findings.

2. Using newspapers or magazines, find examples of citizens using their unalienable rights or practicing responsible citizenship. Cut out five articles to illustrate the points. Mount them and write a one-sentence explanation of each article.

Building Citizenship Skills

Good citizenship skills include **staying informed, solving problems** or **making decisions,** and **taking action.** Every citizen can find ways to build citizenship skills. By showing respect for the law and for the rights of others in your daily life, you promote democracy. You can also work to change conditions in your community to make sure all citizens experience freedom and justice.

How Do You Stay Informed?

Americans can sometimes feel that they have access to too much information. It may seem overwhelming. Even so, you should stay informed on issues that affect your life. Staying informed gives you the information you need to make wise decisions and helps you find ways to solve problems.

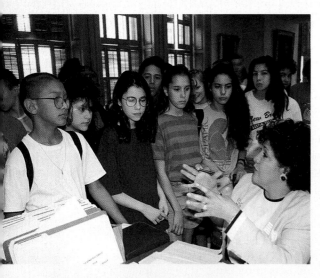

These Texas middle school students are staying informed by talking to their Texas state representative. Many public officials enjoy having students visit and ask them questions about their jobs, and about issues students think are important.

Watch, Listen, and Read

The first step in practicing good citizenship is to know how to find information that you need.

Sources of information include broadcast and print media and the Internet. Public officials and civic organizations are also good sources for additional information. Remember as you are reading to evaluate your sources.

See Citizenship Today: Debating Points of View, p. 456

Evaluate

As you become informed, you will need to make judgments about the accuracy of your news sources. You must also be aware of those sources' points of view and biases. (A bias is a judgment formed without knowing all of the facts.)

You should determine if you need more information. If you do, then decide where to find it. After gathering information, you may be ready to form an opinion or a plan of action to solve a problem.

See Citizenship Today: Detecting Bias in the Media, p. 557

Communicate

To bring about change in their communities, active citizens may need to contact public officials. In today's world, making contact is easy.

You can reach most public officials by telephone, voice mail, fax, or letter. Many public officials also have Internet pages or e-mail that encourages input from the public.

How Do You Make Wise Decisions?

Civic life involves making important decisions. As a voter, whom should you vote for? As a juror, should you find the defendant guilty or not guilty? As an informed citizen, should you support or oppose a proposed government action? Unlike decisions about which video to rent, civic decisions cannot be made by a process as easy as tossing a coin. Instead, you should use a problem-solving approach like the one shown in the chart below. Decision making won't always proceed directly from step to step. Sometimes it's necessary to backtrack a little. For example, you may get to the "Analyze the Information" step and realize that you don't have enough information to analyze. Then you can go back a step and gather more information.

Problem-Solving and Decision-Making Process

Problem-solving and decision-making involves many steps. This diagram shows you how to take those steps. Notice that you may have to repeat some steps depending on the information you gather.

EVALUATE THE SOLUTION
Review the results of putting your solution into action. Did the solution work? Do you need to adjust the solution in some way?

IMPLEMENT THE SOLUTION
Take action or plan to take action on a chosen solution.

CHOOSE A SOLUTION
Choose the solution you believe will best solve the problem and help you reach your goal.

CONSIDER OPTIONS
Think of as many ways as possible to solve the problem. Don't be afraid to include ideas that others might think are unacceptable.

ANALYZE THE INFORMATION
Look at the information and determine what it reveals about solving the problem.

GATHER INFORMATION
Get to know the basics of the problem. Find out as much as possible about the issues.

IDENTIFY THE PROBLEM
Decide what the main issues are and what your goal is.

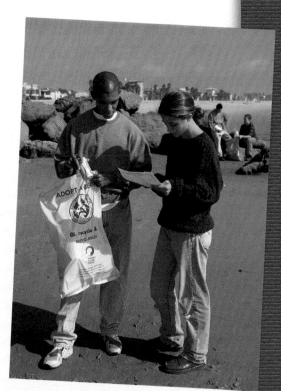

Students working on an environmental project are gathering and analyzing information to help them make decisions.

How Do You Participate in Your Community?

Across the country many young people have come up with ways to make their communities better places to live. Thirteen-year-old Aubyn Burnside of Hickory, North Carolina, is just one example. Aubyn felt sorry for foster children she saw moving their belongings in plastic trash bags. She founded Suitcases for Kids. This program provides used luggage for foster children who are moving from one home to another. Her program has been adopted by other young people in several states. Below are some ways in which you can participate in your community.

See Citizenship Today: Community Service, p. 542

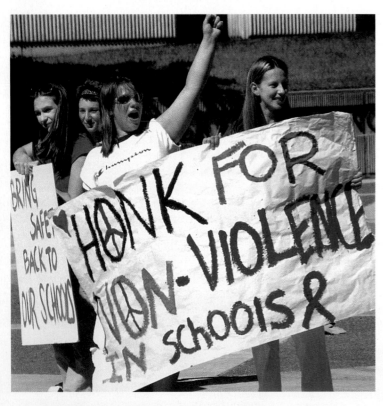

Students participate in a rally to promote safety in their school.

Find a Cause

How can you become involved in your community? First, select a community problem or issue that interests you. Some ideas from other young people include starting a support group for children with cancer, publishing a neighborhood newspaper with children's stories and art, and putting on performances to entertain people in shelters and hospitals.

Develop Solutions

Once you have found a cause on which you want to work, develop a plan for solving the problem. Use the decision-making or problem-solving skills you have learned to find ways to approach the problem. You may want to involve other people in your activities.

Follow Through

Solving problems takes time. You'll need to be patient in developing a plan. You can show leadership in working with your group by following through on meetings you set up and plans you make. When you finally solve the problem, you will feel proud of your accomplishments.

CITIZENSHIP ACTIVITIES

1. Use the telephone directory to make a list of names, addresses, and phone numbers of public officials or organizations that could provide information about solving problems in your community.

2. Copy the steps in the problem-solving and decision-making diagram and show how you followed them to solve a problem or make a decision. Be sure to clearly state the problem and the final decision.

Practicing Citizenship Skills

You have learned that good citizenship involves three skills: staying informed, solving problems, and taking action. Below are some activities to help you improve your citizenship skills. By practicing these skills you can work to make a difference in your own life and in the lives of those in your community.

CITIZENSHIP ACTIVITIES

Stay Informed

CREATE A PAMPHLET OR RECRUITING COMMERCIAL

Ask your school counselors or write to your state department of education to get information on state-run colleges, universities, or technical schools. Use this information to create a brochure or recruiting commercial showing these schools and the different programs and degrees they offer.

KEEP IN MIND

What's there for me? It may help you think about what areas students are interested in and may want to pursue in later life.

Where is it? You may want to have a map showing where the schools are located in your state.

How can I afford it? Students might want to know if financial aid is available to attend the schools you have featured.

Make Wise Decisions

CREATE A GAME BOARD OR SKIT

Study the decision-making diagram on page 285. With a small group, develop a skit that explains the steps in problem solving. Present your skit to younger students in your school. As an alternative, create a game board that would help younger students understand the steps in making a decision.

KEEP IN MIND

What do children this age understand? Be sure to create a skit or game at an age-appropriate level.

What kinds of decisions do younger students make? Think about the kinds of decisions that the viewers of your skit or players of the game might make.

How can I make it interesting? Use visual aids to help students understand the steps in decision making.

Take Action

CREATE A BULLETIN BOARD FOR YOUR CLASS

Do some research on the Internet or consult the yellow pages under "Social Services" to find the names of organizations that have volunteer opportunities for young people. Call or write for more information. Then create a bulletin board for your class showing groups that would like volunteer help.

KEEP IN MIND

What kinds of jobs are they? You may want to list the types of skills or jobs volunteer groups are looking for.

How old do I have to be? Some groups may be looking for younger volunteers; others may need older persons.

How do I get there? How easy is it to get to the volunteer group's location?

The Early Republic

> *"Our country! May she always be in the right; but our country, right or wrong."*
>
> **—Stephen Decatur**

Known as "Old Ironsides," the U.S.S. *Constitution* won more battles than any other early American warship. Today it rests in Boston Harbor.

CHAPTER 9

Launching a New Republic 1789–1800

Section 1 **Washington's Presidency**

Section 2 **Challenges to the New Government**

Section 3 **The Federalists in Charge**

George Washington arrives by boat in New York on April 23, 1789, for his presidential inauguration.

274

Alexander Hamilton, brilliant lawyer and economist, becomes secretary of the treasury.

Thomas Jefferson, farmer, diplomat, and principal author of the Declaration of Independence, becomes secretary of state.

Edmund Randolph, attorney general of Virginia, becomes attorney general of the federal government.

Henry Knox, a general of artillery during the Revolution, becomes secretary of war.

George Washington, general and Revolutionary War hero, is president.

The year is 1789, and George Washington has been inaugurated as the first president of the United States. It quickly becomes obvious to you and to others that the president will need help. He chooses people with different talents and experience to help him govern.

What kind of person would you choose to help you govern?

What Do You Think?

- Why might you want people with different viewpoints in your government?

- How would you go about setting up a government?

- What do you think your biggest challenges would be?

1789
George Washington inaugurated as president.

1791
The first Bank of the United States is established.

1792
Washington re-elected president.

1794
Whiskey Rebellion occurs.

1796
John Adams elected president.

1798
Alien and Sedition Acts

1800
Thomas Jefferson elected president.

USA / World · 1789 — 1800

1789
French Revolution begins.

1791
Slaves revolt in Santo Domingo.

1793
French king Louis XVI executed; Reign of Terror begins in France.

1797
Britain appoints Richard Wellesley Governor-General of India.

1798
French Expedition to Egypt

1800
Napoleon becomes First Consul of France.

BEFORE YOU READ

Inaugural coat buttons, 1789, proclaim the beginning of the Washington presidency.

Previewing the Theme

Democratic Ideals During the Federalist era (1789–1801), the leaders of the United States faced many challenges and difficulties. In this chapter, you will see how the way in which they responded to those obstacles and opportunities established a democratic foundation.

What Do You Know?

What do you think of when you hear the words *democracy* and *republic?* Why do you think the citizens and leaders of the new country wanted to establish a republic governed by laws?

THINK ABOUT
- the experience of the colonists under British rule
- the effect of the Revolutionary War and the period immediately after the war

What Do You Want to Know?

What questions do you have about the people who created the U.S. government? Record your questions in your notebook before you read the chapter.

READ AND TAKE NOTES

Reading Strategy: Identifying and Solving Problems As you read history, try to identify problems in past times and the solutions that people came up with to solve their problems. A graphic organizer such as the chart below can help you to keep track of problems and their solutions. In the middle of the chart, four headings categorize the major issues faced by the young nation. Copy the chart into your notebook and then record problems and the proposed solutions in each category.

 See Skillbuilder Handbook, page R18.

PROBLEMS		SOLUTIONS
	Economics	
	Politics	
	Foreign Affairs	
	Relations with Native Americans	

① Washington's Presidency

TERMS & NAMES
inaugurate
Federal Judiciary
   Act
cabinet
tariff

MAIN IDEA	WHY IT MATTERS NOW
The president and the Congress began to set up the new government.	The strength of the U.S. today is due to the decisions of the Founders about how to organize the government.

ONE AMERICAN'S STORY

Charles Thomson had known George Washington for many years. Thomson had served as secretary of the Continental Congress when delegates from the colonies first met in Philadelphia in 1774.

Now, 15 years later, on April 14, 1789, he had a very different job to do. He had come to Mount Vernon in Virginia with a letter for George Washington. Washington knew the reason for the visit. Thomson's letter was to tell him that he had been elected the nation's first president. Before giving Washington the letter, Thomson made a short speech.

Charles Thomson delivers the letter to Washington announcing his election as president.

A VOICE FROM THE PAST

I have now Sir to inform you that . . . your patriotism and your readiness to sacrifice . . . private enjoyments to preserve the liberty and promote the happiness of your Country [convinced the Congress that you would accept] this important Office to which you are called not only by the unanimous votes of the Electors but by the voice of America.

Charles Thomson, quoted in Washington's Papers, Library of Congress

As you will read in this section, Washington accepted the honor and the burden of his new office. He guided the nation through its early years.

Washington Takes Office

Washington had been elected only a few months before. Each member of the electoral college had written down two names. The top vote-getter, Washington, became president. The runner-up, John Adams, became vice-president. Washington left Mount Vernon on April 16, 1789. He traveled north through Baltimore and Philadelphia to New York City, the nation's capital. On April 30 at Federal Hall, Washington was **inaugurated,** or sworn in, as president. John Adams of Massachusetts was his vice-president.

Launching a New Republic **277**

As the nation's first president, Washington faced a difficult task. He knew that all eyes would be on him. His every action as president would set a precedent—an example that would become standard practice. People argued over what to call him. Some, including John Adams, suggested "His Excellency" or "His Highness." Others argued that such titles would suggest that he was a king. The debate tied up Congress for a month. Finally, "Mr. President" was agreed upon. Congress had to settle other differences about how the new government should be run.

*Reading*History

A. Making Inferences Why were people so concerned about how to address the president?

Setting Up the Courts

The writers of the Constitution had left many matters to be decided by Congress. For example, the Constitution created a Supreme Court but left it to Congress to decide the number of justices. Leaders also argued about how much power the Supreme Court should have. One reason for disagreement was that the states already had their own courts. How would authority be divided between the state and federal courts?

To create a court system, Congress passed the **Federal Judiciary Act** of 1789. This act gave the Supreme Court six members: a chief justice, or judge, and five associate justices. Over time, that number has grown to nine. The act also provided for other lower, less powerful federal courts. Washington appointed John Jay, the prominent New York lawyer and diplomat, as chief justice.

Vocabulary
judiciary: system of courts and judges

Washington's Cabinet

The Constitution also gave Congress the task of creating departments to help the president lead the nation. The president had the power to appoint the heads of these departments, who were to assist the president with the many issues and problems he had to face. These heads of departments became his **cabinet**.

The Congress created three departments. In his first major task as president, Washington chose talented people to run them. For secretary of war, he picked Henry Knox, a trusted general during the Revolution. It was Knox's job to oversee the nation's defenses. For secretary of state, Washington chose Thomas Jefferson. He had been serving as U.S. minister to France. The State Department oversaw relations between the United States and other countries. Washington turned to the brilliant Alexander Hamilton to be the secretary of the treasury. Hamilton had to manage the government's money. The secretary's ties to the president began during the war when he had served as one of Washington's aides. To advise the

Now *and* **then**

THE PRESIDENT'S CABINET
The president's cabinet has more than tripled in size since it began with the secretaries of state, war, and treasury, and the attorney general. As the nation has faced new challenges, the government has added new departments. In 1977, concerns about oil shortages led to the creation of the Department of Energy. The Department of Veterans' Affairs was added in 1989. Today the cabinet (Clinton's cabinet shown below) includes the heads of 14 departments.

government on legal matters, Washington picked Edmund Randolph as attorney general.

These department heads and the attorney general made up Washington's cabinet. The Constitution made no mention of a cabinet. However, Washington began the practice of calling his department heads together to advise him.

Economic Problems

As secretary of the treasury, Alexander Hamilton faced the task of straightening out the nation's finances. First of all, the new government needed to pay its war debts. During the Revolution, the United States had borrowed millions of dollars from France, the Netherlands, and Spain. Within the United States, merchants and other private citizens had loaned money to the government. State governments also had wartime debts to pay back. By 1789, the national debt totaled more than $52 million.

Most government leaders agreed that the nation must repay its debts to win the respect of both foreign nations and its own citizens. Hamilton saw that the new nation must assure other countries that it was responsible about money. These nations would do business with the United States if they saw that the country would pay its debts. If the nation failed to do so, no country would lend it money in the future.

Hamilton came up with a financial plan that reflected his belief in a strong central government. He thought the power of the national government should be stronger than that of the state governments. Hamilton also believed that government should encourage business and industry. He sought the support of the nation's wealthy merchants and manufacturers. He thought that the nation's prosperity depended on them. The government owed money to many of these rich men. By paying them back, Hamilton hoped to win their support for the new government.

AMERICA'S HISTORY MAKERS

ALEXANDER HAMILTON
1755?–1804
Alexander Hamilton was born into poverty in the British West Indies. When he was ten years old, the young Alexander went to work as a clerk. He so impressed his employers that they helped to send him to school at King's College (now Columbia University) in New York.

During the Revolutionary War, he became an aide to General Washington. Hamilton moved up quickly in the army and later in political life. Although of humble origins, Hamilton had little faith in the common people and put his trust in the wealthy and educated to govern.

Why is it odd that Hamilton distrusts the common people to govern?

Reading **History**
B. Making Inferences Why might merchants and manufacturers support a strong central government?

Hamilton's Financial Plan

In 1790, Hamilton presented his plan to Congress. He proposed three steps to improve the nation's finances.

1. paying off all war debts
2. raising government revenues
3. creating a national bank

Hamilton wanted the federal government to pay off the war debts of the states. However, sectional differences arose over repayment of state debts. Virginia, Georgia, and many other Southern states had already repaid their debts and did not like being asked to help Northern states pay theirs.

Hamilton asked Thomas Jefferson of Virginia to help him gain Southern support. They reached a compromise. In exchange for Southern support of the plan, Northerners agreed to place the new nation's capital in the South. The location chosen was on the Potomac River between Virginia and Maryland.

The secretary of the treasury favored tariffs. A **tariff** is a tax on imported goods. It serves two purposes: raising money for the government and encouraging the growth of American industry. The government placed the highest tariffs on foreign goods—such as shoes and textiles—that Americans bought in great quantities. This ensured a steady flow of income to the government. In addition, since tariffs made foreign goods more expensive, they encouraged people to buy American goods.

Hamilton also called for the creation of a national bank. Such a bank would meet many needs. It would give the government a safe place to keep

Economics *in* History

How Banks Work

Why did Hamilton want to create a national bank? He believed that such a bank could help the economy of the new nation. It would create a partnership between the federal government and American business.

Let's say you deposited money into a bank account. Then you went back another day to withdraw some of the money. What happened in the meantime? Did the money just sit in the bank until you wanted it back? No—the bank used your money, and in doing so, helped fuel economic growth. In this way, money flows in a circular path from people like you into the general economy and back to you again. In the process, money can create goods and services, jobs, and profits, as the diagram explains.

CONNECT TO HISTORY

1. **Analyzing Points of View**
Do you think that the people who feared a strong central government supported Hamilton's idea of a national bank? Why or why not?

See Skillbuilder Handbook, page R9.

CONNECT TO TODAY

2. **Making Inferences** How do banks make money?

For more about banking . . .

RESEARCH LINKS
CLASSZONE.COM

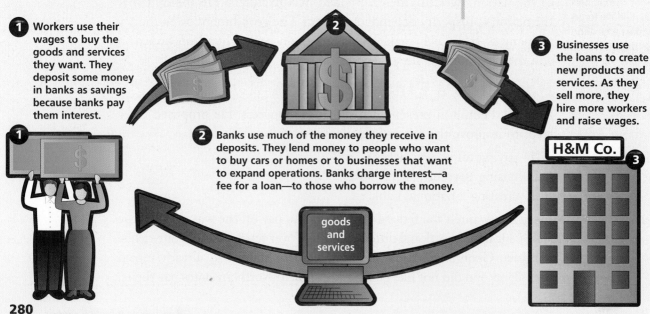

① Workers use their wages to buy the goods and services they want. They deposit some money in banks as savings because banks pay them interest.

② Banks use much of the money they receive in deposits. They lend money to people who want to buy cars or homes or to businesses that want to expand operations. Banks charge interest—a fee for a loan—to those who borrow the money.

③ Businesses use the loans to create new products and services. As they sell more, they hire more workers and raise wages.

goods and services

H&M Co.

money. It would also make loans to businesses and government. Most important, it would issue bank notes—paper money that could be used as currency. Overall, Hamilton's plan would strengthen the central government. However, this worried Jefferson and Madison.

Interpreting the Constitution

Jefferson and Madison believed that the Constitution discouraged the concentration of power in the federal government. The Constitution's writers had tried to make the document general enough so that it would be flexible. As a result, disagreements sometimes arose over the document's meaning.

Two of the first U.S. coins, 1792

The debate over Hamilton's plan for a national bank exposed differences about how to interpret the Constitution. Madison and Jefferson argued that the Constitution did not give the government the power to set up a bank. They believed in the strict construction—narrow or strict interpretation—of the Constitution. They stated that the government has only those powers that the Constitution clearly says it has. Therefore, since the Constitution does not mention a national bank, the government cannot create one.

Hamilton disagreed. He favored a loose construction—broad or flexible interpretation—of the Constitution. Pointing to the elastic clause in the document, he argued that the bank was "necessary and proper" to carry out the government's duties. (See The Living Constitution, page 238.) According to this view, when the Constitution grants a power to Congress, it also grants Congress the "necessary and proper" means to carry out that power. Jefferson and Hamilton argued their positions to Washington. Hamilton won, and the Bank of the United States was set up in 1791. The president, meanwhile, was dealing with other challenges at home and abroad, which you will read about in Section 2.

Reading **History**

C. Contrasting
What is the main difference between strict and loose interpretations of the Constitution?

Section **1** *Assessment*

1. Terms & Names

Explain the significance of:
• inaugurate
• Federal Judiciary Act
• cabinet
• tariff

2. Taking Notes

In a chart, list members of Washington's cabinet and their responsibilities.

Cabinet member	Responsibilities

Which cabinet member had the greatest responsibilities? Explain.

3. Main Ideas

a. What was the purpose of Washington's cabinet?

b. What economic problems did the new government face?

c. How did Hamilton's financial plan attempt to solve the nation's economic problems?

4. Critical Thinking

Contrasting How did Hamilton and Jefferson differ in their interpretation of the Constitution?

THINK ABOUT
• views on the national bank
• views on the role of government

ACTIVITY OPTIONS

LANGUAGE ARTS

ART

Imagine you oppose or support Hamilton's plan for the nation's finances. Write a **letter to the editor** or draw a **political cartoon** expressing your opinion.

2 Challenges to the New Government

TERMS & NAMES
Battle of Fallen
  Timbers
Treaty of
  Greenville
Whiskey Rebellion
French Revolution
neutral
Jay's Treaty
Pinckney's Treaty

MAIN IDEA	WHY IT MATTERS NOW
Washington established central authority at home and avoided war with European powers.	Washington's policies at home and abroad set an example for later presidents.

ONE AMERICAN'S STORY

Pioneers had been moving west since before the Revolution. However, the settlers met fierce resistance from Native Americans. One of their most respected military leaders was Chief Little Turtle of the Miami tribe of Ohio. In 1790 and 1791, he had won decisive victories against U.S. troops.

Now, two years later, the Miami and their allies again faced attack by American forces. At a council meeting, Little Turtle gave a warning to his people about the troops led by General Anthony Wayne.

General Anthony Wayne negotiates with a Miami war chief.

A VOICE FROM THE PAST

We have beaten the enemy twice under different commanders. . . . The Americans are now led by a chief [Wayne] who never sleeps. . . . During all the time he has been marching on our villages . . . we have not been able to surprise him. Think well of it. . . . It would be prudent [wise] to listen to his offers of peace.

Little Turtle, quoted in *The Life and Times of Little Turtle*

While the council members weighed Little Turtle's warning, President Washington was making plans to secure—guard or protect— the western borders of the new nation.

Securing the Northwest Territory

As a general, Washington had skillfully waged war. As the nation's president, however, he saw that the country needed peace in order to prosper. But in spite of his desire for peace, he considered military action as trouble brewed in the Trans-Appalachian West, the land between the Appalachian Mountains and the Mississippi River. The 1783 Treaty of Paris had attempted to resolve the claims. The source of the trouble was competing claims for these lands. Some years later, however, Spain, Britain, the United States, and Native Americans claimed parts of the area as their own.

Spain held much of North America west of the Mississippi. It also claimed Florida and the port of New Orleans at the mouth of the

Mississippi. For American settlers in the West, this port was key to trade. They carried their goods to market by flatboat down the Mississippi to New Orleans. They took Spanish threats to close the port very seriously. The Spanish also stirred up trouble between the white settlers and the Creeks, Choctaws, and other Native American groups in the Southeast.

*Reading*History
A. Making Inferences What expectations might the Native Americans have had of the British as the tribes came into conflict with white settlers?

The strongest resistance to white settlement came from Native Americans in the Northwest Territory. This territory was bordered by the Ohio River to the south and Canada to the north. Native Americans in that territory hoped to join together to form an independent Native American nation. In violation of the Treaty of Paris, the British still held forts north of the Ohio River. The British supported Native Americans in order to maintain their access to fur in these territories. Eventually, Native Americans and white settlers clashed over the Northwest Territory.

Battle of Fallen Timbers

Believing the Northwest Territory was critical to the security and growth of the new nation, Washington sent troops to the Ohio Valley. As you read in One American's Story, this first federal army took a beating from warriors led by Little Turtle in 1790. The chief's force came from many tribes, including the Shawnee, Ottawa, and Chippewa, who joined in a confederation to defeat the federal army.

After a second defeat in 1791 of an army headed by General Arthur St. Clair, Washington ordered another army west. This time Anthony Wayne, known as "Mad Anthony" for his reckless courage, was at its head.

The other chiefs ignored Little Turtle's advice to negotiate. They replaced him with a less able leader. Expecting British help, Native American warriors gathered at British-held Fort Miami. On August 20, 1794, a fighting force of around 2,000 Native Americans clashed with Wayne's troops. The site was covered with trees that had been struck down by a storm. The Native Americans were defeated in what became known as the **Battle of Fallen Timbers**.

The Battle of Fallen Timbers memorial sculpture below shows two American soldiers and a Native American.

The Trans-Appalachian West, 1791–1795

GEOGRAPHY SKILLBUILDER
Interpreting Maps
1. **Region** What does the yellow area of the map represent?
2. **Location** Why might the British forts be located near water?

Land ceded (surrendered) by Native Americans in Treaty of Greenville (1795)
★ Battle
U.S.-held fort
British-held fort

283

The Native Americans retreated to Fort Miami. The British, not wanting war with the United States, refused to help them. The Battle of Fallen Timbers crushed Native American hopes of keeping their land in the Northwest Territory. Twelve tribes signed the **Treaty of Greenville** in 1795. They agreed to cede, or surrender, much of present-day Ohio and Indiana to the U.S. government.

Reading **History**

B. Reading a Map
Use the map on page 283 to see which two states to the south bordered the land ceded by Native Americans.

The Whiskey Rebellion

Not long after the Battle of Fallen Timbers, Washington put another army into the field. The conflict arose over the government's tax on whiskey, part of Hamilton's financial plan. From Pennsylvania to Georgia, outraged farmers resisted the tax. For them, whiskey—and the grain it was made from—were important products.

Because of poor roads, backcountry farmers had trouble getting their grain to market. Crops such as wheat and rye were more easily carried to market in liquid form, so farmers made their grain into whiskey. A farmer's horse could haul only two bushels of rye but could carry two barrels of rye whiskey. This was an amount equal to 24 bushels of the grain. In addition, their customers paid more for whiskey than grain. With little cash to buy goods, let alone pay the tax, farmers often traded whiskey for salt, sugar, and other goods. The farmers used whiskey as money to get whatever supplies they needed.

CITIZENSHIP TODAY

Obeying Rules and Laws

As the Whiskey Rebellion shows, since the earliest days of the republic our government has made laws and punished those who broke them. These laws affect not only adult citizens, but young people as well.

Today, for example, communities across the country are trying to control the problem of juvenile crime by imposing curfews on young people. These laws require minors to be off the streets after a certain time, often ten or eleven at night. Penalties can be harsh. In certain communities, minors who break curfew laws can be detained, and their parents can be fined.

People who favor curfews believe such laws cut crime. Those who oppose curfews think such limits are the responsibility of parents and not the government.

Why Should You Obey Rules and Laws?

1. What are some arguments in favor of curfew laws? What are arguments against them? Make a list of each.

2. Poll your classmates to see how many agree with each position.

3. Write an essay expressing your opinion on this issue.

4. Brainstorm changes or adaptations to curfew laws that you think would make them more flexible.

See Citizenship Handbook, page 267.

For more about young people and the law . . .

 RESEARCH LINKS
CLASSZONE.COM

In the summer of 1794, a group of farmers in western Pennsylvania staged the **Whiskey Rebellion** against the tax. One armed group beat up a tax collector, coated him with tar and feathers, and stole his horse. Others threatened an armed attack on Pittsburgh.

Washington, urged on by Hamilton, was prepared to enforce the tax and crush the Whiskey Rebellion. They feared that not to act might undermine the new government and weaken its authority. Hamilton condemned the rebels for resisting the law.

"Such a resistance is treason."
Alexander Hamilton

A VOICE FROM THE PAST

Such a resistance is treason against society, against liberty, against everything that ought to be dear to a free, enlightened, and prudent people. To tolerate it were to abandon your most precious interests. Not to subdue it were to tolerate it.

Alexander Hamilton, *The Works of Alexander Hamilton*

In October 1794, General Henry Lee, with Hamilton at his side, led an army of 13,000 soldiers into western Pennsylvania to put down the uprising. As news of the army's approach spread, the rebels fled. After much effort, federal troops rounded up 20 barefoot, ragged prisoners. Washington had proved his point. He had shown that the government had the power and the will to enforce its laws. Meanwhile, events in Europe gave Washington a different kind of challenge.

The French Revolution

In 1789, a financial crisis led the French people to rebel against their government. Inspired by the American Revolution, the French revolutionaries demanded liberty and equality. At first, Americans supported the **French Revolution**. By 1792, however, the revolution had become very violent. Thousands of French citizens were massacred. Then, in 1793, Louis XVI, the king of France, was executed.

Other European monarchs believed the revolution threatened their own thrones. France soon declared war on Britain, Holland, and Spain. Britain led the fight against France.

The war between France and Britain put the United States in an awkward position. France had been America's ally in the Revolution against the British.

Connections TO
WORLD HISTORY

EYEWITNESS TO REVOLUTION

In 1789, an American citizen with a strange first name, Gouverneur Morris, went to Paris as a private business agent. Three years later, President Washington appointed him U.S. minister to France. An eyewitness to the French Revolution, Morris kept a detailed record of what he saw, including the execution of the king and queen by guillotine, as shown below.

Here is part of a letter he wrote on October 18, 1793:

"Terror is the order of the Day. . . . The Queen was executed the Day before yesterday. Insulted during her Trial and reviled in her last Moments, she behav'd with Dignity throughout."

A 1778 treaty still bound the two nations together. In addition, many saw France's revolution as proof that the American cause had been just. Jefferson felt that a move to crush the French Revolution was an attack on liberty everywhere. Hamilton, though, pointed out that Britain was the United States' most important trading partner, and British trade was too important to risk war.

In April 1793, Washington declared that the United States would remain **neutral,** not siding with one country or the other. He stated that the nation would be "friendly and impartial" to both sides. Congress then passed a law forbidding the United States to help either side.

Remaining Neutral

Britain made it hard for the United States to remain neutral. Late in 1792, the British began seizing the cargoes of American ships carrying goods from the French West Indies.

Washington sent Chief Justice John Jay to England for talks about the seizure of U.S. ships. Jay also hoped to persuade the British to give up their forts on the Northwest frontier. During the talks in 1794, news came of the U.S. victory at the Battle of Fallen Timbers. Fearing another entanglement, the British agreed to leave the Ohio Valley by 1796. In **Jay's Treaty,** the British also agreed to pay damages for U.S. vessels they had seized. Jay failed, however, to open up the profitable British West Indies trade to Americans. Because of this, Jay's Treaty was unpopular.

Like Jay, Thomas Pinckney helped the United States reduce tensions along the frontier. In 1795, **Pinckney's Treaty** with Spain gave Americans the right to travel freely on the Mississippi River. It also gave them the right to store goods at the port of New Orleans without paying customs duties. In addition, Spain accepted the 31st parallel as the northern boundary of Florida and the southern boundary of the United States.

Meanwhile, more American settlers moved west. As you will read in the next section, change was coming back east as Washington stepped down.

Reading **History**

C. Drawing Conclusions
What sort of U.S. obligation to France did the wartime alliance and treaty of 1778 create?

Reading **History**

D. Evaluating
What were some of the advantages to the new nation of remaining neutral?

Section 2 Assessment

1. Terms & Names

Explain the significance of:
• Battle of Fallen Timbers
• Treaty of Greenville
• Whiskey Rebellion
• French Revolution
• neutral
• Jay's Treaty
• Pinckney's Treaty

2. Taking Notes

Use a chart to record U.S. responses to various challenges.

Challenge	Response
From Spain	
From Britain	
From France	

Which challenge seemed greatest? Why?

3. Main Ideas

a. What military and other actions secured the West for the United States?

b. Why did Washington consider it important to put down the Whiskey Rebellion?

c. How did the French Revolution create problems for the United States?

4. Critical Thinking

Drawing Conclusions
Why was neutrality a difficult policy for the United States to maintain?

THINK ABOUT
• ties with France
• ties with Britain
• restrictions on trade

ACTIVITY OPTIONS

GEOGRAPHY

ART

Make a **map** that describes the Battle of Fallen Timbers, or draw a **scene** from that battle.

3 The Federalists in Charge

TERMS & NAMES
foreign policy
political party
XYZ Affair
Alien and Sedition Acts
states' rights

MAIN IDEA	WHY IT MATTERS NOW
The split between Hamilton and Jefferson led to the growth of political parties.	The two-party system is still a major feature of politics in the United States.

ONE AMERICAN'S STORY

In 1796, President George Washington decided that two terms in office was enough. The president was fed up with political quarreling. He wanted to return to Mount Vernon, his estate in Virginia. But as he left office, he feared the development of political parties would split the nation into enemy camps. With Hamilton's help, in 1796 he wrote a final address to the nation.

This painting portrays Mount Vernon in 1792.

A VOICE FROM THE PAST

Let me now . . . warn you . . . against the [harmful] effects of the spirit of party. . . . This spirit, unfortunately . . . exists in different shapes in all governments . . . but in those of the popular form, it is seen in its greatest rankness and is truly their worst enemy.

George Washington, Farewell Address

In his address, Washington warned of the dangers of political division, or what he termed "the spirit of party." As you will see in this section, few people took his advice.

Washington Retires

Washington had come to the presidency greatly admired by the American people. Throughout his eight years in office (1789–1797), he had tried to serve as a symbol of national unity. In large part, he succeeded. During his second term, however, opponents of Jay's Treaty led attacks on the president. Thomas Paine called Washington "treacherous in private friendship . . . and a hypocrite in public life" because he failed to support the French Revolution.

Washington saw such attacks as the outcome of political disagreements. In his farewell address, he warned that such differences could weaken the nation. Despite his advice, political parties became a part of American politics.

Americans listened more closely to Washington's parting advice on **foreign policy**—relations with the governments of other countries. He urged the nation's leaders to remain neutral and "steer clear of permanent alliances with any portion of the foreign world." He warned that agreements with foreign nations might work against U.S. interests. His advice served to guide U.S. foreign policy into the twentieth century.

Growth of Political Parties

Despite Washington's warning against political parties, Americans were deeply divided over how the nation should be run. During Washington's first term (1789–1792), Hamilton and Jefferson had hotly debated the direction the new nation should take. Then Jefferson returned to Virginia in 1793. During Washington's second term, Madison took Jefferson's place in the debates with Hamilton.

Both sides disagreed on how to interpret the Constitution and on economic policy. Hamilton favored the British government and opposed the French Revolution. Jefferson and Madison were the opposite. Hamilton fought for a strong central government. Jefferson and Madison feared such a government might lead to tyranny. They had different visions of what the nation should become. Hamilton wanted a United States in which trade, manufacturing, and cities grew. Jefferson and Madison pictured a rural nation of planters and farmers.

These differences on foreign and domestic policy led to the nation's first political parties. A **political party** is a group of people that tries to promote its ideas and influence government. It also backs candidates for office. Together, Jefferson and Madison founded the Democratic-Republican Party. The party name reflected their strong belief in democracy and the republican system. Their ideas drew farmers and workers to the new party. Hamilton and his friends formed the Federalist Party. Many Northern merchants and manufacturers became Federalists.

*Reading*History
A. Summarizing
What were the major beliefs of each party?

The First Political Parties

FEDERALISTS	DEMOCRATIC-REPUBLICANS
Strong national government	Limited national government
Fear of mob rule	Fear of rule by one person or a powerful few
Loose construction (interpretation) of the Constitution	Strict construction (interpretation) of the Constitution
Favored national bank	Opposed national bank
Economy based on manufacturing and shipping	Economy based on farming
Supporters: lawyers, merchants, manufacturers, clergy	Supporters: farmers, tradespeople

SKILLBUILDER Interpreting Charts
1. *Which economic interests were served by the Federalists?*
2. *Which party favored a ruling elite? Which put more trust in the common people?*

OBSERVATIONS explanatory of the Plan.

Breadth of the Streets.

SCALE OF POLES.

WASHINGTON, D.C., AND BENJAMIN BANNEKER

Benjamin Banneker was a free African-American farmer. He was a self-taught mathematician and astronomer. He also wrote an almanac (see below). He was named to the survey commission appointed to lay out the boundaries of the nation's new capital. Working with chief planner Pierre L'Enfant, Banneker helped to decide where the White House and Capitol would be located. Their final design is shown at the left.

John Adams Takes Office

In 1796, the United States held its first elections in which political parties competed. The Federalists picked Washington's vice-president, John Adams, as their candidate for president. An experienced public servant, Adams had been a leader during the Revolution and at the Continental Congress. He had also been a diplomat in France, the Netherlands, and Britain before serving with Washington. The Democratic-Republicans chose Jefferson.

In the electoral college, Adams received 71 votes and Jefferson 68. The Constitution stated that the runner-up should become vice-president. Therefore, the country had a Federalist president and a Democratic-Republican vice-president. Adams became president in 1797. His chief rival, Jefferson, entered office as his vice-president. In 1800, Adams became the first president to govern from the nation's new capital city, Washington, D.C.

Problems with France

When Washington left office in 1797, relations between France and the United States were tense. With Britain and France still at war, the French began seizing U.S. ships to prevent them from trading with the British. Within the year, the French had looted more than 300 U.S. ships.

Although some Federalists called for war with France, Adams hoped talks would restore calm. To this end, he sent Charles Pinckney, Elbridge Gerry, and John Marshall to Paris. Arriving there, they requested a meeting with the French minister of foreign affairs. For weeks, they were

American newspapers fueled public anger over the XYZ Affair by publishing editorials and cartoons like this one. Here the five-man group ruling France demands money at dagger point from the three Americans. The American diplomats respond, "Cease bawling, monster! We will not give you sixpence!"

What attitude does the cartoonist have toward France's role in this affair? How can you tell?

ignored. Then three French agents—later referred to as X, Y, and Z—took the Americans aside to tell them the minister would hold talks. However, the talks would occur only if the Americans agreed to loan France $10 million and to pay the minister a bribe of $250,000. The Americans refused. "No, no, not a sixpence," Pinckney shot back.

Adams received a full report of what became known as the **XYZ Affair.** After Congress and an outraged public learned of it, the press turned Pinckney's words into a popular slogan: "Millions for defense, not one cent for tribute!" In 1798, Congress canceled its treaties with France and allowed U.S. ships to seize French vessels. Congress also set aside money to expand the navy and the army.

*Reading*History
B. Drawing Conclusions How did the XYZ Affair show the young nation's growing confidence?

The Alien and Sedition Acts

The conflict with France made Adams and the Federalists popular with the public. Many Democratic-Republicans, however, were sympathetic to France. One Democratic-Republican newspaper called Adams "the blasted tyrant of America." In turn, Federalists labeled Democratic-Republicans "democrats, mobcrats, and other kinds of rats."

Angered by criticism in a time of crisis, Adams blamed the Democratic-Republican newspapers and new immigrants. Many of the immigrants were Democratic-Republicans. To silence their critics, the Federalist Congress passed the **Alien and Sedition Acts** in 1798. These acts targeted aliens—immigrants who were not yet citizens. One act increased the waiting period for becoming a U.S. citizen from 5 to 14 years. Other acts gave the president the power to arrest disloyal aliens or order them out of the country during wartime. A fourth act outlawed sedition, saying or writing anything false or harmful about the government.

With these acts, the Federalists clamped down on freedom of speech and the press. About 25 Democratic-Republican newspaper editors were charged under this act, and 10 were convicted of expressing opinions damaging to the government. A Vermont congressman, Matthew Lyon, was also locked up for saying that the president should be sent "to a mad house." The voters re-elected Lyon while he was in jail.

*Reading*History
C. Making Inferences How might the theory of states' rights undermine the federal government?

The Democratic-Republicans, led by Jefferson and Madison, searched for a way to fight the Alien and Sedition Acts. They found it in a theory called **states' rights**. According to this theory, states had rights that the federal government could not violate. Jefferson and Madison wrote resolutions (or statements) passed by the Kentucky and Virginia legislatures in 1798 and 1799. In the Kentucky Resolutions, Jefferson proposed nullification, the idea that a state could nullify the federal law within the state. In the Virginia Resolutions, Madison said a state could interpose, or place, itself between the federal government and its citizens. These resolutions declared that the Alien and Sedition Acts violated the Constitution. No other states supported Kentucky and Virginia. However, within two years the Democratic-Republicans won control of Congress, and they either repealed the Alien and Sedition Acts or let them expire between 1800 and 1802.

Peace with France

While Federalists and Democratic-Republicans battled at home, the United States made peace with France. Although war fever was high, Adams reopened talks with France. This time the two sides quickly signed the Convention of 1800, an agreement to stop all naval attacks. This treaty cleared the way for U.S. and French ships to sail the ocean in peace.

Adams's actions made him enemies among the Federalists. Despite this, he spoke proudly of having saved the nation from bloodshed. "I desire no other inscription over my gravestone than: 'Here lies John Adams, who took upon himself the responsibility of the peace with France in the year 1800.'" Adams lost the presidential election of 1800 to Thomas Jefferson. You will read more about Jefferson in the next chapter.

Section **3** Assessment

1. Terms & Names

Explain the significance of:
- foreign policy
- political party
- XYZ Affair
- Alien and Sedition Acts
- states' rights

2. Taking Notes

Use a cluster diagram to review details about the Alien and Sedition Acts.

What was the worst effect of the Alien and Sedition Acts? Why?

3. Main Ideas

a. What two pieces of advice did Washington give in his Farewell Address?

b. What led to the rise of political parties?

c. Why did Congress pass the Alien and Sedition Acts? How did Kentucky and Virginia respond?

4. Critical Thinking

Evaluating Do you think Washington's warning about political parties was good advice? Explain.

THINK ABOUT
- roles of political parties
- advantages of parties
- disadvantages of parties

ACTIVITY OPTIONS

TECHNOLOGY

SPEECH

Read more about Benjamin Banneker. Plan part of a **video presentation** on him or present **dramatic readings** of excerpts from the almanac he wrote.

TERMS & NAMES

Briefly explain the significance of each of the following.

1. inaugurate
2. cabinet
3. tariff
4. Battle of Fallen Timbers
5. Whiskey Rebellion
6. neutral
7. foreign policy
8. political party
9. Alien and Sedition Acts
10. states' rights

REVIEW QUESTIONS

Washington's Presidency (pages 277–281)

1. What questions about the judiciary were left open by the Constitution? How were they answered?
2. What financial problems did the new nation face?
3. How did Hamilton and Jefferson interpret the Constitution differently?

Challenges to the New Government (pages 282–286)

4. What did Washington do to secure the West?
5. What were the major arguments regarding taxation under the new government?
6. Why did Washington favor neutrality in the conflict between France and Britain?
7. What problems did the Jay and Pinckney treaties address?

The Federalists in Charge (pages 287–291)

8. Why did Washington oppose political parties?
9. What was the XYZ Affair?
10. Why did Federalists pass the Alien and Sedition Acts? How did Republicans respond?

CRITICAL THINKING

1. USING YOUR NOTES

Using your completed chart, answer the questions.

a. What were the problems that characterized the Federalist era?

b. What do the solutions to these problems reveal about the characteristics of the era?

2. ANALYZING LEADERSHIP

How did Washington's efforts to serve as a symbol of national unity help the new nation?

3. APPLYING CITIZENSHIP SKILLS

How might the farmers in the Whiskey Rebellion have expressed their disapproval of the whiskey tax while staying within the law?

4. THEME: DEMOCRATIC IDEALS

Did the formation of political parties make the nation more or less democratic?

Interact *with* History

How did the challenges of setting up a government that you discussed before you read the chapter compare with the actual challenges you read about?

VISUAL SUMMARY

The First Presidents

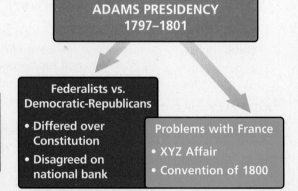

HISTORY SKILLS

1. INTERPRETING CHARTS

The following chart shows the money problems of the new nation between 1789 and 1791. The numbers have been rounded off. Study the chart and then answer the questions.

Financial Problems, 1789–1791

DEBTS	EXPENSES	INCOME
$77,230,000 = total public debt	$4,270,000 budget to run government	$4,400,000 from duties or taxes imposed on imported and exported goods

Source: *Historical Statistics of the United States*

a. What was the government's total income in these years?

b. How much money did the government owe in these same years?

c. How might the government try to raise more money?

2. INTERPRETING PRIMARY SOURCES

In a letter to her sister, John Adams's wife, Abigail, had the following to say about President Washington. Read the quotation and answer the questions.

> He is polite with dignity, affable without familiarity, distant without haughtiness, . . . modest, wise, and good.
>
> **Abigail Adams,** letter of January 5, 1790

a. What qualities seemed to set Washington apart from other political leaders?

b. Is Mrs. Adams's overall impression of Washington positive or negative? Explain your answer.

c. What qualities or characteristics did the people of Washington's time seem to expect in a leader?

ALTERNATIVE ASSESSMENT

1. INTERDISCIPLINARY ACTIVITY: World History

Writing a Letter Imagine that you are a U.S. citizen during the French Revolution. Write a letter to the secretary of state recommending a policy you think the U.S. government should follow. Be sure to use standard grammar, spelling, sentence structure, and punctuation in your letter.

2. COOPERATIVE LEARNING ACTIVITY

Holding a Debate The controversy over the Alien and Sedition Acts deeply divided Federalists and Democratic-Republicans. Were the acts constitutional or an abuse of basic rights? Should criticism of the government be allowed in a time of near war?

Working in three groups, do research on the Alien and Sedition Acts and the positions taken by both political parties on these acts. Then have Federalist and Democratic-Republican groups pick representatives to debate the questions posed above, while the remaining group acts as audience and judge for the debate.

3. TECHNOLOGY ACTIVITY

Creating a Television Commercial People of the eighteenth century had different expectations of their political leaders than do people today. The quotation from Abigail Adams on this page is an example of the different perspective people held in Washington's time. Using the library or the Internet, find pictures of, and quotations about, political leaders of the time.

For more about the first presidents . . .

INTERNET ACTIVITY
CLASSZONE.COM

Create a 30-second television commercial that advertises an American history theme park, using the suggestions below.

- Try to find quotations that suggest the most important qualities of leaders such as Washington, Adams, Hamilton, and Jefferson.

- Try to find more than one image of each leader; find images that suggest different qualities in the person.

- Use quotations from and images of leaders as part of your commercial for a theme park.

- Show your commercial to the class.

4. HISTORY PORTFOLIO

Review your section and chapter assessment activities. Select one that you think is your best work. Then use comments made by your teacher or classmates to improve your work and add it to your portfolio.

Additional Test Practice, pp. S1–S33

TEST PRACTICE
CLASSZONE.COM

CHAPTER 10

The Jefferson Era 1800–1816

Albert Bierstadt's painting, *The Rocky Mountains* (1863), celebrates the beauty of the American West.

This painting gives a more realistic view of the West than that shown at the left.

Explorers often chose to travel by water.

In the early 1800s, it took about 20 seconds to load and fire a gun.

Adult grizzly bears might weigh as much as 900 pounds and run 30 miles per hour.

You have been chosen to participate in an expedition to the West in the early 1800s. You are excited and curious, but also a little scared. You know that you will see and experience many new things. But you know there are risks involved, too.

What dangers will you face on an expedition west?

What Do You Think?

- Notice the land features in these scenes. What problems might they hold for an explorer?
- What other people might you meet on the expedition?
- How will you find food during the long winter?

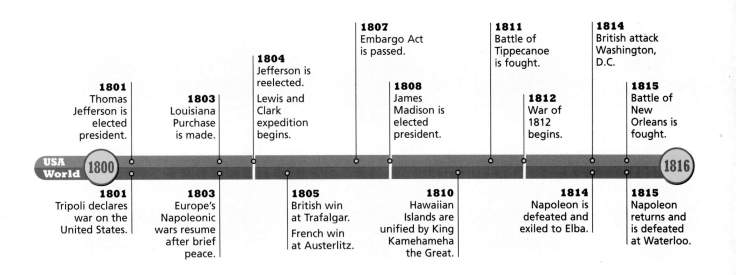

1801 Thomas Jefferson is elected president.

1803 Louisiana Purchase is made.

1804 Jefferson is reelected.
Lewis and Clark expedition begins.

1807 Embargo Act is passed.

1808 James Madison is elected president.

1811 Battle of Tippecanoe is fought.

1812 War of 1812 begins.

1814 British attack Washington, D.C.

1815 Battle of New Orleans is fought.

USA World 1800 — 1816

1801 Tripoli declares war on the United States.

1803 Europe's Napoleonic wars resume after brief peace.

1805 British win at Trafalgar.
French win at Austerlitz.

1810 Hawaiian Islands are unified by King Kamehameha the Great.

1814 Napoleon is defeated and exiled to Elba.

1815 Napoleon returns and is defeated at Waterloo.

BEFORE YOU READ

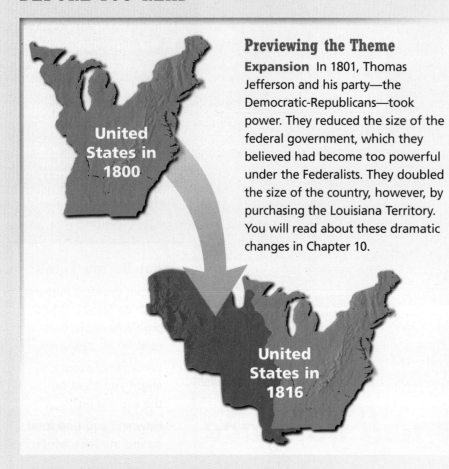

United States in 1800

United States in 1816

Previewing the Theme

Expansion In 1801, Thomas Jefferson and his party—the Democratic-Republicans—took power. They reduced the size of the federal government, which they believed had become too powerful under the Federalists. They doubled the size of the country, however, by purchasing the Louisiana Territory. You will read about these dramatic changes in Chapter 10.

What Do You Know?

What parts of the United States today were not part of the country in 1800? What should leaders consider before they buy land for their countries?

THINK ABOUT
- where the money for the purchase will come from
- what should be done if people already live on the land

What Do You Want to Know?

What details do you need to help you understand the nation's expansion in the early 1800s? Make a list of information you need in your notebook before you read the chapter.

READ AND TAKE NOTES

Reading Strategy: Summarizing When you study history, it is important to clearly understand what you read. One way to achieve a clear understanding is to summarize. When you summarize, you restate what you have read into fewer words, stating only the main ideas and essential details. It is important to use your own words in a summary. Use the chart below to record your summaries of the main ideas and essential details in Chapter 10.

 See Skillbuilder Handbook, page R2.

The Jefferson Era
Summaries
Main Idea: Thomas Jefferson is elected president.   **Details:** Jefferson replaces Federalist policies with his own but has problems with the judiciary.
Main Idea: **Details:**
Main Idea: **Details:**
Main Idea: **Details:**

TERMS & NAMES
radical
Judiciary Act
of 1801
John Marshall
Marbury v.
Madison
unconstitutional
judicial review

MAIN IDEA	WHY IT MATTERS NOW
When Jefferson became president in 1801, his party replaced Federalist programs with its own.	Today's Democratic Party traces its roots to the party of Jefferson, the Democratic-Republicans.

ONE AMERICAN'S STORY

Supporters of John Adams and Thomas Jefferson—competitors in the presidential election of 1800—fought for their candidates with nasty personal attacks. Scottish immigrant James Callender, a Jefferson supporter, wrote some of the harshest criticisms. During the campaign, he warned voters not to reelect President John Adams.

A VOICE FROM THE PAST

In the fall of 1796 . . . the country fell into a more dangerous juncture than almost any the old confederation ever endured. The tardiness and timidity of Mr. Washington were succeeded by the rancour [bitterness] and insolence [arrogance] of Mr. Adams. . . . Think what you have been, what you are, and what, under [Adams], you are likely to become.

James Callender, quoted in *American Aurora*

In the presidential election of 1800, Thomas Jefferson was the candidate of the Democratic-Republican Party. John Adams represented the Federalists.

Adams's defenders were just as vicious. One went so far as to claim that if Jefferson won, "the soil will be soaked with blood, and the nation black with crimes." In spite of the campaign's nastiness, the election ended with a peaceful transfer of power from one party to another. The 1800 election was more than a personal battle, though. It was a contest between two parties with different ideas about the role of government.

The Election of 1800

The two parties contesting the election of 1800 were the Federalists, led by President John Adams, and the Democratic-Republicans, represented by Thomas Jefferson. Each party believed that the other was endangering the Constitution and the American republic.

The Democratic-Republicans thought they were saving the nation from monarchy and oppression. They argued, again and again, that the Alien and Sedition Acts supported by the Federalists violated the Bill of Rights. (See pages 290–291.) The Federalists thought that the nation was about to be ruined by **radicals**—people who take extreme political positions. They remembered the violence of the French Revolution, in which radicals executed thousands in the name of liberty.

When election day came, the Democratic-Republicans won the presidency. Jefferson received 73 votes in the electoral college, and Adams earned 65. But there was a problem. Aaron Burr, whom the Democratic-Republicans wanted as vice president, also received 73 votes.

Background
In 1804, the Twelfth Amendment solved this problem by creating separate ballots for president and vice president.

STRANGE *but* True

HAMILTON-BURR DUEL

In 1804, the Democratic-Republicans replaced Aaron Burr as their candidate for vice president. Burr then decided to run for governor of New York.

Alexander Hamilton questioned Burr's fitness for public office. He wrote that Burr was a "dangerous man . . . who ought not to be trusted with the reins of government."

Burr lost the election. Furious, he challenged Hamilton to a duel. Hamilton went to the duel but resolved not to fire. Burr, however, shot Hamilton, who died the next day.

Breaking the Tie

According to the Constitution, the House of Representatives had to choose between Burr and Jefferson. The Democratic-Republicans clearly intended for Jefferson to be president. However, the new House of Representatives, dominated by Jefferson's party, would not take office for some months. Federalists still held a majority in the House, and their votes would decide the winner.

The Federalists were divided. Some feared Jefferson so much that they decided to back Burr. Others, such as Alexander Hamilton, considered Burr an unreliable man and urged the election of Jefferson. Hamilton did not like Jefferson, but he believed that Jefferson would do more for the good of the nation than Burr. "If there be a man in the world I ought to hate," he said, "it is Jefferson. . . . But the public good must be [more important than] every private consideration."

Over a period of seven days, the House voted 35 times without determining a winner. Finally, two weeks before the inauguration, Alexander Hamilton's friend James A. Bayard persuaded several Federalists not to vote for Burr. On the thirty-sixth ballot, Jefferson was elected president. Aaron Burr, who became vice president, would never forget Hamilton's insults.

People were overjoyed by Jefferson's election. A Philadelphia newspaper reported that bells rang, guns fired, dogs barked, cats meowed, and children cried over the news of Jefferson's victory.

Reading **History**
A. Analyzing Points of View
Why did Hamilton think that Jefferson was the better choice for president?

The Talented Jefferson

In over 200 years, the United States has had more than 40 presidents. Many of them were great leaders. But no president has ever matched Thomas Jefferson in the variety of his achievements.

Jefferson's talents went beyond politics. He was still a young lawyer when he became interested in the architecture of classical Greece and Rome. The look of our nation's capital today reflects that interest. When Washington, D.C., was being built during the 1790s, Jefferson advised its architects and designers.

Jefferson's passion for classical styles can also be seen in his plan of Monticello, his Virginia home. For this elegant mansion, Jefferson designed storm windows, a seven-day clock, and a dumbwaiter—a small elevator that brought bottles of wine from the cellar.

Jefferson was a skilled violinist, horseman, amateur scientist, and a devoted reader, too. His book collection later became the core of the Library of Congress. After his election, Jefferson applied his many talents and ideas to the government of the United States.

Jefferson's Philosophy

The new president had strong opinions about what kind of country the United States ought to be. But his first order of business was to calm the nation's political quarrels.

A VOICE FROM THE PAST

Let us, then, fellow-citizens, unite with one heart and one mind. . . . Every difference of opinion is not a difference of principle. . . . We are all Republicans, we are all Federalists.

Thomas Jefferson, First Inaugural Address

Reading **History**

B. Summarizing
How did Thomas Jefferson try to unite the nation after he was elected?

One way Jefferson tried to unite Americans was by promoting a common way of life. He wanted the United States to remain a nation of small independent farmers. Such a nation, he believed, would uphold the strong morals and democratic values that he associated with country living. He hoped that the enormous amount of available land would prevent Americans from crowding into cities, as people had in Europe.

As president, Jefferson behaved more like a gentleman farmer than a privileged politician. Instead of riding in a fancy carriage to his inauguration, Jefferson walked the two blocks from his boarding house to the Capitol. Though his chef served elegant meals, the president's guests ate at round tables so that no one could sit at the head of the table.

To the end, Jefferson refused to elevate himself because of his office. For his tombstone, he chose this simple epitaph: "Here was buried

The Talented Jefferson

For his Virginia home, Jefferson designed a dumbwaiter to bring bottles from his wine cellar.

Thomas Jefferson was a man of extraordinary talent. His architectural skill can be seen in the design of Monticello, shown here.

Jefferson improved the design of this early copy machine. As a user of the device wrote with one pen, a second pen made an exact copy.

Thomas Jefferson, author of the Declaration of American Independence, of the statute of Virginia for religious freedom, and father of the University of Virginia." Jefferson chose not to list his presidency. His belief in a modest role for the central government is reflected in the changes he made during his presidency.

Background In addition to founding the University of Virginia in 1819, Jefferson designed its buildings and supervised their construction.

Undoing Federalist Programs

Jefferson believed that the federal government should have less power than it had had under the Federalists. During his term of office, he sought to end many Federalist programs.

At the president's urging, Congress—now controlled by Democratic-Republicans—allowed the Alien and Sedition Acts to end. Jefferson then released prisoners convicted under the acts—among them, James Callender. Congress also ended many taxes, including the unpopular whiskey tax. Because the loss of tax revenue lowered the government's income, Jefferson reduced the number of federal employees to cut costs. He also reduced the size of the military.

Jefferson next made changes to the Federalists' financial policies. Alexander Hamilton had created a system that depended on a certain amount of public debt. He believed that people who were owed money by their government would make sure the government was run properly. But Jefferson opposed public debt. He used revenues from tariffs and land sales to reduce the amount of money owed by the government.

Marshall and the Judiciary

Though Jefferson ended many Federalist programs, he had little power over the courts. John Adams had seen to that with the **Judiciary Act of 1801.** Under this act, Adams had appointed as many Federalist judges as he could between the election of 1800 and Jefferson's inauguration in 1801. These last-minute appointments meant that the new Democratic-Republican president would face a firmly Federalist judiciary.

Jefferson often felt frustrated by Federalist control of the courts. Yet because judges received their appointments for life, the president could do little.

Before he left office in 1801, President Adams also appointed a new Chief Justice of the Supreme Court. He chose a 45-year-old Federalist, **John Marshall**. He guessed that Marshall would be around for a long time to check the power of the Democratic-Republicans. He was right. Marshall served as Chief Justice for over three decades. Under Marshall, the Supreme Court upheld federal authority and strengthened federal

AMERICA'S HISTORY MAKERS

JOHN MARSHALL
1755–1835
John Marshall was born, the first of 15 children, in Virginia's back-country. He had little formal schooling. He received most of his education from his parents and a minister who lived with the family one year.

Even so, the lasting strength of the U.S. Constitution is partly due to Marshall's brilliant legal mind. In his long tenure as Chief Justice, John Marshall partici-pated in more than 1,000 deci-sions and wrote 519 of them himself.

How does Marshall's record as Chief Justice demonstrate his decision-making abilities?

Reading **History**
C. Analyzing Causes Why did the Federalists retain a great deal of power even after they were defeated by the Democratic-Republicans?

courts. One of the most important decisions of the Marshall Court was *Marbury v. Madison* (1803).

Marbury v. Madison

Vocabulary
justice of the peace: a low-level official with limited authority, including the power to perform marriages

William Marbury was one of Adams's last-minute appointments. Adams had named him as a justice of the peace for the District of Columbia.

Marbury was supposed to be installed in his position by Secretary of State James Madison. When Madison refused to give him the job, Marbury sued. The case went to the Supreme Court, which ruled that the law under which Marbury sued was **unconstitutional**—that is, it contradicted the law of the Constitution.

Although the Court denied Marbury's claim, it did establish the principle of **judicial review**. This principle states that the Supreme Court has the final say in interpreting the Constitution. In his decision, Marshall declared, "It is emphatically the province and duty of the Judicial Department to say what the law is." If the Supreme Court decides that a law violates the Constitution, then that law cannot be put into effect.

Jefferson and Madison were angry when Marshall seized this new power for the Supreme Court, but they could hardly fight his decision. After all, he had decided *Marbury* v. *Madison* in their favor.

By establishing judicial review, Marshall helped to create a lasting balance among the three branches of government. The strength of this balance would be tested as the United States grew. In the next section, you will read about a period of great national growth.

Now and then

THE SUPREME COURT TODAY

The principle of judicial review is still a major force in American society. In June 1999, the Supreme Court used this power to restrict the ability of the federal government to enforce its laws in the 50 states.

In one case, *Alden* v. *Maine*, the Court ruled that employees of a state government cannot sue their state even when the state violates federal labor laws—such as those that set guidelines for overtime wages.

Section 1 Assessment

1. Terms & Names

Explain the significance of:

• radical
• Judiciary Act of 1801
• John Marshall
• *Marbury* v. *Madison*
• unconstitutional
• judicial review

2. Taking Notes

Use a chart like the one below to list some of the changes made by Jefferson and his party.

Changes made by Democratic-Republicans
1.

What branch of government gave Jefferson trouble?

3. Main Ideas

a. How was the tie between Jefferson and Burr settled after the election of 1800?

b. In what ways did Jefferson's talents reach beyond politics?

c. How did the opinions of Jefferson and Hamilton regarding the public debt differ?

4. Critical Thinking

Making Generalizations
How was Thomas Jefferson's philosophy reflected in his personal life?

THINK ABOUT

• how he behaved after being elected
• how he felt about his presidency later in life

ACTIVITY OPTIONS

TECHNOLOGY

ART

Read more about Thomas Jefferson. Design Jefferson's **Internet home page** showing his inventions or create a **model** of a building he designed.

The Louisiana Purchase and Exploration

TERMS & NAMES
Louisiana Purchase
Meriwether Lewis
William Clark
Lewis and Clark expedition
Sacagawea
Zebulon Pike

MAIN IDEA	**WHY IT MATTERS NOW**
Jefferson purchased the Louisiana Territory in 1803 and doubled the size of the United States.	Thirteen more states were eventually organized on the land acquired by the Louisiana Purchase.

ONE AMERICAN'S STORY

In 1790, Captain Robert Gray became the first American to sail around the world. Two years later, Gray explored a harbor in what is now Washington state. This harbor was later named Gray's Harbor, and Washington's largest river was named after Gray's ship, the *Columbia.*

New England merchants like Captain Gray had to sail all the way around South America to reach the profitable trading regions of the Oregon Country. (See the map on page 304.) In spite of the long trip, merchants from Boston soon began to appear there frequently. They appeared so often that the Native Americans they traded with began calling all white people "Bostons."

Gray's explorations helped to establish U.S. claims to the Pacific Northwest. In this section, you will learn how a lucky land purchase and a daring expedition further hastened westward expansion.

Robert Gray sailed his ship *Columbia* on trading voyages to the Northwest and China.

The West in 1800

In 1800, when Americans talked about the "West," they meant the area between the Appalachian Mountains and the Mississippi River. Thousands of settlers were moving westward across the Appalachians to settle in this region. Many moved onto land long inhabited by Native Americans. Even so, several U.S. territories soon declared statehood. Kentucky and Tennessee had become states by 1800, and Ohio entered the union in 1803.

Although the Mississippi River was the western border of the United States, there was a great deal of activity further west. In 1800, France and Spain were negotiating for ownership of the Louisiana Territory—the vast region between the Mississippi River and the Rocky Mountains.

The Pacific coast region and the Oregon Country, as you read in One American's Story, also attracted increasing attention. In California, Spain had a chain of 21 missions stretching from San Diego to San Francisco. Starting just north of San Francisco, Russian settlements dotted the Pacific coast all the way to Alaska. Great Britain also claimed land in the region.

Reading History

A. Reading a Map Use the map on page 304 to find the location of New Orleans.

As the number of Westerners grew, so did their political influence. A vital issue for many settlers was the use of the Mississippi River. Farmers and merchants used the river to move their products to the port of New Orleans, and from there to east coast markets. Threats to the free navigation of the Mississippi and the use of the port at New Orleans brought America to the brink of war.

Napoleon and New Orleans

"There is on the globe one single spot the possessor of which is our natural and habitual enemy," President Jefferson wrote. That spot was New Orleans. This strategic port was originally claimed by France. After losing the French and Indian War, France turned over the Louisiana Territory—including New Orleans—to Spain. But in a secret treaty in 1800, Spain returned Louisiana and the port to France's powerful leader, Napoleon. Now Napoleon planned to colonize the American territory.

Background In 1799, Napoleon was made the top official of the French Republic. In 1804, he became emperor.

In 1802, these developments nearly resulted in war. Just before turning Louisiana over to France, Spain closed New Orleans to American shipping. Angry Westerners called for war against both Spain and France. To avoid hostilities, Jefferson offered to buy New Orleans from France. He received a surprising offer back. The French asked if the United States wanted to buy all of the Louisiana Territory—a tract of land even larger than the United States at that time.

The Louisiana Purchase

A number of factors may have led Napoleon to make his surprising offer. He was probably alarmed by America's fierce determination to keep the port of New Orleans open. Also, his enthusiasm for a colony in America may have been lessened by events in a French colony in the West Indies. There, a revolt led by Toussaint L'Ouverture (too•SAN loo•vehr•TOOR) had resulted in disastrous losses for the French. Another factor was France's costly war against Britain. America's money may have been more valuable to Napoleon than its land.

Jefferson was thrilled by Napoleon's offer. However, the Constitution said nothing about the president's right to buy land. This troubled Jefferson, who believed in the strict interpretation of the Constitution. But he also believed in a republic of small farmers, and that required land. So, on April 30, 1803, the **Louisiana Purchase** was approved for $15 million—about three cents per acre. The purchase doubled the size of the United States. At the time, Americans knew little about the territory. But that would soon change.

Reading History

B. Making Inferences Why did Jefferson purchase Louisiana even though the Constitution said nothing about the president's right to buy land?

Connections TO WORLD HISTORY

TOUSSAINT L'OUVERTURE

Toussaint L'Ouverture was born in Hispaniola, an island in the West Indies once colonized by both France and Spain. In 1791, L'Ouverture helped to lead a slave revolt against the French-controlled part of Hispaniola. A natural leader, L'Ouverture won admiration when he preached harmony between former slaves and planters.

In 1801, L'Ouverture overran the Spanish part of the island. He then freed all the slaves and put himself in charge of the entire island.

Hoping to regain their territory, the French invaded in 1802. They arrested L'Ouverture but failed to end the rebellion.

Lewis and Clark Explore

Since 1802, Thomas Jefferson had planned an expedition to explore the Louisiana country. Now that the Louisiana Purchase had been made, learning about the territory became even more important.

Jefferson chose a young officer, Captain **Meriwether Lewis,** to lead the expedition. In Jefferson's map-lined study, the two men eagerly planned the trip. Lewis turned to his old friend, Lieutenant **William Clark,** to select and oversee a volunteer force, which they called the Corps of Discovery. Clark was a skilled mapmaker and outdoorsman and proved to be a natural leader. The Corps of Discovery soon became known as the **Lewis and Clark expedition**.

Clark was accompanied by York, his African-American slave. York's hunting skills won him many admirers among the Native Americans met by the explorers. The first black man that many Indians had ever seen, York became something of a celebrity among them.

Lewis and Clark set out in the summer of 1803. By winter, they reached St. Louis. Located on the western bank of the Mississippi River, St. Louis would soon become the gateway to the West. But in 1803, the city was a sleepy town with just 180 houses. Lewis and Clark spent the winter at St. Louis and waited for the ceremony that would mark the transfer of Louisiana to the United States. In March 1804, the American flag flew over St. Louis for the first time.

Vocabulary
corps (kor): a number of people acting together for a similar purpose

The Louisiana Purchase and Explorations, *1804–1807*

The Rocky Mountain summit of Pikes Peak is 14,110 feet high.

GEOGRAPHY SKILLBUILDER Interpreting Maps
1. **Location** *What two rivers met at the starting point of the Lewis and Clark expedition?*
2. **Movement** *How were Lewis and Clark's return routes different from each other?*

AMERICA'S HISTORY MAKERS

MERIWETHER LEWIS
1774–1809

Meriwether Lewis was well qualified for the first overland expedition to the Pacific Northwest. In Virginia, he had become an expert hunter. From 1801 to 1803, he worked for President Jefferson, who had him trained in geography, mineralogy, and astronomy.

The journals Lewis kept tell what the West was like in the early 1800s and are still exciting to read. In one entry, dated September 17, 1804, Lewis describes the "immense herds of Buffaloe, deer Elk and Antelopes which we saw in every direction feeding on the hills and plains."

WILLIAM CLARK
1770–1838

William Clark was an army friend of Meriwether Lewis. Lewis personally chose him to be co-captain of the Corps of Discovery.

Clark's experience in his state militia and the U.S. Army had taught him how to build forts, draw maps, and lead expeditions through enemy territory.

He had less formal training than Lewis, but with his six feet of height and muscular build, he was a more rugged explorer.

Clark's leadership skills smoothed disputes. Also, his artistic skills made the expedition's maps and drawings both accurate and beautiful.

What were the different skills of Lewis and Clark that qualified them as co-leaders of the expedition?

Up the Missouri River

Reading History

C. Making Inferences Why did Lewis and Clark travel on the Missouri River?

The explorers, who numbered about 40, set out from St. Louis in May of 1804. They headed up the Missouri River in one shallow-bottomed riverboat and two pirogues—canoes made from hollowed-out tree trunks. They had instructions from President Jefferson to explore the river and hoped to find a water route across the continent. Lewis and Clark were also told to establish good relations with Native Americans and describe the landscape, plants, and animals they saw.

The explorers inched up the Missouri. The first afternoon, they traveled only about three miles. Sometimes the men had to pull, rather than row or sail, their boats against the current. In late October, they reached the Mandan Indian villages in what is now North Dakota.

The explorers built a small fort and spent the winter with the friendly Mandan. There, they also met British and French-Canadian trappers and traders. They were not happy to see the Americans. They suspected that the Americans would soon compete with them for the rich trade in beaver furs—and they were right.

In the spring of 1805, the expedition set out again. A French trapper, his 17-year-old-wife, **Sacagawea** (SAK•uh•juh•WEE•uh), and their baby went with them. Sacagawea was a Shoshone woman whose language skills and knowledge of geography would be of great value to Lewis and Clark—especially when they reached the area where she was born.

The Jefferson Era **305**

On to the Pacific Ocean

On their way west, the expedition had to stop at the Great Falls of the Missouri. Lewis called this ten-mile-long series of waterfalls "the grandest sight I ever beheld." He described his approach to the falls.

A VOICE FROM THE PAST

I had proceeded on this course about two miles . . . whin my ears were saluted with the agreeable sound of a fall of water and advancing a little further I saw the spray arrise above the plain like a collumn of smoke. . . . (It) soon began to make a roaring too tremendious to be mistaken for any cause short of the great falls of the Missouri.

Meriwether Lewis, quoted in *Undaunted Courage*

Lewis and Clark kept beautiful journals that provided priceless information about the West.

To get around the Great Falls, the explorers had to carry their boats and heavy supplies for 18 miles. They built wheels from cottonwood trees to move the boats. Even with wheels, the trek took nearly two weeks. Rattlesnakes, bears, and even a hailstorm slowed their steps.

As they approached the Rocky Mountains, Sacagawea excitedly pointed out Shoshone lands. Eager to make contact with the tribe, Lewis and a small party made their way overland. Lewis soon found the Shoshone, whose chief recognized Sacagawea as his sister. The chief traded horses to Lewis and Clark, and the Shoshone helped them cross the Rocky Mountains.

The explorers then journeyed to the mighty Columbia River, which leads to the Pacific Ocean. In November 1805, Clark wrote in his journal, "Ocian in view! O! The joy." They soon arrived at the Pacific Coast. There, they spent a rain-soaked winter before returning to St. Louis the following year.

The Lewis and Clark expedition brought back a wealth of scientific and geographic information. Though they learned that an all-water route across the continent did not exist, Americans received an exciting report of what lay to the west.

Reading **History**
D. Finding Main Ideas Why was the Lewis and Clark expedition valuable?

Pike's Expedition

Lewis and Clark explored the northern part of the Louisiana Purchase. In 1806, an expedition led by **Zebulon Pike** left St. Louis on a southerly route. (Refer to the map on page 304.) Pike's mission was to find the sources of the Arkansas and Red rivers. The Red River formed a boundary between Spanish territory and Louisiana.

Pike's party of two dozen men headed westward across the Great Plains. When they reached the Arkansas River, they followed it toward the Rocky Mountains. From 150 miles away, Pike spied the Rocky Mountain peak that would later bear his name—Pikes Peak. However, he failed in his attempt to climb it. Then they turned south, hoping that they would eventually run into the Red River. Instead, they ran into the

Background
The previous year, Pike had led a 5,000-mile expedition to search for the source of the Mississippi River.

EFFECTS: Exploration of the West, 1804–1807

▶ **1. Accurate maps**
Lewis and Clark and Pike produced the first good maps of the Louisiana Territory. Later travelers would use these maps to make their way west.

▶ **2. Growth of fur trade**
Exploration boosted interest in the fur trade. Hunters and trappers would add to the knowledge of the West.

▶ **3. Mistaken view of Great Plains**
Pike inaccurately described the treeless Great Plains as a desert. This led many Americans to believe that the Plains were useless for farming.

SKILLBUILDER Interpreting Charts
Why might Pike's description of the Great Plains have led to the idea that Native Americans east of the Mississippi should be moved there?

Compass used by Lewis and Clark

Vocabulary
Rio Grande: Spanish for *big river*

Rio Grande, which was in Spanish territory. There, they were arrested by Spanish troops.

The explorers returned to the United States after being released by Spanish officials in 1807. Though Pike and his men never explored the Red River, they did bring back valuable descriptions of the Great Plains and the Rio Grande River Valley.

The Effects of Exploration

The first American explorers of the West brought back tales of adventure as well as scientific and geographical information. As the chart above shows, this information would have long-lasting effects.

Early in Jefferson's presidency, events at home occupied much of the new president's time. In the next section, you will learn about foreign affairs during the same time period.

Section 2 Assessment

1. Terms & Names

Explain the significance of:
• Louisiana Purchase
• Meriwether Lewis
• William Clark
• Lewis and Clark expedition
• Sacagawea
• Zebulon Pike

2. Taking Notes

Use a chart like the one below to record the factors that might have led Napoleon to sell the Louisiana Territory.

Causes

Effect

Napoleon sells Louisiana Territory

3. Main Ideas

a. What groups might dispute European land claims in the West?

b. Why was New Orleans important to Americans?

c. How did Sacagawea help Lewis and Clark?

4. Critical Thinking

Recognizing Effects What were some of the effects of the explorations of the West in the 1800s?

THINK ABOUT

• how other people might use the information brought back by the explorers
• the economic effects of the expedition

ACTIVITY OPTIONS

WORLD HISTORY

GEOGRAPHY

Read more about New Orleans. Make an illustrated **time line** of the French, Spanish, and U.S. ownership of the city or create a **map** of its port.

Native Americans on the Explorers' Route

When Thomas Jefferson bought the Louisiana Territory, Native Americans had already been living in that area for thousands of years. Before Lewis and Clark began their trip, Jefferson instructed them to deal with Native Americans in a peaceful manner and to make it clear that the United States wished to be "friendly and useful to them." On their journey, Lewis and Clark met almost 50 different tribes.

Sacagawea

In 1805, the explorers arrived in Shoshone territory near the Rocky Mountains. A Shoshone chief, Cameahwait, confirmed that there was no all-water route to the Pacific. Later, when Cameahwait recognized Sacagawea as his sister, he agreed to sell the explorers the horses they needed to cross the mountains.

① Oto

In 1804, Lewis and Clark met the Oto, a buffalo-hunting people. This was the first formal meeting of U.S. representatives with western Native Americans. Lewis told the Oto that they were "children" of a new great "father"—President Thomas Jefferson.

ARTIFACT FILE

Buffalo Robe Pictured to the right is a section of a Mandan buffalo robe. On it, a Mandan painted a battle scene between the Mandan and the Sioux.

② Mandan

Neighboring tribes as well as exploring Europeans relied on the mainstay of Mandan culture—corn. The Mandan also crafted beautiful leatherwork and pottery. Lewis and Clark spent an entire winter with the Mandan.

③ Teton Sioux

Upon meeting the Teton Sioux, Lewis and Clark showed off an air gun. Known for their aggressiveness, the Teton already viewed the Americans as competitors for trade in this region. As a result, confrontation marked Lewis and Clark's visit.

On-Line Field Trip

The Peabody Museum in Cambridge, Massachusetts, holds an important collection of Native American artifacts. This rain hat was worn by Chinook whalers of the Northwest. The Chinook made these water-repellent hats out of cedar bark and bear grass.

For more about Native American artifacts . . .

RESEARCH LINKS
CLASSZONE.COM

CONNECT TO GEOGRAPHY

1. **Place** What fort was built where the Columbia River empties into the Pacific Ocean?
2. **Location** In what mountain range did the Shoshone tribe live?

🄖 See Geography Handbook, page 4.

CONNECT TO HISTORY

3. **Forming Opinions** What do you think the Native Americans that Lewis and Clark met thought about the explorers?

③ Problems with Foreign Powers

TERMS & NAMES
impressment
Embargo Act of 1807
Tecumseh
War Hawk

MAIN IDEA	WHY IT MATTERS NOW
Jefferson tried to avoid involvement in the problems of other nations.	British interference with the affairs of the United States led to the War of 1812.

ONE AMERICAN'S STORY

In 1804, U.S. Navy Lieutenant Stephen Decatur was on a daring mission overseas. The United States was at war with Tripoli, a state on the North African coast. The war, which began in 1801, was the result of repeated attacks on American merchant ships by African pirates. Decatur's mission was to destroy the U.S. warship *Philadelphia*—which had been captured by Tripoli—so that it could not be used by the enemy.

Decatur bravely sailed into Tripoli's harbor and set fire to the *Philadelphia.* He then managed to escape under enemy fire with only one man wounded. Decatur later issued this rallying cry for all Americans.

> *A VOICE FROM THE PAST*
>
> Our country! In her [relationships] with foreign nations may she always be in the right; but our country, right or wrong.
>
> **Stephen Decatur,** 1816

Stephen Decatur struggles in hand-to-hand combat with African pirates.

Decatur's attack was one of the most celebrated events of the war, which ended in 1805. The conflict showed how hard it was for the United States to stay out of foreign affairs while its citizens participated so heavily in overseas trade. In this section, you will learn how President Jefferson handled problems with other nations.

Jefferson's Foreign Policy

When Thomas Jefferson took office in 1801, he expected to concentrate on domestic concerns. In his inaugural address, he happily noted that America was "kindly separated by nature and a wide ocean from the exterminating havoc [wars] of one quarter of the globe." Jefferson advised the United States to seek the friendship of all nations, but to enter into "entangling alliances with none."

However, the president's desire to keep the United States separated from other nations and their problems was doomed to fail. For one thing, American merchants were busily engaged in trade all over the world. For another, the Louisiana Purchase and the Lewis and Clark expedition were about to open the country to westward expansion. Expansion would bring Americans into closer contact with people from other nations who had already established settlements in the West.

Finally, the United States had little control over the actions of foreign nations—as North African interference with U.S. shipping had shown. Staying out of the ongoing conflict between France and England would be just as difficult.

Reading **History**
A. Analyzing Causes Why was it hard for the United States to avoid other nations' problems?

Problems with France and England

For a long time, the United States managed not to get involved in the European wars that followed the French Revolution. At times, the nation even benefited from the conflict. Busy with affairs in Europe, France sold the Louisiana Territory to the United States. And American shippers eagerly took over the trade interrupted by the war.

By 1805, however, the British began to clamp down on U.S. shipping. They did not want Americans to provide their enemies with food and supplies. After the United States threatened to take action, the British decided to set up a partial blockade. This would only allow some American ships to bring provisions to Europe.

This partial blockade angered France, which enacted its own laws to control foreign shipping. These changes put American merchants in a difficult position. If they obeyed the British rules, their ships could be seized by the French. If they obeyed the French rules, their ships could be seized by the British.

Britain also interfered with U.S. trade by the **impressment,** or kidnapping, of American sailors to work on British ships. Between 1803 and 1812, the British impressed about 6,000 American sailors.

British officers seize an American sailor at gunpoint.

One of the most famous incidents occurred in 1807. The British ship *Leopard* attacked an American naval ship, the *Chesapeake,* off the coast of Virginia. Three Americans lost their lives in the battle. The attack aroused widespread anger. Had Congress been in session, America might have declared war. But Jefferson, who had been re-elected in 1804, decided against it. One critic, furious at the president's caution, called Jefferson a "dish of skim milk curdling at the head of our nation."

Vocabulary
coercion: the practice of forcing someone to act in a certain way by use of pressure or threats

Trade as a Weapon

Instead of declaring war, Jefferson asked Congress to pass legislation that would stop all foreign trade. "Peaceable coercion," as the president described his policy, would prevent further bloodshed.

In December, Congress passed the **Embargo Act of 1807**. Now American ships were no longer allowed to sail to foreign ports. The act also closed American ports to British ships.

Jefferson's policy was a disaster. It was more harmful to the United States than to the British and French. American farmers and merchants were especially hard hit. Southern and Western farmers, for example, lost important markets for their grain, cotton, and tobacco. Shippers lost income, and many chose to violate the embargo by making false claims about where they were going. One New Englander said the embargo was like "cutting one's throat to cure the nosebleed."

The embargo became a major issue in the election of 1808. Jefferson's old friend James Madison won the election. By the time he took office, Congress had already repealed the embargo.

Madison's solution to the problem was a law that allowed merchants to trade with any country except France and Britain. Trade with these countries would start again when they agreed to respect U.S. ships. But this law proved no more effective than the embargo.

Reading **History**
B. Recognizing Effects What were the results of the Embargo Act?

Tecumseh and Native American Unity

British interference with American shipping and impressment of U.S. citizens made Americans furious. They also were angered by Britain's actions in the Northwest. Many settlers believed that the British were stirring up Native American resistance to frontier settlements.

The Shawnee chief Tecumseh led Native American resistance to white rule in the Ohio River Valley.

Since the Battle of Fallen Timbers in 1794 (see page 283), Native Americans continued to lose their land. Thousands of white settlers had swarmed into Ohio and then into Indiana.

Tecumseh, a Shawnee chief, vowed to stop the loss of Native American land. He believed that the reason Native Americans continued to lose their land was because they were separated into many different tribes. He concluded that Native Americans had to do what white Americans had done: unite. Events in 1809 proved him right.

That September, William Henry Harrison, governor of the Indiana Territory, signed the Treaty of Fort Wayne with chiefs of the Miami, Delaware, and Potawatomi tribes. They agreed to sell over three million acres of land. But Tecumseh declared the treaty meaningless.

Reading **History**
C. Forming Opinions Why did Tecumseh declare the Treaty of Fort Wayne meaningless?

A VOICE FROM THE PAST

[Whites] have taken upon themselves to say this [land] belongs to the Miamis, this to the Delawares and so on. But the Great Spirit intended [Native American land] to be the common property of all the tribes, [and it cannot] be sold without the consent of all.

Tecumseh, quoted in *Tecumseh and the Quest for Indian Leadership*

After the Treaty of Fort Wayne, many Native Americans began to answer Tecumseh's call for unity. But his efforts ultimately failed. In November 1811, while Tecumseh was away recruiting tribes for his alliance, the Shawnee were defeated by Harrison's forces at the Battle of

Tippecanoe. It was a severe setback for Tecumseh's movement.

War Hawks

After the battle of Tippecanoe, Tecumseh and his warriors found a warm welcome with the British in Canada. At that point, the Native Americans and the British became allies. Tecumseh's welcome in Canada raised even higher the anti-British feelings in the West.

Leaders such as Congressman Henry Clay of Kentucky angrily demanded war against Britain. Westerners who called for war were known as **War Hawks**. They wanted British aid to Native Americans stopped, and they wanted the British out of Canada. Conquering Canada would open up a vast new empire for Americans.

Other Americans sought war because of the British violations of American rights at sea. Future president Andrew Jackson said hostilities were necessary "for the protection of our maritime citizens impressed on board British ships of war," and to "open a market for the productions of our soil."

Urged on by Jackson and the War Hawks, Congress declared war on Britain on June 18, 1812. In the next section, you will read about the second—and final—war between the United States and Great Britain.

Causes of the War of 1812

Impressment of U.S. Citizens | Interference with American shipping | British support of Native-American resistance

WAR

SKILLBUILDER Interpreting Charts
Which cause of the War of 1812 was not related to activities on the sea?

Section 3 Assessment

1. Terms & Names

Explain the significance of:
- impressment
- Embargo Act of 1807
- Tecumseh
- War Hawk

2. Taking Notes

Use a chart like the one below to record the effects of Jefferson's Embargo Act.

Causes | Embargo Act

Effects | ☐ ☐

Why didn't the act work?

3. Main Ideas

a. How did the British and French interfere with American shipping?

b. How did Jefferson respond to the interference?

c. Why did the War Hawks favor war?

4. Critical Thinking

Analyzing Points of View Why did Tecumseh think it was important for Native Americans to unite?

THINK ABOUT
- what he learned about white men
- what Native Americans would lose if they did not act together

ACTIVITY OPTIONS

ART

SPEECH

Do research on the Battle of Tippecanoe. Draw a **comic strip story** of the battle or hold a **press conference** to describe the battle's outcome.

4 The War of 1812

TERMS & NAMES
Oliver Hazard Perry
Battle of the Thames
Francis Scott Key
Treaty of Ghent

MAIN IDEA	WHY IT MATTERS NOW
Angered by Britain's interference in the nation's affairs, the United States went to war.	The War of 1812 showed that the United States was willing and able to protect its national interests.

ONE AMERICAN'S STORY

The war between the United States and Britain had begun in 1812. Two years later, British troops were marching toward Washington, D.C. Dolley Madison, the president's wife, stayed behind until the last minute. With bombs bursting in the distance, she hurried to save important historical objects from the White House.

A VOICE FROM THE PAST

I have had [a wagon] filled with . . . the most valuable portable articles belonging to the house. . . . I insist on waiting until the large picture of General Washington is secured . . . It is done! and the precious portrait placed in the hands of two gentlemen of New York, for safe keeping.

Dolley Madison, from a letter sent to her sister

When the British troops arrived in the city, they set fire to many public buildings, including the White House and the Capitol. The next day, a violent storm caused even more damage. Fortunately, the heavy rains that accompanied the storm helped put out the fires. You will learn about other events of the War of 1812 in this section.

Before British troops set fire to the president's mansion, Dolley Madison saved priceless historical objects.

The War Begins

Britain did not really want a war with the United States because it was already involved in another war with France. To try to avoid war, the British announced that they would no longer interfere with American shipping. But the slow mails of the day prevented this news from reaching the United States until weeks after June 18th, when Congress approved Madison's request for a declaration of war.

The War of 1812 had two main phases. From 1812 to 1814, Britain concentrated on its war against France. It devoted little energy to the conflict in North America, although it did send ships to blockade the American coast. The second phase of the war began after the British defeated France in April 1814. With their European war nearly at an end, the British could turn their complete attention to the United States.

The United States military was weak when the war was declared. Democratic-Republicans had reduced the size of the armed forces. When the war began, the Navy had only about 16 ships. The army had fewer than 7,000 men. These men were poorly trained and equipped, and were often led by inexperienced officers. A young Virginia army officer complained that the older officers were victims of "sloth, ignorance, or habits of [excessive] drinking."

The First Phase of the War

In spite of its small size, the United States Navy rose to the challenge. Its warships were the fastest afloat. American naval officers had gained valuable experience fighting pirates in the Mediterranean Sea. Early in the war, before the British blockaded the coast, ships such as the *Constitution* and the *United States* won stirring victories. These victories on the high seas boosted American confidence.

The most important U.S. naval victory took place on Lake Erie. In the winter of 1812–1813, the Americans had begun to build a fleet on the shores of Lake Erie. **Oliver Hazard Perry,** an experienced officer, took charge of this infant fleet. In September 1813, the small British force on the lake set out to attack the American ships. Commodore Perry, who had predicted that this would be "the most important day of my life," sailed out to meet the enemy. Perry's ship, the *Lawrence,* flew a banner declaring, "Don't give up the ship."

The War of 1812

BATTLES OF THE WAR

1 **Atlantic Ocean.** British navy blockades American coast, 1813

2 **Lake Erie.** Perry's fleet defeats a British fleet, 1813

3 **Thames River.** Harrison defeats British in Canada, killing Tecumseh, 1813

4 **Washington, D.C.** British burn the capital but later fail to capture nearby Baltimore, 1814

5 **Lake Champlain.** American ships defeat British, who retreat to Canada, 1814

6 **New Orleans.** Jackson's army defeats British in Battle of New Orleans, 1815

← American forces
← British forces
✳ American victory
✳ British victory
🏛 Fort

GEOGRAPHY SKILLBUILDER
Interpreting Maps

1. Location *Where was Fort McHenry located?*

2. Movement *Which battle required American troops to march into Canada?*

For two hours, the British and Americans exchanged cannon shots. Perry's ship was demolished and the guns put out of action. He grabbed his ship's banner and leaped into a rowboat. Under British fire, he and four companions rowed to another ship. In command of the second ship, Perry destroyed two of the enemy's ships and soon forced the British to surrender. After the battle, Perry sent a message to General Harrison: "We have met the enemy and they are ours."

"Don't give up the ship."

Banner on Perry's ship, the *Lawrence*

When General Harrison received Perry's note, he set out to attack the British. But when Harrison transported his army across Lake Erie to Detroit, he discovered that the British had retreated into Canada. Harrison pursued the British forces and defeated them at the **Battle of the Thames** in October. This victory put an end to the British threat to the Northwest—and also claimed the life of Tecumseh, who died in the battle fighting for the British.

*Reading***History**
A. Drawing Conclusions
What was the overall result of the Battle of the Thames?

The Second Phase of the War

After defeating Napoleon in April 1814, Britain turned its full attention to the United States. As you read in One American's Story, British forces burned the Capitol building and the president's mansion in August. The British then attacked Fort McHenry at Baltimore.

The commander of Fort McHenry had earlier requested a flag "so large that the British will have no difficulty in seeing it." Detained on a British ship, a Washington lawyer named **Francis Scott Key** watched the all-night battle. At dawn, Key discovered that the flag was still flying. He expressed his pride in what became the U.S. national anthem.

America's
HERITAGE

THE STAR-SPANGLED BANNER

The "Star-Spangled Banner," inspired by the flag that flew over Fort McHenry (see below), continues to move Americans. On hearing this national anthem, patriotic listeners stand, take off their hats, and put their hands over their hearts. These actions pay respect to the American flag and the song that celebrates it.

Francis Scott Key's song enjoyed widespread popularity for more than 100 years before an act of Congress made it the national anthem in 1931.

A VOICE FROM THE PAST

Oh say can you see by the dawn's early light
What so proudly we hail'd at the twilight's last gleaming,
Whose broad stripes and bright stars through the perilous fight
O'er the ramparts we watch'd were so gallantly streaming?
And the rockets' red glare, the bombs bursting in air,
Gave proof through the night that our flag was still there.
Oh, say does that star-spangled banner yet wave
O'er the land of the free and the home of the brave?

Francis Scott Key, *Star-Spangled Banner*

Meanwhile, in the north, the British sent a force from Canada across Lake Champlain. Its goal was to push south and cut off New England. The plan failed when the American fleet defeated the British in the Battle of Lake Champlain in September 1814.

In the south, the British moved against the strategic port of New Orleans. In December 1814, dozens of ships carrying 7,500 British troops approached Louisiana. To fight them, the Americans patched together an army under the command of General Andrew Jackson.

*Reading***History**
B. Reading a Map
Locate the battles of the second phase of the war on the map on page 315. Note how far apart the sites were.

*Reading*History
C. Making Inferences Why did Jackson fight the British at New Orleans after a peace treaty was signed?

The British attacked Jackson's forces on January 8, 1815. Protected by earthworks, American riflemen mowed down the advancing redcoats. It was a great victory for Jackson. American casualties totaled 71, compared to Britain's 2,000. Though the Battle of New Orleans made Jackson a hero, it was unnecessary. Slow mails from Europe had delayed news of the **Treaty of Ghent,** which ended the War of 1812. It had been signed two weeks earlier, on December 24, 1814.

The Legacy of the War

The treaty showed that the war had no clear winner. No territory changed hands, and trade disputes were left unresolved. Still, the war had important consequences. First, the heroic exploits of men such as Andrew Jackson and Oliver Perry increased American patriotism. Second, the war broke the strength of Native Americans, who had sided with the British. Finally, when war interrupted trade, the Americans were forced to make many of the goods they had previously imported. This encouraged the growth of U.S. manufactures.

The United States had also proved that it could defend itself against the mightiest military power of the era. For perhaps the first time, Americans believed that the young nation would survive and prosper. You will learn about the country's growing prosperity in Chapter 11.

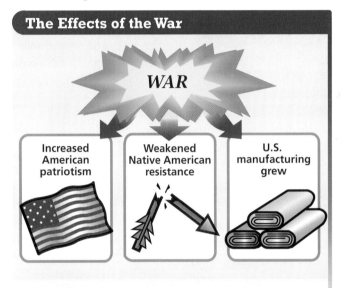

The Effects of the War

WAR

Increased American patriotism | Weakened Native American resistance | U.S. manufacturing grew

SKILLBUILDER Interpreting Charts
Which effect do you think resulted from the war's interruption of U.S. trade?

Section 4 Assessment

1. Terms & Names

Explain the significance of:
- Oliver Hazard Perry
- Battle of the Thames
- Francis Scott Key
- Treaty of Ghent

2. Taking Notes

Use a chart like the one shown to record military events of the War of 1812.

First Phase of War	Second Phase of War
1.	2.

Why was the war divided into two phases?

3. Main Ideas

a. What was the state of the U.S. military when the war began?

b. What were the results of General Harrison's victory at the Battle of the Thames?

c. Where did the British focus their attacks during the second phase of the war?

4. Critical Thinking

Recognizing Effects What was the legacy of the War of 1812?

THINK ABOUT
- Americans' feelings toward their country
- U.S. relations with Native Americans
- possible economic effects

ACTIVITY OPTIONS

LANGUAGE ARTS

ART

Research the U.S.S. *Constitution.* Write a **poem** to commemorate one of its victories or design a **model** to show its parts.

VISUAL SUMMARY

The Jefferson Era

Jefferson Takes Office

Thomas Jefferson and his party, the Democratic-Republicans, win control of the government from the Federalists.

The Louisiana Purchase and Exploration

After Jefferson purchases Louisiana from France, Lewis and Clark are sent to explore the new American territory.

Problems with Foreign Powers

Other countries' interference makes it difficult for Jefferson to stay out of foreign affairs.

The War of 1812

When Britain continues to interfere in American affairs, the two nations battle in the War of 1812.

TERMS & NAMES

Briefly explain the significance of each of the following:

1. *Marbury* v. *Madison*
2. judicial review
3. Louisiana Purchase
4. Lewis and Clark expedition
5. impressment
6. Embargo Act of 1807
7. Tecumseh
8. War Hawk
9. Oliver Hazard Perry
10. Treaty of Ghent

REVIEW QUESTIONS

Jefferson Takes Office (pages 297–301)

1. What were the main parties in the election of 1800, and how did their views differ?
2. How did Jefferson envision the future of America?

The Louisiana Purchase and Exploration (pages 302–309)

3. What was the extent of U.S. territory after the Louisiana Purchase?
4. What difficulties did Lewis and Clark face on their expedition?
5. What troubles did Zebulon Pike have on his 1806-1807 trip?

Problems with Foreign Powers (pages 310–313)

6. Why did Jefferson have difficulty staying out of foreign affairs?
7. How did Tecumseh intend to prevent the loss of Native American land?
8. What were some of the causes of the War of 1812?

The War of 1812 (pages 314–317)

9. Which battle ended the British threat to the U.S. Northwest?
10. What event preceded the second phase of the war?

CRITICAL THINKING

1. USING YOUR NOTES

Using your completed chart, answer the questions below.

The Jefferson Era
Summaries
Main Idea: Thomas Jefferson is elected president.
Details: Jefferson replaces Federalist policies with his own but has problems with the judiciary.
Main Idea:
Details:
Main Idea:
Details:
Main Idea:
Details:

a. What were the major events of the Jefferson era?
b. Based on these events, how would you describe the characteristics of the era?

2. ANALYZING LEADERSHIP

How do you think Thomas Jefferson's behavior as president might have affected the way future presidents viewed the office?

3. THEME: EXPANSION

How did the expansion of the United States affect its foreign policy?

4. RECOGNIZING PROPAGANDA

Before elections, supporters of different candidates sometimes make outrageous claims. How was the election of 1800 an example of this?

5. APPLYING CITIZENSHIP SKILLS

In what ways did Jefferson's behavior as president reflect his idea of good citizenship?

Interact *with* History

How did the dangers you predicted before you read the chapter compare to those experienced by people on expeditions west?

HISTORY SKILLS

1. INTERPRETING GRAPHS

Study the graph. Answer the questions.

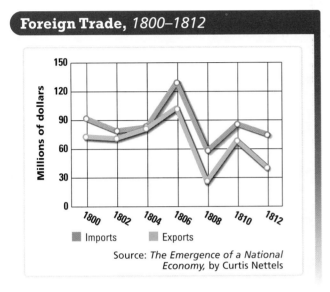

Foreign Trade, *1800–1812*

Millions of dollars

■ Imports ■ Exports

Source: *The Emergence of a National Economy,* by Curtis Nettels

Basic Graph Elements

a. What do the numbers on the left side of the chart indicate?

Interpreting the Graph

b. In what years did the value of U.S. trade decrease dramatically?
c. What was the value of exports in 1806? in 1808?

2. INTERPRETING PRIMARY SOURCES

Examine the cartoon below, which comments on the United States trade policies you read about in Section 3.

D——n it, how he nicks 'em.

Oh! this cursed Ograbme

a. What does *Ograbme* spell when written backwards?
b. What other clues tell you that this cartoon is about the embargo against Great Britain?

ALTERNATIVE ASSESSMENT

1. INTERDISCIPLINARY ACTIVITY: Geography

Making an Outline Make an outline of Section 2 of this chapter using the format from page R7. Review your outline with a partner. Organize and interpret the information from both outlines and write a report about the Louisiana Purchase and the Lewis and Clark expedition.

2. COOPERATIVE LEARNING ACTIVITY

Designing a Plan for Economic Action Form a group that will develop a plan to end British interference with U.S. shipping. Select a leader for your group. Then pick one member of your group to represent farmers, another to represent shippers, and another to speak for those who are demanding war. Discuss the interests of all these groups and then write down your policy statement and present it to the class. Use standard grammar, spelling, sentence structure, and punctuation in your policy statement. Be sure to consider:

• the superior power of the British Navy
• where the farmers will sell their products
• how the shippers will earn their money

3. TECHNOLOGY ACTIVITY

Creating a Multimedia Presentation Use the Internet, books, and other reference materials to create a multimedia presentation on one of the major battles of the War of 1812. Consider including the following:

• paintings or written descriptions of the battle
• pictures of the weapons that were used
• music from the time period
• recorded sound effects
• graphs showing battle statistics

For more about the War of 1812 . . .

INTERNET ACTIVITY
CLASSZONE.COM

4. HISTORY PORTFOLIO

Identify the dates that you consider to be the Jefferson Era. Then identify previous eras in American history and place them all in chronological sequence on a time line. Add your time line to your portfolio.

Additional Test Practice, pp. S1–S33

TEST PRACTICE
CLASSZONE.COM

Making Explorers' Field Notes

On their expedition in the early 1800s, Lewis and Clark filled their journals with field notes—detailed observations and scientific illustrations of the land, plants, and wildlife they saw. Lewis made drawings of plants and animals. Clark drew detailed maps. For many years, their journals were the main source of information about the West.

ACTIVITY Create a journal of field notes that includes illustrations of plants, animals, and terrain found in your neighborhood. Then write a comparison article between your field notes and those of Lewis and Clark.

TOOLBOX

Each group will need:

drawing paper	ruler
poster board for covers	string
pencil and pen	hole punch and hole reinforcers
scissors	

STEP BY STEP

1 **Form groups.** Each group should consist of 3 to 4 students. The members of your group will do the following tasks:

- design and create a handmade journal
- take a walk in your neighborhood and record observations as field notes
- compare the field notes you have created with those of Lewis and Clark

2 **Make your journal.** Your group will need a journal to make field notes on the nature walk. Each page of the journal should be six inches wide and roughly eight inches long, approximately the size of the one used by Lewis and Clark. Cut 10–15 sheets of that size out of the drawing paper. Create a front and back cover for the journal using the poster board.

The scientific and artistic skills of Lewis and Clark made their journals both accurate and beautiful.

3 **Put your journal together.** Punch three holes in the left side of the pages, including the covers. Place hole reinforcers around the holes to ensure that the pages won't tear. Bind the pages and the covers together with string.

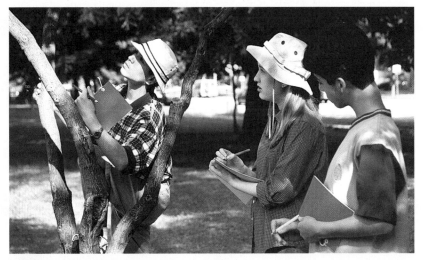

4 **Explore your neighborhood.** Take a walk in your neighborhood, in the area around your school, or in a nearby woods. You might want to divide the tasks of observing, drawing, describing, and mapping among the members of the group.

5 **Model your field notes on those of Lewis and Clark.** In their journals, Lewis and Clark included drawings of animals and plants, as well as detailed observations about them. Remember to draw the plants, insects, and animals as if you have never seen them before.

6 **Make a map of your route.** In addition to the drawings, create a map of your walk. Include any interesting landmarks as well as a detailed description of the terrain. Remember to sketch the route as if it's unexplored territory.

WRITE AND SPEAK

Write and present a paper that compares and contrasts Lewis and Clark's journal with the one your group has completed. Also, explain how your journal might help someone who has just moved to your school or neighborhood.

HELP DESK

For related information, see pages 304–309 in Chapter 10.

Researching Your Project

• You can find copies of Lewis and Clark's journals in many libraries.

• *Undaunted Courage* by Stephen Ambrose gives a fascinating account of the expedition.

For more about Lewis and Clark . . .

RESEARCH LINKS
CLASSZONE.COM

Did You Know?

• The Corps of Discovery sent Jefferson six live specimens of animals, including a prairie dog.

• At one point, the men on the expedition consumed nine pounds of buffalo meat a day.

• Swarms of mosquitoes plagued the expedition. The explorers often found it impossible to eat without inhaling some of the pesky insects.

• Clark estimated that the expedition traveled 4,162 miles. His guess was only 40 miles off the actual distance.

REFLECT & ASSESS

• What process did your group use to observe, draw, and describe your route?

• How did you decide what information to include in your journal?

• How important are the illustrations to understanding the area in which your group took its walk?

CHAPTER 11

National and Regional Growth

1800–1844

Section 1 **Early Industry and Inventions**

Section 2 **Plantations and Slavery Spread**

Section 3 **Nationalism and Sectionalism**

The Erie Canal, which opened in 1825, increased western trade and migration.

Interact *with* History

rotary printing press

steam locomotive

steamboat

telegraph

This Currier and Ives print, *Progress of the Century,* shows some inventions of the 1800s.

From 1790 to 1840, you have seen an explosion of new inventions. These include the cotton gin, the steamboat, the steel plow, and the telegraph. You have also seen neighbors leave their farms to run machines in new factories. You sense that the country is changing.

What Do You Think?

- What would it mean to be able to grow more grain and cotton?
- What would it mean to communicate and travel more quickly?
- How might it feel to do factory work instead of farm work?

How will new inventions change your country?

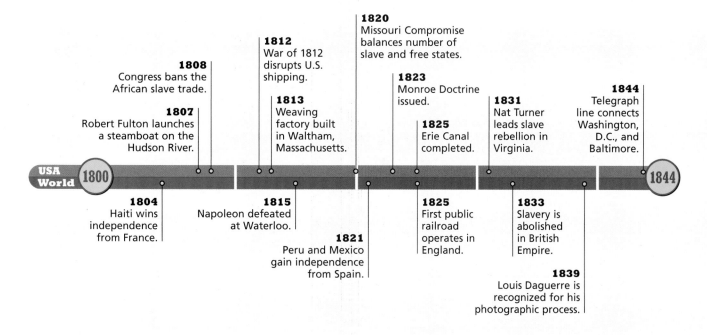

1808
Congress bans the African slave trade.

1807
Robert Fulton launches a steamboat on the Hudson River.

1812
War of 1812 disrupts U.S. shipping.

1813
Weaving factory built in Waltham, Massachusetts.

1820
Missouri Compromise balances number of slave and free states.

1823
Monroe Doctrine issued.

1825
Erie Canal completed.

1831
Nat Turner leads slave rebellion in Virginia.

1844
Telegraph line connects Washington, D.C., and Baltimore.

USA
World 1800 — 1844

1804
Haiti wins independence from France.

1815
Napoleon defeated at Waterloo.

1821
Peru and Mexico gain independence from Spain.

1825
First public railroad operates in England.

1833
Slavery is abolished in British Empire.

1839
Louis Daguerre is recognized for his photographic process.

BEFORE YOU READ

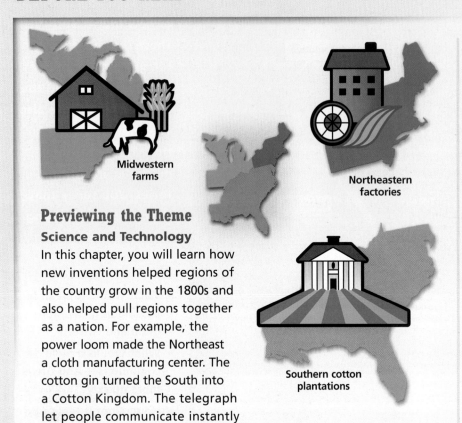

Midwestern farms

Northeastern factories

Southern cotton plantations

Previewing the Theme

Science and Technology
In this chapter, you will learn how new inventions helped regions of the country grow in the 1800s and also helped pull regions together as a nation. For example, the power loom made the Northeast a cloth manufacturing center. The cotton gin turned the South into a Cotton Kingdom. The telegraph let people communicate instantly across regions.

What Do You Know?

What connects you to someone who lives in the same region? When have you felt a bond with someone from a different region?

THINK ABOUT
• the activities of people in different regions
• the things that unite people as a nation

What Do You Want to Know?

What would you ask people from different regions—a factory worker, wheat farmer, plantation owner, or field slave— about their lives in the 1800s? Write these questions in your notebook. Read to see if they are answered in Chapter 11.

READ AND TAKE NOTES

Reading Strategy: Analyzing Causes and Recognizing Effects To help you understand the development of regional growth, sectional tensions, and national unity in Chapter 11, pay attention to causes and effects. Growth, tensions, and unity each had more than one cause. As you read, identify different causes and note them on the chart below. Often a topic sentence at the beginning of a paragraph will state a cause and effect. Be alert for such clue words as "led to," "as a result," or "changed."

S **See Skillbuilder Handbook, page R11.**

Causes

Effects

REGIONAL GROWTH

SECTIONAL TENSIONS

NATIONAL UNITY

Early Industry and Inventions

TERMS & NAMES
Samuel Slater
Industrial Revolution
factory system
Lowell mills
interchangeable parts
Robert Fulton
Samuel F. B. Morse

MAIN IDEA

New machines and factories changed the way people lived and worked in the late 1700s and early 1800s.

WHY IT MATTERS NOW

The industrial development that began more than 200 years ago continues today.

ONE AMERICAN'S STORY

In 1789, the Englishman **Samuel Slater** sailed to the United States under a false name. It was illegal for textile workers like him to leave the country. Britain wanted no other nation to copy its new machines for making thread and cloth. But Slater was going to bring the secret to America. When he got to New York, he wrote a letter to Rhode Island investor Moses Brown.

Samuel Slater's mill was located in Pawtucket, Rhode Island.

A VOICE FROM THE PAST

A few days ago I was informed that you wanted a manager of *cotton spinning* . . . in which business I flatter myself that I can give the greatest satisfaction, in making machinery, making good yarn, either for *stockings* or *twist,* as any that is made in England.

Samuel Slater, quoted in *Samuel Slater: Father of American Manufactures*

With Brown's backing, Slater built the first successful water-powered textile mill in America. You will learn in Section 1 how the development of industries changed the ways Americans lived and worked.

Free Enterprise and Factories

The War of 1812 brought great economic changes to the United States. It sowed the seeds for an Industrial Revolution like the one begun in Britain during the late 18th century. During the **Industrial Revolution,** factory machines replaced hand tools, and large-scale manufacturing replaced farming as the main form of work. For example, before the Industrial Revolution, women spun thread and wove cloth at home using spinning wheels and hand looms. The invention of such machines as the spinning jenny and the power loom made it possible for unskilled workers to produce cloth. These workers, who were often children, could produce more cloth, more quickly.

The **factory system** brought many workers and machines together under one roof. Most factories were built near a source of water to power the machines. People left their farms and crowded into cities where the factories were. They worked for wages, on a set schedule. Their way of life changed, and not always for the better.

Many Americans, such as Thomas Jefferson, did not want the United States to industrialize. But the War of 1812 led the country in that direction. Because the British naval blockade kept imported goods from reaching U.S. shores, Americans had to start manufacturing their own goods. The blockade also stopped investors from spending money on shipping and trade. Instead, they invested in new American industries. Taking advantage of the country's free enterprise system, American businessmen built their own factories, starting in New England. These businessmen and their region grew wealthier.

Vocabulary
industrialize: to develop factories

Reading **History**
A. Recognizing Effects How did the War of 1812 cause economic changes in America?

Factories Come to New England

New England was a good place to set up factories for several reasons. Factories needed water power, and New England had many fast-moving rivers. For transportation, it also had ships and access to the ocean. In addition, New England had a willing labor force. The area's first factory workers were families who were tired of scraping a living from their stony fields.

Samuel Slater built his first spinning mill in Pawtucket, Rhode Island, in 1790. He hired eight children between the ages of 7 and 12, paying them a low wage. Later, he built a larger mill and employed whole families. As Slater influenced others to start mills, his family system of employment spread through Rhode Island, Connecticut, and southern Massachusetts.

The Lowell Mills Hire Women

Lowell girls published a literary magazine.

In 1813, the American textile industry leaped forward when Francis Cabot Lowell built a factory in Waltham, in eastern Massachusetts. This factory not only spun raw cotton into yarn, but wove it into cloth on power looms. Lowell had seen power looms in English mills and had figured out how to build them. Like Samuel Slater, he had brought secrets to America.

The Waltham factory was so successful that Lowell and his partners built a new factory town, Lowell, near the Merrimack and Concord rivers. The **Lowell mills,** textile mills in the village, employed farm girls who lived in company-owned boardinghouses. "Lowell girls" worked 12½-hour days in deafening noise.

Background
Founded in 1826, the town was named for Lowell, who died in 1817.

A VOICE FROM THE PAST

At first the hours seemed very long . . . and when I went out at night the sound of the mill was in my ears . . . . You know that people learn to sleep with the thunder of Niagara [falls] in their ears, and a cotton mill is no worse, though you wonder that we do not have to hold our breath in such a noise.

"Letters from Susan," quoted in the *Lowell Offering*

New England Textile Mill

1 Moving water turns a wheel, which powers the machines through a system of gears and belts.

2 Carding and drawing machines straighten raw cotton fibers and twist them loosely.

3 Spinning machines spin the fibers into yarn, or thread.

4 Power looms weave yarn into cloth.

In 1835, Lowell had 22 mills. In 1855, it had 52 mills employing more than 13,000 workers and producing 2.25 million yards of cotton cloth a week.

Young women came to Lowell in spite of the noise. In the early years, wages were high—between two and four dollars a week. Older women supervised the girls, making them follow strict rules and attend church. Girls read books, went to lectures, and even published a literary magazine—the *Lowell Offering*. Usually they worked for only a few years, until they married. By the 1830s, however, falling profits meant that wages dropped and working conditions worsened for the Lowell girls.

Reading **History**

B. Contrasting How did the Lowell mills differ from Slater's mill?

The Lowell mills and other early factories ran on water power. Factories built after the 1830s were run by more powerful steam engines. Because steam engines used coal and wood, not fast-moving water, factories could be built away from rivers and beyond New England.

A New Way to Manufacture

New manufacturing methods changed the style of work in other industries besides the textile industry. In 1797, the U.S. government hired the inventor Eli Whitney to make 10,000 muskets for the army. He was to have the guns ready in two years. Before this time, guns were made one at a time by gunsmiths, from start to finish. Each gun differed slightly. If a part broke, a new part had to be created to match the broken one.

Whitney sought a better way to make guns. In 1801, he went to Washington with a box containing piles of musket parts. He took a part from each pile and assembled a musket in seconds. He had just demonstrated the use of **interchangeable parts,** parts that are exactly alike.

Robert Fulton invented the *Clermont,* a steamboat.

Machines that produced exactly matching parts soon became standard in industries. Interchangeable parts speeded up production, made repairs easy, and allowed the use of lower-paid, less-skilled workers. But the new system also required a new style of management, with inspectors to make sure each piece was uniform. Workers who were used to more independence disliked such close supervision.

*Reading*History

C. Recognizing Effects What were the effects of using interchangeable parts?

Moving People, Goods, and Messages

New inventions increased factory production. They also improved transportation and communication. Steamboats carried people and goods farther and faster and led to the growth of cities like New Orleans and St. Louis. **Robert Fulton** invented a steamboat that could move against the current or a strong wind. He launched the *Clermont* on the Hudson River in 1807. Its steam engine turned two side paddle wheels, which pulled the boat through the water.

The *Clermont* was dubbed "Fulton's Folly" and described as "looking precisely like a backwoods saw-mill mounted on a scow [boat] and set on fire." But it made the 300-mile trip from New York to Albany and back in a record 62 hours. Even Fulton had not expected to travel so quickly.

> *A VOICE FROM THE PAST*
> I overtook many sloops and schooners, beating to the windward, and parted with them as if they had been at anchor. The power of propelling boats by steam is now fully proved.
> **Robert Fulton,** quoted in *Robert Fulton and the "Clermont"*

In 1811, the first steamship traveled down the Mississippi and Ohio rivers. But its engine was not powerful enough to return upriver, against the current. Henry Miller Shreve, a trader on the Mississippi, designed a more powerful engine. He installed it on a double-decker boat with a paddle wheel in the back. In 1816, he sailed this boat up the Mississippi and launched a new era of trade and transportation on the river.

In 1837, **Samuel F. B. Morse** first demonstrated his telegraph. This machine sent long and short pulses of electricity along a wire. These pulses could be translated into letters of a message. With the telegraph, it took only seconds to communicate with someone in another city. In 1844, the first long-distance telegraph line carried news from Baltimore to Washington, D.C., about who had been nominated for president. Telegraph lines spanned the country by 1861, bringing people closer as a nation. Both the telegraph and the steamboat brought more national unity.

*Reading***History**
D. Recognizing Effects What made the steamboat and telegraph such important inventions?

Technology Improves Farming

Other new inventions increased farm production. In 1836, the blacksmith John Deere invented a lightweight plow with a steel cutting edge. Older cast-iron plows were designed for the light, sandy soil of New England. But rich, heavy Midwestern soil clung to the bottom of these plows and slowed farmers down. Deere's new plow made preparing ground much less work. As a result, more farmers began to move to the Midwest.

The mechanical reaper and the threshing machine were other inventions that improved agriculture. Cyrus McCormick's reaper, patented in 1834, cut ripe grain. The threshing machine separated kernels of wheat from husks.

Vocabulary
patented: protected by a patent, which gives an inventor the sole right to make, use, or sell an invention

John Deere invented the steel plow.

New technologies linked regions and contributed to national unity. With new farm equipment, Midwestern farmers grew food to feed Northeastern factory workers. In turn, Midwestern farmers became a market for Northeastern manufactured goods. The growth of Northeastern textile mills increased demand for Southern cotton. This led to the expansion of slavery in the South, as you will learn in Section 2.

Section 1 Assessment

1. Terms & Names

Explain the significance of:
- Samuel Slater
- Industrial Revolution
- factory system
- Lowell mills
- interchangeable parts
- Robert Fulton
- Samuel F. B. Morse

2. Taking Notes

On a chart like the one below, note new inventions, their dates, and their effects on the United States.

Invention	Date	Effects

Which inventions did most to link the nation? Explain.

3. Main Ideas

a. Why was New England a good place to build early factories?

b. What were working conditions like in Lowell mills?

c. How were different U.S. regions linked economically?

4. Critical Thinking

Evaluating How would you judge Samuel Slater and Francis Lowell, who brought secrets to the United States illegally?

THINK ABOUT
- what they gained
- how they affected the United States and England
- what you believe about keeping technology secret

ACTIVITY OPTIONS

SCIENCE

SPEECH

Explain how an invention from this chapter works, either in an **oral report** or a **labeled diagram**.

Run a Mill Town

You are the owner of a new water-powered textile mill that will soon open in New England. Mills have been around for more than 20 years, and you have studied their operations closely. Even so, you face many problems as you start your business. Machinery failures, labor problems, demanding investors—all will be part of your life from now on.

COOPERATIVE LEARNING On this page are two challenges you face as the owner of a textile mill. Working with a small group, decide how to deal with each challenge. Choose an option, assign a task to each group member, and do the activity. You will find useful information in the Data File. Be prepared to present your solutions to the class.

HEALTH CHALLENGE

"Anna Tripp lost three fingers today."

A neighboring mill owner has just left after sharing some bad news. Today 12-year-old Anna Tripp lost three fingers in one of his machines. Last week, one of his workers was hit and nearly killed by the flying end of a broken belt. Several girls went home because they had trouble breathing. They blamed the closed, damp machine rooms with lint-filled air. How will you reduce the number of costly health problems like these in your mill? Present your plan using one of these options:

• Write a speech to workers outlining the company's safety measures.

• Design a sign for each floor of the mill stating the company's safety rules.

MATH CHALLENGE

"So many applicants for employment"

To make a profit, you must operate at top capacity for the lowest cost. Your mill generates 2 mill power. This dictates how many spinners you can hire. You need about two-and-a-half times that many weavers. What will be your weekly payroll for spinners and weavers? How many men will you hire? Women? Look at the Data File for help. Present your hiring plan for spinners and weavers using one of these options:

• Write a report telling investors whom you plan to hire.

• Design want-ad posters aimed at the workers you are looking for.

Water Power

Potential energy: energy released when water falls from a height.

Kinetic energy: energy provided by fast-moving water.

1 mill power: power produced by 25 cubic feet of water per second dropping over a 30-foot fall; about 60 horsepower.

1 mill power: runs 3,584 spindles.

Waterwheels

Overshot

Undershot

Mid-wheel

Wage Rates

Men: $.85–$2.09 per day, depending on skill

Women: $.52–$.78 per day, depending on skill

Positions

Pickers: clean raw cotton.

Carders: feed cotton into machine that makes a thick strand of fibers.

Spinners: operate a machine that twists thick fibers into yarn and winds it on bobbins fastened to moving spindles. One worker operates 128 spindles.

Dressers: treat finished yarn with a starch paste.

Drawing-in hands: attach dressed yarn to the mechanical loom for weavers.

Weavers: weave dressed yarn into finished cloth. One worker operates two looms.

Work Hours

12 hours per day, 6 days per week, 309 days per year with holidays on Fast Day (spring), the Fourth of July, and Thanksgiving

ACTIVITY WRAP-UP

Present to the Class Meet as a group to review your responses to running a mill town. Pick the most creative solution for each challenge and present these solutions to the class.

For more about textile mills . . .

RESEARCH LINKS
CLASSZONE.COM

Plantations and Slavery Spread

MAIN IDEA	WHY IT MATTERS NOW
The invention of the cotton gin and the demand for cotton caused slavery to spread in the South.	The spread of slavery created lasting racial and sectional tensions.

ONE AMERICAN'S STORY

Catherine Beale was born into slavery in 1838. At the age of 91, in 1929, she recalled her childhood on a Virginia plantation. When asked what games she had played, Catherine replied that enslaved children never played games—they were too busy with chores. Among the tasks were picking and cleaning cotton.

A VOICE FROM THE PAST

We had to work in the field in the day and at night we had to pick out the seed before we went to bed. And we had to clean the wool, we had to pick the burrs and sticks out so it would be clean and could be carded and spun and wove.

Catherine Beale, quoted in *Slave Testimony*

Enslaved workers labor in the cotton fields.

Catherine had to clean cotton by hand because the plantation didn't have a cotton gin. This machine made it easier for enslaved workers to clean cotton. But it also made cotton growing and slave owning more profitable. In this section, you will learn how slavery expanded in the South and how it affected the lives of people living under it.

The Cotton Boom

<u>Eli Whitney</u> invented a machine for cleaning cotton in 1793, after visiting the Georgia plantation of Catherine Greene, the widow of a Revolutionary War general. Mrs. Greene was struggling to make her plantation profitable. English textile mills had created a huge demand for cotton, but the short-fibered cotton that grew in most parts of the South was hard to clean by hand. A worker could clean just one pound of this cotton in a day.

Whitney's <u>cotton gin</u> (short for "engine") made the cotton-cleaning process far more efficient. With the new machine, one worker could now clean as much as 50 pounds of cotton a day. The cotton gin helped set the South on a different course of development from the North. It made

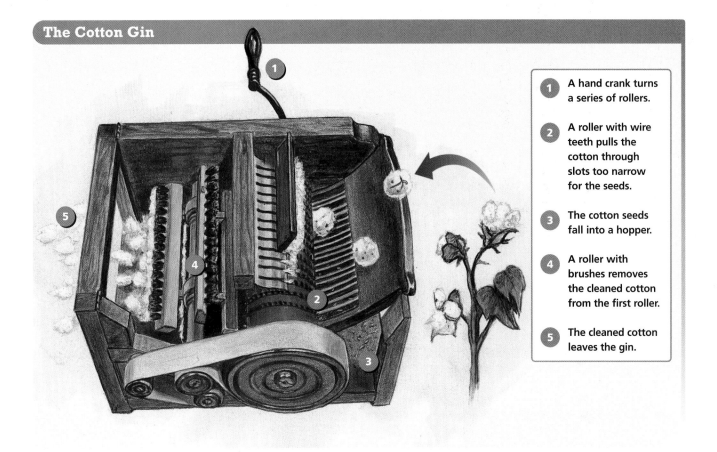

1 A hand crank turns a series of rollers.

2 A roller with wire teeth pulls the cotton through slots too narrow for the seeds.

3 The cotton seeds fall into a hopper.

4 A roller with brushes removes the cleaned cotton from the first roller.

5 The cleaned cotton leaves the gin.

short-fibered cotton a commercial product and changed Southern life in four important ways.

1. It triggered a vast move westward. Cotton farming moved beyond the Atlantic coastal states, where long-fibered, easy-to-clean cotton grew. Cotton plantations began to spread into northern Florida, Alabama, and Mississippi. Then they crossed into Louisiana and Arkansas. After 1840, they reached Texas.

2. Because cotton was valuable, planters grew more cotton rather than other goods, and cotton exports increased.

3. More Native American groups were driven off Southern land as it was taken over for cotton plantations.

4. Growing cotton required a large work force, and slavery continued to be important as a source of labor. Many slaves from the east were sold south and west to new cotton plantations.

Slavery Expands

From 1790 to 1860, cotton production rose greatly. So did the number of enslaved people in the South. Using slave labor, the South raised millions of bales of cotton each year for the textile mills of England and the American Northeast. (See the graph on page 334.) In 1820, the South earned $22 million from cotton exports. By the late 1830s, earnings from cotton exports were nearly ten times greater, close to $200 million.

As cotton earnings rose, so did the price of slaves. A male field hand sold for $300 in the 1790s. By the late 1830s, the price had jumped to

Reading **History**

A. Reading a Map Use the map on page 334 to find cotton-growing areas in 1840.

Reading **History**

B. Recognizing Effects What impact did the cotton gin have on the South?

The Cotton Kingdom, 1840

Cotton-growing areas, 1840

0   250 Miles
0   500 Kilometers

ATLANTIC OCEAN

Gulf of Mexico

VIRGINIA
Norfolk
KENTUCKY
NORTH CAROLINA
Salisbury
Nashville
TENNESSEE
ARKANSAS
SOUTH CAROLINA
ALABAMA
Charleston
Tuscaloosa
GEORGIA
MISSISSIPPI
Jackson
Savannah
LOUISIANA
Montgomery
REPUBLIC OF TEXAS
Natchez
Baton Rouge
30°N
New Orleans
Galveston
FLORIDA TERRITORY

Cotton Production, 1800–1860

Bales of cotton (in millions)

4.0
3.5
3.0
2.5
2.0
1.5
1.0
0.5
0

1800 1820 1840 1860

Source: *Historical Statistics of the United States*

GEOGRAPHY SKILLBUILDER Interpreting Maps

1. **Human-Environment Interaction** *Which five states had the largest areas devoted to growing cotton?*
2. **Human-Environment Interaction** *How far north did people grow cotton?*

$1,000. After 1808, when it became illegal to import Africans for use as slaves, the trading of slaves already in the country increased.

The expansion of slavery had a major impact on the South's economy. But its effect on the people living there was even greater.

Slavery Divides the South

Slavery divided white Southerners into those who held slaves and those who did not. Slaveholders with large plantations were the wealthiest and most powerful people in the South, but they were relatively few in number. Only about one-third of white families owned slaves in 1840. Of these slave-owning families, only about one-tenth had large plantations with 20 or more slaves.

Most white Southern farmers owned few or no slaves. Still, many supported slavery anyway. They worked their small farms themselves and hoped to buy slaves someday, which would allow them to raise more cotton and earn more money. For both small farmers and large planters, slavery had become necessary for increasing profits.

Reading **History**

C. Analyzing Points of View
Why did many white farmers without slaves still support slavery?

African Americans in the South

Slavery also divided black Southerners into those who were enslaved and those who were free. Enslaved African Americans formed about one-third of the South's population in 1840. About half of them worked on large plantations with white overseers. Decades later, a former slave described the routine in an interview.

A VOICE FROM THE PAST

The overseer was 'straddle his big horse at three o'clock in the mornin', roustin' the hands off to the field. . . . The rows was a mile long and no matter how much grass [weeds] was in them, if you [left] one sprig on your row they [beat] you nearly to death.

Wes Brady, quoted in *Remembering Slavery*

*Reading*History
D. Contrasting
How was plantation slavery different from slavery in cities?

Not all slaves faced the back-breaking conditions of plantations. In cities, enslaved persons worked as domestic servants, skilled craftsmen, factory hands, and day laborers. Sometimes they were hired out and allowed to keep part of their earnings. Frederick Douglass, an African-American speaker and publisher, once commented, "A city slave is almost a freeman, compared with a slave on the plantation." But they were still enslaved.

In 1840, about 8 percent of African Americans in the South were free. They had either been born free, been freed by an owner, or bought their own freedom. Many free African Americans in the South lived in cities such as Baltimore and Washington, D.C.

Though not enslaved, free blacks faced many problems. Some states made them leave once they gained their freedom. Most states did not permit them to vote or receive an education. Many employers refused to hire them. But their biggest threat was the possibility of being captured and sold into slavery.

Finding Strength in Religion

An African-American culture had emerged on plantations by the early 1800s. Slaves relied on that culture—with its strong religious convictions, close personal bonds, and abundance of music—to help them endure the brutal conditions of plantation life.

*Reading*History
E. Making Inferences Why would enslaved African Americans be inspired by the biblical story of Moses?

Some slaveholders tried to use religion to make slaves accept their treatment. White ministers stressed such Bible passages as "Servants, obey your masters." But enslaved people took their own messages from the Bible. They were particularly inspired by the story of Moses leading the Hebrews out of bondage in Egypt.

Enslaved people expressed their religious beliefs in **spirituals,** religious folk songs. Spirituals often contained coded messages about a planned escape or an owner's unexpected return. African-American spirituals later influenced blues, jazz, and other forms of American music.

daily*life*

SPIRITUALS

Singing spirituals offered comfort for pain, bound people together at religious meetings, and eased the boredom of daily tasks. This verse came from a spiritual sung by slaves in Missouri.

Dear Lord, dear lord,
  when slavery'll cease
Then we poor souls
  will have our peace;—
There's a better day a coming,
Will you go along with me?
There's a better day a coming,
Go sound the jubilee!

Detail of *Plantation Burial,* (1860), John Antrobus.

Families Under Slavery

Perhaps the cruelest part of slavery was the sale of family members away from one another. Although some slaveholders would not part mothers from children, many did, causing unforgettable grief. When enslaved people ran away, it was often to escape separation or to see family again.

When slave families could manage to be together, they took comfort in their family life. They married, though their marriages were not legally recognized. They tried to raise children, despite interference from owners. Most slave children lived with their mothers, who tried to protect them from punishment. Parents who lived on other plantations often stole away to visit their children, even at the cost of a whipping. Frederick Douglass recalled visits from his mother, who lived 12 miles away.

Reading **History**
F. Recognizing Effects How did slavery harm family life?

A VOICE FROM THE PAST

I do not recollect of [remember] ever seeing my mother by the light of day. She was with me in the night. She would lie down with me, and get me to sleep, but long before I waked she was gone.

Frederick Douglass, *Narrative of the Life of Frederick Douglass*

Douglass's mother resisted slavery by the simple act of visiting her child. Douglass later rebelled by escaping to the North. Other enslaved people rebelled in more violent ways.

A slave auction threatens to split a family apart.

Slave Rebellions

Armed rebellion was an extreme form of resistance to slavery. Gabriel Prosser planned an attack on Richmond, Virginia, in 1800. In 1822, Denmark Vesey planned a revolt in Charleston, South Carolina. Both plots were betrayed, and the leaders were hanged.

The most famous rebellion was led by **Nat Turner** in Virginia in 1831. On August 21, Turner and 70 followers killed 55 white men, women, and children. Later, witnesses claimed that he spoke these words.

> *A VOICE FROM THE PAST*
>
> We do not go forth for the sake of blood and carnage; . . . Remember that ours is not a war for robbery, . . . it is a struggle for freedom.
>
> **Nat Turner,** quoted in *Nat Turner,* by Terry Bisson

Most of Turner's men were captured when their ammunition ran out, and 16 were killed. When Turner was caught, he was tried and hanged.

Turner's rebellion spread fear in the South. Whites killed more than 200 African Americans in revenge. State legislatures passed harsh laws that kept free blacks and slaves from having weapons or buying liquor. Slaves could not hold religious services unless whites were present. Postmasters stopped delivering antislavery publications.

After Turner's rebellion, the grip of slavery grew even tighter in the South. Tension over slavery increased between the South and the North, as you will see in the next section.

*Reading*History
G. Recognizing Effects How did Nat Turner's rebellion affect white Southerners?

AMERICA'S HISTORY MAKERS

NAT TURNER
1800–1831

Nat Turner was born on a plantation in Virginia. As a child, Turner learned to read and write. He became an enthusiastic reader of the Bible. Slaves gathered in forest clearings to listen to his powerful sermons. Turner believed that God wanted him to free the slaves, even if by armed rebellion. He defended the justice of his cause in what came to be known as *Confessions of Nat Turner,* which he dictated to a white lawyer before his execution.

How did Turner justify his rebellion?

Section **2** *Assessment*

1. Terms & Names

Explain the significance of:
• Eli Whitney
• cotton gin
• spirituals
• Nat Turner

2. Taking Notes

In a chart like the one below, note facts about each group of Southerners.

Group	Facts
slaveholding whites	
nonslaveholding whites	
enslaved blacks	
free blacks	

Why do you think many free blacks lived in cities?

3. Main Ideas

a. How did the cotton gin lead to the spread of slavery?

b. How was life different for plantation slaves, city slaves, and free blacks in the South?

c. What were three ways that enslaved people resisted slavery?

4. Critical Thinking

Forming Opinions How do you think slave rebellions affected the institution of slavery?

THINK ABOUT
• Nat Turner's reasons for rebelling
• the reaction of white Southerners and slave owners to Turner's rebellion

---

ACTIVITY OPTIONS

LANGUAGE ARTS

SPEECH

Write a **book report** on a slave narrative, or perform an **oral interpretation** of a passage from one.

TERMS & NAMES
nationalism
Henry Clay
American System
Erie Canal
James Monroe
sectionalism
Missouri
 Compromise
Monroe Doctrine

3 Nationalism and Sectionalism

MAIN IDEA

Patriotic pride united the states, but tension between the North and South emerged.

WHY IT MATTERS NOW

The tension led to the Civil War, and regional differences can still be found in the United States today.

ONE AMERICAN'S STORY

In the early 1800s, as you have read, the North began to industrialize and the South relied more heavily on growing cotton. At the same time, a rising sense of nationalism pulled people from different regions together. **Nationalism** is a feeling of pride, loyalty, and protectiveness toward your country. The War of 1812 sent a wave of nationalist feeling through the United States.

Representative **Henry Clay**, from Kentucky, was a strong nationalist. After the war, President James Madison supported Clay's plan to strengthen the country and unify its different regions.

A VOICE FROM THE PAST

Every nation should anxiously endeavor to establish its absolute independence, and consequently be able to feed and clothe and defend itself. If it rely upon a foreign supply that may be cut off . . . it cannot be independent.

Henry Clay, quoted in *The Annals of America*

Henry Clay

In this section, you will learn how nationalism affected U.S. economic growth and foreign policy. You'll also see how Americans were beginning to be torn between the interests of their own regions and those of the country as a whole.

Nationalism Unites the Country

In 1815, President Madison presented a plan to Congress for making the United States economically self-sufficient. In other words, the country would prosper and grow by itself, without foreign products or foreign markets.

The plan—which Henry Clay promoted as the **American System**—included three main actions.

1. **Establish a protective tariff,** a tax on imported goods that protects a nation's businesses from foreign competition. Congress passed a tariff in 1816. It made European goods more expensive and encouraged Americans to buy cheaper American-made products.

<u>Reading</u>**History**

A. Recognizing Effects How would the three parts of the American System help to make the country self-sufficient?

2. **Establish a national bank** that would promote a single currency, making trade easier. (Most regional banks issued their own money.) In 1816, Congress set up the second Bank of the United States.

3. **Improve the country's transportation systems,** which were important for a strong economy. Poor roads made transportation slow and costly.

Roads and Canals Link Cities

Representative John C. Calhoun of South Carolina also called for better transportation systems. "Let us bind the Republic together with a perfect system of roads and canals," he declared in 1817. Earlier, in 1806, Congress had funded a road from Cumberland, Maryland, to Wheeling, Virginia. By 1841, the National Road, designed as the country's main east-west route, had been extended to Vandalia, Illinois.

Water transportation improved, too, with the building of canals. In fact, the period from 1825 to 1850 is often called the Age of Canals. Completed in 1825, the massive **Erie Canal** created a water route between New York City and Buffalo, New York. The canal opened the upper Ohio Valley and the Great Lakes region to settlement and trade. It also fueled nationalism by unifying these two sections of the country.

The Erie Canal allowed farm products from the Great Lakes region to flow east and people and manufactured goods from the East to flow

Major Canals, *1840*

Canal
National Road

200 Miles
400 Kilometers

CANADA

Lake Huron
Lake Michigan
Lake Ontario
Lake Champlain
Lake Erie

Champlain Canal
Erie Canal
Albany
Buffalo

Hudson R.
Allegheny R.
Susquehanna R.

ATLANTIC OCEAN

Chicago
La Salle
Toledo
Cleveland
Wheeling
Pennsylvania Canal
New York
Columbia
Pittsburgh
Chesapeake and Ohio Canal

Miami and Erie Canal
National (Cumberland) Road
Ohio and Erie Canal
Cumberland
Cincinnati
Portsmouth

Illinois R.
Wabash R.
Miami R.
Ohio R.
Kanawha R.
Potomac R.

Vandalia
Evansville

Mississippi R.

Richmond
James R.

GEOGRAPHY SKILLBUILDER Interpreting Maps
1. **Movement** *By what water route could goods from Cleveland reach New York City?*
2. **Region** *Which region benefited more from canals—the North or the South?*

The Erie Canal was 4 feet deep, 40 feet wide, and 360 miles long.

west. Trade stimulated by the canal helped New York City become the nation's largest city. Between 1820 and 1830, its population swelled from less than 125,000 to more than 200,000.

Around the 1830s, the nation began to use steam-powered trains for transportation. In 1830, only about 30 miles of track existed in the United States. But by 1850, the number had climbed to 9,000 miles. Improvements in rail travel led to a decline in the use of canals.

The Era of Good Feelings

As nationalist feelings spread, people slowly shifted their loyalty away from state governments and more toward the federal government. Democratic-Republican **James Monroe** won the presidency in 1816 with a large majority of electoral votes. The Federalist Party provided little opposition to Monroe and soon disappeared. Political differences gave way to what one Boston newspaper called the Era of Good Feelings.

During the Monroe administration, several landmark Supreme Court decisions promoted national unity by strengthening the federal government. For example, in *McCulloch* v. *Maryland* (1819), the state of Maryland wanted to tax its branch of the national bank. If this tax were allowed, the states could claim to have power over the federal government. The Court upheld federal authority by ruling that a state could not tax a national bank.

James Monroe

Background Maryland also argued that Congress had no power to create the bank, but the Court ruled that it did have such power.

A VOICE FROM THE PAST

The States have no power, by taxation or otherwise, to retard, impede, burden, or in any manner control the operations of the constitutional laws enacted by Congress.

Chief Justice John Marshall, *McCulloch* v. *Maryland* (1819)

Another Court decision that strengthened the federal government was *Gibbons* v. *Ogden* (1824). Two steamship operators fought over shipping rights on the Hudson River in New York and New Jersey. The Court ruled that interstate commerce could be regulated only by the federal government, not the state governments.

The Supreme Court under John Marshall clearly stated important powers of the federal government. A stronger federal government reflected a growing nationalist spirit.

Reading **History**
B. Finding Main Ideas How did the Supreme Court strengthen the federal government?

Settling National Boundaries

This nationalist spirit also made U.S. leaders want to define and expand the country's borders. To do this, they had to reach agreements with Britain and Spain.

Two agreements improved relations between the United States and Britain. The Rush-Bagot Agreement (1817) limited each side's naval

OREGON COUNTRY (claimed by U.S. and Britain)

PACIFIC OCEAN

40°N

BRITISH TERRITORY

CANADA

Claimed by U.S. and Britain

UNITED STATES

ATLANTIC OCEAN

Territory gained:
- Convention of 1818 with Great Britain (including new north border line)
- Adams-Onís Treaty of 1819 with Spain (including new southwest border line)

MEXICO (NEW SPAIN)

Gulf of Mexico

Florida

Spain gave up Florida to the United States after Andrew Jackson invaded the territory to capture raiding Seminoles.

0   500 Miles

0   500 Kilometers

GEOGRAPHY SKILLBUILDER Interpreting Maps

1. **Location** How far west did the Adams-Onís Treaty Line extend?
2. **Region** Who claimed the Oregon Country?

forces on the Great Lakes. In the Convention of 1818, the two countries set the 49th parallel as the U.S.-Canadian border as far west as the Rocky Mountains.

But U.S. relations with Spain were tense. The two nations disagreed on the boundaries of the Louisiana Purchase and the ownership of West Florida. Meanwhile, pirates and runaway slaves used Spanish-held East Florida as a refuge. In addition, the Seminoles of East Florida raided white settlements in Georgia to reclaim lost lands.

In 1817, President Monroe ordered General Andrew Jackson to stop the Seminole raids, but not to confront the Spanish. Jackson followed the Seminoles into Spanish territory and then claimed the Floridas for the United States.

Reading **History**

C. Analyzing Causes Why did Andrew Jackson invade East Florida?

Monroe ordered Jackson to withdraw but gave Spain a choice. It could either police the Floridas or turn them over to the United States. In the Adams-Onís Treaty of 1819, Spain handed Florida to the United States and gave up claims to the Oregon Country. The map above shows boundaries drawn and territories gained in 1818 and 1819.

Sectional Tensions Increase

At the same time nationalism was unifying the country, sectionalism was threatening to drive it apart. **Sectionalism** is loyalty to the interests of your own region or section of the country, rather than to the nation as a whole. Economic changes had created some divisions within the United States. As you have seen, white Southerners were relying more on cotton and slavery. In the Northeast, wealth was based on manufacturing and trade. In the West, settlers wanted cheap land and good transportation. The interests of these sections were often in conflict.

Sectionalism became a major issue when Missouri applied for statehood in 1817. People living in Missouri wanted to allow slavery in their state. At the time, the United States consisted of 11 slave states and 11

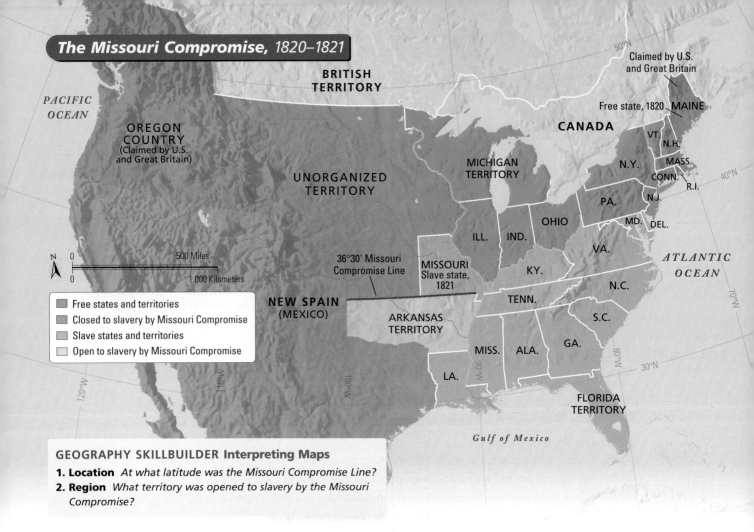

The Missouri Compromise, 1820–1821

PACIFIC
OCEAN

BRITISH
TERRITORY

Claimed by U.S.
and Great Britain

Free state, 1820 MAINE

CANADA

OREGON
COUNTRY
(Claimed by U.S.
and Great Britain)

UNORGANIZED
TERRITORY

MICHIGAN
TERRITORY

VT
N.H.
MASS.
N.Y.
CONN.
R.I.
PA.
N.J.
OHIO
MD. DEL.
ILL. IND.
VA.
36°30' Missouri
Compromise Line

MISSOURI
Slave state,
1821

KY.

ATLANTIC
OCEAN

NEW SPAIN
(MEXICO)

ARKANSAS
TERRITORY

N.C.
TENN.
S.C.
GA.
MISS. ALA.
LA.

FLORIDA
TERRITORY

Gulf of Mexico

500 Miles
1,000 Kilometers

- Free states and territories
- Closed to slavery by Missouri Compromise
- Slave states and territories
- Open to slavery by Missouri Compromise

GEOGRAPHY SKILLBUILDER Interpreting Maps

1. **Location** *At what latitude was the Missouri Compromise Line?*
2. **Region** *What territory was opened to slavery by the Missouri Compromise?*

free states. Adding Missouri as a slave state would upset the balance of power in Congress. The question of Missouri soon divided the nation.

The Missouri Compromise

For months, the nation argued over admitting Missouri as a slave state or a free state. Debate raged in Congress over a proposal made by James Tallmadge of New York to ban slavery in Missouri. Angry Southerners claimed that the Constitution did not give Congress the power to ban slavery. They worried that free states could form a majority in Congress and ban slavery altogether. Representative Thomas Cobb of Georgia expressed the Southerners' point of view when he responded to Tallmadge.

Reading **History**

D. Analyzing Points of View
Why was it so important to Southerners to admit Missouri as a slave state?

A VOICE FROM THE PAST

If you persist, the Union will be dissolved. You have kindled a fire which all the waters of the ocean cannot put out, which seas of blood can only extinguish.

Thomas Cobb, quoted in *Henry Clay: Statesman for the Union*

Meanwhile, Maine, which had been part of Massachusetts, also wanted statehood. Henry Clay, the Speaker of the House, saw a chance for compromise. He suggested that Missouri be admitted as a slave state and Maine as a free state. Congress passed Clay's plan, known as the **Missouri Compromise,** in 1820. It kept the balance of power in the Senate between the slave states and free states. It also called for slavery to be banned from the Louisiana Territory north of the parallel 36° 30', Missouri's southern border.

Thomas Jefferson, nearing 80 years old and living quietly in Virginia, was troubled by the Missouri Compromise. Worried that sectionalism would destroy the country, Jefferson wrote: "In the gloomiest moment of the Revolutionary War I never had any apprehension equal to what I feel from this source."

"If you persist, the Union will be dissolved."
Thomas Cobb

The Monroe Doctrine

Background
Latin America refers to the Spanish- and Portugese-speaking nations of the Western Hemisphere south of the United States.

Background
The ideas in the Monroe Doctrine came from John Quincy Adams, Monroe's secretary of state. Adams delivered a speech against colonization on July 4, 1821—two years before Monroe announced his doctrine.

The nation felt threatened not only by sectionalism, but by events elsewhere in the Americas. In Latin America, several countries had successfully fought for their independence from Spain and Portugal. Some European monarchies planned to help Spain and Portugal regain their colonies, hoping to keep the urge to revolt from reaching Europe. U.S. leaders feared that if this happened, their own government would be in danger.

Russian colonies in the Pacific Northwest also concerned Americans. The Russians entered Alaska in 1784. By 1812, their trading posts reached almost to San Francisco.

In December 1823, President Monroe issued a statement that became known as the **Monroe Doctrine.** (See Interactive Primary Source, page 344.) Monroe said that the Americas were closed to further colonization. He also warned that European efforts to reestablish colonies would be considered "dangerous to our peace and safety." Finally, he promised that the United States would stay out of European affairs. The Monroe Doctrine showed that the United States saw itself as a world power and protector of Latin America.

In Chapter 12, you will learn how a new democratic spirit grew—and how Native Americans suffered—during Andrew Jackson's presidency.

Section 3 Assessment

1. Terms & Names

Explain the significance of:
- nationalism
- Henry Clay
- American System
- Erie Canal
- James Monroe
- sectionalism
- Missouri Compromise
- Monroe Doctrine

2. Taking Notes

On a diagram like the one below, name things that contributed to national unity in the early 1800s.

national unity

Which of these are still important for national unity?

3. Main Ideas

a. How did the Erie Canal help the nation grow?

b. How did the Missouri Compromise resolve a conflict between the North and South?

c. What was the main message of the Monroe Doctrine, and toward whom was it directed?

4. Critical Thinking

Recognizing Effects If the Supreme Court had decided differently in *Gibbons* v. *Ogden* or *McCulloch* v. *Maryland,* what might be one result today?

THINK ABOUT
- if states could interfere with federal laws
- if states controlled interstate commerce

ACTIVITY OPTIONS

LANGUAGE ARTS
ART

In an **editorial** or a **political cartoon,** give your opinion of either the Missouri Compromise or the Monroe Doctrine.

The Monroe Doctrine

Setting the Stage On December 6, 1823, President James Monroe gave a State of the Union address. Part of the speech became known as the Monroe Doctrine. The "allied powers" Monroe refers to are Russia, Prussia, Austria, and France. Earlier in the year, these European monarchies had crushed a revolution in Spain and restored the Spanish king to his throne. They were threatening to help Spain regain its Latin American colonies. See **Primary Source Explorer**

A CLOSER LOOK

NO FUTURE COLONIES

Monroe declares that European countries may not start any new colonies in the Americas.

1. Why might it threaten the United States to have new European colonies near them?

A CLOSER LOOK

NEUTRALITY TOWARD EUROPE

Monroe says that the United States will not take sides in European wars.

2. Why might the United States want to remain neutral toward conflicts in Europe?

[T]he occasion has been judged proper for asserting, as a principle in which the rights and interests of the United States are involved, that the American continents, by the free and independent condition which they have assumed and maintain, are henceforth not to be considered as subjects for future colonization by any European powers. . . .

It was stated at the commencement of the last session that great effort was then making in Spain and Portugal to improve the condition of the people of those countries and that it appeared to be conducted with extraordinary moderation. It need scarcely be remarked that the result has been so far very different from what was then anticipated. . . . The citizens of the United States cherish sentiments the most friendly in favor of the liberty and happiness of their fellowmen on that side of the Atlantic. In the wars of the European powers in matters relating to themselves we have never taken any part, nor does it **comport**[1] with our policy so to do. It is only when our rights are invaded or seriously **menaced**[2] that we resent injuries or make preparation for our defense.

With the movements in this hemisphere we are of necessity more immediately connected, and by causes which must be obvious to all enlightened and impartial observers. The political system of the allied powers is essentially different in this respect from that of America. This difference proceeds from that which exists in their respective governments; and to the defense of our own, which has been achieved by the loss of so much blood and treasure, and matured by the wisdom of their most enlightened citizens, and under which we have enjoyed **unexampled felicity**,[3] this whole nation is devoted. We owe it, therefore, to **candor**[4] and to the **amicable**[5] relations existing between the

---

1. **comport:** agree with.
2. **menaced:** threatened.
3. **unexampled felicity:** the greatest happiness.
4. **candor:** honesty.
5. **amicable:** friendly.

United States and those powers to declare that we should consider any attempt on their part to extend their system to any portion of this hemisphere as dangerous to our peace and safety.

With the existing colonies or dependencies of any European power we have not interfered and shall not interfere. But with the governments who have declared their independence and maintained it, and whose independence we have, on great consideration and on just principles, acknowledged, we could not view any **interposition**[6] for the purpose of oppressing them, or controlling in any other manner their destiny, by any European power in any other light than as the manifestation of an unfriendly disposition toward the United States. In the war between those new governments and Spain we declared our neutrality at the time of their recognition, and to this we have adhered and shall continue to adhere, provided no change shall occur which, in the judgment of the competent authorities of this government, shall make a corresponding change on the part of the United States indispensable to their security.

The late events in Spain and Portugal show that Europe is still unsettled. Of this important fact no stronger proof can be adduced than that the allied powers should have thought it proper, on any principle satisfactory to themselves, to have interposed by force in the internal concerns of Spain. To what extent such interposition may be carried, on the same principle, is a question in which all independent powers whose governments differ from theirs are interested, even those most remote, and surely none more so than the United States.

—*James Monroe*

6. **interposition:**
   interference.

A CLOSER LOOK

A DIFFERENT SYSTEM

Monroe states that the United States will defend its republican form of government and would be threatened if Europeans set up monarchies in the Americas.

3. Why would U.S. citizens want their government to be a republic and not an absolute monarchy?

A CLOSER LOOK

NO INTERFERENCE

Monroe warns that if Europeans invade the newly independent republics in Latin America, this would be considered hostile to the United States as well.

4. What would the United States have to fear if these republics were overthrown?

Interactive Primary Source Assessment

1. Main Ideas

a. Why might the United States want no more European colonies in the Americas, particularly in Latin America?

b. How would staying neutral in European wars protect the United States?

c. How might the U.S. system of government be threatened if Europeans regained control of former colonies in the Americas?

2. Critical Thinking

Making Inferences For decades, the United States lacked the military power to enforce the Monroe Doctrine and depended on the British navy to keep other European powers out of Latin America. Why, then, did the United States proclaim the Monroe Doctrine?

THINK ABOUT

• what the doctrine shows about the values and wishes of the United States

• what it shows about how the country saw itself or wanted to be seen

Early Industry and Inventions

New machines allowed the Northeast to industrialize and the Midwest to increase farm production.

Plantations and Slavery Spread

The cotton gin led to the expansion of plantations and slavery in the South.

Nationalism and Sectionalism

Nationalism drew regions together. At the same time, economic differences created tension between regions.

TERMS & NAMES

Briefly explain the significance of each of the following.

1. Samuel Slater
2. Industrial Revolution
3. Robert Fulton
4. Eli Whitney
5. cotton gin
6. Nat Turner
7. nationalism
8. sectionalism
9. Missouri Compromise
10. Monroe Doctrine

REVIEW QUESTIONS

Early Industry and Inventions (pages 325–331)

1. How did the War of 1812 push the United States to build factories?
2. How did the War of 1812 and free enterprise affect the U.S. economy?
3. What was one effect of the steamboat?
4. How did interchangeable parts transform the manufacturing process?

Plantations and Slavery Spread (pages 332–337)

5. Why did slavery spread in the South?
6. What were three hardships faced by enslaved people on plantations?
7. How did religion help people endure or resist slavery?

Nationalism and Sectionalism (pages 338–345)

8. How did the Supreme Court's ruling in *McCulloch* v. *Maryland* strengthen the federal government?
9. How did the United States gain the territory of Florida?
10. What were the terms of the Missouri Compromise?

CRITICAL THINKING

1. USING YOUR NOTES

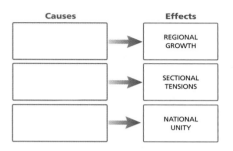

Using your completed chart, answer the questions.

a. What were three causes leading to national unity?
b. What was one cause of sectional tension?

2. THEME: SCIENCE AND TECHNOLOGY

Of all the new inventions mentioned in the chapter, which do you think was most important and why?

3. ANALYZING CAUSES

How did geographic differences between regions lead to economic differences between them?

4. APPLYING CITIZENSHIP SKILLS

Do you think the Missouri Compromise was a wise decision? Consider what might have happened without it, and also why it made Jefferson so uneasy.

5. ANALYZING LEADERSHIP

Think about the Monroe Doctrine and the boundary settlements achieved during the Monroe administration. How would you judge Monroe's foreign policy?

Interact *with* History

Did you predict the ways that new inventions would change the country? What surprised you?

HISTORY SKILLS

1. INTERPRETING MAPS: Region

Study the map. Answer the questions.

Independence in Latin America, *1830*

ATLANTIC OCEAN

Gulf of Mexico

HAITI 1804
MEXICO 1821
SANTO DOMINGO 1821
Caribbean Sea
VENEZUELA 1830
PACIFIC OCEAN
COLOMBIA 1830
ECUADOR 1830
BRAZIL 1822
PERU 1821
PARAGUAY 1811
BOLIVIA 1825
CHILE 1818
URUGUAY 1828
ARGENTINA 1816

Independent republic
Under foreign control
1830 Date of independence

N
0   2,000 Miles
0   4,000 Kilometers

Basic Map Elements

a. What region is the subject of the map?

b. What do the dates on the map mean?

Interpreting the Map

c. What countries were independent by 1823, when the Monroe Doctrine was issued?

d. When did Mexico become independent?

2. INTERPRETING PRIMARY SOURCES

The following verse is from a well-known folk song. Read the verse and answer the questions.

Low Bridge, Everybody Down

I've got a mule and her name is Sal,
Fifteen miles on the Erie Canal.
She's a good old worker and a good old pal,
Fifteen miles on the Erie Canal.
We've hauled some barges in our day,
Filled with lumber, coal, and hay,
And we know every inch of the way
From Albany to Buffalo.

a. In the song, how is the Erie Canal used?

b. What feeling does the song give you about working on the Erie Canal?

ALTERNATIVE ASSESSMENT

1. INTERDISCIPLINARY ACTIVITY: Science

Making a Presentation Do research to learn how inventions of the early 1800s have been improved upon today. For example, learn what kind of engine powers modern boats, and why it works better than a steam engine. Or find out what modern farmers use instead of the McCormick reaper. Share your findings in an oral presentation with visual aids.

2. COOPERATIVE LEARNING ACTIVITY

Planning an Exhibit As a class, plan a museum exhibit to show what slavery was like on cotton plantations. Break into small groups to research different topics—for example, what enslaved people wore, what their houses were like, what rules they lived under, and what stories they told. Bring back your research and decide how you can best share what you learned with an audience. Part of your exhibit might be a model of a plantation or dramatic readings from slave narratives.

3. PRIMARY SOURCE EXPLORER

Planning Foreign Policy The Monroe Doctrine was President Monroe's outline for U.S. foreign policy early in the 19th century. Using the Primary Source Explorer CD-ROM, library, and Internet, find out more about the Monroe Doctrine.

Imagine that you are president of the United States. Come up with four main principles of foreign policy that this country should follow in the 21st century.

- With classmates, talk about broad principles from the Monroe Doctrine. Keeping out of European conflicts would be one example. Protecting free republics would be another.

- Decide whether you agree or disagree with these principles. Think of current U.S. policies that follow or reject them.

- As president, decide how you will communicate U.S. foreign policy for the 21st century to the public. If you make a televised speech, what facts and visual aids would be most persuasive?

4. HISTORY PORTFOLIO

Review the questions you listed for **What Do You Want to Know?** on page 340. In a brief report, write what you learned about the lives of people from different regions in the early 1800s. Be sure to use standard grammar, spelling, sentence structure, and punctuation in your report.

Additional Test Practice, pp. S1–S33

TEST PRACTICE
CLASSZONE.COM

A Changing Nation

Scotts Bluff in Nebraska
became a landmark for
settlers migrating west on
the Oregon Trail.

"*Our manifest destiny is to overspread the continent.*"

—*John L. O'Sullivan*

CHAPTER 12

The Age of Jackson 1824–1840

The people came by the thousands to the White House on Inauguration Day to see their president—Andrew Jackson.

General Andrew Jackson commands his troops in battle.

The year is 1828. You will vote for president for the first time. Important economic, social, and political issues face the country. The favored candidate is Andrew Jackson, a military hero. Before you vote, you should decide what qualities make a strong leader.

What qualities do you think make a strong leader?

What Do You Think?

- What qualities are suggested by this image?
- Which earlier presidents would you consider strong leaders and which not?
- Would qualities that make a military leader also make a good president? Why or why not?

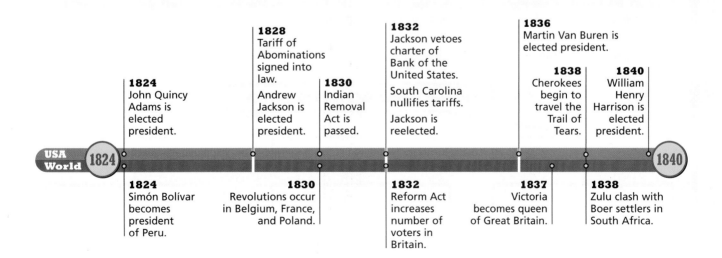

1828
Tariff of Abominations signed into law.

Andrew Jackson is elected president.

1830
Indian Removal Act is passed.

1832
Jackson vetoes charter of Bank of the United States.

South Carolina nullifies tariffs.

Jackson is reelected.

1836
Martin Van Buren is elected president.

1838
Cherokees begin to travel the Trail of Tears.

1840
William Henry Harrison is elected president.

1824
John Quincy Adams is elected president.

**USA
World**   **1824**

1840

1824
Simón Bolívar becomes president of Peru.

1830
Revolutions occur in Belgium, France, and Poland.

1832
Reform Act increases number of voters in Britain.

1837
Victoria becomes queen of Great Britain.

1838
Zulu clash with Boer settlers in South Africa.

BEFORE YOU READ

Previewing the Theme

Economics in History Americans elected Andrew Jackson president in 1828. Many believed that he would bring sweeping changes to the government. This chapter explains how President Jackson made decisions that had far-reaching effects on the American economy and on political life. In fact, because he so dominated the life of the nation, his time in office has been called the Age of Jackson.

What Do You Know?

What do you already know about the issues that faced the nation in the first half of the 19th century? How did presidents before Jackson deal with problems?

THINK ABOUT

• what you have learned about Andrew Jackson from books and movies

• how American life is affected by the actions of a president, by conflicts among different parts of the country, and by the will of the people

What Do You Want to Know?

 What questions do you have about Jackson and his presidency? Record them in your notebook before reading the chapter.

READ AND TAKE NOTES

Reading Strategy: Finding Main Ideas To make it easier for you to understand what you read, learn to find the main idea of each paragraph, topic heading, and section. Remember that the supporting details help explain the main ideas. On the chart below, write down the main ideas about the political, economic, and social changes during Jackson's presidency.

S See Skillbuilder Handbook, page R5.

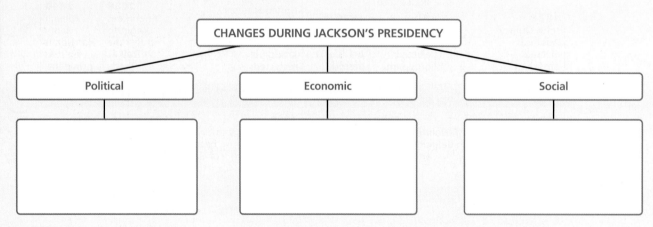

CHANGES DURING JACKSON'S PRESIDENCY

Political   Economic   Social

① **Politics of the People**

TERMS & NAMES
John Quincy
 Adams
Andrew Jackson
Jacksonian
 democracy
spoils system

MAIN IDEA	WHY IT MATTERS NOW
Andrew Jackson's election to the presidency in 1828 brought a new era of popular democracy.	Jackson's use of presidential powers laid the foundation of the modern presidency.

ONE AMERICAN'S STORY

Margaret Bayard Smith was 22 years old when she married and moved to Washington, D.C., in 1800. For the next 40 years, she and her husband, a government official, were central figures in the political and social life of Washington. They entertained presidents from Jefferson to Jackson.

Smith wrote magazine articles and numerous letters describing life in Washington. In 1824, she described how John Quincy Adams reacted to his election as president.

A VOICE FROM THE PAST

When the news of his election was communicated to Mr. Adams by the Committee . . . the sweat rolled down his face—he shook from head to foot and was so agitated that he could scarcely stand or speak.

Margaret Bayard Smith, *The First Forty Years of Washington Society*

Adams had reason to be shaken by his election. It had been hotly contested, and he knew that he would face much opposition as he tried to govern. In this section, you will learn how Adams defeated Andrew Jackson in 1824, only to lose to him four years later.

Margaret Bayard Smith wrote about life in the nation's capital in the first half of the 19th century.

The Election of 1824

In 1824, regional differences led to a fierce fight over the presidency. The Democratic-Republican Party split apart, with four men hoping to replace James Monroe as president. **John Quincy Adams,** Monroe's secretary of state, was New England's choice. The South backed William Crawford of Georgia. Westerners supported Henry Clay, the "Great Compromiser," and **Andrew Jackson,** a former military hero from Tennessee.

Jackson won the most popular votes. But he did not receive a majority of electoral votes. According to the Constitution, if no person wins a majority of electoral votes, the House of Representatives must choose the president. The selection was made from the top three vote getters.

Clay had come in fourth and was out of the running. In the House vote, he threw his support to Adams, who then won. Because Adams

AMERICA'S HISTORY MAKERS

JOHN QUINCY ADAMS
1767–1848

John Quincy Adams was born into wealth and social position. He was the son of President John Adams. Like his father, he had a sharp mind, spoke eloquently, worked tirelessly in public service, and had high principles. But he was sometimes vain, and unwilling to compromise. This made him unpopular with many people and often ineffective. After his presidency, he served with distinction in Congress.

ANDREW JACKSON
1767–1845

Andrew Jackson was the son of a poor farm couple from South Carolina. Orphaned by age 14, he was a wild and reckless youth.

Jackson moved on to become a successful lawyer and plantation owner in Tennessee. But his quick temper still got him into brawls and duels. Bullets in his body from two duels frequently caused him pain.

Jackson's humble background and reputation for toughness endeared him to voters. They considered him one of their own.

Why do you think Jackson was popular but Adams was not?

later named Clay as his secretary of state, Jackson's supporters claimed that Adams gained the presidency by making a deal with Clay. Charges of a "corrupt bargain" followed Adams throughout his term.

Adams had many plans for his presidency. He wanted to build roads and canals, aid education and science, and regulate the use of natural resources. But Congress, led by Jackson supporters, defeated his proposals.

Jacksonian Democracy

Jackson felt that the 1824 election had been stolen from him—that the will of the people had been ignored. Jackson and his supporters were outraged. He immediately set to work to gain the presidency in 1828.

For the next four years, the split in the Democratic-Republican Party between the supporters of Jackson and of Adams grew wider. Jackson claimed to represent the "common man." He said Adams represented a group of privileged, wealthy Easterners. This division eventually created two parties. The Democrats came from among the Jackson supporters, while the National Republicans grew out of the Adams camp.

The election of 1828 again matched Jackson against Adams. It was a bitter campaign—both sides made vicious personal attacks. Even Jackson's wife, Rachel, became a target. During the campaign, Jackson crusaded against control of the government by the wealthy. He promised to look out for the interests of common people. He also promoted the concept of majority rule. The idea of spreading political power to all the people and ensuring majority rule became known as **Jacksonian democracy**.

Actually, the process of spreading political power had begun before Jackson ran for office. When Jefferson was president in the early 1800s,

Reading **History**

A. Analyzing Causes What was the main reason John Quincy Adams was not effective as president?

additional people had gained the right to vote as states reduced restrictions on who could vote. Before, for example, only those who owned property or paid taxes could vote in many states. This easing of voting restrictions increased the number of voters. But voting was still limited to adult white males.

The expansion of voting rights helped Jackson achieve an overwhelming win in the 1828 presidential election. Jackson's triumph was hailed as a victory for common people. Large numbers of Western farmers as well as workers in the nation's cities supported him. Their vote put an end to the idea that the government should be controlled by an educated elite. Now, the common people would be governed by one of their own. (See chart "Changes in Ideas About Democracy," page 357.)

*Reading*History

B. Recognizing Effects What factor made Jackson's appeal to the "common man" especially important in the election of 1828?

The People's President

Jackson's humble background, and his reputation as a war hero, helped make him president. Many saw his rise above hardship as a real American success story. He was the first president not from an aristocratic Massachusetts or Virginia family, and the first from the West.

Jackson indeed had had a hard life. His father died shortly before his birth, and Jackson grew up on a frontier farm in South Carolina. At 13, he joined the militia with his older brother to fight in the Revolutionary War. In 1781, they were taken prisoner by the British. While captive, he allegedly refused when commanded to shine an officer's boots. The officer struck Jackson with a sword, leaving scars on his hand and head. Later, Jackson's mother obtained her sons' release from a military prison, where they had become ill with smallpox. Jackson's brother died, but his mother nursed Jackson back to health. A short time later, she also died. Jackson's experiences during the Revolution left him with a lifelong hatred of the British.

After the war, Jackson moved to the Tennessee frontier. In 1784, he began to study law. He built a successful legal practice and also bought and sold land. Jackson then purchased a plantation near Nashville and ran successfully for Congress. After the War of 1812 broke out, he was appointed a general in the army. At the Battle of New Orleans in 1815, Jackson soundly defeated the British even though his troops were greatly outnumbered. He became a national war hero. He earned the nickname "Old Hickory," after a soldier claimed that he was "tough as hickory."

Jackson Takes Office

Jackson's success in the presidential election of 1828 came at a high price. Shortly after he won, his wife, Rachel, died of a heart attack. Jackson believed that the campaign attacks on her reputation had killed her. She was a private woman who preferred a quiet life. In fact, she had

STRANGE *but* True

ADAMS AND JEFFERSON
John Adams and Thomas Jefferson died on the same day—the Fourth of July, 1826, the 50th anniversary of the adoption of the Declaration of Independence.

Both Adams and Jefferson were founders of the nation, signers of the Declaration, and presidents. They were also political enemies who had become friends late in life.

Adams was 90; Jefferson, 83. Adams's last words were "Jefferson still survives." He was unaware that Jefferson had died hours earlier.

Jackson usually wore this miniature oil portrait of his beloved wife, Rachel, around his neck.

said that she would "rather be a doorkeeper in the house of God than . . . live in that palace at Washington." Margaret Bayard Smith described Rachel's importance to Jackson, saying she "not only made him a happier, but a better man."

Jackson looked thin, pale, and sad at his inauguration on March 4, 1829. But the capital was full of joy and excitement. Thousands of people were there. Senator Daniel Webster wrote about the inauguration.

> ### A VOICE FROM THE PAST
> I have never seen such a crowd before. Persons have come five hundred miles to see General Jackson, and they really seem to think that the country has been rescued from some dreadful danger.
>
> **Daniel Webster,** *Correspondence*

Reading **History**

C. Drawing Conclusions Why did Jackson's supporters react with such enthusiasm at his inauguration?

At the inauguration ceremony, the crowd shouted, waved, applauded, and saluted its hero. He bowed low to the people in turn. A throng followed Jackson to the White House reception. One person described the crowd as containing "all sorts of people, from the highest and most polished, down to the most vulgar and gross in the nation."

The crowd grew rowdy. People broke china and glasses as they grabbed for the food and drinks. The pushing and shoving finally drove the new president to flee the White House. As Supreme Court Justice Joseph Story observed, "The reign of King Mob seemed triumphant."

CITIZENSHIP TODAY

Exercising the Vote

During the Age of Jackson, rules on who could vote were eased. This increased the number of voters. But voting was still limited to adult white males. Over the years, other groups gained the right to vote, including African Americans, women, and Native Americans. Today's elections are open to all citizens aged 18 and over.

Future voters can practice casting their votes in mock, or pretend, elections. The National Student/Parent Mock Election teaches students to be informed voters. Mock presidential elections attract coverage by the media. Television stations may even broadcast live from schools, interviewing student voters.

Students register to vote in a mock election.

One high school student, Charlie Tran from San Jose, California, said, "Students seem to catch the important political events surrounding them. Some students are taking their views . . . to a new level by campaigning for the candidate they support."

How Do You Set Up a Mock Election?

1. Choose issues and candidates and then set up a mock election in your classroom. (You could focus on the national, state, or local level.)

2. Create the materials of an election, such as the polling place, ballots, and posters.

3. Campaign for the candidates or the issues you support.

4. Conduct the voting.

5. Prepare mock media reports on the election's outcome. You may want to interview voters.

See Citizenship Handbook, page 267.

For more about citizenship and voting . . .

CLASSZONE.COM

Changes in Ideas About Democracy

JEFFERSONIAN DEMOCRACY	JACKSONIAN DEMOCRACY
government for the people by capable, well-educated leaders	government by the people
democracy in political life	democracy in social, economic, and political life
championed the cause of the farmer in a mainly agricultural society	championed the cause of the farmer and the laborer in an agricultural and industrial society
limited government	limited government, but with a strong president

SKILLBUILDER Interpreting Charts
1. *What do you think was the most important change in democracy?*
2. *Did Jefferson or Jackson exercise more power?*

A New Political Era Begins

Jackson's inauguration began a new political era. In his campaign, he had promised to reform government. He started by replacing many government officials with his supporters. This practice of giving government jobs to political backers became known as the **spoils system**. The name comes from a statement that "to the victor belong the spoils [possessions] of the enemy." Jackson's opponents charged that the practice was corrupt. But he defended it, noting that it broke up one group's hold on government.

As president, Jackson would face three major issues—the status of Native Americans, the rights of the states, and the role of the Bank of the United States. In the next section, you will learn how Jackson's policies affected Native Americans.

Section 1 Assessment

1. Terms & Names
Explain the significance of:
- John Quincy Adams
- Andrew Jackson
- Jacksonian democracy
- spoils system

2. Taking Notes
Use a chart to identify important biographical information about Andrew Jackson.

Life of Andrew Jackson	
Youthful life	
Road to Congress	
War hero	
Appeal to voters	

3. Main Ideas
a. How did Andrew Jackson react to the election of 1824? Why?

b. What factors helped Jackson win the presidency in 1828?

c. What was the effect of expanding voting rights?

4. Critical Thinking
Analyzing Points of View
What are reasons for and against the spoils system?

THINK ABOUT
- the effects of giving government workers lifetime jobs
- the effects of rewarding political supporters

ACTIVITY OPTIONS

GEOGRAPHY

MATH

Find out which states Jackson and Adams won in the 1828 election. Show the results on a **map** or **chart** that includes vote totals and percentages.

2 **Jackson's Policy Toward Native Americans**

TERMS & NAMES
Sequoya
Indian Removal Act
Indian Territory
Trail of Tears
Osceola

MAIN IDEA	WHY IT MATTERS NOW
During Jackson's presidency, Native Americans were forced to move west of the Mississippi River.	This forced removal forever changed the lives of Native Americans in the United States.

ONE AMERICAN'S STORY

For 12 years, a brilliant Cherokee named <u>**Sequoya**</u> (sih KWOY uh) tried to find a way to "teach the Cherokees to talk on paper like the white man." In 1821, he reached his goal. Sequoya invented a writing system for the Cherokee language without ever having learned to read or write in any other language. Helped by his young daughter, he identified all the sounds in Cherokee and created 86 characters to stand for syllables.

Using this simple system, the Cherokees soon learned to read and write. They even published a newspaper and books in their own language. A traveler in 1828 marveled at how many Cherokees had learned to read and write without schools or even paper and pens.

A VOICE FROM THE PAST

I frequently saw as I rode from place to place, Cherokee letters painted or cut on the trees by the roadside, on fences, houses, and often on pieces of bark or board, lying about the houses.

Anonymous traveler, quoted in the *Advocate*

Sequoya invented a writing system of 86 characters, shown here, for the Cherokee language.

Sequoya hoped that by gaining literacy—the ability to read and write—his people could share the power of whites and keep their independence. But even Sequoya's invention could not save the Cherokees from the upheaval to come. In this section, you will learn about President Jackson's policy toward Native Americans and its effects.

Native Americans in the Southeast

Since the 1600s, white settlers had pushed Native Americans westward as they took more and more of their land. However, there were still many Native Americans in the East in the early 1800s. Some whites hoped that the Native Americans could adapt to the white people's way of life. Others wanted the Native Americans to move. They believed this was the only way to avoid conflict over land. Also, many whites felt that Native Americans were "uncivilized" and did not want to live near them.

By the 1820s, about 100,000 Native Americans remained east of the Mississippi River. The majority were in the Southeast. The major tribes

*Reading*History

A. Reading a Map Use the map on page 360 to locate Native American lands in the Southeast.

were the Cherokee, Chickasaw, Choctaw, Creek, and Seminole. Whites called them the Five Civilized Tribes because they had adopted many aspects of white culture. They held large areas of land in Georgia, the Carolinas, Alabama, Mississippi, and Tennessee.

The Cherokee Nation

More than any other Southeastern tribe, the Cherokee had adopted white customs, including their way of dressing. Cherokees owned prosperous farms and cattle ranches. Some even had slaves. From Sequoya, they acquired a written language, and they published their own newspaper, the *Cherokee Phoenix*. Some of their children attended missionary schools. In 1827, the Cherokees drew up a constitution based on the U.S. Constitution and founded the Cherokee Nation.

A year after the Cherokees adopted their constitution, gold was discovered on their land in Georgia. Now, not only settlers but also miners wanted these lands. The discovery of gold increased demands by whites to move the Cherokees. The federal government responded with a plan to remove all Native Americans from the Southeast.

Jackson's Removal Policy

Andrew Jackson had long supported a policy of moving Native Americans west of the Mississippi. He first dealt with the Southeastern tribes after the War of 1812. The federal government ordered Jackson, then acting as Indian treaty commissioner, to make treaties with the Native Americans of the region. Through these treaties forced on the tribes, the government gained large tracts of land.

Jackson believed that the government had the right to regulate where Native Americans could live. He viewed them as conquered subjects who lived within the borders of the United States. He thought that Native Americans had one of two choices. They could adopt white culture and become citizens of the United States. Or they could move into the Western territories. They could not, however, have their own governments within the nation's borders.

After the discovery of gold, whites began to move onto Cherokee land. Georgia and other Southern states passed laws that gave them the right to take over Native American lands. When the Cherokee and other tribes protested, Jackson supported the states.

To solve the problem, Jackson asked Congress to pass a law that would require Native Americans to either move west or submit to state laws. Many Americans objected to Jackson's proposal. Massachusetts congressman Edward Everett opposed removing Native Americans against their will to a distant land. There, he said, they would face "the

Now and then

CHEROKEE PEOPLE TODAY

Today, there are more than 300,000 Cherokees. They are part of three main groups—the Cherokee Nation of Oklahoma, the United Keetoowah Band in Oklahoma, and the Eastern Band of Cherokee Indians of North Carolina.

Wilma Mankiller, shown below, was the first woman elected principal chief of the Cherokee Nation of Oklahoma. She has said that the "Cherokee people possess an extraordinary ability to face down adversity and continue moving forward. We are able to do that because our culture, though certainly diminished, has sustained us since time immemorial."

Removal of Native Americans, 1820–1840

Removal Routes:
← Cherokee   ← Creek
← Chickasaw ← Seminole
← Choctaw   ← Other tribes

Southeastern People Relocated

= 2,000 Native Americans

(in thousands)

GEOGRAPHY SKILLBUILDER Interpreting Maps
1. **Movement** How long was the Trail of Tears?
2. **Location** What states bordered Indian Territory?

perils and hardships of a wilderness." Religious groups such as the Quakers also opposed forced removal of Native Americans. After heated debate, Congress passed the **Indian Removal Act** in 1830. The act called for the government to negotiate treaties that would require Native Americans to relocate west.

Jackson immediately set out to enforce the law. He thought his policy was "just and liberal" and would allow Native Americans to keep their way of life. Instead, his policy caused much hardship and forever changed relations between whites and Native Americans.

Reading **History**
B. Drawing Conclusions What were reasons for and against the Indian Removal Act?

The Trail of Tears

As whites invaded their homelands, many Native Americans saw no other choice but to sign treaties exchanging their land for land in the West. Under the treaties, Native Americans would be moved to an area that covered what is now Oklahoma and parts of Kansas and Nebraska. This area came to be called **Indian Territory.**

Beginning in the fall of 1831, the Choctaw and other Southeast tribes were removed from their lands and relocated to Indian Territory. The Cherokees, however, first appealed to the U.S. Supreme Court to protect their land from being seized by Georgia. In 1832, the Court, led by Chief Justice John Marshall, ruled that only the federal government, not the states, could make laws governing the Cherokees. This ruling meant that the Georgia laws did not apply to the Cherokee Nation. However, both Georgia and President Jackson ignored the Supreme Court. Jackson said, "John Marshall has made his decision. . . . Now let him enforce it."

A small group of Cherokees gave up and signed a treaty to move west. But the majority of the Cherokees, led by John Ross, opposed the treaty. Jackson refused to negotiate with these Cherokees.

In 1838, federal troops commanded by General Winfield Scott rounded up about 16,000 Cherokees and forced them into camps. Soldiers took people from their homes with nothing but the clothes on their backs. Over the fall and winter of 1838–1839, these Cherokees set out on the long journey west. Forced to march in the cold, rain, and snow without adequate clothing, many grew weak and ill. One-fourth died. The dead included John Ross's wife. One soldier never forgot what he witnessed on the trail.

*Reading*History

C. Recognizing Effects What happened to the Cherokees as a result of the Indian Removal Act?

A VOICE FROM THE PAST

Murder is murder and somebody must answer, somebody must explain the streams of blood that flowed in the Indian country in . . . 1838. Somebody must explain the four-thousand silent graves that mark the trail of the Cherokees to their exile. I wish I could forget it all, but the picture of six-hundred and forty-five wagons lumbering over the frozen ground with their Cargo of suffering humanity still lingers in my memory.

John G. Burnett, quoted in *The Native Americans,* edited by Betty and Ian Ballantine

This harsh journey of the Cherokee from their homeland to Indian Territory became known as the **Trail of Tears**.

HISTORY *through*ART

In 1838, the Cherokees left their homeland by wagon, horse, donkey, and foot, forced to travel hundreds of miles along the Trail of Tears. This painting is by Robert Lindneux, a 20th-century artist.

How does this portrayal of the Trail of Tears reflect continuity and change in 19th-century American life?

Osceola led the
Seminoles in
their fight
against removal.

Native American Resistance

Not all the Cherokees moved west in 1838. That fall, soldiers had rounded up an old Cherokee farmer named Tsali and his family, including his grown sons. On the way to the stockade, they fought the soldiers. A soldier was killed before Tsali fled with his family to the Great Smoky Mountains in North Carolina. There they found other Cherokees. The U.S. Army sent a message to Tsali. If he and his sons would give themselves up, the others could remain. They surrendered, and all except the youngest son were shot. Their sacrifice allowed some Cherokees to stay in their homeland.

Other Southeast tribes also resisted relocation. In 1835, the Seminoles refused to leave Florida. This refusal led to the Second Seminole War. One elderly Seminole explained why he could not leave: "If suddenly we tear our hearts from the homes around which they are twined [wrapped around], our heart strings will snap."

One of the most important leaders in the war was **Osceola** (AHS ee OH luh). Hiding in the Everglades, Osceola and his band used surprise attacks to defeat the U.S. Army in many battles. In 1837, Osceola was tricked into capture when he came to peace talks during a truce. He later died in prison. But the Seminoles continued to fight. Some went deeper into the Everglades, where their descendants live today. Others moved west. The Second Seminole War ended in 1842.

Some tribes north of the Ohio River also resisted relocation. The Shawnee, Ottawa, Potawatomi, Sauk, and Fox were removed to Indian Territory. But in 1832, a Sauk chief named Black Hawk led a band of Sauk and Fox back to their lands in Illinois. In the Black Hawk War, the Illinois militia and the U.S. Army crushed the uprising.

In the next section, you will learn about other issues Jackson faced, especially increasing tensions between various sections of the country.

Background
The Seminoles fought three wars against the U.S. government between 1817 and 1858, when their resistance ended.

Section 2 Assessment

1. Terms & Names

Explain the significance of:
- Sequoya
- Indian Removal Act
- Indian Territory
- Trail of Tears
- Osceola

2. Taking Notes

Use a chart to list the reasons for Jackson's Native American removal policy.

Reasons Native Americans Were Forced West		
Economic	Political	Social

What do you think was the main reason?

3. Main Ideas

a. How did President Jackson justify the Indian Removal Act?

b. In what ways did Native Americans resist the Indian Removal Act?

c. What were the consequences of the Indian Removal Act?

4. Critical Thinking

Recognizing Effects
What were some economic effects of the Indian Removal Act on Native Americans? On whites?

THINK ABOUT
- what the Native Americans lost
- what the white settlers gained

ACTIVITY OPTIONS

GEOGRAPHY
MATH

Use the map on page 376 to estimate the distance traveled by each of the five Southeastern tribes. Show your calculation on a **map** or **chart**.

③ Conflicts Over States' Rights

TERMS & NAMES
John C. Calhoun
Tariff of Abominations
doctrine of nullification
Webster-Hayne debate
Daniel Webster
secession

MAIN IDEA	WHY IT MATTERS NOW
Jackson struggled to keep Southern states from breaking away from the Union over the issue of tariffs.	Disputes about states' rights and federal power remain important in national politics.

ONE AMERICAN'S STORY

Early in his political career, **John C. Calhoun** was hailed as "one of the master-spirits who stamp their name upon the age in which they live." This was praise indeed for someone from the backwoods of South Carolina who had little formal education before age 18. Elected to the U.S. Congress at 28, Calhoun soon was one of its leaders. He supported the need for a strong central government and became something of a hero to the nation's young people. He spoke out against sectionalism.

A VOICE FROM THE PAST

What is necessary for the common good may apparently be opposed to the interest of particular sections. It must be submitted to [accepted] as the condition of our [nation's] greatness.

John C. Calhoun, quoted in *John C. Calhoun: American Portrait* by Margaret L. Coit

But Calhoun's concern for the economic and political well-being of his home state of South Carolina, and the South in general, later caused him to change his beliefs. He became the foremost champion of states' rights, rigid in his views and increasingly bitter.

In this section, you will learn how two strong-willed men—Calhoun and Jackson—came in conflict over the issue of states' rights.

The bitter debate over states' rights took a physical toll on John C. Calhoun. He is shown here in about 1825 and in 1849.

Rising Sectional Differences

Andrew Jackson had taken office in 1829. At the time, the country was being pulled apart by conflicts among its three main sections—the Northeast, the South, and the West. Legislators from these regions were arguing over three major economic issues: the sale of public lands, internal improvements, and tariffs.

The federal government had acquired vast areas of land through conquests, treaties, and purchases. It raised money partly by selling these public lands. However, Northeasterners did not want public lands in the West to be sold at low prices. The cheap land would attract workers who were needed in the factories of the Northeast. But Westerners wanted low land prices to encourage settlement. The more people who moved West, the more political power the section would have.

The issue of internal improvements also pulled the sections apart. Business leaders in the Northeast and West backed government spending on internal improvements, such as new roads and canals. Good transportation would help bring food and raw materials to the Northeast and take manufactured goods to Western markets. Southerners opposed more federal spending on internal improvements because the government financed these projects through tariffs, which were taxes on imported goods. The South did not want any increase in tariffs.

Since 1816, tariffs had risen steadily. They had become the government's main source of income. Northerners supported high tariffs because they made imported goods more expensive than American-made goods. The Northeast had most of the nation's manufacturing. Tariffs helped

Background
During the Jackson era, the West included states that are now considered part of the Midwest.

Economics *in* History

How Tariffs Work

Tariffs are taxes added to the cost of goods imported from another country. There are two kinds of tariffs—revenue tariffs and protective tariffs. **Revenue tariffs** are used to raise money, like the sales taxes that states add to purchases today. These tariffs tend to be fairly low. **Protective tariffs** usually are much higher. They have another goal: to persuade consumers to buy goods made in their own country instead of purchasing foreign-made products. Congress passed a protective tariff in 1828 to help American companies.

The illustration shows how a protective tariff works. A British-made teapot sells for $3.50, and a similar teapot made in the United States sells for $4.00. Most shoppers will buy the British teapot and save 50 cents. But when the government adds a 40 percent tariff to British goods, the price of the British teapot soars to $4.90. The result: consumers buy the now-cheaper American teapots.

CONNECT TO HISTORY
1. **Recognizing Effects** Do consumers benefit from high tariffs? Why or why not?
    See Skillbuilder Handbook, page R11.

CONNECT TO TODAY
2. **Making Inferences** Today, many leaders around the world promote the idea of "free trade." What do you think "free trade" means?

For more about tariffs . . .

RESEARCH LINKS
CLASSZONE.COM

$2.50 to produce in Britain $1.00 profit

+ tariff $4.90

$3.00 to produce in the U.S. $1.00 profit

$4.00

American manufacturers sell their products at a lower price than imported goods.

The South opposed rising tariffs because its economy depended on foreign trade. Southern planters sold most of their cotton to foreign buyers. They were not paid in money but were given credit. They then used the credit to buy foreign manufactured goods. Because of higher tariffs, these foreign goods cost more. Eventually, the tariff issue would lead to conflict between North and South.

Reading **History**
A. Analyzing Causes Why did the three sections of the country differ on the sale of public lands, internal improvements, and tariffs?

Tariff of Abominations

In 1828, in the last months of John Quincy Adams's presidency, Congress passed a bill that significantly raised the tariffs on raw materials and manufactured goods. Southerners were outraged. They had to sell their cotton at low prices to be competitive. Yet tariffs forced them to pay high prices for manufactured goods. Southerners felt that the economic interests of the Northeast were determining national policy. They hated the tariff and called it the **Tariff of Abominations** (an abomination is a hateful thing).

Differences over the tariff helped Jackson win the election of 1828. Southerners blamed Adams for the tariff, since it was passed during his administration. So they voted against him.

Crisis over Nullification

The Tariff of Abominations hit South Carolinians especially hard because their economy was in a slump. Some leaders in the state even spoke of leaving the Union over the issue of tariffs. John C. Calhoun, then Jackson's vice-president, understood the problems of South Carolina's farmers because he was one himself. But he wanted to find a way to keep South Carolina from leaving the Union. The answer he arrived at was the **doctrine of nullification**. A state, Calhoun said, had the right to nullify, or reject, a federal law that it considers unconstitutional.

Reading **History**
B. Summarizing How did the issue of tariffs threaten to tear the Union apart?

Calhoun was not the first person to propose the doctrine of nullification. Thomas Jefferson developed it in 1799 in the Kentucky Resolutions. He argued that the Union was a league of sovereign, or self-governing, states that had the right to limit the federal government. Calhoun extended the doctrine. He said that any state could nullify, or make void, a federal law within its borders. He believed that Congress had no right to impose a tariff that favored one section of the country. Therefore, South Carolina had the right to nullify the tariff. Calhoun's doctrine was an extreme form of states' rights—the theory that states have the right to judge whether a law of Congress is unconstitutional.

In the summer of 1828, Calhoun wrote a document called the "South Carolina Exposition and Protest." It stated his theory. Calhoun allowed the document to be published, but he did not sign his name. He knew his ideas would cause controversy.

A South Carolina woman sews a palmetto emblem (inset) to her hat to show her support for nullification. The palmetto is a South Carolina symbol.

Vocabulary
controversy: a public dispute

"Liberty and Union, now and forever, one and inseparable!"

Daniel Webster of Massachusetts

"The measures of the federal government . . . will soon involve the whole South in . . . ruin."

Robert Y. Hayne of South Carolina

Daniel Webster (standing) and Robert Y. Hayne (seated, with hands extended) debated nullification in the U.S. Senate in 1830.

The States' Rights Debate

Calhoun was right. His ideas added fuel to the debate over the nature of the federal union. This debate had been going on since independence from Britain. More and more people took sides. Some supported a strong federal government. Others defended the rights of the states. This question would be a major political issue from this time until the Civil War was fought to resolve it some 30 years later.

One of the great debates in American history took place in the U.S. Senate over the doctrine of nullification—the **Webster-Hayne debate** of 1830. On one side was **Daniel Webster,** a senator from Massachusetts and the most powerful speaker of his time. On the other was Robert Y. Hayne, a senator from South Carolina. Hayne defended nullification. He argued that it gave the states a lawful way to protest and to maintain their freedom. He also said that the real enemies of the Union were those "who are constantly stealing power from the States, and adding strength to the Federal Government."

Webster argued that it was the people and not the states that made the Union. In words that were printed and spread across the country, Webster declared that freedom and the Union go together.

A VOICE FROM THE PAST

When my eyes shall be turned to behold for the last time the sun in heaven, may I not see him shining on the broken and dishonored fragments of a once glorious Union. . . . Liberty and Union, now and forever, one and inseparable!

Daniel Webster, a speech in the U.S. Senate, January 26, 1830

Jackson had not yet stated his position on the issue of states' rights, even though Calhoun was his vice-president. He got his chance in April at a dinner in honor of the birthday of Thomas Jefferson. Calhoun and other supporters of nullification planned to use the event to win support for their position. Jackson learned of their plans and went to the dinner prepared.

After dinner, Jackson was invited to make a toast. He stood up, looked directly at Calhoun, and stated bluntly, "Our Federal Union—it must be preserved." As Calhoun raised his glass, his hand trembled. Called on to make the next toast, Calhoun stood slowly and said, "The Union—next to our liberty, the most dear; may we all remember that it can only be preserved by respecting the rights of the states and distributing equally the benefits and burdens of the Union." From that time, the two men were political enemies.

*Reading*History

C. Analyzing Points of View What do you think Calhoun meant by "the benefits and burdens of the Union" should be equally distributed?

South Carolina Threatens to Secede

Even though Jackson made it clear that he opposed the doctrine of nullification, he did not want to drive the South out of the Union. He asked Congress to reduce the tariff, and Congress did so in 1832. But Southerners thought the reduced rates were still too high. South Carolina nullified the tariff acts of 1828 and 1832 and voted to build its own army. South Carolina's leaders threatened **secession,** or withdrawal from the Union, if the federal government tried to collect tariffs.

Jackson was enraged. He told a South Carolina congressman that if the state's leaders defied federal laws, he would "hang the first man of them I can get my hands on." Jackson ran for reelection in 1832, this time without Calhoun as his running mate. After he won, he made it clear that he would use force to see that federal laws were obeyed and the Union preserved.

In the Senate, Henry Clay came forward with a compromise tariff in 1833. He hoped that it would settle the issue and prevent bloodshed. Congress quickly passed the bill, and the crisis ended. South Carolina stayed in the Union. In the next section, you will read about another issue of Jackson's presidency—his war on the national bank.

Section **3** Assessment

1. Terms & Names

Explain the significance of:
- John C. Calhoun
- Tariff of Abominations
- doctrine of nullification
- Webster-Hayne debate
- Daniel Webster
- secession

2. Taking Notes

Use a chart to indicate how each section stood on these issues.

	North-east	West	South
Sale of public lands			
Internal improve-ments			
High tariffs			

3. Main Ideas

a. Why did the South oppose high tariffs?

b. What were Calhoun's reasons for proposing the doctrine of nullification?

c. Why did South Carolina threaten secession, and how was the crisis resolved?

4. Critical Thinking

Recognizing Effects In what ways would the doctrine of nullification have made it difficult for the federal government to operate?

THINK ABOUT
- its effect on the enforcement of laws
- its effect on the power of the federal government

ACTIVITY OPTIONS

SPEECH

TECHNOLOGY

Research Daniel Webster's speech; a part of it appears on page 382. Deliver a **speech** for or against nullification to the class, or record it on an **audiocassette.**

Prosperity and Panic

TERMS & NAMES
inflation
Martin Van Buren
Panic of 1837
depression
Whig Party
William Henry Harrison
John Tyler

MAIN IDEA	WHY IT MATTERS NOW
Jackson's policies caused the economy to collapse after he left office and affected the next election.	The condition of the economy continues to affect the outcomes of presidential elections.

ONE AMERICAN'S STORY

Nicholas Biddle was the kind of person that Andrew Jackson neither liked nor trusted. Biddle was wealthy, well educated, and came from a socially prominent Philadelphia family. He was also the influential president of the powerful Second Bank of the United States—the bank that Jackson believed to be a monster of corruption. Jackson declared war on Biddle and the bank during his 1832 reelection campaign. But Biddle felt sure of his political power.

Nicholas Biddle was the president of the powerful Second Bank of the United States, located in Philadelphia.

A VOICE FROM THE PAST

I have always deplored making the Bank a [political] question, but since the President will have it so, he must pay the penalty of his own rashness. . . . [m]y hope is that it will contribute to relieve the country of the domination of these miserable [Jackson] people.

Nicholas Biddle, from a letter to Henry Clay dated August 1, 1832

For his part, Jackson vowed to "kill" the bank. In this section, you will read about his war on the bank and its effect on the economy.

Mr. Biddle's Bank

The Second Bank of the United States was the most powerful bank in the country. It held government funds and issued money. As its president, Nicholas Biddle set policies that controlled the nation's money supply.

Although the bank was run efficiently, Jackson had many reasons to dislike it. For one thing, he had come to distrust banks after losing money in financial deals early in his career. He also thought the bank had too much power. The bank made loans to members of Congress, and Biddle openly boasted that he could influence Congress. In addition, Jackson felt the bank's lending policies favored wealthy clients and hurt the average person.

To operate, the bank had to have a charter, or a written grant, from the federal government. In 1832, Biddle asked Congress to renew the bank's charter, even though it would not expire until 1836. Because 1832 was an election year, he thought Jackson would agree to renewal rather than risk angering its supporters. But Jackson took the risk.

Jackson's War on the Bank

When Congress voted to renew the bank's charter, Jackson vetoed the renewal. In a strongly worded message to Congress, Jackson claimed the bank was unconstitutional. He said the bank was a monopoly that favored the few at the expense of the many. The Supreme Court earlier had ruled that the bank was constitutional. But Jackson claimed elected officials had to judge the constitutionality of a law for themselves. They did not need to rely on the Supreme Court. His veto message also contained this attack on the bank.

A VOICE FROM THE PAST

It is to be regretted that the rich and powerful too often bend the acts of government to their selfish purposes. . . . Distinctions in society will always exist under every just government. . . . [B]ut when the laws undertake to . . . make the rich richer and the potent more powerful, the humble members of society . . . have a right to complain of the injustice of their Government.

Andrew Jackson, veto message, July 10, 1832

Jackson's war on the bank became the main issue in the presidential campaign of 1832. The National Republican Party and its candidate, Henry Clay, called Jackson a tyrant. They said he wanted too much power as president. The Democrats portrayed Jackson as a defender of the people. When he won reelection, Jackson took it as a sign that the public approved his war on the bank.

In his second term, Jackson set out to destroy the bank before its charter ended in 1836. He had government funds deposited in state banks, which opponents called Jackson's "pet banks." Biddle fought back by making it harder for people to borrow money. He hoped the resulting economic troubles would force Jackson to return government deposits to the bank. Instead, the people rallied to Jackson's position. Eventually, the bank went out of business. Jackson had won the war, but the economy would be a victim.

Jackson Fights the Second Bank

In this political cartoon, Jackson fights the many-headed monster—the Second Bank of the United States and its branches—with a cane labeled "VETO."

A President Jackson

B Cane labeled "VETO"

C Nicholas Biddle

D Vice-President Van Buren

Prosperity Becomes Panic

Most of the nation prospered during Jackson's last years in office. Because it was easier to borrow money, people took out loans to buy public lands, and the economy boomed. But the "pet banks" issued too much paper money. The rise in the money supply made each dollar worth less. As a result, prices rose. **Inflation,** which is an increase in prices and decrease in the value of money, was the outcome. To fight inflation, Jackson issued an order that required people to pay in gold or silver for public lands.

Jackson left office proud of the nation's prosperity. But it was a puffed-up prosperity. Like a balloon, it had little substance. Because of Jackson's popularity, his vice-president, **Martin Van Buren,** was elected president in 1836. Within a few months after Van Buren took office, a panic—a widespread fear about the state of the economy—spread throughout the country. It became known as the **Panic of 1837.**

People took their paper money to the banks and demanded gold or silver in exchange. The banks quickly ran out of gold and silver. When the government tried to get its money from the state banks, the banks could not pay. The banks defaulted, or went out of business. A **depression,** or severe economic slump, followed.

The depression caused much hardship. Because people had little money, manufacturers no longer had customers for their goods. Almost 90 percent of factories in the East closed in 1837. Jobless workers had no way of buying food or paying rent. People went hungry. They lived in shelters or on the streets, where many froze in the winter. Every section of the country suffered, but the depression hit hardest in the cities. Farmers were hurt less because they could at least grow their own food. The depression affected politics, too.

The Rise of the Whig Party

In the depths of the depression, Senators Henry Clay and Daniel Webster argued that the government needed to help the economy. Van Buren disagreed. He believed that the economy would improve if left alone. He argued that "the less government interferes with private pursuits the better for the general prosperity." Many Americans blamed Van Buren for the Panic, though he had taken office only weeks before it started. The continuing depression made it almost impossible for him to win reelection in 1840.

Reading **History**

B. Recognizing Effects What were the short-term and long-term effects of Jackson's war on the bank?

Van Buren faced a new political party in that election. During Jackson's war on the national bank, Clay, Webster, and other Jackson opponents had formed the **Whig Party.** It was named after a British party that opposed royal power. The Whigs opposed the concentration of power in the chief executive—whom they mockingly called "King Andrew" Jackson. In 1840, the Whigs chose **William Henry Harrison** of Ohio to run for president and **John Tyler** of Virginia to run for vice-president.

*Reading***History**

C. Making Inferences Why did the Whigs want to nominate a candidate like Harrison, who did not have strong political views?

The Whigs nominated Harrison largely because of his military record and his lack of strong political views. Harrison had led the army that defeated the Shawnees in 1811 at the Battle of Tippecanoe. He also had been a hero during the War of 1812. The Whigs made the most of Harrison's military record and his nickname, "Old Tippecanoe." The phrase "Tippecanoe and Tyler too" became the Whig election slogan.

The Election of 1840

During the 1840 election campaign, the Whigs emphasized personalities more than issues. They tried to appeal to the common people, as Andrew Jackson had done. Harrison was the son of a Virginia plantation owner. However, because he had settled on a farm in Ohio, the Whigs said Harrison was a true Westerner. They used symbols of the frontier, such as a log cabin, to represent Harrison. The Whigs contrasted Harrison with the wealthy Van Buren. Harrison won in a close election.

At his inauguration, the 68-year-old president spoke for nearly two hours in cold March weather with no hat or coat. Later, he was caught in the rain. He came down with a cold that developed into pneumonia. On April 4, 1841, one month after being inaugurated, Harrison died—the first president to die in office. Vice-President Tyler became president.

The election of 1840 showed the importance of the West in American politics. In the next chapter, you'll learn more about the lure of the West and the westward expansion of the United States.

Section Assessment

1. Terms & Names

Explain the significance of:
- inflation
- Martin Van Buren
- Panic of 1837
- depression
- Whig Party
- William Henry Harrison
- John Tyler

2. Taking Notes

Use a diagram to list the events that led to the closing of the Second Bank of the United States.

What was the most significant event?

3. Main Ideas

a. Why did Jackson declare war on the Second Bank of the United States?

b. How did Jackson kill the bank?

c. What role did Jackson's popularity play in the elections of 1836 and 1840?

4. Critical Thinking

Comparing What strategy did the Whig Party use in the 1840 election?

THINK ABOUT
- how Harrison was portrayed
- what group of voters it was trying to attract

ACTIVITY OPTIONS

LANGUAGE ARTS

ART

Imagine yourself as a presidential candidate in 1840. Focusing on the economy as an issue, write a campaign **slogan** or create a **banner** to rally support.

TERMS & NAMES

Briefly explain the significance of each of the following.

1. John Quincy Adams
2. Jacksonian democracy
3. spoils system
4. Sequoya
5. Indian Removal Act
6. Trail of Tears
7. secession
8. inflation
9. depression
10. Whig Party

REVIEW QUESTIONS

Politics of the People (pages 353–357)

1. How was Jackson different from earlier presidents?
2. How did Jackson appeal to voters in his election campaign of 1828?

Jackson's Policy Toward Native Americans (pages 358–362)

3. What were Georgia's policies toward Native Americans?
4. What was Jackson's position on Native Americans in the United States?
5. How did the Indian Removal Act affect Native Americans?

Conflicts over States' Rights (pages 363–367)

6. How did the issue of tariffs divide the country?
7. Why did nullification threaten the nation?
8. How was the nullification crisis resolved?

Prosperity and Panic (pages 368–371)

9. Why did Jackson oppose the Second Bank of the United States?
10. What were the effects of Jackson's war on the bank?

CRITICAL THINKING

1. USING YOUR NOTES

Use your completed chart to answer the questions.

a. What do you think was the most positive change of the Jackson era? Explain.
b. What was the most negative change? Explain.
c. Based on these changes, how would you describe the characteristics of the Jackson era?

2. ANALYZING LEADERSHIP

What was the basis of Andrew Jackson's power as president?

3. APPLYING CITIZENSHIP SKILLS

How did the majority of voters in the presidential elections of 1828 and 1840 exercise their vote in a similar way?

4. THEME: ECONOMICS IN HISTORY

Based on its economic effects, was Jackson's decision to end the national bank a good one? Explain.

5. MAKING INFERENCES

In what ways did Andrew Jackson's policy toward Native Americans reflect bias?

Interact *with* History

Now that you have read the chapter, do you think the qualities that made Jackson a strong military leader made him a good president? Explain your answer.

VISUAL SUMMARY

Major Issues of Jackson's Presidency

POLICY TOWARD NATIVE AMERICANS	CONFLICT OVER STATES' RIGHTS	WAR ON BANK OF THE UNITED STATES
White settlers wanted Native American lands.	Sectional differences developed.	Second Bank of the United States had economic and political power.
Jackson proposed Indian Removal Act of 1830.	Jackson supported strong central government.	Jackson opposed bank and vetoed renewal of its charter.
Thousands of Native Americans removed to Indian Territory.	South Carolina threatened to secede over tariff issue, but compromise reached.	Bank driven out of business, but Jackson's policies eventually led to inflation and depression.

HISTORY SKILLS

1. INTERPRETING GRAPHS

Study the graph. Answer the questions.

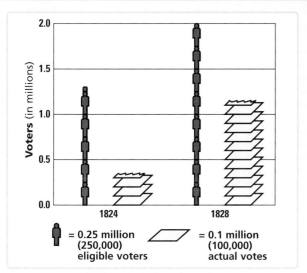

Voter Participation, *1824 & 1828 Elections*

= 0.25 million
(250,000)
eligible voters

= 0.1 million
(100,000)
actual votes

Source: *Historical Statistics of the United States*

Basic Graph Elements

a. What is the subject of the graph?

b. What do the symbols represent?

Interpreting the Graph

c. How many more eligible voters were there in 1828 than in 1824?

d. What percentage of eligible voters cast their ballots in 1824? in 1828?

2. INTERPRETING PRIMARY SOURCES

This is a political cartoon from the 1832 election campaign. It is entitled "King Andrew the First."

a. Is the comparison of Jackson to a king meant as praise or criticism? Explain.

b. What does it mean that he is standing on torn papers entitled "U.S. Constitution" and "U.S. Bank"?

BORN TO COMMAND.

OF VETO MEMORY.

HAD I BEEN CONSULTED.

KING ANDREW THE FIRST.

ALTERNATIVE ASSESSMENT

1. INTERDISCIPLINARY ACTIVITY: Speech

Presenting a Debate Working with a partner, take sides on the doctrine of nullification and prepare a debate for the class.

2. COOPERATIVE LEARNING ACTIVITY

Preparing a Problem-Solving Proposal Plan and write a proposal outlining a solution to the problems between white settlers and Native Americans in the Southeast in the early 1800s. Working in a small group, first brainstorm ideas and make a list. Then identify the positives and negatives of each idea. Agree on an outline for a final plan. Then write, revise, and make a final copy of your proposal. Present your proposal to the class and defend it.

3. TECHNOLOGY ACTIVITY

Designing a Political Campaign Web Site Andrew Jackson was one of the more colorful figures in American history. His election as president brought significant changes to the nation. Plan a Web site for candidate Jackson for the 1828 presidential campaign. Use the Internet or search the library for information on Jackson's life before the presidency and on the 1828 election.

For more about Andrew Jackson . . .

INTERNET ACTIVITY
CLASSZONE.COM

Design the Web site using the suggestions below.

- Include biographical facts.
- Select images that tell Jackson's story.
- Present his views on the major issues of the day using quotations from speeches and other documents.
- Locate appropriate links for visitors to your Web site.

4. HISTORY PORTFOLIO

Option 1 Review your section and chapter assessment activities. Select one that you think was your best work. Then use comments made by your teacher or classmates to improve your work and add it to your portfolio.

Option 2 Review the questions that you wrote for What Do You Want to Know? on page 352. Then write a short report in which you explain the answers to your questions. Be sure to use standard grammar, spelling, sentence structure, and punctuation in your report. Add your work to your history portfolio.

Additional Test Practice,
pp. S1–S33

TEST PRACTICE
CLASSZONE.COM

CHAPTER 13

Manifest Destiny 1810–1853

Weary from their trip west, this pioneer family stops for a rest.

Interact *with* History

The inside of this wagon is only 4 feet by 10 feet—smaller than a modern minivan.

canvas roof with patch

butter churn

kerosene lamp

spinning wheel

chest of silverware

The year is 1844, and you live on a small rocky farm in Massachusetts. Your family has decided to move to Oregon to gain cheap, fertile land. Your father says this move will make your family better off—and give you a brighter future.

What Do You Think?

- What do you think daily life on the trail west might be like?
- What might be the greatest obstacles that you face?
- Notice the necessities packed in this crowded wagon. What might have been left behind?

What might you gain and lose by going west?

1810 — **1853**

USA / World

1815
Napoleon defeated at Waterloo.

1821
Stephen Austin settles in Texas.

1821
Mexico gains independence from Spain.

1824
Jedediah Smith finds South Pass.

1836
Texas declares independence.
Battle of the Alamo fought.
Republic of Texas established.

1839
Opium War fought in China.

1844
James Polk is elected president.

1846
War with Mexico begins.

1847
Mormons migrate to Utah.

1847
Liberia, established by a former American slave, proclaimed an independent nation.

1848
War with Mexico ends.

1849
California gold rush begins.

1853
United States makes Gadsden Purchase.

BEFORE YOU READ

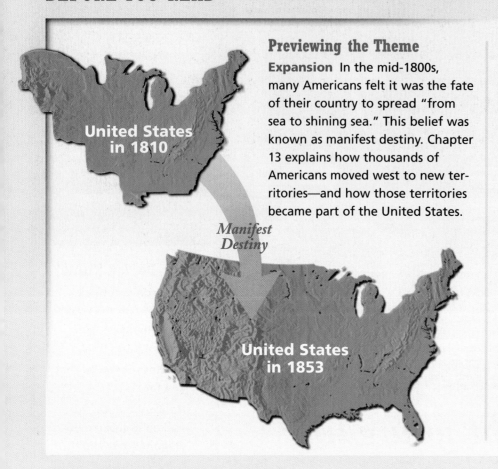

United States in 1810

Manifest Destiny

United States in 1853

Previewing the Theme

Expansion In the mid-1800s, many Americans felt it was the fate of their country to spread "from sea to shining sea." This belief was known as manifest destiny. Chapter 13 explains how thousands of Americans moved west to new territories—and how those territories became part of the United States.

What Do You Know?

What do you think of when you hear the phrase "the West"? Who do you think moved west in the early 1800s? What do you think drew them to the West?

THINK ABOUT
- what you've learned about the West from movies or travel
- reasons that people move to new places today

What Do You Want to Know?

What questions do you have about the westward movement of the 1800s? Record those questions in your notebook before you read the chapter.

READ AND TAKE NOTES

Reading Strategy: Categorizing To help you make sense of what you read, learn to categorize. Categorizing means sorting information into groups. The chart below will help you categorize the information in this chapter about the westward movement. Use the chart to take notes on what groups went west, why they went, and what events brought each territory into the United States.

 See Skillbuilder Handbook, page R6.

	Types of people who traveled there	Why they went there	Key events that brought the territory into the United States
New Mexico			
Utah			
Oregon			
Texas			
California			

① Trails West

TERMS & NAMES
Jedediah Smith
mountain man
Jim Beckwourth
land speculator
Santa Fe Trail
Oregon Trail
Mormon
Brigham Young

MAIN IDEA	WHY IT MATTERS NOW
Thousands of settlers followed trails through the West to gain land and a chance to make a fortune.	This migration brought Americans to the territories that became New Mexico, Oregon, and Utah.

ONE AMERICAN'S STORY

The mountain man **Jedediah Smith** was leading an expedition to find a route through the Rocky Mountains when a grizzly bear attacked. The bear seized Smith's head in its mouth, shredded his face, and partially tore off one ear. Smith's men chased the bear away. Jim Clyman recalled the scene.

A VOICE FROM THE PAST

I asked [Smith] what was best. He said, "One or two go for water and if you have a needle and thread get it out and sew up my wounds around my head." . . . I told him I could do nothing for his ear. "Oh, you must try to stitch it up some way or other," said he. Then I put in my needle and stitched it through and through.

Jim Clyman, quoted in *The West,* by Geoffrey C. Ward

This likeness of Jedediah Smith shows the ruggedness and spirit of the mountain man.

Ten days after this attack, Smith was ready to continue exploring. The following spring, he found what he was looking for—a pass through the Rocky Mountains.

Jedediah Smith was one of the daring fur trappers and explorers known as **mountain men**. The mountain men opened up the West by discovering the best trails through the Rockies. Later, thousands of pioneers followed these trails. In this section, you will learn about the trails—and why people followed them west.

Mountain Men and the Rendezvous

Mountain men survived by being tough and resourceful. They spent most of the year alone, trapping small animals such as beavers. Easterners wanted beaver furs to make the men's hats that were in fashion at the time. To obtain furs, mountain men roamed the Great Plains and the Far West, the regions between the Mississippi River and the Pacific Ocean, and set traps in icy mountain streams.

Because of their adventures, mountain men such as Jedediah Smith and **Jim Beckwourth** became famous as rugged loners. However, they were not as independent as the legends have portrayed them. Instead, they were connected economically to the businessmen who bought their furs.

JIM BECKWOURTH
1798–1867

Jim Beckwourth was born in slavery and set free by his owner. At the age of 25, Beckwourth joined a group of fur traders going west and in time became a daring mountain man.

For several years, Beckwourth lived with a Crow tribe. Later, he worked as an army scout and gold prospector. In 1850, he discovered a mountain pass that became the route into present-day northern California. This pass is still called Beckwourth Pass.

What was Beckwourth's most important contribution to the westward movement?

One businessman, William Henry Ashley, created a trading arrangement called the rendezvous system. Under this system, individual trappers came to a pre-arranged site for a rendezvous with traders from the east. The trappers bought supplies from those traders and paid them in furs. The rendezvous took place every summer from 1825 to 1840. In that year, silk hats replaced beaver hats as the fashion, and the fur trade died out.

Mountain Men Open the West

During the height of the fur trade, mountain men worked some streams so heavily that they killed off the animals. This forced the trappers to search for new streams where beaver lived. The mountain men's explorations provided Americans with some of the earliest firsthand knowledge of the Far West. This knowledge, and the trails the mountain men blazed, made it possible for later pioneers to move west.

For example, thousands of pioneers used South Pass, the wide valley through the Rockies that Jedediah Smith had publicized. Smith learned of this pass, in present-day Wyoming, from Native Americans. Unlike the high northern passes used by Lewis and Clark, South Pass was low, so snow did not block it as often as it blocked higher passes. Also, because South Pass was wide and less steep, wagon trails could run through it.

Smith wrote to his brother that he wanted to help people in need: "It is for this that I go for days without eating, and am pretty well satisfied if I can gather a few roots, a few snails, . . . a piece of horseflesh, or a fine roasted dog."

The Lure of the West

Few of the people who went west shared Smith's noble motive. To many, the West with its vast stretches of land offered a golden chance to make money. The Louisiana Purchase had doubled the size of the United States, and some Americans wanted to take the land away from Native Americans who inhabited this territory.

People called **land speculators** bought huge areas of land. To speculate means to buy something in the hope that it will increase in value. If land value did go up, speculators divided their land holdings into smaller sections. They made great profits by selling those sections to the thousands of settlers who dreamed of owning their own farms.

Manufacturers and merchants soon followed the settlers west. They hoped to earn money by making and selling items that farmers needed. Other people made the trip to find jobs or to escape people to whom they owed money.

Vocabulary
rendezvous
(RAHN•day•voo): meeting; from a French word meaning "present yourselves"

Reading **History**
A. Reading a Map Find South Pass on the map on page 379. Notice which two trails used that pass.

Trails West, 1850

Blackfoot
Nez Perce
Crow
OREGON TERRITORY
CASCADE RANGE
UNORGANIZED TERRITORY
Cheyenne
Pawnee
Ft. Hall
Sublette Cutoff
South Pass
ROCKY MOUNTAINS
Chimney Rock
CALIFORNIA
Pomo
Sacramento
San Francisco
Salt Lake City
UTAH TERRITORY
Great Plains
IOWA
Mississippi R.
Council Bluffs
Nauvoo
ILLINOIS
St. Louis
Independence
MISSOURI
Ute
SIERRA NEVADA
PACIFIC OCEAN
Navajo
Los Angeles
NEW MEXICO TERRITORY
Santa Fe
Cimarron Cutoff
Cherokee
Creek
Seminole
Choctaw
Chickasaw
TEXAS

Chimney Rock, Nebraska, was an important landmark on the Oregon Trail.

0   200 Miles
0   200 Kilometers

Legend:
- Oregon Trail
- California Trail
- Santa Fe Trail
- Old Spanish Trail
- Mormon Trail
- *Crow* Native Americans
- Fort

GEOGRAPHY SKILLBUILDER Interpreting Maps
1. **Place** *What is the length in miles of the Oregon Trail from Independence, Missouri, to Fort Vancouver?*
2. **Human-Environment Interaction** *Why do you think some of the trails ran along rivers?*

The Trail to Santa Fe

Traders also traveled west in search of markets. After Mexico gained independence from Spain in 1821, it opened its borders to American traders, whom Spain had kept out. In response, the Missouri trader William Becknell set out with hardware, cloth, and china for Santa Fe, capital of the Mexican province of New Mexico. By doing so, he opened the **Santa Fe Trail,** which led from Missouri to Santa Fe. Once in Santa Fe, he made a large profit because the New Mexicans were eager for new merchandise.

When Becknell returned to Missouri weeks later, a curious crowd met him. One man picked up one of Becknell's bags and slit it open with a knife. As gold and silver coins spilled onto the street, the onlookers gasped. The news spread that New Mexico was a place where traders could become rich.

The following spring, Becknell headed to Santa Fe again. This time he loaded his trade goods into covered wagons, which Westerners called prairie schooners. Their billowing white canvas tops made them look like schooners, or sailing ships.

Becknell could not haul wagons over the mountain pass he had used on his first trip to Santa Fe. Instead, he found a cutoff, a shortcut that avoided steep slopes but passed through a deadly desert to the south. As his traders crossed the burning sands, they ran out of water. Crazed by

Reading **History**
B. Making Inferences What do you think other Missourians might decide to do after seeing Becknell's wealth?

thirst, they lopped off mules' ears and killed their dogs to drink the animals' blood. Finally, the men found a stream. The water saved them from death, and they reached Santa Fe.

Becknell returned home with another huge profit. Before long, hundreds of traders and prairie schooners braved the cutoff to make the 800-mile journey from Missouri to New Mexico each year.

Oregon Fever

Hundreds of settlers also began migrating west on the **Oregon Trail,** which ran from Independence, Missouri, to the Oregon Territory. The first whites to cross the continent to Oregon were missionaries, such as Marcus and Narcissa Whitman in 1836. At that time, the United States and Britain were locked in an argument about which country owned Oregon. To the Whitmans' great disappointment, they made few converts among the Native Americans. However, their glowing reports of Oregon's rich land began to attract other American settlers.

Amazing stories spread about Oregon. The sun always shone there. Wheat grew as tall as a man. One tale claimed that pigs were "running about, . . . round and fat, and already cooked, with knives and forks sticking in them so you can cut off a slice whenever you are hungry."

Such stories tempted many people to make the 2,000-mile journey to Oregon. In 1843, nearly 1,000 people traveled from Missouri to Oregon. The next year, twice as many came. "The Oregon Fever has broken out," observed a Boston newspaper, "and is now raging."

Vocabulary
converts: people who accept a new religious belief

One Family Heads West

The experiences of the Sager family show how difficult the trail could be. In 1844, Henry Sager, his wife, and six children left Missouri to find cheap, fertile land in Oregon. They had already moved four times in the past four years. Henry's daughter Catherine explained her family's moves.

A VOICE FROM THE PAST
Father was one of those restless men who are not content to remain in one place long at a time. . . . [He] had been talking of going to Texas. But mother, hearing much said about the healthfulness of Oregon, preferred to go there.

Catherine Sager, quoted in *The West,* by Geoffrey C. Ward

The Oregon Trail was dangerous, so pioneers joined wagon trains. They knew their survival would depend on cooperation. Before setting out, the wagon train members agreed on rules and elected leaders to enforce them.

Even so, life on the trail was full of hardship. The Sagers had barely begun the trip when Mrs. Sager gave birth to her seventh child. Two months later, nine-year-old Catherine fell under a moving wagon, which crushed her left leg. Later, "camp fever" killed both of the Sager parents.

Even though the Sager parents had died, the other families in the train cooperated to help the Sager orphans make it to Oregon. There, the Whitmans agreed to adopt them. When Narcissa met them, Catherine recalled, "We thought as we shyly looked at her that she was the prettiest woman we had ever seen."

*Reading*History

C. Finding Main Ideas What difficulties did families like the Sagers face?

The Mormon Trail

While most pioneers went west in search of wealth, one group migrated for religious reasons. The **Mormons,** who settled Utah, were members of the Church of Jesus Christ of Latter-Day Saints. Joseph Smith had founded this church in upstate New York in 1830. The Mormons lived in close communities, worked hard, shared their goods, and prospered.

The Mormons, though, also made enemies. Some people reacted angrily to the Mormons' teachings. They saw the Mormon practice of polygamy—allowing a man to have more than one wife at a time—as immoral. Others objected to their holding property in common.

*Reading*History

D. Analyzing Causes Why did Brigham Young lead the Mormons to Utah?

In 1844, an anti-Mormon mob in Illinois killed Smith. **Brigham Young,** the next Mormon leader, moved his people out of the United States. His destination was Utah, then part of Mexico. In this desolate region, he hoped his people would be left to follow their faith in peace.

In 1847, about 1,600 Mormons followed part of the Oregon Trail to Utah. There they built a new settlement by the Great Salt Lake. Because Utah has little rainfall, the Mormons had to work together to build dams and canals. These structures captured water in the hills and carried it to the farms in the valleys below. Through teamwork, they made their desert homeland bloom.

In the meantime, changes were taking place in Texas. As you will read in Section 2, Americans had been moving into that Mexican territory, too.

 Section 1 Assessment

1. Terms & Names

Explain the significance of:
- Jedediah Smith
- mountain man
- Jim Beckwourth
- land speculator
- Santa Fe Trail
- Oregon Trail
- Mormon
- Brigham Young

2. Taking Notes

Use a cluster diagram like the one shown to review details about the trails west.

Trails West

Which trail would you have wanted to travel? Why?

3. Main Ideas

a. How did the mountain men open up the West for later settlement?

b. What are two examples of pioneer groups who used cooperation to overcome hardship?

c. What economic and social forces drew people to the West?

4. Critical Thinking

Drawing Conclusions Of all the hardships faced by people who went west, what do you think was the worst? Explain.

THINK ABOUT
- the mountain men
- William Becknell
- the Sagers
- the Mormons

ACTIVITY OPTIONS

LANGUAGE ARTS

ART

Research a pioneer from this section and either write a **letter** from his or her point of view to a friend or illustrate a **journal entry** with sights from your journey.

Survive the Oregon Trail!

You are part of a wagon train heading west on the Oregon Trail. During your journey, you will cross endless flat prairies and mountains that climb more steeply than a staircase. You will suffer through blazing heat and icy snowstorms. Food is scarce in the land you travel through—and human settlements are even more scarce.

COOPERATIVE LEARNING On this page are three challenges you will face on your journey. Working with a small group, create a solution for each challenge. To help your group work together, assign a task to each group member. You will find helpful information in the Data File. Be prepared to present your solutions to the class.

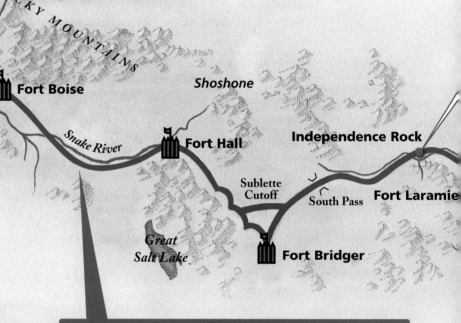

Fort Vancouver

Columbia River

Fort Walla Walla

● **Oregon City**   *Nez Perce*

END

ROCKY MOUNTAINS

Fort Boise

Shoshone

Snake River

Fort Hall

Independence Rock

Sublette Cutoff

South Pass   **Fort Laramie**

Great Salt Lake

Fort Bridger

SCIENCE CHALLENGE

"The most terrible mountains"

One pioneer called the Rockies "the most terrible mountains for steepness." Your oxen have struggled for hours to pull your wagon up a steep slope. Now you have to go down the other side without crashing—and wagon wheels have no brakes. How will you slow your descent? Use the Data File for help. Present your ideas using one of these options:

- Write instructions for climbing and descending the mountain.
- Illustrate your solution in a how-to diagram.

CIVICS CHALLENGE

"A thieving scoundrel"

You wake one morning to the sound of shouting. One of the men in the wagon train has been caught stealing another family's ox—to replace an ox that died from drinking bad water. The wagon train leader asks you to help decide how to punish the thief. Present your decision using one of these options:

- As a group, role-play a discussion of what the punishment should be.
- Write an explanation of a punishment to the wagon train leader.

HEALTH **CHALLENGE**

"A grand blow-out"

On July 4, your wagon train stops near Independence Rock for "a grand blow-out" to celebrate your progress. Each family will bring a dish to the party. What will you cook that is tasty and nutritious? You might use supplies from your wagon and berries or animals from the area. Look at the Data File for help. Present your choice using one of these options:

- Draw a picture of your dish and describe it.
- Write an original recipe.

The Journey

Distance: 2,000 miles

Length: 4–6 months

Average daily distance: 12–15 miles

Best time to travel: April–September

The Wagon

Size of box: 4 x 10 feet

Load: 1,600–2,500 pounds

Oxen needed per wagon: 4–8

Animals Taken

oxen, horses, dairy cows, cattle, chickens, mules, pigs, dogs, cats

Food Supplies

flour, corn meal, salt, baking soda, sugar, crackers, dried beans, rice, dried fruit, bacon, coffee, vinegar

Cooking Equipment

Dutch oven, large kettle, frying pan, bread pan, coffee grinder, rolling pin, tin cups and plates, water kegs, knives, spoons

Other Equipment

bedding, spare wagon parts, tar, rope, chains, pulleys, tools, fishing poles, guns, ammunition, matches, soap, medicines

Trail Hazards

Worst discomforts: heat, cold, wind, rain, dust, mud, mosquitoes, hunger, thirst

Biggest killer: disease

Most common accidents: shooting, drowning, crushing by wagon wheels, injuries from animals

---

For more about the Oregon Trail . . .

RESEARCH LINKS
CLASSZONE.COM

Sioux

Missouri River

Scotts Bluff

Chimney Rock

Platte River

Fort Kearney

START

Independence

ACTIVITY **WRAP-UP**

Present to the class Using the model shown here, ask and answer questions about geographic patterns in the West. Choose the best questions to present to the class.

The Texas Revolution

TERMS & NAMES
Stephen Austin
Tejano
Antonio López
 de Santa Anna
Sam Houston
William Travis
Juan Seguín
Battle of the Alamo
Lone Star Republic

MAIN IDEA	**WHY IT MATTERS NOW**
American and *Tejano* citizens led Texas to independence from Mexico.	The diverse culture of Texas has developed from the contributions of many different groups.

ONE AMERICAN'S STORY

Son of a bankrupt Missouri mine owner, <u>**Stephen Austin**</u> read his mother's letter, written in 1821, in stunned silence. His father, Moses Austin, was dead. In his last moments, she told her son, "He called me to his bedside, . . . he begged me to tell you to take his place . . . to go on . . . in the same way he would have done."

Stephen knew what that meant. Moses Austin had spent the last years of his life chasing a crazy dream. He had hoped to found a colony for Americans in Spanish Texas.

Stephen's dream, though, was to be a lawyer—not a colonizer. Yet as a loving and obedient son, how could he deny his father's dying wish? A week after his father's death, Stephen Austin was standing on Texas soil. From that day on, his father's dream was to be his destiny.

This section explains how Stephen Austin, along with others, worked hard to make the lands of Texas a good place to live. Their spirit would create an independent Texas Republic. Later, Texas would become a state in the United States.

Stephen Austin, shown in this painting, helped fulfill his father's dream by establishing an American colony in Texas.

Spanish Texas

The Spanish land called *Tejas* (Tay•HAHS) bordered the United States territory called Louisiana. The land was rich and desirable. It had forests in the east, rich soil for growing corn and cotton, and great grassy plains for grazing animals. It also had rivers leading to natural ports on the Gulf of Mexico. It was home to Plains and Pueblo Native Americans. Even though *Tejas* was a state in the Spanish colony of New Spain, it had few Spanish settlers. Around 1819, Spanish soldiers drove off Americans trying to claim those lands as a part of the Louisiana Purchase.

In 1821, only about 4,000 *Tejanos* (Tay•HAH•nohs) lived in Texas. <u>*Tejanos*</u> are people of Spanish heritage who consider Texas their home. The Comanche, Apache, and other tribes fought fiercely against Spanish settlement of Texas. The Spanish officials wanted many more settlers to move to Texas. They hoped that new colonists would help to defend against Native Americans and Americans who illegally sneaked into Texas.

Vocabulary
empresarios:
individuals who
agreed to recruit
settlers for the
land

To attract more people to Texas, the Spanish government offered huge tracts of land to *empresarios.* But they were unable to attract Spanish settlers. So, when Moses Austin asked for permission to start a colony in Texas, Spain agreed. Austin was promised a large section of land. He had to agree that settlers on his land had to follow Spanish laws.

Mexican Independence Changes Texas

Shortly after Stephen Austin arrived in Texas in 1821, Mexico successfully gained its independence from Spain. *Tejas* was now a part of Mexico. With the change in government, the Spanish land grant given to Austin's father was worthless. Stephen Austin traveled to Mexico City to persuade the new Mexican government to let him start his colony. It took him almost a year to get permission. And the Mexican government would consent only if the new settlers agreed to become Mexican citizens and members of the Roman Catholic Church.

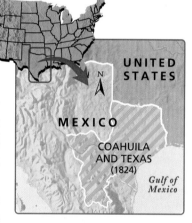

Between 1821 and 1827, Austin attracted 297 families to his new settlement. These original Texas settler families are known as the "Old Three Hundred." He demanded evidence that each family head was moral, worked hard, and did not drink. So law-abiding were his colonists that Austin could write to a new settler, "You will be astonished to see all our houses with no other fastening than a wooden pin or door latch."

The success of Austin's colony attracted more land speculators and settlers to Texas from the United States. Some were looking for a new life, some were escaping from the law, and others were looking for a chance to grow rich. By 1830, the population had swelled to about 30,000, with Americans outnumbering the *Tejanos* six to one.

Posters such as the one above encouraged Americans from the East to settle in Texas. Some people scrawled G.T.T. on their doors to indicate they had "gone to Texas."

Rising Tensions in Texas

Reading **History**
A. Analyzing Causes Why was there growing tension between Americans and *Tejanos?*

As more and more Americans settled in Texas, tensions between them and the *Tejanos* increased. Used to governing themselves, Americans resented following Mexican laws. Since few Americans spoke Spanish, they were unhappy that all official documents had to be in that language. Slave owners were especially upset when Mexico outlawed slavery in 1829. They wanted to maintain slavery so they could grow cotton. Austin persuaded the government to allow slave owners to keep their slaves.

On the other hand, the *Tejanos* found the Americans difficult to live with, too. *Tejanos* thought that the Americans believed they were superior and deserved special privileges. The Americans seemed unwilling to adapt to Mexican laws.

The Mexican government sent an official to Texas to investigate the tensions. He was not happy with what he found. In 1829, he reported to his government, "I am warning you to take timely measures . . . Texas could throw this whole nation into revolution." His advice turned out to be right.

Responding to the warnings, the Mexican government cracked down on Texas. First, it closed the state to further American immigration. Next, it required Texans to pay taxes for the first time. Finally, to enforce these new laws, the government sent more Mexican troops to Texas.

*Reading*History

B. Summarizing
What three actions did the Mexican government take to control Texas?

Texans Revolt Against Mexico

These actions caused angry protests. Some Texans even talked of breaking away from Mexico. Most, however, listened to Austin, who remained loyal to Mexico. In 1833, Austin set off for Mexico City with a petition. This document listed reforms supported by both Americans and *Tejanos*. The most important request was that Texas become a self-governing state within Mexico.

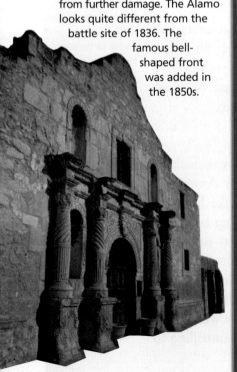

America's HERITAGE

REMEMBER THE ALAMO!
Today the Alamo, shown below, is again under siege. Moisture seeps into the limestone walls and causes them to crumble. Many people view the mission as a memorial to Americans' willingness to fight for freedom, so a Texas group has begun attempts to preserve the Alamo from further damage. The Alamo looks quite different from the battle site of 1836. The famous bell-shaped front was added in the 1850s.

In Mexico City, Austin met General **Antonio López de Santa Anna,** the Mexican president. At first, the general agreed to most of the reforms in Austin's petition. But then Santa Anna learned of a letter Austin had written. The letter said that if the changes weren't approved Austin would support breaking away from Mexican rule. This was rebellion! The general had Austin jailed for an entire year. The Texans were furious and ready to rebel.

Santa Anna's answer to talk of rebellion was to send more troops to Texas. In late September 1835, Mexican soldiers marched to the town of Gonzales. They had orders to seize a cannon used by the Texans for protection against Native Americans. Texas volunteers had hung a flag on the big gun that said, "Come and Take It."

The Mexican troops failed to capture the cannon. Two months later, Texans drove Mexican troops out of an old mission in San Antonio that was used as a fortress. It was called the Alamo. Among the Texas volunteers were free African Americans such as Hendrick Arnold and Greenbury Logan. Angered by these insults, Santa Anna and 6,000 troops headed for Texas.

*Reading*History

C. Analyzing Causes What Texan actions moved Santa Anna to head toward Texas?

The Fight for the Alamo

On March 1–2, 1836, Texans met at a settlement called Washington-on-the-Brazos to decide what to do about Santa Anna's troops. They believed they could do only one thing: to declare Texas a free and independent republic. **Sam Houston,** the only man at the meeting with military experience, was placed in command of the Texas army.

The Texas army hardly existed. At that moment, there were two small forces ready to stand up to Santa Anna's army. One was a company of 420 men, led by James Fannin, stationed at Goliad, a fort in southeast Texas. The second was a company of 183 volunteers at the Alamo. Headed by **William Travis,** this small force included such famous frontiersmen as Davy Crockett and Jim Bowie. In addition, **Juan Seguín** (wahn seh•GEEN) led a band of 25 *Tejanos* in support of revolt.

On February 23, 1836, Santa Anna's troops surrounded San Antonio. The next day, Mexicans began their siege of the Alamo. Two nights later, Travis scrawled a message to the world.

Reading **History**
D. Making Inferences Why would William Travis address his message to all Americans?

A VOICE FROM THE PAST

The enemy has demanded a surrender. . . . I have answered the demand with a cannon shot, and our flag still waves proudly from the walls. I shall never surrender or retreat.

William Travis, "To the People of Texas and all the Americans in the World"

Because Juan Seguín spoke Spanish, he was chosen to carry the plea through enemy lines. Seguín got the message through to other Texas defenders. But when he returned, he saw the Alamo in flames.

The Alamo's defenders held off the Mexican attack for 12 violent days. Travis and the defenders stubbornly refused to surrender. On the 13th day, Santa Anna ordered more than 1,800 men to storm the fortress. The Texans met the attackers with a hailstorm of cannon and gun fire. Then suddenly it became strangely quiet. The Texans had run out of ammunition. At day's end, all but five Texans were dead. The **Battle of the Alamo** was over.

HISTORY *through* ART

The Battle of the Alamo was so intense that Davy Crockett did not have time to reload his gun, which he called "Betsy." He used it as a club. This print is by a 20th-century illustrator, Frederick Yohn.

What does the print reveal about the battle?

JUAN SEGUÍN
1806–1890

Juan Seguín was a *Tejano* hero of the Texas Revolution. It was Seguín who dashed through enemy lines at the Alamo with a last desperate attempt for aid.

And after the war, it was Seguín who arranged for the remains of the Alamo defenders to be buried with full military honors.

Newcomers to Texas who disliked all *Tejanos* falsely accused Seguín of planning rebellion. Fearing for his life, he fled to Mexico in 1842, there "to seek a refuge amongst my enemies."

SAM HOUSTON
1793–1863

Raised by a widowed mother, Sam Houston grew up in Tennessee. He lived with the Cherokee for about three years. Later, he served in the U.S. Army, in Congress, and as the governor of Tennessee.

"I was a General without an army," wrote Houston, after taking command of the Texas forces in 1836. Yet by the time the war was over, he and his troops had defeated Santa Anna's larger army.

Houston was elected the first president of the Republic of Texas. When Texas became a state, he served as a U.S. senator.

In what ways did the experiences of Seguín and Houston differ?

Those men who had not died in the fighting were executed at Santa Anna's command. A total of 183 Alamo defenders died. A few women and children were not killed. Susanna Dickinson, one of the survivors, was ordered by Santa Anna to tell the story of the Alamo to other Texans. He hoped the story would discourage more rebellion. The slaughter at the Alamo shocked Texans—and showed them how hard they would have to fight for their freedom from Mexico.

Victory at San Jacinto

With Santa Anna on the attack, Texans—both soldiers and settlers—fled eastward. Houston sent a message to the men at Goliad, ordering them to retreat. They were captured by Mexican forces, who executed more than 300. The Texans would not soon forget the massacre at Goliad. But even in retreat and defeat, Houston's army doubled. Now it was a fighting force of 800 angry men. It included *Tejanos,* American settlers, volunteers from the United States, and many free and enslaved African Americans.

In late April, Santa Anna caught up with Houston near the San Jacinto (san juh•SIN•toh) River. Late in the afternoon of April 21, 1836, the Texans advanced on the Mexican army "with the stillness of death." When close to Santa Anna's camp, they raced forward, rifles ready, screaming "Remember the Alamo!" "Remember Goliad!"

In just 18 minutes, the Texans killed more than half of the Mexican army. Santa Anna was forced to sign a treaty giving Texas its freedom. With the Battle of San Jacinto, Texas was now independent.

Reading **History**
E. Reading a Map
Use the map on page 389 to see where battles were taking place.

Lone Star Republic

In September 1836, Texans raised a flag with a single star. They adopted a nickname—**Lone Star Republic**—and proclaimed Texas an independent nation. The new nation set up its own army and navy. Sam Houston was elected president of the Lone Star Republic by a landslide.

Many Texans did not want Texas to remain independent for long. They considered themselves Americans and wanted to be a part of the United States. In 1836, the Texas government asked Congress to annex Texas to the Union.

Vocabulary
annex: to join territory to an existing country

Many Northerners objected. They argued that Texas would become a slave state, and they opposed any expansion of slavery. If Texas joined the Union, slave states would outnumber free states and have a voting advantage in Congress. Other people feared that annexing Texas would lead to war with Mexico.

In response, Congress voted against annexation. Texas remained an inde-

Reading **History**
F. Analyzing Causes Why didn't Congress annex Texas?

pendent republic for almost ten years. In the next section, you will learn that the question of annexing Texas did lead to a war between the United States and Mexico.

The Texas Revolution, 1836

GEOGRAPHY SKILLBUILDER Interpreting Maps
1. **Movement** *About how many total miles did Santa Anna travel from Mexico to San Jacinto?*
2. **Movement** *Look at the distances traveled by Mexican forces and those traveled by the Texans. Which side do you think had an advantage? Explain.*

Section 2 Assessment

1. Terms & Names
Explain the significance of:
- Stephen Austin
- *Tejano*
- Antonio López de Santa Anna
- Sam Houston
- William Travis
- Juan Seguín
- Battle of the Alamo
- Lone Star Republic

2. Taking Notes
Use a diagram like the one shown to review events that led to Texan independence and put them in order.

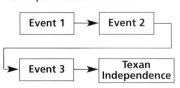

3. Main Ideas
a. Why did Americans want to move to Texas?

b. How did the Mexican government respond to the Texas rebellion?

c. Why did Congress refuse to annex Texas?

4. Critical Thinking
Recognizing Effects How did losing the Battle of the Alamo help the Texans win their independence?

THINK ABOUT
- the Texans' and Americans' shock over the loss of the battle to the Mexicans
- the need to recruit more forces to fight with the Texas army

ACTIVITY OPTIONS

ART
TECHNOLOGY

Research a figure from the Texas Revolution. Create a **trading card** or design that person's **Web page** for the Internet.

3 The War with Mexico

TERMS & NAMES
James K. Polk
manifest destiny
Zachary Taylor
Bear Flag Revolt
Winfield Scott
Treaty of
  Guadalupe
  Hidalgo
Mexican Cession

MAIN IDEA

The United States expanded its territory westward to stretch from the Atlantic to the Pacific coast.

WHY IT MATTERS NOW

Today, one-third of all Americans live in the areas added to the United States in 1848.

ONE AMERICAN'S STORY

Henry Clay sneered, "Who is <u>James K. Polk</u>?" Clay had just learned the name of the man nominated by Democrats to run against him for president in 1844. "A mistake!" answered Washington insiders.

News of Polk's nomination was flashed to the capital by the newly invented telegraph machine. People were convinced that the machine didn't work. How could the Democrats choose Polk? A joke!

Polk was America's first "dark horse," a candidate who received unexpected support. The Democrats had nominated this little-known man only when they could not agree on anyone else.

Still, Polk wasn't a complete nobody. He had been governor of Tennessee and served seven terms in Congress. Polk was committed to national expansion. He vowed to annex Texas and take over Oregon. Americans listened and voted.

When those votes were counted, Clay had his answer. James Knox Polk was the eleventh president of the United States.

During his campaign, Polk's ideas about expanding the country captured the attention of Americans. As you will read in this section, after his election Polk looked for ways to expand the nation.

James Polk's presidential campaign emphasized expansion of the United States.

Americans Support Manifest Destiny

The abundance of land in the West seemed to hold great promise for Americans. Although populated with Native Americans and Mexicans, those lands were viewed by white settlers as unoccupied. Many Americans wanted to settle those lands themselves, and they worried about competition from other nations. Mexico occupied the southwest lands, and Britain shared the northwest Oregon Territory with the United States. Many Americans believed that the United States was destined to stretch across the continent from the Atlantic Ocean to the Pacific Ocean. In 1845, a newspaper editor named John O'Sullivan gave a name to that belief.

A VOICE FROM THE PAST

Our manifest destiny [is] to overspread and possess the whole of the continent which Providence [God] has given us for the development of the great experiment of liberty and . . . self-government.

John O'Sullivan, *United States Magazine and Democratic Review*

---

*Reading***History**

A. Drawing Conclusions
What were the positives and negatives of the idea of manifest destiny?

John O'Sullivan used the word *manifest* to mean clear or obvious. The word *destiny* means events sure to happen. Therefore, **manifest destiny** suggested that expansion was not only good but bound to happen—even if it meant pushing Mexicans and Native Americans out of the way. After Polk's election in 1844, manifest destiny became government policy.

The term "manifest destiny" was new, but the idea was not. By the 1840s, thousands of Americans had moved into the Oregon Territory. Since 1818, Oregon had been occupied jointly by the United States and Britain. In his campaign, Polk had talked of taking over all of Oregon. "Fifty-four forty or fight!" screamed one of his slogans. The parallel of 54° 40' N latitude was the northern boundary of the shared Oregon Territory.

Rather than fight for all of Oregon, however, Polk settled for half. In 1846, the United States and Great Britain agreed to divide Oregon at the 49th parallel. This agreement extended the boundary line already drawn between Canada and the United States. Today this line still serves as the border between much of the United States and Canada.

Oregon, 1846
■ British territory under 1846 treaty
□ U. S. territory under 1846 treaty

"Our manifest destiny [is] to . . . possess the whole of the continent."
John O'Sullivan

Troubles with Mexico

Polk had good reason for avoiding war with Britain over Oregon. By 1846, he had much bigger troubles brewing with Mexico over Texas.

In 1845, Congress admitted Texas as a slave state, in spite of Northern objections to the spread of slavery. However, Mexico still claimed Texas as its own. Mexico angrily viewed this annexation as an act of war. To make matters worse, Texas and Mexico could not agree on the official border between them. Texas claimed the Rio Grande, a river south of San Antonio, as its southern boundary. Mexico insisted on the Nueces (noo•AY•sis) River as the border of Texas. The difference in the distance between the two rivers was more than 100 miles at some points. Many thousands of miles of territory were at stake.

Mexico said it would fight to defend its claim. Hoping to settle the dispute peacefully, Polk sent John Slidell, a Spanish-speaking

*Reading***History**

B. Reading a Map
Use the map on page 392 to find the locations of the disputed border between Texas and Mexico.

ambassador, to offer Mexico $25 million for Texas, California, and New Mexico. But Slidell's diplomacy failed.

Believing that the American people supported his expansion plans, Polk wanted to force the issue with Mexico. He purposely ordered General **Zachary Taylor** to station troops on the northern bank of the Rio Grande. This river bank was part of the disputed territory. Viewing this as an act of war, Mexico moved an army into place on the southern bank. On April 25, 1846, a Mexican cavalry unit crossed the Rio Grande. They ambushed an American patrol and killed or wounded 16 American soldiers.

When news of the attack reached Washington, Polk sent a rousing war message to Congress, saying, "Mexico has invaded our territory and shed American blood upon American soil." Two days later, Congress declared war. The War with Mexico had begun. Thousands of volunteers, mostly from western states, rushed to enlist in the army. Santa Anna, who was president of Mexico, built up the Mexican army.

However, Americans had mixed reactions to Polk's call for war. Illinois representative Abraham Lincoln questioned the truthfulness of the president's message and the need to declare war. Northeasterners questioned the justice of men dying in such a war. Slavery became an issue in the debates over the war. Southerners saw expansion into Texas as an opportunity to extend slavery and to increase their power in Congress. To

Reading **History**
C. Analyzing Causes How did the War with Mexico start?

The War with Mexico, 1846–1847

A symbol of the Bear Flag Revolt, this flag has a grizzly bear and a star made with blackberry juice. The revolt declared California independent from Mexico.

GEOGRAPHY SKILLBUILDER Interpreting Maps
1. **Movement** About how far did General Kearny's troops move to reach San Diego?
2. **Location** Why would defending Texas be much easier than defending Mexico?

prevent this from happening, antislavery representatives introduced a bill to prohibit slavery in any lands taken from Mexico. Frederick Douglass, the abolitionist, summarized the arguments.

A VOICE FROM THE PAST

The determination of our slaveholding President to prosecute the war, and the probability of his success in wringing from the people men and money to carry it on, is made evident, . . . None seem willing to take their stand for peace at all risks; and all seem willing that the war should be carried on in some form or other.

Frederick Douglass in *The North Star,* January 21, 1848

Despite opposition, the United States plunged into war. In May 1846, General Taylor led troops into Mexico. Many Americans thought it would be easy to defeat the Mexicans, and the war would end quickly.

Capturing New Mexico and California

Not long after the war began, General Stephen Kearny (KAHR•nee)—a U.S. Army officer—and his men left Fort Leavenworth, Kansas, with orders to occupy New Mexico. Then they were to continue west to California. As his troops marched along the Santa Fe Trail, they sang songs like this one.

*Reading*History

D. Making Inferences
How does this song support the idea of manifest destiny?

A VOICE FROM THE PAST

Old Colonel Kearny, you can bet,
Will keep the boys in motion,
Till Yankee Land includes the sand
On the Pacific Ocean.

Six weeks and 650 hot and rugged miles later, Kearny's army entered New Mexico. Using persuasion instead of force, he convinced the Mexican troops that he meant to withdraw. This allowed him to take New Mexico without firing a shot. Then Kearny and a small force of soldiers marched on toward California, which had only 8,000 to 12,000 Mexican residents. The remaining force moved south toward Mexico.

In California, Americans led by the explorer John C. Frémont rebelled against Mexican rule in the **Bear Flag Revolt.** They arrested the Mexican commander of Northern California and raised a crude flag showing a grizzly bear sketched in blackberry juice. The rebels declared California independent of Mexico and named it the Republic of California. In the fall, U.S. troops reached California and joined forces with the rebels. Within weeks, Americans controlled all of California.

The Invasion of Mexico

The defeat of Mexico proved far more difficult. The Mexican army was much larger, but the U.S. troops

STRANGE *but* True

SANTA ANNA'S LOST LEG
Santa Anna lost his left leg in a battle with the French. In 1842, he held a funeral for his severed limb. On that day, church and political officials followed the dictator's leg through the streets of Mexico City to its final resting place—an urn placed on a column.

Two years later, an angry mob broke the urn and threw the leg away. The leg was rescued by a loyal soldier who took it home and hid it.

Thirty years later, that soldier visited Santa Anna and returned the bones of his long-lost leg.

were led by well-trained officers. American forces invaded Mexico from two directions.

General Taylor battled his way south from Texas toward the city of Monterrey in northern Mexico. On February 22, 1847, his 4,800 troops met General Santa Anna's 15,000 Mexican soldiers near a ranch called Buena Vista. After the first day of fighting, Santa Anna sent Taylor a note offering him a chance to surrender. Taylor declined. At the end of the second bloody day of fighting, Santa Anna reported that "both armies have been cut to pieces." However, it was Santa Anna who retreated after the Battle of Buena Vista. The war in the north of Mexico was over.

In southern Mexico, fighting continued. A second force led by General **Winfield Scott** landed at Veracruz on the Gulf of Mexico and battled inland toward Mexico City. Outside the capital, Scott met fierce resistance at the castle of Chapultepec (chuh•POOL•tuh•pek). About 1,000 soldiers and 100 young military cadets bravely defended the fortress. Despite their determined resistance, Mexico City fell to Scott in September 1847. As he watched, a Mexican officer sighed and said, "God is a Yankee."

Background
General Winfield Scott had become a national hero during the War of 1812.

The Mexican Cession

On February 2, 1848, the war officially ended with the **Treaty of Guadalupe Hidalgo** (gwah•duh•LOOP•ay hih•DAHL•go). In this treaty, Mexico recognized that Texas was part of the United States, and the

Growth of the United States, *1783–1853*

Ceded to Great Britain, 1818

Ceded by Great Britain, 1818

Ceded by Great Britain, Webster-Ashburton Treaty, 1842

CANADA

OREGON TERRITORY
From Great Britain, 1846

LOUISIANA PURCHASE
Bought from France, 1803

From Great Britain by Treaty of Paris, 1783

MEXICAN CESSION
From Mexico by Treaty of Guadalupe Hidalgo, 1848

Original 13 Colonies

PACIFIC OCEAN

ATLANTIC OCEAN

GADSDEN PURCHASE
Bought from Mexico, 1853

TEXAS ANNEXATION
Annexed Independent Republic, 1845

Ceded by Spain, 1818

1810   1813
Annexed by United States

Gulf of Mexico

FLORIDA CESSION
From Spain, 1819

Modern U.S. boundaries shown.

GEOGRAPHY SKILLBUILDER Interpreting Maps

1. Region *How many states or parts of states were created by all the lands added after Polk's election in 1844?*

2. Region *Which addition to the United States after 1783 added the greatest area of land?*

0   300 Miles
0   600 Kilometers

*Reading*History
E. Finding Main Ideas What were the three main parts of the Treaty of Guadalupe Hidalgo?

Rio Grande was the border between the nations. Mexico also ceded, or gave up, a vast region known as the **Mexican Cession.** This area included the present-day states of California, Nevada, Utah, most of Arizona, and parts of New Mexico, Colorado, and Wyoming. Together with Texas, this land amounted to almost one-half of Mexico. The loss was a bitter defeat for Mexico, particularly because many Mexicans felt that the United States had provoked the war in the hope of gaining Mexican territory.

In return, the United States agreed to pay Mexico $15 million. The United States would also pay the $3.25 million of claims U.S. citizens had against Mexico. Finally, it also promised to protect the 80,000 Mexicans living in Texas and the Mexican Cession.

Mexicans living in the United States saw the conquest of their land differently. Suddenly they were a minority in a nation with a strange language, culture, and legal system. At the same time, they would make important contributions to their new country. They taught new settlers how to develop the land for farming, ranching, and mining. A rich new culture resulted from the blend of many cultures in the Mexican Cession.

*Reading*History
F. Making Inferences Why did the United States pay a large price for the Gadsden Purchase?

"From Sea to Shining Sea"

The last bit of territory added to the continental United States was a strip of land across what is now southern New Mexico and Arizona. The government wanted the land as a location for a southern transcontinental railroad. In 1853, Mexico sold the land—called the Gadsden Purchase—to the United States for $10 million.

On July 4, 1848, in Washington, President Polk laid the cornerstone of a monument to honor George Washington. In Washington's day, the western border of the United States was the Mississippi River. The United States in 1848 now stretched "from sea to shining sea." In August, Polk learned that gold had been found in California. In the next section, you will read about the California gold rush.

Section 3 Assessment

1. Terms & Names

Explain the significance of:
- James K. Polk
- manifest destiny
- Zachary Taylor
- Bear Flag Revolt
- Winfield Scott
- Treaty of Guadalupe Hidalgo
- Mexican Cession

2. Taking Notes

Review the chapter and find five key events to place on a time line as shown.

War with Mexico

1846 — event — event — event — 1848 — event — event

3. Main Ideas

a. How did the acquisitions of Oregon and the Mexican Cession relate to the idea of manifest destiny?

b. Why were some people opposed to the War with Mexico?

c. What does the phrase "sea to shining sea" mean?

4. Critical Thinking

Comparing Compare the different ways land was acquired by the United States in the period of manifest destiny from 1844 to 1853.

THINK ABOUT
- the acquisition of the Oregon Territory
- lands in the Southwest

ACTIVITY OPTIONS

MATH
GEOGRAPHY

In an almanac, find the current population of the states formed from the Mexican Cession. Create a **graph** or a **map** to display the information.

TERMS & NAMES
forty-niner
Californio
Mariano Vallejo
John Sutter
James Marshall
California gold rush

4 The California Gold Rush

MAIN IDEA	WHY IT MATTERS NOW
Gold was found in California, and thousands rushed to that territory. California quickly became a state.	The gold rush made California grow rapidly and helped bring about California's cultural diversity.

ONE AMERICAN'S STORY

Luzena Wilson said of the year 1849, "The gold excitement spread like wildfire." The year before, James Marshall had discovered gold in California. Luzena's husband decided to become a **forty-niner**— someone who went to California to find gold, starting in 1849.

Most forty-niners left their families behind, but Luzena traveled to California with her husband. She later said, "I thought where he could go I could, and where I went I could take my two little toddling babies."

Luzena discovered that women—and their homemaking skills—were rare in California. Shortly after she arrived, a miner offered her five dollars for the biscuits she was baking. Shocked, she just stared at him. He quickly doubled his offer and paid in gold. Luzena realized she could make money by feeding miners, so she opened a hotel.

Like the Wilsons, thousands of people from around the world became forty-niners. In this section, you will read about the forty-niners and what their mining experiences were like. You will learn how the rapid growth of California's population caused problems for the people who lived there before 1849. You will also discover how the gold rush boosted California's economy and changed the nation's history.

This woman is carrying food to miners, just as Luzena Wilson did.

California Before the Rush

Before the forty-niners came, California was populated by as many as 150,000 Native Americans and 6,000 *Californios*—settlers of Spanish or Mexican descent. Most *Californios* lived on huge cattle ranches. They had acquired their estates when the Mexican government took away the land that once belonged to the California missions.

One important *Californio* was **Mariano Vallejo** (mah•RYAH•noh vah•YEH•hoh). A member of one of the oldest Spanish families in America, he owned 250,000 acres of land. Proudly describing the accomplishments of the *Californios*, Vallejo wrote, "We were the pioneers of the Pacific coast . . . while General Washington was carrying on the war of the Revolution." Vallejo himself had been the commander of Northern California when it belonged to Mexico.

Vocabulary
immigration:
the movement
of people into a
country or region
where they were
not born

When Mexico owned California, its government feared American immigration and rarely gave land to foreigners. But **John Sutter,** a Swiss immigrant, was one exception. Dressed in a secondhand French army uniform, Sutter had visited the Mexican governor in 1839. A charming man, Sutter persuaded the governor to grant him 50,000 acres in the unsettled Sacramento Valley. Sutter built a fort on his land and dreamed of creating his own personal empire based on agriculture.

In 1848, Sutter sent a carpenter named **James Marshall** to build a sawmill on the nearby American River. One day Marshall inspected the canal that brought water to Sutter's Mill. He later said, "My eye was caught by a glimpse of something shining. . . . I reached my hand down and picked it up; it made my heart thump for I felt certain it was gold."

Rush for Gold

News of Marshall's thrilling discovery spread rapidly. From all over California, people raced to the American River—starting the **California gold rush.** A gold rush occurs when large numbers of people move to a site where gold has been found. Throughout history, people have valued gold because it is scarce, beautiful, easy to shape, and resistant to tarnish.

Miners soon found gold in other streams flowing out of the Sierra Nevada Mountains. Colonel R. B. Mason, the military governor of California, estimated that the region held enough gold to "pay the cost of the present war with Mexico a hundred times over." He sent this news to Washington with a box of gold dust as proof.

The following year thousands of gold seekers set out to make their fortunes. A forty-niner who wished to reach California from the East had a choice of three routes, all of them dangerous:

1. Sail 18,000 miles around South America and up the Pacific coast—suffering from storms, seasickness, and spoiled food.
2. Sail to the narrow Isthmus of Panama, cross overland (and risk catching a deadly tropical disease), and then sail to California.
3. Travel the trails across North America—braving rivers, prairies, mountains, and all the hardships of the trail.

Because the adventure was so difficult, most gold seekers were young men. "A gray beard is almost as rare as a petticoat," observed one miner. Luzena Wilson said that during the six months she lived in the mining city of Sacramento, she saw only two other women.

Reading **History**
A. Categorizing
What were the three different types of transportation that people took to get to California?

HISTORY through ART

Clipper ship companies used advertising cards such as this one to convince Easterners that their line provided the fastest, most pleasant voyages.

How has the artist tried to project a positive image for sailing west?

Nearly everyone in the United States owns at least one pair of faded, comfortable blue jeans. The first jeans were invented for California miners.

In 1873, a man named Levi Strauss wanted to sell sturdy pants to miners. Strauss made his pants out of the strongest fabric he could buy—cotton denim. He reinforced the pockets with copper rivets so that they could hold heavy tools without ripping.

For more than 125 years, jeans have remained popular. Levi Strauss's pants have proved to be durable in more ways than one.

Life in the Mining Camps

The mining camps had colorful names like Mad Mule Gulch, Hangtown, and Coyote Diggings. They began as rows of tents along the streams flowing out of the Sierra Nevada. Gradually, the tents gave way to rough wooden buildings that housed stores and saloons.

Mining camps could be dangerous. One woman who lived in the region wrote about camp violence.

A VOICE FROM THE PAST

In the short space of twenty-four days, we have had murders, fearful accidents, bloody deaths, a mob, whippings, a hanging, . . . and a fatal duel.

Louise Clappe, quoted in *Frontier Women*

The mining life was hard for other reasons. Camp gossip told of miners who grew rich overnight by finding eight-pound nuggets, but in reality, such easy pickings were rare. Miners spent their days standing knee-deep in icy streams, where they sifted through tons of mud and sand to find small amounts of gold. Exhaustion, poor food, and disease all damaged the miners' health.

Not only was acquiring gold brutally difficult, but the miners had to pay outrageously high prices for basic supplies. In addition, gamblers and con artists swarmed into the camps to swindle the miners of their money. As a result, few miners grew rich.

Reading **History**
B. Making Inferences Why do you think life in the mining camps was so rough?

Miners from Around the World

About two-thirds of the forty-niners were Americans. Most of these were white men—many from New England. However, Native Americans, free blacks, and enslaved African Americans also worked the mines.

Thousands of experienced miners came from Sonora in Mexico. Other foreign miners came from Europe, South America, Australia, and China. Most of the Chinese miners were peasant farmers who fled from a region that had suffered several crop failures. By the end of 1851, one of every ten immigrants was Chinese.

Used to backbreaking labor in their homeland, the Chinese proved to be patient miners. They would take over sites that American miners had abandoned because the easy gold was gone. Through steady, hard work, the Chinese made these "played-out" sites yield profits. American miners resented the success of the Chinese and were suspicious of their different foods, dress, and customs. As the numbers of Chinese miners grew, American anger toward them also increased.

Reading **History**
C. Analyzing Causes Why did some Americans resent Chinese miners?

Surface Mining

Gold is found in cracks, called veins, in the earth's rocky crust. As mountains and other outcrops of rock erode, the gold veins come to the surface. The gold breaks apart into nuggets, flakes, and dust. Flood waters then wash it downhill into stream beds. To mine this surface gold, forty-niners had to use tools designed to separate it from the mud and sand around it. American miners learned some technology from Mexicans who came from the mining region of Sonora.

Miners shoveled dirt into the sluice. The rushing water carried lightweight materials along with it. Heavy gold sank to the bottom and was trapped between the ridges.

A sluice was a series of long boxes with ridges on the bottom. Water ran through the sluice, which angled downward.

Although this photograph shows American and Chinese miners working together, in many places Americans chased the Chinese away.

Mexican miners introduced the use of the pan. A miner would fill a pan with dirt and water. Then he would swirl the pan. Water sloshed over the sides, carrying lightweight minerals with it. Gold settled in the bottom.

CONNECT TO HISTORY

1. **Drawing Conclusions**
   Which mining method could be used by an individual miner and which needed a group of miners? Explain your answer.

   S See Skillbuilder Handbook, page R13.

CONNECT TO TODAY

2. **Researching** How is gold mined today?

For more about the California gold rush . . .

RESEARCH LINKS
CLASSZONE.COM

Conflicts Among Miners

A mixture of greed, anger, and prejudice caused some miners to cheat others. For example, I. B. Gilman promised to free an enslaved African American named Tom if he saved enough gold. For more than a year, Tom mined for himself after each day's work was done. When he finally had $1,000, Gilman gave him a paper saying he was free. The next day, the paper suspiciously disappeared. Even though Tom was certain he had been robbed, he couldn't prove it. He had to work for another year before Gilman would free him.

Once the easy-to-find gold was gone, American miners began to force Native Americans and foreigners such as Mexicans and Chinese out of the gold fields to reduce competition. This practice increased after California became a state in 1850. One of the first acts of the California state legislature was to pass the Foreign Miners Tax, which imposed a tax of $20 a month on miners from other countries. That was more than most could afford to pay. As the tax collectors arrived in the camps, most foreigners left.

*Reading*History
D. Analyzing Causes How did the state government make mining harder for foreigners?

Driven from the mines, the Chinese opened shops, restaurants, and laundries. So many Chinese owned businesses in San Francisco that their neighborhood was called Chinatown, a name it still goes by today.

The Impact of the Gold Rush

By 1852, the gold rush was over. While it lasted, about 250,000 people flooded into California. This huge migration caused economic growth that changed California permanently. The port city of San Francisco grew to become a center of banking, manufacturing, shipping, and trade. Its population exploded from around 400 in 1845 to 35,000 in 1850. Sacramento became the center of a productive farming region.

However, the gold rush ruined many *Californios*. The newcomers did not respect *Californios,* their customs, or their legal rights. In many cases,

CAUSE AND EFFECT: *U.S. Expansion, 1846–1853*

CAUSE		EFFECT
Westward trails move thousands to new territories.	▶	Oregon Territory acquired by the United States.
Austin and others colonize Texas.	▶	Texas Revolution
United States annexes Texas.	▶	War with Mexico
Mexican Cession acquired by the United States.	▶	United States expands "sea to sea."
Transcontinental railroad route needed.	▶	Gadsden Purchase
Thousands of gold seekers rush to California.	▶	California becomes a state.

SKILLBUILDER Interpreting Charts
1. Which two causes are related to transportation?
2. Which cause fulfilled the nation's "manifest destiny"?

Americans seized their property. For example, Mariano Vallejo lost all but 300 acres of his huge estate. Even so, their Spanish heritage became an important part of California culture.

Native Americans suffered even more. Thousands of them died from diseases brought by the newcomers. The miners hunted down and killed thousands more. The reason was the Anglo-American belief that Native Americans stood in the way of progress. By 1870, California's Native American population had fallen from 150,000 to only about 58,000.

A final effect of the gold rush was that by 1849 California had enough people to apply for statehood. Skipping the territorial stage, California applied to Congress for admission to the Union and was admitted as a free state in 1850. Although its constitution outlawed slavery, it did not grant African Americans the vote.

For some people, California's statehood proved to be the opportunity of a lifetime. The enslaved woman Nancy Gooch gained her freedom because of the law against slavery. She then worked as a cook and washerwoman until she saved enough money to buy the freedom of her son and daughter-in-law in Missouri. Nancy Gooch's family moved to California to join her. Eventually, they became so prosperous that they bought Sutter's sawmill, where the gold rush first started.

On a national level, California's statehood created turmoil. Before 1850, there was an equal number of free states and slave states. Southerners feared that because the statehood of California made free states outnumber slave states, Northerners might use their majority to abolish slavery. As Chapter 18 explains, conflict over this issue threatened the survival of the Union.

Reading **History**

E. Recognizing Effects What impact did the gold rush have on the people who lived in California before the forty-niners came?

Mariano Vallejo, unhappy that *Californio* culture was ignored in the new American California, named his home "Tear of the Mountain."

Section 4 Assessment

1. Terms & Names
Explain the significance of:
- forty-niner
- *Californio*
- Mariano Vallejo
- John Sutter
- James Marshall
- California gold rush

2. Taking Notes
Use a chart like the one shown to review and record hardships faced by the forty-niners.

HARDSHIPS	
In the camps	
At work mining	

Which hardships would you have found most difficult?

3. Main Ideas
a. How did the California gold rush get started?

b. Why didn't many forty-niners become rich?

c. How did women and people of different racial, ethnic, or national groups contribute to the California gold rush?

4. Critical Thinking
Recognizing Effects What were some of the effects of the California gold rush?

THINK ABOUT
- changes in San Francisco
- California's bid for statehood

ACTIVITY OPTIONS

SCIENCE

TECHNOLOGY

Research the hazards of mining gold and either plan a **science exhibit** or give an **electronic presentation.**

VISUAL SUMMARY

Manifest Destiny

United States in 1810

Trails West

Mountain men and traders opened trails in the Far West. Pioneers then went west to gain land, wealth, or religious freedom.

The Texas Revolution

Americans moved into the Mexican territory of Texas. Conflicts led those Americans to revolt, and Texas gained independence.

The War with Mexico

President Polk wanted to expand the nation. He negotiated to gain Oregon. The United States fought Mexico to gain much of the Southwest.

The California Gold Rush

The discovery of gold lured thousands of people to California. California's economy and population grew, resulting in statehood.

United States in 1853

TERMS & NAMES

Briefly explain the significance of each of the following.

1. mountain man
2. Oregon Trail
3. Stephen Austin
4. *Tejano*
5. Antonio López de Santa Anna
6. manifest destiny
7. Bear Flag Revolt
8. Mexican Cession
9. forty-niner
10. California gold rush

REVIEW QUESTIONS

Trails West (pages 377–383)

1. What were three reasons why people moved west?
2. What were the three main trails that led to the West?
3. How did the Mormons make the land in Utah productive?

The Texas Revolution (pages 384–389)

4. Why were Texans unhappy with Mexican rule?
5. Why were the battles of the Alamo and San Jacinto important to the Texas Revolution?

The War with Mexico (pages 390–395)

6. What areas did the United States gain as a result of Americans' belief in manifest destiny?
7. How is the Bear Flag Revolt related to the War with Mexico?
8. What lands did the United States acquire as a result of the Treaty of Guadalupe Hidalgo?

The California Gold Rush (pages 396–401)

9. Who were four groups of people who became forty-niners?
10. What were three ways California changed because of the gold rush?

CRITICAL THINKING

1. USING YOUR NOTES

	Types of people who traveled there	Why they went there	Key events that allowed the U.S. to take ownership of the territory
New Mexico			
Utah			
Oregon			
Texas			
California			

Using your completed chart, answer the questions below.

a. In what ways were the reasons people went west similar?
b. Which of the five regions listed on your chart entered the United States peacefully?
c. Which event added the most territory to the United States?

2. ANALYZING LEADERSHIP

Think about the leaders discussed in this chapter. What characteristics did they have that made them good leaders?

3. THEME: EXPANSION

How did the idea of manifest destiny help bring about the expansion of the United States?

4. DRAWING CONCLUSIONS

How did the War with Mexico and the California gold rush contribute to the cultural diversity of the United States?

5. APPLYING CITIZENSHIP SKILLS

What were the different viewpoints that people held about the War with Mexico?

Interact with History

Based on this chapter, what do you think you would have gained or lost by going west?

HISTORY SKILLS

1. INTERPRETING MAPS: Movement

Study the map. Answer the questions.

Settlement of Texas

- Amarillo
- Dallas
- El Paso
- T E X A S
- Austin
- Houston
- San Antonio

Gulf of Mexico

35°N
30°N
25°N
105°W
100°W
95°W

N

Legend:
- Before 1800
- Between 1800 and 1850
- Between 1850 and 1870
- Between 1870 and 1890
- After 1890

Basic Map Elements

a. What is the subject of the map?

b. What years are covered by the map?

c. What do the colors indicate?

Interpreting the Map

d. Which area of Texas was settled first?

e. In what general direction was Texas settled?

2. INTERPRETING PRIMARY SOURCES

This photograph was taken of a man who planned to go to California to find gold. Study the photo carefully. Answer the questions.

a. What does the photo reveal about the man's expectations of danger?

b. What does the photo suggest about how successful he hopes to be?

ALTERNATIVE ASSESSMENT

1. INTERDISCIPLINARY ACTIVITY: Science

Creating a Diagram Do research to learn how gold is deposited into veins in the earth and how erosion later exposes the gold. Draw diagrams showing the processes of gold vein formation and erosion. Share your diagram with the class.

2. COOPERATIVE LEARNING ACTIVITY

Creating a News Magazine Show With the support of President Polk, Congress declared war on Mexico in 1846. Though many Americans supported the decision, some groups felt that war with Mexico was unnecessary and unjust. Working with a small group, create a news magazine show that explores the different viewpoints surrounding the Mexican War. Research these opinions. Then write and perform the news magazine for the class. One student should be the moderator, while the other students in the group should choose one of the following groups to represent.

a. President Polk and his supporters

b. Northerners, including Abraham Lincoln and Frederick Douglass

c. Southerners

3. TECHNOLOGY ACTIVITY

Making a Class Presentation Life in the mining camps was not like life "back east." Information about the camps comes from primary sources, like diaries and newspaper articles. Using the Internet and library, find sources about life in the mining camps.

For more about gold mining . . .

INTERNET ACTIVITY
CLASSZONE.COM

Your sources might include:

- images of mines, miners, or miners' shacks
- images of items that the general store sold to miners
- tales of the gold fields
- information about the diversity of cultures in the camps

4. HISTORY PORTFOLIO

Review the concept of manifest destiny. Then write a brief report listing the political, economic, and social roots of the concept. Be sure to use standard grammar, spelling, sentence structure, and punctuation in your report. Add your report to your portfolio.

Additional Test Practice, pp. S1–S33

TEST PRACTICE
CLASSZONE.COM

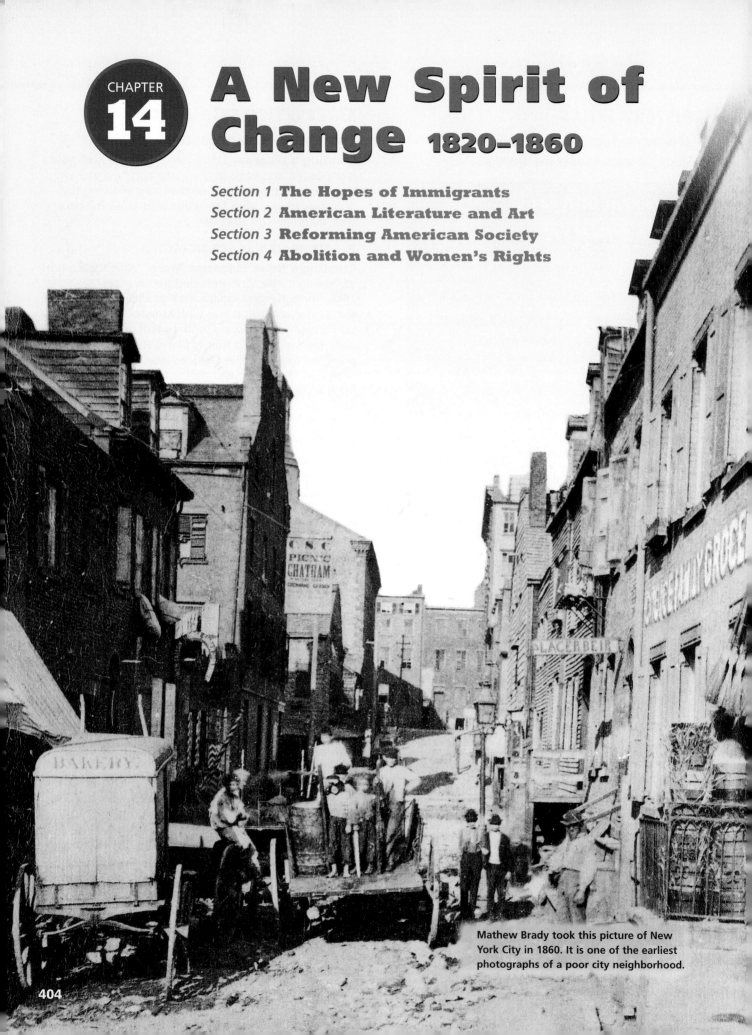

CHAPTER 14

A New Spirit of Change 1820–1860

Section 1 **The Hopes of Immigrants**
Section 2 **American Literature and Art**
Section 3 **Reforming American Society**
Section 4 **Abolition and Women's Rights**

Mathew Brady took this picture of New York City in 1860. It is one of the earliest photographs of a poor city neighborhood.

These immigrants live in New York. This one room is their whole apartment.

Women and children have few legal rights. For example, a married woman's earnings are controlled by her husband.

Many people want to outlaw the sale of alcohol. They believe drinking causes poverty.

Many children do not go to school.

You are a writer who moves to New York in the mid-1800s. A newspaper hires you to write about reform. One day, you hear a speaker call for the end of slavery. Another day you talk to a factory worker whose pay has been cut. In the city, you see great poverty and suffering.

What reforms do you think will most benefit American society?

What Do You Think?

- How might you persuade Americans to change life in the city?
- What are the problems that you see in these two pictures?
- Should reform come about through new laws or through individual actions?

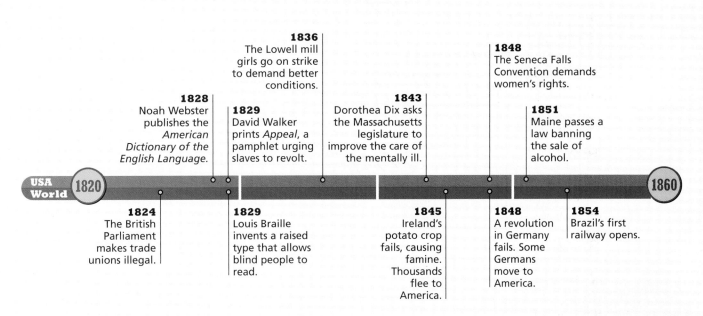

1836
The Lowell mill girls go on strike to demand better conditions.

1848
The Seneca Falls Convention demands women's rights.

1828
Noah Webster publishes the *American Dictionary of the English Language.*

1829
David Walker prints *Appeal*, a pamphlet urging slaves to revolt.

1843
Dorothea Dix asks the Massachusetts legislature to improve the care of the mentally ill.

1851
Maine passes a law banning the sale of alcohol.

USA
World   1820   1860

1824
The British Parliament makes trade unions illegal.

1829
Louis Braille invents a raised type that allows blind people to read.

1845
Ireland's potato crop fails, causing famine. Thousands flee to America.

1848
A revolution in Germany fails. Some Germans move to America.

1854
Brazil's first railway opens.

BEFORE YOU READ

Previewing the Theme

Impact of the Individual In the mid-1800s, millions of Europeans moved to the United States and changed its culture. Writers and artists also shaped American culture. In addition, many individuals worked to reform society in such areas as education and the antislavery movement. Chapter 14 describes how individuals changed America.

This engraving shows a woman teaching a young slave to read, even though it was illegal to do so. The boy grew up, escaped, and became a great reformer—Frederick Douglass.

What Do You Know?

What do you think were the worst problems in the United States in the mid-1800s? How do you think people tried to solve them?

THINK ABOUT
- stories or films that are set in this period
- problems that exist now
- the actions people take to solve today's problems

What Do You Want to Know?

What would you like to learn about the way individuals changed the United States in the mid-1800s? Record your questions in your notebook before you read the chapter.

READ AND TAKE NOTES

Reading Strategy: Comparing To understand the many influences on U.S. culture, learn to compare. Comparing means examining the similarities between people, actions, or ideas. The chart below will help you compare the influences that various people had upon America in the middle of the 19th century. Use the chart to take notes about how people changed America. Also take notes about people who tried to have an influence but failed.

 See Skillbuilder Handbook, page R9.

	How People Influenced America in the Mid-1800s
Immigrants	
Writers	
Reformers	
Abolitionists	
Women	

The Hopes of Immigrants

①

TERMS & NAMES
emigrant
immigrant
steerage
push-pull factor
famine
prejudice
nativist

MAIN IDEA	WHY IT MATTERS NOW
In the mid-1800s, millions of Europeans came to the United States hoping to build a better life.	These Germans, Irish, and Scandinavians had a strong influence on American culture.

ONE AMERICAN'S STORY

In June 1831, Gjert Hovland (YEHRT HAHV•LIHND) and his family left Norway for America. After a few years, Hovland wrote to a friend in Norway. He boasted that in the United States a poor man's vote counted as much as a rich man's vote. Americans could travel and work freely. The United States had so much opportunity that Hovland wondered why anyone would choose to stay hungry in Norway.

A VOICE FROM THE PAST

It would greatly please me to learn that all of you who are in need and have little chance of supporting yourselves and your families have decided to leave Norway and come to America; for, even if many more come, there will still be room here for all. Those who are willing to work will not lack employment or business here.

Gjert Hovland, letter to Torjuls Maeland, April 22, 1835

Advertisements for land attracted immigrants, who came to the United States with only what could fit in trunks like the one shown above.

Millions of people like Hovland decided to become **emigrants,** or people who leave a country. Arriving in the United States, they became **immigrants,** or people who settle in a new country. This section explains how immigrants enriched the United States with their work and their cultures.

Why People Migrated

Most immigrants endured hardships to come to America. Although some, like Hovland, brought their families, many immigrant men came alone and suffered loneliness. Nearly all immigrants made the ocean voyage in **steerage,** the cheapest deck on a ship. In steerage, hundreds of people lived jammed together for ten days to a month. Conditions were filthy. Many passengers became ill or died on the journey.

Despite the hard passage, immigrants flocked to the United States during the mid-1800s. They came from Britain, Ireland, Germany, Scandinavia (Sweden, Denmark, and Norway), and China. Most came from Europe. What made them come to America? Historians talk about

PULL

1. **Freedom**

2. **Economic opportunity**

3. **Abundant land**

PUSH

1. **Population growth**

2. **Agricultural changes**

3. **Crop failures**

4. **Industrial Revolution**

5. **Religious and political turmoil**

push-pull factors. These forces push people out of their native lands and pull them toward a new place. **Push factors** included the following:

1. **Population growth.** Better food and sanitation caused Europe's population to boom after 1750, and the land became overcrowded.

2. **Agricultural changes.** As Europe's population grew, so did cities. Landowners wanted to make money selling food to those cities. New methods made it more efficient to farm large areas of land than to rent small plots to tenants. So landlords forced tenants off the land.

3. **Crop failures.** Poor harvests made it difficult for small farmers to pay their debts. Some of these farmers chose to start over in America. Crop failures also led to hunger, causing people to emigrate.

4. **Industrial Revolution.** Goods produced in factories became cheaper than goods produced by artisans. Suddenly out of work, some artisans took factory jobs. Others emigrated.

5. **Religious and political turmoil.** To escape religious persecution, Quakers fled Norway and Jews left Germany. Also, many Germans came to America after a revolution in Germany failed in 1848.

Immigrants chose the United States because of three main **pull factors**:

1. **Freedom.** As Gjert Hovland wrote, "Everyone has the freedom to practice the teaching and religion he prefers."

2. **Economic opportunity.** Immigrants sought a land where they could support their families and have a better future. Immigration often rose during times of U.S. prosperity and fell during hard times.

3. **Abundant land.** The acquisition of the Louisiana Purchase and the Mexican Cession gave the United States millions more acres of land. To land-starved Europeans, America was a land of opportunity.

Vocabulary
tenant: renter

Vocabulary
artisan: skilled worker

Reading **History**
A. Solving Problems Many of the push factors were problems. Which pull factors were solutions to which problems?

Scandinavians Seek Land

Public land in America was sold for $1.25 an acre, which lured thousands of Scandinavians. At first, their governments tried to keep them at home. A Swedish law of 1768 restricted the right to emigrate. But growing poverty in Scandinavia caused officials to cancel this law in 1840.

Scandinavian clergymen also tried to halt the emigration. At first, they warned their church members against leaving the homeland. Eventually, though, the preachers realized their words had little effect. Some of them even went to America themselves.

Reading History

B. Making Inferences Why do you think Scandinavians moved to places that felt familiar?

In the United States, Scandinavians chose regions that felt familiar. Many settled in the Midwest, especially Minnesota and Wisconsin. These states had lakes, forests, and cold winters like their homelands. A high proportion of Scandinavian immigrants became farmers.

Germans Pursue Economic Opportunity

Like the Scandinavians, many Germans moved to the Midwest. Germans especially liked Wisconsin because the climate allowed them to grow their traditional crop of oats. Some moved to Milwaukee, Wisconsin, because the Catholic bishop there was German. (In the 1800s, German Christian immigrants included both Catholics and Protestants.)

Germans also settled in Texas. In New Braunfels, a group of German nobles bought land and sold it in parcels to German immigrants. The town had to survive poor harvests and conflicts with Native Americans, but it eventually prospered. Germans also founded Fredericksburg, Texas, which still retains its German culture today.

Immigrants from Germany settled in cities as well as on farms or the frontier. German artisans opened businesses as bakers, butchers, carpenters, printers, shoemakers, and tailors. Many German immigrants achieved great success. For instance, in 1853 John Jacob Bausch and Henry Lomb started a firm to make eyeglasses and other lenses. Their company became the world's largest lens maker.

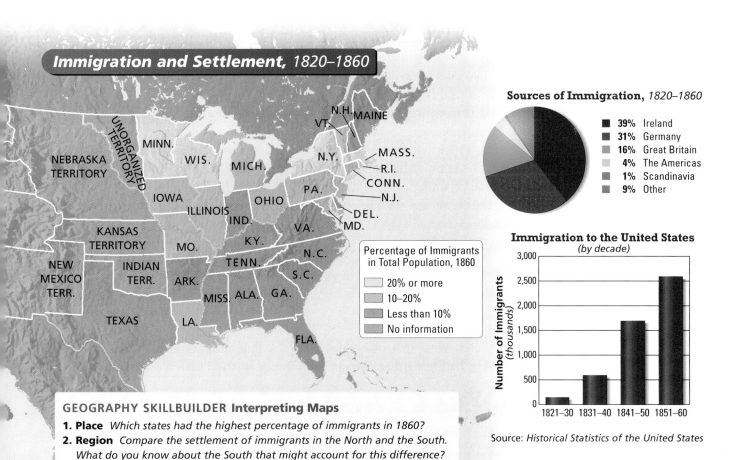

Immigration and Settlement, *1820–1860*

Sources of Immigration, *1820–1860*

- **39%** Ireland
- **31%** Germany
- **16%** Great Britain
- **4%** The Americas
- **1%** Scandinavia
- **9%** Other

Percentage of Immigrants in Total Population, 1860

- 20% or more
- 10–20%
- Less than 10%
- No information

Immigration to the United States
(by decade)

Number of Immigrants *(thousands)* — 1821–30, 1831–40, 1841–50, 1851–60

GEOGRAPHY SKILLBUILDER Interpreting Maps

1. **Place** Which states had the highest percentage of immigrants in 1860?
2. **Region** Compare the settlement of immigrants in the North and the South. What do you know about the South that might account for this difference?

Source: *Historical Statistics of the United States*

Some German immigrants were Jews. Many of them worked as traveling salespeople. They brought pins, needles, pots—and news—to frontier homes and mining camps. In time, some opened their own general stores. Other Jews settled in cities, where many found success. For example, Alexander Rothschild worked as a grocer upon arriving in Hartford, Connecticut, in the 1840s. By 1851, he ran a popular hotel.

The Germans were the largest immigrant group of the 1800s and strongly influenced American culture. Many things we think of as originating in America came from Germany—the Christmas tree, gymnasiums, kindergartens, and the hamburger and frankfurter.

daily life

IMMIGRANT CULTURE

To maintain their culture, immigrants continued many of their traditional activities in the United States. For example, German culture is rich in music. German immigrants put together marching bands, symphony orchestras, and choruses.

In Ireland, many of the Irish had poured their energy into defying the British. This gave them experience with political organization. As a result, Irish immigrants became active in U.S. politics, especially in the cities.

The Irish Flee Hunger

Most Irish immigrants were Catholic. Protestant Britain had ruled Ireland for centuries—and controlled the Catholic majority by denying them rights. Irish Catholics could not vote, hold office, own land, or go to school. Because of the poverty produced by Britain's rule, some Irish came to America in the early 1800s.

Then, in 1845, a disease attacked Ireland's main food crop, the potato, causing a severe food shortage called a **famine**. The Irish Potato Famine killed 1 million people and forced many to emigrate. By 1854, between 1.5 and 2 million Irish had fled their homeland.

In America, Irish farmers became city-dwellers. Arriving with little or no savings, many of these immigrants had to settle in the port cities where their ships had docked. By 1850, the Irish made up one-fourth of the population of Boston, New York, Philadelphia, and Baltimore.

The uneducated Irish immigrants arrived with few skills and had to take low-paying, back-breaking jobs. Irish women took in washing or worked as servants. The men built canals and railroads across America. So many Irishmen died doing this dangerous work that people said there was "an Irishman buried under every [railroad] tie." In 1841, British novelist Charles Dickens observed the huts in which railroad workers lived.

Background
The hamburger and frankfurter are named after the German cities Hamburg and Frankfurt am Main.

Reading **History**
C. Drawing Conclusions How did the effects of British rule make it hard for Irish immigrants to America to find good jobs?

A VOICE FROM THE PAST
The best were poor protection from the weather; the worst let in the wind and rain through the wide breaches in the roofs of sodden grass and in the walls of mud; some had neither door nor window; some had nearly fallen down.

Charles Dickens, quoted in *To Seek America*

The Irish competed with free blacks for the jobs that nobody else wanted. Both groups had few other choices in America in the 1800s.

U.S. Cities Face Overcrowding

Immigrants like the Irish and Germans flocked to American cities. So did native-born Americans, who hoped for the chance to make a better living. Between 1800 and 1830, New York's population jumped from 60,489 to 202,589. St. Louis doubled its population every nine years. Cincinnati grew even faster, doubling every seven years.

Rapid urban growth brought problems. Not enough housing existed for all the newcomers. Greedy landlords profited from the housing shortage by squeezing large apartment buildings onto small lots. Using every inch of space for rooms, these cramped living quarters lacked sunlight and fresh air. Their outdoor toilets overflowed, spreading disease. In such depressing urban neighborhoods, crime flourished.

American cities were unprepared to tackle these problems. In fact, before 1845, New York City had no public police force. Until the 1860s, it had only a volunteer fire department. And in 1857, the rapidly growing city had only 138 miles of sewers for 500 miles of streets.

Reading **History**
D. Identifying Problems What problems were politicians trying to solve by offering to help new immigrants?

Most immigrant groups set up aid societies to help newcomers from their country. Many city politicians also offered to assist immigrants in exchange for votes. The politicians set up organizations to help new arrivals find housing and work.

Some Americans Oppose Immigration

Some native-born Americans feared that immigrants were too foreign to learn American ways. Others feared that immigrants might come to outnumber natives. As a result, immigrants faced anger and prejudice. **Prejudice** is a negative opinion that is not based on facts. For example,

CITIZENSHIP TODAY

Becoming a Citizen

Most immigrants who came to America in the 1800s shared one thing: an appreciation for the nation's values and laws. As a result, many chose to become U.S. citizens.

This trend continues today. In recent decades, more than half a million Vietnamese have immigrated to the United States. Many became citizens of their new country. One of them was Lam Ton, who is a successful restaurant owner in Chicago. Ton viewed U.S. citizenship as both a privilege and a duty. "We have to stick to this country and help it do better," he said.

Each year, immigrants from around the world are sworn in as U.S. citizens on Citizenship Day, September 17. But first they must pass a test on English, the U.S. political system, and the rights and duties of citizenship.

This young immigrant proudly holds up his certificate of citizenship.

How Does Someone Become a Citizen?

1. In a small group, discuss what questions you would ask those seeking to become U.S. citizens.

2. Create a citizenship test using your questions.

3. Have another group take the test and record their scores.

4. Use the McDougal Littell Internet site to link to the actual U.S. citizenship test. Compare it to your test.

See Citizenship Handbook, page 265.

For more about becoming a U.S. citizen . . .

In 1844, a riot took place between Catholics and non-Catholics in Philadelphia. Several people were killed.

some Protestants in the 1800s believed that Catholics threatened democracy. Those Protestants feared that the Pope, the head of the Roman Catholic Church, was plotting to overthrow democracy in America.

Native-born Americans who wanted to eliminate foreign influence called themselves **nativists.** Some nativists refused to hire immigrants and put up signs like "No Irish need apply." In cities like New York and Boston, nativists formed a secret society. Members promised not to vote for any Catholics or immigrants running for political office. If asked about their secret group, they said, "I know nothing about it."

In the 1850s, nativists started a political party. Because of the members' answers to questions about their party, it was called the Know-Nothing Party. It wanted to ban Catholics and the foreign-born from holding office. It also called for a cut in immigration and a 21-year wait to become an American citizen. The Know-Nothings did elect six governors. But they disappeared quickly as a national party. Their northern and southern branches couldn't agree on the issue of slavery.

In spite of such barriers as prejudice, the immigrants of the 1800s had a strong impact on American culture. Writers and artists of the 1800s also shaped American culture. Section 2 discusses their influence.

Background
Protestants feared the Pope because in many European countries, the Catholic Church worked closely with the ruling monarchs.

Section 1 Assessment

1. Terms & Names

Explain the significance of:
- emigrant
- immigrant
- steerage
- push-pull factor
- famine
- prejudice
- nativist

2. Taking Notes

Use a cluster diagram like the one below to record details about immigration, such as which groups came, where they settled, and how they influenced America.

3. Main Ideas

a. What were the push-pull factors that led to immigration?

b. How did the arrival of so many immigrants affect U.S. cities?

c. What was the Know-Nothing Party, and what was its point of view about immigration?

4. Critical Thinking

Analyzing Causes How did the rapid increase in immigration cause conflict?

THINK ABOUT
- why Irish immigrants and free blacks competed for jobs
- the growth of cities and the problems it created
- the prejudices of nativists
- religious differences

ACTIVITY OPTIONS

TECHNOLOGY

ART

Plan a **multimedia presentation** or design a **Web page** that shows immigrants the advantages of settling in the United States.

② American Literature and Art

TERMS & NAMES
romanticism
Hudson River
  school
transcendentalism
civil disobedience

MAIN IDEA	WHY IT MATTERS NOW
Inspired by nature and democratic ideals, writers and artists produced some of America's greatest works.	Nineteenth-century writers such as Hawthorne and Thoreau laid the foundation for American literature.

ONE AMERICAN'S STORY

As a young man, Washington Irving published articles that made fun of society in the early 1800s. Although he studied to be a lawyer, he eventually made writing his full-time career.

Irving wrote some of the first stories to describe America. For example, "Rip Van Winkle" tells of a man in New York State. Rip wakes up after a 20-year nap to find everything changed. He goes to the inn, which once had a picture of King George on its sign.

A VOICE FROM THE PAST

The red coat was changed for one of blue and buff, a sword was held in the hand instead of a sceptre [staff of authority], the head was decorated with a cocked hat, and underneath was painted in large characters, GENERAL WASHINGTON.

Washington Irving, "Rip Van Winkle"

While Rip slept, the Americans had fought and won their revolution!

Irving's work helped to win European respect for American writing for the first time. This section discusses other individuals of the 1800s who created uniquely American literature and art.

In another Irving tale, "The Legend of Sleepy Hollow," a spooky creature—perhaps a ghost from the Revolution—chases a teacher.

Writing About America

Irving and other writers were influenced by a style of European art called **romanticism.** It stressed the individual, imagination, creativity, and emotion. It drew inspiration from nature. American writers turned their interest in nature into a celebration of the American wilderness.

Many books featured the wilderness. James Fenimore Cooper wrote five novels about the dramatic adventures of wilderness scout Natty Bumppo. One that remains popular is *The Last of the Mohicans.* Francis Parkman wrote a travel book, *The Oregon Trail,* about the frontier trail.

HISTORY *through* ART

Asher Durand was a founder of the Hudson River school of painting. His best-known work, *Kindred Spirits,* was painted in 1849. This romantic work shows two artists inspired by a beautiful landscape. The figures in the painting are Durand's friends, the poet William Cullen Bryant and the painter Thomas Cole.

Compare this painting to the one on page 164. What, if any, change in style can you see in Durand's painting?

In addition, writers began to use a more American style. A teacher and lawyer named Noah Webster gave guidelines to that style in his *American Dictionary of the English Language.* Webster first published his dictionary in 1828. He later revised it in 1840. The dictionary gave American, not British, spellings and included American slang.

Other writers besides Irving celebrated America's past. Henry Wadsworth Longfellow wrote many poems that retold stories from history. For example, "Paul Revere's Ride" depicted the Revolutionary hero's ride to warn of a British attack. Generations of students memorized lines from the poem, such as, "One if by land, and two if by sea; / And I on the opposite shore will be."

Creating American Art

European styles continued to influence American artists, but some took these styles in new directions. One group of painters influenced by romanticism worked near the Hudson River in New York State. **Hudson River school** artists painted lush natural landscapes. Several members of this school went west for a change of scenery. For example, Albert Bierstadt took several trips to America's mountainous West. He produced huge paintings that convey the majesty of the American landscape. (See page 294.)

Background
The National
Audubon Society,
whose goal is the
protection of
wildlife today, is
named for John
James Audubon.

Other artists also went west. John James Audubon came to the United States from France at age 18. Traveling across the continent, Audubon sketched the birds and animals of his adopted country.

Enslaved African Americans also contributed to American art. They made beautiful baskets, quilts, and pottery. Most of these slaves remained anonymous, but one did not. David Drake worked in a South Carolina pottery factory and signed the pottery he created. He was the only factory worker to do so.

Following One's Conscience

By the 1840s, Americans took new pride in their emerging culture. Ralph Waldo Emerson, a New England writer, encouraged this pride. He urged Americans to cast off European influence and develop their own beliefs. His advice was to learn about life from self-examination and from nature as well as books.

"No law can be sacred to me but that of my nature."
Ralph Waldo Emerson

Emerson's student, Henry David Thoreau, followed that advice. In 1845, Thoreau moved to a simple cabin he had built by Walden Pond near the town of Concord, Massachusetts. Thoreau furnished it with only a bed, a table, a desk, and three chairs. He wrote about his life in the woods in *Walden*. Thoreau said that people should live by their own individual standards.

*Reading*History
A. Making
Inferences What
do you think it
means to "hear
a different
drummer"?

A VOICE FROM THE PAST

If a man does not keep pace with his companions, perhaps it is because he hears a different drummer. Let him step to the music which he hears, however measured or far away.

Henry David Thoreau, *Walden*

Emerson and Thoreau belonged to a group of thinkers with a new philosophy called **transcendentalism.** It taught that the spiritual world is more important than the physical world. It also taught that people can find the truth within themselves—through feeling and intuition.

Because Thoreau believed in the importance of individual conscience, he urged people not to obey laws they considered unjust. Instead of protesting with violence, they should peacefully refuse to obey those laws. This form of protest is called **civil disobedience.** For example, Thoreau did not want to support the U.S. government, which allowed slavery and fought the War with Mexico. Instead of paying taxes that helped to finance the war, Thoreau went to jail.

Another New England transcendentalist, Margaret Fuller, also called for change. In her magazine, *The Dial,* and in her book, *Woman in the Nineteenth Century,* Fuller argued for women's rights.

Connections TO LITERATURE

"CIVIL DISOBEDIENCE"

In his essay "Civil Disobedience," Thoreau wrote that "Under a government which imprisons any unjustly the true place for a just man is also a prison."

Thoreau did land in prison when he refused to pay his taxes. According to legend, Emerson visited Thoreau in jail and asked, "Why are you here?" Thoreau replied, "Why are you not here?"

In the 20th century, Mohandas K. Gandhi of India and Martin Luther King, Jr., of the United States both used civil disobedience to fight injustice.

Exploring the Human Heart

Like Thoreau, other writers broke with tradition. In 1855, poet Walt Whitman published *Leaves of Grass,* a book that changed American poetry. His bold, unrhymed poems praised ordinary people. Emily Dickinson lived in her family's home almost her entire life. She wrote poems on small pieces of paper that she sewed into booklets. Her subjects include God, nature, love, and death. Most of her 1,775 poems were published only after her death. Both Whitman and Dickinson shaped modern poetry by experimenting with language.

Fiction writers of the 1800s also shaped American literature. Edgar Allan Poe wrote terrifying tales that influence today's horror story writers. He also wrote the first detective story, "The Murders in the Rue Morgue."

Nathaniel Hawthorne depicted love, guilt, and revenge during Puritan times in *The Scarlet Letter.* The novel shows that harsh judgment without mercy can lead to tragedy. Hawthorne may have learned that lesson from his family history. One of his ancestors condemned people at the Salem witchcraft trials.

Herman Melville won fame by writing thrilling novels about his experiences as a sailor. In 1851, Melville published his masterpiece, *Moby Dick.* This novel tells about a man's destructive desire to kill a white whale. Although the novel was not popular when it was published, it is widely read now. Several movie versions exist.

These fiction writers portrayed the harmful effects of cruel actions. Other people thought that individuals could alter society for good. Section 3 describes those reformers.

*Reading*History

B. Recognizing Effects How did Poe influence the fiction that people read today?

Section 2 Assessment

1. Terms & Names

Explain the significance of:

- romanticism
- Hudson River school
- transcendentalism
- civil disobedience

2. Taking Notes

Use a chart like the one below to list important individual writers and artists. For each one, name or describe one of his or her works.

Writer or artist	His or her work

Which one would you like to learn more about? Why?

3. Main Ideas

a. What was romanticism and how did Americans adapt it?

b. What is civil disobedience and what did Thoreau do that is an example of it?

c. How did the writers of the mid-1800s shape modern literature?

4. Critical Thinking

Evaluating Why do you think the literature and art of the mid-1800s are still valued?

THINK ABOUT

- the way they feature U.S. history and culture
- their universal themes— themes that relate to all people in all time periods
- the way they reflect changes happening at that time

ACTIVITY OPTIONS

ART

TECHNOLOGY

Choose an American painting, sketch it, and make it into a **jigsaw puzzle;** or make an **audio recording** of a museum guide's description of it.

③ Reforming American Society

TERMS & NAMES

revival

Second Great Awakening

temperance movement

labor union

strike

Horace Mann

Dorothea Dix

MAIN IDEA	WHY IT MATTERS NOW
In the mid-1800s, several reform movements worked to improve American education and society.	Several laws and institutions, such as public schools, date back to this period.

ONE AMERICAN'S STORY

Anne Newport Royall was a travel writer. In her 1830 book *Letters from Alabama*, Royall recorded America's growing interest in religion. She also described hearing a preacher at a Tennessee **revival**, or meeting to reawaken religious faith.

A VOICE FROM THE PAST

His text was, "He that hath ears to hear, let him hear." The people must have been deaf indeed that could not have heard him. . . . He began low but soon bawled to deafening. He spit in his hands, rubbed them against each other, and then would smite them together, till he made the woods ring.

Anne Newport Royall, *Letters from Alabama*

This revival meeting took place during the Second Great Awakening—a rebirth of religious faith named after the Great Awakening of the 1700s.

Some preachers, like the one Royall saw, were circuit riders. A circuit rider rode from town to town, often holding his meetings in a tent. The preacher gave a sermon urging individuals to give up their sins. This section explains how, in the mid-1800s, many individuals called on Americans to reform, or to improve themselves and their society.

A Spirit of Revival

The renewal of religious faith in the 1790s and early 1800s is called the **Second Great Awakening.** Revivalist preachers said that anyone could choose salvation. This appealed to equality-loving Americans. Revivals spread quickly across the frontier. Settlers eagerly awaited the visits of preachers like Peter Cartwright. At the age of 16, Cartwright had given up a life of gambling and joined a Methodist Church. He became a minister and spent more than 60 years preaching on the frontier.

The revival also traveled to Eastern cities. There, former lawyer Charles Grandison Finney held large revival meetings. He preached that "all sin consists in selfishness" and that religious faith led people to help others. Such teaching helped awaken a spirit of reform. Americans began to believe that they could act to make things better.

Temperance pledges often displayed inspiring pictures and mottoes.

Temperance Societies

Led by churches, some Americans began the **temperance movement,** which is a campaign to stop the drinking of alcohol. Heavy drinking was common in the early 1800s. Some workers spent most of their wages on alcohol—leaving their families without enough money to live on. As a result, many women joined the temperance movement. "There is no reform in which women can act better or more appropriately than temperance," said Mary C. Vaughan.

Some temperance workers handed out pamphlets urging people to stop drinking. Others produced dramas, such as one entitled *The Drunkard,* to dramatize the evils of alcohol. In addition, temperance speakers traveled widely, asking people to sign a pledge to give up alcohol. By 1838, a million people had signed.

Temperance also won the support of business owners. Industry needed workers who could keep schedules and run machines. Alcohol made it hard for workers to do either. New England businessman Neal Dow led the fight to make it illegal to sell alcohol. In 1851, Maine banned the sale of liquor. By 1855, 13 other states passed similar laws. But many people opposed these laws, and most were repealed. Still, the movement to ban alcohol remained strong, even into the 20th century.

Reading **History**
A. Evaluating
How did the temperance movement affect the development of drama?

Vocabulary
repeal: to cancel

Fighting for Workers' Rights

As business owners tried to improve workers' habits, workers called for improvements in working conditions. Factory work was noisy, boring, and unsafe. In the 1830s, American workers began to organize.

The young women mill workers in Lowell, Massachusetts, started a labor union. A **labor union** is a group of workers who band together to seek better working conditions. In 1836, the mill owners raised the rent of the company-owned boarding houses where the women lived. About 1,500 women went on **strike,** stopping work to demand better conditions. Eleven-year-old Harriet Hanson helped lead the strikers.

A VOICE FROM THE PAST

I . . . started on ahead, saying, . . . "I don't care what you do, I am going to turn out, whether anyone else does or not," and I marched out, and was followed by the others. As I looked back at the long line that followed me, I was more proud than I have ever been since.

Harriet Hanson, quoted in *A People's History of the United States*

Other workers called for shorter hours and higher wages. In 1835 and 1836, 140 strikes took place in the eastern United States. Then the Panic of 1837 brought hard times. Jobs were scarce, and workers were afraid to cause trouble. The young labor movement fell apart. Even so, workers achieved a few goals. For example, in 1840 President Martin Van Buren ordered a ten-hour workday for government workers.

Background
President Van Buren's order reduced the workweek from 70 to 60 hours.

Improving Education

In the 1830s, Americans also began to demand better schools. In 1837, Massachusetts set up the first state board of education in the United States. Its head was **Horace Mann.** Mann called public education "the great equalizer." He also argued that "education creates or develops new treasures—treasures never before possessed or dreamed of by any one." By 1850, many Northern states had opened public elementary schools.

Boston opened the first public high school in 1821. A few other Northern cities followed suit. In addition, churches and other groups founded hundreds of private colleges in the following decades. Many were located in states carved from the Northwest Territory. These included Antioch and Oberlin Colleges in Ohio, the University of Notre Dame in Indiana, and Northwestern University in Illinois.

Women could not attend most colleges. One exception was Oberlin. It was the first college to accept women as well as men. In 1849, English immigrant Elizabeth Blackwell became the first woman to earn a medical degree in the United States. Despite such individual efforts, it was rare for a woman to attend college until the late 1800s.

African Americans also faced obstacles to getting an education. This was especially true in the South. There, teaching an enslaved person to read had been illegal since the Nat Turner Rebellion in 1831. Enslaved African Americans who tried to learn were brutally punished. Even in the North, most public schools barred African-American children.

Reading **History**
B. Making Inferences
Why do you think women and African Americans had a hard time getting an education?

Few colleges accepted African Americans. Those that did often took only one or two blacks at a time. The first African American to receive a college degree was Alexander Twilight in 1823. John Russwurm received one in 1826 and later began the first African-American newspaper.

Caring for the Needy

As some people promoted education, others tried to improve society's care for its weakest members. In 1841, **Dorothea Dix,** a reformer from Boston, was teaching Sunday school at a women's jail. She discovered some women who were locked in cold, filthy cells

Mary Jane Patterson was the first African-American woman to earn a college degree. She graduated from Oberlin in 1862 and went on to work as a teacher.

HORACE MANN
1796–1859

Horace Mann once said in a speech to students, "Be ashamed to die until you have won some victory for humanity." Mann had no reason to be ashamed. As a child, he knew poverty and hardship. He educated himself and later fought for public education for other people.

Toward the end of his life, Mann became president of Antioch College. It committed itself to education for both men and women and equal rights for African Americans.

DOROTHEA DIX
1802–1887

At the age of 12, Dorothea Dix left an unhappy home to go live with her grandparents in Boston. Just two years later, she began teaching little children.

In 1841, Dix saw the harsh treatment of mentally ill women. Society frowned upon women traveling alone, but Dix defied custom. She went by train to several places where the mentally ill were housed.

Dix wrote a report about her research. (See page 422.) That report changed the care of the mentally ill.

How might their backgrounds have motivated Dorothea Dix and Horace Mann to become leaders in reform movements?

simply because they were mentally ill. Visiting other jails, Dix learned that the mentally ill often received no treatment. Instead, they were chained and beaten. Dix pleaded with the Massachusetts Legislature to improve the care of the mentally ill. Later, she traveled all over the United States on behalf of the mentally ill. Her efforts led to the building of 32 new hospitals.

Some reformers worked to improve life for people with other disabilities. Thomas H. Gallaudet started the first American school for deaf children in 1817. Samuel G. Howe founded the Perkins School for the Blind in Boston in the 1830s.

Reformers also tried to improve prisons. In the early 1800s, debtors, lifelong criminals, and child offenders were put in the same cells. Reformers demanded that children go to special jails. They also called for the rehabilitation of adult prisoners. Rehabilitation means preparing people to live useful lives after their release from prison.

Reading **History**
C. Recognizing Effects How did reformers change the treatment of the mentally ill, the disabled, and prisoners?

Spreading Ideas Through Print

During this period of reform, Americans began to receive more information about how they should lead their lives. In the 1830s, cheaper newsprint and the invention of the steam-driven press lowered the price of a newspaper to a penny. Average Americans could afford to buy the "penny papers." Penny papers were also popular because, in addition to serious news, they published gripping stories of fires and crimes.

Hundreds of new magazines also appeared. One was the *Ladies' Magazine.* Its editor was Sarah Hale, a widow who used writing to support her family. The magazine advocated education for women. It also suggested that men and women were responsible for different, but equally important, areas of life. The magazine taught that a woman's area was the home and the world of "human ties." A man's area was politics and the business of earning a living for his family. Later, Hale edited *Godey's Lady's Book*, which published poems and stories as well as articles.

Creating Ideal Communities

While magazines sought to tell people how to live and reform movements tried to change society, some individuals decided to start over. They aimed to build an ideal society, called a utopia.

Two attempts at utopias were New Harmony, Indiana, and Brook Farm, Massachusetts. In both, residents received food and other necessities of life in exchange for work. However, both utopias experienced conflicts and financial difficulties. They ended after only a few years.

*Reading*History
D. Forming and Supporting Opinions Why do you think it was hard for utopias to succeed? Give reasons.

Religious belief led to some utopias. For example, the Shakers followed the beliefs of Ann Lee. She preached that people should lead holy lives in communities that demonstrate God's love to the world. When a person became a Shaker, he or she vowed not to marry or have children. Shakers shared their goods with each other, believed that men and women are equal, and refused to fight for any reason. Shakers set up communities in New York, New England, and on the frontier.

People called them *Shakers* because they shook with emotion during church services. Otherwise, Shaker life was calm. Shakers farmed and built simple furniture in styles that remain popular today. The childless Shakers depended on converts and adopting children to keep their communities going. In the 1840s, the Shakers had 6,000 members—their highest number. In 1999, only seven Shakers remained.

In the 1840s and 1850s, reform found a new direction. Many individuals began to try to win rights for two oppressed groups—women and enslaved persons. Section 4 discusses these efforts.

Section 3 Assessment

1. Terms & Names

Explain the significance of:
- revival
- Second Great Awakening
- temperance movement
- labor union
- strike
- Horace Mann
- Dorothea Dix

2. Taking Notes

Create a chart like the one below. Use it to list problems identified by reformers and their solutions to them.

Problem	Reformer's Solution

3. Main Ideas

a. How did the Second Great Awakening influence the reform movement?

b. How did labor unions try to force business owners to improve working conditions?

c. What were women's contributions to the reform movement?

4. Critical Thinking

Recognizing Effects What was the long-term impact of the reform movement that took place in the mid-1800s?

THINK ABOUT
- the changes reformers made in education, temperance, prisons, and the care of the disabled
- which of those changes are still in effect today

ACTIVITY OPTIONS

SPEECH
CIVICS

Think of a modern problem that is similar to an issue discussed in this section. Give a **speech** or write a **letter** to a government official suggesting a reform.

Report to the Massachusetts Legislature

Setting the Stage After traveling to several places where the mentally ill were kept, Dorothea Dix wrote a report describing the conditions she had discovered. In 1843, she presented her report to lawmakers to alert them to the horrible treatment of the mentally ill. This report has been called the "first piece of social research ever conducted in America." An excerpt from Dorothea Dix's report follows. **See Primary Source Explorer** ◎

Report to the Massachusetts Legislature

Gentlemen: . . . I come to present the strong claims of suffering humanity. I come to place before the Legislature of Massachusetts the condition of the miserable, the desolate, the outcast. I come as the **advocate**[1] of helpless, forgotten, insane, and idiotic men and women; of beings sunk to a condition from which the most unconcerned would start with real horror; of beings wretched in our prisons, and more wretched in our **almshouses**.[2]

I must confine myself to a few examples, but am ready to furnish other and more complete details, if required.

I proceed, gentlemen, briefly to call your attention to the *present* state of insane persons confined within this **Commonwealth**,[3] in *cages, closets, cellars, stalls, pens! Chained, naked, beaten with rods,* and *lashed* into obedience.

I offer the following extracts from my notebook and journal.

Springfield: In the jail, one lunatic woman, furiously mad, a state **pauper**,[4] improperly situated, both in regard to the prisoners, the keepers, and herself. It is a case of extreme self-forgetfulness and oblivion to all the decencies of life, to describe which would be to repeat only the grossest scenes. She is much worse since leaving Worcester. In the almshouse of the same town is a woman apparently only needing **judicious**[5] care and some well-chosen employment to make it unnecessary to confine her in solitude in a dreary unfurnished room. Her appeals for employment and companionship are most touching, but the mistress replied "she had no time to attend to her."

Lincoln: A woman in a cage. *Medford:* One idiotic subject chained, and one in a close stall for seventeen years. *Pepperell:* One often doubly chained, hand and foot; another violent; several peaceable now. *Brookfield:* One man caged, comfortable. *Granville:* One often closely confined, now losing the use of his

1. **advocate:** a person who pleads another person's cause.
2. **almshouses:** homes for poor people.
3. **Commonwealth:** one of four U.S. states whose constitution uses this term to describe their form of self-government; in this case, Massachusetts.
4. **pauper:** a person who lives on the state's charity.
5. **judicious:** wise and careful.

limbs from want of exercise. *Charlemont:* One man caged. *Savoy:* One man caged. *Lenox:* Two in the jail, against whose unfit condition there the jailer protests.

Dedham: The insane **disadvantageously**[6] placed in the jail. In the almshouse, two females in stalls, situated in the main building, lie in wooden bunks filled with straw; always shut up. One of these subjects is supposed curable. The overseers of the poor have declined giving her a trial at the hospital, as I was informed, on account of expense.

Besides the above, I have seen many who, part of the year, are chained or caged. The use of cages is all but universal. Hardly a town but can refer to some not distant period of using them; chains are less common; **negligences**[7] frequent; willful abuse less frequent than sufferings proceeding from ignorance, or want of consideration. I encountered during the last three months many poor creatures wandering reckless and unprotected through the country. . . . But I cannot **particularize.**[8] In traversing the state, I have found hundreds of insane persons in every variety of circumstance and condition, many whose situation could not and need not be improved; a less number, but that very large, whose lives are the saddest pictures of human suffering and degradation.

I give a few illustrations; but description fades before reality. . . .

Men of Massachusetts, I beg, I implore, I demand pity and protection for these of my suffering, outraged sex. . . . Become the benefactors of your race, the just guardians of the solemn rights you hold in trust. Raise up the fallen, **succor**[9] the desolate, restore the outcast, defend the helpless, and for your eternal and great reward receive the benediction, "Well done, good and faithful servants, become rulers over many things!"

A CLOSER LOOK

I HAVE SEEN MANY

Notice that Dix cites evidence from many different towns.

3. Why do you think she includes so many specific details in her report?

A CLOSER LOOK

MEN OF MASSACHUSETTS

When Dix says "Men of Massachusetts," she is still speaking to the members of the state legislature.

4. What does Dix want the Massachusetts Legislature to do?

6. **disadvantageously:** harmfully.

7. **negligences:** careless actions.

8. **particularize:** to name in detail.

9. **succor:** to give help during a time of need.

Interactive Primary Source Assessment

1. Main Ideas

a. On what evidence did Dorothea Dix base her report about "suffering humanity"?

b. How were the mentally ill treated in Massachusetts?

c. Who did Dorothea Dix ask to help to improve the care of the mentally ill?

2. Critical Thinking

Evaluating Dix succeeded in convincing the legislature to provide funds for new hospitals. What do you think made her report so persuasive?

THINK ABOUT
• the details included in the report
• how Dix got the information to write her report
• the techniques you would use to persuade someone

4 Abolition and Women's Rights

TERMS & NAMES
abolition
Frederick Douglass
Sojourner Truth
Underground Railroad
Harriet Tubman
Elizabeth Cady Stanton
Seneca Falls Convention
suffrage

MAIN IDEA	WHY IT MATTERS NOW
The spread of democracy led to calls for freedom for slaves and more rights for women.	The abolitionists and women reformers of this time inspired 20th–century reformers.

ONE AMERICAN'S STORY

African-American poet Frances Ellen Watkins Harper was free but grew up in the slave state of Maryland. Harper often wrote about the suffering of enslaved persons. For example, the poem excerpt below describes a woman whose child has been taken from her and sold.

A VOICE FROM THE PAST

They tear him from her circling arms,
Her last and fond embrace.
Oh! never more may her sad eyes
Gaze on his mournful face.

No marvel, then, these bitter shrieks
Disturb the listening air:
She is a mother, and her heart
Is breaking in despair.

Frances Ellen Watkins Harper, "The Slave Mother"

Frances Ellen Watkins Harper impressed audiences with her speaking ability as she called for reform.

In the 1850s, Harper lectured against slavery throughout the North. Later in her life, she called for other reforms, such as the right to vote for women. As this section explains, many individuals in the mid-1800s demanded equal rights for African Americans and women.

Abolitionists Call for Ending Slavery

Abolition, the movement to end slavery, began in the late 1700s. By 1804, most Northern states had outlawed slavery. In 1807, Congress banned the importation of African slaves into the United States. Abolitionists then began to demand a law ending slavery in the South.

David Walker, a free African American in Boston, printed a pamphlet in 1829 urging slaves to revolt. Copies of this pamphlet, *Appeal . . . to the Colored Citizens of the World,* made their way into the South. This angered slaveholders. When Walker heard that his life was in danger, he refused to run away. Shortly afterward, he died mysteriously.

A few Northern whites also fought slavery. In 1831, William Lloyd Garrison began to publish an abolitionist newspaper, *The Liberator,* in

Boston. Of his antislavery stand, he wrote, "I will not retreat a single inch—AND I WILL BE HEARD." Many people hated his views. In 1834, a furious mob in Boston grabbed Garrison and dragged him toward a park to hang him. The mayor stepped in and saved his life.

Two famous abolitionists were Southerners who had grown up on a plantation. Sisters Sarah and Angelina Grimké believed that slavery was morally wrong. They moved north and joined an antislavery society. At the time, women were not supposed to lecture in public. But the Grimkés lectured against slavery anyway. Theodore Weld, Angelina's husband, was also an abolitionist. He led a campaign to send antislavery petitions to Congress. Proslavery congressmen passed gag rules to prevent the reading of those petitions in Congress.

John Quincy Adams ignored the gag rules and read the petitions. He also introduced an amendment to abolish slavery. Proslavery congressmen tried to stop him. Such efforts, however, only weakened the proslavery cause by showing them to be opponents of free speech. Adams also defended a group of Africans who had rebelled on the slave ship *Amistad*. He successfully argued their case before the U.S. Supreme Court in 1841, and in 1842, the Africans returned home.

Eyewitnesses to Slavery

Two moving abolitionist speakers, **Frederick Douglass** and **Sojourner Truth,** spoke from their own experience of slavery. Douglass's courage and talent at public speaking won him a career as a lecturer for the Massachusetts Anti-Slavery Society. Poet James Russell Lowell said of him, "The very look and bearing of Douglass are an irresistible logic against the oppression of his race."

People who opposed abolition spread rumors that the brilliant speaker could never have been a slave. To prove them wrong, in 1845 Douglass published an autobiography that vividly narrated his slave experiences. Afterwards, he feared recapture by his owner, so he left America for a two-year speaking tour of Great Britain and Ireland. When Douglass returned, he bought his freedom. He began to publish an antislavery newspaper.

Sojourner Truth also began life enslaved. Originally named Isabella, Sojourner Truth was born in New York State. In 1827, she fled her owners and went to live with Quakers, who set her free. They also helped her win a court battle to recover her young son. He had been sold illegally into slavery in the South. A devout Christian, Truth changed her name in 1843 to reflect her life's work: to sojourn (or stay temporarily in a place) and "declare the truth to the people." Speaking for abolition, she drew huge crowds throughout the North.

*Reading*History
A. Drawing Conclusions How would the Grimké sisters' background help them as abolitionist speakers?

*Reading*History
B. Comparing How were Frederick Douglass and Sojourner Truth similar as abolitionists?

AMERICA'S HISTORY MAKERS

FREDERICK DOUGLASS
1817–1895

Douglass, born Frederick Bailey, was the son of a black mother and a white father. When he was eight, his owner sent him to be a servant for the Auld family. Mrs. Auld defied state law and taught young Frederick to read.

At the age of 16, Douglass returned to the plantation as a field hand. He endured so many whippings he later wrote, "I was seldom free from a sore back."

In 1838, he escaped to the North by hopping a train with a borrowed pass. To avoid recapture, he changed his last name.

How did Mrs. Auld unknowingly help Douglass become an abolitionist leader? Explain.

The Underground Railroad

Some abolitionists wanted to do more than campaign for laws ending slavery. Some brave people helped slaves escape to freedom along the Underground Railroad. Neither underground nor a railroad, the **Underground Railroad** was actually an aboveground series of escape routes from the South to the North. On these routes, runaway slaves traveled on foot. They also took wagons, boats, and trains.

Some enslaved persons found more unusual routes to freedom. For example, Henry Brown persuaded a white carpenter named Samuel A. Smith to pack him in a wooden box and ship him to Philadelphia. The box was only two and one half feet deep, two feet wide, and three feet long. It bore the label "This side up with care." Despite the label, Brown spent several miserable hours traveling head down. At the end of about 24 hours, Henry "Box" Brown climbed out of his box a free man in Philadelphia. Brown eventually made his way to Boston and worked on the Underground Railroad.

On the Underground Railroad, the runaways usually traveled by night and hid by day in places called stations. Stables, attics, and cellars all served as stations. At his home in Rochester, New York, Frederick Douglass hid up to 11 runaways at a time.

Harriet Tubman

The people who led the runaways to freedom were called conductors. One of the most famous conductors was **Harriet Tubman.** Born into slavery in Maryland, the 13-year-old Tubman once tried to save another slave from punishment. The angry overseer fractured Tubman's skull with a two-pound weight. She suffered fainting spells for the rest of her life but did not let that stop her from working for freedom. In 1849, Tubman learned that her owner was about to sell her. Instead, she escaped. She later described her feelings as she crossed into the free state of Pennsylvania: "I looked at my hands to see if I was the same person now that I was free. There was such a glory over everything."

After her escape, Harriet Tubman made 19 dangerous journeys to free enslaved persons. The tiny woman carried a pistol to frighten off slave hunters and medicine to quiet crying babies. Her enemies offered $40,000 for her capture, but no one caught her. "I never run my train off the track and I never lost a passenger," she proudly declared. Among the people she saved were her parents.

Now and then

THE UNDERGROUND RAILROAD

In 1996, historian Anthony Cohen took six weeks to travel from Maryland to Canada. Cohen followed the paths runaway slaves had taken 150 years earlier. He is shown below arriving in Canada.

Cohen walked, sometimes as much as 37 miles in a day. He also hitched rides on trains and canal boats.

About those long-ago slaves fleeing toward the hope of freedom, Cohen said, "They had no choice. . . . Nobody would do this if they didn't have to."

*Reading*History
C. Reading a Map
The map on page 431 shows the routes of the Underground Railroad. Notice that most of these routes led to Canada.

*Reading*History
D. Forming and Supporting Opinions Why do you think escaped slaves such as Brown, Douglass, and Tubman risked their lives to help free others?

William Lloyd Garrison

Even after being threatened with hanging, Garrison continued to publish his antislavery newspaper, *The Liberator.*

Sojourner Truth and Harriet Tubman

Truth spoke out for both abolition and women's rights. Tubman risked her life leading people to freedom on the Underground Railroad.

Lucretia Mott and Susan B. Anthony

An abolitionist, Mott also helped lead the movement for women's rights. Anthony fought for women's suffrage into the 20th century.

Women Reformers Face Barriers

Vocabulary
delegation: a group that represents a larger group

Other women besides the Grimké sisters and Sojourner Truth were abolitionists. Two of these were Lucretia Mott and **Elizabeth Cady Stanton**. Mott and Stanton were part of an American delegation that attended the World Anti-Slavery Convention in London in 1840. These women had much to say about their work. Yet when they tried to enter the convention, they were not allowed to do so. Men angrily claimed that it was not a woman's place to speak in public. Instead, the women had to sit silent behind a heavy curtain.

To show his support, William Lloyd Garrison joined them. He said, "After battling so many long years for the liberties of African slaves, I can take no part in a convention that strikes down the most sacred rights of all women."

Stanton applauded Garrison for giving up his chance to speak on abolition, the cause for which he had fought so long. "It was a great act of self-sacrifice that should never be forgotten by women."

However, most people agreed with the men who said that women should stay out of public life. Women in the 1800s enjoyed few legal or political rights. They could not vote, sit on juries, or hold public office. Many laws treated women—especially married women—as children. Single women enjoyed some freedoms, such as being able to manage their own property. But in most states, a husband controlled any property his wife inherited and any wages she might earn.

As the convention ended, Stanton and Mott decided it was time to demand equality for women. They made up their minds to hold a convention for women's rights when they returned home.

Elizabeth Cady Stanton's first memory was the birth of a sister when she was four. So many people said, "What a pity it is she's a girl!" that Stanton felt sorry for the new baby. She later wrote, "I did not understand at that time that girls were considered an inferior order of beings."

When Stanton was 11, her only brother died. Her father said, "Oh, my daughter, I wish you were a boy!" That sealed Stanton's determination to prove that girls were just as important as boys.

How did Stanton's childhood experiences motivate her to help other people besides herself?

The Seneca Falls Convention

Stanton and Mott held the **Seneca Falls Convention** for women's rights in Seneca Falls, New York, on July 19 and 20, 1848. The convention attracted between 100 and 300 women and men, including Frederick Douglass.

Before the meeting opened, a small group of planners debated how to present their complaints. One woman read aloud the Declaration of Independence. This inspired the planners to write a document modeled on it. The women called their document the Declaration of Sentiments and Resolutions. Just as the Declaration of Independence said that "All men are created equal," the Declaration of Sentiments stated that "All men and women are created equal." It went on to list several complaints or resolutions. Then it concluded with a demand for rights.

A VOICE FROM THE PAST

Now, in view of this entire disenfranchisement [denying the right to vote] of one-half the people of this country, their social and religious degradation—in view of the unjust laws above mentioned, and because women do feel themselves aggrieved, oppressed, and fraudulently deprived of their most sacred rights, we insist that they have immediate admission to all the rights and privileges which belong to them as citizens of the United States.

Seneca Falls Declaration of Sentiments and Resolutions, 1848

Reading **History**
E. Using Primary Sources Why did the women at the Seneca Falls Convention believe they deserved rights and privileges?

Every resolution won unanimous approval from the group except **suffrage,** or the right to vote. Some argued that the public would laugh at women if they asked for the vote. But Elizabeth Cady Stanton and Frederick Douglass fought for the resolution. They argued that the right to vote would give women political power that would help them win other rights. The resolution for suffrage won by a slim margin.

The women's rights movement was ridiculed. In 1852, the *New York Herald* poked fun at women who wanted "to vote, and to hustle with the rowdies at the polls" and to be men's equals. The editorial questioned what would happen if a pregnant woman gave birth "on the floor of Congress, in a storm at sea, or in the raging tempest of battle."

Continued Calls for Women's Rights

In the mid-1800s, three women lent powerful voices to the growing women's movement. Sojourner Truth, Maria Mitchell, and Susan B. Anthony each offered a special talent.

In 1851, Sojourner Truth rose to speak at a convention for women's rights in Ohio. Some participants hissed their disapproval. Because Truth supported the controversial cause of abolition, they feared her appearance would make their own cause less popular. But Truth won applause with her speech that urged men to grant women their rights.

A VOICE FROM THE PAST

I have heard much about the sexes being equal. I can carry as much as any man, and can eat as much too, if I can get it. I am as strong as any man. . . . If you have woman's rights give it to her and you will feel better. You will have your own rights, and they won't be so much trouble.

Sojourner Truth, quoted by Marius Robinson, convention secretary

This drawing shows a husband and wife fighting over who will "wear the pants in the family"— that is, who will rule the household.

THE DISCORD.

The scientist Maria Mitchell fought for women's equality by helping to found the Association for the Advancement of Women. Mitchell was an astronomer who discovered a comet in 1847. She became the first woman elected to the American Academy of Arts and Sciences.

Susan B. Anthony was a skilled organizer who worked in the temperance and antislavery movements. She built the women's movement into a national organization. Anthony argued that a woman must "have a purse [money] of her own." To this end, she supported laws that would give married women rights to their own property and wages. Mississippi passed the first such law in 1839. New York passed a property law in 1848 and a wages law in 1860. By 1865, 29 states had similar laws. (Anthony also fought for suffrage. See Chapter 22.)

But women's suffrage stayed out of reach until the 1900s, and the U.S. government did not fully abolish slavery until 1865. As you will read in the next chapter, the issue of slavery began to tear the nation apart in the mid-1800s.

Section 4 Assessment

1. Terms & Names

Explain the significance of:
- abolition
- Frederick Douglass
- Sojourner Truth
- Underground Railroad
- Harriet Tubman
- Elizabeth Cady Stanton
- Seneca Falls Convention
- suffrage

2. Taking Notes

On a time line like the one below, record significant individuals and events in the historical development of the abolition movement.

1807   1865

Why does the time line end in 1865?

3. Main Ideas

a. Why were freedom of speech and freedom of the press important to the abolitionist movement?

b. What were Frederick Douglass's contributions to the abolitionist movement?

c. What were Elizabeth Cady Stanton's contributions to the women's rights movement?

4. Critical Thinking

Drawing Conclusions Why do you think that many of the people who fought for abolition also fought for women's rights?

THINK ABOUT
- why they opposed slavery
- the social and economic position of women
- what the two causes had in common

ACTIVITY OPTIONS

TECHNOLOGY

DRAMA

With a partner, act out a meeting between a reformer from Section 3 and one from Section 4. **Videotape** their conversation or **perform** it for the class.

The Underground Railroad

The Underground Railroad was a network of people and places that hid escaping slaves and helped them reach safety in the North or in Canada. One reason slaves often went to Canada is that a U.S. federal law required people to return runaway slaves to their owners. Defying this law, both whites and blacks helped slaves to escape.

The map on page 431 shows the main escape routes. As the map shows, most of the slaves who escaped came from states bordering free states, such as Kentucky and Virginia. Distances from there to the North were relatively short, increasing the chances of reaching freedom. However, the number of slaves who escaped from the Deep South, such as Georgia and South Carolina, was very small, because of the long distances that had to be traveled. While no one knows the exact number, historians estimate that 40,000 to 100,000 people may have used the Underground Railroad on their journey from slavery to freedom.

Among the many people who helped slaves to freedom was former slave Harriet Tubman (far left). She became a well-known guide on the Underground Railroad. She is pictured with her husband (third from left), along with other formerly enslaved people.

ARTIFACT FILE

Identity Tag Enslaved persons were forced to wear tags that identified to whom they belonged.

Freedom Marker The "P" on the rock shown here told slaves that they were in Pennsylvania, a free state.

BRITISH TERRITORY

UNORGANIZED TERRITORY

Lake Superior

CANADA

Montreal

MAINE

VT.

N.H.

MINNESOTA
(Statehood
in 1858)

WISCONSIN

Lake Huron

Collingwood

NEW YORK

MASS.

Boston

MICHIGAN

Niagara Falls

Lake Ontario

CONN. R.I.

Lake Michigan

Detroit

Lake Erie

Erie

New York City

Brooklyn

IOWA

Chicago

Sandusky

PENNSYLVANIA

N.J.

ILLINOIS

INDIANA

OHIO

Baltimore

St. Louis

Cincinnati

MD.

DEL.

MISSOURI

Evansville

Ripley

Washington, D.C.

Ohio River

KANSAS TERRITORY

Cairo

KENTUCKY

VIRGINIA

Free States

Slave states

Routes of the
Underground Railroad

NORTH
CAROLINA

*ATLANTIC
OCEAN*

INDIAN
TERRITORY

ARKANSAS

Mississippi River

TENNESSEE

SOUTH
CAROLINA

ALABAMA

GEORGIA

MISSISSIPPI

N

LOUISIANA

TEXAS

| 0 | 200 Miles |
| 0 | 400 Kilometers |

New Orleans

FLORIDA

MEXICO

Gulf of Mexico

On-Line Field Trip

The National Underground Railroad Freedom Center is being built in Cincinnati, Ohio. Its collections will include artifacts and primary sources like this poster, which shows that substantial rewards were offered for the recapture of slaves.

For more about the Underground Railroad . . .

RESEARCH LINKS
CLASSZONE.COM

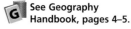

STOP THE THIEF!

One Hundred Dollars Reward.

Stolen from the Plantation of Mrs. E. S.
FARRAR, on the night of Saturday last, two Negro Girls.
One, MARY, low stature, heavy and squarely formed, very straight,
black hair—a very bright Mulatto.
The other named CINTA or CINDERILLA, dark Copper, common
height, has a flesh mole, near the left ear, and is well formed. Mary is
twenty years old and CINTA nineteen.
I will pay a reward of $25 for the apprehension of each, if taken in
the State, and $50 if taken out of it.
My address is Howardsville, Albemarle County, or Rockfish Depot,
Nelson County.

RICHARD T. FARRAR.

September 15, 1862.

CONNECT TO GEOGRAPHY

1. **Place** What geographic feature made it more likely that a slave in Missouri would escape to Michigan than to New York?

2. **Movement** In what way did the Underground Railroad differ from other migrations?

   G See Geography Handbook, pages 4–5.

CONNECT TO HISTORY

3. **Drawing Conclusions** How did the Underground Railroad reflect the American people's division over slavery?

A New Spirit of Change **431**

TERMS & NAMES

Briefly explain the significance of each of the following.

1. immigrant
2. push-pull factors
3. civil disobedience
4. revival
5. Second Great Awakening
6. labor union
7. abolition
8. Underground Railroad
9. Seneca Falls Convention
10. suffrage

REVIEW QUESTIONS

The Hopes of Immigrants (pages 407–412)

1. What factors influenced so many immigrants to come to America in the 1800s?
2. What did Germans contribute to U.S. identity?
3. How did the potato famine affect Irish emigration?

American Literature and Art (pages 413–416)

4. How did American artists display the love of nature in their paintings?
5. What did the transcendentalists believe?

Reforming American Society (pages 417–426)

6. Why did many business owners support the temperance movement?
7. Why was it hard for African Americans to receive an education?

Abolition and Women's Rights (pages 424–431)

8. Who published antislavery writings?
9. How did the Underground Railroad work?
10. What was the Seneca Falls Declaration of Sentiments and Resolutions?

CRITICAL THINKING

1. USING YOUR NOTES

How People Influenced America in the mid-1800s	
Immigrants	
Writers	
Reformers	
Abolitionists	
Women	

Using your chart, answer the questions below.

a. Who influenced America to make reforms?
b. Compare the goals of abolitionists and women. How are they alike?

2. ANALYZING LEADERSHIP

Who is someone from this chapter who exercised leadership by standing up for an unpopular position?

3. THEME: IMPACT OF THE INDIVIDUAL

Judging from what you read in this chapter, what methods can individuals use to influence their society?

4. APPLYING CITIZENSHIP SKILLS

Who in this chapter displayed good citizenship by taking responsibility for their own behavior or by providing for their families? Give examples.

5. FORMING AND SUPPORTING OPINIONS

If someone asked you what was the most important reform of this period, what would you say? Why?

Interact *with* History

Think about the laws you proposed before you read the chapter. Has your opinion changed since you read the chapter?

VISUAL SUMMARY

A New Spirit of Change

The Hopes of Immigrants
Immigrants came to America from many European countries. They strongly influenced American life and culture.

Reforming American Society
Inspired by a religious revival, a reform movement swept the country. It aided schools, the workplace, and the disabled.

IMPACT OF THE INDIVIDUAL

American Literature and Art
American writers and artists of the 1800s produced some of America's greatest works, which are still studied.

Abolition and Women's Rights
Whites and blacks united to fight slavery. Women abolitionists expanded their fight to include women's rights as well.

HISTORY SKILLS

1. INTERPRETING GRAPHS

School Enrollment, 1840–1870

Number of students in millions

8
7
6
5
4
3
2
1
0

1840   1850   1860   1870

Each book equals 1 million students.

Source: *Census of the United States*

Basic Graph Elements

a. On the graph, what does each book stand for?

Interpreting the Graph

b. How did school enrollment change during the period from 1840 to 1870?

c. What is the difference in school enrollment between 1840 and 1870?

2. INTERPRETING PRIMARY SOURCES

Philip Younger escaped from slavery and eventually went to Canada. He dictated this narrative to Benjamin Drew, who included it in his *A North-Side View of Slavery*.

> I served in slavery fifty-five years, and am now nearly seventy-two years old. . . . I got off by skill. I have children and grandchildren in slavery. I had rather starve to death here, being a free man, than to have plenty in slavery. I cannot be a slave any more—nobody could hold me as a slave now, except in irons. Old as I am, I would rather face the Russian fire, or die at the point of the sword, than go into slavery.
>
> **Philip Younger,** quoted in *A North-Side View of Slavery*

a. What do you think Younger means by saying, "I got off by skill"?

b. How important is his freedom to him?

ALTERNATIVE ASSESSMENT

1. INTERDISCIPLINARY ACTIVITY: Literature

Reading a Poem Aloud Choose a poem by Henry Wadsworth Longfellow that includes references to American history. Research the actual event to which the poem refers. Write an introduction that explains whether the poem portrays history accurately. Practice reading the poem until you are comfortable. Then present the poem to the class.

2. COOPERATIVE LEARNING ACTIVITY

Making an Annotated Map Working in a small group, create an annotated map of the Underground Railroad. Make an enlargement of the map of the Underground Railroad on page 431. Then annotate it, using some of the following suggestions.

- Do research to find the stories of slaves who escaped along the Underground Railroad.
- Put brief, typed summaries of a few stories on the map, with arrows connecting them to the right route.
- Draw illustrations of escape narratives and put them on the map.
- Research to discover appropriate songs and create a recording that can play as people view the map.

3. PRIMARY SOURCE EXPLORER

Preparing a Report Dorothea Dix did not just stand before the legislature and talk about her own opinions. She gathered evidence and then wrote a persuasive report. Using the CD-ROM, library, and Internet, find out more about her report. Plan your own report that you could present to the student government.

- Choose a problem in your school that you think needs addressing.
- Find evidence of the problem. This may involve interviewing other students or observing events.
- Decide what you want the student government or school board to do about the problem.
- Write your report. Make sure to refer to the evidence that you gathered.

4. HISTORY PORTFOLIO

Review the questions that you wrote for What Do You Want to Know? on page 406. Write a short report in which you explain the answers to your questions. Be sure to use standard grammar, spelling, sentence structure, and punctuation in your report. If any questions were not answered, do research to answer them. Add your report to your portfolio.

Additional Test Practice, pp. S1–S33

TEST PRACTICE CLASSZONE.COM

Pack Your Trunk

For immigrants, packing up to go to a new land required making hard decisions. Wealthy people could ship belongings ahead. Most immigrants, though, carried their belongings in burlap bags, knotted sheets, large baskets, or small trunks. Even children carried small bundles. Only the very basic items or very precious ones could be taken to the United States. Baggage contained practical items such as tools and household items. But some had personal items such as portraits of loved ones. A few people even carried bags of dirt from their home country!

ACTIVITY Pack a trunk with items needed for a new life in the United States. Explain why you chose the items that you have packed. Finally, write a letter to a friend or relative back in Europe about your journey to the United States.

TOOLBOX

Each group will need:

a shoebox	markers or colored pencils
assorted magazines (optional)	
	3 x 5 note cards
craft sticks	masking tape
drawing paper or posterboard	styrofoam (optional)

STEP BY STEP

1 **Form groups.** Each group should consist of about four or five students. Assign group members the following tasks:

- Do research on what people brought with them when immigrating to the United States.
- Choose ten items that you will need for your new life.
- Present your items in class and give reasons for selecting them.

2 **Research what immigrants brought with them.** In the library or on the Internet (see Researching Your Project on the next page), research what immigrants brought with them to the United States. Make a list of everything you think you'll need for a new life in the United States. Some basic items included

- books
- favorite or special clothing
- toys
- important documents

Real immigrants brought these items to the United States: a mortar and pestle (used to grind spices or medicines), a shoe brush, a coffee grinder, and a paisley shawl.

3 **Create your items.** From your list, choose ten items that you think will be most important to starting a new life. Then draw pictures of the selected items or cut pictures of them out of a magazine. Attach a craft stick to the back of the picture with masking tape.

4 **Write reasons.** Think of why you selected each of the ten items. Write the reasons for each item on a separate 3 x 5 note card. Attach each note card to the back of the corresponding picture.

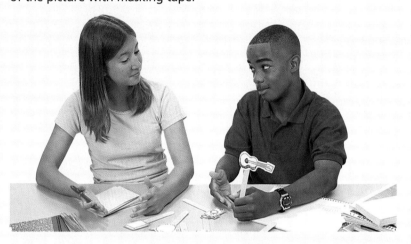

5 **Decorate the shoebox to look like a trunk.** Using the masking tape, affix your pictures to the rim of the shoebox, or use styrofoam in the bottom of the box to insert the pictures.

6 **Examine other groups' trunks.** Walk around the room and examine the contents of the other groups' trunks. Compare your trunk with that of your classmates. Share your reasons for selecting certain items.

WRITE AND SPEAK

Write a descriptive letter. Use the point of view of an immigrant. Write a letter to someone in your homeland describing your journey to the United States. Your letter might also describe what you miss most (personal belongings or people, for example) since the move. Read the letters to others in your class.

HELP DESK

For related information, see pages 407–412 in Chapter 14.

Researching Your Project

- *They Sought a New World* by William Kurdek and Margaret S. Englehart
- *American Immigration* by Edward G. Hartmann

For more about immigration . . .

RESEARCH LINKS
CLASSZONE.COM

Did You Know?

Most immigrants traveled in **steerage** or third class. It was the lowest area of the ship, where a steering mechanism was located. A family "berth," or space allotted, in steerage was about six feet square.

Before World War I, fares in steerage to the United States from Europe were never more than $35 and by 1900 were as low as $10.

Shipping companies often fed herring (a kind of fish) to the immigrants. Herring was cheap and nourishing. It was also thought to help prevent seasickness.

REFLECT & ASSESS

- What priorities did you use in selecting items for your trunk?

- Which items would have to be left behind if you only had a small bag for your belongings?

- Why do you think other groups selected items different from yours?

Civil War to Modern America

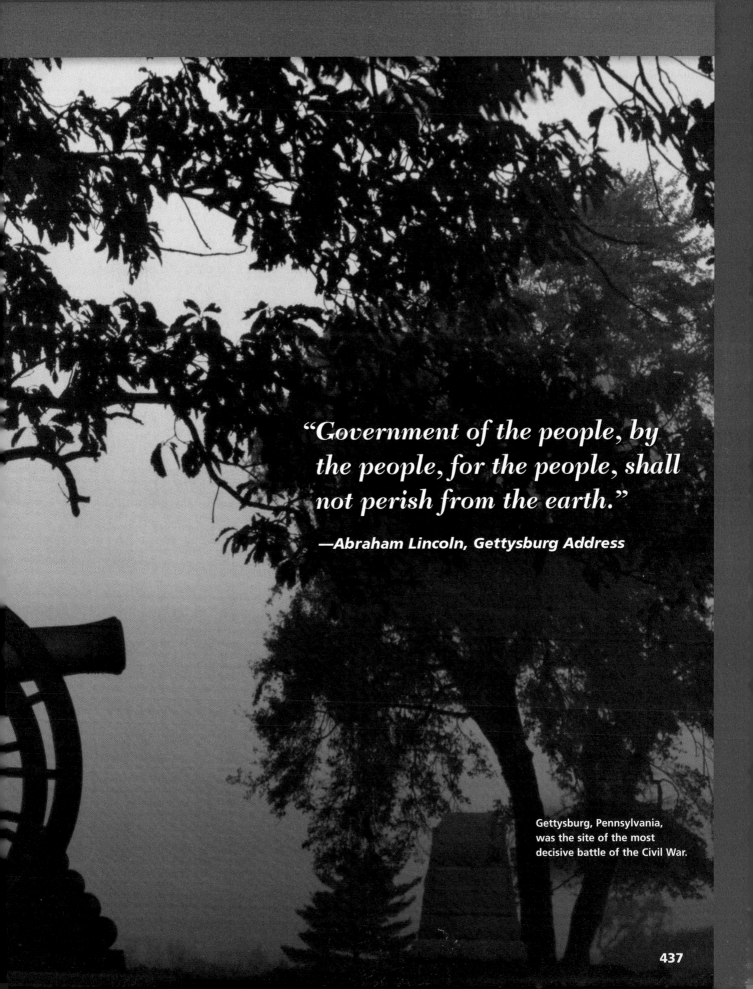

"*Government of the people, by the people, for the people, shall not perish from the earth.*"

—*Abraham Lincoln, Gettysburg Address*

Gettysburg, Pennsylvania, was the site of the most decisive battle of the Civil War.

CHAPTER 15

The Nation Breaking Apart

1846–1861

Abraham Lincoln and Stephen A. Douglas debate the issue of slavery in the 1858 Senate campaign in Illinois.

Disagreements over slavery caused people in the North and the South to lose their tempers. Passions ran so high that fights sometimes broke out between members of Congress.

You are a representative in Congress in the 1850s. The issue of slavery is causing heated debates. Tensions over slavery have risen so high that respectable men have turned to violence to settle their differences. You worry that soon this violence may affect the entire nation.

How would you keep the nation together?

What Do You Think?

- Why do you think people feel so strongly about slavery?

- Do you think debates, such as those between Lincoln and Douglas, could settle emotional issues without leading to violence?

1846 War with Mexico begins. Wilmot Proviso is introduced.

1848 Zachary Taylor is elected president.

1850 President Taylor dies. Millard Fillmore becomes president. Congress passes the Compromise of 1850.

1852 *Uncle Tom's Cabin* is published. Franklin Pierce is elected president.

1854 Congress passes the Kansas–Nebraska Act.

1856 James Buchanan is elected president.

1857 Chief Justice Roger B. Taney delivers his opinion in the *Dred Scott* case.

1860 Abraham Lincoln is elected president.

1861 The Confederate States of America is formed.

USA World | 1846 | 1861

1848 Rebellions erupt across Europe.

1850 Taiping Rebellion begins in China.

1856 War breaks out between Britain and Persia.

1861 Czar Alexander II frees the serfs in Russia.

BEFORE YOU READ

Previewing the Theme

Diversity and Unity As you read in Chapter 14, slavery heightened tensions between Northerners and Southerners. Many people feared that the issue might tear the nation apart. But most Americans hoped that they would be able to solve their problems peacefully. Chapter 15 describes how these tensions led to crisis. It also explains how Americans tried to keep their nation united and how those efforts failed.

What Do You Know?

What do you think about when you hear the terms *slavery* and *abolition?* Why do you think the issue of slavery caused so much anger and resentment?

THINK ABOUT
- what you've learned about differences between the North and the South from books, travel, television, or movies
- reasons people have violent conflicts today

What Do You Want to Know?

What questions do you have about the sectional crisis that led to the Civil War? Record them in your notebook before you read this chapter.

READ AND TAKE NOTES

Reading Strategy: Analyzing Causes Analyzing causes means looking closely at events and describing why they happened. The diagram below will help you analyze some of the causes of secession.

Use the diagram to take notes on how each issue drove the North and the South farther apart.

 See Skillbuilder Handbook, page R11.

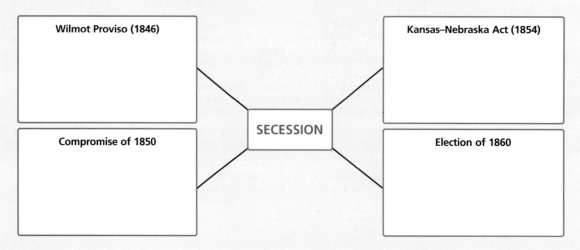

Wilmot Proviso (1846)		Kansas–Nebraska Act (1854)
	SECESSION	
Compromise of 1850		Election of 1860

① Growing Tensions Between North and South

TERMS & NAMES
Wilmot Proviso
Free-Soil Party
Henry Clay
Daniel Webster
Stephen A. Douglas
Compromise of 1850

MAIN IDEA

Disagreements between the North and the South, especially over the issue of slavery, led to political conflict.

WHY IT MATTERS NOW

Regional differences can make national problems difficult to resolve.

ONE EUROPEAN'S STORY

Alexis de Tocqueville [TOHK•vihl] was a young French government official from a wealthy family. In 1831, he set out to study American prisons and politics.

At one point, Tocqueville traveled in a steamship down the Ohio River. The river was the border between Ohio, a free state, and Kentucky, a slave state. Tocqueville noted what he saw on both sides of the river.

A VOICE FROM THE PAST

The State of Ohio is separated from Kentucky just by one river; on either side of it the soil is equally fertile, and the situation equally favourable, and yet everything is different. Here [on the Ohio side] a population devoured by feverish activity, trying every means to make its fortune. . . . There [on the Kentucky side] are people who make others work for them and show little compassion, a people without energy, mettle or the spirit of enterprise. . . . These differences cannot be attributed to any other cause but slavery. It degrades the black population and enervates [saps the energy of] the white.

Alexis de Tocqueville, *Journey to America*

Alexis de Tocqueville

Tocqueville's comment was aimed not at the Southern people as individuals but at the system of slavery itself. In this section, you will read about the differences between the North and the South. You will also learn how slavery led to political tensions that threatened to tear the nation apart.

North and South Take Different Paths

As you read in Chapter 11, the economies of the North and the South developed differently in the early 1800s. Although both economies were mostly agricultural, the North began to develop more industry and commerce. By contrast, the Southern economy relied on plantation farming.

The growth of industry in the North helped lead to the rapid growth of Northern cities. Much of this population growth came from immigration. In addition, immigrants and Easterners moved west and built farms in the new states formed from the Northwest Territory. Most canals and railroads ran east and west, helping the Eastern and

Economics *in* History

Trade

Trade is based on a simple idea. If you have something someone else needs or wants, and that person has something you need or want, you exchange, or trade, those two things. After the trade, you should both be better off than before.

The concept of trade works similarly for groups of people. For example, in the early 1800s, the South had few factories. Planters who wanted manufactured goods usually had to buy them from manufacturers in the North or in Europe. To have the cash to buy those goods, Southerners sold other goods, such as cotton, to the North and other countries. Each sold the goods they could produce in order to get money to buy the goods they could not make.

CONNECT TO HISTORY

1. **Solving Problems** What problem does trade help a country solve? How else could a country solve this problem?

    See Skillbuilder Handbook, page R18.

CONNECT TO TODAY

2. **Comparing** What goods do Americans sell to other countries today? What goods do Americans buy from other countries?

For more about trade . . .

 RESEARCH LINKS
CLASSZONE.COM

Northern States and Other Countries

Southern States

Midwestern states develop strong ties with each other.

The South developed differently than the North. A few wealthy planters controlled Southern society. They made great profits from the labor of their slaves. Much of this profit came from trade. Planters relied on exports, especially cotton. Because these plantations were so profitable, planters invested in slaves instead of industry. As a result, the South developed little industry.

Most Southern whites were poor farmers who owned no slaves. But even many of the nonslaveholding whites supported slavery because it kept them off the bottom of society.

Reading **History**
A. Making Generalizations How did the economies of the North and the South differ?

Antislavery and Racism

The issue of slavery caused tension between the North and the South. In the North, the antislavery movement had slowly been gaining strength since the 1830s. Abolitionists believed that slavery was unjust and should be abolished immediately. Many Northerners who opposed slavery took a less extreme position. Some Northern workers and immigrants opposed slavery because it was an economic threat to them. Because slaves did not work for pay, free workers feared that managers would employ slaves rather than them. Some workers were even afraid that the expansion of slavery might force workers into slavery to find jobs.

Despite their opposition to slavery, most Northerners, even abolitionists, were racist by modern standards. Many whites refused to go to school with, work with, or live near African Americans. In most states, even free African Americans could not vote.

Vocabulary
racist: having prejudice based on race

When Northern attacks on slavery increased, slaveholders defended slavery. Most offered the openly racist argument that white people were superior to blacks. Many also claimed that slavery helped slaves by introducing them to Christianity, as well as providing them with food, clothing, and shelter throughout their lives. Slaveholders were determined to defend slavery and their way of life. In this way, the different ideas about slavery brought the North and the South into conflict.

The Wilmot Proviso

After the Missouri Compromise in 1820, political disagreements over slavery seemed to go away. But new disagreements arose with the outbreak of the War with Mexico in 1846. Many Northerners believed that Southerners wanted to take territory from Mexico in order to extend slavery. To prevent that, Representative David Wilmot of Pennsylvania proposed a bill, known as the **Wilmot Proviso,** to outlaw slavery in any territory the United States might acquire from the War with Mexico.

But slaveholders believed that Congress had no right to prevent them from bringing slaves into any of the territories. They viewed slaves as property. The Constitution, they claimed, gave equal protection to the property rights of all U.S. citizens. The Wilmot Proviso removed the right of slaveholders to take their slaves, which they regarded as property, anywhere in the United States or its territories. Southerners claimed that the bill was unconstitutional.

The Wilmot Proviso divided Congress along regional lines. The bill passed the House of Representatives. But Southerners prevented it from passing the Senate.

Connections TO WORLD HISTORY

EXPANDING SLAVERY

William Walker, a Tennessee-born adventurer, wanted to take over land in Central America. In 1855, he joined an army of Nicaraguan rebels and seized power. Walker declared himself president of Nicaragua in 1856. As president, he legalized slavery there.

Troops from nearby countries drove him from power in 1857. The actions of men like Walker helped to convince Northerners that slaveholders were intent on expanding slavery beyond the U.S. South.

Even though the Wilmot Proviso never became law, it had important effects. It led to the creation of the **Free-Soil Party,** a political party dedicated to stopping the expansion of slavery. The party's slogan expressed its ideals—"Free Soil, Free Speech, Free Labor, and Free Men." The Free-Soil Party won more than ten seats in Congress in the election of 1848. More important, the party made slavery a key issue in national politics. Politicians could ignore slavery no longer.

Reading **History**
B. Recognizing Effects What were the effects of the Wilmot Proviso?

Controversy over Territories

By 1848, the nation's leaders had begun to debate how to deal with slavery in the lands gained from the War with Mexico. The proposed addition of new states threatened the balance in Congress between North and South. The discovery of gold in California brought thousands of people into that territory. There would soon be enough people in California for it to apply for statehood. Most California residents wanted their state to be a free state. But this would tip the balance of power clearly in favor of the North. Southerners wanted to divide California in half, making the northern half a free state and the southern half a slave state.

In 1849, President Zachary Taylor—who opposed the extension of slavery—proposed that California submit a plan for statehood that year, without going through the territorial stage. Taylor's plan gave Southern slaveholders little time to move to California with their slaves.

In March 1850, California applied to be admitted as a free state. With California as a free state, slave states would become a minority in the Senate just as they were in the House. Jefferson Davis, a senator from Mississippi, warned, "For the first time, we are about permanently to destroy the balance of power between the sections."

Background
U.S. land gains from the War with Mexico included all or parts of the future states of California, Nevada, Utah, Arizona, New Mexico, and Colorado.

The Compromise of 1850

California could not gain statehood, however, without the approval of Congress. And Congress was divided over the issue. Behind the scenes, statesmen sought compromise. Taking the lead was Senator **Henry Clay**

This engraving dramatically portrays the Senate debate over the Compromise of 1850.

Henry Clay led the Congress in creating compromises on several important issues during his long career.

John C. Calhoun of South Carolina opposed the Compromise of 1850. He believed the South had no reason to compromise on the issue of slavery.

Daniel Webster spoke eloquently in favor of the compromise.

444

of Kentucky. Clay had helped create the Missouri Compromise in 1820. Now Clay crafted a plan to settle the California problem.

*Reading*History

C. Reading a Map
Look at the map on page 448 to see how the Compromise of 1850 affected the territories open to slavery.

1. To please the North, California would be admitted as a free state, and the slave trade would be abolished in Washington, D.C.
2. To please the South, Congress would not pass laws regarding slavery for the rest of the territories won from Mexico, and Congress would pass a stronger law to help slaveholders recapture runaway slaves.

Many people on both sides felt they had to give up too much in this plan. But others were tired of the regional bickering. They wanted to hold the Union together. **Daniel Webster,** senator from Massachusetts, supported the compromise for the sake of the Union.

A VOICE FROM THE PAST

I wish to speak today, not as a Massachusetts man, nor as a Northern man, but as an American. . . . I speak today for the preservation of the Union. Hear me for my cause.

Daniel Webster, quoted in *The Annals of America*

The job of winning passage of the plan fell to Senator **Stephen A. Douglas** of Illinois. By the end of September, Douglas succeeded, and the plan, now known as the **Compromise of 1850,** became law.

Some people celebrated the compromise, believing that it had saved the Union. But the compromise would not bring peace. In the next section, you will learn how sectional tensions continued to rise.

AMERICA'S HISTORY MAKERS

STEPHEN A. DOUGLAS
1813–1861

Stephen A. Douglas was one of the most powerful members of Congress in the mid-1800s. In fact, he was called the "Little Giant" because he commanded great respect even though he was only five feet four inches tall.

Perhaps the most important issue that Douglas faced during his career was the expansion of slavery into the territories. Douglas privately hated slavery. But he did not believe a debate on morality would do any good. He suggested that the people of each territory should decide whether or not to allow slavery.

What groups of Americans agreed with Douglas's position on slavery?

Section 1 Assessment

1. Terms & Names

Explain the significance of:
- Wilmot Proviso
- Free-Soil Party
- Henry Clay
- Daniel Webster
- Stephen A. Douglas
- Compromise of 1850

2. Taking Notes

Use a chart like the one below to explain the effects of each cause.

Causes	Effects
Abolitionism	
Wilmot Proviso	
California's application for statehood	

Which issue do you think most threatened national unity?

3. Main Ideas

a. What were two ways that the North and the South differed by the mid-1800s?

b. In what ways was racism common in both the North and the South?

c. How did the War with Mexico lead to conflict between the North and the South?

4. Critical Thinking

Comparing and Contrasting How was the Compromise of 1850 similar to and different from the Missouri Compromise?

THINK ABOUT
- the regional tensions at the time the compromises were proposed
- who proposed each bill
- the provisions of the bills

ACTIVITY OPTIONS

TECHNOLOGY

SPEECH

Imagine you are a television news director. Plan a five-minute **documentary** or organize a **panel discussion** on the Compromise of 1850.

② The Crisis Deepens

TERMS & NAMES

Harriet Beecher Stowe

Uncle Tom's Cabin

Fugitive Slave Act

popular sovereignty

Kansas–Nebraska Act

John Brown

MAIN IDEA	WHY IT MATTERS NOW
Turmoil over slavery led to acts of violence.	Violence can make compromise more difficult.

ONE AMERICAN'S STORY

Harriet Beecher Stowe was outraged when she heard about the part of the Compromise of 1850 that would help slaveholders recapture runaway slaves. She described her feelings about the law.

> *A VOICE FROM THE PAST*
>
> Since the legislative act of 1850, when [I] heard . . . Christian and humane people actually recommending the remanding [returning of] escaped fugitives into slavery, as a duty binding on good citizens, . . . [I] could only think, These men and Christians cannot know what slavery is.
>
> Harriet Beecher Stowe, *Uncle Tom's Cabin*

Stowe's anger motivated her to write **Uncle Tom's Cabin,** a novel that portrayed slavery as brutal and immoral. In this section, you will learn how the Compromise of 1850 deepened the division between the North and the South.

Harriet Beecher Stowe

The Fugitive Slave Act

The 1850 law to help slaveholders recapture runaway slaves was called the **Fugitive Slave Act.** People accused of being fugitives under this law could be held without an arrest warrant. In addition, they had no right to a jury trial. Instead, a federal commissioner ruled on each case. The commissioner received five dollars for releasing the defendant and ten dollars for turning the defendant over to a slaveholder.

Southerners felt that the Fugitive Slave Act was justified because they considered slaves to be property. But Northerners resented the Fugitive Slave Act. It required Northerners to help recapture runaway slaves. It placed fines on people who would not cooperate and jail terms on people who helped the fugitives escape. In addition, Southern slave catchers roamed the North, sometimes capturing free African Americans.

The presence of slave catchers throughout the North brought home the issue of slavery to Northerners. They could no longer ignore the fact that, by supporting the Fugitive Slave Act, they played an important role in supporting slavery. They faced a moral choice. Should they obey the law and support slavery, or should they break the law and oppose slavery?

Uncle Tom's Cabin

*Reading*History
A. Analyzing Points of View
How did the play *Uncle Tom's Cabin* affect the development of drama in the United States?

Stowe published *Uncle Tom's Cabin* in 1852. It dramatically portrayed the moral issues of slavery. In fact, a play based on the book increased the popularity of drama as well as abolitionism. The book's main character was Uncle Tom, a respected older slave. The plot centers on Tom's life under three owners. Two of the owners were kind, but the third was cruel. The novel includes dramatic scenes, such as the dangerous escape of a slave named Eliza and her baby across the Ohio River.

A VOICE FROM THE PAST

Eliza made her desperate retreat across the river just in the dusk of twilight. The gray mist of evening, rising slowly from the river, enveloped her as she disappeared up the bank, and the swollen current and floundering masses of ice presented a hopeless barrier between her and her pursuer.

Harriet Beecher Stowe, *Uncle Tom's Cabin*

Stowe's book was wildly popular in the North. But white Southerners believed the book falsely criticized the South and slavery.

The Kansas–Nebraska Act

While the Fugitive Slave Act and *Uncle Tom's Cabin* heightened the conflicts between the North and the South, the issue of slavery in the territories brought bloodshed to the West. In 1854, Senator Stephen A. Douglas of Illinois drafted a bill to organize territorial governments for the Nebraska Territory. He proposed that it be divided into two territories—Nebraska and Kansas.

To get Southern support for the bill, he suggested that the decision about whether to allow slavery in each of these territories be settled by popular sovereignty. **Popular sovereignty** is a system where the residents vote to decide an issue. If this bill passed, it would result in getting rid of the Missouri Compromise by

Background
The Nebraska Territory was part of the Louisiana Purchase. It lay north of the 36° 30′ line, so the Missouri Compromise banned slavery there.

In 1854, Bostonians protested the capture of an African American by federal marshals under the Fugitive Slave Act.

447

Free and Slave States and Territories, *1820–1854*

Compromise of 1850

Missouri Compromise (1820–1821)

Kansas–Nebraska Act (1854)

NEBRASKA
TERRITORY

KANSAS
TERRITORY

- ☐ Free states
- ☐ Territory closed to slavery
- ☐ Slave states
- ☐ Territory open to slavery

GEOGRAPHY SKILLBUILDER Interpreting Maps

1. **Region** *What new free states and slave states entered the Union between 1820 and 1854?*
2. **Region** *How did the Kansas–Nebraska Act change the amount of territory open to slavery?*

allowing people to vote for slavery in territories where the Missouri Compromise had banned it.

As Douglas hoped, Southerners applauded the repeal of the Missouri Compromise and supported the bill. Even though the bill angered opponents of slavery, it passed. It became known as the **Kansas–Nebraska Act**. Few people realized that the act would soon turn Kansas into a battleground over slavery.

"Bleeding Kansas"

Proslavery and antislavery settlers rushed into the Kansas Territory, just west of Missouri, to vote for the territorial legislature. At the time of the election in March 1855, there were more proslavery settlers than antislavery settlers in the territory. But the proslavery forces did not want to risk losing the election. Five thousand Missourians came and voted in the election illegally. As a result, the official Kansas legislature was packed with proslavery representatives.

Antislavery settlers boycotted the official government and formed a government of their own. With political authority in dispute, settlers on both sides armed themselves. In May, a proslavery mob attacked the town of Lawrence, Kansas. The attackers destroyed offices and the

Vocabulary
boycott: refuse to participate in

house of the governor of the antislavery government. This attack came to be known as the Sack of Lawrence.

*Reading*History
B. Sequencing Events What events in Kansas preceded the Pottawatomie Massacre?

Onto this explosive scene came **John Brown,** an extreme abolitionist. To avenge the Sack of Lawrence, Brown and seven other men went to the cabins of several of his proslavery neighbors and murdered five people. This attack is known as the Pottawatomie Massacre, after the creek near where the victims were found. As news of the violence spread, civil war broke out in Kansas. It continued for three years, and the territory came to be called "Bleeding Kansas."

Violence in Congress

While violence was spreading in Kansas in the spring of 1856, blood was also being shed in the nation's capital. In late May, Senator Charles Sumner of Massachusetts delivered a speech attacking the proslavery forces in Kansas. His speech was packed with insults. Sumner even made fun of A. P. Butler, a senator from South Carolina.

Preston Brooks, a relative of Butler, heard about Sumner's speech. To defend Butler and the South, he attacked Sumner, who was sitting at his desk. Brooks hit Sumner over the head with his cane. Sumner tried to defend himself, but his legs were trapped. Brooks hit him 30 times or more, breaking his cane in the assault. (The painting on page 439 shows this event.)

Many Southerners cheered Brooks's defense of the South. But most Northerners were shocked at the violence in the Senate. "Bleeding Kansas" and "Bleeding Sumner" became rallying cries for antislavery Northerners and slogans for a new political party. In the next section, you will learn about the creation of the Republican Party.

STRANGE *but* True

PRESTON BROOKS'S CANE

Many Americans, Northerners and Southerners alike, were ashamed of the behavior of Sumner and Brooks. But sectional tensions were so high at the time that a large number of Southerners cheered Brooks for his actions.

A number of Brooks's supporters sent him new canes to replace the one he had broken while hitting Sumner on the head. Some of the canes were inscribed with mottoes such as "Hit Him Again."

Section 2 Assessment

1. Terms & Names

Explain the significance of:
• Harriet Beecher Stowe
• *Uncle Tom's Cabin*
• Fugitive Slave Act
• popular sovereignty
• Kansas–Nebraska Act
• John Brown

2. Taking Notes

Use a chart like the one below to compare Northern and Southern views of the issues listed.

Northern View	Issue	Southern View
	Fugitive Slave Act	
	Kansas–Nebraska Act	
	"Bleeding Kansas"	

3. Main Ideas

a. How did the book *Uncle Tom's Cabin* influence national politics?

b. Why was the Kansas–Nebraska Act so controversial?

c. What was the cause of "Bleeding Kansas"?

4. Critical Thinking

Solving Problems What would you have done to prevent the violence in Kansas?

THINK ABOUT
• the repeal of the Missouri Compromise
• popular sovereignty
• the actions of John Brown

ACTIVITY OPTIONS

LITERATURE

ART

Read a chapter of *Uncle Tom's Cabin*. Write a **book review** or make a series of **drawings** illustrating the story.

TERMS & NAMES
Republican Party
John C. Frémont
James Buchanan
Dred Scott v. *Sandford*
Roger B. Taney
Abraham Lincoln
Harpers Ferry

③ Slavery Dominates Politics

MAIN IDEA	WHY IT MATTERS NOW
Disagreement over slavery led to the formation of the Republican Party and heightened sectional tensions.	The Democrats and the Republicans are the major political parties of today.

ONE AMERICAN'S STORY

Joseph Warren, editor of the Detroit *Tribune,* wanted the antislavery parties of Michigan to join forces. In 1854, his newspaper pushed them to unite.

A VOICE FROM THE PAST

[A convention should be called] irrespective of the old party organizations, for the purpose of agreeing upon some plan of action that shall combine the whole anti-Nebraska, anti-slavery sentiment of the State, upon one ticket [set of candidates endorsed by a political party].

Detroit *Tribune*, quoted in *The Origins of the Republican Party*

This medal shows an early motto of the Republican Party. It also makes clear the Republican connection to the antislavery position of the Free-Soil Party.

By July, antislavery politicians from various parties, including the Whigs, Free-Soilers, and some Democrats, had settled their differences. On July 6, they met to form a new party "to concentrate the popular sentiment of this state against the aggression of the slave power." In memory of Thomas Jefferson, they called themselves Republicans. In this section, you will learn why the Republican Party was formed and how it changed American politics in the 1850s.

The Republican Party Forms

The creation of the Republican Party grew out of the problems caused by the Kansas–Nebraska Act of 1854. The law immediately caused a political crisis for the Whig Party. Southern Whigs had supported the bill for the same reason that Northern Whigs had opposed it: the bill proposed to open new territories to slavery. There was no room for compromise, so the party split.

The Southern Whigs were destroyed by the split. A few joined the Democratic Party. But most searched for leaders who supported slavery and the Union. The Northern Whigs, however, joined with other opponents of slavery and formed the **Republican Party**.

The Republicans quickly gained strength in the North. "Bleeding Kansas" was the key to the Republican rise. Many people blamed the violence on the Democrats. With the 1856 elections nearing, the

Republicans believed that they had an excellent opportunity to gain seats in Congress and win the presidency.

The Republicans needed a strong presidential candidate in 1856 to strengthen their young party. They nominated **John C. Frémont.** Young and handsome, Frémont was a national hero for his explorations in the West, which earned him the nickname the "Pathfinder."

Republicans liked Frémont for a couple of reasons. He had spoken in favor of admitting both California and Kansas as free states. Also, he had little political experience and did not have a controversial record to defend. Even so, the Republican position on slavery was so unpopular in the South that Frémont's name did not appear on the ballot there.

Reading **History**
A. Summarizing
Why did the Republicans nominate Frémont for president in 1856?

The Election of 1856

The Democrats nominated **James Buchanan** to run for the presidency in 1856. As minister to Great Britain, he had been in England since 1853 and had spoken neither for nor against the Kansas–Nebraska Act.

Buchanan took advantage of his absence from the country. He said little about slavery and claimed that his goal was to maintain the Union. Buchanan appealed to Southerners, to many people in the upper South and the border states, and to Northerners who were afraid that Frémont's election could tear the nation apart.

The American, or Know-Nothing, Party also nominated a presidential candidate in 1856. They chose Millard Fillmore, who had been president, following the death of Zachary Taylor, from 1850 until 1853. But the Know-Nothings were divided over slavery and had little strength.

The 1856 presidential election broke down into two separate races. In the North, it was Buchanan against Frémont. In the South, it was Buchanan against Fillmore. Buchanan won. He carried all the slave states except Maryland, where Fillmore claimed his only victory. Buchanan also won several Northern states.

Although he lost the election, Frémont won 11 Northern states. These results showed two things. First, the Republican Party was a major force in the North. Second, the nation was sharply split over slavery.

The Case of Dred Scott

The split in the country was made worse by the Supreme Court decision in the case of Dred Scott. Scott had been a slave in Missouri. His owner took him to live in territories where slavery was illegal. Then they returned to Missouri. After his owner's death, Scott sued for his freedom. He argued that he was a free man because he had lived in territories where slavery was illegal. His case, ***Dred Scott v. Sandford***, reached the Supreme Court in 1856.

THIRD-PARTY CANDIDATES

American politics has usually been dominated by two parties. Most third-party candidates, such as the Republican Frémont in 1856, lose elections. In 1998, Minnesotans broke that pattern when they elected for governor Jesse Ventura of the Reform Party (below).

One reason for Ventura's victory was his celebrity status. He had been a professional wrestler and the host of a popular radio show. His plain speaking appealed to many Minnesotans who felt the major parties were out of touch with the people.

Ventura was the first Reform Party candidate to gain a major political office.

Dred Scott (above) first sued for his freedom in 1846. The Supreme Court, led by Chief Justice Roger B. Taney (right), did not rule on the case until 1857.

In 1857, the Court ruled against Scott. Chief Justice **Roger B. Taney** [TAW•nee] delivered his opinion in the case. In it, he said that Dred Scott was not a U.S. citizen. As a result, he could not sue in U.S. courts. Taney also ruled that Scott was bound by Missouri's slave code because he lived in Missouri. As a result, Scott's time in free territory did not matter in his case.

In addition, Taney argued that Congress could not ban slavery in the territories. To do so would violate the slaveholders' property rights, protected by the Fifth Amendment. In effect, Taney declared legislation such as the Missouri Compromise unconstitutional.

Southerners cheered the Court's decision. Many Northerners were outraged and looked to the Republican Party to halt the growing power of Southern slaveholders.

Reading **History**
B. Recognizing Effects How did Taney's opinion affect the Missouri Compromise?

Lincoln and Douglas Debate

After the *Dred Scott* decision, the Republicans charged that the Democrats wanted to legalize slavery not only in all U.S. territories but also in all the states. They used this charge to attack individual Democrats. Stephen A. Douglas, sponsor of the Kansas–Nebraska Act, was one of their main targets in 1858. That year, Illinois Republicans nominated **Abraham Lincoln** to challenge Douglas for his U.S. Senate seat. In his first campaign speech, Lincoln expressed the Northern fear that Southerners wanted to expand slavery to the entire nation. He set the stage for his argument by using a metaphor from the Bible.

A VOICE FROM THE PAST

"A house divided against itself cannot stand." I believe this government cannot endure, permanently half slave and half free. I do not expect the Union to be dissolved—I do not expect the house to fall—but I do expect it will cease to be divided. It will become all one thing, or all the other.

Abraham Lincoln, Springfield, Illinois, June 16, 1858

Later in the year, the two men held formal debates across Illinois. The Lincoln–Douglas debates are now seen as models of political debate. At the time, the debates allowed people to compare the short, stocky, well-dressed Douglas with the tall, thin, gawky Lincoln.

The two men squarely addressed the nation's most pressing issue: the expansion of slavery. For Lincoln, slavery was "a moral, a social and a political wrong." But he did not suggest abolishing slavery where it already existed. He argued only that slavery should not be expanded.

Douglas did not share Lincoln's belief that it was the national government's role to prevent the expansion of slavery. Instead, he argued

CITIZENSHIP TODAY

Debating Points of View

Debate has long been an important method of exploring public issues. The Lincoln-Douglas debates drew crowds from all over Illinois to hear Lincoln and Douglas discuss the issues of the day. Debates such as these can help people find out about candidates' views.

Today, the National Forensic League (NFL) sponsors Lincoln-Douglas Debates, competitions for high school students. Many judges, actors, news commentators, and talk show hosts began to develop their debating skills in such competitions.

High school students can benefit from learning to defend their positions in debates. One student explained what she learned from NFL debates. "I learned about how to think really fast and how to respond."

Jessica Bailey of Apple Valley High School in Minnesota won second place in the national Lincoln-Douglas Debates competition in 1998.

How Do You Debate an Issue?

1. Choose a debate opponent and an issue to debate. (One NFL topic for national competition was whether the federal government should establish an educational policy to increase academic achievement in secondary schools in the United States.)
2. Research the topic you chose.
3. Agree on a format for your debate—how many minutes for presentation, rebuttal, and closing.
4. Debate your opponent in front of the class.
5. Find out how many students in the audience agree with each side, then ask for their reasons.

See Citizenship Handbook, page 269.

For more about debating . . .

that popular sovereignty was the best way to address the issue because it was the most democratic method to do so.

But popular sovereignty was a problem for Douglas. The Supreme Court decision in the *Dred Scott* case had made popular sovereignty unconstitutional. Why? It said that people could not vote to ban slavery, because doing so would take away slaveholders' property rights. In the debates, Lincoln asked Douglas if he thought people in a territory who were against slavery could legally prohibit it—despite the *Dred Scott* decision.

Douglas replied that it did not matter what the Supreme Court might decide about slavery because "the people have the lawful means to introduce it or exclude it as they please." Douglas won reelection. Lincoln, despite his loss, became a national figure and strengthened his standing in the Republican Party.

John Brown Attacks Harpers Ferry

In 1859, John Brown, who had murdered proslavery Kansans three years before, added to the sectional tensions. Brown had a plan. He wanted to inspire slaves to fight for their freedom. To do this, he planned to capture the weapons in the U.S. arsenal at **Harpers Ferry,** Virginia.

On October 16, 1859, Brown and 18 followers—13 whites and 5 blacks—captured the Harpers Ferry arsenal. They killed four people in the raid. Brown then sent out the word to rally and arm local slaves.

Reading **History**
C. Making Inferences Why were popular sovereignty and the opinion in the *Dred Scott* case inconsistent?

Vocabulary
arsenal: stock of weapons

HISTORY through ART

John Steuart Curry painted *The Tragic Prelude* between 1937 and 1942. He shows a wild-eyed John Brown standing on the bodies of Civil War soldiers.

What do you think Curry's views were on John Brown's role in U.S. history?

But no slaves joined the fight. The U.S. Marines attacked Brown at Harpers Ferry. Some of his men escaped. But Brown and six others were captured, and ten men were killed.

Brown was then tried for murder and treason. He was convicted and sentenced to hang. On the day he was hanged, abolitionists tolled bells and fired guns in salute. Southerners were enraged by Brown's actions and horrified by Northern reactions to his death.

As the nation headed toward the election of 1860, the issue of slavery had raised sectional tensions to the breaking point. In the next section, you will read about the election of 1860 and its effect on the nation.

Section 3 Assessment

1. Terms & Names

Explain the significance of:

- Republican Party
- John C. Frémont
- James Buchanan
- *Dred Scott* v. *Sandford*
- Roger B. Taney
- Abraham Lincoln
- Harpers Ferry

2. Taking Notes

Use a chart like the one below to take notes on the major events discussed in this section.

Election of 1856	
Dred Scott v. *Sandford*	
Lincoln–Douglas debates	
Harpers Ferry	

3. Main Ideas

a. What issues led to the creation of the Republican Party?

b. What consequences did the *Dred Scott* decision have for free blacks?

c. How did John Brown's attack on Harpers Ferry increase tensions between the North and the South?

4. Critical Thinking

Identifying Facts and Opinions How did Lincoln and Douglas disagree about slavery? Which of their views were facts, and which were opinions?

THINK ABOUT

- Lincoln's speech at Springfield in 1858
- Douglas's support of popular sovereignty

ACTIVITY OPTIONS

MATH

GEOGRAPHY

Do research to find election returns from the 1856 presidential election. Make **graphs** or draw a **map** to illustrate the results.

④ Lincoln's Election and Southern Secession

TERMS & NAMES
platform
secede
Confederate States
  of America
Jefferson Davis
Crittenden Plan

MAIN IDEA	WHY IT MATTERS NOW
The election of Lincoln led the Southern states to secede from the Union.	This was the only time in U.S. history that states seceded from the Union.

ONE AMERICAN'S STORY

In May 1860, Murat Halstead, a reporter for the Cincinnati *Commercial,* traveled to Chicago to cover the Republican convention. Most people assumed that William Seward of New York would win the party's presidential nomination. But there were other candidates, too.

Throughout the convention, candidates tried to win away Seward's delegates. As the other candidates hoped, Seward failed to win the nomination on the first ballot. Throughout the tense voting, Abraham Lincoln, a lesser-known candidate from Illinois, gained strength. Halstead described the scene as Lincoln received the winning votes.

In 1860, the Republican delegates met in Chicago at a convention hall known as the Wigwam.

A VOICE FROM THE PAST

There was a moment's silence. The nerves of the thousands, which through the hours of suspense had been subjected to terrible tension, relaxed, and as deep breaths of relief were taken, there was a noise in the Wigwam [convention hall] like the rush of a great wind [just before] a storm— and in another breath, the storm was there. There were thousands cheering with the energy of insanity.

Murat Halstead, *Caucuses of 1860*

Having won the nomination, Lincoln could turn his attention to winning the general election. In this section, you will learn about the election of 1860 and its role in pushing the nation toward civil war.

Political Parties Splinter

In April, a few weeks before the Republicans nominated Abraham Lincoln, the Democrats held their convention in Charleston, South Carolina. Northern and Southern Democrats disagreed over what to say about slavery in the party's **platform,** or statement of beliefs.

The Southerners wanted the party to defend slavery in the platform.

But Northerners wanted the platform to support popular sovereignty as a way of deciding whether a territory became a free state or a slave state. The Northerners won the platform vote, causing 50 Southern delegates to walk out of the convention.

The remaining delegates tried to nominate a presidential candidate. Stephen A. Douglas was the leading contender, but the Southerners who stayed refused to back him because of his support for popular sovereignty. Douglas could not win enough votes to gain the nomination.

Finally, the Democrats gave up and decided to meet again in Baltimore in June to choose a candidate. But as the Baltimore convention opened, Northerners and Southerners remained at odds. This time, almost all the Southerners left the meeting.

With the Southerners gone, the Northern Democrats nominated Douglas. Meanwhile, the Southern Democrats decided to nominate their own candidate. They chose John Breckinridge of Kentucky, the current vice-president and a supporter of slavery.

As you read in One American's Story on page 455, the Republicans had already nominated Abraham Lincoln. In addition to Lincoln, Douglas, and Breckinridge, a candidate from a fourth party entered the race. This party was called the Constitutional Union Party, and its members had one aim—to preserve the Union. They nominated John Bell of Tennessee to run for president.

*Reading*History

A. Recognizing Effects How did slavery affect U.S. political parties in 1860?

The Election of 1860

The election of 1860 turned into two different races for the presidency, one in the North and one in the South. Lincoln and Douglas were the only candidates with much support in the North. Breckinridge and Bell competed for Southern votes.

Lincoln and Breckinridge were considered to have the most extreme views on slavery. Lincoln opposed the expansion of slavery into the territories. Breckinridge insisted that the federal government be required to protect slavery in any territory. Douglas and Bell were considered moderates because neither wanted the federal government to pass new laws on slavery.

The outcome of the election made it clear that the nation was tired of compromise. Lincoln defeated Douglas in the North. Breckinridge carried most of the South. Douglas and Bell managed to win only in the states between the North and the Deep South. Because the North had more people in it than the South, Lincoln won the election.

This cartoon of the long-legged Abe Lincoln shows him to be the fittest candidate in the 1860 presidential election.

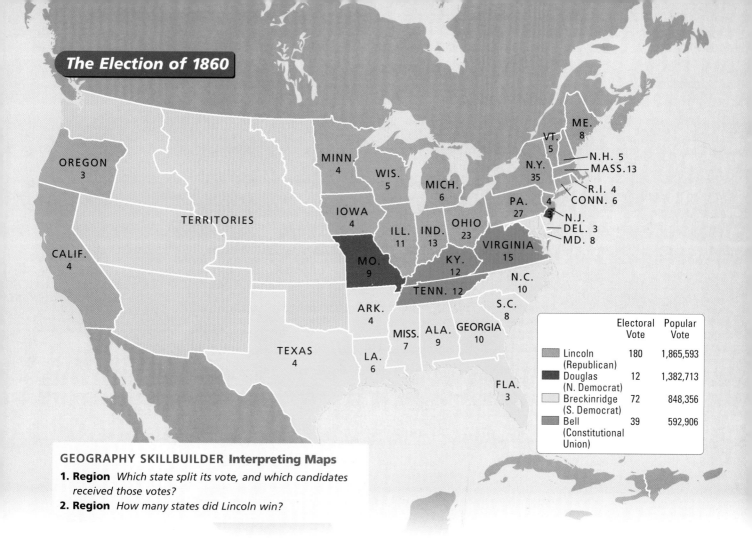

The Election of 1860

		Electoral Vote	Popular Vote
	Lincoln (Republican)	180	1,865,593
	Douglas (N. Democrat)	12	1,382,713
	Breckinridge (S. Democrat)	72	848,356
	Bell (Constitutional Union)	39	592,906

GEOGRAPHY SKILLBUILDER Interpreting Maps

1. **Region** *Which state split its vote, and which candidates received those votes?*
2. **Region** *How many states did Lincoln win?*

Despite Lincoln's statements that he would do nothing to abolish slavery in the South, white Southerners did not trust him. Many were sure that he and the other Republicans would move to ban slavery. As a result, white Southerners saw the Republican victory as a threat to the Southern way of life.

Southern States Secede

Before the 1860 presidential election, many Southerners had warned that if Lincoln won, the Southern states would **secede,** or withdraw from the Union. Supporters of secession based their arguments on the idea of states' rights. They argued that the states had voluntarily joined the Union. Consequently, they claimed that the states also had the right to leave the Union.

On December 20, 1860, South Carolina became the first state to secede. Other states in the Deep South, where slave labor and cotton production were most common, also considered secession. During the next six weeks, Mississippi, Florida, Alabama, Georgia, Louisiana, and Texas joined South Carolina in secession.

In early February 1861, the states that had seceded met in Montgomery, Alabama. They formed the **Confederate States of America.** The convention named **Jefferson Davis** president of the Confederacy.

Background
Before becoming president of the Confederacy, Davis had been a hero during the War with Mexico and a U.S. senator.

Along with naming Davis president, the convention drafted a constitution. The Confederate Constitution was modeled on the U.S. Constitution. But there were a few important differences. For example, the Confederate Constitution supported states' rights. It also protected slavery in the Confederacy, including any territories it might acquire.

Having formed its government, the Confederate states made plans to defend their separation from the Union. Some believed that war between the states could not be avoided. But everyone waited to see what the Union government would do in response.

The Union Responds to Secession

Northerners considered the secession of the Southern states to be unconstitutional. During his last months in office, President James Buchanan argued against secession. He believed that the states did not have the right to withdraw from the Union because the federal government, not the state governments, was sovereign. If secession were permitted, the Union would become weak, like a "rope of sand." He believed that the U.S. Constitution was framed to prevent such a thing from happening.

Vocabulary
sovereign: supreme, self-governing authority

In addition to these issues, secession raised the issue of majority rule. Southerners complained that Northerners intended to use their majority to force the South to abolish slavery. But Northerners responded that Southerners simply did not want to live by the rules of democracy. They complained that Southerners were not willing to live with the election results. As Northern writer James Russell Lowell wrote, "[The Southerners'] quarrel is not with the Republican Party, but with the theory of Democracy."

Efforts to Compromise Fail

With the states in the lower South forming a new government in Montgomery, Alabama, some people continued to seek compromise. Senator John J. Crittenden of Kentucky developed a compromise plan. The **Crittenden Plan** was presented to Congress in late February 1861, but it did not pass.

"We must not be enemies."
Abraham Lincoln

With the hopes for compromise fading, Americans waited for Lincoln's inauguration. What would the new president do about the crisis? On March 4, Lincoln took the oath of office and gave his First Inaugural Address. He assured the South that he had no intention of abolishing slavery there. But he spoke forcefully against secession. Then he ended his speech with an appeal to friendship.

*Reading*History

B. Making Inferences What do you think Lincoln meant by "mystic chords of memory"?

A VOICE FROM THE PAST

We are not enemies, but friends. We must not be enemies. Though passion may have strained, it must not break our bonds of affection. The mystic chords of memory, stretching from every battle-field and patriot grave, to every living heart and hearthstone, all over this broad land, will yet swell the chorus of the Union, when again touched, as surely they will be, by the better angels of our nature.

Abraham Lincoln, *First Inaugural Address*

Lincoln would not press the South. He wanted no invasion. But he would not abandon the government's property there. Several forts in the South, including Fort Sumter in South Carolina, were still in Union hands. These forts would soon need to be resupplied. Throughout March and into April, Northerners and Southerners waited anxiously to see what would happen next. You will find out in the next chapter.

Section 4 Assessment

1. Terms & Names

Explain the significance of:
• platform
• secede
• Confederate States of America
• Jefferson Davis
• Crittenden Plan

2. Taking Notes

Use a time line to fill in the main events that occurred between April 1860 and March 1861.

```
April      June       Feb.
1860       1860       1861
   |        |          |
   |        |          |
      May       Nov.      March
      1860      1860      1861
```

Do you think secession could have been avoided? Why?

3. Main Ideas

a. Who were the candidates in the 1860 presidential election, and what policies did each candidate stand for?

b. Which states seceded right after Lincoln's election? How did they justify this action?

c. What attempts did the North and the South make to compromise? What were the results?

4. Critical Thinking

Analyzing Points of View Do you think the Southern states seceded to protect slavery or states' rights?

THINK ABOUT
• the Southern view of the Fugitive Slave Act
• the Confederate Constitution
• slaveholders' views of the Republican Party

ACTIVITY OPTIONS

SPEECH

TECHNOLOGY

Read Lincoln's First Inaugural Address. Deliver a section of the **speech** before the class or plan an **electronic presentation** about that day and Lincoln's message.

The Nation Breaking Apart

SLAVERY

1846
Wilmot Proviso

Compromise of **1850**

1854
Kansas–Nebraska Act

1855
"Bleeding Kansas"

1856
Caning of Sumner

1857
Dred Scott v. *Sandford*

1859
Attack on Harpers Ferry

Election of **1860**

Secession

TERMS & NAMES

Briefly explain the significance of each of the following.

1. Wilmot Proviso
2. Compromise of 1850
3. *Uncle Tom's Cabin*
4. popular sovereignty
5. Kansas–Nebraska Act
6. John Brown
7. John C. Frémont
8. *Dred Scott* v. *Sandford*
9. secede
10. Confederate States of America

REVIEW QUESTIONS

Growing Tensions Between North and South (pages 441–445)

1. How did the North and the South differ in the 1840s?
2. How did Southerners react to the Wilmot Proviso?
3. What was Stephen A. Douglas's role in passing the Compromise of 1850?

The Crisis Deepens (pages 446–449)

4. How did Northerners react to the Fugitive Slave Act?
5. Why did most Northerners and Southerners disagree about the Kansas–Nebraska Act?
6. How did "Bleeding Kansas" cause problems for Democrats?

Slavery Dominates Politics (pages 450–454)

7. What positions did Lincoln and Douglas take in their debates?
8. What was the result of John Brown's raid on Harpers Ferry?

Lincoln's Election and Southern Secession (pages 455–459)

9. What were the results of the election of 1860, and what did these results show?
10. How did Southerners justify secession?

CRITICAL THINKING

1. USING YOUR NOTES

Using your completed diagram, answer the questions below.

a. What did the Compromise of 1850 and the Kansas–Nebraska Act have in common?
b. Which event do you think caused the most damage to the relationship between the North and the South? Explain.

2. ANALYZING LEADERSHIP

Why were the nation's leaders in 1860 unable to compromise like the leaders in 1820 and 1850? Does their failure to compromise in 1860 mean that they were not as capable as earlier leaders?

3. APPLYING CITIZENSHIP SKILLS

What alternatives did the states in the lower South have to secession? Which of these alternatives do you think would have been the best choice?

4. SOLVING PROBLEMS

How did slavery divide Americans in the 1850s?

5. THEME: DIVERSITY AND UNITY

What could have been done in the 1850s to prevent the Southern states from seceding? What did Americans have in common that could have overcome their differences over slavery?

Interact *with* History

Now that you have read about the sectional crisis of the 1850s, do you think the solution you came up with at the start of the chapter would have helped keep the Union together? Explain.

HISTORY SKILLS

1. INTERPRETING MAPS: Region

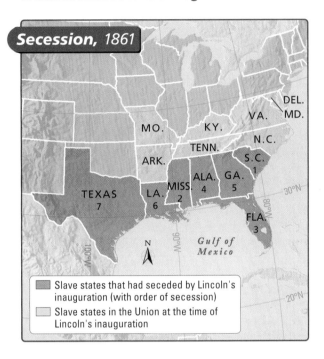

Secession, 1861

DEL.
VA. MD.
MO. KY.
N.C.
TENN.
ARK. S.C. 1
ALA. GA.
MISS. 4 5
TEXAS LA. 2
7 6
FLA.
3
30°N
N Gulf of
Mexico
20°N

☐ Slave states that had seceded by Lincoln's
inauguration (with order of secession)
☐ Slave states in the Union at the time of
Lincoln's inauguration

Basic Map Elements

a. Which states seceded before Lincoln's inauguration in March, 1861?

Interpreting the Map

b. What geographical characteristics did these states have in common?

c. Why do you think these states were the first to secede?

2. INTERPRETING PRIMARY SOURCES

A detail of Thomas Hovenden's painting, *The Last Moments of John Brown* (1884), shows Brown being led to the gallows.

a. How does Brown appear in this image?

b. Based on Hovenden's presentation of Brown, what do you think were the artist's views on Brown?

ALTERNATIVE ASSESSMENT

1. INTERDISCIPLINARY ACTIVITY: Language Arts

Conducting an Interview Pick one of the important people in this chapter, such as Stephen A. Douglas or Harriet Beecher Stowe. Think about what questions you would ask that person in an interview. Then research that person's biographies, speeches, or writings to see how he or she might answer your questions. Write the interview in question-and-answer format. Use direct quotes as often as possible.

2. COOPERATIVE LEARNING ACTIVITY

Presenting a Mock Trial The case of Dred Scott went to the Supreme Court. The Court, led by Chief Justice Roger B. Taney, decided against Scott. Did the court reach the right verdict?

Working in a small group, do research on the Dred Scott case. Present a mock trial of the case. Look for information about the roles of Taney, the other justices, Scott, and the other major participants. Have the class render a verdict at the end of the trial. Compare your verdict with the actual historical results.

3. TECHNOLOGY ACTIVITY

Making a Class Presentation American political parties went through extreme changes in the 1840s and 1850s. Using the Internet or the library, find the election returns of the presidential elections from 1848 to 1860.

For more about presidential elections . . .

INTERNET ACTIVITY
CLASSZONE.COM

Use presentation software to teach your class about U.S. presidential elections. Here are some suggestions.

- Use pie charts to show the percentage of votes that went to each party in each election.
- Use bar graphs to show the growth in total popular vote (nationwide) for each party for each election.

4. HISTORY PORTFOLIO

Review the questions that you wrote for What Do You Want to Know? on page 440. Then write a short report in which you explain the answers to your questions. Be sure to use standard grammar, spelling, sentence structure, and punctuation in your report. If any questions were not answered, do research to answer them. Add your report to your portfolio.

Additional Test Practice, pp. S1–S33

TEST PRACTICE
CLASSZONE.COM

The Nation Breaking Apart **461**

The Civil War Begins 1861–1862

In this vivid engraving, South Carolina shore guns fire on Fort Sumter in Charleston's harbor.

Interact *with* History

This painting shows Fort Sumter from the inside under attack.

damaged fort walls

stockpile of cannon balls

Federal artillery officers inside Fort Sumter witness bombardment.

federal cannon destroyed by Confederate shelling

The date is April 12, 1861. You and other residents of Charleston, South Carolina, watch the bombardment of Fort Sumter by Confederate forces. This event signals the beginning of the Civil War—a war between factions or regions of the same country.

What Do You Think?

- What sort of physical destruction might take place in a civil war?
- What social, political, and economic trouble might be likely to occur in a civil war?
- What might happen when a civil war breaks out?

How might a civil war be worse than other wars?

March 4, 1861
Abraham Lincoln inaugurated as president.

April 12, 1861
Confederate forces fire on Fort Sumter.

July 21, 1861
First Battle of Bull Run (Manassas) occurs.

March 9, 1862
The warships *Monitor* and *Merrimack* (or *Virginia*) clash.

April 6, 1862
Battle of Shiloh takes place.

April 25, 1862
New Orleans falls to Union forces.

September 17, 1862
Battle of Antietam (Sharpsburg) occurs.

USA World — 1861 — 1862

March, 1861
Italy unified under King Victor Emmanuel II.

May 13, 1861
Britain declares neutrality in American Civil War.

April 13, 1862
France annexes Cochin China (southern Vietnam).

May 5, 1862
French troops are defeated at Puebla, Mexico.

June 25, 1862
Imperial decree expels foreigners from Japan.

September, 1862
Bismarck becomes prime minister of Prussia.

Chapter 16 SETTING THE STAGE

BEFORE YOU READ

Union Soldier

Confederate Soldier

Previewing the Theme

Citizenship Secession led to war between the North and South. On both sides, citizens took up arms to defend their regions and ideals. Although most people expected a short war, the American Civil War became a long, bloody struggle. This chapter describes the conflicting demands of citizenship, the early years of the war, and what life was like for the soldiers.

What Do You Know?

What do you think of when you hear the phrase *civil war?* What would it be like to fight in a war of brother against brother? Where and how did the Civil War begin?

THINK ABOUT
- what a civil war is
- what you've learned about the Civil War from movies, television, and books
- reasons that countries threaten to break apart in today's world

What Do You Want to Know?

What details do you need to help you understand the outbreak of the Civil War? Make a list of those details in your notebook before you read the chapter.

READ AND TAKE NOTES

Reading Strategy: Comparing and Contrasting When you compare, you look for similarities between two or more objects, ideas, events, or people. When you contrast, you look for differences. Comparing and contrasting can be a useful strategy for studying the two sides in a war. Use the chart shown here to compare and contrast the North and the South in the early years of the Civil War.

 See Skillbuilder Handbook, page R10.

	North	South
Reasons for fighting		
Advantages		
Disadvantages		
Military strategy		
Battle victories		

TERMS & NAMES
Fort Sumter
Robert E. Lee
border state
King Cotton
Anaconda Plan
blockade
First Battle of Bull Run

MAIN IDEA	WHY IT MATTERS NOW
The secession of the Southern states quickly led to armed conflict between the North and the South.	The nation's identity was in part forged by the Civil War.

ONE AMERICAN'S STORY

Two months before the Civil War broke out, 22-year-old Emma Holmes of Charleston began keeping a detailed diary. Like other South Carolinians, Holmes got caught up in the passions that led her state to secede. From a rooftop, she witnessed the event that started the war. She wrote about South Carolina's attack on Fort Sumter, a federal fort in Charleston's harbor, in her diary.

A VOICE FROM THE PAST

[A]t half past four this morning, the heavy booming of cannons woke the city from its slumbers. . . . Every body seems relieved that what has been so long dreaded has come at last and so confident of victory that they seem not to think of the danger of their friends. . . . I had a splendid view of the harbor with the naked eye. We could distinctly see flames amidst the smoke. All the barracks were on fire. . . . With the telescope I saw the shots as they struck the fort and [saw] the masonry crumbling.

Emma Holmes, *The Diary of Emma Holmes 1861–1866*

This photograph of Emma Holmes was taken in 1900.

Many Southerners expected a short war that they would easily win. Northerners expected the same. In this section, you will learn how the war started, how the states divided, and how each side planned to win.

First Shots at Fort Sumter

As they seceded from the Union (the states loyal to the United States of America during the Civil War), the Southern states took over most of the federal forts inside their borders. President Abraham Lincoln had to decide what to do about the forts that remained under federal control. Major Robert Anderson and his garrison held on to **Fort Sumter** in the harbor of Charleston, South Carolina, but they were running out of supplies.

If Lincoln supplied the garrison, he risked war. If he ordered the troops to leave the fort, he would be giving in to the rebels. Lincoln informed South Carolina that he was sending supply ships to Fort Sumter. Leaders of the Confederacy (the nation formed by Southern states in 1861) decided to prevent the federal government from holding onto the fort by attacking before the supply ships arrived.

At 4:30 A.M. on April 12, 1861, shore guns opened fire on the island fort. For 34 hours, the Confederates fired shells into the fort until Anderson was forced to surrender. No one was killed, but the South's attack on Fort Sumter was the beginning of the Civil War.

Lincoln Calls Out the Militia

Two days after the surrender of Fort Sumter, President Lincoln asked the Union states to provide 75,000 militiamen for 90 days to put down the uprising in the South. Citizens of the North responded with enthusiasm to the call to arms. A New York woman wrote, "It seems as if we never were alive till now; never had a country till now."

In the upper South, however, state leaders responded with anger. The governor of Kentucky said that the state would "furnish no troops for the wicked purpose of subduing her sister Southern States." In the weeks that followed, Virginia, North Carolina, Tennessee, and Arkansas voted to join the Confederacy.

As each state seceded, volunteers rushed to enlist, just as citizens did in the North. A young Arkansas enlistee wrote, "So impatient did I become for starting that I felt like ten thousand pins were pricking me in every part of the body, and started off a week in advance of my brothers." Some feared the war would be over before they got the chance to fight.

With Virginia on its side, the Confederacy had a much better chance for victory. Virginia was wealthy and populous, and the Confederacy in May of 1861 moved its capital to Richmond. Virginia also was the home of **Robert E. Lee**, a talented military leader. When Virginia seceded, Lee resigned from the United States Army and joined the Confederacy. Although Lee opposed slavery and secession, he explained, "I cannot raise my hand against my birthplace, my home, my children." He eventually became the commanding general of the Army of Northern Virginia.

Reading **History**
A. Comparing Why might citizens in both the North and the South have been eager to fight in the Civil War?

Choosing Sides

After Virginia seceded, both sides knew that the border states would play a key role in the war's outcome. The **border states**—Delaware, Maryland, Kentucky, and Missouri—were slave states that bordered states in which slavery was illegal. Because of their location and resources, the border states could tip the scales toward one side.

Keeping Maryland in the Union was important for the North. If Maryland seceded, then Washington, D.C., would be cut off from the Union. To hold on to the state, Lincoln considered arresting Maryland lawmakers who backed the South, but he decided against it.

AMERICA'S HISTORY MAKERS

ABRAHAM LINCOLN
1809–1865
Today, Abraham Lincoln is considered one of the great men of all time. Yet early in his presidency, he was widely criticized and ridiculed. Critics labeled him ignorant, incompetent, and socially crude. As Lincoln grew into his job, however, he gained the respect and affection of many Northerners.

Even as a youth, Lincoln had displayed a gift for public speaking. During the Civil War, through his speeches and writings, Lincoln inspired fellow Americans to "dare to do our duty as we understand it."

Why would the ability to inspire people be important in a wartime leader?

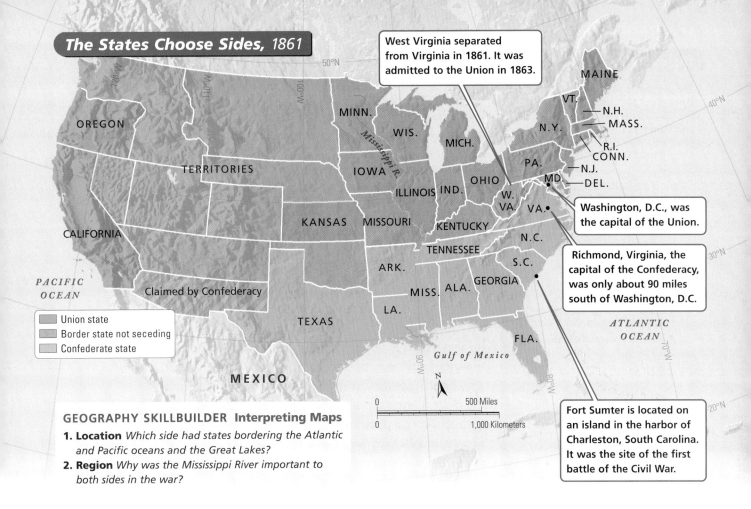

The States Choose Sides, *1861*

West Virginia separated from Virginia in 1861. It was admitted to the Union in 1863.

MAINE
VT.
N.H.
MASS.
N.Y.
R.I.
CONN.
PA.
N.J.
MD.
DEL.

Washington, D.C., was the capital of the Union.

OREGON
MINN.
WIS.
MICH.
TERRITORIES
IOWA
OHIO
ILLINOIS IND.
W. VA.
VA.
CALIFORNIA
KANSAS MISSOURI
KENTUCKY
N.C.
TENNESSEE
S.C.
ARK.
GEORGIA
MISS. ALA.
LA.
Claimed by Confederacy
TEXAS
FLA.

Mississippi R.

Richmond, Virginia, the capital of the Confederacy, was only about 90 miles south of Washington, D.C.

PACIFIC OCEAN

ATLANTIC OCEAN

Union state
Border state not seceding
Confederate state

Gulf of Mexico

MEXICO

N

0   500 Miles
0   1,000 Kilometers

Fort Sumter is located on an island in the harbor of Charleston, South Carolina. It was the site of the first battle of the Civil War.

GEOGRAPHY SKILLBUILDER Interpreting Maps

1. **Location** *Which side had states bordering the Atlantic and Pacific oceans and the Great Lakes?*
2. **Region** *Why was the Mississippi River important to both sides in the war?*

Pro-Union leaders eventually gained control of the Maryland legislature, and the state stayed in the Union.

Kentucky was also important to both sides because of its rivers. For the Union, the rivers could provide an invasion route into the South. For the South, the rivers could provide a barrier. Kentuckians were deeply divided over secession. However, a Confederate invasion in 1861 prompted the state to stay in the Union.

Reading **History**
B. Summarizing Why were the border states critical to the war's outcome?

Both Missouri and Delaware also stayed in the Union. In Virginia, federal troops helped a group of western counties break away. These counties formed the state of West Virginia and returned to the Union. In the end, 24 states made up the Union and 11 joined the Confederacy.

Strengths and Weaknesses

The Union had huge advantages in manpower and resources. The North had about 22 million people. The Confederacy had roughly 9 million, of whom about 3.5 million were slaves. About 85 percent of the nation's factories were located in the North. The North had more than double the railroad mileage of the South. Almost all the naval power and shipyards belonged to the North.

The Union's greatest asset, however, was President Abraham Lincoln. He developed into a remarkable leader. Lincoln convinced Northerners that democracy depended on preserving the Union.

The pie charts show the relative strength of the Union and the Confederacy in population and industry.

Total U.S. Population

29% 71%

■ Union ■ Confederacy

Total U.S. Railroad Mileage

29% 71%

Total U.S. Manufacturing Plants

15%

85%

Total U.S. Industrial Workers

8%

92%

Source: *Encyclopedia Americana*

SKILLBUILDER
Interpreting Charts
1. *Which side had more resources?*
2. *How might the North's railways and factories have helped its armies?*

The Confederacy had some advantages, too. It began the war with able generals, such as Robert E. Lee. It also had the advantage of fighting a defensive war. This meant Northern supply lines would have to be stretched very far. In addition, soldiers defending their homes have more will to fight than invaders do.

The Confederate Strategy

At first, the Confederacy took a defensive position. It did not want to conquer the North—it only wanted to be independent. "All we ask is to be let alone," said Confederate President Jefferson Davis. Confederate leaders hoped the North would soon tire of the war and accept Southern independence.

The South also depended on **King Cotton** as a way to win foreign support. Cotton was king because Southern cotton was important in the world market. The South grew most of the cotton for Europe's textile mills. When the war broke out, Southern planters withheld cotton from the market. They hoped to force France and Britain to aid the Confederate cause. But in 1861, European nations had surplus cotton because of a big crop the year before. They did not want to get involved in the American war.

As the war heated up, the South soon moved away from its cautious plans. It began to take the offensive and try for big victories to wreck Northern morale.

The Union Strategy

The North wanted to bring the Southern states back into the Union. To do this, the North developed an offensive strategy based on General Winfield Scott's **Anaconda Plan.** This plan was designed to smother the South's economy like a giant anaconda snake squeezing its prey.

The plan called for a naval blockade of the South's coastline. In a **blockade,** armed forces prevent the transportation of goods or people into or out of an area. The plan also called for the Union to gain control of the Mississippi River. This would split the Confederacy in two.

One of the drawbacks of Scott's plan was that it would take time to work. But many people, eager for action, were calling for an immediate attack on Richmond, the Confederate capital. Lincoln ordered an invasion of Virginia in the summer of 1861.

*Reading***History**
C. Supporting Opinions At the beginning of the Civil War, which side would you have predicted to win? Why?

Battle of Bull Run

To take Richmond, the Union army would first have to defeat the Confederate troops stationed at the town of Manassas, Virginia. This was a railway center southwest of Washington, D.C.

Background
In the South, the battle was called the First Battle of Manassas. In most cases, the South named a battle after a nearby town. The North used a landmark near the fighting, usually a stream.

On July 21, 1861, Union forces commanded by General Irvin McDowell clashed with Confederate forces headed by General Pierre Beauregard near a little creek called Bull Run north of Manassas. In the North, this battle came to be known as the **First Battle of Bull Run.**

The Confederate Army passes in review before General Pierre Beauregard.

At one point in the battle, a Confederate officer rallied his troops by pointing his sword toward Southern General Thomas J. Jackson. The officer cried, "There is Jackson standing like a stone wall! Rally behind the Virginians!" From this incident, Jackson won the nickname "Stonewall" Jackson. His men held fast against the Union assault.

As fresh troops arrived, the Confederates equaled the Union forces in number and launched a countercharge. Attacking the Union line, they let out a blood-curdling scream. This scream, later called the "rebel yell," caused the Union troops to panic. They broke ranks and scattered.

The Confederate victory in the First Battle of Bull Run thrilled the South and shocked the North. Many in the South thought the war was won. The North realized it had underestimated its opponent. Lincoln sent the 90-day militias home and called for a real army of 500,000 volunteers for three years. In the next section, you will learn what army life was like.

Section 1 Assessment

1. Terms & Names

Explain the significance of:
• Fort Sumter
• Robert E. Lee
• border state
• King Cotton
• Anaconda Plan
• blockade
• First Battle of Bull Run

2. Taking Notes

Use a Venn diagram to compare and contrast the strengths of the North and the South.

3. Main Ideas

a. How did citizens in the North and the South respond to the outbreak of the Civil War?

b. Why were the border states important to both sides in the Civil War?

c. What kind of military strategy did each side develop?

4. Critical Thinking

Comparing How was the South's situation in the Civil War similar to the situation of the Patriots in the Revolutionary War?

THINK ABOUT
• their reasons for fighting
• their opponents' strengths

ACTIVITY OPTIONS

LANGUAGE ARTS
TECHNOLOGY

Read an account of the First Battle of Bull Run. Use the information to write a **news article** or plan the battle's **home page** for the Internet.

from

Across **Five** Aprils

by Irene Hunt

At the beginning of the Civil War, nine-year-old Jethro Creighton and his family live on a farm in southern Illinois. Although Illinois is a free state that remains in the Union, many people in the area have ties to states where slavery is legal. For example, the Creightons have relatives in "Kaintuck," or Kentucky. When this excerpt begins, Jethro has already seen his brother Tom and his cousin Eb go off to fight for the Union. His other brothers, John and Bill, are trying to decide which side to fight for.

A line of wild geese flew southward far overhead, and Jethro stood motionless as he watched them disappear from sight. So **engrossed**[1] he was with the flight of the geese that he did not hear Bill's footsteps until his brother was quite near. He caught his breath at sight of Bill's face, which was swollen and beginning to grow discolored from a deep cut and many bruises.

"What's hurt you, Bill?" he asked, his voice barely **audible,**[2] for he was pretty sure he knew.

"We had a fight, Jeth, about an hour ago. We fit like two madmen, I guess."

"You and John?"

Bill's sigh was almost a moan. "Yes, me and John. Me and my brother John."

Jethro could not answer. He stared at the cut above Bill's right eye, from which blood still trickled down his cheek. Somewhere, far off in another field, a man shouted to his horses, and the shout died away in a cry that ran frightened over the brown water of the creek and into the darkening woods.

He had heard cries often that autumn, all through the countryside. They came at night, wakened him, and then lapsed into silence, leaving him in fear and **perplexity.**[3] Sounds once familiar were no longer as they had seemed in other days—his father calling cattle in from the pasture, the sheep dog's bark coming through the fog, the distant creak of the pulley as Ellen drew water for her chickens—all these once familiar sounds had taken on overtones of wailing, and he seemed to hear an echo of that wailing now. He shivered and looked away from his brother's face.

Bill sat down on the ground beside him. "Did ever Ma tell you, Jeth, about when John and me was little and was goin' to school fer the first time? At night I'd git a book and I'd say to Pa, 'What air that word, Pa?' and when he would tell me, I'd turn to John, jest a scant year older, and I'd say, 'Did Pa call it right, Johnny?' Ma and Pa used to laugh at that, but they was pleased to talk about it. They was always set up at John and me bein' so close."

"I know it." Jethro's words came from a tight throat. "What made you fight, Bill?"

"Hard feelin's that have been buildin' up fer weeks, hard feelin's that fin'ly come out in hard words." He held his hand across his eyes for a minute and then spoke quickly. "I'm leavin', Jeth; it ain't that I want to, but it's that I must. The day is comin' when I've got to fight, and I won't fight fer **arrogance**[4] and big money aginst the southern farmer. I won't do it. You tell Pa that. Tell him, too, that I'm takin' my brown mare—she's mine, and I hev the right. Still, it will leave him short, so you tell him that I'm leavin' money I

---

1. **engrossed:** absorbed; occupied.
2. **audible:** able to be heard.
3. **perplexity:** confusion.
4. **arrogance:** overbearing pride.

made at the sawmill and at corn shuckin'; it's inside the cover of his Bible. You tell him to take it and buy another horse."

Jethro was crying unashamedly in the face of his grief. "Don't go, Bill. Don't do it," he begged.

"Jeth . . ."

"I don't want you to go, Bill. I don't think I kin stand it."

"Listen to me, Jeth; you're gittin to be a sizable boy. There's goin' to be a lot of things in the years ahead that you'll have to stand. There'll be things that tear you apart, but you'll have to stand 'em. You can't count on cryin' to make 'em right."

The colors were beginning to fade on Walnut Hill. A light wind bent the dried grass and weeds. Jethro felt choked with grief, but he drew a sleeve across his eyes and tried to look at his brother without further weeping.

"Where will you go, Bill?"

"To Kaintuck. I'll go to Wilse's place first. From there—I don't know."

"Will you fight fer the Rebs?"

Bill hesitated a few seconds. "I've studied this thing, Jeth, and I've hurt over it. My heart ain't in this war; I've told you that. And while I say that the right ain't all on the side of the North, I know jest as well that it ain't all on the side of the South either. But if I hev to fight, I reckon it will be fer the South."

Jethro nodded. There were things you had to endure. After a while he asked, "Air you goin' tonight, Bill?"

"Right away. I've had things packed in that holler tree fer a couple days. I've knowed that this was comin' on, but I couldn't make myself leave. Now I'm goin'. The little mare is saddled and tied down at the molasses press. I'll go as fur as Newton tonight; in the morning I'll take out early."

He got to his feet. "There's lots of things I want to say, but I reckon I best not talk." Without looking at Jethro he laid his hand on the boy's shoulder. "Git all the larnin' you kin—and take keer of yoreself, Jeth," he said and turned abruptly away.

"Take keer of yoreself, Bill," Jethro called after him.

Across the prairies, through the woods, over the brown water of the creek, there was a sound of crying. Jethro ran to a tree and hid his face. He had heard his mother say that if you watch a loved one as he leaves you for a long journey, it's like as not to be the last look at him that you'll ever have.

Like the Creighton brothers, the Terrill brothers had different loyalties. William Rufus Terrill (left) fought for the Union as an artillery officer at Shiloh. His brother, James Terrill (right), was the commanding officer of a Virginia infantry regiment. Both men died in the war. William was killed at Perryville, Kentucky, in 1862; James was killed in battle in 1864. After the war, the family built a memorial to the brothers, which contained the words, "God Alone Knows Which Was Right."

CONNECT TO HISTORY

1. **Recognizing Effects** How has the Civil War affected the Creighton family? Discuss how the effect reflects what is happening in the country.

 See Skillbuilder Handbook, page R11.

CONNECT TO TODAY

2. **Researching** Where have civil wars or internal rebellions taken place in the recent past?

For more about other civil wars . . .

RESEARCH LINKS
CLASSZONE.COM

2 Life in the Army

TERMS & NAMES
hygiene
rifle
minié ball
ironclad

MAIN IDEA	WHY IT MATTERS NOW
Both Union and Confederate soldiers endured many hardships serving in the army during the Civil War.	The hardships endured led to long-lasting bitterness on both sides.

ONE AMERICAN'S STORY

When the Civil War began, Peter Vredenburgh, Jr., the son of a well-known judge, was working as a lawyer in Eatontown, New Jersey. In 1862, he answered President Lincoln's call for an additional 300,000 soldiers. Nearly 26 years old, Vredenburgh became a major in the 14th Regiment New Jersey Volunteer Infantry. Less than two months after joining the regiment, he wrote a letter urging his parents to keep his 18-year-old brother from enlisting.

Major Peter Vredenburgh, Jr., was an officer in the Union army.

A VOICE FROM THE PAST

I am glad that Jim has not joined any Regt. [regiment] and I hope he never will. I would not have him go for all my pay; it would be very improbable that we could both go through this war and come out unharmed. Let him come here and see the thousands with their arms and legs off, or if that won't do, let him go as I did the other day through the Frederick hospitals and see how little account a man's life and limbs are held in by others and what little return he gets in reputation or money for the risk and privations of enlisting and his ideas of the fun of the thing will vanish in thin air.

Major Peter Vredenburgh, Jr., quoted in *Upon the Tented Field*

On September 19, 1864, Vredenburgh was killed in battle. In this section, you will learn more about other soldiers and what their experiences were like.

Those Who Fought

Like Peter Vredenburgh, the majority of soldiers in the Civil War were between 18 and 30 years of age. But both the Confederate and Union armies had younger and older soldiers. Charles Carter Hay was just 11 years old when he joined an Alabama regiment. William Wilkins was 83 when he became one of the Pennsylvania Home Guards.

Farmers made up the largest group among Civil War soldiers. About half the soldiers on both sides came from farms. Having rarely traveled far from their fields, many viewed going off to war as an exciting adventure. Some rode a train for the first time.

Although the majority of soldiers in the war were born in the United States, immigrants from other countries also served. German and Irish immigrants made up the largest ethnic groups. One regiment from New York had soldiers who were born in 15 foreign countries. The commanding officer gave orders in seven languages.

At the beginning of the war, African Americans wanted to fight. They saw the war as a way to end slavery. However, neither the North nor the South accepted African Americans into their armies. As the war dragged on, the North finally took African Americans into its ranks. Native Americans served on both sides.

In all, about 2 million American soldiers served the Union, and fewer than 1 million served the Confederacy. The vast majority were volunteers. Why did so many Americans volunteer to fight? Many sought adventure and glory. Some sought an escape from the boredom of farm and factory work. Some signed up because their friends and neighbors were doing it. Others signed up for the recruitment money offered by both sides. Soldiers also fought because they were loyal to their country or state.

Reading **History**
A. Summarizing
How did most men in the North and the South feel about going off to war?

Turning Civilians into Soldiers

After enlisting, a volunteer was sent to a nearby army camp for training. A typical camp looked like a sea of canvas tents. The tents were grouped by company, and each tent held from two to twenty men. In winter, the soldiers lived in log huts or in heavy tents positioned on a log base. In the Civil War, Confederate soldiers and soldiers in volunteer units in the Union Army elected their company officers. Both the Union and Confederate armies followed this practice.

A soldier in training followed a set schedule. A bugle or drum awakened the soldier at dawn. After roll call and breakfast, the soldier had the first of several drill sessions. In between drills and meals, soldiers performed guard duty, cut wood for the campfires, dug trenches for latrines (outdoor toilets), and cleaned up the camp.

Shortly after they came to camp, new recruits were given uniforms and equipment. Union soldiers wore

daily*life*

DRILL SESSIONS

"The first thing in the morning is drill. Then drill, then drill again. Then drill, drill, a little more drill. Then drill, and lastly drill." That is the way one soldier described his day in camp.

A soldier in training might have as many as five drill sessions a day, each lasting up to two hours. The soldiers learned to stand straight and march in formation. They also learned to load and fire their guns. Shown drilling below are soldiers of the 22nd New York State Militia near Harpers Ferry, Virginia, in 1862.

yellowish-brown uniforms. Getting a uniform of the right size was a problem, however. On both sides, soldiers traded items to get clothing that fit properly.

Early in the war, Northern soldiers received clothing of very poor quality. Contractors took advantage of the government's need and supplied shoddy goods. Shoes made of imitation leather, for example, fell apart when they got wet. In the Confederacy, some states had trouble providing uniforms at all, while others had surpluses. Because the states did not always cooperate and share supplies, Confederate soldiers sometimes lacked shoes. Like soldiers in the Revolutionary War, they marched over frozen ground in bare feet. After battles, needy soldiers took coats, boots, and other clothing from the dead.

At the beginning of the war, most soldiers in army camps received plenty of food. Their rations included beef or salt pork, flour, vegetables, and coffee. But when they were in the field, the soldiers' diet became more limited. Some soldiers went hungry because supply trains could not reach them.

Background
Before uniforms became standardized, soldiers dressed in outfits supplied from home. This caused confusion on the battlefield.

STRANGE *but* True

DEADLIER THAN BULLETS

"Look at our company—21 have died of disease, 18 have become so unhealthy as to be discharged, and only four have been killed in battle." So a Louisiana officer explained the high death rate in the Civil War.

More than twice as many men died of disease as died of battle wounds. Intestinal disorders, including typhoid fever, diarrhea, and dysentery, killed the most. Pneumonia, tuberculosis, and malaria killed many others. Bad water and food, poor diet, exposure to cold and rain, unsanitary conditions, and disease-carrying insects all contributed to the high rate of disease.

Hardships of Army Life

Civil War soldiers in the field were often wet, muddy, or cold from marching outdoors and living in crude shelters. Many camps were unsanitary and smelled from the odors of garbage and latrines. One Union soldier described a camp near Washington. In the camp, cattle were killed to provide the troops with meat.

A VOICE FROM THE PAST

The hides and [waste parts] of the [cattle] for miles upon miles around, under a sweltering sun and sultry showers, would gender such swarms of flies, armies of worms, blasts of stench and oceans of filth as to make life miserable.

William Keesy, quoted in *The Civil War Infantryman*

Not only were the camps filthy, but so were the soldiers. They often went weeks without bathing or washing their clothes. Their bodies, clothing, and bedding became infested with lice and fleas.

Poor **hygiene**—conditions and practices that promote health—resulted in widespread sickness. Most soldiers had chronic diarrhea or other intestinal disorders. These disorders were caused by contaminated water or food or by germ-carrying insects. People did not know that germs cause diseases. Doctors failed to wash their hands or their instruments. An observer described how surgeons "armed with long, bloody knives and saws, cut and sawed away with frightful rapidity, throwing the mangled limbs on a pile nearby as soon as removed."

*Reading*History
B. Making Inferences What changes could have helped lower the spread of disease among soldiers?

474

The naval duel between the Union *Monitor* and the Confederate *Merrimack* (or *Virginia*) took place on March 9, 1862.

Changes in Military Technology

While camp life remained rough, military technology advanced. Improvements in the weapons of war had far-reaching effects. Battle tactics changed, and casualties soared.

Vocabulary
casualties: number of people killed or injured

Rifles that used minié balls contributed to the high casualty rate in the Civil War. A **rifle** is a gun with a grooved barrel that causes a bullet to spin through the air. This spin gives the bullet more distance and accuracy. The **minié ball** is a bullet with a hollow base. The bullet expands upon firing to fit the grooves in the barrel. Rifles with minié balls could shoot farther and more accurately than old-fashioned muskets. As a result, mounted charges and infantry assaults did not work as well. Defenders using rifles could shoot more of the attackers before they got close.

Reading **History**
C. Drawing Conclusions
Which changes in military technology had an effect on the average soldier? Why?

Ironclads, warships covered with iron, proved to be a vast improvement over wooden ships. In the first ironclad battle, the Confederate *Virginia* (originally named the *Merrimack*) battled the Union *Monitor* off the coast of Virginia in 1862. After hammering away for about four hours, the battle ended in a draw. (See page 476 for more information on ironclads.)

Despite new technology and tactics, neither side gained a decisive victory in the first two years of the war, as you will see in the next section.

Section 2 Assessment

1. Terms & Names

Explain the significance of:
• hygiene
• rifle
• minié ball
• ironclad

2. Taking Notes

Complete the chart below.

The Typical Civil War Soldier	
Age	
Occupation	
Training	
Hardships	

Which hardship do you think would have been most difficult to endure? Why?

3. Main Ideas

a. How were the wartime experiences of Northern and Southern soldiers alike?

b. What factors contributed to the spread of disease among soldiers?

c. How did the use of the rifle and minié ball change combat tactics in the Civil War?

4. Critical Thinking

Forming and Supporting Opinions What were the motives that led individual soldiers to fight in the Civil War?

THINK ABOUT
• the multiple reasons that people had for enlisting
• what you consider valid reasons for fighting

ACTIVITY OPTIONS

LANGUAGE ARTS
ART

Imagine you are a soldier in the Civil War. Write a **letter** home to your parents about your experience or draw an **illustrated map** of your training camp.

Ironclads

They moved through the water, as one observer put it, "like a huge, half-submerged crocodile." To crew members of traditional wooden ships, the ironclads indeed may have seemed like horrible mechanical monsters.

With a powerful iron hull almost entirely under water and a rotating gun turret, or short tower, an ironclad easily destroyed the older vessels it met. When the *Monitor* and the *Merrimack* (or *Virginia*) clashed during the Civil War in the first battle ever waged between ironclads, a new era of naval warfare had begun. Below is a closer look at the Union's *Monitor*.

Steam engines **powered the ship. They were connected by a propeller shaft to a four-blade propeller. Behind the propeller sat the vessel's rudder. This entire area was heavily protected so the ship could keep moving under heavy fire or ramming.**

The **pilothouse, where the captain steered the ship, was a rectangular, reinforced iron box-like structure. A small opening all around the top allowed for full visibility.**

The ship's weapons—two large cannons—were enclosed in a rotating iron **turret. This allowed the guns to fire at an enemy from all directions. Ammunition was passed up to the gunners through a hatch in the floor.**

SCALE AND SIZE OF WARSHIPS				
Class, Name, Launch Date	Length	Weight	Number of Crew	Weaponry
Ironclad (USS *Monitor*) 1862	172 ft.	987 tons	49	two 11-inch smoothbore cannons
Battleship (USS *Maine*) 1889	319 ft.	6,682 tons	374	four 10-inch guns, six 6-inch guns, seven rapid-fire 6-pounders, four torpedo tubes
Nuclear Submarine (USS *Nautilus*) 1954	324 ft.	4,092 tons	105	six torpedo tubes
Aircraft Carrier (USS *Nimitz*) 1972	1,092 ft.	95,000 tons	6,000	24 F-14A Tomcat warplanes, 16 radar guided missiles, six-barrel, 20-millimeter Gatling gun

CONNECT TO HISTORY

1. **Drawing Conclusions** Why would a rotating gun be an advantage in a naval battle?

 See Skillbuilder Handbook, page R13.

CONNECT TO TODAY

2. **Researching** Find out more about modern battleships or aircraft carriers, and write a brief report about their capabilities in battle.

For more about military ships . . .

RESEARCH LINKS
CLASSZONE.COM

③ No End in Sight

TERMS & NAMES
Ulysses S. Grant
Battle of Shiloh
cavalry
Seven Days' Battles
Battle of Antietam

MAIN IDEA	WHY IT MATTERS NOW
In the first two years of the war, neither side gained a decisive victory over the other.	A long war can cause much death and destruction and leave a bitter legacy.

ONE AMERICAN'S STORY

In the summer of 1861, President Lincoln gave George McClellan command of the Union army in the East. The army had recently been defeated at Bull Run. McClellan faced the task of restoring the soldiers' confidence while organizing and training an army that could defeat the Confederates.

Within months, McClellan had accomplished the task and won the devotion of his troops. The entire nation expected great things. In November 1861, Lincoln made McClellan general in chief of the entire Union army. But while Lincoln kept urging him to attack Richmond, McClellan kept drilling his troops.

A VOICE FROM THE PAST

[S]oon as I feel that my army is well organized and well disciplined and strong enough, I will advance and force the Rebels to a battle on a field of my own selection. A long time must elapse before I can do that.

General George McClellan, quoted in *Civil War Journal: The Leaders*

President Lincoln (right) meets with General McClellan (left) on the Antietam battlefield in 1862.

Lincoln said McClellan had "the slows." While McClellan was stalling in the East, another general was winning victories in the West.

Union Victories in the West

That victorious Union general in the West was **Ulysses S. Grant**. In civilian life, he had failed at many things. But Grant had a simple strategy of war: "Find out where your enemy is, get at him as soon as you can, strike at him as hard as you can, and keep moving on."

In February 1862, Grant made a bold move to take Tennessee. Using ironclad gunboats, Grant's forces captured two Confederate river forts. These were Fort Henry on the Tennessee and Fort Donelson on the nearby Cumberland. (See map on next page.) The seizure of Fort Henry opened up a river highway into the heart of the South. Union gunboats could now travel on the river as far as northern Alabama. When the people of Nashville, Tennessee, heard the forts were lost, they fled the city in panic. A week later, Union troops marched into Nashville.

The Battle of Shiloh

After Grant's river victories, Albert S. Johnston, Confederate commander on the Western front, ordered a retreat to Corinth, Mississippi. Grant followed. By early April, Grant's troops had reached Pittsburg Landing on the Tennessee River. There he waited for more troops from Nashville. Johnston, however, decided to attack before Grant gained reinforcements. Marching his troops north from Corinth on April 6, 1862, Johnston surprised the Union forces near Shiloh Church. The **Battle of Shiloh** in Tennessee turned into the fiercest fighting the Civil War had yet seen.

Commanders on each side rode into the thick of battle to rally their troops. One Union general, William Tecumseh Sherman, had three horses shot out from under him. General Johnston was killed, and the command passed to General Pierre Beauregard. By the end of the day, each side believed that dawn would bring victory.

That night, there was a terrible thunderstorm. Lightning lit up the battlefield, where dead and dying soldiers lay in water and mud. During the night, Union boats ran upriver to ferry fresh troops to Grant's camp. Grant then led an attack at dawn and forced the exhausted Southern troops to retreat.

The cost of the Union victory was staggering. Union casualties at Shiloh numbered over 13,000, about one-fourth of those who had fought. The Confederates lost nearly 11,000 out of 41,000 soldiers. Describing

Reading **History**

A. Contrasting
How did Grant differ from McClellan as a military leader?

The Civil War, *1861–1862*

A. Battles of the West

0 100 Miles
0 200 Kilometers

ILLINOIS
INDIANA
WISCONSIN
MICHIG
Mississippi R.
Ohio R.
MINNESOTA
MISSOURI
KENTUCKY
IOWA
Grant
Ft. Donelson
Feb. 1862
INDIANA
ILLINOIS
Pea Ridge
March 1862
Ft. Henry
Feb. 1862
Shiloh
(Pittsburg Landing)
April 1862
TENNESSEE
MISSOURI
KENTUC
Ft. Done
Feb. 186
ARKANSAS
Corinth
A. Johnston
35°N
Ft. Henry
Feb. 1862 TENNES
ARKANSAS
MISSISSIPPI
ALABAMA
Corinth
ALABA

B. Fall of New Orleans

Vicksburg
LOUISIANA
MISSISSIPPI
ALA.
Farragut
Mississippi R.
New Orleans
0 50 Miles
0 100 Kilometers
Gulf of Mexico
30°N
TEXAS
Vicksburg
MISSISSIPPI
LOUISIANA

the piles of mangled bodies, General Sherman wrote home, "The scenes on this field would have cured anybody of war." Congressmen criticized Grant for the high casualties and urged Lincoln to replace him. But Lincoln replied, "I can't spare this man—he fights."

> ## "I can't spare this man— he fights."
> Abraham Lincoln,
> describing General Grant

The Fall of New Orleans

The spring of 1862 brought other bad news for the Confederacy. On April 25, a Union fleet led by David Farragut captured New Orleans, the largest city in the South. Rebel gunboats tried to ram the Union warships and succeeded in sinking one. Farragut's ships had to run through cannon fire and then dodge burning rafts in order to reach the city. Residents stood on the docks and cursed the Yankee invaders, but they were powerless to stop them.

The fall of New Orleans was a heavy blow to the South. Mary Chesnut of South Carolina, the wife of an aide to President Davis, wrote in her diary, "New Orleans gone—and with it the Confederacy. Are we not cut in two?" Indeed, after the victories of General Grant and Admiral Farragut, only a 150-mile stretch of the Mississippi remained in Southern hands. The Union was well on its way to achieving its goal of cutting the Confederacy in two. But guarding the remaining stretch of the river was the heavily armed Confederate fort at Vicksburg, Mississippi.

Reading **History**
B. Recognizing Effects Why was the fall of New Orleans significant?

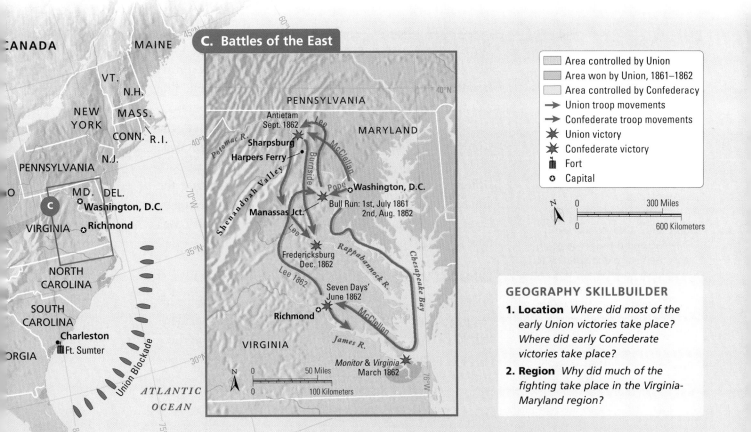

C. Battles of the East

Legend:
- Area controlled by Union
- Area won by Union, 1861–1862
- Area controlled by Confederacy
- → Union troop movements
- → Confederate troop movements
- ✸ Union victory
- ✸ Confederate victory
- Fort
- Capital

GEOGRAPHY SKILLBUILDER

1. **Location** *Where did most of the early Union victories take place? Where did early Confederate victories take place?*

2. **Region** *Why did much of the fighting take place in the Virginia-Maryland region?*

Lee Claims Victories in the East

Meanwhile, also in the spring of 1862, McClellan finally made his move to try to capture Richmond. He planned to attack the Confederate capital by way of a stretch of land between the York and James rivers. McClellan succeeded in bringing his troops within a few miles of Richmond.

But in June 1862, Robert E. Lee took charge of the Army of Northern Virginia and proceeded to turn the situation around. Lee sent Jeb Stuart and his **cavalry**—soldiers on horseback—to spy on McClellan. With about 1,000 men, Stuart rode around the whole Union army in a few days and reported its size back to Lee. Lee then attacked McClellan's army. The two sides clashed for a week, from June 25 to July 1, 1862, in what became known as the **Seven Days' Battles.** The Army of Northern Virginia suffered heavier losses, but it forced McClellan's army to retreat.

In late August, the Confederates won a second victory at Bull Run, and Union troops withdrew back to Washington. Within just a few months, Lee had ended the Union threat in Virginia.

*Reading*History

C. Making Inferences How was Lee's appointment fortunate for the South?

Lee Invades the North

Riding a wave of victories, General Lee decided to invade the Union. He wrote to tell President Davis of his plan. Lee thought it was a crucial time, with the North at a low point. Without waiting for Davis's response, Lee crossed the Potomac with his army and invaded Maryland in early September 1862.

*Reading*History

D. Reading a Map Use the map on page 479 to follow Lee's movements into the North.

Lee had several reasons for taking the war to the North. He hoped a victory in the North might force Lincoln to talk peace. The invasion would give Virginia farmers a rest from war during the harvest season. The Confederates could plunder Northern farms for food.

Lee hoped the invasion would show that the Confederacy could indeed win the war, which might convince Europe to side with the South. By this time, both Britain and France were leaning toward recognizing the Confederacy as a separate nation. They were impressed by Lee's military successes, and their textile industry was now hurting from the lack of Southern cotton.

Bloody Antietam

Soon after invading Maryland, Lee drew up a plan for his campaign in the North. A Confederate officer accidentally left a copy of Lee's battle plans wrapped around three cigars at a campsite. When Union troops stopped to rest at the abandoned campsite, a Union soldier stumbled on the plans. The captured plans gave McClellan a chance to stop Lee and his army.

AMERICA'S HISTORY MAKERS

JEFFERSON DAVIS
1808–1889

Jefferson Davis expected to be given a military command when the Confederacy was formed in 1861. But Davis was chosen President of the Confederacy instead, which stunned and saddened him.

Because of his strong sense of duty and loyalty to the South, Davis accepted the unwelcome post. He had to immediately form a national government and prepare for war at the same time. Davis found it hard to compromise or accept disagreement with his opinions.

How do the qualities required in a military leader differ from those required in a political leader?

McClellan went on the attack, though he moved slowly as always. On September 17, 1862, at Antietam Creek near Sharpsburg, Maryland, McClellan's army clashed with Lee's. The resulting **Battle of Antietam** was the bloodiest day in all of American history. A Confederate officer later described the battle.

Confederate artillery soldiers lie dead after the Battle of Antietam.

A VOICE FROM THE PAST

Again and again . . . by charges and counter-charges, this portion of the field was lost and recovered, until the green corn that grew upon it looked as if it had been struck by a storm of bloody hail. . . . From sheer exhaustion, both sides, like battered and bleeding athletes, seemed willing to rest.

John B. Gordon, quoted in *Voices of the Civil War*

After fighting all day, neither side had gained any ground by nightfall. The only difference was that about 25,000 men were dead or wounded. Lee, who lost as much as one-third of his fighting force, withdrew to Virginia. The cautious McClellan did not follow, missing a chance to finish off the crippled Southern army. Lincoln was so fed up that he fired McClellan in November, 1862. In the next chapter, you will learn about the historic action Lincoln took after the Battle of Antietam.

Section Assessment

1. Terms & Names

Explain the significance of:
- Ulysses S. Grant
- Battle of Shiloh
- cavalry
- Seven Days' Battles
- Battle of Antietam

2. Taking Notes

Review the section and find five key events to place on a time line as shown.

Which of these events do you think was most important?

3. Main Ideas

a. Why were Union victories in the West and the fall of New Orleans significant to the Union cause?

b. Why did Lee go on the offensive against the North?

c. How did the South's fortunes change after Lee took command of the Army of Northern Virginia?

4. Critical Thinking

Making Inferences What does Lee's invasion of the North suggest about his qualities as a general and a leader?

THINK ABOUT
- Lee's military skills and style
- the North's resources

ACTIVITY OPTIONS

GEOGRAPHY
ART

Develop a new military strategy for either the North or the South. Show your strategy on a **map** or in a **diagram** of troop movements.

Chapter 16 ASSESSMENT

TERMS & NAMES

Briefly explain the significance of each of the following.

1. Fort Sumter
2. Robert E. Lee
3. border state
4. blockade
5. hygiene
6. rifle
7. ironclad
8. Ulysses S. Grant
9. Battle of Shiloh
10. Battle of Antietam

REVIEW QUESTIONS

War Erupts (pages 465–471)

1. How and when did the Civil War start?
2. What advantages did the North have at the beginning of the war?
3. What were the war strategies of the two sides?

Life in the Army (pages 472–476)

4. What was the typical Civil War soldier like?
5. Why did so many people volunteer to fight in the Civil War?
6. Why was the incidence of disease so high among Civil War soldiers?
7. How did the use of rifles and minié balls change war tactics?

No End in Sight (pages 477–481)

8. What goal of the Union strategy did Grant further, and how did he do it?
9. Why did the North have such a hard time capturing Richmond, Virginia?
10. How did Lee's appointment to head the Army of Northern Virginia affect the course of the war?

CRITICAL THINKING

1. USING YOUR NOTES

	North	South
Reasons for fighting		
Advantages		
Disadvantages		
Military strategy		
Battle victories		

Using your completed chart, answer the questions.

a. Which side seemed likelier to win the war? Why?
b. Which side followed more closely its original strategy in the first two years of the war?

2. ANALYZING LEADERSHIP

Think about the leaders discussed in this chapter. Choose one. What character traits helped make him an effective leader?

3. APPLYING CITIZENSHIP SKILLS

Which individuals or groups of people demonstrated good and poor citizenship during the war? Explain your choices.

4. THEME: CITIZENSHIP

How could people on both sides of the Civil War believe that they were being good citizens by fighting?

5. MAKING DECISIONS

In your opinion, was Lincoln correct in deciding to go to war to save the Union? Explain your answer.

Interact *with* History

How did the consequences and effects of civil war that you predicted before you read the chapter compare with the actual conditions you read about?

VISUAL SUMMARY

The Civil War, 1861–1862

March 4, 1861 Lincoln inaugurated.

April 12, 1861 Fort Sumter fired upon by rebel forces.

April 15, 1861 Lincoln calls on states to provide 75,000 militiamen.

May 1861 Confederate Congress votes to set up capital in Richmond.

July 21, 1861 First Battle of Bull Run (Manassas)

February 1862 Union forces capture Fort Henry and Fort Donelson.

March 9, 1862 *Monitor* and *Merrimack* (*Virginia*) clash.

April 6, 1862 Battle of Shiloh

April 25, 1862 Fall of New Orleans

June 25 to July 1, 1862 Seven Days' Battles

September 17, 1862 Battle of Antietam (Sharpsburg)

November 1862 Lincoln relieves McClellan of command.

1861 — 1862

HISTORY SKILLS

1. INTERPRETING MAPS: Movement

Study the map and answer the questions.

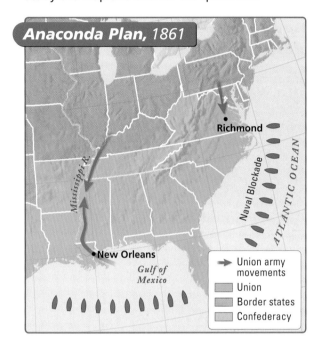

Anaconda Plan, 1861

Basic Map Elements

a. What is the subject of the map?

b. What do the colors of the states indicate?

Interpreting the Map

c. What does the arrow in the East indicate?

d. What two bodies of water did the blockade cover?

2. INTERPRETING PRIMARY SOURCES

The following quotation comes from a letter that Robert E. Lee wrote to his sister after Virginia had seceded from the Union and he had resigned from the U.S. Army. Read the quotation and then answer the questions.

> With all my devotion to the Union and the feeling of loyalty and duty of an American citizen, I have not been able to make up my mind to raise my hand against my relatives, my children, my home. I have, therefore, resigned my commission in the Army, and, save in defense of my native state, with the sincere hope that my poor services may never be needed, I hope I may never be called on to draw my sword.
>
> **Robert E. Lee,** quoted in *The Annals of America*

a. What inner conflict does Lee express?

b. What obligation or loyalty does Lee consider greater than his duty to his country?

ALTERNATIVE ASSESSMENT

1. INTERDISCIPLINARY ACTIVITY: Literature

Reading Letters Using the library or the Internet, find firsthand accounts of the Civil War and read some letters written by soldiers. Choose one letter to read aloud to the class. Then, pretend you are the person receiving the letter, and describe your reaction to it.

2. COOPERATIVE LEARNING ACTIVITY

Developing a Peace Proposal The Civil War broke out because the two sides could not reach a compromise. Work in a small group to develop a compromise that would have resolved the conflict between the North and the South. Have one person in the group take the position of a Northerner, another a Southerner, and the third a mediator between the two. Present your proposal to the class for their comments.

3. TECHNOLOGY ACTIVITY

Making a Class Presentation Life in the army training camps during the Civil War was hard. Information about life in the camps comes from primary sources. Using the library and the Internet, find diaries, letters, photographs, and news articles about daily life.

For more about Civil War army camps . . .

INTERNET ACTIVITY
CLASSZONE.COM

Plan an electronic presentation on army life for your class. Use the list of suggested topics below to begin brainstorming.

- Drawings, maps, and photos that show the design of a typical camp
- Items used for cooking, lodging, sanitation, military drilling, and recreation
- Drills and maneuvers soldiers learned
- Personal belongings of the Yankees and rebels
- Firsthand accounts of camp life from letters and diaries
- Changes in camp life as the war dragged on

4. HISTORY PORTFOLIO

Review the questions that you wrote for What Do You Want to Know? on page 464. Then write a short report in which you explain the answers to your questions. Be sure to use standard grammar, spelling, sentence structure, and punctuation in your report. If any questions were not answered, do research to answer them. Add your report to your portfolio.

Additional Test Practice, pp. S1–S33

TEST PRACTICE
CLASSZONE.COM

CHAPTER 17

The Tide of War Turns 1863–1865

Confederate and Union cavalry clash at Yellow Tavern, Virginia, on May 11, 1864.

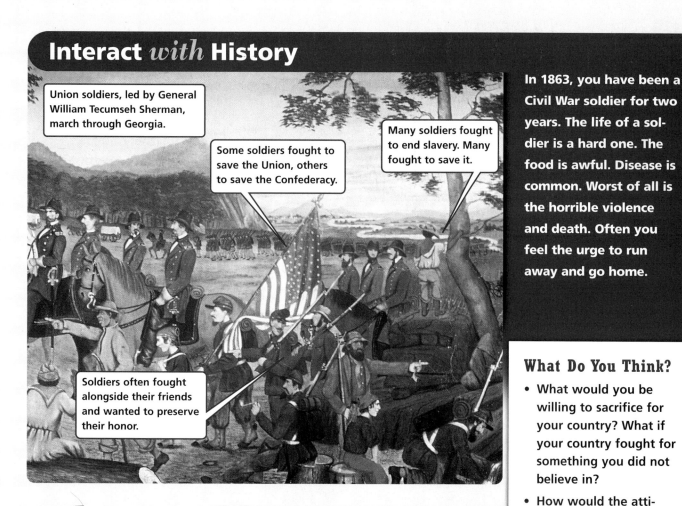

Union soldiers, led by General William Tecumseh Sherman, march through Georgia.

Some soldiers fought to save the Union, others to save the Confederacy.

Many soldiers fought to end slavery. Many fought to save it.

Soldiers often fought alongside their friends and wanted to preserve their honor.

In 1863, you have been a Civil War soldier for two years. The life of a soldier is a hard one. The food is awful. Disease is common. Worst of all is the horrible violence and death. Often you feel the urge to run away and go home.

What would inspire you to keep fighting?

What Do You Think?

- What would you be willing to sacrifice for your country? What if your country fought for something you did not believe in?

- How would the attitudes of fellow soldiers influence your decision?

USA
World **1863**

January 1863
Emancipation Proclamation is issued.

July 1863
Battle of Gettysburg takes place.
Union takes Vicksburg.

March 1864
Grant is put in charge of all Union armies.

Nove...
Li...n...

April 1865
Union takes Richmond.
Lee surrenders at Appomattox Court House.
Lincoln is assassinated.

1866

January 1863
Polish nationalists revolt against Russian rule.

July 1863
Source of Nile River is found at Lake Victoria in present-day Uganda.

June 1864
Archduke Maximilian of Austria becomes emperor of Mexico.

September 1864
First International Workingmen's Association is established, and Karl Marx becomes its leader.

September 1865
English officials arrest *Fenian* leaders of planned uprising in Ireland.

BEFORE YOU READ

Previewing the Theme

Impact of the Individual During the Civil War, thousands of citizens and soldiers acted with great dignity and courage. Leading these men and women were some of the most extraordinary leaders the nation has ever had. You will read more about these citizens and soldiers in Chapter 17.

Robert E. Lee was the military genius at the head of the Confederate armies.

Abraham Lincoln is one of the greatest presidents the United States has ever had.

Jefferson Davis, the Confederate president, had the difficult task of keeping the South united.

Ulysses S. Grant took charge of the Union armies in March 1864.

What Do You Know?

What advantages and disadvantages did the North and the South have? Did particular individuals give either side an advantage during the Civil War?

THINK ABOUT
- what qualities contribute to the success of military leaders
- the importance of obeying orders for soldiers even if it might mean death

What Do You Want to Know?

What questions do you have about the later part of the Civil War and how it ended? Make a list of those questions before you read the chapter.

READ AND TAKE NOTES

Reading Strategy: Comparing and Contrasting
When you study historical events, it is important to compare and contrast the effects that events had on different individuals and groups. A single event might affect two groups of people in completely different ways. Use the chart below to compare and contrast the impact of events on the Union and the Confederacy in the later years of the Civil War.

 See Skillbuilder Handbook, page R10.

	North	South
Emancipation Proclamation		
War's Impact		
Northern Victories in Battle		
Union Wins Civil War		

The Emancipation Proclamation

MAIN IDEA	WHY IT MATTERS NOW
In 1863, President Lincoln issued the Emancipation Proclamation, which helped to change the war's course.	The Emancipation Proclamation was an important step in ending slavery in the United States.

ONE AMERICAN'S STORY

During the Civil War, abolitionists like Frederick Douglass continued their fight against slavery. Douglass urged President Lincoln to emancipate, or free, enslaved Americans. "Sound policy . . . demands the instant liberation of every slave in the rebel states," he declared.

A VOICE FROM THE PAST

To fight against slaveholders, without fighting against slavery, is but a half-hearted business, and paralyzes the hands engaged in it. . . . Fire must be met with water. . . . War for the destruction of liberty [by the South] must be met with war for the destruction of slavery.

Frederick Douglass, quoted in *Battle Cry of Freedom*

During the Civil War, Frederick Douglass offered advice to President Lincoln. He urged the president to make the conflict a war against slavery.

Douglass pointed out that the Confederate war effort depended on slave labor. Enslaved Americans worked in Southern mines, fields, and factories. They also built forts and hauled supplies for rebel armies. For both practical and moral reasons, he said, Lincoln should free the slaves. In this section, you will learn how ending slavery became an important goal of the Civil War.

Calls for Emancipation

Throughout the war, abolitionists such as Frederick Douglass had been urging Lincoln to emancipate enslaved persons. Many criticized the president for being too cautious. Some even charged that Lincoln's lack of action aided the Confederate cause.

Still, Lincoln hesitated. He did not believe he had the power under the Constitution to abolish slavery where it already existed. Nor did he want to anger the four slave states that remained in the Union. He also knew that most Northern Democrats, and many Republicans, opposed emancipation.

Lincoln did not want the issue of slavery to divide the nation further than it already had. Although he disliked slavery, the president's first priority was to preserve the Union. "If I could save the Union without freeing *any* slave I would do it," he declared. "If I could save it by freeing *all* the slaves I would do it; and if I could save it by freeing some and leaving others alone, I would also do that."

By the summer of 1862, however, Lincoln had decided in favor of emancipation. The war was taking a terrible toll. If freeing the slaves helped weaken the South, then he would do it. Lincoln waited, however, for a moment when he was in a position of strength. After General Lee's forces were stopped at Antietam, Lincoln decided to act.

The Emancipation Proclamation

On January 1, 1863, Lincoln issued the **Emancipation Proclamation,** which freed all slaves in Confederate territory. The proclamation had a tremendous impact on the public. However, it freed very few slaves. Most of the slaves that Lincoln intended to liberate lived in areas distant from the Union troops that could enforce his proclamation.

Lincoln presents the Emancipation Proclamation to his cabinet.

A VOICE FROM THE PAST

On the first day of January, in the year of our Lord one thousand eight hundred and sixty-three, all persons held as slaves within any State or designated part of a State, the people whereof shall then be in rebellion against the United States, shall be then, [thenceforth], and forever free.

Abraham Lincoln, from the *Emancipation Proclamation*

Why, critics charged, did Lincoln free slaves only in the South? The answer was in the Constitution. Because freeing Southern slaves weakened the Confederacy, the proclamation could be seen as a military action. As commander-in-chief, Lincoln had this authority. Yet the Constitution did not give the president the power to free slaves within the Union. But Lincoln did ask Congress to abolish slavery gradually throughout the land.

Although the Emancipation Proclamation did not free many enslaved people at the time it was issued, it was important as a symbolic measure. For the North, the Civil War was no longer a limited war whose main goal was to preserve the Union. It was a war of liberation.

Response to the Proclamation

Abolitionists were thrilled that Lincoln had finally issued the Emancipation Proclamation. "We shout for joy that we live to record this righteous decree," wrote Frederick Douglass. Still, many believed the law should have gone further. They were upset that Lincoln had not freed *all* enslaved persons, including those in the border states.

Reading **History**

B. Summarizing
Why did Northern Democrats oppose the Emancipation Proclamation?

Other people in the North, especially Democrats, were angered by the president's decision. Northern Democrats, the majority of whom were against emancipating even Southern slaves, claimed that the proclamation would only make the war longer by continuing to anger the South. A newspaperman in Ohio called Lincoln's proclamation "monstrous, impudent, and heinous . . . insulting to God as to man."

Most Union soldiers, though, welcomed emancipation. One officer noted that, although few soldiers were abolitionists, most were happy "to destroy everything that . . . gives the rebels strength."

White Southerners reacted to the proclamation with rage. Although it had limited impact in areas outside the reach of Northern armies, many slaves began to run away to Union lines. At the same time that these slaves deprived the Confederacy of labor, they also began to provide the Union with soldiers.

African-American Soldiers

In addition to freeing slaves, the Emancipation Proclamation declared that African-American men willing to fight "will be received into the armed service of the United States."

Frederick Douglass had argued for the recruitment of African-American soldiers since the start of the war. He declared, "Once [you] let the black man get upon his person the brass letters, U.S. . . . there is no power on earth which can deny that he has earned the right to citizenship."

Before the proclamation, the federal government had discouraged the enlistment of African Americans, and only a few regiments were formed. After emancipation, African Americans rushed to join the army. By war's end, about 180,000 black soldiers wore the blue uniform of the Union army.

African-American soldiers were organized in all-black regiments, usually led by white officers. They were often given the worst jobs

Thousands of African Americans, such as these men of the 4th U.S. Colored Troops, fought for the Union during the Civil War.

AFRICAN AMERICANS IN THE MILITARY

During the Civil War, no African-American soldier was promoted above the rank of captain. But times have changed. In 1989, General Colin Powell (shown below) was made a four-star general and named chairman of the Joint Chiefs of Staff—the highest position in the military.

General Powell's appointment was the climax of a long struggle to fully integrate American armed forces. From the Civil War through World War II, African-American soldiers were kept apart from white soldiers and denied equal rights. However, in 1948, President Harry Truman ended segregation in the armed forces. Today the American military is fully integrated.

to do and were paid less than white soldiers. Despite these obstacles, African-American soldiers showed great courage on the battlefield and wore their uniforms with pride. More than one regiment insisted on fighting without pay rather than accepting lower pay than the white soldiers.

The 54th Massachusetts

One unit that insisted on fighting without pay was the **54th Massachusetts Regiment,** one of the first African-American regiments organized in the North. The soldiers of the 54th—among whom were two sons of Frederick Douglass—soon made the regiment the most famous of the Civil War.

The 54th Massachusetts earned its greatest fame in July 1863, when it led a heroic attack on Fort Wagner in South Carolina. The soldiers' bravery at Fort Wagner made the 54th a household name in the North and increased African-American enlistment.

The soldiers of the 54th Massachusetts and other African-American regiments faced grave dangers if captured. Rather than take African Americans as prisoners, Confederate soldiers often shot them or returned them to slavery.

The war demanded great sacrifices, not only from soldiers and prisoners, but also from people back home. In the next section, you will read about the hardships that the Civil War placed on the civilian populations in both the North and the South.

Reading **History**

C. Identifying Facts How did many black soldiers protest when they were offered lower pay than white soldiers?

Section 1 Assessment

1. Terms & Names

Explain the significance of:
- Emancipation Proclamation
- 54th Massachusetts Regiment

2. Taking Notes

Use a chart to record responses to the Emancipation Proclamation.

How did the proclamation change Northerners' views of the war?

3. Main Ideas

a. What was Lincoln's reason for not emancipating slaves when the war began?

b. Why was the immediate impact of the Emancipation Proclamation limited?

c. Why did black soldiers often face greater hardships than white soldiers?

4. Critical Thinking

Recognizing Effects How did the Emancipation Proclamation change the role of African Americans in the war?

THINK ABOUT
- how the proclamation changed military policy
- the response of many Southern slaves to the proclamation

ACTIVITY OPTIONS

TECHNOLOGY

MUSIC

Do research on the 54th Massachusetts Regiment. Create a **Web site** for the regiment or write a **song** about the soldiers' heroism at Fort Wagner.

② War Affects Society

TERMS & NAMES
Copperhead
conscription
bounty
income tax
greenback
Clara Barton

MAIN IDEA	WHY IT MATTERS NOW
The Civil War caused social, economic, and political changes in the North and the South.	Some changes, like the growth of industry, affected Americans long after the end of Civil War.

ONE AMERICAN'S STORY

As the Civil War moved into its third year, the constant demand for men and resources began to take its toll back home. Sometimes, the hardships endured by civilians resulted in angry scenes like that witnessed by Agnes, a resident of Richmond, Virginia.

On April 3, 1863, Agnes went for her morning walk and soon came upon a group of hungry women and children, who had gathered in front of the capitol. She described the scene as these women and children were joined by other people who were upset by the shortage of food.

A VOICE FROM THE PAST

The crowd now rapidly increased, and numbered, I am sure, more than a thousand women and children. It grew and grew until it reached the dignity of a mob—a bread riot.

Agnes, quoted in *Reminiscences of Peace and War*

Food became scarce in many places during the Civil War. Here, women demand milk for their hungry families.

The mob then went out of control. It broke into shops and stole food, clothing, and other goods. Only the arrival of Confederate president Jefferson Davis and the threat of force ended the riot.

In this section, you will read more about hardships that the Civil War caused on the home front. These hardships caused changes in civilian society in both the North and the South.

Disagreement About the War

In the spring of 1863, riots like the one in Richmond broke out in a number of Southern towns. Southerners were growing weary of the war and the constant sacrifices it demanded.

Confederate soldiers began to leave the army in increasing numbers. By the end of the year, the Confederate army had lost nearly 40 percent of its men. Some of these men were on leave, but many others were deserters.

In this political cartoon, the Union defends itself against "Copperheads." This was the name given to Northerners who sympathized with the South.

Faced with the difficulties of waging war, the Confederate states fell into disagreement. The same principle of states' rights that led them to break with the Union kept them from coordinating their war effort. As one Southern governor put it, "I am *still* a rebel . . . no matter who may be in power."

Disagreements over the conduct of the war also arose in the North. Lincoln's main opponents were the **Copperheads,** Northern Democrats who favored peace with the South. (A copperhead is a poisonous snake that strikes without warning.) Lincoln had protesters arrested. He also suspended the writ of habeas corpus, which prevents the government from holding citizens without a trial.

Vocabulary
writ: a written order issued by a court of law

The Draft Laws

As the war dragged on, both the North and the South needed more soldiers. As a result, both sides passed laws of **conscription,** also known as the draft. These laws required men to serve in the military.

The Confederates had been drafting soldiers since the spring of 1862. By 1863, all able-bodied white men between the ages of 18 and 45 were required to join the army. However, there were a number of exceptions. Planters who owned 20 or more slaves could avoid military service. In addition, wealthy men could hire substitutes to serve in their place. By 1863, substitutes might cost as much as $6,000. The fact that wealthy men could avoid service caused poor Southerners to complain that it was a "rich man's war but a poor man's fight."

The Union draft law was passed in March 1863. Like the Confederacy, the Union allowed draftees to hire substitutes. However, the North also offered $300 **bounties,** or cash payments, to men who volunteered to serve. As a result, only a small percentage of men in the North were drafted. Most men volunteered and received the bounty.

Reading **History**
A. Drawing Conclusions Why were many soldiers dissatisfied with the draft laws?

Even so, the draft was extremely unpopular. In July 1863, anger over the draft and simmering racial tensions led to the New York City draft riots. For four days, rioters destroyed property and attacked people on the streets. Over 100 people were killed—many of them African Americans.

Economic Effects of the War

Many people suffered economic hardship during the war. The suffering was severe in the South, where most battles were fought, but the North also experienced difficulties.

Food shortages were very common in the South, partly because so many farmers were fighting in the Confederate army. Moreover, food sometimes could not get to market because trains were now being used to carry war materials. The Confederate army also seized food and other supplies for its own needs.

Reading **History**

B. Analyzing Causes Why were economic problems particularly bad in the South?

Another problem, especially in the South, was inflation—an increase in price and decrease in the value of money. The average family food bill in the South increased from $6.65 a month in 1861 to $68 by mid–1863. Over the course of the war, prices rose 9,000 percent in the South.

Inflation in the North was much lower, but prices still rose faster than wages, making life harder for working people. Some people took advantage of wartime demand and sold goods for high prices.

Overall, though, war production boosted Northern industry and fueled the economy. In the short term, this gave the North an economic advantage over the South. In the long term, industry would begin to replace farming as the basis of the national economy.

During the war, the federal government passed two important economic measures. In 1861, it established the first **income tax**—a tax on earnings. The following year, the government issued a new paper currency, known as **greenbacks** because of their color. The new currency helped the Northern economy by ensuring that people had money to spend. It also helped the Union to pay for the war.

Some Southerners in the border states took advantage of the stronger Union economy by selling cotton to Northern traders, in violation of Confederate law. "Yankee gold," wrote one Confederate officer, "is fast accomplishing what Yankee arms could never achieve—the subjugation of our people."

Vocabulary
subjugate: to bring under control or to conquer

Resistance by Slaves

Another factor that affected the South was the growing resistance from slaves. To hurt the Southern economy, slaves slowed their pace of work or stopped working altogether. Some carried out sabotage, destroying crops and farm equipment to hurt the plantation economy. When white

daily *life*

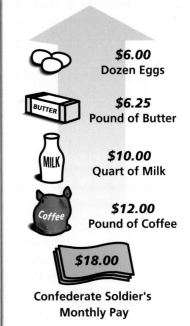

INFLATION IN THE SOUTH
During the Civil War, inflation caused hardship in the North and the South. But inflation was especially severe in the Confederacy, where prices could become outrageously high.

The food prices shown below are from 1864. Consider how many days it took a Confederate soldier to earn enough money to buy each of these foods.

$6.00
Dozen Eggs

$6.25
Pound of Butter

$10.00
Quart of Milk

$12.00
Pound of Coffee

$18.00

Confederate Soldier's Monthly Pay

planters fled advancing Union armies, slaves often refused to go along. They stayed behind, waiting for Union soldiers to free them.

Some enslaved people even rose up in rebellion against their overseers. More commonly, though, slaves ran away from plantations to join the Union forces as they pushed farther into Confederate territory. One Union officer described a common sight.

A VOICE FROM THE PAST

It was very touching to see the vast numbers of colored [African-American] women following after us with babies in their arms, and little ones like our Anna clinging to their tattered skirts. One poor creature, while nobody was looking, hid two boys, five years old, in a wagon, intending, I suppose that they should see the land of freedom if she couldn't.

Union officer, quoted in *The Civil War*

After Lincoln issued the Emancipation Proclamation, the number of slaves fleeing Southern plantations greatly increased. By the end of the war, as many as half a million had fled to Union lines.

Women Aid the War Effort

With so many men away at war, women in both the North and the South assumed increased responsibilities. Women plowed fields and ran farms and plantations. They also took over jobs in offices and factories that had previously been done only by men.

Other social changes came about because of the thousands of women who served on the front lines as volunteer workers and nurses. Susie King Taylor was an African-American woman who wrote an account of her experiences as a volunteer with an African-American regiment. She asked her readers to remember that "many lives were lost,—not men alone but noble women as well."

Relief agencies put women to work washing clothes, gathering supplies, and cooking food for soldiers. Also, nursing became a respectable profession for many women. By the end of the war, around 3,000 nurses had worked under the leadership of Dorothea Dix in Union hospitals. Southern women were also active as nurses and as volunteers on the front.

*Reading*History
C. Summarizing
How did women participate in the Civil War?

Women also played a key role as spies in both the North and the South. Harriet Tubman served as a spy for Union forces along the coast of South Carolina. The most famous Confederate spy was Belle Boyd. Although she was arrested six times, she continued her work through much of the war. At one point, she even sent messages from her jail cell by putting them in little rubber balls and tossing them out the window.

Civil War Prison Camps

Women caught spying were thrown into jail, but soldiers captured in battle suffered far more. At prison camps in both the North and the South, prisoners of war faced terrible conditions.

One of the worst prison camps in the North was in Elmira, New York. Perhaps the harshest feature of a prisoner's life at the camp was the New York winter. One prisoner called Elmira "an excellent summer prison for southern soldiers, but an excellent place for them to find their graves in the winter." In just one year, more than 24 percent of Elmira's 12,121 prisoners died of sickness and exposure to severe weather.

Conditions were also horrible in the South. The camp with the worst reputation was at Andersonville, Georgia. Built to hold 10,000 prisoners, at one point it housed 33,000. Inmates had little shelter from the heat or cold. Most slept in holes scratched in the dirt. Drinking water came from one tiny creek that also served as a sewer. As many as 100 men per day died at Andersonville from starvation, disease, and exposure.

People who saw the camps were shocked by the condition of the soldiers. The poet Walt Whitman—who served as a Union nurse—described a group of soldiers who returned from a prison camp. He exclaimed, "Can those be *men?* . . . are they not really mummied, dwindled corpses?"

Around 50,000 men died in Civil War prison camps. But this number was dwarfed by the number of dead on the battlefronts and even more from disease in army camps. In the next section, you will read about the bloody battles that led to the end of the Civil War.

*Reading*History
D. Making Inferences Why were death rates so high at many Civil War prison camps?

The terrible conditions at Civil War prison camps caused much suffering and death.

Section 2 Assessment

1. Terms & Names

Explain the significance of:

- Copperhead
- conscription
- bounty
- income tax
- greenback
- Clara Barton

2. Taking Notes

Use a diagram like the one below to compare conditions in the North and South during the later years of war.

Conditions During the War

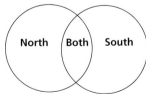

North | Both | South

3. Main Ideas

a. How did the South's principle of states' rights undermine the Confederate war effort?

b. How did the draft laws in the North and South differ?

c. What conditions at prison camps caused so many to suffer behind enemy lines?

4. Critical Thinking

Making Generalizations What economic changes took place during the Civil War?

THINK ABOUT

- the war's effect on prices
- industry and agriculture
- new economic measures begun by the government

ACTIVITY OPTIONS

GEOGRAPHY

SPEECH

Study Civil War prison camps. Make a **map** showing where they were located or give a **speech** explaining why prisoners should be treated better.

③ **The North Wins**

TERMS & NAMES
Battle of Gettysburg
Pickett's Charge
Ulysses S. Grant
Robert E. Lee
Siege of Vicksburg
William Tecumseh Sherman
Appomattox Court House

MAIN IDEA	WHY IT MATTERS NOW
Thanks to victories, beginning with Gettysburg and ending with Richmond, the Union survived.	If the Union had lost the war, the United States might look very different now.

ONE AMERICAN'S STORY

Joshua Lawrence Chamberlain was a 32-year-old college professor when the war began. Determined to fight for the Union, he left his job and took command of troops from his home state of Maine. Like most soldiers, Chamberlain had to get accustomed to the carnage of the Civil War. His description of the aftermath of one battle shows how soldiers got used to the war's violence.

A VOICE FROM THE PAST

It seemed best to [put] myself between two dead men among the many left there by earlier assaults, and to draw another crosswise for a pillow out of the trampled, blood-soaked sod, pulling the flap of his coat over my face to fend off the chilling winds, and still more chilling, the deep, many voiced moan [of the wounded] that overspread the field.

Joshua Lawrence Chamberlain, quoted in *The Civil War*

During the war, Chamberlain fought in 24 battles. He was wounded six times and had six horses shot out from under him. He is best remembered for his actions at the Battle of Gettysburg, where he courageously held off a fierce rebel attack. In this section, you will read about that battle and others that led to the end of the Civil War.

In 1862, Joshua Chamberlain was offered a year's travel with pay to study languages in Europe. He chose to fight for the Union instead.

The Road to Gettysburg

In September 1862, General McClellan stopped General Lee's Northern attack at the Battle of Antietam. But the cautious McClellan failed to finish off Lee's army, which retreated safely to Virginia.

President Lincoln, who was frustrated by McClellan, replaced him with Ambrose Burnside. But Burnside also proved to be a disappointment. At the Battle of Fredericksburg, Virginia, in December 1862, Burnside attacked Confederate troops who had dug trenches. The bloody result was 12,600 Union casualties. This disastrous attack led General Lee to remark, "It is well that war is so terrible—we should grow too fond of it!"

Lincoln replaced Burnside with General Joseph Hooker, who faced Lee the following May at Chancellorsville, Virginia. The result was yet another Union disaster. With half as many men as Hooker, Lee still managed to cut the Union forces to pieces. However, the South paid a high price for its victory. As General "Stonewall" Jackson returned from a patrol on May 2, Confederate guards thought he was a Union soldier and shot him in the arm. Shortly after a surgeon amputated the arm, Jackson caught pneumonia. On May 10, Lee's prized general was dead.

In spite of Jackson's tragic death, Lee decided to head North once again. He hoped that a Confederate victory in Union territory would fuel Northern discontent with the war and bring calls for peace. He also hoped a Southern victory would lead European nations to give diplomatic recognition and aid to the Confederacy.

The Battle of Gettysburg

In late June 1863, Lee crossed into southern Pennsylvania. The Confederates learned of a supply of shoes in the town of Gettysburg and went to investigate. There, on July 1, they ran into Union troops. Both sides called for reinforcements, and the **Battle of Gettysburg** was on.

*Reading***History**

A. Reading a Map Use the map and illustration on pages 498–499 to study Gettysburg's geography.

The fighting raged for three days. On the rocky hills and fields around Gettysburg, 90,000 Union troops, under the command of General George Meade, clashed with 75,000 Confederates.

During the struggle, Union forces tried to hold their ground on Cemetery Ridge, just south of town, while rebel soldiers tried to dislodge them. At times, the air seemed full of bullets. "The balls were whizzing so thick," said one Texan, "that it looked like a man could hold out a hat and catch it full."

The turning point came on July 3, when Lee ordered General George Pickett to mount a direct attack on the middle of the Union line. It was a deadly mistake. Some 13,000 rebel troops charged up the ridge into heavy Union fire. One soldier recalled "bayonet thrusts, sabre strokes, pistol shots . . . men going down on their hands and knees, spinning round like tops . . . ghastly heaps of dead men."

*Reading***History**

B. Making Inferences Why might Lincoln have been disappointed after the Union victory at Gettysburg?

Pickett's Charge, as this attack came to be known, was torn to pieces. The Confederates retreated and waited for a Union counterattack. But once again, Lincoln's generals failed to finish off Lee's army. The furious Lincoln wondered when he would find a general who would defeat Lee once and for all.

Even so, the Union rejoiced over the victory at Gettysburg. Lee's hopes for a Confederate victory in the North were crushed. The North had lost 23,000 men, but Southern losses were even greater. Over one-third of Lee's army, 28,000 men, lay dead or wounded. Sick at heart, Lee led his army back to Virginia.

America's HERITAGE

THE GETTYSBURG ADDRESS

On November 19, 1863, President Lincoln spoke at the dedication of a cemetery in Gettysburg for the 3,500 soldiers buried there. His speech was short, and few who heard it were impressed. Lincoln himself called it "a flat failure."

Even so, the Gettysburg Address has since been recognized as one of the greatest speeches of all time. In it, Lincoln declared that the nation was founded on "the proposition that all men are created equal." He ended with a plea to continue the fight for democracy so that "government of the people, by the people, for the people shall not perish from the earth."

See page 508 for the full text of the Gettysburg Address.

GEOGRAPHY *in* HISTORY

PLACE AND HUMAN-ENVIRONMENT INTERACTION

Battle of Gettysburg

A monument stands today near a ridge at the Gettysburg battlefield. Labeled the "High Water Mark of the Rebellion," it shows how far Confederate troops advanced against Union lines. There, on July 3, 1863, the South came closest to winning the Civil War.

The fighting began on July 1. When a Confederate force captured Gettysburg, Union defenders took up new positions in the hills south of town. The next day, Confederate troops attacked across a wheat field and peach orchard in an attempt to seize the hill called Little Round Top. But Union forces held their ground.

July 3 was the decisive day. Lee, having failed to crack the side of General Meade's Union line, attacked its center. In an assault that came to be known as Pickett's Charge, some 13,000 men charged uphill across an open field toward the Union lines along Cemetery Ridge. Union soldiers covered the field with rifle and cannon fire. "Pickett's Charge" was a Confederate disaster.

PENNSYLVANIA
•Gettysburg
Washington, D.C. ✪

Before beginning the charge named for him, Major General Pickett wrote to his fiancée, "My brave Virginians are to attack in front. Oh, may God in mercy help me."

ARTIFACT FILE

Soldiers' Diaries Many Civil War soldiers wrote about their wartime experiences in personal diaries, such as this one belonging to Sergeant Alfred S. Rowe of Maryland.

Regimental Flag Flags helped soldiers to identify the different sides during battle. Often, a regiment's flag would show the names of battles it had fought. This flag, which belonged to the 28th North Carolina, was captured at Pickett's Charge.

Gettysburg

Culp's Hill

Cemetery Hill

Cemetery Ridge

As in many battles of the Civil War, the outcome at Gettysburg was affected by the landscape. Both sides fought for control of the high ground. Union control of the two "Round Top" hills, Cemetery Ridge and Culp's Hill, gave Meade the advantage.

Peach Orchard

Wheat Field

Devil's Den

Little Round Top

Big Round Top

On-Line Field Trip

The Gettysburg National Military Park Museum contains many objects relating to the Battle of Gettysburg, including this federal bass drum. This heavy drum—two feet in diameter—was harnessed to the neck of a soldier, who beat time with leather-covered wooden mallets.

For more about Gettysburg . . .

RESEARCH LINKS
CLASSZONE.COM

CONNECT TO GEOGRAPHY

1. **Place** How might Confederate positions on low ground have put them at a disadvantage?
2. **Human-Environment Interaction** How might the attitudes of Union soldiers have been affected by fighting in their own territory?

   G See Geography Handbook, pages 4–5.

CONNECT TO HISTORY

3. **Asking Questions** Ask and answer a question about how the geographic patterns of the Gettysburg area affected the battle?

AMERICA'S HISTORY MAKERS

ULYSSES S. GRANT
1822–1885
<u>General Ulysses S. Grant</u> was an unlikely war hero. Although educated at West Point Military Academy, he was a poor student and showed little interest in an army career. With his quiet manner and rumpled uniform, he often failed to impress his fellow officers.

Yet on the battlefield, Grant proved to be a brilliant general. Highly focused and cool under fire, he won the first major Union victories of the war.

Grant was willing to fight Lee—even if the costs were high. He told his generals, "Wherever Lee goes, there you will go also."

ROBERT E. LEE
1807–1870
<u>Robert E. Lee</u> seemed destined for greatness. In his crisp uniform and trim, white beard, Lee was a dashing figure on the battlefield.

Born to a leading Virginia family, Lee was a top student at West Point and won praise for his actions in the Mexican War. General Winfield Scott called him "the very best soldier I have ever seen in the field."

Lee did not want to fight the Union, but he felt he had to stand by Virginia. "I did only what my duty demanded," Lee said. "I could have taken no other course without dishonor."

How did the tough decisions made by Grant and Lee affect the Civil War?

The Siege of Vicksburg

On July 4, 1863, the day after Pickett's Charge, the Union received more good news. In Mississippi, General Ulysses S. Grant had defeated Confederate troops at the **Siege of Vicksburg**.

The previous year, Grant had won important victories in the West that opened up the Mississippi River for travel deep into the South. Vicksburg was the last major Confederate stronghold on the river. Grant had begun his attack on Vicksburg in May 1863. But when his direct attacks failed, he settled in for a long siege. Grant's troops surrounded the city and prevented the delivery of food and supplies. Eventually, the Confederates ran out of food. In desperation, they ate mules, dogs, and even rats. Finally, after nearly a month and a half, they surrendered.

The Union victory fulfilled a major part of the Anaconda Plan. The North had taken New Orleans the previous spring. Now, with complete control over the Mississippi River, the South was split in two.

With the victories at Vicksburg and Gettysburg, the tide of war turned in favor of the North. Britain gave up all thought of supporting the South. And, in General Grant, President Lincoln found a man who was willing to fight General Lee.

Vocabulary
siege: the surrounding of a city, town, or fortress by an army trying to capture it

Background
The Anaconda Plan called for blockading Southern ports, taking control of the Mississippi, and capturing Richmond.

Sherman's Total War

In March 1864, President Lincoln named General Grant commander of all the Union armies. Grant then developed a plan to defeat the Confederacy. He would pursue Lee's army in Virginia, while Union forces under General **William Tecumseh Sherman** pushed through the Deep South to Atlanta and the Atlantic coast.

Battling southward from Tennessee, Sherman took Atlanta in September 1864. He then set out on a march to the sea, cutting a path of destruction up to 60 miles wide and 300 miles long through Georgia.

Sherman waged total war: a war not only against enemy troops, but against everything that supports the enemy. His troops tore up rail lines, destroyed crops, and burned and looted towns.

Reading History
C. **Drawing Conclusions** How might the political situation in the North have been different if Sherman had not taken Atlanta?

Sherman's triumph in Atlanta was important for Lincoln. In 1864, the president was running for reelection, but his prospects were not good. Northerners were tired of war, and Democrats— who had nominated George McClellan—stood a good chance of winning on an antiwar platform.

Sherman's success changed all that. Suddenly, Northerners could sense victory. Lincoln took 55 percent of the popular vote and won re-election. In his second inaugural speech, Lincoln hoped for a speedy end to the war: "With malice towards none; with charity for all; . . . let us strive on to finish the work we are in; to bind up the nation's wounds; . . . to do all which may achieve and cherish a just, and a lasting peace." (See page 509 for more of Lincoln's Second Inaugural Address.)

In December, Sherman took Savannah, Georgia. He then sent a telegram to Lincoln: "I beg to present you, as a Christmas gift, the city of Savannah, with 150 heavy guns and . . . about 25,000 bales of cotton."

> *"Let us strive . . . to bind up the nation's wounds."*
> Abraham Lincoln

The Civil War, 1863–1865

- Area controlled by Union
- Area won by Union, 1863–1865
- Area controlled by Confederacy
- Union troop movements
- Confederate troop movements
- ✷ Union victory
- ✷ Confederate victory

NEW YORK
CONN.
MARYLAND
Washington, D.C.
PENNSYLVANIA
OHIO
Gettysburg July 1863
N.J.
MD.
DEL.
Washington, D.C.
Fredericksburg Dec. 1862
Chancellorsville May 1863
W.V.
Richmond
VIRGINIA
Ohio R.

Wilderness, May 5–6, 1864
Spotsylvania May 8–19, 1864
Cold Harbor, June 1864
VIRGINIA
Richmond
Petersburg, June 1864–Apr. 1865
Appomattox Court House, Apr. 9, 1865 Lee surrenders to Grant
Potomac River
Rappahannock R.
James River
Lee
Grant

MISSOURI
KENTUCKY
Mississippi R.
Grant
ARKANSAS
Nashville
TENNESSEE
Chattanooga Nov. 1863
NORTH CAROLINA
Raleigh
Corinth
Grant
SOUTH CAROLINA
Wilmington
ATLANTIC OCEAN
Columbia
MISSISSIPPI
Atlanta
ALABAMA
Sherman
Charleston
Ft. Wagner July 1863
Union Blockade
Vicksburg July 1863
Montgomery
GEORGIA
Savannah occupied Dec. 1864
N
0   200 Miles
0   400 Kilometers
LOUISIANA
Mobile
Pensacola
St. Augustine
Jacksonville
New Orleans
Gulf of Mexico
FLORIDA

GEOGRAPHY SKILLBUILDER Interpreting Maps
1. **Movement** *About how many miles did Sherman's troops have to march to get from Atlanta to Savannah?*
2. **Location** *At what location did Grant and Lee face off for nearly ten months?*

In 1861, Congress created the Medal of Honor to reward individual bravery in combat.

Grant's Virginia Campaign

After taking Savannah, Sherman moved north through the Carolinas seeking to meet up with Grant's troops in Virginia. Since May 1864, Grant and his generals had been fighting savage battles against Lee's forces. In battle after battle, Grant would attack, rest, then attack again, all the while moving south toward Richmond.

At the Battle of the Wilderness in May 1864, Union and Confederate forces fought in a tangle of trees and brush so thick that they could barely see each other. Grant lost over 17,000 men, but he pushed on. "Whatever happens," he told Lincoln, "we will not retreat."

At Spotsylvania and Cold Harbor, the fighting continued. Again, the losses were staggering. Grant's attack in June, at Cold Harbor, cost him 7,000 men, most in the first few minutes of battle. Some Union troops were so sure they would die in battle that they pinned their names and addresses to their jackets so their bodies could be identified later.

In June 1864, Grant's armies arrived at Petersburg, just south of Richmond. Unable to break through the Confederate defenses, the Union forces dug trenches and settled in for a long siege. The two sides faced off for ten months.

In the end, though, Lee could not hold out. Grant was drawing a noose around Richmond. So Lee pulled out, leaving the Confederate capital undefended. The Union army marched into Richmond on April 3. One Richmond woman recalled, "Exactly at eight o'clock the Confederate flag that fluttered above the Capitol came

*Reading*History

D. Reading a Map Use the map on page 501 to find the locations of the major battles of Grant's Virginia campaign.

HISTORY *through*ART

This photograph shows Union officers before the Battle of the Wilderness. Next to the tree on the right is the photographer Mathew Brady. Photography was still a new art when the Civil War began. Brady's Civil War photos represent one of the first examples of photojournalism.

How might people's attitudes toward war be affected when they can see pictures from the front lines?

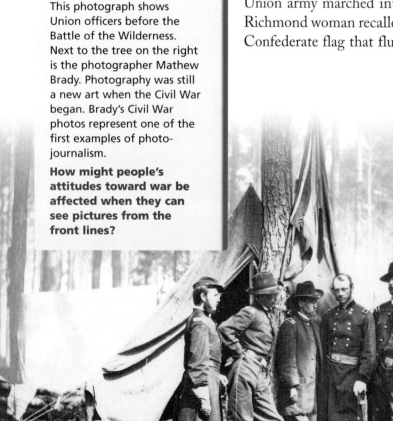

down and the Stars and Stripes were run up. . . . We covered our faces and cried aloud."

Surrender at Appomattox

From Richmond and Petersburg, Lee fled west, while Grant followed in pursuit. Lee wanted to continue fighting, but he knew that his situation was hopeless. He sent a message to General Grant that he was ready to surrender.

On April 9, 1865, Lee and Grant met in the small Virginia town of **Appomattox Court House** to arrange the surrender. Grant later wrote that his joy at that moment was mixed with sadness.

> *A VOICE FROM THE PAST*
>
> I felt like anything rather than rejoicing at the downfall of a foe who had fought so long and valiantly, and had suffered so much for a cause, though that cause was, I believe, one of the worst for which a people ever fought, and one for which there was the least excuse. I do not question, however, the sincerity of the great mass of those who were opposed to us.
>
> **Ulysses S. Grant**, *Personal Memoirs*

Grant offered generous terms of surrender. After laying down their arms, the Confederates could return home in peace, taking their private possessions and horses with them. Grant also gave food to the hungry Confederate soldiers.

After four long years, the Civil War was coming to a close. Its effects would continue, however, changing the country forever. In the next section, you will learn about the long-term consequences of the Civil War.

STRANGE *but* True

WILMER MCLEAN

The first major battle of the Civil War was fought on the property of Wilmer McLean. McLean lived in Manassas, Virginia, the site of the Battle of Bull Run. After the battle, McLean decided to move to a more peaceful place. He chose the village of Appomattox Court House (see map on page 501).

When Lee made the decision to surrender in April 1865, he sent Colonel Charles Marshall to find a location for a meeting with Grant. Marshall stopped the first man he saw in the deserted streets of Appomattox Court House. It was Wilmer McLean.

McLean reluctantly offered his home. Thus, the war that began in McLean's back yard ended in his parlor.

Section 3 Assessment

1. Terms & Names

Explain the significance of:
- Battle of Gettysburg
- Pickett's Charge
- Ulysses S. Grant
- Robert E. Lee
- Siege of Vicksburg
- William Tecumseh Sherman
- Appomattox Court House

2. Taking Notes

Use a time line like the one below to record key events from Section 3.

1862   1866

Which event is considered the turning point of the war?

3. Main Ideas

a. Why was the Battle of Gettysburg important?

b. Why was Northern success in the Siege of Vicksburg important?

c. How did Grant treat Confederate soldiers after the surrender at Appomattox Court House?

4. Critical Thinking

Contrasting How was the Civil War different from wars that Americans had previously fought?

THINK ABOUT
- the role of civilians
- Sherman's military strategy

ACTIVITY OPTIONS

GEOGRAPHY
LANGUAGE ARTS

Research the Siege of Vicksburg. Make a **topographic map** of the area or write an **article** describing the soldiers' hardships during the siege.

4 The Legacy of the War

MAIN IDEA	WHY IT MATTERS NOW
The Civil War brought great changes and new challenges to the United States.	The most important change was the liberation of 4 million enslaved persons.

ONE AMERICAN'S STORY

In the spring of 1864, a year before the end of the Civil War, the Union army was running out of cemetery space to bury its war dead. The secretary of war ordered Quartermaster General Montgomery Meigs to find a new site for a cemetery. Without hesitation, Meigs chose Robert E. Lee's plantation in Arlington, Virginia, just across the Potomac River from Washington, D.C. "The grounds about the mansion are admirably adapted to such a use," wrote Meigs in June 1864.

Meigs was from Georgia and had served under Lee in the U.S. Army before the war. Unlike Lee, however, Meigs remained loyal to the Union and disagreed strongly with Lee's decision to join the Confederacy. His decision to turn Lee's plantation into a Union cemetery was highly symbolic. The Union soldiers who died fighting Lee's army would be buried in Lee's front yard. That site became Arlington National Cemetery.

During the Civil War, the government turned Robert E. Lee's Virginia plantation into a graveyard. That graveyard eventually became Arlington National Cemetery.

Costs of the War

Many Northerners shared Montgomery Meigs's bitter feelings toward the South. At the same time, many Southerners felt great resentment toward the North. After the war, President Lincoln hoped to heal the nation and bring North and South together again. The generous terms of surrender offered to Lee were part of that effort. Hard feelings remained, however, in part because the costs of the war were so great.

The Civil War was the deadliest war in American history. In four years of fighting, approximately 620,000 soldiers died—360,000 for the Union and 260,000 for the Confederacy. Another 275,000 Union soldiers and 260,000 Confederate soldiers were wounded. Many suffered from their wounds for the rest of their lives.

Altogether, some 3,000,000 men served in the armies of the North and South—around 10 percent of the population. Along with the soldiers, many other Americans had their lives disrupted by the war.

*Reading***History**
A. Contrasting
How did government spending during the Civil War compare to that during previous years?

The war also had great economic costs. Together, the North and South spent more than five times the amount spent by the government in the previous eight decades. Many years after the fighting was over, the federal government was still paying interest on loans taken out during the war.

The Thirteenth Amendment

One of the greatest effects of the war was the freeing of millions of enslaved persons. As the Union army moved through the South during and after the war, Union soldiers released African Americans from bondage. One of those released was Booker T. Washington, who later became a famous educator and reformer. He recalled the day a Union officer came to his plantation to read the Emancipation Proclamation.

A VOICE FROM THE PAST

After the reading we were told that we were all free, and could go when and where we pleased. My mother, who was standing by my side, leaned over and kissed her children, while tears of joy ran down her cheeks. She explained to us what it all meant, that this was the day for which she had been so long praying, but fearing that she would never live to see.

Booker T. Washington, quoted in his autobiography, *Up from Slavery*

*Reading***History**
B. Making Inferences Why was an amendment needed to free enslaved persons even after the Emancipation Proclamation?

The Emancipation Proclamation applied primarily to slaves in the Confederacy, however. Many African Americans in the border states were still enslaved. In 1864, with the war still under way, President Lincoln had approved of a constitutional amendment to end slavery entirely, but it failed to pass Congress.

In January 1865, Lincoln urged Congress to try again to end slavery. This time, the measure—known as the **Thirteenth Amendment**—passed. By year's end, 27 states, including eight in the South, had ratified the amendment. From that point on, slavery was banned in the United States.

Lincoln's Assassination

Lincoln did not live to see the end of slavery, however. Five days after Lee's surrender at Appomattox, the president and his wife went to see a play at Ford's Theatre in Washington, D.C. During the play, a Confederate supporter, **John Wilkes Booth,** crept into the balcony where the president sat and shot him in the back of the head. Booth then jumped over the railing and landed on the stage. Although he broke his leg in the leap, he managed to escape the theater.

CONFEDERATE CASUALTIES

UNION CASUALTIES

Source: *World Book; Historical Statistics of the United States; The United States Civil War Center*

ECONOMIC COSTS

- Federal loans and taxes to finance the war totaled $2.6 billion.
- Federal debt on June 30, 1865, rose to $2.7 billion.
- Confederate debt ran over $700 million.
- Union inflation reached 182% in 1864 and 179% in 1865.
- Confederate inflation rose to 9,000% by the end of the war.

SKILLBUILDER
Interpreting Graphs
1. *About how many Confederate soldiers were killed in the Civil War?*
2. *Approximately how many soldiers were wounded in the war?*

That same evening, an accomplice of Booth stabbed Secretary of State William Seward, who later recovered. Another man was supposed to assassinate Vice-President Johnson, but he failed to carry out the attack.

Although Booth had managed to escape after shooting the president, Union troops found and killed him several days later. Soldiers also hunted down Booth's accomplices, whom they either hanged or imprisoned.

After Lincoln was shot, he was carried to a house across the street from the theater. The bullet in his brain could not be removed, however. The next morning, April 15, 1865, the president died. He was the first American president to be assassinated.

Lincoln's murder stunned the nation and caused intense grief. In Washington, D.C., people wept in the streets. One man who mourned the nation's loss was the poet Walt Whitman. In one poem, Whitman considered the president's legacy.

> **A VOICE FROM THE PAST**
> This dust was once the man,
> Gentle, plain, just and resolute, under whose cautious hand,
> Against the foulest crime in history known in any land or age,
> Was saved the Union of these States.
> **Walt Whitman,** *This Dust Was Once the Man*

The loss of Lincoln's vast experience and great political skills was a terrible setback for a people faced by the challenge of rebuilding their nation. In both the North and the South, life would never be the same after the Civil War.

Consequences of the War

In the North, the war changed the way people thought about the country. In fighting to defend the Union, people came to see the United States as a single nation rather than a collection of states. After 1865, people no longer said "the United States *are*" but "the United States *is*."

The war also caused the national government to expand. Before the war, the government was relatively small and had limited powers. With the demands of war, however, the government grew larger and more powerful. Along with a new paper currency and income tax, the government established a new federal banking system. It also funded railroads, gave western land to settlers, and provided for state colleges. This growth of federal power continued long after the war was over.

The war also changed the Northern economy. New industries such as steel, petroleum, food processing, and manufacturing grew rapidly. By

Vocabulary
accomplice: someone who aids a lawbreaker

Reading **History**
C. Summarizing How did Americans react to the assassination of Lincoln?

Background
In the 1850s, an improved way of making steel—the Bessemer process—had been perfected, allowing for the mass production of steel.

CAUSE AND EFFECT: The Civil War, 1861–1865

CAUSES	IMMEDIATE EFFECTS
Conflict over slavery in territories	Abolition of slavery
Economic differences between North and South	Devastation of South
Failure of Congress to compromise	Reconstruction of South
	LONG-TERM EFFECTS
Election of Lincoln as president	Growth of industry
Secession of Southern states	Government more powerful
Firing on Fort Sumter	Nation reunited

SKILLBUILDER Interpreting Charts

1. *What military event is among the causes of the Civil War?*

2. *What effect did the Civil War have on the federal government?*

Background
Some people have called the Civil War the first modern war because of the use of machines, the destructiveness, and the effects on civilians, which would be repeated in later wars.

the late 1800s, industry had begun to replace farming as the basis of the national economy.

For the South, however, the war brought economic disaster. Farms and plantations were destroyed. About 40 percent of the South's livestock was killed. Fifty percent of its farm machinery was wrecked. Factories were also demolished, and thousands of miles of railroad tracks were torn up. Also gone was the labor system that the South had used—slavery.

Before the war, the South accounted for 30 percent of the nation's wealth. After the war it accounted for only 12 percent. These economic differences between the North and the South would last for decades.

The country faced difficult challenges after the war. How would the South be brought back into the Union, and how would four million former slaves be integrated into national life? You will read more about these challenges in the next chapter.

Section 4 Assessment

1. Terms & Names

Explain the significance of:
• Thirteenth Amendment
• John Wilkes Booth

2. Taking Notes

Use a chart like the one below to record the social, economic, and political legacy of the Civil War.

Legacy of the Civil War

Society	Economy	Politics

Is the legacy of the Civil War still apparent today? How?

3. Main Ideas

a. What were some of the human costs of the Civil War?

b. What did the Thirteenth Amendment achieve?

c. What was the state of the Southern economy after the Civil War?

4. Critical Thinking

Making Inferences How do you think the assassination of President Lincoln affected the nation?

THINK ABOUT
• the reaction of ordinary citizens
• its impact on government

ACTIVITY OPTIONS

MATH
TECHNOLOGY

Read about the postwar economy. Create a **database** on industry in the North or make a **storyboard** for a video on the problems in the South.

The Gettysburg Address (1863)

Setting the Stage On November 19, 1863, officials gathered in Gettysburg, Pennsylvania. They were there to dedicate a national cemetery on the ground where the decisive Battle of Gettysburg had taken place nearly five months earlier. Following the ceremony's main address, which lasted nearly two hours, President Lincoln delivered his Gettysburg Address in just over two minutes. In this famous speech, Lincoln expressed his hopes for the nation. **See Primary Source Explorer**

Four **score**[1] and seven years ago our fathers brought forth on this continent a new nation, conceived in liberty, and dedicated to the proposition that all men are created equal.

Now we are engaged in a great civil war, testing whether that nation or any nation so conceived and so dedicated, can long endure. We are met on a great battlefield of that war. We have come to dedicate a portion of that field, as a final resting place for those who here gave their lives that that nation might live. It is altogether fitting and proper that we should do this.

But, in a larger sense, we cannot dedicate—we can not **consecrate**[2]—we can not hallow—this ground. The brave men, living and dead, who struggled here, have consecrated it, far above our poor power to add or **detract.**[3] The world will little note, nor long remember what we say here, but it can never forget what they did here. It is for us the living, rather, to be dedicated here to the unfinished work which they who fought here have thus far so nobly advanced. It is rather for us to be here dedicated to the great task remaining before us—that from these honored dead we **take increased devotion to**[4] that cause for which they **gave the last full measure of devotion**[5]—that we here highly resolve that these dead shall not have died **in vain**[6]—that this nation, under God, shall have a new birth of freedom—and that government of the people, by the people, for the people, shall not perish from the earth.

A CLOSER LOOK

LINCOLN'S MODESTY

Lincoln claimed that what he said at Gettysburg would not be long remembered. However, the address soon came to be recognized as one of the best speeches of all time.

1. What features of Lincoln's address make it so memorable?

A CLOSER LOOK

FIGHTING FOR A CAUSE

Different people fought for different causes during the Civil War. Sometimes, the causes for which people fought changed over the course of the war.

2. What cause is Lincoln referring to in the Gettysburg Address?

1. **score:** a group of 20.
2. **consecrate:** to declare as sacred.
3. **detract:** to take away from.
4. **take increased devotion to:** work harder for.
5. **gave the last full measure of devotion:** sacrificed their lives.
6. **in vain:** for nothing.

Second Inaugural Address (1865)

Setting the Stage President Lincoln delivered his Second Inaugural Address just before the end of the Civil War. In this excerpt, he recalled the major cause of the war and vowed to fight for the restoration of peace and unity. **See Primary Source Explorer** 💿

One-eighth of the whole population were colored slaves. . . . These slaves constituted a peculiar and powerful interest. All knew that this interest was somehow the cause of the war. To strengthen, perpetuate, and extend this interest was the object for which the **insurgents**[1] would rend the Union even by war, while the Government claimed no right to do more than to restrict the territorial enlargement of it. Neither party expected for the war the magnitude or the duration which it has already attained. Neither anticipated that the cause of the conflict might cease with or even before the conflict itself should cease. Each looked for an easier triumph, and a result less fundamental and astounding. Both read the same Bible and pray to the same God, and each invokes His aid against the other. . . . Fondly do we hope, fervently do we pray, that this mighty **scourge**[2] of war may speedily pass away. Yet, if God wills that it continue until all the wealth piled by the **bondsman's**[3] two hundred and fifty years of **unrequited**[4] toil shall be sunk, and until every drop of blood drawn with the lash shall be paid by another drawn with the sword, as was said three thousand years ago, so still it must be said "the judgments of the Lord are true and righteous altogether."

With malice toward none, with charity for all, with firmness in the right as God gives us to see the right, let us strive on to finish the work we are in, to bind up the nation's wounds, to care for him who shall have borne the battle and for his widow and his orphan, to do all which may achieve and cherish a just and lasting peace among ourselves and with all nations.

1. **insurgent:** one that revolts against civil authority.
2. **scourge:** a source of suffering and devastation.
3. **bondsman:** enslaved person.
4. **unrequited:** not paid for.

A CLOSER LOOK

SLAVERY IN TERRITORIES

Before the Civil War, Northern states wanted to prohibit slavery in territories that would eventually become new states. Southern states fought to expand slavery, fearing the prohibition would threaten slavery where it already existed.

1. Why did the Southerners fear that prohibiting slavery in new territories might threaten slavery where it already existed?

A CLOSER LOOK

MALICE TOWARD NONE

As Northerners became more confident in victory, many looked forward to punishing Southerners, whom they blamed for the war. Lincoln, however, urged citizens to care for one another and work for a just and lasting peace.

2. Why do you think that Lincoln believed it would be wiser for Americans not to place blame or seek revenge on one another?

Interactive Primary Sources Assessment

1. Main Ideas

a. Why might President Lincoln have begun the Gettysburg Address by noting that the country was "dedicated to the proposition that all men are created equal"?

b. According to Lincoln's Second Inaugural Address, why did the Confederacy go to war?

c. To what did Lincoln refer with the phrase "the bondsman's two hundred and fifty years of unrequited toil?"

2. Critical Thinking

Making Inferences In 1865, if the South had asked to rejoin the Union without ending slavery, do you think Lincoln would have agreed?

THINK ABOUT

• what Lincoln identifies as the cause of the war
• what might happen if the war ended but slavery did not

TERMS & NAMES

Briefly explain the significance of each of the following.

1. Emancipation Proclamation
2. 54th Massachusetts Regiment
3. conscription
4. Battle of Gettysburg
5. Ulysses S. Grant
6. Robert E. Lee
7. Siege of Vicksburg
8. William Tecumseh Sherman
9. Appomattox Court House
10. Thirteenth Amendment

REVIEW QUESTIONS

The Emancipation Proclamation (pages 487–490)

1. Why did Lincoln issue the Emancipation Proclamation?
2. How did black soldiers aid the war effort?

War Affects Society (pages 491–495)

3. How did events on the home front show the toll that war was taking there?
4. Why did some people say the Civil War was a "rich man's war but a poor man's fight"?
5. How did enslaved persons help the Union?

The North Wins (pages 496–503)

6. Why was the Battle of Gettysburg so important?
7. How did Sherman's march help the Union?
8. How did Grant defeat Lee?

The Legacy of the War (pages 504–507)

9. How was the Thirteenth Amendment different from the Emancipation Proclamation?
10. How did the war change the national economy?

CRITICAL THINKING

1. USING YOUR NOTES

	North	South
Emancipation Proclamation		
War's Impact		
Northern Victories in Battle		
Union Wins Civil War		

a. How did white and black Southerners react to the Emancipation Proclamation?
b. How did inflation affect the North and the South?

2. ANALYZING LEADERSHIP

What qualities made Lincoln an effective leader?

3. THEME: IMPACT OF THE INDIVIDUAL

How did General Grant's actions in the war make a crucial difference to the outcome?

4. FORMING AND SUPPORTING OPINIONS

One Union relief worker said, "The suffering of men in battle is nothing next to the agony that women feel sending forth their loved ones to war." Do you agree with this statement? Explain why or why not.

5. APPLYING CITIZENSHIP SKILLS

How might the behavior of General Grant and President Lincoln toward the Confederacy have helped to begin healing the war-torn nation?

Interact *with* History

Having read about the ferocity of battle during the Civil War, do you still believe that you would be inspired to continue the fighting? Why or why not?

VISUAL SUMMARY

The Civil War, 1863–1865

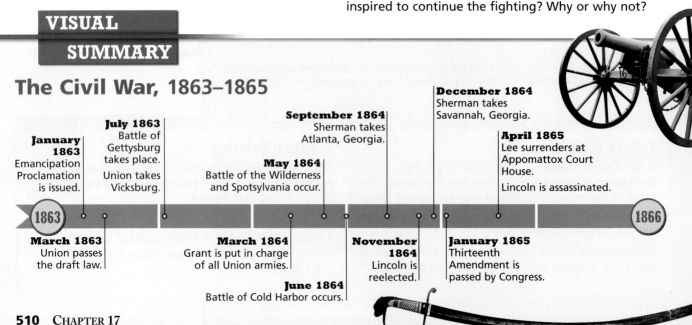

January 1863 Emancipation Proclamation is issued.

July 1863 Battle of Gettysburg takes place. Union takes Vicksburg.

September 1864 Sherman takes Atlanta, Georgia.

May 1864 Battle of the Wilderness and Spotsylvania occur.

December 1864 Sherman takes Savannah, Georgia.

April 1865 Lee surrenders at Appomattox Court House. Lincoln is assassinated.

1863

1866

March 1863 Union passes the draft law.

March 1864 Grant is put in charge of all Union armies.

June 1864 Battle of Cold Harbor occurs.

November 1864 Lincoln is reelected.

January 1865 Thirteenth Amendment is passed by Congress.

HISTORY SKILLS

1. INTERPRETING MAPS: Location

Study the map. Answer the questions.

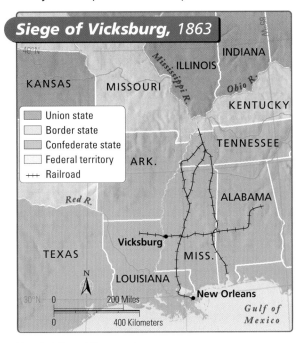

Siege of Vicksburg, 1863

INDIANA
ILLINOIS
KANSAS
MISSOURI
Ohio R.
KENTUCKY
- Union state
- Border state
- Confederate state
- Federal territory
- +++ Railroad
TENNESSEE
ARK.
Red R.
ALABAMA
Vicksburg
TEXAS
MISS.
LOUISIANA
New Orleans
Gulf of Mexico
0   200 Miles
0   400 Kilometers

Basic Map Elements

a. Which color represents Confederate states?

Interpreting the Map

b. Next to what river was Vicksburg built?

c. Why might Vicksburg be important for Southerners supplying the Confederacy from Texas?

2. INTERPRETING SECONDARY SOURCES

Historian Bruce Catton describes a brief meeting between two brothers during the Siege of Vicksburg. Read the passage and answer the questions.

> Both boys [were] from Missouri, one of them in Confederate gray and the other in Federal blue. The Confederate had a roll of bills in his hand and gave them to his brother to send to their mother. . . . He couldn't get things out from Vicksburg through the Union lines, Vicksburg being completely surrounded, so he asked his brother to send them to her, and the brother did. There was no shooting while these arrangements were made, then the brothers shook hands and retired to their individual lines, and the shooting started up again.
>
> **Bruce Catton,** from *Reflections on the Civil War*

a. What does this account say about the nature of war?

b. Why might the fact that the brothers came from Missouri pertain to their fighting for different sides?

ALTERNATIVE ASSESSMENT

1. INTERDISCIPLINARY ACTIVITY: Science

Writing a Report Do research on the advances in military technology during the Civil War. Write a report that describes the new or improved weapons that were used during the war. Be sure to use standard grammar, spelling, sentence structure, and punctuation in your report. Present the report to your class with charts that illustrate the changes and innovations that you describe.

2. COOPERATIVE LEARNING ACTIVITY

Creating a Newspaper Work with a group of classmates to produce a simple newspaper that covers a specific period of the Civil War. With your group, choose the period you want to cover and decide whether you will take a Northern or Southern viewpoint. Research events and conditions during that period, then select the topics you will cover in your newspaper. Articles should include descriptions of the characteristics of the Civil War era. Examples include:

- important battles and military strategies
- political news, including government actions and foreign involvement
- social and economic conditions
- profiles of important figures

3. PRIMARY SOURCE EXPLORER

Use the Internet, books, and other resources to do research for a multimedia presentation on a Civil War battle. Using presentation software, consider including the following content:

- paintings or written descriptions of the battle
- images of the destruction caused by the conflict
- music from the time period
- statistics on casualties
- diary and journal entries

4. HISTORY PORTFOLIO

Review your section and chapter assessment activities. Select one that you think is your best work. Then use comments made by your teacher or classmates to improve your work and add it to your portfolio.

Additional Test Practice, pp. S1–S33

TEST PRACTICE
CLASSZONE.COM

Create a Medal of Honor

In 1782, George Washington established the nation's first award to recognize the bravery of American soldiers. It was a purple heart made of cloth and was called the Badge of Military Merit. But the award was not used much after the Revolutionary War. Then, in 1861, Congress created a new award—the Medal of Honor. In the Civil War, 1,520 Union soldiers, including 20 African Americans, received the medal. Today, that medal is the highest United States military award for individual bravery and is commonly referred to as the Congressional Medal of Honor.

ACTIVITY Create a medal of honor for a hero or heroine from either side of the Civil War. Write a letter recommending your hero for the medal. Then read a speech in class as you award your medal to the deserving individual.

TOOLBOX

Each group will need:

tops of juice cans or cardboard

aluminum foil

pieces of ribbon

safety pins

glue

markers

scissors

writing paper

STEP BY STEP

1 **Form groups.** Each group should consist of three or four students. Each group will:
- identify a Civil War hero or heroine
- create a medal
- write a letter explaining why your group considers that person a hero
- award the medal and read a speech in class

2 **Research a hero.** First, brainstorm characteristics that you think a hero should have. Then, using this chapter, books on the Civil War, or the Internet, select an individual who you think was a hero for either side of the Civil War. Take notes on the actions of the person you selected. The actions should show how that person meets your standards for being a hero.

The Congressional Medal of Honor rewards military personnel who risked their lives, "above and beyond the call of duty." In the Civil War, 1,520 Union soldiers, including 20 African Americans, received the Medal of Honor.

3 **Design your medal.**
Think about the shape, images, and words that you will use to make your medal of honor. You may want to look at the example from Chapter 17 and in Civil War books. Sketch a design of your medal in pencil.

4 **Construct your medal.**
Using art supplies, construct a medal based on your design. First, construct the medal itself by using a juice can lid or a cardboard pattern. Decorate the medal by using foil and markers. Then add a ribbon and pin.

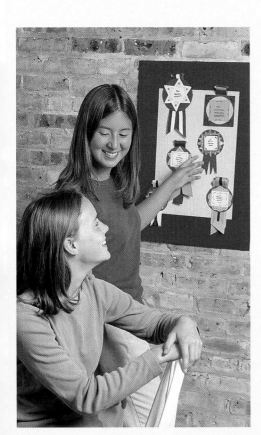

5 **Write a letter.** The letter should be addressed to the Congress of the United States of America or the Congress of the Confederate States of America. Your letter should give reasons for recommending your hero based on the person's actions. Carefully recopy your letter after you have made any corrections.

6 **Pin up the medal.**
Create a Medal of Honor board with other groups in your class. Pin up all the medals you have created. Discuss with other groups the standards your group set for calling a person a hero.

WRITE AND SPEAK

Write a Speech As a Civil War military leader, write a speech praising the courage and bravery of the individual who is receiving the medal. Choose another member of your group to act as the recipient of the award. Read your speech to the class as you award the medal to that person.

HELP DESK

For related information, see page 502 in Chapter 17.

Researching Your Project
Visit the library to learn more about the history of military awards or go to your local historical museum to examine actual medals.

For more about military awards . . .

RESEARCH LINKS
CLASSZONE.COM

Did You Know?
Since the Congressional Medal of Honor was created in 1861, 3,408 persons have received the award. Nineteen persons have received two such awards. Only one woman has received the award.

The Confederate States of America also awarded 43 of its finest men with the Confederate Medal of Honor.

The practice of awarding medals began in Europe during the Middle Ages. Kings realized that giving land to valued knights was too costly, so they gave medals instead.

REFLECT & ASSESS

- What requirements did you set for awarding a medal of honor?

- What reasons did your letter and speech give for awarding the medal?

- What symbols did you use for your medal? Why did you select them?

CHAPTER

18

Reconstruction
1865–1877

Section 1 **Rebuilding the Union**
Section 2 **Reconstruction and Daily Life**
Section 3 **End of Reconstruction**

Freed African Americans stand in the ruins of a Southern city after the Civil War.

In 1874, Congressman Robert B. Elliott of South Carolina made a speech supporting a civil rights bill.

Earlier, former Confederate vice-president Alexander Stephens had spoken against the bill.

Many Southern congressmen ignored Elliott as he spoke.

The Civil War has just ended, and the Southern economy is in ruins. Slavery has been abolished. Northerners and Southerners feel deep anger toward one another. As a member of Congress, you must help rebuild the nation.

How would you rebuild the Union?

What Do You Think?

- What problems would you face in rebuilding the nation?
- How would you ease tensions between North and South?
- How would you help freed African Americans?

1865
Andrew Johnson becomes president after Lincoln's assassination.

Thirteenth Amendment abolishes slavery.

1867
Reconstruction Acts are passed.

1866
Civil Rights Act is passed.

1868
Fourteenth Amendment extends full citizenship to African Americans.

Ulysses S. Grant is elected president.

1870
Fifteenth Amendment guarantees voting rights to African Americans.

1872
Grant is reelected president.

1873
Financial panic leads to an economic depression.

1877
Rutherford B. Hayes is inaugurated as president and ends Reconstruction.

USA
World

1865

1877

1867
Emperor Maximilian is executed in Mexico.

1870
Unification of Italy is completed.

1871
Unification of Germany is completed.

1876
Korea becomes an independent nation.

BEFORE YOU READ

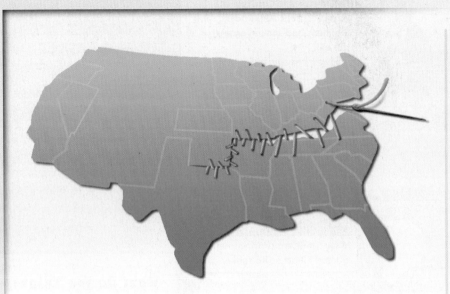

Previewing the Theme

Democratic Ideals After the Union won the war, the nation faced the question of how a democratic government should treat the people who rebelled against it. The Union also faced the question of how to include the millions of freed African Americans in the political process. In this chapter, you will learn how the country struggled to move toward the ideal of equality during Reconstruction.

What Do You Know?

What do you think it means to reconstruct something? What kinds of things did the U.S. government need to reconstruct after the Civil War? Which of these issues do you think was most important?

THINK ABOUT

- what you learned about the Civil War in the last two chapters
- what you've learned about civil rights in the United States from television and movies

What Do You Want to Know?

What questions do you have about Reconstruction? Record those questions in your notebook before you read this chapter.

READ AND TAKE NOTES

Reading Strategy: Identifying and Solving Problems Sometimes, to understand what you read, you must learn to identify problems and solutions. As you read through this chapter, use a diagram like the one below to take notes on the problems the United States faced during Reconstruction and the actions the nation took to solve them.

S See Skillbuilder Handbook, page R18.

Problems		Solutions
Black codes	→	
President Johnson	→	
Education	→	
Economy	→	
Ku Klux Klan	→	
Voting	→	

① Rebuilding the Union

TERMS & NAMES
Radical Republicans
Reconstruction
Freedmen's Bureau
Andrew Johnson
black codes
civil rights
Fourteenth Amendment

MAIN IDEA	WHY IT MATTERS NOW
During Reconstruction, the president and Congress fought over how to rebuild the South.	Reconstruction was an important step in the African-American struggle for civil rights.

ONE AMERICAN'S STORY

After the Civil War, Pennsylvania congressman Thaddeus Stevens became a leader of the **Radical Republicans**. This group of congressmen favored using federal power to create a new order in the South and to promote full citizenship for freed African Americans.

A VOICE FROM THE PAST

The whole fabric of southern society *must* be changed. . . . If the South is ever to be made a safe Republic let her lands be cultivated by the toil of the owners, or the free labor of intelligent citizens.

Thaddeus Stevens, quoted in *The Era of Reconstruction* by Kenneth Stampp

In this section, you will learn how political leaders battled over how to bring the Southern states back into the Union.

Thaddeus Stevens addresses Congress.

Reconstruction Begins

After the Civil War ended in 1865, the South faced the challenge of building a new society not based on slavery. The process the federal government used to readmit the Confederate states to the Union is known as **Reconstruction**. Reconstruction lasted from 1865 to 1877.

In his Second Inaugural Address, in March 1865, Lincoln promised to reunify the nation "with malice [harm] toward none, with charity for all." Lincoln's plan included pardoning Confederate officials. It also called for allowing the Confederate states to quickly form new governments and send representatives to Congress.

To assist former slaves, the president established the **Freedmen's Bureau**. This federal agency set up schools and hospitals for African Americans and distributed clothes, food, and fuel throughout the South.

When Lincoln was killed in April 1865, Vice-President **Andrew Johnson** became president. Johnson was a Democrat. The Republicans had put him on the ticket in 1864 to help win support in the nation's border states. Johnson was a former slaveholder and, unlike Lincoln, a stubborn, unyielding man.

Johnson believed that Reconstruction was the job of the president, not Congress. His policies were based on Lincoln's goals. He insisted that the new state governments ratify the Thirteenth Amendment, which prohibited slavery. He also insisted that they accept the supreme power of the federal government.

Johnson offered amnesty, or official pardon, to most white Southerners. He promised to return their property. In return, they had to pledge loyalty to the United States. At first, the large plantation owners, top military officers, and ex-Confederate leaders were not included in this offer. But they, too, eventually won amnesty.

Rebuilding Brings Conflict

As the Southern states rebuilt, they set up new state governments that seemed very much like the old ones. Some states flatly refused to ratify the Thirteenth Amendment. "This is a white man's government," said the governor of South Carolina, "and intended for white men only."

The Southern states passed laws, known as **black codes,** which limited the freedom of former slaves. In Mississippi, for instance, one law said that African Americans had to have written proof of employment. Anyone without such proof could be put to work on a plantation. African Americans were forbidden to meet in unsupervised groups or carry guns. Because of such laws, many people in the North suspected that white Southerners were trying to bring back the "old South."

When Congress met in December 1865, its members refused to seat representatives from the South. Many of these Southern representatives had been Confederate leaders only months before.

Under the Constitution, Congress has the right to decide whether its members are qualified to hold office. So instead of admitting the Southerners, Congress set up a committee to study conditions in the South and decide whether the Southern states should be represented. By taking such action, Congress let the president know that it planned to play a role in Reconstruction.

Republicans outnumbered Democrats in both houses of Congress. Most Republicans were moderates who believed that the federal government should stay out of the affairs of individuals and the states.

The Radical Republicans, however, wanted the federal government to play an active role in remaking Southern politics and society. Led by Thaddeus Stevens and Massachusetts senator Charles Sumner, the

Background
Not all Confederate leaders were pardoned. Former Confederate president Jefferson Davis, for example, was imprisoned for two years awaiting trial for treason. But he was never tried.

Reading **History**
A. Analyzing Causes What was the main reason Southern states passed black codes?

Vocabulary
moderates: people opposed to extreme views

group also demanded full and equal citizenship for African Americans. Their aim was to destroy the South's old ruling class and turn the region into a place of small farms, free schools, respect for labor, and political equality for all citizens.

The Civil Rights Act

Urged on by the Radicals, Congress passed a bill promoting **civil rights**—those rights granted to all citizens. The Civil Rights Act of 1866 declared that all persons born in the United States (except Native Americans) were citizens. It also stated that all citizens were entitled to equal rights regardless of their race.

Republicans were shocked when President Johnson vetoed the bill. Johnson argued that federal protection of civil rights would lead "towards centralization" of the national government. He also insisted that making African Americans full citizens would "operate against the white race." Congress voted to override Johnson's veto. That is, two-thirds of the House and two-thirds of the Senate voted for the bill after the president's veto, and the bill became law.

The Fourteenth Amendment

*Reading*History

B. Making Inferences How did the Fourteenth Amendment encourage states to give African Americans the vote?

Republicans were not satisfied with passing laws that ensured equal rights. They wanted equality to be protected by the Constitution itself. To achieve this goal, Congress proposed the **Fourteenth Amendment** in 1866. It stated that all people born in the United States were citizens and had the same rights. All citizens were to be granted "equal protection of the laws." However, the amendment did not establish black suffrage. Instead, it declared that any state that kept African Americans from voting would lose representatives in Congress. This meant that the Southern states would have less power if they did not grant black men the vote.

Johnson refused to support the amendment. So did every former Confederate state except Tennessee. This rejection outraged both moderate and Radical Republicans. As a result, the two groups agreed to join forces and passed the Reconstruction Acts of 1867. The passage of these acts began a period known as Radical Reconstruction. From this point on, Congress controlled Reconstruction.

One of the Reconstruction Acts of 1867 divided the South into five military districts, each run by an army commander. Members of the ruling class before the war lost their voting rights. The law also stated that before the Southern states could reenter the Union, they would have to do two things:

1. They must approve new state constitutions that gave the vote to all adult men, including African Americans.
2. They must ratify the Fourteenth Amendment.

The New Southern Governments

In 1867, Southern voters chose delegates to draft their new state constitutions. About three-fourths of the delegates were Republicans. Many of the Republicans were poor white farmers. Angry at planters for starting what they called the "rich man's war," these delegates were called scalawags (scoundrels) for going along with Radical Reconstruction.

Background
Attempts to secure voting rights for African Americans applied only to men. Women were not allowed to vote until 1919.

Another one-fourth of the Republican delegates were known as carpetbaggers—white Northerners who had rushed to the South after the war. Many Southerners accused them, often unfairly, of seeking only to get rich or gain political power.

African Americans made up the rest of the Republican delegates. Of these, half had been free before the war. Most were ministers, teachers, or skilled workers. About 80 percent of them could read.

Background
Carpetbaggers were said to have headed south carrying only a cheap suitcase, known as a carpetbag.

HISTORY *through* ART

His First Vote, an 1868 oil painting by Thomas Waterman Wood, shows a new African-American voter.

How do you think the man felt about voting?

The new constitutions written by these delegates set up public schools and gave the vote to all adult males. By 1870, voters in all the Southern states had approved their new constitutions. As a result, the former Confederate states were let back into the Union and allowed to send representatives to Congress.

During Reconstruction, more than 600 African Americans served in state legislatures throughout the South, and 14 of the new U.S. congressmen from the South were African Americans. Two African Americans served as U.S. senators during this time. One was Hiram Revels of Mississippi, a minister in the African Methodist Episcopal Church. He had recruited African Americans to fight for the Union during the Civil War.

Reading **History**
C. Finding Main Ideas What political gains did African Americans make during Reconstruction?

This is a ticket to the 1868 impeachment trial of President Johnson.

Johnson Is Impeached

INTERNET ACTIVITY
CLASSZONE.COM

President Johnson fought against many of Congress's reform efforts during Radical Reconstruction. For instance, he chose people friendly to ex-Confederates to serve as military commanders in the South. The conflict between Johnson and Congress soon brought a showdown.

In 1867, Congress passed the Tenure of Office Act, which prohibited the president from firing government officials without the Senate's approval. In February 1868, Johnson fired his secretary of war, Edwin Stanton, over disagreements about Reconstruction. Three days later, the House of Representatives voted to impeach the president. This means that the House formally accused him of improper conduct while in office. By removing Johnson from office, they hoped to strengthen Congress's role in Reconstruction.

The case moved to the Senate for a trial. After several weeks of testimony, the senators prepared to vote. George Julian, a 20-year congressman from Indiana, recalled the tension in the air.

Reading **History**

D. Drawing Conclusions Why did Congress decide to impeach President Johnson?

A VOICE FROM THE PAST

The galleries were packed, and an indescribable anxiety was written on every face. Some of the members of the House near me grew pale and sick under the burden of suspense. Such stillness prevailed that the breathing in the galleries could be heard at the announcement of each Senator's voice.

George Julian, quoted in *Grand Inquests*

Vocabulary
acquitted: cleared of a charge

In the end, President Johnson was acquitted by a single vote. But much work remained to be done in rebuilding the South. In the next section, you will learn how African Americans in the South worked to improve their lives.

Section 1 Assessment

1. Terms & Names

Explain the significance of:
- Radical Republicans
- Reconstruction
- Freedmen's Bureau
- Andrew Johnson
- black codes
- civil rights
- Fourteenth Amendment

2. Taking Notes

Use a diagram to review the events that led to Johnson's impeachment.

Event 1 → Event 2
Event 3 → Event 4

Which event seems most important and why?

3. Main Ideas

a. What was Lincoln's Reconstruction plan?

b. How did white Southerners plan to restore the "old South"?

c. What impact did the Reconstruction Acts of 1867 have on the South?

4. Critical Thinking

Evaluating Do you think the House was justified in impeaching President Johnson? Why or why not?

THINK ABOUT
- the clash over Reconstruction policies
- Congress's motives for impeaching Johnson

ACTIVITY OPTIONS

TECHNOLOGY

SPEECH

Research an African American who served in Congress during Reconstruction. Design his Internet **home page**, or make a **speech** about his accomplishments.

Rebuilding Richmond

You live in Richmond, Virginia, the capital of the Confederacy. It is 1865, and the South faces defeat in the Civil War. On April 2, Confederate officials set fire to supplies in Richmond to prevent the approaching Union army from using them. The fire spreads out of control and destroys downtown Richmond. The next day, Union troops march into the city and take command. You must now help rebuild the city.

COOPERATIVE LEARNING On this page are two challenges you face as a resident of Richmond. Working with a small group, decide how to solve one of these problems. Divide the work among the group members. You will find useful information in the Data File. Be prepared to present your solutions to the class.

This picture shows a street in Richmond before the fire.

ARTS CHALLENGE

"We want the burnt district of Richmond to . . . sit proudly again."

The smell of charred wood still floats in the breeze. However, spirit and determination fill the air. Warehouses are opening. Newly cleared streets bustle with activity. The rebuilding of Richmond has begun. How would you design one block of Richmond's new downtown business district? Use the Data File for help. Then present your plan using one of these options:

- Make a model of your new city block.
- Ask and answer questions about how buildings and services should be distributed on the model block.

THE BURNT DISTRICT
- about $30 million damage
- 20 city blocks destroyed, including 900 buildings

Destroyed Property
all banks, 20 law offices, 24 grocery stores, 36 merchant shops, 2 carriage factories, 2 paper mills, 7 book and stationery stores, 2 train depots, 3 bridges, a church, a machine shop, a tin shop, a pottery factory, several flour mills and printing offices

Surviving Property
capitol and city hall, residential areas, ironworks

EMERGENCY SERVICES
Union Army
- distributes 13,000 food rations
- provides medical help
- guards homes; patrols streets

American Union Commission
- hands out food tickets
- distributes 80,000 pounds of flour; feeds soup to 800 people a day
- provides garden seeds and sells shovels at cost to farmers

REBUILDING
April 1865
- rubble is cleared
- markets sell meat, fish, produce
- hotels and bakeries open
- one bridge is rebuilt

May 1865
- two banks open
- gas and telegraph service is restored
- river opens to steamboat traffic

Summer 1865
- horse-drawn buses operate
- city government is reinstated

Fall 1865
- ironworks reopens
- 100 buildings are now under construction

For more about Reconstruction . . .

RESEARCH LINKS
CLASSZONE.COM

CIVICS CHALLENGE

"Open robberies have been perpetrated."

Robberies and assaults are commonplace, especially in the burnt area of the downtown. Groups of orphaned children also roam the city, picking pockets to support themselves. Union military police supposedly protect the public. However, soldiers sometimes commit crimes themselves. What would you do to improve public safety? Use the Data File for help. Present your ideas using one of these options:

- Hold a town meeting to explore possible solutions.
- Create a set of emergency laws, with plans for publicizing them.

ACTIVITY WRAP-UP

Meet as a group to review your responses to rebuilding Richmond. Pick your most creative solution and present it to the class.

② Reconstruction and Daily Life

MAIN IDEA	WHY IT MATTERS NOW
As the South rebuilt, millions of newly freed African Americans worked to improve their lives.	Many important African-American institutions, including colleges, began during Reconstruction.

ONE AMERICAN'S STORY

One day, as the Civil War came to a close, two enslaved women named Mill and Jule saw a fleet of Union gunboats coming up the Mississippi River. Yankee soldiers came ashore and offered them and other slaves passage aboard their boats. On that day, Mill and Jule left the plantation where they had toiled for so long.

A VOICE FROM THE PAST

An' we all got on the boat in a hurry . . . we all give three times three cheers for the gunboat boys, and three times three cheers for big Yankee [soldiers], an' three times three cheers for gov'ment; an' I tell you every one of us, big and little, cheered loud and long and strong, an' made the old river just ring ag'in.

Mill and Jule, quoted in *We Are Your Sisters*

Freed people and a federal soldier pose on a South Carolina plantation.

The Union's victory in the Civil War spelled the end of slavery in America and a new beginning for the nation's millions of newly freed African Americans. In this section, you will learn about the gains and setbacks of former slaves during Reconstruction.

Responding to Freedom

African Americans' first reaction to freedom was to leave the plantations. No longer needing passes to travel, they journeyed throughout the region. "Right off colored folks started on the move," recalled one freedman. "They seemed to want to get closer to freedom, so they'd know what it was—like it was a place or a city." Some former slaves returned to the places where they were born. Others went looking for more economic opportunity. Still others traveled just because they could.

African Americans also traveled in search of family members separated from them during slavery. One man walked 600 miles from Georgia to North Carolina to find his family. To locate relatives, people placed advertisements in newspapers. The Freedmen's Bureau helped many families reunite. A Union officer wrote in 1865, "Men are taking

*Reading*History
A. Analyzing Causes For what reasons did former slaves move?

their wives and children, families which had been for a long time broken up are united and oh! such happiness."

Freedom allowed African Americans to strengthen their family ties. Former slaves could marry legally. They could raise families without fearing that their children might be sold. Many families adopted children of dead relatives and friends to keep family ties strong.

Starting Schools

With freedom, African Americans no longer had to work for an owner's benefit. They could now work to provide for their families. To reach their goal of economic independence, however, most had to learn to read and write. As a result, children and adults flocked to **freedmen's schools** set up to educate newly freed African Americans. Such schools were started by the Freedmen's Bureau, Northern missionary groups, and African-American organizations. Freed people in cities held classes in warehouses, billiard rooms, and former slave markets. In rural areas, classes were held in churches and houses. Children who went to school often taught their parents to read at home.

*Reading*History
B. Finding Main Ideas Why did freed people desire an education?

In the years after the war, African-American groups raised more than $1 million for education. However, the federal government and private groups in the North paid most of the cost of building schools and hiring teachers. Between 1865 and 1870, the Freedmen's Bureau spent $5 million for this purpose.

More than 150,000 African-American students were attending 3,000 schools by 1869. About 10 percent of the South's African-American adults could read. A number of them became teachers. Northern teachers, black and white, also went South to teach freed people. Many white Southerners, however, worked against these teachers' efforts. White racists even killed teachers and burned freedmen's schools in some parts of the South. Despite these setbacks, African Americans kept working toward an education.

Background Most African Americans were illiterate because teaching slaves to read and write had been illegal.

America's HERITAGE

BLACK COLLEGES

Some of today's African-American colleges and universities date back to Reconstruction. The Freedmen's Bureau and other societies raised funds to build many of the schools. Howard University, shown in this photograph, opened in 1867. It was named for General Oliver Otis Howard, head of the Freedmen's Bureau. During Reconstruction, these colleges offered courses ranging from basic reading and writing to medicine and law. They also trained much-needed teachers.

African-American families hoped to own land but were often disappointed.

40 Acres and a Mule

More than anything else, freed people wanted to own land. As one freedman said, "Give us our own land and we take care of ourselves, but without land, the old masters can hire us or starve us, as they please."

As the Civil War ended, General William T. Sherman suggested that abandoned land in coastal South Carolina be split into 40-acre parcels and given to freedmen. The rumor then spread that all freedmen would get 40 acres and a mule. Most African Americans thought they deserved at least that much. In the end, however, most freedmen never received land. Those who did often had to return it to its former owners after the owners were pardoned by President Johnson. One freedman, Bayley Wyat, protested.

> **A VOICE FROM THE PAST**
>
> Our wives, our children, our husbands, [have] been sold over and over again to purchase the lands we now [locate] upon; for that reason we have a divine right to the land. . . . And then didn't we clear the land, and raise the crops of corn, of cotton, of tobacco, of rice, of sugar, of everything.
>
> **Bayley Wyat,** quoted in *Reconstruction: America's Unfinished Revolution*

Radical Republican leaders Thaddeus Stevens and Charles Sumner pushed to make land reform part of the Reconstruction Acts of 1867. Stevens proposed a plan to Congress that would have taken land from plantation owners and given it to freed people.

Many moderate Republicans and even some Radicals were against the plan. They believed that new civil and voting rights were enough to give African Americans a better life.

Supporters of the plan argued that civil rights meant little without economic independence. Land could provide that independence, they claimed. However, Congress did not pass the land-reform plan.

Reading **History**

C. Analyzing Points of View What were some arguments in favor of giving land to freed people?

The Contract System

Without their own property, many African Americans returned to work on plantations. They returned not as slaves but as wage earners. They and the planters both had trouble getting used to this new relationship. "It seems humiliating to be compelled to bargain and haggle with our own servants about wages," wrote the daughter of a Georgia plantation owner. For their part, many freed workers assumed that wages were extra. They thought that the planters still had to house and feed them.

After the Civil War, planters desperately needed workers to raise cotton, still the South's main cash crop. African Americans reacted to this demand for labor by choosing the best contract offers. The contract system was far better than slavery. African Americans could decide whom to work for, and planters could not abuse them or split up families.

The contract system still had drawbacks, however. Even the best contracts paid very low wages. Workers often could not leave the plantations

Background Civil War deaths and the departure of slaves from plantations created a labor shortage in the South.

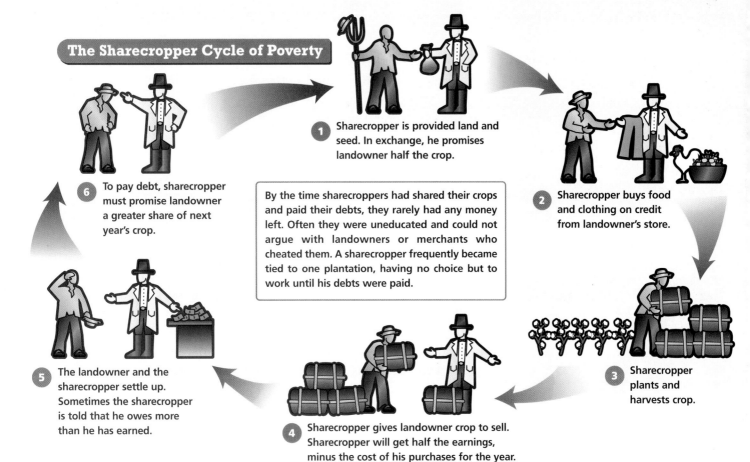

The Sharecropper Cycle of Poverty

1 Sharecropper is provided land and seed. In exchange, he promises landowner half the crop.

2 Sharecropper buys food and clothing on credit from landowner's store.

3 Sharecropper plants and harvests crop.

4 Sharecropper gives landowner crop to sell. Sharecropper will get half the earnings, minus the cost of his purchases for the year.

5 The landowner and the sharecropper settle up. Sometimes the sharecropper is told that he owes more than he has earned.

6 To pay debt, sharecropper must promise landowner a greater share of next year's crop.

By the time sharecroppers had shared their crops and paid their debts, they rarely had any money left. Often they were uneducated and could not argue with landowners or merchants who cheated them. A sharecropper frequently became tied to one plantation, having no choice but to work until his debts were paid.

without permission. Many owners cheated workers out of wages and other benefits. Worse yet, laws punished workers for breaking their contracts, even if the plantation owners were abusing or cheating them. These drawbacks made many African Americans turn to sharecropping.

Sharecropping and Debt

Under the **sharecropping** system, a worker rented a plot of land to farm. The landowner provided the tools, seed, and housing. When harvest time came, the sharecropper gave the landowner a share of the crop. This system gave families without land a place to farm and gave landowners cheap labor.

But problems soon arose with the sharecropping system. One cause of these problems was that farmers and landowners had opposite goals. Farmers wanted to grow food to feed their families, but landowners forced them to grow cash crops, such as cotton. As a result, farmers had to buy food from the local store—which was usually owned by the landlord. Most farmers did not have the money to pay for goods. As a result, many were caught in a cycle of debt, as shown in the diagram above. Often farmers had to use one year's harvest to pay the previous year's bills.

White farmers also became sharecroppers. Many had lost their land in the war. Others had lost it to taxes. By 1880, one-third of the white farmers in the Deep South worked someone else's land.

No matter who worked the plantations, much of what they grew was cotton. After the war, the value of cotton dropped. Southern planters responded by trying to produce more of the cash crop—a move that

Reading **History**
D. Recognizing Effects What were some problems with the sharecropping system?

drove down prices even further. Growing cotton exhausted the soil and reduced the amount of land available for food crops. As a result, the South had to import half its food. Relying on cotton was one reason the Deep South experienced years of rural poverty.

The Ku Klux Klan

African Americans in the South faced other problems besides poverty. They also faced violent racism. Many planters and former Confederate soldiers did not want African Americans to have more rights. In 1866, such feelings spurred the rise of a secret group called the **Ku Klux Klan.** The Klan's goals were to restore Democratic control of the South and keep former slaves powerless.

These Ku Klux Klan members were arrested after an 1868 riot in Alabama.

The Klan attacked African Americans. Often it targeted those who owned land or had become prosperous. Klansmen rode on horseback and dressed in white robes and hoods. They beat people and burned homes. They even **lynched** some victims, killing them on the spot without a trial as punishment for a supposed crime. The Klan also attacked white Republicans.

Klan victims had little protection. Military authorities in the South often ignored the violence. President Johnson had appointed most of these authorities, and they were against Reconstruction.

The Klan's terrorism served the Democratic Party. As gun-toting Klansmen kept Republicans away from the polls, the Democrats increased their power.

In the next section you will see how planters took back control of the South. You also will learn how they blocked African Americans' attempts to win more rights.

*Reading*History
E. Finding Main Ideas What were the goals of the Ku Klux Klan?

Section **2** Assessment

1. Terms & Names

Explain the significance of:
• freedmen's school
• sharecropping
• Ku Klux Klan
• lynch

2. Taking Notes

Use a cluster diagram like the one below to review details about sharecropping.

For farmers, what were the advantages and disadvantages of sharecropping?

3. Main Ideas

a. How did freedom help strengthen African-American families?

b. How were African Americans educated during Reconstruction?

c. What were the main reasons African Americans wanted their own land?

4. Critical Thinking

Analyzing Causes
Despite greater civil rights, why did African Americans still face difficulty in improving their lives?

THINK ABOUT
• the defeat of the land-reform bill
• the Ku Klux Klan's rise
• the attitude of military authorities in the South

ACTIVITY OPTIONS

SPEECH

ART

Make a **speech** to President Johnson or design a **mural** explaining why land should be given to newly freed African Americans.

③ End of Reconstruction

TERMS & NAMES
Fifteenth Amendment
Panic of 1873
Compromise of 1877

MAIN IDEA	WHY IT MATTERS NOW
As white Southerners regained power, Reconstruction ended, as did black advances toward equality.	Reforms made during Reconstruction made later civil rights gains possible.

ONE AMERICAN'S STORY

Robert B. Elliott was a U.S. congressman from South Carolina during Reconstruction. In 1874, he made a stirring speech supporting a civil rights bill that would outlaw racial discrimination in public services. (See Interact with History, page 515.)

A VOICE FROM THE PAST

The passage of this bill will determine the civil status, not only of the negro but of any other class of citizens who may feel themselves discriminated against. It will form the capstone of that temple of liberty begun on this continent.

Robert B. Elliott, quoted in *The Glorious Failure*

Robert B. Elliott lost his political office when Reconstruction ended.

Elliott was elected South Carolina's attorney general in 1876. He began his term in 1877, just as Reconstruction was ending. That year, federal troops left the South. White Southerners took back control of the region. Quickly, they forced African Americans, including Elliott, out of office.

In this section, you will learn about the events that ended Reconstruction. You will also see how Reconstruction's end meant setbacks in the fight for civil rights and equality.

The Election of Grant

The Republican Party seemed stronger than ever in 1868. That year, its candidate, General Ulysses S. Grant, won the presidency. During the campaign, the Democrats attacked the Republicans' Reconstruction policies. They blamed the party for granting rights to African Americans.

On Election Day, however, the Republicans won. Grant received 214 electoral votes. His Democratic opponent received only 80. The popular count was much closer. Grant had a majority of only 306,000 votes.

Grant would not have had such a majority without the freedmen's vote. Despite attacks by the Ku Klux Klan, about 500,000 African Americans voted in the South. Most cast their ballots for Grant.

The Fifteenth Amendment

After Grant's victory, Radical Republicans worried that the Southern states might try to keep African Americans from voting in future elections. To prevent this, Radical leaders proposed a new constitutional amendment.

The **Fifteenth Amendment** stated that citizens could not be stopped from voting "on account of race, color, or previous condition of servitude." (This amendment, like the Fourteenth Amendment, did not apply to Native Americans on tribal lands.) The amendment was ratified in 1870.

The Fifteenth Amendment was not aimed only at the South. African-American men could not vote in 16 states. "We have no moral right to impose an obligation on one part of the land which the rest will not accept," one Radical wrote. With the Fifteenth Amendment, the nation again turned toward democracy.

The Fifteenth Amendment did not apply to women. This made many white women angry. Why couldn't they vote when black men—former slaves—could? Suffragist Elizabeth Cady Stanton protested the idea of uneducated immigrants and freedmen "who never read the Declaration of Independence" making laws for educated white women. Most African-American women were not as angry. To Frances E. W. Harper, a black suffragist and writer, it was important for African Americans to gain voting rights, even if that meant only men at first.

*Reading*History

A. Comparing How was the Fifteenth Amendment a step beyond the Fourteenth Amendment?

Vocabulary **suffragist:** someone who favors equal voting rights, especially for women

Grant Fights the Klan

Despite gaining the vote, African Americans in the South continued to be terrorized by the Ku Klux Klan. In 1871, to stop the terror, President Grant asked Congress to pass a tough law against the Klan. Joseph Rainey, a black congressman from South Carolina, had received death threats from the Klan. He urged his fellow lawmakers to support the bill.

> *A VOICE FROM THE PAST*
>
> When myself and colleagues shall leave these Halls and turn our footsteps toward our southern home we know not but that the assassin may await our coming. Be it as it may we have resolved to be loyal and firm, and if we perish, we perish! I earnestly hope the bill will pass.
>
> **Joseph Rainey,** quoted in *The Trouble They Seen*

Congress approved the anti-Klan bill. Federal marshals then arrested thousands of Klansmen. Klan attacks on African-American voters declined. As a result, the 1872 presidential election was both fair and peaceful in the South. Grant won a second term.

Scandal and Panic Weaken Republicans

Under the Grant administration, support for the Republicans and Reconstruction weakened. Scandals hurt the administration and caused divisions in the Republican Party. A financial panic further hurt the Republicans and turned the country's attention away from Reconstruction.

President Grant did not choose his advisers well. He put his former army friends and his wife's relatives in government positions. Many of these people were unqualified. Some Grant appointees took bribes. Grant's private secretary, for instance, took money from whiskey distillers who wanted to avoid paying taxes. Grant's secretary of war, General William Belknap, left office after people accused him of taking bribes.

Reading History
B. Making Inferences How did Republican scandals hurt Reconstruction?

Such scandals deeply outraged many Republicans. In 1872, some Republican officials broke away and formed the new Liberal Republican Party. The Republicans, no longer unified, became less willing to impose tough Reconstruction policies on the South.

In 1873, political corruption and Republican quarreling gave way to a more serious problem. When several powerful Eastern banks ran out of money after making bad loans, a financial panic swept the country. In the **Panic of 1873,** banks across the land closed. The stock market temporarily collapsed. The panic caused an economic depression, a time of low business activity and high unemployment. The railroad industry, which relied on banks for loans, suffered. Within a year, 89 of the country's 364 railroads went broke. Railroad failures left Midwestern farmers with no way to move their crops, and many farmers were ruined.

The depression, which lasted about five years, touched nearly all parts of the economy. By 1875, more than 18,000 companies had folded. Hundreds of workers had lost their jobs. Many Americans blamed the crisis on the Republicans—the party in power. As a result, Democrats won victories in the 1874 congressional and state elections. In the middle of the depression, Americans grew tired of hearing about the South's problems. The nation was losing interest in Reconstruction.

Reading History
C. Recognizing Effects What resulted from the Panic of 1873?

This cartoon from *Puck* magazine shows President Grant weighed down by corruption in his administration.

Supreme Court Reversals

To make matters worse for the Republicans, the Supreme Court began to undo some of the changes that had been made in the South. In an 1876 case, *U.S. v. Cruikshank,* the Court ruled that the federal government could not punish individuals who violated the civil rights of African Americans. Only the states had that power, the Court declared. Southern state officials often would not punish those who attacked African Americans. As a result, violence against them increased.

In the 1876 case *U.S. v. Reese,* the Court ruled in favor of white Southerners who barred African Americans from voting. The Court stated that the Fifteenth Amendment did not give everyone the right to vote—it merely listed the grounds on which states could not deny the vote. In other words, states could prevent African Americans from voting for other reasons. States later imposed poll taxes and literacy tests to restrict the vote. These Court decisions weakened Reconstruction and blocked African-American efforts to gain full equality.

Reading **History**

D. Recognizing Effects
How did the Reese and Cruikshank rulings affect African Americans' efforts to gain civil rights?

Reconstruction Ends

The final blow to Reconstruction came with the 1876 presidential election. The Democrats nominated Samuel J. Tilden, governor of New York. The Republicans chose Rutherford B. Hayes, governor of Ohio. The race was very close. Victory depended on the electoral votes of South Carolina, Louisiana, and Florida. The votes in those states were so close that both the Democrats and the Republicans claimed victory. A special commission of eight Republicans and seven Democrats made a deal. Under the **Compromise of 1877,** Hayes became president. In return, the Republicans compromised with the Southern Democrats on several issues.

This cartoon from *Harper's Weekly* shows a federal soldier as the freedman's only defense against white Southerners.

1. The government would remove federal troops from the South.
2. The government would provide land grants and loans for the construction of railroads linking the South to the West Coast.
3. Southern officials would receive federal funds for construction and improvement projects.
4. Hayes would appoint a Democrat to his cabinet.
5. The Democrats promised to respect African Americans' civil and political rights.

Reading **History**

E. Summarizing
What events led to a weakening of support for Reconstruction?

Abolitionist Wendell Phillips was against the compromise. He doubted that the South would respect black rights. "The whole soil of the South is hidden by successive layers of broken promises," he said. "To trust a Southern promise would be fair evidence of insanity."

After the 1876 presidential election, the Reconstruction governments in the South collapsed. The Democrats returned to power, believing that they were the redeemers, or rescuers, of the South.

Reconstruction: Civil Rights Amendments and Laws

Civil Rights Act of 1866	• Granted citizenship and equal rights to all persons born in the United States (except Native Americans)
Fourteenth Amendment (1868)	• Granted citizenship and equal protection of the laws to all persons born in the United States (except Native Americans)
Fifteenth Amendment (1870)	• Protected the voting rights of African Americans
Civil Rights Act of 1875	• Outlawed racial segregation in public services • Ensured the right of African Americans to serve as jurors

SKILLBUILDER Interpreting Charts

1. *Which amendment and law are most similar?*
2. *Which amendment specifically protects voting rights?*

The Legacy of Reconstruction

Historians still argue about the success of Reconstruction. The nation did rebuild and reunite. However, Reconstruction did not achieve equality for African Americans.

After Reconstruction, most African Americans still lived in poverty. Legally, they could vote and hold public office. But few took part in politics. They continued to face widespread violence and prejudice.

During this period, however, African Americans did make lasting gains. Protection of civil rights became part of the U.S. Constitution. The Fourteenth and Fifteenth amendments would provide a legal basis for civil rights laws of the 20th century. Black schools and churches begun during Reconstruction also endured. Reconstruction changed society, putting African Americans on the path toward full equality. In the next unit, you will learn about other changes in American society after the Civil War.

Section 3 Assessment

1. Terms & Names

Explain the significance of:
- Fifteenth Amendment
- Panic of 1873
- Compromise of 1877

2. Taking Notes

Review the chapter and find five significant individuals and events to place on a time line as shown.

Which event or person was most important and why?

3. Main Ideas

a. What did the Fifteenth Amendment declare?

b. What effect did scandals in the Grant administration have on the Republican Party?

c. What demands did Southern Democrats make in the Compromise of 1877?

4. Critical Thinking

Drawing Conclusions
Why do you think the Republicans were willing to agree to the Compromise of 1877 and end Reconstruction?

THINK ABOUT
- the election of 1876
- the Panic of 1873
- the Supreme Court rulings

ACTIVITY OPTIONS

LANGUAGE ARTS
CIVICS

Research Ku Klux Klan activities barring African Americans from voting. Then write a protest **letter to the editor** or propose a **law** to protect voting rights.

TERMS & NAMES

Briefly explain the significance of each of the following.

1. Reconstruction
2. Andrew Johnson
3. black codes
4. civil rights
5. Fourteenth Amendment
6. sharecropping
7. lynch
8. Fifteenth Amendment
9. Panic of 1873
10. Compromise of 1877

REVIEW QUESTIONS

Rebuilding the Union (pages 517–523)

1. What was the Freedmen's Bureau?
2. What were the main parts of President Johnson's Reconstruction plan?
3. Who were scalawags and carpetbaggers?
4. What reason did the House give for impeaching President Johnson?

Reconstruction and Daily Life (pages 524–528)

5. Why did Congress not pass a land-reform plan?
6. What new systems of labor developed in the South after the Civil War?
7. How did the Ku Klux Klan serve the Democratic Party?

End of Reconstruction (pages 529–533)

8. Why did the Fifteenth Amendment arouse anger in many women?
9. What caused an economic depression in the 1870s?
10. How did Supreme Court rulings during Reconstruction help weaken African Americans' civil rights?

CRITICAL THINKING

1. USING YOUR NOTES

Problems		Solutions
Black codes	➤	
President Johnson	➤	
Education	➤	
Economy	➤	
Ku Klux Klan	➤	
Voting	➤	

Using your diagram, answer the following questions.

a. What was the solution to the problem of educating African Americans?

b. What was the solution to the problem of Ku Klux Klan violence?

2. ANALYZING LEADERSHIP

Why might Reconstruction be considered a time in which the presidency was weak?

3. THEME: DEMOCRATIC IDEALS

How did the Fourteenth and Fifteenth amendments promote greater equality for African Americans? How were the amendments limited?

4. APPLYING CITIZENSHIP SKILLS

What were the different viewpoints of Elizabeth Cady Stanton and Frances E. W. Harper regarding the Fifteenth Amendment's failure to give women an important right of citizenship—the right to vote?

5. ANALYZING CAUSES

What aspect of the Compromise of 1877 likely played the greatest role in ending Reconstruction?

Interact with History

How did your solutions to rebuilding the nation compare with the actual solutions carried out?

VISUAL SUMMARY

Reconstruction

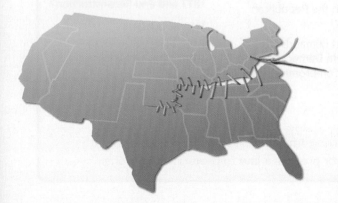

Rebuilding the Union

During Reconstruction, Congress decided how the Southern states would be readmitted to the Union and passed laws to improve conditions for freed people.

Reconstruction and Daily Life

After slavery ended, freed African Americans reunited their families, attended school, and began working for pay. Racist violence and lack of land slowed their progress.

End of Reconstruction

In the 1870s, hostile Supreme Court decisions, the Southern Democrats' return to power, and the withdrawal of federal troops from the South ended Reconstruction.

HISTORY SKILLS

1. INTERPRETING MAPS: Region

Study the map and then answer the questions.

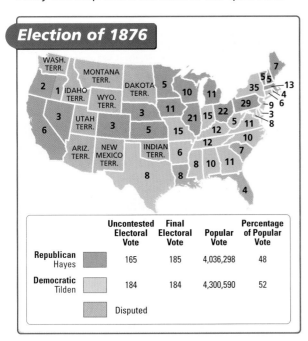

Election of 1876

	Uncontested Electoral Vote	Final Electoral Vote	Popular Vote	Percentage of Popular Vote
Republican Hayes	165	185	4,036,298	48
Democratic Tilden	184	184	4,300,590	52
	Disputed			

Basic Map Elements
a. What is the subject of the map?

Interpreting the Map
b. In what region of the country were most of the disputed votes located?

c. What regions voted mostly Republican?

2. INTERPRETING PRIMARY SOURCES

This political cartoon shows the effect of the Ku Klux Klan on African-American families in the South. Study the cartoon carefully and then answer the questions.

a. Based on the cartoon, what were the goals of the Ku Klux Klan?

b. Does the image reflect any bias on the part of the artist? Explain.

ALTERNATIVE ASSESSMENT

1. INTERDISCIPLINARY ACTIVITY: Language Arts

Writing Letters Write letters that you imagine the following three people would write about Reconstruction: 1) a member of the old Southern upper class; 2) a newly freed African American; and 3) a white Northern carpetbagger. Be sure to use standard grammar, spelling, sentence structure, and punctuation in your letters.

2. COOPERATIVE LEARNING ACTIVITY

Conducting an Impeachment Trial The impeachment trial of Andrew Johnson was a dramatic and colorful event. Many officials pleaded their case either for or against the president.

Working in a small group, research the trial using resources such as diaries, journals, autobiographies, letters, and books. Each group member should choose an official who spoke at the trial and collect some of his quotes. The group should then perform its own trial in front of the class, with each member portraying the official he or she chose. Some possible officials include Thaddeus Stevens, Edmund G. Ross, James W. Grimes, Benjamin Butler, and Chief Justice Samuel Chase.

3. TECHNOLOGY ACTIVITY

Making an Electronic Presentation Life under the sharecropping system was not easy. Information about sharecropping comes from a variety of sources. Using the library or the Internet, find diaries, memoirs, images, and news articles about life as a sharecropper.

For more about sharecropping . . .

INTERNET ACTIVITY
CLASSZONE.COM

Use presentation software to share your information about sharecropping. Consider the suggestions below to get started.
- images or descriptions of a sharecropper's shack
- examples of the crops that were grown by a sharecropper
- facts and quotations about a sharecropper's life

4. HISTORY PORTFOLIO

Identify the dates that you consider to be the era of Reconstruction. Then identify previous eras in American history and place them all in chronological sequence on a time line. Add your time line to your portfolio.

Additional Test Practice, pp. S1–S33

TEST PRACTICE
CLASSZONE.COM

CHAPTER
19
EPILOGUE

The United States, 1860–1920

Crowds of people walk, work, and shop on Mulberry Street in New York's Lower East Side.

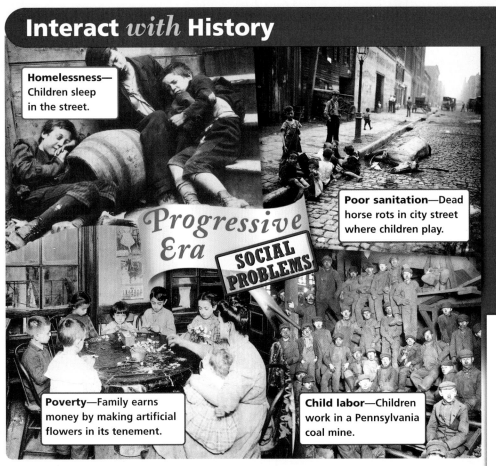

Homelessness—Children sleep in the street.

Poor sanitation—Dead horse rots in city street where children play.

Progressive Era

SOCIAL PROBLEMS

Poverty—Family earns money by making artificial flowers in its tenement.

Child labor—Children work in a Pennsylvania coal mine.

It is 1901, and the nation is at a crossroads. Its population and economy are growing. It is also gaining territories and becoming a world power. But there are serious problems at home. You're anxious to see how your national leaders will address these issues.

What Do You Think?

• Which problem shown in the collage is most important?

• Are domestic issues more important than international ones?

• What should government, business, or other organizations do to address these issues?

How would you solve these problems?

1898
United States defeats Spain in Spanish–American War.

1896
Supreme Court establishes "separate but equal" doctrine in *Plessy* v. *Ferguson* decision.

1901
President William McKinley is assassinated and Theodore Roosevelt becomes president.

1917
United States enters World War I.

1882
Thomas Edison installs electric lights in New York City.

1892
Immigration center opens on Ellis Island.

1912
Woodrow Wilson is elected president.

1920
19th Amendment ensures women the right to vote.

1862
The Homestead Act encourages western settlement.

1876
Rutherford B. Hayes wins disputed election and becomes president.

USA World 1860

1920

1869
Suez Canal opens in Egypt.

1885
Berlin Conference on African affairs divides Africa among European nations.

1896
First modern Olympic games are held in Athens, Greece.

1900
Boxer Rebellion against foreigners begins in China.

1910
Mexican Revolution begins.

1914
First World War breaks out in Europe.

1918
Allies defeat Central Powers to win World War I.

BEFORE YOU READ

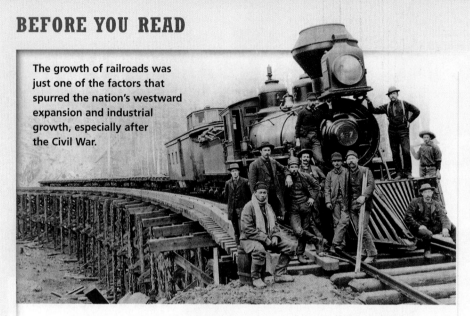

The growth of railroads was just one of the factors that spurred the nation's westward expansion and industrial growth, especially after the Civil War.

Previewing the Theme

Expansion This chapter examines the tremendous growth the United States experienced during the late 1800s and early 1900s. The nation expanded physically as Americans settled in the West, built an overseas empire, and increased their influence around the globe. Meanwhile, the nation experienced industrial and population growth, created new ways of life, and renewed efforts to improve conditions for its citizens.

What Do You Know?

What do you think of when you hear the following terms associated with the late 1800s and early 1900s: "wild west," "industrialization," "progressivism," "imperialism?"

THINK ABOUT

• what you already know about these terms from your reading or experience with them from the popular media

• why they might be associated with an era in which America underwent dramatic changes

What Do You Want to Know?

What questions do you have about the United States at the turn of the century? Record these questions in your notebook before you read the chapter.

READ AND TAKE NOTES

Reading Strategy: Sequencing Events
Sequencing means putting events in the order in which they happen in time. In learning about U.S. history between the Civil War and World War I, it will be helpful to list important events in the order

in which they occurred. You might record the event and its date in a graphic organizer such as the one below. Copy this organizer in your notebook. Fill it in as you read the chapter.

S See Skillbuilder Handbook, page R4.

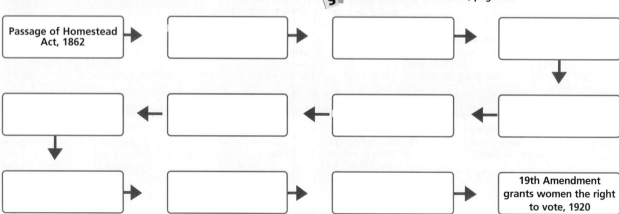

Passage of Homestead Act, 1862 →

19th Amendment grants women the right to vote, 1920

① A Time of Growth

TERMS & NAMES
frontier
Great Plains
Homestead Act
Dawes Act
Gilded Age
urbanization
new immigrants

MAIN IDEA	WHY IT MATTERS NOW
During the second half of the 19th century, the nation experienced tremendous growth.	The changes that the United States underwent helped transform it into the modern nation it is today.

ONE AMERICAN'S STORY

Nat Love was born a slave in Tennessee in 1854. After the Civil War, he was one of thousands of African Americans who left the South and went west. In 1869, Love headed for Dodge City, Kansas. He was 15 and now free.

Love's horse-taming skills landed him a job as a cowhand. For 20 years, he took part in the cattle drives that brought Texas cattle to Kansas stockyards. He became well known for his expert horsemanship. In his autobiography, Love offered a lively but exaggerated account of his life. He told how he braved hailstorms, wild animals, and human attackers.

A VOICE FROM THE PAST

I carry the marks of fourteen bullet wounds on different parts of my body, most any one of which would be sufficient to kill an ordinary man. . . . Horses were shot from under me, men killed around me, but always I escaped with a trifling wound at the worst.

Nat Love, *The Life and Adventures of Nat Love*

Nat Love was an African-American cowhand who became a rodeo star.

During the second half of the 19th century, the United States underwent a time of tremendous growth. Americans such as Nat Love contributed to this growth.

Westward Expansion

In the decades following the Civil War, more Americans began to settle on the **frontier.** The frontier was the sparsely populated area on the western side of the nation. Aside from Native Americans, few people lived there. It included the **Great Plains,** the area from the Missouri River to the Rocky Mountains.

American settlers migrated westward for several reasons. The discovery of gold in California drew numerous fortune seekers to the West. A growing demand for beef in the nation's cities prompted ranchers to seek land for raising cattle. In addition, thousands of families sought to start a new life as frontier farmers.

The federal government encouraged western settlement by passing the **Homestead Act** in 1862. This law offered 160 acres of free land to anyone who agreed to live on the land for five years and improve it.

Railroads also played a key role in extending U.S. control over Western lands. Trains carried the natural resources of the West—minerals, timber, crops, and cattle—to markets in the East. In turn, trains brought miners, ranchers, and farmers west to develop these resources further.

This western movement forced changes to Native American ways of life. As white settlers continued to move farther onto the frontier, they frequently clashed with Native Americans over land and resources. By the 1880s, most Native American tribes had been forced onto reservations, land set aside for them by the U.S. government.

Many well-meaning reformers felt that assimilation was the only way for Native Americans to survive. In other words, the reformers wanted Native Americans to adopt the culture of white Americans. Passed in 1887, the **Dawes Act** was intended to encourage Native Americans to give up their traditional cultures and become farmers. The U.S. government sent many Native American children to boarding schools to be "Americanized." In the end, the Dawes Act did little to benefit Native Americans. Not all of them wanted to be farmers. Those who did lacked the tools, money, or other resources to be successful.

*Reading*History
A. Making Inferences Why were railroads so important to the West?

The Growth of Industry

As thousands of Americans forged new lives in the West, much of the rest of the nation experienced the Industrial Revolution. In the years after the Civil War, a number of factors boosted the pace of industrialization in the United States.

1. **Plentiful natural resources.** The United States had abundant raw materials, including forests, water, coal, iron, copper, silver, and gold.
2. **Improved transportation.** Since the early 1800s, steamboats, canals, and railroads made it ever easier to ship items over long distances.

These laborers are working in a foundry, a place where metal is cast.

3. **Growing population.** From 1860 to 1900, the U.S. population grew from 31.5 million to 76 million—due in large part to a wave of immigration. This increase provided millions of workers to make products and consumers to buy them.

4. **New inventions.** New technologies and inventions made industry more efficient.

Vocabulary
capital: money and property used in a business

5. **Investment capital.** Banks and wealthy people invested in businesses so they could improve factories and equipment. Such improvements made business more successful. The government also provided help, such as subsidies, to businesses wishing to expand.

Industrialization led to the rise of powerful businessmen. John D. Rockefeller, for example, led the oil industry. Andrew Carnegie controlled the steel industry. They and others made millions—often through ruthless tactics.

The late 1800s become known as the **Gilded Age.** To gild is to coat an object with gold leaf. Gilded decorations were popular during the era. But the name has a deeper meaning. Just as gold leaf can disguise an object of lesser value, so did the wealth of a few people mask society's problems, including corrupt politics and widespread poverty.

Many of the nation's poor were workers who labored in factories. Eventually, angry workers organized to try to

Vocabulary
negotiate: to discuss something in order to reach an agreement

improve their lives. They formed labor unions—groups of workers that negotiated with business owners to obtain better wages and working conditions. By standing up to employers, unions won shorter working hours and better pay for workers.

Business leader John D. Rockefeller is shown as a wealthy king. Notice which industries are the "jewels in his crown."

Cities Grow and Change

The Industrial Revolution, which transformed how people worked, also changed where people worked. During the late 1800s, more and more people moved to cities to find jobs.

Factories sprouted in cities because they offered good transportation and plentiful workers. Increasing numbers of factory jobs appeared in U.S. cities, followed by more workers to fill those jobs. The growth of cities that resulted from these changes is called **urbanization.**

As people flocked to cities, overcrowding became a serious problem. Many poor families lived in rented apartments or tenements. A tenement is an apartment house that is usually run-down and overcrowded. Many tenements were dangerous and unhealthy places to live.

Many Americans were disgusted by the poverty and slums in the cities. Some people, known as urban reformers, sought changes that could solve these problems. Some reformers helped to ease the problems

Community Service

Since the United States began, citizens have shared concerns about their communities. Many citizens have identified problems and proposed solutions to them.

In 1993, sixth-grader David Levitt asked his principal if the leftover food from the school cafeteria could be sent to a program to feed needy people. David was told that many restrictions prevented giving away the food.

Determined to get food to people who needed it, David talked to the school board, the state health department, and private companies to convince them to back his program. Today, more than 500,000 pounds of food from schools has been given to hungry people in the Seminole, Florida, area.

David Levitt carries supplies for his food pantry program.

How Do You Participate in Your Community?

1. In a small group, think about problems within your community. Make a list of those problems.

2. Choose one problem to work on.

3. Gather information about the problem. Keep a log of your sources to use again.

4. After you gather information, brainstorm solutions to the problem. Create a plan to carry out one solution.

5. Present the problem and your plan to the class.

 See the Citizenship Handbook, page 270.

For more about community service . . .

 RESEARCH LINKS
CLASSZONE.COM

---

of urban life by opening settlement houses. These facilities offered services such as daycare, education, and health care to needy people in slum neighborhoods.

Political machines were another type of organization that addressed the problems of the city. A political machine is an organization that influences enough votes to control a local government. Although often corrupt, political machines did some good things for cities. They built parks, sewers, schools, roads, and orphanages in many cities. In addition, machine politicians often helped city dwellers find jobs or homes.

The New Immigrants

Many of those who lived in the nation's growing cities were immigrants. Throughout the late 1800s and early 1900s, the United States experienced a wave of immigration. Until the 1890s, most immigrants to the United States came from northern and western Europe. But after 1900, fewer northern Europeans immigrated, and more southern and eastern Europeans did. This later group of immigrants came to be known as the **new immigrants**.

Immigrants settled where they could find jobs. Many found work in U.S. factories. They tried to assimilate, or become part of American

Reading **History**
B. Comparing and Contrasting
How were settlement houses and political machines similar? How were they different?

society. At the same time, however, they also were changing America. Immigrants did not give up their cultures right away. Bits and pieces of immigrant languages, foods, and music worked their way into the rest of American culture.

Despite their efforts to assimilate, immigrants faced prejudice from native-born Americans. Many native-born Americans feared they would have to compete with immigrants for jobs. In 1882, Congress passed laws to restrict immigration. Nonwhites faced deeper prejudice than European immigrants did. Asians faced some of the worst prejudice. In 1882, Congress passed the Chinese Exclusion Act. It banned Chinese immigration for ten years. The Chinese Exclusion Act was renewed in 1892. In 1902, Congress made the ban permanent. It was not repealed until 1943.

The Chinese Exclusion Act was not the only example of prejudice in the United States around 1900. As you will read in the next section, racial discrimination was very much a part of life in American society at the dawn of the 20th century.

U.S. Immigration, *1841–1900*

Origins of Immigrants

1841–1860

0.7%
1%
2%
3.3%
93%

1881–1900

0.5%
1.5%
6%
31%
61%

- Northern and western Europe
- Southern and eastern Europe
- Americas
- Asia
- All others

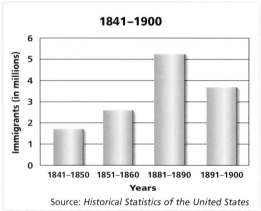

1841–1900

Immigrants (in millions)

Years: 1841–1850, 1851–1860, 1881–1890, 1891–1900

Source: *Historical Statistics of the United States*

SKILLBUILDER Interpreting Graphs

1. *About how many immigrants came to the United States from 1841 to 1860?*
2. *About how many southern and eastern European immigrants came to the United States from 1881 to 1900?*

Section Assessment

1. Terms & Names

Explain the significance of:
- frontier
- Great Plains
- Homestead Act
- Dawes Act
- Gilded Age
- urbanization
- new immigrants

2. Taking Notes

Use a cluster diagram like the one below to list the factors that contributed to industrial growth in the United States.

Factors

3. Main Ideas

a. What drew large numbers of people to the West in the decades after 1860?

b. What urban problems did reformers try to solve?

c. How were the new immigrants different from earlier immigrants?

4. Critical Thinking

Recognizing Effects How were the effects of the Dawes Act different from what was intended?

THINK ABOUT
- the goals of the act
- the impact on the land use and independence of the Plains people

---

ACTIVITY OPTIONS

MATH

GEOGRAPHY

Research immigration to your city or state. Create a **spreadsheet** of this information or draw a **map** showing immigration routes.

Industry in the Midwest

The Midwest is the region around the Great Lakes and the Upper Mississippi Valley. The region saw explosive growth during the 1800s. The first wave came after 1825, when the Erie Canal linked the East with the Great Lakes region. The second wave, caused by investments in products related to the Civil War (1861–1865), saw a boom in mining, farming, forestry, and meat-packing. By 1890, 29 percent of the country's manufacturing employment was in the Midwest, and the next big wave of growth was just beginning. New industries included steel and steel products, such as train rails and skyscraper beams.

Transportation and resources spurred the region's growth. Coal, oil, iron ore, limestone, and lumber were abundant, and the land was fertile. Trains, rivers, and lakes connected the Midwest to markets in the East and South and brought in raw materials from the West. The map on page 545 shows the resources of the lower Great Lakes and how transportation by rail and water joined regions.

The industries of the Midwest used raw materials that came both from their own region and from other regions of the country. For example, the cattle in this photograph of the Chicago stockyards came by rail from the ranches of the West. In contrast, the logs being floated down the river came from the pine forests of Michigan and Wisconsin.

ARTIFACT FILE

A Quick Dinner Midwestern meat-packing companies advertised canned meats as a way to save time feeding a hungry family.

ARMOUR'S
Veribest
CANNED MEATS

Affordable Housing People began to build with wooden siding over a frame of wooden two-by-fours. These homes were cheap and quick to construct.

Iron ore from the Lake Superior region and coal from southern Illinois were used to manufacture steel.

On-Line Field Trip

The Chicago Historical Society
in Chicago, Illinois, contains photographs, documents, and artifacts such as this Western Electric typewriter, made in 1900. Typewriters enabled office workers to produce neat, clean documents quickly.

For more about the Midwest . . .

CONNECT TO GEOGRAPHY

1. **Region** What advantages did the Midwest have that helped it become highly industrialized?

2. **Human-Environment Interaction** How did the development of railroads add to the region's advantages?

   See Geography Handbook, pages 4–5.

CONNECT TO HISTORY

3. **Analyzing Causes** Chicago was a big meatpacking center. Why do you think that industry chose to locate there?

Life at the Turn of the Century

TERMS & NAMES
mass culture
leisure
vaudeville
ragtime
Jim Crow
segregation
Plessy v. *Ferguson*
NAACP

MAIN IDEA	**WHY IT MATTERS NOW**
Around the turn of the century, mass culture emerged and the nation continued to grapple with racism.	Americans continue to participate in a mass culture and issues of race continue to affect society.

ONE AMERICAN'S STORY

Abigail Scott was born in Illinois in 1834. She was told that her mother remarked at the time, "Poor baby! She'll be a woman some day! . . . A woman's lot is so hard!" At 17, Abigail moved to Oregon by wagon train with her family. Her mother died on the journey. In Oregon, Abigail taught school until she married a farmer named Benjamin Duniway in 1853. When he was disabled in an accident, Abigail assumed the support of her family. She wrote about a day on a pioneer farm with its endless chores.

A VOICE FROM THE PAST

[W]ashing, scrubbing, churning . . . preparing . . . meals in our lean-to kitchen . . . [having] to bake and clean and stew and fry; to be in short, a general pioneer drudge, with never a penny of my own, was not pleasant business.

Abigail Scott Duniway, in her autobiography, *Path Breaking*

Like Abigail Scott Duniway, this pioneer woman worked long and hard. She is shown here with buffalo chips she has collected on the treeless prairie to use as fuel.

The long days of hard work for the frontier pioneers represented only one example of life in the United States at the turn of the 20th century. In the East, industrialization and new technologies were creating a distinct urban culture. At the same time, racial minorities across the country continued to face discrimination.

Life in the West

Life in the West was tough. Farmers, such as Abigail Duniway, faced many challenges. The Plains were nearly treeless. Farmers were forced to build their first homes from blocks of sod, or prairie soil. For fuel, the farmers burned corn cobs or "cow chips" (dried manure). In many places, farmers had to dig wells more than 280 feet deep to reach the only water. Blizzards, prairie fires, hailstorms, tornadoes, grasshoppers, and drought added to the misery of life on the plains.

New inventions helped farmers to meet some of these challenges. The steel plow, for example, sliced through the tough sod. Windmills adapted to the plains pumped water from deep wells to the surface. Barbed wire allowed farmers to fence in land and livestock. Meanwhile, reapers made the harvesting of crops much easier, and threshers helped farmers to separate grain or seed from straw. These inventions also made farm work more efficient. For example, from 1860 to 1890, farmers doubled their production of wheat.

Reading **History**

A. Summarizing
What inventions helped farmers to meet the challenges of the prairie?

The West was also home to numerous cowhands, who helped herd cattle. The cowhands drove the cattle to cow towns, where they would be shipped on trains to the meat markets of the East. Cowhands spent most of their days in the saddle. They ate around campfires and slept under the stars.

In addition to farms and ranches, a number of cities grew in the West. Gold and silver strikes made instant cities of places like Denver in the Colorado Territory and brought new life to sleepy towns like San Francisco in California. These cities prospered while much of the area around them remained barely populated. San Francisco grew from a small town to a city of about 25,000 in just one year following the 1849 gold rush.

The railroads also brought rapid growth to some towns in the West. Omaha, Nebraska, flourished as a meat-processing center for cattle ranches in the region. Portland, Oregon, became a regional market for fish, grain, and lumber.

Population of Western Cities		
CITY	*1860*	*1890*
Denver	2,603*	106,713
Omaha	1,883	140,452
Portland	2,874	46,385
San Francisco	56,802	298,997

SKILLBUILDER Interpreting Charts
Which city had the largest increase in number of people from 1860 to 1890?

*1861 Territorial Census
Sources: *Population Abstract of the United States; Colorado Republic*

San Francisco, 1847

San Francisco, 1850

Women in the West

Western life provided a few new opportunities for women. Most women who worked held traditional jobs. They were teachers or servants or helped support their families by taking in sewing or laundry. However, a few became sheriffs, gamblers, and even outlaws. In mining camps and cow towns, some women ran dance halls and boarding houses.

Western lawmakers recognized the contributions women made to Western settlement by giving women more legal rights than they had in the East. In most territories, women could own property and control their own money. In addition, in 1869, the Wyoming Territory led the nation in giving women the vote.

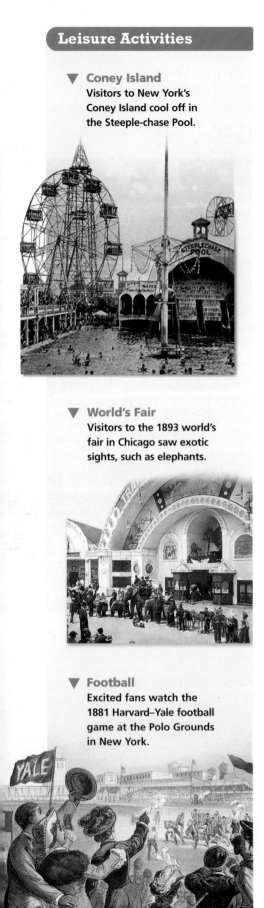

▼ **Coney Island**
Visitors to New York's Coney Island cool off in the Steeple-chase Pool.

▼ **World's Fair**
Visitors to the 1893 world's fair in Chicago saw exotic sights, such as elephants.

▼ **Football**
Excited fans watch the 1881 Harvard–Yale football game at the Polo Grounds in New York.

Society and Mass Culture

Far from the frontier, life for residents of the nation's urban centers was rapidly changing. During the late 1800s, the growth of large cities and other changes helped create an American **mass culture**—a common culture experienced by large numbers of people.

In what became one of the nation's most popular shared activities, more and more Americans began to read newspapers. Newspapers had a wide influence on American life, including the rise of modern advertising. Advertisers used images of celebrities in newspapers and magazines to tempt people to buy products. Advertisements also helped people learn about new products. At the turn of the century, new inventions, such as the electric washing machine, promised to help people do their household chores more easily. Because women did most of these chores as well as most of the shopping, manufacturers marketed these new devices to women.

New Leisure Activities

Advertising and shopping were not the only daily activities changing at this time. **Leisure,** or free time, activities also changed. In cities, new parks provided entertainment for people. The increasing number of people who worked in factories and offices liked to go to parks for sunshine and fresh air. Parks helped bring grass and trees back into city landscapes.

Central Park in New York City is the nation's best-known urban park. Opened in 1876, Central Park was built to look like the country. Trees and shrubs dotted its gently rolling landscape. Winding walkways let city dwellers imagine they were strolling in the woods. People could also ride bicycles and play sports in the park.

In addition to urban parks, amusement parks provided a place people could go for fun. World's fairs provided another wildly popular form of entertainment for Americans. Between 1876 and 1916, several U.S. cities, including Philadelphia, Chicago, St. Louis, and San Francisco, hosted world's fairs.

During this time, spectator sports also became popular entertainment. Baseball, football, boxing, and many other sports drew thousands of people to fields and gymnasiums around the country as spectators as well as participants.

In addition to sports, other forms of live entertainment attracted large audiences. **Vaudeville,** for example, featured a mixture of song, dance, and comedy. New types of music also began to be heard. **Ragtime,** a blend of African-American and European musical forms, was an important new type of music. Early in the 20th century, movies began to compete with live entertainment. The first movies were silent and were added as the final feature of a vaudeville show. Soon, storefront theaters appeared that showed only movies.

*Reading*History
B. Making Inferences How do you think movies contributed to mass culture?

Segregation and Discrimination

Many Americans at the turn of the century enjoyed the freedom to participate in the emerging mass culture. For the nation's racial minorities, however, racism and segregation often limited their economic, political, and social freedom. As you read in earlier chapters, racist attitudes had been developing in America for centuries. Such attitudes led whites to discriminate against nonwhites around the country. The most obvious examples of racial discrimination were in the South. African Americans experienced political power in the South during Reconstruction. (See Chapter 18.) But when Reconstruction ended in 1877, Southern states passed laws to restrict African Americans' rights.

For example, Southern states passed laws that set up literacy, or reading, tests and poll taxes to prevent blacks from voting. White officials made sure that blacks failed the tests by giving unfair exams. For instance, white officials might give blacks tests written in Latin.

In addition to voting restrictions, African Americans faced **Jim Crow** laws. Jim Crow laws enforced **segregation,** or separation, of white and black people in public places. As a result, separate schools, restrooms, and seating in public places were common throughout the South. In 1896, the Supreme Court upheld the practice of segregation in its decision in ***Plessy v. Ferguson*** by declaring that "separate but equal" facilities did not violate the Fourteenth Amendment.

Segregation often forced African Americans to use separate entrances from whites.

African Americans Organize

A number of African-American leaders worked to overcome discrimination. Booker T. Washington, a former slave, urged blacks to improve their lives by learning trades and gaining economic strength. In 1881, he founded Tuskegee Institute in Alabama to achieve this goal. At Tuskegee, Washington hired talented teachers and scholars, such as George Washington Carver.

To gain white support, Washington did not openly challenge segregation. Some black leaders, however, disagreed with this approach.

Reading **History**

C. Making Inferences In what way did Washington and Du Bois disagree about how to achieve African American progress?

AMERICA'S HISTORY MAKERS

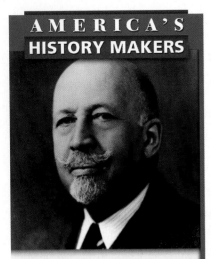

W. E. B. DU BOIS
1868–1963

W. E. B. Du Bois grew up in a middle-class home. He went to college and earned his doctorate at Harvard. Du Bois became one of the most distinguished scholars of the 20th century.

Du Bois fought against segregation. He believed that the best way to end it would be to have educated African Americans lead the fight. He referred to this group of educated African Americans as the "Talented Tenth"—the most educated 10 percent of African Americans.

Why do you think Du Bois believed the Talented Tenth should lead the fight against segregation?

W. E. B. Du Bois (doo•BOYS) encouraged African Americans to reject segregation.

A VOICE FROM THE PAST

Is it possible . . . that nine million men can make effective progress in economic lines if they are deprived of political rights? . . . If history and reason give any distinct answer to these questions, it is an emphatic NO.

W. E. B. Du Bois, *The Souls of Black Folk*

In 1909, Du Bois and other reformers founded the National Association for the Advancement of Colored People, or the **NAACP**. The NAACP played a major role in ending segregation in the 20th century.

Discrimination in the West

Other minorities also faced discrimination in the United States. Chinese immigrants who came to the American West in the late 1800s endured low wages and even violence. In 1885, white workers in Rock Springs, Wyoming, refused to work in the same mine as Chinese workers. The white people stormed through the Chinese part of town, shooting Chinese people and burning buildings. During the attack, 28 Chinese were killed and 15 were wounded.

As difficult as life was for the country's minorities, they were not the only ones who struggled. As you will read in the next section, the nation's farmers fought for a stronger voice in government. And a number of Americans strove to improve conditions for workers and reform many of society's ills during the late 1800s and early 1900s.

Section 2 Assessment

1. Terms & Names

Explain the significance of:
• mass culture
• leisure
• vaudeville
• ragtime
• Jim Crow
• segregation
• *Plessy* v. *Ferguson*
• NAACP

2. Taking Notes

Use a diagram such as the one below to note what factors contributed to the emergence of a mass culture at the turn of the century.

3. Main Ideas

a. How did life on the frontier provide greater opportunities for women?

b. What were Jim Crow laws?

c. What did Chinese immigrants and Mexican immigrants have in common?

4. Critical Thinking

Solving Problems What could have been done to end racial discrimination against nonwhites in the United States around 1900?

THINK ABOUT
• attitudes of whites about nonwhites
• the efforts of nonwhites to find jobs and security
• competition for jobs

ACTIVITY OPTIONS

LANGUAGE ARTS

TECHNOLOGY

Research a civil rights leader from the turn of the century. Write a short **biography** of that person or design a **Web site** devoted to the work of that person.

MAIN IDEA	WHY IT MATTERS NOW
During the late 1800s and early 1900s, Populists and progressives worked for social reform.	Many of the reforms supported by Populists and progressives remain in place today.

Nellie Bly

ONE AMERICAN'S STORY

Journalist Nellie Bly worked for *The New York World*. In 1887, Bly wanted to investigate the Women's Lunatic Asylum in New York City. An asylum is a place where people with an illness can get help. She faked mental illness and fooled doctors so that she could become a patient there. After spending ten days in the asylum, Bly wrote a newspaper article about what she had witnessed. She described being forced to take ice cold baths.

A VOICE FROM THE PAST

My teeth chattered and my limbs were goose-fleshed and blue with cold. Suddenly I got, one after the other, three buckets of water over my head—ice-cold water, too—into my eyes, my ears, my nose and my mouth.

Nellie Bly, quoted in *Nellie Bly: Daredevil, Reporter, Feminist*

Bly also wrote about poor conditions in slums, factories, prisons, and nursing homes—all in an attempt to right the wrongs of American society. She was not alone. During the late 1800s and early 1900s, many Americans worked to reform American institutions and improve life in the United States.

The Rise of Populism

By the 1870s, many of the nation's farmers faced serious economic problems. Aided by new tools and techniques, farmers grew increasing amounts of food. As supplies of farm products grew, their prices fell. At the same time, farmers had to spend more to run a farm. New farm machinery and railroad rates were especially costly. Railroads, for example, charged the farmers high fees to carry their crops to market.

Farmers eventually began to work together to seek solutions to their problems. In 1890, several farm groups organized to try to gain political power. They formed the **Populist Party**, or People's Party. The Populists wanted the government to adopt a free silver policy, that is, the unlimited coining of silver. Since silver was plentiful, more money would be put in circulation. Populists believed that increasing the supply of money would raise crop prices. Higher prices would help farmers pay back the money that they had borrowed to improve their farms.

Opponents of free silver wanted to keep the gold standard. Under the gold standard, the government backs every dollar with a certain amount of gold. Since the gold supply is limited, fewer dollars are in circulation. This protects the value of money and keeps prices down.

In 1892, the Populist Party platform called for free silver, government ownership of railroads, shorter working hours, and other economic reforms. The Populist presidential candidate, James B. Weaver won more than a million votes. But he still finished a distant third behind Republican Benjamin Harrison, the incumbent president, and Democrat Grover Cleveland, who won the election.

Economics *in* History

Supply and Demand

Farmers in the West faced serious economic problems in the 1880s. The supply of food was increasing rapidly, but consumer demand was growing slowly. To attract more consumers, farmers had to drop the prices of their products.

The farmers were confronting the **law of supply and demand**. The amount of economic goods available for sale is the **supply**. The willingness and ability of consumers to spend money for goods and services is **demand**. The price of goods is set by the supply of that good and the demand for that good.

At a lower price, businesses produce less of a good because they will make less money. As the price rises, they produce more. Consumer demand works in the opposite way. Consumers want to buy more of the good when the price is lower—after all, it costs them less. They buy less when the price is higher. The actual price of a good results from a compromise—how much consumers are willing to pay and how little businesses are willing to take for the good.

CONNECT TO HISTORY

1. **Recognizing Effects** Suppose farmers found a new market for their wheat—the people in another country, for instance. What effect would that have on price? Why?

 See Skillbuilder Handbook, page R11.

CONNECT TO TODAY

2. **Comparing** How does the price of blue jeans show the law of supply and demand?

For more about supply and demand . . .

RESEARCH LINKS
CLASSZONE.COM

1 Prices are high.

2 Producers want to increase supply.

3 More goods push price down.

4 Demand increases.

5 Producer increases supply.

6 Price decreases again.

7 Producer supplies less.

8 Prices increase and demand falls

The Election of 1896

In 1893, the nation experienced a depression that lasted until 1897. In the face of tough economic times, the Democrats nominated **William Jennings Bryan** of Nebraska for president in 1896. In a speech at the Democratic convention, Bryan urged his listeners to support free silver.

*Reading*History

A. Analyzing Points of View What point was William Jennings Bryan making about the importance of farms?

A VOICE FROM THE PAST

Burn down your cities and leave our farms, and your cities will spring up again as if by magic; but destroy our farms and the grass will grow in the street of every city in the country. . . . [We] . . . answer their demand for a gold standard by saying . . . : You shall not press down upon the brow of labor this crown of thorns. You shall not crucify mankind upon a cross of gold.

William Jennings Bryan, "Cross of Gold" speech, July 8, 1896

The Populists hoped the weak economy would increase support for their candidate in the 1896 presidential election. Because Bryan, the Democratic nominee, supported free silver, the Populists joined the Democrats in supporting Bryan. Meanwhile, the Republicans nominated Ohio governor William McKinley. Although Bryan received heavy support from farmers in the South and the West, McKinley won the election. Bryan's defeat marked the beginning of the end for the Populist Party.

Progressivism Emerges

As you saw in Section 1, the rapid growth of cities and industries in the United States at the turn of the century brought many problems. Among them were poverty, the spread of slums, and poor conditions in factories. In addition, corrupt political machines had won control of many city and state governments. Big corporations had gained power over the economy and government. To attack these problems, a varied set of reform movements emerged. These reform movements are commonly grouped under the label **progressivism.**

The progressive reformers shared at least one of three basic goals: first, to reform government and expand democracy; second, to promote social welfare; third, to create economic reform.

In the 1890s and early 1900s, progressive leaders in a number of states sought to expand democracy. They proposed reforms that gave voters more control over their government. For example, an Oregon newspaperman pushed his state to accept three reforms known as the initiative, the referendum, and the recall. The initiative and the referendum allowed voters to propose and pass laws directly without going through the legislature. The

*Reading*History

B. Finding Main Ideas What was the main goal behind the progressive reforms of government?

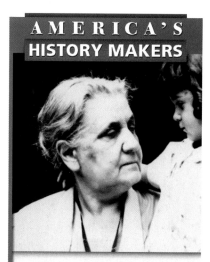

AMERICA'S HISTORY MAKERS

JANE ADDAMS
1860–1935

Jane Addams founded Hull House as an "effort to aid in the solution of the social and industrial problems which are [caused] by the modern conditions of life in a great city."

In addition to her involvement with Hull House, Addams was active in many other areas. She fought for the passage of laws to protect women workers and outlaw child labor. She also worked to improve housing and public health. In 1931, she was awarded a share of the Nobel Peace Prize for her efforts.

Why did Jane Addams found Hull House?

recall allowed the people to vote an official out of office. In addition, reformers pushed for the direct primary, which allowed voters rather than party conventions, to choose candidates to run for public office.

To promote social welfare, progressives tackled problems such as poverty, unemployment, and poor working conditions. For example, Jane Addams was leader in the settlement house movement. Settlement houses aimed to help people, such as immigrants and the poor, overcome the social problems they faced.

The third progressive goal was to create economic reform. Economic reform often meant limiting the power of big business and regulating its activities. The Sherman Antitrust Act of 1890 made it illegal for corporations to form trusts. Trusts were combinations of businesses that could control a market and squeeze out competition.

An important aspect of progressivism was the role that women played in the movement. Educated middle-class women led many of the social reform movements of the era. As these women worked to better the lives of others, they also sought to improve their own status in society. Many women progressives were active in the struggle for woman suffrage, or the right to vote. They finally achieved this goal in 1920, when the states ratified the Nineteenth Amendment to the Constitution.

Progressive Presidents

Many Americans supported progressive reforms and they elected presidents who also supported reform. The first progressive president was **Theodore Roosevelt**. Roosevelt saw government as an umpire. Its purpose was to ensure fairness, or a "square deal," for workers, consumers, and business.

Roosevelt began his reforms with an effort to break up trusts. He thought industries should be regulated for the public interest. He acted to regulate the meatpacking industry and signed the Pure Food and Drug Act. This law banned the sale of impure foods and medicines. Roosevelt also fought for conservation to protect America's natural resources. He preserved more than 200 million acres of public lands and doubled the number of national parks in the United States.

Roosevelt's successor, **William Howard Taft,** had a reputation as a conservative. But he also advanced some progressive causes. During his four years in office, Taft pursued almost twice as many antitrust suits as Roosevelt had in nearly eight years in office.

Taft also oversaw the passage of two progressive amendments to the Constitution. The Sixteenth Amendment, passed in 1909 and ratified in 1913, gave Congress the power to establish income taxes. It was

THEODORE ROOSEVELT
1858–1919
From his youth on, Theodore Roosevelt lived what he called the "strenuous life." He rode horses, hiked, boxed, wrestled, and played tennis. In winter, he swam in the icy Potomac River. He hunted rhinoceros in Africa, harpooned devilfish in Florida, and boated down the Amazon.

Americans loved reading of his exploits and affectionately referred to him as "Teddy" or "T.R." Once, on a hunting trip, he refused to shoot a bear cub. News of the event resulted in a new toy—the teddy bear.

How did Roosevelt's active style of living carry over into his presidency?

Background
Theodore Roosevelt became president after McKinley was assassinated in 1901. Roosevelt was reelected in 1904.

intended to spread the cost of government more fairly among the people. The Seventeenth Amendment also was ratified in 1913. This amendment provided for the direct election of U.S. senators by the voters in each state. It gave people a more direct voice in the government.

Woodrow Wilson was elected president in 1912. He also established a progressive record. At Wilson's urging, Congress passed the Clayton Antitrust Act of 1914. This law banned business practices that reduced competition. In addition, during Wilson's tenure, reform of the nation's financial system took effect. The Federal Reserve Act was passed in 1913. It improved the nation's monetary and banking system.

Reading **History**
C. Drawing Conclusions Why are the Sixteenth and Seventeenth amendments considered progressive?

What Wilson and the other progressive presidents failed to do, however, was try to improve life for African Americans. In fact, Wilson approved the segregation of black and white employees in the federal government. Throughout the Progressive Era, few white politicians promoted civil rights for African Americans.

Shown at the left is Upton Sinclair's novel, *The Jungle,* which discussed dangerous and unhealthy meat-packing practices. The photograph shows immigrant workers stuffing sausages in a Chicago meat-packing house.

Section 3 Assessment

1. Terms & Names

Explain the significance of:
- Populist Party
- William Jennings Bryan
- progressivism
- Theodore Roosevelt
- William Howard Taft
- Woodrow Wilson

2. Taking Notes

Use a chart to list examples of progressive reforms.

Goals	Reforms
To expand democracy	
To protect social welfare	
To create economic reform	

3. Main Ideas

a. What problems in the late 1800s led farmers to take political action?

b. What did President Roosevelt mean by a "square deal" and how did he try to achieve it?

c. What were three progressive amendments and what did each do?

4. Critical Thinking

Recognizing Effects
In what ways do the reforms that Theodore Roosevelt promoted affect your life today?

THINK ABOUT
- the quality of the food you eat
- natural resources that have been preserved

ACTIVITY OPTIONS

ART
GEOGRAPHY

Do research on one of the natural areas that President Roosevelt preserved. Create a **travel brochure** or an **illustrated map** of the area.

④ Becoming a World Power

TERMS & NAMES
imperialism
Spanish-American War
yellow journalism
Platt Amendment
Panama Canal
Roosevelt Corollary
Fourteen Points
Great Migration

MAIN IDEA	WHY IT MATTERS NOW
The United States extended its global influence and fought with the Allies in World War I.	The United States continues to be a global power today.

ONE AMERICAN'S STORY

Alfred Thayer Mahan joined the U.S. Navy in the 1850s and served for nearly 40 years. In the 1890s, he made use of his decades of experience to write several books on the historical importance of sea power. In one passage, he discussed the economic importance of trading stations and colonies.

A VOICE FROM THE PAST

The trading-station . . . [was] the same as the . . . colony. In both cases the mother-country had won a foothold in a foreign land, seeking a new outlet for what it had to sell, a new sphere for its shipping, more employment for its people, and more comfort and wealth for itself.

Alfred Thayer Mahan, *The Influence of Sea Power upon History, 1660–1805*

Naval historian Alfred Thayer Mahan at the turn of the century

Mahan encouraged government officials to build up American naval forces so that the United States could compete with other powerful nations. In this section, you will learn how the United States began to extend its influence beyond its boundaries and become a world power.

Growth of U.S. Imperialism

By the 1880s, several European nations were expanding their overseas empires. Many Americans believed the United States should also follow a policy of **imperialism**—the policy of extending economic, political, or military control over other nations. Three factors helped to fuel the development of American imperialism.

1. **Economic Interests.** Economic leaders argued that expansion would increase U.S. financial prosperity. Many business leaders saw new colonies as a potential source of cheap raw materials and new markets for their products.

2. **Military Interests.** In his books, Mahan had argued that economic interests went hand-in-hand with military interests. Foreign policy

experts agreed. They urged U.S. leaders to follow the European example and establish a military presence overseas.

3. **Belief in Cultural Superiority.** Many white Americans believed that their government, religion, and even race were superior to those of other societies. Some people hoped to spread democracy and Christianity overseas.

During the late 19th century, the United States began to gain control over more territories. In 1867, the United States purchased Alaska from Russia. In 1893, U.S. Marines helped American planters in Hawaii overthrow the Hawaiian queen and set up their own government. The United States annexed Hawaii in 1898.

The Spanish-American War

America's overseas empire grew dramatically as a result of the **Spanish-American War** of 1898. The war began after Cubans rose up in rebellion against Spain, who had colonized the island. The United States joined the side of the Cuban rebels. Americans were influenced in part by newspaper stories that described—and often exaggerated—news about Spanish cruelty. This sensational style of reporting the news became known as **yellow journalism**.

The war was fought on Spain's colonies in the Caribbean and the Philippine Islands. One of the more famous American fighting units

---

CITIZENSHIP TODAY

Detecting Bias in the Media

Modern journalists try to report the news without bias—that is, without letting their personal opinions or those of their employer influence what they write. Unbiased reporting is one of the responsibilities of a free press. It allows citizens to weigh the facts and come to their own understanding of issues and events.

As you have read, journalists and their employers do not always avoid bias. In fact, in the 1890s, journalists were not concerned with bias. Before the United States declared war on Spain in 1898, 'yellow journalists' exaggerated stories to help sell newspapers. These stories helped turn U.S. public opinion in favor of war against Spain. They used words and images to reflect their bias that the United States should declare war on Spain—and sell more papers along the way.

William Randolph Hearst ran this headline in his *New York Journal* before authorities had a chance to determine the cause of the *Maine*'s explosion.

Can You Find Bias in the Media?

1. With a small group, collect news stories from different sources that cover the same issue or event.

2. Record any differences in the way a specific issue or event is covered by the oral, written, or visual sources you have selected.

3. Review the differences and decide whether any of the authors of the sources showed bias in their coverage.

4. Write a report that describes any bias you might detect. Explain why the biased source might have reported the story the way it did.

 See Citizenship Handbook, page 268.

For more about the news media . . .

 RESEARCH LINKS
CLASSZONE.COM

The explosion of the *Maine* and accounts of the event by yellow journalists led many Americans to favor war against Spain.

was known as the Rough Riders. Led by Theodore Roosevelt, its recruits included cowboys, miners, college students, New York policemen, athletes, and Native Americans. The Rough Riders helped the Americans capture Santiago, a key Spanish stronghold in southern Cuba.

Within months, Spain surrendered. As a result of the war, the United States gained the Spanish colonies of Puerto Rico, Guam, and the Philippines. While Cuba won its freedom, the United States insisted that Cubans add the **Platt Amendment** to their constitution. This amendment gave the United States the right to intervene in Cuban affairs anytime the U.S. government believed "life, property, and individual liberty" were in danger.

Some Americans opposed the taking of colonies. They formed the Anti-Imperialist League. Members of the League believed that Americans should not deny other people the right to govern themselves. Most Americans, however, favored the creation of an overseas empire and the power and prestige it brought.

*Reading*History

B. Finding Main Ideas Why did the Anti-Imperialist League oppose U.S. efforts to establish colonies

U.S. Influence Expands

In the years following the Spanish-American War, the United States increased its presence on the world stage. It did so by expanding its influence in Asia and Latin America.

During the late 1800s, the United States joined other countries in competing for access to China. In 1899, Secretary of State John Hay asked nations interested in the region to follow an Open Door Policy. This policy intended that the nations with interests in China leave open the door for other nations to trade with China. Although some people did not think Hay's policy would work, no nation rejected it.

Meanwhile, the United States became more involved in the affairs of Latin America. In 1904, the United States began construction of the **Panama Canal** to create a shorter trade route between the Atlantic and

How the Panama Canal Works

Engineers faced a problem in building the Panama Canal. Because of the region's different landscape elevations, no waterway would remain level. They solved this dilemma by building three sets of *locks*—water-filled chambers that raise or lower ships to match a canal's different water levels.

1 The lock gates open on one end to allow the ship to enter.

2 The gates close, and water is pumped in or out depending on whether the ship is moving up or down.

3 Once the water in the chamber and the canal ahead is level, the second gate opens and the ship moves on.

The locks, whose steel gates rise six stories high, can hold as much as 26 million gallons of water—enough to supply a major U.S. city for one day.

Gatún Locks   Culebra Cut   Pedro Miguel Locks
Gatún   Miraflores
Lake   Lake   Miraflores
Atlantic   Locks
Ocean   Pacific
                            Ocean

◄——— 51 miles ———►

This cross-section shows the different elevations and locks that a ship moves through on the 8–9 hour trip through the canal. Before the canal was built, a trip around South America could take two months.

CONNECT TO HISTORY

1. **Drawing Conclusions** Why did the United States want a shorter route between the Atlantic and Pacific oceans?

CONNECT TO TODAY

2. **Researching** What is the economic and political status of the Panama Canal today?

For more about the Panama Canal . . .

RESEARCH LINKS
CLASSZONE.COM

Pacific oceans. In addition, numerous U.S. businesses began establishing relationships with Latin American countries.

As economic interests drew the United States deeper into Latin America, U.S. leaders took a more active role in influencing the region's political affairs. In 1904, President Roosevelt added the **Roosevelt Corollary** to the Monroe Doctrine—the U.S. policy opposing European intervention in Latin America. The Roosevelt Corollary extended the Monroe Doctrine to authorize the United States to intervene in Latin American domestic affairs if the United States believed it was necessary to maintain stability.

Vocabulary
corollary: a statement that follows logically from an earlier statement

World War I

By the early 1900s, the United States had become a global power. Perhaps nothing demonstrated this more than the decisive role the nation played in deciding the outcome of the greatest conflict the world had yet seen—World War I.

The war began in 1914. On one side were the Central Powers: Austria-Hungary, Germany, the Ottoman Empire, and Bulgaria. On the other side were the Allied Powers, or Allies, including Serbia, Russia, France, Great Britain, and Italy. The war had several long-term causes. Competition for colonies, an intense arms race, and growing feelings of nationalism had combined to raise international tensions in Europe. These tensions eventually led to war.

When the war first broke out, the United States announced a policy of neutrality, refusing to take sides in the war. As time passed, many

Vocabulary
nationalism: devotion to the interests and culture of one's nation

Soldiers scramble out of their trench to attack the enemy during a World War I battle.

The Western Front, 1914–1918

- Deepest German advance, July 18, 1918
- → Allied drive, late summer and autumn 1918
- Armistice line, November 1918
- ✵ Major battle sites, 1914–1918

Brussels

English Channel

Ypres, 1st battle, 1914
2nd battle, 1915
3rd battle, 1917

Lille

BELGIUM

GERMANY

Rhine R.

Somme R.

50°N

Somme, 1916

Amiens

Cantigny, 1918

Meuse R.

LUXEMBOURG

Moselle R.

Seine R.

FRANCE

Aisne R.

Meuse-
Argonne,
1918

N

ARGONNE
FOREST

Verdun,
1916

0   50 Miles

Marne, 2nd battle, 1918

St. Mihiel, 1918

Metz

0   100 Kilometers

Belleau Wood, 1918

Château-Thierry, 1918

Marne R.

Marne, 1st battle, 1914

Paris

GEOGRAPHY SKILLBUILDER Interpreting Maps
1. **Location** *What three battles occurred closest to the Armistice line?*
2. **Movement** *In what two directions did the Allied drives move?*

Americans developed a greater sympathy for the Allies. And, in 1917, the United States entered the war on the side of the Allies. U.S. forces tipped the balance in favor of the Allies. In 1918, the Allies were clearly winning the war. In November, Germans mutinied and their emperor gave up the throne. The new German government asked for peace.

World War I had been the most devastating conflict the world had yet known. About 8.5 million soldiers died in the war, and about 21 million were wounded. The war also lead to the deaths of millions of civilians in Europe, Asia, and Africa—often due to starvation and disease.

Postwar America

During the war, President Woodrow Wilson had announced a plan for a lasting peace. The plan became known as the **Fourteen Points.** Most of the points dealt with specific border placements. Others proposed rules for international relations, such as banning secret agreements. For Wilson, the fourteenth point mattered most. It called for an association of nations to settle disputes peacefully. The other Allied leaders did not support much of Wilson's plan. However, the Treaty of Versailles, which ended the war, still provided for an international organization to address disputes between countries. This organization was called the League of Nations.

Many U.S. citizens and legislators, however, opposed the League. They feared that further involvement in Europe would lead them into more conflicts. As a result, the U.S. Senate refused to ratify the Treaty of Versailles. The nation instead made a separate peace agreement with Germany.

*Reading*History
C. Analyzing Causes Why didn't the United States ratify the Treaty of Versailles?

After the war, Americans wanted to focus on domestic affairs. Shortly after the war ended, the United States experienced a number of labor strikes. Some Americans saw efforts to organize labor unions as the work of radicals, people who favor extreme measures to bring about change. The strikes sparked fears of a communist revolution. In 1919–1920, this fear created a wave of panic called the Red Scare. (Communists were often called Reds.)

Now and then

THE FLU EPIDEMIC

In 1918, flu victims often came down with pneumonia and died within a week. Today, bacterial infections such as pneumonia resulting from the flu can be controlled with antibiotics.

The 1998 discovery of the frozen remains of a 1918 flu victim in an Alaskan cemetery may one day lead to a better understanding of the virus. Scientists have found a genetic link between the 1918 flu virus and swine flu, a virus first found in pigs. The Alaskan find may help scientists develop vaccines to protect against future flu outbreaks.

Americans also saw a rise in racial tensions after the war. For a few decades, African Americans had been leaving the rural South to escape Jim Crow. During the war, this movement, known as the **Great Migration,** grew as African Americans filled war-related jobs in cities, especially in the North. African Americans enjoyed better-paying jobs and the relative lack of segregation in the North. But in cities where blacks settled in large numbers, racial tensions rose over housing, job competition, and segregation. During the summer of 1919, race riots flared in 25 cities around the country.

By 1920, when the nation held its presidential election, Americans were ready for a break from turmoil at home and abroad. Republican candidate Warren G. Harding of Ohio offered them one. He promised the nation a "return to normalcy" and the voters responded. Harding won a landslide victory. In the next chapter, you will learn about American life in the 1920s and beyond.

Section 4 Assessment

1. Terms & Names

Explain the significance of:
- imperialism
- Spanish-American War
- yellow journalism
- Platt Amendment
- Panama Canal
- Roosevelt Corollary
- Fourteen Points
- Great Migration

2. Taking Notes

Use a chart like the one shown here to record causes of U.S. expansion overseas in the late 1800s.

Causes   Effect

United States expansion

3. Main Ideas

a. How did the Roosevelt Corollary change U.S. foreign policy?

b. What were the long-term causes of World War I?

c. Why did many Americans oppose joining the League of Nations?

4. Critical Thinking

Forming Opinions Did the United States betray its democratic principles when it established overseas colonies?

THINK ABOUT
- the public's response to yellow journalists and U.S. military victories
- the work of the Anti-Imperialist League

ACTIVITY OPTIONS

SCIENCE

MATH

Research the Panama Canal. Build a simple **model** of the canal or create a **graph** that shows how many ships use the canal each year.

The Fourteen Points

Setting the Stage Nine months after the United States entered World War I, President Wilson delivered to Congress a statement of war aims. This statement became known as the "Fourteen Points." In the speech, President Wilson set forth 14 proposals for reducing the risk of war in the future. Numbers have been inserted to help identify the main points, as well as those omitted. **See Primary Source Explorer**

All the peoples of the world are in effect partners . . . , and for our own part we see very clearly that unless justice be done to others it will not be done to us. The program of the world's peace, therefore, is our program; and that program, . . . as we see it, is this:

[1] Open **covenants**[1] of peace, openly arrived at, after which there shall be no private international understandings of any kind but diplomacy shall proceed always frankly and in the public view.

[2] Absolute freedom of navigation upon the seas . . . in peace and in war. . . .

[3] The removal, so far as possible, of all economic barriers and the establishment of an equality of trade conditions among all the nations. . . .

[4] Adequate guarantees given and taken that national **armaments**[2] will be reduced. . . .

[5] A free, open-minded, and absolutely impartial adjustment of all colonial claims, based upon . . . the principle that . . . the interests of the populations concerned must have equal weight with the . . . claims of the government whose title is to be determined.

[6–13: These eight points deal with specific boundary changes.]

[14] A general association of nations must be formed under specific covenants for the purpose of affording mutual guarantees of political independence and territorial **integrity**[3] to great and small states alike.

—*Woodrow Wilson*

1. **covenants:** binding agreements.
2. **armaments:** weapons and supplies of war.
3. **integrity:** the condition of being whole or undivided; completeness.

A CLOSER LOOK

THE VALUE OF OPENNESS

The first of Wilson's points attempts to solve one of the problems that caused the outbreak of World War I—agreements between nations arrived at in secret.

1. How might agreements arrived at in public prevent another world war?

A CLOSER LOOK

BALANCING CLAIMS

Wilson frequently appeals to fairness, balance, and impartiality in settling competing claims.

2. What might be unusual about a leader such as Wilson calling for an impartial adjustment of colonial claims?

A CLOSER LOOK

LEAGUE OF NATIONS

Wilson proposes that nations join a formal organization to protect one another.

3. Why did Wilson believe that such an organization would benefit the world?

Interactive Primary Source Assessment

1. Main Ideas

a. Why should diplomacy avoid private dealings and proceed in public view?

b. How might equality of trade be important to keeping the peace?

c. What must nations join together to guarantee?

2. Critical Thinking

Evaluating The first five points address issues that Wilson believed had caused the war. How successful do you think Wilson's ideas have been in the rest of the 20th century?

THINK ABOUT
• other conflicts since World War I
• peacekeeping efforts around the world

TERMS & NAMES

Briefly explain the significance of each of the following.

1. frontier
2. Homestead Act
3. mass culture
4. Jim Crow
5. *Plessy* v. *Ferguson*
6. Populist Party
7. progressivism
8. imperialism
9. Roosevelt Corollary
10. Fourteen Points

REVIEW QUESTIONS

A Time of Growth (pages 539–545)

1. What caused conflict between Native Americans and white settlers on the Great Plains?
2. Why was the late 1800s known as the Gilded Age?
3. Where did most immigrants to the United States come from around 1900?

Life at the Turn of the Century (pages 546–550)

4. What is mass culture?
5. Why was *Plessy v. Ferguson* an important Supreme Court decision?

An Era of Reform (pages 551–555)

6. Why did farmers favor a free silver policy?
7. What problems did progressivism address?

Becoming a World Power (pages 556–563)

8. Why did Americans become interested in overseas expansion in the late 1800s?
9. What territories did the United States take control of as a result of the Spanish-American War?
10. Why did the U.S. Senate reject the Treaty of Versailles?

CRITICAL THINKING

1. USING YOUR NOTES

Using your completed chart, answer the questions.

a. Why were the Sixteenth and Seventeenth amendments considered progressive?
b. Why did some Americans oppose the taking of overseas colonies?

2. THEME: EXPANSION

How did U.S. expansion at the end of the 19th century compare with expansion that occurred earlier?

3. ANALYZING LEADERSHIP

Think about the actions of Booker T. Washington and W. E. B. Du Bois. Which approach did each take against discrimination? Whose approach was more effective?

4. APPLYING CITIZENSHIP SKILLS

What issues did progressive reformers address around 1900? What issues would they address today?

5. FORMING OPINIONS

How did "yellow journalism" influence U.S. foreign policy at the turn of the century? How does modern media, such as television, shape public opinion today?

Interact *with* History

How did your solution to one of the problems of the Progressive Era compare with those proposed by reformers?

VISUAL SUMMARY

The United States, 1860–1920

Western Migration
Miners, ranchers, cowhands, and farmers settle in the West; Native Americans are forced onto reservations.

Reform Movements
Americans increase their efforts to reform society's ills and improve conditions for farmers, workers, and other Americans.

EXPANSION

Industrial Growth
Numerous factors, such as natural resources and inventions, lead to industrialization, which prompts the growth of cities.

A Global Power
The United States becomes a global power as it expands its influence in other lands and helps the Allies win World War I.

HISTORY SKILLS

1. INTERPRETING GRAPHS

Study the graph below. Then answer the questions that follow.

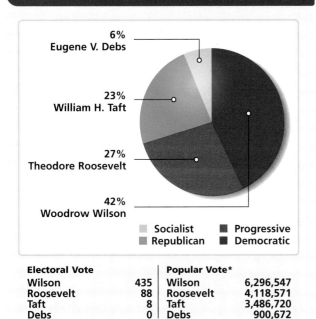

Election of 1912

6%
Eugene V. Debs

23%
William H. Taft

27%
Theodore Roosevelt

42%
Woodrow Wilson

■ Socialist   ■ Progressive
■ Republican   ■ Democratic

Electoral Vote		Popular Vote*	
Wilson	435	Wilson	6,296,547
Roosevelt	88	Roosevelt	4,118,571
Taft	8	Taft	3,486,720
Debs	0	Debs	900,672

*Other candidates received about 2% of the popular vote.

a. What percentage of the popular vote did Eugene V. Debs win?

b. How many electoral votes did Woodrow Wilson win?

c. Who won the second greatest total of popular votes?

2. INTERPRETING PRIMARY SOURCES

Following is an excerpt from Woodrow Wilson's first inaugural address, delivered on March 4, 1913. Read the excerpt and then answer the questions that follow.

> There can be no equality of opportunity . . . if men and women and children be not shielded in their lives . . . from the consequences of great industrial and social processes which they cannot alter, control, or singly cope with. . . . Sanitary laws, pure-food laws, and laws determining conditions of labor which individuals are powerless to determine for themselves are intimate parts of the very business of justice and legal efficiency.
>
> **Woodrow Wilson,** First Inaugural Address, March 4, 1913

a. What is Wilson promoting in this passage?

b. What values are reflected in this passage?

ALTERNATIVE ASSESSMENT

1. INTERDISCIPLINARY ACTIVITY: Math

Making a Graph Do research to determine the number of immigrants who came from various countries between 1880 and 1914. Find out where immigrants come from today. Make a graph that displays your findings. Explain your graph to the class.

2. COOPERATIVE LEARNING ACTIVITY

Performing Dramatic Readings Drawing on the many journals, diaries, and other primary sources left by sodbusters, create a Voices of the Plains play. Working in small groups, have students research such topics as "the journey west," "first impressions," "dugouts and soddies," "farming the plains," and "women's work and worries." Within groups, members can create presentations using these suggestions.

- Choose and research a topic.
- Select quotations related to the topic.
- Pick writers to compose lines to introduce and make transitions between quotations, and choose readers to perform readings.

3. ⊚ TECHNOLOGY ACTIVITY

Creating a Multimedia Presentation World War I was the most destructive war the world had yet seen. Use the Internet, books, and other resources to develop a multimedia presentation on the war.

For more information about World War I . . .

INTERNET ACTIVITY
CLASSZONE.COM

Using presentation software, consider including the following content:
- descriptions or images of battles
- the views of American troops as well as the troops of other nations
- public opinion about the war in the United States and other nations
- statistics of casualties suffered by all sides during the conflict

4. HISTORY PORTFOLIO

Review the questions that you wrote for What Do You Want to Know? on page 538. Then write a short report in which you explain the answers to your questions. If any questions were not answered, do research to answer them. Add your answers to your portfolio.

Additional Test Practice,
pp. S1–S33

TEST PRACTICE
CLASSZONE.COM

CHAPTER 20
EPILOGUE

The United States Since 1919

20th Century

21st Century

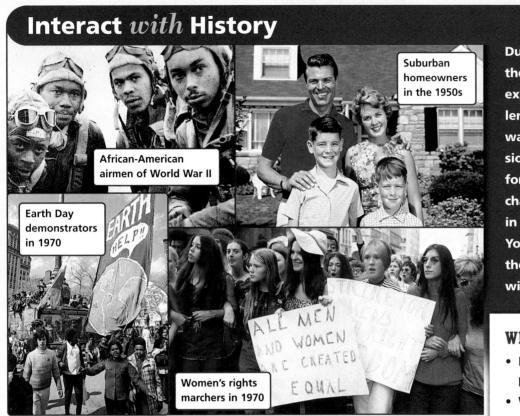

African-American airmen of World War II

Suburban homeowners in the 1950s

Earth Day demonstrators in 1970

Women's rights marchers in 1970

During the 20th century, the United States has experienced many challenges. These include war, economic depression, and the struggle for equal rights. New challenges await you in the 21st century. You must decide what they are and how you will respond.

What Do You Think?

- How will technology play a part in your life?

- What are your talents, and how could you use them to benefit yourself and society?

- What do you think the United States and the world need most from your generation?

How do you think the 21st century will differ from the 20th century?

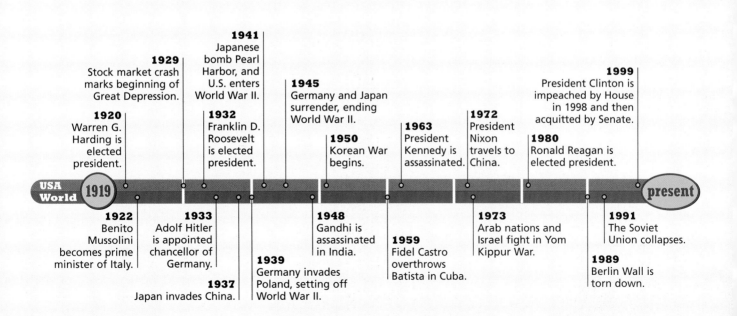

1929 Stock market crash marks beginning of Great Depression.

1920 Warren G. Harding is elected president.

1941 Japanese bomb Pearl Harbor, and U.S. enters World War II.

1932 Franklin D. Roosevelt is elected president.

1945 Germany and Japan surrender, ending World War II.

1950 Korean War begins.

1963 President Kennedy is assassinated.

1972 President Nixon travels to China.

1999 President Clinton is impeached by House in 1998 and then acquitted by Senate.

1980 Ronald Reagan is elected president.

USA / World — 1919 — present

1922 Benito Mussolini becomes prime minister of Italy.

1933 Adolf Hitler is appointed chancellor of Germany.

1948 Gandhi is assassinated in India.

1959 Fidel Castro overthrows Batista in Cuba.

1973 Arab nations and Israel fight in Yom Kippur War.

1991 The Soviet Union collapses.

1939 Germany invades Poland, setting off World War II.

1989 Berlin Wall is torn down.

1937 Japan invades China.

Chapter 20 Epilogue SETTING THE STAGE

BEFORE YOU READ

Previewing the Theme

America in the World During the 20th century, the United States took a more prominent place in the world. This chapter explains how the nation's domestic life and politics, as well as its relations with the rest of the world, changed during the century.

In this political cartoon published in the *Washington Post* in the 1930s, Uncle Sam turns his back on Europe.

What Do You Know?

What do you think of when you hear the phrase "the Great Depression"? Who do you think fought in World War II? How can a war be a "Cold War"?

THINK ABOUT

• what you've learned about any of these topics from movies, television, or travel
• how great events shape the lives of individuals

What Do You Want to Know?

What questions do you have about great events of the 20th century? Record these questions in your notebook before you read the chapter.

READ AND TAKE NOTES

Reading Strategy: Categorizing To help you make sense of what you read, learn to categorize. Categorizing means sorting information into groups. The chart below will help you to categorize the information in this chapter. Use the chart to take notes on important political, economic, and social events of selected decades of this century.

 See Skillbuilder Handbook, page R6.

The 20th Century	Political Events	Economic Events	Social Events
1920–1939			
1940–1959			
1960–1979			
1980–1999			

Prosperity and the Great Depression

1

TERMS & NAMES
Warren G. Harding
Calvin Coolidge
jazz
Harlem Renaissance
Great Depression
Franklin D. Roosevelt
New Deal

MAIN IDEA	WHY IT MATTERS NOW
The stock market crash of 1929 and the Great Depression led to Franklin D. Roosevelt's New Deal.	The New Deal increased the role of the federal government.

ONE AMERICAN'S STORY

Louis Armstrong grew up in New Orleans, the birthplace of jazz. As a child, Armstrong often listened to jazz music played at funeral processions, dance halls, saloons, and lawn parties. He learned to play the cornet and trumpet, and became a great jazz musician. In 1922, he accepted a job offer to play jazz with a Chicago band.

A VOICE FROM THE PAST

When I left New Orleans to go up North in 1922 the toughest Negro . . . his name is Slippers . . . he gave me a pep talk. . . . He loved the way I played those Blues. . . . When he found out that I was leaving to go to Chicago, he was the first one to congratulate me. . . . He said, "I love the way you blow that Quail." Of course he meant the cornet.

Louis Armstrong, quoted in *Louis: The Louis Armstrong Story*

Louis Armstrong greatly influenced the development of jazz.

Armstrong and other jazz musicians spread jazz to other parts of the country. In this section, you will read about popular culture, the Harlem Renaissance, the artists of the Lost Generation, and the stock market crash of 1929.

The Roaring Twenties' Business Boom

By the start of the 1920s, Americans were turning away from progressive reforms. World War I was over. Americans were disappointed with the Treaty of Versailles. This, and the terrible human cost of the war, made them unwilling to fight "other people's wars." Now they wanted to help themselves. Americans were ready for a decade-long buying spree.

Earlier in the century, presidents like Roosevelt and Taft had sought to place tighter controls on business. Under presidents **Warren G. Harding** and **Calvin Coolidge,** the government put into practice pro-business policies. These policies made business growth easier and more profitable. President Coolidge came into office in 1923. He spoke for many when he said, "the chief business of the American people is business."

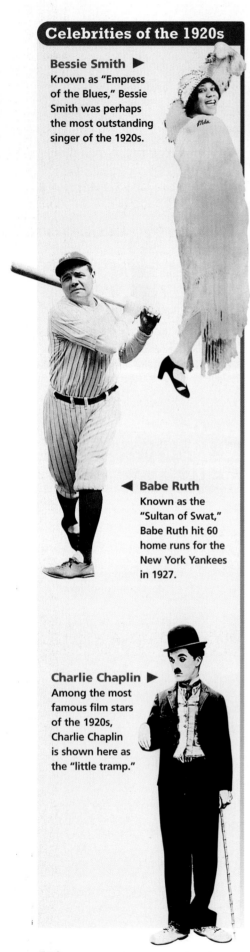

Giant business empires such as the automobile industry made the economy boom. Between 1920 and 1930, the number of cars in the United States almost tripled from about 8 million to 23 million. Car sales fueled demand for steel, oil, rubber, gasoline, and glass. Tourism thrived as more people took vacations by car. Improvements in methods of mass production made it possible to turn out products faster and cheaper. As a result, prices fell for such goods as washing machines and refrigerators. At the same time, the nation's wealth grew. During the 1920s, the income of the average American rose by almost 40 percent. People had both more money to spend and more goods to buy.

The Rise of Popular Entertainment

After the sacrifices of World War I, Americans wanted to enjoy themselves. Radio, movies, and sports gained in popularity. Big-city dwellers flocked to nightclubs where they learned hot new dances like the Charleston and the shimmy. The 1920s also introduced more Americans to a musical form called **jazz**. The new jazz music sprang up in cities such as New Orleans and Chicago. It blended African and European musical traditions. Trumpeter Louis Armstrong and composer and bandleader Duke Ellington drew crowds to jazz clubs and speakeasies. Singer Bessie Smith, known as "Empress of the Blues," thrilled audiences wherever she performed.

Audiences for movies grew throughout the decade. Even small towns had a movie theater. In 1922, people bought tickets to see such stars as Clara Bow and Charlie Chaplin on the silent screen. In 1925, Chaplin charmed audiences with his portrayal of the "little tramp" in silent films such as *The Gold Rush*. Two years later, Al Jolson's *The Jazz Singer* became the first talking picture. By the end of the decade, over 100 million people a year were packing movie theaters for talking pictures.

The growing popularity of radio helped put sports in the spotlight. Radio spread the fame of such teams as the New York Yankees and the Chicago Cubs. It made national heroes out of sports figures like Babe Ruth, who was baseball's home-run king. Baseball, boxing, and football all gained wider audiences.

In literature, such writers as Ernest Hemingway, F. Scott Fitzgerald, and Edna St. Vincent Millay were

Vocabulary
speakeasies: places for illegal sale and consumption of alcoholic drinks during the 1920s

able to capture the feelings of disillusionment and rebellion that some young people felt at the end of World War I. In the Harlem section of New York City, the 1920s were a time of great creativity for African-American artists. Writers such as Langston Hughes, Countee Cullen, and Zora Neale Hurston belonged to the cultural movement known as the **Harlem Renaissance.** Hughes used jazz rhythms and dialect in his writings to celebrate black urban life and to call for social change.

Stock Market Crash and Great Depression

During the 1920s, the stock market soared. Ordinary people saw buying stocks as a safe, quick way to get rich. Many ordinary people invested their life savings. Most did not understand the risks of investing. Many investors even borrowed money to buy shares. Then, in October 1929, the stock market crashed.

"The chief business of the American people is business."

President Coolidge

The crash sparked a chain reaction. First, banks demanded that customers pay back the money they had borrowed to buy stock. When people could not repay these loans, the banks ran short of money. Fearing that banks would close, customers lined up to withdraw their money. Since banks rarely keep enough cash on hand to pay all their customers at once, many banks shut down. The **Great Depression,** a time of great economic hardship, had begun.

As banks failed or cut back on loans to businesses, factories produced fewer goods and therefore laid off workers. With more people out of work, spending declined. Businesses let more workers go and factories closed. By 1932, one-fourth of the nation's workers were jobless.

Everywhere, sales of farm products fell sharply. In the Midwest and Great Plains, farmers not only faced economic losses but also suffered a terrible drought that lasted for years. Poor farming methods and over-farming of the land led to massive soil erosion, making it impossible to grow crops. Winds carried away dry soil over millions of acres, creating the Dust Bowl. Thousands were forced to abandon their farms and leave the Great Plains.

Republican President Herbert Hoover took office early in 1929. When the stock market crashed in October 1929, he urged Americans to be patient. He warned that government programs would only make things worse. Relief, or government aid to the hungry and homeless, would make Americans dependent on government handouts. In the 1932 election, they voted for a leader who promised another way.

Background
The stock market crash came on October 29, 1929. On that day, the prices of stocks fell dramatically.

*Reading***History**
A. Analyzing Causes Why did some banks shut down during the Depression?

*Reading***History**
B. Summarizing What was Hoover's attitude toward government action?

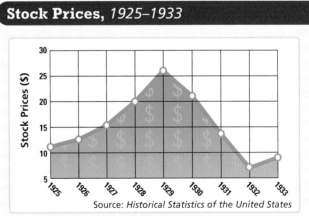

Stock Prices, *1925–1933*

Source: *Historical Statistics of the United States*

SKILLBUILDER Interpreting Charts
1. *In what year did stock prices begin their decline?*
2. *In what year did prices begin to rise again after the crash?*

The New Deal's Federal Arts Project commissioned murals for post offices and other public buildings. This mural, entitled *Construction of a Dam,* was painted by William Gropper (1897–1977). It was painted in the Department of the Interior building in Washington, D.C.

What does the painting reveal about the value of work in a time of both economic depression and unemployment?

Roosevelt's New Deal

When Democrat **Franklin D. Roosevelt,** also known as FDR, took over as president, millions of families lacked food or shelter. People searched in garbage dumps for food or stood for hours in long lines for soup. Former business executives sold apples on streetcorners. Blaming Hoover for the hard times, the homeless called their tin-and-cardboard shacks "Hoovervilles." Roosevelt set out to restore hope and confidence both in government and in the American economy. His inaugural address expressed his optimism.

A VOICE FROM THE PAST

This great nation will endure as it has endured, will revive and will prosper. So, first of all, let me assert my firm belief that the only thing we have to fear is fear itself.

Franklin D. Roosevelt, Inaugural Address, March 4, 1933

Roosevelt promised immediate action, and he kept his word. His first target was the bank crisis. Calling for a "bank holiday," he ordered a brief shutdown of all banks. Federal officials went to work examining bank records. They decided which ones could reopen at once and which needed government help to do so. FDR's confidence persuaded Americans to put their money back into the banks.

With the public and Congress firmly supporting him, Roosevelt began a bold new program to end the Great Depression. It was called the **New Deal.** During a period known as the "Hundred Days," Congress passed with little debate almost all the bills the White House sent over. Even Republican lawmakers admired FDR's decisiveness.

Roosevelt's New Deal had three major goals, known as the "three R's":

1. **Relief programs** to help the hungry and jobless
2. **Recovery programs** to help agriculture and industry
3. **Reform of the economy** to ensure that a crisis like the Great Depression did not happen again

Not all of FDR's policies worked, and many angered business leaders because they led to higher taxes. Still, most Americans believed his policies were effective, and they reelected him to office in 1936.

Lasting New Deal Changes

The New Deal made lasting changes in American society and government. It increased the power of the federal government. It encouraged presidents and Congress to practice deficit spending during economic hard times. This means spending more money than the government raises in taxes. Many New Deal programs were financed by deficit spending. The New Deal created Social Security, unemployment insurance, and other federal programs to care for the elderly, jobless, and needy. Roosevelt believed in using the power of government to help those in need. Government-supported social programs were the centerpiece of the New Deal.

*Reading*History

C. Summarizing What were some of the accomplishments of the New Deal?

Full economic prosperity did not return until the United States entered World War II in 1941. Even so, the New Deal restored Americans' faith in democracy. In the decade ahead, Americans put their lives on the line to preserve democracy abroad.

Section 1 Assessment

1. Terms & Names

Explain the significance of:
- Warren G. Harding
- Calvin Coolidge
- jazz
- Harlem Renaissance
- Great Depression
- Franklin D. Roosevelt
- New Deal

2. Taking Notes

Fill in the diagram with some causes of the Depression.

Which cause was most important? Why?

3. Main Ideas

a. How did the boom times of the 1920s lead to the stock market crash?

b. What happened to farm prices during the Great Depression?

c. What were the three goals of FDR's New Deal?

4. Critical Thinking

Making Inferences Why might the Great Depression have caused people to consider changes in the role of government?

THINK ABOUT
- aims of democracy
- fears sparked by the Depression
- attitudes toward government

ACTIVITY OPTIONS

LANGUAGE ARTS

MUSIC

Prepare a short **essay** on a writer of the Harlem Renaissance or make a **class presentation** about jazz of the 1920s in which you play recordings of the music.

The Rise of Dictators and World War II

TERMS & NAMES
Benito Mussolini
fascism
Adolf Hitler
Nazi
World War II
Dwight D. Eisenhower
Holocaust

MAIN IDEA	WHY IT MATTERS NOW
In the 1930s, the rise of dictators and their military aggression led to World War II.	Lessons learned in fighting aggression in World War II continue to influence American foreign policy.

ONE AMERICAN'S STORY

Margaret Bourke-White was a photographer before the era of instant news. Beginning in the 1930s, her powerful pictures in magazines and books helped Americans understand the events of their time. As one of *Life* magazine's first photographers, she traveled to the Dust Bowl in the 1930s to photograph drought victims. During the same decade, she recorded the terrible living conditions of sharecroppers in the South.

As you will read in this section, during the 1940s the United States joined Britain in fighting a war against Nazi Germany. As the first female photographer attached to U.S. forces, Bourke-White risked her life to send home vivid images of combat. At war's end, she crossed into Germany with some of the first U.S. troops. She joined stunned soldiers entering Nazi concentration camps. She became one of the first photographers to record the horrors they saw there.

Margaret Bourke-White (shown above in both pictures) photographed the Manhattan skyline and events of World War II.

Dictators Take Power

The Great Depression spread around the world. In Germany and Italy, dictators appealed to desperate citizens by promising to restore prosperity. In Italy, **Benito Mussolini** built a political movement called **fascism**—a system under which the government rules through terror and by appealing to racism and nationalism. Using black-shirted followers to enforce his rule, Mussolini became prime minister in 1922. He won over nationalists by promising to turn Italy into a new Roman Empire. In 1935 his fascist troops invaded Ethiopia in Africa. The League of Nations had been formed to halt such aggression. However, it had little success.

In Germany, **Adolf Hitler** joined the National Socialist German Workers', or **Nazi**, Party. He tapped the bitter anger many Germans felt about the unfairness of the peace agreement ending World War I. The treaty required Germany to pay millions for war damages. Hitler skillfully blamed the nation's economic woes on Jews and other groups. After coming to power in 1933, he jailed critics. His expansion of German territory began with a violation of the World War I peace agreement. He sent troops into the Rhineland, a part of Germany near the French border. In

1938, he invaded Austria and attached it to Germany. Prime Minister Neville Chamberlain of Britain met with Hitler in Munich, Germany, in September, 1938. Chamberlain agreed to allow Germany to take parts of Czechoslovakia. In return, Hitler promised not to demand any more land.

During this same period, dictator Joseph Stalin controlled the Soviet Union. Communist parties loyal to the Soviet Union had followers throughout Europe. Both Nazis and Fascists won many supporters by opposing the Communists. People feared Communist governments would seize their businesses and outlaw private property.

In Japan, military leaders held a powerful position in the government. In 1931, Japan invaded Manchuria, a province of China. This signaled the beginning of a planned Asian expansion. The League of Nations did little. In 1940, Japan, Italy, and Germany formed the Axis Powers.

War Breaks Out in Europe

On September 1, 1939, the Nazis invaded Poland. Germany's massive air and ground attack finally made Britain and France understand that Hitler could only be stopped by force. Two days later, Britain and France declared war on Germany. <u>**World War II**</u> had begun.

The early war years were dark ones for the Allies, which included Britain, France, and the Soviet Union, among others. The German military seemed unstoppable. In the spring of 1940, German troops conquered Norway, Denmark, the Netherlands, and Belgium. Paris and much of France fell to the Germans in June.

Reading **History**
A. Interpreting Time Lines
Which of the steps leading to World War II took place in Asia?

In 1941, German forces smashed through Eastern Europe and invaded the Soviet Union. Great Britain now stood alone against Hitler. Despite nightly bombings of London and other cities by the Germans, Britain's prime minister, Winston Churchill, inspired Britons to hold on. In the United States, isolationists still urged Americans to stay out of European affairs and avoid war.

Surprise Attack on Pearl Harbor

Roosevelt began his third term in 1941. He was the first and only president to serve more than two terms. He believed that failure to stop the

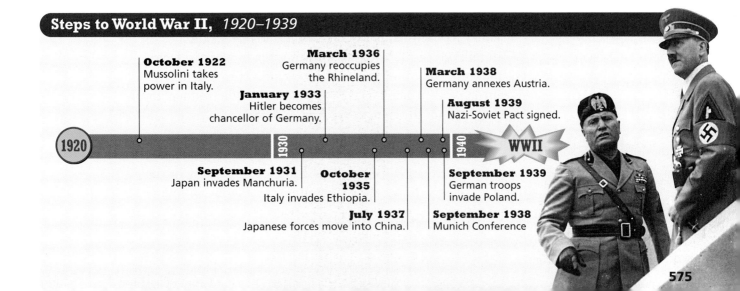

Steps to World War II, *1920–1939*

October 1922
Mussolini takes power in Italy.

January 1933
Hitler becomes chancellor of Germany.

March 1936
Germany reoccupies the Rhineland.

March 1938
Germany annexes Austria.

August 1939
Nazi-Soviet Pact signed.

1920 — 1930 — 1940 — WWII

September 1931
Japan invades Manchuria.

October 1935
Italy invades Ethiopia.

July 1937
Japanese forces move into China.

September 1939
German troops invade Poland.

September 1938
Munich Conference

U.S.S. *ARIZONA* MEMORIAL

The U.S.S. *Arizona* suffered extensive damage during the attack on Pearl Harbor. The ship sank, and 1,177 of its crew died. The nation chose not to raise the battleship. Instead, officials created a memorial that sits above the sunken hull (see below). The names of all the crewmen who perished are carved on the memorial.

To commemorate the 50th anniversary of the attack against the U.S. naval base at Pearl Harbor, President George Bush visited the site in 1991.

Nazis and Fascists would endanger the United States. In early 1941, he gave a speech to Congress to prepare the public to aid the Allies.

A VOICE FROM THE PAST

We look forward to a world founded upon four . . . human freedoms. The first is freedom of speech and expression—everywhere in the world. The second is freedom of every person to worship God in his own way. . . . The third is freedom from want. . . . The fourth is freedom from fear . . . anywhere in the world.

Franklin D. Roosevelt, State of the Union speech, January 6, 1941

Freedom required arms for its defense. Congress enacted the Lend-Lease Act in 1941. This law allowed the United States to ship arms and supplies, without immediate payment, to Britain and its Allies.

On December 7, 1941, Japan launched an attack against the U.S. naval base in Pearl Harbor, Hawaii. Calling December 7 "a date which will live in infamy," FDR requested and Congress passed a declaration of war against Japan. Japan's allies—Italy and Germany—then declared war on the United States.

In 1942, the Axis Powers (Germany, Italy, Japan) seemed close to victory. By this time, the Soviet Union had joined the Allied Powers, following Germany's invasion of its territory in June 1941.

The Home Front in America

Once the United States entered the war, its automobile plants and other factories were turned into defense plants. Airplanes, ships, weapons, and other supplies rolled off production lines at a rapid pace. By 1944, American assembly lines were producing 50 percent more armaments than those in the Axis nations combined.

Poster of factory worker during World War II

Americans put up with wartime shortages so that resources such as steel, tin, and rubber could be redirected to military uses. Gasoline was in short supply. So were meat, butter, coffee, cheese, and sugar. Every family received ration books of stamps to buy goods.

With millions of men at war, women went to work in factories, shipyards, and offices. At first, heavy industries resisted hiring female workers, but by 1944 some 3.5 million stood on assembly lines turning out cargo ships and bombers.

As they had during World War I, hundreds of thousands of African Americans left the South for such cities as Cleveland, Chicago, and Detroit. More than 2 million took jobs in the defense industry. Roosevelt outlawed discrimination in industries with federal contracts.

Reading History

B. Summarizing
What were some of the activities and challenges faced by women and minorities on the home front?

On the home front, Japanese Americans on the West Coast faced harsh treatment. By executive order, over 100,000 loyal Japanese Americans were forced to leave their jobs, businesses, and homes. They were sent to internment (prison) camps throughout the West.

War Continues in Europe and Asia

The invasion of Italy got underway with an attack on the island of Sicily in July 1943. The Allies forced the Germans out of Sicily and then swept into Italy. By this time, the Italians had imprisoned Mussolini. The new Italian government surrendered to the Allies in September 1943.

Meanwhile, in August 1942, German forces attacked the Russian city of Stalingrad, an important industrial center. A brutal battle took place. Soviet forces encircled and trapped the German army. As winter approached, the German commander begged Hitler to let him retreat. The *Führer* (or "leader") refused. The trapped Germans had no food or supplies. Each day, thousands of Nazi soldiers froze or starved to death. In late January of 1943, the German troops surrendered. Each side had suffered staggering losses. With its defeat at Stalingrad, Germany's hopes of conquering the Soviet Union ended.

Another turning point in World War II came on June 6, 1944, known as D-Day. About 70,000 American troops crossed the English Channel and landed on the beaches of Normandy in northern France. They were

World War II in Europe and Asia, 1942–1945

Legend:
- Axis Powers
- Axis-controlled
- Allied Powers
- Neutral nations
- Allied advances
- Allied victories

GEOGRAPHY SKILLBUILDER Interpreting Maps

1. **Region** Which three countries on the western fringes of Europe remained neutral?
2. **Movement** Which battle was fought closest to Japan?

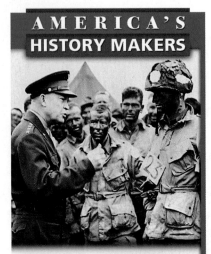

AMERICA'S HISTORY MAKERS

DWIGHT D. EISENHOWER
1890–1969

If ever there was a general who cared about his troops, it was General Dwight D. Eisenhower (at left, above). As Allied forces battled in Italy, Ike learned that he and another general were scheduled to stay in two large villas. "That's *not* my villa!" he exploded. "And that's not General Spaatz's villa! None of those will belong to any general as long as I'm Boss around here. This is supposed to be a rest center—for combat men—not a playground for the Brass [officers]!"

How might Eisenhower's concern for the common man have affected his standing with the troops?

part of a vast Allied invasion under the command of American General **Dwight D. Eisenhower.** British and American forces advanced on Germany from the west. The Soviets closed in from the east. In early May of 1945, Germany surrendered.

In the Pacific, the Japanese fought on. After 12 years as president, FDR died suddenly in April 1945, making Harry S. Truman the president. Truman decided to end the war before an invasion of Japan caused huge losses. In August 1945, American bombers dropped atomic bombs on Hiroshima and Nagasaki. In Hiroshima about 70,000 people died instantly. On September 2, 1945, Japan surrendered.

The War Is Over

World War II had been the costliest and most destructive war in history. Approximately 55 million people died. Among them were some 6 million Jews, or almost two-thirds of Europe's Jews. Victims were shot, gassed, and worked to death in Nazi concentration camps, death camps, and slave labor camps. This systematic mass murder of 6 million Jews and other ethnic minorities by the Nazis became known as the **Holocaust.**

At war's end, the United States joined the United Nations, the international peacekeeping organization that replaced the League of Nations. New York City became its headquarters. The Soviet Union joined as well. Nevertheless, conflict between the former allies would lead to a new era of tension, as you will read in the next section.

*Reading*History
C. Reading a Map
Use the map on page 577 to point out the locations of Hiroshima and Nagasaki on the Japanese mainland.

Section 2 Assessment

1. Terms & Names

Explain the significance of:
• Benito Mussolini
• fascism
• Adolf Hitler
• Nazi
• World War II
• Dwight D. Eisenhower
• Holocaust

2. Taking Notes

Arrange these events with their dates on a time line:

event 2   event 4

event 1   event 3   event 5

• Normandy Invasion
• U.S. bombs Hiroshima
• Germany invades Russia
• Pearl Harbor bombed
• Germany invades Poland

3. Main Ideas

a. What events following World War I led to the rise of Hitler and Mussolini?

b. Why were Americans reluctant to go to war? What made them change their minds?

c. What ended the war in the Pacific?

4. Critical Thinking

Analyzing Causes What elements in Nazi thinking might have contributed to the Holocaust?

THINK ABOUT
• wartime fears
• attitudes towards minorities
• prejudice

ACTIVITY OPTIONS

LANGUAGE ARTS
TECHNOLOGY

Research women working in wartime factories. Write a **diary entry** of one woman's experiences or plan the contents of a **Web page** about women in World War II.

③ The Cold War

TERMS & NAMES
Harry S. Truman
Cold War
containment
John F. Kennedy
Lyndon B. Johnson
Vietnam War
Richard M. Nixon
Watergate scandal

MAIN IDEA

After World War II, the United States and the Soviet Union entered into a deadly struggle for world power.

WHY IT MATTERS NOW

This struggle affected American foreign policy for almost half a century.

ONE AMERICAN'S STORY

When World War II ended in 1945, Europe lay in ruins. War had destroyed roads, bridges, mines, and railroads. Factories lacked fuel and raw materials. Tensions between the Soviet Union and the United States were rising. U.S. leaders wanted to help the European economies. At the same time, they opposed Communist expansion. George C. Marshall was secretary of state under President **Harry S. Truman**. Marshall came up with a plan to put Europe back on its feet. The plan offered billions of dollars in aid to Europe.

President Truman and George C. Marshall meet at the White House.

A VOICE FROM THE PAST

[The] United States should do whatever it [can] to assist in the return of . . . economic health in the world, without which there can be no political stability and no. . . peace. Our policy is directed . . . against hunger, poverty, desperation, . . . chaos.

George C. Marshall, speech at Harvard University, June 5, 1947

As you will read in this section, the Marshall Plan helped make Western and Southern Europe stable again.

The Cold War Begins

After World War II, fear and mistrust between the superpowers grew. The United States had hoped Eastern European nations would become democracies. Stalin feared that Eastern Europe could again become an invasion route into his country. For this reason, Stalin and the Soviets helped Communist governments come to power throughout Eastern Europe in the late 1940s.

President Truman and his advisers feared the spread of communism and looked for ways to stop it. This struggle marked the start of the **Cold War** between the superpowers. It was called a Cold War because there was no actual, direct fighting between the superpowers. This conflict was waged mainly with threats, spying, propaganda, and war in other countries.

Truman's anti-Soviet policy was called **containment.** It sought to contain, or stop, the Soviet Union from gaining influence outside its borders. Containment became the foundation of American foreign policy.

The Marshall Plan and the North Atlantic Treaty Organization (NATO) were key elements of containment. The Marshall Plan helped pay for Western and Southern Europe's recovery. Under the NATO agreement, Western allies formed a defense pact. The members pledged to protect one another in case of attack. The Soviet Union and its allies formed the Warsaw Pact.

The Korean War and McCarthyism

In 1949, the Communists led by Mao Zedong took power in China. In 1950, troops from Communist North Korea, supplied by the Soviet Union, invaded American-backed South Korea. U.S. troops made up most of a UN force commanded by General Douglas MacArthur. The UN force drove the North Koreans out of the South and back into North Korea.

Fighting continued after General Dwight D. Eisenhower became the new U.S. president in 1953. He soon arranged a truce that ended the three-year war. The national boundaries of the two Koreas had changed very little. However, the United States had shown that the free world would fight Communist aggression.

In the postwar United States, public fears of communism allowed Senator Joseph McCarthy of Wisconsin to gain great power. He claimed that hundreds of government workers were Communists or Communist supporters. His hunt for Communists ruined many lives. A new word—McCarthyism—described the use of unproven charges against opponents and innocent citizens. By 1954, however, the public had turned away in disgust from McCarthy. His power quickly faded.

*Reading*History

A. Recognizing Effects What effect did the Communist takeover in China and Communist aggression in Korea have on American political life?

Nuclear Threat and Superpower Conflicts

In 1945, the United States had dropped two atomic bombs on Japan to end World War II. Four years later, the Soviets built their own atomic bomb. A deadly arms race had begun. Both superpowers stockpiled nuclear weapons. By the end of the decade, both sides were developing missiles to carry bombs to each other's doorsteps.

Vocabulary
stockpiled: maintained a supply for future use

Neither superpower wanted to risk an all-out war. Instead, they pursued their rivalry indirectly by supporting opposite sides in conflicts in the Third World. These were the poorer nations of Latin America, Asia, and Africa. One such conflict brought the superpowers to the brink of war. In Cuba, Fidel Castro led a revolution that brought a Communist government to power in 1959. Attempts by the United States to topple Castro failed.

This photograph shows a Soviet ship thought to be carrying nuclear missiles to Cuba.

The U.S. flag is planted on the surface of the moon in July 1969.

Then, in 1962, President **John F. Kennedy** learned that the Soviets were supplying Cuba with missiles. U.S. navy ships blockaded the island. The threat of nuclear war seemed very real. The world waited to see if the Soviets would remove all missiles and missile bases from Cuba. Finally, the Soviet Union agreed to remove them.

By the 1960s the superpowers were in a space race as well as an arms race. Americans were stunned in 1957 when the Soviets sent *Sputnik,* a man-made satellite, into orbit around the earth. Alarm deepened as a Soviet cosmonaut took the first manned space flight. Throughout the 1960s, the two nations raced to see who would be first to put a person on the moon. Americans cheered as Neil Armstrong and Buzz Aldrin made the first lunar landing in 1969.

In 1963, Kennedy was assassinated in Dallas, Texas. Kennedy's vice-president, **Lyndon B. Johnson,** succeeded him as president. Under Johnson, the United States became more deeply involved in conflict in the Southeast Asian countries of North and South Vietnam.

*Reading*History
B. Summarizing What are some examples of superpower rivalry?

War in Vietnam

In 1954, Vietnam was divided in two. The Communists controlled North Vietnam and the non-Communists controlled South Vietnam. The **Vietnam War** began in 1957 when Communist forces attacked the government in the south. American presidents Eisenhower, Kennedy, and Johnson all feared a Communist victory in South Vietnam. Experts argued that if South Vietnam fell to the Communists, other Southeast Asian nations would soon fall.

Background The idea that if one nation fell to the Communists, others would soon follow, was called the "domino theory."

By 1968, more than 500,000 American troops were serving in Vietnam. U.S. planes dropped thousands of tons of bombs on the North. The large, well-equipped U.S. military faced a disciplined North Vietnamese force. Communist soldiers used hit-and-run guerrilla tactics. They sometimes relied on civilians for shelter and supplies. American soldiers won many battles, but they were stuck in an unwinnable war.

By 1968, the war had divided the United States. Strong criticism of Johnson's Vietnam policy contributed to his decision not to run for reelection. **Richard M. Nixon,** who was elected president in 1968, pledged to end the war. Over the next four years, he expanded the air war into neighboring Cambodia and Laos. At the same time, Nixon withdrew U.S. ground troops from South Vietnam. A 1973 ceasefire brought American troops home. Two years later, South Vietnam fell to the Communists. In 1976, the two Vietnams were united under Communist rule.

daily*life*

THE "TELEVISION WAR"
The Vietnam War was the first "television war," broadcast each night on the evening news. Reports rarely showed actual battles, partly because much of the fighting occurred off and on and at night, between small units.

Networks also tried to avoid gruesome scenes because they did not want to offend viewers. In addition, the networks agreed not to show any American dead or wounded so that their families would not recognize them on screen. Still, the images of war shocked viewers.

CAUSE AND EFFECT: *The Cold War, 1945–1991*

CAUSES		IMMEDIATE EFFECTS	LONG-TERM EFFECTS
Soviet domination of Eastern Europe		Truman Doctrine and Marshall Plan	Arms race between United States and Soviet Union
Communist victory in China	THE COLD WAR	East-West tension	
Distrust between United States and Soviet Union		Founding of NATO and Warsaw Pact	Rivalry between United States and Soviet Union for world power

SKILLBUILDER Interpreting Charts

1. Which of the causes was not centered in Europe?
2. Which alliance was founded by the Soviet Union and its allies?

Nixon as President

In the early 1970s, President Nixon took steps to improve relations with the Soviet Union and Communist China. In 1972, Nixon visited China. He reopened direct communication between the two nations after a 21-year break. After Nixon's visit to the Soviet Union, the superpowers signed an agreement limiting nuclear arms.

The **Watergate scandal** took up much of Nixon's second term as president. People who worked for Nixon carried out illegal activities. These included wiretapping telephones and breaking into the Democratic Party headquarters in the Watergate building in Washington, D.C. An investigation showed that Nixon had ordered his staff to cover up White House involvement in these crimes.

In 1974, a congressional committee wanted to impeach Nixon. Rather than face impeachment, Nixon resigned. He became the only U.S. president to do so. Gerald Ford succeeded Nixon as president and eventually pardoned him.

Foreign Policy of the 1970s and 1980s

Jimmy Carter won the 1976 presidential election, defeating Gerald Ford. He made human rights a cornerstone of his foreign policy. In 1977, Carter signed a treaty to turn the Panama Canal over to Panama in 2000. Carter also negotiated the Camp David Accords—a peace agreement between Egypt and Israel.

In 1979, the Soviet Union invaded Afghanistan to prop up a pro-Communist government. Ronald Reagan, who became president in 1980, took a tough stance toward the Soviet Union. Reagan increased U.S. defense spending and pledged to oppose communism in Central America. For several years, U.S.-Soviet relations became more tense.

By the late 1980s, however, U.S.-Soviet relations improved. A new Soviet leader, Mikhail Gorbachev, tried to reform the Soviet government and economy. Reagan and Gorbachev signed treaties agreeing to destroy some of their nations' nuclear weapons.

Reading **History**

C. Summarizing What were Reagan's policies toward the Soviet Union?

Meanwhile, many people in Communist nations wanted more freedom. They overthrew Communist rulers and formed democratic governments. In 1991, Communist leaders also lost power in the Soviet Union. The country split into independent states. Russia remained the largest of these states. The collapse of the Soviet Union ended the Cold War.

New Threats to the United States

As the Soviet Union fell apart, the United States stood as the world's only superpower. But major issues still challenged the nation. In 1990, Iraq invaded Kuwait. President George H. W. Bush organized a coalition of nations to drive Iraq out of Kuwait. In 1991, the coalition defeated Iraq in the Persian Gulf War and freed Kuwait of Iraqi control.

Smoke billows from the World Trade Center buildings after the terrorist attack of September 11, 2001.

Then, in 2001, Americans faced a more direct threat. On September 11, 2001, terrorists hijacked commercial airplanes and crashed them into the World Trade Center in New York City and the Pentagon outside Washington, D.C. Within hours, both World Trade Center towers collapsed. Thousands were buried in the rubble. Meanwhile, the Pentagon was badly damaged. In both attacks, nearly 3,000 people died. Across the nation, Americans mourned for the victims and yearned to bring the terrorists to justice.

President George W. Bush vowed to hunt down the attackers and end terrorism. "This battle will take time and resolve," Bush declared. "But make no mistake about it: we will win." Meanwhile, many Americans lost forever their sense of security. As *The New York Times* wrote the next day, "We look back at sunrise yesterday through pillars of smoke and dust, and we understand that everything has changed."

Section 3 Assessment

1. Terms & Names

Explain the significance of:
- Harry S. Truman
- Cold War
- containment
- John F. Kennedy
- Lyndon B. Johnson
- Vietnam War
- Richard M. Nixon
- Watergate scandal

2. Taking Notes

Use a diagram to summarize America's Cold War policy.

COLD WAR Containment

3. Main Ideas

a. How did the goals of the Soviet Union and the United States for Eastern Europe differ after World War II?

b. What were the space race and the arms race?

c. How did the breakup of the Soviet Union change U.S.-Soviet relations?

4. Critical Thinking

Comparing How were the Korean War and the Vietnam War similar and different?

THINK ABOUT
- American goals
- those who fought on each side
- the outcome of each struggle

ACTIVITY OPTIONS

SPEECH

SCIENCE

Give an **oral presentation** on one scientific challenge of landing on the moon or create a **diagram** of the lunar module.

Life in America Since 1945

TERMS & NAMES
baby boom
Dr. Martin Luther
  King, Jr.
Great Society
counterculture

MAIN IDEA	**WHY IT MATTERS NOW**
Since World War II, civil rights, economic growth, and social change have dominated American life.	Prosperity, equality, and rapid change will remain important issues in the 21st century.

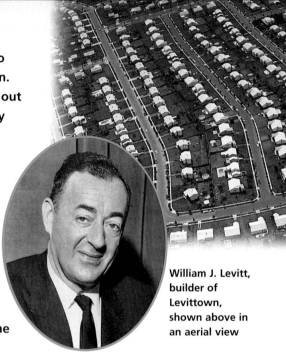

ONE AMERICAN'S STORY

When World War II ended, Americans were eager to return to normal life. Couples had put off marrying and having children. Now newlyweds and young families were looking for a way out of crowded city apartments. They wanted cheap single-family houses, and they wanted them fast.

Builder William J. Levitt had the answer. He built cheap houses using assembly-line methods. All of a sudden, many Americans could afford to buy homes. On 1,000 acres of farmland on New York's Long Island, Levitt built more than 17,000 homes in Levittown. It was America's first suburban housing development. As Cold War tensions grew, Levitt liked to brag that his home building was helping to win the war against Communism. "No man who owns his own house and lot," he said, "can be a Communist. He has too much to do." As you will read, in the 1950s a home in the suburbs became a part of the American dream.

William J. Levitt, builder of Levittown, shown above in an aerial view

Economic Boom and Baby Boom

After World War II, the U.S. economy boomed. The GI Bill offered returning soldiers schooling and job training. The Veterans Administration provided low-interest mortgages to home buyers. Rising demand for homes made possible the rapid growth of the suburbs. Other home builders were soon copying the building methods pioneered by Levitt. Car sales soared, too. Suburban families needed cars. They drove to work, to shopping centers, to movie theaters, and to restaurants.

During the late 1940s and the 1950s, the population grew rapidly. Americans were having more children, a trend known as the **baby boom**. Many people moved from the cities to the suburbs. They also moved from the Northeast to the Sunbelt—the states of the South and the Southwest.

As Americans earned more, they spent more. Television appeared in almost every home. Americans eagerly bought the cars, electrical appliances, and other goods advertised on television and in magazines.

Not all Americans shared in the new prosperity, however. In the 1950s, African Americans and other minorities continued to face discrimination, as did working women. In rural areas and inner cities, many people struggled to survive.

The Civil Rights Movement

In the 1950s, reformers began to win legal victories to end segregation in the South. In 1954, in *Brown* v. *Board of Education of Topeka*, the Supreme Court ruled that segregated public schools were illegal. Two years later, after a black-led boycott of the Montgomery, Alabama, bus system, the Court ruled that segregated public transportation was against the law.

By the early 1960s, a young minister named **Dr. Martin Luther King, Jr.,** led a strong civil rights movement. Despite attacks by whites, the movement for equal rights remained largely nonviolent. At the 1963 March on Washington, King inspired more than 200,000 supporters with his words.

A VOICE FROM THE PAST

I have a dream that my four little children will one day live in a nation where they will not be judged by the color of their skin but by the content of their character. I have a dream today.

Martin Luther King, Jr., "I Have a Dream," August 28, 1963

In 1964, President Johnson pushed a Civil Rights Act through Congress. It banned discrimination in employment and voter registration. It also banned discrimination in public places such as restaurants, motels, and gas stations. Four years later, the Fair Housing Act outlawed discrimination in housing. Many of these changes were inspired by the leadership of Dr. King. King's assassination in Memphis, Tennessee, on April 4, 1968, stunned the nation.

Laws now guarantee African Americans and other minority groups equal treatment. With a growing number of African Americans elected to local, state, and federal offices, they have a greater voice in government.

*Reading*History

A. Recognizing Effects What goals did Dr. Martin Luther King, Jr., help to achieve in civil rights?

The Great Society

In 1964, President Lyndon B. Johnson convinced Congress to fund his War on Poverty. This effort created many government and private agencies to fight poverty. Some agencies provided job training. Others sent volunteers to teach in poor rural communities and rundown urban neighborhoods. Some programs funded part-time jobs for needy college students. Others offered preschool classes to give poor children a head

AMERICA'S HISTORY MAKERS

DR. MARTIN LUTHER KING, JR.
1929–1968

Dr. King (shown below) became leader of the Montgomery bus boycott. Fresh out of school, he had been in Montgomery about a year. But his courage and eloquence made him the perfect person to lead the movement.

King learned about nonviolence by studying religious writers and thinkers. He came to believe that only love could convert people to the side of justice. He described the power of nonviolent resisters: "We will wear you down by our capacity to suffer. And in winning our freedom . . . we will win you in the process."

How might King's beliefs have supported his leadership of a nonviolent protest?

start on learning. In 1965, Johnson got Congress to set aside millions for health care for the poor, elderly, and disabled. These health-care programs were called Medicare and Medicaid.

Reducing poverty, extending civil rights, and expanding medical care were all parts of Johnson's plan for a better America. He called it the **Great Society**. Like FDR's New Deal, the Great Society reflected Johnson's belief that government can improve people's lives. Johnson's social programs were costly. However, they attempted to reduce the poverty rate during the 1960s. As the U.S. role in the Vietnam War grew, though, fewer dollars were directed to Great Society programs.

Rights for All

In the 1960s, minorities and women struggled for equal rights. Native Americans turned to the courts to fight for their land rights. They held protests highlighting the federal government's failure to honor treaties. One of the most outspoken Native American groups was the American Indian Movement (AIM).

In the early 1960s, César Chávez began organizing poorly paid Mexican-American farm workers in California. He led a five-year-long strike by grape pickers. Then Chávez formed the nation's first successful union of farm workers. It became the United Farm Workers of America. Chávez's success inspired other Mexican Americans to work for change. In 1969–1970, they formed La Raza Unida—"the united people." This group worked to improve the lives of Mexican Americans and others.

In 1963, Betty Friedan wrote a best-selling book called *The Feminine Mystique.* This book led many women to rethink their roles. In 1966, Friedan and other activists founded the National Organization for Women (NOW). NOW and other women's groups such as Working Women and the American Association of University Women have worked to change laws that discriminate against women. They have helped to reform property rights and hiring. They continue working for equal pay and fair treatment in the workplace.

César Chávez organized the United Farm Workers of America during the 1960s.

Reading **History**
B. Comparing and Contrasting What was similar and different about the struggles of various groups for their rights?

Youth Protests and the Counterculture

No controversy was more heated than that over the Vietnam War. Opponents of the war argued that it was a civil war between Communists and non-Communists for control of Vietnam. They stated that the United States had no right to interfere. The war's supporters considered these opponents to be traitors who were undermining the war effort. Antiwar protests brought millions of Americans into the streets. Shouting matches and flag burnings followed. Some protests turned violent. Antiwar activists clashed with supporters of the war. At Ohio's Kent State University in 1970, National Guardsmen fired their weapons and killed four students.

Vietnam widened the gap between younger and older Americans. Differences in beliefs and values between generations eventually gave rise to the **counterculture.** These were groups of people seeking new ways of living. One of the central values for members of the counterculture was a concern for the environment. Environmentalists sought to protect the environment by fighting pollution of the country's natural resources. Some younger Americans had different values from those of the mainstream. "Hippies" emphasized the importance of love and freedom. They celebrated at music festivals such as the one at Woodstock, New York, in 1969. Critics such as President Nixon charged that hippies and antiwar protesters were tearing the nation apart. Many critics spoke out against the way young people questioned American values. Despite such concerns, in 1971 the Twenty-Sixth Amendment lowered the voting age to 18.

Protesters march in 1969 in opposition to the war in Vietnam.

Reagan, Bush, and Conservatism

Throughout the 1960s and 1970s, Democratic presidents such as Jimmy Carter had favored a strong role for government in the economy. They favored regulation of big business, support for organized labor, and public spending on the poor.

Ronald Reagan, a former movie actor and governor of California, was elected president in 1980, defeating Jimmy Carter. Reagan wanted to reduce the role of government in American life. "Government," he said, "is not the solution to our problem. Government is the problem." He sharply cut taxes and slashed spending on social programs for the poor. At the same time, he greatly increased military spending.

The tax cuts, coupled with heavy defense spending, caused the national debt to skyrocket. The government was borrowing more money to pay for spending than it was taking in through taxes. As a result, the national debt doubled in size from 1981 through 1986.

*Reading*History

C. Summarizing
What are some examples of how Reagan limited the role of government in economic affairs?

Reagan pushed pro-business economic policies. He abolished thousands of government regulations on business. After a recession in 1982, the economy sharply improved. A new wealthy class of young people emerged, whom reporters labeled "yuppies" (from "young urban professionals").

Reagan's successor, George Bush, shared his conservative outlook. In the early 1990s, after his successful management of the Persian Gulf War, Bush's popularity surged. However, when the country headed into a recession, Bush's approval ratings fell sharply. The causes of the weak economy included the nation's growing national debt, rising oil prices as a result of the Persian Gulf War, and shrinking factory production. In 1992, Bush was defeated in his bid for a second term by Bill Clinton, the governor of Arkansas.

(From left) Presidents Clinton, Bush, Reagan, Carter, and Ford at the funeral for President Nixon on April 27, 1994.

The Clinton Presidency

During his first term, Bill Clinton focused on domestic issues. To reduce the deficit, he supported tax increases and spending cuts. To fight crime, he pushed gun-control laws through Congress. Clinton's boldest move was his attempt to overhaul the U.S. health-care system. This effort, led by Hillary Rodham Clinton, failed to pass Congress.

In 1994, the Democrats lost control of Congress to the Republicans. The new Congress pushed for deeper cuts in taxes and social programs than Clinton would support. At first, the two sides failed to reach a budget agreement. Then, a compromise led to deep cuts in some government social programs but protected some spending for education, welfare, and health care programs for the needy. The nation's strong economy helped Clinton win reelection in 1996.

Reading **History**

D. Contrasting What effect did the economy have on the elections of 1992 and 1996?

Clinton's second term in office was marred by scandal. An investigation into Clinton's finances revealed that he had had an improper relationship with a White House intern. And he allegedly had lied about it under oath. The charges led to his impeachment in 1998. Despite the charges, Clinton remained popular. The Senate opened its trial of President Clinton in January 1999. Nearly a month later, the Senate acquitted him on both charges, and Clinton remained in office.

The 2000 Presidential Election

In 2000, the nation held a presidential election to choose Clinton's successor. The Democrats nominated Vice-President Al Gore as their candidate. The Republicans chose Texas governor George W. Bush, the son of the former president. Gore argued he was the best candidate to keep the nation's economy healthy. Meanwhile, Bush campaigned on a plan to give Americans huge tax cuts.

The 2000 election was one of the closest in U.S. history. By the morning after Election Day, Gore held a narrow lead in the popular vote. However, he did not have enough electoral votes to claim the presidency. Bush led in Florida by a few hundred votes, which promised to give him enough electoral votes to win the election. For five weeks, the two campaigns fought legal battles over recounts of the Florida ballots. Finally, on December 12, the U.S. Supreme Court voted 5 to 4 to stop the recounts, ensuring that Bush would win the presidency.

Immigrants and the New Millennium

From 1981 to 1996, nearly 13.5 million people came to the United States. These new immigrants increased U.S. diversity. Most of the immigrants who arrived in America during earlier periods had come from Europe. Nearly 85 percent of the most recent arrivals came from Latin America or

Asia. The Census Bureau predicts that by 2020 the U.S. Hispanic population will increase from 11 percent to 16 percent. At the same time, the Asian population is expected to climb from 3 percent to nearly 6 percent.

One cause of the recent surge in immigration is the Immigration Act of 1965. It allowed people from a greater variety of countries to enter the United States. The lure of America also plays a role. As with previous waves of immigration, many of the newcomers came to the United States seeking economic opportunity and political freedom.

While immigrants bring their culture to America, they also have embraced many American traditions. Most wear American clothes, adopt American customs, and learn English. Furthermore, they share with other Americans a belief in democracy and freedom.

Citizens of all races and backgrounds will play a vital role in shaping America. So will today's students. You have a part to play in helping the United States embrace people from every culture and land. You are the generation that will create the America of the future.

The American People

Origins of Immigrants, 1981–1996	Numbers of Immigrants*
1. Mexico	3,300,000
2. Philippines	840,000
3. China°	730,000
4. Vietnam	720,000
5. Dominican Republic	510,000
6. India	500,000
7. Korea	450,000
8. Soviet Union†	420,000
9. El Salvador	360,000
10. Jamaica	320,000

* Numbers rounded to nearest 10,000.
° China includes Taiwan.
† The Soviet Union broke apart in 1991. This figure includes the former Soviet republics.

Source: *U.S. Bureau of the Census*

SKILLBUILDER Interpreting Charts

1. *From which European countries were there still substantial numbers of immigrants in the 1980s and 1990s?*
2. *From what regions of the world do most recent immigrants come?*

Section 4 Assessment

1. Terms & Names

Explain the significance of:
- baby boom
- Dr. Martin Luther King, Jr.
- Great Society
- counterculture

2. Taking Notes

Use the chart to examine the aims of groups that protested in the 1960s.

	Goal	Success
African Americans		
Mexican Americans		
Native Americans		
Women		

3. Main Ideas

a. How did the civil rights movement of the 1960s lessen discrimination against African Americans?

b. What were the goals of President Johnson's Great Society programs?

c. How did Reagan attempt to reduce the role of government in American life?

4. Critical Thinking

Supporting Opinions Do any youth countercultures exist today? Why or why not?

THINK ABOUT
- music and the arts
- politics
- religion
- values

ACTIVITY OPTIONS

LANGUAGE ARTS
MATH

Find out about voters' attitudes toward politicians. Create a survey, conduct a poll, and either write a **report** or display your results in a **graph**.

Protecting the Environment

The nation has made great strides over the past several decades in taking better care of the environment. However, much work remains to be done. As the United States embarks on a new century, the country continues to face such controversial issues as global warming, and the problems of water pollution and a growing amount of waste.

COOPERATIVE LEARNING You have recently joined a local organization whose goal is to find solutions to the environmental challenges that affect your community. On these pages are three challenges you face as a member of the organization. Working with a small group, decide how to deal with each challenge. Choose an option, assign a task to each group member, and do the activity. You will find useful information in the Data File. Present your solutions to the class.

ECONOMICS CHALLENGE

"from a feel-good issue to a bottom-line issue"

A growing number of businesses have begun taking steps to curb the amount of trash they produce. These companies have found that scaling back on waste helps to save money. How can you convince businesses in your community to follow this trend? Use the Data File for help. Use one of these options:

- Create an economic report showing companies ways they can cut back on waste while saving money.
- Write a proposal outlining further ways companies can reduce waste.

ART CHALLENGE

"very troubled waters"

In the decades after the Clean Water Act of 1972, many of the nation's rivers grew cleaner. Recently, however, the government has had to name more waterways as unsuitable for fishing or swimming.

The main pollutants include pesticide and sewage runoff from large farms, runoff from city and suburban sewer systems, and chemical waste from mining. How can you alert people in your community to these problems? Use the Data File for help. Present your information using one of these options:

- Design a poster showing one or more types of pollutants reaching a river.
- Create a graphic for town officials that depicts the Data File information about contaminated rivers.

MATH CHALLENGE

"the seas would rise . . . and whole forest types could disappear"

Global warming remains a controversial problem. Many—but not all—scientists believe that air pollutants create a ceiling that traps heat near the earth's surface. Foremost among the pollutants is carbon dioxide, which is generated by factories, automobiles, and common household appliances. Help people become more aware of their carbon dioxide output. Use the Data File for help. Present your information using one of these options:

• Make a graph showing the yearly carbon dioxide output of various household items.

• Write a report detailing ways in which a household could reduce its carbon dioxide output.

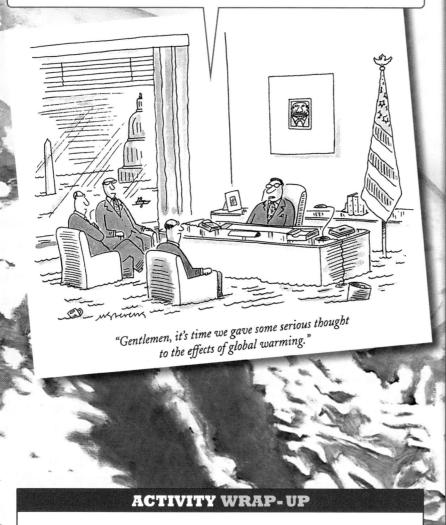

"Gentlemen, it's time we gave some serious thought to the effects of global warming."

ACTIVITY WRAP-UP

Present to the Class Meet as a group to review your responses to various environmental challenges. Pick the most creative solution for each challenge and present these solutions to the class.

Global Warming

Average U.S. Household's Yearly Output of Carbon Dioxide (in pounds):

Human respiration (2.6 persons)—1,950
Television—510
Range—933
Dishwasher—1,038
Lighting—1,045
Refrigerator—1,136
Dryer—1,177
Washer—1,199
Oil-fired water heater—4,476
Oil-fired space heater—12,958
Car—20,956

What's in Our Dirty Rivers

From a 1998 study: 36 percent of U.S. rivers are contaminated. Percentage of contaminated rivers affected by following pollutants:

• Toxic chemicals—9%

• Waste and chemicals from mining—13%

• City/suburban run-off (trash, chemical fertilizers)—13%

• Treated sewage (nitrogen and phosphorus)—14%

• Silt and sediment (from construction projects)—37%

• Agriculture run-off (dirt, manure, chemical fertilizers)—70%

Corporate Conservation

• Colonial Pacific Leasing Corp. in Oregon cut $5,200 from its yearly electrical bill by using energy-efficient light bulbs.

• Stonyfield Farm Inc. in New Hampshire saved $60,000 one year by reducing the amount of plastic packaging on products.

• Mercer Color Corp. in Ohio made $8,000 one year by selling its waste for recycling.

• Xerox saves more than $200 million a year by reusing print and toner cartridges.

For more about conservation . . .

RESEARCH LINKS
CLASSZONE.COM

VISUAL SUMMARY

The United States Since 1919

1920s:
Prosperity; increased income and leisure

1930s:
Great Depression; New Deal; rise of dictators

1940s:
World War II; beginning of Cold War

1950s:
Prosperity; growth of suburbs; baby boom

1960s:
Civil rights movement; Vietnam War

1970s:
Détente; Vietnam War ends; Nixon resigns

1980s:
Soaring federal deficit; U.S.-Soviet relations improved

1990s:
Collapse of Soviet Union; prosperity

TERMS & NAMES

Briefly explain the significance of each of the following.

1. Great Depression
2. New Deal
3. fascism
4. World War II
5. Holocaust
6. Harry S. Truman
7. Cold War
8. containment
9. baby boom
10. Great Society

REVIEW QUESTIONS

Prosperity and the Great Depression (pages 569–573)

1. What role did the market crash play in the Great Depression?
2. What was the purpose of Roosevelt's bank holiday?
3. What problems did FDR's New Deal address?

The Rise of Dictators and World War II (pages 574–578)

4. How did Hitler and the Nazi Party gain the support of Germans in the 1930s?
5. How did the role of the United States in World War II change between 1939 and 1945?

The Cold War (pages 579–583)

6. What differences between the Soviet Union and the United States fueled the Cold War?
7. What strategies did the United States use to carry out its containment policy?
8. How did the end of the Cold War change the United States' role in world affairs?

Life in America Since 1945 (pages 584–589)

9. What methods did civil rights activists use?
10. How did the views of presidents Johnson and Reagan differ on the role of government?

CRITICAL THINKING

1. USING YOUR NOTES

The 20th Century	Political Events	Economic Events	Social Events
1920–1930			
1940–1950			
1960–1970			
1980–1990			

Using your completed chart, answer the questions below.

a. What was an important political event in the period 1940–1950?
b. What was an important social event in the period 1960–1970?
c. What was an important economic event in the period 1980–1990?

2. APPLYING CITIZENSHIP SKILLS

How has the African-American struggle for civil rights changed since the 1960s?

3. THEME: AMERICA IN THE WORLD

As the world's most powerful nation, does the United States have a special responsibility to intervene in conflicts around the world? Why or why not?

4. ANALYZING LEADERSHIP

How do the leadership skills of a president differ in times of war and in times of peace and prosperity? Explain your answer.

5. FORMING AND SUPPORTING OPINIONS

Should the government's focus today be on domestic issues or on foreign affairs? Explain your answer.

Interact with History

Now that you've read the chapter, what are some ways the 21st century may be the same as and different from the 20th century? Explain your ideas.

HISTORY SKILLS

1. INTERPRETING MAPS: Location

Study the map and then answer the questions.

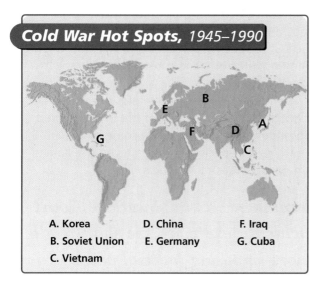

Cold War Hot Spots, *1945–1990*

A. Korea   D. China   F. Iraq
B. Soviet Union   E. Germany   G. Cuba
C. Vietnam

Basic Map Elements

a. What is the subject of the map?

b. In which hemisphere are most of these countries located?

Interpreting the Map

c. Why might the United States have been concerned about missiles in Cuba?

d. Which Cold War hot spot was located in Europe?

2. INTERPRETING PRIMARY SOURCES

Ken Burns, a documentary filmmaker, argues that a shared belief in the ideals of democracy and civil rights makes America unique in the world.

> There is no other country on Earth that is configured like ours. Every other nation is there because of race, religion, language, ethnicity, or geography. We are here only because we agreed to subscribe to the words on four pieces of paper—the U.S. Constitution. Unlike every other country, which sees itself as an end unto itself, we see ourselves as evolving. We're not satisfied. We're not willing to rest on our laurels. We think we can get better. We think we've got someplace to go.
>
> **Ken Burns,** quoted in *America West*

a. Does Burns's comment imply a hopeful view of the future? Why or why not?

b. What might be some of the advantages and disadvantages of changing and adapting to meet the future?

ALTERNATIVE ASSESSMENT

1. INTERDISCIPLINARY ACTIVITY: World History

Creating a Linking Time Line Make a dual time line for the period 1920–2000. Divide the time line into eight segments, one for each decade. On one side, list key events from world history during this period. On the other side, note major events from American history. Pick a decade and give a talk explaining how the events on the time line are connected.

2. COOPERATIVE LEARNING ACTIVITY

Analyzing Social Issues Working in groups, make a list of social issues that concern Americans today, such as pollution, drugs, crime, or school violence. Decide which problem the group thinks is most important. Create presentations using these suggestions.

- Research and write a description of the problem.
- Make a list of at least three alternative ways experts suggest for solving the problem.
- Pick the solution your group considers most practical and likely to be effective and write an action statement explaining the reasons for your choice.

3. TECHNOLOGY ACTIVITY

Making an Electronic Presentation During the 1920s, there was a dramatic rise in popular entertainment. Using the library and the Internet, find information about important celebrities of the time, such as Babe Ruth, Bessie Smith, or Charlie Chaplin.
For more about the 1920s . . .

RESEARCH LINKS
CLASSZONE.COM

Use presentation software to create a program about celebrities of the 1920s. Use the suggestions below to get started.

- the 1927 championship boxing match between Jack Dempsey and Gene Tunney
- important events in the baseball career of Ty Cobb or Babe Ruth
- recordings of jazz greats
- facts about movie celebrities of the 1920s

4. HISTORY PORTFOLIO

Review your section and chapter assessment activities. Select one that you think is your best work. Then use comments made by your teacher or classmates to improve your work and add it to your portfolio.

Additional Test Practice, pp. S1–S33

TEST PRACTICE
CLASSZONE.COM

The Supreme Court

The task of the Supreme Court, according to Chief Justice John Marshall, is "to say what the law is." The Court reviews appeals of decisions by lower courts. It judges whether federal laws or government actions violate the Constitution. And it settles conflicts between state and federal laws.

By interpreting the law, the Supreme Court wields great power, for its decisions affect practically every aspect of life in the United States. In the following pages, you'll learn about some of the Supreme Court's landmark cases—decisions that altered the course of history or brought major changes to American life.

"When we have examined . . . the Supreme Court and the [rights] which it exercises, we shall readily admit that a more imposing judicial power was never constituted by any people."

— ALEXIS DE TOCQUEVILLE, *DEMOCRACY IN AMERICA* (1835)

Chief Justice John Marshall established the principle of judicial review.

The development of steamships led to Supreme Court decisions on interstate commerce.

McCulloch v. *Maryland* decided if a state had the power to tax a federal agency.

1803	1824	1896
Marbury v. *Madison*	*Gibbons* v. *Ogden*	*Plessy* v. *Ferguson*
Judicial Review	State Versus Federal Authority	Segregation

1819	1857
McCulloch v. *Maryland*	*Dred Scott* v. *Sandford*
Powers of Congress and States' Rights	Citizenship

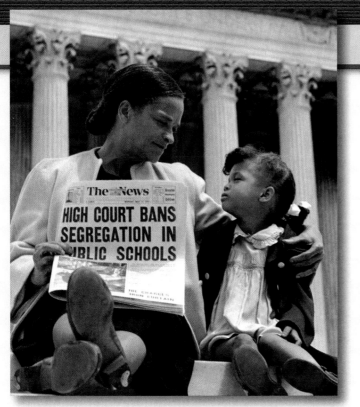

Landmark decisions on school desegregation helped give rise to the civil rights movement.

TABLE OF CONTENTS

BEFORE YOU READ

Think About It Why is there a need for a judicial authority "to say what the law is"? How might the history of the United States be different if the Supreme Court had not taken on this role?

Find Out About It Use library resources or the Internet to find out what issues the Supreme Court is presently reviewing. How might the Court's decisions on these issues affect you?

For more information on the Supreme Court . . .

RESEARCH LINKS CLASSZONE.COM

Opinions written by Justice Oliver Wendell Holmes, Jr. helped to set standards for free speech.

The Court has reviewed several affirmative-action cases in recent years.

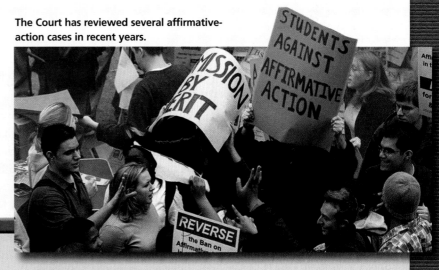

1919
Schenck v. *United States*
Freedom of Speech

1954
Brown v. *Board of Education of Topeka*
School Desegregation

1964
Reynolds v. *Sims*
One Person, One Vote

1978
Regents of the University of California v. *Bakke*
Affirmative Action

Marbury v. Madison (1803)

THE ISSUE Judicial Review

ORIGINS OF THE CASE In 1801, just before he left office, President John Adams appointed dozens of Federalists as judges. Most of these "midnight justices" took their posts before Thomas Jefferson, Adams's Democratic-Republican successor, took office. Jefferson ordered his secretary of state, James Madison, to block the remaining appointees from taking their posts. One of these appointees, William Marbury, asked the Supreme Court to issue an order forcing Madison to recognize the appointments.

THE RULING The Court ruled that the law under which Marbury had asked the Supreme Court to act was unconstitutional.

LEGAL Sources

U.S. CONSTITUTION/LEGISLATION

Article 3, Section 2 (1789)
"In all cases affecting ambassadors, other public ministers and consuls, and those in which a state shall be party, the Supreme Court shall have original jurisdiction. In all other cases . . . the Supreme Court shall have appellate jurisdiction."

Judiciary Act, Section 13 (1789)
"The Supreme Court . . . shall have power to issue . . . writs of *mandamus,* in cases warranted by the principles and usages of law."

RELATED CASES

Fletcher v. Peck (1810)
For the first time, the Supreme Court ruled a state law unconstitutional.

Cohens v. Virginia (1821)
For the first time, the Court overturned a state court decision.

The Legal Arguments

Chief Justice John Marshall wrote the Court's opinion, stating that Marbury had every right to receive his appointment. Further, Marshall noted, the Judiciary Act of 1789 gave Marbury the right to file his claim directly with the Supreme Court. But Marshall questioned whether the Court had the power to act. The answer, he argued, rested on the kinds of cases that could be argued directly in the Supreme Court without first being heard by a lower court.

Article 3 of the Constitution clearly identified those cases that the Court could hear directly. A case like Marbury's was not one of them. The Judiciary Act, therefore, was at odds with the Constitution. Which one should be upheld? Marshall's response was clear:

> . . . [T]he particular phraseology of the Constitution of the United States confirms and strengthens the principle . . . that a law repugnant to the Constitution is void; and that *courts* . . . are bound by that instrument.

Since Section 13 of the Judiciary Act violated the Constitution, Marshall concluded, it could not be enforced. The Court, therefore, could not issue the order. With this decision, Marshall appeared to limit the powers of the Supreme Court. In fact, the decision increased the Court's power because it established the principle of judicial review. This holds that the courts—most notably the Supreme Court—have the power to decide if laws are unconstitutional.

William Marbury received his appointment as a reward for his loyal support of John Adams in the 1800 presidential election.

Why Did It Matter Then?

The principle of judicial review had been set down in earlier state and lower federal court decisions. However, Marshall did not refer to those cases in *Marbury.* Rather, he based his argument on logic.

For a written constitution to have any value, Marshall stated, it is logical that any "legislative act [that is] contrary to the Constitution is not law." Only then could the Constitution be—as Article VI calls it—"the supreme law of the land." Who, then, decides that a law is invalid? Marshall declared that this power rests only with the courts:

> It is, emphatically, the province and duty of the judicial department to say what the law is. Those who apply the rule to particular cases must of necessity expound and interpret that rule. If [the Constitution and a law] conflict with each other, the courts must decide on the operation of each.

Not only did the courts have this power, Marshall said, it was "the very essence of judicial duty" for them to exercise it.

Why Does It Matter Now?

Over the years, judicial review has become a cornerstone of American government. The principle plays a vital role in the system of checks and balances that limits the powers of each branch of the federal government. For example, since 1803 the Court has struck down more than 125 acts of Congress as unconstitutional.

The Court has cited *Marbury* more than 250 times to justify its decisions. In *Clinton* v. *Jones* (1997), for example, the Court found that presidents are not protected by the Constitution from lawsuits involving actions in their private lives. The Court supported this finding by pointing to its power "to say what the law is." More recently, in *United States* v. *Morrison* (2000), the Court ruled that Congress went beyond its constitutional bounds by basing a federal law banning violence against women on the Fourteenth Amendment and the Commerce Clause of the Constitution. The opinion pointed out that "ever since *Marbury* this Court has remained the ultimate [explainer] of the constitutional text."

John Marshall, a Federalist, was practically a "midnight justice." John Adams appointed him chief justice in January 1801, just two months before Thomas Jefferson took office.

CONNECT TO HISTORY

1. Making Decisions Marshall was a Federalist, and many people expected him to act quickly on Marbury's case. What do you think might have been the consequences if Marshall had found for Marbury?

 See Skillbuilder Handbook, page R14.

CONNECT TO TODAY

2. Researching Find a recent instance of a law or administrative action that was ruled unconstitutional by the Supreme Court. What were the Court's reasons for the ruling, and what impact did the decision have? Prepare a summary of your findings.

For more information on judicial review . . .

RESEARCH LINKS
CLASSZONE.COM

McCulloch v. Maryland
(1819)

THE ISSUES Balance of power between the federal and state governments

ORIGINS OF THE CASE The second Bank of the United States (BUS) was established by an act of Congress in 1816. It set up branches nationwide. But many states objected to the bank's policies and wanted to limit its operations. In fact, Maryland set a tax on the currency issued by the Baltimore branch. The bank could avoid the tax by paying an annual fee of $15,000. However, James McCulloch, the branch cashier, refused to pay either the tax or the fee. The state sued McCulloch, and the Maryland courts ordered him to pay. McCulloch appealed the case to the Supreme Court.

THE RULING The Court ruled that Congress had the power to establish a national bank and that the Maryland tax on that bank was unconstitutional.

The Legal Arguments

The Court first addressed Maryland's argument that the act establishing the BUS was unconstitutional. Chief Justice John Marshall wrote that the Constitution listed the specific powers of Congress. These included collecting taxes, borrowing money, and regulating commerce. In addition, the Elastic Clause gave Congress the authority to make all "necessary and proper" laws needed to exercise those powers. Establishing a bank, he concluded, was necessary for Congress to carry out its powers. The BUS, then, was constitutional.

Next, Marshall addressed whether Maryland had the power to tax the BUS. Marshall acknowledged that the states had the power of taxation. But he said:

> [T]he constitution and the laws made in pursuance thereof are supreme . . . they control the constitution and laws of the respective states, and cannot be controlled by them.

So, to give a state the power to tax a federal agency created under the Constitution would turn the Supremacy Clause on its head. Further, Marshall observed, "the power to tax involves the power to destroy." If a state could tax one federal agency, it might tax others. This eventually "would defeat all the ends of government." He added that the framers of the Constitution certainly did not intend to make the national government subject to the states:

> [T]he States have no power, by taxation or otherwise, to retard, impede, burden, or in any manner control, the operations of the constitutional laws enacted by Congress to carry [out its] powers.

The Maryland tax, therefore, was unconstitutional.

LEGAL *Sources*

U.S. CONSTITUTION/LEGISLATION

Article 1, Section 8 (1789)
"The Congress shall have the power to . . . make all laws which shall be necessary and proper for carrying into execution the [specific powers given to Congress]."

Article 6 (1789)
"This Constitution, and the laws of the United States . . . shall be the supreme law of the land; . . . anything in the Constitution or laws of any state to the contrary notwithstanding."

RELATED CASES

Fletcher v. Peck (1810)
Noting that the Constitution was the supreme law of the land, the Supreme Court ruled a state law unconstitutional.

Gibbons v. Ogden (1824)
The Court ruled that the federal Congress—not the states—had the power to regulate interstate commerce.

Why Did It Matter Then?

At the time of the *McCulloch* case, there was considerable debate over what powers Congress held. Some people took a very limited view. They suggested that Congress's powers should be restricted to those named in the Constitution. Others pointed out that the Elastic Clause implied that Congress had much broader powers.

The *McCulloch* opinion followed this second view. Marshall wrote:

> Let the end be [lawful], let it be within the scope of the Constitution, and all means which are appropriate, which are plainly adapted to that end, which are not prohibited, but consist with the letter and spirit of the Constitution, are constitutional.

In other words, Congress could exercise the powers it considered appropriate to achieve its lawful goals.

Marshall's broad view of congressional power strengthened the federal government. And this stronger government reflected and encouraged the growing nationalist spirit in the early 1800s.

Why Does It Matter Now?

Since Marshall's time, the United States has undergone many changes. Over the course of the 19th and 20th centuries, the country has grown dramatically. The population has increased and moved. In Marshall's day, the United States was predominantly rural. Today, most people live in urban areas, where economic and leisure activities abound.

The economy of the United States, too, has changed. The country has moved from an agricultural economy to one based on industry and, later, service and information.

During this time, the federal government has stretched its powers to meet the needs of the ever-changing American society. Programs like Franklin Roosevelt's New Deal and Lyndon Johnson's Great Society came about through this expanding of powers. Marshall's broad reading of the Elastic Clause in the *McCulloch* opinion, in large part, laid the groundwork for this growth in the size and power of the federal government.

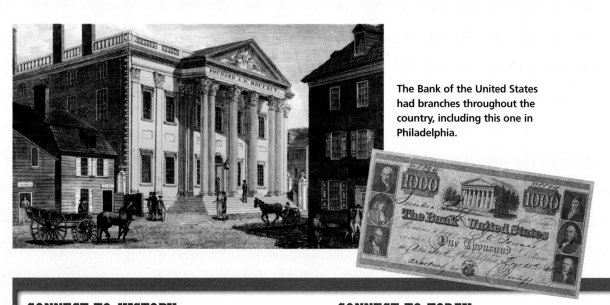

The Bank of the United States had branches throughout the country, including this one in Philadelphia.

CONNECT TO HISTORY

1. **Forming and Supporting Opinions** Chief Justice John Marshall considered the *McCulloch* decision the most important that he made. Why do you think he considered it such an important decision? Give reasons for your answer.

 See Skillbuilder Handbook, page R17.

CONNECT TO TODAY

2. **Researching** One issue addressed in *McCulloch* was states' rights and federal authority. Do research to find a recent Supreme Court case that has dealt with this issue. Write a paragraph describing the basis of the case and the Court's decision.

For more information on states' rights and federal authority . . .

RESEARCH LINKS
CLASSZONE.COM

HISTORIC DECISIONS *OF THE SUPREME COURT*

Gibbons v. *Ogden* (1824)

THE ISSUE Federal power to regulate interstate commerce

ORIGINS OF THE CASE Aaron Ogden ran steamboats between New York City and New Jersey. The New York state legislature granted him a monopoly—the right to operate this service without any competition. However, Thomas Gibbons ran a competing service. He had a license to sail under the federal Coasting License Act of 1793. Ogden sued Gibbons for violating his monopoly. When the New York state courts found in Ogden's favor, Gibbons appealed to the United States Supreme Court.

THE RULING In a unanimous decision, the Court ruled that where state and federal laws on interstate commerce conflict, federal laws are superior.

LEGAL *Sources*

U.S. CONSTITUTION/LEGISLATION

Article 1, Section 8 (1789)
"The Congress shall have power to . . . regulate commerce with foreign nations, and among the several states, and with the Indian tribes."

Coasting License Act (1793)
All ships licensed under this act, "and no others, shall be deemed ships or vessels of the United States, entitled to the privileges of ships or vessels employed in the coasting trade or fisheries."

RELATED CASES

Fletcher v. Peck (1810)
Citing the Supremacy Clause, the Court ruled that a state law was unconstitutional.

McCulloch v. Maryland (1819)
The Court established that states had no authority to tax federal agencies.

The Legal Arguments

Chief Justice John Marshall wrote the Court's unanimous opinion, which found for Gibbons. Since the Constitution gave Congress the power to regulate commerce among the states, Marshall began, it would be useful to decide what the word *commerce* meant. In arguments before the Court, Ogden's lawyers had said that it simply referred to the buying and selling of goods. Marshall disagreed, suggesting that it also included the navigation necessary to move goods from one place to another. He wrote:

> The word used in the Constitution comprehends . . . navigation within its meaning; and a power to regulate navigation is as expressly granted as if that term had been added to the word "commerce."

Marshall then pointed to the Supremacy Clause of the Constitution. This is Article 6, Section 2, which states, "This Constitution, and the laws of the United States . . . shall be the supreme law of the land."

The New York monopoly law denied Gibbons the right to sail in New York waters. The federal Coasting License Act, however, gave him the right to sail *all* U.S. waters. According to the Supremacy Clause, the Constitution and federal laws were the supreme law of the land. So, Marshall concluded, the Coasting License Act was "the supreme law of the land," and the New York monopoly was void.

Aaron Ogden obtained a monopoly on steamship operation between New York and New Jersey in 1815.

600

Why Did It Matter Then?

At the time of the *Gibbons* case, navigation of the waters around New York was difficult. To encourage companies to provide water transportation, New York granted monopolies to the companies. Some states set up their own. Other states passed laws preventing New York steamboats from entering their waters. Obviously, such a situation was not good for trade among the states. By making it clear that the federal government regulated commerce among the states, the *Gibbons* decision brought order to interstate commerce. And this helped the national economy to grow.

Unlike other decisions of the Marshall Court that strengthened the federal government, *Gibbons* proved popular. Most Americans—even New Yorkers—were opposed to the New York steamboat monopoly. They saw any kind of monopoly as a limit to economic competition. As a result, the *Gibbons* decision was well received throughout the country. One newspaper reported the following incident:

> **Yesterday the Steamboat *United States*, [commanded by] Capt. Bunker, from New Haven, entered New York in triumph, with streamers flying and a large company of passengers [celebrating] the decision of the United States Supreme Court against the New York monopoly. She fired a salute which was loudly returned by [cheers] from the wharves.**

After the first voyage of Robert Fulton's *Clermont* in 1807, it soon became clear that operating steamships could be a profitable business.

Why Does It Matter Now?

Marshall defined "commerce" very broadly in the *Gibbons* decision. Over the years, Congress has used Marshall's definition to expand its authority over interstate commerce. Today, Congress regulates practically every activity that affects or is connected to commerce.

In 1964, for example, Congress used the Commerce Clause to justify the passage of the Civil Rights Act. This law banned racial discrimination in hotels, restaurants, theaters, and other public places.

The Supreme Court rejected two challenges to the Civil Rights Act—in *Heart of Atlanta Motel, Inc.* v. *United States* (1964) and *Katzenbach* v. *McClung* (1964). In both cases, the Court noted that racial discrimination could harm interstate commerce.

CONNECT TO HISTORY

1. **Drawing Conclusions** Many of Chief Justice John Marshall's opinions contributed to the growth of the nationalist spirit in the early 1800s. How do you think the *Gibbons* v. *Ogden* decision might have helped to build national unity?

   S See Skillbuilder Handbook, page R13.

CONNECT TO TODAY

2. **Researching** Use library resources and the Internet to find recent Supreme Court cases that involved interstate commerce. Write a brief summary of one of these cases, noting whether it expanded or contracted Congress's power to regulate commerce.

   For more information on interstate commerce . . .

RESEARCH LINKS
CLASSZONE.COM

601

Dred Scott v. Sandford (1857)

THE ISSUE The definition of citizenship

ORIGINS OF THE CASE Dred Scott was an enslaved African American who had lived for a while in Illinois and in the Wisconsin Territory, both of which banned slavery. Scott sued for his freedom, arguing that since he had lived in a free state and a free territory, he was a free man. In 1854, a federal court found against Scott, ruling that he was still a slave. Scott's lawyers appealed to the Supreme Court, which heard arguments in 1856 and delivered its decision the following year.

THE RULING The Court ruled that no African American could be a citizen and that Dred Scott was still a slave. The Court also ruled that the Missouri Compromise of 1820 was unconstitutional.

The Legal Arguments

Chief Justice Roger Taney wrote the majority opinion for the Court. He began by addressing the issue of citizenship. He pointed out that since colonial times African Americans had been looked on as inferior and "had no rights which the white man was bound to respect." Taney added that where African Americans were mentioned in the Constitution, they were referred to as property—slaves. African Americans, whether enslaved or free, he continued:

> . . . are not included, and were not intended to be included, under the word 'citizens' in the Constitution, and can therefore claim none of the rights and privileges which that instrument provides for and secures to citizens of the United States.

Since Scott was not a citizen, Taney concluded, he had no right to use the courts to sue for his freedom.

Taney then went further, claiming Scott was still a slave because he had never been free. Congress had gone beyond its power when it passed the Missouri Compromise, he argued. The Constitution guaranteed the right to own property, and slaves were property. By banning slavery from the territories, Congress was, in effect, taking away private property without due process of the law. This action violated the Fifth Amendment. The Missouri Compromise was, Taney charged, "not warranted by the Constitution, and . . . therefore void." As a result, Scott remained a slave, regardless of where he lived.

Two justices disagreed with the majority on both grounds. They pointed to precedents—earlier legal rulings—that indicated that African Americans could, indeed, be citizens. They also argued that the Constitution gave Congress the power to establish rules and regulations for the territories.

LEGAL Sources

U.S. CONSTITUTION/LEGISLATION

Article 4, Section 3 (1789)
"No person held to service or labor in one state, . . . escaping into another, shall, in consequence of any law or regulation therein, be discharged from such service or labor. . . ."

Fifth Amendment (1791)
"No person shall be . . . deprived of life, liberty, or property, without due process of law."

Missouri Enabling Act (1820)
"[I]n all that territory . . . north of 36° 30' N latitude, . . . slavery . . . shall be . . . forever prohibited." Also known as the Missouri Compromise.

RELATED CASE

Ableman v. Booth (1858)
The Court ruled that laws passed in Northern states that prohibited the return of fugitive slaves were unconstitutional.

Why Did It Matter Then?

Dred Scott contributed to the growing dispute over slavery that led to the Civil War. White Southerners praised the ruling, seeing it as a spirited defense of their right to own slaves. Many Northerners, however, viewed it with alarm. They feared that if Congress could not ban slavery in the territories, slavery would spread. If this happened, slave states eventually would outnumber free states and would control Congress.

Stephen A. Douglas, a Northern Democrat, disagreed with the Court's finding. He favored leaving the issue of slavery to the voters in each territory. Most Southern Democrats, however, did not agree with him. As a result, the Democratic Party divided along sectional lines in the 1860 presidential election. Northern Democrats supported Douglas, while Southern Democrats backed a pro-slavery candidate. Because of this split, Abraham Lincoln of the antislavery Republican Party won the election. Soon after, many slave states seceded, and the Civil War began.

Northern abolitionists held meetings to show their support for Scott (shown here) and their opposition to the Supreme Court decision.

Why Does It Matter Now?

The issues addressed by *Dred Scott* were resolved by the Thirteenth and Fourteenth amendments to the Constitution. The Thirteenth Amendment, which was ratified in 1865, abolished slavery in the United States. The Fourteenth Amendment, ratified three years later, made it very clear who was a citizen:

> **All persons born or naturalized in the United States, and subject to the jurisdiction thereof, are citizens of the United States and of the state wherein they reside.**

This amendment went on to guarantee all citizens "equal protection of the laws" and the right to due process. These amendments meant the rulings in *Dred Scott* no longer had the force of law.

Today, *Dred Scott* is not used as a precedent. Instead, it is pointed to as an example of how the Supreme Court can make mistakes. In fact, many legal scholars think it is the worst decision the Court has ever handed down.

CONNECT TO HISTORY

1. **Forming and Supporting Opinions** The *Dred Scott* decision was just one in a long line of events that led to the Civil War. Write an editorial about the case in which you evaluate its importance in bringing about the war.

 See Skillbuilder Handbook, page R17.

CONNECT TO TODAY

2. **Researching** Use library sources and the Internet to research a contemporary Court decision that affects civil rights. Use newspaper indexes, periodical guides, and library catalogs, for example, to locate sources of this information. Create a public service brochure to report your findings.

For more information on citizenship . . .

Plessy v. Ferguson (1896)

THE ISSUE Segregation

ORIGINS OF THE CASE By the 1890s, most Southern states had begun to pass laws enforcing segregation—the separation of the races—in public places. One Louisiana law called for "equal but separate accommodations for the white and colored races" on trains. On June 7, 1892, Homer Plessy, who was part African American, took a seat in a train car reserved for whites. When a conductor told him to move, Plessy refused. Plessy was convicted of breaking the "separate car" law. He appealed the case, saying that the law violated his rights under the Thirteenth and Fourteenth amendments.

THE RULING The Court ruled that "separate but equal" facilities for blacks and whites did not violate the Constitution.

LEGAL *Sources*

U.S. CONSTITUTION/LEGISLATION

Thirteenth Amendment (1865)
"Neither slavery nor involuntary servitude . . . shall exist within the United States, or any place subject to their jurisdiction."

Fourteenth Amendment (1868)
"No state shall make or enforce any law which shall abridge the privileges or immunities of citizens of the United States; nor shall any state deprive any person of life, liberty, or property, without due process of law; nor deny to any person within its jurisdiction the equal protection of the laws."

RELATED CASE

***Cumming v. Board of Education of Richmond County* (1899)**
The Court ruled that because education is a local issue, the federal government could not stop school districts from having separate facilities for black and white students.

The Legal Arguments

The Court's opinion, written by Justice Henry Billings Brown, rejected Plessy's appeal. Brown first answered Plessy's claim that the separate car law created a relationship between whites and blacks similar to that which existed under slavery. The Thirteenth Amendment simply ended the ownership of one person by another, Brown wrote. Louisiana's law did not reestablish this system of ownership.

Brown then turned to Plessy's claim that the Fourteenth Amendment was designed to ensure the equality of the races before the law. Brown wrote that the amendment "could not have been intended to abolish distinctions based on color." A law that treated the races differently did not brand one race as inferior. If a law made people feel inferior, it was because they chose to see it that way. Summing up, Brown stated:

> A [law] which implies merely a legal distinction between the white and colored races . . . has no tendency to destroy the legal equality of the two races.

Justice John Marshall Harlan strongly disagreed with the majority view. In a bitter dissent, he wrote that the "thin disguise" of separate but equal facilities would fool no one, "nor atone for the wrong this day done."

In his dissent, Justice Harlan stated that "our constitution is color-blind, and neither knows nor tolerates classes among citizens."

Why Did It Matter Then?

Plessy was one of several cases in the late 1800s involving the civil rights of African Americans. In these cases, the Court misread the Fourteenth Amendment and let stand state laws that denied African Americans their rights. *Plessy* has come to stand for all of these decisions because it said that "separate but equal" facilities for blacks and whites did not violate the Constitution.

Although the *Plessy* decision dealt only with public transportation, state governments across the South applied it to all areas of life. In time, "Jim Crow" laws forced African Americans to use separate restaurants, hotels, train cars, parks, schools, and hospitals. Signs reading "For Colored Only" and "Whites Only" ruled everyday life in the South for years to come.

Why Does It Matter Now?

After *Plessy,* many African Americans and some whites looked for ways to fight segregation. Some of these people helped to found the National Association for the Advancement of Colored People (NAACP).

Throughout the first half of the 20th century, lawyers working for the NAACP chipped away at segregation laws. Their greatest victory came in 1954, in *Brown* v. *Board of Education.* In this decision, the Supreme Court ruled that separate educational facilities were "inherently unequal" and, therefore, unconstitutional. Southern state and local governments had used the *Plessy* decision to build a system of legal segregation. In the same way, civil rights workers used the *Brown* ruling to dismantle it.

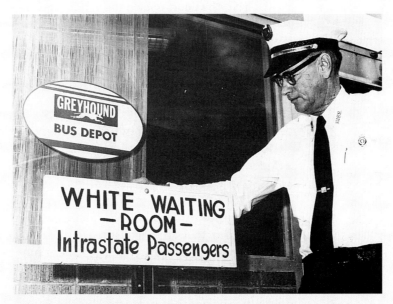

After the *Plessy* decision, signs designating separate facilities for whites and African Americans became a common sight throughout the South.

CONNECT TO HISTORY

1. **Drawing Conclusions** Read the section of the Fourteenth Amendment reprinted in the "Legal Sources" section on page 604. Based on that passage, what do you think "equal protection of the laws" means? How does it apply to the *Plessy* case?

 See Skillbuilder Handbook, page R13.

CONNECT TO TODAY

2. **Researching** Use library resources and the Internet to find information on Supreme Court cases that dealt with segregation. Present your findings in a three-column chart. Use "Case," "Brief Description of Issues Involved," and "Decision" as column headings.

For more information on segregation and the law . . .

RESEARCH LINKS
CLASSZONE.COM

Schenck v. United States
(1919)

THE ISSUE Freedom of Speech

ORIGINS OF THE CASE In August 1917, Charles Schenck, a Socialist Party official, distributed several thousand anti-war leaflets throughout the city of Philadelphia. The leaflets called the draft a crime and urged people to work for the repeal of the Selective Service Act. Schenck was found guilty of violating the Espionage Act of 1917 and sentenced to prison. He appealed his conviction, arguing that the language in the leaflets was protected by the First Amendment.

THE RULING The Court upheld the verdict against Schenck, noting that the leaflets presented "a clear and present danger" to the country during wartime.

LEGAL Sources

U.S. CONSTITUTION/LEGISLATION

First Amendment (1791)
"Congress shall make no law . . . abridging the freedom of speech, or of the press . . ."

The Espionage Act (1917)
"[Anyone who] shall wilfully obstruct . . . the recruiting or enlistment service of the United States . . . shall be punished by . . . fine . . . or imprisonment . . . or both."

RELATED CASES

Debs v. United States (1919)
Upheld the conviction of Socialist Party leader Eugene V. Debs for violating the Espionage Act.

Frohwerk v. United States (1919)
Confirmed the guilty verdict against a newspaper publisher for printing articles opposing U. S. involvement in World War I.

Abrams v. United States (1919)
Upheld convictions of five people under the Espionage Act. Holmes dissented, arguing that their action did not present "a clear and present danger."

The Legal Arguments

Justice Oliver Wendell Holmes, Jr., wrote the Court's unanimous opinion. In ordinary times, Holmes noted, Schenck's claim of First Amendment rights might well be valid. "But the character of every act depends upon the circumstances in which it is done," Holmes added. Schenck distributed the leaflets during wartime, when "many things that might be said in time of peace . . . will not be endured." Holmes suggested that Schenck's "impassioned" appeal for people to oppose the draft was just like someone "falsely shouting fire in a theatre and causing a panic." The First Amendment certainly did not protect such behavior.

Holmes then went on to offer a guide for judging when speech is protected by the First Amendment:

> The question in every case is whether the words used are used in such circumstances and are of such a nature as to create a clear and present danger that they will bring about the . . . evils that Congress has a right to prevent.

Schenck's words, Holmes charged, did pose "a clear and present danger" to the United States war effort. Therefore, they did not merit protection under the First Amendment.

Justice Holmes's opinions in the Espionage Act cases set the standard for free speech.

Why Did It Matter Then?

The Supreme Court decisions in *Schenck* and other Espionage Act cases considered the limits of free speech during wartime. In *Schenck,* Justice Holmes stated that speech that presented "a clear and present danger" to the country's well being was not protected. As he looked at other cases, however, Holmes began to refine this view.

In *Frohwerk* v. *United States* (1919), decided just a week after *Schenck,* the Court again upheld a conviction under the Espionage Act. However, Holmes noted that anti-government speech uttered during wartime is not always a crime. "We do not lose our right to condemn either measures or men because the country is at war," he wrote.

Holmes broadened this statement in his dissent to the majority opinion in *Abrams* v. *United States* (1919). The government's power to limit speech during wartime undoubtedly is greater, he noted, "because war opens dangers that do not exist at other times." However, the basic principles of free speech are the same in war as in peace:

It is only the present danger of immediate evil or an intent to bring it about that warrants Congress in setting a limit to the expression of opinion.

All opinions, even ones we find hateful, should be heard, Holmes concluded.

During the Vietnam War, some Americans vigorously challenged government policies.

Why Does It Matter Now?

The Supreme Court has been asked to decide on free speech issues dozens of times since *Schenck.* In making these decisions, the Court has attempted to heed Justice Holmes's words and strike a balance between protecting free speech and maintaining political and social order.

Over the years, the Court has applied this balance test to free speech questions in many settings, including schools. In *Tinker* v. *Des Moines Independent Community School District* (1969), the Court upheld students' right to protest in school. However, the Court added that in certain circumstances school officials might limit the exercise of such rights—if the students' actions disrupt the work of the school, for example.

In two later cases, *Bethel School District No. 403* v. *Fraser* (1986) and *Hazelwood School District* v. *Kuhlmeier* (1988), the Court felt that such circumstances existed. In *Bethel,* the Court upheld the suspension of a student who, during a school assembly, gave a speech that included inappropriate language. The Court ruled that the school could punish behavior that "interferes with the educational process." In *Hazelwood,* the Court ruled that school officials could censor the content of a student newspaper if it was "inconsistent with [the school's] educational mission."

CONNECT TO HISTORY

1. **Making Inferences** The Supreme Court decided *Schenck* and other Espionage Act cases during the Red Scare. Do you think the timing of the cases influenced the Court's decisions? Why or why not?

 See Skillbuilder Handbook, page R12.

CONNECT TO TODAY

2. **Researching** Working with a group of two or three other students, identify and research recent court cases involving free speech issues. Present your findings in a brief oral report to the class.

For more information on free speech . . .

 RESEARCH LINKS CLASSZONE.COM

Brown v. Board of Education of Topeka (1954)

THE ISSUE School Desegregation

ORIGINS OF THE CASE In September 1950, Oliver Brown tried to enroll his seven-year-old daughter, Linda, at the neighborhood grade school. The school principal rejected Brown's request because Linda was an African American. The school was for white students only. Linda ended up attending a school an hour's bus ride away. Brown filed suit against the school board, demanding that Linda be allowed to go to the neighborhood school. The Supreme Court heard arguments in the *Brown* case in 1952 and 1953.

THE RULING A unanimous court ruled that segregation in education was unconstitutional.

LEGAL *Sources*

U.S. CONSTITUTION/LEGISLATION

Fourteenth Amendment (1868)
"No state shall . . . deprive any person of life, liberty, or property, without due process of law; nor deny to any person within its jurisdiction the equal protection of the laws."

RELATED CASES

Plessy v. Ferguson (1896)
Upheld Louisiana laws that segregated railroad passenger cars according to race. Established the doctrine of "separate but equal."

Brown v. Board of Education of Topeka (May, 1955)
Ordered that desegregation take place "with all deliberate speed." Often called "*Brown II.*"

The Legal Arguments

Chief Justice Earl Warren wrote the Court's decision. He began by reviewing the history of the Fourteenth Amendment. Its equal protection clause was the basis for the decision. The Court had ruled in *Plessy* v. *Ferguson* (1896) that "separate but equal" facilities for blacks and whites did not violate this amendment. However, Warren pointed out that *Plessy* involved transportation, not education. He then stressed the importance of education for society:

> It is doubtful that any child may reasonably be expected to succeed in life if he is denied the opportunity of an education.

Warren went on to suggest that segregation denied African-American children that opportunity. He concluded with *Brown's* most famous statement:

> . . . [I]n the field of public education the doctrine of "separate but equal" has no place. Separate educational facilities are inherently unequal.

The Court expected whites in the South, where segregation was dominant, to resist the ruling. Therefore, it delayed orders on how to put the decision into action for several months.

Thurgood Marshall was one of the team of lawyers that represented Oliver Brown. In 1967, Marshall became the first African American appointed as a Supreme Court justice.

Why Did It Matter Then?

The Fourteenth Amendment had guaranteed African Americans equal rights as citizens. In the late 1800s, however, many Southern states passed "Jim Crow" laws, which enforced separation of the races in public places. In 1896, the Supreme Court upheld a "Jim Crow" law in *Plessy* v. *Ferguson.* In the Court's view, "separate but equal" rail cars did not violate the Fourteenth Amendment.

Brown, however, stated that segregated schools denied African Americans the "equal protection of the laws" guaranteed by the Fourteenth Amendment. Segregation, therefore, had no place in school systems.

As the Court expected, the decision met opposition. One Southern politician accused the Court of "a flagrant abuse of judicial power." Even after *Brown II,* many school districts, particularly in the South, dragged their feet on desegregation. Some 10 years later, segregation was still the rule in most Southern school districts. Even so, the impact of the *Brown* decision on American society was immense. It marked the beginning of the civil rights movement.

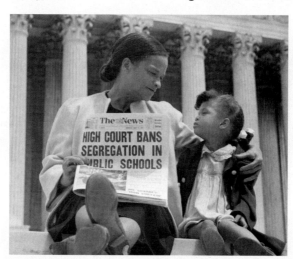

The *Brown* decision was a front-page story in newspapers across the United States.

Why Does It Matter Now?

Throughout the 1960s and 1970s, the Supreme Court continued to review the issue of school segregation. In *Green* v. *New Kent County* (1968), the Court called for the end of the dual school system—one white and one black. This involved integrating not only students, but also teachers, support staff, and services.

In *Swann* v. *Charlotte-Mecklenburg* (1971), the Court ruled that busing could be used to achieve school desegregation. Later, in *Milliken* v. *Bradley* (1974), the Court ruled that students might be bused between school districts to achieve this goal. However, this step could be taken only in very exceptional circumstances.

In recent years, the Court has moved away from enforcing desegregation. Still, the *Brown* decision brought about far-reaching changes. The statement that separate facilities are "inherently unequal" proved a powerful weapon against segregation in all areas of American life. Indeed, the Court's opinion in *Brown* provided the basis for most of the civil rights laws passed in the late 1950s and 1960s.

CONNECT TO HISTORY

1. **Analyzing Points of View** Chief Justice Earl Warren wanted the *Brown* opinion to be unanimous. He even pressured Justice Stanley Reed, a southerner, not to file a dissenting opinion. Why do you think Warren insisted that all the justices agree to the *Brown* decision?

 See Skillbuilder Handbook, page R9.

CONNECT TO TODAY

2. **Researching** Working with a group of two or three other students, conduct research to find out about efforts to desegregate another part of American society, such as the military, the workplace, or colleges. Report your findings to the class.

For more information on civil rights today . . .

Reynolds v. Sims (1964)

THE ISSUE One Person, One Vote

ORIGINS OF THE CASE Most state constitutions require a redrawing of legislative districts every 10 years, based on the latest U.S. Census figures. By the 1960s, however, many states had not redrawn their districts for decades. For example, Alabama's last redrawing—in 1901—did not reflect the great population changes that had taken place. In 1962, a group of Alabama voters sued to have their legislative map redrawn. When a federal court found for the voters, the Alabama state legislature appealed to the Supreme Court.

THE RULING The Court firmly established the principle of "one person, one vote." It ruled that Alabama must redraw its legislative districts so that each district had about the same number of people.

LEGAL Sources

U.S. CONSTITUTION/LEGISLATION

Fourteenth Amendment (1868)
"No state shall . . . deprive any person of life, liberty, or property, without due process of law; nor deny to any person within its jurisdiction the equal protection of the laws."

Alabama Constitution, Article 9, Section 198 (1901)
"The members of the house of representatives shall be apportioned by the legislature among the several counties of the state, according to the number of inhabitants in them, respectively, as ascertained by the decennial census of the United States."

RELATED CASES

Baker v. Carr (1962)
Ruled that federal courts could intervene in state legislative districting issues.

Gray v. Sanders (1963)
Ruled that when counting votes in primary elections, states should follow the principle of "one person, one vote."

The Legal Arguments

The Court's ruling, written by Chief Justice Earl Warren, clearly stated the issue:

> The right to vote freely for the candidate of one's choice is of the essence of a democratic society, and any restrictions on that right strike at the heart of representative government.

Weakening the power of an individual's vote, Warren added, was as much a restriction as preventing that individual from voting.

"Legislators represent people, not trees or acres," Warren continued. Population, therefore, had to be the determining factor in redrawing legislative districts. Warren based his argument squarely on the Fourteenth Amendment:

Chief Justice Earl Warren considered *Reynolds* v. *Sims* one of the most important opinions he had written.

> We hold that as a basic constitutional standard, the Equal Protection Clause requires that seats in . . . a . . . state legislature must be apportioned on a population basis. . . . [T]he Equal Protection Clause requires that a State make an honest and good faith effort to construct districts . . . as nearly of equal population as is practicable.

John Marshall Harlan—the grandson of the justice who wrote the famous dissent to *Plessy* v. *Ferguson*—dissented. He claimed that the Constitution did not give the Court the power to interfere in how states decide on their legislative districts.

Why Did It Matter Then?

Reynolds was one of several voting rights cases that the Court heard in the 1960s. In the first, *Baker* v. *Carr* (1962), the Court broke with past decisions and said that federal courts had the power to make sure that states drew legislative districts fairly. A year later, in *Gray* v. *Sanders* (1963), the Court applied the principle of "one person, one vote" for the first time. The Court observed that the vote of someone living in one part of a state should count as much as that of someone living in another part.

In *Reynolds,* the court extended the "one person, one vote" principle to the drawing of state legislative districts. In time, the *Reynolds* ruling forced most states to draw new district boundaries. As a result, there was a shift in political power in state legislatures. The number of state representatives from cities, which had larger populations, increased. In contrast, the number from rural areas, where fewer people lived, declined.

Why Does It Matter Now?

During the 1990s, the Court faced a new redistricting issue. The Voting Rights Act of 1965 urged states to increase minority representation in the legislatures. To do so, many states created districts where minorities made up a voting majority. However, some white voters challenged these districts under the Fourteenth Amendment.

In several cases—*Bush* v. *Vera* (1996), for example—the Court ruled that such districts were unconstitutional. Since these districts were drawn *solely* based on race, the Court said, they violated the Fourteenth Amendment's equal protection clause. In *Lawyer* v. *Department of Justice* (1997), the Court upheld a Florida district drawn to include several African-American communities. The Court found that in this case, race was only one of several factors used to draw district boundary lines.

After the U.S. Census of 2000, the states began a new round of redistricting. As a result, the Supreme Court probably will revisit this issue over the next few years.

Representation in the Alabama State Legislature, 1962		
COUNTY	POPULATION	NUMBER OF HOUSE REPRESENTATIVES
Bullock	13,462	2
Henry	15,286	2
Mobile	314,301	3
Jefferson	634,864	7

Source: *U.S. Supreme Court, Reynolds v. Sims, 377 U.S. 533 (1964)*

In 1962, the rural counties of Bullock and Henry had less than one-thirtieth of the population of the urban counties of Mobile and Jefferson. Even so, they returned close to half as many state representatives as did the two urban counties.

CONNECT TO HISTORY

1. **Finding Main Ideas** Use library or Internet resources to locate a copy of the majority opinion in *Reynolds* v. *Sims.* Make a chart listing the main idea and details for each part of the opinion. Make a similar chart for Harlan's dissenting opinion in this case.

 See Skillbuilder Handbook, page R5.

CONNECT TO TODAY

2. **Researching** Conduct research to find news stories about a recent Supreme Court decision on the issue of redistricting. Write a summary of the background of the case, the ruling the Court made, and the legal reasoning behind that ruling.

For more information on the Supreme Court and redistricting . . .

Regents of the University of California v. Bakke (1978)

THE ISSUE Affirmative Action

ORIGINS OF THE CASE In 1970, the medical school of the University of California at Davis adopted an "affirmative action" admissions policy. The policy set a quota calling for 16 percent of each year's incoming students to be minority students. Allan Bakke, a white applicant, had better test scores and grades than most of the students accepted under the affirmative action plan. However, he was not admitted. Bakke sued, arguing that he had been rejected because of his race. The California Supreme Court ordered the school to admit Bakke. The school appealed the case to the U.S. Supreme Court.

THE RULING The Court ruled that the school could use race as one of several factors in making admissions decisions but that setting racial quotas was unconstitutional.

LEGAL *Sources*

U.S. CONSTITUTION/LEGISLATION

Fourteenth Amendment (1868)
"No state shall . . . deprive any person of life, liberty, or property, without due process of law; nor deny to any person within its jurisdiction the equal protection of the laws."

Civil Rights Act, Title VI (1964)
"[N]o person in the United States shall, on the ground of race, color, or national origin, be excluded from participation in . . . any program or activity receiving Federal financial assistance."

RELATED CASE

Fullilove v. Klutznick (1980)
The Court upheld the Public Works Employment Act of 1977, which required that minority-owned businesses receive 10 percent of all federal funds for public works projects.

The Legal Arguments

The Court upheld the California Supreme Court decision on a 5-4 vote. Four of the five majority justices maintained that holding a set number of admission slots for minority students violated the Civil Rights Act of 1964. The fifth justice, Justice Lewis Powell, noted that racial quotas violated the Fourteenth Amendment. Powell wrote:

> The guarantee of equal protection cannot mean one thing when applied to one individual and something else when applied to a person of another color. If both are not accorded the same protection, then it is not equal.

However, the Court did not reject affirmative action completely. By a different 5-4 majority, the Court ruled that race could be used as one of several factors in college admissions. Powell, who again provided the deciding vote, thought that race should be considered in order to promote a "diverse student body."

Allan Bakke graduated from the University of California at Davis with a medical degree in 1982.

Why Did It Matter Then?

African Americans made many gains in civil rights during the 1950s and 1960s. President Lyndon Johnson, however, thought more needed to be done. He explained why:

> You do not take a person who for years has been hobbled by chains and . . . bring him up to the starting line of a race and then say, "you are free to compete with all the others" and still justly believe that you have been completely fair.

In 1965, Johnson urged companies to increase the hiring and promoting of minorities.

In time, many businesses, colleges, and other organizations set up affirmative-action programs. Not everyone was happy with this development, however. Some whites felt that affirmative action amounted to little more than "reverse discrimination." That is, they felt that they would be denied jobs or college places because of their race.

With the Bakke ruling, the Supreme Court took a compromise position on affirmative-action programs. They were acceptable, the Court said, as long as they did not use strict racial quotas.

Why Does It Matter Now?

Since *Bakke,* the Court has ruled on several affirmative-action cases. In *Metro Broadcasting* v. *Federal Communications Commission* (1990), for example, the Court upheld a policy that gave preference to minority broadcasters. However, in *Adarand Constructors* v. *Peña* (1995), the Court struck down a similar affirmative-action program.

The standing of affirmative action in college admissions is somewhat clearer, however. Some states have abandoned the policy altogether. In California, for example, voters approved a 1996 referendum banning the state's universities from using affirmative action in admissions.

Washington voters passed a similar measure in 1998. These and other states are looking for new ways to help minority students attend college. One method—adopted by California, Florida, and Texas—guarantees admission to state universities for the top students from each high school graduating class.

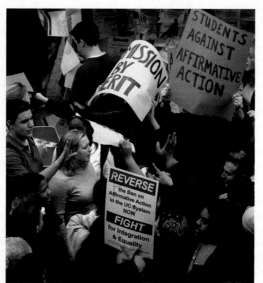

The affirmative-action debate, at times, has been quite bitter. Here, supporters and opponents of affirmative action confront each other at a demonstration on the campus of the University of California at Berkeley.

CONNECT TO HISTORY

1. **Making Inferences** In the *Bakke* case, the Supreme Court issued six separate opinions. Also, the voting on the two issues in the case was 5-4. From this information, what inferences can you draw on the Court's attitudes on affirmative action?

 See Skillbuilder Handbook, page R12.

CONNECT TO TODAY

2. **Researching** The state university system of Michigan recently has faced court challenges to its affirmative-action program. Track the progress of these challenges and write a few paragraphs comparing the arguments and court findings in Michigan to those in the *Bakke* case.

For more information on affirmative action . . .

RESEARCH LINKS
CLASSZONE.COM

The War on Terrorism

Reporter's Notes
By Kevin McCoy

NEW YORK— First came a deep rumble. Then a roar like a giant speeding train. But the sound came crashing from the sky, not along steel tracks. In an instant, a warm, sunny September morning at the World Trade Center in Lower Manhattan became a darkened moonscape of choking cement dust and swirling paper, wailing sirens and screaming victims.

"I heard the rumbling and I looked up, and one of the towers was coming down," said Sergeant Moises Cruz, a New York City police officer who ran for his life with other survivors of the most horrible terrorist attack in U.S. history. Lower Broadway, normally a bustling checkerboard of financial traders, government officials, businessmen and tourists, lay silenced under a three-inch carpet of gritty gray dust.

"I can't even describe it, it was so awful," said Wilbert, a 50-year-old elevator maintenance worker. "All I could do was run."

News reporters who covered the attacks knew instinctively this was the most significant story of a lifetime.

The twin towers of the World Trade Center in New York City, before (inset) and after the terrorist attacks of September 11, 2001

The Attack on America

Flight Path of the Hijacked Airliners, September 11, 2001

L. Michigan

MICHIGAN

L. Ontario

NEW YORK

NEW HAMPSHIRE

Boston

ATLANTIC OCEAN

MASSACHUSETTS

L. Erie

Cleveland

New York City

RHODE ISLAND
CONNECTICUT

INDIANA

OHIO

PENNSYLVANIA
Pittsburgh

• Shanksville

NEW JERSEY

0   50   100 miles
0   50 100 kilometers
Azimuthal Equal–Area Projection

Dulles   **Pentagon**

return path undetermined

DELAWARE

MARYLAND

KENTUCKY

WEST VIRGINIA

WASHINGTON, D.C.

VIRGINIA

N
W   E
S

American Flight 11
American Flight 77
United Flight 93
United Flight 175

McCoy's reporter's instincts were right. Before the day was over, there would be more than 3,000 victims of the most destructive act of terrorism in modern history. **Terrorism** is the calculated use of, or threatened use of, violence against individuals or property for the purpose of intimidating or causing fear for political or social ends.

The terrorist attacks on September 11 were aimed at well-known symbols of the economic and military power of the United States. But what they mainly destroyed was something Americans value much more—the lives of thousands of individual citizens.

UNIMAGINABLE HORROR

On the morning of September 11, 2001, many New Yorkers were heading for work or school when 19 Arab terrorists hijacked four airliners from East Coast airports. The first plane crashed into the upper floors of the north tower of the World Trade Center and exploded into flames. About 20 minutes later, the second plane sliced into the south tower.

Desks, chairs, paper—and people—blew out of the windows of the twin towers. People on the streets below watched in horror as more than a dozen workers on the upper floors jumped from the blazing buildings to their deaths. Other workers poured out of the towers to escape the fire.

Less than an hour after the twin towers were hit, the third hijacked plane rammed into the southwest side of the Pentagon in Arlington, Virginia. It tore a 75-foot gash in the five-sided, five-story building.

That crash site, too, immediately became engulfed in flames. Meanwhile, passengers on the fourth hijacked plane had used their cell phones and had heard about the other plane crashes. Some of the passengers rushed the hijackers and prevented them from striking their intended target, thought to be either the White House or the Capitol.

Because of these heroic efforts, the plane crashed not into a crowded building but into an empty field in Pennsylvania. No one will ever know how many lives the passengers saved as they gave up their own.

Recovery efforts continue on the collapsed section of the Pentagon's southwest side two days after the attack.

The Destruction The planes were loaded with fuel. They became destructive missiles when they crashed into the World Trade Center and the Pentagon. As one investigator noted, the hijackers "couldn't carry anything—other than an atom bomb—that could be as bad as what they were flying."

The explosions and fires so weakened the damaged skyscrapers that they crumbled to the ground less than two hours after impact. The fire and raining debris caused nearby buildings to collapse as well. Nine buildings in New York City's financial district completely or partially collapsed. Six others suffered major damage. The disaster area covered 16 acres. The damage at the Pentagon, though extensive, was confined to one wing of the building.

But it was the toll in human lives that most grieved Americans and others around the world. About 3,000 people died in the attacks. All passengers on the four planes were killed, as well as workers and visitors in the World Trade Center and the Pentagon. The dead included more than 300 New York City firefighters and 40 police officers who rushed to the scene and were buried in the rubble when the skyscrapers collapsed.

Grieving Families and Companies "Please tell the children I love them," said a father of three from the World Trade Center before the phone line went dead. From the burning towers and the hijacked planes,

men and women used their last moments to call and to speak with their families for the last time.

In the first hours and days after the September 11 attacks, family members and friends of people in the World Trade Center frantically tried to find their loved ones. They checked hospitals and posted pictures of the missing on lampposts and walls. The thousands of people who escaped before the towers collapsed were reunited with their families. But only a few survivors were pulled from the wreckage of the buildings. For thousands of people, loved ones never returned home. Also, several businesses with offices in the towers lost large numbers of employees.

The horror of September 11 has haunted more than just the survivors and witnesses of the attacks, although they were the hardest hit. Millions of Americans watched the events on television shortly after they occurred. They, too, would have difficulty forgetting those horrifying images.

RESCUE EFFORTS

Amidst the brutal destruction at the World Trade Center, the courage, selflessness, and noble actions of New York City's firefighters, police officers, and rescue workers stood as a testament. Many of the first

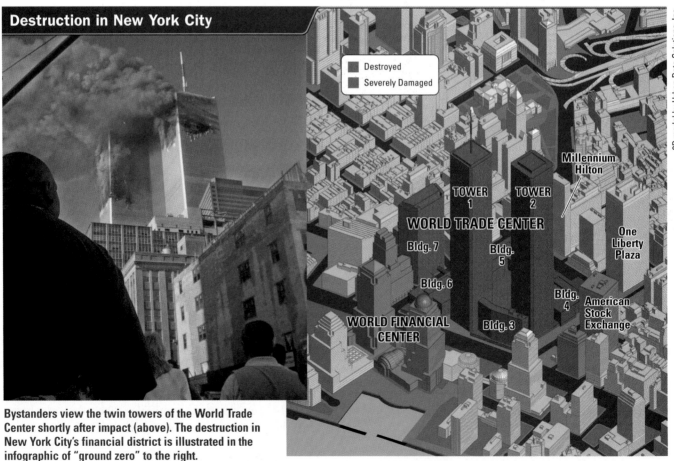

Destruction in New York City

Destroyed
Severely Damaged

Millennium Hilton

TOWER 1   TOWER 2

WORLD TRADE CENTER

Bldg. 7   Bldg. 5

One Liberty Plaza

Bldg. 6

Bldg. 4   American Stock Exchange

WORLD FINANCIAL CENTER   Bldg. 3

3D model by Urban Data Solutions, Inc.

Bystanders view the twin towers of the World Trade Center shortly after impact (above). The destruction in New York City's financial district is illustrated in the infographic of "ground zero" to the right.

How the debris is removed

Truck staging area
Fifty-four city sanitation trucks, parked at 55th and West Side Highway, are dispatched along secure routes to the site to pick up any debris considered still sensitive by the FBI. Separate, privately owned trucks are picking up debris from ConEd and the Transit Authority.

Truck capacity:
6 tons or more

Total debris moved in one day:
6,000 to 10,000 tons

Hudson River

MANHATTAN

55th Street

— Broadway

30th Street

14th Street

— First Avenue

West Street

E. Houston Street

Warren Street

Hot Zone

Broadway

Rector Street

East River

Makeshift morgue where medical examiners inventory and catalog human remains for identification

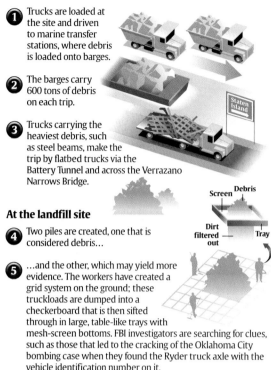

1 Trucks are loaded at the site and driven to marine transfer stations, where debris is loaded onto barges.

2 The barges carry 600 tons of debris on each trip.

3 Trucks carrying the heaviest debris, such as steel beams, make the trip by flatbed trucks via the Battery Tunnel and across the Verrazano Narrows Bridge.

Staten Island

At the landfill site

4 Two piles are created, one that is considered debris...

5 ...and the other, which may yield more evidence. The workers have created a grid system on the ground; these truckloads are dumped into a checkerboard that is then sifted through in large, table-like trays with mesh-screen bottoms. FBI investigators are searching for clues, such as those that led to the cracking of the Oklahoma City bombing case when they found the Ryder truck axle with the vehicle identification number on it.

Screen Debris
Dirt filtered out Tray

Sources: City of New York; Federal Emergency Management Agency; Caterpillar; Mueser Rutledge Consulting Engineers

Reporting by Debbie Howlett and Martha Moore, USA TODAY ®; graphic by Frank Pompa, Robert Ahrens, Adrienne Lewis and Dave Merrill, USA TODAY ®

firefighters at the scene disappeared into the burning buildings to help those inside and never came out again. Entire squads were lost. New York City Fire Department chaplain, Father Mychal Judge, was killed by falling debris just after giving the last rites of the Catholic Church to a firefighter at the scene.

Firefighters worked around the clock trying to find survivors in the wreckage. They had to contend with shifting rubble and smoky, ash-filled air. Medical workers from the area rushed to staff the city's trauma centers. But after the first wave of injured, there were few survivors to treat. One emergency medical technician said, "We were set up for any emergency. It was a great site, full of surgeons. But we were treating firemen and police who needed their eyes washed."

A flood of volunteers assisted rescue workers. Ironworkers helped cut through steel beams, while high school students helped provide water and food for the rescue workers. From around the country, people sent donations of blood, food, and money to New York City. The city kept functioning in the hours and days that followed the attack under the direction of its mayor, Rudy Giuliani.

The Cleanup After the first few days, the work at "ground zero," the World Trade Center disaster site, shifted to recovering bodies and removing the massive amount of debris. The twin towers alone contained more than 200,000 tons of steel, 425,000 cubic yards of concrete, and 14 acres of glass—an estimated 2 billion pounds.

SEARCH FOR TERRORISTS BEGINS

In the weeks that followed, the U.S. government organized a massive effort to identify those responsible for the attacks. Officials concluded that Osama bin Laden, a Saudi Arabian millionaire, directed the terrorists. He had been exiled from his native country because of suspected terrorist activities. Bin Laden was hiding in Afghanistan, protected there by the strict Islamic government known as the Taliban. The effort to bring him to justice would lead the United States to begin military action against Afghanistan in October, as the next section explains.

Thinking Critically

CURRENT EVENTS
CLASSZONE.COM

• Why were the specific targets of the September attacks selected by the terrorists?

• What might cause individuals to use terrorist tactics to attempt to change situations they think are a problem?

AFGHANISTAN— I entered Afghanistan from the north on an aging ferry boat at dusk on October 22. All I could see in the encroaching darkness were silhouettes of Northern Alliance fighters with Kalishnikov weapons slung loosely on their shoulders. My passport was stamped in a small mud hut under a dim lantern, then I was off to the village of Hoja Baddahuin, where the Northern Alliance had set up headquarters after the Taliban had taken over most of the country.

The United States had entered the war in Afghanistan after the terrorist attacks on September 11, 2001. Covering the war in Afghanistan has been the single most challenging experience of my career as a reporter at USA TODAY.

The most dangerous part of the experience was traveling through the front lines as I made my way to Kabul. My jeep had to cross minefields and the most narrow mountain roads imaginable. At Taloqan, the first city to be restored to the Northern Alliance, I wrote my stories while gunfire erupted outside my walled compound. I paid two men to stay inside with their machine guns and to answer the door should someone come knocking. Taliban fighters were still hiding out in houses just down the street. Through it all, I learned to stay calm by doing the best I could to ensure both my safety and the safety of my team, and to leave the rest to a healthy dose of faith.

Selected Terrorist Attacks Around the World Since 1972

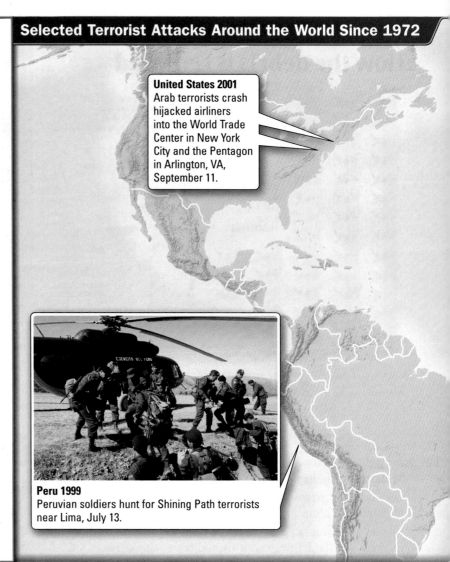

United States 2001
Arab terrorists crash hijacked airliners into the World Trade Center in New York City and the Pentagon in Arlington, VA, September 11.

Peru 1999
Peruvian soldiers hunt for Shining Path terrorists near Lima, July 13.

Hunting for the Terrorists

Terrorism is not new. Reporters like Tim Friend have been covering terrorist attacks across the globe for the last three decades. Throughout history, individuals, small groups, and governments have used terror tactics to try to achieve political or social goals— whether it be to bring down a government, eliminate opponents, or promote a cause.

In recent times, however, terrorism has become an international problem. Since the late 1960s, more than 14,000 terrorist attacks have occurred worldwide. International terrorist groups have carried out increasingly destructive, high-profile attacks to attract global attention. Many countries also face domestic terrorists who oppose their governments' policies or have special interests to promote.

The reasons for modern terrorism are many. The traditional motives, such as gaining independence, expelling foreigners, or changing society, still drive various terrorist groups around the world. These terrorists use violence to force concessions from their enemies, usually the governments in power. But other kinds of terrorists, driven by radical religious motives, began to emerge in the late 20th century.

The goal of these terrorists is the destruction of what they consider the forces of evil. This evil might be located in their own countries or in other parts of the world. These terrorists often threaten to use weapons of mass destruction, such as chemical, biological, or nuclear weapons, to kill their enemies.

West Germany 1972
Israeli athletes are killed after being taken hostage by Arab terrorists at the Summer Olympics in Munich, September 5.

Japan 1995
The Tokyo subway system is attacked with deadly nerve gas by the Aum Shinrikyo cult, March 20.

Northern Ireland 1979
Irish Republican Army assassinates Lord Mountbatten, a member of the British royal family, by blowing up his boat off the Irish coast, August 30.

Israel 2001
Suicide bombings by Hamas terrorists in Jerusalem and Haifa kill and wound many civilians, December.

India 2001
Kashmiri terrorists attack the Indian Parliament Building in New Delhi, with guns and grenades, December 13.

Kenya 1998
U.S. Embassy personnel in Nairobi, Kenya, evacuate area after Arab terrorists detonate truck bombs at embassy buildings there, and in Tanzania, August 7.

TERRORISM AROUND THE WORLD

The problem of international terrorism first came to world attention in a shocking way during the 1972 Summer Olympic Games in Munich, Germany (then West Germany). Eight members of a Palestinian terrorist group called Black September killed two Israeli athletes and took nine others hostage. Five of the terrorists, all the hostages, and a police officer were later killed in a bloody gun battle. The attack became known as the Munich Massacre. Since then, few regions of the world have been spared from terrorist attacks.

The Middle East Like Black September, many terrorist organizations have their roots in the Israeli-Palestinian conflict over land in the Middle East.

("Middle East" is the political term for the geographic region of Southwest Asia.) Arab terrorist groups such as the Palestine Islamic Jihad, Hamas, and Hizballah have sought to prevent a peace settlement between Israel and the Palestinians. They want a homeland for the Palestinians on their own terms, with the most extreme among them denying Israel's right to exist. In a continual cycle of violence, the Israelis retaliate after each terrorist attack, and the terrorists attack again.

Among Muslims in the Middle East, the Israeli-Palestinian violence has bred widespread Arab anger at Israel—and at the United States for supporting Israel. For example, the Lebanese-based group Hizballah seeks to eliminate all non-Islamic influences in Muslim countries. It is thought to have been responsible for bombing the U.S. embassy and marine barracks in Beirut in 1983 and the U.S. embassy annex in Beirut in 1984.

In December 2001, terrorist attacks on Israeli civilians in Jerusalem and Haifa killed 27 people and wounded more than 200. Hamas claimed responsibility, and the Israelis responded with military strikes against Palestinian targets.

Israel then declared a "war on terrorism," patterned after the U.S. response to the September 11 attacks. Moderates in the region believe that the only long-term solution is a compromise between Israel and the Palestinians over the issue of land.

Europe Many countries in Europe—including Great Britain, Germany, and Italy—have been targets of domestic terrorists who oppose government policies. For example, for decades the Irish Republican Army engaged in terrorist attacks against Britain because it opposed British control of Northern Ireland. By 2001, however, the British and the IRA were peacefully negotiating for greater autonomy for Northern Ireland.

Both Germany and Italy have suffered terrorist attacks by extreme left-wing and right-wing domestic groups. In general, left-wing groups oppose capitalism, and right-wing groups support capitalism and oppose government regulation.

These groups sometimes join forces with other terrorist organizations when it suits their purposes. In 1975, for example, West Germany's Red Army Faction and Italy's Red Brigades cooperated with the Palestine Liberation Organization to kidnap officials at a meeting of the Organization of Petroleum Exporting Countries (OPEC) in Vienna, Austria.

South Asia and East Asia South Asia has become another hotbed of terrorism in recent years. Afghanistan became a haven for international terrorists after the extremist Muslim Taliban came to power in 1996. In that year, Osama bin Laden moved to Afghanistan and began using mountain hideouts in that country as a base of operations for his global network of Muslim terrorists known as al-Qaeda.

Muslim extremists from all over the world came to al-Qaeda training camps. Bin Laden and these other extremists were opposed to American influence in Muslim lands. Bin Laden called for terrorist attacks against Americans and U.S. allies.

Terrorist groups have arisen in East Asia, as well. Japanese terrorist groups include the Aum Shinrikyo (Supreme Truth Sect) and the Japanese Red Army. The Aum Shinrikyo (called Aleph since 2000) is a religious cult that wants to control Japan. In 1995, it released sarin, a deadly nerve gas, in subway stations in Tokyo. Twelve people were killed and more than 5,700 injured. This attack brought global attention to the threat of biological and chemical agents as terrorist weapons.

Africa Civil unrest and regional wars were the root causes of most terrorist activity in Africa at the end of the 20th century. But al-Qaeda cells operated in

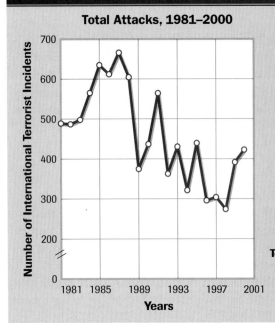

International Terrorist Attacks

Total Attacks, 1981–2000

International Casualties of Terrorism, 1995–2000

	Africa	Asia	Euroasia	Latin America	Middle East	North America	Western Europe
1995	8	5369	29	46	445	0	287
1996	80	1507	20	18	1097	0	503
1997	28	344	27	11	480	7	17
1998	5379	635	12	195	68	0	405
1999	185	690	8	9	31	0	16
2000	102	898	103	20	69	0	4
Totals	5782	9713	199	299	2190	7	1232

Source: U.S. Department of State

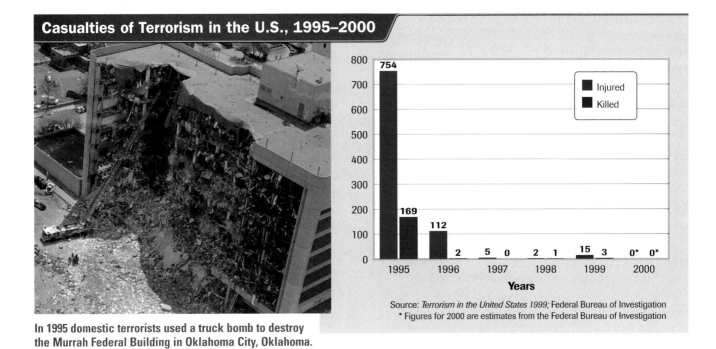

Casualties of Terrorism in the U.S., 1995–2000

In 1995 domestic terrorists used a truck bomb to destroy the Murrah Federal Building in Oklahoma City, Oklahoma.

Source: *Terrorism in the United States 1999;* Federal Bureau of Investigation
* Figures for 2000 are estimates from the Federal Bureau of Investigation

many African countries, and several major attacks against U.S. personnel and facilities in Africa were linked to al-Qaeda.

For example, a 1993 attack on U.S. soldiers in Somalia killed 18. In 1998, bombings at the U.S. embassies in Kenya and Tanzania left 301 dead and more than 5,000 people injured. The United States responded to these attacks with missile strikes on suspected terrorist facilities in Afghanistan, and in Sudan where bin Laden was based from 1991 to 1996.

Latin America In 2000, more terrorist attacks occurred in Latin America than in any other region of the world. Terrorist activity was particularly heavy in Colombia, a country where powerful narcotics organizations have frequently turned to violence. The Revolutionary Armed Forces of Colombia (FARC) is a left-wing guerrilla group responsible for numerous bombings, hijackings, and kidnappings of Colombians and foreign citizens. It has attacked Colombian political, military, and economic targets, as well as those with American ties. FARC is linked to narcotics traffickers.

The region where the borders of Argentina, Brazil, and Paraguay meet has become a center of Islamic extremism and terrorist financing. The Israeli embassy in Buenos Aires, Argentina, was bombed in 1992, and another Israeli target was hit in 1994.

The United States Before September 11, the most destructive act of terrorism on American soil had been the 1995 truck bombing of the Murrah Federal Building in Oklahoma City, Oklahoma. That attack killed 168 people, but it was an act of domestic terrorism. It was carried out by an antigovernment extremist named Timothy McVeigh. Such domestic terrorists are motivated by the belief that the government has too much power to regulate people's lives.

The longest-lasting terrorist campaign by an individual in U.S. history was conducted by Theodore Kaczynski, who was known as the Unabomber. From 1978 to 1995, Kaczynski mailed bombs to business executives and scientists because he opposed the effects of modern technology on society. He killed 3 people and injured 23 others.

The attack on the World Trade Center on September 11 was not the first to have occurred there. A previous attack took place in 1993, when a van filled with explosives was detonated in the center's parking garage. Six people died and more than 1,000 were injured. The person responsible, Ramzi Yousef, was captured and imprisoned, but Osama bin Laden was suspected of being part of the plot. Another bin Laden-linked attack was the bombing of the destroyer USS *Cole* in Yemen in October 2000.

FINDING THOSE RESPONSIBLE

Immediately after the September 11 attacks, the Bush administration launched the largest criminal investigation in U.S. history. The FBI searched across the country—and the world—for clues to the identities of the suicide hijackers and those who aided them.

In an address to Congress and the nation, President George W. Bush pledged, "Whether we bring our enemies to justice or bring justice to our enemies, justice will be done." He called the terrorist attacks "acts of war" and declared that the United States would wage a war to end global terrorism. He vowed that as a part of that war, "We will pursue nations that provide aid or safe haven to terrorism. Every nation in every region now has a decision to make. Either you are with us, or you are with the terrorists."

Seven nations were on a U.S. government list of state sponsors of terrorism in 2001—Iran, Iraq, Syria, Libya, Cuba, North Korea, and Sudan. In addition, Afghanistan, Pakistan, Lebanon, and Yemen were considered major centers of terrorist activity. After the September 11 attacks, however, some of these countries, including Pakistan and Sudan, began to cooperate with the United States in hunting down those responsible.

The investigation into the September 11 attacks soon showed that top leaders in the al-Qaeda network were responsible for planning the attacks. The U.S. government then undertook a worldwide hunt for terrorists linked to al-Qaeda.

The United States built an international coalition, or alliance, to fight the war on terrorism. Canada, China, Great Britain, Pakistan, Russia, and many other nations joined the coalition. They agreed to share intelligence information, to arrest terrorists operating within their borders, and to seize the financial assets of terrorist groups. The coalition also gave support to U.S. military action in Afghanistan.

Great Britain took an especially active role in the coalition. One Londoner left a card at the U.S. embassy that reflected the surge of support that the United States received immediately after the devastating attacks: "Dear America, You supported us in two world wars. We stand with you now."

The War in Afghanistan

The U.S. government first focused its military response on Afghanistan, because that country was the home base of Osama bin Laden's al-Qaeda network. The strict Islamic regime that controlled most of Afghanistan—the Taliban—had harbored bin Laden and al-Qaeda since 1996. In return, bin Laden helped keep the Taliban in power by providing fighters in their civil war against the Northern Alliance, a coalition of anti-Taliban Afghan groups.

The United States demanded that the Taliban turn over bin Laden. After they refused, the United States began military action. The U.S. goals were to find bin Laden, to destroy al-Qaeda, and to end Taliban rule.

USA TODAY first appeared in print 10/16/2001

The corporate structure of Terror Inc.

Osama bin Laden's terrorist organization, al-Qaeda, is organized like a business. Here is a flow chart of its structure, as of the terrorist attacks on September 11, 2001:

Emir
Osama bin Laden

A key member of the military committee is Muhammad Atef, also known as Abu Hafs el Masry. The second-ranking person in al-Qaeda, he was indicted in the U.S. embassy bombings in Kenya and Tanzania in 1998. Atef was killed during the bombing of Afghanistan.

Shura council
A policymaking council of about 30 top aides, business associates and religious scholars.

Ayman al-Zawahri

A key member of the shura council is Ayman al-Zawahri, bin Laden's top aide. The Egyptian-born surgeon, sentenced to death for terrorism in his native country, reportedly slipped into the United States in 1995 as Abdel Moez for a fundraising tour. He supplied $250,000 in 1991 for the purchase of a farm for al-Qaeda in Sudan.

Military committee Atef
Responsible for training, weapons acquisition and planning attacks.

Money/business committee
Runs al-Qaeda business operations. Key members include Abu Fadhl al Makkee and Abu Hammam al Saudi.

Media committee
Ran now-defunct al-Qaeda newspaper, *Newscast*, and did public relations.

Islamic study/fatwah committee
Issues *fatwahs*, or religious edicts, such as an edict in 1998 telling Muslims to kill Americans.

Travel office
Provides plane tickets and fake passports.

Payroll office
Pays al-Qaeda members.

Management office
Oversees money-making businesses (banks, farms).

Abu Fadhl and Abu Hammam managed the business operations and deployed assets and al-Qaeda members. Abu Fadhl was identified in court papers as "the man who bought bin Laden a salt farm in Sudan." Abu Hammam did advance work on the move to Sudan.

Source: Reported by Dennis Cauchon, USA TODAY®

By Dave Merrill, USA TODAY®

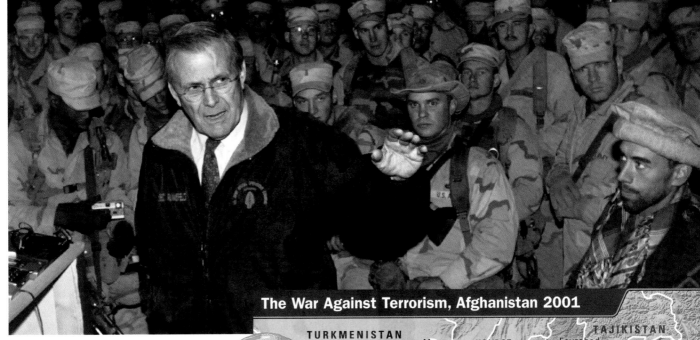

Secretary of Defense Donald Rumsfeld addresses U.S. troops in Afghanistan.

The War Against Terrorism, Afghanistan 2001

TURKMENISTAN

TAJIKISTAN

Mazar-e Sharif
KONDOZ
Feyzabad
TAKHAR
JOWZJAN
BALKH
Konduz
BADAKHSHAN
Baghlan
Talogan
Meymaneh
SAR-E-POL
BAGHLAN
LAGHMAN
SAMANGAN
KAPISA
KONAR
FARYAB
PARVAN
KABUL
BADGHIS
Bamian
BAMIAN
Herat
VARDAK
Kabul
Jalalabad
INDIA
HERAT
GHOWR
LOWGAR
NANGARHAR
Islamabad
AFGHANISTAN
PAKTIA
Shindand
ORUZGAN
GHAZNI
Khowst
FARAH
PAKTIKA
Farah
ZABOL
PAKISTAN
HELMAND
Qandahar
NIMRUZ

IRAN

QANDAHAR

Estimated area of Northern Alliance control
■ Suspected training camps/militia bases
◆ Taliban army bases
✈ Military and/or civilian airfields
Province boundaries

0   100   200 miles
0   100   200 kilometers
Conformal Conic Projection

N   W   E   S

In October 2001, the United States began bombing Taliban air defenses, airfields, and command centers, as well as al-Qaeda training camps. On the ground, the United States relied on anti-Taliban groups—first, the Northern Alliance and later, the Eastern Alliance—to do most of the fighting against the Taliban. These Afghan groups were assisted by U.S. air strikes against Taliban military positions and by a small number of U.S. special-forces troops and marines.

In December, the Taliban were driven from power, but the fight to destroy al-Qaeda continued. Meanwhile, the United Nations worked with the Northern Alliance and other Afghan groups to establish an interim government to replace the Taliban.

A number of nations in the antiterrorism coalition actively assisted the United States in Afghanistan, including Pakistan. The Pakistanis shared intelligence information and allowed the United States to stage military operations from their country.

Pakistan, a Muslim country, took a political risk by giving support to the United States. The Pakistani government's actions were opposed by groups within Pakistan who believed the antiterrorism campaign to be anti-Islamic.

The United States tried to make it clear to Muslim nations that the antiterrorism campaign was *not* anti-Islamic and that Americans respected the religion of Islam. For the United States, maintaining the support of moderate Muslim leaders was important to the long-term success of the war against terrorism—a war that in its next phase would target other nations that supported international terrorism.

Thinking Critically

CURRENT EVENTS
CLASSZONE.COM

• How will the graph on page US8 change when the statistics for the year 2001 are added?

• What are some of the reasons for domestic terrorism in the various regions of the world?

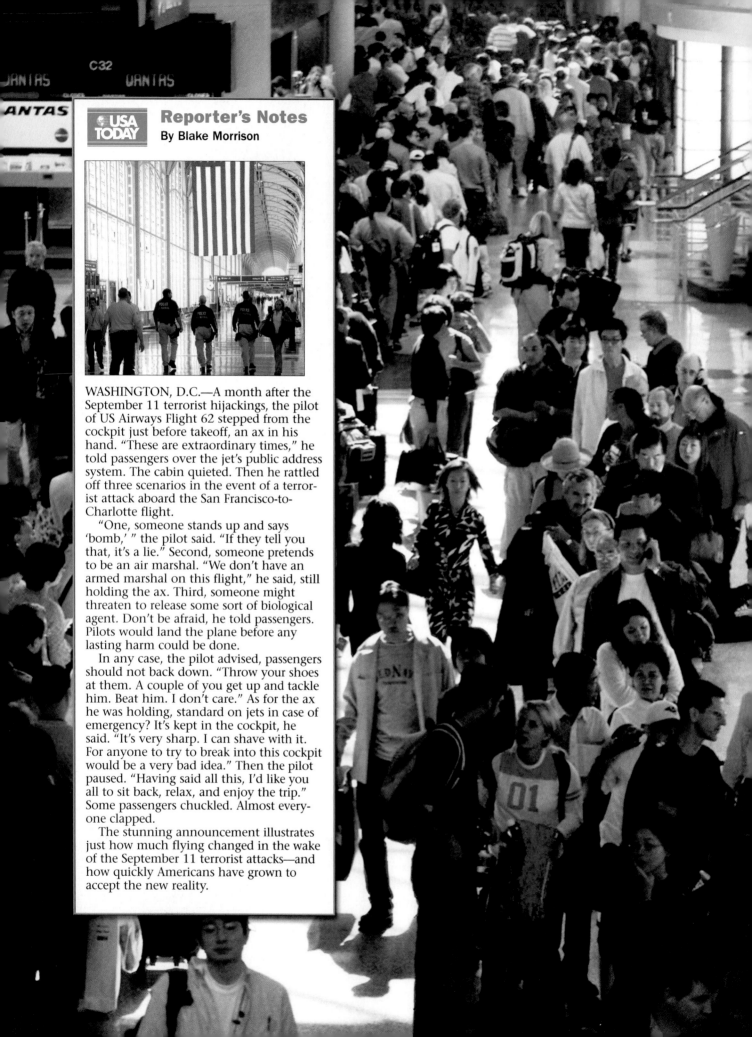

WASHINGTON, D.C.—A month after the September 11 terrorist hijackings, the pilot of US Airways Flight 62 stepped from the cockpit just before takeoff, an ax in his hand. "These are extraordinary times," he told passengers over the jet's public address system. The cabin quieted. Then he rattled off three scenarios in the event of a terrorist attack aboard the San Francisco-to-Charlotte flight.

"One, someone stands up and says 'bomb,'" the pilot said. "If they tell you that, it's a lie." Second, someone pretends to be an air marshal. "We don't have an armed marshal on this flight," he said, still holding the ax. Third, someone might threaten to release some sort of biological agent. Don't be afraid, he told passengers. Pilots would land the plane before any lasting harm could be done.

In any case, the pilot advised, passengers should not back down. "Throw your shoes at them. A couple of you get up and tackle him. Beat him. I don't care." As for the ax he was holding, standard on jets in case of emergency? It's kept in the cockpit, he said. "It's very sharp. I can shave with it. For anyone to try to break into this cockpit would be a very bad idea." Then the pilot paused. "Having said all this, I'd like you all to sit back, relax, and enjoy the trip." Some passengers chuckled. Almost everyone clapped.

The stunning announcement illustrates just how much flying changed in the wake of the September 11 terrorist attacks—and how quickly Americans have grown to accept the new reality.

The Impact on American Life

 first appeared in print 9/18/2001

Airport security tightens up

As the nation's 400 airports get back to business, passengers around the country are finding tighter security. Since the Sept. 11 hijacking of four U.S. airliners, the procedures from ticket counter to gate are stiffer. Airlines are recommending that passengers arrive between two and four hours early for flights. Security measures and wait times varied widely, according to USA TODAY® reporters.

Security
Passengers, and their families and friends, could all go to the gate. Keys, cell phones and change could be dropped into plastic dishes or cups to one side of the metal detectors. Hand-held sensors were used if metal still detected, or sometimes a manual pat-down.

Check in
Photo ID required. Ticket agent asks "Have your bags been in your possession since you packed them?"

Curb-side luggage check-in permitted

No curb-side luggage check permitted.

Carry-on
Bags are placed on a conveyor belt and contents displayed on a screen. Security employees are trained to spot suspicious objects.

Increased use of bomb-sniffing dogs. Dogs and police officers were highly visible at Newark International.

Before security checkpoint
Passengers asked to show tickets and photo IDs again.

Security
Only passengers beyond this point. Cell phones, keys, pagers and other loose objects have to be put on the conveyor belts, where they are screened, according to passengers at San Francisco and Chicago airports Monday. Knives and cutting tools prohibited. Overhead metal detectors are being used in addition to hand-held units. In Baltimore, some bags were checked for bomb dust.

Before the Sept. 11 attack

After the attack

Check in
Baggage checked randomly. Photo ID required. In some cases, passengers had to exchange e-tickets for paper tickets. Passengers still asked if they have had their bags in their possession since packing.

Sources: FAA; reporting by Jack Gruber, Debbie Howlett, Martin Kasindorf, USA TODAY®; and Reed Stacey

By Frank Pompa, USA TODAY®

After the September 11 attacks, many Americans reported feeling that everything had changed—that life would never be the same. Before, Americans had viewed war as something that happened in other countries. Now they felt vulnerable, and the threat of terrorism began to affect many aspects of American life—as the experience of those on Flight 62 showed.

THE AIRLINES AND THE ECONOMY

In the wake of the terrorist attacks, the Federal Aviation Administration (FAA) shut down all airports in the United States for the first time in the nation's history. They did so to prevent any other hijackings. When the airports reopened and flights resumed a few days later, the airlines had few passengers. Some people did not feel safe flying, and others did not want to face the delays caused by tighter airport security.

The number of passengers dropped 43 percent in the days after flights resumed. The airline industry lost an estimated $5 billion in September and cut more than 100,000 jobs to reduce their costs. Congress quickly passed a $15-billion-aid package to help the industry get through the crisis. After September, airline business partially recovered. But even months later, the passenger airfleet was still flying well below capacity.

Industries related to the airlines also suffered. Travel agents, hotels, resorts, and theme parks all lost business. Also hard hit was the insurance industry, which would have to pay billions in death and property loss claims due to the attacks.

The New York Stock Exchange and other stock markets closed after the attacks and did not reopen until the following Monday. The last time the New York exchange had shut down for more than three days was in 1914, at the start of World War I. After the stock markets reopened, the Dow Jones Industrial Average suffered its biggest weekly drop since the Great Depression—14.3 percent.

Over the next few weeks, the markets began to rebound, but the economy continued to decline. Consumers spent less, and unemployment rose. Experts believed that the attacks had only worsened an economic slowdown that had begun early in 2001. They agreed that the nation was in a recession.

THE ANTHRAX THREAT

Not long after September 11th, terrorism struck America again, but in a different form. Letters containing spores of a bacterium that causes the disease anthrax were sent to persons in the news media and to members of Congress in Washington, D.C.

Anthrax bacteria can cause illness when they come in contact with skin or when inhaled. The skin form of anthrax is usually not fatal. But if anthrax bacteria are inhaled, the poisons they produce can damage body tissues. If not treated quickly, inhalation anthrax can cause death.

The threat of biological warfare became real when letters containing the anthrax bacterium (right) were sent to some members of the U.S. Congress in Washington D.C. (below) and persons in the news media after the September 11 attacks.

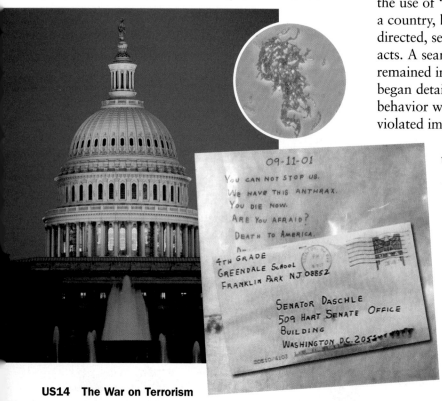

Five people who came in contact with spores from the tainted letters died of inhalation anthrax. Two were postal workers. Many others contracted the skin form of the disease. Thousands who were exposed to anthrax were treated with antibiotics.

The anthrax scare frightened many Americans. The U.S. Postal Service warned Americans to be suspicious of mail without return addresses or in strange packages and to wash their hands after handling mail. Many businesses began taking precautions.

Investigators did not immediately find a link between the anthrax letters and the September 11 attacks. Some experts believed that the anthrax letters might be the work of a lone terrorist rather than an organized group. The anthrax scare not only made Americans fearful of the mail but also of the threat of other biological or chemical weapons, such as the smallpox virus or the nerve gas sarin.

ANTITERRORISM MEASURES

The federal government warned Americans that additional terrorist attacks were likely. It then took actions to prevent such attacks. The Office of Homeland Security was created to coordinate national efforts against terrorism. Antiterrorism measures included a search for terrorists in the United States, the passage of an antiterrorism law, and the adoption of new aviation security regulations.

Searching for Terrorists The al-Qaeda network was able to carry out its terrorist attacks partly through the use of "sleepers." These are agents who move to a country, blend into a community, and then, when directed, secretly prepare for and carry out terrorist acts. A search to find any al-Qaeda terrorists who remained in the United States was started. Officials began detaining and questioning Arabs whose behavior was considered suspicious or who had violated immigration regulations.

Because the hijackers had been Arabs, the government held that the actions were justified. But some critics charged that detaining these men was unfair to the innocent and violated their civil rights. In one incident, Mohammed Irshaid, a Jordanian-born civil engineer who had lived in the United States for more than 20 years, was jailed for three weeks without being charged. His three children were American citizens. Although the incident humiliated him, he said that it "doesn't change my love of America."

President George W. Bush discusses the war against terrorism with advisers, including Vice President Dick Cheney (left) and Secretary of State Colin Powell (right).

More than three million Arab Americans live in the United States, and many were viewed with distrust by other Americans after the September 11 attacks. In one incident, three Arab Americans were taken off a plane when other passengers refused to fly with them. After questioning the men, officials allowed them to take a later flight.

Such incidents sparked debate about the need to respect civil rights while conducting searches for terrorists. The government argued that it was not unusual to curtail civil liberties during wartime in order to protect national security. This argument was also used to justify a proposal to try some terrorist suspects in military tribunals rather than in criminal courts.

Antiterrorism Law On October 26, 2001, President Bush signed into law an antiterrorism bill. The law allowed the government to
- detain foreigners suspected of terrorism for seven days without charging them with a crime
- tap all phones used by suspects and monitor their e-mail and Internet use
- make search warrants valid across states
- order U.S. banks to investigate sources of large foreign accounts
- prosecute terrorist crimes without any time restrictions or limitations

Again, critics warned that these measures would let the government infringe on people's civil rights.

Aviation Security The federal government also increased its involvement in aviation security. The Federal Aviation Administration ordered airlines to install bars on cockpit doors to prevent passengers from gaining control of planes, as the hijackers had done. Sky marshals were assigned to fly on planes; National Guard troops began patrolling airports.

In November 2001, a new aviation-security law made airport security the responsibility of the federal government. Previously, individual airports had been responsible. The law provided for a federal security force that would inspect passengers and carryon bags. It also required the screening of checked baggage.

Airline and government officials debated these and other measures for making air travel more secure. Major concerns were long delays at airports and respect for passengers' privacy. It also became clear that public debate over security measures would continue as long as the United States fights terrorism and tries to balance national security with civil rights.

Thinking Critically

- Is it important for the U.S. government to respect people's civil rights as it wages a war against terrorism? Why or why not?
- What has been the greatest impact of terrorism on American life, aside from the tragic deaths caused by the September 11 attacks?

RAND MCNALLY
World Atlas

CONTENTS

Complete Legend for Physical and Political Maps

Symbols

 Lake

 Salt Lake

 Seasonal Lake

 River

\ Waterfall

—— Canal

△ Mountain Peak

▲ Highest Mountain Peak

Cities

■ Los Angeles   City over 1,000,000 population

▣ Calgary   City of 250,000 to 1,000,000 population

• Haifa   City under 250,000 population

✹ *Paris*   National Capital

★ Vancouver   Secondary Capital (State, Province, or Territory)

Type Styles Used to Name Features

CHINA   Country

ONTARIO   State, Province, or Territory

PUERTO RICO (U.S.)   Possession

ATLANTIC OCEAN   Ocean or Sea

A l p s   Physical Feature

Borneo   Island

Boundaries

 International Boundary

 Secondary Boundary

Land Elevation and Water Depths

Land Elevation

Meters	Feet
3,000 and over --	-- 9,840 and over
2,000 - 3,000 --	-- 6,560 - 9,840
500 - 2,000 --	-- 1,640 - 6,560
200 - 500 --	-- 656 - 1,640
0 - 200 --	-- 0 - 656

Water Depth

Less than 200 --	-- Less than 656
200 - 2,000 --	-- 656 - 6,560
Over 2,000 --	-- Over 6,560

ARCTIC OCEAN

GREENLAND (Den.)

Baffin Bay

Arctic Circle

RUSSIA   ALASKA
          Yukon (U.S.)
Anchorage•

ICELAND

FAROE IS. (Den.)

Hudson Bay

UNITED KINGDOM

IRELAND
London

CANADA

Aleutian Islands

Vancouver

Missouri

Montréal•
Ottawa⊛

Chicago•

Newfoundland

FRANCE

UNITED STATES

Colorado

New York•
Washington D.C.⊛

Azores (Port.)

PORTUGAL
Madrid
SPAIN

Los Angeles•

Casablanca

MOROCCO

Houston•

ATLANTIC

MIDWAY IS. (U.S.)

Tropic of Cancer

MEXICO

Gulf of Mexico

BAHAMAS

Canary Islands (Sp.)

W. SAHARA

Hawaiian Islands (U.S)

Mexico City⊛

CUBA

DOM. REP.

MAURITANIA

MALI

CAPE VERDE

PACIFIC

BELIZE
GUAT. HOND.
EL. SAL. NIC.

HAITI   PUERTO RICO (U.S.)
JAMAICA

Caribbean Sea

SENEGAL
GAMBIA
GUINEA-BISSAU

Niger

BURK.
FASO
GUINEA

COTE
D'IVOIRE

SIERRA LEONE

LIBERIA

COSTA RICA

Caracas⊛

TRINIDAD AND TOBAGO

PANAMA

VENEZUELA

GUYANA

SURINAME
FRENCH GUIANA

COLOMBIA

KIRIBATI

Equator

Galapagos Islands (Ecuador)

ECUADOR

Amazon

OCEAN

PERU
Lima⊛

BRAZIL

OCEAN

SAMOA

AMERICAN SAMOA

BOLIVIA

ST. HELENA (U.K.)

COOK ISLANDS (N.Z.)

TONGA

FRENCH POLYNESIA

Tropic of Capricorn

PARAGUAY

Rio de Janeiro•

Easter Island (Chile)

ARGENTINA

URUGUAY

Santiago⊛

CHILE

Buenos⊛
Aires

N

0   1000   2000 Miles
0 1000 2000 3000 Kilometers
Copyright by Rand McNally & Co.
Robinson Projection

FALKLAND IS. (U.K.)

South Georgia (U.K.)

South Orkney Is. (U.K.)

Antarctic Circle

South Shetland Is. (U.K.)

Weddell Sea

ARCTIC OCEAN

Franz Josef
Land

pitsbergen
(Nor.)

Novaya
Zemlya

75°

ORWAY

FINLAND

SWEDEN

DEN.

EST.
LAT.
LITH.

BELARUS

Yenisey

Ob'

Lena

R U S S I A

60°

Bering
Sea

GERMANY

POLAND

CZ.
AUS. SLVK.
SWITZ. HUNG.
CRO
BOS. ROM.
SER. BUL.

UKRAINE

MOLD.

Volga

Moscow

Novosibirsk

Sea of Okhotsk

45°

ITALY

ALB. MA.
GREECE

GEO.
ARM. AZER.

Black Sea

KAZAKHSTAN

M O N G O L I A

NORTH
KOREA

Sea of Japan

JAPAN

Rome

TURKEY

CYPRUS LEB.
SYRIA

UZBEKISTAN

KYRG.

Beijing

SOUTH
KOREA

Tokyo

Crete

TUNISIA

Mediterranean Sea

ISRAEL
JORDAN

IRAQ

TURKMENISTAN

TAJIK.

C H I N A

Shanghai

30°

PACIFIC

Tropic of Cancer

LGERIA

LIBYA

EGYPT

Cairo

KUWAIT

SAUDI

QATAR

IRAN

AFGHANISTAN

Ganges

NEPAL

BHU.

Chang Jiang
Yangtze

TAIWAN

NORTHERN
MARIANA ISLANDS
(U.S.)

WAKE ISLAND
(U.S.)

NIGER

CHAD

ARABIA

U.A.E.

PAKISTAN

Kolkata
(Calcutta)

BNGL.

Guangzhou

MYANMAR

15°

SUDAN

Red Sea

OMAN

YEMEN

Mumbai
(Bombay)

I N D I A

Arabian
Sea

Bay of
Bengal

LAOS

THAILAND

South China
Sea

PHILIPPINES

GUAM (U.S.)

O C E A N

NIGERIA

Lagos

CENTRAL
AFRICAN
REPUBLIC

Addis
Ababa

DJIBOUTI

ETHIOPIA

SRI LANKA

Bangkok

CAMBODIA

VIETNAM

PALAU

FED. STATES OF
MICRONESIA

MARSHALL
ISLANDS

CAMEROON

QUATORIAL
GUINEA

Congo

UGANDA

KENYA

SOMALIA

MALDIVES

BRUNEI

MALAYSIA

GABON

RWANDA

SINGAPORE

Borneo

New Guinea

SOLOMON
ISLANDS

0°

Equator

REP. OF
CONGO

DEM. REP.
OF CONGO

BURUNDI

TANZANIA

SEYCHELLES

Sumatra

Jakarta

INDONESIA

PAPUA
NEW GUINEA

Java

EAST TIMOR

ANGOLA

ZAMBIA

COMOROS

I N D I A N

Darwin

15°

Coral Sea

VANUATU

NAMIBIA

ZIMBABWE

MOZAMBIQUE

MADAGASCAR

MAURITIUS

REUNION
(Fr.)

NEW CALEDONIA
(Fr.)

FIJI

Tropic of Capricorn

BOTSWANA

MALAWI

O C E A N

A U S T R A L I A

SOUTH
AFRICA

SWAZILAND

LESOTHO

Perth

Darling

Sydney

30°

Cape Town

Melbourne

NEW ZEALAND

Tasmania

Wellington

Kerguelen
Islands
(Fr.)

45°

60°

Antarctic Circle

A N T A R C T I C A

75°

15° 30° 45° 60° 75° 90° 105° 120° 135° 150° 180°

⊛ National Capital

• Major Cities

ARCTIC OCEAN

Baffin
Bay

Greenland

Jan Maye

Baffin
Island

Arctic Circl

Iceland

Faroe Is.

Yukon

Mt. McKinley △
20,320 Ft.
6,194m

Mackenzie

Canadian Shield

Hudson
Bay

British
Isle

Londo

Aleutian Islands

Vancouver

NORTH
AMERICA

Newfoundland

Rocky Mountains

Great Plains

St. Lawrence

Iberian
Peninsu

Los Angeles

Colorado

Mississippi

Appalachian Mts.

Washington D.C.

Azores

Cape Hatteras

ATLANTIC

Atlas
Mts.

Midway Is.

Tropic of Cancer

Baja
California

Gulf of Mexico

Canary
Islands

Hawaiian
Islands

Yucatan
Peninsula

Cuba

Hispaniola

Puerto Rico

Cape
Verde
Islands

15°

Jamaica

Caribbean
Sea

Cape Verde

PACIFIC

Orinoco

Trinidad

Niger

OCEAN

Palmyra

0°
Equator

Galapagos Islands

Amazon

Amazon

Kiribati

SOUTH

Basin

OCEAN

Marquesas Is.

Andes

AMERICA

Samoa
Islands

15°

Mato Grosso
Plateau

St. Helena

Tonga
Is.

Cook
Islands

Tahiti

Tropic of Capricorn

Andes

Rio de Janeiro

Easter Island

Paraná

N

30°

△ Mt. Aconcagua
22,831 Ft.
6,959m

Archipiélago
Juan Fernández

Buenos Aires

Chatham Is.

Patagonia

45°

0   1000   2000 Miles

Falkland Is.

South
Georgia

0   1000   2000   3000 Kilometers

Tierra del Fuego

South
Sandwich Is.

Copyright by Rand McNally & Co.
Robinson Projection

Cape Horn

South
Orkney Is.

60°

South
Shetland Is.

Antarctic
Peninsula

Weddell
Sea

Antarctic Circle

75°

Ross
Sea

Marie
Byrd
Land

△ Vinson Massif
16,066 Ft.
4,897m

ARCTIC OCEAN

75°

Spitsbergen
Franz Josef Land
Novaya Zemlya
North Cape
Scandinavian Peninsula
North Sea
Yenisey
Ob'
Lena
Siberia
60°
Bering Sea
Sea of Okhotsk
Kamchatka Peninsula

EUROPE
Alps
Volga
Moscow
Ural Mts.
Don
Caucasus
Black Sea
Mt. Elbrus 18,510 Ft. 5,642m
Sardinia
Balkan Peninsula
Sicily
Crete
Cyprus
Zagros Mts.
Cairo
Sahara Desert
Arabian Peninsula
Nile
Red Sea
Altai Mts.
ASIA
Pamir
Indus
Plateau of Tibet
Himalayas
Mt. Everest 29,035 Ft. 8,850m
Ganges
Gobi Desert
Beijing
Huang
Yangtze
Amur
Sakhalin
Hokkaidō
Sea of Japan
Honshū
Kyūshū
East China Sea
45°
Mariana Islands
PACIFIC
Tropic of Cancer
30°
Wake Island
Guam
OCEAN

AFRICA
Sahel
Gulf of Guinea
Congo
Congo Basin
Rift Valley
Ethiopian Plateau
Kilimanjaro 19,340 Ft. 5,895m
Zambezi
Kalahari Desert
Mumbai (Bombay)
Arabian Sea
Deccan Plateau
Socotra
Lakshadweep
Maldive Islands
Sri Lanka
Bay of Bengal
Mekong
Hainan Island
South China Sea
Taiwan
Luzon
Mindanao
Malay Peninsula
Sumatra
Borneo
Celebes
Java
Timor
New Guinea
Palau Islands
Caroline Islands
Solomon Islands
Marshall Islands
15°
Equator
0°

Seychelles
INDIAN
Madagascar
Mauritius
Reunion
OCEAN
Cocos Island
New Hebrides
New Caledonia
Fiji Is.
Coral Sea
Great Sandy Desert
AUSTRALIA
Great Dividing Range
Darling
Cape Leeuwin
Sydney
North Island
Aoraki (Mt. Cook) 12,316 Ft. 3,754m
Tasmania
South Island
Tropic of Capricorn
30°
45°

Cape of Good Hope
Cape Town

Kerguelen Islands

Queen Maud Land
Enderby Land
Wilkes Land
Victoria Land
60°
Antarctic Circle
75°

ANTARCTICA

15° 30° 45° 60° 75° 90° 105° 120° 135° 150° 180°

Land Elevation		
Meters		Feet
3,000		9,840
2,000		6,560
500		1,640
200		656
0		0

Water Depth		
0		0
200		656
2,000		6,560

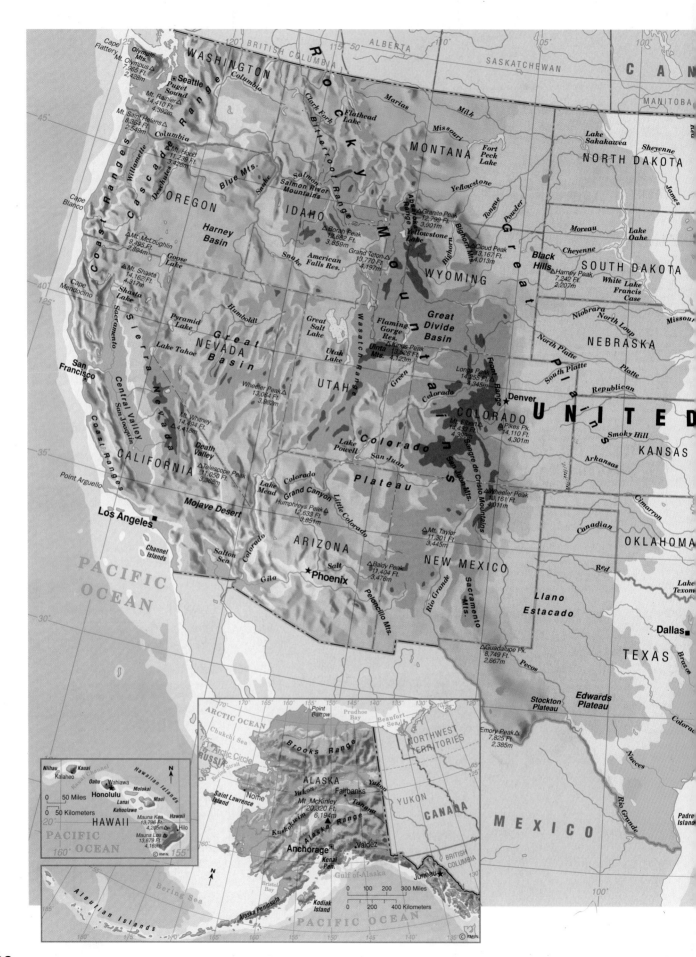

PACIFIC OCEAN

WASHINGTON

Cape Flattery
Olympic Mts.
Mt. Olympus
7,965 Ft.
2,428m
Seattle
Puget Sound
Mt. Rainier
14,410 Ft.
4,392m
Mt. Saint Helens
8,364 Ft.
2,549m
Columbia

BRITISH COLUMBIA
ALBERTA
SASKATCHEWAN

Columbia

Clark Fork
Bitterroot Range
Flathead Lake
Marias
Milk
Missouri
Fort Peck Lake

MONTANA
Yellowstone
Tongue
Powder

Moreau
Lake Oahe

NORTH DAKOTA
Sheyenne
James
Lake Sakakawea

MANITOBA
C A N

Mt. Hood
11,239 Ft.
3,426m
Deschutes

OREGON
Blue Mts.
Salmon
Salmon River Mountains

IDAHO
Borah Peak
12,662 Ft.
3,859m
Snake
American Falls Res.
Grand Teton
13,770 Ft.
4,197m

Absaroka Range
Granite Peak
12,799 Ft.
3,901m
Yellowstone Lake

Bighorn
Cloud Peak
13,167 Ft.
4,013m
Bighorn Mts.

WYOMING

Great

Moreau

Cheyenne

SOUTH DAKOTA

Black Hills
Harney Peak
7,242 Ft.
2,207m
White Lake Francis Case

Niobrara
North Loup
Missouri

Cape Blanco
Mt. McLoughlin
9,495 Ft.
2,894m
Goose Lake

Harney Basin

Snake

Cascade Ranges

Coast Ranges

Willamette

Cape Mendocino
Mt. Shasta
14,162 Ft.
4,317m
Shasta Lake

Pyramid Lake
Humboldt

Lake Tahoe

Great
NEVADA
Basin

Great Salt Lake
Utah Lake

Wasatch Range
Flaming Gorge Res.
Uinta Mts.
13,528 Ft.
4,123m
Kings Peak

Great Divide Basin

Green

Front Range
Longs Peak
14,255 Ft.
4,345m

North Platte

South Platte

Platte
Republican

NEBRASKA

San Francisco

Sierra Nevada

Wheeler Peak
13,064 Ft.
3,982m

Mt. Whitney
14,494 Ft.
4,418m

UTAH

Lake Powell

Colorado

Denver
Mt. Elbert
14,433 Ft.
4,399m
Pikes Pk.
14,110 Ft.
4,301m
COLORADO

Sangre de Cristo Mountains
San Juan
Wheeler Peak
13,161 Ft.
4,011m

U N I T E D
Smoky Hill

KANSAS
Arkansas

Central Valley
San Joaquin

Death Valley
Telescope Peak
11,050 Ft.
3,368m

CALIFORNIA

Lake Mead

Colorado
Grand Canyon
Humphreys Peak
12,633 Ft.
3,851m
Little Colorado

Colorado Plateau

San Juan

Mt. Taylor
11,301 Ft.
3,445m

Canadian

OKLAHOMA

Red

Coast Ranges

Point Arguello

Los Angeles

Channel Islands

Mojave Desert

Salton Sea

Colorado

Gila

Salt
Phoenix

ARIZONA

Baldy Peak
11,404 Ft.
3,476m

Rio Grande

Sacramento Mts.

NEW MEXICO

Pecos

Llano Estacado

Canadian

Cimarron

Lake Texoma

TEXAS
Dallas

Brazos

PACIFIC OCEAN

Peloncillo Mts.

Guadalupe Pk.
8,749 Ft.
2,667m

Pecos

Stockton Plateau

Edwards Plateau

Emory Peak
7,825 Ft.
2,385m

Colorado

Nueces

Rio Grande

M E X I C O

Padre Island

HAWAII inset:
Niihau
Kalaheo
Kauai
Oahu
Wahiawa
Honolulu
Molokai
Lanai
Maui
Kahoolawe
Hawaiian Islands
Kauai Channel
0 50 Miles
0 50 Kilometers
HAWAII
Mauna Kea
13,796 Ft.
4,205m
Hawaii
Hilo
Mauna Loa
13,679 Ft.
4,169m
PACIFIC OCEAN

ALASKA inset:
ARCTIC OCEAN
Chukchi Sea
Point Barrow
Prudhoe Bay
Beaufort Sea
NORTHWEST TERRITORIES
RUSSIA
Bering Strait
Arctic Circle
Brooks Range
Saint Lawrence Island
Nome
ALASKA
Yukon
Fairbanks
Tanana
Yukon
Kuskokwim
Mt. McKinley
20,320 Ft.
6,194m
Alaska Range
YUKON
CANADA
Anchorage
Valdez
Kenai Pen.
Gulf of Alaska
BRITISH COLUMBIA
Juneau
Bristol Bay
Kodiak Island
Alaska Peninsula
Aleutian Islands
Bering Sea
PACIFIC OCEAN
0 100 200 300 Miles
0 200 400 Kilometers

CANADA

MINNESOTA

Minneapolis

Minnesota

Lake of the Woods

Lake Winnipeg

Lake Superior

Isle Royale

Keweenaw Peninsula

Whitefish Point

Great Lakes

ONTARIO

Lake Nipigon

QUEBEC

St. Lawrence

Montréal

Toronto

NEW BRUNSWICK

MAINE

Mt. Katahdin 5,268 Ft. 1,606m

Moosehead Lake

Kennebec

VERMONT

White Mts.

Mt. Washington 6,288 Ft. 1,917m

NEW HAMPSHIRE

Lake Champlain

Green Mts.

Connecticut

MASS. ★Boston

Cape Cod

Nantucket Island

WISCONSIN

Lake Winnebago

Wisconsin

Chippewa

MICHIGAN

Upper Peninsula

Bruce Peninsula

Georgian Bay

Lake Huron

Lower Peninsula

Muskegon

Grand

Saginaw Bay

Lake Michigan

Lake Ontario

Niagara Falls

Allegheny Plateau

Catskill Mts.

Hudson

NEW YORK

Adirondack Mountains

Long Island

CONNECTICUT R.I.

New York

IOWA

Iowa

Des Moines

Chicago

Detroit

Lake Erie

Maumee

INDIANA

OHIO

Ohio

Scioto

Wabash

PENNSYLVANIA

Appalachian Mountains

Susquehanna

Philadelphia

NEW JERSEY

Delaware Bay

DELAWARE

MARYLAND

ATLANTIC OCEAN

S T A T E S

Kansas

ILLINOIS

Illinois

White

Missouri

Lake of the Ozarks

St. Louis

Mississippi

MISSOURI

Ozark Plateau

Neosho

nt Hills

Boston Mts.

White

Arkansas

Ouachita Mts.

ARKANSAS

Ouachita

Sabine

Sam Rayburn Res.

Toledo Bend Res.

Red

Trinity

LOUISIANA

Houston

New Orleans

Atchafalaya Bay

Mississippi Delta

GULF OF MEXICO

WEST VIRGINIA

VIRGINIA

Washington D.C.

James

Chesapeake Bay

Roanoke

Albemarle Sound

Cape Hatteras

Pamlico Sound

KENTUCKY

Green

Cumberland

Cumberland Lake

Kentucky Lake

Cumberland Plateau

Mississippi

Yazoo

Tennessee

TENNESSEE

Appalachian

Blue Ridge

Mt. Mitchell 6,684 Ft. 2,037m

Piedmont

NORTH CAROLINA

Cape Lookout

Cape Fear

Pee Dee

SOUTH CAROLINA

Clarks Hill Lake

Santee

Coastal Plain

MISSISSIPPI

Pearl

ALABAMA

Alabama

Tombigbee

GEORGIA

★Atlanta

Flint

Chattahoochee

Altamaha

Savannah

Sea Islands

Suwannee

Cape San Blas

Apalachee Bay

FLORIDA

Tampa Bay

Lake Okeechobee

The Everglades

Cape Canaveral

Miami

Cape Sable

Florida Keys

N

Land Elevation

Meters		Feet
3,000		9,840
2,000		6,560
500		1,640
200		656
0		0

Water Depth

0		0
200		656
2,000		6,560

0   100   200   300 Miles

0   100   200   300   400 Kilometers

Copyright by Rand McNally & Co.
Alber's Conic Equal Area Projection

ATLANTIC OCEAN

Arecibo

San Juan

Mayagüez

Caguas

Ponce

PUERTO RICO (U.S.)

0   25   50 Miles

0   25   50 Kilometers

Caribbean Sea

RAND McNALLY

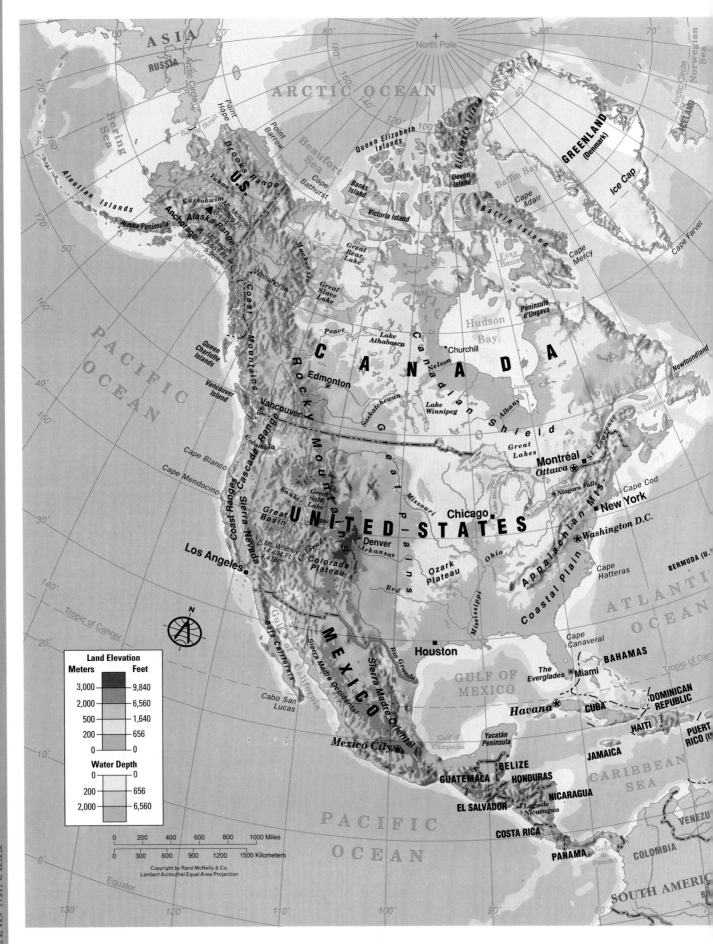

ASIA
RUSSIA
Arctic Circle

ARCTIC OCEAN
North Pole

Point Hope
Point Barrow
Prudhoe Bay
Cape Bathurst
Banks Island
Victoria Island
Queen Elizabeth Islands
Ellesmere Island
Devon Island
Baffin Bay
GREENLAND (Denmark)
Ice Cap
Cape Adair
Baffin Island
Cape Mercy
Cape Farvel
Norwegian Sea
ICELAND
Arctic Circle

Bering Sea
Bering Strait
U.S.
Brooks Range
Yukon
Kuskokwim
Mt. McKinley 20,320 Ft. 6,194m
Alaska Range
Anchorage
Mt. Logan 19,551 Ft. 5,959m

Aleutian Islands
Alaska Peninsula
Gulf of Alaska

PACIFIC OCEAN

Whitehorse
Coast Mountains
Mackenzie
Great Bear Lake
Great Slave Lake
Peace
Lake Athabasca
Nelson
Churchill
Hudson Bay
Foxe Basin
Péninsule d'Ungava

Queen Charlotte Islands
Vancouver Island
Vancouver
Cascade Range
Columbia
Rocky Mountains
Edmonton
Saskatchewan
Lake Winnipeg
CANADA
Canadian Shield
Great Lakes
James Bay
Albany
Gulf of St. Lawrence
Newfoundland

Cape Blanco
Cape Mendocino
Coast Ranges
Sierra Nevada
Snake
Great Salt Lake
Great Basin
Great Plains
Missouri
Chicago
Lake Superior
Lake Michigan
Montréal
Ottawa
St. Lawrence
Niagara Falls
Appalachian Mts.
Cape Cod
New York
Washington D.C.

Los Angeles
Mt. Whitney 14,494 Ft. 4,418m
Colorado
Colorado Plateau
UNITED STATES
Arkansas
Red
Ozark Plateau
Ohio
Mississippi
Coastal Plain
Cape Hatteras
BERMUDA (U.
ATLANTIC OCEAN

Tropic of Cancer
N
Gulf of California
Baja California
MEXICO
Sierra Madre Occidental
Sierra Madre Oriental
Rio Grande
Houston
Cape Canaveral
The Everglades
Miami
BAHAMAS
Tropic of Can

Cabo San Lucas
GULF OF MEXICO
Havana
CUBA
DOMINICAN REPUBLIC
HAITI
PUERTO RICO (U.

Land Elevation

Meters		Feet
3,000		9,840
2,000		6,560
500		1,640
200		656
0		0

Water Depth

0		0
200		656
2,000		6,560

Gulf of Campeche
Yucatán Peninsula
Mexico City
BELIZE
GUATEMALA
HONDURAS
JAMAICA
CARIBBEAN SEA
EL SALVADOR
NICARAGUA
Lago de Nicaragua
COSTA RICA
VENEZU
PANAMA
Golfo de Panamá
COLOMBIA
SOUTH AMERIC

0   200   400   600   800   1000 Miles
0   300   600   900   1200   1500 Kilometers

Copyright by Rand McNally & Co.
Lambert Azimuthal Equal Area Projection

PACIFIC OCEAN

Equator

GULF OF MEXICO

NORTH AMERICA

CUBA
Greater Antilles
JAMAICA
HAITI
DOMINICAN REPUBLIC
PUERTO RICO (U.S.)

MEXICO
BELIZE
GUATEMALA
HONDURAS
Gulf of Honduras
EL SALVADOR
NICARAGUA
COSTA RICA
PANAMA
Gulf of Panama

CARIBBEAN SEA

Lesser Antilles

ATLANTIC OCEAN

Cristóbal Colón Peak
18,948 Ft.
5,775m

Caracas

TRINIDAD AND TOBAGO

Llanos
Orinoco
VENEZUELA
GUYANA
SURINAME
FRENCH GUIANA
Cape Orange

Magdalena
Bogotá
COLOMBIA

Galapagos Islands (Ec.)

ECUADOR
Chimborazo
20,703 Ft.
6,310m

Putumayo
Japurá
Negro
Amazon
Manaus
Amazon
Ilha de Marajó
Belém

Equator

Amazon
Basin
Juruá
Madeira
Tapajós
Tocantins

B R A Z I L

Selvas
Selvas
Ucayali

Andes

PERU

Mt. Huascarán
22,133 Ft.
6,746m

Lima

Recife

Mato Grosso
Plateau

Mt. Illampu
21,066 Ft.
6,421m

Lake Titicaca

Cordillera Oriental

BOLIVIA

Brasília

São Francisco

Serra do Espinhaço

Mt. Sajama
21,463 Ft.
6,542m

Gran Chaco

Atacama Desert

Andes

PARAGUAY

Paraná

São Paulo
Rio de Janeiro

Tropic of Capricorn

PACIFIC OCEAN

Isla San Ambrosio (Chile)

Isla San Felix (Chile)

Mt. Ojos del Salado
22,615 Ft.
6,893m

Paraná

URUGUAY

Archipiélago Juan Fernández (Chile)

Santiago

CHILE

ARGENTINA

Andes

Mt. Aconcagua
22,831 Ft.
6,959m

Buenos Aires

Pampas

Río de la Plata

N

Land Elevation

Meters		Feet
3,000		9,840
2,000		6,560
500		1,640
200		656
0		0

Water Depth

0		0
200		656
2,000		6,560

San Matías Gulf
Península Valdés

Chiloé

Patagonia

San Jorge Gulf

Point Medanoso

ATLANTIC OCEAN

| 0 | 200 | 400 | 600 | 800 | 1000 Miles |
| 0 | 300 | 600 | 900 | 1500 Kilometers |

Copyright by Rand McNally & Co.
Lambert Azimuthal Equal Area Projection

Grand Bay
West Falkland
FALKLAND ISLANDS (U.K.)
East Falkland
Strait of Magellan

Tierra del Fuego
Cape Horn

Drake Passage

South Georgia (U.K.)

South Shetland Islands (U.K.)
South Orkney Islands (U.K.)
South Sandwich Islands (U.K.)

ATLANTIC
OCEAN

FRANCE
EUROPE
PORTUGAL
SPAIN
ITALY
AUS HUNG 20°
ROMANIA
YUGO
BOS
BUL.
ALB
GREECE
Mediterranean Sea
MALTA
UKRAINE
Black Sea
GEORGIA
TURKEY
CYPRUS
SYRIA
LEBANON
ISRAEL
RUSSIA
ARM
AZER.
IRAQ
JORDAN
KAZ.
Aral 60
Sea
UZBEK.
TURKMENISTAN
ASIA
IRAN
KUWAIT
QATAR
U.A.E.

Azores
(Port.)

Madeira
Islands
(Port.)

Strait of Gibraltar

Canary
Islands
(Spain)

Algiers

MOROCCO
Atlas Mountains
Great
Western
Desert
TUNISIA
Great
Eastern
Desert

Qattara
Depression
Cairo

Persian Gulf

SAUDI ARABIA
Red Sea

WESTERN
SAHARA
(MOROCCO)
Tropic of Cancer

Ijafene
Tahat
9,541 Ft.
2,908m
Ahaggar
Mts.

Sahara
Desert

ALGERIA
LIBYA
EGYPT
Libyan
Desert
Lake
Nasser

Nubian
Desert

YEMEN
Gulf of Aden
Cape
Gward

CAPE VERDE

MAURITANIA
MALI
Air (Mts.)
NIGER
Tibesti
Massif
Mt. Koussi
11,204 Ft.
3,415m
Ennedi
CHAD
Lake
Chad
Sahel

Cape
Verde
Dakar
SENEGAL
GAMBIA
GUINEA-
BISSAU
GUINEA
BURKINA
FASO

Sénégal
Niger
Niger

CENTRAL AFRICAN
REPUBLIC

Khartoum
SUDAN
As Sudd
White Nile
Blue Nile
Nile
Lake
Tana
Ethiopian
Plateau

ERITREA
DJIBOUTI
ETHIOPIA
SOMALIA

SIERRA LEONE
LIBERIA
COTE
D'IVOIRE
GHANA
TOGO
BENIN
Lake
Volta
Niger
Benue
NIGERIA
Jos
Plateau

Lagos
CAMEROON
Mt. Cameroon
13,451 Ft.
Bioko 4,100m
Gulf of Guinea
EQUATORIAL
GUINEA
SAO TOME AND
PRINCIPE
GABON
REP. OF
CONGO
Congo
Congo
Basin
Ubangi
Uele

Great Rift Valley
Lake
Turkana
UGANDA
KENYA
Mt. Kenya
17,058 Ft.
5,199m
Nairobi
Lake
Victoria
RWANDA
Serengeti
BURUNDI
Plain
Kilimanjaro
19,340 Ft.
5,895m
Masai
Steppe
Zanzibar
SEYCHE

Mountain Nile

Equator

N

Ascension
(St. Helena)

Kinshasa
Kwango
Kasai
DEM. REP.
OF CONGO
Lake
Tanganyika
TANZANIA

Great Rift Valley

Cuanza

ATLANTIC

St. Helena
(U.K.)

OCEAN

Cuango
Cunene
ANGOLA
Okavango
ZAMBIA
Victoria
Falls
Lake
Kariba
Zambezi
MALAWI
Lake Nyasa
Cape Amb

Mayotte
(Fr.)
COMOROS
MOZAMBIQUE

Mozambique Channel

MADAGASCAR
MAUR

Reunion
(Fr.)

Tropic of Capricorn
Namib
Desert
NAMIBIA
BOTSWANA
Kalahari
Desert
ZIMBABWE
Limpopo

Barra Point

Cape Sainte-Marie

Cape of
Good Hope
Cape Agulhas
Orange
Vaal
Johannesburg
SWAZILAND
LESOTHO
SOUTH
AFRICA
Drakensberg

Prince Edward
Islands
(S. Af.)

Crozet Islands
(Fr.)

INDIAN
OCEAN

Land Elevation
Meters   Feet
3,000   9,840
2,000   6,560
500   1,640
200   656
0   0

Water Depth
0   0
200   656
2,000   6,560

Tristan da
Cunha Group
(St. Helena)

0   200 400 600 800 1000 Miles
0 300 600 900 1200 1500 Kilometers
Copyright by Rand McNally & Co.
Lambert Azimuthal Equal Area Projection

Legend

National Capital ⊛

Secondary Capital ★
(State, Province, or Territory)

City over 1,000,000 population ■

City of 250,000 to 1,000,000 population ▣

City under 250,000 population •

Land Elevation

Meters	Feet
3,000	9,840
2,000	6,560
500	1,640
200	656
0	0

Water Depth

0	0
200	656
2,000	6,560

N

International Date Line

PACIFIC OCEAN

Tropic of Cancer

Equator

Tropic of Capricorn

Hawaiian Islands

Hawaii

Kiritimati

Line Islands

Marquesas Is.

FRENCH POLYNESIA

Tuamotu Archipelago

Tahiti

Society Islands

Austral Is.

PITCAIRN (U.K.)

P O L Y N E S I A

Northern Cook Islands

COOK ISLANDS (N.Z.)

Southern Cook Islands

NIUE (N.Z.)

TOKELAU (N.Z.)

AMERICAN SAMOA

SAMOA

TONGA

WALLIS AND FUTUNA (FR.)

FIJI

Koro Sea

TUVALU

KIRIBATI

M I C R O N E S I A

MARSHALL ISLANDS

NAURU

M E L A N E S I A

SOLOMON ISLANDS

VANUATU

NEW CALEDONIA (FR.)

New Caledonia

Coral Sea

NORFOLK ISLAND (Austl.)

Kermadec Islands (N.Z.)

Auckland

Wellington

North Island

NEW ZEALAND

South Island

Mt. Cook 12,316 Ft. 3,754 m

Chatham Islands

Tasman Sea

CHINA

Taipei

TAIWAN

Luzon Strait

Manila

PHILIPPINES

Luzon

Mindoro

Mindanao

South China Sea

Sulu Sea

Philippine Sea

Celebes Sea

Celebes

Halmahera

Ceram

Moluccas

INDONESIA

Banda Sea

EAST TIMOR

Timor

Timor Sea

Arafura Sea

New Guinea

Puncak Jaya 16,503 Ft. 5,030 m

PAPUA NEW GUINEA

Mount Wilhelm 2,509m 14,793 Ft.

Port Moresby

Bismarck Sea

Solomon Sea

NORTHERN MARIANA ISLANDS (U.S.)

GUAM (U.S.)

PALAU

FEDERATED STATES OF MICRONESIA

Torres Strait

Cape York Peninsula

Gulf of Carpentaria

Great Barrier Reef

A U S T R A L I A

Great Sandy Desert

Gibson Desert

Kimberley Plateau

Great Victoria Desert

Great Australian Bight

GREAT DIVIDING RANGE

Darling

Murray

Brisbane

Sydney

Canberra

Mount Kosciuszko 7,310 Ft. 2,229m

Melbourne

Bass Strait

Tasmania

0 200 400 600 800 1000 Kilometers

0 200 400 600 800 Miles

Copyright by Rand McNally & Co.
Lambert Azimuthal Equal Area Projection

⊛ RAND McNALLY

A13

Land Elevation

Meters	Feet
3,000	9,840
2,000	6,560
500	1,640
200	656
0	0

Water Depth

0	0
200	656
2,000	6,560

N

0   100   200   300   400 Miles

0   200   400   600 Kilometers

Copyright by Rand McNally & Co.
Lambert Conformal Conic Projection

ICELAND

Horn
Fontur
Surtsey

FAROE ISLANDS
(Den.)

Arctic Circle

NORWEGIAN SEA

Lofoten Islands

Kebnekaise
6,926 Ft.
2,111m

Scandinavian Peninsula

NORWAY   SWEDEN

Galdhøpiggen △
8,100 Ft.
2,469m

Glåma

Klarälven

Umeälven

Dalälven

Gulf of Bothnia

Stockholm ⊛

Vänern

Vättern

Öland

ATLANTIC OCEAN

Hebrides

Orkney Islands

Grampian Mts.

UNITED KINGDOM

Cheviot Hills

NORTH SEA

DENMARK

Skagerrak

Bornholm
(Den.)

BALTIC SEA

RUSSIA

IRELAND

Irish Sea

Great Britain

St. George's Channel

Thames

London ⊛

NETHERLANDS

Northern Euro

Berlin ⊛

Elbe

Oder

POLAND

Wisla

English Channel

Strait of Dover

BELGIUM

Rhine

GERMANY

LUX.

CZECH REPUBLIC

Bohemian Forest

SLOVAKIA

Paris ⊛
Paris Basin

Seine

Loire

FRANCE

Saône

Jura

Danube

AUSTRIA

HUNGARY

Great Hungarian Plain

Bay of Biscay

Dordogne

Massif Central

Rhône

Mt. Blanc
15,771 Ft.
4,808m

SWITZERLAND

LIECH.

A l p s

SLOVENIA

Drava

CROATIA

Cantabrian Mts.

Pyrenees

ANDORRA

Po

SAN MARINO

Dinaric Alps

ADRIATIC SEA

BOSNIA AND HERZEGOVINA

Balka

YUGOSLAV

Douro

Duero

Ebro

Iberian Mts.

MONACO

Corsica
(Fr.)

Apennines

Rome ⊛

ITALY

ALBANIA

MACEDON

Lisbon ⊛

PORTUGAL

Tagus

Iberian Peninsula

SPAIN

Sierra Morena

Balearic Islands

Minorca

Ibiza   Majorca

Sardinia
(It.)

△ Vesuvius
4,190 Ft.
1,277m

Pindus

Strait of Gibraltar

GIBRALTAR
(U.K.)

Algiers

TYRRHENIAN SEA

Mt. Etna
10,902 Ft.
3,323m △
Sicily

IONIAN SEA

MOROCCO

AFRICA

ALGERIA

TUNISIA

MEDITERRANE

MALTA

■ Murmansk

Kola
Peninsula
Ponoy

WHITE SEA

Timan Ridge

Pechora

Ob'

Irtysh

FINLAND

Mezen

Onega

Northern Dvina

Northern Uvals
(Uplands)

Kama

U r a l   M o u n t a i n s

Lake
Onega

Sukhona

Lake
Ladoga

⊕ Helsinki

f of Finland

Rybinsk
Res.

R U S S I A

A S I A

STONIA

Lake
Peipus

Valdai
Hills

❉ Moscow

Oka

Don

Khopër

50°

LATVIA

ITHUANIA

a-n   P l a i n

Central
Russian
Upland

Ural

Neman

BELARUS

Pripyat

Dnieper   Lowland

Den

KAZAKHSTAN

Caspian Depression

Aral Sea

UZBEKISTAN

Syr Darya

Kiev ⊛

UKRAINE

Dnieper

Donets Basin

Dnieper

Volga

60°

40°

Dniester

MOLDOVA

C
A
S
P
I
A
N

TURKMENISTAN

Amu Darya

rpathian Mts

OMANIA

sylvanian Alps

Sea of Azov

Crimean
Peninsula

C a u c a s u s

Mt. Elbrus
18,510 Ft.
5,642m

GEORGIA

Baku

S
E
A

Danube

eninsula

B L A C K   S E A

ARMENIA

AZERBAIJAN

AZER.

BULGARIA

■ Istanbul

TURKEY

⊛ Tehran

IRAN

t. Olympus
,570 Ft.
,917m

GREECE

EGEAN SEA

30

IRAQ

Euphrates

Tigris

30°

Rhodes

NORTH
CYPRUS

SYRIA

LEBANON

40°

50°

Crete

SEA

CYPRUS

ATLANTIC OCEAN

ARCTIC OCEAN

ICELAND

Arctic Circle

Barents Sea

IRELAND

UNITED KINGDOM

London

FAROE ISLANDS (Den.)

North Sea

DENMARK

NORWAY

SWEDEN

FINLAND

Severnaya Zemlya

Kara Sea

Novaya Zemlya

Yamal Pen.

PORTUGAL

SPAIN

FRANCE

GERMANY

NETH.
BEL.

POLAND

RUS.

ESTONIA
LATVIA
LITH.
BELARUS

Ob

Ural Mountains

West Siberian Lowland

Novosibirsk

MOROCCO

GIBRALTAR (U.K.)
ANDORRA
MONACO

ITALY

AUSTRIA
SLOVENIA
CZECH
SLOVAKIA
HUNGARY

CROATIA
BOS.
YUGO.
S. MAR.

UKRAINE

ROMANIA

MOLD.

Moscow

Volga

KAZAKHSTAN

Astana

Ishim

Irtysh

Ob

ALGERIA

TUNISIA

Mediterranean Sea

GREECE

ALB.
MAC.
BULGARIA

Black Sea

Caspian Depression

Caucasus

GEORGIA

Aral Sea

Ust-Urt Plateau

Syr Darya

Lake Balkhash

Tian Shan

LIBYA

Ankara

TURKEY

Mount Ararat 16,940 Ft. 5,165m

ARM.
AZER.

Caspian Sea

UZBEKISTAN

Amu Darya

Kara Kum (Desert)

TURKMENISTAN

KYRGYZSTAN

N. CYPRUS
CYPRUS

LEBANON

SYRIA

Tigris

Euphrates

Tehran

TAJIKISTAN

Pamirs

Tarim Basin

K2 (Qogir Feng) 28,250 Ft. 8,611m

Altun Sha

EGYPT

Cairo

Nile

ISRAEL

Sinai Pen.

JORDAN

IRAQ

Zagros Mts.

IRAN

Dasht-e Kavir

Hindu Kush

Kunlun Mts.

CHAD

An-Nafud

SAUDI ARABIA

KUWAIT

Persian Gulf

BAHRAIN

QATAR

AFGHANISTAN

HIMALAYA MTS.

SUDAN

Red Sea

Arabian Peninsula

U.A.E.

Gulf of Oman

PAKISTAN

Indus

New Delhi

Ganges

NEPAL

Mt. Everest 29,035 Ft. 8,850m

Great Indian Desert

Rub Al-Khali

OMAN

ERITREA

YEMEN

Godavari

INDIA

ETHIOPIA

DJIBOUTI

Gulf of Aden

Mumbai (Bombay)

Deccan Plateau

Western Ghats

Eastern Ghats

Bay of Benga

DEM. REP. OF THE CONGO (ZAIRE)

Socotra (Yem.)

Arabian Sea

UGANDA

RWANDA

KENYA

SOMALIA

N

Lakshadweep (India)

SRI LANKA

BURUNDI

MALDIVES

TANZANIA

0   200   400   600   800 Miles

0   200 400 600 800 1000 Kilometers

Copyright by Rand McNally & Co.
Lambert Azimuthal Equal Area Projection

INDIAN OCEAN

ZAMBIA

MALAWI

MOZAMBIQUE

Land Elevation

Meters		Feet
3,000		9,840
2,000		6,560
500		1,640
200		656
0		0

Water Depth

0		0
200		656
2,000		6,560

New Siberian Islands

Laptev Sea

Taymyr Peninsula

East Siberian Sea

Indigirka

Kolyma

Bering Sea

Aleutian Islands (U.S.)

Central Siberian Uplands

Angara

Lena

Verkhoyansk Mts.

Stanovoy Range

Kamchatka Peninsula

RUSSIA

Siberia

Lake Baikal

Sayan Mountains

Altai Mts.

Amur

Greater Khingan Range

Sikhote-Alin Mts.

Sea of Okhotsk

Sakhalin

Tatar Strait

Kuril Islands

Hokkaido

Sea of Japan

Honshu

MONGOLIA

Gobi Desert

⊛Beijing

NORTH KOREA

SOUTH KOREA

Tokyo⊛

Mt. Fuji 12,388 3,776m

JAPAN

Shikoku

Kyushu

PACIFIC OCEAN

Tropic of Cancer

Qilian Shan

Yellow Sea

Huang

Qinling Shandi

Chang (Yangtze)

CHINA

Shanghai

East China Sea

TAIWAN

Philippine Sea

NORTHERN MARIANA ISLANDS (U.S.)

GUAM (U.S.)

BHUTAN

Brahmaputra

Xi

Himalayas

Irrawaddy

Salween

Mekong

Red

Gulf of Tonkin

Hainan Island

Luzon Strait

Luzon

PHILIPPINES

South China Sea

Manila⊛

Mindanao

PALAU

FEDERATED STATES OF MICRONESIA

NGL

MYANMAR

LAOS

VIETNAM

THAILAND

Bangkok⊛

CAMBODIA

Andaman Islands (India)

Andaman Sea

Gulf of Thailand

Sulu Sea

Celebes Sea

Moluccas

Equator

Nicobar Islands (India)

Str. of Malacca

MALAY PENINSULA

MALAYSIA

BRUNEI

MALAYSIA

Celebes

Ceram

New Guinea

PAPUA NEW GUINEA

Singapore⊛

Borneo

Banda Sea

Arafura Sea

Gulf of Carpentaria

Coral Sea

Sumatra

Greater Sunda Islands

INDONESIA

Java Sea

EAST TIMOR

Timor

Jakarta⊛

Java

Timor Sea

AUSTRALIA

Guam

Philippine Sea

144°45'
145°

13°30'

Agana ★ · Tamuning

GUAM
(U.S.)

PACIFIC
OCEAN

13°15'

| 0 | 2 | 4 | 6 | 8 | 10 Miles |
| 0 | 5 | 10 | 15 Kilometers |

Copyright by Rand McNally & Co.
Lambert Conformal Conic Projection

144°45'
145°

ICELAND
NORWAY SWEDEN FINLAND
UNITED KINGDOM
IRELAND DEN.
NETH. GERMANY POLAND BELARUS
FRANCE ROM. UKRAINE
SPAIN ITALY BUL.
GREECE TURKEY
TUNISIA SYRIA
GERIA LIBYA EGYPT ISRAEL JORDAN
NIGER CHAD SUDAN
NIGERIA
CENTRAL AFRICAN REPUBLIC ETHIOPIA
CAMEROON
GABON CONGO DEM. REP. OF CONGO RWANDA BURUNDI KENYA
SAO TOME PRINCIPE TANZANIA
ANGOLA ZAMBIA
NAMIBIA ZIMBABWE MOZAMBIQUE
BOTSWANA

RUSSIA
KAZAKHSTAN MONGOLIA
UZBEKISTAN KYRG.
TURKMENISTAN TAJIK.
AFGHANISTAN CHINA
IRAN PAKISTAN NEPAL
KUWAIT
SAUDI ARABIA INDIA MYANMAR (BURMA) LAOS
QATAR OMAN THAILAND VIETNAM
YEMEN CAMBODIA
DJIBOUTI
SOMALIA SRI LANKA

NORTH KOREA
SOUTH KOREA JAP

TAIWAN
NORTH MARIA ISLAN
PHILIPPINES GUAM
PALAU
BRUNEI
MALAYSIA
SINGAPORE

INDONESIA
EAST TIMOR (UN Admin.)
PAP NEW GUI

Arctic Circle
Tropic of Capricorn

INDIAN
OCEAN

COMOROS
MADAGASCAR
MAURITIUS
REUNION (Fr.)

AUSTRALIA

| 0 | 1000 | 2000 Miles |
| 0 | 1000 | 2000 | 3000 Kilometers |

Copyright by Rand McNally & Co.
Robinson Projection

ANTARCTICA

Samoa

171°
170°

| 0 | 5 | 10 | 15 | 20 | 25 Miles |
| 0 | 10 | 20 | 30 | 40 Kilometers |

Copyright by Rand McNally & Co.
Lambert Conformal Conic Projection

PACIFIC
OCEAN

14°

N

AMERICAN
SAMOA

Ofu ⊳ Olosega
Tau

Pago Pago
Aunuu

Tutuila

Manua Islands

Pacific Islands

140° 150° 160° 170° 180° 170° 160° 150° 140° 130°

PACIFIC OCEAN

HAWAII

N

NORTHERN MARIANA ISLANDS (U.S.)
GUAM (U.S.)
CAROLINE ISLANDS
MARSHALL ISLANDS
FEDERATED STATES OF MICRONESIA
★ Koror
PALAU

INTERNATIONAL DATE LINE

| 0 | 200 | 400 | 600 | 800 | 1000 Miles |
| 0 | 300 | 600 | 900 | 1200 | 1500 Kilometers |

Copyright by Rand McNally & Co.
Lambert Azimuthal Equal Area Projection

Equator

INDON.
NAURU
KIRIBATI
PHOENIX ISLANDS
PAPUA NEW GUINEA
Port Moresby ★
SOLOMON ISLANDS
★ Honiara
TUVALU
TOKELAU (N.Z.)
SANTA CRUZ ISLANDS
WALLIS AND FUTUNA (Fr.)
SAMOA
Apia ★
AMERICAN SAMOA
COOK ISLANDS (N.Z.)
FRENCH POLYNESIA

CORAL SEA
Cairns
Gulf of Carpentaria
VANUATU
FIJI
Port Vila ★
Suva ★
TONGA
NIUE (N.Z.)

AUSTRALIA
NEW CALEDONIA (Fr.)
Nouméa ★

140° 150° 160° 170° 180° 170° 160° 150° 140° 130°

20° 10° 0° 10° 20°

165° 180° 165° 150° 135° 120° 105° 90° 75° 60° 45°

ARCTIC OCEAN

GREENLAND
(Den.)

75°

Arctic Circle

CANADA

60°

International Date Line

UNITED STATES

45°

ATLANTIC

MIDWAY
ISLANDS

Tropic of Cancer

MEXICO

30°

BERMUDA (U.K)

OCEAN

WAKE
ISLAND

Johnston
Atoll

CUBA

BAHAMAS

HAITI

DOM. REP.
PUERTO RICO
U.S. VIRGIN ISLANDS

15°

PACIFIC

MARSHALL
ISLANDS

Palmyra Atoll   Kingman Reef

BELIZE
GUAT. HOND.
EL. SAL. NIC.

JAMAICA

Navassa
Island

STATES
OF
MICRONESIA

Howland Island
Baker Island   Jarvis Island

Equator

COSTA
RICA

PANAMA

VENEZUELA

TRINIDAD AND TOBAGO

GUYANA
SURINAME
FRENCH GUIANA

0°

NAURU   KIRIBATI

COLOMBIA

OCEAN

ECUADOR

N

SOLOMON
ISLANDS   TUVALU

TOKELAU
(N.Z.)

PERU

BRAZIL

15°

SAMOA

VANUATU

AMERICAN
SAMOA

NEW
CALEDONIA
(FR.)   FIJI

NIUE
(N.Z.)   COOK
ISLANDS
(N.Z.)

TONGA

FRENCH POLYNESIA

BOLIVIA

Tropic of Capricorn

PARAGUAY

NORFOLK
ISLAND
(Austl.)

ARGENTINA

30°

URUGUAY

NEW ZEALAND

45°

FALKLAND ISLANDS
(U.K)

60°

Antarctic Circle

75°

165° 180° 165° 150° 135° 120° 105° 90° 75° 60° 45°

Symbol	Description
✪	National Capital
★	Secondary Capital (State, Province, or Territory)
■	City over 1,000,000 population
⊡	City of 250,000 to 1,000,000 population
·	City under 250,000 population

Puerto Rico and the U.S. Virgin Islands

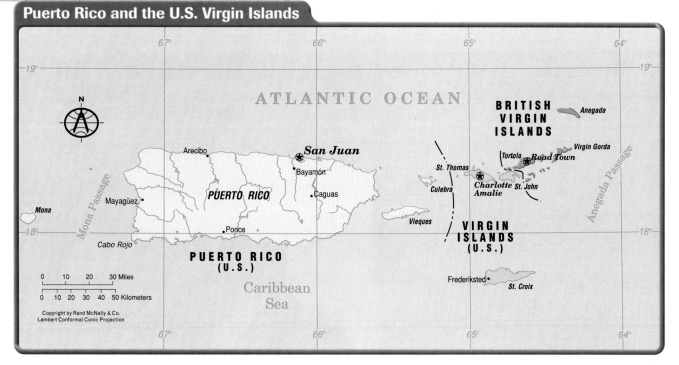

67°   66°   65°   64°

19°   19°

ATLANTIC OCEAN

N

BRITISH
VIRGIN
ISLANDS

Anegada

Arecibo

San Juan

Virgin Gorda

Tortola   Road Town

Bayamón

St. Thomas

Anegada Passage

Mona
Passage

PUERTO RICO

Caguas

Culebra

Charlotte
Amalie   St. John

Mona   Mayagüez

Ponce

Vieques

VIRGIN
ISLANDS
(U.S.)

18°   18°

Cabo Rojo

PUERTO RICO
(U.S.)

Caribbean
Sea

Frederiksted   St. Croix

0 10 20 30 Miles
0 10 20 30 40 50 Kilometers

Copyright by Rand McNally & Co.
Lambert Conformal Conic Projection

67°   66°   65°   64°

Ceded to Great Britain, 1818

Line of Treaty of 1846 with Great Britain

Boundary adjusted by Convention of 1818 with Great Britain

Ceded by Great Britain 1818

WASHINGTON

MONTANA

NORTH DAKOTA

Missouri River

Joint occupation by United States and Great Britain 1818-1846 (Claim abandoned by Russia, 1824)

OREGON TERRITORY
From Great Britain, 1846

OREGON

IDAHO

Columbia River

Snake River

Yellowstone River

SOUTH DAKOTA

WYOMING

N. Platte River

Line of Adams-Onis Treaty with Spain, 1819

NEVADA

Great Salt Lake

NEBRASKA

S. Platte River

LOUISIANA PURCHASE
Bought from France, 1803

CALIFORNIA

UTAH

COLORADO

KANSAS

Arkansas River

MEXICAN CESSION
From Mexico by Treaty of Guadalupe Hidalgo, 1848

Colorado River

ARIZONA

NEW MEXICO

OKLAHOMA

Red River

Rio Grande

Claimed by Texas and ceded by Mexico, 1848

PACIFIC OCEAN

Gila River

GADSDEN PURCHASE
Bought from Mexico, 1853

Line of Treaty of Guadalupe Hidalgo with Mexico, 1848

TEXAS

TEXAS ANNEXATION

Independent Texas Republic annexed, 1845

HAWAII
Annexed, 1898

ARCTIC OCEAN

ALASKA
From Russia, 1867

PACIFIC OCEAN

© RMcN.

PACIFIC OCEAN

Tropic of Cancer

PACIFIC OCEAN

© RMcN.

Lake of the Woods

Boundary adjusted by Webster-Ashburton Treaty with Great Britain, 1842

From Great Britain, 1842

Boundary adjusted by Webster-Ashburton Treaty with Great Britain, 1842

From Great Britain, 1842

MINNESOTA

Lake Superior

MAINE

VT.

N.H.

MICHIGAN

WISCONSIN

Lake Michigan

Lake Huron

Lake Ontario

NEW YORK

MASS.

CONN.

R.I.

Mississippi River

Lake Erie

PENNSYLVANIA

Hudson River

IOWA

ILLINOIS

INDIANA

OHIO

From Great Britain by Treaty of Paris, 1783

THE UNITED STATES

IN

WEST VIRGINIA

1783

NEW JERSEY

DEL.

MARYLAND

Missouri River

Ohio River

MISSOURI

KENTUCKY

VIRGINIA

ATLANTIC OCEAN

Cumberland River

TENNESSEE

NORTH CAROLINA

ORIGINAL 13 COLONIES

Tennessee River

ARKANSAS

SOUTH CAROLINA

Red River

MISSISSIPPI

ALABAMA

GEORGIA

Mississippi River

LOUISIANA

From Spain, 1795

Boundary adjusted by Pinckney's Treaty with Spain, 1795

Ceded by Spain, 1818

1810   1813
Annexed by the United States

FLORIDA

FLORIDA CESSION
From Spain by Adams-Onis Treaty, 1819

GULF OF MEXICO

0   100   200   300 Miles
0   100   200   300   400 Kilometers

Copyright by Rand McNally & Co.
Alber's Conic Equal Area Projection

Creating America
A History of the United States

Skillbuilder HANDBOOK

Table of Contents

1.1 Summarizing

Defining the Skill

When you **summarize,** you restate a paragraph, passage, or chapter in fewer words. You include only the main ideas and most important details. It is important to use your own words when summarizing.

Applying the Skill

The passage below tells about Harriet Tubman, a prominent member of the Underground Railroad. She helped runaway slaves to freedom. Use the strategies listed below to help you summarize the passage.

How to Summarize

Strategy ① Look for topic sentences stating the main idea. These are often at the beginning of a section or paragraph. Briefly restate each main idea—in your own words.

Strategy ② Include key facts and any numbers, dates, amounts, or percentages from the text.

Strategy ③ After writing your summary, review it to see that you have included only the most important details.

> ### HARRIET TUBMAN
>
> ① One of the most famous conductors on the Underground Railroad was Harriet Tubman. ② Born into slavery in Maryland, the 13-year-old Tubman once tried to save another slave from punishment. The angry overseer fractured Tubman's skull with a two-pound weight. She suffered fainting spells for the rest of her life but did not let that stop her from working for freedom. When she was 25, Tubman learned that her owner was about to sell her. Instead, ② she escaped.
>
> After her escape, ② Harriet Tubman made 19 dangerous journeys to free enslaved persons. The tiny woman carried a pistol to frighten off slave hunters and medicine to quiet crying babies. Her enemies offered $40,000 for her capture, but ② no one caught her. "I never run my train off the track and I never lost a passenger," she proudly declared. Among the people she saved were her parents.

Write a Summary

You can write your summary in a paragraph. The paragraph at right summarizes the passage you just read.

Practicing the Skill

Turn to Chapter 6, Section 2, "Colonial Resistance Grows." Read "The Boston Tea Party" and write a paragraph summarizing the passage.

③ Harriet Tubman was one of the most famous conductors on the Underground Railroad. She had been a slave, but she escaped. She later made 19 dangerous journeys to free other slaves. She was never captured.

1.2 Taking Notes

Defining the Skill

When you **take notes,** you write down the important ideas and details of a paragraph, passage, or chapter. A chart or an outline can help you organize your notes to use in the future.

Applying the Skill

The following passage describes President Washington's cabinet. Use the strategies listed below to help you take notes on the passage.

How to Take and Organize Notes

Strategy ❶ Look at the title to find the main topic of the passage.

Strategy ❷ Identify the main ideas and details of the passage. Then summarize the main idea and details in your notes.

Strategy ❸ Identify key terms and define them. The term *cabinet* is shown in boldface type and underlined; both techniques signal that it is a key term.

Strategy ❹ In your notes, use abbreviations to save time and space. You can abbreviate words such as *department (dept.), secretary (sec.), United States (U.S.),* and *president (pres.)* to save time and space.

> ❶ **WASHINGTON'S CABINET**
>
> ❷ The Constitution gave Congress the task of creating departments to help the president lead the nation. The ❷ president had the power to appoint the heads of these departments, which became his ❸ <u>cabinet.</u>
>
> Congress created three departments. Washington chose talented people to run them. ❷ For secretary of war, he picked Henry Knox, a trusted general during the Revolution. ❷ For secretary of state, Washington chose Thomas Jefferson. He had been serving as ambassador to France. The State Department oversaw U.S. foreign relations. For secretary of the treasury, Washington turned to the brilliant ❷ Alexander Hamilton.

Make a Chart

Making a chart can help you take notes on a passage. The chart below contains notes from the passage you just read.

❷ Item	Notes
1. ❸ cabinet	heads of ❹ depts; ❹ pres. appoints heads
a. War Dept.	Henry Knox; ❹ sec. of war; former Revolutionary War general
b. State Dept.	Thomas Jefferson; sec. of state; oversees relations between ❹ U.S. and other countries
c. Treasury Dept.	Alexander Hamilton; sec. of the treasury

Practicing the Skill

Turn to Chapter 3, Section 3, "Founding the Middle and Southern Colonies." Read "Maryland and the Carolinas" and use a chart to take notes on the passage.

1.3 Sequencing Events

Defining the Skill

Sequence is the order in which events follow one another. By being able to follow the sequence of events through history, you can get an accurate sense of the relationship among events.

Applying the Skill

The following passage describes the sequence of events involved in Britain's plan to capture the Hudson River Valley during the American Revolution. Use the strategies listed below to help you follow the sequence of events.

How to Find the Sequence of Events

Strategy ① Look for specific dates provided in the text. If several months within a year are included, the year is usually not repeated.

Strategy ② Look for clues about time that allow you to order events according to sequence. Words such as *day, week, month,* or *year* may help to sequence the events.

BRITAIN'S STRATEGY

Burgoyne captured Fort Ticonderoga in ① July 1777. From there, it was 25 miles to the Hudson River, which ran to Albany. ② Burgoyne took three weeks to reach the Hudson. On ① August 3, Burgoyne received a message from Howe. He would not be coming north, Howe wrote, because he had decided to invade Pennsylvania to try to capture Philadelphia and General Washington. "Success be ever with you," Howe's message said. But General Burgoyne needed Howe's soldiers, not his good wishes. Howe did invade Pennsylvania. In ① September 1777, he defeated —but did not capture—Washington at the Battle of Brandywine.

Make a Time Line

Making a time line can help you sequence events. The time line below shows the sequence of events in the passage you just read.

July 1777: Burgoyne captures Fort Ticonderoga.

August 3, 1777: Howe writes that he will not join Burgoyne.

Three weeks after the capture of Fort Ticonderoga: Burgoyne reaches the Hudson.

September 1777: Howe defeats Washington at Brandywine.

Practicing the Skill

Turn to Chapter 10, Section 4, "The War of 1812." Read the section and make a time line showing the sequence of major events in the war.

1.4 Finding Main Ideas

Defining the Skill

The **main idea** is a statement that summarizes the main point of a speech, an article, a section of a book, or a paragraph. Main ideas can be stated or unstated. The main idea of a paragraph is often stated in the first or last sentence. If it is the first sentence, it is followed by sentences that support that main idea. If it is the last sentence, the details build up to the main idea. To find an unstated idea, you must use the details of the paragraph as clues.

Applying the Skill

The following paragraph describes the role of women in the American Revolution. Use the strategies listed below to help you identify the main idea.

How to Find the Main Idea

Strategy ❶ Identify what you think may be the stated main idea. Check the first and last sentences of the paragraph to see if either could be the stated main idea.

Strategy ❷ Identify details that support that idea. Some details explain the main idea. Others give examples of what is stated in the main idea.

> **WOMEN IN THE REVOLUTION**
>
> ❶ Many women tried to help the army. Martha Washington and other wives followed their husbands to army camps. ❷ The wives cooked, did laundry, and nursed sick or wounded soldiers. ❷ A few women even helped to fight. ❷ Mary Hays earned the nickname "Molly Pitcher" by carrying water to tired soldiers during a battle. ❷ Deborah Sampson dressed as a man, enlisted, and fought in several engagements.

Make a Chart

Making a chart can help you identify the main idea and details in a passage or paragraph. The chart below identifies the main idea and details in the paragraph you just read.

Main Idea: Women helped the army during the Revolution.

Detail: They cooked and did laundry.
Detail: They nursed the wounded and sick soldiers.
Detail: They helped to fight.
Detail: One woman, Molly Pitcher, carried water to soldiers during battles.

Practicing the Skill

Turn to Chapter 5, Section 1, "Early American Culture." Read "Women and the Economy" and create a chart that identifies the main idea and the supporting details.

1.5 Categorizing

Defining the Skill

To **categorize** is to sort people, objects, ideas, or other information into groups, called categories. Historians categorize information to help them identify and understand patterns in historical events.

Applying the Skill

The following passage contains information about the reasons people went west during the mid-1800s. Use the strategies listed below to help you categorize information.

How to Categorize

Strategy ❶ First, decide what kind of information needs to be categorized. Decide what the passage is about and how that information can be sorted into categories.

For example, find the different motives people had for moving west.

Strategy ❷ Then find out what the categories will be. To find why many different groups of people moved west, look for clue words such as *some, other,* and *another.*

Strategy ❸ Once you have chosen the categories, sort information into them. Of the people who went west, which ones had which motives?

> ### THE LURE OF THE WEST
>
> ❶ People had many different motives for going west. ❷ One motive was to make money. ❷ *Some* people called speculators bought huge areas of land and made great profits by selling it to thousands of settlers. ❷ *Other* settlers included farmers who dreamed of owning their own farms in the West because land was difficult to acquire in the East. ❷ *Another* group to move west was merchants. They hoped to earn money by selling items that farmers needed. Finally, ❷ *some* people went west for religious reasons. These people included ❷ missionaries, who wanted to convert the Native Americans to Christianity, and Mormons, who wanted a place where they could practice their faith without interference.

Make a Chart

Making a chart can help you categorize information. You should have as many columns as you have categories. The chart below shows how the information from the passage you just read can be categorized.

Motives	Money	Land	Religion
❸ Groups	• speculators • merchants	• farmers	• missionaries • Mormons

Practicing the Skill

Turn to Chapter 14, Section 3, "Reforming American Society." Read "Improving Education" and make a chart in which you categorize the changes happening in elementary, high school, and college education.

1.6 Making Public Speeches

Defining the Skill

A speech is a talk given in public to an audience. Some speeches are given to persuade the audience to think or act in a certain way, or to support a cause. You can learn how to **make public speeches** effectively by analyzing great speeches in history.

Applying the Skill

The following is an excerpt from the "I Have a Dream" speech delivered by Martin Luther King, Jr., in 1963 in Washington, D.C. Use the strategies listed below to help you analyze King's speech and prepare a speech of your own.

How to Analyze and Prepare a Speech

Strategy ❶ Choose one central idea or theme and organize your speech to support it. King organized his speech around his dream of equality.

Strategy ❷ Use words or images that will win over your audience. King referred to the Declaration of Independence when he used the words "all men are created equal."

Strategy ❸ Repeat words or images to drive home your main point—as if it is the "hook" of a pop song. King repeats the phrase "I have a dream."

> ### I HAVE A DREAM
>
> ❶ I have a dream that one day this nation will rise up and live out the true meaning of its creed—we hold these truths to be ❷ self-evident that all men are created equal.
>
> ❸ I have a dream that one day on the red hills of Georgia the sons of former slaves and the sons of former slave owners will be able to sit down together at the table of brotherhood.
>
> ❸ I have a dream that my four little children will one day live in a nation where they will not be judged by the color of their skin but by the content of their character.
>
> ❸ I have a dream today!

Make an Outline

Making an outline like the one to the right will help you make an effective public speech.

Practicing the Skill

Turn to Chapter 12, Section 2, "Jackson's Policy Toward Native Americans." Read the section and choose a topic for a speech. First, make an outline like the one to the right to organize your ideas. Exchange your outline with a partner. Organize and interpret information from that outline to write a speech.

Title: I Have a Dream

I. Introduce Theme: I have a dream
    A. This nation will live up to its creed
    B. Quote from the Declaration of Independence: that all men are created equal

II. Repeat theme: I have a dream
    A. Sons of former slaves and slave owners will sit together in brotherhood
    B. My four children will be judged by their character, not by their skin color

III. Conclude: I have a dream

1.7 Writing for Social Studies

Defining the Skill

Writing for social studies requires you to describe an idea, situation, or event. Often, social studies writing takes a stand on a particular issue or tries to make a specific point. To successfully describe an event or make a point, your writing needs to be clear, concise, and factually accurate.

Applying the Skill

The following passage describes Stephen A. Douglas. Notice how the strategies below helped the writer explain Douglas's historical importance.

How to Write for Social Studies

Strategy ❶ Focus on your topic. Be sure that you clearly state the main idea of your piece so that your readers know what you intend to say.

Strategy ❷ Collect and organize your facts. Collect accurate information about your topic to support the main idea you are trying to make. Use your information to build a logical case to prove your point.

Strategy ❸ To express your ideas clearly, use standard grammar, spelling, sentence structure, and punctuation when writing for social studies. Proofread your work to make sure it is well organized and grammatically correct.

STEPHEN A. DOUGLAS, 1813–1861

❶ Stephen A. Douglas was one of the most powerful members of Congress in the 1850s. In fact, ❷ he was called the "Little Giant" because he commanded great respect even though he was only five feet four inches tall. The most important issue that Douglas faced in his career was slavery in the territories. ❷ He played a key role in the passage of the Compromise of 1850 as well as the Kansas–Nebraska Act, which addressed this issue. In 1858, his famous debates with Abraham Lincoln also focused on slavery in the territories. ❷ When Douglas ran for president in 1860, his position on slavery was critical to his defeat.

Practicing the Skill

Turn to Chapter 15, Section 1, "Growing Tensions Between North and South." Read the section and use the strategies above to write your answer to Question 4 in the Chapter 15 Section 1 Assessment.

2.1 Analyzing Points of View

Defining the Skill

Analyzing points of view means looking closely at a person's arguments to understand the reasons behind that person's beliefs. The goal of analyzing a point of view is to understand a historical figure's thoughts, opinions, and biases about a topic.

Applying the Skill

The following passage describes the Panic of 1837 and two politicians' points of view about it. Use the strategies listed below to help you analyze their points of view.

How to Analyze Points of View

Strategy ① Look for statements that show you a person's view on an issue. For example, Van Buren said he believed the economy would improve if he took no action. Clay thought the government should do something to help the people.

Strategy ② Use information about people to validate them as sources and understand why they might disagree. What do you know about Clay and Van Buren that might explain their own biases and disagreements with each other?

Strategy ③ Write a summary that explains why different people took different positions on the issue.

> **THE PANIC OF 1837**
>
> The Panic of 1837 caused severe hardship. People had little money, so manufacturers had few customers for their goods. Almost 90 percent of factories in the East closed. Jobless workers could not afford food or rent. Many people went hungry.
>
> ① Whig senator Henry Clay wanted the government to do something to help the people. ① President Van Buren, a Democrat, disagreed. He believed that the economy would improve if left alone. He argued that "the less government interferes with private pursuits the better for the general prosperity." Many Americans blamed Van Buren for the Panic, though he had taken office only weeks before it started. The continuing depression made it difficult for him to win reelection in 1840.

Make a Diagram

Using a diagram can help you analyze points of view. The diagram below analyzes the views of Clay and Van Buren in the passage you just read.

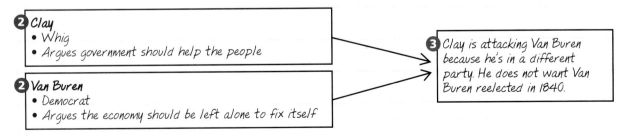

② Clay
• Whig
• Argues government should help the people

② Van Buren
• Democrat
• Argues the economy should be left alone to fix itself

③ Clay is attacking Van Buren because he's in a different party. He does not want Van Buren reelected in 1840.

Practicing the Skill

Turn to the Interactive Primary Sources at the end of Chapter 8, Section 3. Read the selections by James Madison and George Mason. Use their language, information from other sources, and information about each man to validate them as sources. Then make a chart to analyze their different points of view on the Constitution.

2.2 Comparing and Contrasting

Defining the Skill

Comparing means looking at the similarities and differences between two or more things. **Contrasting** means examining only the differences between them. Historians compare and contrast events, personalities, behaviors, beliefs, and situations in order to understand them.

Applying the Skill

The following paragraph describes the American and British troops during the Revolutionary War. Use the strategies listed below to help you compare and contrast these two armies.

How to Compare and Contrast

Strategy ① Look for two aspects of the subject that may be compared and contrasted. This passage compares the British and American troops to show why the Americans won the war.

Strategy ② To contrast, look for clue words that show how two things differ. Clue words include *by contrast, however, except,* and *yet.*

Strategy ③ To find similarities, look for clue words indicating that two things are alike. Clue words include *both, like, as,* and *similarly.*

> ### WHY THE AMERICANS WON
>
> ① By their persistence, the Americans defeated the British even though they faced many obstacles. The Americans lacked training and experience. They were often short of supplies and weapons. ② *By contrast,* the British forces ranked among the best trained in the world. They were experienced and well-supplied professional soldiers. ② *Yet,* the Americans also had advantages that enabled them to win. These advantages over the British were better leadership, foreign aid, a knowledge of the land, and motivation. Although ③ *both* the British and the Americans were fighting for their lives, ② the Americans were also fighting for their property and their dream of liberty.

Make a Venn Diagram

Making a Venn diagram will help you identify similarities and differences between two things. In the overlapping area, list characteristics shared by both subjects. Then, in the separate ovals, list the characteristics of each subject not shared by the other. This Venn diagram compares and contrasts the British and American soldiers.

American Soldiers:
- lacked experience and training
- short of supplies and weapons
- had better leadership
- received foreign aid
- had knowledge of the land
- fought for liberty and property

Both:
fought for their lives

British Soldiers:
- best trained in the world
- experienced
- well-supplied

Practicing the Skill

Turn to Chapter 5, Section 1, "Early American Culture." Read "Young People at Work" and make a Venn diagram showing the similarities and differences between the roles of boys and girls in colonial America.

2.3 Analyzing Causes; Recognizing Effects

Defining the Skill

A **cause** is an action in history that makes something happen. An **effect** is the historical event that is the result of the cause. A single event may have several causes. It is also possible for one cause to result in several effects. Historians identify cause-and-effect relationships to help them understand why historical events took place.

Applying the Skill

The following paragraph describes events that caused changes in Puritan New England. Use the strategies listed below to help you identify the cause-and-effect relationships.

How to Analyze Causes and Recognize Effects

Strategy ❶ Ask why an action took place. Ask yourself a question about the title and topic sentence, such as, "What caused changes in Puritan society?"

Strategy ❷ Look for effects. Ask yourself, "What happened?" (the effect). Then ask, "Why did it happen?" (the cause). For example, What caused the decline of Puritan religion in New England?

Strategy ❸ Look for clue words that signal causes, such as *cause* and *led to.*

Strategy ❹ One way to practice recognizing effects is to make predictions about the consequences that will result from particular actions. Then, as you read, look to see if your predictions were accurate.

---

❶ **CHANGES IN PURITAN SOCIETY**

❶ The early 1700s saw many changes in New England society. ❷ One of the most important changes was the gradual decline of the Puritan religion in New England. There were a number of reasons for that decline.

❸ One *cause* of this decline was the increasing competition from other religious groups. Baptists and Anglicans established churches in Massachusetts and Connecticut, where Puritans had once been the most powerful group. ❸ Political changes also *led to* a weakening of the Puritan community. In 1691, a new royal charter for Massachusetts granted the vote based on property ownership instead of church membership.

Make a Diagram

Using a diagram can help you understand causes and effects. The diagram below shows two causes and an effect for the passage you just read.

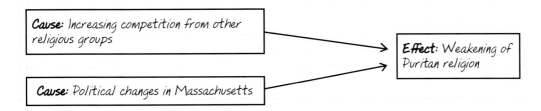

Practicing the Skill

Turn to Chapter 13, Section 3, "The War with Mexico." Read the section and make a diagram about the causes and effects of the war.

2.4 Making Inferences

Defining the Skill

Inferences are ideas that the author has not directly stated. **Making inferences** involves reading between the lines to interpret the information you read. You can make inferences by studying what is stated and using your common sense and previous knowledge.

Applying the Skill

The passage below describes the strengths and weaknesses of the North and the South as the Civil War began. Use the strategies listed below to help you make inferences from the passage.

How to Make Inferences

Strategy ❶ Read to find statements of facts and ideas. Knowing the facts will give you a good basis for making inferences.

Strategy ❷ Use your knowledge, logic, and common sense to make inferences that are based on facts. Ask yourself, "What does the author want me to understand?" For example, from the facts about population, you can make the inference that the North would have a larger army than the South. See other inferences in the chart below.

ADVANTAGES OF THE NORTH AND THE SOUTH

The North had more people and resources than the South. ❶ The North had about 22 million people. ❶ The South had roughly 9 million, of whom about 3.5 million were slaves. In addition, ❶ the North had more than 80 percent of the nation's factories and almost all of the shipyards and naval power. The South had some advantages, too. ❶ It had able generals, such as Robert E. Lee. ❶ It also had the advantage of fighting a defensive war. Soldiers defending their homes have more will to fight than invaders do.

Make a Chart

Making a chart will help you organize information and make logical inferences. The chart below organizes information from the passage you just read.

❶ Stated Facts and Ideas	❷ Inferences
The North had about 22 million people. The Confederacy had about 9 million, less the 3.5 million slaves.	The North would have a larger army than the South.
The North had more factories, naval power, and shipyards.	The North could provide more weapons, ammunition, and ships for the war.
The Confederacy had excellent generals.	The Confederacy had better generals, which would help it overcome other disadvantages.
The Confederacy was fighting a defensive war.	Confederate soldiers would fight harder because they were defending their homes and families.

Practicing the Skill

Turn to Chapter 11, Section 1, "Early Industry and Inventions." Read "Free Enterprise and Factories" and use a chart like the one above to make inferences about early industry.

2.5 Drawing Conclusions

Defining the Skill

Drawing conclusions means analyzing what you have read and forming an opinion about its meaning. To draw conclusions, look at the facts and then use your own common sense and experience to decide what the facts mean.

Applying the Skill

The following passage presents information about the Intolerable Acts and the colonists' reactions to them. Use the strategies listed below to help you draw conclusions about those acts.

How to Draw Conclusions

Strategy ① Read carefully to identify and understand all the facts, or statements, that can be proven true.

Strategy ② List the facts in a diagram and review them. Use your own experiences and common sense to understand how the facts relate to each other.

Strategy ③ After reviewing the facts, write down the conclusion you have drawn about them.

THE INTOLERABLE ACTS

① In 1774, Parliament passed a series of laws to punish the Massachusetts colony and serve as a warning to other colonies.

① These laws were so harsh that colonists called them the **Intolerable Acts.** One of the acts closed the port of Boston. Others banned committees of correspondence and allowed Britain to house troops wherever necessary.

In 1773, Sam Adams had written, "I wish we could arouse the continent." ① The Intolerable Acts answered his wish. Other colonies immediately offered Massachusetts their support.

Make a Diagram

Making a diagram can help you draw conclusions. The diagram below shows how to organize facts and inferences to draw a conclusion about the passage you just read.

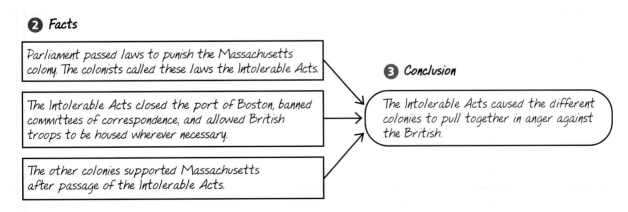

❷ *Facts*

Parliament passed laws to punish the Massachusetts colony. The colonists called these laws the Intolerable Acts.

The Intolerable Acts closed the port of Boston, banned committees of correspondence, and allowed British troops to be housed wherever necessary.

The other colonies supported Massachusetts after passage of the Intolerable Acts.

❸ *Conclusion*

The Intolerable Acts caused the different colonies to pull together in anger against the British.

Practicing the Skill

Turn to Chapter 3, Section 2, "New England Colonies." Read "The Salem Witchcraft Trials" and use the diagram above as a model to draw conclusions about the trials.

2.6 Making Decisions

Defining the Skill

Making decisions involves choosing between two or more options, or courses of action. In most cases, decisions have consequences, or results. Sometimes decisions may lead to new problems. By understanding how historical figures made decisions, you can learn how to improve your decision-making skills.

Applying the Skill

The following passage describes Lincoln's decisions regarding federal forts after the Southern states seceded. Use the strategies listed below to help you analyze his decisions.

How to Make Decisions

Strategy ① Identify a decision that needs to be made. Think about what factors make the decision difficult.

Strategy ② Identify possible consequences of the decision. Remember that there can be more than one consequence to a decision.

Strategy ③ Identify the decision that was made.

Strategy ④ Identify actual con- sequences that resulted from the decision.

> **FIRST SHOTS AT FORT SUMTER**
>
> ① Lincoln had to decide what to do about the forts in the South that remained under federal control. A Union garrison still held **Fort Sumter**, but it was running out of supplies. ② If Lincoln supplied the garrison, he risked war. ② If he withdrew the garrison, he would be giving in to the rebels. ③ Lincoln informed South Carolina that he was sending supply ships to Fort Sumter. ④ Confederate leaders decided to prevent the federal government from holding on to the fort by attacking before the supply ships arrived. No one was killed, but ④ the South's attack on Fort Sumter signaled the beginning of the Civil War.

Make a Flow Chart

A flow chart can help you identify the process of making a decision. The flow chart below shows the decision-making process in the passage you just read.

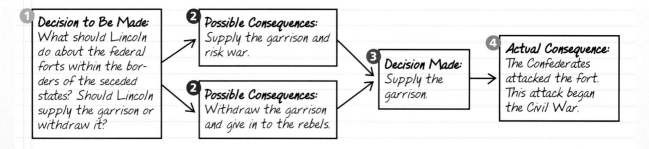

① Decision to Be Made: What should Lincoln do about the federal forts within the borders of the seceded states? Should Lincoln supply the garrison or withdraw it?

② Possible Consequences: Supply the garrison and risk war.

② Possible Consequences: Withdraw the garrison and give in to the rebels.

③ Decision Made: Supply the garrison.

④ Actual Consequence: The Confederates attacked the fort. This attack began the Civil War.

Practicing the Skill

Turn to Chapter 6, Section 1, "Tighter British Control." Read "The Colonies Protest the Stamp Act" and make a flow chart to identify a decision and its consequences described in that section.

2.7 Recognizing Propaganda

Defining the Skill

Propaganda is communication that aims to influence people's opinions, emotions, or actions. Propaganda is not always factual. Rather, it uses one-sided language or striking symbols to sway people's emotions. Modern advertising often uses propaganda. By thinking critically, you will avoid being swayed by propaganda.

Applying the Skill

The following political cartoon shows Andrew Jackson dressed as a king. Use the strategies listed below to help you understand how it works as propaganda.

How to Recognize Propaganda

Strategy ❶ Identify the aim, or purpose, of the cartoon. Point out the subject and explain the point of view.

Strategy ❷ Identify those images on the cartoon that viewers might respond to emotionally and identify the emotions.

Strategy ❸ Think critically about the cartoon. What facts has the cartoon ignored?

Make a Chart

Making a chart will help you think critically about a piece of propaganda. The chart below summarizes the information from the anti-Jackson cartoon.

❶	Identify Purpose	The cartoon portrays Jackson negatively by showing him as a king.
❷	Identify Emotions	The cartoonist knows that Americans like democracy. So he portrays Jackson as a king because kings are not usually supporters of democracy. He also shows Jackson standing on a torn U.S. Constitution—another thing that Americans love.
❸	Think Critically	The cartoon shows Jackson vetoing laws. But it ignores the fact that those actions were not against the Constitution. The president has the power to veto legislation. In this case, Jackson was exercising the power of the presidency, not acting like a king.

Practicing the Skill

Turn to Chapter 6, Section 2, "Colonial Resistance Grows," and look at the engraving *The Bloody Massacre* on the third page of the section. Use a chart like the one above to think critically about the engraving as an example of propaganda.

2.8 Identifying Facts and Opinions

Defining the Skill

Facts are events, dates, statistics, or statements that can be proved to be true. **Opinions** are the judgments, beliefs, and feelings of a writer or speaker. By identifying facts and opinions, you will be able to think critically when a person is trying to influence your own opinion.

Applying the Skill

The following passage tells about the Virginia Plan for legislative representation offered at the Constitutional Convention of 1787. Use the strategies listed below to help you distinguish facts from opinions.

How to Recognize Facts and Opinions

Strategy ❶ Look for specific information that can be proved or checked for accuracy.

Strategy ❷ Look for assertions, claims, and judgments that express opinions. In this case, one speaker's opinion is expressed in a direct quote.

Strategy ❸ Think about whether statements can be checked for accuracy. Then, identify the facts and opinions in a chart.

> ### ANTIFEDERALIST VIEWS
>
> ❶ Antifederalists published their views about the Constitution in newspapers and pamphlets. ❶ They thought the Constitution took too much power away from the states and did not protect the rights of the people. They charged that the Constitution would destroy American liberties. As one Antifederalist wrote, ❷ "It is truly astonishing that a set of men among ourselves should have had the [nerve] to attempt the destruction of our liberties."

Make a Chart

The chart below analyzes the facts and opinions from the passage above.

Statement	❸ Can It Be Proved?	❸ Fact or Opinion
Antifederalists published their views in newspapers and pamphlets.	Yes. Check newspapers and other historical documents.	Fact
They thought the Constitution took too much power away from the states.	Yes. Check newspapers and other historical documents.	Fact
It is astonishing that some Americans would try to destroy American liberties.	No. This cannot be proved. It is what one speaker believes.	Opinion

Practicing the Skill

Turn to Chapter 11, Section 3, and read the section entitled "The Missouri Compromise." Make a chart in which you analyze key statements to determine whether they are facts or opinions.

2.9 Forming and Supporting Opinions

Defining the Skill

When you **form opinions,** you interpret and judge the importance of events and people in history. You should always **support your opinions** with facts, examples, and quotes.

Applying the Skill

The following passage describes events that followed the gold rush. Use the strategies listed below to form and support your opinions about the events.

How to Form and Support Opinions

Strategy ❶ Look for important information about the events. Information can include facts, quotations, and examples.

Strategy ❷ Form an opinion about the event by asking yourself questions about the information. For example, How important was the event? What were its effects?

Strategy ❸ Support your opinions with facts, quotations, and examples. If the facts do not support the opinion, then rewrite your opinion so it is supported by the facts.

> ### THE IMPACT OF THE GOLD RUSH
>
> By 1852, the gold rush was over. ❶ While it lasted, about 250,000 people flooded into California. ❶ This huge migration caused economic growth that changed California. ❶ The port city San Francisco grew to become a center of banking, manufacturing, shipping, and trade. ❶ However, the gold rush ruined many *Californios. Californios* are the Hispanic people of California. The newcomers did not respect *Californios,* their customs, or their legal rights. ❶ In many cases, Americans seized their property.
>
> Native Americans suffered even more. ❶ Thousands died from diseases brought by the newcomers. ❶ Miners hunted down and killed thousands more. ❶ By 1870, California's Native American population had fallen from 150,000 to only about 30,000.

Make a Chart

Making a chart can help you organize your opinions and supporting facts. The following chart summarizes one possible opinion about the impact of the gold rush.

❷	Opinion	The effects of the gold rush were more negative than positive.
❸	Facts	Californios were not respected, and their land was stolen.
		Many Native Americans died from diseases, and others were killed by miners. Their population dropped from 150,000 to about 30,000.

Practicing the Skill

Turn to Chapter 11, Section 3, "Nationalism and Sectionalism." Read "The Missouri Compromise" and form your own opinion about the compromise and its impact. Make a chart like the one above to summarize your opinion and the supporting facts and examples.

2.10 Identifying and Solving Problems

Defining the Skill

Identifying problems means finding and understanding the difficulties faced by a particular group of people during a certain time. **Solving problems** means understanding how people tried to remedy those problems. By studying how people solved problems in the past, you can learn ways to solve problems today.

Applying the Skill

The following paragraph describes problems that the Constitutional Convention faced on the issues of taxation, representation, and slavery. Use the strategies listed below to help you see how the Founders tried to solve these problems.

How to Identify Problems and Solutions

Strategy ❶ Look for the difficulties, or problems, people faced.

Strategy ❷ Consider how the problem affected people with different points of view. For example, the main problem described here was how to count the population of each state.

Strategy ❸ Look for solutions people tried to deal with each problem. Think about whether the solution was a good one for people with differing points of view.

> **SLAVERY AND THE CONSTITUTION**
>
> Because the House of Representatives would have members according to the population of each state, ❶ the delegates had to decide who would be counted in the population of each state. The Southern states had many more slaves than the Northern states had. ❷ Southerners wanted the slaves to be counted as part of the general population for representation but not for taxation. ❷ Northerners argued that slaves were not citizens and should not be counted for representation, but that slaves should be counted for taxation. ❸ The delegates decided that three-fifths of the slave population would be counted in the population to determine both representation and taxes.

Make a Chart

Making a chart will help you identify and organize information about problems and solutions. The chart below shows problems and solutions included in the passage you just read.

❶ Problem	❷ Differing Points of View	❸ Solution
Northerners and Southerners couldn't agree on how to count population because of slavery in the South.	Southerners wanted slaves counted for representation but not for taxation. Northerners wanted slaves counted for taxation but not for representation.	Delegates decided that three-fifths of the slave population should be counted.

Practicing the Skill

Turn to Chapter 8, Section 2, "Creating the Constitution." Read "The Delegates Assemble" and "The Virginia Plan." Then make a chart that summarizes the problems faced by the delegates at the Constitutional Convention and the solutions they agreed on.

2.11 Evaluating

Defining the Skill

To **evaluate** is to make a judgment about something. Historians evaluate the actions of people in history. One way to do this is to examine both the positives and negatives of a historical action, then decide which is stronger—the positive or the negative.

Applying the Skill

The following passage describes Susan B. Anthony's fight for women's rights. Use the strategies listed below to evaluate how successful she was.

How to Evaluate

Strategy ① Before you evaluate a person's actions, first determine what that person was trying to do. In this case, think about what Anthony wanted to accomplish.

Strategy ② Look for statements that show the positive, or successful, results of her actions. For example, Did she achieve her goals?

Strategy ③ Also look for statements that show the negative, or unsuccessful, results of her actions. Did she fail to achieve something she tried to do?

Strategy ④ Write an overall evaluation of the person's actions.

SUSAN B. ANTHONY

① Susan B. Anthony was a skilled organizer who fought for women's rights. ② She successfully built the women's movement into a national organization. Anthony believed that a woman must have money of her own. To this end, she supported laws that would give married women rights to control their own property and wages. ② Mississippi passed the first such law in 1839. New York passed a property law in 1848 and a wages law in 1860. ③ Anthony also wanted to win the vote for women but failed to convince lawmakers to pass this reform in her lifetime. This reform did go through in 1920, 14 years after her death.

Make a Diagram for Evaluating

Using a diagram can help you evaluate. List the positives and negatives of the historical person's actions and decisions. Then make an overall judgment. The diagram below shows how the information from the passage you just read can be diagrammed.

② *Positive Results:*
- *women's movement became a national organization*
- *Mississippi and New York passed property and wage laws*

③ *Negative Results:*
- *failed to win vote for women in her lifetime*

④ *Evaluation:*
She was a successful reformer. Even the one reform she failed to achieve in her life did pass shortly after her death.

Practicing the Skill

Turn to Chapter 18, Section 3, "The End of Reconstruction." Read the section and make a diagram in which you evaluate Grant's presidency.

2.12 Making Generalizations

Defining the Skill

To **make generalizations** means to make broad judgments based on information. When you make generalizations, you should gather information from several sources.

Applying the Skill

The following three passages contain different views on George Washington. Use the strategies listed below to make a generalization about these views.

How to Make Generalizations

Strategy ❶ Look for information that the sources have in common. These three sources all discuss George Washington's ability as a military leader.

Strategy ❷ Form a generalization that describes Washington in a way that all three sources would agree with. State your generalization in a sentence.

> ### WASHINGTON'S LEADERSHIP
>
> ❶ Washington learned from his mistakes. After early defeats, he developed the strategy of dragging out the war to wear down the British. ❶ Despite difficulties, he never gave up.
>
> —*Creating America*
>
> ❶ [Washington] was no military genius. . . . But he was a great war leader. Creating an army out of unpromising material, he kept it in being against great odds.
>
> —*The Limits of Liberty*
>
> ❶ [Washington] certainly deserves some merit as a general, that he . . . can keep General Howe dancing from one town to another for two years together, with such an army as he has.
>
> —*The Journal of Nicholas Cresswell, July 13, 1777*

Make a Chart

Using a chart can help you make generalizations. The chart below shows how the information you just read can be used to generalize about people's views of Washington.

Practicing the Skill

Turn to Chapter 16, Section 1, "War Erupts." Read "Choosing Sides." Also read the excerpt from *Across Five Aprils* at the end of Section 1. Then use a chart like the one above to make a generalization about how the outbreak of the Civil War affected Americans.

3.1 Using Primary and Secondary Sources

Defining the Skill

Primary sources are materials written or made by people who lived during historical events and witnessed them. Primary sources can be letters, journal entries, speeches, autobiographies, or artwork. Other kinds of primary sources are government documents, census surveys, and financial records. **Secondary sources** are materials written by people who did not participate in an event. History books are secondary sources.

Applying the Skill

The following passage contains both a primary source and a secondary source. Use the strategies listed below to help you read them.

How to Read Primary and Secondary Sources

Strategy ① Distinguish secondary sources from primary sources. The first paragraph is a secondary source. The Declaration of Independence is a primary source. The secondary source explains something about the primary source.

Strategy ② Analyze the primary source and consider why the author produced it. Consider what the document was supposed to achieve and who would read it.

Strategy ③ Identify the author of the primary source and note when and where it was written.

> ① The core idea of the Declaration is based on the philosophy of John Locke. This idea is that people have unalienable rights, or rights that government cannot take away. Jefferson stated this belief in what was to become the Declaration's best-known passage.
>
> ② We hold these truths to be self-evident, that all men are created equal, that they are endowed by their Creator with certain unalienable Rights, that among these are Life, Liberty and the pursuit of Happiness.
>
> ③ —Thomas Jefferson, *The Declaration of Independence*, 1776

Make a Chart

Making a chart will help you summarize information from primary sources and secondary sources. The chart below summarizes the information from the passage you just read.

Author	Thomas Jefferson
Document	The Declaration of Independence
Notes on Primary Source	The Declaration says that "all men are created equal." It also says that people have "unalienable rights." These rights include the right to life and the right to liberty, as well as a right to pursue happiness.
Notes on Secondary Source	Jefferson based his ideas on those of John Locke. Locke had written about rights that governments could not take away from the people.

Practicing the Skill

Turn to Chapter 6, Section 3, "The Road to Lexington and Concord." Read "Between War and Peace" and make a chart like the one above to summarize the information in the primary source and the secondary source.

3.2 Interpreting Graphs

Defining the Skill

Graphs use pictures and symbols, instead of words, to show information. Graphs are created by taking information and presenting it visually. The graph on this page takes numerical information on immigration and presents it as a bar graph. There are many different kinds of graphs. Bar graphs, line graphs, and pie graphs are the most common. Bar graphs compare numbers or sets of numbers. The length of each bar shows a quantity. It is easy to see how different categories compare on a bar graph.

Applying the Skill

The bar graph below shows numbers of immigrants coming to the United States between 1821 and 1860. Use the strategies listed below to help you interpret the graph.

How to Interpret a Graph

Strategy ① Read the title to identify the main idea of the graph. Ask yourself what kinds of information the graph shows. For example, does it show chronological information, geographic patterns and distributions, or something else?

Strategy ② Read the vertical axis (the one that goes up and down) on the left side of the graph. This one shows the number of immigrants in thousands. Each bar represents the number of immigrants during a particular decade.

Strategy ③ Read the horizontal axis (the one that runs across the bottom of the graph). This one shows the four decades from 1821 to 1860.

Strategy ④ Summarize the information shown in each part of the graph. Use the title to help you focus on what information the graph is presenting.

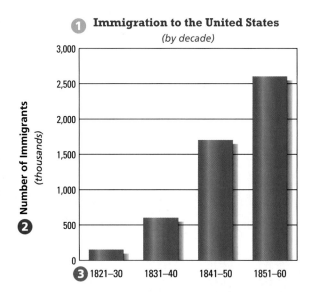

① **Immigration to the United States**
(by decade)

② **Number of Immigrants** *(thousands)*

③ 1821–30   1831–40   1841–50   1851–60

Write a Summary

Writing a summary will help you understand the information in the graph. The paragraph to the right summarizes the information from the bar graph.

④ *Immigration to the United States increased between 1821 and 1860. Between 1821 and 1830, fewer than 200,000 immigrants arrived. In the next decade, more than 500,000 immigrants came. During the 1840s, more than 1.5 million immigrants arrived, and that number increased to more than 2.5 million in the 1850s.*

Practicing the Skill

Turn to Chapter 16, Section 1, "War Erupts." Look at the graphs entitled "Resources, 1860." Write a paragraph in which you summarize what you learned from these graphs.

3.3 Interpreting Charts

Defining the Skill

Charts, like graphs, present information in a visual form. Charts are created by organizing, summarizing, and simplifying information and presenting it in a format that makes it easy to understand. Tables and diagrams are examples of commonly used charts.

Applying the Skill

The chart below shows the number of slaves who were imported to the Americas between 1601 and 1810. Use the strategies listed below to help you interpret the information in the chart.

How to Interpret a Chart

Strategy ① Read the title. It will tell you what the chart is about. Ask yourself what kinds of information the chart shows. For example, does it show chronological information, geographic patterns and distributions, or something else?

Strategy ② Read the labels to see how the information in the chart is organized. In this chart, it is organized by region and years.

Strategy ③ Study the data in the chart to understand the facts that the chart intends to show.

Strategy ④ Summarize the information shown in each part of the chart. Use the title to help you focus on what information the chart is presenting.

1601–1810

① Slaves Imported to the Americas (in thousands)

② REGION/COUNTRY	1601–1700	1701–1810
③ British N. America	*	348
British Caribbean	263.7	1,401.3
French Caribbean	155.8	1,348.4
Spanish America	292.5	578.6
Dutch Caribbean	40	460
Danish Caribbean	4	24
Brazil (Portugal)	560	1,891.4

*= less than 1,000

Source: Philip D. Curtin, *The Atlantic Slave Trade*

Write a Summary

Writing a summary can help you understand the information given in a chart. The paragraph to the right summarizes the information in the chart "Slaves Imported to the Americas, 1601–1810."

Practicing the Skill

Turn to Chapter 17, Section 4, and look at the charts entitled "Costs of the Civil War." Study the charts and ask yourself what geographic patterns and distributions are shown on them. Then write a paragraph in which you summarize what you learned from the charts.

④ The chart shows how many slaves were imported to the Americas between 1601 and 1810. It divides the Americas into seven regions. It also divides the time period into two parts: 1601–1700 and 1701–1810. The number of slaves imported increased greatly from the 1600s to the 1700s. More slaves were imported to Brazil than to any other region.

3.4 Interpreting Time Lines

Defining the Skill

A **time line** is a visual list of events and dates shown in the order in which they occurred. Time lines can be horizontal or vertical. On horizontal time lines, the earliest date is on the left. On vertical time lines, the earliest date is often at the top.

Applying the Skill

The time line below lists dates and events during the presidencies of John Adams, Andrew Jackson, and Martin Van Buren. Use the strategies listed below to help you interpret the information.

How to Read a Time Line

Strategy ❶ Read the dates at the beginning and end of the time line. These will show the period of history that is covered. The time line below is a dual time line. It includes items related to two topics. The labels show that the information covers U.S. events and world events.

Strategy ❷ Read the dates and events in sequential order, beginning with the earliest one. Pay particular attention to how the entries relate to each other. Think about which events caused later events.

Strategy ❸ Summarize the focus, or main idea, of the time line. Try to write a main idea sentence that describes the time line.

1828 Tariff of Abominations signed into law.

Andrew Jackson is elected president.

❷ **1824** John Quincy Adams is elected president.

❶

1830 Indian Removal Act is passed.

1832 Jackson vetoes charter of Bank of the United States.

South Carolina nullifies tariffs.

Jackson is reelected.

1836 Martin Van Buren is elected president.

1838 Cherokees begin to travel the Trail of Tears.

1840 William Henry Harrison is elected president.

USA World

1824 — 1840

❷ **1824** Simón Bolívar becomes president of Peru.

1830 Revolutions occur in Belgium, France, and Poland.

1832 Reform Act increases number of voters in Britain.

1837 Victoria becomes queen of Great Britain.

1838 Zulu clash with Boer settlers in South Africa.

Write a Summary

Writing a summary can help you understand information shown on a time line. The summary to the right states the main idea of the time line and tells how the events are related.

Practicing the Skill

Turn to Chapter 15 and look at the time line at the beginning of the chapter. Then write a summary of the information shown on the time line.

❸ *The time line covers the period between 1824, when John Quincy Adams was elected president, and 1840, when William Henry Harrison was elected president. During that period of time, Andrew Jackson and Martin Van Buren also served as president. The time line shows that the important issues in the United States were tariffs, banking, and relations with Native Americans.*

3.5 Reading a Map

Defining the Skill

Maps are representations of features on the earth's surface. Some maps show political features, such as national borders. Other maps show physical features, such as mountains and bodies of water. By learning to use map elements and math skills, you can better understand how to read maps.

Applying the Skill

The following map shows the Battle of Yorktown during the Revolution. Use the strategies listed below to help you identify the elements common to most maps.

How to Read a Map

Strategy ① Read the title. This identifies the main idea of the map.

Strategy ② Look for the grid of lines that forms a pattern of squares over the map. These numbered lines are the lines of latitude (horizontal) and longitude (vertical). They indicate the location of the area on the earth.

Strategy ③ Read the map key. It is usually in a box. This will give you the information you need to interpret the symbols or colors on the map.

Strategy ④ Use the scale and the pointer, or compass rose, to determine distance and direction.

Make a Chart

A chart can help you organize information given on maps. The chart below summarizes information about the map you just studied.

Title	Battle of Yorktown, 1781
Location	between latitude 40° N and 35° N, just east of longitude 80° W
Map Key Information	blue = American and allied forces, red = British forces
Scale	7/16 in. = 100 miles, 9/16 in. = 200 km
Summary	British commanders Graves and Hood sailed south from New York. They were defeated by De Grasse at the Battle of the Capes. British commander Cornwallis marched north from Wilmington, North Carolina, to Virginia, where he was defeated by American forces.

Practicing the Skill

Turn to Chapter 7, Section 1, "The Early Years of the War." Read the map entitled "War in the Middle States, 1776–1777" and make a chart to identify information on the map.

3.6 Reading a Special-Purpose Map

Defining the Skill

Special-purpose maps help people focus on a particular aspect of a region, such as economic development in the South. These kinds of maps often use symbols to indicate information.

Applying the Skill

The following special-purpose map indicates the products of the Southern colonies. Use the strategies listed below to help you identify the information shown on the map.

How to Read a Special-Purpose Map

Strategy ❶ Read the title. It tells you what the map is intended to show.

Strategy ❷ Read the legend. This tells you what each symbol stands for. This legend shows the crops that were grown in various Southern colonies.

Strategy ❸ Look for the places on the map where the symbols appear. These tell you the places where each crop was grown.

❶ **The Southern Colonies, 1750**

❷ Corn
Indigo
Naval stores
Pigs
Rice
Tobacco

Make a Chart

A chart can help you understand special-purpose maps. The chart below shows information about the special-purpose map you just studied.

	Corn	Indigo	Naval stores	Pigs	Rice	Tobacco
Maryland						x
Virginia	x			x		x
North Carolina	x		x	x	x	x
South Carolina	x	x	x	x	x	
Georgia		x		x	x	

Practicing the Skill

Turn to Chapter 4, Section 1, "New England: Commerce and Religion." Look at the special-purpose map entitled "The New England Colonies, 1750" and make a chart that shows information about products from New England.

3.7 Creating a Map

Defining the Skill

Creating a map involves representing geographical information. When you draw a map, it is easiest to use an existing map as a guide. On the map you draw, you can show geographical information. You can also show other kinds of information, such as data on climates, population trends, resources, or routes. Often, this data comes from a graph or a chart.

Applying the Skill

Below is a map that a student created to show information about the number of slaves in 1750. Read the strategies listed below to see how the map was created.

How to Create a Map

Strategy ❶ Select a title that identifies the geographical area and the map's purpose. Include a date in your title.

Strategy ❷ Draw the lines of latitude and longitude using short dashes.

Strategy ❸ Create a key that shows the colors.

Strategy ❹ Draw the colors on the map to show information.

Strategy ❺ Draw a compass rose and scale.

❶ Slave Population of the Southern Colonies, 1750

❸
- Fewer than 300,000
- 300,000–400,000
- 400,000–450,000
- More than 450,000

Practicing the Skill

Make your own map. Turn to the Chapter 3 Assessment and study the chart entitled "The 13 Colonies." Use the strategies described above to create a map that shows the 13 colonies and the dates that they were founded.

3.8 Interpreting Political Cartoons

Defining the Skill

Political cartoons are cartoons that use humor to make a serious point. Political cartoons often express a point of view on an issue better than words do. Understanding signs and symbols will help you to interpret political cartoons.

Applying the Skill

The cartoon below shows Abraham Lincoln and the other candidates running for the presidency in 1860. Use the strategies listed below to help you understand the cartoon.

How to Interpret a Political Cartoon

Strategy ❶ Identify the subject by reading the title of the cartoon and looking at the cartoon as a whole.

Strategy ❷ Identify important symbols and details. The cartoonist uses the image of a running race to discuss a political campaign. The White House is the finish line.

Strategy ❸ Interpret the message. Why is Lincoln drawn so much taller than the other candidates? How does that make him the fittest candidate?

Make a Chart

Making a chart will help you summarize information from a political cartoon. The chart below summarizes the information from the cartoon above.

Subject	"A Political Race" (The Election of 1860)
Symbols and Details	Running is a symbol for a political campaign. Lincoln is the tallest and fastest candidate.
Message	❸ Lincoln is pulling ahead of the other candidates in the campaign for the presidency.

Practicing the Skill

Turn to Chapter 18, Section 3, "End of Reconstruction." Look at the political cartoon under "Scandal and Panic Weaken Republicans." It shows a cartoonist's view of corruption in President Grant's administration. Use a chart like the one above and the strategies outlined to interpret the cartoon.

3.9 Creating a Model

Defining the Skill

When you **create a model,** you use information and ideas to show an event or a situation in a visual way. A model might be a poster or a diagram that explains how something happened. Or, it might be a three-dimensional model, such as a diorama, that depicts an important scene or situation.

Applying the Skill

The following sketch shows the early stages of a model of three ways that people could have traveled from the eastern United States to California during the gold rush. Use the strategies listed below to help you create your own model.

How to Create a Model

Strategy ① Gather the information you need to understand the situation or event. In this case, you need to be able to show the three routes and their dangers.

Strategy ② Visualize and sketch an idea for your model. Once you have created a picture in your mind, make an actual sketch to plan how it might look.

Strategy ③ Think of symbols you may want to use. Since the model should give information in a visual way, think about ways you can use color, pictures, or other visuals to tell the story.

Strategy ④ Gather the supplies you will need and create the model. For example, you will need a globe and art supplies, such as yarn, for this model.

Strategy ⑤ Write and answer a question about the California gold rush, as shown in this model.

The California Gold Rush
Dangerous Routes West

Wagon:
Dangers from hardships of the trail, mountains, rivers

Boat/overland:
Dangers from tropical sickness

Boat:
Dangers from sickness, storms, spoiled food

Practicing the Skill

Read the History Workshop called "Pack Your Trunk" at the end of Chapter 14. Follow the step-by-step directions to create a model of a trunk that shows what immigrants might have decided to bring with them when they came to America.

4.1 Using an Electronic Card Catalog

Defining the Skill

An **electronic card catalog** is a library's computerized search program that will help you find information about the books and other materials in the library. You can search the catalog by entering a book title, an author's name, or a subject of interest to you. The electronic card catalog will give you information about the materials in the library. This information is called bibliographic information. You can use an electronic card catalog to create a bibliography (a list of books) on any topic you are interested in.

Applying the Skill

The screen shown below is from an electronic search for information about Thomas Jefferson. Use the strategies listed below to help you use the information on the screen.

How to Use an Electronic Card Catalog

Strategy ❶ Begin searching by choosing either subject, title, or author, depending on the topic of your search. For this search, the user chose "Subject" and typed in the words "Jefferson, Thomas."

Strategy ❷ Once you have selected a book from the results of your search, identify the author, title, city, publisher, and date of publication.

Strategy ❸ Look for any special features in the book. This book is illustrated, and it includes bibliographical references and an index.

Strategy ❹ Locate the call number for the book. The call number indicates the section in the library where you will find the book. You can also find out if the book is available in the library you are using. If not, it may be in another library in the network.

Search Request:

❶ Subject   Title   Author

Find Options Locations Backup Startover Help

❷ Miller, Douglas T. Thomas Jefferson and the creation of America. New York: Facts on File, 1997.

❷ AUTHOR: Miller, Douglas T.
  TITLE: Thomas Jefferson and the creation of America/Douglas T. Miller.
❷ PUBLISHED: New York: Facts on File, ©1997.
❸ PAGING: vi, 122p. : ill ; 24 cm.
  SERIES: Makers of America.
❸ NOTES: Includes bibliographical references (p. 117-118) and index.
❹ CALL NUMBER: 1. 973.46 N61T 1997–Book Available–

Practicing the Skill

Turn to Chapter 10, "The Jefferson Era," and find a topic that interests you, such as the Federalists, the Louisiana Purchase, the Lewis and Clark expedition, or the War of 1812. Use the SUBJECT search on an electronic card catalog to find information about your topic. Make a bibliography of books about the subject. Be sure to include the author, title, city, publisher, and date of publication for all the books included.

4.2 Creating a Database

Defining the Skill

A **database** is a collection of data, or information, that is organized so that you can find and retrieve information on a specific topic quickly and easily. Once a computerized database is set up, you can search it to find specific information without going through the entire database. The database will provide a list of all information in the database related to your topic. Learning how to use a database will help you learn how to create one.

Applying the Skill

The chart below is a database for the significant battles of the Civil War. Use the strategies listed below to help you understand and use the database.

How to Create a Database

Strategy ① Identify the topic of the database. The keywords, or most important words, in this title are "Civil War" and "Battles." These words were used to begin the research for this database.

Strategy ② Ask yourself what kind of data you need to include. For example, what geographic patterns and distributions will be shown? Your choice of data will provide the column headings for your database. The key words "Battle," "Date," "Location," and "Significance" were chosen to focus the research.

Strategy ③ Identify the entries included under each heading.

Strategy ④ Use the database to help you find information quickly. For example, in this database you could search for "Union victories" to find a list of significant battles won by the North.

① LOCATION OF SIGNIFICANT CIVIL WAR BATTLES			
② BATTLE	DATE	② LOCATION	SIGNIFICANCE
③ Fort Sumter	April 12, 1861	Charleston, SC	Beginning of the Civil War
First Battle of Bull Run (Manassas)	July 21, 1861	Virginia	Confederate victory
Shiloh	April 6–7, 1862	Tennessee (near Shiloh Church)	④ Union victory
Antietam	September 17, 1862	Sharpsburg, MD	No clear victory; considered bloodiest battle of war
Gettysburg	July 1–3, 1863	Gettysburg, PA	Retreat of Confederacy
Vicksburg	Three-month siege ending July 3, 1863	Vicksburg, MS	Union gained control of Mississippi River
Chattanooga	November 23–25, 1863	Chattanooga, TN	④ Union victory
Atlanta	September 2, 1864	Atlanta, GA	④ Union victory; helped convince Confederacy of defeat

Practicing the Skill

Create a database for U.S. presidents through the Civil War that shows each president's home state, political party, and years served as president. Use the information in "Presidents of the United States" at the end of the book to provide the data. Use a format like the one above for your database.

4.3 Using the Internet

Defining the Skill

The Internet is a computer network that connects to universities, libraries, news organizations, government agencies, businesses, and private individuals throughout the world. Each location on the Internet has a home page with its own address, or URL (universal resource locator). With a computer connected to the Internet, you can reach the home pages of many organizations and services. The international collection of home pages, known as the World Wide Web, is a good source of up-to-date information about current events as well as research on subjects in history.

Applying the Skill

The Web page below shows the links for Chapter 6 of *Creating America.* Use the strategies listed below to help you understand how to use the Web page.

How to Use the Internet

Strategy ❶ Go directly to a Web page. For example, type classzone.com in the box at the top of the screen and press ENTER (or RETURN). The Web page will appear on your screen. Then click on the link to *Creating America.*

Strategy ❷ Explore the *Creating America* links. Click on any one of the links to find out more about a specific subject. These links take you to other pages at this Web site. Some pages include links to related information that can be found at other places on the Internet.

Strategy ❸ When using the Internet for research, you should confirm the information you find. Web sites set up by universities, government agencies, and reputable news sources are more reliable than other sources. You can often find information about the creator of a site by looking for copyright information.

Practicing the Skill

Turn to Chapter 14, Section 2, "American Literature and Art." Read the section and make a list of topics you would like to research. If you have Internet access, go to classzone.com. There you will find links that provide more information about the topics in the section.

4.4 Creating a Multimedia Presentation

Defining the Skill

Movies, CD-ROMs, television, and computer software are different kinds of media. To **create a multimedia presentation,** you need to collect information in different media and organize them into one presentation.

Applying the Skill

The scene below shows students using computers to create a multimedia presentation. Use the strategies listed below to help you create your own multimedia presentation.

How to Create a Multimedia Presentation

Strategy ❶ Identify the topic of your presentation and decide which media are best for an effective presentation. For example, you may want to use slides or posters to show visual images of your topic. Or, you may want to use CDs or audiotapes to provide music or spoken words.

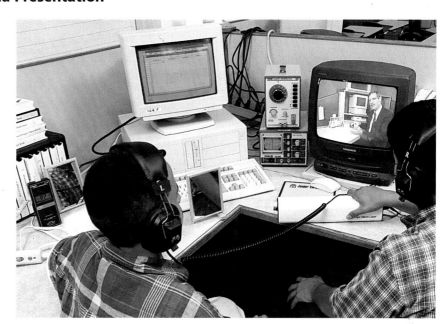

Strategy ❷ Research the topic in a variety of sources. Images, text, props, and background music should reflect the historical period of the event you choose.

Strategy ❸ Write the script for the oral portion of the presentation. You could use a narrator and characters' voices to tell the story. Primary sources are an excellent source for script material. Make sure the recording is clear so that the audience will be able to understand the oral part of the presentation.

Strategy ❹ Videotape the presentation. Videotaping the presentation will preserve it for future viewing and allow you to show it to different groups of people.

Practicing the Skill

Turn to Chapter 15, "The Nation Breaking Apart." Choose a topic from the chapter and use the strategies listed above to create a multimedia presentation about it.

Alabama
4,352,000 people
52,237 sq. mi.
Rank in area: 30
Entered Union in 1819

Florida
14,916,000 people
59,928 sq. mi.
Rank in area: 23
Entered Union in 1845

Louisiana
4,369,000 people
49,650 sq. mi.
Rank in area: 31
Entered Union in 1812

Alaska
614,000 people
615,230 sq. mi.
Rank in area: 1
Entered Union in 1959

Georgia
7,642,000 people
58,977 sq. mi.
Rank in area: 24
Entered Union in 1788

Maine
1,244,000 people
33,741 sq. mi.
Rank in area: 39
Entered Union in 1820

Arizona
4,669,000 people
114,006 sq. mi.
Rank in area: 6
Entered Union in 1912

Hawaii
1,193,000 people
6,459 sq. mi.
Rank in area: 47
Entered Union in 1959

Maryland
5,135,000 people
12,297 sq. mi.
Rank in area: 42
Entered Union in 1788

Arkansas
2,538,000 people
53,182 sq. mi.
Rank in area: 28
Entered Union in 1836

Idaho
1,229,000 people
83,574 sq. mi.
Rank in area: 14
Entered Union in 1890

Massachusetts
6,147,000 people
9,241 sq. mi.
Rank in area: 45
Entered Union in 1788

California
32,667,000 people
158,869 sq. mi.
Rank in area: 3
Entered Union in 1850

Illinois
12,045,000 people
57,918 sq. mi.
Rank in area: 25
Entered Union in 1818

Michigan
9,817,000 people
96,705 sq. mi.
Rank in area: 11
Entered Union in 1837

Colorado
3,971,000 people
104,100 sq. mi.
Rank in area: 8
Entered Union in 1876

Indiana
5,899,000 people
36,420 sq. mi.
Rank in area: 38
Entered Union in 1816

Minnesota
4,725,000 people
86,943 sq. mi.
Rank in area: 12
Entered Union in 1858

Connecticut
3,274,000 people
5,544 sq. mi.
Rank in area: 48
Entered Union in 1788

Iowa
2,862,000 people
56,276 sq. mi.
Rank in area: 26
Entered Union in 1846

Mississippi
2,752,000 people
48,286 sq. mi.
Rank in area: 32
Entered Union in 1817

Delaware
744,000 people
2,397 sq. mi.
Rank in area: 49
Entered Union in 1787

Kansas
2,629,000 people
82,282 sq. mi.
Rank in area: 15
Entered Union in 1861

Missouri
5,439,000 people
69,709 sq. mi.
Rank in area: 21
Entered Union in 1821

District of Columbia
523,000 people
68 sq. mi.

Kentucky
3,936,000 people
40,411 sq. mi.
Rank in area: 37
Entered Union in 1792

Montana
880,000 people
147,046 sq. mi.
Rank in area: 4
Entered Union in 1889

Sources: U.S. Bureau of the Census, 1998 population estimates.
World Almanac and Book of Facts, 1999
Statistical Abstract of the United States, 1998

Nebraska
1,663,000 people
77,359 sq. mi.
Rank in area: 16
Entered Union in 1867

Ohio
11,209,000 people
44,828 sq. mi.
Rank in area: 34
Entered Union in 1803

Texas
19,760,000 people
267,277 sq. mi.
Rank in area: 2
Entered Union in 1845

Nevada
1,747,000 people
110,567 sq. mi.
Rank in area: 7
Entered Union in 1864

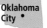

Oklahoma
3,347,000 people
69,903 sq. mi.
Rank in area: 20
Entered Union in 1907

Utah
2,100,000 people
84,904 sq. mi.
Rank in area: 13
Entered Union in 1896

New Hampshire
1,185,000 people
9,283 sq. mi.
Rank in area: 44
Entered Union in 1788

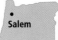

Oregon
3,282,000 people
97,132 sq. mi.
Rank in area: 10
Entered Union in 1859

Vermont
591,000 people
9,615 sq. mi.
Rank in area: 43
Entered Union in 1791

New Jersey
8,115,000 people
8,215 sq. mi.
Rank in area: 46
Entered Union in 1787

Pennsylvania
12,001,000 people
46,058 sq. mi.
Rank in area: 33
Entered Union in 1787

Virginia
6,791,000 people
42,326 sq. mi.
Rank in area: 35
Entered Union in 1788

New Mexico
1,737,000 people
121,598 sq. mi.
Rank in area: 5
Entered Union in 1912

Rhode Island
988,000 people
1,231 sq. mi.
Rank in area: 50
Entered Union in 1790

Washington
5,689,000 people
70,637 sq. mi.
Rank in area: 19
Entered Union in 1889

New York
18,175,000 people
53,989 sq. mi.
Rank in area: 27
Entered Union in 1788

South Carolina
3,836,000 people
31,189 sq. mi.
Rank in area: 40
Entered Union in 1788

West Virginia
1,811,000 people
24,232 sq. mi.
Rank in area: 41
Entered Union in 1863

North Carolina
7,546,000 people
52,672 sq. mi.
Rank in area: 29
Entered Union in 1789

South Dakota
738,000 people
77,121 sq. mi.
Rank in area: 17
Entered Union in 1889

Wisconsin
5,224,000 people
65,500 sq. mi.
Rank in area: 22
Entered Union in 1848

North Dakota
638,000 people
70,704 sq. mi.
Rank in area: 18
Entered Union in 1889

Tennessee
5,431,000 people
42,145 sq. mi.
Rank in area: 36
Entered Union in 1796

Wyoming
481,000 people
97,819 sq. mi.
Rank in area: 9
Entered Union in 1890

United States: *Major Dependencies*

- American Samoa—63,786 people; 90 sq. mi.
- Guam—151,716 people; 217 sq. mi.
- Commonwealth of Puerto Rico—3,887,652 people; 3,508 sq. mi.
- Virgin Islands of the United States—119,827 people; 171 sq. mi.
- Midway Islands—no indigenous inhabitants; 2 sq. mi.
- Wake Atoll—no indigenous inhabitants; 3 sq. mi.

PRESIDENTS of the UNITED STATES

Here are some little-known facts about the presidents of the United States:

- Only former president to serve in Congress: John Quincy Adams
- First president born in the new United States: Martin Van Buren (eighth president)
- Only president who was a bachelor: James Buchanan
- First left-handed president: James A. Garfield
- Largest president: William H. Taft (6 feet 2 inches, 326 pounds)
- Youngest president: Theodore Roosevelt (42 years old)
- Oldest president: Ronald Reagan (77 years old when he left office in 1989)
- First president born west of the Mississippi River: Herbert Hoover (born in West Branch, Iowa)
- First president born in the 20th century: John F. Kennedy (born May 29, 1917)

1 **George Washington**
1789–1797
No Political Party
Birthplace: Virginia
Born: February 22, 1732
Died: December 14, 1799

2 **John Adams**
1797–1801
Federalist
Birthplace: Massachusetts
Born: October 30, 1735
Died: July 4, 1826

3 **Thomas Jefferson**
1801–1809
Democratic-Republican
Birthplace: Virginia
Born: April 13, 1743
Died: July 4, 1826

4 **James Madison**
1809–1817
Democratic-Republican
Birthplace: Virginia
Born: March 16, 1751
Died: June 28, 1836

5 **James Monroe**
1817–1825
Democratic-Republican
Birthplace: Virginia
Born: April 28, 1758
Died: July 4, 1831

6 **John Quincy Adams**
1825–1829
Democratic-Republican
Birthplace: Massachusetts
Born: July 11, 1767
Died: February 23, 1848

7 **Andrew Jackson**
1829–1837
Democrat
Birthplace: South Carolina
Born: March 15, 1767
Died: June 8, 1845

8 **Martin Van Buren**
1837–1841
Democrat
Birthplace: New York
Born: December 5, 1782
Died: July 24, 1862

9 **William H. Harrison**
1841
Whig
Birthplace: Virginia
Born: February 9, 1773
Died: April 4, 1841

10 **John Tyler**
1841–1845
Whig
Birthplace: Virginia
Born: March 29, 1790
Died: January 18, 1862

11 **James K. Polk**
1845–1849
Democrat
Birthplace: North Carolina
Born: November 2, 1795
Died: June 15, 1849

12 **Zachary Taylor**
1849–1850
Whig
Birthplace: Virginia
Born: November 24, 1784
Died: July 9, 1850

13 Millard Fillmore
1850–1853
Whig
Birthplace: New York
Born: January 7, 1800
Died: March 8, 1874

14 Franklin Pierce
1853–1857
Democrat
Birthplace: New Hampshire
Born: November 23, 1804
Died: October 8, 1869

15 James Buchanan
1857–1861
Democrat
Birthplace: Pennsylvania
Born: April 23, 1791
Died: June 1, 1868

16 Abraham Lincoln
1861–1865
Republican
Birthplace: Kentucky
Born: February 12, 1809
Died: April 15, 1865

17 Andrew Johnson
1865–1869
National Union
Birthplace: North Carolina
Born: December 29, 1808
Died: July 31, 1875

18 Ulysses S. Grant
1869–1877
Republican
Birthplace: Ohio
Born: April 27, 1822
Died: July 23, 1885

19 Rutherford B. Hayes
1877–1881
Republican
Birthplace: Ohio
Born: October 4, 1822
Died: January 17, 1893

20 James A. Garfield
1881
Republican
Birthplace: Ohio
Born: November 19, 1831
Died: September 19, 1881

21 Chester A. Arthur
1881–1885
Republican
Birthplace: Vermont
Born: October 5, 1829
Died: November 18, 1886

22 24 Grover Cleveland
1885–1889, 1893–1897
Democrat
Birthplace: New Jersey
Born: March 18, 1837
Died: June 24, 1908

23 Benjamin Harrison
1889–1893
Republican
Birthplace: Ohio
Born: August 20, 1833
Died: March 13, 1901

25 William McKinley
1897–1901
Republican
Birthplace: Ohio
Born: January 29, 1843
Died: September 14, 1901

26 Theodore Roosevelt
1901–1909
Republican
Birthplace: New York
Born: October 27, 1858
Died: January 6, 1919

27 William H. Taft
1909–1913
Republican
Birthplace: Ohio
Born: September 15, 1857
Died: March 8, 1930

28 Woodrow Wilson
1913–1921
Democrat
Birthplace: Virginia
Born: December 28, 1856
Died: February 3, 1924

29 Warren G. Harding
1921–1923
Republican
Birthplace: Ohio
Born: November 2, 1865
Died: August 2, 1923

30 **Calvin Coolidge**
1923–1929
Republican
Birthplace: Vermont
Born: July 4, 1872
Died: January 5, 1933

31 **Herbert C. Hoover**
1929–1933
Republican
Birthplace: Iowa
Born: August 10, 1874
Died: October 20, 1964

32 **Franklin D. Roosevelt**
1933–1945
Democrat
Birthplace: New York
Born: January 30, 1882
Died: April 12, 1945

33 **Harry S. Truman**
1945–1953
Democrat
Birthplace: Missouri
Born: May 8, 1884
Died: December 26, 1972

34 **Dwight D. Eisenhower**
1953–1961
Republican
Birthplace: Texas
Born: October 14, 1890
Died: March 28, 1969

35 **John F. Kennedy**
1961–1963
Democrat
Birthplace: Massachusetts
Born: May 29, 1917
Died: November 22, 1963

36 **Lyndon B. Johnson**
1963–1969
Democrat
Birthplace: Texas
Born: August 27, 1908
Died: January 22, 1973

37 **Richard M. Nixon**
1969–1974
Republican
Birthplace: California
Born: January 9, 1913
Died: April 22, 1994

38 **Gerald R. Ford**
1974–1977
Republican
Birthplace: Nebraska
Born: July 14, 1913

39 **James E. Carter, Jr.**
1977–1981
Democrat
Birthplace: Georgia
Born: October 1, 1924

40 **Ronald W. Reagan**
1981–1989
Republican
Birthplace: Illinois
Born: February 6, 1911

41 **George H. W. Bush**
1989–1993
Republican
Birthplace: Massachusetts
Born: June 12, 1924

42 **William J. Clinton**
1993–2001
Democrat
Birthplace: Arkansas
Born: August 19, 1946

43 **George W. Bush**
2001–
Republican
Birthplace: Connecticut
Born: July 6, 1946

The Gazetteer identifies important places and geographical features in this book. Entries include a short description, often followed by two page numbers. The first number refers to a text page on which the entry is discussed, and the second, in italics, refers to a map where the place appears. (The reference *Atlas* is to the section of U.S. and world maps on pages A1–A21.) In addition, some entries include rounded-off geographical coordinates. There are entries for all U.S. states (with capital cities).

Africa world's second largest continent. *Atlas*

Alabama 22nd state. Capital: Montgomery. *Atlas*

Alamo Texas mission in San Antonio captured by Mexico in 1836. (29°N 98°W), 387, *m389*

Alaska 49th state. Capital: Juneau. *Atlas*

Antarctica continent at the South Pole. *Atlas*

Antietam Maryland creek; site of bloodiest day's fighting in the Civil War. (39°N 77°W), 481, *m479*

Appalachian Mountains mountain range running from Alabama into Canada. 110, *m111*

Appomattox Court House town near Appomattox, Virginia, where Lee surrendered to Grant on April 9, 1865. (37°N 79°W), 503, *m511*

Arizona 48th state. Capital: Phoenix. *Atlas*

Arkansas 25th state. Capital: Little Rock. *Atlas*

Asia world's largest continent. *Atlas*

Atlantic Ocean ocean forming east boundary of the United States. *Atlas*

Australia island country between Indian and Pacific oceans; also the world's smallest continent. *Atlas*

Austria-Hungary one of the Central Powers in World War I; after the war, divided into smaller countries. 560

Aztec Empire former region of Mexico once under Aztec control. 30, *m30*

Backcountry identification for former undeveloped region beginning in the Appalachian Mountains and extending west. 110, *m111*

Baltimore Maryland city on Chesapeake Bay. (39°N 77°W), 316, *m315*

Bay of Pigs (Bahía de Cochinos) inlet on south coast of Cuba; site of 1961 ill-fated, U.S.-backed Cuban invasion attempt. (22°N 81°W), 822

Beringia former land bridge connecting Asia with North America and now under waters of Bering Strait. (66°N 169°W), 27

Berlin capital of Germany; divided into East and West Berlin, 1948–1989. (53°N 13°E), *m577*

Boston capital of Massachusetts; site of early colonial unrest and conflict. (42°N 71°W), 149, *m156*

Bull Run stream 30 miles southwest of Washington, D.C.; site of first land battle of Civil War. (39°N 78°W), 469, *m479*

Bunker Hill hill now part of Boston; its name misidentifies Revolutionary War battle fought at nearby Breed's Hill. (42°N 71°W), 161

Cahokia Illinois Mound Builders site; village taken from British by Clark in 1778. (39°N 90°W), *m187*

California 31st state. Capital: Sacramento. *Atlas*

Canada nation sharing northern U.S. border. *Atlas*

Caribbean Sea expanse of the Atlantic Ocean between the Gulf of Mexico and South America. *Atlas*

Central America area of North America between Mexico and South America. *m60, Atlas*

Charleston as Charles Town, largest Southern colonial city; South Carolina site of first Civil War shots, at offshore Fort Sumter. (33°N 80°W), 465, *m467*

Charlestown former town, now part of Boston; site of both Bunker and Breed's hills. (42°N 71°W), 161, *m156*

Chicago large Illinois city on Lake Michigan. (42°N 88°W), 544, *m545, Atlas*

China large nation in Asia. *Atlas*

Colorado 38th state. Capital: Denver. *Atlas*

Concord Massachusetts city and site of second battle of the Revolutionary War. (42°N 71°W), 156, *m156*

Confederate States of America nation formed by 11 Southern states during the Civil War. Capital: Richmond, Virginia. 457, 466, *m467*

Connecticut 5th state. Capital: Hartford. *Atlas*

Cuba Caribbean island south of Florida. 558, *Atlas*

Delaware 1st state. Capital: Dover. *Atlas*

District of Columbia (D.C.) self-governing federal district between Virginia and Maryland, made up entirely of the city of Washington, the U.S. capital. (39°N 77°W), 289, *Atlas*

Dominican Republic nation sharing the island of Hispaniola with Haiti. *Atlas*

England southern part of Great Britain. *Atlas*

English Channel narrow waterway separating Great Britain from France. 57

Erie Canal all-water channel dug out to connect the Hudson River with Lake Erie. 339, *m339*

Europe second smallest continent, actually a peninsula of the Eurasian landmass. *Atlas*

Florida 27th state. Capital: Tallahassee. *Atlas*

Fort McHenry fort in Baltimore harbor where 1814 British attack inspired U.S. national anthem. (39°N 77°N), 316, *m315*

Fort Sumter fort in Charleston, South Carolina, harbor where 1861 attack by Confederates began the Civil War. (33°N 80°W), 465, *m467*

France nation in western Europe; it aided America in the Revolutionary War. *Atlas*

Gadsden Purchase last territory (from Mexico, 1853) added to continental United States. 395, *m394*

Georgia 4th state. Capital: Atlanta. *Atlas*

Germany nation in central Europe; once divided into West and East Germany, 1949–1990. *Atlas*

Gettysburg Pennsylvania town and site of 1863 Civil War victory for the North that is considered war's turning point. (40°N 77°W), 497, *m498*

Ghana first powerful West African trading empire. 34, *m34*

Great Britain European island nation across from France; it consists of England, Scotland, and Wales. *Atlas*

Great Lakes five connected lakes—Ontario, Erie, Huron, Michigan, and Superior—on the U.S. border with Canada. 339, *m339*

Great Plains vast grassland region in the central United States. 377, *m379*

Gulf of Mexico body of water forming southern U.S. boundary from east Texas to west Florida. *Atlas*

Haiti nation sharing the island of Hispaniola with Dominican Republic. *Atlas*

Harpers Ferry village today in extreme eastern West Virginia where John Brown raided stored U.S. weapons in 1859. (39°N 78°W), 453, *m479*

Hawaii 50th state. Capital: Honolulu. *Atlas*

Hiroshima Japanese city destroyed by U.S. atomic bomb dropped to end World War II. (34°N 132°E), 578, *m577*

Hispaniola West Indies island (shared today by Dominican Republic and Haiti) that Columbus mistook for Asia. 42, *m41*

Hudson River large river in eastern New York. 84, *m79*

Idaho 43rd state. Capital: Boise. *Atlas*

Illinois 21st state. Capital: Springfield. *Atlas*

Indiana 19th state. Capital: Indianapolis. *Atlas*

Indian Territory area, mainly of present-day Oklahoma, that in the 1800s became land for relocated Native Americans. 360, *m360*

Iowa 29th state. Capital: Des Moines. *Atlas*

Iran Middle East nation. *Atlas*

Iraq Middle East nation whose 1990 invasion of Kuwait led to the Persian Gulf War. *Atlas*

Ireland island country west of England whose mid-1800s famine caused more than one million people to emigrate to America. 410, *Atlas*

Israel Jewish nation in the Middle East. *Atlas*

Italy nation in southern Europe. *Atlas*

Jamestown community in Virginia that was the first permanent English settlement in North America. 71, *m71*

Japan island nation in east Asia. *Atlas*

Kansas 34th state. Capital: Topeka. *Atlas*

Kentucky 15th state. Capital: Frankfort. *Atlas*

Kosovo province of the Yugoslavian republic of Serbia. *Atlas*

Kuwait tiny, oil-rich Middle East nation. *Atlas*

Latin America region made up of Mexico, Caribbean Islands, and Central and South America, where Latin-based languages of Spanish, French, or Portuguese are spoken. 343

Lexington Massachusetts city and site of first Revolutionary War battle in 1775. (42°N 71°W), 157, *m156*

Little Rock capital of Arkansas and site of 1957 school-desegregation conflict. *Atlas*

Los Angeles 2nd largest U.S. city, on California's coast. *Atlas*

Louisiana 18th state. Capital: Baton Rouge. *Atlas*

Louisiana Purchase land west of the Mississippi River purchased from France in 1803. 303, *m314*

Lowell Massachusetts city built in early 1800s as planned factory town. (43°N 71°W), 326

Maine 23rd state. Capital: Augusta. *Atlas*

Mali early West African trading empire succeeding Ghana empire. 34, *m35*

Maryland 7th state. Capital: Annapolis. *Atlas*

Massachusetts 6th state. Capital: Boston. *Atlas*

Mexico nation sharing U.S. southern border. *Atlas*

Michigan 26th state. Capital: Lansing. *Atlas*

Minnesota 32nd state. Capital: St. Paul. *Atlas*

Mississippi 20th state. Capital: Jackson. *Atlas*

Mississippi River second longest U.S. river, south from Minnesota to the Gulf of Mexico. 130, *m137*

Missouri 24th state. Capital: Jefferson City. *Atlas*

Missouri River longest U.S. river, east from the Rockies to the Mississippi River. 305, *m304*

Montana 41st state. Capital: Helena. *Atlas*

Montgomery Alabama capital and site of 1955 African-American bus boycott. (32°N 86°W), *m334*

Nagasaki Japanese port city, one-third of which was destroyed by U.S. atomic bomb dropped to end World War II. (33°N 130°E), 578, *m577*

Nebraska 37th state. Capital: Lincoln. *Atlas*

Nevada 36th state. Capital: Carson City. *Atlas*

New England northeast U.S. region made up of Maine, New Hampshire, Vermont, Massachusetts, Rhode Island, and Connecticut. 93, *m94*

New France first permanent French colony in North America. 58, *m132*

New Hampshire 9th state. Capital: Concord. *Atlas*

New Jersey 3rd state. Capital: Trenton. *Atlas*

New Mexico 47th state. Capital: Santa Fe. *Atlas*

New Netherland early Dutch colony that became New York in 1664. 58

New Orleans Louisiana port city at mouth of the Mississippi River. *Atlas*

New Spain former North American province of the Spanish Empire, made up mostly of present-day Mexico and the southwest United States. 59, *m60*

New York 11th state. Capital: Albany. *Atlas*

New York City largest U.S. city, at the mouth of the Hudson River; temporary U.S. capital, 1785–1790. *Atlas*

Normandy region of northern France where Allied invasion in 1944 turned tide of World War II. 577

North America continent of Western Hemisphere north of Panama-Colombia border. *Atlas*

North Carolina 12th state. Capital: Raleigh. *Atlas*

North Dakota 39th state. Capital: Bismarck. *Atlas*

North Korea Communist country in Asia, bordering eastern China. *Atlas*

North Vietnam northern region of Vietnam, established in 1954; reunified with South Vietnam in 1975 after Vietnam War. 581

Northwest Territory U.S. land north of the Ohio River to the Great Lakes and west to the Mississippi River; acquired in 1783. 207, *m210*

Ohio 17th state. Capital: Columbus. *Atlas*

Ohio River river that flows from western Pennsylvania to the Mississippi River. *Atlas*

Oklahoma 46th state. Capital: Oklahoma City. *Atlas*

Oregon 33rd state. Capital: Salem. *Atlas*

Oregon Country former region of northwest North America claimed jointly by Britain and the United States until 1846. 302, *m304*

Oregon Trail pioneer wagon route from Missouri to the Oregon Territory in the 1840s and 1850s. 380, *m379*

Pacific Ocean world's largest ocean, on the west coast of the United States. *Atlas*

Panama Canal ship passageway cut through Panama in Central America, linking Atlantic and Pacific oceans. (8°N 80°W), 558, 559

Pearl Harbor naval base in Hawaii; site of surprise Japanese aerial attack in 1941. (21°N 158°W), 575–576

Pennsylvania 2nd state. Capital: Harrisburg. *Atlas*

Persian Gulf waterway between Saudi Arabia and Iran, leading to Kuwait and Iraq. 587, *Atlas*

Philadelphia large port city in Pennsylvania; U.S. capital, 1790–1800. (40°N 76°W), 213, *Atlas*

Philippine Islands Pacific island country off the southeast coast of China. 557, *Atlas*

Plymouth town on Massachusetts coast and site of Pilgrim landing and colony. (42°N 71°W), 77, *m79*

Portugal nation in southwestern Europe; leader in early oceanic explorations. 39, *m41*

Potomac River historic river separating Virginia from Maryland and Washington, D.C. 480, *m479*

Puerto Rico Caribbean island that has been U.S. territory since 1898. 558, *Atlas*

Quebec major early Canadian city; also a province of eastern Canada. 130, *m132*

Rhode Island 13th state. Capital: Providence. *Atlas*

Richmond Virginia capital that was also the capital of the Confederacy. (38°N 77°W), 466, *m467*

Rio Grande river that forms part of the border between the United States and Mexico. *Atlas*

Roanoke Island island off the coast of North Carolina; 1585 site of the first English colony in the Americas. (36°N 76°W), 69, *m71*

Rocky Mountains mountain range in the western United States and Canada. *Atlas*

Russia large Eurasian country, the major republic of the former Soviet Union (1922–1991). *Atlas*

St. Augustine oldest permanent European settlement (1565) in the United States, on Florida's northeast coast. (30°N 81°W), 56, 57, *m56*

St. Lawrence River Atlantic-to-Great Lakes waterway used by early explorers of mid-North America. 130, *m132*

St. Louis Missouri city at the junction of the Missouri and Mississippi rivers. (39°N 90°W), 304, *Atlas*

San Antonio Texas city and site of the Alamo. (29°N 99°W), 386, *m389*

San Francisco major port city in northern California. (38°N 123°W), 400, *Atlas*

San Salvador West Indies island near the Bahamas where Columbus first landed in the Americas. (24°N 74°W), 42, *m41*

Santa Fe Trail old wagon route from Missouri to Santa Fe in Mexican province of New Mexico. 379, *m379*

Songhai early West African trading empire succeeding Mali empire. 34–35, *m34*

South America continent of Western Hemisphere south of Panama-Colombia border. *Atlas*

South Carolina 8th state. Capital: Columbia. *Atlas*

South Dakota 40th state. Capital: Pierre. *Atlas*

South Korea East Asian country bordering North Korea. *Atlas*

South Vietnam southern region of Vietnam, established in 1954; reunified with North Vietnam in 1975 after Vietnam War. 581

Soviet Union country created in 1922 by joining Russia and other republics; in 1991, broken into independent states. 576, *m577*

Spain nation in southwestern Europe; early empire builder in the Americas. 40, *m41*

Tennessee 16th state. Capital: Nashville. *Atlas*

Tenochtitlán Aztec Empire capital; now site of Mexico City. 53, *m56*

Texas 28th state. Capital: Austin. *Atlas*

Utah 45th state. Capital: Salt Lake City. *Atlas*

Valley Forge village in southeast Pennsylvania and site of Washington's army camp during winter of 1777–1778. (40°N 75°W), 186, *m193*

Vermont 14th state. Capital: Montpelier. *Atlas*

Vicksburg Mississippi River site of major Union victory (1863) in Civil War. (32°N 91°W), 500, *m501*

Vietnam country in Southeast Asia; divided into two regions (1954–1975), North and South, until end of Vietnam War. 581, *Atlas*

Virginia 10th state. Capital: Richmond. *Atlas*

Washington 42nd state. Capital: Olympia. *Atlas*

Washington, D.C. capital of the United States since 1800; makes up whole of District of Columbia (D.C.). (39°N 77°W), 289, *Atlas*

West Africa region from which most Africans were brought to the Americas. 33, *m34*

Western Hemisphere the half of the world that includes the Americas. 62, *m62*

West Indies numerous islands in the Caribbean Sea, between Florida and South America. 95, *m95*

West Virginia 35th state. Capital: Charleston. *Atlas*

Wisconsin 30th state. Capital: Madison. *Atlas*

Wyoming 44th state. Capital: Cheyenne. *Atlas*

Yorktown Virginia village and site of American victory that sealed British defeat in Revolutionary War. (37°N 77°W), 193, *m193*

abolition (AB uh LIHSH uhn) *n.* the movement to end slavery. (p. 424)

abridge (uh BRIHJ) *v.* to reduce. (p. 250)

affirmation (AF uhr MAY shuhn) *n.* a statement declaring that something is true. (p. 241)

African Diaspora (AF rih kuhn dy AS puhr uh) *n.* the forced removal of Africans from their homelands to serve as slave labor in the Americas. (p. 61)

Albany Plan of Union *n.* the first formal proposal to unite the American colonies, put forth by Benjamin Franklin. (p. 133)

Alien and Sedition (si DISH uhn) **Acts** *n.* a series of four laws enacted in 1798 to reduce the political power of recent immigrants to the United States. (p. 290)

ally (AL eye) *n.* a country that agrees to help another country achieve a common goal. (p. 184)

American System *n.* a plan introduced in 1815 to make the United States economically self-sufficient. (p. 338)

Anaconda (AN uh KAHN duh) **Plan** *n.* a strategy by which the Union proposed to defeat the Confederacy in the Civil War. (p. 468)

Antifederalist (AN tee FED uhr uh list) *n.* a person who opposed the ratification of the U.S. Constitution. (p. 218)

Appalachian (AP uh LAY chee uhn) **Mountains** *n.* a mountain range that stretches from eastern Canada south to Alabama. (p. 110)

appellate (uh PEL it) *adj.* having power to review court decisions. (p. 244)

Appomattox (AP uh MAT uhks) **Court House** *n.* the Virginia town where Robert E. Lee surrendered to Ulysses S. Grant in 1865, ending the Civil War. (p. 503)

apprentice (uh PREN tis) *n.* a beginner who learns a trade or a craft from an experienced master. (p. 121)

appropriation (uh PROH pree AY shuhn) *n.* public funds set aside for a specific purpose. (p. 237)

Articles of Confederation *n.* a document, adopted by the Continental Congress in 1777 and finally approved by the states in 1781, that outlined the form of government of the new United States. (p. 206)

artillery (ahr TIL uhr ee) *n.* a cannon or large gun. (p. 161)

artisan (AHR ti zuhn) *n.* a skilled worker, such as a weaver or a potter, who makes goods by hand; a craftsperson. (p. 101)

baby boom *n.* the term for the generation born between 1946 and 1961, when the U.S. birthrate sharply increased following World War II. (p. 584)

Backcountry *n.* a colonial region that ran along the Appalachian Mountains through the far western part of the New England, Middle, and Southern colonies. (p. 93)

Bacon's Rebellion *n.* a revolt against powerful colonial authority in Jamestown by Nathaniel Bacon and a group of landless frontier settlers that resulted in the burning of Jamestown in 1676. (p. 73)

bail (bayl) *n.* money paid as security by arrested persons to guarantee they will return for trial. (p. 252)

Battle of Antietam (an TEE tuhm) *n.* a Civil War battle in 1862 in which 25,000 men were killed or wounded. (p. 481)

Battle of Fallen Timbers *n.* in 1794, an American army defeated 2,000 Native Americans in a clash over control of the Northwest Territory. (p. 283)

Battle of Gettysburg (GET eez BURG) *n.* an 1863 battle in the Civil War in which the Union defeated the Confederacy, ending hopes for a Confederate victory in the North. (p. 497)

Battle of Quebec (kwi BEK) *n.* a battle won by the British over the French, and the turning point in the French and Indian War. (p. 134)

Battle of Shiloh (SHY loh) *n.* an 1862 battle in which the Union forced the Confederacy to retreat in some of the fiercest fighting in the Civil War. (p. 478)

Battle of Yorktown *n.* the last major battle of the Revolutionary War, which resulted in the surrender of British forces in 1781. (p. 194)

Battle of the Alamo (AL uh MOH) *n.* in 1836, Texans defended a church called the Alamo against the Mexican army; all but five Texans were killed. (p. 387)

Battle of the Thames (temz) *n.* an American victory over the British in the War of 1812, which ended the British threat to the Northwest Territory. (p. 316)

Battles of Saratoga (SAR uh TOH guh) *n.* a series of conflicts between British soldiers and the Continental Army in 1777 that proved to be a turning point in the Revolutionary War. (p. 183)

bayonet (BAY uh net) *n.* a long steel knife attached to the end of a gun. (p. 186)

Bear Flag Revolt *n.* the 1846 rebellion by Americans against Mexican rule in California. (p. 393)

bill of attainder (uh TAYN duhr) *n.* a law that condemns a person without a trial in court. (p. 239)

Bill of Rights *n.* the first ten amendments to the U.S. Constitution, added in 1791, and consisting of a formal list of citizens' rights and freedoms. (p. 221)

black code *n.* a law passed by Southern states that limited the freedom of former slaves. (p. 518)

blockade *n.* when armed forces prevent the transportation of goods or people into or out of an area. (p. 468)

border state *n.* a slave state that bordered states in which slavery was illegal. (p. 466)

Boston Massacre (MAS uh kuhr) *n.* a clash between British soldiers and Boston colonists in 1770, in which five of the colonists, including Crispus Attucks, were killed. (p. 149)

Boston Tea Party *n.* the dumping of 342 chests of tea into Boston Harbor by colonists in 1773 to protest the Tea Act. (p. 151)

bounty (BOWN tee) *n.* a reward or cash payment given by a government. (pp. 255, 492)

boycott (BOI kot) *n.* a refusal to buy certain goods. (p. 145)

buck *n.* a buckskin from an adult male deer was a unit of money for settlers. (p. 111)

C

cabinet *n.* a group of department heads who serve as the president's chief advisers. (p. 278)

California gold rush *n.* in 1849, large numbers of people moved to California because gold had been discovered there. (p. 397)

caravel (KAR uh vel) *n.* a ship with triangular sails that allowed it to sail into the wind and with square sails that carried it forward when the wind was at its back. (p. 39)

cash crop *n.* a crop grown by a farmer to be sold for money rather than for personal use. (p. 99)

cavalry *n.* soldiers on horseback. (p. 480)

charter *n.* a written contract issued by a government giving the holder the right to establish a colony. (p. 71)

checks and balances *n.* the ability of each branch of government to exercise checks, or controls, over the other branches. (p. 230)

civil disobedience (DIS uh BEE dee uhns) *n.* peacefully refusing to obey laws one considers unjust. (p. 415)

civilization (SIV uh li ZAY shuhn) *n.* a form of culture characterized by city trade centers, specialized workers, organized forms of government and religion, systems of record keeping, and advanced tools. (p. 28)

civil rights *n.* rights granted to all citizens. (p. 519)

clan *n.* a large group of families that claim a common ancestor. (p. 111)

Cold War *n.* the state of hostility, without direct military conflict, that developed between the United States and the Soviet Union after World War II. (p. 579)

Columbian (kuh LUM bee uhn) **Exchange** *n.* the transfer of plants, animals, and diseases between the Western and the Eastern hemispheres. (p. 62)

committee of correspondence *n.* a group of people in the colonies who exchanged letters on colonial affairs. (p. 150)

common law *n.* a system of law developed in England, based on customs and previous court decisions. (p. 252)

Compromise of 1850 *n.* a series of Congressional laws intended to settle the major disagreements between free states and slave states. (p. 445)

Compromise of 1877 *n.* the agreement that resolved an 1876 election dispute: Rutherford B. Hayes became president and then removed the last federal troops from the South. (p. 532)

compulsory process *n.* a required procedure. (p. 251)

Conestoga (KON i STOW guh) **wagon** *n.* a vehicle with wide wheels, a curved bed, and a canvas cover used by American pioneers traveling west. (p. 101)

Confederate States of America *n.* the confederation formed in 1861 by the Southern states after their secession from the Union. (p. 457)

conquistador (kon KWIS tuh DAWR) *n.* a Spaniard who traveled to the Americas as an explorer and a conqueror in the 16th century. (p. 53)

conscription (kuhn SKRIP shuhn) *n.* a law that required men to serve in the military or be drafted. (p. 492)

Constitutional Convention *n.* a meeting held in 1787 to consider changes to the Articles of Confederation; resulted in the drafting of the Constitution. (p. 213)

containment (kuhn TAYN muhnt) *n.* the blocking by one nation of another nation's attempts to spread influence—especially the efforts of the United States to block the spread of Soviet Communism during the late 1940s and early 1950s. (p. 580)

Continental Army *n.* a colonial force authorized by the Second Continental Congress in 1775, with George Washington as its commanding general. (p. 161)

convene (kuhn VEEN) *v.* to call together. (p. 243)

Copperheads *n.* Abraham Lincoln's main political opponents; they favored peace with the South. (p. 492)

cotton gin *n.* a machine invented in 1793 that cleaned cotton much faster and far more efficiently than human workers. (p. 332)

counterculture (KOWN tuhr KUL chuhr) *n.* a group of young people with values and lifestyles in opposition to those of the established culture. (p. 587)

Crittenden (KRIT uhn duhn) **Plan** *n.* a compromise introduced in 1861 that might have prevented secession. (p. 459)

Crusades (kroo SAYDZ) *n.* a series of wars to capture the Holy Land, launched in 1096 by European Christians. (p. 36)

culture (KUL chuhr) *n.* a way of life shared by people with similar arts, beliefs, and customs. (p. 28)

Dawes (dawz) **Act** *n.* a law, enacted in 1887, that distributed reservation land to individual owners. (p. 540)

Declaration of Independence *n.* the document, written in 1776, in which the colonies declared independence from Britain. (p. 164)

depression *n.* a severe economic slump. (p. 370)

desert (di ZURT) *v.* to leave military duty without intending to return. (p. 187)

diversity (di VUR si tee) *n.* a variety of people. (p. 101)

doctrine of nullification (NUL uh fi KAY shuhn) *n.* a right of a state to reject a federal law that it considers unconstitutional. (p. 365)

domestication (doh MES ti KAY shuhn) *n.* the practice of breeding plants or taming animals to meet human needs. (p. 28)

Dred Scott* v. *Sandford *n.* an 1856 Supreme Court case in which a slave, Dred Scott, sued for his freedom because he had been taken to live in territories where slavery was illegal; the Court ruled against Scott. (p. 451)

due process of law *n.* fair treatment under the law. (p. 251)

elector *n.* a voter. (p. 233)

Emancipation (i MAN suh PAY shuhn) **Proclamation** *n.* an executive order issued by Abraham Lincoln on January 1, 1863, freeing the slaves in all regions in rebellion against the Union. (p. 488)

Embargo (em BAHR goh) **Act of 1807** *n.* an act that stated that American ships were no longer allowed to sail to foreign ports, and it also closed American ports to British ships. (p. 312)

emigrant (EM i gruhnt) *n.* a person who leaves a country. (p. 407)

encomienda (en koh mee YEN duh) *n.* a grant of Native American labor. (p. 233)

English Bill of Rights *n.* an agreement signed by William and Mary to respect the rights of English citizens and of Parliament, including the right to free elections. (p. 128)

enlightenment (en LYT n muhnt) *n.* an 18th-century movement that emphasized the use of reason and the scientific method to obtain knowledge. (p. 124)

enumeration (i NOO muh RAY shuhn) *n.* an official count, such as a census. (p. 124)

equity (EK wi tee) *n.* a system of justice not covered under common law. (p. 253)

Erie (EER ee) **Canal** *n.* completed in 1825, this waterway connected New York City and Buffalo, New York. (p. 339)

European Middle Ages *n.* a period from the late 400s to about the 1300s, during which Europeans turned to feudalism and the manor system. (p. 35)

ex post facto (EKS pohst FAK toh) **law** *n.* a law that would make an act a criminal offense after it was committed. (p. 239)

factory system *n.* a method of production that brought many workers and machines together into one building. (p. 325)

fall line *n.* the point at which a waterfall prevents large boats from moving farther upriver. (p. 110)

famine (FAM in) *n.* a severe food shortage. (p. 410)

fascism (FASH iz uhm) *n.* a political philosophy that advocates a strong, centralized, nationalistic government headed by a powerful dictator. (p. 574)

federalism *n.* a system of government where power is shared among the central (or federal) government and the states. (pp. 218, 229)

Federalists *n.* supporters of the Constitution. (p. 218)

Federalist Papers *n.* a series of essays defending and explaining the Constitution. (p. 219)

Federal Judiciary (joo DISH ee ER ee) **Act** *n.* it helped create a court system and gave the Supreme Court six members. (p. 278)

felony (FEL uh nee) *n.* a serious crime. (p. 237)

feudalism (FYOOD l iz uhm) *n.* a political system in which the king allows nobles the use of his land in exchange for their military service and their protection of people living on the land. (p. 35)

Fifteenth Amendment *n.* passed in 1870, this amendment to the U.S. Constitution stated that citizens could not be stopped from voting "on account of race, color, or previous condition of servitude." (p. 530)

54th Massachusetts Regiment *n.* one of the first African-American regiments organized to fight for the Union in the Civil War. (p. 490)

First Battle of Bull Run *n.* an 1861 battle of the Civil War in which the South shocked the North with a victory. (p. 469)

foreign (FAWR in) **policy** *n.* relations with the governments of other countries. (p. 288)

Fort Sumter *n.* a federal fort located in the harbor of Charleston, South Carolina; the Southern attack on Fort Sumter marked the beginning of the Civil War. (p. 465)

forty-niner *n.* a person who went to California to find gold, starting in 1849. (p. 396)

Fourteen Points *n.* President Woodrow Wilson's goals for peace after World War I. (p. 561)

Fourteenth Amendment *n.* an amendment to the U.S. Constitution, passed in 1868, that made all persons born or naturalized in the United States—including former slaves—citizens of the country. (p. 519)

First Continental Congress *n.* a meeting of delegates in 1774 from all the colonies except Georgia to uphold colonial rights. (p. 155)

Freedmen's Bureau *n.* a federal agency set up to help former slaves after the Civil War. (p. 517)

freedmen's school *n.* a school set up to educate newly freed African Americans. (p. 525)

Free Soil Party *n.* a political party dedicated to stopping the expansion of slavery. (p. 443)

French and Indian War *n.* a conflict in North America from 1754 to 1763 that was part of a worldwide struggle between France and Britain; Britain defeated France and gained French Canada. (p. 131)

frontier (frun TEER) *n.* unsettled or sparsely settled area occupied largely by Native Americans. (p. 539)

Fugitive Slave Act *n.* an 1850 law to help slaveholders recapture runaway slaves. (p. 446)

French Revolution *n.* in 1789, the French launched a movement for liberty and equality. (p. 285)

Fundamental Orders of Connecticut *n.* a set of laws that were established in 1639 by a Puritan congregation who had settled in the Connecticut Valley and that expanded the idea of representative government. (p. 79)

G

Gilded (gil did) **Age** *n.* an era during the late 1800s of fabulous wealth. (p. 541)

"Glorious Revolution" *n.* the overthrow of English King James II in 1688 and his replacement by William and Mary. (p. 128)

Great Awakening *n.* a revival of religious feeling in the American colonies during the 1730s and 1740s. (p. 123)

Great Compromise *n.* the Constitutional Convention's agreement to establish a two-house national legislature, with all states having equal representation in one house and each state having representation based on its population in the other house. (p. 216)

Great Depression *n.* a period, lasting from 1929 to 1941, in which the U.S. economy was in severe decline and millions of Americans were unemployed. (p. 571)

Great Migration *n.* the movement of Puritans from England to establish settlements around the world, including 20,000 who sailed for America (p. 78); the movement of African Americans between 1910 and 1920 to northern cities from the South. (p. 562)

Great Society *n.* a program started by President Lyndon Johnson that provided help to the poor, the elderly, and women, and also promoted education and outlawed discrimination. (p. 586)

greenback *n.* paper currency issued by the federal government during the Civil War. (p. 493)

gristmill (GRIST MIL) *n.* a mill in which grain is ground to produce flour or meal. (p. 99)

guerrilla (guh RIL uh) *n.* a soldier who weakens the enemy with surprise raids and hit-and-run attacks. (p. 191)

H

Harlem Renaissance *n.* a flowering of African-American artistic creativity during the 1920s, centered in the Harlem community of New York City. (p. 571)

Harpers Ferry *n.* a federal arsenal in Virginia that was captured in 1859 during a slave revolt. (p. 469)

Holocaust (HOL uh KAWST) *n.* the systematic killing by Germany during World War II of about six million Jews as well as millions from other ethnic groups. (p. 578)

Homestead Act *n.* passed in 1862, this law offered 160 acres of land free to anyone who agreed to live on and improve the land for five years. (p. 540)

House of Burgesses *n.* created in 1619, the first representative assembly in the American colonies. (p. 72)

Hudson River school *n.* a group of artists living in the Hudson River Valley in New York. (p. 414)

hygiene (HY JEEN) *n.* conditions and practices that promote health. (p. 474)

immigrant *n.* a person who settles in a new country. (p. 407)

immunity *n.* legal protection. (p. 246)

impeachment *n.* the process of accusing a public official of wrongdoing. (p. 233)

imperialism *n.* the policy by which stronger nations extend their economic, political, or military control over weaker nations or territories. (p. 556)

impressment *n.* the act of seizing by force. (p. 311)

inaugurate (in AW gyuh RAYT) *v.* to swear in or induct into office in a formal ceremony. (p. 277)

income tax *n.* a tax on earnings. (p. 493)

indentured servant *n.* a person who sold his or her labor in exchange for passage to America. (p. 72)

Indian Removal Act *n.* this 1830 act called for the government to negotiate treaties that would require Native Americans to relocate west. (p. 360)

Indian Territory *n.* present-day Oklahoma and parts of Kansas and Nebraska to which Native Americans were moved under the Indian Removal Act of 1830. (p. 360)

indictment (in DYT muhnt) *n.* a written statement issued by a grand jury charging a person with a crime. (p. 234)

indigo *n.* a plant grown in the Southern colonies that yields a deep blue dye. (p. 105)

individual right *n.* a personal liberty and privilege guaranteed to U.S. citizens by the Bill of Rights. (p. 231)

Industrial Revolution *n.* in late 18th-century Britain, factory machines began replacing hand tools and manufacturing replaced farming as the main form of work. (p. 325)

inferior court *n.* a court with less authority than the Supreme Court. (p. 244)

inflation *n.* an increase in the price of goods and services and a decrease in the value of money. (p. 370)

inoperative *adj.* no longer in force. (p. 258)

insurrection (IN suh REK shuhn) *n.* open revolt against a government. (p. 255)

interchangeable part *n.* a part that is exactly like another part. (p. 327)

Intolerable Acts *n.* a series of laws enacted by Parliament in 1774 to punish Massachusetts colonists for the Boston Tea Party. (p. 154)

ironclad *n.* a warship covered with iron. (p. 475)

Iroquois (IR uh KWOH) **League** *n.* a 16th-century alliance of the Cayuga, Mohawk, Oneida, Onondaga, and Seneca Native American groups living in the eastern Great Lakes region. (p. 31)

Islam (is LAHM) *n.* a religion founded by the prophet Muhammad in the 600s, which teaches that there is one God, named Allah. (p. 34)

Jacksonian democracy *n.* the idea of spreading political power to all the people, thereby ensuring majority rule. (p. 354)

Jamestown *n.* the first permanent English settlement in North America. (p. 71)

Jay's Treaty *n.* the agreement that ended dispute over American shipping during the French Revolution. (p. 286)

jazz *n.* a new kind of music in the 1920s that captured the carefree spirit of the times. (p. 570)

Jim Crow *n.* laws meant to enforce separation of white and black people in public places in the South. (p. 549)

joint-stock company *n.* a business in which investors pool their wealth in order to turn a profit. (p. 70)

judicial (joo DISH uhl) **review** *n.* the principle that the Supreme Court has the final say in interpreting the Constitution. (p. 301)

Judiciary (joo DISH ee ER ee) **Act of 1801** *n.* a law that increased the number of federal judges, allowing President John Adams to fill most of the new spots with Federalists. (p. 300)

Kansas-Nebraska Act *n.* an 1854 law that established the territories of Kansas and Nebraska and gave their residents the right to decide whether to allow slavery. (p. 448)

King Cotton *n.* cotton was called king because cotton was important to the world market, and the South grew most of the cotton for Europe's mills. (p. 468)

King Philip's War *n.* a war between the Puritan colonies and Native Americans in 1675–1676. (p. 80)

Ku Klux Klan *n.* a group formed in 1866 that wanted to restore Democratic control of the South and to keep former slaves powerless. (p. 528)

labor union *n.* a group of workers who band together to seek better working conditions. (p. 418)

Land Ordinance of 1785 *n.* a law that established a plan for surveying and selling the federally owned lands west of the Appalachian Mountains. (p. 207)

land speculator *n.* a person who buys huge areas of land for a low price and then sells off small sections of it at high prices. (p. 378)

leisure (LEE zhuhr) *n.* free time. (p. 548)

Lewis and Clark expedition *n.* a group led by Meriwether Lewis and William Clark who explored the lands of the Louisiana Purchase beginning in 1803. (p. 304)

Lexington and Concord *n.* sites in Massachusetts of the first battles of the American Revolution. (p. 157)

limited government *n.* the principle that requires all U.S. citizens, including government leaders, to obey the law. (p. 231)

Lone Star Republic *n.* the nickname of the republic of Texas, given in 1836. (p. 389)

Louisiana (loo EE zee AN uh) **Purchase** *n.* the 1803 purchase of the Louisiana Territory from France. (p. 303)

Lowell mills *n.* textile mills located in the factory town of Lowell, Massachusetts, founded in 1826. (p. 326)

Loyalist *n.* an American colonist who supported the British in the American Revolution. (p. 157)

M

Magna Carta *n.* "Great Charter;" a document guaranteeing basic political rights in England, approved by King John in 1215. (p. 125)

manifest destiny *n.* the belief that the United States was destined to stretch across the continent from the Atlantic Ocean to the Pacific Ocean. (p. 391)

Marbury* v. *Madison *n.* an 1803 case in which the Supreme Court ruled that it had the power to abolish laws by declaring them unconstitutional. (p. 301)

mass culture *n.* a common culture experienced by large numbers of people. (p. 548)

Mayflower Compact *n.* an agreement established by the men who sailed to America on the *Mayflower*, which called for laws for the good of the colony and set forth the idea of self-government. (p. 77)

mercantilism (MUHR kuhn tee LIZ uhm) *n.* an economic system in which nations increase their wealth and power by obtaining gold and silver and by establishing a favorable balance of trade. (p. 51)

mercenary (MUR suh NER ee) *n.* a professional soldier hired to fight for a foreign country. (p. 179)

Mexican Cession (sesh uhn) *n.* a vast region given up by Mexico after the War with Mexico; it included the present-day states of California, Nevada, Utah, most of Arizona, and parts of New Mexico, Colorado, and Wyoming. (p. 395)

middle passage *n.* the middle leg of the triangular trade route—the voyage from Africa to the Americas—that brought captured Africans into slavery. (p. 61)

militia (muh LISH uh) *n.* a force of armed civilians pledged to defend their community during the American Revolution. (p. 154); an emergency military force that is not part of the regular army. (p. 238)

minié (MIN ee) **ball** *n.* a bullet with a hollow base. (p. 475)

Minuteman *n.* a member of the colonial militia who was trained to respond "at a minute's warning." (p. 154)

misdemeanor (mis di MEE nuhr) *n.* a violation of the law. (p. 243)

Missouri Compromise *n.* a series of laws enacted in 1820 to maintain the balance of power between slave states and free states. (p. 342)

Monroe Doctrine *n.* a policy of U.S. opposition to any European interference in the Western Hemisphere, announced by President Monroe in 1823. (p. 343)

Mormon *n.* a member of a church founded by Joseph Smith in 1830. (p. 381)

Mound Builder *n.* an early Native American who built large earthen structures. (p. 29)

mountain man *n.* a fur trapper or explorer who opened up the West by finding the best trails through the Rocky Mountains. (p. 377)

Muslim (MUZ luhm) *n.* a follower of Islam. (p. 34)

N

nationalism *n.* a feeling of pride, loyalty, and protectiveness toward one's country. (p. 338)

nativist *n.* a native-born American who wanted to eliminate foreign influence. (p. 412)

natural-born citizen *n.* a citizen born in the United States or a commonwealth of the United States or to parents who are U.S. citizens living outside the country. (p. 241)

naturalization *n.* a way to give full citizenship to a person born in another country. (pp. 237, 254)

Navigation Acts *n.* a series of laws passed by Parliament, beginning in 1651, to ensure that England made money from its colonies' trade. (p. 96)

navigator *n.* a person who plans the course of a ship while at sea. (p. 39)

Nazi (NAHT see) **Party** *n.* the National Socialist German Workers' Party; came to power under Adolf Hitler in the 1930s. (p. 574)

neutral (NOO truhl) *adj.* not siding with one country or the other. (p. 288)

New Deal *n.* President Franklin Roosevelt's programs to fight the Great Depression. (p. 572)

New France *n.* a fur-trading post established in 1608 that became the first permanent French settlement in North America. (p. 58)

new immigrant *n.* a person from southern or eastern Europe who entered the United States after 1900. (p. 542)

New Jersey Plan *n.* a plan of government proposed at the Constitutional Convention in 1787 that called for a one-house legislature in which each state would have one vote. (p. 215)

Northwest Ordinance *n.* it described how the Northwest Territory was to be governed and set conditions for settlement and settlers' rights. (p. 207)

Northwest Territory *n.* territory covered by the Land Ordinance of 1785, which included land that formed the states of Ohio, Indiana, Michigan, Illinois, Wisconsin, and part of Minnesota. (p. 207)

O

Oregon Trail *n.* a trail that ran westward from Independence, Missouri, to the Oregon Territory. (p. 380)

overseer *n.* a worker hired by a planter to watch over and direct the work of slaves. (p. 106)

P

pacifist (PAS uh fist) *n.* a person morally opposed to war. (p. 193)

Panama (PAN uh MAH) **Canal** *n.* a shortcut through Panama that connects the Atlantic and the Pacific oceans. (p. 558)

Panic of 1837 *n.* a financial crisis in which banks closed and the credit system collapsed. (p. 370)

Panic of 1873 *n.* a financial crisis in which banks closed and the stock market collapsed. (p. 531)

Parliament (PAHR luh muhnt) *n.* England's chief lawmaking body. (p. 126)

Patriot *n.* an American colonist who sided with the rebels in the American Revolution. (p. 157)

patroon (puh TROON) *n.* a person who brought 50 settlers to New Netherland and in return received a large land grant and other special privileges. (p. 85)

Pickett's Charge *n.* General George Pickett led a direct attack on Union troops during the 1863 Civil War battle at Gettysburg; the attack failed. (p. 497)

piedmont *n.* a broad plateau that leads to the foot of a mountain range. (p. 110)

Pilgrim *n.* a member of the group that rejected the Church of England, sailed to America, and founded the Plymouth Colony in 1620. (p. 76)

Pinckney's (PINGK neez) **Treaty** *n.* a 1795 treaty with Spain that allowed Americans to use the Mississippi River and to store goods in New Orleans; made the 31st parallel the southern U.S. border. (p. 286)

plantation *n.* a large farm that raises cash crops. (p. 60)

platform *n.* a statement of beliefs. (p. 455)

Platt Amendment *n.* a result of the Spanish-American War, which gave the United States the right to intervene in Cuban affairs when there was a threat to "life, property, and individual liberty." (p. 558)

Plessy* v. *Ferguson *n.* an 1896 case in which the Supreme Court ruled that separation of the races in public accommodations was legal. (p. 549)

Pontiac's (PON tee AKS) **Rebellion** *n.* a revolt against British forts and American settlers in 1763, led in part by Ottawa war leader Pontiac, in response to settlers' claims of Native American lands and to harsh treatment by British soldiers. (p. 135)

popular sovereignty (SOV uhr in tee) *n.* a government in which the people rule (p. 228); a system in which the residents vote to decide an issue. (p. 135)

Populist Party *n.* also known as the People's Party and formed in the 1890s, this group wanted a policy that would raise crop prices. (p. 551)

prejudice (PREJ uh dis) *n.* a negative opinion that is not based on facts. (p. 411)

privateer (PRY vuh TEER) *n.* a privately owned ship that has government permission during wartime to attack an enemy's merchant ships. (p. 188)

Proclamation (PRAHK luh MAY shuhn) **of 1763** *n.* an order in which Britain prohibited its American colonists from settling west of the Appalachian Mountains. (p. 135)

progressivism (pruh GREHS ih VIHZ uhm) *n.* an early 20th-century reform movement seeking to return control of the government to the people, to restore economic opportunities, and to correct injustices in American life. (p. 553)

proprietary (pruh PRY ih TEHR ee) **colony** *n.* a colony with a single owner. (p. 85)

pro tempore (proh TEHM puh ree) *adv.* Latin phrase meaning "for the time being." (p. 234)

Puritan *n.* a member of a group from England that settled the Massachusetts Bay Colony in 1630 and sought to reform the practices of the Church of England. (p. 78)

push-pull factor *n.* a factor that pushes people out of their native lands and pulls them toward a new place. (p. 408)

Q

Quaker (KWAY kuhr) *n.* a person who believed all people should live in peace and harmony; accepted different religions and ethnic groups. (p. 85)

quarter *v.* to give a place to stay. (p. 251)

Quartering Act *n.* a law passed by Parliament in 1765 that required the colonies to house and supply British soldiers. (p. 144)

quorum (KWAWR uhm) *n.* the minimum number of members that must be present for official business to take place. (p. 235)

R

racism (RAY sihz uhm) *n.* the belief that some people are inferior because of their race. (p. 62)

radical (RAD ih kuhl) *n.* a person who takes extreme political positions. (p. 297)

Radical Republican (rih PUHB lih kuhn) *n.* a congressman who, after the Civil War, favored using the government to create a new order in the South and to give African Americans full citizenship and the right to vote. (p. 517)

ratification (RAT uh fih KAY shuhn) *n.* official approval. (p. 248)

Reconstruction *n.* the process the U.S. government used to readmit the Confederate states to the Union after the Civil War. (p. 517)

Reformation *n.* a 16th-century religious movement to correct problems in the Roman Catholic Church. (p. 37)

Renaissance (REHN ih SAHNS) *n.* a period of European history, lasting from the 1300s to 1600, that brought increased interest in art and learning. (p. 36)

rendezvous (RAHN day VOO) *n.* a meeting. (p. 181)

reprieve (rih PREEV) *n.* a delay or cancellation of punishment. (p. 243)

republic (rih PUHB lihk) *n.* a government in which people elect representatives to govern for them. (p. 206)

republicanism (rih PUHB lih keh NIHZ uhm) *n.* the belief that government should be based on the consent of the people; people exercise their power by voting for political representatives. (pp. 198, 229)

Republican Party *n.* the political party formed in 1854 by opponents of slavery in the territories. (p. 450)

revenue (REHV uh noo) *n.* income a government collects to cover expenses. (pp. 144, 236)

revival (rih VY vuhl) *n.* a meeting designed to reawaken religious faith. (p. 417)

rifle *n.* a gun with a grooved barrel that causes a bullet to spin through the air. (p. 475)

robber baron *n.* a business leader who became wealthy through dishonest methods. (p. 578)

romanticism (roh MAN tih sihz uhm) *n.* a European artistic movement that stressed the individual, imagination, creativity, and emotion. (p. 413)

Roosevelt Corollary (KAWR uh lehr ee) *n.* a 1904 addition to the Monroe Doctrine allowing the United States to be the "policeman" in Latin America. (p. 560)

royal colony *n.* a colony ruled by governors appointed by a king. (p. 87)

S

salutary (SAL yuh TEHR ee) **neglect** *n.* a hands-off policy of England toward its American colonies during the first half of the 1700s. (p. 128)

Santa Fe (SAN tuh FAY) **Trail** *n.* a trail that began in Missouri and ended in Santa Fe, New Mexico. (p. 379)

secede (sih SEED) *v.* to withdraw. (p. 457)

secession (sih SEHSH uhn) *n.* withdrawal. (p. 367)

Second Continental Congress *n.* a governing body whose delegates agreed, in May 1775, to form the Continental Army and to approve the Declaration of Independence. (p. 161)

Second Great Awakening *n.* the renewal of religious faith in the 1790s and early 1800s. (p. 417)

sectionalism (SEHK shuh nuh LIHZ uhm) *n.* the placing of the interests of one's own region ahead of the interests of the nation as a whole. (p. 341)

segregation (SEHG rih GAY shuhn) *n.* separation, especially of races. (p. 549)

Seneca (SEHN ih kuh) **Falls Convention** *n.* a women's rights convention held in Seneca Falls, New York, in 1848. (p. 428)

separation of powers *n.* the division of basic government roles into branches. (p. 230)

servitude (SUR vih TOOD) *n.* a state of belonging to an owner or master. (p. 254)

Seven Days' Battles *n.* an 1862 Civil War battle in which the Confederacy forced the Union to retreat before it could capture the Southern capital of Richmond. (p. 480)

sharecropping *n.* a system in which landowners gave farm workers land, seed, and tools in return for a part of the crops they raised. (p. 527)

Shays's (SHAY zuhz) **Rebellion** *n.* an uprising of debt-ridden Massachusetts farmers in 1787. (p. 209)

Siege (seej) **of Vicksburg** *n.* an 1863 Union victory in the Civil War that enabled the Union to control the entire Mississippi River. (p. 500)

slash-and-burn agriculture (ag rih kuhl chuhr) *n.* a farming method in which people clear fields by cutting and burning trees and grasses, the ashes of which fertilize the soil. (p. 31)

slavery *n.* the practice of holding a person in bondage for labor. (p. 60)

smuggle *v.* to illegally import or export goods. (p. 96)

Sons of Liberty *n.* a group of colonists who formed a secret society to oppose British policies at the time of the American Revolution. (p. 145)

Spanish-American War *n.* a war in 1898 that began when the United States demanded Cuba's independence from Spain. (p. 557)

Spanish Armada (ahr MAH duh) *n.* a fleet of ships sent in 1588 by Philip II, the Spanish king, to invade England and restore Roman Catholicism. (p. 57)

spiritual *n.* a religious folk song. (p. 335)

spoils system *n.* the practice of winning candidates giving government jobs to political backers or supporters. (p. 357)

Stamp Act *n.* a 1765 law passed by Parliament that required all legal and commercial documents to carry an official stamp showing a tax had been paid. (p. 144)

states' rights *n.* theory that said that states had the right to judge when the federal government had passed an unconstitutional law. (p. 291)

steerage *n.* the cheapest deck or place on a ship. (p. 407)

Stono (STOH noh) **Rebellion** *n.* a 1739 uprising of slaves in South Carolina, leading to the tightening of already harsh slave laws. (p. 107)

strategy *n.* an overall plan of action. (p. 180)

strike *v.* to stop work to demand better working conditions. (p. 418)

subsistence farm *n.* a farm that produces enough food for the family with a small additional amount for trade. (p. 94)

suffrage *n.* the right to vote. (pp. 246, 428)

Sugar Act *n.* a law passed by Parliament in 1764 that placed a tax on sugar, molasses, and other products shipped to the colonies; also called for harsh punishment of smugglers. (p. 144)

T

tariff *n.* a tax on imported goods. (p. 280)

Tariff of Abominations *n.* an 1828 law that raised the tariffs on raw materials and manufactured goods; it upset Southerners who felt that economic interests of the Northeast were determining national economic policy. (p. 365)

technology *n.* the use of tools and knowledge to meet human needs. (p. 29)

Tejano (tuh HAH noh) *n.* a person of Spanish heritage who considered Texas his or her home. (p. 384)

temperance movement *n.* a campaign to stop the drinking of alcohol. (p. 418)

tender *n.* money. (p. 239)

Thirteenth Amendment *n.* an amendment to the U.S. Constitution, adopted in 1865, banning slavery and involuntary servitude in the United States. (p. 505)

Three-Fifths Compromise *n.* the Constitutional Convention's agreement to count three-fifths of a state's slaves as population for purposes of representation and taxation. (p. 216)

Townshend (TOWN zuhnd) **Acts** *n.* a series of laws passed by Parliament in 1767 that suspended New York's assembly and established taxes on goods brought into the British colonies. (p. 147)

Trail of Tears *n.* the tragic journey of the Cherokee people from their homeland to Indian Territory between 1838 and 1839; thousands of Cherokee died. (p. 361)

transcendentalism (TRAN sen DEN tl iz uhm) *n.* a 19th-century philosophy that taught the spiritual world is more important than the physical world and that people can find truth within themselves through feeling and intuition. (p. 415)

Treaty of Ghent (gent) *n.* treaty, signed in 1814, which ended the War of 1812; no territory exchanged hands and trade disputes were not resolved. (p. 317)

Treaty of Greenville *n.* a 1795 agreement in which 12 Native American tribes surrendered much of present-day Ohio and Indiana to the U.S. government. (p. 284)

Treaty of Guadalupe Hidalgo (GWAHD loop hi DAH goh) *n.* the 1848 treaty ending the U.S. war with Mexico; Mexico ceded nearly one-half of its land to the United States. (p. 394)

Treaty of Paris *n.* the 1763 treaty that ended the French and Indian War; Britain gained all of North America east of the Mississippi River. (p. 134)

Treaty of Paris of 1783 *n.* the treaty that ended the Revolutionary War, confirming the independence of the United States and setting the boundaries of the new nation. (p. 196)

Treaty of Tordesillas (TAWR duh SEE uhs) *n.* the 1494 treaty in which Spain and Portugal agreed to divide the lands of the Western Hemisphere between them and moved the Line of Demarcation further west. (p. 51)

triangular trade *n.* the transatlantic system of trade in which goods, including slaves, were exchanged between Africa, England, Europe, the West Indies, and the colonies in North America. (p. 95)

tribunal (try BYOO nuhl) *n.* a court. (p. 237)

U

unanimous (yoo NAN uh muhs) **consent** *n.* complete agreement. (p. 248)

Uncle Tom's Cabin *n.* a novel published by Harriet Beecher Stowe in 1852, which portrayed slavery as brutal and immoral. (p. 446)

unconstitutional *n.* something that contradicts the law of the Constitution. (p. 301)

Underground Railroad *n.* a series of escape routes used by slaves escaping the South. (p. 426)

urbanization *n.* growth of cities resulting from industrialization. (p. 541)

V

vaudeville (VAWD vil) *n.* a form of live stage entertainment with a mixture of songs, dance, and comedy. (p. 549)

Vietnam War (vee ET NAHM) *n.* a military conflict from 1957 to 1975 between the North Vietnam Communists and the non-Communist forces of South Vietnam supported by the United States. (p. 581)

vigilante (vij uh LAN tee) *n.* a person willing to take the law into his or her own hands. (p. 545)

Virginia Plan *n.* a plan proposed by Edmund Randolph, a delegate to the Constitutional Convention in 1787, that proposed a government with three branches and a two-house legislature in which representation would be based on a state's population or wealth. (p. 215)

W

War Hawk *n.* a westerner who supported the War of 1812. (p. 313)

Watergate scandal *n.* a scandal resulting from the Nixon administration's attempt to cover up its involvement in the 1972 break-in at the Democratic National Committee headquarters in the Watergate apartment complex in Washington, D.C. (p. 582)

Webster-Hayne debate *n.* an 1830 debate between Daniel Webster and Robert Hayne over the doctrine of nullification. (p. 366)

Whig (hwig) **Party** *n.* a political party organized in 1834 to oppose the policies of Andrew Jackson. (p. 371)

Whiskey Rebellion *n.* a 1794 protest against the government's tax on whiskey, which was valuable to the livelihood of backcountry farmers. (p. 285)

Wilderness Road *n.* the trail into Kentucky that woodsman Daniel Boone helped to build. (p. 205)

Wilmot (WIL muht) **Proviso** (pruh VY zoh) *n.* an 1846 proposal that outlawed slavery in any territory gained from the War with Mexico. (p. 443)

World War II *n.* a war fought from 1939 to 1945, in which Great Britain, France, the Soviet Union, the United States, and other allies defeated Germany, Italy, and Japan. (p. 575)

writ (rit) **of assistance** *n.* a search warrant that allowed British officers to enter colonial homes or businesses to search for smuggled goods. (p. 148)

X

XYZ Affair *n.* a 1797 incident in which French officials demanded a bribe from U.S. diplomats. (p. 290)

Y

yellow journalism *n.* a style of journalism that exaggerates and sensationalizes the news. (p. 557)

abolition [abolición] *s.* movimiento para eliminar la esclavitud. (p. 424)

abridge [abreviar] *v.* reducir. (p. 250)

affirmation [afirmación] *s.* declaración de que algo es cierto. (p. 241)

African Diaspora [diáspora africana] *s.* traslado forzado de los africanos, desde su patria a las Américas para trabajar allí como esclavos. (p. 61)

Albany Plan of Union [Plan de la Unión de Albany] *s.* primera propuesta formal para unir las colonias norteamericanas, presentado por Benjamín Franklin. (p. 133)

Alien and Sedition Acts [leyes de Extranjeros y Sedición] *s.* serie de cuatro leyes promulgadas en 1798 para reducir el poder político de inmigrantes recién llegados a Estados Unidos. (p. 290)

ally [aliado] *s.* país que acuerda ayudar a otro país a alcanzar un objetivo común. (p. 184)

American System [Sistema Americano] *s.* plan presentado en 1815 para hacer autosuficiente a Estados Unidos. (p. 338)

Anaconda Plan [Plan Anaconda] *s.* estrategia de tres pasos mediante la cual la Unión se proponía derrotar a la Confederación durante la guerra civil estadounidense. (p. 468)

Antifederalist [antifederalista] *s.* persona que se oponía a la ratificación de la Constitución de los Estados Unidos. (p. 218)

Appalachian Mountains [montes Apalaches] *s.* cadena de montañas que se extiende desde el este de Canadá hacia el sur, hasta Alabama. (p. 110)

appellate [de apelación] *adj.* que tiene el poder de reexaminar decisiones de las cortes. (p. 244)

Appomattox Court House [Appomattox] *s.* pueblo de Virginia donde Robert E. Lee se rindió a Ulysses s. Grant en 1865, finalizando así la guerra civil. (p. 503)

apprentice [aprendiz] *s.* joven que aprende un oficio o una artesanía de un maestro experto. (p. 121)

appropiation [apropiación] *s.* fondos públicos que se reservan para un propósito específico. (p. 237)

Articles of Confederation [Artículos de Confederación] *s.* documento, adoptado por el Congreso Continental en 1777 y finalmente aprobado por los estados en 1781, que delineaba la forma de gobierno de los nuevos Estados Unidos. (p. 206)

artillery [artillería] *s.* cañón o arma grande. (p. 161)

artisan [artesano] *s.* obrero especializado, como un tejedor a telar o un alfarero, que hace artículos a mano; artífice. (p. 101)

baby boom *s.* término para la generación que nació en Estados Unidos entre 1946 y 1961, cuando el índice de natalidad aumentó marcadamente después de la segunda guerra mundial. (p. 584)

Backcountry [tierras fronterizas] *s.* región colonial que se extendía a lo largo de los montes Apalaches a través de la sección oeste de Nueva Inglaterra y las colonias del centro y del sur. (p. 93)

Bacon's Rebellion [Rebelión de Bacon] *s.* levantamiento contra la poderosa autoridad colonial de Jamestown por Nathaniel Bacon y un grupo de habitantes de la frontera que resultó en la quema de Jamestown en 1676. (p. 73)

bail [fianza] *s.* dinero que pagan como fianza las personas arrestadas para garantizar que van a regresar para el juicio. (p. 252)

Battle of Antietam [batalla de Antietam] *s.* batalla de la guerra civil, en 1862, en que murieron o resultaron heridos 25,000 hombres. (p. 481)

Battle of Fallen Timbers *s.* en 1794 el ejército estadounidense derrotó a 2,000 amerindios en un enfrentamiento por el control del territorio del Noroeste. (p. 283)

Battle of Gettysburg [batalla de Gettysburg] *s.* batalla de 1863 de la guerra civil en que la Unión derrotó a la Confederación, poniendo fin a la esperanza de una victoria confederada en el Norte. (p. 497)

Battle of Quebec [batalla de Quebec] *s.* batalla en la que los británicos derrotaron a los franceses y cambio decisivo en la guerra Francesa y Amerindia. (p. 134)

Battle of Shiloh [batalla de Shiloh] *s.* batalla de 1862 en que la Unión obligó a la Confederación a retroceder; fue una de las batallas más encarnizadas de la guerra civil. (p. 478)

Battle of Yorktown [batalla de Yorktown] *s.* última batalla importante de la guerra Revolucionaria que resultó en la capitulación de las fuerzas británicas en 1781. (p. 194)

Battle of the Alamo [batalla de El Álamo] *s.* en 1836 los texanos defendieron contra el ejército mexicano una misión llamada El Álamo; sobrevivieron sólo cinco texanos (p. 387)

Battle of the Thames [batalla de Thames] *s.* victoria estadounidense sobre los británicos en la guerra de 1812 que puso fin a la amenaza británica en el Territorio del Noroeste. (p. 316)

Battles of Saratoga [batallas de Saratoga] *s.* serie de conflictos en 1777, entre soldados británicos y el Ejército Continental que resultó en un cambio decisivo en la guerra Revolucionaria. (p. 183)

bayonet [bayoneta] *s.* largo cuchillo de acero colocado en el extremo de un arma de fuego. (p. 186)

Bear Flag Revolt [revuelta de la Bandera del Oso] *s.* rebelión de 1846 por los estadounidenses contra el dominio mexicano en California. (p. 393)

bill of attainder [decreto de proscripción] *s.* ley que condena a una persona sin juicio ante un tribunal. (p. 239)

Bill of Rights [Carta de Derechos] *s.* diez primeras enmiendas a la Constitución de Estados Unidos, adoptadas en 1791, que consisten en una lista formal de los derechos y libertades de los ciudadanos. (p. 221)

black code [código negro] *s.* ley pasada por los estados sureños que limitaba la libertad de los antiguos esclavos. (p. 518)

blockade [bloqueo] *s.* acción de las fuerzas armadas que impide la entrada o salida de mercaderías o personas. (p. 468)

border state [estado fronterizo] *s.* estados esclavistas fronterizos a estados en que la esclavitud era ilegal. (p. 466)

Boston Massacre [Matanza de Boston] *s.* choque en 1770 entre soldados británicos y colonos de Boston en que perecieron cinco de los colonistas, incluso Crispus Attucks. (p. 149)

Boston Tea Party [Motín del Té de Boston] *s.* como protesta contra el Acta del té, en 1773 los colonos arrojaron al puerto de Boston 342 cajones de té. (p. 151)

bounty [gratificación] *s.* recompensa o pago en dinero que da un gobierno. (pp. 255, 492)

boycott [boicot] *v.* negarse a comprar ciertos productos. (p. 145)

buck [ciervo] gamuza obtenida de la piel de un ciervo adulto, o unidad de dinero de los colonos. (p. 111)

C

cabinet [gabinete ministerial] *s.* grupo de ministros que actúan como los asesores princpales del presidente. (p. 278)

California gold rush [fiebre del oro de California] *s.* en 1849 gran cantidad de gente se fue a California porque allí se había descubierto oro. (p. 397)

caravel [carabela] *s.* barco con velas triangulares que le permitían navegar hacia el viento y con velas cuadradas que lo llevaban hacia delante cuando soplaba viento en popa. (p. 39)

cash crop [cultivo comercial] *s.* cultivo que produce un agricultor para venderlo por dinero y no para su uso personal. (p. 99)

cavalry [caballería] *s.* soldados montados a caballo. (p. 480)

charter [cédula] *s.* contrato escrito que concede un gobierno otorgando al que lo recibe el derecho a establecer una colonia. (p. 71)

checks and balances [frenos y cortapisas] *s.* capacidad de cada rama del gobierno de usar frenos o controles sobre las otras ramas. (p. 230)

civil disobedience [desobediencia civil] *s.* negarse pacíficamente a obedecer leyes que uno considera injustas. (p. 415)

civilization [civilización] *s.* forma de cultura caracterizada por ciudades con centros de comercio, trabajadores especializados, formas de gobierno y religión organizadas, sistemas de mantener registros, y herramientas avanzadas. (p. 28)

civil rights [derechos civiles] *s.* derecho otorgado a todos los ciudadanos. (p. 519)

clan [clan] *s.* grupo grande de familias procedentes de un antepasado común. (p. 111)

Cold War [guerra fría] *s.* estado de hostilidad, sin conflicto militar directo, que se desarrolló entre Estados Unidos y la Unión Soviética después de la segunda guerra mundial. (p. 579)

Columbian Exchange [transferencia colombina] *s.* transferencia de plantas, animales y enfermedades entre el hemisferio occidental y el oriental. (p. 62)

committee of correspondence [comité de correspondencia] *s.* grupo de personas de las colonias que se intercambiaban cartas sobre asuntos coloniales. (p. 150)

common law [derecho consuetudinario] *s.* sistema de leyes desarrollado en Inglaterra, basado en costumbres y decisiones jurídicas anteriores. (p. 252)

Compromise of 1850 [Acuerdo de 1850] *s.* serie de medidas del Congreso para resolver los desacuerdos principales entre los estados libres y los esclavistas. (p. 445)

Compromise of 1877 [Acuerdo de 1877] *s.* acuerdo que resolvió la disputa sobre las elecciones de 1876: se declaró presidente a Rutherford B. Hayes, quien entonces retiró las tropas federales que quedaban en el Sur. (p. 532)

compulsory process [proceso obligatorio] *s.* procedimiento requerido. (p. 251)

Conestoga wagon [carreta conestoga] *s.* vehículo que tenía ruedas anchas, caja de carro curvada y capota de lona y se usaba para transportar gente y artículos. (p. 101)

Confederate States of America [Estados Confederados de América] *s.* confederación constituida en 1861 por los estados sureños después de separarse de la Unión. (p. 457)

conquistador [conquistador] *s.* español que en el siglo XVI viajó a las Américas para explorar y conquistar. (p. 53)

conscription [conscripción] *s.* ley que requería que los hombres sirvieran en las fuerzas armadas o que fueran reclutados. (p. 492)

Constitutional Convention [Convención Constitucional] *s.* reunión realizada en 1787 para considerar cambios a los Artículos de Confederación, que resultó en la redacción de la Constitución. (p. 217)

containment [contención] *s.* bloqueo de una nación en la expansión de la influencia de otras naciones, especialmente los esfuerzos de Estados Unidos por bloquear la expansión de la influencia soviética hacia fines de los años cuarenta y comienzos de los cincuenta. (p. 580)

Continental Army [Ejército Continental] *s.* fuerzas coloniales autorizadas en 1775 por el segundo Congreso Continental, con George Washington como su comandante en jefe. (p. 161)

convene [convocar] *v.* llamar a reunión. (p. 243)

Copperheads [víboras cobrizas] *s.* los principales adversarios políticos de Abraham Lincoln; abogaban por la paz con el Sur. (p. 508)

cotton gin [desmontadora de algodón] *s.* máquina inventada en 1793 que limpiaba el algodón con mucha más rapidez y eficiencia que los obreros humanos. (p. 332)

counterculture [contracultura] *s.* grupo de jóvenes con valores morales y modos de vida contrarios a los de la cultura establecida. (p. 587)

Crittenden Plan [Plan de Crittenden] *s.* acuerdo presentado en 1861 que podría haber evitado la secesión. (p. 459)

Crusades [cruzadas] *s.* serie de guerras para capturar la Tierra Santa, iniciada en 1096 por cristianos europeos. (p. 36)

culture [cultura] *s.* manera de vida compartida por gente que tiene artes, creencias y costumbres semejantes. (p. 28)

Dawes Act [ley Dawes] *s.* ley, aprobada en 1887, que distribuía la tierra de las reservas amerindias a dueños individuales. (p. 540)

Declaration of Independence [Declaración de Independencia] *s.* documento, escrito en 1776, en que las colonias declararon su independendia de Gran Bretaña. (p. 164)

depression [depresión] *s.* aguda crisis económica. (p. 370)

desert [desertar] *v.* abandonar el servicio militar sin intenciones de regresar. (p. 187)

diversity [diversidad] *s.* variedad de gente. (p. 101)

doctrine of nullification [doctrina de la invalidación] *s.* derecho de un estado a rechazar una ley federal que considerase inconstitucional. (p. 365)

domestication [domesticación] *s.* práctica de criar plantas o amansar animales para satisfacer las necesidades humanas. (p. 28)

Dred Scott v. Sandford [Dred Scott contra Sandford] *s.* caso de 1865 de la Corte Suprema en que un esclavo, Dred Scott, entabló juicio por su libertad porque su amo lo había llevado a vivir en territorios donde la esclavitud era ilegal; la Corte dictaminó contra Scott. (p. 451)

due process of law [proceso legal debido] *s.* tratamiento justo bajo la ley. (p. 251)

Elector [elector] *s.* votante. (p. 233)

Emancipation Proclamation [Proclama de Emancipación] *s.* orden ejecutiva dictada por Abraham Lincoln el 1.° de enero de 1863, que liberaba a los esclavos de todas las regiones insurgentes contra la Unión. (p. 504)

Embargo Act of 1807 [ley de Embargo de 1807] *s.* ley que dictaminaba que los barcos estadounidenses ya no estaban autorizados para ir a puertos extranjeros y que también cerraba los puertos de Estados Unidos a los barcos británicos. (p. 488)

emigrant [emigrante] *s.* persona que abandona un país. (p. 407)

encomienda [encomienda] *s.* concesión del trabajo de los amerindios. (p. 60)

English Bill of Rights [Carta de Derechos Ingleses] *s.* acuerdo firmado por Guillermo y María por el que prometían respetar los derechos del Parlamento y los ciudadanos ingleses, incluso el derecho a elecciones libres. (p. 128)

enlightenment [Ilustración] *s.* movimiento del siglo XVIII que enfatizaba el uso de la razón y el método científico para obtener conocimiento. (p. 124)

enumeration [enumeración] *s.* recuento oficial, como un censo. (p. 233)

equity [equidad] *s.* sistema de justicia no cubierto bajo la ley común. (p. 253)

Erie Canal [canal de Erie] *s.* completado en 1825, esta vía navegable conectaba a la ciudad de Nueva York con Buffalo, New York. (p. 339)

European Middle Ages [Edad Media europea] *s.* período desde fines del siglo V hasta aproximadamente el siglo XIV, durante el cual los europeos adoptaron el feudalismo y el sistema señorial. (p. 35)

ex post facto law [ley ex post facto] *s.* ley que hace que un acto sea una ofensa criminal aprobada después de cometido el acto. (p. 239)

factory system [sistema fabril] *s.* un método de producción que juntó a obreros y máquinas en el mismo edificio. (p. 325)

fall line *s.* punto a partir del cual una catarata impide que los barcos grandes continúen río arriba. (p. 110)

famine [hambruna] *s.* severa escasez de alimentos. (p. 410)

fascism [fascismo] *s.* filosofía política que propugna un fuerte gobierno nacionalista centralizado, con un dictador poderoso a la cabeza. (p. 574)

federalism [federalismo] *s.* sistema de gobierno en que el poder está dividido entre el gobierno central (o federal) y los estados. (pp. 218, 229)

Federalists [federalistas] *s.* partidarios de la Constitución. (p. 218)

Federalist Papers [El federalista] *s.* serie de ensayos que defienden y explican la Constitución, escritos por Alexander Hamilton, James Madison y John Jay. (p. 219)

Federal Judiciary Act [ley de la Judicatura Federal] *s.* ayudó a establecer un sistema de tribunales; le dio al Tribunal Supremo seis miembros. (p. 278)

felony [felonía] *s.* delito grave. (p. 237)

feudalism [feudalismo] *s.* sistema político en que el rey concedía a sus nobles el uso de sus tierras a cambio de su prestación militar y la protección de la gente que vivía en esas tierras. (p. 35)

Fifteenth Amendment [Enmienda Decimoquinta] *s.* aprobada en 1870, esta enmienda a la Constitución de Estados Unidos declaraba que a los ciudadanos no se les podía impedir que votaran "por motivo de raza, color ni condición anterior de esclavitud". (p. 530)

54th Massachusetts Regiment [54.° Regimiento de Massachusetts] *s.* regimientos afroamericano organizado para luchar por la Unión en la guerra civil. (p. 490)

First Battle of Bull Run [primera batalla de Bull Run] *s.* una batalla de la guerra civil, de 1861, en que el Sur horrorizó al Norte con una victoria. (p. 469)

foreign policy [política exterior] *s.* relaciones con los gobiernos de otros países. (p. 288)

Fort Sumter [fuerte Sumter] *s.* fuerte federal ubicado en el puerto de Charleston, Carolina del Sur; el ataque sureño al fuerte Sumter marcó el comienzo de la guerra civil. (p. 465)

forty-niner [buscador de ventura del 49] *s.* persona que fue a California en búsqueda de oro, empezando en 1849. (p. 396)

Fourteen Points [Catorce puntos] *s.* los objetivos del presidente Woodrow Wilson para la paz que siguió a la primera guerra mundial. (p. 561)

Fourteenth Amendment [Enmienda Decimocuarta] *s.* enmienda a la Constitución de Estados Unidos, aprobada en 1868, que hizo ciudadanos del país a todas las personas nacidas en Estados Unidos o naturalizadas, incluso a los antiguos esclavos. (p. 519)

First Continental Congress [primer Congreso Continental] *s.* reunión en 1774 de delegados de todas las colonias, excepto Georgia, para defender los derechos coloniales. (p. 155)

Freedmen's Bureau [Agencia de Manumisos] *s.* agencia federal establecida para ayudar a los antiguos esclavos después de la guerra civil. (p. 517)

freedmen's school [escuela para los manumisos] *s.* escuela establecida por la Agencia de Manumisos para educar a los recientes libertos afroamericanos. (p. 525)

Free Soil Party [Partido del Suelo Libre] *s.* partido político dedicado a parar la expansión de la esclavitud. (p. 443)

French and Indian War [guerra Francesa y Amerindia] *s.* conflicto en Norteamérica, entre 1754 y 1763, que fue parte de una lucha mundial entre Francia y Gran Bretaña y que terminó con la derrota de Francia y el traspaso del Canadá francés a Gran Bretaña. (p. 131)

frontier [frontera] *s.* región sin o con muy pocos asentamientos ocupada mayormente por amerindios. (p. 539)

Fugitive Slave Act [ley de los Esclavos Fugitivos] *s.* ley de 1850 para ayudar a los dueños de esclavos a recapturar los esclavos fugados. (p. 446)

French Revolution [Revolución francesa] *s.* en 1789 los franceses iniciaron un movimiento por la libertad y la igualdad. (p. 285)

Fundamental Orders of Connecticut [Órdenes Fundamentales de Connecticut] *s.* conjunto de leyes establecidas en 1639 por una congregación puritana que se había asentado en el valle del río Connecticut y que ampliaban la idea de un gobierno representativo. (p. 79)

Gilded Age [Edad Dorada] *s.* época de fines del siglo XIX de fabulosa riqueza. (p. 541)

"Glorious Revolution" [Revolución gloriosa] *s.* derrocamiento, en 1688, del rey inglés Jacobo II y su substitución por Guillermo y María. (p. 128)

Great Awakening [Gran Despertar] *s.* renovación del sentimiento religioso en las colonias norteamericanas durante las décadas de 1730 a 1750. (p. 123)

Great Compromise [Gran Compromiso] *s.* acuerdo en la Convención Constitucional que estableció una legislatura nacional de dos cámaras; en una de estas cámaras, todos los estados tendrían representación igual, en la otra, cada estado tendría representación basada en su población. (p. 216)

Great Depression [gran depresión] *s.* período que duró desde 1929 hasta 1941, en que la economía de Estados Unidos declinó severamente y millones de estadounidenses estaban sin empleo. (p. 571)

Great Migration [Gran Emigración] *s.* movimiento de puritanos que salieron de Inglaterra para establecer asentamientos por todo el mundo, incluyendo a 20,000 que partieron para América (p. 78); el movimiento de afroamericanos entre 1910 y 1920 del Sur hacia las ciudades del Norte. (p. 562)

Great Society [gran sociedad] *s.* programa iniciado por Lyndon Johnson para ayudan a los pobres, los ancianos y las mujeres y también promovía la educación, prohibía la discriminación racial y protegía el medio ambiente. (p. 586)

greenback [billete verde] *s.* papel moneda emitido por el gobierno federal durante la guerra civil. (p. 493)

gristmill [molino harinero] *s.* molino en que el grano se muele para producir cualquier tipo de harina. (p. 99)

guerrilla [guerrillero] *s.* soldado que debilita al enemigo con asaltos inesperados y ataques relámpagos. (p. 191)

Harlem Renaissance [renacimiento de Harlem] *s.* florecimiento de la creatividad artística afroamericana durante los años veinte, centrada en la comunidad de Harlem de la ciudad de Nueva York. (p. 571)

Harpers Ferry *s.* arsenal federal en Virginia, capturado en 1859 durante un levantamiento de esclavos. (p. 469)

Holocaust [Holocausto] *s.* matanza sistemática en Alemania, durante la segunda guerra mundial, de unos seis millones de judíos así como millones de otros grupos étnicos. (p. 578)

Homestead Act [ley de Residencia] *s.* aprobada en 1862, esta ley ofrecía 160 acres de tierra gratis a cualquiera que acordara ocuparla y trabajarla por cinco años. (p. 540)

House of Burgesses [Cámara de los Burgueses] *s.* creada en 1619, la primera asamblea representativa de las colonias norteamericanas. (p. 72)

Hudson River school [Escuela del río Hudson] *s.* grupo de artistas que vivían en el valle del río Hudson del estado de New York. (p. 414)

hygiene [higiene] *s.* condiciones y prácticas que fomentan la buena salud. (p. 474)

immigrant [inmigrante] *s.* persona que se establece en un país nuevo. (p. 407)

immunity [inmunidad] *s.* protección legal. (p. 246)

impeachment [imputación] *s.* proceso de acusar a un funcionario público de un delito en el desempeño de sus funciones. (p. 233)

imperialism [imperialismo] *s.* política por la cual las naciones más poderosas extienden su control económico, político o militar sobre territorios o naciones más débiles. (p. 556)

impressment [secuestro] *s.* el acto de capturar personas a la fuerza. (p. 311)

inaugurate [investir] *v.* conferir un cargo oficial en una ceremonia formal. (p. 277)

income tax [impuesto sobre la renta] *s.* impuesto sobre los ingresos. (p. 493)

indentured servant [siervo escriturado] *s.* persona que vendía su trabajo a cambio de pasaje a Norteamérica. (p. 72)

Indian Removal Act [ley del Traslado de los Indígenas] *s.* esta ley de 1830 requería que el gobierno negociara tratados para el traslado de los amerindios al oeste. (p. 360)

Indian Territory [territorio Indio] *s.* lo que hoy son Oklahoma y partes de Kansas y Nebraska a la cual se trasladó a los amerindios bajo la ley del Traslado de los Indígenas de 1830. (p. 360)

indictment [acusación] *s.* declaración escrita dictada por un jurado de acusación que inculpa a una persona de un delito. (p. 234)

indigo [añil] *s.* planta que cultivaban las colonias sureñas de la cual se obtiene un colorante azul oscuro. (p. 105)

individual right [derecho individual] *s.* libertad y privilegio personal que garantiza a los ciudadanos estadounidenses la Carta de Derechos. (p. 231)

Industrial Revolution [revolución industrial] *s.* en la Inglaterra de fines del siglo XVIII, las maquinarias de fábrica empezaron a reemplazar las herramientas manuales, y la producción de bienes manufacturados reemplazó la agricultura como el principal modo de trabajo. (p. 325)

inferior court [tribunal inferior] *s.* corte con autoridad menor que la del Tribunal Supremo. (p. 244)

inflation [inflación] *s.* subida en el precio de los productos y los servicios y disminución del valor del dinero. (p. 370)

inoperative [inoperante] *adj.* que no está vigente. (p. 258)

insurrection [insurrección] *s.* levantamiento abierto contra un gobierno. (p. 255)

interchangeable part [parte intercambiable] *s.* parte que es exactamente igual a otra parte. (p. 327)

Intolerable Acts [leyes Intolerables] *s.* serie de leyes aprobadas en 1774 por el Parlamento para castigar a Massachusetts por el Motín del Té de Boston. (p. 154)

ironclad [acorazado] *s.* buque de guerra cubierto de hierro. (p. 475)

Iroquois League [Liga Iroquesa] *s.* alianza del siglo XVI entre los pueblos amerindios cayuga, mohawk, oneida, onondaga y seneca, que vivían en la región oriental de los Grandes lagos. (p. 31)

Islam [islam] *s.* religión fundada por el profeta Mahoma en el siglo VII, que enseña que hay un solo Dios: Alá. (p. 34)

Jacksonian Democracy [democracia jacksoniana] *s.* idea de extender el poder político a toda la gente asegurando de ese modo el gobierno de la mayoría. (p. 354)

Jamestown *s.* primer asentamiento inglés permanente en Norteamérica. (p. 71)

Jay's Treaty [Tratado de Jay] *s.* el acuerdo que puso fin a la disputa sobre los derechos marítimos estadounidenses durante la Revolución francesa. (p. 286)

jazz [jazz] *s.* tipo nuevo de música en los años veinte que capturó el despreocupado espíritu de la época. (p. 570)

Jim Crow [ley Jim Crow] *s.* ley que imponía la separación entre la gente blanca y la de piel negra en los lugares públicos del Sur. (p. 549)

joint-stock company [sociedad por acciones] *s.* empresa en que los inversionistas colocan su dinero en un fondo común con la intención de sacar ganancias. (p. 70)

judicial review [revisión judicial] *s.* principio de que el Tribunal Supremo tiene la última palabra en la interpretación de la Constitución. (p. 301)

Judiciary Act of 1801 [ley Judicial de 1801] *s.* ley que aumentó el número de jueces federales, permitiéndole al presidente John Adams cubrir la mayoría de los puestos nuevos con federalistas. (p. 300)

Kansas-Nebraska Act [ley de Kansas-Nebraska] *s.* ley de 1854 que estableció los territorios de Kansas y Nebraska y otorgó a sus habitantes el derecho a decidir si querían o no permitir la esclavitud. (p. 448)

King Cotton [rey Algodón] *s.* al algodón se lo llamaba rey porque era importante en el mercado mundial y el Sur cultivaba la mayor parte del algodón que usaban las fábricas textiles de Europa. (p. 468)

King Philip's War [guerra del rey Felipe] *s.* guerra entre las colonias puritanas y los amerindios que se libró entre 1675 y 1676. (p. 80)

Ku Klux Klan *s.* grupo constituido en 1866 que quería restaurar el control del Sur a los demócratas y mantener sumisos a los antiguos esclavos. (p. 528)

labor union [sindicato laboral] *s.* obreros que se unen para tratar de conseguir mejores condiciones de trabajo. (p. 418)

Land Ordinance of 1785 [Ordenanza de Tierras de 1785] *s.* ley que establecía un plan para la agrimensura y venta de las tierras públicas al oeste de los montes Apalaches. (p. 207)

land speculator [especulador en tierras] *s.* persona que compra grandes extensiones de terreno a precio bajo y luego vende secciones pequeñas a precios altos. (p. 378)

leisure *s.* tiempo libre. (p. 548)

Lewis and Clark expedition [expedición de Lewis y Clark] *s.* grupo dirigido por Meriwether Lewis y William Clark que exploró las tierras de la Compra de Luisiana empezando en 1803. (p. 304)

Lexington and Concord *s.* escenarios, en Massachusetts, de las primeras batallas de la Revolución norteamericana. (p. 157)

limited government [gobierno limitado] *s.* principio que requiere que todos los ciudadanos estadounidenses, incluso los líderes gubernamentales, obedezcan la ley. (p. 231)

Lone Star Republic [República de la Estrella Solitaria] *s.* apodo de la República de Texas, que se le dio en 1836. (p. 389)

Louisiana Purchase [Compra de Luisiana] *s.* en 1803, la compra a Francia del Territorio de Luisiana. (p. 303)

Lowell mills [fábricas de Lowell] *s.* fábricas textiles ubicadas en el pueblo manufacturero de Lowell, Massachusetts, fundado en 1826. (p. 326)

Loyalist [realista]. *s.* colono norteamericano que apoyaba a los británicos durante la Revolución norteamericana. (p. 157)

Magna Carta [Carta Magna] *s.* "Gran Cédula Real"; documento que garantizaba los derechos políticos básicos en Inglaterra, aprobada por el rey Juan en el año 1215. (p. 125)

manifest destiny [destino manifiesto] *s.* creencia de que era el destino de Estados Unidos extenderse por todo el continente, desde al océano Atlántico al océano Pacífico. (p. 391)

Marbury v. *Madison* [Marbury contra Madison] *s.* caso de 1803 en que el Tribunal Supremo dictaminó que tenía el poder de invalidar leyes declarándolas inconstitucionales. (p. 301)

mass culture [cultura de masas] *s.* cultura común compartida por grandes números de personas. (p. 548)

Mayflower Compact [Pacto del Mayflower] *s.* acuerdo firmado por los hombres que viajaron a América en el Mayflower, que requería leyes para el bien de la colonia y establecía el concepto de autogobierno. (p. 77)

mercantilism [mercantilismo] *s.* sistema económico en que las naciones tratan de aumentar su riqueza y poder obteniendo oro y plata y estableciendo una balanza comercial favorable. (p. 51)

mercenary [mercenario] *s.* soldado profesional contratado para luchar por un país extranjero. (p. 179)

Mexican Cession [Cesión mexicana] *s.* extensa región cedida por México después de la guerra con México; incluía los actuales estados de California, Nevada, Utah, la mayor parte de Arizona y partes de Nuevo México, Colorado y Wyoming. (p. 395)

middle passage [travesía intermedia] *s.* parte intermedia de la ruta del comercio triangular (el viaje de África a las Américas) que traía africanos capturados a la esclavitud. (p. 61)

militia [milicia] *s.* fuerza de civiles armados comprometidos a defender su comunidad durante la Revolución norteamericana. (p. 154); fuerza militar de emergencia, que no es parte del ejército profesional. (p.238)

minié ball [bala minié] *s.* bala con base hueca. (p. 475)

Minuteman [minutero] *s.* miembro de la milicia colonial entrenado para responder "con un minuto de aviso". (p. 154)

misdemeanor [fechoría] *s.* violación de la ley. (p. 243)

Missouri Compromise [Acuerdo de Missouri] *s.* serie de leyes aprobadas en 1820 para mantener el equilibrio del poder político entre los estados esclavistas y los libres. (p. 342)

Monroe Doctrine [Doctrina Monroe] *s.* política de oposición estadounidense a cualquier interferencia europea en el hemisferio occidental, proclamada por el presidente Monroe en 1823. (p. 347)

Mormon [mormón] *s.* miembro de una iglesia fundada por Joseph Smith en 1830. (p. 381)

Mound Builder [constructor de túmulos] *s.* amerindio primitivo que construía grandes estructuras de tierra. (p. 29)

mountain man [hombre de las montañas] *s.* trampero o explorador que abrió el oeste hallando sendas a través de las montañas Rocosas. (p. 377)

Muslim [musulmán] *s.* adherente del islam. (p. 34)

nationalism [nacionalismo] *s.* sentido de orgullo, lealtad y protección hacia el país de uno. (p. 338)

nativist [nativista] *s.* estadounidense nativo que quería eliminar toda influencia extranjera. (p. 412)

natural-born citizen [ciudadano nato] *s.* ciudadano nacido en Estados Unidos o en un estado asociado o dependencia de Estados Unidos, o a padres que son ciudadanos estadounidenses que viven fuera del país. (p. 241)

naturalization [naturalización] *s.* manera de darle ciudadanía completa a una persona nacida en otro país. (pp. 237,254)

Navigation Acts [Actas de Navegación] *s.* serie de leyes aprobadas por el Parlamento, empezando en 1651, para asegurarse Inglaterra de que el comercio de sus colonias le rindiera ganancias económicas. (p. 96)

navigator [oficial de derrota] *s.* persona que planea el rumbo de un barco mientras está en el mar. (p. 39)

Nazi Party [Partido Nazi] *s.* partido Alemán Nacionalsocialista de los Trabajadores, llegó al poder bajo Adolfo Hitler en 1930. (p. 574)

neutral [neutral] *adj.* que no apoya ni a un país ni al otro. (p. 288)

New Deal [Nuevo Trato] *s.* programas de Franklin Roosevelt para luchar contra la depresión. (p. 572)

New France [Nueva Francia] *s.* puesto para el comercio de las pieles establecido en 1608 que se convirtió en el primer asentamiento francés permanente en Norteamérica. (p. 58)

new immigrant [inmigrante nuevo] *s.* persona del sur y el este de Europa que entró a Estados Unidos después de 1900. (p. 542)

New Jersey Plan [Plan de Nueva Jersey] *s.* plan de gobierno propuesto en 1787 en la Convención Constitucional que proponía una cámara legislativa única en que cada estado tendría un solo voto. (p. 215)

Northwest Ordinance [Ordenanza del Noroeste] *s.* describe cómo se iba a gobernar el territorio del Noroeste y establecía las condiciones para el asentamiento, así como los derechos de los colonos. (p. 207)

Northwest Territory [territorio del Noroeste] *s.* territorio organizado por la Ordenanza de Tierras de 1785, que incluía tierras que formaron los estados de Ohio, Indiana, Michigan, Illinois, Wisconsin y parte de Minnesota. (p. 207)

O

Oregon Trail [Camino de Oregón] *s.* camino hacia el oeste que iba de Independence, Missouri, al territorio de Oregón. (p. 380)

overseer [capataz] *s.* persona contratada por el dueño de una plantación para vigilar a los esclavos y dirigir su trabajo. (p. 106)

P

pacifist [pacifista] *s.* persona moralmente opuesta a la guerra. (p. 193)

Panama Canal [canal de Panamá] *s.* atajo a través de Panamá que conecta los oceános Atlántico y Pacífico. (p. 558)

Panic of 1837 [pánico de 1837] *s.* crisis financiera con clausura de bancos y colapso del sistema crediticio, que resultó en muchas quiebras y serio desempleo. (p. 370)

Panic of 1873 [pánico de 1873] *s.* crisis financiera en que los bancos se clausuraron y la bolsa de comercio se derrumbó. (p. 531)

Parliament [Parlamento] *s.* el cuerpo legislativo principal de Inglaterra. (p. 126)

Patriot [patriota] *s.* colono norteamericano que durante la Revolución norteamericana estaba a favor de los rebeldes. (p. 157)

patroon [patrono] *s.* persona que traía 50 colonos a Nueva Holanda y a cambio recibía una gran concesión de tierras y otros privilegios especiales. (p. 85)

Pickett's Charge [carga de Pickett] *s.* en 1863 el general George Pickett dirigió una carga frontal contra las fuerzas de la Unión durante la batalla de la guerra civil en Gettysburg; el ataque fracasó. (p. 497)

piedmont [tierras bajas] *s.* ancha extensión de tierra llana al pie de una cadena de montañas. (p. 110)

Pilgrim [peregrino] *s.* miembros del grupo que rechazó la Iglesia de Inglaterra, viajó a América y fundó la colonia de Plymouth en 1620. (p. 76)

Pinckney's Treaty [Tratado de Pinckney] *s.* tratado de 1795 con España que otorgaba a Estados Unidos el uso del río Mississippi y el derecho a depositar bienes en Nueva Orleans; creó el paralelo 31 como el límite sur de Estados Unidos. (p. 286)

plantation [plantación] *s.* finca grande para cultivos comerciales. (p. 60)

platform [plataforma] *s.* declaración de creencias. (p. 455)

Platt Amendment [Enmienda Platt] *s.* resultado de la guerra entre Estados Unidos y España, dio a Estados Unidos el derecho a intervenir en los asuntos de Cuba cuando existiera amenaza a la "vida, propiedad y libertad individual". (p. 558)

Plessy* v. *Ferguson [Plessy contra Ferguson] *s.* caso de 1896 en que el Tribunal Supremo dictaminó que la separación de las razas en las instalaciones públicas era legal. (p. 549)

Pontiac's Rebellion [rebelión de Pontiac] *s.* rebelión de 1763 contra los fuertes británicos y los colonos norteamericanos, dirigida en parte por el líder ottawa Pontiac, en reacción a los colonos que demandaban las tierras de los amerindios, así como a la severidad con que trataban a éstos los soldados británicos. (p. 135)

popular sovereignty [soberanía popular] *s.* gobierno en que gobierna la gente (p. 228); sistema en que los ciudadanos votan para decidir un asunto. (p. 447)

Populist Party [Partido Populista] *s.* también conocido como el Partido del Pueblo y constituido en 1890, este grupo quería una política que aumentara el precio de lo que cultivaban los granjeros. (p. 551)

prejudice [prejuicio] *s.* opinión negativa no basada en los hechos. (p. 411)

privateer [corsario] *s.* barco de propiedad particular autorizado por un gobierno que está en guerra a atacar los barcos de la marina mercante enemiga. (p. 188)

Proclamation of 1763 [Proclama de 1763] *s.* orden por la cual Gran Bretaña les prohibía a los colonos norteamericanos establecer asentamientos al oeste de los montes Apalaches. (p. 135)

progressivism [progresismo] *s.* movimiento reformista de principios del siglo XX que buscaba devolver el control del gobierno al pueblo, restablecer oportunidades económicas y corregir las injusticias de la vida estadounidense. (p. 553)

proprietary colony [colonia de propietario] *s.* colonia de un único dueño. (p. 85)

pro tempore *adv.* latín para "por el momento". (p. 234)

Puritan [puritano] *s.* miembro de un grupo de Inglaterra que se asentó en la Colonia de la bahía de Massachusetts en 1630 y trató de reformar las prácticas de la Iglesia de Inglaterra. (p. 78)

push-pull factor *s.* factor que empuja a la gente a irse de su tierra natal y las atrae a un lugar nuevo. (p. 408)

Q

Quaker [cuáquero] *s.* persona que creía que todas las personas debieran vivir en paz y armonía; aceptaba a religiones y grupos étnicos diferentes. (p. 85)

quarter [acuartelar] *v.* dar alojamiento. (p. 251)

Quartering Act [ley de Acuartelamiento] *s.* ley aprobada por el Parlamento en 1765 que requería que las colonias alojaran a los soldados británicos y los aprovisionaran. (p. 144)

quorum [quórum] *s.* número mínimo de miembros que deben estar presentes para que pueda empezar a deliberar oficialmente una asamblea. (p. 235)

racism [racismo] *s.* creencia de que alguna gente es inferior a causa de su raza. (p. 62)

radical [radical] *s.* persona que adopta posiciones políticas extremas. (p. 297)

Radical Republican [republicano radical] *s.* diputado que después de la guerra civil estaba a favor de usar el gobierno para crear un nuevo orden en el Sur y dar la ciudadanía total y derecho al voto a los afroamericanos. (p. 517)

ratification [ratificación] *s.* aprobación oficial. (p. 248)

Reconstruction [Reconstrucción] *s.* proceso que usó el gobierno de Estados Unidos para readmitir a los estados confederados a la Unión después de la guerra civil. (p. 517)

Reformation [Reforma] *s.* movimiento religioso del siglo XVI para corregir los problemas de la Iglesia Católica Romana. (p. 37)

Renaissance [Renacimiento] *s.* período de la historia europea que duró desde el siglo XIV hasta comienzos del XVII y que acrecentó el interés por el arte y el saber. (p. 36)

rendezvous [encuentro] *s.* reunión. (p. 181)

reprieve [indultar] *n.* cancelación de un castigo. (p. 243)

republic [república] *s.* gobierno en que el pueblo elige representantes para que lo gobiernen. (p. 206)

republicanism [republicanismo] *s.* creencia de que el gobierno se debe basar en el consentimiento del pueblo; el pueblo ejercita su poder votando por representantes políticos. (pp. 198, 229)

Republican Party [Partido Republicano] *s.* el partido político constituído en 1854 por los que se oponían a la esclavitud en los territorios. (p. 450)

revenue [rentas públicas] *s.* entradas que recibe un gobierno para cubrir sus gastos. (pp. 144, 236)

revival [renacimiento religioso] *s.* reunión diseñada para revivir la fe religiosa. (p. 417)

rifle [rifle] *s.* arma de barril estriado que hace que la bala vaya girando por el aire. (p. 475)

robber baron [capitalista inescrupuloso] *s.* líder industrial que se hizo acaudalado usando medios deshonestos. (p. 578)

romanticism [romanticismo] *s.* movimiento artístico europeo que acentuaba al individuo, la imaginación, la creatividad y la emoción. (p. 413)

Roosevelt Corollary [Corolario de Roosevelt] *s.* la adición en 1904 a la Doctrina Monroe permitiendo a los Estados Unidos a actuar de "policía" en Latinoamérica. (p. 560)

royal colony [colonia real] *s.* colonia regida por gobernadores nombrados por un rey. (p. 87)

salutary neglect [indiferencia beneficiosa] *s.* política de no interferir Inglaterra en los asuntos de sus colonias norteamericanas durante la primera mitad del siglo XVIII. (p. 128)

Santa Fe Trail [Camino de Santa Fe] *s.* camino hacia el oeste que iba de Missouri a Santa Fe, New Mexico. (p. 379)

secede [separarse] *v.* retirarse. (p. 457)

secession [secesión] *s.* separarse como parte de Estados Unidos. (p. 367)

Second Continental Congress [segundo Congreso Continental] *s.* organismo de gobierno cuyos delegados acordaron en mayo de 1775 organizar el Ejército Continental y aprobar la Declaración de Independencia. (p. 161)

Second Great Awakening [segundo Gran Despertar] *s.* renovación de la fe religiosa durante fines del siglo XVIII y comienzos del XIX. (p. 417)

sectionalism [seccionalismo] *s.* colocar los intereses de la región propia por encima de los de la nación como unidad. (p. 341)

segregation [segregación] *s.* separación. (p. 549)

Seneca Falls Convention [convención de Seneca Falls] *s.* convención sobre los derechos de la mujer llevada a cabo en Seneca Falls, New York, en 1848. (p. 428)

separation of powers [separación de poderes] *s.* división de las funciones básicas del gobierno en tres ramas. (p. 230)

servitude [servitud] *s.* práctica de pertenecer a un dueño o amo. (p. 254)

Seven Days' Battles [batallas de los Siete Días] *s.* batalla de 1862 de la guerra civil en que la Confederación forzó a la Unión a retroceder después de un intento fracasado de capturar la capital sureña de Richmond. (p. 480)

sharecropping [aparcería] *s.* sistema en que los terratenientes daban a los agricultores tierra, semilla y herramientas a cambio de parte de la cosecha. (p. 527)

Shays's Rebellion [revuelta de Shay] *s.* sublevación de granjeros adeudados de Massachusetts en 1787. (p. 209)

Siege of Vicksburg [sitio de Vicksburg] *s.* victoria unionista de 1863, durante la guerra civil que le permitió a la Unión controlar todo el río Misisipí. (p. 500)

slash-and-burn agriculture [agricultura de corte y quema] *s.* método agrícola en que la gente preparaba los campos cortando y quemando árboles y pastos, cuyas cenizas fertilizaban la tierra. (p. 31)

slavery [esclavitud] *s.* sistema de servidumbre humana involuntaria. (p. 60)

smuggle [contrabandear] *v.* importar o exportar mercancías ilegalmente. (p. 96)

Sons of Liberty [Hijos de la Libertad] *s.* grupo de colonos que formaron una sociedad secreta para oponerse a las políticas británicas en los tiempos de la revolución norteamericana. (p. 145)

Spanish-American War *s.* guerra de 1898 que comenzó cuando Estados Unidos demandó que España le concediera la independencia a Cuba. (p. 557)

Spanish Armada [Armada española] *s.* flota de buques enviada en 1588 por el rey español Felipe Segundo para invadir a Inglaterra y restaurar allí el catolicismo romano. (p. 57)

spiritual [canción espiritual] *s.* canción folklórica religiosa. (p. 335)

spoils system [sistema de prebendas] *s.* práctica de otorgar los candidatos elegidos empleos gubernamentales a los simpatizantes políticos. (p. 357)

Stamp Act [ley del Timbre] *s.* ley aprobada por el Parlamento en 1765 que requería que todos los documentos comerciales y legales llevaran un timbre oficial que indicaba que se había pagado un impuesto. (p. 144)

states' rights [derechos estatales] *s.* teoría que sostenía que los estados tenían el derecho a decidir cuándo el gobierno federal había pasado una ley inconstitucional. (p. 291)

steerage [tercera clase] *s.* nivel o lugar más barato de un barco. (p. 407)

Stono Rebellion [Rebelión de Stono] *s.* sublevación de esclavos de 1739, en Carolina del Sur, que resultó en que se hicieran aún más estrictas las leyes que controlaban a los esclavos. (p. 107)

strategy [estrategia] *s.* plan general de acción. (p. 180)

strike [declararse en huelga] *v.* suspender los obreros el trabajo para tratar de conseguir condiciones de trabajo mejores. (p. 418)

subsistence farm *v.* una granja que produce bastante alimento para la familia con sólo una pequeña cantidad para vender. (p. 94)

suffrage [sufragio] *s.* derecho a votar. (pp. 246, 428)

Sugar Act [ley del Azúcar] *s.* ley aprobada por el Parlamento en 1764 que impuso impuestos al azúcar, la melaza y otros productos que llegaban a las colonias; también establecía severos castigos para los contrabandistas. (p. 144)

T

tariff [arance aduanero] *s.* impuesto a las mercancías importadas. (p. 280)

Tariff of Abominations [arancel de las Abominaciones] *s.* ley de 1828 que subió los aranceles de las materias primas y las manufacturas; alteró a los sureños, quienes sentían que la política económica nacional la estaban determinando los intereses económicos del noreste. (p. 365)

technology [tecnología] *s.* uso de herramientas y conocimiento para satisfacer las necesidades humanas. (p. 29)

Tejano [tejano] *s.* persona de ascendencia española que consideraba a Texas su hogar. (p. 384)

temperance movement [movimiento de la templanza] *s.* campaña para acabar con el consumo de las bebidas alcohólicas. (p. 418)

tender *s.* dinero (p. 239)

Thirteenth Amendment [Enmienda Decimotercera] *s.* enmienda a la Constitución de Estados Unidos adoptada en 1865 que abolía la esclavitud y la servidumbre involuntaria en Estados Unidos. (p. 505)

Three-Fifths Compromise [Acuerdo de los Tres Quintos] *s.* acuerdo de la Convención Constitucional que establecía que, para efectos de la representación y del cobro de impuestos, se contarían como parte de la población tres quintos de los esclavos de un estado. (p. 216)

Townshend Acts [leyes de Townshend] *s.* serie de leyes aprobadas por el Parlamento en 1767 que suspendieron la Asamblea de Nueva York y establecieron impuestos a las mercancías importadas a las colonias británicas. (p. 147)

Trail of Tears [Sendero de las Lágrimas] *s.* trágica marcha del pueblo cherokee desde sus tierras hasta el Territorio Indio, entre 1838 y 1839; miles de cherokees murieron. (p. 361)

transcendentalism [trascendentalismo] *s.* filosofía del siglo XIX que enseñaba que el mundo espiritual es más importante que el mundo físico y que las personas pueden hallar la verdad dentro de sí mismas mediante los sentimientos y la intuición. (p. 415)

Treaty of Ghent [Tratado de Gante] *s.* tratado firmado en 1814 que puso fin a la guerra de 1812; no cambió de dueño ningún territorio ni se resolvieron los conflictos comerciales. (p. 317)

Treaty of Greenville [Tratado de Greenville] *s.* acuerdo de 1795 por el cual 12 tribus amerindias cedieron al gobierno de Estados Unidos gran parte de lo que hoy son los estados de Ohio e Indiana. (p. 284)

Treaty of Guadalupe Hidalgo [Tratado de Guadalupe Hidalgo] *s.* tratado de 1848 que puso fin a la guerra estadounidense con México; México cedió California y Nuevo México a los Estados Unidos. (p. 394)

Treaty of Paris [Tratado de París] *s.* tratado de 1763 que puso fin a la guerra Francesa y Amerindia; Inglaterra entregó toda norteamérica del este del río Mississippi. (p. 134)

Treaty of Paris of 1783 [Tratado de París de 1783] *s.* tratado que puso fin a la guerra Revolucionaria, confirmó la independencia de Estados Unidos y estableció los límites de la nueva nación. (p. 196)

Treaty of Tordesillas [Tratado de Tordesillas] *s.* tratado de 1494 por el cual España y Portugal acordaron repartirse las tierras del hemisferio occidental y movieron la línea de demarcación hacia el oeste. (p. 51)

triangular trade [comercio triangular] *s.* sistema de comercio transatlántico en que se intercambiaban mercancías, incluso esclavos, entre África, Inglaterra, Europa, las Antillas y las colonias de Norte América. (p. 95)

tribunal [tribunal] *s.* corte. (p. 237)

unanimous consent [consentimiento unánime] *s.* acuerdo completo. (p. 248)

Uncle Tom's Cabin [La cabaña del tío Tom] *s.* novela publicada por Harriet Beecher Stowe en 1852, que mostraba la esclavitud como brutal e inmoral. (p. 446)

unconstitutional [inconstitucional] *adj.* que contradice la ley de la constitución. (p. 301)

Underground Railroad [ferrocarril clandestino] *s.* serie de rutas de escape que usaban los esclavos para escaparse del Sur. (p. 426)

urbanization [urbanización] *s.* crecimiento de las ciudades como resultado de la industrialización. (p. 541)

vaudeville [vodevil] *s.* tipo de espectáculo teatral en vivo con mezcla de canciones, baile y comedia. (p. 549)

Vietnam War [guerra de Vietnam] *s.* conflicto militar que duró desde 1954 hasta 1975, entre el Vietnam del Norte comunista, apoyado por China y la Unión Soviética y las fuerzas no comunistas de Vietnam del Sur, apoyadas por Estados Unidos. (p. 581)

vigilante [vigilante] *s.* persona dispuesta a tomar la ley en sus propias manos. (p. 545)

Virginia Plan *s.* plan presentado por Edmund Randolph, delegado a la Convención Constitucional de 1787, que proponía un gobierno de tres ramas y una legislatura bicameral en la que la representación se basaría en la población o la riqueza de un estado. (p. 215)

War Hawk *s.* habitante de las regiones del oeste que apoyaba la guerra de 1812. (p. 313)

Watergate Scandal [escándalo de Watergate] *s.* escándalo que resultó de los esfuerzos del gobierno de Nixon por encubrir su participación en el allanamiento de la Sede Central del Partido Demócrata en el edificio de apartamentos Watergate. (p. 582)

Webster-Hayne debate [debate Webster-Hayne] *s.* debate de 1830 entre Daniel Webster y Robert Hayne sobre la doctrina de la invalidación. (p. 366)

Whig Party [Partido Whig] *s.* partido político organizado en 1834 en oposición a las políticas de Andrew Jackson. (p. 371)

Whiskey Rebellion [rebelión del Whisky] *s.* protesta de 1794 contra el impuesto que impuso el gobierno al whisky, valioso medio económico de los granjeros de la frontera. (p. 285)

Wilderness Road [Camino al Desierto] *s.* sendero a Kentucky que ayudó a construir el pionero Daniel Boone. (p. 205)

Wilmot Proviso [Claúsula de Wilmot] *s.* propuesta de 1846 que excluía la esclavitud de cualquier territorio adquirido como resultado de la guerra con México. (p. 443)

World War II [segunda guerra mundial] *s.* guerra que se libró entre 1939 y 1945, en que Gran Bretaña, Francia, la Unión Soviética, Estados Unidos, China y otros aliados derrotaron a Alemania, Italia y Japón. (p. 575)

writ of assistance [mandato judicial de transferencia] *s.* orden de registro que permitía a los oficiales británicos entrar en los hogares o comercios coloniales en busca de contrabando. (p. 148)

XYZ Affair [asunto XYZ] *s.* incidente de 1797 en que funcionarios franceses demandaron que los diplomáticos estadounidenses les pagaran un soborno. (p. 290)

yellow journalism [periodismo amarillo] *s.* estilo de periodismo que usa la exageración y el sensacionalismo para presentar las noticias. (p. 557)

INDEX

An *i* preceding a page reference in italics indicates that there is an illustration, and usually text information as well, on that page. An *m* or a *c* preceding an italic page reference indicates a map or a chart, as well as text information on that page.

branches of government, 206, 215
visual summary of, *i262*
Brant, Joseph, *i181*
Brazil, 51
Breckinridge, John, 456, *m457*
Brook Farm, 421
Brooks, Preston, 449
Brown, John, 449, 453, *i461*
Brown v. *Board of Education of Topeka,* 585
Bryan, William Jennings, 553
bubonic plague, 36
Buchanan, James, 451, 458, R37
Buena Vista, Battle of, 394
buffalo, *i113, i308*
Bull Run, Battle of, 469
Bunker Hill, Battle of, 161
Burgoyne, John, 180–181, 182, 183
Burnett, John G., 361
Burnside, Ambrose, 496
Burr, Aaron, *i298*
Bush, George H. W., 583, 587, *i588,* R38
Bush, George W., 588, R38
antiterrorism and, US15
war against terrorism and, US9–US10
business
Great Depression and, 571–573
reform movements and, 554
Sherman Antitrust Act and, 554
supply and demand in, *c552*
Butler, A. P., 449
Butler, Benjamin F., *i519*
Byrd, William, II, *i105,* 111

C

cabinet, 278, *i278*
Cabot, John, 55
Cabrillo, Juan Rodríguez, 54
Cajuns, *i133*
Calhoun, John C.
nullification, doctrine of, 365–367
opposition to sectionalism by, *i363*
in slavery debate, *i444*
and transportation, 339
California, *m21*
Bear Flag Revolt in, *i392,* 393
exploration of, 302

facts about, R34
gold rush in, 395, 396–401
slavery and, 443–444
Spanish colonization of, 60
states' rights and, 252
in War with Mexico, 393
California Trail, *m379*
Californios, 396
Callender, James, 297
Camden, S.C., 191
Cameahwait, *i308*
Camp David Accords, 582
Canada
British settlement of, 313
Oregon Territory and, 391
as refuge for Loyalists, 197
canals, 339, *i339,* 340
cannon, *i192*
Cape of Good Hope, 39
capital punishment. *See* death penalty.
captivity narrative, 122
caravel, 39
Caribbean, *mR39*
Columbus in, 42
Spanish-American War in, 557–558, *m557*
Carnegie, Andrew, 541
Carolina, 86–87
carpetbaggers, 520
Carter, Jimmy, 582, 587, *i588,* R38
Cartier, Jacques, 56
Carver, George Washington, 549
Castro, Fidel, 580
categorizing, *c376, c568,* R6
cattle, 547
causes and effects, analyzing, *c36, c582,* R11
cavalry, 480
Central America, R39
Central Park, 548
Central Powers, 560
Chamberlain, Joshua Lawrence, *i496*
Chamberlain, Neville, 575
Champlain, Samuel de, 58
Chaplin, Charlie, *i570*
Charles II (English monarch), 73
Charleston (Charles Town), S.C., 86–87, 104, 190–191, *m193*
charter, 71
charts, interpreting, R23
Chávez, César, *i586*
checks and balances, 230, *c245*
chemical weapons. *See* weapons of mass destruction.

Cherokee people, 359–362, *m360, i361*
writing system of, 358, 359
Chesapeake, 311
Chesapeake Bay, 71
Chestnut, Mary, 479
Chicago, Ill.
stockyards in, *i544*
world's fair in, 548
Chicago Historical Society, 545
Chickasaw people, 31, 359, *i360*
child labor, *i537*
children in colonial life, 120–121
China, 580, 582
Chinatown, 400
Chinese Exclusion Act, 543
Chinese immigrants, 543, 550
in California gold rush, 398, *i399,* 400
Chinook people, *i309*
Choctaw people, 31, 358–359, *i360*
Churchill, Winston, 575
Church of Jesus Christ of Latter-Day Saints, 381
circuit rider, 417
cities
growth of, 541–542, 547, *c547*
immigration and overcrowding in, 410–411
industrialization and, 325–326, 441
reform movements in, 553
citizenship, 264–271
debating and, 453
definition of, 264
naturalization and, 265, 411
Patriots and, 176
responsibilities of, 267, 284
rights of, 126, 182, 246, 266, 356, 519
Citizenship Day, 411
civil disobedience, 415
civilization, 28
civil rights
Arab Americans and, US15
Arabs and, US14
citizenship and, 266
constitutional amendments and, 254, 519
movement for African Americans', 585–586
Reconstruction and, 519, *c533*
Civil Rights Act of 1866, 519
Civil Rights Act of 1964, 585

contrasting. *See* comparing and
    contrasting.
Convention of 1800, 291
Convention of 1818, 341
Conyers, John, *i530*
Coolidge, Calvin, 569, R38
Cooper, James Fenimore, 413
Copperheads, 492
Coral Pink Sand Dunes, *i10*
corn, 63
Cornwallis, Charles, 193–194
Coronado, Francisco Vázquez de,
    54
corporations, 554
Corps of Discovery, 304–305
Cortés, Hernando, 53, *i53*
cotton, 332–334, *m334*, 468
    in North-South exchange of
        goods, *c442*
    in Reconstruction, 527–528
cotton gin, 332–333, *i333*
counsel, 251
counterculture, 587
cowhands, 547
Creek people, 358–359, *i360*
Creoles, 59
Crèvecoeur, Michel Guillaume
    Jean de, 98
Crittenden, John J., 459
Crittenden Plan, 459
Crusades, 36
Cuba
    missile crisis and, *i580*, 581
    in Spanish-American War,
        557–558
culture, 28
curfews, 284
Currier and Ives, *i323*
Czechoslovakia
    in World War II, 575

D

dame schools, 122
Dare, Virginia, 69
database, creating, R31
Daughters of Liberty, *i148*
Davis, Jefferson, 468
    imprisonment of, 518
    leadership of Confederacy,
        i480, 486
    and secession, 457
Dawes, William, *m156*

Dawes Act, 540
D-Day, 577
deafness, 420
Deane, Silas, *i206*
death penalty, *i252*
debates
    Lincoln-Douglas, 452–453
    National Forensic League and,
        i453
    Webster-Hayne, *i366*
Decatur, Stephen, *i310*
decisions, making, 214, *c269*, R14
Declaration of Independence
    drafting and adoption of, *i164*,
        164–165
    text of, 166–169
Declaration of Rights, 223
Declaration of Sentiments and
    Resolutions, 428
Declaratory Act, 146
Deere, John, 329
Deganawida, 31–32
de Kalb, Baron, 185–191
Delaware
    as border state, 466, 467
    facts about, R34
    founding of, 85, 86
Delaware River, 100
delegated powers, 229
delta, *i14*
Deming, Edward, 130
democracy
    early American culture and,
        118
    and establishment of federal
        government, *i204*
    in new republic, 276
Democratic Party
    development of, *i370*
    division of, 603
    in election of 1860, *m457*
    Jacksonian democracy and, 354
    Ku Klux Klan and, 528
    in Reconstruction, 518
Democratic-Republican Party
    development of, *i370*
    Jefferson and, 289, 297–298,
        300
    opposition to Federalists,
        288, 291
    split in, 291
    support of France by, 290
Denver, Colo., *c547*
depression. *See also* Great
    Depression.

Panic of 1837 and, 370–371
Panic of 1873 and, 531
desegregation, 585, 608–609
desert, *m12*, 13, *i14*
de Soto, Hernando, 54
despotism, 166
Dias, Bartolomeu, 39, *m41*
Dickens, Charles, 410
Dickinson, Emily, 416
Dickinson, John, 148, 215
dictionary, 414
direct election of senators, 256
direct primary, 554
diseases
    in Civil War deaths, *i474*, 495,
        i495
    in Jamestown, 71
    Native Americans and, 62–63
    urbanization and, 541–542
    at Valley Forge, 186
District of Columbia
    facts about, R34, R40
    as seat of U.S. government, 238
    voting in, 259
Dix, Dorothea, *i420*
    in Civil War, 494
    as prison and mental health
        reformer, 419–420, 422–423
domestication, 28
Douglas, Stephen A., 603
    and Compromise of 1850, *i445*
    debates with Lincoln, *i438*,
        452–453
    in election of 1860, *m457*
    popular sovereignty and, 453,
        456
Douglass, Frederick, 335, 336,
        393, 428, 488
    and abolition movement, *i425*,
        426, *i487*
draft
    in Civil War, 492–493
Drake, David, 415
Drake, Francis, 57–58
Dred Scott v. *Sandford*, 451–453,
        602–603
dual citizenship, 265
dual sovereignty, 229
Du Bois, W. E. B., 550, *i550*
due process of law, 251
Durand, Asher, *i414*
Dust Bowl, 571, 574
Dutch immigrants, 99

Adams and, 289, 297–298, 300
at Constitutional Convention, 218–221, *c219*
opposition to Democratic-Republican Party, *c288,* 291
Federal Judiciary Act, 278
federal law, 278
Federal Reserve Act, 555
felonies, 236, 237
Ferdinand (Spanish monarch), 40–41
Ferris wheel, *i548*
feudalism, 35–37, *i36*
Fifteenth Amendment, 255, 530, 533
Fifth Amendment, 251
"Fifty-four forty or fight!" 391
54th Massachusetts Regiment, 490
filibustering, 235
Fillmore, Millard, 451, R37
First Amendment, 250, 606
First Continental Congress, 155
fishing, 95
Fitzgerald, F. Scott, 570, 571
five freedoms, 266
Flag Day, *i183*
Florida
acquisition from Spain, 341
expansionism and, *m394*
exploration of, 54
facts about, R34
in French and Indian War, 134
human movement and, *m18*
Seminole resistance in, 362
Stono Rebellion in, 107
flu epidemic of 1918, 562
Folger, Peleg, 93
Fontaine, John, 110
Ford, Gerald R., 582, R38
Foreign Miners Tax, 400
forests, *m17,* 95
Fort Duquesne, 132
Forten, James, 188
Fort McHenry, 316
Fort Necessity, 132
forts, 113
Fort Sumter, 459, *i462, i463,* 465, *m467*
Fort Ticonderoga, 160, 180
Fort Wagner, 490
Fort Wayne, Treaty of, 312
forty-niners, 396, 397–398, *i399*
four freedoms, 576
Fourteen Points, 561–562

text of, *i563*
Fourteenth Amendment, 254–255, 519, 533, 603–604, 608–609
Fourth Amendment, 251
4th U.S. Colored Troops, *i489*
France
in American Revolution, 184–185
balance of trade and, 52
in Civil War, 480
conflicts with England, 113, 285
control of New Orleans by, 303
and Convention of 1800, 291
exploration of Americas by, 56, 58, 291
in French and Indian War, 130–135, *m132*
Jefferson and, 311
revolution in, 285–286
in World War I, 560
in World War II, 575, 577
and XYZ Affair, 289–290
Franklin, Benjamin, *i124,* 133, *i184, i196, i203,* 213
Fredericksburg, Battle of, 496
Free African Society, 199
free blacks, 335
in Reconstruction, 516, 517, 518, 520, 524–525, *i524*
Freedman's Bureau, 517, 524–525
freedmen's schools, 524–525
freedom of assembly, *c250*
freedom of religion, *c250*
freedom of speech, 182, *c250*
Alien and Sedition Acts and, 290
protection of, 606–607
in schools, 607
freedom of the press, *c250*
Alien and Sedition Acts and, 290
Zenger Trial and, 129
freedom to petition, *c250*
free enterprise, *c198*
Freeman, Elizabeth, *i199*
free silver, 551–553
Free-Soil Party, 443, *i450*
Frémont, John C., 393, 451
French and Indian War, 129–134, *m132*
results of, 134–135, *m134,* 143, 184
French Revolution, 285–286, *i285*
Friedan, Betty, 586

frontier
American Revolution on, 187
conflicts with Native Americans on, 540
farming and populism on, 539–540
life on western, 539–540, 546–547
miners, ranchers, and cowhands on, 539–540, 547
Fugitive Slave Act, 446
Fuller, Margaret, 415
Fulton, Robert, 328, *i328*
Fundamental Orders of Connecticut, 79
text of, 82–83
fur trade
in Backcountry, 113
Lewis and Clark Expedition and, *c307*
mountain men and, 378
in New France, 130–131

G

Gadsden Purchase, *m394–395*
Gage, Thomas, 154, 156, 160–161
galleons, 57
Gálvez, Bernardo de, 185
Gama, Vasco da, 39, *m51*
Garfield, James A., R37
Garrison, William Lloyd, 424–425, 427
Gates, Horatio, 182, 191
Gaullaudet, Thomas H., 420
General Assembly, 127
generalizations, making, R20
geography, 2–21
George III (British monarch), 144, 154, 168
Georgia
facts about, R34
forced migration of Cherokees from, 359, 360, 361
slavery in, 105
German immigrants, 99, 100, 101, 409, *m409*
in World War I, 410
Germany
in World War I, 560–561
in World War II, 574–578
Gettysburg, Battle of, 497–499, *m498*
Gettysburg Address, 497

industrialization and, 544–545, *m545*
Navajo people, 29
navigation, 39–43
Navigation Acts, 96, 127
Navy, U.S.
  in American Revolution, 188–189
  in War of 1812, 315–316
  in World War II, 576
Nazi Party, 574–578
Nebraska, 360, R35
Nebraska Territory, 447
Netherlands, 58
neutrality, 286, 560
Nevada, R35
New Amsterdam, 58, 84
New Bedford Whaling Museum, *i109*
New Braunfels, Tex., 409
New Deal, 572–573
New England
  commerce in, 93–97, *m94*
  economy of, 108–109
  establishment of colonies in, 77, *m79, m86*
  factories in, 326
New France, *m30,* 58
New Hampshire, facts about, R35
New Harmony, Ind., 421
New Jersey, 85, R35
New Jersey Plan, 215, *c216*
New Mexico
  exploration of, 54
  facts about, R35
  Gadsden Purchase and, 395
  Santa Fe Trail and, 379–380
  Spanish colonization of, 60
  in War with Mexico, 393
New Netherland, 58, 84–86
New Orleans, Battle of, 316–317
New Orleans, La.
  in Civil War, *m478,* 479
  claimed by Spain, 282–283
  treaty with Spain, 286
  use for commerce, 303
  in War of 1812, 316
New Spain, 59–63, *m60,* 384
newspapers, 122–123, 420, 548
New Sweden, 85
New York (state), 58, 85
  American Revolution in, 179
  Antifederalists from, 220–221
  facts about, R35
New York City, 100, 102, *i404,*

i536. See also September 11 terrorist attack.
  Central Park in, 548
  draft riots in, 493
  Erie Canal and, 339–340
  Harlem Renaissance in, 571
  prejudice against immigrants in, 412
  as U.S. financial center, US2
New-York Weekly Journal, i129
NFL, *i453*
Nigeria, 35
Niña, 41
9–11 terrorist attack. *See* September 11 terrorist attack.
Nineteenth Amendment, 257, *i257*
Ninth Amendment, 252
Nixon, Richard M., *i231, i242,* 581–582, R38
nonviolence, 585
Normandy, 577
North
  abolition movement in, 424–425
  after Civil War, 504–507
  draft laws in, 492
  federalism and, 288
  Fugitive Slave Act and, 446
  industrialization in, 441–442
  Kansas-Nebraska Act and, 447
  pre-Civil War tensions and, 441–457
  Three-Fifths Compromise and, 216–217
North America
  early map of, *m45*
  land bridge to, 27
North Atlantic Treaty Organization, 580
North Carolina
  in American Revolution, 193
  establishment of, 87
  facts about, R35
  Lumbee people in, 70
  ratification of U.S. Constitution by, 221
  secession of, 466
North Dakota, R35
Northeast
  Jackson and, 363, 364
  manufacturing in, 326
  sectionalism and, 341
Northern Alliance, US6, US10
  as U.S. allies, US11

North Korea, 580
North Vietnam, 581
Northwest Coast People, 29
Northwest Ordinance, 207
Northwest Passage, 55, 56
Northwest Territory, 207, *m210, i211,* 282–283, *m283,* 441
notes, taking, *c50, c92, c118, c142, c176, c204, c296, c324, c352, c376, c406, c440, c464, c486, c516, c538,* R3
NOW, 586
nuclear weapons, 581
Nueces River, 391
nullification, 291, 365
nursing, 494

oasis, *i14*
Oberlin College, *i419*
"Objections to the Constitution of Government Formed by the Convention," 223
Office of Homeland Security, US14
Ogden, Aaron, 600, *i600*
Oglethorpe, James, 87, *i87*
Ohio, R35
Ohio River valley
  in American Revolution, 187
  Battle of Fallen Timbers in, 283
  Erie Canal and, 339
  in French and Indian War, 131
  steamboat travel in, 329–330
oil. *See* petroleum.
Oklahoma, 360
  facts about, R35
"Old Hickory." *See* Jackson, Andrew.
"Old Ironsides," *i272–273*
Old Spanish Trail, *m379*
"Old Three Hundred," 385
Olive Branch Petition, 162, 168
Olmec people, 28
Omaha, Neb., *c547*
Open Door Policy, 558
opinions
  forming and supporting, R17
  identifying, R16
Oregon, R35
Oregon Country, 302, 341, *i341*
Oregon Territory, 390–391, *m391, m394*

Sherman, William Tecumseh, 478–479, 485, 500–503
Sherman Antitrust Act, 554
Shiloh, Battle of, 478–479
shipping, 100
Shoshone people, 306, *i308*
Shreve, Henry Miller, 328–329
Sierra Nevada, 397
silver, 540, 547
Sixteenth Amendment, 256, 554–555
Sixth Amendment, 251
skills for studying history
 analyzing, R8, R11
 categorizing, *c376, c568,* R6
 causes and effects, analyzing, *c38, c80, c92, c307, c313, c317, c324, c400, c440, c507, c568, c582,* R11
 charts, interpreting, R23
 comparing and contrasting, *c406, c464, c486,* R10
 conclusions, drawing, 28, R13
 contrasting, R10
 database, creating, R31
 decisions, making, 214, *c269,* R14
 electronic card catalog, using, R30
 evaluating, R19
 facts, identifying, R16
 generalizations, making, R20
 graphs, interpreting, R22
 inferences, making, 43, 283, R12
 Internet, using, R32
 main ideas, finding, *c118, c352,* R5
 maps, creating, R27
 maps, reading, R25–R26
 model, creating a, R29
 multimedia presentation, creating, R33
 notes, taking, *c68, c92, c118, c142, c176, c204, c296, c324, c352, c376, c406, c440, c464, c486, c516, c538, c568,* R3
 opinions, forming and supporting, R17
 opinions, identifying, R16
 points of view, analyzing, *c440,* 453, R9
 political cartoons, interpreting, R28
 primary sources, using, R21
 problems, identifying and solving, *c204, c276, c516,* R18
 propaganda, recognizing, R15
 public speeches, making, R7
 secondary sources, using, R21
 sequencing, *c68, c142, c176, c538,* R4
 summarizing, *c296,* R2
 time lines, interpreting, R24
 writing for social studies, R8
slash-and-burn agriculture, 31
Slater, Samuel, *i325,* 326
slave auction, *i336*
slave codes, 62, 107
slave rebellions, 107, 337
slavery, *c104,* 602–603
 abolition movement and, 424–425
 annexation of Texas and, 389, 391, 392
 California gold rush and, 401
 in Civil War, 493–494
 Confederate Constitution and, 458
 congressional debate of, 439
 cotton farming and, 333–334
 Declaration of Independence and, 165
 and *Dred Scott v. Sandford,* 602–603
 and election of 1860, 456–457
 Free-Soil Party and, 443
 Fugitive Slave Act and, 446
 Kansas-Nebraska Act and, 447
 Lincoln and, 452–453, 459, 487–489, 509
 in Middle Colonies, 102
 Missouri Compromise and, 341–342, *m342*
 in New England, 96–97
 plantation life under, 103, 105, *i106,* 107, *i335,* 335–337
 Southern farming and, 442
 states allowing, *m448*
 Thirteenth Amendment and, 254, 505
 Tocqueville's view of, 441
 Underground Railroad and, 430–431, *m431*
slave trade
 origins of, 60–62
 ships used in, *i61*
 triangular trade and, *m95,* 95–96
Slidell, John, 391–392
sluicing, 399
slums, 541, 553
smallpox, 53, 62–63, 135
Smith, Bessie, *i570*
Smith, Jedediah, *i377*
Smith, John, 71
Smith, Margaret Bayard, *i353*
smuggling, 96
Society of Friends. *See* Quakers.
soldiers. *See* armed forces; military.
Solomon, Haym, *i177*
solving problems, 204, 276, 516
Songhai, 35
Sons of Liberty, 145, *i172*
South. *See also* Confederate States of America.
 agriculture in, *i329,* 332–334, 441–442
 at beginning of Civil War, 466
 black codes in, 518–519
 after Civil War, 504–507
 pre-Civil War tensions and, 441–457
 secession of, 457–458
 sectionalism and, 341, 363, 364, 365
South America
 ancient artifacts in, 27
 early map of, *m45*
 gold rush and, 397
 migration and, *m28*
 Portuguese exploration of, 51
South Carolina
 in American Revolution, 193
 establishment of, 87
 facts about, R35
 nullification and, 365, *i365*
 secession of, 457
 slavery in, 105
 tariffs and, 365, 367
"South Carolina Exposition and Protest," 365
South Dakota, R35
Southeast, *i3*
 Native American cultures of, 31
Southern Colonies, 86–87, *m86*
 American Revolution in, *m193*
 economy of, 108–109
 farming in, *m104*
South Korea, 580
South Pass, 378
South Vietnam, 581
Southwest, early civilizations in, 29

ACKNOWLEDGMENTS

TEXT ACKNOWLEDGMENTS

Chapter 6, pages 174–175: Excerpt from *Johnny Tremain* by Esther Forbes. Copyright © 1943 by Esther Forbes Hoskins, copyright renewed by Linwood M. Erskine, Jr., executor of the Estate of Esther Forbes Hoskins. Reprinted by permission of Houghton Mifflin Company. All rights reserved.

Chapter 9, page 300: "Obeying Rules and Laws," from *Government in America* by Richard J. Hardy. Copyright © 1995 by Houghton Mifflin Company. All rights reserved. Reprinted by permission.

Chapter 16, pages 486–487: Excerpt from *Across Five Aprils* by Irene Hunt. Copyright © 1964 by Irene Hunt. All rights reserved. Reprinted by permission of Shirley Beem on behalf of the author.

Chapter 17, pages 508, 509, 510, 512, 513, 516, 518, 519: Excerpts from *The Civil War* by Kenneth Burns, Ric Burns, and Geoffrey Ward. Copyright © 1990 by American Documentaries, Inc. Reprinted by permission of Alfred A. Knopf, a division of Random House, Inc.

Chapter 20 Epilogue, page 585: Excerpt from "I Have a Dream" by Martin Luther King, Jr. Copyright © 1963 by Martin Luther King, Jr., copyright renewed 1991 by Coretta Scott King. Reprinted by arrangement with The Heirs to the Estate of Martin Luther King, Jr., c/o Writers House, Inc., as agent for the proprietor.

page 593: Quote by Ken Burns from "Of documentaries and storytelling, historical awareness and arrogance, heroes and villains . . . a conversation with Ken Burns" by Sam Stall, *America West Airlines Magazine,* November 1997. Reprinted by permission of America West Airlines Magazine and Sam Stall.

ART CREDITS

Cover and Frontispiece

cover background Copyright © Bob Gelberg/SharpShooters. *frontispiece background* The Granger Collection, New York.

Abraham Lincoln: The Library of Congress.

Zitkala-Šă: Negative no. Mss 299, William F. Hansen Collection, Photographic Archives, Harold B. Lee Library, Brigham Young University, Provo, Utah.

Sam Houston: The Texas State Library and Archives Commission.

Abigail Adams: *Portrait traditionally said to be Abigail Adams* (about 1795), artist unknown. Oil on canvas, 30 1/4" × 26 1/2", N-150.55. Photo by Richard Walker. Copyright © New York State Historical Association, Cooperstown, New York.

Juan Seguín: Detail of *Juan Seguin* (1838), Jefferson Wright. Texas State Library and Archives Commission.

Harriet Tubman: James Gensheimer/NGS Image Collection.

Elizabeth Cady Stanton: The Granger Collection, New York.

Crispus Attucks: Copyright © Stock Montage.

Andrew Jackson: *Andrew Jackson* (1845), Thomas Sully. The Granger Collection, New York.

George Washington: Corbis.

Table of Contents

viii–xvii *background* The Granger Collection, New York; **viii** *top* Smithsonian Institution, Washington, D.C.; *bottom* The Granger Collection, New York; **ix** *top* Copyright © Michael Gadomski/Photo Researchers, Inc.; *center* The Granger Collection, New York; *bottom* Library of Congress; **x** *top* Copyright © R. Kord/H. Armstrong Roberts; *center George Washington in the Uniform of a British Colonial Colonel,* 1772, by Charles Willson Peale. Washington-Custis-Lee Collection, Washington and Lee University, Lexington, VA; *bottom* Illustration by Bill Cigliano; **xi** *bottom right* Copyright © John E. Fletcher & Arlan R. Wiler/NGS Image Collection; *bottom* Corbis; **xii** *top* Copyright © 1998 North Wind Pictures; *center* National Museum of American History, Smithsonian Institution; *bottom* Illustration by Patrick Whelan; **xiii** *top* From the collections of the Minnesota Historical Society;

bottom left Copyright © 1998 Louis Psihoyos/Matrix; *bottom right* The Granger Collection, New York; **xiv** *top* Copyright © George Peter Alexandre Healy/Wood River Gallery/PNI; *center* Courtesy, *Soldier* magazine, U.S. Army; *bottom* The Granger Collection, New York; **xv** *top,* Northern Pacific Railroad. *The Pioneer Route to Fargo Moorhead Town Bismark Dakota and Montana and the Famous Valley of the Yellowstone* (about 1885), Creator–Poole Brothers, Printers. Broadside. Chicago Historical Society; *bottom left* NASA; *bottom right* From the Collection of David J. and Janice L. Frent.

Voices from the Past

xix *left The Last Voyage of Henry Hudson,* (1881) John Collier. Tate Gallery, London/Art Resource, NY; *right* The Granger Collection, New York; **xx** Copyright © 1999 North Wind Pictures; **xxi** *top left* Corbis; *bottom left* Illustration from *The Headless Horseman* by Natalie Standiford. Illustration Copyright © 1992 by Donald Cook, Reprinted by permission of Random House, Inc.; *right* Corbis/Bettmann; *right* Library of Congress; **xxii** *top left* National Archives; *center right* Copyright © 1963 Bob Adelman/Magnum Photos; *bottom right* Survey Compass, accession number 1982–145. Colonial Williamsburg Foundation.

Themes of American History

xxviii *top* Copyright © 1999 PhotoDisc, Inc.; *center* Photo by Howard Sochrer/*Life* Magazine, Copyright © Time Inc.; *bottom* Michael S. Yamashita/Corbis; **xxix** *top* Library of Congress; *bottom* National Museum of American History/Smithsonian Institution.

Geography Handbook

2 *top right* Copyright © H. Abernathy/H. Armstrong Roberts; *center left* Copyright © Warren Morgan/H. Armstrong Roberts; *bottom* Copyright © 1996 Denver A. Bryan; **3** *top* Copyright © Nathan Benn/Stock Boston; *bottom right* Copyright © Andy Sacks/Tony Stone Images; **4–5** The Granger Collection, New York; **4** *top* Copyright © 1997 David Noble/FPG International; **5** *top* Copyright © John Coletti/Stock Boston; *center* Copyright © Bill Horsman/Stock Boston; **6** *top* Copyright © George Mobley/NGS Image Collection; *center* Copyright © Lowell Georgia/NGS Image Collection; *bottom left* The Granger Collection, New York; **10** *top* Copyright © T. Algire/H. Armstrong Roberts; *bottom* Copyright © Ken Graham/Tony Stone Images; **11** *top* Copyright © SuperStock; *bottom* Copyright © Tom Dietrich/Tony Stone Images; **12** *top* Copyright © Zane Williams/Tony Stone Images; *bottom* Copyright © Eastcott/Momatiuk/Tony Stone Images; **13** *top* Copyright © SuperStock; *bottom* Copyright © F. Sieb/H. Armstrong Roberts; **14–15** Illustration by Ken Goldammer; **16** *top* Copyright © M. Schneiders/H. Armstrong Roberts; *bottom* Copyright © D. Frazier/H. Armstrong Roberts; **17** *top left* Copyright © Ron Levy/Liaison Agency; *top right,* center right, *bottom right* Copyright © Steve Adams/NGS Image Collection; *bottom left* Copyright © Cathlyn Melloan/Tony Stone Images; **18** *bottom* Copyright © J. Marshall/The Image Works; **19** *left* Culver Pictures; *right* Copyright © Santi Visalli/The Image Bank.

Unit 1

22–23 Copyright © R. Kord/H. Armstrong Roberts.

Chapter 1

24, 25 The Granger Collection, New York; **26** *top* Werner Forman/Art Resource, New York; *center* Copyright © Aldona Sabalis/Photo Researchers, Inc.; *bottom* Copyright © Stuart Dee/The Image Bank; **27** Courtesy of Rock Art Foundation, San Antonio, Texas; **28** Copyright © Francois Gohier/Photo Researchers, Inc.; **29** Smithsonian Institution, Washington, D.C.; **33** Copyright © Thomas D. W. Friedmann/Photo Researchers, Inc.; **34** *left* Copyright © Aldona Sabalis/Photo Researchers, Inc.; **35** PNI; **37** *School of Athens* (1508), Raphael (Raffaello Santi). Stanza della Segnatura, Vatican City, Vatican. Photo copyright © Erich Lessing/Art Resource, New York; **39** Detail of *St. Vincent Polyptych* (date unknown), Nuno Gonçalves. Museu Nacional de

Arte Antiga, Lisbon, Portugal. Copyright © Scala/Art Resource, New York; **40** *Portrait of a Man, Called Christopher Columbus* (1519), Sebastiano del Piombo. Oil on canvas, 42″ × 34 3/4″. The Metropolitan Museum of Art, gift of J. Pierpont Morgan, 1900; **42** Archivio Fotografico del Museo Preistorico Etnografico L. Pigorini, Rome. Photo by Lorenzo de Masi; **43** Cliché Bibliothèque nationale de France, Paris; **45** *bottom* Courtesy of John Goss; **46** Copyright © Francois Gohier/Photo Researchers, Inc.; **47** Photos by Sharon Hoogstraten.

Chapter 2

48, 49 The Granger Collection, New York; **51** Detail of *Pope Alexander VI Borgia Kneeling in Prayer* (date unknown), Bernardino Pinturicchio. Sala die Misteri della Fede, Apparta-mento Borgia, Vatican Palace, Vatican State/Scala/Art Resource, New York; **53** Corbis; **54** The Granger Collection, New York; **55** *top, The Last Voyage of Henry Hudson* (1881), John Collier. Tate Gallery, London/Art Resource, New York; **57** PNI; **59** The Granger Collection, New York; **61** *right* The Newberry Library, Chicago; *left, Slaves Below Deck of Albanez* (date unknown), Francis Meynell. Copyright © National Maritime Museum Picture Library, London.

Chapter 3

66 The Granger Collection, New York; **67** Colonial Williamsburg Foundation; **69** British Museum; **71** AP/Wide World Photos; **72** *Pocahontas* (1616), Simon van de Passe. Engraving, 6 7/8″ × 4 3/4″ (17.5 cm × 12 cm). Published in the *Baziliologia,* London, 1618. National Portrait Gallery, Smithsonian Institution/Art Resource, New York; **73** The Granger Collection, New York; **74-75** Illustration by Ivan Lapper. Copyright © The Reader's Digest Association; **76** The Granger Collection, New York; **77** *The Mayflower in Plymouth Harbor* (1882), William Halsall. Courtesy of the Pilgrim Society, Plymouth, Massachusetts; **78** *top* Copyright © SuperStock; *bottom* Copyright © Andrew J. Martinez/Photo Researchers, Inc.; **79** *bottom* The Granger Collection, New York; **80** *left* Courtesy of American Antiquarian Society; *right* The New York Public Library; **81** *Trial of George Jacobs for Witchcraft, 1692* (1855), T. H. Matteson. Oil on canvas, acc. #1246. Peabody Essex Museum, Salem, Massachusetts. Photo by Mark Sexton; **84** Detail of *Peter Stuyvesant and the Trumpeter (The Wrath of Peter Stuyvesant)* (1835), Asher B. Durand. Oil on canvas, 24 1/4″ × 30 1/4″, accession no. 1858.28. Copyright © Collection of The New-York Historical Society; **85** Copyright © Tom Dietrich/Tony Stone Images; **87** Brown Brothers; **89** Colonial Williamsburg Foundation.

Chapter 4

90, 91 The Granger Collection, New York; **93** *Sperm Whaling: No. 2, The Capture* (1862), A. Van Best and R. S. Gifford. Lithograph by Endicott and Company, corrected by Benjamin Russell, 16 3/4 × 25 3/4″ (43 cm × 65 cm). N.M.A.H., Harry Peters "America on Stone" Lithography Collection; **94** *right* Copyright © Thomas Neill; **96** North Carolina Collection, University of North Carolina Library at Chapel Hill; **98** Detail of *Quaker Meeting* (date unknown), Egbert Van Heemskerk. The Quaker Collection, Haverford (Pennsylvania) College Library; **99** *right* Historic Hudson Valley, Tarrytown, New York; **100** The Granger Collection, New York; **102** Library of Congress; **103** Detail of *George Mason* (1811), Dominic W. Boudet. Oil on canvas, 30″ × 25″ (76.2 cm × 63.5 cm). Virginia Museum of Fine Arts, Richmond. Gift of David K. E. Bruce. Photo by Ron Jennings. Copyright © Virginia Museum of Fine Arts; **104** *right* Copyright © Chip Henderson/Tony Stone Images; **105** Virginia Historical Society, Richmond, Virginia; **106** The Granger Collection, New York; **108** *bottom left* Smithsonian Institution, Washington, D.C.; *bottom right background* Photo copyright © Dorothy Miller; *bottom right* foreground Copyright © The New York Botanical Garden; **109** *bottom center* Copyright © Old Dartmouth Historical Society, New Bedford (Massachusetts) Whaling Museum; **110** The Granger Collection, New York; **111** *right* Copyright © Michael Gadomski/Photo Researchers, Inc.; **112** Copyright © Mark McGehearty/AllSport; **113** *Catching the Wild Horse* (date unknown), George Catlin. Oil on canvas, 12 1/4″ ×

16 1/4″. The Thomas Gilcrease Institute of American History and Art, Tulsa, Oklahoma.

Chapter 5

116 Virginia Historical Society, Richmond, Virginia; **117** Library of Congress; **120, 122** The Granger Collection, New York; **124** Corbis; **125** Detail of *Increase Mather* (1688), John Vander Spriett. Courtesy of the Massachusetts Historical Society; **126** Courtesy of Knox County, Illinois Teen Court; **127** The Granger Collection, New York; **129** *left* Corbis; *right* The Newberry Library, Chicago; **130** Detail of *Braddock's Defeat* (1903), Edward Deming. State Historical Society of Wisconsin Museum Collection; **131** Library of Congress; **133, 135** The Granger Collection, New York.

Unit 2

138–139 Copyright © William Johnson/Stock Boston.

Chapter 6

140, 141 The Granger Collection, New York; **142** *top* Colonial Williamsburg Foundation; *center* Detail of *The Battle of Princeton* (date unknown), William Mercer. The Historical Society of Pennsylvania; *bottom* The Granger Collection, New York; **143** *James Otis Arguing Against the Writs of Assistance in the Old Towne House* (1901), Robert Reid. Courtesy Commonwealth of Massachusetts Art Commission; **144** *top* Rare Books Division, The New York Public Library. Astor, Lenox, and Tilden Foundations; *bottom* Emmet Collection, Manuscripts and Archives Division, The New York Public Library. Astor, Lenox, and Tilden Foundations; **145, 146** The Granger Collection, New York; **147** Copyright © Stock Montage; **148** Copyright © Collection of The New-York Historical Society; **149** The Granger Collection, New York; **150** *left* The Granger Collection, New York; *right, John Adams* (date unknown), John Trumbull. National Portrait Gallery, Smithsonian Institution/Art Resource, New York; **151** The Granger Collection, New York; **152–153** Copyright © McDougal Littell Inc.; **154** Copyright © Paul Mozell/Stock Boston; **157** Copyright © Charles Winters/Stock Boston; **158** Copyright © McDougal Littell Inc.; **159** The Granger Collection, New York; **160** *Portrait traditionally said to be Abigail Adams* (about 1795), artist unknown. Oil on canvas, 30 1/4″ × 26 1/2″, N-150.55. Photo by Richard Walker. Copyright © New York State Historical Association, Cooperstown, New York; **161** Detail of *The Death of General Warren at the Battle of Bunker's Hill, 17 June 1775* (date unknown), John Trumbull. Oil on canvas. Yale University Art Gallery, Trumbull Collection; **162** Library of Congress; **163** *top* The Granger Collection, New York; *bottom* Library of Congress; **164** *top* Detail of *The Declaration of Independence, 4 July 1776* (date unknown), John Trumbull. Oil on canvas. Yale University Art Gallery, Trumbull Collection; *bottom* Copyright © R. Kord/H. Armstrong Roberts; **165, 166** The Granger Collection, New York; **171** *bottom* Clement Library, University of Michigan; **172** The Granger Collection, New York; **173** Photos by Sharon Hoogstraten.

Chapter 7

174 *March to Valley Forge* (1883), William B. T. Trego. Courtesy of Stacey Swigart, The Valley Forge Historical Society; **175, 176** The Granger Collection, New York; **177** Haym Salomon Home for Nursing and Rehabilitation, Brooklyn, New York. Courtesy of American Jewish Historical Society, Waltham, Massachusetts, and New York, New York; **178** *George Washington in the Uniform of a British Colonial Colonel* (1772), Charles Willson Peale. Washington-Custis-Lee Collection. Washington and Lee University, Lexington, Virginia; **179** *top* From *American Story: The Revolutionaries.* Courtesy of the Jamestown-Yorktown Educational Trust. Photo by Katherine Wetzel. Copyright © 1996 Time-Life Books Inc.; **180** *The Passage of the Delaware* (1819), Thomas Sully. Oil on canvas, 146 1/2″ × 207″ (372.11 cm × 525.78 cm.). Copyright © Museum of Fine Arts, Boston. Gift of the Owners of the old Boston Museum; 03.1079; **181** *bottom* The Granger Collection, New York; **182** Copyright © Michael Newman/PhotoEdit/PNI; **183** *Two American Flags Flown* by John Paul Jones in 1779 (date unknown), unknown Dutch artist. Watercolor. Chicago Historical Society; **184, 185** The Granger Collection, New York; **186** From *American Story: The Revolutionaries.* Courtesy of the Jamestown-Yorktown Educational Trust. Photo by Katherine Wetzel. Copyright © 1996 Time-Life Books Inc.; **189** The Granger Collection, New York; **190** Library of Congress; **191** Defense Visual Information Center, Linda Delatorre, Researcher; **192** Illustration by Bill Cigliano; **194** *Surrender of Lord Cornwallis at Yorktown* (date unknown), John Trumbull. Yale University Art Gallery, Trumbull Collection; **195** Private collection; **196** The Granger Collection, New York; **199** Courtesy of the Massachusetts Historical Society; **200** Private collection.

Chapter 8

202 The Granger Collection, New York; **203** *The Signing of the Constitution* (date unknown), H. C. Chandler. Art Resource, New York; **205** Detail of *Daniel Boone Escorting Settlers Through the Cumberland Gap* (1851–1852), George Caleb Bingham. Oil on canvas, 36 1/2″ × 50 1/4″. Washington University Gallery of Art, St. Louis (Missouri). Gift of Nathaniel Phillips, 1890; **206, 209** top The Granger Collection, New York; **209** bottom Copyright © Thad Samuels Abell II/NGS Image Collection; **210** bottom left Copyright © John E. Fletcher & Arlan R. Wiler/NGS Image Collection; bottom right William L. Clements Library, Map Division, University of Michigan;
211 top The Granger Collection, New York; bottom Courtesy of the Shelby County (Ohio) Historical Society; **212** Corbis; inset Library of Congress; **213** Copyright © Joseph Nettis/Tony Stone Images; **214** The Granger Collection, New York; **231** PNI; **218** The Granger Collection, New York; **219** left, *Portrait of John Jay* (c. 1783, 1804–1808), Gilbert Stuart, believed to have been begun by and finished by John Trumbull. National Portrait Gallery, Smithsonian Institution/Art Resource, New York; **219** right, **220** The Granger Collection, New York.

Constitution Handbook

226 left The Granger Collection, New York; right Copyright © Ivan Massar/Black Star; **227** top Copyright © Bob Daemmrich/The Image Works; center Copyright © Topham/The Image Works; bottom Courtesy of The New York Times; **228** bottom Copyright © J. L. Atlan/Sygma; **229** top Copyright © Robert E. Daemmrich/Tony Stone Images; **231** top Copyright © 1973 Engelhardt in the *St. Louis Post-Dispatch*/Reprinted with permission; bottom Copyright © Patrick Forden/Sygma; **232** background The Granger Collection, New York; **232** inset, **241** AP/Wide World Photos; **242** top right Copyright © Archive Photos; top left Culver Pictures; center right Copyright © 1972 Magnum Photos, Inc.; center left AP/Wide World Photos; bottom right Courtesy Ronald Reagan Library; **248** AP/Wide World Photos;
249 Copyright © Collection of The New-York Historical Society; **251** Copyright © Baron Wolman/ Tony Stone Images; **252** left Copyright © Jean-Marc Giboux/Liaison Agency; right Copyright © Bob Dremmrich/Sygma; **254** Copyright © 1993 Ron Rovtar/FPG International; **272** The Granger Collection, New York; **257** left Copyright © 1998 FPG International; right Copyright © Cynthia Johnson/Liaison Agency; **258** Franklin D. Roosevelt Library; **261** Copyright © Rock the Vote Inc.

Citizenship Handbook

264 AP/Wide World Photos; **265** background Copyright © Bob Daemmrich; foreground Copyright © 1994 Mark Harmel/FPG International; **268** Copyright © Bob Daemmrich/The Image Works; **269** Copyright © David Young-Wolff/Tony Stone Images; **270** AP/Wide World Photos.

Unit 3

272–273 Copyright © Marvin E. Newman/The Image Bank.

Chapter 9

274 The Granger Collection, New York; **275** *Washington's First Cabinet* (date unknown), Alonzo Chappel. Courtesy of CNA; **276** Washington inaugural buttons, 1789. National Museum of American History, Smithsonian Institution; **278** AP/Wide World

Photos; **279** *Portrait of Alexander Hamilton* (about 1796), James Sharples (the Elder). National Portrait Gallery, Smithsonian Institution/Art Resource, New York;
281 Copyright © Larry Stevens/Nawrocki Stock Photo Inc.; **282** Chicago Historical Society; **283** right Ohio Historical Society; **285** *Execution of Louis XVI* (18th century), anonymous. Colored engraving. Musée de la Ville de Paris, Musée Carnavalet, Paris, France/Giraudon/Art Resource, NY; **287** Mount Vernon Ladies Association; **289** top The Granger Collection, New York; center right Maryland Historical Society; **290** The Granger Collection, New York.

Chapter 10

294 *The Rocky Mountains, Lander's Peak* (1863), Albert Bierstadt (1830–1902). Oil on canvas, 73 1/2″ × 120 3/4″. The Metropolitan Museum of Art, Rogers Fund, 1907 (07.123). Photograph copyright © 1979 The Metropolitan Museum of Art; **295** From the Collection of Gilcrease Museum, Tulsa;
297 left, *Thomas Jefferson* (date unknown), Rembrandt Peale. Copyright © Collection of the New-York Historical Society; right Boston Athenaeum; **298** The Granger Collection, New York; **299** center right Kirby Collection of Historical Paintings, Lafayette College; bottom background Monticello/Thomas Jefferson Memorial Foundation, Inc.; bottom center Polygraph, 1806. John Isaac Hawkins, Charles Willson Peale. University of Virginia. Photo courtesy of Monticello/Thomas Jefferson Memorial Foundation, Inc.; **300** Boston Athenaeum; **301** Copyright © James Blair/NGS Image Collection; **302, 303** The Granger Collection, New York; **304** inset Copyright © Addison Geary/Stock Boston/PNI; **305** *Lewis and Clark at Three Forks* (date unknown), E. S. Paxson. Mural in the Montana State Capitol. Courtesy of the Montana Historical Society. Photo by John Reddy; **306** Copyright © 1998 North Wind Pictures; **307** National Museum of American History, Smithsonian Institution; **308** center left Copyright © Stock Montage; center right, *The Surrounder, Chief of the Tribe* (1833), George Catlin. Oto tribe. National Museum of American Art, Smithsonian Institution/Art Resource, New York; bottom center, bottom right Peabody Museum of Archeology and Ethnology, Harvard University. Copyright © President and Fellows of Harvard College. Photo by Hillel Burger; **309** center left, *Mink, a Pretty Girl* (1832), George Catlin. National Museum of American Art, Smithsonian Institution/Art Resource, New York; center right, *Steep Wing, a Brave of the Bad Arrow Points Band* (1832), George Catlin. Teton Dakota (Western Sioux). National Museum of American Art, Smithsonian Institution/Art Resource, New York; bottom Whaling Chief's Hat, Makah or Nootka. Cedar bark, bear grass, unidentified mammal hair, remnant feathers, leather thong. H 22 cm, D 27 cm. PM# 99-12-10/53080. Peabody Museum of Archeology and Ethnology, Harvard University. Copyright © President and Fellows of Harvard College. Photo by Hillel Burger; **310** Detail of *Decatur Boarding the Tripolitan Gunboat* (date unknown), Dennis Malone Carter. Oil on canvas. Courtesy of the Naval Historical Foundation; **311** Library of Congress; **312** The Granger Collection, New York; **314** left White House Collection. Copyright © White House Historical Association; right The Granger Collection, New York; **316** National Museum of American History, Smithsonian Institution; **318** top, *Thomas Jefferson* (date unknown), Rembrandt Peale. Copyright © Collection of the New-York Historical Society; bottom National Museum of American History, Smithsonian Institution; **319** "Ograbme, or, The American Snapping Turtle" (1807), D. Longworth. Negative no. 7278. Copyright © Collection of The New-York Historical Society; **320** left Elk skin bound journal (1805), William Clark. Ink on paper. Missouri Historical Society; right, bottom Copyright © 1998 North Wind Pictures;

321 Photos by Sharon Hoogstraten.

Chapter 11

322, 323, 325 Corbis-Bettmann; **326** The Granger Collection, New York; **327** Illustration by Patrick Whelan; **328** Corbis-Bettmann; **329** Copyright © Stock Montage;
330–331 Illustrations by Randal Birkey; **332** The Granger Collection, New York; **333** Illustration by Patrick Whelan; **335**

Jan White Brantley; **336** Corbis-Bettmann; **337** *The Granger Collection*, New York; **338** Corbis-Bettmann; **339** *right inset* The Granger Collection, New York; **340, 341** *right inset* Corbis-Bettmann.

Unit 4

348–349 Layne Kennedy/Corbis.

Chapter 12

350 The Granger Collection, New York; **351** Chicago Historical Society; **352** Copyright © Collection of the New-York Historical Society; **353** Redwood Library and Athenaeum, Newport, Rhode Island; **354** *left, John Quincy Adams* (1858), George Healy. Oil on canvas, 62″ × 47″. White House Collection. Copyright © White House Historical Association; *right, Andrew Jackson* (1845), Thomas Sully. The Granger Collection, New York; **355** The Hermitage: Home of President Andrew Jackson, Nashville, Tennessee. Photo of ribbon by Sharon Hoogstraten; **356** Copyright © *The News-Sentinel*, Fort Wayne, Indiana; **357** *left* The Granger Collection, New York; *right* Culver Pictures; **358** *Sequoyah, Indian Statesman* (date unknown), anonymous, after Charles Bird King. Hand-colored lithograph, J. T. Bowen lithography company. National Portrait Gallery, Smithsonian Institution/Art Resource, New York; **359** Copyright © J. Pat Carter/Liaison Agency; **361** *The Trail of Tears* (date unknown), Robert Lindneux. Woolaroc Museum, Bartlesville, Oklahoma; **362** The Granger Collection, New York; **363** *top, John Caldwell Calhoun* (about 1818–1825), attributed to Charles Bird Kind. Oil on canvas, 76.2 cm × 63.5 cm. National Portrait Gallery, Smithsonian Institution/Art Resource, New York; **363** *bottom,* **365** *top* The Granger Collection, New York; *bottom* The Museum of the Confederacy, Richmond, Virginia. Photo by Katherine Wetzel; **366** Detail of *Webster's Reply to Hayne* (date unknown), George Healy. Courtesy Boston Art Commission; **368** *top* The Granger Collection, New York; *bottom inset, Nicholas Biddle* (1839), Henry Inman. Oil on canvas [1978.2]. The Historical Society of Pennsylvania; **369** The Granger Collection, New York; **370** Copyright © Collection of The New-York Historical Society; **373** Library of Congress.

Chapter 13

374 Denver Public Library, Western History Department; **375** National Archives; **376** *Jedediah Smith in the Badlands* (date unknown), Harvey Dunn. The South Dakota Art Museum Collection; **378** Copyright © United States Postal Service; **379** *inset* Copyright © Ric Ergenbright; **380** Skillet, negative no. OrHi 97119. Oregon Historical Society; **384** The Granger Collection, New York; **385** *top* Broadsides Collection, The Center for American History, The University of Texas at Austin; **386** Copyright © Bob Daemmrich/Stock Boston/PNI; **387** *The Battle of the Alamo* (about 1913), Frederick C. Yohn. Courtesy Continental Insurance; **388** *left* Texas State Library and Archives Commission; **388** *right,* **390** The Granger Collection, New York; **392** *inset,* **396** Courtesy of the California History Room, California State Library, Sacramento, California; **397** Copyright © Collection of The New-York Historical Society; **398** Courtesy of Levi Strauss Company; **399, 401** Courtesy of the California History Room, California State Library, Sacramento, California; **403** *bottom* From the collections of the Minnesota Historical Society.

Chapter 14

404 Courtesy Meserve-Kunhardt Collection, Mount Kisco, New York; **405** The Granger Collection, New York; **406** The New York Public Library; **407** *background* From the collections of the Minnesota Historical Society; *foreground* Copyright © Collection of The New-York Historical Society; **408** *center* The Granger Collection, New York; **411** Michael S. Yamashita/Corbis; **412** The Granger Collection, New York; **413** From *The Headless Horseman* by Natalie Standiford, illustrated by Donald Cook. Illustration copyright © 1992 Donald Cook. Reprinted by permission of Random House, Inc.; **414** The Granger Collection, New York; **416** *background* Photo by Simon Marsden/The Marsden Archive; **417** The Granger Collection, New York; **434** Copyright © Archive Photos; **419** Department of Archives, Oberlin (Ohio) College; **420, 424** The Granger Collection, New York; **425** Chester County

Historical Society, West Chester, Pennsylvania; **426** Copyright © 1996 Wayne Sorce; **427** *from left to right* The Granger Collection, New York; The Granger Collection, New York; The Granger Collection, New York; Corbis-Bettmann; **428** The Granger Collection, New York; **429** *The Discord* (1885), F. Heppenheimer. Color lithograph, negative no. 51038. Copyright © Collection of The New-York Historical Society; **430** *center* Sophia Smith Collection, Smith College; *bottom right, bottom left* Copyright © 1998 Louis Psihoyos/Matrix; **431** *bottom* From the Collections of the National Underground Railroad Freedom Center, Cincinnati, Ohio; **434** From the collections of the Minnesota Historical Society; **435** Photos by Sharon Hoogstraten.

Unit 5

436–437 Corbis.

Chapter 15

438, 439, 441, 444 The Granger Collection, New York; **445** Corbis; **446** Hulton-Deutsch Collection/Corbis; **447** *left* The Granger Collection, New York; *right* Corbis-Bettmann; **450** From the Collection of David J. and Janice L. Frent; **451** AFP/Corbis; **452, 455** The Granger Collection, New York; **456** Lloyd Ostendorf Collection; **458** *background* Hulton-Deutsch Collection/Corbis; *inset* Copyright © George Peter Alexandre Healy/Wood River Gallery/PNI; **461** *The Last Moments of John Brown* (1884), Thomas Hovenden. Oil on canvas, 77 3/8″ × 63 1/4″. The Metropolitan Museum of Art, gift of Mr. and Mrs. Carl Stoeckel, 1897. Photograph copyright © 1982 The Metropolitan Museum of Art.

Chapter 16

462, 463 The Granger Collection, New York; **464** *top left, top right* Library of Congress; *bottom left, bottom right* The Granger Collection, New York; **466** The Lincoln Museum, Fort Wayne, Indiana. #0-43; **469** Copyright © H. Armstrong Roberts; **470** Copyright © McDougal Littell Inc.; **471** *left* Courtesy of Brian C. Pohanka; *right* Massachusetts Commandery Military Order of the Loyal Legion and the U.S. Army Military History Institute; **472** Bureau of Archives and History, New Jersey State Library; **473** Corbis-Bettmann; **474** Culver Pictures; **475** The Granger Collection, New York; **476** Illustration by Alexander Verbitsky; **477** Library of Congress; **478** U.S. Signal Corps photo no. 111-B-4146 (Brady Collection) in the National Archives; **481** Chicago Historical Society; **482** *left* Photograph copyright © High Impact Photography. Courtesy 103rd ENG.; *center* Courtesy, Museum of the Confederacy, Richmond, Virginia; *bottom right* Fort Sumter National Park.

Chapter 17

484 *Cavalry Charge at Yellow Tavern, Virginia, May 11, 1864* (1871), H. W. Chaloner. Oil on canvas, 31″ × 47 7/8″. Garbisch no. 61.1, purchased from Kenneth E. Snow by Garbisches (1961). Presented by the Estate of Edgar William and Bernice Chrysler Garbisch. Photo by West Point Museum Collections, United States Military Academy; **485** Corbis-Bettmann; **486** *top left, top right, bottom left* Library of Congress; *bottom right* The Granger Collection, New York; **487** Corbis; **488** The Granger Collection, New York; **489** *top* Copyright © Archive Photos; *bottom* Library of Congress; **490** Defense Visual Information Center, Linda Delatorre, Researcher; **491** Culver Pictures; **492** The Granger Collection, New York; **494** American Red Cross; **495** *background* Corbis; *foreground* Massachusetts Commandery Military Order of the Loyal Legion and the U.S. Army Military History Institute; **496** The Pejepscot Historical Society; **497** Copyright © 1994 Kunio Owaki/The Stock Market; **498–499** *background* Illustration by Ken Goldammer; **498** *center* Library of Congress; *bottom left* Courtesy, Gettysburg National Military Park Museum. Photograph by Eric Long; *bottom right* The Museum of the Confederacy, Richmond, Virginia. Photo by Katherine Wetzel; **499** *bottom* Courtesy, Gettysburg National Military Park Museum. Photograph by Eric Long; **500** Library of Congress; **502** *top left* Courtesy, *Soldier* magazine, U.S. Army; *bottom* Courtesy, Meserve-Kunhardt Collection, Mount Kisco, New York; **504** Copyright © Robert M. Anderson/Uniphoto, Inc.; **506** National Archives; **510** *top right* Photograph copyright © High Impact Photography. Courtesy,

Virginia Military Institute; *bottom right* Collection of Old Capitol Museum of Mississippi History; **512** *left* Cruz Collection, New Bedford Historical Society; *center* National Archives; *right* Courtesy, *Soldier* magazine, U.S. Army; **513** Photos by Sharon Hoogstraten.

Chapter 18

514 Corbis-Bettmann; **515** *The Shackle Broken—by the Genius of Freedom.* Color lithograph. Pub. by E. Sachs & Co., Baltimore, 1874. Chicago Historical Society; **517, 518** The Granger Collection, New York; **519** Corbis; **520** *His First Vote* (1868), Thomas Waterman Wood. Oil on board. Cheekwood Museum of Art, Nashville, Tennessee; **521, 522–523** *background* The Granger Collection, New York; **522** *top right,* **524, 525** Corbis; **526** Library of Congress; **528** The Granger Collection, New York; **529** Library of Congress; **530, 531** The Granger Collection, New York; **532** Library of Congress; **535** *bottom* The Granger Collection, New York.

Chapter 19 Epilogue

536 The Granger Collection, New York; **537** *top left, Street Arabs in Sleeping Quarters at Night* (date unknown), photo by Jacob A. Riis. The Jacob A. Riis collection, Museum of the City of New York; *top right* Library of Congress; *bottom left, Family Making Artificial Flowers* (about 1910), photo by Jessie Tarbox Beals. The Jacob A. Riis Collection, Museum of the City of New York; *bottom right* Library of Congress; **538** Special Collections Division, University of Washington Libraries. Negative no. 2315; **539** Denver Public Library; **540** Detail of *Forging the Shaft* (1874–1877), John Ferguson Weir. Oil on canvas, 52" x 73 1/4" (132.1 cm × 186.1 cm). Painted at West Point Foundry at Cold Spring, New York. The Metropolitan Museum of Art, Purchase, Lyman G. Bloomingdale Gift, 1901 (01.7.1). Photograph copyright © 1983 The Metropolitan Museum of Art; **541** The Newberry Library, Chicago; **544** *top right* Library of Congress; *center left* Chicago Historical Society; *bottom right* Library of Congress; **544** *bottom left,* **545** *center left* Corbis-Bettmann; *bottom* Chicago Historical Society; **546** The Kansas State Historical Society, Topeka, Kansas; **547** *top, View of San Francisco [Formerly Yerba Buena]* (1847), attributed to Victor Prevost. Oil on canvas, 25" x 30". California Historical Society, gift of the Ohio Historical Society; *bottom* The Bancroft Library, University of California, Berkeley; **548** *top* Lake County Museum/Corbis; *center, bottom* The Granger Collection, New York; **549** Joseph Schwartz Collection/Corbis; **550** Library of Congress; **551** Library of Congress; **553** Corbis-Bettmann; **554** *Theodore Roosevelt* (date unknown), John Singer Sargent. White House Collection. Copyright © 1992 White House Historical Association; **555** *right* Brown Brothers; l*eft inset* Doubleday, Page and Company, New York, 1906, second issue; **556** Corbis; **557** The Granger Collection, New York; **558** Chicago Historical Society; **559** Illustration by Nick Rotando; *center left* Corbis-Bettmann; **560** The Granger Collection, New York.

Chapter 20 Epilogue

566 *top, left to right* Copyright © Illustration House, Inc.; The Granger Collection, New York; National Archives; U.S. Air Force Photo; *bottom, left to right* Elvis Presley Enterprises, Inc. Used by permission; Copyright © James Blair/NGS Image Collection; Photo by Larry Burrows/*Life* Magazine, copyright © Time Inc.; Copyright © Sentinel Star/Sygma; **567** *top left* Corbis-Bettmann; *top right* Copyright © H. Armstrong Roberts; *center left, center right* Copyright © 1999 Werner Wolff/Black Star; **568** Copyright © The Washington *Post.* Reprinted with permission; **569** Brown Brothers; **570** *top* Culver Pictures; *center* Copyright © Blank Archives/Archive Photos; *bottom* Movie Still Archives; **572** National Museum of American Art, Smithsonian Institution/Art Resource, New York; **573** Photo by Margaret Suckley/Franklin D. Roosevelt Library; **574** *top* Photo courtesy of Margaret Bourke-White Estate/*Life* Magazine, copyright © 1934 Time Inc.; *bottom* Photo courtesy of Margaret Bourke-White Estate/*Life* Magazine, copyright © Time Inc.; **575** Copyright © Hulton Getty/Liaison

Agency; **576** *top* Copyright © 1999 Owen H. K./Black Star; *bottom* The Granger Collection, New York; **578** UPI/Corbis-Bettmann; **579** AP/Wide World Photos; **580** U.S. Air Force Photo; **581** *top* NASA; *bottom* UPI/Corbis-Bettmann; **583** Patrick Sison/AP/Wide World Photos; **584** *top* Copyright © 1970 Elliott Erwitt/Magnum Photos, Inc.; *bottom* AP/Wide World Photos; **585** Copyright © 1963 Bob Adelman/Magnum Photos, Inc.; **586** Copyright © 1978 George Ballis/Take Stock; **587** *top* Wally McNamee/Corbis; *bottom* From the Collection of David J. and Janice L. Frent; **588** AP/Wide World Photos; **589** Copyright © Robert Brenner/PhotoEdit/PNI; **590–591** *background* NASA; **590** *top right* Copyright © 1996 The Stock Market; *bottom left* Copyright © Scott McKlernan/Zuna Images/The Stock Market; **591** *center* Copyright © The New Yorker Collection 1999 Mick Stevens from cartoonbank.com. All rights reserved.

Supreme Court

732 *top left* Corbis; *bottom left* Copyright © 1994 North Wind Pictures; *bottom center* The Granger Collection, New York; *bottom right* Copyright © 1999 North Wind Pictures; **733** *top* Corbis; *bottom left* Corbis-Bettmann; *bottom right* AP/Wide World Photos; **734** *top left* Corbis; *bottom right* The Granger Collection, New York; **735** Copyright © 1994 North Wind Pictures; **736** Corbis; **737** *left* Culver Pictures; *right* The Granger Collection, New York; **738** Corbis; *bottom right* The Granger Collection, New York; **739** Copyright © 1999 North Wind Pictures; **740** Corbis; **741** *left* The Granger Collection, New York; *right* Lincoln University Archives, Langston Hughes Memorial Library, Lincoln University, Penn.; **742** *top left* Corbis; *bottom right* The Granger Collection, New York; **743** AP/Wide World Photos; **744** *top left* Corbis; **745** Wally Mcnamee/Corbis; **746** *top left* Corbis; *bottom right* AP/Wide World Photos; **747** Corbis; **748** *top left* Corbis; *bottom right* Corbis-Bettmann; **750** *top left* Owen Franken/Corbis; *bottom right,* **751** AP/Wide World Photos.

The War on Terrorism

US2 Copyright © AFP/Corbis; *inset* Copyright © John Annerino/TimePix; **US3** *top* MapQuest.com; *bottom* Susan Walsh/AP/Wide World Photos; **US4** *left* AP/Wide World Photos; *right* MapQuest.com; **US5** USA TODAY®; **US6–US7** MapQuest.com; **US6** *inset* Copyright © Reuters NewMedia Inc./Corbis; **US7** *top inset* Katsumi Ksashara/AP/Wide World Photos; *bottom inset* Sayyid Azim/AP/Wide World Photos; **US9** *left* AP/Wide World Photos; **US10** USA TODAY®; *top inset* AP/Wide World Photos; *middle inset* Al-Jazeera/AP/Wide World Photos; *bottom inset* AP/Wide World Photos; **US11** *top* Copyright © David Hume Kennerly/Corbis Sygma; *bottom* MapQuest.com; **US12** Copyright © Jeff Christensen/Reuters/TimePix; *inset* Copyright © Greg Mathieson/MAI/TimePix; **US13** USA TODAY®; **US14** *left* Copyright © Digital Stock/Corbis; *top inset* Copyright © Kent Wood/Photo Researchers; *bottom* FBI/AP/Wide World Photos; *bottom inset* Justice Department/AP/Wide World Photos; **US15** Copyright © Eric Draper/The White House/TimePix.

SkillBuilder Handbook

R15 Library of Congress; **R28** Courtesy of the Lloyd Ostendorf Collection.

Presidents of the United States

R36–R38 The Oval Office Collection™ except Clinton AP/Wide World Photos, George W. Bush Bush-Cheney 2000, Inc.

Maps created by Mapping Specialists

McDougal Littell has made every effort to locate the copyright holders of all copyrighted material in this book and to make full acknowledgment for its use.

lol
lmao
Rolmao
faclmao
Roflmao